ANTIQUE SHOPS & DEALERS U.S.A.

D1479375

Second Edition

A comprehensive guide to antique shops and dealers in the United States

ILLUSTRATED, Furniture Edition

Editor — Joseph Derum

Distributed by
CROWN PUBLISHERS, INC.,
New York

and published by
DRIVERDALE COMPANY, Publishers
Dallas

The editor and the editorial staff have made no judgment regarding the quality or the authenticity of any items listed. Since the information contained within these pages has been supplied by the individual dealers themselves, the publishers can assume no responsibility for its accuracy.

© 1979 by Driverdale Company
All rights reserved. No part of this book may be reproduced or utilized in any form or by any means, electronic or mechanical, including photocopying, recording, or by an information storage and retrieval system, without permission from the publisher.
Inquiries should be addressed to
Driverdale Company, Publishers, P. O. Box 12577, Dallas, Texas 75225

ISBN: 0-517-535238

Printed in the United States of America

INTRODUCTION
to First Edition

My idea for the *Antique Shops & Dealers, U.S.A.* came as a personal thing. I enjoy shopping for antiques, and finding little out-of-the-way shops has always been one of the extra joys of vacations or even all-day shopping sprees, spent with friends. I believe I am quite average in my interests and number more "antique hounds" among my friends than I do those who have no interest in them at all.

When traveling on the expressways during our vacations the past few years, I have often wondered what quaint and interesting shops were in the area, but not knowing definitely that there were any in the immediate vicinity, we have not ventured forth off the well-traveled highways to search. Last summer, the idea came to me of a book, listing at least some of the many such shops throughout the country; the little out-of-the-way shops as well as the city shops — with directions to help the tourists and travelers find their way.

With this book, I have attempted to do just this, and I, along with the rest of the antique-lovers in the nation, can pack it along with our other vacation necessities and visit antiques shops all along our vacation routes. Wonder what terrific bargains we will find!

I wish to thank all the kind dealers who helped so much to make this volume possible, by sending me information, not only about their own shops, but others in their areas.

EVIE DOHERTY

Editor of the
First Edition

ABOUT THE WRITER

Colonel James Q. Erwin is an Instructor in
the Schools of Continuing Education for
both Southern Methodist University, Dallas,
and Texas Christian University, Fort Worth.

DESIGNS   Virginia Wrenn Jones

DRAWINGS   Kem Ormand

PHOTOGRAPHY

C. Alan Crabtree

Pete Petrisky / Image 35

PREFACE

It is our hope that you, our reader, will find enjoyment in the use of our Second Edition. This book has been made completely current and has been revised on a very large scale. Many more shops have chosen to be listed in the appreciably enlarged Specialties section.

To undertake a task without incurring debts of gratitude to a remarkably large number of people is impossible. We are greatly obliged to the many antique merchants who have offered quite valuable suggestions and help. The dozen young women comprising the production staff for the manuscript of this publication are deserving of thanks by this editor in so many ways that even a simple beginning seems insurmountable. Their diligence and attentiveness to digesting information from thousands of listing questionnaires has engendered my complete respect.

Perhaps the only way to say thank you to so many people is to express our goal. Ways to improve the utility of the Specialties Index will be continually sought. We shall strive to make each edition the most complete listing possible of antique shops in this nation.

Joseph Derum

PICTURE ACKNOWLEDGMENTS

Empire and Victorian Furniture

Old City Park, A Museum of Cultural History
Dallas County Heritage Society, Inc.
Dallas, Texas

Jacobean to Empire Furniture   *James Q. Erwin, Antiques, Dallas*

TABLE OF CONTENTS

The information in this book is first organized by states, then by cities and finally by the names of the antique shops. All are presented alphabetically.

x

The Basics of
ANTIQUE FURNITURE

by James Q. Erwin

Welcome to the world of antiques. Your having purchased this book is evidence enough that you are entertaining the idea of becoming a better collector. This writer, who has been both a collector and a dealer, would like to share some thoughts with you.

I once met an old fellow from New England who possessed an extremely fine collection of antiques and was a very shrewd trader as well. He gave me one of my first important pieces of advice. "When you meet an expert on antiques, beware!" The school-of-hard-knocks has taught me how true that was. Antiques comprise such a large and all-encompassing field that one really never learns enough. You must learn enough to become your own expert. The field of antiques is fluid because new things are constantly becoming old enough to enter the market. Therefore, learning in order to make your knowledge current is never ending. Limited knowledge is truly a dangerous thing. If you are not completely informed, you are vulnerable to all sorts of unknowns. Study and become aware, so that your searches for antiques will be made up of happy and profitable adventures, rather than misadventures.

In the following paragraphs I will discuss all the major periods of American antique furniture styles. Regardless of what you collect, it should fall within one of these periods. Great detail is not possible in so limited a presentation, but it is my hope to give you a very good beginning. More space will be devoted to the more recent styles for they are the majority of the present inventories in antique shops. Their prevalence also means that these more recent periods will be the most reasonably affordable.

The first interval of interest to us, as collectors, is referred to as the "Pilgrim Century". It identifies furniture used by the early settlers at Jamestown and Plymouth. They brought very little with them. That which they made after they were here was very limited in quantity and lacking in glamour. It was very utilitarian, very uncomfortable and most of it was literally used up. Very little of it exists today. One must go to museums to see authentic examples.

(Continued on page 11)

STATE OF ALABAMA

Anniston

ANNISTON GALLERIES
915 Wilmer Ave   36201
205 236-3741   Est: 1950
Proprietor: Frank & Helen
Jones
Hours: Daily, Also By Appt
Types & Periods: 18th &
19th Century American,
European & Oriental
Furniture; Porcelains &
Bibelots
Appraisal Service Available
   Directions: From Hwy 120,
   Turn N on 421 to Quintard
   Ave; Turn W on 9th St

Athens

OLD RAIL ANTIQUES
101 E Washington St
                           35611
205 232-3218   Est: 1972
Proprietor: James M Igou
Hours: Open Tues &
Thurs thru Sat
Types & Periods: Queen
Anne, Chippendale, Empire,
Victorian, Primitives
   Directions: 1/2 Block from
   Court House Sq

**THE RESTORATION
SHOPPE**
119 Monroe St   35611
205 232-8554   Est: 1972
Proprietor: Ford J. Caudle
Hours: Tues thru Sat,
10-5:30
Hours: Daily, 10-5:30,
Closed Sun & Mon
Types & Periods: General
Line
Specialties: Pictures, Prints,
Mirrors
   Directions: 1 Block from
   Court House, Across RR
   from Depot

Bessemer

MARTHA'S ANTIQUES
913 Hall Ave   35020
205 822-2195   Est: 1973
Proprietor: Martha I Bell

Hours: By Appointment,
By Chance
Types & Periods: General
Line, Glass, China,
Furniture, Collectables
   Directions: State Hwy 150,
   Turn on Hall Ave, Approx
   4 Blks on Left

Birmingham

BIRMINGHAM CLUSTER
Directions: No Real
Cluster, Several Shops on
Cobb Lane

**CINDERELLA ANTIQUE
SHOPPE**
1932 Bessemer Rd   35208
205 786-5613
Proprietor: J Morris
Hours: Daily
Types & Periods: "Anything
old and beautiful in china,
glass & furniture"
   Directions: One Mile W of
   Fairgrounds on US 11

**COBB LANE FLOWERS &
INTERIORS**
1 Cobb Lane   35205
205 933-8304   Est: 1971
Proprietor: Wm W
Whesenant
Hours: Daily, 9:30-5
Types & Periods: Antique
Wicker Furniture
   Directions. 1318 20th St
   South

COX ANTIQUES
1820 Greensprings Hwy
                           35205
205 322-1881   Est: 1972
Proprietor: C D Cox
Hours: Daily, Closed Sun
Types & Periods: English
Imports
Specialties: Oriental
Appraisal Service Available

**C M GEORGE INTERIORS
INC**
2330 7th Ave S   35233
205 322-1704   Est: 1970
Proprietor: C M George
Hours: Daily, 9-5
Types & Periods: Various
Periods

Directions: South of Town,
Exit on Red Mountain
Expwy, Bear Right to 24th
St, Turn Right to 7th Ave

GRIER ANTIQUES
2407 2nd Ave N   35203
205 251-7882   Est: 1960
Proprietor: Edward M
Grier
Hours: Mon thru Sat, 9-5
Types & Periods: European
& Oriental Antiques,
Bric-A-Brac, Chinese
Porcelains
Specialties: Oriental
(Porcelain)
Appraisal Service Available
   Directions: "We are
   located directly downtown,
   conveniently accessible
   from any direction"

IRON ART INC
2901 Cahaba Rd   35223
205 879-0529   Est: 1949
Proprietor: Mrs Katherine
M McTyeire
Hours: Mon thru Sat, 9-5;
Nights or Sun By
Appointment
Types & Periods: 18th &
19th Century English &
French Furniture, Old Books
Specialties: Books,
Chandeliers, Furniture,
Paintings
Appraisal Service Available
   Directions: Old 280 Hwy, 2
   Miles S of Birmingham in
   Mountain Brook Village

**THE KING'S HOUSE
ANTIQUES**
2418 Montevallo Rd 35223
205 871-5787   Est: 1973
Proprietor: Mrs J M Kidd
Jr & Mrs J L Glasser
Hours: Mon thru Fri,
9:30-5; Sat, 10-4
Types & Periods: 18th
Century English, French,
Oriental & American
Furniture & Accessories;
Oriental Rugs
Specialties: Rugs, Furniture
Appraisal Service Available
   Directions: Corner of
   Montevallo Rd & Culver,
   Mountain Brook Village

Birmingham Cont'd

THE NIDDY-NODDY
Hwy 119 S Cahaba Valley
Rd   35243
205 967-3178   Est: 1974
Proprietor: Mr Carl W
Stapleton & Miss Julie
Stapleton
Hours: Tues thru Sun
Types & Periods: Furniture,
American, Primitives
Directions: Hwy 119 S
between Hwy 31 S & Hwy
280 E

POTPOURRI ANTIQUES
3373 Overbrook Rd 35213
205 879-6064   Est: 1972
Proprietor: Betty Jackson
Hours: By Appointment
Types & Periods: "Potpourri
means a little bit of
everything"

PUMP HOUSE ANTIQUES
3279 Cahaba Heights Rd
                       35243
205 967-2855   Est: 1972
Proprietor: Buzz Gaissert
& Jane Malone
Hours: Mon--Tues, 10-4;
Thurs-Fri, 10-4; Sat & Sun
By Appointment
Types & Periods: General
Line
Directions: Cahaba
Heights Exit Off Hwy 280

**ROBERTA'S BROWSE 'N
BUY**
7303 1st Ave N   35206
205 836-7624   Est: 1969
Proprietor: Roberta & J W
Hawkins
Hours: Tues-Sat, 8:30-5
Types & Periods: Cut Glass,
China, Silver, Jewelry,
American Furniture
Directions: "Easy to find
address on main Hwy 11
through city"

**SEEDS 4 ANTIQUES
(NEVER BEFORE STORE)**
2327 2nd Ave N   35203
205 425-1605   Est: 1968
Proprietor: Jim Anderson
Hours: Mon-Sat, 10-6
Types & Periods:
Hard-To-Find Off-Beat
Furniture (All Periods),
Oriental Accessories,
Nostalgia Items, Interior
Design

Specialties: Country French
Appraisal Service Available
Directions: Between 23rd
& 24th St on 2nd Ave N,
Convenient to All
Interstates Through City

**THE WRENS NEST
ANTIQUES**
948 41st St   35208
205 785-4381   Est: 1956
Proprietor: Sue Wren
Hours: Daily, Eves By
Appointment
Types & Periods: Jewelry,
General Line
Specialties: Furniture,
Jewelry
Appraisal Service Available
Directions: 4 Blocks Off
I-59

Brownsboro

LYDA'S ANTIQUES
Rt 1   35741
205 776-2160
Proprietor: Will E Lyda
Hours: Tues-Sat, 10-5;
Sun, 1-5
Types & Periods: General
Line-Southern
Directions: Hwy 72 E,
Approx 10 Miles E of
Huntsville

Cullman

THE COLLECTORS SHOP
1348 3rd St SE   35055
205 739-1430   Est: 1971
Proprietor: R H Brown
Hours: By Appointment
Types & Periods: Clocks,
Glass, China
Specialties: Clocks (Repair)
Directions: Hwy 278 E

Daphine

**THOMPSON HOUSE
ANTIQUES**
Rt 3 Box 322   36526
205 626-1310
Proprietor: Agnew
Thompson Jr
Hours: Flea Market
Weekends

Types & Periods: General
Line
Directions: Mobile
Causeway

Decatur

**DANCY-POLK HOUSE
ANTIQUES**
824 Bank St NE   35601
Proprietor: Mr & Mrs T E
Anderson
Hours: Mon-Tues;
Thurs-Sat; Wed & Sun By
Appointment
Types & Periods: 18th &
19th Century American &
English Furniture &
Accessories
Specialties: Authentic Early
American & Southern
Furniture
Appraisal Service Available
Directions: In a Restored
Turn-of-the-Century
Building in the Oldest Part
of Town

THE GASLIGHT
1414 Fifth Ave SE   35601
                   Est: 1972
Proprietor: Mrs Mary
Cannon
Hours: Mon-Sat, 12-4:30
Types & Periods: Country,
Middle & Late 1800s & Early
1900; Emphasis on Kitchen
Specialties: Furniture &
Small Items
Directions: Turn West at
Intersection Rte 31 & 11th
St, Go 1 Block, Turn Right

H & H ANTIQUES
22 2nd St SW   35601
Hours: Wed-Fri, 10-4; Sat,
12-5
Types & Periods: Furniture,
Glass, Brass

**INGLIS HOUSE OF BANK
STREET**
806 Bank St NE   35601
205 355-6118
Proprietor: Netta & Fred
Inglis
Hours: Mon-Sat, 10-5
Types & Periods: China,
Furniture, Glass, Lamp Parts

MURPHY CUSTOM CRAFTS
603 Bank St NE   35601
205 350-0141

Proprietor: D L & Irene
Murphy
Hours: Mon-Fri, 9-5; Sat,
9-12
Types & Periods: Doll
Hospital, Dolls, Miniature
Furniture
Specialties: Furniture

**PRICEVILLE ANTIQUES &
FLEA MARKET**
Hwy 67 E & I-65   35601
205 355-9973
Proprietor: Mr & Mrs
Campbell
Hours: Tues-Sun, 10-5;
Mon By Appointment
Types & Periods: Furniture,
China, Glass, Wicker, Lamps

**SMITH'S ANTIQUES &
COLLECTABLES**
1206 5th Ave SE   35601
205 355-5176
Proprietor: Jim & Audrey
Smith
Hours: Daily 12-5 or By
Appointment
Types & Periods: Wicker &
Oak Furniture, Glass, China,
Lamps

WYNELLE'S ANTIQUES
906 6th Ave SE   35601
205 350-1978
Proprietor: Wynelle & Bill
Lyle
Hours: Mon-Fri, 10-5; Sun
By Appointment
Types & Periods: Clocks,
Lamps, Primitives, Period
Furniture

Dothan

THE ANTIQUE CORNER
Hwy. 231-N & By-Pass
36301
205 792-5181   Est: 1967
Proprietor: Bea Blumberg
Hours: Seven Days a
Week, 9-9
Types & Periods: 19th &
20th Century Porcelains,
Silver, Glass; Also Limited
Number of Collectables
Appraisal Service Available
Directions: In Lobby of
Quality Inn Carousel,
Adjacent to Shopping Mall

Eight Mile

BLEASDALE ANTIQUES
4913 St Stephens Rd
36613
205 457-1132
Proprietor: Mrs J R
(Claudia) Bleasdale
Types & Periods: Primitives,
Pressed Glass

Elba

FARMER'S ANTIQUE SHOP
Rt 2 Box 269E   36323
205 897-6456   Est: 1971
Proprietor: Doris Farmer
Hours: Tues-Sun
Types & Periods: General
Line
Specialties: Glass
Directions: Taylor Mill Rd

Enterprise

**LEJON'S ANTIQUES &
LAMPS**
605 Northside Dr   36330
Est: 1970
Proprietor: John O
Gilliland
Hours: Mon-Sat, 9-5; By
Appointment, By Chance
Types & Periods: General
Line, Aladdin and Other
Kerosene Lamps & Parts
Specialties: Aladdin Lamps
& Parts, Lamp Repair
Appraical Service Available
Directions: Northern
Section of City Near
Dauphin St School

Eufaula

EUFAULA ANTIQUE SHOP
136 Front St   36027
205 687-3859   Est: 1970
Proprietor: Mrs Bill
Garrison
Hours: By Chance, 10-12
& 2-5
Types & Periods: Victorian &
Oak Pieces, Primitive
Ironware
Specialties: Glass
Directions: Off Hwy 82
Across From Holiday Inn

Fairhope

MAGGIE'S ANTIQUES
450 S Section St   36532
205 928-5602
Proprietor: Mrs Maggie
Sislak
Types & Periods: General
Line

**SQUARE-RIGGER
ANTIQUES**
131 Fairhope Ave   36532
205 928-7416
Proprietor: Elsie & Wallace
Milham
Types & Periods: Furniture,
General Line

STIMSON'S ANTIQUES
PO Box 98   36532
205 928-5811
Proprietor: Mr & Mrs W D
Stimson
Types & Periods: 18th &
19th Century Furniture
Directions: Truck Rte 93

Florence

**CABIN ANTIQUES/FLYING
CARPET**
458 N Court   35630
205 764-1852   Est: 1927
Proprietor: Mrs H W
Wright & W P Wright
Hours: Mon-Tues, 10-5;
Thurs-Sat, 10-5
Types & Periods: Complete
Line
Specialties: Oriental Rugs
Appraisal Service Available
Directions: S of University
of Alabama

LAZY DAZY ANTIQUES
1123 N Wood   35630
205 764-6551   Est: 1967
Proprietor: Mrs Koleta W
Lewis
Hours: Mon thru Sat; By
Appointment, By Chance
Types & Periods: Oriental
Furniture, Porcelains,
Screens, Paintings,
Embroideries, English &
American Furniture
Specialties: Antique Jewelry
Appraisal Service Available
Directions: Next Door to
Norwood Grill

Florence   Cont'd

SARA ANN'S ANTIQUE SHOPPE
Florence Blvd,
Rt 8, Box 66   35630
205 766-5334   Est: 1967
Proprietor: Mrs Ivan Gist
Hours: Mon-Sat,
12:30-4:30; Sun By
Appointment, By Chance
Types & Periods: General
Line
Specialties: Lamps & Parts
of All Kinds
Directions: Hwy 72-43 E

Greenville

SOLOMONS ANTIQUES
215 College   36037
205 382-3224   Est: 1964
Proprietor: Frances B &
Kenneth Solomons III
Hours: Daily; Mon by
Appointment Only
Types & Periods:
Chippendale, Queen Anne,
Victorian, French
Specialties: Furniture
Directions: One Block S
From Stablers Clinic

Gulf Shores

FISH HOUSE ANTIQUES
                   36542
205 968-7701
Proprietor: Mrs Vivian C
Peed
Types & Periods: General
Line

FRIENDSHIP HOUSE
Hwy 180 at Intracoastal
Canal   36542
205 968-7477   Est: 1959
Proprietor: Norman N
Coles
Types & Periods: Cut Glass,
18th & 19th Century English
& American Furniture,
China, English & Chinese
Cloisonne
Specialties: Jewelry,
Primitives American
Appraisal Service Available
Directions: One Block E
Off Intracoastal Canal
Bridge

Homewood

MARY ADAMS ANTIQUES
1822 29th Ave S   35209
205 871-7131   Est: 1948
Proprietor: Mary S Adams
Hours: Mon-Fri, 8-5; Sat,
8:30-12:30
Types & Periods: Furniture,
Rugs, Chandeliers
Appraisal Service Available
Directions: Suburb of
Birmingham, Off Hwy 31 S

Hueytown

FOUR SEASONS ANTIQUES
3031 Devon Rd   35020
205 491-6561   Est: 1971
Proprietor: Susie W
Fulmer
Hours: Daily, 10-5; Also By
Appointment, By Chance
Types & Periods: French,
English, American, Chinese,
Queen Anne, Chippendale,
18th & 19th Century
Specialties: Furniture,
Mirrors, Bric-A-Brac
Directions: Exit I-59, Go
1.2 Miles

Huntsville

HUNTSVILLE CLUSTER
Directions: Several Shops
on Whitesburg Dr SE
(2000 Block), Also on
Madison S (500 Block)

MADELYN HEREFORD INTERIORS
2332 Whitesburg Dr 35801
205 539-4429   Est: 1972
Proprietor: Madelyn
Hereford
Hours: Daily, By
Appointment
Types & Periods: 18th &
19th Century Furniture &
Accessories
Directions: Approximately
2 Miles SE of Downtown

MADISON ANTIQUES
405 Franklin St   35801
205 534-2851   Est: 1972
Proprietor: Valerie
Fursdon
Hours: Tues-Sun, 11-5

Types & Periods: 18th &
Early 19th Century English
Only Furniture- Brass &
Pewter, Silver
Appraisal Service Available
Directions: 1821 House in
Historic District One Block
Off Square

TWICKENHAM ANTQUES
2338 Whitesburg Dr 35801
205 534-5794   Est: 1972
Proprietor: J E Fikes, Mgr
Hours: Mon-Sat; Sun By
Appointment
Types & Periods: Complete
Line
Appraisal Service Available
Directions: 3 Blocks S of
Huntsville Hospital

Irondale

HAPPY HOUSE OLDTIQUES
2009 1st Ave N   35210
205 956-3123   Est: 1974
Proprietor: C Grigsby & O
Dial
Hours: Tues-Sat
Types & Periods: Largely
Country Oak
Specialties: Furniture
Refinishing
Directions: One Mile E of
Eastwood Mall in
Birmingham

Locust Fork

STERLING ANTIQUES INC
Box 46   35097
205 681-3591   Est: 1972
Proprietor: W E Hatley
Hours: Daily
Types & Periods: General
Line, Furniture, Glass
Specialties: Dealers Only

Midway

SUZIE'S ANTIQUES
Rte 82   36053
205 529-3949   Est: 1976
Proprietor: Sue & Dennis
Gallimore
Hours: Daily; By
Appointment, By Chance

Types & Periods: Dishes,
Glass, Guns, Needlework,
Pictures, Furniture, General
Line
Specialties: Needlework,
Glass
Appraisal Service Available
Directions: On Rte 82
Downtown, Across from
PO

Mobile

MOBILE CLUSTER
Directions: Western
Section of City, Bounded
by Telegraph Rd on the
Eastland Azalea Rd,
becoming McGregor Ave
on the West between
Government Street &
Springhill Ave

**ANTHONY'S ANTIQUES &
GIFTS**
350 Dauphin St   36602
205 452-1862   Est: 1972
Proprietor: Roy R
Atchison
Hours: Daily
Types & Periods: General
Line

**ANTIQUE EMPORIUM &
GIFT SHOP**
2208 Airport Blvd   36606
205 479-8750   Est: 1974
Proprietor: Howard L
Morgan
Hours: Daily
Types & Periods: Primitives,
Drass, Copper, Wooden,
Iron, All Periods
Specialties: Books
Directions: 2 Miles E I-65
on Airport Blvd, 1 Block N
of Hwy 90

ANTIQUITY SHOP
141 Tuscaloosa St   36607
205 471-2752
Proprietor: Harold &
Suzanne Drew
Types & Periods: Oriental
Rugs, Furniture

APPLESEED ANTIQUES
1502 Wolfridge Rd   36618
205 342-1113
Proprietor: Mrs Nancy
Dodd
Types & Periods: American
Country Furniture

ASHLAND ANTIQUES
2401 Old Shell Rd   36607
205 479-1024
Proprietor: Mrs Barbara
Corcoran
Types & Periods: English
Imports

**AL ATCHISON COURTYARD
ANTIQUES**
601 Government St 36602
205 432-8423   Est: 1946
Proprietor: A O Atchison
& Sons
Hours: Mon-Sat, 9-6
Types & Periods: English &
American Antiques
Appraisal Service Available
Directions: Corner
Government & Warren,
Downtown Mobile

AUNT KATHY'S ANTIQUES
3750 Government St
                            36609
205 478-8900
Proprietor: Mrs Katherine
(Harvey) Singer
Types & Periods: Primitives

**B J'S ANTIQUES &
COLLECTIBLES**
3750 Government St
                            36609
205 478-8900
Proprietor: Jeanie Boland
& Carolyn Jones
Types & Periods: General
Line

J CHAMBERLIN ANTIQUES
368 Michigan Ave   36604
205 432-2478
Proprietor: A J & Louise
Chamberlin
Types & Periods: Silver,
Maps, Prints

**COLONIAL MOBILE
ANTIQUES**
1407 Government St
                            36604
205 473-2847
Proprietor: Mrs Martha
Hamilton
Types & Periods: Oriental
Rugs, Furniture

COSBY'S ANTIQUES
1568 Dauphin St   36604
205 479-7504
Proprietor: Mrs C R Cosby
Types & Periods: General
Line, Silver, Jewelry

ELIZABETH'S ANTIQUES
3750 Government St
                            36609
205 478-8900
Proprietor: Walt &
Elizabeth Baldwin
Types & Periods: Lamps,
General Line

FIVE POINTS ANTIQUES
1325 Spring Hill Ave 36604
205 473-5619   Est: 1974
Proprietor: Thomas W
Ryan
Hours: Mon-Sat, By
Appointment
Types & Periods: American
Oak, Pine, Iron, Primitives,
Depression Glass, Brass,
Copper, Furniture, General
Line
Directions: 2 Blocks E of
Providence Hospital

**MAURINE HAAS ANTIQUES
"THE MAGNOLIAS"**
1624 Springhill Ave 36604
205 432-6268   Est: 1930
Proprietor: Mrs Maurine
Haas
Hours: Mon-Sat, 9-5
Types & Periods: 18th
Century English, American,
French, Porcelains, Silver
Directions: On Hwy 98
One Block W of Catherine
St

**HAVILAND HOUSE
ANTIQUES**
3750 Government St
                            36609
205 478-8900
Proprietor: Mrs Clinton L
Hines
Types & Periods: Haviland
Matching Service

**HERITAGE HOUSE
ANTIQUES**
1000 Dauphin St   36604
205 432-0842
Proprietor: Tommy & Zela
Grubbs
Types & Periods: Mirrors,
Furniture, Glass

**BAXTER HOOPER
ANTIQUES**
952 Government St 36604
205 432-6221   Est: 1964
Proprietor: Madge &
Baxter Hooper
Hours: By Appointment,
By Chance

Mobile   Cont'd

BAXTER HOOPER   Cont'd
Types & Periods: General
Line, Bronze, Orientals,
Small Cabinet Collectibles
Appraisal Service Available
    Directions: On Hwy 90 in
    Midtown Mobile

JAN & THEA ANTIQUES
4072-B Old Shell Rd 36608
205 344-9065
Proprietor: Jan Stone &
Thea Atkinson
Types & Periods: Silver,
Primitives, Traditionals

JORDAN'S ANTIQUES
457 Dauphin St   36602
Proprietor: Raymond
Jordan
Types & Periods: General
Line

KEARNEY'S ANTIQUES
1004 Government St
                       36604
205 438-9984
Proprietor: Mrs Maude
Kearney
Types & Periods: General
Line

LAND & SEA ANTIQUES
3750 Government St
                       36609
205 478-8900
Proprietor: Frank Lundell
Types & Periods: Oriental,
Nautical, General Line

MAC'S ANTIQUES
3750 Government St
                       36609
205 478-8900
Proprietor: Dot Huey &
Willie McRaney
Types & Periods: General
Line

MC CRORY'S JEWELRY & ANTIQUES
2961 Springhill Ave   36607
205 479-2292   Est: 1948
Proprietor: Andrew L
McCrory
Hours: Mon-Tues, 9-6;
Thurs-Sat, 9-6
Types & Periods: General
Line
Specialties: Clocks
    Directions: On Hwy 98 W

MOBILE ANTIQUE MART & FLEA MARKET
614 Michigan Ave   36605
205 432-4854   Est: 1972
Proprietor: Gerald & Betty
Koors
Hours: Wed-Fri, 10-3; Sun,
12-6
Types & Periods: Furniture,
Glassware, Primitives,
Bric-A-Brac, Silver, Jewelry,
Clocks
    Directions: Michigan Ave
    Exit off I-10, Five Blocks
    after Second Stop Light

MURRAY'S ANTIQUES
959 Dauphin St   36604
205 433-6362
Proprietor: C H (Doc) &
Rosemary Murray
Types & Periods: Art Glass,
General Line

PINE TREE ANTIQUES & COLLECTIBLES
156 N McGregor Ave
                       36608
                 Est 1973
Proprietor: Mrs Mary
Frances Jenkins
Hours: Tues-Thurs, also
Sat
Types & Periods: Collectible
Glass
Specialties: Research &
Appraisal
Appraisal Service Available

PLANTATION ANTIQUE GALLERY
3750 Government Blvd
                       36609
205 478-8900   Est: 1974
Proprietor: J Gulas & F
Lundell
Hours: Mon-Sat, 10-5;
Sun, 1-5
Types & Periods: Period
Furniture, Oriental Rugs,
Bric-A-Brac, Cut Glass,
Nautical Items, Haviland
China Matching Service
Appraisal Service Available
    Directions: On Hwy 1/2
    Mile W of I-65

STEADMAN ANTIQUES
1650 Government St
                       36604
205 473-4616
Proprietor: Miss Ruby Lee
Steadman
Types & Periods: Cut Glass,
Lamps, General Line

VIRGINIA STICKNEY ANTIQUES
1464 Church St   36604
205 478-4312
Proprietor: Mrs Virginia
Stickney
Types & Periods: Period
Furniture, Orientals

A TOUCH OF GLASS
3750 Government St
                       36609
205 478-8900
Proprietor: Cortez Fowler
& Ed Campbell
Types & Periods: Stained
Glass, Wicker

Montgomery

MONTGOMERY CLUSTER
    Directions: Clayton to Clay
    (S-N), Goldwaite to
    Hanrick (E-W)

BODIFORD'S ANTIQUES MALL
919 Hampton St   36106
205 265-4220   Est: 1969
Proprietor: Charlie
Bodiford
Hours: Daily
Types & Periods: Primitives,
Oak, Victorian, Glassware,
Silver
    Directions: Exit Forest or
    Mulberry Sts from I-85

BOHART'S ANTIQUES
321 Clayton St   36104
205 263-4156   Est: 1973
Proprietor: Col & Mrs Chet
Bohart USAF Ret
Hours: Mon-Sat, 10-4;
Also by Appointment
Types & Periods: Furniture,
China, Glassware, Pictures,
Clocks, General Line
Appraisal Service Available
    Directions: I-65 Herron St
    Exit to Goldwaite, Turn R
    to Clayton, Turn L

COLLECTOR'S II
309 N Hull St   36104
205 263-4679   Est: 1971
Proprietor: B & E von
Gohren & H Keller
Hours: Mon-Sat

Types & Periods: American,
European & Oriental
Furniture & Decorator
Accessories, 17th-19th
Centuries
Specialties: Furniture
(American Country)
Appraisal Service Available
  Directions: In Restored
  DeWolf-Cooper Cottage,
  Exit I-65 on Herron St,
  Through Town to Hull,
  Left on Hull, Corner
  House Next Block, White
  Picket Fence, Gazebo

**GEORGE E GRIFFITH &
ASSOCIATES**
  317 Clayton   36104
  205 269-4818   Est: 1975
  Proprietor: George Griffith
  & Gerald Darby
  Hours: Mon-Sat, 10-5
Types & Periods: Furniture
& Accessories of the
17th-19th Centuries,Oriental
Rugs
Appraisal Service Available
  Directions: Herron St Exit
  Off I-65 Going Downtown,
  Turn Right on Goldwaite
  St, Then Left on Clayton

**HERRON HOUSE
ANTIQUES**
  422 Herron St   36104
  205 265-2063   Est: 1971
  Proprietor: P Thames & J
  Louden
  Hours: Mon-Sat, 10-5; Sun
  By Appointment
Types & Periods: 18th &
19th Century Furniture,
Crystal, China & Silver,
Oriental Rugs, Primitives
Appraisal Service Available
  Directions: Exit Herron Off
  I-65, Located in Cottage
  Hill District

THE JOGGLING BOARD
  220 N Hull   36104
  205 269-5977
  Proprietor: Elizabeth
  Vaughan
  Hours: Daily
Types & Periods: Primitives,
Oak, Late 19th & Early 20th
Century Collectibles
  Directions: 2 Blocks N of
  Dexter Ave on N Hull

MEMORY LANE ANTIQUES
  2124 Gibson   36110
  205 264-2570   Est: 1968
  Proprietor: Sara D Mitchell
  Hours: Tues-Sat, 10-5
Types & Periods: General
Line
Specialties: Glass, Jewelry,
Silver
Appraisal Service Available
  Directions: Directly Behind
  Garrett Coliseum, US 231

THE PERIOD SHOP
  1814 Midway St   36110
  205 263-7738   Est: 1973
  Proprietor: John R George
  Hours: Daily
Types & Periods: Period &
Reproductions, Chippendale,
Victorian

POLLARD'S ANTIQUES
  102 Marshall St   36104
  205 262-2171   Est: 1955
  Proprietor: George &
  Margaret Pollard
  Hours: By Appointment,
  By Chance
Types & Periods: American
Primitives, Some Period
Furniture, Unusual Collector
Items
Appraisal Service Available
  Directions: Off Court St,
  1600 Block

Mooresville

**COUNTRY STORE OF
MOORESVILLE**
  Box 28   35649
  205 355 4911   Est: 1975
  Proprietor: A Carter & J
  Vollmer
  Hours: Daily
Types & Periods: Old
Grocery Store Items &
Primitives
  Directions: Hwy 20, 4
  Miles E of Decatur

Newville

BRACKIN INC ANTIQUES
  Hwy 173   36353
  205 889-4514   Est: 1969
  Proprietor: Mrs U L
  Brackin

Hours: Mon-Wed, Open
Thur A.M., Fri & Sat,
Closed Sunday
Types & Periods: Early
Period Furniture, Round Oak
China Cabinets,
Washstands, Bowl & Pitcher
Sets, China & Marble-Top
Tables
  Directions: SE Corner of
  AL Hwy 173, Fifteen Miles
  N of Dothan

Northport

ADAMS ANTIQUES
  426 Main Ave   35476
  205 758-8651   Est: 1973
  Proprietor: Carl Adams
  Hours: Mon-Fri, 8-5:30;
  Sat, 8-12; Also By
  Appointment
Types & Periods: 18th
Century, Lap Desks, Tea
Caddies, Work Boxes, etc
  Directions: Old Downtown
  Portion of Northport,
  Cross Hugh Thomas
  Bridge From Tuscaloosa,
  Take First Right, Go
  Under Highway & To
  Second Light,Turn Left

Opelika

BETTY'S BARN
  Rte 4, Box 265-3B 36801
  205 749-9419   Est: 1974
  Proprietor: Betty
  Woodward
  Hours: Tues-Sat, 10-5
Types & Periods: Late 19th
& Early 20th Century Pine &
Oak, Ice Boxes, Hall Trees,
Dining Tables, Cabinets,
Primitives
Specialties: Furniture
  Directions: Hwy 280-431
  Two Miles E of I-85 &
  Four Miles E of Downtown
  Opelika

**HERITAGE HOUSE
ANTIQUES**
  714 Second Ave   36801
  205 745-4805   Est: 1965
  Proprietor: V Magee & R
  Crook
  Hours: Mon-Sat, 10-5

HERITAGE HOUSE
ANTIQUES Cont'd
Types & Periods: 17th, 18th
& 19th Century Furniture,
Fine Glass, Sterling Silver
Specialties: Furniture, Silver
  Directions: Off I-85, Take
  Hwy 29 into Opelika

JACKSON ANTIQUES
1807 Frederick Dr   36801
205 749-0939   Est: 1974
Proprietor: Janet & Walter
Jackson
Hours: Mon-Tues,
Thurs-Sat
Types & Periods: General
Line, Oak, Pine & Primitive
Furniture
Specialties: Furniture
Appraisal Service Available
  Directions: Between
  Opelika & Auburn, 2 Miles
  Off I-85

MARTHA'S VINEYARD
5 N 8th St   36801
205 745-4481   Est: 1971
Proprietor: Martha Mills
Hours: Daily, 9-5
Types & Periods: "We like
all types & periods & handle
furniture, glass, china,
jewelry, clocks &
collectibles"
  Directions: Downtown
  Opelika, 2 Blocks Off
  Hwys 280 & 29

Owens Cross Roads

B & S ANTIQUES
Manns Rd   35763
205 725-4535   Est: 1974
Proprietor: C W Sneed
Hours: Daily
Types & Periods: General
Line
Specialties: Furniture (Oak)
Appraisal Service Available

Ozark

AMERICAN EAGLE
ANTIQUES
US 231 S   36360
205 774-4330   Est: 1970
Proprietor: Russell A West
Hours: Mon-Sat, 9-5:30

Types & Periods: 18th &
19th Century American, Also
Wholesale
Appraisal Service Available

COACH & CARRIAGE
Rte 2, 231 N   36360
205 774-8877   Est: 1969
Proprietor: H M Luckfield
Hours: Mon-Fri, 8-5;
Sat-Sun, 9-5
Types & Periods: American
& English Furniture; Cut,
Pressed & Pattern Glass; Art
Glass; Brass; Primitives
Specialties: Clocks,
Furniture
Appraisal Service Available
  Directions: 3 Miles N of
  Ozark on Main Hwy 231

HANEYS ANTIQUES
US 231 N   36360
205 774-4618   Est: 1974
Proprietor: Howard & Lois
Haney
Hours: Mon-Sat; Nights By
Appointment
Types & Periods: Early
American, Cherry & Walnut
Furniture; Victorian
Furniture; Oak; China; Cut &
Pressed Glass; Antique Colt
Winchester Guns
Specialties: Antique Guns
Appraisal Service Available
  Directions: 2 1/2 Miles N
  of Ozark

Pell City

DOLL HOUSE ANTIQUES
116 N 21st St   35125
205 338-2826
Proprietor: Anne G Riser
Types & Periods: General
Line

KILGROE'S ANTIQUES
2212 3rd Ave N   35125
205 338-7923   Est: 1953
Proprietor: Mr & Mrs Joe
W Kilgroe
Hours: Seven Days a
Week, 10-5; Also By
Appointment
Types & Periods: 18th &
19th Century Furniture
Specialties: Oriental &
English Porcelain
  Directions: 1 Block W of
  Hwy 235

Pinson

ANTIQUE & GIFT SHOPPE
N Main St   35126
205 681-2566   Est: 1973
Proprietor: Faye &
Eugenia Price
Hours: Mon-Thurs, Sat; Fri
& Sun By Appointment
Types & Periods: General
Line
  Directions: Between Hwy
  75 & 79, Three Miles From
  Birmingham

Prattville

HOUSE OF EXOTICA
967 S Memorial Dr   36067
205 365-0601   Est: 1967
Proprietor: C P & P C
Jones
Hours: Mon-Sat, 9-6; Sun
By Appointment
Types & Periods: Middle &
Far East Antiques,
Samovars, Wood Carvings,
Stone, Jade, Porcelain
Statues, Oriental Carpets
Specialties: Oriental
Appraisal Service Available
  Directions: Next to Skyline
  Shopping Center on Hwy
  31 in Prattville

Pritchard

HOUSE OF LAMPS
1112 Telegraph Rd 36610
205 457-7326   Est: 1951
Proprietor: Lamar L
Davidson
Hours: Daily, 9-5
Types & Periods: Lamps
  Directions: 3 Miles N of
  Mobile & Hwy 43

Tanner

HUDSON'S ANTIQUES &
AUCTION
Rte 1, Box 102   35671
205 355-7773   Est: 1967
Proprietor: Frank Hudson
Hours: By Appointment
Types & Periods: General
Line, Monthly Auctions

Appraisal Service Available
 Directions: Just Off I-65
 on Hwy 31, Four Miles N
 of Decatur

Tuscaloosa

BLOSSOM TOP FARM
 Jug Factory Rd   35401
 205 345-5224   Est: 1970
 Proprietor: Cherry Austin
 Hoyt
 Hours: Mon-Sat, 10-5;
 Also By Appointment
Types & Periods: 17th, 18th
& 19th Century Continental
& Chinese Antiques
Specialties: Oriental
(Chinese)
 Directions: Between
 McFarland Blvd &
 Greensboro Rd

BOYKIN ANTIQUES
 1109 21st Ave   35401
 205 759-5231   Est: 1926
 Proprietor: Frank & Sara
 Boykin
 Hours: Mon--Fri, 8-5; Sat,
 8-1

Types & Periods: Large
stock of wide variety of
furniture & bric-a-brac
Appraisal Service Available
 Directions: 1 Block From
 Main Post Office

THE COLLECTORS SHOP INC
 1118 21st Ave   35401
 205 752-4379   Est: 1970
 Proprietor: Mrs Robert W
 Poellnitz
 Hours: Mon-Sat, 9-5
Types & Periods: Mostly
English, Sideboards, Chests,
Secretaries, Chairs, 18th &
19th Century Oriental
Porcelain & Chests, English
Porcelain, Some Chinese
Exports
 Directions: One Block
 From Junior High

LITTLEJOHN'S ANTIQUES
 3601 University Blvd E
                      35401
 205 553-0671   Est: 1948
 Proprietor: Mr & Mrs W K
 Littlejohn
 Hours: Mon-Fri, 8-5; Sat,
 8-12
Types & Periods: General
Line
Appraisal Service Available

MC CRORY ANTIQUES
 1913 8th St   35401
 205 752-4474   Est: 1970
 Proprietor: Sue McCrory
 Hours: Daily
Types & Periods: 17th, 18th
& 19th Century Furniture &
Accessories

Whistler

KATHRYN ADAMS ANTIQUES
 352 N Gould Ave   36612
 205 452-1008
 Proprietor: Miss Kathryn
 Adams
Types & Periods: General
Line

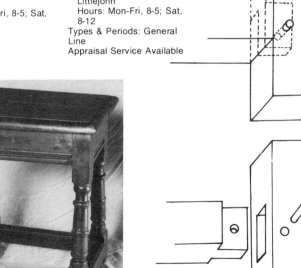

The strenth of the mortise & tenon system diagrammed has made it possible for this 17th century Jacobean Joint Stool to pose for this portrait.

STATE OF ALASKA

Anchorage

BLACK EAGLE ANTIQUES
3801 Patricia Lane 99504
907 333-4290   Est: 1972
Proprietor: Della & Bud
Graves
Hours: by chance
Types & Periods: New
England Primitives & Oak
Specialties: Toys & Clocks
Directions: In Scenic Park
near Tudor & Muldoon Rd
intersection

EAST-WEST PRIMITIVES
2928 Byrn Mawr Ct 99503
907 333-1775
Proprietor: Caryl & Bill
Lewis
Hours: by appointment
Types & Periods: General
Line

HOLLIE'S ANTIQUES
University Center   99503
907 274-5912
Hours: Mon-Fri, 11-7; Sat,
11-6
Types & Periods: General
Line
Appraisal Service Available

LOG CABIN TRADING CO.
106 E. Fireweed Ln 99503
907 276-2807   Est: 1977
Proprietor: John H Daley
Hours: Mon-Sat, 10-6
Types & Periods: All
Antiques & Collectables
Appraisal Service Available
Directions: One Block
East of Sports Arena

**SPINNING WHEEL
ANTIQUES**
4117 Mt View Dr   99504
907 272-0341   Est: 1972
Proprietor: Ralph Blakely
Hours: Mon-Sat, 10-5
Types & Periods: General
Line
Specialties: Furniture; Oak &
Country
Appraisal Service Available
Directions: In Mt View
Shopping Center

YE OLDE PINE SHOP
1809 Skilak Circle   99504
907 333-7658
Proprietor: Don & Lou
Rehrer
Hours: by appointment &
by chance
Types & Periods: General
Line
Specialties: Furniture; Hand
Crafted Pine

Juneau

HOMER'S AUCTION
Rte 5, Box 5278, Mile 10
99803
907 789-9611   Est: 1973
Proprietor: Homer R
Beedle
Hours: Mon-Sun
Types & Periods: Anything &
Everything
Appraisal Service Available
Directions: Mile 10,
Glacier Hwy

Soldotna

**GLASS MENAGERIE
ANTIQUES**
Box 1026   99669
901 262-4297   Est: 1975
Proprietor: Susie Keating
Hours: by chance
Types & Periods: Glass,
China, Copper, Primitives &
Furniture
Directions: In center of
town directly behind Nat'l
Bank of Alaska, in my
home (2 story tan house
with pillars), Farnsworth
Blvd

Willow

**KASHWITNA HOMESTEAD
STORE**
MILE 795 Anchorage-
Fairbanks Hwy   99688
Proprietor: Charles &
Thelma Brock
Hours: Mon-Sun,
May-Sept
Types & Periods: Bottles &
Collectibles

(Continued from page x)

Simultaneously with the pilgrims, the first prevalent period of furniture to be encountered is the Jacobean. This name refers to the time of James I (1566-1625) who followed Queen Elizabeth (1533-1603) on the throne of England. It is called Jacobean because James becomes Jacobus in Latin. The oak furniture of this period is characterized by unusally heavy proportions. It was extensively decorated with relief carving and "split turnings". Split turnings were made by shaping a piece of wood on a lathe, then cutting it lengthwise into half-sections or quarter-sections. Aside from tables, chairs and beds; there were coffer-type chests and wall cupboards. Clothes were kept on shelves in large cupboards, which solved one storage function since early houses were virtually without closets. The basic piece of furniture was the coffer chest which later evolved into the chest-of-drawers as we know it today. (See pages 42 & 43).

Canopy beds were developed in Jacobean times. The canopy was not for beauty's sake, but to keep out the night air. Cold drafts invaded the houses when fires died down in the fireplaces. Since most of the members of a family slept in one room, the canopy also provided at least some privacy for the occupants of the bed.

Chairs of this time were straight and very uncomfortable. Benches and stools were most commonly used for seating. During this period the "joint" stool was developed and remains popular today. (See page 9). Upholstery was used only by the wealthy because of limited availability and therefore very great cost. One finds needlepoint, velvet, brocades and leather being used in upholstering. Chairs in the average houshold had only rush, cane or ordinary board seats. Rush was woven from swamp plants such as the cattail. Cane seats were also woven by using split, wood-like materials. Of course, the easiest way was to merely attach a board or plank. These boards were sometimes shaped by handwork into a concaved saddle effect to conform more comfortably to one's natural shape.

It was during the Jacobean period that the "gate leg" table was developed. Gatelegs are unique in that the swinging leg which supports the dropleaf is braced like a gate at both the bottom and top. This is in opposition to the usual "swing leg" table which has no stretcher, or brace, across the bottom. (See page 74).

The Jacobean style had a resurgence of popularity in the 1920's and was manufactured in large quantities. As a result, a lot of the Jacobean in antique shops today is not the 17th, but of the 20th Century. One must learn to look Continued on page 24)

STATE OF ARIZONA

Chandler

SUDEE'S ANTIQUES
809 N Arizona Ave   85224
602 963-6901   Est: 1965
Proprietor: SuDee Burris
Hours: Winter: Mon-Fri,
11-5; Summer: 10-2; Other
by appt
Types & Periods: General
Line of Furniture, China,
Clocks, Silver, Pewter,
Copper & Brass
Specialties: Copper & Brass
Appraisal Service Available
Directions: Main St of
Chandler

Eloy

**MYERS PICACHO PEAK
ANTIQUES**
Box 835   85231
602 466-3793
Proprietor: Robert J Myers
Hours: Tues-Sun, 8-6
Types & Periods: General
Line, Carnival Glass &
Primitives
Directions: I-10, Picacho
Peak Exit

Flagstaff

A-1 ANTIQUES
2001 N Main St   86001
602 774-2633   Est: 1971
Proprietor: Mr & Mrs
Oscar Maier
Hours: Mon-Sat, 9-6
Types & Periods: Primitives,
Lamps, Wagon Wheels &
Oak Furniture
Specialties: Refinishing
Furniture
Directions: 4 blocks N of
Hwy 66, in East Flagstaff
(Greenlaw Area)

SIERRA TREASURES
2708 N 4th St   86001
602 526-3695   Est: 1976
Proprietor: Gloria
Aguinaga
Hours: Mon-Sat, 10-5:30
Types & Periods: General
Line, Furniture & Glassware

Directions: Between K
Mart & Cedar Pines
Shopping Center on 4th St
in E Flagstaff

Glendale

THE OLD OR ODD SHOP
6828 Grand Ave   85001
602 939-9211
Hours: Tues-Sat, 10-5
Types & Periods: Glass,
China, Brass, Furniture &
Primitives

Mesa

BROWN HOUSE ANTIQUES
141 W 1st Ave   85201
602 969-5823
Proprietor: Donna
Johnson
Hours: Mon thru Wed, Fri
& Sat, 11-5
Types & Periods: Period
furniture, signed art glass,
porcelain, Bronze, Dolls &
toys.
Directions: 1 blk S of
Main. 2 blks E of Country
Club Rd

COLLECTOR'S CORNER
919 E Broadway   85203
602 969-0081   Est: 1961
Proprietor: Maxine Lines
Hours: Winter: Mon-Fri,
11-5, Sat 11-3; Summer:
10-2; Later by appt
Types & Periods: American
& English Primitives, Pine
Furniture, Clocks, General
Line of Colored Glass & Fine
Porcelains
Specialties: Copper, Brass,
Wood, Lamps & Clocks
Appraisal Service Available
Directions: Broadway,
between Horne & Stapley

**FLORENCE'S UNIQUE
COUNTRY ANTIQUES**
910 W Broadway   85202
602 969-0654   Est: 1956
Proprietor: Florence &
Ralph Welekle
Hours: Mon-Sat, 9-5:30;
Sun 12-5:30

Types & Periods: Primitives
& Oak & Country Furniture
Specialties: Furniture
Appraisal Service Available
Directions: 15 miles E of
Phoenix

**JACK'S COINS, CURRENCY
& ANTIQUES**
6826 E Main St   85207
602 985-6381   Est: 1968
Proprietor: Jack &
Blossom Schumm
Hours: Tues-Sat, 9-5
Types & Periods: Small
Items, China, Cut Glass &
Silver
Appraisal Service Available
Directions: Corner of Bush
Hwy & Main St; or Hwy 60
& 70

KILEY'S ANTIQUES
1547 W University   85201
602 969-1666   Est: 1969
Proprietor: Billie L Kiley
Hours: by appt or by
chance
Types & Periods: General
Line, Collectibles & Rampant
Nostalgia
Appraisal Service Available

RED SLEIGH ANTIQUES
9536 E Apache Tr   85207
602 986-1856   Est: 1964
Proprietor: Al Odegard
Hours: By Appointment
Mon-Wed, Fri-Sat, 10-5
Types & Periods: Glassware,
Furniture, Jewelry, Primitives
& Clocks
Specialties: Furniture
Directions: US 60 & 96th
St, 15 miles E. of Mesa

Phoenix

PHOENIX CLUSTER
Directions: N 7th St
(1000-6000 block), E
Indian School Rd
(900-9000 block), E
Camelback Rd (700-900
block)

THE ANTIQUARY
3044 N 24th St   85016
602 955-8881   Est: 1969
Proprietor: Grant & Betty
Zimmerman
Hours: Mon-Fri, 10-5; Sat
10-6
Types & Periods: Furniture,
Glass, China, Pottery,
Primitives, Paper Americana
& Collector Items

**BANKER'S SECOND HAND
STORE**
1309 E Van Buren   85006
602 253-5010   Est: 1960
Proprietor: Edward Reed,
Jr
Hours: Mon-Sat, 9-5
Types & Periods: All types
of Furniture & Glassware

BOBBI'S ANTIQUES
3838 N 7th St   85012
602 279-7768   Est: 1968
Proprietor: L E & Bobbie
Phillips
Hours: Tues-Sat, 10-5
Types & Periods: Furniture,
Glass, China, Jewelry, Oak,
Art Glass & Primitives
Appraisal Service Available
Directions: Come off Frwy
at 7th St exit & go N
approximately 3 miles

ANN CLARK SHOWCASE
2927 N 24th St   85016
602 955-7580   Est: 1947
Proprietor: Ann Clark
Hours: Daily
Types & Periods: Furniture,
Oil Paintings, Glassware &
Old Indian Jewelry & Rugs
Specialties: Indian Jewelry
Appraisal Service Available

**CLASSIC CARRAIGE
HOUSE**
5552 E Washington 85034
602 275-6825   Est: 1958
Proprietor: Russ & Brian
Jackson
Hours: Mon-Sat
Types & Periods: Antique,
Classic & Collectible Cars
Directions: 5 minutes from
Phoenix Internat'l Airport

THE 4 WALLS
417 E Roosevelt St 85004
602 253-7180   Est: 1978
Proprietor: James & Ruth
Algis

Hours: Tues-Sat, 10-5 &
by appt
Types & Periods: European
Paintings, Watercolors,
Prints Decorative
Accessories & Old Frames
Specialties: Wholesale &
Retail
Directions: Corner of N
5th & E Roosevelt

THE GLASS URN
5235 N 7th St   85014
602 274-1712   Est: 1971
Proprietor: Fran
McClendon
Hours: Mon-Sun
Types & Periods: General
Line
Specialties: Glass: Pattern,
Cut, Etched & Engraved
Appraisal Service Available
Directions: 3 blocks N of
Camelback

THE JUNQUE SHOP
2021 E Washington 85034
602 254-8204
Proprietor: John &
Barbara Williams
Hours: Mon-Fri, 10-3; Sat
10-1
Types & Periods: Furniture,
Iron, Copper, Brass, Silver,
Glass, China

KAY'S ANTIQUES
2545 W Northern Avenue
85021
602 995-1187   Est: 1974
Proprietor: K M Chapman
Hours: Mon-Sat, 10-5:
July-Sept by chance
Types & Periods: Depression
Glass, Victorian, Oak &
Collectibles
Specialties: Depression
Glass
Appraisal Service Available
Directions: 1 block W of
Black Canyon Frwy on
Northern Ave

LILLIAN'S ANTIQUES
609 W Osborn Rd   85013
602 279-9619   Est: 1967
Proprietor: Lillian & Ben
Feiler
Hours: Mon-Sat, 10-6
Types & Periods: Furniture,
Jewelry, Clocks, Watches,
China, Glassware, Books &
Dolls

Specialties: Watches, Cut
Glass & Jewelry.
Directions: Between
Thomas Rd & Indian
School Rd

MARGARET'S ANTIQUES
2521 W Northern   85021
602 995-0449   Est: 1962
Proprietor: J D Dickens
Hours: Mon-Sun
Types & Periods: Complete
Line
Directions: Corner of W
Northern Ave & Blacy
Canyon Hwy, which is I-17
N

**PHOENIX LAMPS &
ANTIQUES**
2225 E Indian School Rd
85016
602 955-5640   Est: 1946
Proprietor: Olney & Naomi
Craig
Hours: Mon-Sun, 9-5
Types & Periods: Lamps,
China, Glass, Art Objects,
Furniture, Chimneys & Ball
Shades (Reproductions)
Specialties: Gone With The
Wind, Tiffany type Lamps &
Lamp parts
Appraisal Service Available
Directions: between Indian
School & Scottsdale Rd

POCKET KNIFE SWAPPER
3514 S Central Ave 85041
602 268-4561   Est: 1974
Proprietor: Roger K Emery
Hours: By appt & by
chance
Types & Periods: Collector
Pocket Knives, Edged
Weapons & other small
items
Appraisal Service Available
Directions: 1 mile S of I-10

RED HOUSE ANTIQUES
914 E Camelback Rd
85018
602 265-7795
Hours: Mon-Sat, 10-5
Types & Periods: General
Line
Specialties: Primitives

**SADIES QUILTS &
ANTIQUES**
914 E Camelback Rd
85014
602 274-5775   Est: 1973
Proprietor: Sadie Haines

Phoenix   Cont'd

SADIES QUILTS   Cont'd

Hours: Mon-Sat
Types & Periods: General
Line
Specialties: Embroidery &
Needlework (Quilts)
Directions: In the Camelot
Building

THE SELECTIVE SALVAGE COMPANY

1651 E. Camelback Rd
85016
602 265-2850   Est: 1975
Proprietor: Danny
Alspach, Linda Shore
Hours: Mon-Sat, 10-5;
Sun, 12-5
Types & Periods: American
Oak & Pine Furniture,
stained glass & antique
hardware, decorative wood
& metal
Specialties: Printer's
Drawers, antique wooden
type & copper printing
plates.
Directions: adjacent to
greenhouse at rear of
Berridge Nursery.

SEVENTH STREET SHOPPE

1510 N 7th St   85006
602 252-1069   Est: 1962
Proprietor: Verna Drosky
Hours: Daily, 9-5
Types & Periods: Cut Glass
& Antique Furniture
Specialties: Furniture &
Glass

STUFF ANTIQUES

407 E Roosevelt   85004
602 252-0612   Est: 1969
Proprietor: Joe & Robbie
Weaver
Hours: Sept-May: Sat only
10-5; June-Aug: Tues-Sat,
10-5
Types & Periods: Tiffany &
Tiffany Type Lamps, Stained
Glass, Lamp Restoration &
Stained Glass Repair
Appraisal Service Available
Directions: Downtown
near Civic Center

SYLVIAS' DOLLS & ANTIQUES

3602 N 24th St   85016
602 957-0545

Hours: Mon-Fri, 9:30-2:30;
Sat 9:30-5; Also by
appointment
Types & Periods: Miniatures,
Primitives & Furniture
Specialties: Dolls

THOSE WERE THE DAYS

4628 E Van Buren   85008
602 267-0453   Est: 1973
Hours: Mon-Sun
Types & Periods: Golden
Oak Era, Advertising &
Leaded Lamps & Windows
Appraisal Service Available
Directions: From I-10, 48th
St exit N to Van Buren,
then 2 blocks W

TOY COTTAGE ANTIQUES

4242 N 7th Ave   85013
602 274-3731   Est: 1951
Proprietor: George & June
Bradbury
Hours: Daily
Types & Periods: English,
American & Oriental
Furniture & Accessories;
General Line.
Specialties: Oriental
Furniture
Appraisal Service Available
Directions: Between Indian
School Rd & Camelback

UNEEDA ANTIQUES

931 E Indian School 85014
602 279-2488   Est: 1974
Proprietor: Rick & Sharon
Hamilton
Hours: Mon-Sat, 11-5:30
Types & Periods: Oak &
Wicker Furniture, Country
Store & Advertising Items
Specialties: Coca Cola
Advertising
Appraisal Service Available
Directions: Centrally
located; only 12 minutes
from Scottsdale & Tempe

UPTOWN ANTIQUES

4411 N 7th St   85014
602 266-6105
Proprietor: Frank Donnelly
& John Sullivan
Hours: Mon-Sat, 10-5
Types & Periods: Brass
Beds, Beer Steins, Oriental
Rugs & Bric-A-Brac
Specialties: China &
Furniture

UPTOWN ANTIQUES

809 N 13th Ave   85006
602 266-2049
Proprietor: F J Donnelly &
J J Sullivan
Hours: Wed-Sat, 10-4
Types & Periods: China,
Furniture, Bric-A-Brac &
Oriental Rugs

Prescott

AMERICA'S ATTIC

235 N Pleasant   86301
602 445-0212   Est: 1963
Proprietor: Terrel Hohman
Hours: Daily, by chance
Types & Periods: Estate
Objects & Collectibles
Appraisal Service Available
Directions: 4 blocks E
from center of town

PAUL-MAR ANTIQUES

346 S Montezuma   86301
602 445-0606   Est: 1968
Proprietor: Paul V DeVore
Hours: Daily
Types & Periods: Victorian
Furniture, China & Clocks
Specialties: China: Flow
Blue
Appraisal Service Available
Directions: State Rte 89, 3
blocks S of Court House

Scottsdale

ANTIQUES FOREVER

7019 Main St   85251
602 945-4171   Est: 1975
Proprietor: Kathy Harris
Hours: Mon-Sat, 10-5.
Types & Periods: General
line, Turn-of-century Oak
Specialties: Oak furniture,
ice boxes, roll-top desks
Appraisal Service Available
Directions: Main St, 2
blocks W of Scottsdale Rd

ATTIC ANTIQUITY

4017 N 69th St   85251
602 945-0825
Hours: Daily
Types & Periods: General
Line of Furniture, Glass &
China

BULLOCK'S ANTIQUES
4300 Craftsman's Ct 85251
602 994-5147
Proprietor: Mrs Fred
Bullock
Hours: Mon-Sat, 12-5
Types & Periods: Silver,
Brass, Oriental Objects,
Porcelain & Furniture

THE CLOISTERS
7040 Fifth Ave   85251
602 994-9359   Est: 1972
Proprietor: Dick Paine
Hours: Mon-Sat, 10-6;
Closed Mon, June-Sept
Types & Periods: General
Line, 18th-Early 20th
Century Furniture, Art Glass
& Pottery
Directions: NE corner Fifth
Ave & 70th St

**JOANNA'S ANTIQUE
BOUTIQUE**
7125 Main St   85251
Est: 1969
Proprietor: Joanna
Guilmette
Hours: Mon-Sat,
10:30-5:30, & by appt.
Types & Periods: American,
European & Oriental
Miniatures, Bronze, Silver,
Cut Glass, China & Jewelry
Specialties: Glass
Directions: In the heart of
Old Town Scottsdale

**JOANNA LOKEY ANTIQUE
FURNITURE**
7000 5th Ave   85251
602 994-0010   Est: 1975
Hours: Mon-Sun, 10-5;
also by appointment
Types & Periods: English,
French & Rare Americana &
17th to turn of century
Antique Chinese Porcelain
Specialties: Orientals
Directions: Heart of
Scottdale's 5th Ave shops

**MARSHA'S GIFTS OF THE
MOST UNUSUAL**
7121 5th Ave   85251
602 946-0141   Est: 1958
Proprietor: Marsha de
Berge
Hours: Tues-Sat, 10-5
Types & Periods: Oriental
Art Objects, Bronzes, Jade,
Cloisonne, Porcelains &
Ivories
Directions: Kiva Craft
Center

REDDY'S ANTIQUES
7091 5th Ave   85251
602 946-0381   Est: 1965
Proprietor: Dennis M
Fritch
Hours: Winter: Mon-Sat,
10-5; Summer: Mon-Sat,
10-4
Types & Periods: Pre-1900,
General Line
Specialties: Jewelry Glass &
Porcelain
Appraisal Service Available
Directions: Next to Trader
Vic's

**THE ROSEMARY ANTIQUE
SHOP**
Box 115   85251
Est: 1937
Proprietor: Avie Kalker
Hours: by appt
Types & Periods: General
Line
Specialties: Glass & China;
Research & Finders Service
Appraisal Service Available

ROSE TREE ANTIQUES
6901 First St   85251
602 946-8874   Est: 1975
Proprietor: Rose
Delmonico
Hours: Tues & Sat or
anytime by appt
Types & Periods: Victorian,
Early American, China,
Glass, Crystal, Art & Art
Objects
Directions: Corner of 69th
St & 1st St, next to
Ramada Inn

SURREY ANTIQUES
7014 First Ave   85251
602 947-6663   Est: 1970
Proprietor: Ruth E
Lownsbury
Hours: Tues-Sat, 10-5
Types & Periods: American
& European Furniture,
China, Porcelain, Glass,
Silver, Brass & Clocks
Appraisal Service Available
Directions: Two blocks W
of N Scottsdale Rd & 1
block S of Indian School
Rd

**YE OLDE CURIOSITY
SHOPPE**
7245 E. First Ave   85251
602 947-3062   Est: 1964
Proprietor: Evelyn Doyer
Hours: Mon-Sat, 10:30-5

Types & Periods: Victorian
Jewelry, 1850-1940 Glass,
Antique Dolls, Post Cards &
Antique Clothing &
Accessories (1850 & Up)
Specialties: Antique clothing
Appraisal Service Available
Directions: Old Town
Scottsdale

Sedona

THE ANTIQUE GALLERY
89A & 179 Hwys, Box 20
86336
602 282-5874   Est: 1975
Proprietor: Marilyn A
Reynolds
Hours: Daily
Types & Periods: Victorian &
Western American Furniture,
Clocks, Silver, Cut Glass &
Collectibles
Specialties: Nippon,
Staffordshire & Oak
Furniture
Appraisal Service Available
Directions: At the ''Y''
upstairs in the Hayloft

THE DELIGHTFUL MUDDLE
PO Box 967   86336
602 282-4343   Est: 1968
Proprietor: Zoula N Foley
Hours: Sun-Fri, 11-5
Types & Periods: Jewelry,
Silver & General Line, circa
1850-1910
Specialties: Jewelry
Appraisal Service Available
Directions: At the ''Y'' at
Hwys 179 & 89A

ESTEBAN'S
Tlaquepaque   86336
602 282-4686   Est: 1974
Proprietor: Steve & Nancy
Scagnelli
Hours: Tues-Sun, 10-5
Types & Periods: Pine &
Golden Oak Primitives
Directions: Tlaquepaque
Shopping Complex on
Hwy 179, space 102 & 103

**HOUSE OF TRASH &
TREASURE**
211 Jordan Rd   86336
602 282-5512   Est: 1975
Proprietor: Maj D E
Williams USMC, retired
Hours: Mon-Sun

HOUSE OF TRASH & TREASURE   Cont'd
Types & Periods: Depression Glass, Small Furniture, Kitchen Items & Farm Primitives
Specialties: Arms & Armor (Militaria: US & Foreign)
  Directions: Located behind the Arizona Bank

THINGS UNLIMITED
Box 453   86336
602 282-7413   Est: 1962
Proprietor: Viola V Johnson
Hours: Mon-Sat, 10-5; Sun 1-5
Types & Periods: Furniture, Lamps & Glassware
Specialties: Glass, Furniture & Toy Train Items
  Directions: I-17, 15 miles NW of Sedona cut off

Tempe

REVERIE ANTIQUES
516 Mill Ave   85281
602 967-4729   Est: 1970
Hours: Mon-Sun
Types & Periods: Oak Furniture, Stained Glass Windows, Architectural & Wicker
  Directions: I-10 to 48th St N exit, N to University then E on Mill Ave, 3 blocks N

Thatcher

RED LAMP ANTIQUES
313 Main St   85552
602 428-3382   Est: 1963
Proprietor: Bill Swift & R.D. Coffey
Hours: Mon-Sat
Types & Periods: General Line
Specialties: Ceramics & China (Wedgwood, Belleek & Meissen)
  Directions: 3 miles W of Safford on US 70

Tucson

TUCSON CLUSTER
Directions: Heavy concentration on E Speedway Blvd (200-4000 block), adjacent streets N Country Club Rd (300 block), E Broadway (2000 block), intersected by N Stone Ave (1000-2000 block)

ANTIQUE FURNITURE GALLERY
1045 N Jerrie Blvd   85711
602 327-6441   Est: 1957
Proprietor: Halden E Birt
Hours: Mon-Sat, 10-5
Types & Periods: 18th & 19th Century, Art & Cut Glass & Bric-A-Brac
Specialties: Glass
Appraisal Service Available
  Directions: 1 block E of Columbus & 1 block S of Speedway

ANTIQUE PATCHWORK QUILTS
P.O. Box 42964   85733
602 793-8714
Proprietor: Marcia Spark
Hours: by appt
Types & Periods: Quilts, Hooked Rugs & Folk Art

ELEGANT JUNK SHOP
2828 N Stone Ave   85705
602 622-8773   Est: 1972
Proprietor: Mr & Mrs Wayne Olson
Hours: Mon-Sat, 10:00-5:30
Types & Periods: General Line
Specialties: "Fun shop to look around"
  Directions: Freeway, E on Grant & N on Stone Ave

HAYDEN'S DISTINCTIVE FURNITURE CO
3305 N Freeway   85703
602 888-5000   Est: 1946
Proprietor: Ken Hayden, FASID
Hours: Mon-Sat, 9:30-5:30
Types & Periods: 17th & 18th Century English, Spanish & Italian Furniture, "We buy in Europe and do our own importing"

Specialties: Furniture
Appraisal Service Available
  Directions: Prince Rd exit off I-10

LASTENIA'S ANTIQUES
2550 N Stone   85705
602 622-1194   Est: 1956
Proprietor: James H & Mary L Madison
Hours: Mon-Sun, 10-5:30
Types & Periods: Furniture, Glass, China & Books
Specialties: China, Glass & Silver
Appraisal Service Available
  Directions: W Tucson; 2 1/2 blocks N of Grant Rd

KAY MALLEK ANTIQUES
1208 N Alvernon Way
                          85712
602 326-1642   Est: 1947
Proprietor: Kay Mallek
Hours: Mon-Sat
Types & Periods: Full line including collectibles
Specialties: Christmas Plates & Navajo Items
Appraisal Service Available
  Directions: Central Tucson

KAY MALLEK ANTIQUES NO 2
3644 E Ft Lowell Rd
602 327-6118
Proprietor: Kay Mallek
Types & Periods: Full line including collectibles
  Directions: In Rams Shopping Center

KAY MALLEK ANTIQUES NO 3
6541 E Tanque Verde Rd
                          85715
Proprietor: Kay Mallek
Types & Periods: Commemoritive Plates only

NETTIE'S TREASURES
217 E Congress   85702
602 624-9051   Est: 1969
Proprietor: Nettie Frazier
Hours: Mon-Sun, 10:30-6; also by appt
Types & Periods: Glass, China, Pictures, Jewelry, Imports & Collectors Items
Specialties: Glass
  Directions: Downtown between 5th & 6th Ave

OPPORTUNITY HOUSE
445 E Prince Rd   85705
602 887-5761   Est: 1954
Proprietor: Alice Bronson
Hours: Oct-May: Mon-Sun
Types & Periods: General Line, Antique Lamps & Crystal
Appraisal Service Available

BARBARA SKILTON'S ANTIQUES
119 E Wetmore Rd 85705
602 887-2140   Est: 1958
Proprietor: Barbara Skilton
Hours: Mon-Sat
Types & Periods: General Line
Specialties: Carnival Glass
Appraisal Service Available
Directions: 2 blocks N of Roger Rd, between First Ave & Oracle

PHYLISS C SPAGNOLA
1918 E Prince Rd   85719
602 326-5712   Est: 1962
Proprietor: Phyliss C Spagnola
Hours: Mon-Sun
Types & Periods: China, Indian Jewelry & Small Furniture
Specialties: Ceramics, China & Glass
Appraisal Service Available
Directions: near Campbell Rd

West Sedona

THE SAWMILL ANTIQUES
3173 W Hwy 89A   86340
602 282-5804   Est: 1969
Proprietor: L Tifft & E Bertalan
Hours: Mon-Sun
Types & Periods: General line, Glass, China, Pottery, Silver, Furniture, Primitives & Collectibles
Appraisal Service Available
Directions: 3 miles W of Downtown Sedona

Wickenburg

NANCY'S TRADING POST & ANTIQUES
596 Whipple   85358
602 684-7005   Est: 1973
Proprietor: Nancy L Dorgan
Hours: Daily
Types & Periods: General Line, Leaded Shades, Tools, Wooden Indians, Souvenirs, Primitives, Bottles & Glass
Specialties: Indian Jewelry & Crafts
Appraisal Service Available
Directions: Hwy 60 W of town

THE PLUM TREE
1001 Whipple   85358
602 684-7418   Est: 1972
Proprietor: Myrtis Pierson
Hours: Mon-Sun
Types & Periods: Furniture, Clocks & Bric-A-Brac
Appraisal Service Available
Directions: Hwy 80 W

THE WOODSHED
Box 999 (Moonlight Mesa)   85358
602 684-7221   Est: 1973
Proprietor: Sally Bassett
Hours: Sept-June: Sun-Tues, by appt & Wed-Sat, 10-6; July-Aug by chance
Types & Periods: Furniture, Clocks, Primitives & Mid 19th Century & WW II Advertising
Appraisal Service Available
Directions: 4 1/2 miles N on Hwy 89, right 1/2 mile past Milepost 256, 1 mile to shop

Yuma

ART'S PAWNS & ANTIQUES
2255 4th Ave   85364
602 782-4693   Est: 1974
Proprietor: Art & Goldie Smart
Hours: Mon-Sun by appt; Closed Sat during Summer
Types & Periods: General Line
Directions: Off Interstate 8

SHERMAN'S ANTIQUES & COLLECTIBLES
600 Orange Ave   85364
602 783-8913   Est: 1975
Proprietor: Wayne Sherman
Hours: Mon-Fri, 12-5:30; Sat, 10-6
Types & Periods: Furniture, particularly Oak; primitives, pressed & depression glass
Appraisal Service Available
Directions: 1 blk off 4th Ave (Hwy 80), corner of 6th St & Orange

To smooth by hand plane

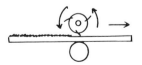

TOOL MARKS

To smooth by machine

STATE OF ARKANSAS

Alexander

SCHROEDER'S ANTIQUES, INC
Rte 2, Box 486   72002
501 847-3542   Est: 1945
Proprietor: Carl & Mary Bea Schroeder
Hours: Tues-Sat, 8:30-5; Sun 2-5; Closed Mon
Types & Periods: European & American Furniture, Clocks, General Line
Specialties: April & Sept Auctions, Fri-Sat
Appraisal Service Available
Directions: 12 Miles W of Little Rock on Hwy 67

Bald Knob

CASH DISCOUNT ANTIQUES
67 Hwy N   72010
501 724-5741   Est: 1971
Proprietor: W C & Omah Pearrow
Hours: Mon-Sat, 9-5; Sun 1-5
Types & Periods: General Line, Furniture, Glass
Directions: Hwy N in City

Batesville

MARGARET'S ANTIQUES
Box 2757   72501
501 793-5268   Est: 1961
Proprietor: Margaret Miller
Hours: Daily
Types & Periods: Art, Cut & Pressed Glass, Silver, Pictures, Primitives, Victorian & American Empire Furniture, China
Specialties: Cut Glass & China
Appraisal Service Available
Directions: 2 Miles S of Batesville on Hwy 167 S

Benton

DEN OF ANTIQUITY
409 Algood   72015
501 778-3203   Est: 1968
Proprietor: Mae Reeves
Hours: Weekends; Week Days By Chance
Types & Periods: All Types of Glass & China; Some Furniture
Specialties: Lamps
Directions: East Side of Downtown Benton

Bentonville

PERSIAN MARKET
807 NW 2nd St   72712
501 273-3138   Est: 1971
Proprietor: Mrs J D Thornton
Hours: Daily
Types & Periods: China, Copper, Brass, Pewter; Prior to 1842 to Present
Specialties: Metalwork
Directions: One Block N and One Block E of 4-Way Stop on Hwy 71 Going N From Bentonville

Blytheville

BOB WHITE'S ANTIQUES
1533 N 61 Hwy   72315
501 763-7112   Est: 1972
Proprietor: Bob White
Hours: Mon-Sat; Closed Sun
Types & Periods: Victorian, Queen Anne, Chippendale, Early Oak & Wicker, Some Primitives, General Line
Specialties: Furniture
Appraisal Service Available
Directions: First Blytheville Exit Off I-55, Stay on Hwy 61 N, In City Limits

Brinkley

CAMP ANTIQUE SALES
Hwy 17 N   72021
501 734-4304   Est: 1964
Proprietor: Mr & Mrs H L Camp
Hours: Daily
Types & Periods: General Line of Furniture & Glass
Specialties: Cut Glass & Crystal
Appraisal Service Available
Directions: 1/4 Mile N of I-40 on Hwy 17

Carlisle

COOK'S ANTIQUE HOUSE
221 Court St   72024
501 552-3761   Est: 1973
Proprietor: Rose Cook
Hours: Mon-Sat, 9-5; Closed Sun; Also By Appointment
Types & Periods: General Line, Art Glass, Depression Glass, Pottery, Books, Primitives, Curios
Specialties: Glass
Directions: Between I-40 & Hwy 70 on Hwy 13; 'Large Old House Full of Memories'

MILLER'S ANTIQUES
221 Center   72024
501 552-7716   Est: 1959
Proprietor: C C Miller
Hours: Daily; By Appointment; By Chance
Types & Periods: Furniture, Glass, China, Lamps, Primitives
Specialties: China
Directions: Six Blocks E of Hwy 13

Conway

ANTIQUES IN THE RED BARN
I-40 & Hwy 64   72032
501 329-9608   Est: 1973
Proprietor: Frank & Jane Lambert
Hours: Mon-Sat, 10-5:30; Sun 1-5:30; Also By Appointment
Types & Periods: Primitives, Farm Equipment & General Line

Specialties: Furniture
Directions: Exit 127, I-40,
behind Ramada Inn at
Conway

DeWitt

GALLERY 'G' ANTIQUES
200 Court Square   72042
501 946-2593   Est: 1967
Proprietor: Mrs Leon J
Garat
Hours: Daily, 8:30-5:30
Types & Periods: Cut Glass
Brilliant Period, R S Prussia,
Art Glass, China, Furniture,
Silver
Specialties: Glass, Jewelry
Directions: 25 Miles S of
Stuttgart, on Hwy 11 on
The Square

Eureka Springs

OLIVE ELLIS ANTIQUES
73 Spring St   72632
501 253-9893
Proprietor: Olive Ellis
Hours: Daily, 8-4
Types & Periods: Pattern
Glass, Bric-A-Brac, China,
General Line

Fayetteville

POPPA BEAR'S ANTIQUES
1430 S School   72701
501 521-4400   Est: 1972
Proprietor: Bruce & Rosa
Lee Lunsford
Hours: Mon-Sat, 9-5; Sun
By Appointment; Call
442-7629
Types & Periods: Victorian,
Oak & Walnut, Primitives,
Glass, Dishes, Silver, Brass,
Copper
Directions: Two Doors N
of Intersection of 15th St
& U S 71 S

Forrest City

CRICKET ON THE HEARTH
407 Cleveland   72325
501 633-2580   Est: 1972
Proprietor: Wm E Mills

Hours: Daily
Types & Periods: Period
Accessories
Directions: S Off I-40, S
on Washington St to
Cleveland, Turn E

Fort Smith

ELKINS ANTIQUES
714 Garrison   72901
501 783-9023   Est: 1966
Proprietor: Mr & Mrs
Woodrow Elkins
Hours: Daily, 9-5:30
Types & Periods: Carnival &
Cut Glass, Furniture
Directions: Downtown on
Main St

FERNE'S ANTIQUES
1704 S Houston   72901
501 646-3594   Est: 1962
Proprietor: Ferne Davis
Hours: Daily; Weekends;
'Call and I will be there'
Types & Periods: Lamps,
China, Glass, Marble Top
Furniture
Specialties: Ceramics,
China, Lamps
Directions: Just Off
270-271 S, Turn off
Fresco, Go 5-6 Blocks to
Jenny Lind, Right to First
St, Right Second Block on
Left, Houston

THE HOUSE OF TIME
Rte 4, Box 220   72901
501 646-9031   Est: 1966
Proprietor: George Brown
Hours: Daily
Types & Periods: Clocks,
Mantle, Kitchen, Wall &
Grandfather, 'All at least 50
years old'
Specialties: Pocket Watches
Appraisal Service Available
Directions: 1/2 Mile E of
Oklahoma Arkansas Line
on Hwy 271

Greenland

HANK'S TRADING POST
PO Box 70   72737
501 442-6991   Est: 1968
Proprietor: Henry H Miller
Hours: Daily & Weekends,
8-5

Types & Periods: All Types
Glass, Primitives, Tools,
Bottles; 'Largest Selection of
78 rpm Records in Area, All
Catalogued'
Directions: U S HWY 71 S
of Fayetteville, Two miles
at the Blinking Hwy Light

Hardy

MR CHRISTOPHER SHOP
Main Street   72542
501 856-3688   Est: 1972
Proprietor: Herman E
Benton
Hours: Mon-Sat, 10-5; Sun
1-5
Types & Periods: Porcelain,
Depression Glass, Primitives,
Bottles, Beer Cans, Pattern
Glass, Furniture, Quilts,
Handcrafts and Gifts
Specialties: Bottles,
Ceramics, Glass
Appraisal Service Available

Harrison

DESMOND'S ANTIQUES
US 62-65   72601
Proprietor: Mrs R M
Desmond
Hours: Daily, 9-5
Types & Periods: General
Line, Furniture, Glass, China
Directions: Two miles S of
Harrison on US 62-65

Heber Springs

GWALTNEY'S, INC
Rte 4, Box 4   72543
501 362-3139   Est: 1974
Proprietor: Mary Gwaltney
Hours: Daily; 8-5 Except
Sun
Types & Periods: General
Line, Nippon, Depression,
Furniture
Specialties: Glass
Directions: Hwy 25 N,
Seven Blocks N of Main
St

Helena

EDELWEISS ANTIQUES
516 Cherry   72342
501 338-8031   Est: 1975
Proprietor: Martha Bieri
Hours: Mon-Fri, 10-5:30,
Sat 12-5
Types & Periods: Mostly
furniture dating from late
1700's to 1910, A lot of Oak
and English Imports
Specialties: Furniture
  Directions: Downtown
  Helena

Hope

**WORTHEY'S ANTIQUES
AND GIFTS**
Rte 4, Box 131A   71801
501 777-4837   Est: 1970
Proprietor: Mrs H F
Worthey
Hours: Daily
Types & Periods: Mostly
Glass
Specialties: Depression
Glass
  Directions: Hwy 4 N 2 1/2
  Miles N of I-30

Hot Springs

RUBYE BARBER
P O Box 521   71901
501 623-5788   Est: 1963
Proprietor: Dorothy
Sandeafer
Hours: Daily; Weekends;
9:30-5; After Hours By
Chance
Types & Periods: Jewelry,
Porcelain, Bronze, Cut Glass
Specialties: Silver
Appraisal Service Available
  Directions: Downtown

CLINTON'S ANTIQUES
112 Central Ave   71901
501 623-0216   Est: 1964
Proprietor: Janet E Clinton
Hours: Daily
Types & Periods: General
Line
Specialties: Haviland China
Appraisal Service Available

Directions: Hwy 7
becomes Central Ave in
Hot Springs; We are at the
Intersection of Whittington
Park & Central at Fountain

MAGGIE'S ANTIQUES
2914 Albert Pike   71901
501 767-3313   Est: 1972
Proprietor: Edward B
Holland
Hours: Mon-Sat, 8-4;
Cosed Sun
Types & Periods:
Collectibles, Furniture
  Directions: 1 Mile Past
  Junction of 70W & 270W,
  Stay on 270W, Right Side
  of Hwy

ROYAL ARMS GIFT SHOP
508 W Grand   71901
501 623-0918   Est: 1971
Proprietor: F W Pathmann
Jr
Hours: Mon-Sat,
Types & Periods: Jewelry,
Silver, Furniture
  Directions: Center of
  Town, Three Blocks W of
  Central Ave, (Main St) on
  Hwys 70 & 270

WATSON'S ANTIQUES
962 Airport Road   71901
501 767-2103   Est: 197l
Proprietor: Mr & Mrs
Aaron L. Watson
Hours: Mon-Sun; By
Appointment
Types & Periods: General
Line, Furniture, Glass,
China, Brass, Iron, Jewelry,
Depression Glass, Art Glass
Specialties: Furniture, Glass
  Directions: Hwy 70 W in
  Hot Springs

**YESTERDAY'S BOOKS,
ETC**
258 Whittington Ave 71901
501 624 2216   Est: 1974
Proprietor: Miss Rose
Edwards
Hours: Mon-Sat, 10-5
Types & Periods: Old and
Rare Books, Prints,
Postcards
Specialties: Free Book
Search Service, We
specialize in Arkansas Items;
Books mailed any place in
the U S

Directions: N on Central
Ave to Fountain in the
Center of Street, Turn Left
on Whittington, Go
approximately four Blocks

Jasper

THE PRIMITIVE HOUSE
Hwy 7   72641
501 446-2344   Est: 1968
Proprietor: Marian J
Velflick
Hours: By Chance
Types & Periods: Primitives;
Quilts
Specialties: Needlework,
Quilts
  Directions: 1 1/2 Blocks
  from Jasper Square on
  Hwy 7

Judsonia

**SCHRAND'S GIFTS AND
ANTIQUES**
Rte 2, Hwy 67 N   72081
501 729-3581   Est: 1955
Proprietor: Mr & Mrs
Claude Schrand
Hours: Daily; Weekends
Types & Periods: Glassware,
Dolls, Furniture, Jewelry,
Pottery
Specialties: Glass, Toys, &
Automata
  Directions: Three Miles N
  on Hwy 67

Keo

MORRIS ANTIQUES
Box 127   72083
501 842-3531   Est: 1968
Proprietor: Dean Morris
Hours: Wed-Sun, 12-5:30;
Closed Mon & Tues
Types & Periods: Victorian &
American Furniture,
Glassware, Primitives
  Directions: Three Blocks
  W off Hwy 130; 20
  Minutes from Little Rock

Lake Hamilton

DORA DAVIS' ANTIQUES
P O Box 315   71951
501 525-1381   Est: 1969
Proprietor: Dora Davis
Hours: Daily
Types & Periods: General
Line, Player Pianos,
Furniture
Specialties: Furniture
   Directions: Hwy 7 S Hot
   Springs, 1/2 Mile Past
   Lake Hamilton Post Office

Little Rock

LITTLE ROCK CLUSTER
Directions: Cluster of
Shops on Kavanaugh Blvd
(2000-5000 Block); Some
Shops on W 12
(2000-8000 Block)

ANTIQUE HOUSE
905 Autumn Road   72211
501 225-3696   Est: 1973
Proprietor: Paul E & Jane
Anne Emerson
Hours: Mon-Sat, 10-5:30
Types & Periods: 18th &
19th Century French,
English, & American
Furniture, Porcelain, Cut
Glass & Other Objects of Art
Appraisal Service Available
   Directions: Off Exit 6,
   I-430 to Kanis Road, West
   4/10 Mile to Autumn
   Road, Right on Autumn
   Road to Business

ANTIQUES LIMITED
8109 Cantrell Road 72207
501 227-7788   Est: 1976
Proprietor: Mrs H Leland
Gunn
Hours: Mon-Sat, 10-5
Types & Periods: 18th &
19th Century English
Antiques, Antique Jewelry,
Leather Books, Ivory,
Oriental Appointments,
Chinese Silk Embroidery,
Oriental Rugs,
Reproductions, Gifts &
Accessories
Specialties: Jewelry, English
Furniture
   Directions: 1 Mile East of
   I-430 at Cantrell Exit

BLACKBURN'S ANTIQUES
3608 Kavanaugh Blvd
                    72205
501 666-6862   Est: 1951
Proprietor: Mr & Mrs C R
Blackburn
Hours: Tues-Sat, 9:30-5;
Closed Sun & Mon
Types & Periods: Period
Furniture, Glassware, Art,
Cut & Pressed Glass, China,
Brass, Copper, Pewter, Oils,
Bric-a-Brac, Collectors Items
Specialties: Glasses &
Lamps
   Directions: 1 1/2 Blocks N
   of St Mary's Academy

FIELD'S SELECT ANTIQUES
Rte 5, Box 423B   72207
501 868-5124   Est: 1964
Proprietor: Frances Fields
Hours: Wed-Sat, 9:30-5
Types & Periods: Furniture,
Porcelain, Glass
Specialties: Furniture
Appraisal Service Available
   Directions: Three Miles W
   of I-430 on Hwy 10

FINDER'S KEEPER'S ANTIQUES
3610 Kavanaugh   72205
501 666-7945
Proprietor: Finkbeiner,
Finkbeiner, & Smith
Hours: Mon-Sat
Types & Periods: American
Primitives, 18th Century
English, Oriental
Appointments, Paintings,
Oriental Rugs

FINER THINGS COMPANY-ANTIQUES & ACCESSORIES
5110 Kavanaugh   72207
501 664-4793   Est: 1978
Proprietor: James L
Couch
Hours: Tues-Sat
Types & Periods: 18th &
19th Century English
Furniture, Antique &
Reproduction Gift Items
   Directions: North on
   Kavanaugh 2 Blocks from
   the Intersection of
   Kavanaugh & Hwy 10

KAYLIN'S ANTIQUE GALLERIES, INC
2917 Kavanaugh   72205
501 664-3728   Est: 1972

Proprietor: Dr & Mrs L R
Pyles
Hours: Mon-Sat, 10-5
Types & Periods: 18th &
19th Century Antique
Furniture, Art Glass, Cut
Glass, Silver, Porcelains,
Bronze, Russian Paintings
Appraisal Service Available
   Directions: Hillcrest
   Decorative Center, Spruce
   & Kavanaugh

KAZUKO ORIENTAL ARTS
2917 Kavanaugh Blvd
                    72205
501 663-6210   Est: 1966
Proprietor: Richard E
Boles
Hours: Mon-Sat, 10-5;
Closed Sun
Types & Periods: Oriental
Antiques Only
Specialties: Furniture,
Oriental
Appraisal Service Available
   Directions: In Hillcrest
   Antique & Decorator
   Center, Two Blocks From
   Mount St Mary's Academy

LAMPS-N-TIQUES
4325 W 12th   72204
501 663-3930   Est: 1975
Proprietor: Lois & Carl
Corley
Hours: Tues-Sat, 9-5
Types & Periods: American
Oak Furniture, American
Clocks, Lamps, General Line
Specialties: Antique Brass
Light Fixtures
   Directions: Four Blocks
   South and Four Blocks
   West Off Cedar St, Exit on
   I-630

LOCATOR'S, INC
908 Rock St   72202
                 Est: 1973
Types & Periods: A
Matching Registry For
American And English Out
Of Production China, Crystal
and Silver
Appraisal Service Available
   Directions: No Warehouse
   or Goods; All Mail Orders

QUEEN ANNE'S ANTIQUES
Rte 5, Box 443BB   72212
501 868-9144   Est: 1977
Proprietor: Julie Nelson &
Lois Morrissy

QUEEN ANNE'S   Cont'd

Types & Periods: American,
General Line of Antiques,
Furniture, Glassware
  Directions: Hwy 10, 3 1/2
  Miles West of I-430

Magnolia

**RALPH JENNINGS
AUCTION SERVICES INC**
  211 S Washington   71753
  501 234-1170   Est: 1968
  Proprietor: Ralph Jennings
  Hours: Antique Auctions
  Held Most Sat Nights-6
Types & Periods: American
Antique Furniture, Old
Glassware, Pottery,
Primitives
  Directions: One Block S of
  Magnolia's Square

Marvel

RED HOUSE ANTIQUES
  210 Midway Drive   72366
  501 829-3108   Est: 1971
  Proprietor: Roy-Leta
  Kemmer
  Hours: By Appointment;
  By Chance
Types & Periods: Oak,
Walnut, Victorian Furniture
Specialties: Cut Glass,
Antique Jewelry, RS Prussia
  Directions: 85 Miles SW
  Memphis, Tenn
  110 Miles E Little Rock
  Hwy 49

Mena

MONTEGA ANTIQUES
  Rte 3, Box 466   71953
  501 394-2062   Est: 1974
  Proprietor: Guy & Anna
  Mae DuVall
  Hours: Daily
Types & Periods: Furniture,
Primitives, Guns, Clocks
  Directions: U S 71 N 4
  Miles

Monticello

NELL GIBSON ANTIQUES
  314 S Main   71655
  501 367-2594   Est: 1956
  Proprietor: Nell Gibson
  Hours: Daily
Types & Periods: China,
Pressed & Cut Glass,
Furniture, Books, Prints
  Directions: Three Blocks S
  of Downtown

STUCKEY'S ANTIQUES
  849 N Main   71655
  501 367-5153   Est: 1967
  Proprietor: Mr & Mrs
  Monroe Stuckey
  Hours: By Chance
Types & Periods: General
Line

Mountain Home

THE OX YOKE
  R R 6, Box 110   72653
  501 492-5125   Est: 1960
  Proprietor: Margaret E
  Wilhm
  Hours: Daily except during
  Jan and Feb; Open by
  Appointment During Jan
  and Feb
Types & Periods: General
Line, Primitives, Furniture,
Cut & Pattern Glass, Paper
Goods, Especially Post
Cards
Appraisal Service Available
  Directions: Four Miles
  East of Mountain Home on
  Hwy 62 Toward Free Ferry
  Over Lake Norfork at
  Junction of Cranfield Road

Newport

**MINOR SHOPS, INC (Ye
Old Antiques)**
  111 Walnut   72112
       Est: 1972
  Proprietor: Mrs A F Minor
  Jr
  Hours: Mon-Sat, 10-5
Types & Periods: Oriental,
English Sheraton, Queen
Ann, Victorian, Early Attic
Primitives
  Directions: Two Blocks Off
  Hwy 67

PEDDLER'S ANTIQUES
  311 Laurel St   72112
  501 523-2186   Est: 1975
  Proprietor: Bea Crews
  Hours: Mon-Sat, 9-5: Sun
  By Appointment
Types & Periods: General
Line, American, Victorian
  Directions: 1/2 Block Off
  Hwy 67

North Little Rock

BETTY'S ANTIQUES
  1901 Main St   72114
  501 375-7051   Est: 1971
  Proprietor: Betty Berry
  Hours: 10-5; Open Sat
Types & Periods: Furniture,
China, Glass, Brass,
Accessories, Clocks,
Pictures, Mirrors
Specialties: Furniture
  Directions: 19 Blocks N of
  the Arkansas River

**COUNTRY STORE
JUNKTIQUES**
  3301 E Broadway   72114
  501 945-0780   Est: 1973
  Proprietor: Dorothy
  Fortner
  Hours: Mon-Sat, 10:30-5;
  Closed Sun
Types & Periods: 1885 to
1930 Oak Furniture,
Victorian Furniture, China,
Glass
Specialties: Primitives
  Directions: I-30 to
  Broadway Exit, Turn Right

HENSON'S ANTIQUES
  416 Remount Road   72116
  501 758-1426   Est: 1973
  Proprietor: Virginia & Max
  Henson
  Hours: Daily, Weekends,
  Sun & Wed, 1-5
Types & Periods: Depression
Glass, China Cabinets,
Furniture, Aladdin Lamps,
Collectibles
  Directions: Levy Exit Off
  I-40 in N Little Rock to
  Camp Robinson Rd; 3
  Miles N to Remount Rd; 1
  Mile N to Henson's
  Antiques

POT LUCK ANTIQUES
   4321 E Broadway   72117
   501 945-9968   Est: 1973
   Proprietor: Georgia
   Craig-Frances Jones
   Hours: Thurs-Sun
Types & Periods: Primitives,
Depression Glass, Oak
Furniture
Specialties: Primitives
   Directions: Rose City
   Section of N Little Rock

Paragould

**NINA'S ANTIQUES AND
GIFTS**
   1250 West Main   72450
   501 236-6213   Est: 1974
   Proprietor: Nina Martin
   Hours: Mon-Sun
Types & Periods: Early 18th
& 19th Century Small
Accent Pieces in Oak,
Walnut & Cherry
Specialties: Matching Crystal
or China in Discontinued
Patterns
Appraisal Service Available
   Directions: One Block
   East of Hwy 1 Bypass

Pine Bluff

THE HITCHING POST
   6305 Dollarway   71601
   501 247-1643
   Proprietor: Mary Stovall
   Hours: Tues-Sun, 9-5;
   Closed Mon
Types & Periods: General
Line

SISSY'S LOG CABIN INC
   4016 Mirimar   71601
   501 879-3040   Est: 1971
   Proprietor: Sissy Jones
   Hours: Mon-Sat
Types & Periods: Victorian
Furniture, Wicker, Glass,
Jewelry
Appraisal Service Available
   Directions: Hwy 79 S

Rogers

HOUSE OF VALUE
   Rte 3   72756
   Proprietor: Alice Durr
   Hours: Daily; except
   Closed from Dec 21 to
   April 1, By Chance Only
Types & Periods: General
Line
Specialties: Depression
Glass
   Directions: Six Miles N of
   Rogers on Hwy 62

Springdale

PAT'S ANTIQUES
   1506 Johnson Road 72764
   501 751-6703
   Proprietor: Pat Baskin
   Hours: Daily
Types & Periods: Early
American Country Furniture
& Accessories-17th & 18th
Century
Specialties: Unusual
Accessory Pieces
   Directions: Two Blocks Off
   Hwy 68 W on Johnson
   Road

Van Buren

PORTER'S ANTIQUES
   3912 Alma Hwy   72956
   501 474-3143   Est: 1960
   Proprietor: Thelma Porter
   Hours: Tues-Sat; Closed
   Sun & Mon
Types & Periods: Victorian,
Primitives, General Line
   Directions: Three Miles E
   on Hwy 64 & 71 N off I-40
   & I-540

West Fork

**PEDDLER'S WAGON
ANTIQUE SHOP**
   Rte 2, Box 207A   72774
   501 839-3301   Est: 1975
   Proprietor: Margaret
   Rogers
   Hours: Daily
Types & Periods: Small
Primitives, Bottles, Lamps,
Glassware & Some Furniture
Specialties: Primitives
   Directions: Located on U
   S Hwy 71 at North City
   Limit Sign of West Fork,
   Arkansas

West Memphis

BACK ROOM ANTIQUES
   205 S Worthington Dr
      72301
   501 735-1044
   Proprietor: Mildred F Fall
   Hours: Daily, 4-8; Other
   Hours By Appointment
Types & Periods: Furniture,
China, Glass, Bric-A-Brac

Bun foot,
Jacobean Period

Inverted Trumpet leg,
William & Mary Period

24

(Continued from page 11) for distinguishing characteristics to be able to determine from which century it is derived. One help in determining the age of a piece of furniture is to see if it was made by hand tools or mechanically powered tools. In the case of furniture, we think of the industrial revolution as beginning roughly between 1840 and 1860. In this period were introduced the basic woodworking machines found in cabinet shops today. The only real difference being that early machinery was powered by steam engines using belts, pulleys and shafts; whereas today's machinery is powered by electric motors. The marks left by these differently powered machine tools are identical. Therefore, one looks for tool marks to help in determining the age of a piece. Early furniture made prior to the industrial revolution would have different tool marks from that made after the use of machinery. To remove the saw marks after cutting a plank from the log, the early cabinetmaker would use a hand propelled smoothing plane. It would leave distinctive concave marks running with the length of the plank and parallel to the grain of the wood. Boards planed by the use of machinery will have concave marks running across the grain, or width, of the plank which denotes sharp rotating blades have created marks as they revolved during the act of smoothing the board. (See page 17).

Prior to the advent of decent glues, early cabinetmakers were known as "joiners" because of the way they put things together with various joints. Among others, lasting joints with no glue were made by the use of the mortise and tenon system. Such joints were pinned with a dowel, or peg, to secure them. (See page 9). Because of the mortise and tenon's strength, a very large number of 17th and 18th Century antiques are quite sound and usable today.

Cabinetmakers began making the "bun" foot to go on Jacobean furniture. The bun foot did not cease with that period, but continued on due to acceptability, familiarity and also the ease of making it. (See page 23). Communications were slow in that day, so new styles spread slowly. Regardless of the period being discussed here, one must remember that any given style will have persisted from its inception to the present day. Simply being of a certain style does not in itself date a piece. One must be able to establish a date based upon the method of joining, and whether there are hand tool or machine tool marks.

The relatively short William and Mary Period from 1689 to 1702 is the next strong influence on design. It was a time influenced

(Continued, page 63)

STATE OF CALIFORNIA

Anaheim

ANAHEIM CLUSTER
Directions: Heavy
concentration around
State College Area,
Orange & Glassel Circle;
Other Shops scattered
throughout City

Atwater

**BUSTAMENTE
ENTERPRISES INC**
5100 Crest Dr   95301
209 358-3134
Proprietor: Elias E
Bustamente
Hours: By Appointment
Types & Periods: General
Line
Specialties: Glass

Bakersfield

**BETTYS BARN OF
ANTIQUES**
4811 Marro Dr   93307
805 366-5620   Est: 1955
Proprietor: Betty Sadler
Hours: Wed-Sat, 1-5; Also
by Appointment
Types & Periods: Victorian
Furniture, Glassware, Silver,
Jewelry
Specialties: Furniture
(Victorian)
Appraisal Service Available
Directions: 1st St E off
Fairfax Exit on Frwy 58

CLEO'S ATTIC
1888 S Chester   93304
805 832-8202   Est: 1963
Proprietor: Cleo Foran
Hours: Thurs-Sat, by
Appointment
Types & Periods: Art Glass,
Furniture, Old Pattern Glass,
Porcelain
Specialties: Good Art Glass
Appraisal Service Available
Directions: Ming St off
ramp, Hwy 99, East to So
Chester; 1 Blk S

**CREATIVE ARTS &
ANTIQUES**
1101 S ' H' St   93304
805 834-1191   Est: 1974
Proprietor: Martha Brock
Hours: Mon-Sun, by
Appointment
Types & Periods: General
Line
Directions: From US 99
Take Ming Ave Off Ramp
E to H St Turn N

DR ANN'S ANTIQUES
305 S Chester   93304
803 831-0108   Est: 1950
Proprietor: Pat Johnson
Hours: Tues-Sat
Types & Periods: China,
Small Furniture, Primitives,
mostly 19th Century
Specialties: Early American
Pattern Glass
Appraisal Service Available
Directions: 3 Houses
South of Freeway 58 on
Chester

DUSTY TOMES
322 Chester Ave   93301
805 322-4814
Proprietor: Clara & Wm
Marr
Types & Periods: Books

EDISON ANTIQUES
2227 Edison Hwy   93307
805 322-6174   Est: 1965
Proprietor: L A Bliss & H
C Malouf
Hours: Daily
Types & Periods: Furniture,
Primitives, Glass, China,
Hanging Lamps, Leaded
Windows
Specialties: Phonographs &
Records
Directions: Hwy 58, 1 Block
E of Mt Vernon Overpass

GOLDBERG & LAND LTD
1514 18th St   93301
805 324-4444   Est: 1974
Proprietor: Shirley
Goldberg
Hours: Mon-Sat
Types & Periods: Victorian &
French Furniture
Specialties: Jewelry
Appraisal Service Available
Directions: Downtown

SAM'S
2491 Edison Hwy   93307
805 323-3798   Est: 1966
Proprietor: Sam Lelemsis
Hours: Tues-Sun, 10-6
Types & Periods: Victorian,
Turn of Century & Newer
Specialties: China Cabinets
Directions: Oswell off
ramp from Freeway 58 to
Edison; L on Edison 3
Blocks

Banning

FLEA MART
210 N San Gorgonio
                    92220
714 849-9014   Est: 1975
Proprietor: Dallas Lee
Hours: Mon-Sat, 9-5
Types & Periods: General
Line
Appraisal Service Available
Directions: Downtown
Banning

OLE'S ANTIQUE SHOP
255 E Ramsey   92220
714 849-6962   Est: 1966
Proprietor: Harry J Garten,
Sr
Hours: Mon-Sat
Types & Periods: Glassware,
Furniture, China, General
Line
Specialties: Restoration
Appraisal Service Available
Directions: Located on
Main St in Downtown
Banning on 110 & 60
Frwys

Beaumont

**THE GYPSY HOUSE
ANTIQUES**
507 E 6th St   92223
714 845-1827   Est: 1934
Proprietor: Iris D Meek
Hours: Tues-Sun,
Afternoons
Types & Periods: General
Line
Directions: Downtown,
Corner of Magnolia & 6th
St

Benecia

THE DIALS
190 West J St   94045
707 745-2552   Est: 1969
Proprietor: Ray Hackett,
George & Nola Theobald
Hours: Daily
Types & Periods: Clocks,
Music Boxes, Phonographs,
Records, Furniture
Specialties: Records, Discs,
Rolls
    Directions: Opposite the
    Post Office, I Block from
    the Main St

LUNDIN HOUSE
101 E J St   94510
707 745-1554   Est: 1947
Proprietor: Frieda Lundin
Hours: Mon-Sat, Sun by
Appointment
Types & Periods: Unusual
Jewelry, General Line
Specialties: Jewelry
Appraisal Service Available
    Directions: Corner 1st &
    East J

Berkeley

BERKELEY CLUSTER
Directions: Cluster of
Streets Bounded on North
by Solano, West by San
Pablo, East by Piedmont &
South by Grand; Look for
College Ave., MacArthur,
Bancroft, Telegraph &
Adeline. These streets
have many shops

COLLECTORS ITEMS SHOP
1317 Gilman St   94706
415 525-6269   Est: 1964
Proprietor: Fred W
Borcher
Hours: Mon-Wed, Fri, Sat,
12-5
Types & Periods: Small
Collectibles, Campaign
Buttons, Post Cards, Menus,
Railroadiana, Medals, Sheet
Music, Baseball Cards,
Stamps
Appraisal Service Available
    Directions: In N Central
    Berkeley

WILLIAM KALWAY
305 The Uplands   94705
415 848-5177   Est: 1948
Proprietor: William Kalway
Types & Periods: Furniture;
Porcelains, Crystal, I7th-19th
Centuries

Beverly Hills

**SHADOW HILLS ANTIQUES
AND FINE ARTS GALLERY**
8621 Wilshire Blvd   90211
213 652-3398
Proprietor: Annette and
Sol Zwirn
Hours: Mon-Sat, 11-5
Types & Periods: Art Glass,
Bronzes, Porcelain, Fine
Paintings, Period Furniture,
Jewelry
Specialties: Same as above
    Directions: Wilshire Blvd
    between La Cienega &
    Robertson

Big Pine

MARY K'S ANTIQUES
173 S Main St   93513
714 938-2451   Est: 1969
Proprietor: Mary K Mann
Hours: By Chance
Types & Periods: 1900
Coins, Bric-a-Brac
Specialties: Glass, Coins
    Directions: Located on US
    Hwy 395, Rear of Country
    Kitchen Restaurant

Bishop

**HIGH COUNTRY WESTERN
ART GALLERY AND
ANTIQUES**
2293 No. Sierra Hwy
                              93514
714 873-5203   Est: 1968
Proprietor: Georgi Ana
Smith & Nora Jean
Wagoner
Hours: Daily, 10-5
Types & Periods: Art Glass,
Victorian and Early
American; Western Art;
Indian Baskets
Appraisal Service Available
    Directions: Two Miles N of
    Bishop on Hwy 395

Brawley

BRAWLEY ANTIQUES
141 N 5th   92227
714 344-1941   Est: 1963
Proprietor: Richard Kaiser
Hours: Daily
Types & Periods: Furniture,
Glass, Collectables
Specialties: Furniture (Oak),
Pressed Glass
Appraisal Service Available
    Directions: 5th & E Sts, 1
    Blk N of Main St

Buellton

THE GRAND MANOR
85 Hwy 246 W   93427
805 688-3466   Est: 1969
Proprietor: Esther
Anderson
Hours: Wed-Sun
Types & Periods: Period
Furniture, Silver
Specialties: Furniture
    Directions: Off Hwy 101
    Near Famous Pea Soup
    Andersen Restaurant in
    Buellton, 40 Miles N of
    Santa Barbara

THIS 'N THAT SHOPPE
272 Ave of Flags   93427
805 688-6006   Est: 1968
Proprietor: Charles L
Letson
Hours: Sat-Thurs
Types & Periods: General
Line, Turn-of-the-Century
Specialties: Glass
    Directions: On Same Side
    & Just S of Split Pea
    Andersen's

Burbank

**CRIPES ANTIQUES &
CLOCK SHOPPE**
309 W First St   91502
213 849- 7362
Proprietor: Bob & Ethel
Cripes
Hours: Mon-Sat, 10-5
Types & Periods: Clocks,
Watches, Furniture,
Primitives

Burlingame

KEN PRAG
P O Box 531   94010
415 343-0242   Est: 1972
Proprietor: Ken Prag
Hours: By Appointment
Types & Periods: Paper
Collectors Items: Old Stock
Certificates & Bonds, Old
Post Cards, Railroad Passes
& Timetables, Stereopticon
Views, Obsolete Currency
Specialties: Stock
Certificates & Post Cards
Apprasial Service Available

**THE SIMPSONS'
COLLECTORS SHOP**
1127 Howard Ave   94010
415 343-5031
Hours: Mon, Wed-Sat,
10:30-5
Types & Periods: English,
French & American Period
Furniture, Accessories

Camino

REYNOLD'S EUREKA MINE
3200 Hwy 50 E   95729
916 644-2803   Est: 1971
Proprietor: Frank & Edith
Dunn
Hours: Daily
Types & Periods: General
Line of Furniture, Primitive,
Victorian, Oak; China, Glass
Directions: US 50, 5 Miles
E of Placerville at Carson
Rd Turnoff

**WAYSIDE VILLAGE
ANTIQUES**
3200 Hwy 50 E   95729
916 644-2803   Est: 1971
Proprietor: Frank & Edith
Dunn
Hours: Daily
Types & Periods: General
Line of Furniture, Primitives,
Victorian, Oak, China, Glass
Directions: US 50 , 5 Miles
E of Placerville at Carson
Rd Turnoff

Canyon Country

ALESAVIT'S ANTIQUES
16385 Sierra Hwy   91351
805 252-2487   Est: 1962
Proprietor: Ed & Alesavit
Navroth
Hours: Daily
Types & Periods: American
Oak Furniture, Lamps,
China, Primitives, General
Line
Specialties: Repairing &
Refinishing Old Furniture,
Sheet Caning
Directions: 3.2 Miles N of
Soledad Canyon & Sierra
Hwy

Carlsbad

BLUE GARRET
425 Elm Ave   92008
714 729-4227
Proprietor: Jack & Shauna
Whitworth
Hours: Tues-Sat, 10-4:30
Types & Periods: General
Line
Directions: Elm Ave off I-5

Carmel

**DAVIS-HOLDSHIP
ANTIQUES**
P O Box 5908   93921
408 624-5757
Proprietor: Wm E & Grace
Davis
Hours: Mon-Sat, 10:30-5
Types & Periods: 18th
Century Porcelain, Art & Art
Objects
Apprasial Service Available
Directions: Mission Near
6th

GEORGE E MONTGOMERY
Mission at 5th   93921
Hours: Daily, 10-5
Types & Periods: American
& English Period Furniture,
Accessories

**RICHARD S GORMAN
ANTIQUES**
Mission at Seventh   93921
408 625-1770

Proprietor: Richard S
Gorham
Hours: Mon-Sat, 9:30-5
Types & Periods: 18th
Century Furniture, Porcelain
Directions: 2nd Shop at
San Carlos & 7th

Carpinteria

**TREASURE HOUSE
ANTIQUES**
3755 Santa Claus Lane
                        93013
805 684-4317   Est: 1960
Proprietor: Nadine Pusey
Rittiman
Hours: Tues-Sun
Types & Periods: General
Line
Specialties: Clocks
Directions: 8 Miles S of
Santa Barbara, 85 Miles N
of Los Angeles

Cathedral City

**DESERT AUCTION
GALLERY**
670 1st St   92234
714 328-6589   Est: 1969
Proprietor: Steve &
Joyce Quinlan
Hours: Thurs-Mon, 1-4,
Auctions Fri-Sun, 7 pm
Types & Periods: Furniture,
Crystal, Porcelains, Jade,
Oriental, Paintings, Jewelry,
Estate Sales, China, Art
Glass, Etc
Specialties: Jewelry
Appraisal Service Available
Directions: Hwy 111
East Border of Palm
Springs

Chula Vista

HIDDEN HOUSE ANTIQUES
288 Del Mar Ave   92010
714 420-9848
Proprietor: Sally Casey
Hours: Tues-Fri, 11-4
Types & Periods: General
Specialties: Antique
Christmas
Directions: E Street Off
Ramp of both 805 & 5,
South two Blocks on Del
Mar

MCMURRAY'S ANTIQUES
204 Glover Ave   92010
714 426-7772
Proprietor: Roger &
Virginia McMurray
Hours: Tues-Sat, 10-5
Types & Periods: General
Line Collectables, Oak
Furniture, Glass, Silver

Clovis

**HERITAGE ANTIQUES &
REFINISHING**
754 3rd St   93612
209 298-8441   Est: 1974
Proprietor: Larry R Hayes
Hours: Mon-Sat, 8-5
Types & Periods: American
Oak of 1800's
Specialties: Restoration,
Refinishing, Caning
Directions: Corner of 4th
& Pollasky St

Columbia

CHEAP CASH STORE
Main St   95310
209 532-6694   Est: 1972
Proprietor: Roger & Bettie
Holmberg
Hours: Daily
Types & Periods: Clocks,
Phonos, Novelties,
Collectables
Specialties: Clocks
Directions: Columbia State
Historic Park, Located on
main street

49'ER ANTIQUES
Box 569   95310
209 532-9898
Hours: Daily
Types & Periods: General
Line
Directions: Parrots Ferry
Rd until the 49'er Sign, At
49'er Trailer Ranch

ROAD RUNNER ANTIQUES
P O Box 649   95310
209 532-3544   Est: 1973
Proprietor: Dick & Edna
Palmer
Hours: Mon-Fri, 9-5
Types & Periods: American
& European Furnishings,
Lamps

Specialties: China, Clocks,
Glass (cut & art)
Directions: Located 1
Block on Right from
Columbia Grammar
School on Parrots Ferry
Rd

Corona Del Mar

JANES'S ANTIQUES
2721 E. Coast Highway
          92625
714 673-5752   Est: 1966
Proprietor: Sandra McNeill
Hours: Mon-Fri, 10-4; Sat,
11-5
Types & Periods: General
Line
Directions: Sea side of
Coast Hwy between
Fernleaf & Goldenrod

Corte Madera

TRIFLES AND TREASURES
305 Montecito Dr   94925
415 924-2171   Est: 1964
Proprietor: Sonia &
Richard DeLew
Hours: Tues-Sat, By
Appointment
Types & Periods: California
Paintings in all Medias,
General Line
Specialties: California Art of
early Artists
Directions: Corte Madera
is 14 Miles N of San
Francisco, off Hwy 101

Costa Mesa

ARTHUR YATES
P O Box 1980   92626
714 639-1966
Proprietor: Arthur Yates
Hours: By Appointment
Types & Periods: Japanese
Art, Arms, Armour

Coulterville

SHERLOCK'S AMERICANA
6 Main St   95311
209 878-3621   Est: 1973
Proprietor: Neal & Mary
Sherlock
Hours: Daily
Types & Periods: Old
American Glass, Lamps,
Jewelry, Cutlery, Uniques,
Furnishings, Pictures
Directions: Hiways 49
&132

**GEORGINA STOUT
ANTIQUES**
5023 Main St   95311
209 878-3630   Est: 1975
Proprietor: Ron &
Georgina Stout
Hours: Sun-Thurs
Types & Periods: Match
Safes, Beer Steins, China,
and Glass
Directions: 1 1/2 Blocks
up Main St off Hwy 49
"Mother Lode Hwy"

Covina

SALLY'S ANTIQUES
402 E San Bernardino Rd
          91722
213 339-2435
Proprietor: Sally & Philip
Roberts
Types & Periods: Cut Glass,
Silver, Jewelry, General Line

Culver City

**ARELL'S ANTIQUES N'
THINGS**
10762 Washington Blvd
          90230
213 838-0600   Est: 1969
Proprietor: R L & Lee
Hodges
Hours: Tues-Sat, 11-6
Types & Periods: Glass,
China, Clocks, Jewelry,
Primitives, Dolls
Specialties: Antique Clock
Repair
Directions: One Block W
of MGM Studio

Daly City

BOB'S ANTIQUES
6775 Mission   94014
415 756-5084   Est: 1968
Proprietor: Robert Archini
Hours: Daily
Types & Periods: General
Line
Specialties: Victorian
Clothes
Directions: "Next Door to
San Francisco"

SOUTHSIDE GOODIES
6626 Mission St   94014
415 992-7923   Est: 1973
Proprietor: Tim & Loni
Bonnici
Hours: Daily
Types & Periods: Oak
Furniture, Depression Glass,
Prints, Carnival Glass
Directions: "Top of the
Hill"

Dana Point

LA MARINA ANTIQUES LTD
34146 Coast Hwy   92629
714 496-9486   Lot: 1000
Proprietor: Henry Zunigh
Hours: Daily
Types & Periods:
Turn-of-the-Century Oak;
English, Dutch & Austrian
Furniture
Specialties: Rolltop Desks,
Swivel Chairs, Halltrees

El Cerrito

**COLLECTORS' ITEMS
SHOP**
10542 San Pablo Avenue
94530
415 525-6269   Est: 1964
Proprietor: Fred Borcher
Hours: Mon-Sat, 11-5; Fri
until 8
Types & Periods: Small
Collectibles, Campaign
Buttons, Post Cards, Menus,
Railroadiana, Medals, Sheet
Music, Baseball Cards,
Stamps

Specialties: Campaign
Buttons & Baseball Cards
Appraisal Service Available
Directions: Central El
Cerrito, 2 Blocks S of El
Cerrito City Hall (6 Blocks
E of I-80)

El Segundo

**GOLDEN MOVEMENT
EMPORIUM**
607 Nash   90405
213 640-1603   Est: 1968
Proprietor: John Wilson
Hours: 2 Auctions & 2
Sales Per Year
Types & Periods: Stained
Glass Windows; Doors, Bars
Appraisal Service Available
Directions: San Diego
Frwy to Imperial Frwy W;
S on Nash by International
Airport

Fairfax

CORBETTS ANTIQUES
1621 Sir Francis Drake
94930
415 456-9565   Est: 1954
Proprietor: Blanche
Corbett
Hours: Wed-Sun, 11-4; By
Appointment Only
Specialties: Period &
Primitive Furniture
Appraisal Service Available
Directions: Marin Co. Hwy
17 Approx 20 Miles North
of San Francisco

**MERLE L THOMAS
ANTIQUES**
6 Madrone Rd   94930
415 456-4948
Hours: By Appointment
Types & Periods: General
Line

Fairoaks

CAPPS ANTIQUES
10239 Fair Oaks Blvd
95628
916 961-2933

Proprietor: Lex & Lillian
Capps
Hours: Tues-Sat, 12-4
Types & Periods: General
Line

Fallbrook

ALTIM'S ANTIQUE ATTIC
725 Sutter St   95630
916 985-7666
Proprietor: Al & Tim Lane
Hours: Tues-Sun, 10-5
Types & Periods: Roll Top
Desks, Cut Glass, Silver,
General Line

**ROBERTA COLLISTER'S
ANTIQUES**
3137 S Mission Rd   92028
714 728-2742
Proprietor: Roberta
Collister
Hours: Wed-Sun, 11-4
Types & Periods: Clocks,
European, American

Forest Knolls

CONNIE'S ANTIQUES
6828 Sir Francis
Drake Blvd   94933
415 488-0764   Est: 1955
Proprietor: Connie & Ed
Wood
Hours: Daily, By
Appointment
Types & Periods: Victorian
Early American, Accessories
Appraisal Service Available
Directions: 10 Miles W of
San Rafael

Frazier Park

**FRAZIER ANTIQUES &
UNIQUES**
373 Mt Pinos Way,
P O Box 66   93225
805 245-3659   Est: 1970
Proprietor: Louise & Leo
Gentry
Hours: Sat & Sun, 11-5;
By Appointment
Types & Periods: Primitives,
Books, Paper, Glass, Silver,
Tins, Collectibles, Etc
Directions: Next to Market
in Town on Mt Pinos Way

Fremont

FREEMONT CLUSTER
Directions: Concentration
on Mission Blvd
(20,000-40,000 Block);
Niles Blvd (37,000 Block)

Fresno

FRESNO CLUSTER
Directions: Heavy
Concentration on E Olive
Ave (200-800 Block); Also
on E Belmont Ave
(200-4,000 Block)

**AUBERRY VALLEY
ANTIQUES**
7163 N Blackstone 93650
209 431-3722   Est: 1968
Proprietor: Don & Barbara
Rose
Hours: Daily, 10-5 unless
at Show or on Buying Trip
Types & Periods: Furniture,
Primitives
Directions: Hwy 4 1/2
Blocks N of Herndon

STAPLES ANTIQUES
725 E Belmont   93701
209 485-1970
Proprietor: Penny & Jim
Price
Hours: Wed-Sat, 11-5
Types & Periods: Art Glass,
Cut Glass, China, Jewelry,
Furniture

Fullerton

COLONY ARTS ANTIQUES
129 N Euclid Ave   92632
714 526-4311   Est: 1964
Proprietor: Otto & Mattie L
Pike
Hours: Tues-Sat, 10-5
Types & Periods: Cut &
Pressed Glass, China,
Furniture
Appraisal Service Available

Garden Grove

GARDEN GROVE CLUSTER
Directions: 24 Shops
located on Main St;
Others scattered
throughout City

DEBB'S ANTIQUES INC
8322 Garden Grove Blvd
92644
Est: 1970
Proprietor: L & M
Burleson, L Harrison
Hours: Tues-Sat, 9-5
Types & Periods: European
Directions: 35 Miles S of
LA

Gilroy

PATS USED FURNITURE
7428 Monterey Rd   95020
408 842-9050
Proprietor: Patrick Ramey
Hours: Tues-Sat, 9:30-5:30
Types & Periods: General
Line
Directions: Hwy 109 to
Gilroy

Glendale

GLENDALE CLUSTER
Directions: 1500 E
Colorado Ave, S Brand
(500-600 Blocks), Other
Shops scattered
throughout City

MARION & MILTS
1340 E Wilson   91206
213 240-5677
Proprietor: Milton &
Marion Guttman Jr
Hours: Tues-Sat
Types & Periods: Glass

NINA'S ANTIQUES
454 W Colorado St 91204
213 247-1805   1966
Proprietor: Nina & Norm
Jamison
Hours: Tues-Fri, 11-4; 1st
Sat & Sun each Month
Types & Periods: Art Glass,
Cut Glass, Heisey, Pattern
Glass, Pottery, Sterling,
China

Specialties: Glass of all
Types
Directions: Two Blocks E
off I-5 at Colorado St Off
Ramp

PERIOD FURNITURE
612 E Glenoaks Blvd
91207
213 241-2031
Proprietor: Kenneth &
Marion Ross
Types & Periods: Period
Furniture, Victorian

SHEVAUNS ANTIQUES
1546 E Colorado Blvd
91205
213 243-2082
Proprietor: Shevaun
O'Sullivan
Types & Periods: Post
Cards, Glass, General Line

Glendora

**HAMILTON HOUSE
ANTIQUES**
1030 E Alosta Ave   91740
213 335-3805
Proprietor: Jane Hamilton
Torf
Hours: Wed-Sat, 12-5
Types & Periods: Glass,
China, Silver, Furniture,
Jewelry

Goleta

WESTMINSTER ANTIQUES
449 S Kellogg Way 93017
805 967-3889   Est: 1959
Proprietor: A Stone
Hours: Tues-Sun
Types & Periods: English,
American, Victorian,
Edwardian
Directions: 10 Minutes W
of Santa Barbara; between
Patterson & Fairview Exits
off 101

Hayward

AULD LANG SYNE
20035 Western Blvd 94541
415 276-3831   Est: 1967
Proprietor: Eleanor B
Thomas

Hours: By Appointment
Types & Periods: French
and American China: Sets &
Pieces, over 15,000 Pieces
Specialties: Chocolate Sets,
Pots & Pitchers
Appraisal Service Available
Directions: Directions
given at time of
Appointment

IRVING ANTIQUES
1540 Stafford Ave   94541
415 537-2124
Proprietor: Gerald & Ruth
Irving
Hours: By Appointment
Types & Periods: Porcelains,
Glass, Bibelots

Hollywood

**GEORGE GEORGES &
SONS**
1757 N Highland Ave
90028
213 465-3941   Est: 1933
Proprietor: Mrs George
Georges ,Jr
Hours: Daily, 9-5
Types & Periods: Louis XV
&XVI, Empire & Provincial
Furniture, Marble Mantels,
Mirrors, Crystal Chandeliers
Specialties: French Imports

Inglewood

**ANTIQUE FURNITURE
PALACE-RESTORATION
SERVICE CENTER**
4173 W Imperial Hwy
90304
213 671-2134   Est: 1970
Proprietor: Don & Bonnie
Barnard
Hours: Mon-Sat, 10-6
Types & Periods: Furniture,
Glassware
Specialties: Authentic
Restoration
Directions: On Imperial
Hwy; 5 Minutes E of Los
Angeles International
Airport in Hawthorne

Jamestown

EMPORIUM ANTIQUES
Box 413   95327
209 984-8923   Est: 1972
Proprietor: Jacob
Barendregt III
Hours: Fri-Sun; By Chance
Types & Periods:
Architectural Items,
Furniture (1820-1950), Dolls,
Arcade & Slot Machines,
Books, Oddities, Advertising,
Refinishing
Specialties: Oddities &
One-of-a-Kind
Appraisal Service Available
Directions: Main St; Off
Hwy 49, 6 Miles from
Columbia State Park, 1/2
Mile from Sierra Railroad,
Jamestown's Rail Town

**JIMTOWN TRADING
COMPANY**
18207 Main St   95327
209 984-8946   Est: 1974
Proprietor: John S Marrs
Hours: Wed-Sun, Mon &
Tues by Appointment
Types & Periods: Oak
Furniture, Wood Stoves,
Western Primitives, Mining
Equipment, Lamps,
Lanterns, Trunks & Old
Pawn Turquoise
Directions: Hwy 108 to
Jamestown; 2 Blocks on
Right, Next Door to
Jamestown Drug Store

THE POTPOURRI HOUSE
Box 156   95327
Est: 1974
Proprietor: Anja P Kenyon
Hours: Sat, Sun
Types & Periods: Glassware,
Collectibles, Pictures,
Tapestries, Beads, Period
Clothing
Directions: Main St Royal
Hotel; 3 Miles from
Sonora, in Mother Lode
Country

**SUNDBORG'S ANTIQUE
BARN**
P O Box 739   95327
209 984-3750
Home: 984-5965
Proprietor: Gus & Wanda
Sundborg
Hours: Fri-Tues

Types & Periods: General
Line, Antiques &
Collectibles, Oak Furniture,
China, Glass, Primitives,
Small Collectibles; All Ages!
Specialties: Hand Painted
Old Plates & China
Directions: 1 1/2 Blocks
from Sierra Railroad at 9th
& Seco; Large Red
Building

WEATHERVANE ANTIQUES
18145 Main St   95327
209 984-5147   Est: 1965
Proprietor: Helen Barnes
Hours: Sun-Sat, Closed
Some Weekends
Types & Periods: China,
Silver, Furniture, Primitives
Specialties: Flow Blue &
Childrens Items
Directions: Hwy 49, 3
Miles from Sonora

La Canada

**JOANNA'S CURIOSITY
SHOPPE**
925 Foothill Blvd   91011
213 790-0026   Est: 1971
Proprietor: Joanna M
Lindberg
Hours: Tues-Sat, 10-5
Types & Periods: Victorian,
French, American Oak; 18th
& 20th Centuries
Specialties: Collectibles;
Glass, cut & pressed; Hand
Painted China
Appraisal Service Available
Directions: Exit Angelus
Crest off 210 Freeway;
Left to Foothill, E to Shop

Laguna (South)

CHATEAU DE MAISON
31576 Scenic Dr S   92677
714 499-2865   Est: 1960
Proprietor: A J Maison
Hours: By Appointment
Types & Periods: French,
English; Unusual Decorator
Items, Bric-a-Brac
Appraisal Service Available
Directions: Off Coast Hwy;
Up 2nd Ave at Top of Hill

**MOLL'S ANTIQUES &
ORIENTAL RUGS**
31660 S Coast Hwy 92677
714 499-1901   Est: 1970
Proprietor: George &
Helene Moll
Hours: Tues-Sun, 10-5
Types & Periods: General
Line
Specialties: Oriental (Rugs &
Carpets)
Appraisal Service Available
  Directions: "Easy to find
  on Coast Hwy"

THIRD HAND SHOP
4th at Coast Hwy   92677
714 499-1040   Est: 1963
Proprietor: Rock
Thompson, Curator
Hours: Thurs-Sun, 11-5
Types & Periods: "Exclusive
Junk"

Laguna Beach

ANCIENT ART
860 Glenneyre St   92651
714 494-2478   Est: 1943
Proprietor: Leonard
Kaplan, Richard Dreaper,
Assoc
Hours: Wed-Sun, 11-5
Types & Periods: Ancient,
Oriental, European &
Spanish Colonial; Prior to
18th Century
  Directions: Between Thalia
  & St Ann Sts

ECLECTIC
326 Glenneyre   92651
714 497-2020   Est: 1974
Proprietor: Ron Edwards
Hours: By Appointment
Types & Periods:
Architectural Antiques
Specialties: Doors, Windows,
Columns, Hardware

GALLERY ONE
1220 North Coast Hwy
                 92651
714 494-4444   Est: 1976
Proprietor: Ken Uranga &
Jerry Hall
Hours: Daily

Types & Periods: American
& European: Jewelry,
Paintings, Silver, Watches,
Clocks, Bronzes; Oriental
Items: Ivory & Jade,
Netsukes, Porcelains,
Cloisonne, Rugs, Copper &
Brass; 18th & 19th Century
Furniture
Specialties: Glass (Art &
Cut), China, Watches,
Oriental Collections, Jade &
Ivory Carvings, Jewelry
Appraisal Service Available
  Directions: North Coast
  Hwy 1

**ROBERTA GAUTHEY
ANTIQUES**
1290 North Coast Hwy
                 92651
714 494-9925   Est: 1967
Proprietor: Roberta
Gauthey
Hours: Tues-Sat, By
Chance, By Appointment
Types & Periods: Early
American Pine, Victorian
Furniture; Glass: Pressed,
Sandwich, Art & Cut; Silver
& Jewelry
Appraisal Service Available
  Directions: N End of
  Laguna Beach, by
  Emerald Bay

GOLDIES OLDIES
490 S Coast Hwy   92651
714 837-4752
Proprietor: Marvin M &
Eileen Cary
Types & Periods: Furniture,
Glass

**WARREN IMPORTS-FAR
EAST FINE ARTS**
1910 South Coast Blvd
                 92651
714 494-6505   Est: 1937
Proprietor: Maxine & Harry
J Lawrence
Hours: Mon-Sat, 9-5
Types & Periods: Chinese,
Japanese, Korean 10th to
19th Century
Specialties: Jewelry, Jade
Appraisal Service Available
  Directions: Main Blvd in
  Laguna Beach

**RICHARD YEAKEL
ANTIQUES**
1099 South Coast Hwy
                 92651
714 494-5526   Est: 1940

Proprietor: Richard Yeakel
Hours: Tues-Sat; By
Appointment
Types & Periods: 15th, 16th,
17th & 18th Century
Furniture. Three stores,
each with a different Period
  Directions: Oak St &
  Coast Hwy

Laguna Niguel

HOUSE OF SECONDS
27635 G Forbes Rd 92677
714 831-2350   Est: 1967
Proprietor: Tom Becknell
Hours: Mon-Sat, 11-5
Types & Periods: Furniture
from 1850 to 1930's
Specialties: Hand Carved
Cameo's in Sea Shells
  Directions: San Diego
  Freeway & Crown Valley
  Offramp

La Jolla

**CENTURY HOUSE
ANTIQUES**
7401 La Jolla Blvd   92037
714 459-8467   Est: 1970
Proprietor: Kay Miner &
Mel Manarrino
Hours: Mon -Sat, 12-5
Types & Periods: Jewelry,
bronze & oriental
Specialties: Jewlery, oriental
Appraisal Service Available

TROSBY GALLERIES
7442 Girard Ave   92037
714 454-5525   Est: 1951
Proprietor: Norman Trosby
Hours: Daily
Types & Periods: General
Line, All Periods & Types
Specialties: Oil Paintings
  Directions: W on Torrey
  Pines Road, then Left
  on to Girard

Lake Elsinore

THE CHIMES
201 W Graham   92330
714 674-3456   Est: 1950
Proprietor: Lory O &
Wilma L Watts
Hours: Weekends

Types & Periods: General
Line
Specialties: Clocks &
Watches, Jewelry
Directions: 1 Block off
Main St

Lakeside

H R B ANTIQUES
9242 Wintergardens Blvd
92040
714 561-0910
Proprietor: Hal & Harriet
Betcher
Hours: Wed-Sat, 10-5; Sun
12-5
Types & Periods: Primitives,
Oak
Directions: Near Corner of
Magnolia & Wintergardens

La Mesa

FRIQUE & FRAQUE
8326 La Mesa Blvd 92041
714 461-1262
Proprietor: Kay Black &
Grace Lundeen
Hours: Wed-Sat, 11-5;
Tues By Chance
Types & Periods: Primitives,
Oak, General Line
Directions: Between
University & Rte 98

Larkspur

**SHADOWS OF FORGOTTEN
ANCESTORS**
503 Magnolia   94939
415 924-9303   Est: 1972
Proprietor: Charles & Jean
Stewart
Hours: Mon-Sat, 1-6
Types & Periods: Victorian &
Edwardian Clothing, Jewelry,
American Indian Baskets
Specialties: Authentic Folk
Costumes
Directions: Old Downtown
10 Miles N of San
Francisco on Hwy 101

La Verne

STEVEN'S ANTIQUES
2157 5th   91750
Proprietor: Ralph McGee
& Steven Shannon
Hours: Daily
Types & Periods: Jewelry,
Belleek, China, Glass

Lee Vining

**TIOGA LODGE ANTIQUES
& SALOON**
Box 130   93541
714 647-6551   Est: 1919
Proprietor: Jim & Dot
Hathaway
Hours: Daily, Weekends;
April-Oct   Furniture,
Gold Rush Items,
Turquoise Jewelry
Specialties: Antique
Furniture Refinishing
Appraisal Service Available
Directions: Hwy 395 on
Mono Lake (Gateway to
Yosemite; 3 Miles S)

Lemon Grove

**ANTIQUE INVESTMENTS
(HOLDINGS) LTD**
7945 Broadway   92045
714 469-4140   Est: 1976
Proprietor: Andrew W Kerr
Hours: Daily, 12-5, By
Appointment
Types & Periods: Early Pine,
Roll Top Desks, Oak,
Clocks, Carriages, Pewter,
Copper, English & French
Furniture
Specialties: Pewter &
Copper
Appraisal Service Available
Directions: 11 Miles E of
San Diego on Hwy 94

ANTIQUES BY MARY KAY
3338 Main   92045
714 460-5533
Proprietor: Mary Kay
Hours: Mon-Sat, 12-6
Types & Periods: General
Line
Directions: Between
Broadway & Mt Vernon

HIGH HOPE ANTIQUES
7921 Broadway   92045
714 465-7830   Est: 1971
Proprietor: Ruby Goodwin
Hours: Mon, Sat & By
Appointment
Types & Periods: Early
American Pine, Oak and
Victorian Furniture, Dolls,
Glass, China, Brass &
Copper, Woodenware
Directions: Suburb of San
Diego; take Freeway 94
East

**PA KERR'S COUNTRY
STORE**
7945 Broadway   92045
714 469-4140
Proprietor: Lillian Kerr
Hours: Tues, Thus & Sat,
12-5
Types & Periods: Clocks,
Early American, Pine,
Pressed Glass

LILLIAN'S ANTIQUES
2046 Berry St   92045
714 469-1454
Proprietor: Lillian Kerr
Hours: Mon, Wed & Sun,
11-5
Types & Periods: English
Furniture, Cut Glass,
Paintings, Stevengraphs
Directions: S off Mt
Vernon

RICK'S RELICS
3340 Main St   92045
714 463-8306   Est: 1960
Proprietor: Fern Dunkel
Hours: Mon-Sat
Types & Periods: Depression
Glass, Jewelry, Furniture,
Primitives, New Books on
Antiques, General Line
Specialties: Depression
Glass, New Books on
Antiques
Appraisal Service Available
Directions: Center of
Lemon Grove by The
Lemon at Broadway &
Imperial

**YEARS OF YESTERDAY
ANTIQUE SUPER MART**
7895 Broadway   92045
Proprietor: Freda Joyal
Hours: Mon-Sat, 11-5
Types & Periods: Furniture,
China, Glass, Toys, Dolls,
Lamps, Clocks, Jewelry,
Pictures

Lemon Grove   Cont'd

YEARS OF YESTERDAY
                    Cont'd
Appraisal Service Available
   Directions: Approx 5 Miles
   E of San Diego off
   Highway 94, Lemon Grove
   Ave Exit; Broadway
   between Imperial & Grove

Lockeford

**LOCKEFORD CLOCK
COMPANY, INC**
   13356 E Hwy 88
   P O Box 521   95209
   209 727-5624   Est: 1974
   Proprietor: Nancy Walker
   Hours: Sat & Sun
Types & Periods: Austrian
Clocks & Furniture
Specialties: Clocks:Vienna
Regulators
   Directions: Hwy 88, about
   40 Miles S of Sacramento

Lodi

LAKESIDE ANTIQUES
   1102 W Turner Rd   95240
   209 368-9400   Est: 1973
   Proprietor: Everett &
   Dagny Fox
   Hours: Daily; By
   Appointment
Types & Periods: Formal
Period & European
Furniture, Cut Glass
Specialties: Glass, Persian
Rugs
Appraisal Service Available
   Directions: Rte 99 N thru
   Lodi or 99 S; Turn Off at
   Turner Rd

**MOEHRING'S REFINISHERS
& ANTIQUES**
   500 S Central   95240
   209 369-5011   Est: 1968
   Proprietor: Frank &
   Barbara Moehring
   Hours: Tues-Sat, 9-5; By
   Appointment Sun & Mon
Types & Periods: Early
American Furniture, Glass,
Metal Objects, Lamps

Specialties: Refinish &
Restore Furniture, Polish
Brass & Copper
Appraisal Service Available
   Directions: Corner of Flora
   & Central

Long Beach

LONG BEACH CLUSTER
   Directions: E 4th St
   (200-4000 Block); Long
   Beach Blvd (300-5000
   Block); E Broadway
   (200-4000 Block); Atlantic
   Ave 600-4000 Block;
   Redondo Ave (200-800
   Block)

BETTY'S ANTIQUES
   1092 E Wardlow Rd 90807
   213 424-1135
   Proprietor: Betty Davison
   Hours: Thurs-Mon
Types & Periods: Furniture,
Clocks, General Line

DEBB'S ANTIQUES INC
   5201 Long Beach Blvd
                       90805
   213 422-0925   Est: 1970
   Proprietor: Lenora
   Harrison
   Hours: Mon-Sat
Types & Periods: European
Specialties: Furniture;
WHOLESALE ONLY
   Directions: N of Delamo
   Blvd

DOROTHY V GRACE
   1152 E Wardlow Road
                       90807
   213 424-8921
   Hours: Tues-Sat, 12-5
Types & Periods: General
Line
Appraisal Service Available

**GREEN DOOR BOOKS &
ANTIQUES**
   3850 E Ocean Blvd 90803
   213 438-8740
   Proprietor: Ray & Blanche
   Pryor
   Hours: Mon-Sat, 11-5
Types & Periods: Games,
Machines, Americana

LESLIE'S TREASURE COVE
   1090 E Wardlow Rd 90807
   213 426-0087

Proprietor: L Gabrielson &
F Miller
Hours: Fri-Tues, 11-5:30
Types & Periods: R S
Prussia, Art & Cut Glass,
Lamps, Furniture

Los Altos

CONNOISSEUR ANTIQUES
   398 State St   94022
   415 948-3731
   Proprietor: Geraldine W
   Kavanaugh
   Hours: Mon-Sat, 10-5
Types & Periods: Furniture,
Jewelry, Silver, General Line

**GERANIUM HOUSE
ANTIQUES**
   371 First St   94022
   415 941-2620
   Proprietor: Wen Staskus
   Hours: Tues-Sat, 11-5
Types & Periods: Furniture,
General Line

Los Angeles

LOS ANGELES CLUSTER
   Directions: Melrose
   (7000-9000 Blocks, Others
   scattered throughout City,
   Heavy Concentration in
   Suburban Areas

**ANTIQUE MART OF LOS
ANGELES**
   809 North La Cienega Blvd
                       90069
   213 652-1282   Est: 1936
   Proprietor: Murray
   Braunfeld
   Hours: Mon-Sat, by
   Appointment
Types & Periods: 18th
Century, American, English
& French Furniture &
Objects of Art; Paintings,
18th & 19th Centuries
Specialties: 18th Century
American Furniture
Appraisal Service Available
   Directions: Restaurant
   Row

IAN ARUNDEL
   8629 Melrose Ave   90069
   213 393-6155   Est: 1953
   Proprietor: Ian Arundel

Hours: Daily, 2:30-5:30,
Also by Appointment
Types & Periods: Primitive
Tribal Art, Old Master
Paintings
Specialties: Pre-Columbian,
African, American Indian &
Oceanic Art
Appraisal Service Available
Directions: 4 1/2 Blocks
W of La Cienega

**DON BADERTSCHER
IMPORTS**
716 N La Cienega Blvd
90069
213 652-0286
Proprietor: Don
Bedertscher
Hours: Daily, 9-5
Types & Periods: Victorian
European to Date,
Primitives, Rustic Americana
Directions: Between Santa
Monica Blvd & Melrose

BALDACCHINO
919 N La Cienega Blvd
90069
213 657-6810   Est: 1964
Proprietor: Gerald Decker
& Robert Kelly
Hours: Daily
Types & Periods: English,
French, Continental, 18th
Century
Directions: Restaurant
Row Area

BEAUSEJOUR ANTIQUES
1832 Sepulveda Blvd
90025
213 477-3069   Est: 1970
Proprietor: Richard &
Serge Agraphiotis
Hours: Mon-Sat, 10-6
Types & Periods: 17th &
18th Century French
Country Furniture, Paintings,
Bronzes, China
Specialties: Louis XV &
Empire of the Period
Furniture
Appraisal Service Available
Directions: Between Santa
Monica & Olympic Blvds;
Santa Monica Blvd Exit
from San Diego Frwy

BEVERLY ANTIQUES
8827 Beverly Blvd   90048
213 271-8517   Est: 1938
Proprietor: Grace Elliott
Hours: Mon-Fri, 10-5; Sat
10-4

Types & Periods: Silver,
Early Porcelain
Specialties: Silver (Sterling
Matching Service)
Appraisal Service Available
Directions: Just W of
Robertson Blvd

**BRADBURY GENERAL
STORE**
304 So Broadway   90013
213 626-0231   Est: 1967
Proprietor: Shevaun
O'Sullivan
Hours: Mon-Fri, 11-5
Types & Periods: Ephemera,
General Line,
Turn-of-the-Century
Directions: Located in the
Historic Bradbury Bldg

BRETON HOUSE
8630 Sunset Blvd   90069
213 655-5335   Est: 1956
Proprietor: J Saggsser &
B Diamond
Hours: Mon-Sat, 10:30-5
Types & Periods: Paper
Ephemera, Toys, Doll
Houses, Political, Theatre,
Turn-of-the-Century,
Nostalgia, Movies
Specialties: Furniture
(Miniature), Paper Goods
Directions: Between La
Cienega & Doheny Blvd
on Sunset Strip

CARAVAN BOOK STORE
605 S Grand Ave   90017
213 626-9944   Est: 1954
Proprietor: Morris
Bernstein
Hours: Mon-Fri 10:30-6;
Sat 11-5

**J F CHEN,
ANTIQUE ORIENTALIA**
8414 Melrose Ave   90069
213 655-6310   Est: 1973
Proprietor: Joel Chen
Hours: Mon-Fri, 10-5
Types & Periods: Period
Oriental Antique porcelains
and furniture, including
Large Fish Bowls,
Jardinaires, Vases,
Lacquerware & Bronzes
Specialties: Cater to Interior
Design Trade
Appraisal Service Available
Directions: Between La
Cienega Blvd & Orlando

DENNIS & LEEN INC
612 N Robertson Blvd
90069
213 652-0855   Est: 1959
Hours: Daily
Types & Periods: 18th
Century French, Italian,
English Classic Glass, 18th
Century Stone & Marble
Mantels
Directions: W Hollywood

THE EAGLE'S NEST
3715 Sunset Blvd   90026
213 665-9103   Est: 1966
Proprietor: Will Hoffeld
Hours: Fri & Sat, 10-6
Types & Periods: Guns,
Swords, Military Relics
Appraisal Service Available
Directions: 3 Miles From
Downtown

**JOHN C ELLIOTT
ANTIQUES**
8827 Beverly Blvd   90048
213 271-8517
Proprietor: J C Elliott
Hours: Mon Fri, 10-5; Sat,
10-4
Types & Periods: General
Line, Oriental

GRACE ELLIS ANTIQUES
731 N LaCienega   90069
215 652-1688   Est: 1923
Proprietor: Grace Ellis
Hours: Daily, 11-5; By
Appointment
Types & Periods: French &
English Furniture, Lamps,
Accessories
Directions: Antique &
Restaurant Row Wilshire
Blvd to Santa Monica Blvd

KENT ERLE ANTIQUES
8110 Melrose Ave   90046
213 655-6665   Est: 1969
Proprietor: Kent Erle
Sokolow
Hours: Tues-Sat, 10-6
Directions: Melrose Ave
off Hollywood Freeway or
La Cienega off San Diego
Frwy

MARGOT FLATAU
721 N LaCienega Blvd
90069
213 652-1623   Est: 1948
Proprietor: Margot Flatau
Hours: Daily, by
Appointment

Los Angeles   Cont'd

MARGOT FLATAU   Cont'd
Types & Periods: French &
English; Accessories,
Original Posters, Art
Nouveau
Appraisal Service Available

FONG'S
939-943 Chungking Rd
90012
213 626-5904   Est: 1920
Proprietor: Gim & Shirley
Fong
Hours: Tues-Sat, 11-5 &
7-9; Sun, 3-9
Types & Periods: Oriental
Items, Ivory Carvings,
Cloisonne, Stoneware,
Collectibles
Appraisal Service Available
Directions: North Hill &
College Sts

FOSTER'S
1101 Glendon Ave   90024
213 479-3739   Est: 1930
Proprietor: Newby Foster
& Van Foster, Jr
Hours: Tues-Sat, 10-5
Types & Periods: English
Silver, Chinese & Japanese
Porcelains

GALLERY ARTASIA
8380 Melrose Ave   90069
213 658-7320   Est: 1975
Proprietor: Gerald
Stockton
Hours: Sun-Fri, 10-5; Sat
by Appointment
Types & Periods: East
Asian, Tang & Ming;
Burmese Buddhistic
Sculptures; Cambodian
Stone Sculpture; Japanese
Screens
Specialties: Oriental
Directions: 2 Blocks E of
La Cienega Blvd, Corner
of Orlando

GAZEBO
8264 Melrose Ave   90046
213 658-7110   Est: 1973
Proprietor: Hall
Halverstadt & David R
Williams
Hours: Mon-Sat, 10:30-5
Types & Periods: 19th
Century English & French
Pine, Victorian English
Bamboo, Wicker

Specialties: Baskets
Directions: Between La
Cienega & Crescent
Heights

GERBER'S ANTIQUES
7965 1/2 Melrose Ave
90046
213 653-1050   Est: 1963
Proprietor: Jessie S
Gerber
Hours: Mon-Sat, 11-5
Types & Periods: General
Line
Directions: Between
Fairfax & La Cienega Blvd

GLORIA'S POTPOURRI
2310 Hyperion Ave   90027
213 662-1483   Est: 1970
Proprietor: Gloria Samario
Hours: Mon-Thurs, 1:30-7:
Fri & Sat 12-6:30
Types & Periods:
Turn-of-the-Century
Bric-a-Brac, Depression
Glass, American Art Pottery,
Collectibles
Specialties: Depression
Glass & Depression Era
Pottery
Directions: E of Sunset
Blvd; Los Feliz-Silverlake
Area

**HAMMOND HOUSE
ANTIQUES**
7415 Melrose Ave   90046
213 651-0772   Est: 1974
Proprietor: Jeffrey & Bea
Goldstein
Hours: Mon-Sat, 10-5
Types & Periods: American
Oak Furniture &
Accessories:
Turn-of-the-Century, 1900
Specialties: Oak Furniture,
Refinishing
Directions: In West
Hollywood, between
Fairfax & La Brea

HANDLEBAR ANTIQUES
7966 Melrose Ave   91201
213 655-6997
Proprietor: Kenneth J
Leach & E E Bustamente
Types & Periods: Art
Nouveau, Art Deco, Oriental
Accessories

HARVEY'S
8168 Melrose Ave   90048
213 658-6229   Est: 1969

Proprietor: Harvey
Schwartz
Hours: Mon-Sat, 11-6
Types & Periods: Art Deco,
Art Nouveau, Jewelry,
Rattan
Specialties: Art Deco, Art
Nouveau
Directions: Near La
Cienega Blvd

**IRON N' ANTIQUE
ACCENTS**
342 N La Brea   90036
213 934-3953   Est: 1968
Proprietor: Ray Ferra
Hours: Mon-Sat
Types & Periods: Old
Lighting Fixtures: Lamps, Oil
Lamps, Brass Student
Lamps, Persian Beaded
Lamps
Specialties: Green Shades
Directions: 3 Stop Lights
N of Wilshire

JEAN ANTIQUES
4616 Eagle Rock Blvd
90041
213 257-8653
Types & Periods: General
Line

JEAN'S ACCENTS
128 1/2 N Larchmont
90004
213 467-6565   Est: 1964
Proprietor: Mrs Evelyn
Jean
Hours: Tues-Sat, 10:30-5
Types & Periods: Oriental,
Silver, Dolls, Miniatures
Directions: Between
Beverly & First St, 3
Blocks E of Rossmore

JEWELL'S ANTIQUES
3719 Sunset Blvd   90026
213 662-4786
Proprietor: Joe & Jewell
Serrani
Hours: Wed-Sat
Types & Periods: Furniture,
China

**H FRANK JONES
ARTS DECO**
8101 Melrose Ave   90046
213 852-9359
Proprietor: H Frank Jones
& Walter Yows
Hours: Daily

Types & Periods: Arts Deco
Appraisal Service Available
Directions: On the Melrose
Walk

KINGS CABINET
622 N La Peer Dr   90069
213 657-7878   Est: 1970
Proprietor: Charles Belden
Hours: Daily, 10-5
Types & Periods: Country
French & European
Specialties: Furniture,
German & French Farm
Tables
Appraisal Service Available
Directions: 1 Block from
Pacific Design Center

LEISURE TIME INC
4323 W Pico Blvd   90019
213 937-7666   Est: 1866
Proprietor: Marvin Miller
Hours: Daily, 10-6, Mon &
Thurs 'til 9
Types & Periods: Some of
the world's most unusual
clocks
Specialties: Clocks
Appraisal Service Available
Directions: 2 Blocks W of
Crenshaw Blvd on Pico
Blvd

YVETTE LIARDET
646 N Robertson   90069
213 652-3192   Est: 1954
Proprietor: Andre Liardet
Hours: Mon-Fri, 8-5;
Weekends by Appointment
Types & Periods: English,
French, Spanish;
Accessories, all over 120
Years Old
Directions: On Robertson
between Melrose & Santa
Monica Blvd

LIGHTFOOT HOUSE
8251 Melrose Ave   90048
213 643-1600   Est: 1965
Proprietor: Beebe &
Lightfoot
Hours: Mon-Sat, 10-5
Types & Periods: American
Wicker, Furniture
Directions: 2 Miles W of
Hollywood Frwy Melrose
Off Ramp; Between
Crescent Heights & La
Cienega Blvd

LOREN'S ANTIQUES
3902 Sunset Blvd   90039
213 666-1828   Est: 1974
Proprietor: Loren Sims
Hours: Daily, 12-5
Types & Periods: 20th &
19th Century Furniture,
Porcelain, Silver, Americana
Specialties: Oriental
Appraisal Service Available
Directions: N of Silverlake
Turnoff of Hollywood
Freeway

MARCO POLO
123 S Western Ave 90004
213 387-8689   Est: 1971
Proprietor: Lois Moffett
Hours: Tues-Sat, 12-6
Types & Periods: Oriental:
Jewelry, Jade
Appraisal Service Available
Directions: Between 1st &
2nd Streets

FRANCES MOORE
7373 Melrose Ave   90046
213 653-5242
Proprietor: Frances Moore
Hours: Mon-Fri, 10-5
Types & Periods: French &
English; Accessories, Prints,
Original Drawings

MR RICK'S ANTIQUES
5300 Venice Blvd   90019
213 935-6141   Est: 1971
Proprietor: Mr Rick
Hours: Tues-Sat, 12-5
Types & Periods: Oak
Furniture, Guns, Furniture of
the 30's & 40's
Specialties: Oak Furniture
Directions: Near Santa
Monica Frwy, between La
Brea Ave & La Cienega
Blvd at Venice Blvd &
Dunsmuir

**THE NEW MANILA
IMPORTING CO**
8438 Melrose Ave   90069
213 655-5348
Proprietor: Richard
Gervais
Hours: Mon-Sat
Types & Periods: Southeast
Asian, Philippine,
Indonesian, Mainland China
Specialties: Philippine Native
& Domestic Antiques
Directions: Near La
Cienega; in Melrose Area

NOB HILL ANTIQUES
8627 Melrose Ave   91401
213 657-2729   Est: 1963
Proprietor: David Lord
Hours: Mon-Sat, 10-6
Types & Periods: 17th, 18th
& 19th Century French
Specialties: Bird Cages,
Smoking Paraphernalia

ODD'S N' END'S
4437 Fountain Ave   90029
213 665-2521   Est: 1966
Proprietor: R P Tommy
Thompson
Hours: Tues-Sun
Types & Periods: General
Line
Appraisal Service Available
Directions: In Hollywood;
Off the Corner of Fountain
& Virgil

OLD WORLD IMPORTS INC
8226 W Third St   90048
213 653-1400   Est: 1946
Proprietor: Leonard Gazin
Hours: Thurs-Sat,
9:30-5:30
Types & Periods: General
Line, Furniture, Paintings,
Chandeliers, Bric-a-Brac,
Bronzes
Specialties: Glass (French
Cameo, Early Bohemian),
Beer Steins
Appraisal Service Available
Directions: 5 Blocks W of
Farmers Market

**OLDEN TYMES OFFICE
INTERIORS**
10850 Tennessee Ave
90064
213 475-9737   Est: 1974
Proprietor: Lorne &
Richard Hirsch
Hours: Daily, 9-5 By
Appointment
Types & Periods: 19th
Century &
Turn-of-the-Century Chairs,
Oak File Cabinets, Desks,
Bookcases, Tables
Specialties: Office
Equipment
Directions: W Los Angeles
between Olympic & Pico
Blvds at Westwood Blvd

Los Angeles   Cont'd

MOREY PALMER ASSOCIATES
8457 Melrose Place 90069
213 658-6444   Est: 1971
Proprietor: Morey Palmer
Hours: Mon-Fri, 8:30-5
Types & Periods: 18th & 19th Century English Furniture

WALDO PEDERSEN'S ANTIQUES
12237 Wilshire Blvd 90025
213 820-3014
Proprietor: Waldo Pedersen
Hours: Mon-Fri, 10-5; Also by Appointment
Types & Periods: French, Italian & English Furniture & Accessories

PENNINGTON MUSEUM TREASURES
8440 Melrose Ave   90069
213 852-0081   Est: 1975
Proprietor: M & M Pennington, S den Hartog, D Evans
Hours: Tues-Sat, 12-4, Also by Appointment
Types & Periods: 18th & 19th Century Paintings, Sculptures; French Furniture
Appraisal Service Available
Directions: One Block E of La Cienega

PERSIAN GALLERY & BIAZAR'S ANTIQUE SHOP
318 N Robertson Blvd
P O Box 480087   90048
213 645-5454   Est: 1974
Proprietor: Mohamad Biazar
Hours: Tues-Fri; By Appointment
Types & Periods: 19 Different Countries; Some Close to 900 Years Old
Specialties: Persian & Oriental; Some Special Items from America
Appraisal Service Available
Directions: Intersection of Beverly Hills, Hollywood & Los Angeles; 1 Block from Pacific Design Center

THE PHANTOM
8115 Melrose Ave   90046
213 653-0976   Est: 1974
Proprietor: Sandra Spines

Hours: Daily, 11-5:30; By Appointment
Types & Periods: Art Deco, Furniture, Porcelain, Jewelry, Signed Bronzes, Clocks
Directions: 1 Block W of Cresant Heights Blvd in Heart of Antique District

PROPINQUITY
8915 Santa Monica Blvd   90069
213 652-2963
Proprietor: John & Dudley Geiger
Hours: Mon-Thur, 9:30-11; Fri & Sat, 9:30-12; Sun, 12-6
Types & Periods: Art Deco, Art Nouveau, Advertising Pieces
Appraisal Service Available
Directions: Between La Cienega & Doheny

DON QUIXOTE ANTIQUES
5011 Hollywood Blvd   90027
213 666-1167   Est: 1969
Proprietor: Dolly Frank
Hours: Wed-Sat, 10:30-4:45
Types & Periods: China, Crystal, Silver, Furniture
Specialties: Jewelry
Appraisal Service Available
Directions: Between Vermont & Normandie

ROYCE'S OLD FURNITURE
2214 Sunset Blvd   90026
213 413-3065   Est: 1988
Proprietor: Royce & Mary Perkins
Hours: Daily, 10-6
Types & Periods: Furniture
Appraisal Service Available
Directions: Echo Park-Silver Lake Area; 2 Blocks from Alvarado

J ROBERT SCOTT & ASSOCIATES INC
8727 Melrose Ave   90069
213 659-4910   Est: 1971
Proprietor: Bernard Lewis
Hours: Daily
Types & Periods: Orientals, Ivory, Lacquers
Specialties: Oriental Screens & Scrolls
Directions: W Hollywood between San Vicente Blvd & N Robertson Blvd

SPEIRS & PAANAKKER LTD
915 N La Cienega Blvd   90069
213 653-4600
Hours: Mon-Fri, 9-5
Types & Periods: English & Continental

STUDIO FURNITURE
7313 Santa Monica Blvd   90046
213 874-8870   Est: 1962
Proprietor: Ronnie Tino
Hours: Daily, 10:30-6
Types & Periods: Turn-of-Century, Imports, Bric-a-Brac
Directions: 5 Blocks E of La Brea in Hollywood

CHARLOTTE UHLS ANTIQUES
716A N La Cienega Blvd   90069
213 659-0265
Proprietor: Charlotte Uhls
Hours: Daily, 10:30-4
Types & Periods: Glass, Lamps, General Line

UNUSUAL ANTIQUES A TO Z
7555 Sunset Blvd   90046
213 876-7331   Est: 1969
Proprietor: Christopher Marra
Hours: Daily
Types & Periods: Furniture, American, European, Bronzes, Prints, Paintings, Dolls, Crystal, Oriental Rugs
Specialties: Glass (Art)
Directions: Between La Brea & Fairfax

VIRGINIA'S
7223 Melrose   90046
213 934-4524   Est: 1973
Proprietor: Virginia Jacks
Hours: Daily
Types & Periods: Art Deco, Rattan, Oriental, Mission
Directions: 2 Blocks W of La Brea in W Hollywood

WITS END
1997 Hyperion   90027
213 665-2579   Est: 1970
Proprietor: John Gorman
Hours: Fri-Mon, 1-6 during Summer; Also by Chance

Types & Periods:
Collectibles, Art Deco,
Pottery, Black Americana,
Hollywood Items, Depression
Glass, Orphaned &
Distressed Materials
Specialties: Doll House
Miniatures
    Directions: Silverlake Area

Los Gatos

**HERITAGE STUDIO
ANTIQUES**
101 W Main St   95030
Proprietor: Herb & Naomi
Chittick
Hours: Wed-Mon, 10-5;
Also by Appointment
Types & Periods: 19th
Century Furniture,
Accessories
Appraisal Service Available

MARY MITCHELL
140 W Main St   95030
408 354-3484
Proprietor: Mary Mitchell
Hours: Daily, 11-5
Types & Periods: Oriental,
Colored Glass

MONTGOMERY ANTIQUES
262 E Main St   95030
408 354-1825   Est: 1948
Proprietor: Jean
Montgomery
Hours: Tues-Sat, 11-5
Types & Periods: Early
American
Appraisal Service Available

THE OPERA HOUSE
140 W Main St   95030
408 354-3484
Types & Periods: General
Line

PATTERSON'S
91 W Main St   95030
408 354-1718
Proprietor: Pat Patterson
Hours: Daily, 11-5
Types & Periods: General
Line

Mammoth Lakes

THE ANTIQUE SHOPPE
Hwy 203 (Main St)   93546
714 934-2118   Est: 1972
Proprietor: Florence &
Don Sharp & Joe Reeves
Hours: Daily, 'til 5
Types & Periods: Furniture,
Primitives, Silver,
Collectibles
Specialties: Furniture (Oak &
Early Pine)
    Directions: Across from
    Pea Soup Anderson; Little
    Red Cottage

Menlo Park

THE DOLPHIN
605 Cambridge Ave 94025
415 325-4409
Hours: Tues-Sat, 9:30-4:30
Types & Periods: 18th
Century American, English &
French Furniture; Silver,
Accessories

Mill Valley

COUNTRY COMFORT
149 Throckmorton   94941
415 383-0777   Est: 1975
Proprietor: Ron
Vandenbrock & Mark Root
Hours: Tues-Sun
Types & Periods:
Turn-of-the-Century
American Oak Furniture,
Lighting
    Directions: Mill Valley Exit
    from Hwy 101

TOM PEPPER ANTIQUES
34 Sunnyside Ave   94941
415 388-5207   Est: 1973
Proprietor: Roland Sarfert
Hours: Daily
Types & Periods: 18th
Century American &
European Furniture, Folk
Art, Americana
Specialties: Folk Art
Appraisal Service Available
    Directions: Downtown Mill
    Valley

YESTERYEAR ANTIQUES
154 Throckmorton   94941
415 388-2725   Est: 1968
Proprietor: Barbara J
Stockham
Hours: Tues-Sat,
1:30-5:30; By Appointment
Types & Periods: American,
Victorian, Oriental China,
Post Cards
Appraisal Service Available
    Directions: Downtown Mill
    Valley; Corner of
    Throckmorton & Madson

Montecito

ROBERT MAUL ANTIQUES
1086 Coast Village Rd
                    93108
805 969-0210
Hours: Mon-Sat, 10-5
Types & Periods: Period
Furniture, Oriental Rugs,
Accessories

Murphys

**CARRIAGE TRADE
ANTIQUES**
434 Main St   95247
209 728-3688   Est: 1969
Proprietor: Francis & Mary
Nicholson
Hours: Wed-Mon
Types & Periods: Orientals,
Paintings, Porcelains, Cut
Glass, American & European
Furniture, American Indian
Baskets, Rugs, Jewelry
Appraisal Service Available
    Directions: Calaveras
    County; 8 Miles from
    Angels Camp

GOLD TRAILS ANTIQUES
Pennsylvania Gulch Rd
                    95247
209 728-2182   Est: 1969
Proprietor: Dixie L Wilcock
Hours: Daily
Types & Periods: General
Line
Specialties: Furniture,
Lamps, Primitives
    Directions: Hwy 4 E from
    Angels Camp to Murphys;
    Right on P A Gulch Rd,
    Left at Woodland Dr; 1/4
    Mile from Hwy

MARIAN MEDLIN'S ANTIQUES
472 Main St   95247
209 728-3350   Est: 1953
Proprietor: Marian Medlin
Hours: Wed-Mon, 11-
Types & Periods: Victorian
Furniture, Cut Glass, China
Directions: 8 Miles from
Angels Camp Off Hwy 4

Murrieta

THE BLACK HORSE
41450 Los Alamos Rd
                            92362
714 677-5096   Est: 1972
Proprietor: Richard
Rossiter Tetrow
Hours: Daily
Types & Periods: Western
Collectibles, Carriages,
Horse-Drawn Farm
Equipment
Directions: Between
Elsinore &
Temecula-Rancho Area; W
of Hwy 71

Newport Beach

ALMA'S ANTIQUES
113 Via Eboli   92663
714 673-2734
Proprietor: Alma Lou
Wilson
Hours: By Appointment
Types & Periods: Cut Glass,
Art Glass, Porcelain

Niles

THE CABOOSE ANTIQUES
37659 Niles Blvd   94536
415 462-3790   Est: 1974
Proprietor: Suzanne & Jim
Hacker
Hours: Tues-Sun, 11-4
Types & Periods:
Turn-of-the-Century Oak
Furniture, Collectibles,
Clocks
Specialties: Scales; Brasses
of all kinds
Appraisal Service Available
Directions: SE of Oakland;
Niles Blvd E Off Rte 17

Northridge

COBWEB COLLECTION
8353 Gladbeck Ave 91329
213 349-2212
Proprietor: Betty Gausman
Types & Periods: General
Line

Novato

SCHEHERAZADE GALLERIES INC
881 Grant Ave   94947
415 897-7950   Est: 1971
Proprietor: I Mohtashem
Hours: Daily
Types & Periods: General
Line
Specialties: Rugs (Oriental)

Oakhurst

ABBY HOUSE ANTIQUES
Box 776   93644
209 683-5755   Est: 1966
Proprietor: Andrea Piene
Hours: Wed-Sat; Sun by
Chance
Types & Periods: Pine,
Walnut, Oak, 1800-1910;
China, Glass, Jewelry
Appraisal Service Available
Directions: Corner of Hwy
41 & Hwy 49

Oakland

OAKLAND CLUSTER
Directions: Heavy
Concentration on:
MacArthur Blvd
(2000-7000 Blocks),
Telegraph Ave (5000-6000
Block), Piedmont Ave
(3000-4000 Block), College
Ave (5000 Block),
Bancroft Ave (3000-5000
Block)

ANTIQUES EXCLUSIVELY
4068 Piedmont Ave 94611
415 655-2914   Est: 1973
Proprietor: Ron & Carole
Silva
Hours: Tues-Sat,
11:30-5:30

Types & Periods: Victorian
Furniture, Bric-a-Brac,
Collectibles
Appraisal Service Available
Directions: N of McArthur
Blvd off Hwy 680

THE AVENUE ANTIQUES
5815 College Ave   94618
415 658-7778   Est: 1965
Proprietor: Fred L Taber
Hours: Wed-Sat, 12:30-5
Types & Periods: American
Primitives, Lamps, Baskets
Appraisal Service Available
Directions: Rockridge Area
Near Bart Station

BETTY'S ANTIQUES
5387 Bancroft Ave   94602
415 261-9292
Proprietor: Betty & Knud
Danild
Hours: Tues, Fri, Sat,
10:30-4:30; Wed, Thurs,
12-4:30
Types & Periods: General
Line, Paintings

COLLECTABLES
4197 Park Blvd   94602
415 531-7170   Est: 1974
Proprietor: Ed & Ellamae
Cannell
Hours: Daily, by
Appointment
Types & Periods:
Bric-a-Brac, Small Furniture,
Early American, Pictures,
Memorabilia
Specialties: Collectibles
Directions: Take 13 Park
Blvd Off Ramp from
Warren Freeway, or the
580 Park Blvd Off Ramp
from MacArthur Freeway

DOROTHY'S FLEA MARKET
3241 Grand Ave   94610
415 444-5596   Est: 1968
Proprietor: Dorothy C
Seaboyer & Wayne
Holmberg
Hours: Mon-Sat
Types & Periods: China,
Glass, Jewelry, Furniture,
Collectibles
Appraisal Service Available

DRAGON ARTS
5811 College Ave   94618
415 654-6742
Proprietor: George Y Lee
Hours: Mon-Fri, 9:30-5;
Weekends by Appointment

Types & Periods: Oriental Art, Jade, Snuff Bottles, Cloissone, Paper Weights, Seals, Stands, Porcelain, Netsuke
Specialties: Oriental

FORTY-TWO ELEVEN ANTIQUES
4211 Piedmont Ave 94610
415 654-4477   Est: 1970
Proprietor: Richard Myrick
Hours: Mon-Sat, 9-6
Types & Periods: 1840-1920; American Pine, Walnut, Mahogany, Oak, Turn-of-the-Century Furnishings
Directions: 7 Blocks N of Broadway & Piedmont

FRUITVALE ANTIQUES
1669 Fruitvale Ave 94601
415 534-6278   Est: 1974
Proprietor: Geo & Valerie Nilacek
Hours: By Appointment
Types & Periods: Cut Glass, Plates, Limoges, Furniture
Directions: Between MacArthur & Nimetz Freeways

LINCOLN'S PARLOR ANTIQUES
5316 Fairfax   94601
415 261-4522   Est: 1972
Proprietor: Annitta L Rudkosky (Patti)
Hours: Tues-Sat, by Appointment
Types & Periods: General Line; Glass, China, Furniture, Lamps, Collectibles (Tins, Signs, Games, Toys, Dolls, Iron & other Metal Items), Silver, Some Jewelry, Old Linens & Quilts
Specialties: Kitchen Collectibles, Primitives, Americana, Prints, Mirrors
Appraisal Service Available
Directions: Oakland Antiques Center, intersection of Bancroft & Fairfax Ave (between Foothill & Bancroft)

Ojai

THE HALL CLOSET
952 E Ojai Ave   93023
805 646-5377   Est: 1965
Proprietor: Meg & Gene Hovley
Hours: Wed-Sun, or by Appointment
Types & Periods: American Country Furniture, Primitives, Paper Americana
Directions: On Main Hwy, E end of Village

THE VILLAGE FLORIST
242 E Ojai Ave   93023
805 646-4145   Est: 1965
Proprietor: David M Mason
Hours: Daily
Types & Periods: Glass, China, Silver
Specialties: Silver
Directions: Center Store in Downtown Ojai's Arcade

Orange

A ANTIQUE HOUSE
711 W Chapman   92668
714 633-7786
Proprietor: Jim & Shirley McDonald
Hours: Tues-Sat
Types & Periods: General Line

DRURY LANE ANTIQUES
512 W Chapman Ave
                          92668
Proprietor: Tony & Ednabelle (Drury) Menditto
Hours: Tues-Sat, 11:30-5
Types & Periods: 4 Centuries of Furniture, including Country Kitchen; also Access & Guaranteed Clocks
Specialties: Restoration of Clocks & Period Furniture
Directions: 30 Minutes S of LA; 5 Blocks W of Downtown Circle

SHERRY'S ANTIQUES
605 W Chapman   92668
714 639-6401
Proprietor: Sherry Woodington
Hours: Tues-Sat
Types & Periods: General Line, Art & Cut Glass

Palm Desert

NETTIE WOLF ANTIQUES
73-255 El Paseo   92260
714 346-8510   Est: 1971
Proprietor: Nettie Wolf
Hours: Tues-Sat, by Appointment; Closed in Summer
Types & Periods: Over 120 Years Old; English & Oriental
Specialties: Oriental
Directions: 1 Block S of Hwy 111, 1 Block E of Hwy 74, Malaga Square Bldg

Palo Alto

LYONS LTD
Box 11151   94306
415 493-6300
Hours: By Appointment
Types & Periods: Original Etchings, Engravings & Lithographs

Pasadena

PASADENA CLUSTER
Directions: E Colorado Blvd (2000-3000 Blocks), 100 E Colorado Blvd to W Colorado Blvd, California Blvd & Arroyo Area, Others scattered throughout City

MARY AYER INTERIORS & ANTIQUES
225 S Los Robles   91101
213 795-4181
Proprietor: Mary Ayer Schwyner
Hours: Sun-Fri, 9-4
Types & Periods: American, French, Italian, English; Jewelry, Crystal, Silver, Porcelain
Specialties: Jewelry
Directions: Across from Pasadena Hilton

BURCH'S CHANGIN' TIMES ANTIQUES
257 So Rosemead Blvd
                          91107
213 449-6602   Est: 1967

Coffer Chest, early 17th Century Jacobean. Ancestor of the Hope Chest. By the addition of drawers beneath, it became parent to . . . . .

Pasadena   Cont'd

BURCH'S CHANGIN' TIMES ANTIQUES   Cont'd
 Proprietor: Margaret & Gardner Burch
 Hours: Mon-Sat
Types & Periods: Dolls, Toys, Miniatures, Collectibles, General Line
 Directions: S of Colorado Blvd at Del Mar

GISELE'S ANTIQUES
 256 S Rosemead Blvd 91107
 213 795-7449
 Proprietor: Art & Gisele Mahfuz
 Hours: Tues-Sat, 1-5
Types & Periods: French Furniture; Curio Cabinets, Paintings, Mirrors, Chandeliers, Colored Glass, Cut Glass, Russian En, Art Glass
Appraisal Service Available
 Directions: Rosemead Blvd Off State Hwy 10 or Hwy 210; between California Blvd & Del Mar Blvd

MARTHA'S ANTIQUES
 995 E Green 91106
 213 796-1373   Est: 1976
 Hours: Daily
Types & Periods: American, English; General Line
Specialties: Books, Oak Furniture
 Directions: S of Frwy 134 thru Town, 1 1/2 Blocks E of Lake St

THE SOHO SHOPPE-ANTIQUES
 49 N Altadena Dr 91107
 213 793-6509   Est: 1952
 Proprietor: Michael & Elizabeth Soho
 Hours: Mon-Sat, 11-5
Types & Periods: Fine Antique Furniture, General Line
Specialties: Furniture; Furniture Repair & Restoration
 Directions: 1 Block N of 2500 Block of Colorado Blvd, between San Gabriel Blvd & Sierra Madre Blvd

T L SUN COMPANY
 230 S Lake Ave 91101
 213 792-9406   Est: 1970
 Proprietor: Richard Sun & Sophie Sun
 Hours: Tues-Sat 10:30-5:30; also by Appointment
Types & Periods: Oriental Art, Neolithic to Ch'ing Dynasty (1644-1911)
Specialties: Oriental
Appraisal Service Available
 Directions: Between California & Colorado Blvds

SWISHER'S HERITAGE ANTIQUES
 2220 E Colorado Blvd 91106
 213 287-7148
 Proprietor: Ken & Marge Swisher
 Hours: Wed-Sat, 12-4
Types & Periods: General Line; Early American, Victorian

THOSE WERE THE DAYS
 283 N. Lake Ave.   91101
213 792-1665
Proprietor: Margaret Blair
Hours: Daily
Types & Periods:
Collectibles, China, Glass,
American Oak, Clocks
Specialties: China (Haviland)
 Directions: 1/2 Block S of
 210 Freeway

Pleasanton

JJ'S ANTIQUES
 249 Spring St   94566
415 462-3174   Est: 1974
Proprietor: Jewell Johnson
& Betty Cook
Hours: Tues-Sat, 10-5
Types & Periods: Furniture,
Glassware, Dolls, Lamps,
Primitives, Jewelry
 Directions: 1/2 Block from
 Main St, Downtown

Redlands

**AMERICAN WAY
ANTIQUES**
 Hwy 10 S   92373
714 794-3514
Proprietor: Steven Whaley
Hours: Mon-Sun, 9-5
Types & Periods: General
Line

KREPS CARRIAGE BARN
 31181 Outer Hwy 10 92373
714 794-3919   Est: 1952
Proprietor: Mrs. N Maxine
Kreps
Hours: Mon-Sat, 10-5:30;
Sun by Appointment, by
Chance
Types & Periods: General
Line
Appraisal Service Available
 Directions: Yucaipa Blvd
 Off Ramp of I-10

MEMORY LANE ANTIQUES
 31773-75 I-10   92373
714 794-3511
Proprietor: H Ellis & L
Teal
Hours: Thurs-Tues
Types & Periods: General
Line

Redondo Beach

HATHAWAY HOUSE
 415 Faye Lane   90277
213 379-0119   Est: 1919
Proprietor: Jim & Dot
Hathaway
Hours: Daily, by
Appointment
Types & Periods: Primitives,
Depression Glass, Oak &
Victorian Furniture, Gold
Rush Items, Silver &
Turquoise Jewelry
 Directions: Corner of Faye
 Lane & Pearl

. . . . . the Jacobean Chest of Drawers.

Rio Vista

THE ODDITY
35 N Front St   94512
707 374-5677   Est: 1975
Proprietor: The Danas
Hours: Tues-Sat
Types & Periods: American,
English, Victorian Pieces;
Jewelry, Bottles
Directions: Near the
Waterfront; Off Hwy 12
between Fairfield &
Stockton

THE TREASURE CHEST
100 S 2nd St   94571
707 374-6632   Est: 1973
Proprietor: Paul Hamby
Hours: Tues-Sat
Types & Periods: General
Line
Directions: Corner of 2nd
& Montezuma Sts

Riverside

ANDER'S ATTIC
14080 Hwy 395   92504
714 653-3001   Est: 1962
Proprietor: Joe & Lorraine
Anders
Hours: By Chance
Types & Periods: Books,
Paper, Americana, General
Line
Specialties: Books, Post
Cards
Directions: Next to March
Air Force Base

BAKER'S ANTIQUES
5964 Mission Blvd   92509
714 686-5200
Hours: Sat, Sun Afternoon
or By Chance
Types & Periods: General
Line

Sacramento

SACRAMENTO CLUSTER
Directions: J (100-3000
Blocks), Stockton Blvd
(2000-4000 Blocks), 57th
Ave (800 Block)

ARDELL'S ANTIQUES
810 K St Mall   95814
916 441-3646   Est: 1973
Proprietor: Dorothy &
Raymond Marshall
Hours: Mon-Sat, 10-5:30
Types & Periods: Orientals,
Cut Glass, Furniture, Coins,
Paper, Collectibles
Specialties: Art Deco
Directions: Downtown, on
the Mall, 8th & K Sts, 4
Blocks from the State
Capitol

**ESTATES AUCTION
GALLERY**
2419 K St   95816
916 443-1622   Est: 1953
Proprietor: Isabelle V Grey
& Alex Sabbadini
Hours: Daily, 9-5; Auction
Thurs Night, 7:30
Types & Periods: General
Line
Appraisal Service Available
Directions: Center of Town
Close to Historical Fort
Sutter

**LOVELL'S ANTIQUE
FURNITURE GALLERIES**
2114-2116 P St   95818
916 452-1749
Proprietor: Verl Lovell,
Norma Becker
Hours: Mon-Sat, 10-5
Types & Periods: General
Line: Furniture, Old Stained
and Leaded Glass; Also
Lessons
Appraisal Service Available
Directions: On P St
between 21st & 22nd

LOVELL'S ANTIQUE SHOPS
2121 21st St   95818
916 452-1749   Est: 1950
Proprietor: Mrs Verl J
Lovell
Hours: By Appointment
Only
Types & Periods: Art Glass,
Clocks, Dolls, China,
Objects of Art, Bronzes,
Paintings, Furniture, Music
Boxes
Appraisal Service Available
Directions: On 21st St
between U & V Sts

LOVELL'S WINDO-ART
2114-2116 P St   95818
Proprietor: Verl Lovell &
Norma Becker

Hours: Mon-Sat, 10-5
Types & Periods: General
Line, Stained & Leaded
Glass
Specialties: Stained &
Leaded Glass
Appraisal Service Available
Directions: P St between
2lst & 22nd

ODOM'S ANTIQUES
4905 Franklin Blvd   95820
916 452-4694   Est: 1973
Proprietor: Bob & Jean
Odom
Hours: Wed-Sat, 11-5:30;
Sun, 11-3
Types & Periods: American
Oak & Walnut Furniture,
Glassware, Primitives
Specialties: Furniture
Appraisal Service Available
Directions: South
Sacramento, Off Hwy 99
at Fruitridge West or 12th
Ave West

PERRAULT'S ANTIQUES
3840 Stockton Blvd   95820
916 452-1343   Est: 1965
Proprietor: Philomene A
Perrault
Hours: Tues-Sat, 9-5
Types & Periods: General
Line
Specialties: Glass (Carnival
& Depression)

PLUNDER INN ANTIQUES
2300 Capitol Ave   95816
916 446-1100   Est: 1969
Proprietor: Sue Whitfield
Hours: Tues-Sat, 12-5;
Also by Appointment
Types & Periods: Victorian &
Edwardian; Art & Cut Glass,
Furniture, Lamps, Clocks,
General Line
Appraisal Service Available
Directions: Located in one
of Sacramento's Elegant
Victorian Homes, Corner
of 23rd St & Capitol Ave;
8 Blocks E of the State
Capitol & 3 Blocks W of
Historic Sutter's Fort

JON QUINN GALLERY
1002 10th St   95814
916 446-1788   Est: 1963
Proprietor: L Jon & Mae
Quinn
Hours: Daily, 10-4; Also by
Appointment

Types & Periods: Cut Glass,
Art Nouveau, Silver,
Oriental, Original Oils &
Watercolors
Specialties: Coins
Appraisal Service Available
 Directions: 10th & J Sts,
 Downtown

**SACRAMENTO ANTIQUE
CENTER**
 866 57th St   95819
 916 455-3409   Est: 1970
 Proprietor: Marvin &
 Roberta Bagwell
 Hours: Tues-Sat,
 10;30-4:30
Types & Periods: 11
Shops Specializing in
American Antiques
Specialties: Oak Furniture,
Clocks, Oriental
 Directions: Off H St on
 57th

**SACRAMENTO FLEA
MARKET**
 7713 Folsom Blvd   95826
 916 383-4012   Est: 1962
 Proprietor: Robert & Julia
 Beckett
 Hours; Tues-Fri, 12-4; Sat
 by Appointment
Types & Periods: All Periods
of Furniture
Specialties: Furniture
(Chairs)
Appraisal Service Available
 Directions: US Hwy 50,
 Exit Howe Ave & Power
 Inn Rd

NORMAN SOLGAS
 810 K St   95814
 916 442-3646
 Proprietor: Norm Solgas
 Hours: Mon-Sat
Types & Periods: Early
American
Specialties: Outside Horn
Phonographs, Records,
Sheet Music, Musical
Instruments
 Directions: Downtown
 Sacramento on the Mall

TRUESDELL'S AUCTION
 1417 Del Paso Blvd 95834
 916 925-8547   Est: 1965
 Proprietor: Patrick D
 Truesdell
 Hours: Daily

Types & Periods: Victorian,
Early American; Art Deco,
Art Nouveau, Jewelry, Silver,
Gold Coins
Specialties: Estates
Appraisal Service Available
 Directions: Off Hwy 80 to
 Arden Way to Del Paso
 Blvd

WEST ANTIQUES
 5210 Bradshaw   95826
 916 362-1270   Est: 1970
 Proprietor: Mary & Floyd
 West
 Hours: By Appointment,
 By Chance
Types & Periods: American
Furniture, Household Items,
Collectibles, Primitives
 Directions: Off US 50 at
 Bradshaw to Jackson Rd
 (Hwy 16)

St Helena

THE ARBOR
 1095 Lodi Lane   94574
 707 963-2288
 Proprietor: Ruth Titus
 Hours: Tues-Sun, 12-5
Types & Periods: General
Line

THE CARRIAGE HOUSE
 3431 St Helena Hwy N
                       94574
 707 963-7917
 Proprietor: Marjorie Arroyo
 Hours: Tues-Sat, 11-4
Types & Periods: China,
Glassware, Collectibles
Specialties: Furniture (Oak &
Victorian)

CHALET BERNENSIS
 225 St Helena Hwy   94574
 707 963-4423
 Proprietor: Jack Essie &
 Steve Doty
 Hours: Daily, 10-5
Types & Periods: Early
American & Victorian
Furniture, Glass, China,
Clocks

CONNECTICUT YANKEE
 1344 Main St   94574
 707 963-7200
 Proprietor: Cheryl &
 Nadine Rossi

Hours: Mon-Sat, 10-5;
Sun, 12-4
Types & Periods: Furniture,
China, Glass, Primitives,
Jewelry

**THE NOW AND THEN
SHOP**
 3000 St Helena Hwy N
                       94574
 707 963-7129
 Proprietor: Jean Rothlin
 Hours: Tues-Sun, 11-5
Types & Periods: China,
Glass, Furniture

THE SILK PURSE
 115 Main St   94574
 707 963-7377   Est: 1968
 Proprietor: C W & Patricia
 I Snyder
 Hours: Tues-Sat
Types & Periods: Pine &
Oak Early American
Furniture
Specialties: Furniture
Restoring & Refinishing
 Directions: S Side of Town
 on Hwy 29

SKYHAWK GALLERY
 1478 Railroad Ave   94574
 707 963-9251
 Proprietor: Frank D Stout
 Hours: Thurs-Sat, By
 Appointment
Types & Periods: Oriental
Ceramics, Furniture,
Woodblock Prints;
Contemporary Stoneware
 Directions: 1 Block E of
 Main St, Next to Old S P
 Depot

WILLIAMS' ANTIQUES
 61 Main St   94574
 707 963-3235
 Proprietor: Edward &
 Pearl Williams
 Hours: Tues-Sun, 9-5 (Live
 Next Door)
Types & Periods: Glassware,
Pottery, Jewelry, Primitives,
Collectibles, Silver
Specialties: Heisey,
Cambridge, Carnival &
Depression Glass: Large
Selection
 Directions: On Main St

San Anselmo

THE IBEX
202 Sir Francis Drake Blvd
94960
415 456-9070   Est: 1973
Proprietor: Jeanne R
Carlson
Hours: Thurs-Sun, Tues
Types & Periods: General
Line
Directions: Hwy 101 N
from San Francisco; San
Anselmo Turnoff

MOSDEN'S
1525 San Anselmo Ave
94960
415 456-9464   Est: 1972
Proprietor: Kit Mosden
Hours: Mon-Sat, 10-5
Specialties: Antique
Restoration & Chair Caning
Directions: San Anselmo
Exit Off Hwy 101; West
End of Town between
Center Blvd & Sir Francis
Drake Blvd

THE OLD & THE YOUNGS
232 Sir Francis Drake Blvd
94960
415 456-5914   Est: 1970
Proprietor: John &
Meredyth Young
Hours: Mon-Sat, 11-4;
Sun, 12-4; By
Appointment
Types & Periods: 19th
Century English, Oriental
Rugs, Clocks, Paintings
Specialties: Jewelry
Appraisal Service Available
Directions: Known as Old
Bank Building

SALLY'S BAND BOX
332 Sir Francis Drake Blvd
94960
415 456-8216
Proprietor: Sarah M Trube
Hours: Wed-Sat, 11-5; Sun
1-5
Types & Periods: General
Line
Specialties: American Indian
Art

SAN ANSELMO ANTIQUES
721 Sir Francis Drake Blvd
94960
415 456-7851   Est: 1970
Proprietor: Roy Theobald
Hours: Daily

Types & Periods: Victorian,
American & European
Furniture
Specialties: Clocks,
Furniture

U & I TRADING POST
15 Ross   94960
415 454-2467   Est: 1951
Proprietor: Frank Secondo
Hours: Mon-Sat, 8-4
Types & Periods: Pine &
Oak; Bathroom Pull Chain
Toilets
Specialties: Antique
Plumbing, Building Supplies
Directions: 1 Block Off
Main St; Across from
Santa Barbara Savings &
Loan

WITHERSPOON & POSTLETHWAITE
411 San Anselmo Ave
94960
415 456-1849   Est: 1974
Proprietor: Kent & Sheila
Diehl
Hours: Mon-Sat, 11-5:30
Types & Periods: General
Line, Oriental Rugs, Jewelry,
Postcards
Specialties: Post Cards,
Rugs (Persian)
Appraisal Service Available
Directions: Center of San
Anselmo in Old West
Arcade next to Bank of
America

San Clemente

COLBY ANTIQUES
149 Ave Del Mar   92672
714 492-5130
Proprietor: Mary E Colby
Hours: 11-5:30
Types & Periods: 18th &
19th Century Furniture, Art
Objects

San Diego

SAN DIEGO CLUSTER
Directions: Heavy
Concentration on Adams
(2000-3000 Blocks),
Washington, Running E-W
(200-800 Blocks) Adjacent
Streets, University &
Fairmont

A-1 ANTIQUES
2816 Adams Ave   92116
714 295-8232
Proprietor: Mae Halpenny
Hours: Daily, 1-5
Types & Periods: General
Line
Directions: Corner of
Adams Ave & Park

ANTIQUE CLOCKS & WATCHES
448 West Market St 92101
714 232-7961   Est: 1976
Proprietor: Joe Sherman
Hours: Thurs-Mon, 11-5:30
Types & Periods:
Timepieces
Specialties: Timepieces
Directions: 1 Cracker
Barrel Road in Olde
Cracker Factory

ANTIQUE TYME SHOP
3017 Adams Ave   92116
714 283-3095
Proprietor: Stanley &
Verna Heaton
Hours: Tues-Sat, 11-4:30
Types & Periods: General
Line, Jewelry, China,
Furniture
Directions: Between I-805
& Park

AS TIME GOES BY
3549 University   92104
714 280-9062   Est: 1975
Proprietor: Gloria Selingen
Hours: Tues-Sat, 11-5;
Mon by Chance
Types & Periods: 20's &
30's Funky Items,
Overstuffed Furniture,
European
Turn-of-the-Century
Furniture, Bric-a-Brac
Appraisal Service Available
Directions: Between 35 &
36, 2 Blocks E of Hwy 805

AUBREY'S ANTIQUES
4622 Park Blvd   92116
714 296-6464
Proprietor: Aubrey Melius
Hours: Wed-Sat, 12-5;
Also by Appointment
Types & Periods: Clocks,
Furniture
Directions: Near Corner of
Park & El Cajon

BEN GUN
3495 University Ave 92104
714 282-9015   Est: 1966
Proprietor: Ben Ramer
Hours: Mon-Sat, 11-5:30
Types & Periods: Guns,
Swords, Medals, War Relics,
Games, Western Relics,
Indian Relics
Appraisal Service Available

BOK-HOF GALLERY
1903 Adams Ave   92116
714 295-3714   Est: 1967
Proprietor: D L Hoffmaster
Hours: Daily, 5-7pm; Also
by Appointment
Types & Periods: Anything
before 1920 AD
Directions: 2 Miles N of
Zoo

**BOB BROWN'S TREASURE
SPOT**
226 W Washington St
                    92103
714 298-3368
Proprietor: Bob Brown
Hours: Mon-Sat, 12-5
Types & Periods: General
Line, Furniture, Bric-a-Brac
Directions: N of Dalboa
Park, W of Rte 163

BUCKINGHAM GALLERIES
10125 San Diego
Mission Rd   92108
714 283-7286   Est: 1968
Proprietor: Chester
Whalen
Hours: Exhibitions Mon,
12-8, Auctions,
Tues Eve, 7
Types & Periods: Victorian &
Prior
Specialties: European
Imports

**CANDY COTTAGE & BEA
HIVE**
448 West Market St 92101
714 232-7961   Est: 1976
Proprietor: Bea Hartman
Hours: Thurs-Mon, 11-5:30
Types & Periods: Sweets &
Antiques
Directions: 15 Oreo Ave In
Olde Cracker Factory

CANNON'S ANTIQUES
448 West Market St 92101
714 232-7961   Est: 1976
Proprietor: Marie & Clay
Cannon

Hours: Thurs-Mon, 11-5:30
Types & Periods: Furniture,
Glass
Directions: 1 Nabisco Dr
in Olde Cracker Factory

**THE CHOPPING BLOCK
ANTIQUES**
3827 30th St   92104
714 299-0996   Est: 1974
Proprietor: The Bartlett
Family
Hours: Mon-Sat, 11-5
Types & Periods: American
& European Furniture,
Depression Glassware,
Collectibles
Specialties: Furniture
(Rolltop Desks)
Directions: North Park

COLLECTABLES CORNER
705 6th Ave   92101
714 235-6000   Est: 1973
Proprietor: Mrs Karen
Smith
Hours: Daily
Types & Periods: California
Nostalgia, Glassware,
Furniture
Specialties: Future
Collectibles
Directions: 3 Blocks from
Broadway, Corner of G St

**COLLECTORS BOOK
SHOPPE**
448 West Market St 92101
714 232-7961   Est: 1976
Proprietor: Joe Sherman
Hours: Thurs-Mon, 11-5:30
Types & Periods: Collectors
Books
Directions: 1 Cracker
Barrel Road in Olde
Cracker Factory

**COLLECTORS OF
MEMORABILIA**
448 West Market St 92101
714 232-7961   Est: 1976
Proprietor: Bob & Ella
Salmi
Hours: Sun, Mon, Thurs,
Fri, Sat; Closed Tues, &
Wed.
Types & Periods: Oak,
Americana, Memorabilia
Directions: 3rd Floor, Olde
Cracker Factory

THE CONNOISSEUR
3165 Adams Ave   92116
714 284-1132

Proprietor: Jacqueline &
Trigg Stewart
Hours: Sun-Fri, 12:30-4:30;
Sat, 11-4:30
Types & Periods: 18th &
19th Century American &
English

**COUNTRY COUSINS
ANTIQUES**
448 West Market St 92101
714 232 7961   Est: 1976
Proprietor: Mary McAlister
& Margaret Stacey
Hours: Mon, Thurs, Fri,
Weekends 11-5:30; Closed
Tues & Wed.
Types & Periods: Early
Country
Directions: 17 Oreo Ave in
Olde Cracker Factory

**DAVENPORT
ENTERPRISES ANTIQUES**
7636 Clairemont
Mesa Blvd   92111
714 560-5808   Est: 1974
Proprietor: Robert L
Davenport
Hours: Wed-Sun, 11-5
Types & Periods: English
Victorian Furniture
Directions: Between
Freeways 805 & 100

DESIGNING DAMES
448 West Market   92101
714 232-7961   Est: 1976
Proprietor: Joanne
Brennan
Hours: Thurs-Mon, 11-5:30
Types & Periods: Victorian;
Walnut, Pine, Cherry
Directions: 0 Bishop Blvd
in Olde Cracker Factory

ETC ANTIQUES
448 West Market St 92101
714 232-7961   Est: 1976
Proprietor: Ed Conlon
Hours: Thurs-Mon, 11-5:30
Types & Periods: Miniatures,
Art Glass
Directions: 2 Sesame St in
Olde Cracker Factory

LOLA FORD ANTIQUES
4121 Ashton   92110
714 276-1081   Est: 1956
Proprietor: Lola Ford
Hours: Mon, Tues,
Thurs-Sat, 11-5, Wed by
chance.

San Diego   Cont'd

LOLA FORD   Cont'd
Types & Periods: Furniture,
Glass, China, Brass, Copper,
Jewelry
Specialties: Primitives
Directions: Off Moreno
Blvd

THE FRANCIS FAMILY INC
310 5th Ave   92101
714 232-6561   Est: 1969
Proprietor: The Francis
Family
Hours: Tues-Thurs, 10-5;
Fri & Sat, 10-8; Sun, 12-5
Types & Periods: 19th &
20th Century Austrian,
French & English Furniture;
Bric-a-Brac, Player Pianos,
Stained Glass, Clocks,
Silver, Cars
Directions: Corner of 5th
& K, across from Old
Spaghetti Factory
Restaurant

GASLAMP ANTIQUES
448 West Market St 92101
714 232-7961   Est: 1976
Proprietor: Bud Kader
Hours: Thurs-Mon, 11-5:30
Types & Periods: Furniture
& Funky Junque
Directions: 3 Bishop Blvd
in Olde Cracker Factory

GINGERBREAD COTTAGE
1331 Garnet Ave   92109
714 272-0180   Est: 1974
Proprietor: Alana & Mel
Booth
Hours: Mon-Fri, 10-5; Sat
& Sun, 12-5
Types & Periods: Fancy
Turn-of-the-Century
American Oak Furniture,
Gifts, Frames, Collectibles
Directions: Pacific Beach;
From I-5 head West Go W
on Garnet Ave

**GRANNY'S HADDIT
ANTIQUES**
7644 Clairmont Mesa Blvd
92111
714 292-1455
Proprietor: Myron &
Marilee Smith
Hours: Daily, 9:30-6

Types & Periods: American
Oak
Directions: Between US
395 & I-805; N Side of St

**THE HAWTHORNE'S
ANTIQUES**
448 W Market St   92101
714 232-7961   Est: 1976
Proprietor: John C.
Hawthorne & Melissa
Clarke
Hours: Thurs-Mon,
11-5:30; Evenings by
Appointment
Types & Periods: General,
Coins, Old Picture
Postcards, Political Buttons
Specialties: Old Picture
Postcards
Directions: 3rd Floor, in
Olde Cracker Factory

**MAMIE HOGAN ANTIQUES
& MEMORABILIA**
2940 Adams Ave   92116
714 282-2811
Proprietor: Mamie Hogan
Hours: Mon, Wed-Sat,
11:30-5
Types & Periods: General
Line, Collectibles

**HOOK & LADDER
ANTIQUES**
806 W Washington St
92103
714 295-3867
Proprietor: L W Tuttle
Hours: Daily, 11-5
Types & Periods: Furniture,
Oriental Rugs, Silver,
General Line
Directions: NE of Balboa
Park

HOUSE OF HEIRLOOMS
801 University Ave   92103
714 298-0502   Est: 1972
Proprietor: Trend
Industries Inc & Ruth L
Schulman
Hours: Mon-Sat, 9:30-5
Types & Periods: 17th to 1st
Quarter of 20th Century;
General Line
Directions: 3 Miles N of
City Center in Hillcrest
Area

**HOUSE'S EMPORIUM
ANTIQUES**
3260 Adams Ave   92116
Proprietor: Betty House
Hours: Tues-Sat

Types & Periods:
Collectibles, Primitives,
Depression Glass
Directions: Next to Post
Office, Between 33rd St &
Bancroft

**HUMBERSTON'S
ANTIQUES**
228 W Washington St
92103
714 298-1522
Proprietor: Peg & Ken
Humberston
Hours: Tues-Sat, 11-5
Types & Periods: Art Glass,
General Line
Directions: N of Balboa
Park, Near Corner of Rte
163 & W Washington

KANTOR'S ANTIQUES
448 West Market St 92101
714 236-0099   Est: 1976
Proprietor: Edna &
Benjamin Kantor
Hours: Thurs- Mon,
11-5:30
Types & Periods: Collectors
Items, Objets D'Art
Directions: 2nd Floor, Olde
Cracker Factory

KELLY'S RELICS
1621 W Lewis St   92103
714 298-1404   Est: 1964
Proprietor: La Trelle Kelly
Hours: Tues-Sat, 12-5
Types & Periods: General
Line
Specialties: Jewelry
Appraisal Service Available
Directions: Mission Hills

**BLANCHE KOEHMSTEDT
ANTIQUES**
4187 Fairmount Ave 92105
714 281-8939   Est: 1956
Proprietor: Blanche
Koehmstedt
Hours: Mon-Sat, 12:30-5
Types & Periods: China,
Early American, Pressed
Glass, Flint & Cut Glass,
Primitives, Paper Americana
Specialties: Post Cards,
Glass
Directions: 1 Block S of El
Cajon Blvd

THE KRACKER KRUMM
448 W Market St   92101
714 232-7961   Est: 1976
Proprietor: Pat Krumm
Hours: Thurs-Mon, 11-5:30

Types & Periods: General
Line
Directions: 10 Ritz Rd in
Olde Cracker Factory

KROPP'S ANTIQUES
1441 Garnet   92109
714 272-0840
Proprietor: Pat & Linda
Kropp
Hours: Daily
Types & Periods: 1880-1910
American Oak Furniture
Directions: Pacific Beach;
1 1/2 Miles W of I-5

**LAMB ANTIQUES &
APPRAISAL SERVICE**
3436 30th St   92104
714 291-6588   Est: 1959
Proprietor: L O & M R
Lamb
Hours: By Appointment,
By Chance
Types & Periods: Art Glass,
Bronzes, Dolls, French,
Lamps, Period Furniture,
Jewelry, Oriental, Rugs,
Sterling, Porcelains, Rare
Antiques, Victorian
Specialties: Art Glass,
Bronzes, Dolls, Jewelry,
Lamps, Porcelains, Rugs,
Sterling
Appraisal Service Available
Directions: 805 Frwy S;
Exit at University Ave; Go
E to 30th St, then S 4
Blocks

LAMPLIGHTER ANTIQUES
3020 Adams Ave   92116
714 282-0877
Proprietor: Lloyd G.
Davies
Hours: Daily, 10-5, Sun
12-5
Types & Periods: General
Line
Directions: From 805 S,
Exit at Adams Ave
Off-ramp; from 163, Take
El Cajon Blvd; Adams Ave
is 4 Blocks N of El Cajon
Blvd

LIZ-BETH'S ANTIQUES
3260 Adams Ave   92116
714 283-2681
Proprietor: Elizabeth
Prater
Hours: Tues-Sat, 10:30-5
Types & Periods: Art Glass,
China, General Line

LOUISE'S
448 W Market St   92101
714 232-7961   Est: 1976
Proprietor: Louise Glaeser
Hours: Thurs-Mon, 11-5:30
Types & Periods:
Collectibles
Directions: 11 Ritz Rd in
Olde Cracker Factory

NANCY MORRIS ANTIQUES
320 W Washington St
                      92103
714 291-2366
Proprietor: Nancy & Jack
Morris
Hours: Tues-Sat, 11-5
Types & Periods: Silver,
Victorian, Paintings,
Orientals

NEWCOMB'S ANTIQUES
448 W Market St   92101
714 232-7961   Est: 1976
Proprietor: Elva Newcomb
Hours: Thurs-Mon, 11-5:30
Types & Periods: Glassware
in Miniature
Directions: 5 Saltine Trail
in Olde Cracker Factory

NEW ENGLAND IMAGES
448 W Market St   92101
714 232-7961   Est: 1970
Proprietor: Kathleen Derby
Hours: Thurs-Mon, 11-5:30
Types & Periods: General
Line
Specialties: Pen & Ink
Drawings
Directions: Olde Cracker
Factory, 6 Premium Plaza

NOSTALGIA
1908 Cable St   92107
714 224-8866   Est: 1974
Proprietor: Gary &
Maureen Karlson
Hours: Mon-Fri, 11-5; Sat,
10-5
Types & Periods:
1850's-1950's
Specialties: Furniture
Directions: Ocean Beach;
Take I-8 to Sunset Cliffs
Blvd, Right on Newport to
Cable

OLDE CRACKER FACTORY
448 W Market   92101
714 232-7961   Est: 1976
Proprietor: Joe & Ruth
Sherman
Hours: Thurs-Mon, 11-5:30

Types & Periods: Complete
Range of Antiques &
Collectibles: Over 40
Antique & Collectible Shops
in the Old Bishop Cracker
Factory
Specialties: Antique Clock
Museum
Appraisal Service Available
Directions: Downtown San
Diego, SW Harbor Corner;
Two Blocks from the
Police Station; Corner of
Colombia & Market

OUR COUNTRY ANTIQUES
448 West Market   92101
714 232-7961   Est: 1976
Proprietor: Doris Shelley
Hours: Thurs-Mon, 11-5:30
Types & Periods: Early
American Pine, Cherry &
Walnut Furniture; Early
Accessories
Directions: 3rd Floor in
Olde Cracker Factory

PAPER ANTIQUITIES
448 W Market St   92101
714 232-7961   Est: 1976
Proprietor: Alan Witty
Hours: Thurs-Mon, 11-5:30
Types & Periods:
Newspapers, Magazines,
Postcards
Directions: 14 Oreo Ave in
Olde Cracker Factory

PARKER'S CORNER
448 W Market St   92101
714 232-7961   Est: 1976
Proprietor: Bernice Parker
Hours: Thurs-Mon, 11-5:30
Types & Periods: European,
American
Directions: 5 Graham Lane
in Olde Cracker Factory

THE PHOTOGRAPHER
448 W Market St   92101
714 232-7961   Est: 1976
Proprietor: Natalie
Johnson
Hours: Thurs-Mon, 11-5:30
Types & Periods: Old Time
Photos
Directions: 13 Ritz Rd in
Olde Cracker Factory

FRANK PRINCE ANTIQUES
2922 Adams Ave   92116
714 283-3039
Proprietor: Frank Prince
Hours: Mon-Sat

San Diego Cont'd

FRANK PRINCE Cont'd
Types & Periods: Whatever
is Available
Specialties: Light Fixtures
Appraisal Service Available
Directions: 30th & Adams

THE RED LION ANTIQUES
448 W Market   92101
714 232-1819   Est: 1976
Proprietor: Mary Rose
O'Connor
Hours: Thurs-Mon, 11-5:30
Types & Periods: Early
American Pine, Country
Primitives, Pewter,
Bennington, Lightings, Guns,
Oils, Crocks
Specialties: Early 18th
Century Pine
Directions: Bishop Blvd in
Olde Cracker Factory

SCHENCK'S ANTIQUES
448 W Market St   92101
714 232-7961   Est: 1976
Proprietor: Mary Beth
Schenck
Hours: Thurs-Mon, 11-5:30
Types & Periods: General
Line
Directions: 16 Oreo Ave in
Olde Cracker Factory

THE SECOND STORY
448 W Market St   92101
714 232-7961   Est: 1976
Proprietor: Lucy
Fernandez
Hours: Thurs-Sun, 11-5:30
Types & Periods: General
Line & Collectibles
Directions: 1 Sesame St in
Olde Cracker Factory

SKI'S TRADING POST
3530 University Ave 93204
714 281-1247   Est: 1969
Proprietor: John
Malinowski
Hours: Mon-Sat, 11-6
Types & Periods: Clocks,
Watches, Jewelry, Lamps,
Swords, Military Medals,
Furniture
Specialties: Clocks, Watches
Appraisal Service Available
Directions: 3 Blocks E of
Hwy 805

SLAVIC FOLK ART
448 West Market St 92101
714 232-7961   Est: 1976
Proprietor: Vladimir
Gurevich
Hours: Thurs-Mon, 11-5:30
Types & Periods: Slavic Folk
Art, Collectibles
Directions: 3 Sesame St in
Olde Cracker Factory

SMITH'S ANTIQUES
930 W Washington   92103
714 291-1758   Est: 1955
Proprietor: Ermin M Smith
Hours: Tues-Sat
Types & Periods: Georgian
& Early American Silver,
Porcelains, Jewelry
Directions: 4 Blocks E of
I-5 on Washington
Off-Ramp

**T & R ANTIQUES
WAREHOUSE INC**
4630 Santa Fe St   92109
714 272-0437   Est: 1970
Proprietor: Ray & Trude
Gitler
Hours: Mon-Fri, 9-6; Sat &
Sun, 10-5
Types & Periods: Imports
from 5 European Countries;
French & Country French

TREASURES TO TRASH
448 W Market St   92101
714 232-7961   Est: 1976
Proprietor: Kelly Espey
Hours: Thurs-Mon, 11-5:30
Types & Periods: Oak, Glass
Directions: 12 Ritz Road in
Olde Cracker Factory

THE TREE HOUSE
448 W Market St   92101
714 232-7961   Est: 1976
Proprietor: Bob Smith
Hours: Thurs-Mon, 11-5:30
Types & Periods: Greenery
Among Antiques
Directions: 2 Bishop Blvd
in Olde Cracker Factory

TUCKER'S MUSIC BOX
310 Fifth Ave   92101
714 281-0636   Est: 1972
Proprietor: Mr & Mrs
Charles J Tucker
Hours: Tues-Thurs, 10-5;
Fri & Sat, 10-8; Sun, 12-5
Types & Periods: Music
Boxes, Player Pianos,

Nickelodeons, Orchestrions
& Other Automated Musical
Instruments
Specialties: Music Boxes
Appraisal Service Available
Directions: Second Floor,
Francis Family Bldg;
Corner of 5th & K in the
Gaslamp District

20'S UNLIMITED
448 W Market St   92101
714 232-7961   Est: 1976
Proprietor: Linda Moss &
Richard Avey
Hours: Thurs-Mon,11-5:30
Types & Periods: Art Deco
Directions: 7 Uneeda Way
in Olde Cracker Factory

**UNICORN COMPANY
ANTIQUES**
660 2nd Ave   92101
714 234-0721   Est: 1974
Proprietor: Ron Maikovich
Hours: Daily, 11-5:30
Types & Periods: European
& English Victorian &
Edwardian Furniture, Clocks
& Bric-a-Brac
17,000 Sq Ft of Showroom
Space
Specialties: Complete Clock
Sales & Service Dept;
Complete Refinishing &
Restoration Dept
Appraisal Service Available
Directions: Corner of 2nd
& G; Downtown

**UNIQUE ANTIQUES &
GIFTS**
7119 Navajo Rd   92119
714 461-7780   Est: 1974
Proprietor: Betty Mabee &
Carol Ulrey
Hours: Mon-Sat, Open
Shop
Types & Periods: Furniture,
Glass, China, Silver,
Primitives; New Books on
Antiques; 4,000 Sq Ft
Specialties: Matching
Service for Old French
Haviland & Lennox China
Directions: Off Hwy 8 at
College Ave, N to Navajo
Rd, 2 Miles E on Navajo

**VANCE'S MIZ MOON'S
HANGUP**
448 W Market St   92101
714 232-7961   Est: 1976
Proprietor: Ellie Vance
Hours: Thurs-Mon, 11-5:30

Types & Periods: General
Line, Collectibles
   Directions: 9 Saltine Trail
   in Olde Cracker Factory

WATSON'S TIQUES N' TRIVIA
   448 W Market St   92101
   714 232-7961   Est: 1976
   Proprietor: Lucille &
   Walter Watson
   Hours: Thurs-Mon, 11-5:30
Types & Periods: Glass,
Furniture
   Directions: 2 Plaza in Olde
   Cracker Factory

WEEDS 'N' THINGS
   448 W Market St   92101
   714 236-1927   Est: 1976
   Proprietor: Shirley Klein &
   Don Pyke
   Hours: Thurs-Mon, 11-5:30
Types & Periods: Oak
Furniture, Copper & Brass
Pots
Specialties: Dried & Silk
Florals in Antique Containers
& Trunks
   Directions: 6 Uneeds Way
   in Olde Cracker Factory

THE WRIGHT PLACE
   448 West Market St 92101
   714 232-7961   Est: 1976
   Proprietor: David Wright
   Hours: Thurs-Mon, 11-5:30
Types & Periods: Small
Items, Collectibles
   Directions: 8 Saltine Trail
   in Olde Cracker Factory

YVETTE'S ANTIQUES
   4636 Mission Blvd   92109
   714 488-6050
   Proprietor: Ken & Yvette
   Moore
   Hours: Mon-Sat, 11-4
Types & Periods: European,
American
   Directions: In Pacific
   Beach

San Francisco

SAN FRANCISCO CLUSTER
   Directions: Union St:
   Franklin St W to Fillmore,
   Shops on Adjacent
   Streets; Sacramento:
   Divisadero St W to Maple;
   Jackson Square; Sutter
   St: Powell St W to Gough;
Polk St: Geary St N to
Filbert; Clement St:
Arquello Blvd W to Park;
Presidio

ALESIA
   1640 Union   94123
   415 441-5520   Est: 1976
   Proprietor: Darlene Green
   Hours: Mon-Sat, 11-5;
   Also by Appointment
Types & Periods: 18th
Century Furniture,
Accessories
Specialties: Furniture
(Empire, Louis XV & XVI)
   Directions: Between
   Franklin & Gaugh

THE ANTIQUE TRADERS
   4314 California St   94118
   415 668-4444   Est: 1974
   Proprietor: Alan Schneider
   Hours: By Appointment,
   By Chance
Types & Periods: Early
American, Stained Glass
Windows

ANTIQUES & COTTAGE CRAFTS AT LIVINGSTONS
   100 Grant Ave   94108
   415 362-2054   Est: 1975
   Proprietor: Evelyn Alesnin
   Hours: Daily
Types & Periods: English &
French Furniture,
Porcelains, Silver
   Directions: Grant Ave &
   Geary St, Just Off Union
   Sq

ANTIQUES UNLIMITED
   219 Monterey Blvd   94131
   415 585-7100   Est: 1969
   Proprietor: Mrs Muriel E W
   Cassell
   Hours: Daily
Types & Periods: Early
American & European
Furniture, China, Silver
   Directions: James Lick
   Freeway (101) to Daly City
   Freeway (280); 3rd Turn is
   Monterey Blvd

ARGONAUT BOOK SHOP
   786-792 Sutter St   94109
   415 474-9067   Est: 1941
   Proprietor: Robert D
   Haines, Jr
   Hours: Tues-Sat; by
   Appointment

Types & Periods: Fine &
Rare books in all Fields, with
an Emphasis on Areas of
Specialty
Specialties: Books: Western
American History, Early
American Exploration,
Voyages of Discovery,
Cartography, Historical
Works with Hand Colored
Plates
Appraisal Service Available
   Directions: Corner of
   Sutter & Jones; 3 Blocks
   from Downtown San
   Francisco

ASIAN ART
   500 Beach St   94133
   415 885-5010
   Proprietor: Hun Lee &
   Juana T Lee
   Hours: Daily
Types & Periods: Chinese &
Japanese Jade, Pottery,
Ivory, Netsukes, Snuff
Bottles
Specialties: Jade Articles
from China, Netsukes &
Snuff Bottles
Appraisal Service Available
   Directions: Beach & Jones
   Sts, Fisherman's Wharf

ASIAN ART
   165 Jefferson St   94133
   415 771-9049
   Proprietor: Hun Lee &
   Juana T Lee
   Hours: Daily
Types & Periods: Jade,
Bronze, Ceramics, Ivory,
Netsuke, Oriental
Appraisal Service Available

JOHN HUDSON AVERY
   2953 Fillmore   94123
   415 563-1560   Est: 1966
   Proprietor: John H Avery
   Hours: By Appointment
Types & Periods: Unusual
Oriental, European &
American Furniture,
Paintings & Art Objects
Specialties: Textiles, Rugs &
Silver
Appraisal Service Available
   Directions: Near Union St

BELKNAP & PURCELL
   1546 California St   94109
   415 776-0756   Est: 1976
   Proprietor: Pamela R
   Scheu
   Hours: Tues-Sat, 10-6

San Francisco   Cont'd

BELKNAP & PURCELL
                    Cont'd
Types & Periods: English
1800's, Furniture, Silver,
Crystal, Accessories
   Directions: Between Polk
   & Larkin Sts; Calif St
   Cable Car

BETTIE BOOPS
   1342 9th Ave   94122
   415 665-5624   Est: 1973
   Proprietor: Elizabeth
   Bloom
   Hours: Daily, 12-6
Types & Periods: General
Line
Specialties: Jewelry
   Directions: Between Judah
   & Irving Sts; 2 Blocks
   from Golden Gate Park;
   An underground antique
   shop

BLACKWELL ANTIQUES
   563 Sutter   94102
   415 433-4886   Est: 1926
   Hours: Mon-Sat
Types & Periods: Jewelry
Specialties: Jewelry
Appraisal Service Available
   Directions: Downtown

BLUE SWAN GALLERY
   575 Sutter St   94102
   415 981-5366   Est: 1973
   Proprietor: W E Davis
   Hours: Tues-Sat, 11-5 and
   by Appointment
Types & Periods: Art
Nouveau, Furniture & Objets
D'Art
   Directions: Sutter St
   between Powell (Cable
   Car Line) & Mason

**ROBERT K BORMAN
ANTIQUES**
   1843 Union St   94123
   415 922-9411   Est: 1957
   Proprietor: Robert Borman
   Hours: Daily, 11:30-5; Also
   by Appointment
Types & Periods: 18th &
19th Century Country &
French
Specialties: Bird Cages,
American Quilts

LEONARD BOWMAN
   555 Sutter   94102
   415 781-2327   Est: 1945
   Proprietor: Leonard
   Bowman
   Hours: Mon-Fri, by
   Appointment
Types & Periods: Russian,
Oriental; Rare Items of
Antiquity
Specialties: Appraiser for W
R Hearst's San Simeon
Appraisal Service Available
   Directions: Downtown, 2
   Blocks from Union Square

**BUTTERFIELD &
BUTTERFIELD
AUCTIONEERS**
   1244 Sutter St   94109
   415 673-1362   Est: 1865
   Proprietor: Bernard Osher
   Hours: Mon-Fri, 9-5; Sat &
   Sun,Preview Days;
   Monthly Auctions
Types & Periods: Fine
English, American &
Continental Furniture,
Furnishings, Porcelain,
Paintings, Silver, Jewelry &
Carpets
Appraisal Service Available
   Directions: Between Polk
   & Van Ness (Hwy 101 thru
   San Francisco)

**CARUSO ANTIQUES &
ACCESSORIES**
   1400 Green St   94109
   415 673-8912   Est: 1969
   Proprietor: Gilbert Caruso
   Hours: Mon-Sat, 12-6
Types & Periods: American,
French, Italian & English
Paintings, Porcelain; Oriental
Art
Specialties: Oriental
   Directions: Green St at
   Polk St

**DILLINGHAM & BROWN,
LTD**
   3485 Sacramento St 94118
   415 563-1976   Est: 1973
   Proprietor: Gaylord
   Dillingham & Janet Brown
   Dillingham
   Hours: Mon-Sat, 10-5 or
   by Appointment
Types & Periods: 17th, 18th
& Early 19th Century English
Furniture, Pottery, Porcelain
& Metalware; 18th & 19th
Century Primitive Paintings

Specialties: Furniture,
Metalware, Pottery (pre
1830)
   Directions: 2 Blocks W of
   Presidio Ave

**JOHN DOUGHTY
ANTIQUES INC**
   619 Sansome St   94111
   415 398-6849   Est: 1948
   Proprietor: John Doughty
   Hours: Mon-Fri, by
   Appointment
Types & Periods: Fine 17th
& 18th Century English
Furniture, Works of Art &
Decorative Accessories
Appraisal Service Available
   Directions: Jackson Sq
   between Washington &
   Jackson

FABULOUS THINGS LTD
   831 Montgomery   94133
   415 391-6565   Est: 1967
   Proprietor: Harlan G Koch
   Hours: Mon-Fri, 10:30-5:30
Types & Periods: Korean
Chests, Thai Temple
Carvings, Buddhas,
Paintings, Carved Beds, Silk,
Batiks, Ch'ing Dynasty
Specialties: Oriental
   Directions: Also Store
   at Kahala Mall,
   Honolulu

FABULOUS THINGS LTD
   1974 Union St   94133
   415 346-0346   Est: 1967
   Proprietor: Harlan G Koch
   Hours: Daily, 10:30-5:30
Types & Periods: 14th-19th
Century Thai & Burmese
Buddhas & Buddha Heads
(Bronze, Wood & Lacquer);
18th & 19th Century Thai
Temple Carvings (Teak);
19th Century Chinese
Temple Carvings (Camphor
Wood); 19th Century (Tao
Kuang) Blue & White
Porcelains; 19th Century
original Korean Cabinets &
Chests; Antique Chinese
Silver Jewelry; 30-70 Yr Old
Japanese Obis made into
Table Runners
30-70 Yr Old Chinese
Puppets

Specialties: Oriental
Appraisal Service Available
Directions: Between
Laguna & Buchanan

FAR EAST FINE ARTS INC
518 Sutter St   94102
415 421-0932   Est: 1973
Proprietor: Jung Ying
Tsao
Hours: Mon-Sat, 10-5
Types & Periods: Paintings,
Jade, Lacquer, Ceramics,
Bronze
Specialties: Oriental
Appraisal Service Available
Directions: Between
Powell & Mason, 1 Block
from Union Square

FILIA
437 Grant Ave   94108
415 391-5224   Est: 1970
Proprietor: E Dang
Hours: Daily
Types & Periods: Orientals
Specialties: Oriental (Jade)

FILIPELLO ANTIQUES
1632 Market St   94102
415 861-5100   Est: 1962
Proprietor: John Filipello
Hours: Daily, 9:30-6
Types & Periods: 17th, 18th
& 19th Century French,
Austrian & English, Some
American
Specialties: Clocks
Directions: 2 Blocks N of
Van Ness and Market

**PETER FRIES ANTIQUE
CHURCHPLATE**
64 Vicksburg St   94114
415 826-8015
Proprietor: Rev Peter Fries
Hours: By Appointment
Types & Periods: Christian
Sacred Vessels,
Monstrances, Reliquaries,
Vestments, Carvings,
Manuscripts
Appraisal Service Available

GAY'S ANTIQUES
3029 Clement   94121
415 221-6036   Est: 1967
Proprietor: Jack Lewis
Hours: Mon-Fri
Types & Periods: General
Appraisal Service Available
Directions: Between 31st
& 32nd Ave's on Clement
St.

GEORGE V ANTIQUES
915-1100 Battery St 94111
415 788-4900   Est: 1970
Proprietor: George A
Vasilaidis
Hours: Daily, 10-6, Also by
Appointment
Types & Periods: English,
French, Austrian, Belgian,
American; General Line
Specialties: Architectural
Items, European
Copperware
Directions: Between Union
& Lombard, Off Broadway

THE GILDED AGE
450 Castro St   94114
415 621-0609   Est: 1968
Proprietor: Ian F Ingham
Hours: Daily
Types & Periods: 2 Huge
Floors of English &
American Antiques
Directions: 1/2 Block from
Market St

GRANDMA'S HOUSE
2200 Polk St   94109
415 441-5561   Est: 1971
Proprietor: Sam Du Vall
Hours: Tues-Sat, 12-6;
Sun, 1-5
Types & Periods: Stained
Glass, Spanish Furniture,
Brass, English Leather
Chairs, Sofas, Candelabra
Directions: Corner of
Vallejo & Polk

**EMILY L HARVEY
ANTIQUES**
1680 Market St   94103
415 626-2216   Est: 1975
Proprietor: Emily L Harvey
Hours: Daily, 10-6
Types & Periods: All;
American & European
Furniture, Tapestry, China,
Glass, Collectibles, Brass,
Copper; Asian Rugs, Etc
Specialties: European
Antiques
Appraisal Service Available
Directions: Market St near
Van Ness Avenue

HOUSE OF WICKER
4117 19th St   94114
415 626-1017   Est: 1973
Proprietor: Frank G Stagg
Hours: Tues-Sat, 12-6

Types & Periods: Wicker,
Silk & Beaded Lamps, Art
Deco, Art Nouveau,
Furniture
Specialties: Furniture
(Wicker)
Appraisal Service Available
Directions: 19th St off
Castro, 2 Blocks from
Market St

RONALD JAMES
1201 Sutter St   94109
415 771-9330   Est: 1967
Proprietor: Ronald
Schwarz & James Artman
Hours: Mon-Fri, 10-5; Sat,
11-4
Types & Periods: 18th &
19th Century Porcelains,
Silver, Glass
Specialties: Porcelains
Appraisal Service Available
Directions: Corner of
Sutter & Polk

TOM KAYE ANTIQUES
2044 Union St   94123
415 921-0300   Est: 1966
Proprietor: Tom Kaye
Hours: Mon-Sat, 10:30-5
Types & Periods: Marine
Artifacts, Barometers;
Desks, Oil Paintings
Specialties: Furniture (18th
Century English)

KINGS ANTIQUES
1255 Sansome St   94111
415 986-7770   Est: 1972
Proprietor: Ken King
Hours: Daily, 10-5
Types & Periods: French: All
Periods & Styles, 18th
Century to Art Deco
Specialties: Furniture
Directions: Hwy 101 to
Broadway Exit; Turn
Right; 1 Block to Sansome
St; 4 Blocks on Left

KUROMATSU
722 Bay St   94109
415 474-4027
Proprietor: J Edward Cook
Hours: Mon-Sat, 10-5
Types & Periods: Oriental
Antiques & Accessories

J M LANG ANTIQUES
361 Sutter St   94108
415 982-2213   Est: 1973
Proprietor: Jarmila M Lang
Hours: Mon-Sat, 10-5

San Francisco   Cont'd

J M LANG   Cont'd
Types & Periods: Antique
Jewelry & Objects of Art
Directions: Near Union
Square Hyatt House;
between Stockton & Grant

WALTER LARSEN ANTIQUES
533 Sutter St   94102
415 391-2180
Proprietor: Walter C
Larsen
Hours: Daily, 11-4
Types & Periods: General
Line, Silver, Pottery, China,
Art Glass, Bronze

K H LENGFELD
1409 Sutter   94109
415 775-3040   Est: 1937
Hours: Daily, 9-5
Types & Periods: 17th, 18th
& 19th Century French,
Italian & English
Specialties: Country French
Directions: Near
Downtown

M IVAN MALNEKOFF
760 Market, Suite 251
94102
415 981-1545   Est: 1970
Proprietor: M Ivan
Malnekoff
Hours: Daily
Types & Periods: Jade
Carvings, Ch'ing Dynasty
Directions: Downtown

COL JOHN MALONEY ANTIQUES
1695 Market St   94103
415 626-2133   Est: 1976
Proprietor: John Maloney
Hours: Mon-Fri, 9-6; Sat,
9-5
Types & Periods: General
Antiques, Collectibles &
Reproductions; All Periods
Appraisal Service Available
Directions: Located where
Valencia, Haight & Gough
Sts Intersect Market St

WALKER MC INTYRE ANTIQUES
3615 Sacramento St 94118
415 563-8024   Est: 1977
Proprietor: Walker
Mc Intyre

Hours: Tues-Fri, 11-5; Sat,
12-5
Types & Periods: English
Antiques
Specialties: Oriental Rugs,
Decorative Accessories,
Silver, Mahogany, Oak &
Walnut Furniture
Directions: Between
Locust & Spruce

MERRYVALE INC
3640 Buchanan St   94123
415 567-0615
Hours: Mon-Fri, 9-5:30
Types & Periods: 18th
Century English & French
Furniture, Garden
Accessories

JEAN MILLER
3108 Fillmore St   94123
415 567-1778   Est: 1972
Proprietor: Jean Miller
Hours: Daily, 9-5
Types & Periods: French &
Italian Country Furniture &
Accessories
Specialties: Oriental
Directions: Off the Union
St Shopping Area

MONTGOMERY & SON ANTIQUES
470 Jackson St   94111
415 989-7693
Hours: Mon-Fri, 10-5
Types & Periods: 18th
Century English &
Continental Furniture

G L MORRIS
547 Sutter St   94102
415 989-4709   Est: 1972
Proprietor: Gary Morris
Hours: Mon-Sat, 10-5
Types & Periods: European
& Oriental; Small Curio
Pieces, Ivories, Porcelains,
Objet D'Art & Objet De
Virtu, Antique Jewelry,
Pocket Watches
Specialties: Prints of Paul
Jacoulet
Directions: Between
Powell & Mason,
Downtown, 1 1/2 Blocks
from Union Square

THE NEW MANILA IMPORTING COMPANY
1549 California St   94109
415 776-4835   Est: 1970
Proprietor: Richard
Gervais

Hours: Mon-Sat, 10-6
Types & Periods: Southeast
Asian, Philippine,
Indonesian, Mainland China
Specialties: Philippine Native
& Domestic Antiques
Directions: On California
Near Polk St

NGAN'S ANTIQUES
704 Kearny St   94109
415 781-6729   Est: 1976
Proprietor: Bill Ngan
Hours: Daily
Types & Periods: Chinese
Furniture, Jade
Specialties: Ceramics,
Paintings
Directions: Near Financial
Dist of SF between Clay
St & Kearny

NOSTALGIA EXPRESS
2535 Irving St   94122
415 665-0867   Est: 1973
Proprietor: Angelo & Carol
Abbate
Hours: Daily
Types & Periods: 19th &
20th Century American
Specialties: China, Glass
Directions: Between 26th
& 27th Aves; Sunset
District near Golden Gate
Park

OLD STUFF ANTIQUES
1728 Divisadero St 94115
415 931-8860   Est: 1975
Proprietor: Clifford Glover
Hours: Daily, 9:30-6:30
Types & Periods: 1850-1920,
Furniture, Light Fixtures
Appraisal Service Available
Directions: Between Sutter
& Bush Near Pacific
Heights

OLD WAGON WHEEL ANTIQUES
1125 Clement St   94118
415 752-2117   Est: 1948
Proprietor: Florence
McColly
Hours: Tues-Sat
Types & Periods: General
Line
Specialties: Furniture, Silver,
Crystal, Porcelains
Directions: Richmond
District near the Presidio

PAINTED LADY
1838 Divisadero   94115
415 563-1073   Est: 1971
Proprietor: Diane Breivis
Hours: Mon-Sat, 11-6
Types & Periods: 1900-1940;
Clothing, Jewelry, Furniture,
Accessories
Specialties: Unusual
Jewelry, Evening Clothes
Directions: Between Pine
& Bush

PARSE RUG CO
1100 Sutter St   94109
415 673-2777   Est: 1973
Proprietor: Ahmed
Ebrahimi
Hours: Daily
Types & Periods: Persian
Rugs, Oriental Rugs
Appraisal Service Available
Directions: Corner of
Larkin & Sutter

PETERSEN'S ANTIQUES
1866 Union St   94123
415 567-6260
Hours: By Appointment
Types & Periods: General
Line

R & F H POSTLETHWAITE
792 Bay St   94109
415 885-5878   Est: 1948
Proprietor: R & F H
Postlethwaite
Hours: Tues-Sat, 10-4:30
Types & Periods: English,
Early Oak
Specialties: Treen,
Staffordshire Figurines &
Cottages
Directions: Corner of Bay
& Hyde; Cable Car Line

RED ANCHOR
872 North Point   94109
415 673-3436   Est: 1977
Proprietor: Jerry Posner
Hours: Tues-Sat
Types & Periods:
Consignment Shop
Exclusively, Deals in All
Phases of the Decorative
Arts
Specialties: 18th Century
English & Continental
Porcelain, Silver & Furniture
Appraisal Service Available

REPEAT PERFORMANCE
2223 Fillmore St   94115
415 563-3123

Proprietor: San Francisco
Symphony Ass'n
Hours: Mon, 1-4;
Tues-Sat, 10-4
Types & Periods: Small
Furniture Items, Art, Silver,
Etc donated by Friends of
the Symphony
Appraisal Service Available
Directions: Pacific Heights
Neighborhood; Take 22
Fillmore St Bus or 3
Jackson Bus to
Sacramento & Fillmore Sts

**BRUCE ROGERS
ANTIQUES**
432 Jackson St   94111
415 771-3390
Proprietor: Louis Fenton
Hours: Mon-Fri
Types & Periods: Rare
European English & Oriental
Furniture & Porcelain Objet
D'Art; 18th Century & Earlier
Directions: Between
Montgomery & Sansome

SAMARKAND
1235 Sutter St   94109
415 441-0755   Est: 1969
Proprietor: W R Roalfe &
R B Steele
Hours: Daily
Types & Periods: Oriental
Rugs, Textiles
Appraisal Service Available
Directions: Between Polk
& Van Ness

SERVICE-KNOLLE
551 Pacific Ave   94133
415 981-7717
Proprietor: Anne Service &
W Allen Knolle
Hours: Mon-Fri, 9-4:30
Types & Periods: Oriental
Antiques: Furniture,
Screens, Scrolls, Decorative
Accessories from Japan,
China, Thailand, Southeast
Asia
Specialties: Coromandel
Screens & Japanese Folding
Screens
Directions: Located in
Jackson Square

**SHIABATA ART STUDIO-
THE DAIBUTSU**
3028 Fillmore St   94123
415 567-1530
Hours: Mon-Sat, 10:30-5
Types & Periods: Chinese &
Japanese Art Objects

**SHINGLE SHACK
ANTIQUES**
1772 Haight   94117
415 752-4301   Est: 1967
Proprietor: Ken Lemekon
Hours: Daily, 12-5
Types & Periods: Glass
Shades, Furniture, Primitives
Specialties: American Oak
Furniture
Directions: Between Cole
& Shrader St

T Z SHIOTA
3131 Fillmore St   94123
415 929-7979   Est: 1897
Proprietor: Paul Shiota
Hours: Mon-Sat, 9-5:30
Types & Periods: Chinese &
Japanese Potteries,
Porcelains, Bronzes, Wood
Block Prints, Paintings; 18th
& 19th Century
Specialties: Japanese Wood
Block Prints, Netsuke
Directions: Between Filbert
& Greenwich Sts; 1 1/2
Blocks from Union St

SOLANNE ANTIQUES
2238 Polk St   94109
415 775-1653   Est: 1959
Proprietor: Anne Dublin
Hours: Tues-Sat, 10-6
Types & Periods: Diversified,
including Furniture,
Paintings, Chandeliers,
Hardware, Frames, Clocks
Specialties: Frames,
Chandeliers, Hardware
Directions: 1 Block E of
Van Ness Ave (101),
between Vallejo & Green
Sts; 2 Blocks W of Hyde
St Cable Car; Municipal
Bus 19 Runs in Front of
Shop

SYLVAR GALLERY
1216 Polk St   94109
415 776-0300   Est: 1970
Proprietor: Gerald M
Sylvar (& John Harms)
Hours: Tues-Sat, 11-5; By
Appointment
Types & Periods:
Pre-Columbian Art (Ancient
Mexico), Egyptian
Antiquities, Japanese Prints;
Antique & Fine Silver; Works
of Art
Specialties: Pre-Columbian
Art & Fine Silver

San Francisco   Cont'd

SYLVAR GALLERY   Cont'd
Appraisal Service Available
Directions: Between Sutter
& Bush Sts; From
Downtown take any Sutter
St Bus, or use the Polk St
Bus

TAKAHASHI IMPORTS INC
59 Grant Ave   94108
415 397-4475   Est: 1948
Proprietor: Mrs Tami
Takahashi
Hours: Mon-Sat, 10-6
Types & Periods: Japanese
Wooden Bridal Chests
(Tansu), Sea Captains'
Chests, Sewing Boxes, Imari
Sometsuke, Imari Multi-color
Brocade (Nishiki), Lacquer
Pieces, Screens
Directions: 1 Block from
Union Sq Garage; Located
near Corner of Geary &
Grant

THINGS OF YORE
538 Sutter St   94102
                  Est: 1976
Proprietor: W J J
Scoggins
Hours: Mon & Tues,
Thurs-Sat, 10-5
Types & Periods: General
Line, Western Emphasis

CLAIRE THOMPSON
2274 Union St   94123
415 346-5144   Est: 1929
Proprietor: Claire
Thompson
Hours: Daily, 10-5; Also by
Appointment or by Chance
Types & Periods: Queen
Anne, Sheraton,
Chippendale, Hepplewhite,
English Furniture
Directions: Between
Filmore & Steiner

TOBY ANTIQUES
3315 Sacramento   94118
415 563-0929   Est: 1970
Proprietor: Bruce Ledman
Hours: Daily, 11-5
Types & Periods: Furniture,
General Line
Specialties: Toby Jugs
Directions: Near Presidio
Ave

UP TO SNUFF
4238 18th St   94114
415 626-1717   Est: 1974
Proprietor: Mo Core & Ric
Kelly
Hours: Mon-Sat, 10-7
Types & Periods: American
& Oriental; Jewelry
Directions: Take Market W
to Castro; Turn Left up
Castro to 18th; Right
1 1/2 Blocks; Upstairs

URBAN ANTIQUES AT SEAWALL B
1861 Union   94123
415 931-7063   Est: 1965
Proprietor: Ray Hackett,
George & Nola Theobald
Hours: Daily, 10-6
Types & Periods: Huge
Stock; Furniture &
Bric-a-Brac from Every
Period
Specialties: Clocks,
Watches, Musical Automata
Directions: Between
Laguna & Octavia;
in one of the most
unique Areas of City

JOSEPH VINGO ANTIQUES & DECORATIONS
872 N Point St   94109
415 928-0771   Est: 1973
Proprietor: Joseph Vingo
Types & Periods: European
Furniture, Oriental Items
Directions: Between Hyde
& Larken St

JAMES HENRY WALKER ANTIQUES
710 Sansome St   94111
415 392-2833   Est: 1970
Proprietor: James Henry
Walker
Hours: Daily, 9-5
Types & Periods: English &
French Furniture
Specialties: Furniture
(Italian)
Appraisal Service Available
Directions: Jackson
Square Area

WALLACE EDWARD ANTIQUES
1799 Union St   94123
415 928-2919   Est: 1973
Proprietor: Wallace E
Garthe
Hours: Mon-Sat, 10-6;
Evenings by Appointment

Types & Periods: 18th &
19th Century European &
English Furniture,
Porcelains, Clocks &
Accessories
Specialties: Vienna
Regulator Wall Clocks
Directions: Corner of
Octavia & Union Sts

JAMES WASTE ANTIQUES
463 Jackson St   94118
415 986-5060   Est: 1970
Proprietor: James Waste
Hours: Mon-Fri, 9-5
Types & Periods: 18th &
19th Century English
Specialties: Arms & Armor
Appraisal Service Available
Directions: 1 Block from
Transamerica Pyramid on
Jackson Square; Between
Montgomery & Sansome

WILLIAMS ANTIQUES
532 Sutter St   94102
415 981-4300
Hours: Mon-Sat, 10-5:30
Types & Periods: English
Furniture & Accessories

WINFIELD WINSOR
458-460 Jackson St 94111
415 362-0613
Hours: Mon-Fri, 9-5
Types & Periods: English,
French

San Jose

SAN JOSE CLUSTER
Directions: Heavy
Concentration on S 1st
(600-1000 Blocks), Lincoln
Ave (800-2000 Blocks)

ANTIQUES FROM FREUND'S
1731 Park Ave   95126
408 292-8528   Est: 1950
Proprietor: Rabbi & Mrs
Iser L Freund
Hours: Mon-Fri, Except
Sat & Sun by Appointment
Only
Types & Periods: General
Line
Specialties: Oriental Art
Objects
Appraisal Service Available
Directions: Rose Garden
Area

BRASS WASHBOARD
894 S 2nd   95112
408 297-0581   Est: 1974
Proprietor: Frank Milward
Hours: Daily, by
Appointment, by Chance
Types & Periods: General
Line, Furniture, Clocks
Specialties: Musical
Instruments (Pump Organs
& Record Players)
Directions: 2 Blocks S of
New 280 Frwy

CLASSIC ANTIQUES
2210 Lincoln Ave   95125
408 264-0604
Proprietor: H Keith
Kinkade
Hours: Daily; 10-5 by
appointment
Types & Periods: Furniture,
American & French
Specialties: Cut Glass,
China, Silver, Art Glass
Appraisal Service Available
Directions: Corner of
Lincoln & Curtner, 1/2
Block N

**INDIANA ANTIQUES &
DOLLS**
890 2nd St   95112
408 295-4407   Est: 1950
Proprietor: E Milton
Hours: Fri-Wed, 11-5:30
Types & Periods: Victorian
Furniture, Dolls, Art Glass,
Collectibles, H P Plates
Specialties: Dolls, Quality
Victorian Items
Appraisal Service Available
Directions: Downtown,
Between Virginia & Martha

**VICTORIAN HOUSE
ANTIQUES & GARDEN
RESTAURANT**
476 S First St   95113
408 286-1770
Proprietor: Patrick
Mormon
Hours: Sun-Thurs, 11-10;
Fri & Sat, 11-11
Types & Periods: Victorian
Furniture, Glass, China
Appraisal Service Available
Directions: Downtown

San Juan Capistrano

G R DURENBERGER
31431 Camino   92675
714 493-1283
Proprietor: G R
Durenberger
Hours: Tues-Sat, 11-5
Types & Periods: 17th &
18th Century English &
French; Decorative
Accessories

**MANNING'S COLLECTORS
SHOP**
31761 Camino   92675
714 496-7551   Est: 1968
Proprietor: Helen & Art
Manning
Hours: Daily, 11-5
Types & Periods: Miniatures,
Dolls, Antique Jewelry,
China, Glass, Antique Guns,
Civil & Indian War Items,
Oriental & Indian Artifacts;
Collectibles
Specialties: Museum of Civil
War & Early Western Items
for Display Only
Directions: Catercorner
from the Mission San
Juan, in Capistrano Plaza;
Corner of Ortego Hwy &
Camino Capistrano

San Mateo

PEDESTAL SHOPPE
201 B St   94401
415 342-5070
Proprietor: Mildred & Jim
McCarty
Hours: Tues-Sat, 12-5
Types & Periods: Furniture,
General Line

**TREASURE HOUSE OF
U V S**
30 2nd Ave   94401
415 343-3663
Proprietor: Helen Lengfeld
Hours: Tues-Thurs,
10-4:30; Fri by Chance
Types & Periods: General;
Glass, Art & Cut; Silver,
Porcelain, Bronzes, Pottery,
Furniture, Pictures, Oriental,
French, English, Americana,
Etc
Directions: Downtown San
Mateo; Off El Camino Real

San Pedro

THE BLUE QUAIL
458 W 6th St   90731
Types & Periods: General
Line

San Rafael

ANTIQUE ALLEY
638 5th Ave   94901
415 456-5282   Est: 1967
Proprietor: Lee Sexton
Hours: Tues-Sat, 12-5
Types & Periods: Oak &
Victorian Furniture, China,
Jewelry, Paintings, Doll
House Miniatures
Specialties: Period Clothing
& Accessories, 1880-1935
Appraisal Service Available
Directions: On the
Railroad Tracks at 5th Ave

NOW & THEN ANTIQUES
1205 3rd St   94901
415 453-4296   Est: 1975
Proprietor: Louis & Sandra
Lum
Hours: Daily
Types & Periods: English
Oak Furnishings;
Turn-of-the-Century
American Pieces
Specialties: Furniture
Refinished or Restored
Directions: Downtown Off
B St

Santa Ana

DOROTHY'S ANTIQUES
405 W McFadden St 92707
714 543-7342
Proprietor: Dorothy &
Warren Billingsley
Hours: By Appointment
Types & Periods: General
Line
Specialties: Jewelry

ELZ FARGO & CO
830 S Main St   92701
714 544-4021   Est: 1953
Proprietor: Robert G Elz
Hours: Mon-Sat, 10-6
Types & Periods:
Automobiles, Jewelry, Guns
& Armor, Furniture
Appraisal Service Available

EMPIRE GALLERIES LTD
2722 N Main St   92701
714 547-7384   Est: 1975
Proprietor: Carl Marcus
Hours: Daily, for
Inspection; Auctions Held
Every Other Mon & Tues
Nights
Types & Periods: Furniture,
Crystal, Oriental, Tiffany, Art
Glass, Sevres, Paintings,
Antique Autos, China,
Porcelain, Jade, Jewelry
Appraisal Service Available
  Directions: Santa Ana or
  Garden Grove Frwys; Main
  St Offramp; Next to
  Bullocks Fashion Sq

Santa Barbara

ADOBE ANTIQUES
707 Anacapa St   93101
805 963-4516
Proprietor: Helen & Cliff
Jameson
Hours: By Appointment
Types & Periods: General
Line, Oriental Art, Jade,
Ivories

CAVALIER'S STUDIO 5
812 State St   93102
805 965-2022
Proprietor: Suzanne
Cavalier
Types & Periods: Jewelry,
General Line

EMILEE'S ANTIQUES
528 Brinkerhoff   93101
805 966-3492
Proprietor: Emilee Salvini
Hours: Daily, 12-5
Types & Periods: Post
Cards, Advertising, Glass,
General Line

J MAIN ANTIQUES
1336 State St   93101
805 962-7710
Proprietor: Jim & Edwina
Main
Hours: Mon-Sat, 9:30-5
Types & Periods: General
Line

Santa Cruz

I M CHAIT GALLERY
2409 Wilshire Blvd   90403
213 465-6469
Proprietor: M Chait
Hours: Mon-Wed, Fri &
Sat, 11-5
Types & Periods: Oriental
Arts, Jade, Porcelain,
Ivories, Jewelry; Ancient to
Antique
Appraisal Service Available
  Directions: Wilshire & 24th

**RICHARD GOULD
ANTIQUES LTD**
216 26th St   90402
213 395-0724
Proprietor: Richard M
Gould
Hours: Mon-Sat, 10-5
Types & Periods: 17th, 18th
& Early 19th Century
Country English Furniture;
18th & 19th Century Chinese
& English Porcelains;
Decorative Accessories
Specialties: Chinese
Porcelains, Lamp Bases
  Directions: 1st Block S of
  San Vicente Blvd; Across
  from Brentwood Country
  Mart

HALL'S SURREY HOUSE
708 Water St   95060
408 423-2475
Proprietor: M A Hall & A R
Remme
Hours: Wed-Mon,11-4:30
Types & Periods: Tiffany
Lamps, Jewelry, Glass;
Victorian

THE RAGAMUFFIN
2717 Main St   90405
213 399-4544
Proprietor: Londa Columb
Hours: Wed-Sun,
12:30-5:30
Types & Periods: Dolls,
Toys, Miniatures
Specialties: French &
Character Dolls
Appraisal Service Available
  Directions: Pico Blvd to
  Main toward Beach; L on
  Main

L H SELMAN LTD
761 Chestnut St   95060
408 427-1177
Proprietor: L H Selman

Hours: Mon-Fri
Types & Periods: Glass
Paperweights from Mid 19th
Century
Specialties: Paperweights,
Antique & Contemporary
Appraisal Service Available
  Directions: Please
  telephone

**WAY BACK WHEN
ANTIQUES**
52 Front St   95060
408 423-4892
Proprietor: David D
Karmann
Hours: Wed-Mon
Types & Periods: Victorian
Specialties: Cut Glass &
Oriental
Appraisal Service Available
  Directions: One Block
  from Fisherman's Wharf

Santa Rosa

ARACK'S ANTIQUES
2150 Grace St   95404
707 542-8830
Proprietor: George &
Phyllis Arack
Hours: By Appointment
Types & Periods: Lamps,
Phonos, Music Boxes, Art
Glass, Porcelain

**HARRY BARNETT
ANTIQUES**
5680 Sonoma Hwy   95405
707 539-9083
Proprietor: Harry Barnett
Types & Periods: General
Line

THE PAPERMILL
228 Ricardo Ave   95401
707 544-3455   Est: 1970
Proprietor: Richard Chase
Hours: By Appointment,
by Mail Order (Catalog
available upon request)
Types & Periods: 19th &
20th Century Paper
Collectibles: Books, Posters,
Photographs, Post Cards,
Prints
Specialties: Thousands of
Paper Items
  Directions: Just off Santa
  Rosa Ave, or P O Box
  6556

Saratoga

THE BLUE CANDLESTICK
20375 Saratoga   95070
408 354-7474   Est: 1962
Proprietor: Isabel Pool
Hours: Mon-Sat,
10:30-5:30; Other times by
Appointment
Types & Periods: Early
American Country, Period &
Early 19th Century, including
Queen Ann, Chippendale &
Shaker
Specialties: Windsor Chair,
Grandfather Clocks,
Spongeware, Canopy Beds,
Long Tables, Rare
Cupboards
Appraisal Service Available
Directions: Large White
Georgian Style House on
Hwy 9 in Saratoga, 1
Block S of Center of
Town; Hwy 9 is reached
from Hwy 17 or I-280

CORINTHIAN STUDIOS
20550 Saratoga,
Los Gatos Rd   95070
408 867-4630
Proprietor. D Kongsli & V
Halcomb
Hours: Mon-Sat, 9-5:30,
Sun, 12-5
Types & Periods: Furniture,
Jewelry, General Line

BILLIE NELSON ANTIQUES
20450 Saratoga,
Los Gatos Rd   95070
400 067 2363
Proprietor: Billie & Denny
Nelson
Hours: Mon-Sat, 10-5
Types & Periods: Jewelry,
Furniture, General Line

Sausalito

ANTIQUA
777 Bridgway   94965
415 332-9020   Est: 1974
Proprietor: Alberto Pinto
Hours: Daily
Types & Periods: 19th
Century &
Turn-of-the-Century;
European
Appraisal Service Available
Directions: At the Village
Fair

JOHN STANFORD GORHAM
205 2nd St   94965
415 332-4854   Est: 1973
Proprietor: John Stanford
Gorham
Hours: Daily, 9-5
Types & Periods: 18th &
19th Century Antiques,
American Furniture, Chinese
Export Porcelain
Appraisal Service Available
Directions: Main & 2nd St

INTERIORS BY ALBERT
493 Bridgeway   94965
415 332-4644   Est: 1970
Proprietor: Albert D Moses
Hours: Mon-Sat, 9:30-5
Types & Periods: Antiques &
Collectibles, Furniture,
China, Glass, New & Old
Directions: S End of
Bridgeway Facing
Sausalito Bay

NOWELL'S, INC
490 Gate Five Road 94965
415 332-4286   Est: 1954
Proprietor: C E & Helene
Nowell, Barbara
Mendenhall
Hours: Tues-Sat, 9:30-5
Types & Periods: General
Line
Specialties: Restoration &
Parts for Lamps & Lighting
Fixtures; Manufacture a very
fine line of Reproduction
Victorian Chandeliers &
Sconces
Directions: Harbor Dr to
Gate 5 Rd, Turn Left

PORTO BELLU
21 Princess St   94965
415 332-3336   Est: 1975
Proprietor: Mary Hall
Hours: Daily, 11-5:30
Types & Periods:
Turn-of-the-Century
American, European,
Oriental Accessories &
Furniture; Jewelry
Appraisal Service Available

Seal Beach

ANTIQUE SHOP
1520 Pacific Coast Hwy
90740
213 430-9014

Proprietor: Betty Stepp
Hours: Daily, 12-5:30
Types & Periods: Furniture,
Jewelry, General Line

AUDREY'S ANTIQUES
142 Main St   90740
213 430-7213
Proprietor: Audrey Barnes
Peters
Hours: Mon-Sat, 11-6
Types & Periods: Silver,
Jewelry, General Line

Sherman Oaks

ARNOLDS ANTIQUES
13743 Ventura Blvd 91413
213 784-4449
Proprietor: Dorothy & Jack
Arnold
Hours: Mon-Sat,
10:30-5:30; Sun, 1-4
Types & Periods: General
Line

THE UPSTAIRS STORE
14534 Ventura Blvd 91403
213 783-4144
Proprietor: Mildred Bard
Hours: Mon-Sat, 10-5:30
Types & Periods: Furniture,
Art Objects, Jewelry,
Fixtures
Appraisal Service Available
Directions: S of Ventura
Freeway

Solana Beach

BLUE QUAIL ANTIQUES
209 S Hwy 101   92075
Types & Periods: General
Line

**INTERNATIONAL
ANTIQUES**
215 S Hwy 101   92075
714 755-6602   Est: 1969
Hours: Daily, 9-5; also by
Appointment
Types & Periods: French,
English & American; 18th &
19th Century Furniture
Specialties: Bronzes,
Enamels, Porcelains
Appraisal Service Available
Directions: Hwy 101, 2
Blocks N of Del Mar
Racetrack

Solvang

**THE CHIMNEY SWEEP
ANTIQUES**
530 Alisal Rd   93463
805 688-3137   Est: 1969
Proprietor: Mr & Mrs
Kenneth G FitzGerald
Hours: Wed-Sun
Types & Periods: Cut Glass,
Early American Pattern
Glass, Porcelain, Victorian
Furniture
Appraisal Service Available
Directions: US 101 to
Buellton; 246 to Solvang

OLDEN TYMES
1588 Mission Dr   93463
805 688-5110   Est: 1970
Proprietor: Mr & Mrs Jim
Hitt & Mr & Mrs Harold
Tegge
Hours: Daily, 10-5
Types & Periods: American
& Danish Furniture
Specialties: Christmas
Plates, Old Royal
Copenhagen

Sonora

ARBEE'S ANTIQUES
Rte 6 Box 20   95370
209 532-3084
Hours: By Appointment
Types & Periods: China,
Glass, Silver, Furniture
Directions: 2 Miles from
Town on Lime Kiln Rd

HOUSE OF CANE
226 W Jackson St   95370
209 532-4218   Est: 1972
Proprietor: Bob & Pat
Norris
Hours: Mon-Wed, Closed
Thurs, Fri-Sun
Types & Periods: American
Furniture, Glass, China,
Collectibles
Specialties: Antique
Furniture Restored &
Refinished, Cane Weaving

JEAN'S ANTIQUES
Shaws Flat Rd   95370
Mail: Box 951
Columbia   95310
209 532-6171

Proprietor: Jean Pardina
Hours: Daily
Types & Periods: Dolls,
Lamps, General Line

TRINKETS 'N TREASURES
132 N Washington St
                      95370
209 532-1782   Est: 1966
Proprietor: Louise & Jack
Perry
Hours: Daily; Closed
Jan-mid Feb, Thanksgiving
& Christmas
Types & Periods: General
Line
Specialties: Miniatures, Doll
House Furniture
Directions: N End of
Washington Near Red
Church

South Pasadena

**SOUTH PASADENA
CLUSTER**
Directions: Mission
(1100-1200 Blocks),
Others scattered
throughout City

Stockton

STOCKTON CLUSTER
Directions: Scattered
throughout City; Some
Shops on East Main
(300-3000 Blocks)

ROBERT M SOARES
999 N Lincoln St   95203
209 464-1752
Proprietor: R M Soares
Hours: By Appointment
Types & Periods: General
Line
Specialties: Clocks

Studio City

COUNTRY ANTIQUES
3746 Willowcrest Ave
                      91604
213 980-2813   Est: 1953
Proprietor: Virginia F
Smith
Hours: By Chance

Types & Periods: Toys,
Banks, American Furniture,
Pine, Maple, Birch, Canton,
Rose Medallion, Wooden
Utensils, Candle Sticks,
Fireplace Andirons
Specialties: Furniture,
American
Appraisal Service Available

Sunol

**SUNOL WHISTLE STOP
ANTIQUES**
11853 Main St   94586
415 862-9901   Est: 1970
Proprietor: Co-op
Hours: Tues-Sun, 11-4:30,
Closed Holidays
Types & Periods: Oak
Furniture, Dolls, Toys,
Bottles, China, Glass,
Lamps, Wicker, Primitives
Specialties: 18 Rooms of
Antiques
Directions: E Bay Area;
Off Hwy 680, between
Pleasanton & Mission San
Jose

Tarzana

JOANNE'S ANTIQUES
18531 Ventura   91356
213 344-6015   Est: 1974
Proprietor: Joanne Tappa
Hours: Mon-Sat,
10:30-5:30
Types & Periods: American
& English Oak, Primitives,
Accessories
Specialties: Victorian Prints
Directions: 1 Block W of
Reseda Blvd

SHARON'S ANTIQUES
18584 Ventura Blvd 91356
213 881-2014
Proprietor: Sharon
Fernandez
Hours: Tues-Sat, 10-5
Types & Periods: Clocks,
Jewelry, General Line

Tulare

THE WHITE HOUSE
315 North N St   93274
209 686-1462
209 686-2407

Proprietor: Virginia E
Lewis
Hours: Tues-Fri, 11-4; and
By Appointment
Types & Periods: Victorian,
Empire, & Early California
Furniture; China, some
Haviland; Silver Holloware &
Flatware (Sterling & Plated);
Postcards; Paper Goods
Appraisal Service Available
   Directions: 2 1/2 Blocks N
   of Tulare Ave & about 6
   Blocks from Frwy 99

Tuolumne

BLUE JAY ANTIQUES
   Rte 1 Box 950   95379
   209 928-4424
   Proprietor: Carl & Dottie
   Eickmeyer
   Hours: Daily
Types & Periods: Furniture,
General Line, Collectibles
   Directions: 2 Miles W of
   Tuolumne on Cherokee
   Rd

Tustin

**FISHER & CHATHAM
ANTIQUES**
   405 El Camino Real 92680
   714 832-5101
   Proprietor: Katherine F
   Fisher & Pearl Shiffman
Types & Periods: Clocks,
Jewelry, Furniture, Silver,
Porcelain

**SHADOW HILLS ANTIQUES
& ART GALLERY**
   215 W 1st St   92680
   714 832-7771
   Proprietor: Annette & Sal
   Zwirn
   Hours: Mon-Sat, 11-5;
   Sun, 12-5
Types & Periods: Art Glass,
Porcelains, Bottles,
Paintings, Furniture

Twain Harte

ANDY'S ANTIQUES
   Box 800   95383
   209 586-5359   Est: 1971
   Proprietor: Andy & John
   Schlarb

Hours: Thurs-Mon, 10-6
Types & Periods: Victorian
Golden Oak & Early
American Primitive
Furniture, Clocks, China,
Glass
Specialties: Restoration &
Refinishing
   Directions: Twain Harte Dr
   at Hillcrest, Business Rte
   108

EARLY'S ANTIQUES
   E Ave   95383
   209 586-3057
   Proprietor: Helyn &
   George Santos
   Hours: Daily
Types & Periods: Furniture,
General Line
   Directions: E Ave & Twain
   Harte Dr

Ventura

AGNES ASHBY ANTIQUES
   871 E Thompson   93001
   805 643-8766
   Proprietor: Agnes Ashby
   Hours: Wed-Sat, 11-4;
   Other Hours by
   Appointment
Types & Periods: General
Line, English & American

CANDY'S BAZAAR
   1474 East Main St   93003
   805 643-8313   Est: 1976
   Proprietor: Candace L
   Hardin
   Hours: Mon-Sat, 11-6;
   Sun, 1-4
Types & Periods: Victorian,
Oak & General
Appraisal Service Available
   Directions: At the Y of
   Santa Clara & Main St

THIS OLD HOUSE
   1042 E Main St   93001
   805 648-7256   Est: 1975
   Proprietor: Lila L Fletcher
   & Shirley B Shirley
   Hours: Mon-Sat, 11-5
Types & Periods: Victorian,
Art Glass, Silver, China,
Oriental
Specialties: Victorian
Appraisal Service Available
   Directions: Between Ann
   St & Laurel St

Vista

HILL TOP ANTIQUES
   728 Escondido Ave 92083
   714 726-3790
   Proprietor: Kay Ehrhart
   Hours: Wed-Sat, 10-5
Types & Periods: Glass,
China, Furniture
   Directions: Near Corner of
   Escondido Ave & Rte 78

Wasco

PAUL'S ANTIQUES
   804 7th   93280
   805 758-6252   Est: 1973
   Proprietor: Paul Grones
   Hours: Daily
Types & Periods: Furniture,
Glass, Farm Items, Brass
Cash Register
Appraisal Service Available
   Directions: 20 Miles N, 7
   Miles W Bakersfield off
   Hwy 466

Whittier

ANTIQUE ARTS
   13415 E Whittier Blvd
                 90605
   213 696-6117
   Proprietor: Don & Barbara
   Nolan
Types & Periods: General
Line

Yountville

ANTIQUE FAIR
   6512 Washington St 94599
   707 944-8440
   Proprietor: Alice & George
   Rothwell
   Hours: Tues-Fri, 10-4; Sat
   & Sun, 10-5
Types & Periods: Oak,
Walnut, Pear, Pine Furniture,
of all Periods
Specialties: Bedroom Sets,
Brass, & all Types Furniture
Appraisal Service Available
   Directions: Near Vintage
   1870

Yountville   Cont'd

ARTHUR'S ANTIQUES
6500 Washington St 94599
Proprietor: Marge Harer
Hours: Daily, 11-5
Types & Periods: Furniture
& Accessories

BURGUNDY HOUSE
6711 Washington St 94599
707 944-2711
Proprietor: Mary Keeman
Hours: Daily
Types & Periods: General
Line
   Directions: "Country Inn"

CLOCKS UNLIMITED
Washington St   94599
707 944-8242
Hours: Tues-Sun
Types & Periods: Clocks,
Music Boxes
Specialties: Clocks, Clock
Restoration & Repair
   Directions: Yount Square

GOLDEN EAGLE BAZAAR
Vintage 1870
P O Box 2554   94599
707 944-2667   Est: 1969
Proprietor: Merle & Grace
Harris
Hours: Tues-Sun, 10-5
Types & Periods: China &
Glassware
Appraisal Service Available
   Directions: Located in
   Vintage 1870; 9 Miles N of
   Napa on Hwy 29

IRON HORSE
6432 Washington St 94599
707 944-8212
Hours: Wed-Sun
Types & Periods: English,
American Furniture
   Directions: E on California
   Ave to Washington St;
   Turn Right; Left Side of
   Street

TOUCH OF SILVER
6500 Washington St 94559
Proprietor: Carles Pellau &
Joe Thompson
Hours: Daily, 11-5
Types & Periods: Furniture,
Jewelry, Silver, China,
Glassware

TWIN TURRET ANTIQUES
6500 Washington St 94599
Proprietor: Marge Harer,
Charles Pellau & Joe
Thompson
Hours: Daily, 11-5
Types & Periods: Furniture,
China, Glassware, Jewelry

THE VICTORIAN LADY
6428 Washington St 94599
707 944-2063
Hours: Tues-Sun, 11-4
Types & Periods:
Americana, Oak, Walnut,
Wicker
Specialties: Furniture

VINTAGE LAMP STUDIO
Washington St   94599
707 944-2933
Types & Periods: Glass,
China, Wine Bottles
Specialties: Lamps, Parts &
Repair

Yuba City

ANTIQUE CENTER
826 Plumas St   95991
916 673-9298
Proprietor: Hal & Opal
Dietzel
Hours: By Appointment
Types & Periods: Clocks,
Furniture, Jewelry, General
Line

Yucca Valley

BOUTIQUE ANTIQUES
7323 Sage Ave   92284
714 365-9525
Proprietor: Daisy M
Westlund
Hours: Thurs-Sun, 10-5;
By Chance
Types & Periods: Art Glass,
Lamps, Porcelains, Furniture
Specialties: Art Glass &
Lamps
Appraisal Service Available
   Directions: Next to Vons &
   Thrifty Plaza

Queen Anne Lowboy. Notice the square
cabriole legs and trifid feet.

(From page 24) by the Dutch, for William had been Prince of Orange before marrying Mary. The elements of the design were intended to produce greater comfort with a lightened, more graceful appearance. The furniture can be characterized by its inverted trumpet-shaped leg. (See page 23). One begins to find the introduction of curved lines, hooded tops, shaped stretchers, and more ornamental turnings applied to furniture. Walnut replaced oak as the main wood. More intricate cabinetwork was produced by the use of veneering, especially on mirror frames and cased pieces. Much decorative trim required inlaid woods to execute the design. Built-up lacquer finishes were introduced from the Orient. The use of upholstery greatly increased because technological advances in textile manufacture increased its availability. Brass drawer pulls appeared in tear-drop shapes as well as the "bail" style. A bail is the handle of a bucket; therefore, the drawer pull resembled a bucket handle. During this time appeared the chest-on-frame, the highboy, the butterfly table and the grandfather clock.

The Queen Anne Period is one of the most lasting and popular styles. Her reign in England was from 1702 until 1714. Walnut was the primary wood used by the cabinetmakers in England during this period. It must be remembered that an American cabinetmaker in New Hampshire could just as well make a chair from his native birch or maple. Examples of this style may therefore be seen in any type of hardwood depending upon the locality of the cabinetmaker. Queen Anne furniture may be characterized by use of the "cabriole", an S-shaped, curved leg. (See page 97). The cabriole usually terminated in a pad foot, slipper foot or trifid foot. (See page 125). Lacquer work and decorative painting are found along with natural finishes. Upholsteries consisted of needlepoint, damask and leather. The turned or coiled metal springs we now enjoy did not exist at that time. Upholstering was done with webbing as a foundation which was then covered over by a padding of horse hair or moss to give it some softness, and an upholstery material was placed over it all. Possibly it would be topped off with a separate cushion of feathers or of down for further comfort. The simple lines and graceful proportions of the Queen Anne make it one of the most pleasing with which to live. Its beauty has caused it to be among the most copied of designs, so look very closely when determining its age.

A period that is well to remember is termed the Georgian. It applies primarily to the time from 1715 until 1800 during which

(Continued, page 112)

64

STATE OF COLORADO

Allenspark

THE TOP SHELF
Box 43, Hwy 7   80510
Proprietor: Pearl & Don
Yost
Hours: Daily, 9-5 June,
July, Aug; Closed Tues
Types & Periods: General
Line, China, Glass

Arriba

**SHULLS PIANOS &
ANTIQUES**
Box 108   80804
303 768-3468
Proprietor: Sterling C
Shull
Hours: Daily
Types & Periods: Cut Glass,
Furniture, General Line

Arvada

**WHITT'S ATTIC FURNITURE
& WORLD OF BOOKS**
7505 Grandview   80002
303 423-2824   Est: 1973
Proprietor: Mr & Mrs
Ballard Whitt
Hours: Daily, I0-5; Sat by
Appointment; By Chance
Types & Periods: Furniture,
Glass, Oriental Objects,
Books of Collector's Interest
Directions: N of I-70

Aspen

MARJORIE'S BARN
3776 McLean Flats Rd
    81611
303 925-7008
Proprietor: Marjorie B
Stein
Hours: By Appointment
Types & Periods: American
& English
Specialties: Silver
Directions: Red Butte
Ranch 2 1/2 miles NW

**ANN TAYLOR MC INTYRE
ANTIQUES**
675 E Cooper St   81611
303 925-9845
Proprietor: Anne Taylor
McIntyre
Hours: Daily; Weekends,
11-6; Closed Sun
Types & Periods: 18th
Century to Golden Oak,
Collectibles, Clothing

**TOWN & COUNTRY
ANTIQUES & UNIQUES**
205 S Mill St   81611
303 925-2999   Est: 1973
Proprietor: Karen
Troobnick
Hours: Daily; Weekends
Types & Periods: "Unusual
from around the world"
Appraisal Service Available
Directions: Downtown in
"Mill St Station"

Aurora

EUROPA ANTIQUES
1405 Florence St   80010
303 344-3142   Est: 1973
Proprietor: Mr & Mrs
Howard J Frase
Hours: Mon thru Sat
9:30-5:30; Closed Sun
Types & Periods: 19th
Century English and
American Furniture,
Porcelain, Glass, Pewter,
Prints
Specialties: European
Porcelain
Appraisal Service Available
Directions: Corner 14th &
Florence St, Central
Business District

Basalt

**ALL AMERICANA
ANTIQUES**
137 Midland Ave   81621
303 927-3903   Est: 1972
Proprietor: Margaret H
Wilson
Hours: Daily, I0:30-5; Sun
by Appointment

Types & Periods: Furniture,
Glass, China, Primitives
Specialties: American
Historic Material on the
West
Directions: Off Hwy 82
Midway Btwn Glenwood
Springs & Aspen

Boulder

**ANTIQUES APPRAISALS &
BROKERAGE**
2436 6th St   80302
Proprietor: Elise C Hersey
Hours: Daily; By
Appointment; By Chance
Types & Periods: Broker for
18th thru early 20th
Centuries Furniture
Specialties: Period Pieces,
Primitives, Locator Service
Appraisal Service Available
Directions: N of Mapleton
Ave on 6th St

ARIEL'S ANTIQUES
2210 Pearl   80302
303 443-1073   Est: 1970
Hours: Daily; Weekends
Types & Periods: China,
Glass, Pottery, Porcelain
Specialties: Glass
Directions: Six Blocks W
of 28th St on Pearl

THE CARPET SHOPS LTD
4900 E Pearl   80303
303 442-7545   Est: 1954
Proprietor: Elliot Smollan
Hours: Daily; Weekends
Types & Periods: Oriental &
Navajo Rugs
Specialties: Rugs (Navajos,
Preceding 1940)
Appraisal Service Available

Canon City

TRADING POST ANTIQUES
305 Main St   81212
303 275-6972   Est: 1971
Proprietor: Nicholas L
Brown
Hours: Mon thru Sat 9-5

Types & Periods: Glassware,
Furniture, Primitives, Bottles,
General Line
Directions: One Block N of
Hwy 50 on W End of Main
St

Central City

ALPINE ANTIQUES
430 Lawrence   80427
303 582-5846   Est: 1973
Proprietor: Olga Hiratsuka
Hours: Daily, II-5
Types & Periods: "I try to
have almost all types"
Directions: 2 Miles W of
Hwy 119 on Main Road

Colorado Springs

**COLORADO SPRINGS
CLUSTER**
Directions: Tejon (l00-600
Blocks), Colorado Ave
(2000-2200 Blocks), Other
Shops scattered
throughout City

AUGUSTIN GALLERIES
618 N Tejon   80903
303 471-8073   Est: 1969
Proprietor: J P L Augustin
Hours: Daily
Types & Periods: Bronzes,
Chandeliers, Clocks,
Cloisonne, Ivories, Marble
Statuary, Oriental Rugs,
Paintings, 18th & 19th
Centuries Porcelain, Silver
Objects de Vertu
Appraisal Service Available
Directions: Turn off I-25 at
the Unitah Intersection,
Follow Unitah to Cascade
Ave, Right 4 Blocks to
Monument, Left I Block,
Right 1/2 Block

COBWEB ANTIQUES
2624 W Colorado Ave
                   80934
303 634-5494   Est: 1949
Proprietor: Wesley &
Katherine Walker
Hours: Daily, By
Appointment; By Chance
Types & Periods: American
& English Silver,
Accessories

Specialties: Lamps, Stained
Glass
Directions: W on Hwy 2A
via Midland Exprwy to
26th St Exit

DOWN SOUTH
1778 S Nevada   80906
303 471-2300   Est: 1975
Proprietor: Sherm
Connolly
Hours: Mon thru Sat
l0:30-5
Types & Periods: General
Line, Small Items on
Consignment
Directions: 2 Blocks N of
S Gate Shopping Center

**FLEA MARKET CITY
AUDITORIUM**
Kiowa & Weber Sts 80902
303 475-7324   Est: 1967
Proprietor: Harvey Black
Hours: Ist Weekend of
Each Month, Sat 9-6; Sun
l0-5:30
Types & Periods: Furniture,
Art Glass, Coins, Primitives,
Watches, Banks, Indian
Items, Paintings, Guns
Appraisal Service Available
Directions: Downtown

THIS OLD HOUSE
318 E Pikes Peak   80903
303 632-4836   Est: 1974
Proprietor: Annette
Lesikar
Hours: Mon-Sat, Summer
l0:00-6:00; Winter
9:30-5:30; Closed Sun
Types & Periods: Antiques,
Gifts, Furniture, Used &
Rare Books
Specialties: Costume
Rentals & Sales
Directions: Downtown,
Next Door to Telephone
Co Bldg, 1 1/2 Blocks
from City Auditorium

TUCK BOX
111 E Bijou   80903
303 634-0651   Est: 1973
Proprietor: Brozyna's
Hours: Daily, l0-5
Types & Periods: Copper &
Brass
Directions: Downtown
across from Acacia Park

Cortez

NANNY'S LITTLE SHACK
S Hwy 666   81321
303 565-8010   Est: 1969
Proprietor: Merle M Parker
Hours: By Appointment;
By Chance
Types & Periods: Early
Americana
Specialties: Oak Furniture,
Dolls, Primitives
Appraisal Service Available
Directions: 10 Miles W of
Mesa Verde National Park

Cripple Creek

RIIS JOHNSON
259 E Bennett Ave 80813
303 689-2523   Est: 1968
Proprietor: R W Johnson
Hours: Daily
Types & Periods: General
Line
Directions: Center of
Downtown

Del Norte

GOLDEN FLEECE
560 Grande   81132
303 657-3740   Est: 1975
Proprietor: Mark & Greta
Allison
Hours: Daily
Types & Periods: Furniture,
Dishes
Specialties: Victorian Era
Antiques
Appraisal Service Available
Directions: Across Street
from Only Bank in Town
on Hwy 160

LOG CABIN ANTIQUES
20642 W Hwy 160   81132
303 657-2377   Est: 1975
Proprietor: John & Jackie
Botsford
Hours: Daily 9-5; Evenings
by Appointment
Types & Periods: Americana
Collectibles, Depression
Glass, Art Pottery, China,
Silver, Crystal, Beams,
Avons, Oak Furniture
Directions: 1/2 between
South Fork & Del Norte

Denver

DENVER CLUSTER
Directions: Btwn Federal &
Kipling (E-W) & 29th &
44th Ave; Federal to
University (W-E);
Hampden to Almeda

**ALEXANDER'S ANTIQUE
SHOP**
3827 W 32nd Ave   80211
303 477-9634   Est: 1952
Proprietor: William & Ellen
E Alexander
Hours: Daily; Weekends;
By Chance
Types & Periods: Furniture,
Ornamental Iron Pieces,
Glass, China, General Line
Directions: 3200 N & 3900
W at 32nd & Osceola Sts

ALICE'S ATTIC
5020 W 29th Ave   80212
303 458-0396   Est: 1973
Proprietor: Alice Simons
Hours: Daily; Weekends
Types & Periods: Victorian &
Turn-of-the-Century
Furniture, Glass, China,
Primitives
Directions: In N Denver 1
Block E of Sheridan Blvd

**ANTIQUE CLOCK SHOP
INC**
9700 E Colfax   80202
303 366-1494
Hours: Daily; Weekends
11-6, Sat 10-5; Closed Sun
Types & Periods: Clocks,
Repair

ANTIQUE TRADER
1760 S Broadway   80210
303 777-7070   Est: 1972
Proprietor: Martin Boxer
Hours: Daily, 9:30-5:30;
Sun 12-5
Types & Periods: General
Line, Furniture
Appraisal Service Available
Directions: 9 Blocks S
from Hwy 25

ANTIQUE TRADER
2227 E Colfax   80206
303 333-4292   Est: 1966
Proprietor: Martin Boxer
Hours: Mon-Sat 9:30-5:30;
Sun 12-5

Types & Periods: General
Line, Oak & Victorian
Furniture, Brass Beds
Specialties: Furniture
Appraisal Service Available
Directions: Intersection
Colfax (US 40) & York Sts

ANTIQUES CENTER
1219 E 4th Ave   80218
Est: 1967
Proprietor: J Robert Welch
Hours: Tues-Sat,
10:00-4:00
Types & Periods: General
Line
Appraisal Service Available
Directions: Between
Downing & Marion Streets

ANTIQUES ETC
1421 Larimer Sq   80202
303 623-0050   Est: 1974
Proprietor: John C
Donohue
Hours: Daily,11-10; Sun 12-6
Types & Periods: American
Oak Furniture, Metal &
Wood Primitives, Collectibles
Directions: Lower
Downtown in Historic
Larimer Sq

ASHLEE'S ANTIQUES
5010 W 29th Ave   80212
303 458-1504   Est: 1970
Proprietor: George Ashlee
Johnson
Hours: Daily; Weekends
Types & Periods: General
Line, China, Glass,
Furniture, Clocks
Specialties: Books
Appraisal Service Available
Directions: NW Denver

BEE'S ANTIQUES
4166 Tennyson St   80212
303 458-5010   Est: 1974
Proprietor: Barbara
Connors & Beverly Miller
Hours: Wed-Sat, 11-5
Types & Periods: Victorian &
Oak Furniture, Collectibles,
China, Bottles, Tins,
Primitives
Specialties: Kitchen
Collectibles, Paper
Americana
Directions: 3 Blocks N of
Elitch's Amusement Park

BLUE LION ANTIQUES
1452 S Broadway   80210
303 777-5633   Est: 1971
Proprietor: Lee Graves
Hours: Daily, 12-5
Types & Periods: Glass,
China, Jewelry, Dolls, Silver,
Furniture, Primitives
Appraisal Service Available
Directions: I-25 to
Broadway Exit then 6
Blocks S

BORGMAN'S ANTIQUES
1211 E 4th Ave   80218
303 777-4623
Proprietor: Alice I
Borgman
Hours: Daily, 10-4; Sat 10-1;
Closed Sun
Types & Periods: Art Glass,
China, General Line

CARRIAGE HOUSE II
18 W Arkansas   80210
Proprietor: Thomas L
Pomeleo
Hours: Sun, Tues-Sat;
Closed Mon
Types & Periods: Cut Glass,
Art Glass, China, Home
Decorative Accessories,
Hobby Items, General Line
Furniture, Kitchen Primitives
& Tools
Appraisal Service Available

COPPER & BRASS
1425 Historic Larimer Sq
80202
303 892-0741
Types & Periods: Copper,
Brass, Lamps, Bed, Boilers

**DENVER ANTIQUE
MARKET**
2727 W 27th Ave   80211
303 455-9175   Est: 1973
Proprietor: Andy & Sally
Burnett
Hours: Weekends, 10-6
Types & Periods: General
Line
Specialties: Furniture,
Jewelry, Glass
Appraisal Service Available
Directions: Near
Downtown off I-25 at N
Speer Exit

GRANDMA'S HOUSE
3308 W 38th Ave   80211
303 458-1100   Est: 1970
Proprietor: John J White

Hours: Daily; Summer,
Fall, Winter; Weekends by
Appointment
Types & Periods: Victorian &
Oak Furniture, Railroadiana,
Primitives
Specialties: Railroadiana,
Paper Goods
Appraisal Service Available
Directions: 5 Min W of
Historic Larimer Sq or the
Federal Exit of I-70

**GRANDPA SNAZZYS
ANTIQUES**
1832 S Broadway   80210
303 935-3269   Est: 1972
Proprietor: S L Gustafson
& B C Hupper
Hours: Daily 10-4:30; Sat
12-4; Closed Sun
Types & Periods:
Collectibles, Furniture
Hardware, Phone Parts
Specialties: "15,000 Back
Magazines 1837-1960"
Appraisal Service Available

**HAN'SOM HORSE
ANTIQUES**
800 E 6th Ave   80218
303 744-1544
Proprietor: Doris Pearson
Hours: Daily 10-5:30
Types & Periods: Porcelain,
Glass, Metal, American
Furniture, Bibelots

**IGOTATHINGABOUT
ANTIQUES**
3027 E 2nd Ave   80206
303 222-7070   Est: 1970
Proprietor: Jeanne &
Garland Richardson
Hours: Mon-Sat 10-5
Types & Periods: General
Line of Fine Antiques
Specialties: Fine Furniture,
Clocks, Woodworking Tools,
Unusual Decorative
Accessories, Primitives
Appraisal Service Available
Directions: In Cherry
Creek N Shopping Area
Btwn Milwaukee & St Paul
Sts on 2nd Ave

K-JAY KOLLECTABLES
5724 E Colfax   80220
303 322-8632   Est: 1971
Proprietor: Jean
Brunemeier
Hours: Daily 10-6; Sat 10-5

Types & Periods: General
Line, Collectibles, Golden
Oak Furniture
Appraisal Service Available
Directions: Btwn Jay &
Ivanhoe Sts

**NIKKI KRAMER'S
THINGS II**
310 Holly St   80220
303 399-2322   Est: 1968
Proprietor: Nikki Kramer
Hours: Daily
Types & Periods: Furniture,
Silver, Porcelain, Decorative
Items
Specialties: Lecture Series
on Antiques & Related
Subjects
Appraisal Service Available
Directions: Crestmoor
Area, E of Cherry Creek

LAVENDER & OLD LACE
1404 S Broadway   80210
303 744-7777   Est: 1965
Proprietor: Eli H Sobol
Hours: Daily 10-5;
Closed Sun
Types & Periods: General
Line
Specialties: American Indian
Artifacts
Directions: S of I-25
Broadway Exit

**MEMORABILIA/COLORADO
ART GLASS WORKS**
1516 Blake St   80202
303 825-8801   Est: 1969
Proprietor: John & Carol
Fryer
Hours: Daily 11-5:30
Types & Periods:
Architectural Antiques;
WHOLESALE ONLY
Specialties: Glass Sheet,
Leaded Stained Glass
Appraisal Service Available
Directions: Two Blocks N
of Larimer Sq

**ROBERT MOORE
ANTIQUES**
1524 15th St   80202
303 623-5537   Est: 1973
Proprietor: Robert J
Moore
Hours: Mon-Fri 9-5; Sat
10-2
Types & Periods: Restaurant
Oriented Antiques
Directions: Corner of 15th
& Wazee Sts

PETER NATAN GALLERY
1550 California St   80202
303 534-4629   Est: 1963
Proprietor: Peter Natan
Hours: Daily 10-5;
Closed Sun
Types & Periods: Eskimo
Pre-Columbian African
Oceanic & American Indian
Tribal Art, Jewelry
Specialties: Talks on
Primitive Art
Appraisal Service Available
Directions: Heart of
Downtown btwn 15th &
16th Sts

**NEUHART'S ANTIQUES &
IMPORTS**
1415 Market St   80202
303 571-5149   Est: 1963
Proprietor: Francis H &
Janice M Neuhart
Hours: Mon-Sat 9:30-5:30
Types & Periods: European
& Oriental Furniture, Rugs,
Accessories, Brass Items,
Far East Indian Miniatures,
Wood Carvings, American
Indian Rugs
Specialties: Oriental Rugs
Appraisal Service Available
Directions: Lower
Downtown, Corner of
Speer Blvd & Market St

THE NOSTALGIA SHOP
2431 S University Blvd
    80210
Proprietor: L G Cantwell &
Rodney White
Hours: Tues-Fri 10-5; Sun
& Sat 12-5; Closed Mon
Types & Periods: Items from
'20s, '30s & '40s Art Deco,
Period Clothing, Magazines
before 1945, Photographs,
"Out of Print" 78 rpm
Records, Movie Materials,
Furnishings, "Out of Print"
Books, Maintain Customer
"Want" Book
Specialties: Vintage
Phonographs, 78 rpm
Recordings
Appraisal Service Available
Directions: On University
Blvd between Harvard &
Wesley, 4 Blks from
University of Denver

Denver   Cont'd

OK ANTIQUE PLATING CO INC
3500 E 12th Ave   80206
303 377-0361
Types & Periods: Metal,
Victorian Silver, Iron,
Copper, Brass
  Directions: At Madison

REMEMBER WHEN ANTIQUES
1401 S Broadway   80210
303 733-1086   Est: 1974
Proprietor: Maril & Tom
Bice
Hours: Daily; Weekends
Types & Periods: Victorian
(Walnut), Turn-of-the-Century
Furniture, Collectibles
Specialties: Restoring &
Refinishing
  Directions: Corner of S
  Broadway & Arkansas Ave
  on "Denver's Famous
  Antique Row"

SECOND NATURE RESTORATION & ANTIQUES
2009 Market   80205
Proprietor: Michael Green
Hours: Mon-Sat l0-5
Types & Periods:
Turn-of-the-Century Antiques
& Lighting, Interior &
Exterior Architectural Goods
Specialties: Custom
Woodworking & Finishing,
Antiques & Collectibles
Restored, Refinished &
Re-created, Interior House
Restoration
  Directions: Located in
  historic lower Downtown
  Denver near Union Station
  on corner of 20th &
  Market St

SILVER DOLLAR TRADING CO
1446 S Broadway   80210
303 733-0500   Est: 1970
Proprietor: William R
McCoy
Hours: Daily, l0-5; Closed
Sun
Types & Periods: Victorian,
Mission, Golden Oak
Furniture, Antique Pool
Tables, Light Fixtures
Specialties: Pool Tables,
Light Fixtures

Appraisal Service Available
  Directions: S Broadway
  Exit from I-25, Go 1 1/2
  Miles S

TREASURES & TRIFLES
8350 N Washington 80229
303 288-8011   Est: 1968
Proprietor: Marv & Marge
Grosz
Hours: Daily l-5; Closed
Sun & Mon
Types & Periods: Glass,
Books, General Line
  Directions: N on Valley
  Hwy to 84th St Turnoff,
  East 5 Blocks to
  Washington, S 1/2 Block

VINTAGE '76
2467 S Broadway   80210
303 777-3854   Est: 1974
Proprietor: Beverly & Ron
Nelson
Hours: Mon-Sat 10-5;
Closed Sun
Types & Periods: Clothing &
Textiles, 1950's & Older
Appraisal Service Available
Specialties: Costume Parties
& Tintypers
  Directions: 15 Blocks S on
  Broadway Exit of I-25

YESTERYEARS ANTIQUES
4840 W 29th Ave   80212
303 455-0888
Proprietor: George &
Dorothy White
Hours: Daily; Weekends;
Closed Fri
Types & Periods: Furniture,
Primitives, Cut Glass, Tools,
General Line

Eckert

GOOD'S ANTIQUES
R 1, Box 245   81418
303 835-3289   Est: 1964
Proprietor: Doris & Max
Good
Hours: Daily Summer;
Tues-Sun, Closed Mon,
Winter
Types & Periods: Art, Cut,
Pressed Glass, Furniture,
Silver, Primitives
Specialties: Furniture
Restoration
Appraisal Service Available
  Directions: Btwn Delta &
  Cedaredge on Hwy 65

Englewood

CARRIAGE HOUSE I
3016 S Broadway   80110
Proprietor: Dr Hardendorf
Hours: Tues-Sun; Closed
Mon
Types & Periods: Cut Glass,
Art Glass, China, Home
Decorative Accessories,
Hobby Items, General Line
Furniture, Kitchen Primitives
& Tools
Appraisal Service Available
  Directions: S Broadway
  Antique Row

GATEWAY ANTIQUES
2910 S Tejon   80110
303 761-0659   Est: 1960
Proprietor: James W
Chandler
Hours: Mon-Fri; By
Appointment
Types & Periods: Bronzes,
Porcelains, American,
French & English, 18th
Century Furniture, Tiffany
Specialties: Tiffany,
Meissen/American
Paintings-Will buy or locate
specific items
Appraisal Service Available
  Directions: SW Denver
  near Cinderella City

MYAN'S PO'POURRI
3663 S Broadway   80110
303 781-7724   Est: 1969
Proprietor: John & Marian
Swartz
Hours: Mon-Sat l0-5;
Sun-Summer Adv
Appointment; Sun-Winter
l-5
Types & Periods: Furniture,
Primitives, Glass, China,
Collectibles, Bath Fixtures &
Accessories
Specialties: Footed Tubs,
Oak Toilet Seats, Oak Water
Tanks, Marble & China
Lavatories of l920's with
appropriate trims in polished
brass

ROCKY MOUNTAIN CLOCK REPAIR
2739 S Broadway   80110
303 789-1573
Hours: Mon-Sat 9-5:30
Types & Periods: Clocks,
Watches, Music Boxes, Gear
Cutting

Estes Park

THE JOLLY DROVER
361 Moraine   80517
303 586-4050
Proprietor: James &
Nancy Swickard
Hours: Daily 9-9 Summer;
9-5 Winter
Types & Periods: Art Glass,
Primitive

Evergreen

D C ALMQUIST JEWELERS & WATCHMAKERS
80439
303 674-5222   Est: 1970
Proprietor: Larry L
Lipstein
Hours: Daily 9-5:30; Sat
9-12; Closed Sun
Types & Periods: American
Pocket Watches, Fobs,
Chains, Jewelry
Specialties: Repairs,
Restorations, Parts,
Remanufacturing
Appraisal Service Available
Directions: High Country
Sq, N Evergreen, Rte 74,
1 Mile N of Lake
Evergreen

YANKEE DOODLER
Evergreen N Shopping Ctr,
Box 1664   80439
303 674-7444   Est: 1974
Proprietor: Marcille Hawley
Hours: Daily 10-5:30; Sat
10-5
Types & Periods: Furniture,
Accessories
Directions: 4 Miles N of
Downtown, 4 Miles S of
I-70 on Hwy 74, Take Exit
57A from I-70; 12 Miles W
of Golden

Fort Collins

A-I SALVAGE
2104 E Lincoln   80521
303 493-4000   Est: 1968
Proprietor: R Bruce Grant
Hours: Daily 8-6; Sun 11-5
Types & Periods: Primitives,
Doors, Windows, Flooring
Appraisal Service Available
Directions: One Block S
Valley Airport

ANNE'S ANTIQUES & DECORATOR FURNISHINGS
131 1/2 Lincoln   80521
303 482-4558
Proprietor: M Anne
Harden
Hours: By Appointment;
By Chance
Types & Periods: Haviland,
Art Glass, Silver
Appraisal Service Available

FLORENCE CARROLL
411 W Oak   80521
303 482-3022
Proprietor: Florence
Carroll
Types & Periods: Glass,
China, Furniture

THE COLONIAL SHOP
147 W Oak St   80521
303 482-7577   Est: 1955
Proprietor: Martha B
Jordan
Hours: Tues, Thur, Fri; By
Appointment
Types & Periods: Art Glass,
Pattern Glass, China, Brass,
Copper, Clocks
Directions: Downtown Fort
Collins

SALISBURY AUCTIONS LTD
2028 SE Frontage Rd
80521
303 493-9072   Est: 1970
Proprietor: Jack Salisbury
Hours: Daily 9:30-5:30
Types & Periods: General
Line, By Consignment
Appraisal Service Available
Directions: Take
Prospect Exit off I-25,
Right-Hand UTurn, Go 1/2
Miles S on E Frontage Rd

SILENT WOMAN ANTIQUES
132 W Mountain   80521
303 493-3255   Est: 1974
Proprietor: Joann & Bob
Montgomery
Hours: Daily; Weekends,
10-5; Closed Sun
Types & Periods: General
Line, American Furniture,
Glassware, Primitives,
Stained Glass

TRIMBLE COURT ARTISANS
114 Trimble Ct   80521
303 493-9579   Est: 1971

Proprietor: Mrs Carl
Bruere
Hours: Daily, Closed Sun
& Mon
Types & Periods: Ranch &
Farm Tools, Chairs, Tables,
Dolls, Kitchen Items
Specialties: Caning, Wood
Repair, Quilting

Franktown

AYERS OF FRANKTOWN
80116
303 688-3827   Est: 1963
Proprietor: David W Ayers
Hours: By Appointment
Types & Periods: 17th &
18th Centuries English &
American Furniture &
Decorative Arts
Directions: Btwn Denver &
Colorado Sprgs on Hwy
83, 6 Miles E of Exit 80,
I-25

Frisco

LAVENDER & OLD LACE SHOPPE
503 Main St   80443
303 468-2122
Hours: Daily; Weekends
10-6; Sun 11-5; By
Appointment
Types & Periods: General
Line, Indian Jewelry & Arts,
Furniture, Glass, China,
Primitives
Directions: Denver Phone
303 222-5018

Georgetown

BLUE SPRUCE ANTIQUES
412 Sixth   80444
303 569-2370
Proprietor: Barbara Clark
Hours: Daily 9-5:30
Types & Periods: Glass,
Furniture, Jewelry

Glenwood Springs

WESTERN QUEEN ANTIQUES
4845 Road 154   81601
303 945-5363   Est: 1963

WESTERN QUEEN ANTIQUES   Cont'd
Proprietor: Vivian Carver
Hours: Daily; Weekends;
By Appointment; By
Chance
Types & Periods: Early
Pressed Glass, Hand
Painted China, Cut Glass,
Crystal, Victorian Furniture
Appraisal Service Available
Directions: 6 Miles S of
Glenwood Sprgs on Old
Hwy 82, On the River

Golden

LAMPLIGHTER ANTIQUES
15801 W Colfax   80401
303 279-3188
Proprietor: Earl & Marian
Stiegelmeyer
Hours: Daily; Weekends;
Closed Mon & Tues
Types & Periods: General
Line, Music Boxes, Clocks
Directions: Denver Area

Grand Junction

BURTON'S FURNITURE & ANTIQUES
826 N 1st St   81501
303 242-8095   Est: 1963
Proprietor: Hugh & Mary
Ann Burton
Hours: Daily
Types & Periods: Furniture,
Glass, China, Silver, General
Line
Specialties: Lamps, Lamp
Parts
Appraisal Service Available
Directions: 1st St W Side
of Town

CHINA CLOSET ANTIQUES
1025 N 5th   81501
303 243-2046
Types & Periods: China,
Glass, Silver

LOUISA'S ANTIQUES
961 Main St   81501
303 242-6317   Est: 1974
Proprietor: Bob & Louisa
Lewis
Hours: Daily; Weekends;
Eves by Appointment

Types & Periods: General
Line, Furniture, China,
Glass, Collectibles,
Primitives
Appraisal Service Available
Directions: Corner of 10th
& Main

MOTOR INN TREASURE HUT
2812 North Ave   81501
303 243-2711
Proprietor: Paul L
Donovan
Hours: Sun-Sat, 9-5
Types & Periods: Antique
Furniture, Old Relics,
Buggies, Wagons, China,
Unusual Items, Turquoise,
Silver

PARKVIEW ANTIQUES
1430 N Ave   81501
303 242-6458
Proprietor: Mr & Mrs Glen
Cox
Types & Periods: Indian
Jewelry, Buggies, Lamps,
Furniture

WATERMAN'S SWAP SHOP
418 S 7th St   81501
303 243-4500
Proprietor: Tunney & Betty
Waterman
Types & Periods:
Collectibles, Furniture,
China, Glass, Primitives,
Pottery, Indian Jewelry,
Rugs, Baskets

Greeley

BAR-F ANTIQUES
2221 1st Ave   80631
303 352-3552   Est: 1972
Proprietor: Fred & Barbara
Hahnbaum
Hours: Tues-Sat
Types & Periods: General
Line
Directions: 22nd St Exit
off US 85 Bypass Greeley

LITTLE RED HOUSE ANTIQUES
1005 95 Ave   80631
303 352-3534   Est: 1963
Proprietor: Hubbard &
Mildred Rinearson
Hours: Daily

Types & Periods: Cut Glass,
Dolls, Miniatures, Period
Clothing, General Line
Specialties: Glass, (Cut),
Miniatures
Appraisal Service Available
Directions: Bus Hwy 34, 7
Miles W of Greeley, I3
Miles E of Loveland Hwy
34

SARAH'S ANTIQUES
1329 9th St   80631
303 352-9204   Est: 1970
Proprietor: Eddie Foster
Hours: Tues-Sat I0-5; By
Appointment
Types & Periods: China,
Clocks, Glass, Primitives,
Furniture, Collectibles
Specialties: Clocks
Appraisal Service Available

Lamar

ANTIQUE MERCANTILE
1301 N Main   81052
303 336-9621   Est: 1974
Proprietor: Jo Swenson
Hours: Mon-Sat; By
Appointment
Types & Periods: General
Line
Specialties: Furniture, Music
Items, Primitives
Directions: On Main Hwy
287, N Edge of Town in
Cow Palace Motel

Limon

LIMON TRADING POST
760 First St   80828
303 775-2378   Est: 1969
Proprietor: Ardith Reagan
Hours: Daily; Closed Sun
Types & Periods: General
Line
Directions: "At only stop
light in town turn S two
blocks then E I 1/2
blocks"

Littleton

VERA L PHILLIPS
6427 S Prince St   80120
303 794-4135   Est: 1967
Proprietor: Vera L Phillips
Hours: Daily, Weekends,
Also by Appointment
Types & Periods: French &
American Haviland Chinas
Appraisal Service Available
Directions: Denver Suburb

THE PROSPECTOR
2529 W Main St   80120
303 798-5552   Est: 1972
Proprietor: Mel & Robin
Moore
Hours: Daily 9:30-5:30;
Except Sun; Also by
Appointment
Types & Periods: American
Pine Primitives, Tools,
Railroad Items, General Line
Specialties: Books,
Americana & Poetry
Appraisal Service Available
Directions: "Near Corner
of Nevada & Main St, Old
Downtown Littleton"

Loveland

THE ANTIQUE CENTRE
908 Cleveland   80537
303 667-8127   Est: 1973
Proprietor: Herena
Burkette
Hours: "Most time
Mon-Sat l0-5"
Types & Periods: Period
Furniture, General Line
Appraisal Service Available
Directions: 50 Miles N of
Denver on I-25, 4 Miles W
on 34

**COUNTRY MOUSE
ANTIQUES**
1326 N Carter Lake Rd
80537
303 669-0415
Proprietor: Lowell &
Sharon Brady
Hours: Sun, Mon,
Wed-Sat; Closed Tues
Types & Periods: Furniture,
General Line
Appraisal Service Available
Directions: 7 Miles W of
Loveland on US 34, 1/4
Mile S on Carter Lake Rd

POTPOURRI ANTIQUES
225 E 10th   80537
Est: 1971
Proprietor: D Heffington
Hours: Daily l0-5
Types & Periods: Period
Furnishings, Paintings,
Orientals, Metals, Primitives,
General Line of English &
American
Appraisal Service Available
Directions: Hwy 34 into
Loveland as far as
Cleveland, Follow to 10th,
E One Block

**SILVER BELL ANTIQUES
SHOP**
1127 E 4th St   80537
303 667-4007
Proprietor: Raymon & Lois
Swartz
Hours: By Appointment;
By Chance
Types & Periods: Glass,
China, Jewelry

SUNSET ANTIQUES
2803 W Eisenhower 80537
Est: 1937
Proprietor: Ruth M Setzler
Hours: Daily, Weekends
Types & Periods: General
Line
Directions: Hwy 34 into
Estes Park, 2 Miles W of
Loveland

Lyons

ANTIQUE LYONS LAIR
400 Main   80540
303 823-6788   Est: 1974
Proprietor: Edith & Lee
Proctor
Hours: Mon-Sat l0-5;
Sun 1-5
Types & Periods: General
Line
Appraisal Service Available
Directions: Only Stop
Light; Store Downstairs

ANTIQUES & JUNQUE
433 High   80540
303 823-6783   Est: 1972
Proprietor: Ron & Phyllis
Wheaton
Hours: Mon-Sat
Types & Periods: Furniture,
Primitives, Books, Linens,
Miniatures, China, Glass

Directions: 15 Miles N of
Boulder on Hwys 66 & 36,
Enroute to Estes Park

BLUE WILLOW ANTIQUES
436 High   80540
303 823-6080
Proprietor: Sylvia Link &
Hope Firkins
Hours: Mon-Sat; Closed
Sun
Types & Periods: Jewelry,
Oriental, Glass, Fine
Porcelain, Books & Prints
Appraisal Service Available
Directions: Junction
36 & 66

**CARRIAGE HOUSE
ANTIQUES**
324 Main   80580
303 823-6414   Est: 1972
Proprietor: D R
Hardendorf
Hours: Daily
Types & Periods: General
Line

HONEYMAN'S ANTIQUES
Jcts 36 & 66   80540
303 823-6759
Types & Periods: Furniture,
Cut Glass, Jewelry, Dolls,
General Line

REVA'S MOUNTAIN HOME
Raymond's Resort   80540
303 747-2247
Proprietor: Reva M
Woolley & Richard W
Woolley
Hours: Daily, July 1 to
Sept 1; Otherwise By
Appointment
Types & Periods: Pressed
Glass, Art Glass, China,
French Dolls, Miniatures
Specialties: Glass, China,
French Dolls & Miniatures
Directions: 15 Miles N of
Lyons in S St Urain
Canyon

Mancos

ANTIQUE ACCENTS
192 S Main   81328
303 533-7484   Est: 1966
Proprietor: Steve & Betty
Exum
Hours: Mon-Sat

ANTIQUES ACCENTS
Cont'd
Types & Periods: Glass,
China, Furniture, Car Parts,
Old Bottles, Trash &
Treasures
  Directions: 7 Miles from
  Entrance to Mesa Verde
  Nat'l Pk, E on Bus Rte
  thru Town, 1 Block S

Merino

D & J COUNTRY ANTIQUES
Rte 2, Box 29   80741
Proprietor: Dorothy & Jake
Leis
Hours: Daily; By
Appointment; By Chance
Types & Periods: Oak &
Walnut Furniture, General
Line
  Directions: 10 Miles E of
  Merino Overpass, 32039
  Co Rd 3l

Monte Vista

MANSION ANTIQUES
1030 Park Ave   81144
303 852-3353   Est: 1972
Proprietor: Paul & Donna
Hall
Hours: Daily; Weekends
Types & Periods: Victorian,
Early American, Primitives,
Turquoise Jewelry
Specialties: Jewelry
(Turquoise)
Appraisal Service Available
  Directions: Rtes 160 & 285

Niwot

THE ANTIQUE PLACE
190 Second Ave   80544
303 772-4131   Est: 1970
Proprietor: Paul D
Vandruff
Hours: Daily
Types & Periods: Furniture,
1800-1915
Specialties: Refinishing
Appraisal Service Available
  Directions: 7 Miles from
  Boulder, Seven Other
  Small Antique Shops in
  Town

Palisade

OLETA'S ANTIQUES
688 Brentwood Dr   81526
303 464-7824   Est: 1960
Proprietor: Oleta & Harvey
Leach
Hours: Daily; Weekends
9-5; By Appointment; By
Chance
Types & Periods: China,
Glass, Furniture, Primitives,
Dolls
Appraisal Service Available
  Directions: 1 Block S of
  Stoplight on Hwy 6

Pueblo

ANTIQUE COLLECTOR'S
KORNER
209 S Union St   81003
303 543-0073   Est: 1972
Proprietor: William DeBaca
Hours: Mon-Thurs
Types & Periods: General
Line
  Directions: 2 Blocks S of
  City Hall

COLLECTORS EXCHANGE
325 S Union   81004
303 561-8201   Est: 1975
Proprietor: Mrs Pat
Griffeth
Hours: Daily; Weekends;
By Appointment
Types & Periods:
Turn-of-the-Century Oak,
Oriental, Glassware, Jewelry,
China
Appraisal Service Available
  Directions: 1/2 Block from
  Union Depot

GREEN'S ANTIQUES
25281 South Rd   81006
303 545-3624   Est: 1964
Proprietor: George & Doris
Green
Hours: By Appointment;
By Chance
Types & Periods: Vintage
Clothing & Accessories,
1880-1940, Linens, Dolls,
China, Bisque, Composition
& Collectibles, Primitives,
Glass, Buttons
Appraisal Service Available

Directions: Old Hwy 50 E
to 25th Lane, S to 2nd
Stop Sign, Left on South
Rd to 2nd House

HOUSE OF THE GOLDEN
HARP
325 South Union Ave
                     81003
303 544-1251   Est: 1899
Proprietor: Roderick D
Myers
Hours: Mon-Sat l0-5; By
Appointment
Types & Periods: Museum
Pieces, European, American,
& Oriental Antiques, Art,
Indian Jewelry, Blankets,
Pottery, Rugs, Antique &
Unique Jewelry, Primitives
Appraisal Service Available
  Directions: In "Old
  Pueblo", Exit 1st St from
  Hwy 25 to Union Ave

LENORE JOHNSON
ANTIQUES & ELEGANT
JUNQUE
207 S Union Ave   81003
303 545-7191
Hours: Daily; Weekends
ll-5; Closed Sun
Types & Periods: General
Line
  Directions: 2 Blocks S of
  City Hall

Rocky Ford

THE SHOP
912 Swink Ave   81067
303 254-6687   Est: 1968
Proprietor: Emily
Mendenhall
Hours: Daily; By
Appointment; Closed Tues
Types & Periods: General
Line
  Directions: 1/2 Block
  Beyond Stoplight on Hwy
  50 going W

Silverton

THE LEMON TREE
PO Box 3   81433
303 387-5471   Est: 1969
Proprietor: June & George
Bradbury

Hours: Daily; Weekends,
l0-5
Types & Periods: Country &
Oriental, Tools
Appraisal Service Available
  Directions: "Blue building
  on Green Street"

Snowmass Village

**C LEIGH ANTIQUES &
GALLERY**
  PO Box 5228   81615
  303 923-3987   Est: 1978
  Proprietor: Ms Carey
  Leigh
  Hours: By Appointment
  Only
Types & Periods: Oriental
Art, Cloisonne, Porcelain,
Bronze, Furniture, Antique
Rugs
Specialties: Pottery
  Directions: Will be given
  when you call for
  Appointment

Steamboat Springs

**THE LITTLE RED SLEIGH
ANTIQUES**
  PO Box 817   80477
  303 879-4385   Est: 1975
  Proprietor: Toni Lanza &
  Suzanne Cowen
  Hours: Tues-Fri, l0-5; Sat,
  Sun & Mon by
  Appointment
Types & Periods: Furniture,
China, Glass, Tole
Specialties: Furniture
(Country)
  Directions: At Steamboat
  Villa btwn Town & Ski
  Area on Hwy 40

**PLAZA GALLERY/SHOP
LIMITED**
  Steamboat Village Plaza
                      80477
  303 879-2679   Est: 1972
  Proprietor: Emily Ingram
  Hours: Daily
Types & Periods: 1850's
Stained Glass Windows, Oak
Wash Stands, Cupboards,
Copper Containers, Bottles,
Prints, Jewelry, Collectibles
  Directions: Mt Werner Ski
  Area back of Steamboat
  Village Inn

Sterling

THE RELIC SHOP
  102 N Division Ave 80751
  303 522-5546   Est: 1972
  Proprietor: Jean Kircher
  Hours: Daily; By
  Appointment; Closed Sun
Types & Periods: Turn of
the Century & Late 1800
Furniture, Primitives,
Collectibles
  Directions: "Just off Main
  St on corner of Main & N
  Division"

Trinidad

**ANTIQUE JUNK & STUFF
TRADING POST**
  210-212 N Commercial
                      81082
  303 846-7579   Est: 1976
  Proprietor: Betty A Warren
  Hours: Mon-Sat l0-5:30;
  By Appointment
Types & Periods: Furniture,
Collectibles
Appraisal Service Available
  Directions: One of the
  Main Sts in Trinidad, Easy
  to find

THE FALLEN ANGEL
  120 W Main St   81082
                  Est: 1965
  Proprietor: Olga Azar
  Hours: Mon-Sat
Types & Periods: Primitives,
Victorian, Miscellaneous-
Different Periods
Appraisal Service Available
  Directions: Located on
  Main St in Town, Easy to
  Find

Walsenburg

THE FALLEN ANGEL
  623 Main St   81089
  303 738-2510   Est: 1965
  Hours: Daily
Types & Periods: General
Line, Victorian Furniture,
Glass, China
Appraisal Service Available
  Directions: On Main St of
  Town, Easy to find

Wheat Ridge

BARLOW'S ANTIQUES
  6390 W 44th   80033
  303 424-1531
  Proprietor: Ray R Barlow
  Hours: Sat l0-5; By
  Appointment
Types & Periods: Lamps &
Parts, Carnival & Cut Glass,
China

**MC KINLEY & HILL
ANTIQUES**
  4340 Harlan   80033
  303 424-1102
  Proprietor: Hogue W
  McKinley & H K Hill
  Hours: Mon-Sat l0:30-6:00;
  Closed Sun
Types & Periods: 18th
Century English & American
Furniture & Accessories, Art
Glass, Wedgwood
Specialties: Art Glass,
Wedgwood, Chinese
Porcelains
Appraisal Service Available
  Directions: Denver Metro
  Area, Off I-70 W at Harlan
  St Exit

THE OLDE SAGE PLACE
  3785 Marshall St   80033
  303 422-7934   Est: 1976
  Proprietor: Betty Loye
  Hours: Tues-Sat l-5
Types & Periods: General
Line, "Personally Selected
Antiques & Country
Collectibles"
  Directions: Exit from I-70
  at Harlan St, S to 38th
  Ave, W to Marshall St

**WHEATRIDGE COUNTRY
MART**
  9970 W 44th Ave   80033
  303 422-3538
  Proprietor: Bernice B
  Hansen
  Hours: Daily; Weekends,
  l2-5; Closed Sun & Mon
Types & Periods: Furniture,
Silver, Paintings, Prints

YANKEE PEDDLER
  9970 W 44th Ave   80033
  Proprietor: Virginia Snow
  Hours: Tues-Sat l0-5
Types & Periods: Country;
Primitives

Woodland Park

**HERITAGE STUDIO
ANTIQUES**
   Rte 2310   80863
   303 687-9426
   Proprietor: Herb & Naomi
   Chittick
   Hours: Daily; Weekends,
   l0-5; Closed Mon
Types & Periods: 19th
Century American Furniture
& Accessories

LOG CABIN ANTIQUES
   US Hwy 24   80863
   303 687-2150   Est: 1972
   Proprietor: Hans & Irene
   Baden
   Hours: Daily, Summer;
   Closed Mon, Winter; By
   Appointment
Types & Periods: General
Line
   Directions: 20 Miles W
   Colorado Sprgs, US Hwy
   24

**SPINNING WHEEL
ANTIQUES**
   414 W Midland   80863
   303 687-9102
   Proprietor: Curtis & Hazel
   Hanawalt
   Hours: Daily; Weekends,
   11-5 June 15-Sept 1;
   Closed Sun & Mon
Types & Periods: General
Line, Cut Glass

**SPINNING WHEEL
ANTIQUES**
   Hwy 24   80863
   303 687-9102
   Proprietor: Curtis & Hazel
   Hanawalt
   Hours: June I thru Sept I;
   Closed Sun & Thurs
Types & Periods: Primitives,
Cut Glass, General Line
   Directions: 20 Miles W of
   Colorado Sprgs

Gateleg Table, Jacobean, dropleaf

Swing Leg Table, 19th Century, dropleaf

STATE OF CONNECTICUT

Andover

THE WELLSWEEP
Hebron Rd   06232
203 742-8952
Proprietor: Evelyn P Clark
Hours: By Appointment,
By Chance
Types & Periods: Early
American

Avon

HERITAGE ANTIQUES
87 Paper Chase Trail
          06001
203 673-0787
Proprietor: Garland &
Frances Pass
Hours: By Shows & Mail
Order Only
Types & Periods: 17th, 18th
& Early 19th Century Base
Metal Antiques
Specialties: Pewter and
Period Brass
Appraisal Service Available

THE QUILT PATCH
45 Old Mill Rd   06001
203 673-2117
Proprietor: Lori Berti
Hours: By Appointment
Types & Periods: Patchwork
Quilts & Coverlets, Some
Accessories and Related
Items
Specialties: Antique Quilts &
Coverlets
Directions: Rte 44, West
of Hartford

Bantam

BANTAM ANTIQUES
Rt 202 Main St   06750
203 567-9025
Proprietor: Dorothy
MacDonald
Hours: Daily, 10-5
Types & Periods: 18th &
19th Century Furniture &
Accessories

**GOOSEBORO BROOK
ANTIQUES**
Old Turnpike Rd   06750
203 567-5245
Proprietor: Mrs Carolyn
Butts
Hours: Sun-Sat 10-5
Types & Periods: General
Line of Antiques from 18th
Century to 20th Century
Collectibles
Specialties: Country Items:
Woodenware, Stoneware,
Tools, Tinware, Primitives
Appraisal Service Available
Directions: 500 Yards off
US Rte 202 (5 Miles West
of Historic Litchfield)

Berlin

RED HOUSE ANTIQUES
2248 Wilbur Cross Hwy
          06037
203 828-9650
Proprietor: H & B
Cummings
Hours: Daily, I-5
Types & Periods: Americana

Bethel

ELEPHANT & CASTLE
127 Greenwood Ave 06801
203 748-0116
Proprietor: E G Ziolinski
Hours: Daily 12-5, Closed
Sun & Mon
Types & Periods: China,
Glassware, Silver

J THOMAS MELVIN
10 Wooster St   06801
203 744-5244   Est: 1950
Proprietor: J Thomas
Melvin
Hours: Tues-Sat 11-5,
Also By Appointment
Types & Periods: Oriental
Porcelains, Period Furniture,
General Line
Specialties: Glass, Oriental
Appraisal Service Available
Directions: 20 Minutes N
of Westport

OLD FAVORITES
92 Greenwood Ave 06801
203 797-0857
Proprietor: Rita Barg
Hours: Wed-Sat
Types & Periods: Oak,
Mahogany, Country English
Furniture, Wicker, Oils, Early
Prints, Collectibles
Directions: I-84 Exit 8, Rte
6, Right to Old Hawleyville
Rd, Stop Sign Turn Right,
Follow Signs to Bethel
Business District

**ROLF VIGMOSTAD
ANTIQUES GALLERY**
Greenwood Ave   06801
203 743-6644
Proprietor: Rolf Vigmostad
Hours: By Appointment
Types & Periods: 18th &
Early 19th Century American
& English Furniture
Directions: Greenwood
Ave & Depot Place, Old
Opera House

Branford

THE TRADING POST
80 N Main St   06405
203 488-1876   Est: I965
Proprietor: Dorothy
Wallace
Hours: Daily 10-5, Closed
Mon
Types & Periods: General
Line
Directions: Boston Post
Road (Rte 1)

Bridgeport

BRIDGEPORT CLUSTER
Directions: On Post Rd
(1000 Block) Main St
(I000-3000 Blocks) Park
Ave (99-I000 Blocks)

ALBERTO'S ANTIQUES
1223 Park Ave   06604
203 367-6962
Proprietor: Evelyn Oropal
Hours: Tues thru Sat I0-5
Types & Periods: Clocks,
Furniture, Glass, Collectibles

THE PARK AVEUNE CURIO SHOPPE
1399 Park Ave   06604
203 333-6896
Proprietor: Lenny Zetomer
Hours: Daily l0-5
Types & Periods: Victorian & Oak Furniture, Rockers, Glass, China

VILLAGE BARN ANTIQUES
222 Wood Ave   06604
203 366-1750
Proprietor: D Ross Potter
Hours: Daily 9:30-4:30
Types & Periods: General Line

Bristol

ABC ANTIQUES
370 Burlington Ave   06010
203 582-7397
Proprietor: A B Colella
Hours: By Appointment
Types & Periods: China, Glass

DICK'S ANTIQUES
670 Lake Ave   06010
203 584-2566   Est: l962
Proprietor: Richard Blaschke
Hours: By Appointment
Types & Periods: Walnut & Oak Furniture, Lamps, Clocks
Directions: Off Exit 31 I-84

INTERNATIONAL HOBBIES
799 Farmington Ave 06010
203 582-0496   Est: l968
Proprietor: Wilbur Muller
Hours: Daily, l0-l2 & l- 5, Closed Tues & Wed
Types & Periods: Prints, Documents, Books, Stamps, Coins
Appraisal Service Available
Directions: On Rte 6

OLE' LAMPLIGHTER ANTIQUES
200 Wolcott Rd   06010
203 583-5395   Est: l965
Proprietor: Dick Semprini
Hours: Daily, 1-5, Sat by Appointment or Chance
Types & Periods: Furniture, General Line, Lamp Parts

Specialties: Victorian Lighting & Furniture, Replacement Lamp Parts
Appraisal Service Available
Directions: Rte 6 & 202 to Rte 69 S

Brookfield

THE BROOKFIELD SHOP
Rt 7   06804
203 775-3003   Est: l96l
Proprietor: Harold H Schramm
Hours: Weekends, By Appointment
Types & Periods: General Line
Appraisal Service Available
Directions: 9 Miles N of Danbury

ORIENTAL RUG BARN
Station Rd   06804
203 775-2838
Proprietor: Amber R Harrington
Hours: By Appointment
Types & Periods: Oriental Rugs
Directions: Jct of Rte 7 & 25

Brooklyn

HEIRLOOM ANTIQUES
Winding Rd   06234
203 774-7017   Est: 1974
Proprietor: Catharine H Williams & Marcia LaPorte
Hours: Daily 12-5, Closed Wed
Types & Periods: General Line
Specialties: Early Lamps & Furniture
Appraisal Service Available
Directions: Center of Brooklyn, Just Off Rte 169, Rear of Firehouse

Canton

BALCONY ANTIQUES
140 Albany Tnpk   06019
203 693-2996
Hours: Mon-Sat 10-5:30

Types & Periods: General Line
Directions: At the Finishing Touch

BRASS BED BOUTIQUE
Rte 44   06019
203 693-0333   Est: l972
Proprietor: John Perrino
Hours: Thurs-Sun, By Appointment
Types & Periods: Victorian Oak & Walnut
Specialties: Brass Beds
Appraisal Service Available
Directions: At Intersections of Rts 44 & 177

THE COB-WEB
Jct Rte 44 at Rte l02   06019
203 693-2658   Est: l968
Proprietor: Doris Rudder
Hours: Sat & Sun 11:30-5, or By Appointment
Types & Periods: General Line, Triffels & Treasures
Specialties: Flea Market Next to Shop Sun May-Sept (50 Dealers) 8:30 to Dusk
Directions: 2 Miles W of the Green

THE FRAME UP
162 Albany Trnpk   06019
203 693-4698   Est: l967
Proprietor: Martha S Simmons
Hours: Mon, Wed, Thurs, Sat, Also By Appointment
Types & Periods: Country Thru Art Deco, Baskets, Woodenware, Silver, Small Furniture
Specialties: Paper Goods, Picture Frames
Appraisal Service Available
Directions: W from Hartford on Rte 44 (Albany Trnpk) Just E of Canton Green

Centerbrook

JUNE & BEN CARDE
Main St   06409
203 767-0222
Proprietor: June & Ben Carde

Hours: Thur 10-5 Also By
Appointment or By
Chance
Types & Periods: General
Line

CHAS W THILL ANTIQUES
Main St   06409
203 767-1696
Proprietor: Chas W Thill
Hours: Daily 10-5, Closed
Mon, Also By Appointment
Types & Periods: General
Line
Directions: Factory Bldg

Cheshire

BERNIE MC MANUS
ANTIQUES
200 S Main St   06410
203 272-0745
Proprietor: Bernie
McManus
Hours: Fri, Sat, & Sun,
12-5
Types & Periods: General
Line
Directions: Rte 10

Chester

ONE OF A KIND
4 Water St in the Center
                       06412
203 526-9736
Proprietor: The Perry
Family
Hours: Daily Mon-Sun, 10-5
Types & Periods: Large
Variety Everything from
Primitives to Victorian &
Turn of the Century,
Especially Oak, Walnut,
Mahogany, Some Pine,
Some Wicker, Lamps,
Accessories
Specialties: Fine Quality
Furniture all Periods
Covered, also Lamps, China,
Glassware, Collectibles
Appraisal Service Available
Directions: From Hartford
& Points N take I-91 S to
Rte 9, Exit 6, 1 Mile to
center of Chester From
New York, New Haven or
Rhode Island, take I-95 to
Exit 69 (to Rte 9) take Exit
6, 1 Mile to Center

WALT KILLAM ORIENTAL
ARTS
122 Middlesex Tpk   06412
203 526-2967
Proprietor: Betty & Walt
Killam
Hours: Daily 11-4 & By
Appointment
Types & Periods: Oriental
Netsuke, Swords, Prints,
Porcelain, Bronzes
Appraisal Service Available
Directions: Rte 9A

Clinton

ANTIQUES BY WILLIS
146 E Main St   06413
203 669-9828
Proprietor: Esther & David
Willis
Hours: Daily, Weekends
10-5, Closed Mon & Tues
Types & Periods: Country
Furniture, Primitives

TIZ-ANTIQUES ET AMIES
173 Glenwood Rd   06413
203 669-9070
Proprietor: Betty Killian
Hours: Daily, By
Appointment 10:30-4
Types & Periods: Primitives,
Pressed Glass

Colchester

NATHAN LIVERANT &
SONS
48 S Main St   06415
203 537-2409   Est: 1925
Proprietor: Israel E
Liverant
Hours: Daily, Closed Sun
Types & Periods: Early
American Furniture, 18th &
19th Century Paintings,
Decorative Items
Specialties: Early American
Appraisal Service Available
Directions: On Rte 85
Junction of Rte 2

Cornwall Bridge

THE BRASS BUGLE
Rt 45   06754
203 672-6535   Est: 1961
Proprietor: Louise M
Hoffman

Hours: Daily 9-5,
April-Nov Otherwise By
Appointment or By
Chance
Types & Periods: Primitives,
Furniture, China, Glass
Specialties: Glass & Lamps
Directions: Large Barn on
Rte 45, 1/2 Mile from
Intersection of Rte 7

HOLMES ANTIQUES
Rts 7 & 45   06754
203 672-6427
Proprietor: Gunnar K
Holmes
Hours: Daily 8-8, Closed
Wed
Types & Periods: Early
American, Mostly Furniture
in Pine, Maple & Cherry,
Mahogany Also Accessories,
Including Dolls (Antique),
Toys, & Bric-a-brac
Specialties: Furniture
Directions: Rte 7, 35 Miles
N of Danbury, 35 Miles S
of Pittsfield, Mass, 35
Miles W of Hartford, & 35
Miles E of Poughkeepsie,
N Y

HARRY HOLMES
ANTIQUES
Rte 7 & Carter Rd   06754
203 927-3420   Est: 1950
Proprietor: Harry &
Jeanette Holmes
Hours: Daily
Types & Periods: 18th
Century Furniture &
Accessories
Specialties: Clocks,
Furniture
Directions: 4 Miles N of
the Village of Kent, At the
Corner of Rte 7 &
Carter Rd

ARCHIE M JAMGOTCHIAN
West Rd   06754
203 672-6014
Proprietor: Archie M
Jamgotchian
Hours: By Appointment
Types & Periods: Oriental
Rugs

Coventry

OLD COUNTRY STORE ANTIQUES
ll40 Main St   06238
203 742-9698
Proprietor: Barbara & Burt Baver
Hours: Sun-Sat I0-5:30, Closed Mon
Types & Periods: General Antiques & Collectibles
Directions: Rte 31

Cromwell

BROYLES' BARN
521 Main St (Rt 99) 06416
203 635-5957   Est: 1969
Proprietor: Chuck & Anne Broyles
Hours: Wed-Sat 12-4:30, By Appointment & By Chance
Types & Periods: Miniatures to Furniture, Very Diversified

RUSTY HINGE ANTIQUES
6 Oak Rd   06410
203 635-1017   Est: 1970
Proprietor: Lorraine Merrill
Types & Periods: Clocks, Victorian & Primitive Furniture
Specialties: Clocks
Directions: Exit 21 Off I-91, Go W 2nd Right Follow Signs

THE TIN PEDDLAR
29 Franklin Rd   06416
203 635-4270   Est: 1974
Proprietor: Gertrude Wyer
Hours: By Appointment, By Chance
Types & Periods: Tinware, Kitchen, Insulators, General Line
Directions: Exit 19 Off Rte 9, 1 Block

WANDA'S ANTIQUES
39 Elm Rd   06416
203 635-4287   Est: 1976
Proprietor: Ralph & Wanda Waters
Hours: Weekends, Also by Appointment
Types & Periods: Glass, Tin, Lamps, Bric-A-Brac, Mid 1800 to Early 1900

Specialties: Kerosene Lamps
Directions: Rte 9 N Exit 18 to Rte 99, Left at South St 1 Mile

Danbury

MRS MC GILLICUDDY'S SHOPPE
82 King St   06810
203 748-0041
Proprietor: Ruth & Jim Tibbets
Hours: Weekdays By Appointment, Sat I0-4, Sun "Noon till dark"
Types & Periods: Clocks, Primitives, Furniture, Glass, Bric-A-Brac, China, Picture Framing, Use Only Old Frames
Specialties: Fine Old Clocks-Mantle & Wall, Picture Framing, we Use Only Old Frames-Hundreds to Choose From
Appraisal Service Available
Directions: 3 Miles N of Interste 84, off at Exit 5, Take Rte 39 N 3 Miles & Left on King St for I.3 Miles

MIMI'S ANTIQUES
49 South St   06810
Est: 1973
Proprietor: Mimi Peterson
Hours: 11-4, Closed Wed Sat & Sun, Also By Appointment
Types & Periods: General Line, Estate Jewelry
Appraisal Service Available
Directions: South St is Rte 302, On Main Rte to Bethel

STONE HOUSE ANTIQUES
68 Sugar Hollow Rd (Rt 7)
06810
203 748-9417
Proprietor: Mary Ann Lenahan & Gwen Franco
Hours: Daily I0-5, Also By Appointment
Types & Periods: Flow Blue, Primitive Furniture

Danielson

M & C ANTIQUES
Blackrock Ave   06239
203 774-5552
Proprietor: Mitchell Phaiah & Chuck Touchette
Hours: By Appointment
Types & Periods: Oriental

Darien

THE COLLECTOR'S BARN
770 Post Rd   06820
203 655-7576   Est: I976
Proprietor: Carol Morgan & Emy Jones
Hours: Mon-Sat I0-5, Sun I-5
Types & Periods: English & Victorian Furntiure, Art Glass, Silver, Minatures, Tools, Toys, Quilts, Primitives, Porcelain, Paintings, Baskets, Clocks, Collector's Boxes
Appraisal Service Available
Directions: From N Y C Rte 95 (Conn Tpke) Exit 11 (Post Rd-Rte 1) Turn Left

DEACON'S HORSE ANTIQUES
70 Hollow Tree Ridge Rd
06820
203 838-2950
Proprietor: Sally Case & Nancy Fox
Hours: By Appointment
Types & Periods: General Line

HABITAT ANTIQUES
52 Locust Hill Rd   06820
203 655-8626
Proprietor: Ethel A Brady
Hours: By Appointment
Types & Periods: Furniture, Collectibles, Children's Furniture

CHARLES STUART & CO
1 Tokeneke Rd   06820
203 655-3555   Est: I970
Proprietor: Charles E Dinger & J D Pickering
Hours: Daily I0-5, Sun I-4

Types & Periods: American, English & Continental Porcelain, China, Silver, Jewelry, Paintings, Bronzes, China
Appraisal Service Available
Directions: Corner of Tokeneke Rd & Boston Post Rd

Deep River

THE COUNTRY SHOP
94 Main St   06417
203 526-9069
Proprietor: Charles Rozhon
Hours: Daily 11-6, Closed Sun
Types & Periods: Books, Framed Prints

WINTHROP CORNERS ANTIQUES
Rte 80   06417
203 526-9462
Proprietor: W B Gottlieb
Hours: Daily 12:30-5:30 or By Appointment
Types & Periods: English & Continental Furniture, Books

East Granby

THE KNOTTY PINE ANTIQUE SHOP
186 Hartford Ave   06026
203 653-2274
Proprietor: Wilfred Lennon
Hours: Daily 10-5, Also By Appointment
Types & Periods: General Line

East Haddam

L'ATELIER
Main St   06423
203 873-9198
Proprietor: Raymond & Diane Cummings
Hours: Wed-Sun 11-5, Also By Appointment
Types & Periods: 18th & Early 19th Century Americana
Directions: Rte 149

JIM MILLER ANTIQUES
Rte 82 Town St   06423
203 873-8286
Proprietor: Louise R Miller
Hours: Sun & Sat, By Chance
Types & Periods: General Line

Easton

DOROTHY BROOKS OF WEATPORT
69 Wedgewood Dr   06425
203 374-7939   Est: 1966
Proprietor: Dorothy Brooks Levine
Hours: By Appointment
Types & Periods: Antique Jewelry
Appraisal Service Available

MICHAEL FRIEDMAN ANTIQUES
10 Mile Common   06430
203 255-4486
Proprietor: Michael Friedman
Hours: By Appointment
Types & Periods: American Antiques & Folk Art of the 18th & 19th Century
Specialties: To The Trade & Advanced Collectors Emphasis on Country & Painted Furniture

OLD EASTON CENTER ANTIQUES
299 Center Rd   06425
203 268-9551
Proprietor: Richard Greiser
Hours: Mon-Fri 9-5, Sat 9-1, Sun By Appointment
Types & Periods: 19th Century Clocks, Cut Glass, Primitives, Furniture, Prints, General Line
Specialties: Stained Glass
Appraisal Service Available
Directions: Intersection Rte 136 & Center Rd, PO Bldg

East Putnam

COUNTRY SQUIRE ANTIQUES SHOP
Rte 44   06260
203 928-3239   Est: 1951

Proprietor: James F Melia
Hours: Daily 10-5, Sun 12-5, Closed Mon
Types & Periods: General Line
Specialties: Lamp Parts
Directions: 3 Miles E of Rte 52 at Exit 97

East Windsor

FRINGE TREE ANTIQUES
115 Bridge St   06028
203 623-8317
Proprietor: Lois Guckin
Hours: Wed-Sun 10-6
Types & Periods: Country Furniture
Directions: Warehouse Point

Ellington

TARRY A WHILE ANTIQUES
122 Main St   06029
203 875-7285
Proprietor: Germaine Peltier
Hours: April 1-Dec 1, 8:00-5:00, Also By Appointment
Types & Periods: Country Furniture, Primitives, China, Glass, Collectibles

Essex

AMERICAN HERITAGE ANTIQUES
Rte 153 Westbrook Rd   06426
203 767-8162
Hours: Daily 10-Dark
Types & Periods: General Line

BEALEY AMERICAN ANTIQUES
35 Main St   06426
203 767-0220
Hours: Wed-Sat 10-5:30, Also By Appointment
Types & Periods: General Line

CONNECTICUT MARINER
Griswold Sq   06426
203 767-8198   Est: 1973
Proprietor: Alan Bish

Essex   Cont'd

CONNECTICUT MARINER
                      Cont'd
Hours: Daily & by
appointment
Types & Periods: 19th
Century Marine Paintings,
Scrimshaw, Nautical Items
Specialties: Nautical Items
Appraisal Service Available
Directions: CT Turnpike
Exit 69 to Essex then end
of Main St Opposite
Griswold Inn

OLIVE DRAKE ANTIQUES
Rte 9A   06426
203 767-1568
Proprietor: Olive Drake
Hours: Mon-Sat l0-3, Sun
l2-3 or By Appointment
Types & Periods: Early
American China, Glass,
Silverplate
Specialties: Lamps
Appraisal Service Available
Directions: Rte 9A Essex
Rd to Saybrook

JAS E ELLIOTT ANTIQUES
8 N Main St   06426
203 767-1600   Est: 1960
Proprietor: James (Jim)
Elliott
Hours: Daily ll-4, Sun &
Mon By Appointment,
Appointment Suggested
Jan-March
Types & Periods: Empire &
Regency Furniture, British
Pottery & Porcelain, Blown
& Pattern Glass
Specialties: Staffordshire
Appraisal Service Available
Directions: Just Off
Square in Essex Village

ESSEX SHOWCASE
16 Main St   06426
203 767-1612
Hours: Daily l0-5, Closed
Sun
Types & Periods: General
Line

**FOREFATHER'S SHOP
ANTIQUES**
Saybrook Rd   06426
203 767-8962
Proprietor: Marian Dock
Hours: By Appointment,
By Chance

Types & Periods: Country
Furniture, Decoys, Tools
Directions: Corner of
Saybrook Rd & S Main St,
Saybrook is Rte 9A

THE GOLDEN APPLE
Essex Sq   06426
203 767-0324
Hours: Daily ll-5, Sun 2-5
Types & Periods: General
Line

**HASTINGS HOUSE
ANTIQUES**
Essex Sq   06426
203 767-0014
Hours: Tue-Sat 10:30-5:30,
Closed Sun & Mon, Also
By Appointment
Types & Periods: General
Line

HONORE
1 Griswold Sq Main St
                          06426
203 767-1271   Est: 1973
Proprietor: Ronald &
Honore Kaplan
Hours: Weekends
Types & Periods: Jewelry,
Artifacts
Directions: Across From
Griswold Inn

THE LAMP SHOP
Middlesex Trnpk   06426
203 767-1568
Hours: By Appointment
Types & Periods: Lamps
Directions: Rte 9A

MRS WALTER SANDS
Saybrook Rd Rte A 06426
203 767-1218
Proprietor: Mrs Walter
Sands
Hours: Daily l0-4:30
Types & Periods: General
Furniture, Glass, China

ROBERT SPENCER
Essex Square   06426
203 767-8655   Est: 1959
Proprietor: Robert
Spencer
Hours: Daily
Types & Periods: 18th
Century American Furniture
& English Pottery, Porcelain,
Silver
Specialties: Scrimshaw
Appraisal Service Available
Directions: I-95 to Rte 9 to
Exit 3

IRENA URDAND'S DETOUR
34 N Main St   06426
203 767-0505
Proprietor: Irena Urdand
Hours: By Appointment
Types & Periods: General
Line

VALLEY FARM ANTIQUES
Rte 154   06426
203 767-8555   Est: 1947
Proprietor: Ellsworth E
Stevison
Hours: Mon-Sat 10-5,
Closed Sun
Types & Periods: Furniture,
Glass, China, Steins,
Pewter, Guns, Swords,
Oriental, Indian Baskets &
Rugs, Nautical, Whaling,
Clocks, Phonographs, Toys
all Periods
Appraisal Service Available
Directions: Exit 3 Off Rte
9 or Exit 67 Off Rte I 95

Fairfield

BANKS HOUSE ANTIQUES
Banks North Rd   06430
203 259-7332
Proprietor: Patty Gagarin
Hours: By Appointment,
By Chance
Types & Periods: Primitive
Furniture, Folk Art, Paintings
& Decorative Accessories
Specialties: Painted
Furniture
Directions: Call For Simple
Directions

JAMES BOK ANTIQUES
1954 Post Rd   06430
203 255-6500   Est: 1950
Proprietor: James S Bok
Hours: Daily, By
Appointment
Types & Periods: Country &
Formal Furniture &
Accessories
Appraisal Service Available
Directions: On Hwy 1

JUSTINIUS OF FAIRFIELD
2 Reef Rd   06430
203 255-3887
Proprietor: Ivan & Dorothy
Justinius
Hours: Daily, l0-4, Closed
Sun
Types & Periods: Furniture,
Accessories

Appraisal Service Available
Directions: Exit 21 CT
Trpk, 1 Block to Post Rd,
Corner of Post & Reef
Rds

Falls Village

THREE RAVENS
Rte 63   06031
203 824-0041
Proprietor: Mr & Mrs
Harold H Corbin Jr
Hours: Daily, Weekends,
9-6, "Appointment
Advisable"
Types & Periods: American
Period Accessories & Folk
Art

Farmington

**THE ATTIC ANTIQUES AND
FLEA MARKET**
Rte 6   06032
203 677-7287   Est: 1973
Proprietor: Mrs Lillian
Cartwright
Hours: Daily 11-4,
Weekends 11 6
Types & Periods: Furniture,
Collectibles
Specialties: Outdoor Flea
Market in Summer
Directions: W from
Hartfield 8 Miles off I-84 to
Rte 10 N to 6 W

LILLIAN BLANKLEY COGAN
22 High St   06032
203 677-9259
Proprietor: Lillian Cogan
Hours: By Appointment
Types & Periods: Only
Museum Quality Pilgrim
Century American Furniture
& Appropriate 18th & 17th
Century, Pewter, Brass,
Silver, English Delft, Fabrics,
Iron, Woodenware
Specialties: American
Furniture of the Early Period
1680 to 1750 in Original
Condition of New England
Origin
Appraisal Service Available
Directions: Rte 84 Exit 39
Farmington, to Weston-4,
Left Turn at Blinker Light
(High St) Located in
Middle of Block

REMAINS TO BE SEEN
127 Main St   06032
203 677-9553
Proprietor: Robert M
Hoffman
Hours: By Appointment
Types & Periods: Pre-1900
Railroadiana, Pre-1930
Sheet Music

JOSEPH WEI GALLERY INC
246 Main St   06032
203 677-9404   Est: 1969
Proprietor: Joseph Wei
Hours: Tue-Sat 10-6, Sun
2-6, Closed Mon, Also By
Appointment
Types & Periods: Oriental
Works of Art, Emphasis on
Chinese, Japanese, Korean
& Himalayan
Specialties: Oriental
Appraisal Service Available
Directions: 10 Miles W of
Hartford off Rte 84, I/4
Mile S of Farmington
Center on Rte 10

Gales Ferry

GALES FERRY ANTIQUES
1561 Rt 12   06335
203 464-2318   Est: 1975
Hours: By Appointment
Types & Periods: General
Line
Appraisal Service Available
Directions: From I-95
Gales Ferry Exit N on Rte
12 for 5 Miles

Gaylordsville

**THE YELLOW HOUSE
ANTIQUES & GIFTS**
Kent Rd   06755
203 354-1944   Est: 1971
Proprietor: Ruth J Helmus
Hours: Mon-Fri 1:30-5:30,
Sat & Sun 10-5:30
Types & Periods: General
Line
Directions: 7 Miles N of
New Milford on Rte 7
"Yellow Victorian House"

Georgetown

PRETTY PENNY ANTIQUES
Rte 7   06829
Proprietor: Richard F
Venner
Hours: Weekends 11-5,
Also By Appointment
Types & Periods: Primitives,
Country Furniture, General
Line

Goshen

BARRETTS ANTIQUES
North St   06756
203 491-2436
Proprietor: Walter M
Barrett
Types & Periods: Clocks,
Watches, Americana

FRANCESCA'S ANTIQUES
Rte 4   06756
203 491-3515
Proprietor: Frances
Zampaglione
Hours: Daily 10-5
Types & Periods: Furniture,
Bric-A-Brac

**TRANQUIL ACRES
ANTIQUES**
North St Rte 63   06756
203 491-3716
Proprietor: Jeanne
Dautrich
Hours: Daily 11-5,
Weekends 12-5, Closed
Tue, Closed Dec-May 1
Types & Periods: Early
American Furniture of
Mid-I800's, Empire &
Victorian, Tinware, Sterling
& Coin Silver, Jewelry,
Tools, Glass, Cook Books,
China & Collectible
Nostalgia Items
Specialties: Coin Silver &
Jewelry
Appraisal Service Available
Directions: Rte 63, 1 Mile
From Center Rotary,
Opposite Catholic Rectory

Greenwich

**DENNY MUSHKIN
ANTIQUES**
403 Stanwich Rd   06830

DENNY MUSHKIN ANTIQUES   Cont'd
203 661-0749
Proprietor: Denny Mushkin
Hours: By Appointment
Types & Periods: American, Furniture, Folk Art, Paintings

PUTNAM ANTIQUE SHOP
40 W Putnam Ave   06830
203 869-3160   Est: 1940
Proprietor: Max Zaretsky
Hours: Daily 9-5, Closed Sun, Closed Mon July & Aug
Types & Periods: 18th & 19th Century Furniture, Objects of Art
Appraisal Service Available
Directions: In Business Dist of Greenwich

KATE YONKMAN ANTIQUES
60 Mildwood Rd   06830
203 661-8836
Proprietor: Kate Yonkman
Hours: By Appointment
Types & Periods: Furniture, Lamps, Doll Furniture, Dishes

Groton

TOLL GATE BARN ANTIQUES
381 Tollgate Rd   06340
203 445-0533   Est: 1973
Proprietor: Ed & Bette McLaughlin
Hours: Daily 9-5, Sun 12-5
Types & Periods: Primitives, Victorian
Specialties: Restoration
Directions: US Sub Base Exit off I-95, 1/2 Mile on Rte 12

JUNE'S ANTIQUES & COLLECTABLES
64 Hamilton Ave   06340
203 445-7523   Est: 1971
Proprietor: June Franciosi
Hours: By Chance
Types & Periods: General Line from Furniture to Glassware, Jewelry
Specialties: Lamps & Lamp Parts
Appraisal Service Available

Directions: N on 95 1st Exit on Groton Side of Bridge, Left at Rotary, Right Before 3rd Red Light

Guilford

SCUTTLE-BUTT HAS IT
85 Whitfield St   06437
203 453-6881
Proprietor: Janet Doane
Hours: Mon-Sat 9:30-5:30
Types & Periods: Nauticals
Directions: On the Green

YE OLDE CLOCK SHOPPE
50 York St   06437
203 453-4306   Est: 1967
Proprietor: Steven Phillips
Hours: Daily, Weekends
Types & Periods: Restorations, Repeaters, Tallcase, French Carriages & Tower Clocks
Specialties: Clocks
Appraisal Service Available
Directions: Conn Trpk Exit 58, Right to Rte 1 1/4 Mile

Haddam

HOBART HOUSE
Saybrook Rd Rte 9-A
06438
203 345-2525   Est: 1965
Proprietor: Malcolm Stearns Jr.
Hours: By Appointment
Types & Periods: Pre-1830 English, Irish, Portuguese & American Silver, Pre-1850 English & American Needlework
Specialties: Small Georgian Collectibles, Tea Caddy, Scoops, Nutmeg, Graters, Wine Labels, Vinegarettes
Appraisal Service Available
Directions: From Rte 9 Exit 8 I.8 Mile to 9-A, Immediately on Left in Heart of Haddam Village

Hadlyme

THE BLACK WHALE
Rte 82   06439
203 526-5895

Proprietor: Philip W Schwartz
Hours: Weekends, Also By Appointment or By Chance
Types & Periods: 18th & 19th Century Furniture, Nautical Antiques, Folk Art, Paintings, Prints
Specialties: Marine Items, Ship Models, Ship Paintings, Navigational Instruments
Appraisal Service Available
Directions: Five Miles S of Goodspeed Opera House on Conn Rte 82

VILLAGE STORE
Ferry Rd   06439
203 526-5146   Est: 1962
Proprietor: Patricia J Fulton
Hours: By Appointment
Types & Periods: Furniture & Accessories Found in 18th & 19th Century New England Homes, Paintings, Match Safes
Specialties: Scientific Instruments
Appraisal Service Available
Directions: 10 Miles N from Exit 70 CT Turnpike

Hamden

THE CROWNED HARP
222 Blake Rd   06514
203 787-2933
Proprietor: J D Kernan
Hours: By Appointment
Types & Periods: Silver

OLD PECK PLACE
3584 Whitney Ave Rte 10
06518
Est: 1960
Proprietor: Vi Hostetler
Hours: Daily
Types & Periods: 18th & Early 19th Century Furniture & Accessories
Specialties: Pewter
Directions: Approx 3 Miles N, Exit on Merrit Pkwy

JOSEPH PARI ANTIQUES
3846 Whitney Ave   06518
203 248-4951
Proprietor: Joseph Pari
Hours: By Appointment

Types & Periods: American
from Colonial Period to
Turn-of-theCentury

POLLY'S ANTIQUES
2964 Dixwell   06518
203 248-3788   Est: 1965
Proprietor: Polly Jolly
Hours: Mon-Fri 10:30-3
Types & Periods: General
Line
Directions: Exit 61 Wilbur
Cross Pkwy at Town Hall

**WHITCO HOBBY
EXCHANGE**
2582 Whitney Ave   06518
203 281-1137   Est: 1962
Proprietor: M L Sager
Hours: Daily By
Appointment, By Chance
Types & Periods: Political
Memorabilia, Historical,
Documents, Medals, Books
Specialties: Colonial Coins &
Paper Money, Civil War
Period
Appraisal Service Available
Directions: Exit 61 Wilbur
Cross Pkwy, Exit 10 CT
Trnpk

Hanover

JOHN CARL THOMAS
Saltrock Rd   06350
203 822-9260
Proprietor: John Carl
Thomas
Hours: By Appointment
Types & Periods: Early
Pewter, Country Furniture

Hartford

HARTFORD CLUSTERS
Directions: Shops
Scattered Throughout
City, Concentration on
Park Ave (50-2000 Blocks)
Maple Ave (100 Block)

A ANTIQUES
1619 Park St   06l06
203 233-5240   Est: 1961
Proprietor: Edmond
Theriault
Hours: Daily 9-7, Except
Sun

Types & Periods: 19th
Century Victorian & Oak,
Marble Top Tables, Rugs
Specialties: Clocks
Appraisal Service Available
Directions: W on I-84,
Take Sission Ave Exit, Go
Left to end of Sission
Which Runs Into Park St

ARTISTIC INVESTMENTS
Box 6   06101
203 523-9821
Proprietor: Diane E Dogan
Hours: By Appointment
Types & Periods: Glass

GRACE DYAR-DOLLS
20 Vernon St   06106
203 247-4381   Est: 1956
Proprietor: Grace Dyar
Hours: By Chance
Types & Periods: Dolls,
Toys, Miniatures, Children's
Books
Specialties: Toys &
Automata, (Dolls)
Appraisal Service Available
Directions: 2 Blocks from
Trinity College

EMMET R GEMME
159 Wethersfield Ave
                       06100
203 525-3853   Est: 1938
Proprietor: Emmet R
Gemme
Hours: Daily, Weekends,
By Appointment
Types & Periods: American
& European
Appraisal Service Available

HONORE INC
1 Civic Ctr Plaza   06103
203 527-2747
Proprietor: Ronald &
Honore Kaplan
Hours: Daily
Types & Periods: Jewelry,
Victorian, Noveau Art, Deco
Art, Primitive, Ethnic,
Contemporary
Directions: North Mall,
Second Level, Near
Sheraton Hotel

**A LITTLE BEFORE YOUR
TIME**
16 Union Pl   06103
203 527-7989   Est: 1973
Proprietor: Deborah Rule
& John Westinghouse
Hours: Mon-Wed 11-7,
Thurs-Sat 11-12, Sun 12-5

Types & Periods: Varied
Selection of Nouveau,
Primitives & Early Americana
Specialties: Boxes, Brass &
Walnut
Directions: 2 Blocks W of
Hartford Civic Center
Opposite Train Station

THE UNIQUE ANTIQUE
Civic Ctr Shops   06103
203 522-9094   Est: 1974
Proprietor: Chuck & Pat
Snyder
Hours: Daily 10-9,
Sat 10-6
Types & Periods: Victorian
Furniture, Leaded Lamps,
Paintings, Art Glass, Jewelry
Directions: Located at
Civic Center 1 Block from
Intersection Rts 84 & 91

VASALIE ANTIQUES
123-129 Maple Ave 06114
203 246-9679   Est: 1965
Proprietor: Pete M &
Jewell V Vasalie
Hours: Mon-Sat 10-5,
Closed Sun
Types & Periods: General
Line, 18th & 19th Century
Furniture & Accessories,
20th Century Oak, Clocks
Directions: Close to
Hartford Hospital

Harwinton

HOWARD BLUM
                       06790
203 482-6062
Proprietor: Howard Blum
Hours: By Appointment
Types & Periods: American

RYANS ANTIQUES
South Rd   06790
203 489-8958
Proprietor: Susan & David
Ryan
Hours: Mon, Tues, & Fri,
Also By Appointment
Types & Periods: Primitives,
Small Collectibles

Higganum

SLEEPY HOLLOW ANTIQUES
Killingworth Rd 06441
203 345-8995
Proprietor: Joseph W Bentz
Hours: Daily 10-4, Sat & Sun 10-6
Types & Periods: Furniture, Primitives, Glassware

Hitchcocksville

ELIZABETH WINSOR McINTYRE ANTIQUES
Rt 20 Riverton 06065
203 379-0846 Est: 1950
Proprietor: Elizabeth McIntyre
Hours: Daily 11-5
Types & Periods: 18th & 19th Century Furniture, Pottery, Glass, China, Primitives
Specialties: Toys, (Dolls, Miniatures)
Appraisal Service Available
Directions: 30 Miles NW of Hartford

Huntington

MIZZENTOP FARM ANTIQUES
215 Ripton Rd 06484
203 929-7142
Proprietor: J F Louv
Hours: By Appointment, By Chance
Types & Periods: Canton, Furniture, General Line

Kent

FORRER'S ANTIQUES
RR 1 Box 115 06757
203 927-3612 Est: 1966
Proprietor: Mr & Mrs Edward E Forrer
Hours: By Appointment, By Chance
Types & Periods: Pewter, Tools, Banks, Toys

Specialties: Mechanical & Still Banks, Historical Blue Staffordshire
Appraisal Service Available
Directions: Rte 7, 3 Miles N of Kent

THE GOLDEN THISTLE
Rte 7 06757
203 927-3923
Proprietor: George F Ewald Jr
Hours: Mon-Sun 11:30-5:30
Types & Periods: General Line, Furniture
Directions: At RR Crossing

SIDE DOOR ANTIQUES
Main St 06757
203 927-3288
Proprietor: Elizabeth S Mankin
Hours: Mon-Sat 11-5, Closed Sun
Types & Periods: American Period Furniture, Paintings, Ceramics, Folk Art

TINKER'S BAZAAR
Box 70 Rt 7 06757
203 927-3192 Est: 1973
Proprietor: Stephen M Weill
Hours: Daily
Types & Periods: General Line, Collectibles
Appraisal Service Available
Directions: Rte 7

VICTORIAN SHOP
Main St 06757
203 927-4146 Est: 1973
Proprietor: Paul Slason
Hours: Daily
Types & Periods: Victorian Era, Primitives, Tools
Directions: Center of Kent

Killingworth

GLADHAND ANTIQUES
Rt 80 06417
203 663-1102
Proprietor: Jean Bishop Fiore
Hours: Fri, Sat, & Sun 12-6, Also By Appointment
Types & Periods: Carnival Glass, Silver

Appraisal Service Available
Directions: Exit 63 Off I-95 N to Circle of Rte 80 & 81, 1/4 Mile E on Rte 80

CAROLE & RICHARD PLEINES
Pea Hill Rd
227-1 RFD 2 06417
203 663-2214
Proprietor: Carole & Richard Pleines
Hours: By Appointment
Types & Periods: Nantucket Baskets, General Line
Specialties: Nantucket Baskets
Appraisal Service Available

LEWIS W SCRANTON
Roast Meat Hill 06417
203 663-1060 Est: 1968
Proprietor: Lewis W Scranton
Hours: By Appointment, By Chance
Types & Periods: Early American Furniture & Related Accessories
Specialties: New England Redware Pottery, Painted New England Furniture & Early Iron
Appraisal Service Available
Directions: CT Tpke (I-95) Exit 63 N 5 Miles to Rte 80 E 1 Mile, Turn Right

Lakeville

THE VICKERS
Main St 06039
203 435-9384
Proprietor: John Vickers
Hours: By Appointment, By Chance
Types & Periods: Collectibles

Lisbon

JEROME W. BLUM
Ross Hill Rd 06351
Proprietor: Jerome W Blum
Hours: By Appointment
Types & Periods: Authentic American 18th & 19th Century Country Furniture & Accessories Used in the Period, American Folk Art

Specialties: Lighting,
Fireplace Equipment,
Weathervanes
Appraisal Service Available
   Directions: Off the CT
   Trpk Rte 52, Exit 84
   Jewett City, CT

Litchfield

HARRY W STROUSE ANTIQUES
   Maple St   06789
   203 567-0656   Est: 1971
   Proprietor: Harry W
   Strouse
   Hours: Daily-By Chance
Types & Periods: General
Line, Town & Country, 17th,
18th & 19th Century
Furniture & Appointments,
Unusual & Rare Items
Specialties: Antique
American Coin Silver &
Silver from England &
Europe, Antique Sheffield
Silver Plate
Appraisal Service Available
   Directions: 1 1/2 Miles N
   Off Rte 202, Large White
   Colonial House, Built 1749

THOMAS D & CONSTANCE R WILLIAMS
   Brush Hill Rd   06759
   203 567-8794
   Hours: By Appointment
Types & Periods: 18th &
19th Century American
Decorative Arts
Specialties: Furniture,
Pewter, Paintings, Porcelain,
Fireplace Equipment
Appraisal Service Available
   Directions: 1 1/2 Miles W
   on Rte 202, 4th Rd on
   Left (Brush Hill Rd)
   Continue 1 1/2 Miles

Madison

AT THE CRATE
   724 Boston Post Rd 06444
   203 245-4920   Est: 1965
   Proprietor: Vincent J
   O'Brien
   Hours: Daily 9:30-5
Types & Periods: General
Line, Furniture
Appraisal Service Available
   Directions: Exit 61 off New
   England Tnpk

FANTASY ANTIQUES
   873 Boston Post Rd 06443
   203 245-9926   Est: 1971
   Proprietor: Carmen
   Martone
   Hours: Daily 11-5
Types & Periods: General
Line
Specialties: Restoring &
Repairing
   Directions: Exit 61, I-95 N
   onto Rte 1, Boston
   Post Rd

MILDRED ROSS
   294 Boston Post Rd 06443
   203 245-7122   Est: 1974
   Proprietor: Mildred Ross
   Hours: Daily
Types & Periods: General
Line

SCHAFER ANTIQUES
   82 Bradley Rd   06443
   203 245-4173   Est: 1969
   Proprietor: Susan Schafer
   Hours: Daily
Types & Periods: General
Line, Music Boxes
Specialties: Music Boxes
   Directions: Exit 61 Off Rte
   95 toward Madison, Turn
   Left at Stop Light

SLEPPY HOLLOW ANTIQUES & COLLECTIBLES
   1336 Boston Post Rd
                       06443
   203 245-9421
   Proprietor: Cliff Doorley Sr
   Hours: Mon-Sun, May
   1-Sept 30 9-5:30, Oct-Dec
   By Chance
Types & Periods: Glass,
China, Furniture, Primivites,
Collectibles

Manchester

ANTIQUES ET CETERAS
   115 Spruce St   06040
   203 649-5051   Est: 1968
   Proprietor: Arthur &
   Elizabeth Carpenter
   Hours: Daily 4-8,
   Weekends 10-6, Closed
   Mon
Types & Periods: Old Glass,
Heisey, Art Glass, China,
Clocks, Lamps, Scrimshaw,
Silver, Bronzes

Specialties: Ceramics
(Dresden & Meissen)
Appraisal Service Available
   Directions: Exit 92 off I-84,
   1 Block E of Main

PARKER HOUSE ANTIQUES (TRADER WORLD)
   397 Tolland Tnpk   06040
   203 646-9288
   Proprietor: Trader World
   Antiques
   Hours: Mon-Thur 10-3, Fri
   10-9, Sat-Sun 10-5
Types & Periods: Oak,
Walnut, & Pine, Furniture,
Lamps, Clocks, Jewelry,
Primitives, Old Tools, Tole &
Wooden Ware, Glass,
Collectibles, Post Cards,
General Line
   Directions: Exit 94 off I-86

Mansfield Center

MULBERRY HOUSE
   187 Wormwood Hill Rd
                       06250
   203 419-4114   Est: 1963
   Proprietor: Juanita M
   Dorwart
   Hours: Sun 10-8, Also By
   Appointment
Types & Periods: Oriental
Art & Accessories
   Directions: Near University
   of CT

Marble Dale

DON ABARBANEL
   Box 76 Rt 202   06761
   203 868-2436
   Proprietor: Don Abarbanel
   Hours: Daily 11-4, Closed
   Mon
Types & Periods: General
Line from 18th & 19th
Century

LORETTA ROVINSKY
   Rte 202   06777
   203 868-7287   Est: 1963
   Proprietor: L Rovinsky
   Hours: Daily 11-4,
   Weekends 11-4, By
   Appointment, By Chance

LORETTA ROVINSKY Cont'd

Types & Periods: Six
Shops with Wide Selection
of Antiques, 18th & 19th
Century Memorabilia,
Collectibles, Much Furniture,
Toys, Dolls, Books, Glass
Specialties: Toys, Dolls,
Banks, Furniture
   Directions: 12 Miles S of
   Litchfield CT on Rte 202

Meriden

DOLLY'S ANTIQUES
   74 S Broad St Rte 5 06450
   203 237-9151   Est: 1968
   Proprietor: Mr & Mrs
   Anthony Gibas
   Hours: Daily 11-6, Closed
   Mon
Types & Periods: General
Line, Primitives
Specialties: China, Furniture
Appraisal Service Available
   Directions: Off Rte 91 to
   Rte 5 in Meridan, 1/2 Mile
   from Yale Motor Inn
   Going N

Montville

**CRICKET ON THE HEARTH
ANTIQUES**
   1499 Rte 85   06353
   203 443-7191
   Proprietor: Ralph & Pat
   Lanzetti
   Hours: Daily, Weekends
   11-5, Sun & Mon By
   Chance or By
   Appointment
Types & Periods: General
Line

Morris

**T'OTHER HOUSE
ANTIQUES**
   Litchfield Rd (Rte 63)
                 06763
   203 567-9283
   Proprietor: Margaret &
   David Gardiner
   Hours: By Appointment,
   By Chance

Types & Periods: General
Line
   Directions: Exit 17 Off I-84

Mount Carmel

JOSEPH PARI ANTIQUES
   3846 Whitney Ave   06518
   203 248-4951
   Proprietor: Joseph Pari
   Hours: By Appointment,
   Also By Shows
Types & Periods: General
Line
   Directions: Suburb of New
   Haven

Mystic

THE QUEEN'S TASTE
   Olde Mistick Village 06355
   203 536-8789   Est: 1972
   Proprietor: Patrica M
   Haines
   Hours: Daily 10-5:30,
   Open till 9 in Summer
Types & Periods: General
Line
Specialties: Victorian
   Directions: Intersection of
   I-95 & Connecticut 27

TROLLEY BARN ANTIQUES
   17 Water St   06355
   203 536-1289   Est: 1972
   Proprietor: Raymond
   Izbicki
   Hours: Mon-Sun, Closed
   Tue
Types & Periods: Folk Art,
Paintings, Jewelry, Silver,
China, Glassware, Primitive
Tools, Unusual Decorative
Pieces, "Items Brought by
Clipper Ship Captains during
19th Century"
Specialties: Folk Art,
Paintings, Jewelry
Appraisal Service Available
   Directions: Downtown
   Near Bank Square

WATER STREET ANTIQUES
   10 Water St   06355
   203 536-1969
   Proprietor: Ms Eaton &
   Krulisch
   Hours: Tue-Sat 11-5,
   Closed Sun & Mon

Types & Periods: Coin
Silver, Miniatures,
Collectibles

THE WHAT-NOT SHOP
   2 Greenmanville Ave
                 06355
   203 536-6668   Est: 1970
   Proprietor: Doris M
   Newman
   Hours: Daily 10-5, Closed
   Mon
Types & Periods: Cut Glass,
Oriental Rugs, Small
Furniture Pieces,
(Victorian-Empire)
Appraisal Service Available
   Directions: S Of Mystic
   Seaport on Rte 27

Naugatuck

ADELE SCAVONE
   407 Rubber Ave   06770
   203 729-5934
   Proprietor: Adele Scavone
   Hours: Sat 11-5, Sun 1-5
Types & Periods: Furniture

New Britain

RITA BROWN
   227 Brook St   06051
   203 229-0201   Est: 1956
   Proprietor: Rita Brown
   Hours: By Appointment or
   Mail Order
Types & Periods: Lamps:
Victorian, Student,
Gone-With-The-Wind, Angle,
Banquet, Store, Miniature,
Lanterns, Library, Many
More
Appraisal Service Available
   Directions: 1 Mile from Rte
   72, 84 & 15

TRADER HORN
   44 Rockwell Ave   06052
   203 223-4183   Est: 1974
   Proprietor: Karl Ludi
   Hours: Daily 10-5
Types & Periods: Furniture,
Collectibles, Glass,
Silverware
   Directions: 1 Block from
   Old New Britain High
   School, Corner of
   Rockwell Ave & Glen St

WANDERER'S DEN
120 North St   06051
203 223-6196   Est: 1975
Proprietor: Thomas
Giarnella
Hours: Tue-Sat 10-4
Types & Periods: 19th &
20th Century Oak,
Mahogony, & Walnut
Furniture
Specialties: Furniture
Directions: Off Main St

YANKEE TRADER
182 S Main St   06051
203 229-7909   Est: 1965
Proprietor: Charles A
Ravickas
Hours: Daily, By Chance
Types & Periods: General
Line
Directions: Center of Town

New Canaan

JERI BLAIR INTERIORS
125 Main St   06840
203 966-2822
Proprietor: Jeri Blair
Hours: Daily 9-5
Types & Periods: Furniture
& Accessories

**CAROLYN GAMBER
ANTIQUES**
370 Oenoke Ridge   06540
203 966-1035
Proprietor: Carolyn
Gamber
Hours: By Appointment
Types & Periods: Country
Furniture, General Line

HILBERT BROS
120 Main St   06840
203 966-1463   Est: 1936
Proprietor: Harry & N
Valdemar Hilbert
Hours: Daily 9-5:30,
Closed Sun & Wed
Types & Periods: General
Line
Specialties: Furniture,
Paintings, Decorations
Appraisal Service Available
Directions: At Main &
Elm St

JAN & LARRY MALIS
PO Box 211   06840
203 966-8510
Proprietor: Jan & Larry
Malis

Hours: By Appointment
Types & Periods: Paper
Americana, Old & Rare
Books, Selected American
Antiques & Toys, 18th &
19th Century
Specialties: Books & Toys
Appraisal Service Available

SHAKER HOUSE ANTIQUES
104 Shaker Rd   06840
203 966-3047
Proprietor: Carl & Lee
Male
Hours: By Appointment
Types & Periods: Shaker,
Primitive American
Furniture, Tools, Flow Blue
China, Glass

New Hartford

**THE HOUSE ON MAIN
STREET**
1846 Main St   06057
203 379-8315
Proprietor: Kalman Le
Bow & William Marinelli
Hours: Daily, Weekends;
11-6
Types & Periods: General
Line

New Haven

NEW HAVEN CLUSTER
Directions: Heavy
Concentration on Whalley
Ave (500 1000 Blocks),
Some Shops on Boston
Post Rd (700-2000 Blocks)

**EDWIN C AHLBERG
ANTIQUES**
442 Middletown Ave 06473
203 624-9076
Proprietor: Ed & Fred
Ahlberg
Hours: Daily 8-5,
Sat 8-12, Sun 1-5,
Sept-May
Types & Periods: Furniture
Directions: Exit 81-91

THE ANTIQUES MARKET
881 Whalley Ave   06515
203 389-5440   Est: 1968
Proprietor: Aaron Levine
Hours: Daily 10:30-5

Types & Periods: English
Imports
Specialties: Furniture
Appraisal Service Available
Directions: Exit 59 Merrit
Parkway

CARMEN ANTIQUES
247 Crown St.   06511
Est: 1959
Proprietor: Carmine
Centanni
Hours: Daily 9-6
Types & Periods: Empire,
Queen Anne, Jewelry,
Lamps
Specialties: Statues

THOMAS COLVILLE
Box 1323 Yale Station
06520
203 787-2816
Proprietor: Thomas
Colville
Hours: By Appointment
Types & Periods: Paintings,
Drawings, American &
European 19th Century

DE LEW'S ANTIQUES INC
514 Whalley Ave   06473
203 389-4893
Hours: Daily 11-5,, Closed
Wod
Types & Periods:
WHOLESALE ONLY

ESTHER'S INC
201 Crown St   06510
Proprietor: L E Jacobsen
Hours: Daily 9:30-5:30
Types & Periods: General
Line

HAIG RUGS
535 Whalley Ave   06511
203 389-0111   Est: 1933
Proprietor: Jack Haig
Hours: Daily, Weekends
Types & Periods: General
Line
Specialties: Oriental (Rugs)
Appraisal Service Available

KASOWITZ ANTIQUES
895 Whalley Ave   06473
203 934-2511
Proprietor: Milton &
Bernice Kasowitz
Hours: Daily 11-5, Sun
1-4, Eve By Appointment
Types & Periods: General
Line

NOSTALIGIC ERA ANTIQUES
912 1/2 Whalley Ave
06515
203 934-8083
Proprietor: Steve & Sherry Somma
Hours: Daily 10-5:30
Types & Periods: American, Oak Furniture, Lamps, Collectibles

Newington

HI VIEW ANTIQUES
174 Lamplighter Ln   06111
203 666-9353
Proprietor: Al & Betty Barnett
Hours: Tue, Wed, & Thur 12-4 & 7-9, Weekends By Chance
Types & Periods: Country Furniture & Accessories

New London

THE FERRY SLIP
123 Pequot Ave   06320
203 442-8873   Est: 1965
Proprietor: Millie & Bill Andrews
Hours: Daily, Closed Wed, Closed Dec-March
Types & Periods: Colonial, Victorian, Furniture, Glass, Bric-A-Brac
Specialties: Clocks, Watches & Barometers
Appraisal Service Available
Directions: Across From Terminal of the Orient Point-Long Island Ferry

HEMPSTEAD HOUSE ANTIQUES
110 Hempstead St   06320
203 447-2311
Proprietor: Ward Young
Hours: By Appointment
Types & Periods: English & American, Unusual & Rare Furniture & Objects, Chinese & Japanese Porcelains & Objects
Specialties: Oriental
Appraisal Service Available
Directions: CT 95 to New London, Turn off Broad St to Hempstead

MANACHESTER'S ANTIQUE CLOCKS
35 Georgianna St   06320
203 447-1570   Est: 1960
Proprietor: Bill Manachester
Hours: Daily
Types & Periods: Furniture, Glass, Clocks
Appraisal Service Available
Directions: Right Off Broad St Which is Rte 85

New Milford

ECLECTIQUE
49 Bridge St   06776
203 355-1400
Proprietor: Jocelyn & Al
Hours: Tue-Sat 11-4:30, Sun By Appointment
Types & Periods: China, Art Glass, Furniture, Collectibles

PENNY PINCHER
53 Bridge St   06776
203 355-0500   Est: 1971
Proprietor: Lynn Baecht
Hours: Daily, Weekends
Types & Periods: General Line
Specialties: Furniture
Appraisal Service Available

SCARLET LETTER ANTIQUES & BOOKS
Candlewood Mt Rd   06776
203 354-4181
Proprietor: Kathleen & Michael Lazare
Hours: By Appointment
Types & Periods: Books, Prints, Silver, Glass, Figural Silver Plate, Out of Prod Royal Doulton, China
Specialties: Books & Prints
Appraisal Service Available
Directions: Rte 7 N to Rte 37, First Left off Rte 37

THE TULIP TREE
4 Railroad St   06776
203 354-1982   Est: 1970
Hours: Daily 11-5, Closed Sun
Types & Periods: Orientals from 5000 BC-19th Century, 18th Century American & English Furniture
Appraisal Service Available
Directions: Across Street from RR Station

New Preston

GRAMPA SNAZZY'S LOG CABIN ANTIQUES
Rte 25 Woodville   06777
203 868-7153   Est: 1965
Proprietor: Elisabeth Graves
Hours: Daily
Types & Periods: General Line, Glass, China, Furniture, Pottery, Prints
Specialties: Pewter
Appraisal Service Available
Directions: Corner of Rte 202 & 341

Newton

BUTTONSHOP ANTIQUES
271 S Main St Rte 25
06470
203 426-6698   Est: 1973
Proprietor: C Bevensee & P Parker
Hours: Daily 11-5, Closed Thur & Fri
Types & Periods: Silver, Jewerly, China, Glass, Small Furniture, Unusual Items From Victorian thru Art Deco
Specialties: China, Glass, Jewelry
Appraisal Service Available
Directions: Rte 25 Corner of Buttonshop Rd, 3 Miles S of Flagpole

THE COUNTRY SHOP
Church Hill Rd   06470
203 426-2704   Est: 1954
Proprietor: Darl Gulick
Hours: Daily
Types & Periods: Primitives, Early American
Directions: Exit 10 on I-84 Newton & Sandy Hook

Newtown

FORD ENTERPRISES
54 S Main St Rte 25
06470
Est: 1958
Proprietor: Elwood Ford
Hours: Daily
Types & Periods: General Line, Furniture, Lamps, Clocks

Directions: Rte 25, 20
Miles N Bridgeport, 1 Mile
from I-84, Exit 10

POVERTY HOLLOW ANTIQUES
Poverty Hollow Rd   06470
203 426-2388
Proprietor: Margaret
Bennett
Hours: Thur-Sun 9:30-5
Types & Periods: Furniture,
Lamps, Shades, China,
Glass

Niantic

THE BEE HIVE FRAMING CENTER
8 W Main St   06357
203 739-0384   Est: 1976
Proprietor: John & Lois
Monchester
Hours: Mon-Sat 9-5
Types & Periods: Small
Items, Collectibles, General
Line
Directions: Across from
Niantic Centre School

EAST LYNN ANTIQUES
22 Fairhaven Rd   06357
203 739-9197   Est: 1961
Proprietor: Lynn
Krauthamer
Hours: By Appointment
Types & Periods: Victorian
Furniture & Decorative
Accessories
Directions: Exit 72 on CT
Trpk (I-95), Left on Rte
150 Approx 1 1/4 Miles,
Right on Fairhaven Rd

FIRESIDE ANTIQUES & COLLECTIBLES
41 W Main St Rte 156   06357
203 442-1041
Proprietor: Stenberg
Family
Hours: Summer: Tue-Sun
11-5, Winter: 12-5, or By
Appointment
Types & Periods: General
Line
Specialties: Shells From
Around the World, Stamps
Directions: 1/2 Mile W
from Niantic Center on
Rte 156 (Shore Route)

NOSTALGIA LTD
41 W Main St   06357
203 739-7315 or 442-0834
Proprietor: Terry L
Gouette
Hours: Wed-Sun, Closed
Mon & Tue
Types & Periods: Jewelry,
Silver, Timepieces, Estate
Diamond Jewelry, Gold &
Silver Jewelry, also many
Handmade Creations
Directions: Exit 72 off I-95
Turn Left onto Rte 156,
travel 2 Miles to the Barn
Shoppes of Niantic

SAM & LEE WHOLESALE IMPORT MERCHANTS
404 Main St   06357
203 739-8817   Est: 1954
Proprietor: Sam & Lee
Smith
Hours: By Appointment,
By Chance
Types & Periods: General
Line, Collectibles,
WHOLESALE ONLY
Specialties: Early Country
Pine Furniture & Utensils
Appraisal Service Available
Directions: Exit 74 CT
Trnpk, Between
Pharmacy & Baptist
Church

Northford

FARM RIVER ANTIQUE SHOP
269 Forest Rd Rt 22   06472
203 484-0327
Proprietor: M Yuhas & G
Morgio
Hours: Sun, By
Appointment, By Chance
Types & Periods: Victorian,
Walnut & Oak Furniture,
Brass Beds, Glass Shade
Lamps & Nice Mahogany &
Wicker Furniture
Specialties: Wholesale &
Retail
Directions: CT Rte 22,
Between Rte 17 & 80

Norwalk

WARREN & RUBY BAUR
Silvermine Ave   06850
203 847-3310   Est: 1969
Proprietor: Warren & Ruby
Baur
Hours: By Appointment
Types & Periods: Victorian
Lighting Devices, Old Tools,
Tins, Kitchen Items
Specialties: Victorian
Lighting Devices
Directions: 0.4 Miles N of
Merrit Parkway Over Pass

Old Greenwich

WILLIAM'S ANTIQUE SHOP
Post Rd   06870
203 637-1022   Est: 1938
Proprietor: William
Richmond
Hours: Daily, By
Appointment
Types & Periods: American
& English Furniture
Appraisal Service Available
Directions: Exit 5 CT
Thruway 1/2 Mile to the
Right

Old Lyme

ANTIQUES AND
Lyme St   06371
203 434-5995 &
338-5409   Est: 1968
Proprietor: Peggy Carboni
& Ella Smith
Hours: Mon, Wed, Fri &
Sat 10-4, or By
Appointment
Types & Periods: Victorian,
Oak & Wicker Furniture,
Primitives, Decorations &
Accessories
Specialties: Old Wicker
Directions: Exit 70 E &
Exit 71 W Off Rte 95 to
Lyme St

FALCONS ROOST ANTIQUES
4 Mile River Rd   06371
203 739-5879   Est: 1969
Proprietor: The Bierylo's
Hours: Daily By Chance,
Weekends 9-5

**FALCON'S ROOST
ANTIQUES** Cont'd

Types & Periods: Primitive &
Period American Furniture,
Pewter, Clocks, Accessories
Specialties: Clocks,
Furniture
Appraisal Service Available
  Directions: Exit 71 CT
  Trnpk (I-95), Left 1/2 Mile
  to Junction of Rte 156

RIVERWOOD ANTIQUES
  Neck Rd   06371
  203 434-7555   Est: 1968
  Proprietor: Ann & Frank
  Hefner
  Hours: Daily 1-6, Closed
  Mon, By Appointment
Types & Periods: 18th &
19th Century American &
English Furniture
  Directions: Rte 156

Old Mystic

OLD MYSTIC ANTIQUES
  46 Main St   06372
  203 536-1841   Est: 1950
  Proprietor: George L
  Armstrong, Jr
  Hours: Daily, Closed Mon
  & Tue, By Chance
Types & Periods: 18th &
19th Century, William &
Mary, Queen Anne,
Chippendale, Sheraton,
Hepplewhite & Early
Victorian, American &
English Antiques, Silver,
Pewter, Ship Paintings,
Glassware
Specialties: Period Furniture,
Ship Paintings, Silver &
Glassware
Appraisal Service Available
  Directions: One Mile N of
  Rte 95, Exit 90, Between
  Methodist Church & Old
  Mystic Book Store

STONE CELLAR ANTIQUES
  Rte 27 (126)   06372
  203 536-4344   Est: 1975
  Proprietor: Karl Thayer
  Hours: By Appointment,
  By Chance
Types & Periods: Country
Furniture & Primitives, 18th
& 19th Century
  Directions: 1 Mile N of
  Mystic Seaport Off I-95

Old Saybrook

**BOSTON WHALER
ANTIQUES**
  88 Sheffield St   06475
  203 388-5840
  Hours: Sun 1-5, Also By
  Appointment
Types & Periods: General
Line

**CORNER CUPBOARD
ANTIQUES**
  Middlesex Trnpk   06475
  203 388-0796   Est: 1957
  Proprietor: Iola H Wright
  Hours: Daily, Closed Tue,
  Out Of State By
  Appointment
Types & Periods:
Americana, Kitchen Items,
Collectibles
  Directions: Tri State Bldg,
  Middlesex Trnpk,
  Old Rte 9

FALLA'S ANTIQUES
  15 N Main St   06475
  203 388-3344
  Hours: Daily, Closed Mon
Types & Periods: General
Line

**THE HOUSE OF PRETTY
THINGS**
  49 Sherwood Terrace
                      06475
  203 388-5920   Est: 1975
  Proprietor: Dot & Frank
  Burton
  Hours: Mon-Sat 10-5,
  Closed Sun
Types & Periods: General
Line, Glass, China,
Porcelains, Furniture, Rugs,
Silver, Primitives
Appraisal Service Available
  Directions: One Mile from
  I-95, Exit 66-69, Rte 1 to
  Rte 154 (Main St) W at
  Firehouse 1st Right

PATRIOT ANTIQUES
  8 Vista Terrace   06475
  203 399-6752   Est: 1973
  Proprietor: Betty Silvestri
  Hours: Daily
Types & Periods: Furniture,
Glassware, Tinware,
Woodenware, Pictures,
Crocks
Appraisal Service Available
  Directions: CT Trnpk, Exit
  66 to Rte 1

RED ROSE ANTIQUES
  Boston Post Rd   06475
  203 388-9898
  Proprietor: Leona Leone
  Hours: Fri-Mon 10-5
Types & Periods: Oak,
Walnut & Wicker Furniture
  Directions: On Rte 1

WILSON'S ANTIQUES
  One Hammock Rd   06475
  203 388-9547   Est: 1945
  Proprietor: Jane Wilson
  Hours: By Appointment,
  By Chance
Types & Periods: Canton
China, 18th Century
American Furniture &
Accessories, Animal
Paintings
Specialties: Canton China
Appraisal Service Available
  Directions: One Mile off
  CT Trnpk, Exit 66

Oxford

**LEISURE HOUSE COUNTRY
STORE**
  100 Oxford Rd   06483
  203 888-2507   Est: 1961
  Proprietor: B H Kolbert
  Hours: Daily, Weekends
Types & Periods: Weapons,
Coins, Clocks, Watches,
Autos, Toys, Trains
Specialties: Arms, Coins
Appraisal Service Available
  Directions: On Rte 67
  8 1/2 Miles W of New
  Haven Just off Rte 8

Plainville

**ROBERT T BARANOWSKY
ANTIQUE SHOP**
  337 New Britian Ave
  (Rte 72)   06062
  203 747-3833   Est: 1975
  Proprietor: Robert T
  Baranowsky
  Hours: Tue-Sun 12-4:30,
  Closed Mon
Types & Periods: Oak,
Victorian & Antique
Furnishings
Specialties: Furniture
  Directions: Exit 34 Off
  I-84, Across from
  Drive-In Theatre (End of
  Exit)

PLAINVILLE RAIL ROAD STATION ANTIQUE CENTER

Rte 72   06062
203 747-1018 or
747-9094   Est: 1971
Proprietor: Cookie
Bartosewicz
Hours: Weekends
Types & Periods: General
Line, Anything & Everything
Collectible
Specialties: Depression
Glass, Postcards, Furniture
Directions: Rte 72, Exit 34
Off I-84 Center of Town

Plantsville

PLANTSVILLE GENERAL STORE

780 S Main   06489
203 621-5255   Est: 1973
Proprietor: Dwight W
Blakeslee, Jr
Hours: Daily Mon-Sun
Types & Periods: Furniture,
China, Glassware, Silver,
Tools
Appraisal Service Available
Directions: Exit 30 off I-84,
Rte 10

YE OLDE DOORSTOP

857 S Main St   06479
203 628-6159
Proprietor: Marge Newell
Hours: Daily 11-4,
Thur to 9
Types & Periods: Furniture,
Glass, Clocks, Lamps,
Collectibles
Directions: Rte 10 Exit 30
off I-84, 3 Dealers

Ridgefield

SILVER SPRING FARM

318 Silver Spring Rd
                           06877
203 438-7713   Est: 1973
Proprietor: Judy Lenett
Hours: Daily, Weekends,
By Appointment
Types & Periods: American
Folk Art & Furniture
Specialties: Folk Art
Directions: 1/4 Mile off
Rte 35

Riverside

ANN TEEKS

1185 Post Rd   06878
203 637-9431   Est: 1972
Proprietor: Annie Moffat
Hours: Daily Mon-Sun, or
By Appointment
Types & Periods: Victorian
Furniture, Cloisonne,
Jewelry, Clocks, Glass
Directions: Exit 5 off Rte
95 (CT Trnpk), Left at
Light opp Hess Gas Stn

Rockville

SPINNING WHEEL

Rte 83   06066
203 875-4925
Proprietor: Jill T Hatch
Hours: Daily, Weekends
10-5, Thur & Fri 10-8,
Closed Sun
Types & Periods: General
Line

Rowayton

LADIES DAY ANTIQUES

Box 27   06853
203 866-1021
Proprietor: Sue Anderson
& Mary Cohn
Hours: By Appointment
Types & Periods: 18th &
19th Century Glass & China
Collectibles

YESTERDAY ANTIQUES

143 Rowayton Ave   06853
203 853-8111   Est: 1972
Proprietor: Nicholas
Geraci
Hours: Daily 12-5, Closed
Mon
Types & Periods: 18th, 19th
& 20th Century American &
English
Specialties: Leaded Glass
Shades of the Victorian
Period

Salem

CLIFFORD O DEVINE

Rte 82   06415
203 859-1899   Est: 1956
Proprietor: Clifford O
Devine
Hours: Weekends, By
Appointment, By Chance
Types & Periods: Early
Primitives, Period Furniture,
Folk Art, Prints, Paintings,
Collectibles
Specialties: Primitives
Appraisal Service Available
Directions: In Front of
Gardner Lake 6 Miles W
Exit 80

Sandy Hook

CHURCH HILL GALLERIES

Church Hill Rd   06482
203 426-9104
Proprietor: Dorothy
Soloway
Hours: By Appointment,
By Chance
Types & Periods: 17th, 18th
& Early 19th Century
Furniture, General Line
Directions: Exit 10 off I-84

Scotland

DEVOTION HOUSE ANTIQUES

Rte 97   06264
203 456-0452   Est: 1970
Proprietor: Lillian & Don
Glugover
Hours: Daily, Mon-Sun, By
Appointment, By Chance
Types & Periods: 18th &
19th Century
Furniture-Country & Formal,
Pottery, Folk Art &
Appropriate Accessories
Appraisal Service Available
Directions: Rte 97

LINDEN HALL ANTIQUES

Gager Hill Rd   06264
203 423-8192
Proprietor: Albert &
Catherine Linden
Hours: By Appointment
Types & Periods: English,
European
Directions: Misty Hollow
Farm

Sharon

ESTATES BOUTIQUE
Gay St   06069
203 364-5396
Proprietor: Diana S Fowler
Hours: Daily 1-5, By
Appointment
Types & Periods: Furniture,
Paintings, Porcelains

**SHARON CLOCK &
ANTIQUE SHOP**
Cornwall Bridge Rd 06069
203 364-0352
Proprietor: Walter H Rick
Hours: By Appointment
Types & Periods: General
Line, Clocks

Shelton

GALLERY ON THE HILL
160 Grove St   06484
203 734-2323
Proprietor: Pat Inzero
Hours: By Appointment,
Eves Only
Types & Periods: Prints,
Jewelry

Sherman

**PENNY PINCHER
ANTIQUES**
Rte 37   06784
203 355-9916
Proprietor: Audrey Baccht
Hours: Daily, Weekends
Types & Periods: China,
Glass, Silver, Small Furniture

Simsbury

**ABBY'S TREASURES &
ANTIQUES**
213 Bushy Hill Rd 06070
203 658-4913
Proprietor: Abby & Tom
Griffin
Hours: By Appointment,
By Chance
Types & Periods: Woods,
Prints & Good Miscellaneous
Specialties: Wallace Nutting

**FARMINGTON ANTIQUE
GALLERY**
535 Bushy Hill Rd   06070
203 658-0868
Proprietor: Edith V
Carlson
Hours: By Appointment
Types & Periods: General
Line

Somers

HELEN HAYES
611 Main St
PO Box 303   06071
203 749-7745
Proprietor: Hazel Hayes
Hours: By Appointment
Types & Periods: Shakers

Southbury

RAVENWOOD ANTIQUES
Spruce Brook Rd   06488
Proprietor: Lili Loftus
Hours: By Appointment
Types & Periods: Primitive,
Country & Period
Furniture 1675-1840
Specialties: Fireplace
Cooking Iron & Tin
Appraisal Service Available
Directions: Exit 14 off I-84,
Take Rte 172 to Spruce
Brook Rd go 1 Mile to
Fork in Road, take Right,
First House on Right, or
Call For Directions

South Kent

THE GOLDEN THISTLE
S Kent Rd   06785
203 354-5801
Proprietor: George Ewald
Hours: Sat, Sun &
Holidays 10-6, Also By
Appointment
Types & Periods: Glass,
Hanging Fixtures, Small
Furniture, Paintings
Directions: 2 Miles off
Rte 7

Southport

THE KEEPING ROOM
2600 Post Rd   06490
203 255-6087
Proprietor: Tom Sheridan
& Kerry Fuller
Hours: Daily, Closed Tues
Types & Periods: General
Line
Directions: Inside
Freedman's

**J B RICHARDSON
GALLERY**
362 Pequot Ave   06490
203 259-1903
Proprietor: J B Richardson
Hours: Tues-Sat 10-5
Types & Periods: Country
American Furniture &
Accessories

South Windsor

THE ANTIQUE COBWEBB
John Fitch Blvd Rte 5
06074
203 289-6165
Proprietor: Rod Clarke
Hours: Daily, Weekends
11-5, Closed Sat
Types & Periods: Primitive,
Oak, Walnut Furniture, Post
Cards

Stamford

**ANTIQUARIANS &
APPRAISERS**
60 Mill Rd   06903
Est: 1946
Proprietor: Mr & Mrs
Gardiner
Hours: By Appointment
Types & Periods: Books,
Prints, Newspapers, Oil
Paintings, Tools
Appraisal Service Available
Directions: 4 Miles N Of
Exit 34 Merritt Pkwy

ANTIQUE SUPERMARKET
866 High Ridge Rd 06903
203 329-8244   Est: 1971
Proprietor: Laitman,
Nedvin, Popper,
Spiegelman
Hours: Tues-Sat 10-4:30,
Sun 1-5

Types & Periods:
Collectibles, Old Toys,
Clocks, Primitives
Appraisal Service Available

ANTIQUES ET CETERA
3020 High Ridge Rd 06903
203 322-9288
Proprietor: Mona Sawyer
Hours: By Appointment
Types & Periods: Brass,
Cooper, Silver, Jewelry

BOOKS FOR COLLECTORS
60 Urban St   06905
203 323-1726   Est: 1938
Proprietor: Jacqueline
Levine
Hours: Mail Order Only
Types & Periods: Rare
Out-Of-Print Books
Specialties: Limited Editions
Club, Maritime, Books on
Books, Fine Bindings
Appraisal Service Available

FINDERS SEEKERS
1087 Hope St   06907
203 329-8039
Proprietor: Eileen C
Abbott
Hours: Daily 11-4, Closed
Cun, Mon & Wed
Types & Periods: General
Line

**GEORGE'S JEWELERS
ARTS & TREASURES**
20 6th St Ridgeway Ctr
06905
203 324-0204   Est: 1974
Proprietor: George
Feldman
Hours: Daily
Types & Periods: General
Line
Specialties: Clocks
Appraisal Service Available

**STAMFORD ANTIQUES
ASSOCIATION**
83 Hope St   06907
203 329-0009
Proprietor: 7 Dealers
Hours: Daily, Weekends
11-4, Fri till 7
Types & Periods: General
Line, Collectibles

Stonington

**VIVIAN MEYER
FAIRBROTHER ANTIQUES**
122 Water St   06378
203 535-1749   Est: 1965
Proprietor: Mrs Fairbrother
Hours: Daily, Closed Sun
Types & Periods: 18th &
19th Century Furniture
Directions: Rte 95, N Main
St, Stonington Village Exit

N PENDERGAST JONES
Box 228   06378
203 599-2206
Hours: By Appointment
Types & Periods: American
& English Furniture,
Paintings, Porcelain

MARGUERITE RIORDAN
8 Pearl St   06378
203 535-2511   Est: 1962
Proprietor: Marguerite
Riordan
Hours: By Appointment
Types & Periods: New
England Furniture & Works
of Art
Specialties: Primitive
Paintings & Folk Art
Appraisal Service Available

**STONINGTON ANTIQUE
SHOP**
148 Water St   06378
203 535-1458   Est: 1945
Proprietor: Mrs Olga B
Fraser
Hours: Daily 9-4:30
Types & Periods: General
Lino
Directions: "Borough of
Stonington"

Stafford

ARNOLD T SMALL
67 Peck   06075
203 378-2345   Est: 1962
Hours: Daily
Types & Periods: Pottery,
Brass, Tools, Collectibles,
Glass
Specialties: Tools

Storrs

BUTTON BOX ANTIQUES
Gurleyville Rd   06268
203 429-6623   Est: 1960
Proprietor: Rita Heinige
Hours: Daily, Weekends
Types & Periods: General
Line
Appraisal Service Available
Directions: 1 Mile from
Storrs Campus

Stratford

THE ANTIQUE SHOP
919 Stratford Ave   06497
203 378-4870   Est: 1957
Proprietor: Blanche
Hallquist
Hours: Daily 11-4
Types & Periods: General
Line
Specialties: Books, China,
Glass
Directions: Btwn Main &
Elm

BON-AN'S SHOPPE
119 Nichols Terr   06497
203 378-5415 &
378-1075   Est: 1966
Proprietor: Bonnie L Arlio
Hours: Sat & Sun, By
Appointment, By Chance
Types & Periods: General
Line, Glass, China, Nearly
New Collectibles
Directions: Barnum Ave to
Nichols Ave, 2nd Right
Turn After Nichols School

MARCUS ANTIQUES
221 Honeyspot Rd   06497
203 377-2231
Proprietor: Aaron Marcus
Hours: Daily 10-5, Sat 1-5
Types & Periods: General
Line
Directions: At CT Turnpike
Exit 31

Suffield

MARY LOU'S CORNER
32 Randall Dr   06078
203 668-7994
Proprietor: Mrs Edward
Lane
Types & Periods: Victorian
Furniture, Art Glass, Silver

Torrington

BARREDO'S ANTIQUES & USED FURNITURE
2496 S Main St   06790
203 482-0627   Est: 1962
Proprietor: Joseph &
Evelyn Barredo
Hours: Tue-Sat
Types & Periods: "Anything
& Almost Everything We
Can Obtain", Glassware,
Brassware, Clocks, Jewelry,
Huge Coffee Grinders,
Senate Desks, Horse Drawn
Wagons, Sleighs
Specialties: Oak, Walnut,
Victorian Furniture, Bean
Bottle Collection
Appraisal Service Available
Directions: 1/2 Mile From
Exit 42 Going Toward
Torrington On Old Rte 8

Tylerville

THE LANGHAMMER SHOP
Saybrook Rd   06438
203 345-2675
Hours: Daily 9-6
Types & Periods: General
Line
Directions: Rte 9A & 82

Warren

RAWBURN HALL
Rte 341, Brick School Rd
06754
203 868-7173 & 868-0049
Est: 1930
Proprietor: Cyril Bernfeld
Hours: Tues-Sun 10-5
Types & Periods: General
Line
Specialties: Jewelry, Silver
Appraisal Service Available

Washington Depot

**SILVER
GUILD-MEMORABILIA**
Rte 109   06794
203 868-0190
Proprietor: Cyril Bernfeld
Hours: Tue-Sun 10-5,
Closed Mon

Types & Periods: General
Line
Specialties: Jewelry, Silver
Appraisal Service Available

Waterbury

WATERBURY CLUSTER
Directions: Shops
scattered throughout City,
Concentration on Main St
(Running N-S)

**MC DUFF'S SURPLUS
SALVAGE ANTIQUE FLEA
MARKET**
71 Homer St   06714
203 753-6654   Est: 1964
Proprietor: Mc Duff
Hours: Mon-Sat 11-5, Sun
11-3
Types & Periods: General
Line

SHIRL & DON'S ANTIQUES
1405 Highland Ave   06712
203 756-6493
Proprietor: Shirley
Tremaglio
Hours: Tue, Wed & Thur
10-5, By Appointment May
1st to Oct 30th
Types & Periods: Small
Collectibles, General Line

Waterford

**ANTIQUES OF
CONNECTICUT**
357 Rope Ferry Rd   06385
203 443-5556
Proprietor: Eileen Myers
Hours: Sat & Sun 10-5, By
Appointment
Types & Periods: Victorian,
General Line
Specialties: Antique Clocks

Westbrook

ANOTHER ANTIQUE SHOP
W Pond Meadow Rd
06498
203 399-7240   Est: 1975
Proprietor: Marilyn &
Haskel Frankel
Hours: Daily, By Chance
Types & Periods: General
Line, Collectibles

Directions: Located at the
Site of "Stuff For Sale",
Exit 64 from I-95 & Turn
Left Onto Rte 145, Go
About 3 Miles to Cross Rd
& Turn Right, At End of
Cross Turn Right & Go
About 1 Mile

**CONTINENTAL ANTIQUES
& GIFTS**
Rte 1   06498
203 399-9485   Est: 1954
Proprietor: Walter Karliner
Hours: Mon-Sun, By
Appointment
Types & Periods: China,
Glass, Collectors Plates,
Hummels
Appraisal Service Available
Directions: Ct Trnpk Exit
66, to Rte 1,
Westbrook-Saybrook Town
Line

MAKE ME AN OFFER
Post Rd   06498
203 399-9628
Proprietor: Gary Amara
Hours: Daily, Weekends
Types & Periods: General
Line
Appraisal Service Available
Directions: Just Outside
Center of town

THE WHITE CARRIAGE
Essex Rd   06498
203 399-6463   Est: 1946
Proprietor: Maude A
Bisaccia
Hours: Weekends, By
Chance
Types & Periods: General
Line, Collectibles, New
England
Appraisal Service Available
Directions: 500 Ft N of
Exit 65, I-95

West Cornwall

**DOROTHY'S DOLL
HOSPITAL**
RD 1 Box 178   06796
203 672-6569
Proprietor: Dorothy Maar
Hours: Daily, By
Appointment, Closed Wed
Types & Periods: Doll
Furniture
Specialties: Toys, (Dolls)

OUTSVILLE BARN
Rte 128   06796
203 672-6708
Proprietor: Joan Stall &
Elaine Ludermann
Hours: Daily 10-6,
April-Dec
Types & Periods: General
Line, Collectibles, Furniture

West Hartford

NOW & THEN
10 LaSalle Rd   06017
203 233-l070   Est: 1974
Proprietor: Barbara Duffy
Hours: Daily 11-5, By
Appointment
Types & Periods: American
& Victorian Furniture, Art
Noveau, Jewelry, Clocks, Oil
Paintings, Accessories
Directions: Off Farmington
Ave in W Hartford Center

Westport

**CARPETBAGGER
ANTIQUES**
179 Post Rd West   06880
203 226-9665   Est: 1970
Proprietor: Michael J
Lundquist
Hours: Daily 10-6
Types & Periods: Tools,
Country Furniture &
Accessories
Specialties: Tools
Appraisal Service Available
Directions: Exit 17 Off I-95
onto US 1, Left at the
Woodshed

**THE COUNTRY
COLLECTOR**
Whippoorwill Lane   06880
203 226-0591   Est: 1972
Proprietor: William
Gladstone
Hours: By Appointment
Types & Periods: Country
Furniture, Decorator Items,
American Military
Photography, Photographica
Specialties: Civil War
Photography

ILLUSTRATION HOUSE
7 Belaire Dr   06880
203 227-6910
Proprietor: Walt Reed
Hours: By Appointment
Types & Periods: Illustration
Originals

**LOCK STOCK & BARREL
ESTATE SALES**
47 Imperial Ave   06880
203 227-2923   Est: 1973
Proprietor: Irene
Marcenaro
Hours: Weekends, By
Appointment
Types & Periods: General
Line
Appraisal Service Available
Directions: Each Sale Held
At Different Location

SUNFLOWER
47 Riverside Ave   06880
203 227-3343
Proprietor: Ann Laredo
Hours: Tues-Sat 11-4
Types & Periods: General
Line, Especially Decorative
Accessories, Painted
Furniture
Directions: Next to
Attractive Restaurant,
Center Westport
Overlooking River

**THREE BEARS ANTIQUE
SHOP**
333 Wilton Rd   06880
203 227-7219
Proprietor: Stephen C
Vazzano
Hours: By Appointment
Types & Periods: Art Glass

TODBURN ANTIQUES
243 Post Rd W   06880
203 226-3859   Est: 1966
Proprietor: G G Anderson
& D W Jobe
Hours: Daily 10-6, Closed
Sun, Also By Appointment
Types & Periods: General
Line, Wicker
Appraisal Service Available
Directions: I-95 Exit 17
Left

YE OLDE LAMP SHOPPE
315 Main St   06880
203 226-3140   Est: 1969
Proprietor: William & Judy
Langton
Hours: Tues-Fri 10-6, Sat
10-4

Types & Periods: "Victorian
Lighting of all Types", Brass
& Iron Beds, Wicker & Oak
Furniture, Brass Bathroom
Fixtures, Clocks
Directions: 3/4 Mile N of
US Rte 1

Wethersfield

THE LITTLE STORE
285 Main   06109
203 529-8719   Est: 1975
Proprietor: A M Officer
Hours: Wed-Sat 11-4
Types & Periods: General
Line, Collectibles
Specialties: Hand Carvings
by Kit Larson
Directions: 1 Block N of
Famous Webb House

Wilton

IVORY TOWER ANTIQUES
2 E Meadow Rd   06897
203 762-3888   Est: 1974
Proprietor: Mrs Gertrude
Gordon
Hours: By Appointment
Types & Periods: Pattern
Glass, China & Ceramics
Specialties: Stick Spatter
Directions: Phone For
Instructions

KNAPP HOUSE ANTIQUES
Box 384   06897
203 762-2044
Proprietor: Helen Schwindt
Hours: By Appointment
Types & Periods: American
& English Country Furniture

**SALANDER GALLERIES
INC**
392 Danbury Rd Rte 7
                    06897
203 762-0616
Proprietor: Larry &
Barbara Salander
Hours: Daily 10:30-3, Sat
& Sun By Appointment
Types & Periods: American,
English, Furniture, Paintings,
Oriental Rugs

TOBY HOUSE
526 Danbury Rd   06897
Proprietor: Melvin P Wiser
Hours: Mon-Sat 9:30-6,
Sun 12:30-6
Types & Periods: General
Line

WAYSIDE EXCHANGE
300 Danbury Rd   06897
203 762-3183
Proprietor: D Lochridge &
B Steele
Hours: Daily 10:30-5
Types & Periods: General
Line, Bric-A-Brac

Windham

**EDWARD & JOAN
STECKLER**
Webb Hill   06280
203 423-2665
Proprietor: Edward & Joan
Steckler
Hours: By Appointment
Types & Periods: American
Country Furniture, Doll
House Miniatures,
Needlework Tools
Directions: Webb Hill &
Rte 203

Windham Center

THE UPPER CRUST SHOP
Rte 203   06280
203 423-9351
Proprietor: Virginia
McDonald
Hours: Daily 11-4
Types & Periods: American
18th & 19th Century

Windsor

ANTIQUES & THINGS
141 Grove St   06095
203 688-5415
Proprietor: Don & Lorraine
Marcin
Hours: By Appointment
Types & Periods: General
Line, Collectibles

Windsor Locks

BOYNTON ANTIQUES
4 Copper Dr   06096
203 623-9533
Proprietor: Mr & Mrs Allen
Boynton
Hours: By Appointment
Types & Periods: 2 Wheel
Coffee Grinders, Deldare

Winsted

THE GLASS ROOM
48 Walnut St   06098
203 379-0114
Proprietor: Mrs W G
Hughes
Hours: By Appointment,
By Chance
Types & Periods: Early
American Pattern Glass
Directions: 1 Block Off
Main St (Rte 44)

Wolcott

M & H ANTIQUES
59 Lewis Ave   06716
203 879-4054
Proprietor: M Crandall
Hours: Daily, Also By
Appointment
Types & Periods: General
Line

Woodbury

COOP ANTIQUE SHOP
245 Main St N   06798
203 263-2428
Proprietor: Jean Rozenski
Hours: Daily 9-5
Types & Periods: Glass,
General Line

COUNTRY BAZAAR
451 Main St S   06798
203 263-2228   Est: 1968
Proprietor: Jerry Madans
Hours: Tue-Sun,Closed
Mon
Types & Periods:
Americana, Primitives,
Furniture, Pictures,
Accessories, Advertising,
Memorabilia, Wicker,

Baskets, Copper, Brass,
Iron, Dealers Welcome
Appraisal Service Available
Directions: 4 Miles N of
Exit 15 (I-84) on Rte 6,
Red Bldg

ROGER S DAVIS INC
480 Main St S   06798
203 263-5700   Est: 1973
Proprietor: Roger Davis
Hours: By Appointment,
By Chance
Types & Periods: American
& European Antique Clocks
Specialties: Weight & Crystal
Regulators, Howards,
Carriage Clocks
Appraisal Service Available
Directions: 4 Miles E on
Rte 6 From Exit 15 I-84, 2
Doors From Curtis House

DAVID DUNTON
Weekeepeemee Rd   06798
203 263-5355
Proprietor: David Dunton
Hours: By Appointment
Types & Periods: American
& English Furniture

**BRUCE M GILBERT
ANTIQUES**
1917 Main St N   06798
203 274-4098   Est: 1940
Proprietor: Bruce W
Gilbert
Hours: Daily 9-5,
Weekends, By
Appointment
Types & Periods:
Collectibles, General Line
Appraisal Service Available
Directions: Rte 6-Main St

GRASS ROOTS ANTIQUES
12 Main St N   06798
203 263-3983   Est: 1971
Proprietor: N Fierberg & E
Greenblatt
Hours: Daily, Closed Mon
Types & Periods: General
Line
Appraisal Service Available
Directions: Junction of
Rts 6 & 47

**KENNETH HAMMITT
ANTIQUES**
Main St.   06798
Proprietor: Kenneth F
Hammitt
Hours: Mon-Sat 10-5:30

Types & Periods: American
18th & 19th Century,
Accessories
Appraisal Service Available
  Directions: From New York
  Exit 15 off I-84 3 Miles on
  Rte 6. From Hartford Exit
  17 off I-84, 7 Miles on
  Rte 64

MILL HOUSE ANTIQUES
  Rte 6   06798
  203 263-3446.   Est: 1964
  Hours: Daily, Weekends,
  Closed Tues
Types & Periods: 17th & 18th
Century Furniture, Paintings,
Garden Ornaments
Specialties: Furniture, Large
Chair Sets, Welsh Dressers
  Directions: Exit 15 from
  I-84, 7 Miles E on Rte 6

OLD TIMERS
  139 Main St N.   06798
  203 263-5777
  Proprietor: Willard K
  Denton
  Hours: Daily 11-5
Types & Periods: Clocks,
Watches
  Directions: Rte 6

TIQUE MART
  Rte 6   06798
  203 758-1571   Est: 1967
  Proprietor: R H Sprano
  Hours: Flea Market Every
  Sat 9-5 & On Memorial
  Day, July 4th & Labor Day
Types & Periods: General
Line, Collectibles
  Directions: Exit 15 on
  I-84 to Rte 6, Near A & W
  Root Beer Stand

TURN O' THE CENTURY
  434 Main St.   06798
  203 263-2829   Est: 1973
  Proprietor: W & R
  Kurzmann
  Hours: Thur-Sun 10-6,
  Also By Appointment
Types & Periods: Oak &
Wicker Furniture, Clocks,
Glass, China
Specialties: Stained Leaded
Glass
  Directions: 4 Miles N of
  I-84 Exit 15 on US Rte 6

**MADELINE WEST
ANTIQUES**
  Main St.   06798
  203 263-4604
  Proprietor: Madeline West
  Hours: Mon-Sun 10-6
Types & Periods: 19th
Century Furniture, Paintings,
Prints, Oriental Rugs,
Porcelains
  Directions: Main St At
  War Memorial

THE CABRIOLE LEG

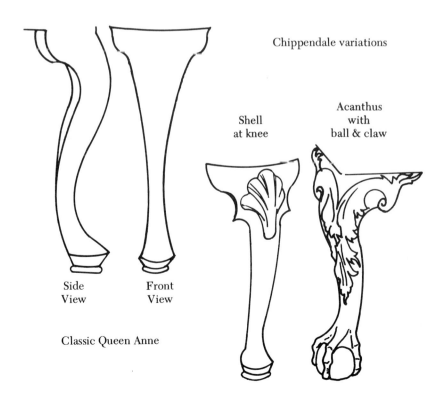

Chippendale variations

Shell at knee

Acanthus with ball & claw

Side View   Front View

Classic Queen Anne

STATE OF DELAWARE

Centerville

THE COLLECTOR
5716 Kennett Pike   19807
302 654-0786   Est: 1970
Proprietor: Ruth Lescaud
Hours: Tues-Sat, 11-4
Types & Periods: Furniture,
Antique Jewelry & Accessories
Specialties: Furniture,
Jewelry
  Directions: Located on
  Rte 52, 1 mile N of
  Winterthur Museum

Dewey Beach

**STUDIO GIFTS & ANTIQUE
SHOP**
Ocean Hwy   19971
302 227-2181
Proprietor: Fred & Lynn
Vogel
Hours: June 1-Sept 30,
Mon-Sat 1-5, Sun 12-4;
Off Season By
Appointment or By
Chance
Types & Periods: Primitives,
Lamps, Glass, Small
Furniture
Specialties: Decoys
  Directions: At Van Dyke
  St, Near Rehoboth Beach

Dover

FLAMM ANTIQUES INC
RD 4 Box 155   19901
302 734-5623   Est: 1949
Proprietor: Mrs James I
Flamm
Hours: Daily
Types & Periods: Pressed,
Cut, Art Glass; China; Silver;
Furniture; Period; Victorian;
Oak
Specialties: Glass (Cut &
Pressed)
Appraisal Service Available
  Directions: DuPont Hwy 4
  Miles N of Town

**MEETING HOUSE SQUARE
ANTIQUES**
305 S Governors Ave
    19901

302 678-1853
Proprietor: Susan Redden
Hours: Sat 10-5;
Appointment Anytime
Types & Periods: Furniture,
China, Brass, Books,
Textiles, Primitives, Trunks
  Directions: Across from
  State Museum

OLD DOVER ANTIQUES
666 S Dupont Hwy   19901
302 736-1345   Est: 1974
Proprietor: Mary J Truitt &
W C Torbert
Hours: Tues-Sun, 10-5
Types & Periods: Furniture,
China, Collectables, Junque
Specialties: Flow Blue, China
  Directions: On
  Rte 13 next to Saint Jones
  River Bridge in S Bound
  Lane

ROBERTS ANTIQUE LAMPS
2035 S DuPont Hwy 19901
302 697-3414
Hours: Mon-Sat, 8-4:30;
Sun, 1-4
Types & Periods: Lamps,
Country Furniture, Primitives
  Directions: Pine Shop is in
  Back of Roberts Antique
  Lamps

Fenwick Island

SEASIDE COUNTRY STORE
Ocean Hwy   19944
302 539-6110
Proprietor: Mr & Mrs David
Bates
Hours: Daily 10-10, May
1st thru Oct
Types & Periods: General
Line of Early Americana
  Directions: At Georgetown
  St

Georgetown

**EDWIN L & OLETA SMITH
ANTIQUES & GADGETS**
422 N Race St   19947
302 856-6004

Proprietor: Edwin L &
Oleta Smith
Hours: By Chance
Types & Periods: General
Line

Greenwood

RUTH MERVINE
Rte 1 Box 72   19950
302 349-4282
Proprietor: Ruth Mervine
Hours: Mon-Sat, 10-5
Types & Periods: Cut, Art &
Pattern Glass; China,
Lamps; Furniture; Jewelry
  Directions: 1/4 Mile E of
  Greenwood Rte 36 on
  Milford-Greenwood Rd

Harbeson

BRICK BARN ANTIQUES
Rte 18   19951
302 684-8220
Proprietor: Bill & Evelyn
Smith
Hours: Sat-Thurs,
9:30-5:30, April thru
December
Types & Periods: Glass,
China, Furniture, Primitives,
Jewelry
  Directions: Between
  Georgetown & Lewes

Laurel

CULVER'S ANTIQUES
Rte 9   19956
302 875-7673
Proprietor: Bob & Minnie
Culver
Hours: By Appointment,
By Chance
Types & Periods: Glassware,
Furniture
Specialties: Lamps
  Directions:
  Laurel-Georgetown Hwy, 3
  1/3 Miles E of US 13

**FIVE POINTS ANTIQUES
SHOP**
Rte 13   19956

302 875-5254
Proprietor: Mimi Alexander
Hours: Seven Days a
Week, 10-6
Types & Periods: General
Line

THE GOLDEN DOOR
214 E Market St   19956
302 875-5084   Est: 1968
Proprietor: Aiko & Leroy
Phillips
Hours: Daily, 10-10
Types & Periods: American,
Oriental, European Objets
d'Art; Folk Art; Pewter;
Brass; Silver; Glass; Lamps;
Porcelain; Collectibles;
Furniture

VAL'S ANTIQUES
304 4th St   19956
Proprietor: Valeria Litwak
Hours: Daily, 10-9
Types & Periods:
Bric-A-Brac, Bronzes, Brass,
China, Paintings, Porcelains,
Art Glass, Furniture

Lewes

**OLD RUSSELL FARM
HOUSE**
410 Pilot Town Rd   19958
302 645-6561
Proprietor: Reba R Lynch
Hours: Daily, 10-5
Types & Periods: China,
Glass, Small Furniture
Directions: On the Canal

Middletown

G W THOMAS ANTIQUES
RD 2 Box 73   19709
302 378-2414   Est: 1930
Proprietor: George W
Thomas
Hours: By Chance, 9-5
Most Days
Types & Periods: 18th &
Early 19th Century Furniture,
Glass, China, Pewter
Appraisal Service Available
Directions: 2 Miles N of
Odessa on US 13

Milton

**YORK'S HOMESTEAD
ANTIQUES**
Rte 9   19968
302 684-3262   Est: 1974
Proprietor: Harlan G
York Sr
Hours: Tues-Sun, 10-5
Types & Periods: Furniture,
Glass, Collectibles,
Primitives, Art, Lamps
Directions: Coolspring,
Lewis-Georgetown Hwy

New Castle

**THE CARPENTER'S TOOL
CHEST**
11-13 E 2nd St   19720
302 322-3921
Proprietor: Robert &
Margaret Dean
Hours: By Appointment
Types & Periods:
Woodworking Tools, Sewing
Tools, Country Furniture,
Primitives

**JACKSON-MITCHELL/WILLIS
MOORE INC**
3rd & Delaware St   19720
302 322-4365   Est: 1975
Proprietor: James Parker,
Stuart Horn & Willis Moore
Hours: Seven Days a
Week
Types & Periods: Period
English Furniture &
Accessories
Specialties: Marine
Paintings, Brass, Copper
Appraisal Service Available
Directions: "Across the
green in historic New
Castle, minutes from I-95"

QUALITY HOUSE
124 Delaware St   19720
Proprietor: Vernon Hagan
Hours: Mon thru Sat
Types & Periods: Pressed &
Blown Glass, Period
Furniture
Directions: Rte 141, 5
Miles S of Wilmington

Ocean View

ANTIQUE CITY
Rte 26   19970
302 539-7521
Proprietor: Mr & Mrs Perry
Alexander
Hours: Daily, 10-6
Types & Periods: Tiffany,
Orientals, Art Glass,
Primitives, Furniture
Directions: 2 Miles W of
Bethany Beach

IRON AGE ANTIQUES
Central Ave & Daisey St
    19970
302 539-5344
Proprietor: Debby, Mike &
Bill Gichner
Hours: Daily, 10-10
Types & Periods: Iron,
Primitives, Tools, General
Line
Specialties: Blacksmithing
Equipment

Rehoboth Beach

**DINNER BELL INN
ANTIQUE BARN**
2 Christian St   19971
302 227-2561
Proprietor: Mr & Mrs
David Deibler
Hours: Daily, April thru
Nov, 11-9
Types & Periods: Nostalgic
Items, Furniture, Glass,
China

THE HUDSON HOUSE
Rte 1 & Benson St   19971
302 227-2487   Est: 1972
Proprietor: Earl &
Catherine Hudson
Hours: Seven Days a
Week, March thru Oct; By
Chance Nov thru April
Types & Periods: Country
Primitive & Victorian
Furniture, Antique Tools,
Guns & Accessories
Specialties: Tools &
Country Furniture
Directions: Rte 1 on
Dewey Beach Cutoff
Opposite State Police
Station on Benson St

THE HUDSON HOUSE
Rte 1 & Airport Rd   19971
Proprietor: Earl &
Catherine Hudson
Hours: Seven Days a
Week, March thru Oct; By
Chance, Nov thru April
Types & Periods: Country
Primitive & Victorian
Furniture, Antique Tools,
Guns, Accessories
Specialties: Tools, Country
Furniture
    Directions: On Rte 1 N of
    Rehoboth

Seaford

BLUE HEN FARM
ANTIQUES
Rd 541   19973
302 629-7718
Proprietor: Lulu O'Day
Hours: By Appointment,
By Chance
Types & Periods: General
Line
    Directions: 4 Miles W of
    Town off Stein Hwy Rte
    20 on Rd 541

MC CALLISTER'S ANTIQUE
SHOP
Rte 13 N   19973
302 629-6996
Proprietor: Bill & Jody
McCallister
Hours: Mon-Sat, 10-5; Sun
By Appointment
Types & Periods: Furniture
& Accessories
    Directions: 3 Miles S of
    Seaford

VICKI'S ANTIQUES
Willey St   19973
302 629-9595
Proprietor: Victorine &
Frank Joseph
Hours: Daily
Types & Periods: Furniture,
Glass, China, Clocks, Lamps
    Directions: Corner W
    Spruce & Willey St, Turn
    off Stein Hwy at Texaco
    Station

Shelbyville

SEAPORT ANTIQUE
VILLAGE
Rte 1 Box 299   19975
302 436-8962
Proprietor: Mrs Kit Lyman
Hours: Daily
Types & Periods: Furniture,
Glass, China, Wicker,
General Line
    Directions: W on Rte 54 at
    Fenwick Light, 4 Blocks at
    Bridge

Smyrna

EILEEN GANT ANTIQUES
Rte 13   19977
302 653-8996   Est: 1954
Proprietor: Eileen C Gant
Hours: Mon-Fri, 10-4; Sat,
10-5; Sun, 12-5
Types & Periods: Country &
Formal Furniture, Pewter,
Porcelain
Specialties: China (Canton &
Rose Medallion)
    Directions: Approximately
    1 Mile N of Town, S Lane
    Across from State Rest
    Area

PEACOCK PLUME INC
RD 2 Box 1034   19977
302 653-8635   Est: 1969
Proprietor: Mrs Dietrich
Hours: Mon-Sat, 9-5
Types & Periods: General
Line, "Early Attic"
    Directions: 1 Mile N of
    Smyrna on Rte 13 S
    Bound

Wilmington

BRANDYWINE ANTIQUES
2116 N Market St   19802
302 655-9826   Est: 1967
Proprietor: Jean Condon
Hours: Daily, By Chance
Types & Periods: General
Line, Collectibles, Jewelry
Appraisal Service Available

1818 ANTIQUES
1818 Marsh Rd   19810
302 475-1815   Est: 1974

Proprietor: Mr & Mrs F
Hayward & Mrs R B
Weatherby
Hours: Tues-Sat
Types & Periods: Country
Furniture, Accessories
Specialties: Primitives, Folk
Art
Appraisal Service Available
    Directions: 1 Mile from
    Marsh Rd, Exit Off I-95 or
    3 Miles from Rte 202 via
    Silverside Rd, Next to
    Bran Mar Plaza Shopping
    Center

GREENWOOD BOOK SHOP
110 W 9th St   19801
302 654-6237   Est: 1920
Proprietor: Colwyn S
Krussman
Hours: Mon-Fri, 9:30-5:30;
Sat, 10-4
Types & Periods: Chinese
Porcelain, Snuff Bottles,
Netsukes, Rare & Out of
Print Books, Maps
    Directions: Downtown

DAVID STOCKWELL INC
3701 Kennett Pike   19807
Proprietor: David
Stockwell
Hours: Mon-Fri, 9:30-5
Types & Periods: 18th &
Early 19th Century American
Furniture & Accessories
Specialties: Americana
    Directions: Rte 52 near
    Junction of Rte 141

DISTRICT OF COLUMBIA

Washington

ADAMS DAVIDSON GALLERIES INC
3233 P St NW   20007
202 965-3800   Est: 1967
Proprietor: Theodore A
Cooper
Hours: Tues-Fri 10-5,
Sat 11-5
Types & Periods: American
Paintings, Watercolors,
Drawings from 19th & Early
20th Centuries, European
Master Paintings
Specialties: "Hudson River
School, Impressionists, Ash
Can School"
Appraisal Service Available
Directions: Located in
Georgetown just off
intersection of Wisc Ave &
P St NW

AMERICAN FOLK ART SHOP
3214 O St NW   20007
202 338-8250
Proprietor: Janet & John
Wallach
Hours: Tues thru Sat 11-5
Types & Periods:
Weathervanes, Wood
Carvings, Quilts, Trade
Signs, Coverlets

ANTON GALLERY
415 E Capitol   20003
202 546-2071   Est: 1961
Proprietor: Florence Anton
Hours: Weekends, By
Appointment
Types & Periods: General
Line
Specialties: Russian Objets
d'Art
Appraisal Service Available
Directions: Near Fulger
Library

ARPAD ANTIQUES, INC
3222 O St NW   20007
202 337-3424   Est: 1953
Proprietor: Michael Arpad
Hours: Mon-Fri 8-5,
Sat 9-5
Types & Periods: 17th-19th
Centuries Furniture,
Furnishings, Silver, Pewter,
Paintings, Porcelains, Glass

Specialties: Restorations to
Silver, Brass, Pewter,
Porcelain
Appraisal Service Available
Directions: Georgetown, 1
block W of Wisconsin
Ave NW

THE ATLANTIC GALLERY
1055 Thomas Jefferson
St NW   20007
202 337-2299   Est: 1976
Proprietor: Malcolm
Henderson
Hours: Mon-Wed, Fri-Sat
10-6, Thurs 10-9, Sun 1-5,
By Appointment
Types & Periods: 18th &
19th Centuries Paintings,
Watercolors, Etchings &
Prints
Specialties: English Maritime
Paintings
Appraisal Service Available
Directions: The Foundry
Bldg, 1 block below M St
in Georgetown

BARBARA'S PLACE
2424 37th St NW   20007
202 965-2042   Est: 1976
Proprietor: Barbara Bastin
Hours: Sun, Fri & Sat
Types & Periods: 19th &
20th Centuries Furniture,
Glass, China, Silver,
Jewelry, Textiles,
Collectibles
Directions: In NW
Washington on 37th St
just past the intersection
of Calvert St & Wisconsin
Ave in Smallest House in
Wash., D C

PETER MACK BROWN ANTIQUES
1525 Wisconsin Ave NW
          20007
202 338-8484   Est: 1964
Proprietor: Peter Mack
Brown
Hours: Mon-Sat
Types & Periods: 18th
Century French &
Continental Furniture,
Related Objects
Specialties: Chinese Export
Porcelain
Appraisal Service Available
Directions: Georgetown,
D C

CALVERT GALLERY
2311 Calvert St NW
          20009
202 387-5177   Est: 1973
Proprietor: Peter A
Cocasante
Hours: Daily, Weekends,
10:30-6:30, 5 Days in July
& Aug
Types & Periods: 18th
Century Period, American,
English Furniture, Oriental
Carpets, Japanese &
Chinese Export Porcelains,
Paintings
Specialties: China
(Cloisonne)
Appraisal Service Available
Directions: Just E of
Corner of Calvert &
Connecticut about 1000 ft
E of Shoreham Americana
Hotel

THE CANAL CO OF GEORGETOWN
1055 Thomas Jefferson
NW   20007
202 338-1332   Est: 1976
Proprietor: Jeffrey J Yudin
Hours: Mon Wed, Fri-Sat
10-6, Thurs 10-9, Sun 12-6
Types & Periods: Quilts
(1850-1930), Office Furniture
(1870-1930), Architectural
Items (Mantels, Chandeliers,
Door Knobs, Brass
Bathroom Hardware, from
Victorian era), Miscellaneous
Items
Specialties: Quilts, Office
Furniture, Architectural
Items, Lighting Fixtures
Directions: Located in the
Foundry Shopping Mall
adjacent to the C & O
Canal between 30th &
31st Sts, NW in Historic
Georgetown

THE CANDLER COMPANY
2805 M St NW   20007
202 338-6508   Est: 1970
Proprietor: Charles Z
Candler III
Hours: Daily 10-6:30, Sun
By Appointment
Types & Periods: General
Line
Specialties: Early American
Country

CHANDLER CO   Cont'd

Directions: In Georgetown where Penn Ave intersects M St

CHERISHABLES

1823 Jefferson Place
20036
202 785-4087   Est: 1974
Proprietor: Marilyn Hannigan & Marston Luce
Hours: Mon-Fri 11-6, Sat 11-5
Types & Periods: American Country Furniture, Early 19th Century, Quilts, Samplers, Baskets, Crocks, Jewelry, Silver
Specialties: Quilts
Directions: 1/2 block off Connecticut Ave & 19th St, parallel between "M" & "N" Sts

ANTONY CHILDS ASSOCIATES

1670 Wisconsin Ave NW
20007
202 337-1100   Est: 1968
Proprietor: Antony Childs, Robert Mondin, Roger Newman
Hours: Mon-Fri, By Appointment
Types & Periods: Continental & English Furniture, French & Oriental Porcelain, Assorted Decorative Pieces & Accessories
Directions: At Intersection of Wisconsin Ave, 33rd St & Reservoir Rd, 1 block below R St in Georgetown

THE COLLECTORS GALLERY

1710 Connecticut Ave NW
20009
202 483-3100   Est: 1975
Proprietor: Jeffery N Cohen
Hours: Mon-Fri, By Appointment
Types & Periods: American Scrimshaw, Dolls, American Folk Art
Specialties: Scrimshaw, Dolls, Folk Art

M DARLING LIMITED

3213 O St NW   20007
202 337-0096   Est: 1964
Proprietor: Macy M Darling
Hours: Tues-Sat 11-6, June-Aug Mon-Fri 11-6, By Appointment
Types & Periods: 17th thru Early 19th Centuries English Furniture & Works of Art
Appraisal Service Available
Directions: In Georgetown Area

DEJA VU

1675 Wisconsin Ave
20007
202 965-1988   Est: 1973
Proprietor: J Elizabeth Ford
Hours: Mon-Sat
Types & Periods: Art Nouveau, Art Deco
Specialties: Vintage Clothes & Accessories, Jewelry
Appraisal Service Available
Directions: Top of Hill in Georgetown

DUNCAN & DUNCAN CHINESE GALLERY

1509-11 Connecticut Ave NW   20036
202 232-4884
Proprietor: P Harrison & Miriam C Fisher
Hours: Mon-Fri 10-6, Sat 10-5, By Appointment
Types & Periods: Furniture, Rugs, Porcelains, Statues, Embroidery Screens, Carvings, Snuff Bottles, Jewelry, Wood Cuts, Paintings, Scrolls
Appraisal Service Available
Directions: 4 Doors above Dupont Circle and 4 blocks from the White House

EARLY AMERICAN SHOP

1319 Wisconsin Ave NW
20007
202 333-5843   Est: 1947
Proprietor: Elizabeth Y Webb
Hours: Mon-Sat 11-5:30
Types & Periods: American & English Furniture, Late 1600's to Early 1800's

Specialties: 18th Century Furniture, Historical Engravings
Directions: In the Center of Georgetown

CYNTHIA FEHR ANTIQUES

3214 O St NW   20007
202 338-5090   Est: 1965
Proprietor: Cynthia Fehr & Niente Robertson
Hours: Mon-Sat 11-5
Types & Periods: Period English & American Furniture, Accessories
Directions: First block W of Wisconsin Ave on O St in Georgetown

FISHER GALLERIES

1509-11 Connecticut Ave NW   20036
202 265-6255
Proprietor: P Harrison & Miriam C Fisher
Hours: Mon-Fri 10-6, Sat 10-5, By Appointment
Types & Periods: Antique Paintings, Drawings, Watercolors, Lithos & Etchings, Sculpture
Appraisal Service Available
Directions: 4 Doors above Dupont Circle & 4 blocks from the White House

VICTORIA FORTUNE INC

2035 P St NW   20036
202 659-9345   Est: 1974
Proprietor: Victoria Fortune
Hours: Mon-Sat, By Appointment, By Chance
Types & Periods: Art Deco, Art Nouveau
Specialties: Jewelry & Posters
Appraisal Service Available
Directions: One block off Massachusettes Ave at 21st St

GEORGETOWN TEMPTATIONS

3210 O St NW   20007
202 338-2336   Est: 1966
Proprietor: Martha B McTigue
Hours: Mon-Sat 9:30-5:30
Types & Periods: Small Furniture, Tables, Chairs, Shelves, Magazine Racks, Bookends, Boxes (All kinds, Lap desks, Jewelry, Tea Caddy), Inkwells

Specialties: Boxes &
Stationary
Directions: Near Corner of
Wisconsin & O Sts NW

GERALDINE'S
4105 Wisconsin Ave NW
20016
202 686-5050   Est: 1976
Proprietor: Geraldine
Ricketts
Hours: Tues-Sat 12-6
Types & Periods: Vintage
Clothing, Victorian thru
1950's Plus Accessories of
Every Kind, Jewelry
Directions: Located in an
Apartment Bldg, 1 Mile N
of National Cathedral on
Wisconsin Ave NW

HERMES
2000 S St NW   20009
202 332-2067   Est: 1977
Proprietor: Douglas M
Haller & Helen S Coutts
Hours: Tues-Sat 11-6:30
Types & Periods: l9th & 20th
Centuries Glass, China,
Prints, Jewelry, Books,
Furniture, Collectibles
Directions: Located in the
Heart of the Dupont Circle
Art Center off Connecticut
Ave on S St

LAUNAY E CO INC
2410 18th St NW   20009
202 483-0907   Est: 1962
Proprietor: Raymond B
Launay
Hours: Mon-Sat
Types & Periods: 18th
Century Continental & Some
American
Specialties: Antique
Restoration of Furniture,
Coromandel Screens, Gold
Leaf, Inlay
Directions: Below
Columbia Rd on 18th St
NW

**LAW-FORD HOUSE
ANTIQUES**
1608 Wisconsin Ave
20007
202 965-4676   Est: 1970
Proprietor: Ford A Kalil Jr
Hours: Daily, Weekends,
Closed Sun

Types & Periods: English,
French & Oriental Furniture,
Porcelain, Silver, Brass,
Copper
Directions: In Georgetown
at Wisconsin Ave & Q St
NE

**LOUISE'S LES CHAMPS
GALLERY**
600 N Hampshire Ave NW
20037
202 333-3220
Proprietor: Louise M Pilitt
Hours: Daily 11-8
Types & Periods: Period
French & English Furniture
& Accessories

MARKET ROW ANTIQUES
311 7th St SE   20003
202 543-3773   Est: 1973
Proprietor: Richard
McMullen
Hours: Sun, Tues-Sat,
Types & Periods: Victorian
Specialties: Oak
Directions: On Capitol Hill

**MARTIN'S OF
GEORGETOWN**
1304 Wisconsin Ave NW
20007
202 338-6144   Est: 1930
Hours: Daily, Weekends
10-6, Closed Sun
Types & Periods: Georgian
Silver, Victorian Plate,
China, Oriental & European
Odd Bits & Pieces
Specialties: Silver
Directions: Main St
(Wisconsin Ave),
Georgetown Section of
the District

MASON ANTIQUES
2651 Connecticut Ave NW
20008
202 462-3001   Est: 1970
Proprietor: Dolores D
Mason
Hours: Daily, Weekends
10-6
Types & Periods: American,
European, 18th-19th
Centuries, Porcelains,
Bronzes, Furniture, Jewelry,
Oriental Rugs, Oil Paintings,
Silver
Appraisal Service Available
Directions: Cleveland Park
Area btwn Calvert St NW
& Woodley Rd NW

MC DONALD GALLERY
725 E Capitol St SE
20003
202 544-6578   Est: 1975
Proprietor: George J
McDonald
Hours: Weekends, By
Appointment
Types & Periods: 18th &
19th Centuries American
Paintings, Furniture &
Furnishings
Directions: Capitol Hill, 8
blocks E of US Capitol
Bldg

OLD ANTIQUE HOUSE
817 Pennsylvania Ave NW
20004
202 628-5699   Est: 1884
Proprietor: Simon &
Stanley Krupsaw
Hours: Mon-Sat, Except
July & Aug
Types & Periods: British &
Continental Antique
Furniture & Art Objects,
Handmade Furniture
Reproductions, Carved
Semi-Precious Stone
Figures, Paperweights,
Paintings, Chandeliers,
Fireplace Equipment
Specialties: Full Service on
Most Furniture Items,
Custom Cabinetmaking
Appraisal Service Available
Directions: Downtown
Washington, D C

ROSE BROS JEWELERS
3317 Connecticut Ave NW
20008
202 363-3681   Est: 1938
Proprietor: Lyons & Julian
Rose
Hours: Daily 9-5, Sat
9-4:30
Types & Periods: Clocks,
Jewelry
Specialties: Bottles (19th
Century Music)
Appraisal Service Available
Directions: Upper NW, 2
blocks above Nat'l
Zoological Park

SEGAL'S ANTIQUES
  1339 Wisconsin Ave NW
    20007
  202 333-6161   Est: 1906
  Proprietor: Israel & Percy
  Segal
  Hours: Daily 9:30-4, Sat by
  Appointment
Types & Periods: American
& English Furniture,
American Silver, China
Specialties: Furniture, Silver
Appraisal Service Available
  Directions: In Old
  Georgetown at Dumbarton
  Ave NW

C G SLOAN & CO INC
  715 Thirteenth St NW
    20005
  202 628-1468   Est: 1891
  Proprietor: Mrs Jennie E
  O'Brien
  Hours: Daily, By Auction
Types & Periods: General
Line
Appraisal Service Available
  Directions: In Downtown
  Nat'l Capitol at 13th & G
  Sts, 3 blocks E of White
  House

TESORO TRADING POST
  5117 MacArthur Blvd NW
    20016
    Est: 1975
  Proprietor: Virginia Brown
  & Ted Musial
  Hours: Mon-Sat 12-6
Types & Periods:
Americana, Oak, Maple,
Pine, Iron Implements,
Stoneware, English &
European 18th & 19th
Centuries Furniture, Crystal,
China
Specialties: Americana,
Furniture Repaired and
Refinished
  Directions: Btwn Dana Pl
  and Arizona Ave on the
  2nd Floor above Hungry
  Hilda's Gourmet Carryout

TINY JEWEL BOX INC
  1143 Connecticut Ave NW
    20036
  202 393-2747   Est: 1944
  Proprietor: James
  Rosenheim
  Hours: Daily
Types & Periods: 18th &
19th Centuries American &
Western European Jewelry
Appraisal Service Available
  Directions: NW btwn L &
  M Sts

UNIVERSITY ANTIQUES
  3428 O St NW   20007
  202 238-3149   Est: 1972
  Proprietor: Roy H Jones
  Hours: Daily, Weekends
  11-5, Closed Sun
Types & Periods: 17th, 18th
& 19th Centuries Furniture &
Accessories
Specialties: Furniture
(English)
  Directions: In Georgetown,
  2 blocks from Georgetown
  Univ

**JULES H VAN MARKEN
INC**
  950 Upshur St NW   20011
  202 829-0418   Est: 1971
  Proprietor: Jules H
  Van Marken & John C
  Summer
  Hours: Daily 9-5,
  Weekends by Appointment
Types & Periods:
Architectural Artifacts,
Stained Glass
Specialties: Architectural
Artifacts
  Directions: 1½ Miles S of
  Walter Reed

**VIP ANTIQUES OF
GEORGETOWN**
  1658 33rd St NW   20007
  202 965-0700   Est: 1974
  Hours: Daily 11-6, By
  Appointment
Types & Periods: Furniture
(Assorted Periods), Silver,
Porcelain, Jewelry, Snuffs,
Collectibles, Lamps &
Chandeliers, Miscellaneous
  Directions: At Intersection
  of Wisconsin Ave, btwn Q
  & R Sts

cross section

Fluted leg, Sheraton

Apalachicola

THE CHESNUT TREE
88 Market St   32320
904 653-8443   Est: 1973
Proprietor: Wesley
Chesnut
Hours: Daily
Types & Periods: General
Line
Specialties: Furniture
Directions: Hwy 98,
Downtown

Avon Park

**M & M ANTIQUES &
TRADING CENTER**
108 S Forest Ave   33825
813 453-6095   Est: 1971
Proprietor: Mary Louise
Bucche

Belleair Bluffs

BELLEAIR COINS
778 N Indian Rocks
                   33540
813 585-4502   Est: 1973
Proprietor: Art Arbutine
Hours: Daily
Types & Periods: Oriental
Art, Jewelry, Bangkok Gold
Chains
Specialties: Odd & Curious
Money
Appraisal Service Available
Directions: N of St
Petersburg between Largo
& Clearwater

MASTER JEWELERS
416 Indian Rocks Rd N
                   33540
513 585-7031   Est: 1923
Proprietor: Aaron Masters
Hours: By Appointment
Types & Periods: Jewelry,
Victorian; All Periods
Specialties: Jewelry
Appraisal Service Available
Directions: 6 Miles from
Clearwater

Blountstown

THE FOXFIRE SHOP
720 W Central Ave   32424
904 674-5811   Est: 1973
Proprietor: Jo House
Hours: Mon-Sat, 9-5
Types & Periods: General
Line
Specialties: Primitives
Directions: Hwy 20W
(Main St of Town)

Boca Raton

THE FINDERS
3360 N Federal Hwy
                   33431
305 392-9404
Types & Periods: General
Line, Art, Collectibles
Specialties: China &
Porcelain Repair
Directions: In Boca Plaza

**JULIE'S FINE
APPOINTMENTS**
6099 N Federal Hwy
                   33431
305 278-7083
Hours: Tues-Sat, 10-5
Types & Periods: General
Line
Directions: US 1

MAYBE SHOP ANTIQUES
351 E Palmetto Park Rd
                   33432
305 392-5680
Types & Periods: General
Line, Orientals
Appraisal Service Available

Bradenton

THE BIZARRE BAZAAR
8615 Cortez Rd W   33505
813 792-8222   Est: 1962
Proprietor: T C Stebbings
Hours: Tues-Sun, 10-5
Types & Periods: General
Line
Specialties: Coins, Ivory, Old
Pocket Watches
Appraisal Service Available

Directions: Cortez Rd W
from Town toward Gulf of
Mexico, Located across
from Antique City

**FOXHALL ANTIQUE
GALLERY**
8500 Cortez Rd   33505
813 756-6622   Est: 1971
Proprietor: Mr & Mrs Dan
Sexton
Hours: Tues-Sun, 9-5
Types & Periods: General
Line, Glass, China, Silver,
Furniture, Jewelry, Clocks,
Paintings, Bronzes, Oriental
Rugs
Specialties: Auction Service
Available
Appraisal Service Available
Directions: US 41 to
Bradenton to Cortez Rd W

**KOUNTRY KITCHEN
ANTIQUES**
5831 15th St E   33507
813 755-7484   Est: 1949
Proprietor: E R & Anne
Adams
Hours: Daily
Types & Periods: Coins,
Jewelry, General Line
Appraisal Service Available
Directions: Hwy 301 S of
Onelo, Half-Way between
Sarasota & Bradenton

Carrabelle

MILLER'S SEAHORSE
Star Rte   32322
904 697-3751   Est: 1956
Proprietor: W B Miller III
Hours: Daily
Types & Periods: Primitives
to Contemporary
Appraisal Service Available
Directions: US 98, 5 Miles
E of Town on the Beach

Clearwater

COLLECTORS' CORNER
1935 Drew St   33515
813 447-8788   Est: 1970
Proprietor: Paul O
Germann

Clearwater   Cont'd

COLLECTORS' CORNER
Cont'd
Hours: Mon, Wed & Sat,
11-4, Also by Appointment
Types & Periods: Unusual
Antiques, Collectibles &
Decor Items
Directions: Approximately
2 Miles W of US 19 on
Drew

CHARLOTTE FERRARA
ANTIQUES &
COLLECTIBLES
1614 N Ft Harrison   33515

813 446-4309   Est: 1975
Proprietor: Charlotte
Ferrara
Hours: Mon-Fri, 9:30-5;
Sat & Eves by
Appointment
Types & Periods: General
Line, Glass, Silver, China,
Pottery, Furniture, Clocks,
Brass, Pictures, Lighting
Specialties: Jewelry
Appraisal Service Available
Directions: Alt 19, 1 1/2
Miles N Rte 60

KAREN'S KORNER
2444 Timbercrest Cir West
33515
813 733-0104   Est: 1973
Proprietor: Barbara
Flowers
Hours: By Appointment,
by Chance, Mail Order
Types & Periods: Depression
Glass, Heisey, Cambridge,
Art Pottery, Nippon
Specialties: Depression,
Heisey & Cambridge Glass,
Art Pottery, Nippon
Directions: Near the
Intersection of Fla 580 &
US 19

KYLE'S CLOCK SHOP
1454 Gulf-to-Bay Blvd
33515
813 442-7466   Est: 1967
Proprietor: Victor Kyle
Hours: Mon-Fri, 9-5:30;
Sat until 12; By
Appointment
Types & Periods: Clocks,
Furniture
Appraisal Service Available
Directions: Gulf-to-Bay
Blvd is Rte 60

OAKRIDGE ANTIQUES
2039 Highridge Dr   33515
813 734-7747
Proprietor: Mr & Mrs Loris
Webster
Hours: By Appointment
Types & Periods: Jewelry,
Dolls, Miniatures, Glass,
General Line

PORTOBELLO ANTIQUES
1029 1/2 Charles St
33515
813 441-9301   Est: 1970
Proprietor: Gladys
(Mickey) Doyne
Hours: By Appointment,
by Chance
Types & Periods: General
Line
Specialties: China (Flow
Blue), Dolls
Appraisal Service Available
Directions: 3 Blocks N of
Sunset Point Rd & Alt
US 19

WEE BIT O'HEATHER
520 Cleveland St   33515
813 443-0353   Est: 1972
Proprietor: Harold G Day
Hours: Mon-Sat, 10-5
Types & Periods: General
Line
Specialties: Furniture, Art
Glass
Appraisal Service Available
Directions: Rte 60
Downtown Clearwater

Cocoa

THE ANTIQUE GARDEN
304 B Brevard Ave   32922
305 631-0718   Est: 1973
Proprietor: Marianne T
Elam
Hours: Tues-Sat
Types & Periods: Wicker,
Oak Furniture, Glass, China,
Pottery, Primitives, Etc
Appraisal Service Available
Directions: Off Hwy 1, E
on 520 to Brevard Ave; in
Cocoa Village

FORGET-ME-NOT
ANTIQUES
402 Brevard Ave   32922
305 632-4700   Est: 1973
Proprietor: Nancy Benard
Hours: Mon-Sat

Types & Periods: Antique &
Quality Jewelry, China,
Glass, Furniture, Collectibles
& Silver
Specialties: Jewelry
Directions: 2 Blocks E of
US 1, just off 520; In
Cocoa Village

PAT'S ANTIQUES
643 Brevard Ave   32922
Est: 1973
305 637-8784
Proprietor: Pat Durham
Hours: Tues-Sat, 10-4
Types & Periods: General
Line & Collectibles
Specialties: China,
Glassware
Directions: 2 Block E of
US 1 in Downtown Cocoa

THE VILLAGE PLATE
COLLECTOR
219 King St   32922
305 636-6914   Est: 1975
Proprietor: Lois Epstein
Hours: Mon-Sat, 10-5
Types & Periods: Limited
Edition Collectibles
Specialties: China
Appraisal Service Available
Directions: State Rd 520
(King St in Village) &
Brevard Ave in Cocoa
Village

Cocoa Beach

EDYTHE CARLL'S ETC
SHOP
260 N Orlando Ave   32931
305 783-5370
Proprietor: Edythe Carll
Hours: Daily
Types & Periods: General
Line, Books, Collectibles
Directions: E of Rockledge

Coconut Grove

FOREIGN UNLIMITED ART
GALLERY
3315 Rice St   33133
305 444-3848   Est: 1972
Proprietor: Charles E
Warren
Hours: Mon-Sat

Types & Periods: Coins,
Pre-Columbian Art, Colonial
Art, World Maps, Prints,
Documents, Roman &
Egyptian
Appraisal Service Available
Directions: Across from
the Fire Station on Corner
of Oak & Rice

**HEART OF THE
ARTICHOKE**
3300 Rice St   33133
305 442-8131   Est: 1975
Proprietor: Alan & Vicki
Hours: Tues-Sat
Types & Periods: Oak &
Other American Furniture,
General Line, Collectibles
Specialties: Golden Oak
Furniture, Brass
Directions: Corner of Oak
Ave & Rice St

Coral Gables

**JOSEPH TUDISCO
ANTIQUES**
2906 Douglas Rd   33134
305 446-5466   Est: 1969
Proprietor: Joseph
Tudisco
Hours: Mon-Sat, 10:30-5
Types & Periods: American,
English, Continental
Furniture, Porcelains, Silver,
Paintings; 17th, 18th & 19th
Centuries
Specialties: Furniture
Appraisal Service Available
Directions: 5 Blocks S of
Miracle Mile between
Palermo & Malaga Sts

JIM WILLS DESIGN
4944 LeJeune Rd S
                   33146
305 666-2579   Est: 1962
Proprietor: James M
Wills III
Hours: Daily, 9-5
Types & Periods: 12th &
13th Century Siamese
Artifacts; Canton, Rose
Medallion, English &
American Chests &
Breakfronts; French Bonnet
Chests, Provincial
Breakfronts, Bombe Desks;
Primitive Oils; Wall
Hangings; Sterling

Appraisal Service Available
Directions: 1 Block S of
Dixie Hwy (US 1) on
LeJeune Rd

Dade City

LONGFRITZ'S ANTIQUES
1206 W Coleman Ave
                   33525
904 567-3804   Est: 1945
Proprietor: Mrs LeRoy
Longfritz
Hours: Daily, 10-5
Types & Periods: General
Line, China, Glass,
Primitives
Specialties: Pattern Glass
Directions: 10 Miles from
I-75

MALTBY
992 S Hwy 98   33525
904 567-3815   Est: 1955
Proprietor: Z R Maltby
Hours: Daily
Types & Periods: General
Line
Directions: 4 Miles S of
Dade City, 1/4 Mile off
301 on 98 S

ROBERTS BARN ANTIQUES
621 Roberts Barn Rd
                   33525
904 567-3570   Est: 1951
Proprietor: Carrie Mae
Roberts
Hours: By Appointment,
by Chance "I live next to
shop"
Types & Periods: General
Line
Specialties: Glass
Appraisal Service Available
Directions: 3 Miles W of
Dade City on St Joe Rd; R
on Roberts Barn Rd, 2nd
Driveway

Dania

AN WISE ANTIQUES
233 N Federal Hwy 33004
305 925-5551   Est: 1925
Types & Periods: China, Cut
Glass, Silver, Furniture,
Jewelry, Paintings, Oriental
Rugs
Directions: In Dania Plaza

ATHENA GALLERY
19 S Federal Hwy   33004
305-921-7697   Est: 1975
Hours: Mon-Sat, 10-4
Types & Periods: Art Glass,
Sculpture, China, Bronzes,
Orientals, Lamps, Cut Glass,
Clocks
Directions: On Rte US 1

BROWNER ANTIQUES
233 N Federal Hwy 33004
305 925-1433   Est: 1973
Proprietor: Arthur Browner
Hours: Mon-Fri, by
Appointment
Types & Periods: French,
European & American,
17th-20th Century: Bronze
Sculpture, European &
American Tiffany Lamps &
Glass, Art Noveau & Art
Deco, Cameo & Art Glass,
Enamels, Paintings, Stained
Glass, Works of Art; Estate
Auction Service
Specialties: Sculpture,
Tiffany Lamps, Glass,
Enamels
Appraisal Service Available
Directions: I-95 to Griffin
Rd Exit, E to Federal Hwy;
2 Blocks S of Griffin Rd
on W side of Federal Hwy

CAMEO ANTIQUES
18 N Federal Hwy   33004
305 922-0358   Est: 1969
Proprietor: Ellen Smith
Hours: Daily
Types & Periods: Clocks,
English & American
Furniture
Directions: "Antique
Center of the South"

**DANIA ANTIQUE &
JEWELRY EXCHANGE**
19 N Federal Hwy   33004
305 925-8827
Proprietor: E Moskowitz,
Mgr
Hours: Mon-Sat, 10-5
Types & Periods: 17
Air-Conditioned Shops
Featuring Jewelry,
Bric-a-Brac, Objets D'Art

ELY ANTIQUE SHOP
246 S Federal Hwy 33004
305 922-5590
Proprietor: Willard &
Genevieve Ely

Dania Cont'd

ELY ANTIQUE SHOP Cont'd
Hours: Mon-Sat, 10-6
Types & Periods: General
Line, Lamps

THE HITCHING POST ANTIQUES SHOP
62 N Federal Hwy 33004
305 923-2690 Est: 1958
Proprietor: Ellen Gaines
Mulford
Hours: Mon-Sat
Types & Periods: 18th &
19th Century Furniture,
China, Glassware, Silver
Directions: On US Hwy 1,
20 Miles N of Miami, 45
Miles S of Palm Beach

HODGE-PODGE ANTIQUES
26 NE 1st Ave 33004
305 925-2161
Hours: Daily
Types & Periods: General
Line, Orientals, Collectibles

MARDON ANTIQUES
17 N Federal Hwy 33004
305 921-0474 Est: 1978
Proprietor: Donald Rose
Hours: Mon-Sat, 10-5
Types & Periods: General
Line

MAXINE'S
26 N Federal Hwy 33004
Hours: Mon-Sat, 10-5
Types & Periods: General
Line, Jewelry, Collectibles
Directions: US 1

ORANGE MILL ANTIQUES
645 S Federal Hwy 33004
305 922-2238 Est: 1937
Proprietor: Gabriel J
Cardell
Hours: Daily
Types & Periods: French,
American & English
Furniture, China, Jewelry,
Silver, Glass
Appraisal Service Available
Directions: Corner of S
Federal Hwy (US I) &
7th St

SIGN OF THE RAM
214 Dania Plaza,
N Federal Hwy 33004
305 925-8073 Est: 1970
Proprietor: Bernice Brody
Hours: Mon-Sat, 9-5:30

Types & Periods: Jewelry,
Bronzes, Silver, Art,
Porcelains, Jade, Ivory
Appraisal Service Available
Directions: US Hwy 1, S of
Hollywood Ft Lauderdale
Airport

MARGARET TRIMBLE ANTIQUES
30 N Federal Hwy 33004
305 524-9274 Est: 1948
Proprietor: Margaret
Trimble
Types & Periods: General
Line

T'S TERRITORY ANTIQUES
8 N Federal Hwy 33004
305 923-2989
Hours: Thurs-Tues, 10-5
Types & Periods: General
Line, Guns, Pocket Knives &
Swords
Directions: US 1

VERONICA'S ANTIQUES 'N JEWELRY
33 N Federal Hwy 33004
305 587-0769
Proprietor: Veronica
Gregory
Hours: Daily, 11-4
Types & Periods: General
Line, Jewelry

WEDGEWOOD OF CANTEBURY
17 N Federal Hwy 33004
305 962-3247
Hours: By Appointment
Types & Periods: General
Line, Commemoratives
Specialties: Wedgewood
China
Directions: US 1

Daytona Beach

WINFRED HARNED ANTIQUES
648 Ridgewood Ave 32014
904 253-6808
Proprietor: Winfred
Harned
Hours: Daily
Types & Periods: Period
Furniture, General Line

KAY'S ANTIQUES
186 Broadway 32018
904 253-5047 Evenings
Est: 1969
Proprietor: Kay Schaur
Hours: Mon-Sat, 11-5,
Also by Appointment
Types & Periods: 18th &
19th Century Oriental
Porcelains, Cloisonne,
Bronzes, Ivories, Lacquer,
Furniture, Woodblock Prints,
Netsuke; 19th Century &
Other Furniture, Glass,
China, Silver, Paintings,
Books, Prints
Specialties: Oriental
Antiques, Furniture, Prints
Appraisal Service Available
Directions: On Hwy 92,
Beachside

De Bary

FRANK D GUARINO
3 Madera Rd 32713
305 668-8174 Est: 1973
Proprietor: Frank D
Guarino
Hours: By Appointment
Types & Periods: Civil War
Items, Photographica
Specialties: Civil War
Hardware
Appraisal Service Available
Directions: I-4 to Sanford
Exit to Hwy 17/92; L to
De Bary to Highbanks
Ave, R on Madera

Deerfield Beach

ANTIQUES BY JO
819 S Federal 33441
305 421-2121 Est: 1940
Proprietor: Josephine R
Powis
Hours: By Appointment
Types & Periods: General
Line

DeLand

ANGEVINE'S ANTIQUES
Hwy 17-92 South 32720
904 734-6347 Est: 1959
Proprietor: Shirley
Angevine

Hours: Mon, Tues, Fri &
Sat, 9-5:30; Sun, 2-5:30
Types & Periods: Jewelry,
Sterling Silver (Obsolete
Patterns Included) Cut
Glass, Art Glass, China,
Guns, Edged Weapons,
Coins, Stamps
Specialties: Jewelry, Sterling
Silver Flatware Matching,
Guns
   Directions: 3 Miles S of
   DeLand

APPLE ANNIE'S ANTIQUES
   2235 N Kepler   32720
   305 736-2059   Est: 1972
   Proprietor: Jane Marshall
   Hours: By Appointment,
   by Chance
Types & Periods: General
Line, Primitives, Children's
Items
   Directions: W Side on Hwy
   17-92 in the Middle of
   DeLeon Springs

CAROUSEL ANTIQUES
   110 East Church   32720
   904 734-8091   Est: 1970
   Proprietor: Anna Lee
   Croone
   Hours: Mon-Sat, 9:30-5
Types & Periods: Complete
Line
Appraisal Service Available
   Directions: East Church at
   N Blvd

D & E ANTIQUES
   1303 N Blvd   32720
   904 734-2160   Est: 1969
   Proprietor: D C & Eileen
   Daugherty
   Hours: Mon-Sat, 9:30-5
Types & Periods: Early
Empire, Victorian, American
Oak, Collectibles
Appraisal Service Available

**CORNELIA MOSELEY
ANTIQUES**
   121 E Rich Ave   32720
   904 734-6326   Est: 1936
   Proprietor: Cornelia
   Moseley McIntosh
   Hours: Daily; By
   Appointment, by Chance
Types & Periods: 18th
Century Empire & Victorian
Oil Paintings, Glass, China
Specialties: Dolls
Appraisal Service Available

RICKSHA ANTIQUES
   200 S Spring Garden Ave
                  32720
   904 734-3575   Est: 1960
   Proprietor: Mildred T &
   Elmer T Blomberg
   Hours: Daily, 10-4
Types & Periods: General
Line

**SERENDIPITY ANTIQUES &
FURNITURE CO, INC**
   1430 E New York Ave
                  32720
   904 736-2837   Est: 1970
   Proprietor: Kay or Terry
   Hours: Mon-Fri, 9:30-6;
   Sat, 9:30-5
Types & Periods: General
Line, primarily Furniture
Specialties: Oak Furniture,
St Clair Glass
Appraisal Service Available
   Directions: New York Ave
   is Hwy 44

Delray Beach

ANTIQUES & SOFORTH
   2213 N Federal Hwy
                  33444
   305 272-1812
   Hours: Daily
Types & Periods: "Buying
from a Plate to an Estate"
   Directions: Delray Antique
   Mall

**ANTIQUES BY DAVID &
PATRICIA**
   136 N Federal Hwy 33444
   305 272-1064   Est: 1968
   Proprietor: David Dobkin
   Hours: Mon-Sat; Sun by
   Appointment
Types & Periods: Oriental,
Jewelry, General Line
Specialties: Oriental &
Jewelry
Appraisal Service Available
   Directions: Across from
   Howard Johnsons

ANTIQUES ET CETERA
   514 E Atlantic Ave   33444
   305 278-6490   Est: 1969
   Proprietor: Elizabeth
   Weintraub
   Hours: Mon-Sat; Closed
   July & Aug
Types & Periods: General
Line, Collectibles

Appraisal Service Available
   Directions: Main St
   Downtown

BARLOW ANTIQUES
   128 N E 6th Ave   33444
   305 272-7544   Est: 1975
   Proprietor: Dudley &
   Marjory Barlow
   Hours: Daily, Nov-May
   (Will be found at Hwy 107,
   Glenville, NC, 28736,
   June-Oct)
Types & Periods: General
   Directions: US 1 N

**THE CAPTAIN'S
QUARTERS**
   330 Atlantic Ave   33444
   305 272-8668
Types & Periods: General
Line, Scrimshaw

**ALFRED COUSINS
ANTIQUES**
   130 N E 6th Ave   33444
   305 278-2098   Est: 1971
   Proprietor: Alfred Cousins
   Hours: Mon-Sat,
   sometimes Sun
Types & Periods: General
Line, Lamps, Clocks
Appraisal Service Available
   Directions: US Hwy 1

DANIELLE OF DELRAY INC
   343 NE 5th Ave   33444
   305 276-4532   Est: 1973
   Proprietor: Danielle Harris
   Hours: Daily, Nov-Apr
Types & Periods: 18th &
19th Century British
Porcelains & Pottery
   Directions: On Federal
   Hwy S; 4 Blocks N of
   Atlantic Ave

**DELRAY BEACH THIEVES
MARKET**
   2399 N Federal Hwy
                  33444
   305 732-3744
   Proprietor: David & Marion
   Davis
   Hours: Weekends, 9-5
Types & Periods: 75 Antique
Dealers under One Roof;
General Line
   Directions: On US 1, just
   above Delray Beach

Delray Beach   Cont'd

**FRANTIQUES BY FRAN &
ANN**
2213 N Federal Hwy 33444
305 968-8447
Hours: Fri, Sat & Sun in
Season
Types & Periods: Art Glass,
Jewelry, Furniture, Lamps,
Oriental Rugs, General Line
Directions: Delray Antique
Mall

GARRISON ANTIQUES
1201 N Federal Hwy 33444
305 278-9685   Est: 1972
Proprietor: Audrey Watts
Kelch
Hours: Daily
Types & Periods: General
Line
Specialties: Wicker
Directions: On Rte 1

LUCILLE'S ANTIQUES
328 E Atlantic Ave   33444
305 272-4477
Hours: Daily, 10-5
Types & Periods: General
Line
Specialties: Porcelain,
Miniatures on Ivory

MATTIE'S ANTIQUES
2213 N Federal Hwy 33444
305 427-2081
Types & Periods: Depression
& Carnival Glass, Old Lamps
& Shades, General Line
Directions: In Delray
Antique Mall

THE PICKET FENCE
2213 N Federal Hwy 33444
305 272-4024
Hours: Mon-Sat, 10-5;
Sun 'til 9
Types & Periods: Furniture,
Collectibles, Jewelry
Directions: Delray Antique
Mall

**ST JAMES ENGLISH
ANTIQUES**
404 N E 2nd St   33444
305 278-4357   Est: 1972
Proprietor: Peggy
Johnston & Vera Nelson
Hours: Mon-Sat; By
Appointment

Types & Periods: Mainly
English Antiques; All Periods
Furniture, China, Glass,
Silver, Brass & Copper
Specialties: Brass & Copper
from England (English Tea
Shoppe adjoining)
Appraisal Service Available
Directions: Drive N from
Atlantic Ave 2 Blocks;
Traffic Light, take a L,
cross the Hwy; On the L

TAYLOR ANTIQUES
128 N E 6th Ave   33444
305 276-3344
Hours: Daily, 10-4:30
Types & Periods: Tiffany,
Quezel, Steuben, Durand
Glass, Silver, Bronze, Brass,
Furniture

TAYLOR MANTIQUES
210 N E 3rd Ave   33444
305 276-5237
Hours: Mon-Fri, 7-4:30,
Sat 'til Noon
Types & Periods: Trains,
Toys, Steam Engines,
Primitives, Cutlery, Guns,
Nautical, Brass, Bronze,
Collectibles

TREASURES OF TIME LTD
707 Bond Way, Box 1437
33444
305 272-7342   Est: 1974
Proprietor: Joe Emkjer
Hours: Oct-May, Mon-Sat,
10-5; June-Sept, Thurs-Sat
Types & Periods: General
Line
Specialties: Clocks, Repair,
Restoration, & Sale of
European Clocks
Appraisal Service Available
Directions: 1 Block off
Federal Hwy across from
Int'l Pancake House

Eaton Park

**THE CHEEK HOUSE
ANTIQUES**
Box C   33840
813 686-2313
Proprietor: Betty L Cheek
Hours: Tues-Sat, 10 5;
Sun & Mon by Chance
Types & Periods: Glass,
China, Furniture, Primitives
Directions: US 98 at 33 A,
1 Mile S of Lakeland

Eustis

BLUE FROG ANTIQUES
23 Orange Ave   32726
904 357-1569   Est: 1960
Proprietor: Lea Rader
Hours: Daily
Types & Periods: Furniture
1800-1920; Primitives,
Collectibles, Oriental,
Pattern & Cut Glass, China,
Lamps
Appraisal Service Available
Directions: Heart of Eustis,
32 Miles N of Orlando

BLANCHE M WILDER
315 W Charlotte Ave
32726
305 357-2801
Proprietor: Blanche M
Wilder
Hours: Daily
Types & Periods: Art Glass,
China, Jewelry
Directions: W of Orange
City on US Hwy 92

Fern Park

**MONTGOMERY'S
ANTIQUES**
Hwy 17/92, Box 34 32730
305 339-1999
Hours: Sun-Fri
Types & Periods: Early
American & Period Furniture
Directions: Between
Winter Park & Casselberry

Fort Lauderdale

**FORT LAUDERDALE
CLUSTER**
Directions: Heavy Cluster
on S Federal Hwy
(1000-2000 Blocks) to N
Federal Hwy (800-3000
Blocks), E Las Olas Blvd
(700-2000 Blocks), Davie
Blvd (2000-3000 Blocks)

**AMERICANA GALLERIES
INC**
4307 N Federal Hwy
33308
305 771-8447
Types & Periods: Paper
Money, Autographs, Prints,
Documents, Stocks, Bonds,

Maps, Medals, Civil War,
Jade, Ivory, Paintings,
Coins
   Directions: Room
   202-4 in the Colonial Bldg

THE ARGO GALLERY
   2497 Stirling Rd   33312
   305 961-9197
   Hours: Mon-Thurs, Sat,
   9-6; Fri, 9-9
Types & Periods: Paintings,
Graphics, Prints, Sculpture,
Silver
   Specialties: Silver, Jewish &
   Israeli Artists, Objets d'Art

ARTS & TREASURES
   4250 Galt Ocean Dr
                        33308
   305 564-5566
   Proprietor: Mrs. S H
   Nordlinger
   Hours: By Appointment
Types & Periods: French
Furniture, European
Porcelains

AVENUE ANTIQUES
   637 N E 3rd Ave   33304
   305 763-5294   Est: 1960
   Proprietor: Mr & Mrs J
   Nelson Wagner
Types & Periods: General
Line, Crystal & Art Glass,
Jewelry
   Directions: 6 Blocks from
   Center of Ft Lauderdale

**BASS & HOLBROOK
ANTIQUES**
   2128 S Federal Hwy
                        33316
   305 525-7072   Est: 1956
   Proprietor: Paul E Bass
   Hours: Daily; By
   Appointment, by Chance
Types & Periods: General
Line, Silver, Porcelain,
Oriental, Art Glass, Furniture
Appraisal Service Available
   Directions: Rte US 1 is S
   E 6th Ave

BRASS BEDS LTD
   5551 N State Rd 7   33313
   305 484-7730
   Hours: Mon-Sat, 10-5:30
   Specialties: Brass Beds

CARS UNLIMITED
   701 N Federal Hwy   33304
   305 764-1400

Types & Periods: Classic &
Special Interest Cars &
Parts
   Directions: US 1

D S CLARKE
   1880 S Federal Hwy
                        33316
   305 523-2278   Est: 1935
   Proprietor: D S Clarke
   Hours: Daily
Types & Periods: General
Line
   Specialties: Nautical Items
Appraisal Service Available
   Directions: Fed Hwy 1 & S
   19th

**CLIFF'S COINS &
COLLECTIBLES**
   1137 S Federal Hwy
                        33316
   305 527-1992
Types & Periods: US &
Foreign Coins, General Line,
Indian Relics

DAVID "A" MUSEUM
   P O Box 2352   33316
   305 524-3465   Est: 1960
   Proprietor: David A
   Jacobson
   Hours: Mon-Sat; By
   Appointment (524-3465
   Evenings)
Types & Periods: Antique
Cars, Toys, Banks, Music
Boxes. Political, Edged
Weapons, Guns, Coins,
Paper Currency, Military,
Advertising, Negro Items,
Indian Relics, Restraints,
Marbles, Radio Premiums,
Coin Operated Machines,
Beer Cans, Thimbles, Dolls
   Specialties: Unusual
   Collectors Items
Appraisal Service Available
   Directions: 2 Blocks N of
   State Rd 84, 1 Mile N of
   Ft Lauderdale Int Airport
   2132 S Federal Hwy
   (US 1)

**FORT LAUDERDALE
RESTORING & TRADING
ASSOCIATION**
   186 NE Prospect Rd
                        33334
   305 564-4731
   Hours: Mon-Fri, 10-4;
   Sat, 9-12

Types & Periods: General
Line, Collectibles,
Bric-a-Brac

**JEFF GLAUSIER'S
ANTIQUE SHOPPE**
   2102 SE 6th Ave   33316
   305 524-3524   Est: 1968
   Proprietor: Marge & Jeff
   Glausier
   Hours: Daily, 11-6; By
   Appointment
Types & Periods: Victoriana,
Lamps, Phonographs, Art &
Cut Glass
Appraisal Service Available
   Directions: 3 Blocks N of
   SR-84 on US 1

KARS CO
   3418 NE 2nd Ave   33334
   305 564-0098
   Specialties: Classic &
   Antique Auto Restoration

LAS OLAS FLEA MARKET
   304 SE 11th Ave   33301
   305 462-8078
   Hours: Daily, 10-4
Types & Periods: General
Line
Appraisal Service Available

Y K MA & SONS INC
   3361 NE 33rd St   33308
   305 564-4804
Types & Periods: Chinese
Art Objects, Accessories,
Furniture, General Line
   Directions: On Galt Ocean
   Mile

MAC'S
   219 SW 1st Ave   33301
   305 462-1933
Types & Periods: Silver, Old
Jewelry, Diamonds, General
Line

RON MALOUF ANTIQUES
   2114 S Federal Hwy
                        33316
   305 527-4829   Est: 1965
   Proprietor: Ron Malouf
   Hours: Daily
Types & Periods: Jewelry,
China, Glass, Silver,
Furniture
   Directions: N of St Rd 84

(From page 63)
there were three Kings George on the throne of England. An advanced collector might look for small details that would characterize a piece as distinctly from one particular George, but to the average collector it is simply a term that applies to English furniture of the whole period. It is an excellent name to remember and have available for use. Furniture of these early periods was usually custom produced. A customer might go to a cabinet shop and possibly say, "I want a chair with a Queen Anne back and Chippendale legs." The cabinetmaker might protest that he would be combining various styles. The customer might reply, "I don't mind. That is what I want. I am paying for it, so make me what I ask." The cabinetmaker, having to earn his living, would yield and produce the hybrid design. We as modern collectors seeing this chair with the characteristics of two well known periods wouldn't really know by which period to call it. It wouldn't be necessary to display our confusion to everyone around us. We may stand with confidence and simply refer to that chair as a fine example of the "Georgian period".

In the last half of that time the Golden Age of furniture bloomed magnificently. It was the age of great furniture makers such as Chippendale, Sheraton and Hepplewhite. It was a zenith in elegant designs, exotic woods, the finest of detail and superb craftsmanship.

Thomas Chippendale received prominence through the publication in England of his book *Gentleman and Cabinet-maker's Directory* in 1762. It was filled with beautiful designs for the Georgian homes of the last half of the 18th Century and is still being reprinted. The styles are as crisp and exciting now as when they first appeared. They remain unexcelled. He was the first to use mahogany to any great extent. Both in England and America, mahogany then came to be imported in greater quantities for use in executing his designs. Chippendale's early period is characterized by using the Queen Anne styles, but embellishing them to achieve more decorative feeling. As an example, he placed acanthus leaves or a shell on the knee of the Queen Anne cabriole leg and replaced its padded foot with a ball and claw motif. (See page 97). After having added carving all over the chairs, he began piercing the splats of their backs as well. This approach may be seen in his famous "ribbon back" chairs. He emphasized the bracket base on case goods and introduced the ogee bracket base. (See page 160). He introduced the serpentine-front cabinet and fine carving emphasizing the "C" curve. In his later years, (Continued, page 212).

Fort Lauderdale   Cont'd

**MITCHELL'S HOUSE OF
ANTIQUES &
COLLECTIBLES**
2126 S Federal Hwy
                     33316
305 523-0483
Types & Periods: Diamonds,
Watches, Clocks, Toys, RR
Memorabilia, Model Ships

OLD FEDERAL SHOP
2130 S Federal Hwy
                     33316
305 523-1345
Proprietor: Louis E Ahlen '
Hours: Mon-Sat, Noon-5
Types & Periods: Toys,
Mechanical Banks, Political,
Edged Weapons, Military,
Advertising, Dolls, Beer
Cans, Coins, Radio
Premiums, Indian Relics,
General Line
Directions: US 1

DAVID PEPPER LTD
2214-18 S Federal Hwy
                     33316
305 525-3729
Types & Periods: China,
Bric-a-Brac, Furniture,
Paintings, Oriental Rugs,
Silver, General Line
Appraisal Service Available

H M POLINER ANTIQUES
2067 S Federal Hwy
                     33316
305 523-4633   Est: 1961
Proprietor: H M Poliner
Hours: Mon-Sat, 10-5
Types & Periods: 18th &
19th Century French,
English, American, Oriental
Furniture & Accessories,
Paintings, Rugs, Ivories,
Jewels
Specialties: Chandeliers,
Enamels
Appraisal Service Available
Directions: 1 1/2 Miles N
of Ft Lauderdale Airport
on US 1

JASON REISS ANTIQUES
703 East Las Olas Blvd
                     33301
305 467-1031   Est: 1967
Proprietor: Jason Reiss
Hours: Daily

Types & Periods: Jewelry,
French & Oriental Porcelains
& Enamels, Clocks,
Paintings, Furniture, Bronzes
Directions: Between US 1
& AIA Ocean Blvd

ROSS-PLUMMER LTD
2909 E Commercial Blvd
                     33308
305 491-4060   Est: 1975
Proprietor: Patricia Ross &
Ann Plummer
Hours: Mon-Sat, 10-5,
Other times by
Appointment
Types & Periods: General
Line, Concentration on
English Pottery & Porcelain;
18th & 19 Century Furniture
Specialties: American &
English Pewter,
Appraisal Service Available
Directions: E off I-95 at
Commercial Blvd Exit,
almost to Intracoastal on
N side of St

**JOHN R SELL ASSOCIATES
INC**
920 E Las Olas Blvd
                     33301
305 463 6436   Est: 1966
Proprietor: John Sell
Hours: Mon-Fri; Sat by
Appointment
Types & Periods: French &
Early American Accessories,
Silver, Bronze Dore,
Scrimshaw, Leather Books,
Furniture, Oriental, Nautical
& Primitive
Appraisal Service Available
Directions: Between
Beach & Downtown

R SINES ANTIQUES
1233 E Las Olas Blvd
                     33301
305 463-2489   Est: 1941
Proprietor: Ron & Virginia
Sines
Hours: Daily
Types & Periods: 18th
Century Furniture, Paintings,
Oriental Rugs, Silver, Glass,
China, Collectibles
Specialties: Furniture,
Paintings
Appraisal Service Available
Directions: 6 Blocks E of
US 1 Tunnel

**TREASURES OF THE
WORLD INC**
2215 S Federal Hwy
                     33316
305 522-3095   Est: 1961
Hours: By Chance
Types & Periods: China,
American Sterling
Specialties: Haviland China

**ED TURNER'S GUN
TRADING POST**
4139 N Dixie Hwy   33334
305 565-0768
Proprietor: Ed Turner
Hours: Daily, 10-6, Fri 'til 9
Types & Periods: Guns,
Collectibles

VANTIQUES
3020 N Federal Hwy
                     33306
305 564-8237
Hours: Mon-Sat,
10:30-4:30
Types & Periods: General
Line, Collectibles, Furniture
Directions: No 9 Times Sq

Fort Myers

**PALM BEACH BLVD FLEA
MARKET**
4852 Palm Beach Blvd
                     33905
813 694-4743   Est: 1970
Proprietor: Barbara Felske
Hours: Wed-Fri; Outside
Dealers on Weekends
Directions: 4 Miles from
Downtown on Rte 80

PURPLE BARN ANTIQUES
2320 Cleveland Ave
                     33901
813 334-4852   Est: 1959
Proprietor: Yvonne
Salvesen
Hours: Mon-Fri, 9-4; Sat,
9-12
Types & Periods: General
Line
Directions: US 41 S of Old
Fort Myers

TURSCHWELL ANTIQUES
2124 1st St   33901
813 334-4325
Proprietor: Mrs Mary
Turschwell
Hours: Daily

TURSCHWELL ANTIQUES
Cont'd
Types & Periods: General
Line, Furniture, Porcelain,
Glass, Silver, Jewelry,
Oriental Art Objects,
Collectors Items
  Directions: Downtown
  between Monroe &
  Broadway, 1st St is the
  Main Downtown St

Fort Myers Beach

THE ANNEX ANTIQUES
  1051 San Carlos Blvd
                    33931
  813 463-4355   Est: 1968
  Proprietor: Marion Potter
  & Barbara Dyer
  Hours: Daily
Types & Periods: General
Line
Appraisal Service Available
  Directions: "On main road
  to beach"

Fort Walton Beach

RUTH BAILEYS ANTIQUES
  136 Miracle Strip Pkwy
  NW   32548
  904 244-2424   Est: 1963
  Proprietor: Ruth Bailey
  Hours: Daily, 10-5
Types & Periods: Art Glass,
Porcelain, Silver
Specialties: Victorian
Furniture
Appraisal Service Available
  Directions: Downtown on
  Hwy 98; Between
  Pensacola & Panama City

Gainesville

THEN & NOW SHOP
  P O Box 94   32602
  904 372-1682   Est: 1961
  Proprietor: Eugene W
  Barnes
  Hours: By Appointment;
  May be out of town during
  show
Types & Periods: General
Line

Goulds

TRASH & TREASURE
HOUSE INC
  22601 US Hwy 1   33170
  305 247-3127   Est: 1965
  Proprietor: Chuck
  Bannister ·
  Hours: Mon-Sat, 9-5:30
Types & Periods: Glass,
China, Furniture, Collectibles
Appraisal Service Available
  Directions: 7 Miles N of
  Homestead on US 1

Greenville

BERMUDA HOUSE
ANTIQUES
  US Hwy 90   32331
  904 948-6831   Est: 1971
  Proprietor: Robert M
  Spieker
  Hours: Daily, 9-5
Types & Periods: General
Line
  Directions: 40 Miles E of
  Tallahassee; 1 Mile W of
  Greenville (Greenville Exit
  of I-10)

Haines City

THE CALICO CAT
ANTIQUES
  106 S First St   33844
  813 422-3752
  Proprietor: Billie O Loucks
  Hours: Sat-Mon, Wed &
  Thurs; Tue & Fri by
  Chance
Types & Periods: General
Line

Hialeah

HIALEAH CLUSTER
  Directions: Many Antique
  Shops; Heaviest
  Concentration on NE 2nd
  Ave (1000-8000 Blocks),
  Coral Way (2000 Block),
  Bird Ave (3000 Block)

JERRY'S COIN SHOP
  170 Hialeah Dr   33010
  305 887-6873
  Hours: Daily, 9:30-5

Types & Periods: Coins,
Stamps, Miniatures on Ivory,
Watches, Bronzes, US &
Foreign Paper Money,
Political Americana

Hobe Sound

WILLIAM D HOCKER, INC
  P O Box 746   33455
  305 546-7007   Est: 1968
  Proprietor: William D
  Hocker
  Hours: Mon-Sat, Late Dec
  to Early April
Types & Periods: Marine
Antiques, 18th Century
Copper & Brass, Georgian
Furniture
  Directions: Corner of A1A
  & Olympus, Hobe Sound

Hollywood

ALFREDO'S ANTIQUES
  2832 Stirling Rd   33020
  305 925-7410
  Hours: Daily
Types & Periods: Furniture,
Bric-a-Brac, Paintings,
Clocks, General Line
  Directions: 1 Block E of
  I-95

Homestead

BARGAIN BARN
FURNITURE INC
  28610 SW 192 St   33030
  305 248-1624   Est: 1957
  Proprietor: Joe M Page
  Hours: Mon-Sat
Types & Periods: General
Line
Appraisal Service Available
  Directions: 3 Miles N of
  Homestead & 25 Miles S
  of Miami on US 1

Jupiter

EARLY ATTIC
  1516 Cypress Dr   33458
  305 746-9418   Est: 1974
  Proprietor: Dorothy B
  Koster

Hours: Summer: Mon-Fri,
10-5; Oct-Apr: Mon-Sat,
10-5
Types & Periods: Primitives,
Period Furniture; Pressed,
Art & Pattern Glass;
Porcelain, Spode
Specialties: Ceramics,
Furniture, Silver
Appraisal Service Available
Directions: Cypress Dr
Runs Parallel to Rte 1 & is
1st St past Railroad
Tracks; Turn W at Light
on Rte 1 & Tequesta Dr to
Cypress Dr

Key West

THE ANTIQUES SHOP
210 Duval St   33040
305 296-6700   Est: 1953
Proprietor: E P Brown
Hours: Daily
Types & Periods: General
Line
Directions: Main St

Lakeland

THE COUNTRY STORE
Lake Miriam Square
4814 S Fla Ave,   33803
813 646-9401   Est: 1978
Proprietor: William Van
Steenburg
Hours: Mon-Sat, 10-6
Types & Periods: Oak, Pine,
Advertising Items
Specialties: Amish Foods
Directions: S Florida Ave
is Rte 37

Lake Worth

**MARQUETTE'S GIFTS &
ANTIQUES**
18 South J St   33460
305 586-4570
Types & Periods: General
Line, Bric-a-Brac
Specialties: Arms

Largo

GULF ROYAL IMPORTS
13128 Indian Rocks Rd
                     33540
                Est: 1969
Proprietor: Jane Paulson
Hours: Daily
Types & Periods: European
Furniture, Far East Metals &
Porcelains
Specialties: Oriental
(Chinese Batik Prints)
Directions: 1 Mile S of
I-688

H & H ANTIQUES
11193 Seminole Blvd
                     33540
813 392-2076   Est: 1964
Proprietor: Harold A
Batsford
Hours: Mon-Sat
Types & Periods:
Chippendale, Victorian,
Music Boxes, Primitives,
Furniture, Glassware,
Bronzes, Guns, Clocks,
Buggies, Weathervanes,
Imports, General Line
Specialties: Nautical, Music
Boxes, Oriental Rugs, Period
Furniture
Appraisal Service Available
Directions: Between 110th
Ave & 114th Ave N

**THE MART (THE
BOULEVARD MART INC)**
106 W Bay Dr   33540
813 581-6940   Est: 1971
Proprietor: Dorothy L
Boxman
Hours: Tues-Sat, 9:30-4;
Sun, 12-4
Types & Periods: Glass,
Furniture, Primitives, China,
Jewelry
Appraisal Service Available
Directions: Located next
to Post Office

TRASH 'N TREASURES
12790 66th St N   33540
813 531-8072   Est: 1963
Proprietor: Richard F
Wacha & Albert Karsch
Hours: Tues-Sat
Types & Periods: General
Line, Collectibles
Specialties: Glass, Paintings
Appraisal Service Available
Directions: N of St
Petersburg; 1 1/2 Miles
from US 19

**THE WAGON WHEEL
ANTIQUES**
1203 Ridge Road SW
                     33540
813 584-3634   Est: 1949
Proprietor: Bruce W &
Carol Bechtel
Hours: Tues-Fri, 10-4; Sat
& Mon, by Appointment
Types & Periods: General
Line
Specialties: Refinishing
Appraisal Service Available
Directions: 1 Mile S of W
Bay Dr

Lutz

BISHOP'S ANTIQUES
18833 US 41   33549
813 949-3183   Est: 1972
Proprietor: Harry L Bishop
Hours: Daily, 10-5
Types & Periods: General
Line
Specialties: Furniture
Appraisal Service Available
Directions: Downtown Lutz

Maitland

SADLER'S ANTIQUES
201 W Horatio Ave   32751
305 644-2398
Hours: Daily
Types & Periods: Glass,
China, Furniture, Lamps
Directions: W at Royal
Castle, 1 1/2 Blocks off
Hwy 17-92

Malabar

**ANTIQUE & COIN
COLLECTORS MALL**
US 1   32935
305 724-0100   Est: 1970
Proprietor: Virginia
Matlock
Hours: Thurs-Tues, 10-5
Types & Periods: Coins,
Furniture, Art Glass, Silver,
Jewelry, Collectibles, Dolls,
Paintings
Appraisal Service Available
Directions: 5 Miles S of
Melbourne

ANTIQUE COLLECTORS MALL
US 1   32950
305 724-0100   Est: 1972
Proprietor: Bernard
Stadtmiller
Hours: Daily, 10-5
Types & Periods: Coins,
Postcards, Furniture, Gold,
Antique Jewelery, Orientals,
Porcelains, Art Glass, Etc
Specialties: Heisey & Art
Glass
Appraisal Service Available
Directions: 6 Miles S of
Melbourne

LYNN'S ANTIQUES
US Hwy 1   32950
305 724-2868   Est: 1973
Proprietor: A Lynn Charon
Hours: Daily
Types & Periods: Furniture,
Glass, Jewelry
Specialties: Glass (Art,
Depression, Occupied
Japan)
Appraisal Service Available
Directions: In Palm
Terrace Motel 6 Miles S of
Melbourne

Margate

THE ORIENTAL SHOP
PO Box 4095   33063
305 972-3201
Proprietor: Victor H Semet
Hours: By Appointment
Types & Periods: Chinese &
Japanese Pieces

Miami

MIAMI CLUSTER
Directions: Heavy
concentration throughout
city especially Coral Way,
NE 2nd Ave, Bird Rd, W
Dixie Hwy, Federal Hwy
N-S to Dania

ABACUS HOUSE HOBBIES
218 NE 1st Ave   33132
305 377-8700
Proprietor: G Raymond
Lyles
Hours: Daily

Types & Periods: Stamps,
Coins, Books, Sea Shells,
Comics, Post Cards, Medals,
General Line, Bottles,
Buttons

COLLECTORS' CORNER
2665 Cor of 27th Ave &
Coral Way   33145
305 854-6788
Hours: Daily, 10:30-3
Types & Periods: General
Line, Furniture, Jewelry,
Guns, Old Gold & Silver

COUNCIL LTD
2391 Coral Way   33145
305 854-6067
Hours: Mon-Sat, 10-4
Types & Periods: Furniture,
Glass, Paintings, Orientals,
Ceramics, Collectibles

CONNIE GEE'S ANTIQUES
1965 NW 193 Terrace
                     33055
305 624-9155   Est: 1965
Proprietor: Connie Gee
Hours: By Chance
Types & Periods: English
Items, Early Americana,
Jewelry, Collectibles
Directions: NW Miami
Gardens; Go N on NW
22nd Ave to 193 Terrace,
E to 1965

GREAT THINGS, INC
2333 Coral Way   33145
(SW 22nd St)
305 854-8273   Est: 1974
Proprietor: Joseph Hoyt,
Richard Troutner
Hours: Mon-Sat, 10-6, by
Appointment Sun
Types & Periods: Ceiling
Fans (antique & modern),
Brass Beds, Stained Glass
(panels & lamp shades),
Bathroom Items (sinks,
toilets, tubs), Oriental Rugs,
Roll-top Desks, Bookcases,
Office Equipment
Specialties: "Large stock of
genuine old ceiling fans,
expertly restored & repaired;
complete polishing &
electroplating service"
Directions: Rte I-95 S to
Rte 1 to SW 22nd Ave;
Turn R to Coral Way (SW
22nd); Turn L, in Second
Block on R

I CHING ORIENTAL ANTIQUE GALLERY
3035 Grand Ave   33133
305 448-3111   Est: 1971
Proprietor: M Frey
Hours: Daily
Types & Periods: All Periods
& Types of Oriental Art:
Japan, China, Tibet, India,
Southeast Asia
Specialties: Porcelains,
Cloisonne, Satsuma,
Netsuke, Bronzes, Jade,
Furniture, Silver
Appraisal Service Available
Directions: 10 Minutes S
of Downtown Miami in
Center of the Coconut
Grove Business Area

LAURAINE DESIGNS
130 NE 82 St   33138
305 758-7174   Est: 1959
Proprietor: Lauraine Dunn
Hours: Mon-Fri, 9:30-5;
Sat, 9:30-12
Types & Periods: French,
English, American, Oriental,
predominantly; German &
Russian when Available
Specialties: "Expert Witness,
Admitted to Courts of
Florida"
Appraisal Service Available
Directions: One-way
West-bound Arterial Feeds
to I-95; S Side of St

LIBERTY ANTIQUES COINS & STAMPS
1235 SW 8th St   33135
305 858-0522   Est: 1974
Proprietor: Luis Pita
Hours: Daily
Types & Periods:
Spanish-American War &
Civil War Items
Specialties: Post Cards,
Jewelry, Documents &
Medals
Appraisal Service Available

MAIN JEWELRY & TRADING CO
301 N Miami Ave   33128
305 374-4385   Est: 1962
Proprietor: Si Kaplan
Hours: Daily
Types & Periods: Jewelry,
Objets D'Art
Specialties: Jewelry
Appraisal Service Available
Directions: Center of
Downtown

ORIENTAL ACCESSORY HOUSE
2385 Coral Way 33145
305 854-7323 Est: 1959
Proprietor: Clifford M
Sundstrom
Hours: Daily, 10-4; Closed
Mon during Summer
Types & Periods: Oriental
Porcelains, Chinese
Furniture; 17th, 18th & 19th
Centuries
Appraisal Service Available
Directions: I-95 S to Miami
US 1; Left at SW 22nd
Ave to Coral Way, Left

PACKER'S ANTIQUES
7317 Collins Ave 33141
305 864-9112 Est: 1960
Proprietor: Morris & Della
Packer
Hours: Daily
Types & Periods: Victorian
Bric-a-Brac, Glass, China,
Bronzes
Directions: Main St on
Miami Beach & 73rd St

RIKKI'S STUDIO, INC
2256 Coral Way 33145
305 856-6741 Est: 1948
Proprietor: Mr & Mrs
Richard Wm Hall
Hours: Mon-Fri; Sat, 1/2
Day
Types & Periods: Oriental,
American, European
Furniture, Porcelain,
Painting, Art Objects,
African Art, Pre-Columbian
Specialties: Paintings,
Oriental Antiques; Restorers
of Art, Porcelain, Wood,
Paintings
Appraisal Service Available
Directions: Main
Thoroughfare, SW 22 Sts
& 22nd Ave

SIDNEY SCHAFFER ANTIQUES
2223 Coral Way 33145
305 856-6291
Proprietor: Barbara &
Sidney Schaffer
Hours: Mon-Sat, Except
Jun-Aug
Types & Periods: "Top
Quality Items from all
Periods"
Specialties: Leaded Glass
(Stained & Beveled), Sterling
Silver, Cloisonne
Appraisal Service Available

J WAYNE TAYLOR INC
3848 Bird Rd 33146
305 446-0152 Est: 1960
Proprietor: J Wayne Taylor
& Jay Rumbaugh
Hours: Mon-Sat, 9-5
Types & Periods: Paintings,
Furniture, Bric-a-Brac,
General Line
Appraisal Service Available
Directions: 2 Blocks W of
US 1; Between Coral
Gables & Coconut Grove

TIMACARTHY ANTIQUES
11958 W Dixie Hwy 33161
305 893-3441
Hours: Tues-Sat, 11-5
Types & Periods: Furniture,
Silver, China, Glassware,
Collectibles

TROPICAL TRADER
2600 Biscayne Blvd 33137
503 573-1885 Est: 1941
Proprietor: R C Kinsloe
Hours: Mon-Sat, 9-4
Types & Periods: Wood
Carvings, Masks, West
Coast Africa & New Guinea
Specialties: Arms & Armor,
Ceramics, Machinery, Coins
Appraisal Service Available
Directions: US Hwy 1, 20
Blocks N of Downtown

YE OLDE MANTEL SHOPPE
3800 NE 2nd Ave 33137
305 576-0225 Est: 1879
Hours: Daily, 9-5
Types & Periods: Marble &
Wood Mantels, Accessories

Miami Beach

CIRCLE ART & ANTIQUES
1014 Lincoln Rd Mall
33139
305 531-1859 Est: 1970
Proprietor: Sherna Brody
Hours: Mon-Fri, 9-4
Types & Periods: European,
Oriental, American
Accessories, Paintings,
Furniture; Oriental Rugs
Specialties: Decorative
Items, Bronzes, Jewelry
Directions: 2 Blocks off
Alton Rd on Lincoln Rd
Mall in 1000 Bldg; Main St

Micanopy

LEWIS ANTIQUES
32667
904 466-3061 Est: 1972
Proprietor: Sylva & Jerry
Lewis
Hours: Mon-Sat, 10-6;
Sun, 1-6
Types & Periods: General
Line
Directions: Center of
Micanopy

Mt Dora

ALEXANDRA'S ANTIQUES
132 W 5th Ave 32757
904 357-5691 Est: 1968
Proprietor: Ted & Grace
Gottfried
Hours: Mon-Sat; By
Appointment
Types & Periods: Pattern
Glass, Some Cut Glass,
Limoges, Haviland, Nippon,
Orientals, Sterling Flatware,
Jewelry, Primitives, Some
Furniture
Specialties: Dolls, Doll
Accessories & Doll Houses
Directions: 30 Miles NW of
Orlando on Rte 441

WILLIAM G SCHWAB ANTIQUES
426 N Donnelly St 32757
904 383-6030
Proprietor: William G
Schwab
Hours: Daily
Types & Periods: 10th &
19th Century Furniture,
Clocks, Oriental Rugs,
Glass, China, Silver
Directions: W of Orange
City

Mulberry

HAMMOCK'S ANTIQUES
Box 6 33860
813 425-2859
Proprietor: Frank &
Margaret Hammock
Hours: Daily
Types & Periods: China,
Lamps, Furniture, Primitives
Directions: Hwy 37 N,
Turn at Freezette, 1/2
Block

Naples

BARGAIN DEPOT
3315 Radio Rd   33940
305 774-2777   Est: 1968
Proprietor: T B Moore
Hours: Daily
Types & Periods: Eclectic,
Period 1830's, Victorian
Directions: Corner Airport
& Radio Rds; At Airport
Entrance

Nokomis

**COLONIAL ANTIQUES &
COLLECTABLES**
102 E Nippino Tr   33555
813 485-0195   Est: 1972
Proprietor: C M Koisa &
Frank Koisa, Jr.
Hours: Mon-Sat, 9:30-5;
Sun, 1-5
Types & Periods: 1881 to
Depression Era; Glass,
China, Primitives, Furniture
& Pottery
Specialties: Miniature Shop;
Doll Houses, Mini Electric &
Lumber, Accessories
Directions: Behind Service
Station, US 41 & Nippino
Trail East

**THE CONNOISSEUR'S
SHOP**
104 E Nippino Trail 33555
813 488-7516   Est: 1957
Proprietor: D R Lanius
Hours: Daily, also by
Appointment
Types & Periods: General
Line, 19th Century Furniture,
China, Glass, Silver
Appraisal Service Available

North Miami

ANTIQUE TREASURES
1695 NE 123rd St   33181
305 893-2291   Est: 1960
Proprietor: L Clark
Hours: Mon-Sat, 10-5, also
by Appointment
Types & Periods: General
Line
Specialties: Oil Paintings &
Porcelains
Appraisal Service Available

Directions: Near Fed Hwy
1 & Broad Causeway to
Miami Beach

**HOLBROOK ARMS
MUSEUM**
12953 Biscayne Blvd
                    33161
305 891-1806
Types & Periods: Military,
Collectible, Coins
Appraisal Service Available

**NORTH MIAMI ANTIQUE &
FURNITURE EXCHANGE**
1695 NE 123rd St   33181
305 893-2291   Est: 1961
Proprietor: Leonard Oleck
Hours: Mon-Sat, also by
Appointment
Types & Periods: General
Line
Specialties: Furniture
Appraisal Service Available
Directions: 4 Doors W on
Rte 1, near Broad
Causeway to Miami Beach

**BLISS VAN DEN HEUVEL
ANTIQUES**
12740-50 W Dixie Hwy
                    33161
305 891-7662
Hours: Daily, 10-9
Types & Periods: "Oldies
But Goodies"
Appraisal Service Available

Ocala

THE ANTIQUE MUSEUM
1525 NE 22nd Ave   32670
904 732-2194   Est: 1974
Proprietor: Bob & Joyce
Alabeck
Hours: Mon, Tues,
Thurs-Sat, 10:30-5
Types & Periods: General
Line
Specialties: Stoneware,
Music Boxes, Phonographs,
Primitives
Appraisal Service Available
Directions: I-75 to Rte 40
to 25th Ave; N to 14th St,
L to 22nd Ave

THE GREEN DOOR STORE
30 SE Wenona Ave 32670
904 629-3642   Est: 1965
Proprietor: W F &
Margaret Sterchl

Hours: Mon-Sat
Types & Periods: General
Line
Specialties: Primitives
Appraisal Service Available
Directions: 3 Doors off
Silver Springs Blvd

Oneco

R W MADDOX
5305 15th St E   33507
813 755-9103   Est: 1967
Proprietor: Dick & Mae
Maddox
Hours: Mon-Sat, 9:30-5
Types & Periods: General
Line
Directions: Hwy 301, 3
Miles S of Bradenton;
Corner of 301 & 53rd Ave
E at Traffic Light

Orange City

**THE CARRIAGE WHEEL
ANTIQUES**
P O Box 7   32763
904 775-2231   Est: 1961
Proprietor: Helen
O'Connor
Hours: Daily, Except when
away buying in Oct
Types & Periods: General
Line, Furniture, Art &
Pressed Glass, Orientals,
Collections of Goss
Miniatures, Christmas
Plates, Open Salts, China
Appraisal Service Available
Directions: 2 Blocks E of
Hwys 17 & 92, Corner of
Oak & Graves

GRINDOL'S ANTIQUES
651 S Volusia   32763
904 775-4848   Est: 1969
Proprietor: J T & S D
Grindol
Hours: Tues-Sat
Types & Periods: General
Line
Specialties: Victorian
Appraisal Service Available
Directions: On Hwy
17 & 92

Orange Springs

JULE'S ANTIQUES
P O Box 37   32682
904 546-5491   Est: 1963
Proprietor: Juliana M
Chapman
Hours: Sun, Wed & Fri,
also by Appointment
Types & Periods: Cut & Art
Glass, 19th Century
Furniture, Hand Painted
China, General Line
Specialties: Toby Mugs &
Figurines
Appraisal Service Available
Directions: 22 Miles N of
Silver Springs, on Rte 315

Orlando

ANTIQUE ACCENTS
2900 N Orange Ave
                        32804
305 898-4962   Est: 1970
Proprietor: William & Ed
Lewis
Hours: Mon-Sat, 9-5
Types & Periods: General
Line, American & European
Furniture
Specialties: Furniture, Glass
Appraisal Service Available
Directions: Off I-4

COAT OF ARMS
1213 N Orange Ave
                        32804
305 898-2066   Est: 1975
Proprietor: Joan McDaniel
Hours: Mon-Sat, 9-6
Types & Periods:
Collectibles; a Bit of
Everything
Specialties: Primitives
Appraisal Service Available
Directions: Exit I-4 at
Princeton, E to Orange, R
Turn on Orange; Approx
1/2 Mile to Ivanhoe
Antique Row

CORDELIER ANTIQUES
3414 Fairway Lane   32804
305 423-7789
Hours: Mon-Sat, also by
Appointment
Types & Periods:
Pre-Columbian to Pre-War
Specialties: "Dog Antiques"
Appraisal Service Available

HANCOCK'S ANTIQUES
715 N Garland Ave   32801
305 425-7914
Proprietor: Billie Hancock
Hours: Daily
Types & Periods: Furniture,
Glass, China, Silver, Jewelry
Directions: Rtes 50 & I-4

**DOROTHY HICK'S
ANTIQUES**
5644 Edgewater Dr   32803
305 298-7210
Proprietor: Dorothy Hick
Hours: Daily
Types & Periods: Furniture,
Silver, China, Glass

**IVANHOE ANTIQUE
MINI-MALL**
1219 N Orange Ave
                        32804
                        Est: 1976
Proprietor: 15 Dealers
Hours: Mon-Sat; Dec-Mar,
Sun 1-5
Types & Periods: English
Furniture & Accessories,
Orientals, General Line
Specialties: 18th & 19th
English Furniture, 19th
Century English Copper &
Brass
Appraisal Service Available
Directions: Ivanhoe Blvd
Exit off I-4, 2 Minutes
away

**THE POTPOURRI ANTIQUE
SHOP**
1217 1/2 N Orange Ave
                        32801
                        Est: 1975
Proprietor: June Williams
Hours: Mon-Sat, 10-4
Types & Periods: Furniture,
Collectibles, Orientals,
Jewelry, Bric-a-Brac
Specialties: English Items
Directions: On Ivanhoe
Antique Row

**THE POTPOURRI ANTIQUE
SHOP**
5644 Edgewater Rd   32810
305 843-3493   Est: 1975
Proprietor: June Williams
Hours: Mon-Sat, 10-4
Types & Periods: General
Line
Directions: I-4 to Lee Rd,
W to Edgewater Dr, N to
5644; On L Hand Side

MARIAN SMITH ANTIQUES
1115 N Mills Ave   32803
305 896-7251
Proprietor: Marian Smith
Hours: Daily
Types & Periods: Small
Items, General Line
Directions: Frame
Bungalow, Hwy 17-92

WESCHE'S ANTIQUES
480 N Orange Ave   32801
305 425-6481   Est: 1942
Proprietor: Charlotte E
Wesche
Hours: Mon-Fri, 9:30-5
Types & Periods: General
Line
Specialties: Matching
Service in Sterling Flatware
Appraisal Service Available

Ormond Beach

LONDON SHOP
1224 Ocean Shore Blvd
                        32074
904 677-5056   Est: 1947
Proprietor: Tony Brennan
Hours: Daily, 9-5; Also by
Appointment
Types & Periods: Victorian,
Jewelry, Silver, Paintings,
Orientals, Furniture, Cut
Glass
Specialties: Imports
Appraisal Service Available
Directions: 2 Miles N of
Ormond Beach, in
Ormond Mall Shopping
Center

**SURFVIEW ANTIQUES &
UNIQUE NAUTICALS**
2120 Ocean Shore Blvd
                        32074
904 672-1853   Est: 1951
Proprietor: Muriel DeLucia
& Lance Lenart
Hours: Mon-Sat, 9-6;
Sun, 12-6
Types & Periods: General
Line, "From Tiffany &
Diamonds to everyday
collectibles"
Specialties: Nautical
Appraisal Service Available
Directions: 6 Miles N of
Daytona on A1A on the
Oceanfront

Palm Beach

ANTIQUE MEISSEN
16 Viamizner   33480
305 655-2193   Est: 1970
Proprietor: Lee & George
Ionescu
Hours: Daily, 10-5
Types & Periods: 18th &
19th Century Porcelain
Specialties: Meissen &
Derby
Appraisal Service Available
Directions: Off Worth Ave

THE ELEPHANT'S FOOT
116 N County Rd   33480
305 832-0170   Est: 1959
Proprietor: Marvin H Ray
Hours: Mon-Sat, Oct-Jun;
By Appointment, Jun-Oct
Types & Periods: 18th &
19th Century Furniture,
Oriental Rugs, Paintings,
Silver, Porcelains, Jewelry
Appraisal Service Available

HARTMAN GALLERIES INC
234 Worth Ave   33480
305 655-6114   Est: 1969
Proprietor: Alan Hartman
Hours: Daily
Types & Periods: English
Silver, Porcelains, Oriental
Art Objects, Jade, Furniture
Specialties: Chinese Snuff
Bottles, Netsuke
Appraisal Service Available

DOUGLAS LORIE, INC
334 Worth Ave   33480
305 655-0700   Est: 1934
Proprietor: Charles P
Muldoon
Hours: Mon-Fri, 10-5
Types & Periods: Silver,
Porcelain, Crystal
Specialties: Dorothy Doughty
Birds, Royal Worcester,
Cybis Porcelains
Appraisal Service Available

BRIAN RIBA GALLERY
308 Peruvian Ave   33480
305 655-1067
Proprietor: Brian Riba
Types & Periods: American
Paintings, Folk Art, Pottery

STARITA ANTIQUES
313A Peruvian Ave 33480
305 655-1879   Est: 1949
Proprietor: Rudy Starita
Hours: Daily

Types & Periods: English,
French & European
Porcelains, Bric-a-Brac,
Silver, Wedgwood, Chinese
Export
Specialties: Chinese Export
Appraisal Service Available
Directions: "Next St from
Worth Ave"

YETTA OLKES ANTIQUES
255 Sunrise Ave   33480
305 655-2800   Est: 1947
Proprietor: Yetta Olkes
Hours: Daily
Types & Periods: General
Line, 18th & 19th Century
Appraisal Service Available
Directions: Near St
Edwards Church

Palmetto

COUNTRY FAIR
P O Box 609   33561
813 722-5633   Est: 1967
Proprietor: Col Roland &
Col Jan Creel
Hours: Sat, Sun & Wed
Types & Periods: General
Line
Appraisal Service Available
Directions: 30 Miles S of
St Petersburg on US 301
at US 41

**GILMORE'S HOUSE OF
TREASURES**
Rte 1, Box 90   33561
813 722-3650   Est: 1965
Proprietor: Duane & Mary
Gilmore
Hours: Mon-Sat, Closed
Holidays
Types & Periods: General
Line
Directions: Hwy 41 at Jct
19 N

Panama City

**ST ANDREW ANTIQUE
SHOP**
1428 Beck Ave   32401
904 763-3721   Est: 1965
Proprietor: Kate & Emily
Hobecht & Linda Hughes
Hours: Daily
Types & Periods: General
Line

Specialties: Cut & Art Glass,
Tiffany Style Lamps
Appraisal Service Available
Directions: On Business
98 in St Andrew

Pensacola

CLELAND ANTIQUES
412 E Zarragossa St
                    32501
904 932-9933   Est: 1959
Proprietor: Ora Lee
Cleland
Hours: Mon-Sat
Types & Periods: 18th
Century Americana,
Primitive & Formal
Appraisal Service Available
Directions: Seville Square

GARTH'S ANTIQUES
3930 Navy Blvd   32507
904 456-7192
Proprietor: Winston F
Garth, Jr
Hours: Mon-Sat
Types & Periods: 18th &
19th Century American
Country & Formal Furniture,
Guns, Brass Beds, Round
Oak Tables, Oriental Rugs
Specialties: Oak Furniture,
Oriental Rugs
Appraisal Service Available
Directions: Hwy Alternate
98, Approx 3 Miles from
Downtown

**HAMILTON HOUSE
ANTIQUES**
503 S Adams   32501
904 438-9350   Est: 1974
Proprietor: Lorene
Rodgers & Zelma Neal
Hours: Daily
Types & Periods: Primitives
& Country
Directions: Historic Seville
Square

VEAZIE'S ANTIQUE SHOP
1110 N Palafox   32501
904 432-7017   Est: 1973
Proprietor: Wm H Veazie
Hours: By Appointment,
by Chance
Types & Periods: Early
American, Primitives,
Copper, Brass
Specialties: Furniture
Appraisal Service Available
Directions: N on Rte 29

Plant City

HEIRLOOM ANTIQUES LTD INC
404 N Frontage Rd 33566
813 754-7070
Proprietor: Jas T Leigh
Hours: Daily, 9-5
Types & Periods: Furniture, American & Imports

Plantation

THE PURSE STRING
6931 1/2 W Broward Blvd
33317
305 792-6020
Hours: Mon-Sat, 10-5:30
Types & Periods: General Line, Jewelry, China, Crystal, Art Objects
Directions: Inside the Plantation Towne Mall

Pampano Beach

AUNT BESSIE'S
1320 S Dixie Hwy W
33060
305 942-8470
Hours: Daily, 11-5
Types & Periods: General Line
Specialties: Silver

BELL BOOK & CANDLE ANTIQUES
221 SW 6th St   33060
305 782-6508
Hours: Tues-Sat, 10-5
Types & Periods: Glass, China, General Line

COUNTRY COTTAGE ANTIQUES & GIFTS
1003 E Atlantic Blvd
33060
305 781-7990
Hours: Mon-Sat, 10-5
Types & Periods: Country, Early American, Primitive, Victorian Furniture, Bric-a-Brac, General Line

THE LAMP DOCTOR INC
4649 N Dixie Hwy   33060
305 946-6355
Hours: Tues-Fri, 9:30-5:30; Sat, 9:30-1

Types & Periods: Lamps, Chandeliers
Specialties: Glass, Shade & Chandelier Replacements

MAGIC DREAM CASTLES
1321 S Dixie Hwy E,
Suite 3E   33060
305 942-9620
Proprietor: Phyllis Tutor Malineux
Types & Periods: Art Nouveau, Art Deco, Oak Furniture
Specialties: Stained Glass Windows

NAUTICAL HOME FURNISHINGS INC
191 SW 11th Ave   33062
305 781-3650
Hours: Daily
Types & Periods: General Line

M P STUUT RARE COIN INC
12 NE 28th Ave   33060
305 785-0080
Hours: Daily, Sept 15-May 1
Types & Periods: Rare Coins & Currency
Directions: 28th at Atlantic Blvd

Port Orange

COLLECTOR'S SHOP, INC
708 Ridgewood   32019
904 761-0592   Est. 1970
Proprietor: W C Nacelli & W E King
Hours: Mon-Sat
Types & Periods: General Line, Jewelry, Clocks, Coins
Appraisal Service Available
Directions: US Hwy 1 in Downtown Port Orange

Princeton

CAMPBELL'S COUNTRY STORE
24847 South Dixie Hwy
33030
305 247-1024   Est: 1975
Proprietor: Joyce Olsen & Carol Campbell

Hours: Tues-Sat; 10-4, by Appointment
Types & Periods: American
Specialties: Glass
Directions: 25 Miles S of Miami on US 1

Reddick

WAYSIDE ANTIQUES, INC
RD 1 Irvine   32686
904 591-2001   Est: 1971
Proprietor: Thomas W Gates
Hours: Mon-Sat 9-5:30, Sun 10-5:30
Types & Periods: Imports from Many Countries Period to Quality Reproductions
Specialties: "The Unique in Antique Furnishings, Objects of Art, Jewelry"
Appraisal Service Available
Directions: 20 Miles S of Gainesville on I-75 at the Irvine Exit

Rockledge

VILLAGE TREASURE HOUSE
880 Searstown Plaza
32955
305 632-8320   Est: 1973
Proprietor: Doris Butcher
Hours: Mon-Sat, 10-5
Types & Periods: General Line
Directions: US 1 near Coooa & Space Ctr at Cape Kennedy

WOMAN'S EXCHANGE
20 Barton Ave   32955
305 636-2346
Proprietor: Bernice A Stefurak
Hours: Tues-Sat, 10:30-4:30; Sun & Mon by Appointment
Types & Periods: General Line
Directions: 2 Blocks E of US 1

St Petersburg

ST PETERSBURG CLUSTER
Directions: Central Ave
(900-7000 Blocks), 4th St
N (1000-5000 Blocks), 9th
St N (300-2000 Blocks)

**GRANDMA'S ATTIC
ANTIQUES**
716 2nd St N   33701
Est: 1969
Proprietor: Johnson &
Speakman
Hours: Mon-Sat, 10-5
Types & Periods: American,
Oriental, Continental
Specialties: Glass (Early
American)
Appraisal Service Available
Directions: 7 Blocks from
Downtown on 2nd St

JONATHAN'S ANTIQUES
7283 46th Ave N   33709
813 544-2075
Proprietor: Martin J &
Irene A Brice
Hours: Mon-Sat, 9-5
Types & Periods: Furniture,
Paintings, Primitives,
Caning, General Line

Sarasota

VIOLA MAYBERRY
2304 Ringling Blvd   33577
Est: 1955
Hours: By Appointment
Types & Periods: Art Glass,
Porcelain, China, 1800
Lamps
Appraisal Service Available
Directions: Off Rte
41 & 103

METHUSELAH'S ANTIQUES
322 S Washington Blvd
33577
813 366-2218   Est: 1973
Proprietor: John
Herschman
Hours: Mon-Sun 10-6
Types & Periods:
Turn-of-the-Century Oak &
Walnut Furniture, Primitives
Specialties: Oak Furniture
Appraisal Service Available
Directions: Washington
Blvd is Hwy 301

**JANET F POST JEWELRY
INC**
19 N Blvd of Presidents
33577
813 388-3979   Est: 1978
Proprietor: Janet F Post &
Carmen A Gianforte
Hours: Mon-Sat 10-5
Types & Periods: Jewelry,
Related Items, Estate &
Collectibles
Specialties: Gemology
Appraisal Service Available
Directions: Ringling
Causeway from Sarasota
Mainland to St Armands
Key

**THE YELLOW BIRD OF ST
ARMAND'S INC**
468 John Ringling Blvd
33577
813 388-1823   Est: 1970
Proprietor: Joann Carmel
& Hazel Glenn
Hours: Mon-Sat 11-5
Types & Periods: General
Line
Specialties: Toys, Miniatures
Directions: US 41 to John
Ringling Causeway to St
Armand's Circle

Sebring

ANTIQUES & THINGS
2249 Hwy 27 S   33870
813 385-8660   Est: 1970
Proprietor: Evelyn Morgan
Hours: Tues-Sun, Mon By
Chance
Types & Periods: Glass,
Furniture, Primitives, Jewelry
Specialties: Oriental
Appraisal Service Available
Directions: N of Southgate
Shopping Center on Hwy
27 S

**FOSTER'S TRADING
CENTER**
4803 Hwy 27 S   33870
813 385-5824   Est: 1972
Proprietor: Alma &
Benjamin Foster
Hours: Daily 10-5, Closed
Mon & Wed, Sun 12-5
Types & Periods: General
Line
Specialties: China, Glass,
Toys

Seminole

THE BUTERBAUGH'S
10,000 Park Blvd   33603
Est: 1946
Proprietor: The
Buterbaugh's
Hours: By Appointment,
By Shows
Types & Periods: Jewelry,
Paperweights, Art Glass,
Doulton Figurines & Jugs,
Postcards, Furniture,
Orientals
Specialties: Shows
Appraisal Service Available

Shalimar

ANTIQUES & UNIQUES INC
Box 15 Eglin Pkwy 32579
904 651-1931   Est: 1969
Proprietor: Geneva
utnam
Hours: Tues-Sat
10:30-4:30
Types & Periods: Americana
Appraisal Service Available
Directions: Near Ft Walton
Beach

South Miami

ANTIQUE PARADISE
5833 Sunset Dr   33143
305 666-1135   Est: 1974
Proprietor: Jim Wood
Hours: Mon-Sat 10:30-6,
Sun 1-5 During Season
Types & Periods: Clocks,
Furniture, American Brilliant
Cut Glass, Jewelry, China
Specialties: Cut Glass,
Clocks
Appraisal Service Available
Directions: 1 Block E of
US 1 (Dixie Hwy) on SW
72nd St (Sunset Dr)

JOAN FREDERICKS
5738 Sunset Dr   33143
305 665-0002   Est: 1976
Proprietor: Joan H Epstein
Hours: Tues-Sat 10:30-5
Types & Periods: Jewelry,
Nautical, 18th & 19th
Century English Furniture,
Boxes & Small Wood

Pieces, 18th & 19th Century
Glass Porcelain Pottery
(English & French)
Directions: Heart of City of
S Miami

GARDINER'S GARRET
5833 Sunset Dr   33143
305 666-1135   Est: 1969
Proprietor: C Barnes
Gardiner
Hours: Tues-Sat 12-5
Types & Periods: English &
American Furniture, Clocks,
Quilts, Brass, Copper, Iron,
Baskets, Primitives,
Pre-1850 Era
Specialties: Clocks, Quilts
Appraisal Service Available
Directions: Near Corner of
Red Rd & Sunset Dr

**GOLDEN HAND ANTIQUE
BOUTIQUE**
5841 SE 73rd St   33143
305 665-2492
Types & Periods: Ivory,
Silver, General Line, Jewelry

Surfside

DECOR INC
9446 Harding Ave   33154
305 866-0905   Est: 1956
Proprietor: Braddy
Bernstein
Hours: Mon-Sat
Types & Periods: Oriental &
European Antique
Accessories, 18th & 19th
Century Paintings &
Furniture
Specialties: Oriental
Embroideries on Silk
Directions: Btwn 94th &
95th Sts, 1 Block W of
Collins Ave on Harding

Tallahassee

YESTERYEAR SHOP
2906 Ivanhoe Rd   32303
904 385-2054   Est: 1969
Proprietor: Elizabeth
Shannon
Hours: By Appointment
Types & Periods: Colored
Glass, Small Items, China,
Brass, Iron
Appraisal Service Available

Tampa

TAMPA CLUSTER
Directions: Heavy
Concentration On El
Prado Blvd (4000 Block),
Along S MacDill Ave
(600-3000 Blocks)

BEAUFEL'S ANTIQUES INC
4243 El Prado Blvd   33609
813 839-0820   Est: 1963
Proprietor: Mr Joseph P
Bodo, Sr
Hours: Mon-Sat 8-5
Types & Periods: Furniture,
Crystal, China, Silver
Specialties: Furniture,
Oriental
Appraisal Service Available
Directions: Where El
Prado Intersects Dale
Mabry, 5 Blocks W

CHASE ANTIQUES
4307 El Prado Blvd   33609
813 837-2631   Est: 1968
Proprietor: Louise Chase
Hours: Tues-Sat 11-4:30
Types & Periods: European,
American, Collectibles, Early
20th Century Furniture
Specialties: Primitives
Directions: Bayshore Blvd
to El Prado Blvd Past Dale
Mabry Hwy to El Prado
Antique Ctr

**LARRY R ENGLE
ANTIQUES**
4303 El Prado Blvd   33609
813 839-0611   Est: 1968
Proprietor: Larry R Engle
Hours: Tues-Sat
10:30-4:30
Types & Periods: General
Line
Specialties: Jewelry, Silver,
Paperweights
Appraisal Service Available
Directions: W on El Prado
off S Dale Mabry Hwy, In
Tampa Antique Ctr

**GOLDEN EAGLE ANTIQUES
INC**
4328 El Prado Blvd   33609
813 839-0580   Est: 1965
Proprietor: Angela & Jim
Leigh
Hours: Mon-Sat 10:30-5

Types & Periods: General
Line, 18th & 19th Century
European & American
Furniture, Bric-A-Brac,
Paintings
Specialties: European
Porcelains, Art & Cut Glass,
Silver
Appraisal Service Available
Directions: SE Corner of
El Prado Blvd &
Manhattan Ave

GRANDMA'S PLACE
4305 El Prado   33609
813 839-7098   Est: 1965
Proprietor: Emily & Ashby
Moody
Hours: Daily
Types & Periods: General
Line
Specialties: Miniatures
Appraisal Service Available
Directions: In El Prado
Antiques Center

HENSEL'S ANTIQUES
2707 S MacDill Ave   33609
813 839-2900   Est: 1971
Proprietor: Richard &
Norma Hensel
Hours: Mon-Fri 10-5,
Sat 10-3
Types & Periods: General
Line, Primitives, Pattern &
Art Glass, China, Prints,
Paintings, Jewelry, Silver,
Furniture
Specialties: Clocks, Lamps
Appraisal Service Available
Directions: 3 Blocks N of
Bay to Bay Blvd

LA PETITE GALERIE INC
4245 El Parado Blvd
                     33609
813 839-2077
Proprietor: Helga L Zipser
Hours: Mon-Sat 10:30-5
Types & Periods: General
Line

LAW ANTIQUES
4321 El Prado Blvd   33609
813 839-7148   Est: 1971
Proprietor: Lloyd & Nikki
Wiggins
Hours: Mon-Sat 10:30-5
Types & Periods: General
Line
Specialties: English

Tampa Cont'd

MRS GEO A MC CLELLAND ANTIQUES
4521 Azeele St   33609
813 876-7395
Proprietor: Mr & Mrs
George A McClelland
Hours: By Appointment,
By Chance
Types & Periods: Art & Cut
Glass, China, Silver

O'NEIL ANTIQUE SHOP
2708 Gandy Blvd   33611
813 839-8053   Est: 1972
Proprietor: Helen O'Neil
Hours: Daily
Types & Periods: Grand Dad
Clocks from 1699,
Secretaries, Hutch's, Desks,
Lamps
Specialties: Oriental Rugs
Directions: Corner of
Gandy & Bayshore Blvd

PATRICIA'S ANTIQUES & GIFTS
2510 S MacDill Ave 33609
813 831-9671   Est: 1972
Proprietor: Patricia
Reynolds
Hours: Wed-Sat 10-4
Types & Periods: General
Line
Directions: S of Kennedy
Blvd & I-4, Palma Ceia
Area

SMITH'S TRADING POST
1781 W Hillsboro Ave
             33603
813 935-8889   Est: 1966
Proprietor: Mary B Smith
Hours: Daily 10-5:30
Types & Periods: General
Line
Appraisal Service Available
Directions: Btwn Rome &
Armenea on Hillsboro Ave

TAMPA'S ANTIQUES & COLLECTABLES
415 S Dale Mabry   33609
813 935-8889   Est: 1977
Proprietor: M Betty Smith
Hours: Mon-Fri, 10-5,
Sat, 10-3

Types & Periods: Glass,
China, Victorian Furniture,
Primitives, Pottery
Specialties: Complete
Estates Sold
Appraisal Service Available
Directions: 5 Blocks S of
Kennedy Blvd

A TIFANEY & SON
715 E Bird St   33604
813 935-0183   Est: 1964
Proprietor: Jay M
Weisman
Hours: Daily 9:30-4:30
Types & Periods: General
Line
Specialties: Jewelry, Silver
Appraisal Service Available
Directions: Pan American
Bank Bldg

TOP VALUE FLEA MARKET
8120 Anderson Rd   33614
813 884-7810   Est: 1968
Proprietor: H J Gardner
Hours: Sat & Sun
Types & Periods: 50 Antique
Dealers, Furniture,
Primitives, Glass
Appraisal Service Available
Directions: Corner of W
Waters Ave & Anderson
Rd

WALTER'S MEMORY LANE ANTIQUES
2202 S MacDill   33609
813 251-6004   Est: 1972
Proprietor: Verda & Walter
Horton
Hours: Mon-Sat 9-5, Sun
1-5, Also By Appointment
Types & Periods: General
Line
Specialties: Clocks
Directions: 2 Miles S of
Kennedy Blvd, Corner of
San Nicolas & MacDill

Tequesta

THE ADMIRALS ATTIC INC
354 Cypress Dr   33458
305 746-5610   Est: 1975
Proprietor: Jo Ann
Setterfield & Deborah
Gooch
Hours: Daily
Types & Periods: Stained
Glass Architectural Pieces,
Primitives, Stoneware, Brass

Beds, Nautical Pieces, Oak
Furniture, Wagons & Farm
Equipment
Directions: Take Tequesta
Dr Over the RR Tracks,
Make a Left on Cypress
Dr, Approx 1 Block on the
Left

THE DRUMMER BOY
385 Tequesta Dr   33458
305 746-4129   Est: 1969
Proprietor: Marion R
Alexander
Hours: Daily
Types & Periods: General
Line
Appraisal Service Available
Directions: N End Palm
Beach County, 4 Blocks W
of Rt 1, Gallery Sq N
Shopping Ctr

KATHRYN ROOS POTTS ANTIQUES
1615 Cypress Jupiter
             33458
305 746-0385   Est: 1965
Proprietor: Kathryn Roos
Potts
Hours: Tues-Fri, Also By
Appointment
Types & Periods: Furniture,
Accessories, Paintings

Treasure Island

ARTEMIS ANTIQUITIES
136 107th Ave   33740
813 367-3444   Est: 1967
Proprietor: Maj C H
Schroeder AUS Ret
Hours: Daily, Also By
Appointment
Types & Periods: Ancient
Greek & Roman Coins,
Pottery, Lamps, Statuettes
Specialties: Coins
Appraisal Service Available
Directions: Treasure Isle
Plaza Shopping Center
out Central from St
Petersburg

Warrington

GARTH'S ANTIQUES
   3930 Navy Blvd   32507
   904 456-7192
   Proprietor: Winston &
   Debby Garth
   Hours: Tues-Sun 10-5
   Types & Periods: General
   Line, Furniture, Glass,
   Oriental Rugs, Oils

West Palm Beach

ANTIQUE WAREHOUSE INC
   415 Belvedere Rd   33405
   305 659-7275
   Types & Periods: Furniture,
   Bric-A-Brac, Stained Glass
   Windows, General Line

Wildwood

THE CLAUSE HOUSE
   500 Gray Ave   32787
   904 748-1887
   Proprietor: Mrs A G
   Clause
   Hours: Daily
   Types & Periods: General
   Line
   Directions: From 301 Take
   Cleveland St, 8 Blocks
   Right on Gray

Winter Park

COBWEB ANTIQUES
   348 Park Ave N   32789
   305 647-5004
   Proprietor: R T
   Rademacher
   Hours: Daily
   Types & Periods: Porcelains,
   Metals, Colored Glass
   Directions: Hidden Park

FERRIS GALLERIES
   214 Park Ave N   32789
   305 647-0273
   Hours: Daily
   Types & Periods: European
   Directions: N of Orlando

Slipper
or shoe
foot

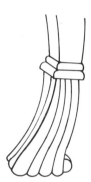

Brush
foot

Pad
foot

Trifid
or drake
foot

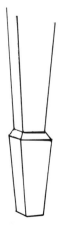

Spade
foot

STATE OF GEORGIA

Albany

RAY'S ANTIQUES
517 W Broad   31701
912 435-7333   Est: 1976
Proprietor: Ray Maltby
Hours: Mon-Sat
Types & Periods: American
& European Furniture
Specialties: Antique Wicker
Directions: Downtown, 1
Block N of US 319

Alpharetta

DIFFERENT THINGS INC
735 Midbroadwell Rd
                        30201
404 475-5961   Est: 1977
Proprietor: Ferne & Gene
Housel
Hours: Mon-Fri, 10-5; Sat,
10-6; Sun,1-6
Types & Periods: American
Primitive Oak, Pine, Walnut
& Cherry Furniture;
American & European
Copper & Brass
Specialties: Custom Building
of Lamps & Lamp Repairs,
Copper & Brass Polishing
Directions: 5 Miles N of
Roswell at Flashing Red
Light on Hwy 372

Athens

HOMEPLACE
1676 S Lumpkin St 30606
404 549-0829   Est: 1971
Proprietor: Barbara Fuller
Hours: Mon-Sat
Types & Periods: American
Country Pieces before 1900
Specialties: Southern
American Traditional
Handicrafts
Directions: 5 Points Area

Atlanta

ATLANTA CLUSTER
Directions: NE SECTION:
Peachtree Rd NE
(1000-5000 Blocks); Paces
Ferry Rd (100-500 Blocks);
Piedmont Ave NE
(1000-3000 Blocks);
DOWNTOWN: Peachtree
St NE (100 Block); Spring
St NW (1400 Block)

ALMARK JEWELRY MANUFACTURING & ANTIQUES
6075 Roswell Rd,
Suite 631   30328
404 252-1185   Est: 1970
Proprietor: Ida Geller
Hours: Daily
Types & Periods: Jewelry,
Restoration, Colored Stones
Specialties: Antique Jewelry
Repair
Appraisal Service Available
Directions: Take 285 to
Roswell Rd in Sandy
Springs, go N approx 1/2
Mile to C & S Bank Bldg

ANTHONY & STICKNEY
110 E Andrews Dr N W
                        30305
404 261-7546   Est: 1969
Proprietor: Paul Anthony,
Paul Stickney
Hours: Daily
Types & Periods: General
Specialties: English Pub
Tables
Directions: Cates Center,
2 Blocks from Governor's
Mansion

ANTIQUES LIMITED
511 E Paces Ferry Rd NE
                        30305
404 233-4672   Est: 1970
Proprietor: Vernon G
Abrams Jr
Hours: Mon-Fri, 10:30-5;
Sat, 1-5
Types & Periods: 18th &
19th Century English
Furniture & Porcelain,
Oriental Porcelain &
Accessories
Specialties: Oriental
(Porcelain)

Appraisal Service Available
Directions: Buckhead
Section between
Peachtree & Piedmont

ATLANTA ANTIQUES EXCHANGE
1185 Howell Mill Rd NW
                        30318
404 351-0727   Est: 1973
Proprietor: Alan Kolodkin
& Bob London
Hours: Mon-Sat, 10-5
Types & Periods: General
Line; English & Oriental 18th
& 19th Century Porcelain,
European Furniture
Specialties: Porcelain
Directions: Just N of the
Corner of 14th St &
Howell Mill Rd

BENCHMARK ANTIQUES
514 E Paces Ferry Rd NE
                        30305
404 261-3415   Est: 1972
Proprietor: Mrs James
Kincaid
Hours: Mon-Fri, 11-4;
Weekends by Appointment
Types & Periods: American
Country Pine & Cherry
Furniture, Pressed Glass,
Brass, Copper & Iron
Accessories
Specialties: Furniture
Directions: In Buckhead 1
Block off Peachtree Rd

SHARON BENNETT
3 Peachtree Ave NE 30305
404 233-0124   Est: 1973
Hours: Tues-Thurs, by
Appointment, by Chance
Types & Periods: Antique
Prints, Paintings, Southern
American Primitive Furniture
Specialties: Same
Directions: In Buckhead, R
off Peachtree Rd;
Restored Old House with
High Pickett Fence

LILA BENTON ANTIQUE DOLLS
311 A Lakemoore Dr NE
                        30342
404 252-6817   Est: 1956
Proprietor: Lila Benton
Hours: By Appointment,
By Chance

Types & Periods: Restore,
Buy, Sell Antique Dolls Only
Specialties: Dolls
Appraisal Service Available
Directions: 1 1/4 Blocks
from Roswell Rd;
Lakemoore Colony
Condominium 311A

THE BRASS GALLERY
2833 Peachtree St NE
30305
404 231-0887
Proprietor: Patti Crenshaw
Hours: Mon-Sat, by
Appointment
Types & Periods: Large
Selection of Brass Beds,
1880-1910; New
Reproductions Available
Specialties: Brass Beds
Directions: In Buckhead

**CABBAGES & KINGS
CONSIGNMENT SHOP**
5 Mountain St   30339
404 434-1228   Est: 1975
Proprietor: Mimi Ralls
Hours: Mon-Sat,
10:30-4:30; Sun, 2-5
Types & Periods: Many
Different Kinds Available
from 4 Shops: Cabbages &
Kings, Vinings Antique
Shop, The Designing Eye,
The Antiquary
Directions: Vinings Village,
NW of City of Atlanta

CAINS HILL, LTD
56 E Andrews Dr   30305
404 233-9489   Est: 1976
Proprietor: Ruth Siegel
Hours: Mon-Sat, By
Appointment, By Chance
Types & Periods: Mostly
Small Collectibles such as
Ivories, Porcelains, Crystal,
Objets d'Art
Appraisal Service Available
Directions: In Andrews Sq,
in the Heart of Buckhead
Andrews Dr Runs
between W Paces Ferry &
Roswell Rd

**THE CENTURY SHOP-
RENNAISSANCE BLDG**
3317 Piedmont Rd   30327
404 262-2634   Est: 1971
Proprietor: Jane S Taylor,
Caroline W Fowler
Hours: Tues-Sat, 11-5;
Sun, 1-5

Types & Periods: Furniture,
Brass, Crystal, Porcelain,
Silver
Directions: Near
Peachtree Intersection in
the Old R L Hope School
Bldg

**A COLLECTORS CHOICE
INC**
317 Buckhead Ave 30305
404 237-8871   Est: 1972
Proprietor: Dorothy
(Trotty) Miller
Hours: Mon-Sat; Sun by
Appointment
Types & Periods: Late 17th,
18th & Early 19th Century
English Antiques &
Accessories; some American
Furniture of 18th & 19th
Centuries; English &
Chinese Export Porcelains
Specialties: Chinese Export
Armorial Porcelain, Treen
Appraisal Service Available
Directions: 2 Blocks off
Peachtree Rd in Heart of
Buckhead Area

**COOK'S ANTIQUES &
STUFF**
111 Broad St SW   30303
404 524-9157   Est: 1945
Proprietor: Tom Cook
Hours: Daily
Types & Periods: General
Line
Directions: 4 Blocks from
Underground Atlanta

CRAWLEY STILES & MAY
288 E Paces Ferry Rd NE
30305
404 233-3598   Est: 1968
Proprietor: G Crawley, M
Stiles & A May
Hours: Mon-Sat, 10-5
Types & Periods: General
Line
Directions: Buckhead
Section, 1 1/2 Blocks off
Peachtree Rd

JOHN A DAVIS INC
3500 Peachtree St NE
30326
404 237-6751   Est: 1974
Proprietor: John A Davis
Hours: Daily
Types & Periods: Oriental
Porcelains, English &

American Furniture,
Paintings, Jewelry
Directions: Phipps Plaza,
Peachtree Rd NE

J H ELLIOTT ANTIQUES
537-39 Peachtree St NE
30308
404 872-8233   Est: 1922
Proprietor: J H Elliott Jr
Hours: Mon-Fri, 9:30-4:30;
and by Appointment
Types & Periods: Choice
18th & 19th Century
American & English
Furniture, Paintings,
Porcelain & Silver
Specialties: Fine Porcelains
& Silver, Furniture
Appraisal Service Available
Directions: Located in
Victorian Brick Mansion
on Peachtree St, 1 Block
Off I-85 and I-75, Exit
Peachtree St

**GALLERY OF
ARCHITECTURAL DETAIL
INC**
660 Ponce de Leon NE
30308
404 872-7834   Est: 1972
Proprietor: Kenneth A
McDonald
Hours: Mon-Sat, 9-4:30
Types & Periods:
Architectural Detail, Mantels,
Doors, Lighting, Windows
Hardware, Ornamental Iron,
Moldings, Stone Figures &
Fountains, Balusters, Accent
Pieces
Specialties: Hardware
Appraisal Service Available
Directions: In Central Part
of Town

GERALD'S ANTIQUES
490 E Paces Ferry Rd NE
30305
Est: 1973
Proprietor: Gerald R
Brown
Hours: Mon-Sat
Types & Periods: 18th &
19th Century English,
American, French & Chinese
Porcelain
Specialties: English
Porcelain
Directions: Between
Piedmont & Peachtree Rd

Atlanta   Cont'd

**GOLD'S ANTIQUES &
AUCTION GALLERY**
1149 Lee St SW   30310
404 753-1493   Est: 1967
Proprietor: Wilbur G Gold
Hours: Mon-Fri, 9-5:30;
Sat, 10-3:30
Types & Periods: English,
French, American
Specialties: Large
Commercial Type Antiques
for Offices, Restaurants,
Hotels, Etc
  Directions: SW Atlanta,
  1 1/2 Miles S of I-20 at
  Lee St Exit

HOLLAND & COMPANY INC
351 Peachtree Hills Ave
                       30305
404 233-2091   Est: 1971
Proprietor: H Leslie
Holland
Hours: Daily, 9-5
Types & Periods: 18th &19th
Century English &
Continental Furniture,
Porcelain, Rugs, Paintings,
Accessories
Specialties: Furniture
(English Walnut & Yew
Wood)
Appraisal Service Available
  Directions: Off Peachtree
  Rd in Residential Area

**INTERNATIONAL ART
PROPERTIES, LTD**
56 E Andrews Dr   30305
404 237-6990   Est: 1975
Proprietor: Ms Boone M
Smith
Hours: Mon-Sat
Types & Periods: Chinese
Porcelain, Jade, Bronzes,
Embroideries, Etc from the
Ming & Ch'ing Dynasties
Specialties: A very Broad
Selection of Chinese
Porcelain from the Ch'ing
Dynasty
  Directions: In NW Atlanta,
  Just off the Intersection of
  Roswell Rd, Peachtree Rd
  & W Paces Ferry

**KINGS & QUEENS
ANTIQUES**
514 E Paces Ferry Rd
                       30305
404 237-7980   Est: 1972
Proprietor: M J Hide

Hours: Mon-Sat, 10-5
Types & Periods: 17th, 18th
& Early 19th Century English
Furniture & Accessories
Specialties: Refinishing &
Restoration Service
Appraisal Service Available
  Directions: Corner of E
  Paces Ferry Rd &
  Maple Dr

JOSEPH KONRAD, INC
3278 Peachtree Rd 30305
Hours: Mon-Sat
Types & Periods: Furniture,
Porcelains, Lamps, Paintings
Specialties: Early 19th
Century English Porcelains
& Ironstone
  Directions: Buckhead

**THE LITTLE SHOPPE
(ANTIQUES), INC**
3174 Peachtree Rd, NE
                       30305
404 233-0060   Est: 1965
Proprietor: Leon E
Jackson, Jr
Hours: Mon-Sat, 10-5; Sun
by Appointment
Types & Periods: 18th &
Early 19th Century English &
American Furniture, Oriental
& English Porcelains &
Complimentary Accessories
& Furnishings
Specialties: Chinese Export
Porcelain, Staffordshire
Figures, American Quilts &
Baskets
  Directions: Buckhead
  Area; between West
  Paces Ferry Rd
  (Governor's Mansion) &
  Lenox-Phipps Shopping
  Center (Sak's Fifth
  Avenue & Neiman-Marcus)

**JANE J MARSDEN
ANTIQUES & INTERIORS**
2299 Peachtree St NE
                       30309
                  Est: 1975
Proprietor: Jane Marsden
Hours: Daily
Types & Periods: 18th &
19th Century English &
Continental Furniture,
Paintings, Porcelain
Specialties: English &
Chinese Export Porcelain
Appraisal Service Available
  Directions: Between
  Downtown & Buckhead

THE MAXWELL HOUSE
1385 Spring St NW 30309
404 876-0194   Est: 1975
Proprietor: Jesse N
Maxwell
Hours: Mon-Fri
Types & Periods: Furniture,
Crystal, Porcelain & Other
Bric-a-Brac
Specialties: American
Brilliant Period Cut Crystal
(1890-1905)
Appraisal Service Available
  Directions: Between 16th
  & 18th Sts

THE MAXWELL HOUSE
2424 Piedmont Ave 30309
                  Est: 1975
Proprietor: Jesse N
Maxwell
Hours: Fri, Sat & Sun
12-9:30
Types & Periods: Furniture,
Crystal, Porcelain
  Directions: Located at the
  intersection of Piedmont
  Ave & Lindbergh Dr
  "Atlanta Flea Market"

**NOBLE PIECES LTD,
ANTIQUES**
291 Techwood Dr NW
                       30313
404 524-1100
404 688-6642   Est: 1976
Proprietor: James A Roper
Hours: Mon-Fri, 10-5:30;
most Saturdays, 10-4; also
by appointment
Types & Periods: 18th &19th
Century English & American
Furniture
Specialties: Sets of
Chippendale & Queen Anne
Dining Room Chairs,
Secretaries, Chests of
Drawers
Appraisal Service Available
  Directions: At Baker St, 2
  Blocks W of Merchandise
  Mart; Exit from I-75 or I-85

THE PACESETTERS
290 Paces Mill Rd   30339
404 435-2940   Est: 1973
Proprietor: Helen
Christiansen & Nancy
Bean
Hours: Tues-Sat, 11-4:30
Types & Periods: English &
Continental Furniture,
Porcelains, Paintings; Gift
Items

Directions: W Paces Ferry Rd to Paces Ferry Rd, cross over Chattahoochee River; We're at the stoplight, green & white awning over door; Or I-285, take Vinings Exit to Paces Mill

SANDY SPRINGS GALLERIES

233 Hilderbrand Dr NE
30328
404 252-3244   Est: 1971
Proprietor: Jim & Eloise Pickard
Hours: Mon-Sat, 9-5; and by Appointment
Types & Periods: 18th & 19th Century American & European Furniture, Mirrors & Old Prints
Specialties: Restored Brass, Wood, & Crystal Chandeliers & Sconces
Directions: 1/2 Mile N of I-285 on US 19

SECOND HAND ROSE'S, INC

959 Peachtree St, NE
30309
404 876-5333
Proprietor: Jeffrey A Hill, Jeremiah L Gordon
Hours: Mon-Fri, 11-7; Sat, 11-6
Types & Periods: Assorted
Directions: Between 8th & 10th Sts, Across from Peachtree Place

BEVERLY SCOTT, LTD

1189 Howell Mill Rd 30318
404 351-7034   Est: 1976
Proprietor: Beverly Scott
Hours: Mon-Sat, 10-5
Types & Periods: All sorts; We receive regular shipments from England, all shipments hand-picked by proprietor; we have a warehouse & deal primarily with wholesale
Specialties: Period Pine, Country Furniture, Collectibles & Decorative Accessories
Directions: Between 14th St & the Water Works, Next Door to Atlanta Antiques Exchange

SLATER'S ANTIQUES

7869 Roswell Rd NE
30338
404 992-4920   Est: 1972
Proprietor: Sam, Joan, Steven, Susan Slater
Hours: Daily, 10-5:30
Types & Periods: American Furniture & Wicker
Specialties: Wicker, American Furniture, Fine Restoration
Appraisal Service Available
Directions: 4 1/2 Miles N of 285 Perimeter Hwy at Roswell Rd-Sandy Springs Exit

THE TOBY HOUSE ANTIQUES

517 E Paces Ferry Rd NE
30305
404 233-2161   Est: 1974
Proprietor: Mrs Joanne Pirkle
Hours: Daily; By Appointment
Types & Periods: 18th &19th Century Furniture & Accessories
Specialties: Furniture (Country Pine & English Oak), Ironstone, Staffordshire
Directions: Main St in Atlanta, 4 Blocks Off Peachtree St

TRADER DOY'S

2424 Piedmont Rd   30324
404 231-0052   Est: 1956
Proprietor: Doy Miller
Hours: Fri-Sun, 12-9; Daily by Chance or Appointment
Types & Periods: All Types & Periods
Specialties: Large Wardrobes & Pub Tables
Appraisal Service Available
Directions: South End of the Atlanta Flea Mkt

TURNAGE PLACE, LTD

1001 Brady Sue   30318
404 872-4100   Est: 1970
Proprietor: Helen F Nagel
Hours: Mon-Sat, 10-5
Types & Periods: English Antiques & Accessories
Appraisal Service Available
Directions: Corner of 10th St & Brady Ave, Near Georgia Tech

VICTORIA GALLERIES

3193 Roswell Rd NW
30305
404 261-8900   Est: 1971
Proprietor: Robert J Stebbins, Sr
Hours: Daily; by Appointment
Types & Periods: Period English & French Paintings, Accessories
Specialties: 18th & 19th Century Painting
Appraisal Service Available
Directions: 2 Blocks out of Buckhead

THE WALKERS ANTIQUES

222 Westminster Dr 30309
404 872-2784   Est: 1971
Proprietor: Robert C Walker
Hours: By Appointment
Types & Periods: American Cut Glass, Art Glass, Art Pottery; Tiffany
Appraisal Service Available
Directions: Home, Downtown Atlanta

CAROL WALTZ INC

526 E Paces Ferry Rd NE
30306
404 261-4455   Est: 1963
Proprietor: Carol & Robert Waltz
Hours: Mon-Fri, 10-5; Sat, 1-5
Types & Periods: 18th & 19th Century Antiques, Oriental Porcelains & Art Objects
Specialties: Design Service
Directions: In Buckhead Section, Near Lenox Shopping Ctr & Phipps Plaza; N of City off Peachtree Rd

WE HAD IT YESTERDAY ANTIQUES

1040 N Highland Ave NE
30306
404 872-9592   Est: 1977
Proprietor: J W Holbrook & B H Grube
Hours: Daily
Types & Periods: All Types
Directions: Ponce de Leon to N Highland, N on Highland, 1/2 Block Past Intersection with Virginia Ave

Atlanta Cont'd

E R WILKERSON INC
3300 Piedmont Rd NE
30305
404 261-4413 Est: 1933
Proprietor: E R Wilkerson
Hours: Daily, 9-4:30
Types & Periods: 17th &
18th Century Furniture &
Accessories
Directions: Buckhead

**WILLIAM WORD ANTIQUES
INC**
3107 Early St NW 30342
404 233-6890
Proprietor: William Word
Hours: Mon-Fri, 9-5; Sat,
10-4
Types & Periods: 18th &
19th Century English &
Continental Antiques,
Paintings; Oriental & English
Porcelains, Oriental Rugs
Specialties: English &
Continental Furniture, fully
Restored
Directions: Buckhead;
Early St crosses W Paces
Ferry Rd

WILLIAM'S ANTIQUES INC
4010 Peachtree Rd NE
30319
404 233-4072 Est: 1966
Proprietor: Don & Jane
Pierce
Hours: Mon-Sat, 10-5;
Sun, 1-5
Types & Periods: 18th &
Early 19th Century English,
French & American
Furniture
Appraisal Service Available
Directions: NE Atlanta, 1
1/2 Miles N of Lenox
Square

**THE WRECKING BAR OF
ATLANTA INC**
292 Moreland Ave NE
30307
404 525-0468 Est: 1969
Proprietor: Wilma Stone
Hours: Mon-Sat, 9-5
Types & Periods: Doors,
Entranceways, Mantels,
Brass Hardware, Lighting,
Wrought Iron Gates,
Carvings, Beveled Glass,
Bronze Lanterns

Directions: 1 Mile Off I-20
Expy E; Located in One of
Atlanta's Early Mansions
10 Minutes from
Downtown

YESTERYEAR BOOK SHOP
256 E Paces Ferry Rd NE
30305
404 237-0163 Est: 1971
Proprietor: Frank Ogden
Walsh, III
Hours: Mon-Sat; Sun by
Appointment
Types & Periods: Old Prints
& Maps, Rare & Out-of-Print
Books (Americana,
Children's Books, Military
History, Cookbooks,
Gardening, Architecture,
Leather Bindings, Etc)
Specialties: Books: Southern
History, First Editions
Appraisal Service Available
Directions: 6 Miles N of
Downtown Atlanta, 11/2
Blocks E of Peachtree Rd,
in the Buckhead Shopping
Community

Augusta

**GEORGIA-CAROLINA
SALES CO**
472 Broad St 30902
404 724-4447 Est: 1963
Proprietor: Paul R Blue
Hours: Thurs-Sat;
Mon-Wed by Appointment
Types & Periods: 18th &
19th Century Furniture,
Glass & China
Specialties: Clocks
Appraisal Service Available
Directions: E Broad St at
Intersection of Hwy
25-1-78

**MERRY'S TRASH &
TREASURES**
1236 Broad St 30902
404 722-3244 Est: 1962
Proprietor: Wm B Merry
Hours: Daily
Types & Periods: General
Line
Directions: Downtown

**OLD HUB ANTIQUE
VILLAGE**
3623 Old Petersburg Rd
30907
404 863-7142 Est: 1960

Proprietor: Mr & Mrs Tom
Ayers & Nicky
Hours: Wed-Mon, 1-6; and
by Appointment
Types & Periods: Furniture,
Empire Victorian, Primitive,
Silver, Glass, Jewelry, China
Appraisal Service Available
Directions: 1/2 Mile from
Martinez Post Office, out
Washington Rd from
Augusta; Turn R at the
Piggly Wiggly, 2 Blocks

Bainbridge

THE COACH HOUSE
915 Old Albany Rd 31717
912 246-4152 Est: 1963
Proprietor: Mary E Rollins
Hours: Mon-Sat; Sun by
Appointment, Sat by
Chance
Types & Periods: Late 18th
& 19th Century Furniture &
Bric-a-Brac: Primitive,
Victorian, Empire, Sheraton;
China, Silver, Glass
Appraisal Service Available
Directions: Hwy 97 N
within City Limits

Bogart

FLO'S ANTIQUES
Cleveland Rd 30622
404 725-7436 Est: 1971
Proprietor: Flo Clubertson
Hours: Thurs-Tues, 12-5
Types & Periods: General
Line
Specialties: Oak Ice Boxes
Directions: Hwy 29; Turn
on Cleveland Rd, go 9/10
Mile

Bolingbroke

BRICE ANTIQUES
Hwy 41 31004
912 994-9353 Est: 1973
Proprietor: Mike Brice
Hours: Mon-Sat, 10-6;
Sun, 1-6
Types & Periods: Furniture
Specialties: Furniture
Directions: 10 Miles N of
Macon

Carrollton

HAY'S MILL ANTIQUES
111 City Hall Ave   30117
404 832-7177   Est: 1973
Proprietor: Mrs J E Hay &
Mrs B R Talley
Hours: Mon, Tues, Thurs
& Fri, 11-5
Types & Periods: General
Line
Specialties: China, Furniture,
Glass
   Directions: 1 Block Off
   Square N

Cave Spring

THE GINGHAM SHOP
Box 401   30124
404 777-3608   Est: 1975
Hours: Thurs-Tues
Types & Periods: General
Line
Directions: On Broad St

Chamblee (Atlanta)

ANTIQUE ROW
3509 Broad St   30341
404 455-1139   Est: 1974
Proprietor: Peggy & Harry
Davidson
Hours: Mon-Sat
Types & Periods: American
Oak & Primitive Furniture
Specialties: Stripping &
Refinishing
Appraisal Service Available
   Directions: Interstate 285;
   Exit E on Peachtree
   Industrial; Left on
   Broad St

**OLD BLANTON HOUSE
ANTIQUES**
5449 Peachtree Rd 30324
404 458-1453   Est: 1972
Proprietor: Erma Anderson
Hours: Mon-Sat, 10:30-5;
Sun 1-5:30
Types & Periods: American
Oak, Victorian & Primitive
Furniture, Brass & Iron
Beds, Spindle Back Chairs,
Glassware, China,
Collectibles, Accessories,
Etc
   Directions: In Chamblee's
   Antique Row in North
   Atlanta

REESE'S ANTIQUES
2050-C Carroll Ave   30341
404 458-0119   Est: 1950
Proprietor: S Gaber
Hours: Daily; By
Appointment
Types & Periods: General
Line, Furniture, Porcelain,
Silver
Appraisal Service Available
   Directions: Across from
   Peachtree Dekalb Airport

Clarkesville

APPALACHIAN ANTIQUES
Rte 2 US 441 N   30523
    Est: 1973
Proprietor: Claude & Alice
Hunter
Hours: Weekends; By
Chance
Types & Periods: Primitives,
Cast Iron, Country Store,
Dolls, Bottles, Fruit Jars,
Glass, Furniture, Collectibles
Specialties: Primitives from
NE Georgia Area
   Directions: 6 Miles N of
   Town

**HABERSHAM ANTIQUE
SHOP**
Hwy 197, Lake Burton Rd
    30523
404 754-6138   Est: 1974
Proprietor: Grant &
Suwannee Watson
Hours: Mon, Wed-Sat; Sun
from 12:30
Types & Periods: General
Line
Specialties: Chair Caning
   Directions: 2 Miles off Hwy
   441 N toward Clayton

Clayton

THE FENCE RAIL
Box 232, Derrick &
Church Sts   30525
404 782-3595   Est: 1973
Proprietor: Marion Gilbert
Hours: Daily, 10-5
Types & Periods: Primitive
Mountain Crafted Furniture,
Allied Mountain Crafts,
Quilts, Coverlets

Specialties: Needlework
(Quilts & Coverlets)
   Directions: Downtown,
   behind Dillard Motor
   Lodge

Clermont

**SARA HERNDON'S
COLONY HOUSE**
Old Clermont Hotel 30527
404 983-3501   Est: 1959
Proprietor: Sara Herndon
Hours: Tues-Sat, 10-6;
Sun, 2-6
Types & Periods: English,
Primitive
Specialties: Room Settings
   Directions: 2 Blocks off
   Hwy 129 Going N toward
   Helen & Unicoa

Columbus

COLUMBUS CLUSTER
Directions: No Cluster,
however Wynnton Rd
(1000-2000 Blocks) has
several Shops

CENTURY ANTIQUES
4405 Armour Rd   31904
404 322-0947   Est: 1972
Proprietor: Dianne &
Gordon Estes
Hours: Mon-Fri, 10:30-4;
Weekends by Appointment
Types & Periods: 18th &
19th Century Furniture &
Accessories; Direct
Importers of Fine English
Antiques
Specialties: Furniture,
Oriental Porcelain for
Collectors & Trade
Appraisal Service Available
   Directions: 1 Block E of
   I-85 just Off Hwy 80

DERUMS ANTIQUE SHOP
4022 Cody Rd   31907
404 563-1293   Est: 1974
Proprietor: Karl Derums &
Oren Hallonquist
Hours: Mon-Sat
Types & Periods: American
& European Period
Appraisal Service Available
   Directions: Opposite
   Columbus College

MADDOX ANTIQUES
   2214 Wynnton Rd   31906
   404 323-9497   Est: 1968
   Proprietor: Mr & Mrs Otis
   Maddox
   Hours: Daily; By
   Appointment
Types & Periods: 18th
Century Period American,
Victorian, Country Oak
Furniture, Glassware
   Directions: Wynnton Rd is
   Hwy 22

**MILLER'S ANTIQUES &
WHAT-KNOTS**
   4044 Cody Rd   31907
   404 563-8958   Est: 1974
   Proprietor: Liz & Jim Miller
   Hours: Mon-Sat, 10-6
Types & Periods: General
Line including Glass,
Pottery, Jewelry, Watches,
Clocks
Specialties: Clocks
Appraisal Service Available
   Directions: University
   Plaza Shopping Ctr across
   from Columbus College

Cordele

JOSEPH OLIVER HURT JR
   410 14th Ave   31015
   912 273-7704   Est: 1962
   Proprietor: Oliver Hurt Jr
   Hours: By Appointment
Types & Periods: Furniture:
American, English, French,
Chinese; Folk Art; Chinese
Porcelain

**THE NOOK ANTIQUE
SHOPPE**
   US 280 & I-75 Hwys 31015
   912 273-4421   Est: 1961
   Proprietor: Mrs Sam
   Hendley
   Hours: Mon-Fri, & Sat
   Morning
Types & Periods: Furniture,
China, Crystal, Silver,
Jewelry, Cut & Art Glass
Appraisal Service Available
   Directions: Across from
   Holiday Inn, behind Gulf
   Station, on the Way to
   Plains

Cornelia

**WOODY'S TRADING POST
& ANTIQUES**
   Hwy's 441 & 23 N   30531
   404 778-7549   Est: 1969
   Proprietor: Woody & Alma
   Browning
   Hours: Wed-Mon
Types & Periods: Cut &
Pressed Glass, Furniture,
Farm Tools, General Line
Appraisal Service Available
   Directions: 2 Miles N of
   Cornelia, N side of Bypass

Covington

**W H HARRIS WAREHOUSE
SALES**
   3181 Emory St NW 30209
   404 786-1877   Est: 1972
   Proprietor: Walter H Harris
   Hours: Mon-Sat
Types & Periods: General
Line
   Directions: Covington -
   Oxford Exit from I-20 E;
   Turn Left at 1st Traffic
   Light; 1st Bldg on the
   Left; Corner of Hwy 278 &
   Emory

Cuthbert

**WIGGINS FRAME &
ANTIQUE SHOP**
   Rte 2 Box 41, US 275
                    31740
   912 732-2068   Est: 1965
   Proprietor: W Roberts
   Wiggins
   Hours: Daily; By
   Appointment
Types & Periods: Furniture,
Cut Glass
Appraisal Service Available
   Directions: 1 1/4 Miles S
   of Public Square on
   Blakely Rd, U S 27

Decatur

PAUL BARON CO
   2825 E College   30030
   404 292-2779   Est: 1944
   Proprietor: Wenonah
   Chambers
   Hours: Mon-Sat, 10-5

Types & Periods: General,
Primarily Porcelain & Glass
Specialties: Porcelain, Glass,
Oil Painting, Restorations
Appraisal Service Available
   Directions: Twin Oak
   Shopping Center,
   Suburban Atlanta

THE CHINA CLOSET
   3334 N Druid Hills Rd NE
                    30033
   404 633-4743   Est: 1975
   Proprietor: W D
   Theodorow
   Hours: Daily
Types & Periods: Furniture,
Cut Glass, Brass, Copper,
Bronzes, Bric-a-Brac,
Primitives
Appraisal Service Available
   Directions: Approx 3 Miles
   Off I-85; N Druid Hills Rd
   Exit

JACK THE STRIPPER
   115 Church St   30030
   404 378-0007   Est: 1970
   Proprietor: John L Dale
   Hours: Daily
Types & Periods: Early
American
Specialties: Roll Top Desks
   Directions: 1 Block E &
   2 1/2 Blocks S of Old
   Court House in Decatur

**WEBB'S ANTIQUES &
ACCENTS**
   1677 Church St   30033
   404 292-0863   Est: 1966
   Proprietor: Mrs Leatha
   Webb
   Hours: Mon-Thurs & Sat
Types & Periods: Porcelains,
Glass (Cut, Art, Pressed &
Depression), Silver, Jewelry,
Candlesticks, Bronze, 18th &
19th Century Furniture,
Primitives & Oak
Specialties: Porcelains &
Bronze, but Prefer Diversity
to Specialties
   Directions: Near Scott
   Blvd Church St & Dekalb,
   Ind Blvd Intersection; from
   Atlanta: E on Ponce de
   Leon to Church St, Turn L
   onto Church St

Douglas

CATO'S ANTIQUES
617 S Peterson   31533
912 384-3468   Est: 1935
Proprietor: Riley W Cato
Hours: Daily, 8-6
Types & Periods: Oak,
Mahogany, Halltrees, Round
Tables, Chairs, Ice Boxes
Appraisal Service Available
Directions: Located on
Hwy 441 S

Eatonton

CHARLEY'S ANTIQUES
Rte 1 Box 172   31024
404 485-8365   Est: 1975
Proprietor: Charley Brooks
Hours: Daily
Types & Periods: General
Line, 19th & Early 20th
Century American,
Collectibles
Specialties: Country Store
Items, Advertising Items
Appraisal Service Available
Directions: 8 Miles S of
Town on US Hwy 441

Evans

THE COUNTRY HOUSE
Georgia Hereford Farm Rd
   30809
404 863-7761
Proprietor: Claire West
Types & Periods: General
Line

WALNUT HILL FARM
Rte 1 Box 268C Cox Rd
   30809
404 863-1131
Proprietor: Mary Byrd
Types & Periods: General
Line

Fitzgerald

COLONY CITY ANTIQUES
509 S Grant St   31750
912 423-9984   Est: 1974
Proprietor: W M Patrick

Hours: Mon & Tues,
Thurs-Sat, 10-6; Wed
Afternoon & Sun by
Appointment
Types & Periods: General
Line
Appraisal Service Available
Directions: 18 Miles E of
I-75; Grant St Main N-S
Rte through Fitzgerald

Gainsville

DUNNS ANTIQUES
1859 Thompson Bridge Rd
   30501
404 532-8467   Est: 1958
Proprietor: Mrs Sandra
Dunn
Hours: Daily, 10-5:30
Types & Periods: Cut Glass,
Nippon, Brassware, Victorian
Furniture, Hepplewhite,
Sheraton, 18th Century
Queen Anne, Lamps
Appraisal Service Available
Directions: 52 Miles N of
Atlanta on Connector
Hwy 365

Gay

MITCHEM'S ANTIQUES
P O Box 105   30218
404 538-6323   Est: 1971
Proprietor: Billy & Ann
Mitchem
Hours: Daily
Types & Periods: Fine
Furniture; 18th & 19th
Century Chippendale,
Sheraton, Queen Anne
Specialties: American
Country Furniture, English
Pine & Early 18th Century
Oak; Restored & Refinished
Directions: Hwy 85, 45
Miles from Atlanta & 50
Miles from Columbus

Georgetown

**GRADDY'S ANTIQUES &
WORKSHOP**
Hwy 82   31754
912 334-5083   Est: 1961
Proprietor: Mr & Mrs Dean
Graddy

Hours: Daily; Shop is in
Home
Types & Periods: General
Line, Primitives
Directions: In Town

Grantville

RUBY HALL
Rte 1 Grandma Branch Rd
   30220
   Est: 1973
Proprietor: Ruby Hall
Hours: By Appointment
Types & Periods: General
Line

Griffin

BRANNON ANTIQUES INC
1031 W Taylor St   30223
404 227-2300   Est: 1968
Proprietor: J H Brannon Jr
Hours: Mon & Tues,
Thurs-Sat, 9-5; Sun by
Appointment
Types & Periods: Furniture,
Architectural Items, Oriental
Rugs, Brassware,
Porcelains, Paintings
Specialties: Chinese &
Japanese Porcelain & Art
Appraisal Service Available
Directions: On Hwys
41 & 19

THE TREASURE CHEST
312 S 8th St   30223
404 228-8472
Proprietor: Dot Ellis
Hours: Mon & Tues,
Thurs-Fri, 9-5; Wed &
Sat, 9-12
Directions: 1 1/2 Blocks S
off Hwy 41

Hiawassee

**THE MOUNTAIN
HOMESTEAD**
Hwy 76   30546
404 896-2568   Est: 1969
Proprietor: Mrs Jane K
Head
Hours: Daily; Closed Jan
1st to April 1st; Phone

MOUNTAIN HOMESTEAD
                    Cont'd
Types & Periods: American
& Victorian; Golden Oak,
General Line of Bric-a-Brac,
Quilts, Potted Herbs & Home
Cured Hams
Specialties: Jewelry, Dolls,
Clocks, Quilts
   Directions: On US 76, 110
   Miles N of Atlanta; 1 Mile
   from N Carolina between
   I-75 & I-85

Indian Springs

**HALL ANTIQUES & FLEA
MARKET**
   Hwy 42   30231
   404 775-5686   Est: 1968
   Proprietor: T J & Frances
   Hall
   Hours: By Appointment;
   Open Sat, Sun & Holidays
Types & Periods: General
Line
Specialties: Furniture (Oak)
   Directions: Jackson Exit
   Off I-75; Go through
   Jackson to Hwy 42; 5
   Miles S to Indian Springs

Jackson

**CENTURY HOUSE
ANTIQUES**
   236 W 3rd St   30233
   404 775-5776   Est: 1974
   Proprietor: Mary Frances
   Daniel
   Hours: Weekends; By
   Appointment
Types & Periods: American,
Victorian, Primitives
Specialties: Clocks, Brass
Beds, Rolltop Desks
Appraisal Service Available
   Directions: 8 Miles Off
   I-75, Jackson Exit

Kennesaw

**M RINGEL & SON ANTIQUE
CO, INC**
   US Hwy 41 Box 327 30144
   404 428-2967   Est: 1939
   Proprietor: Morris &
   Michael Ringel

Hours: Mon-Sat, 9-5;
Sun, 2-5
Types & Periods: Early
American & European,
Indian Relics, Confederate
Items
Specialties: Stripping &
Refinishing; Violins,
Advertising Mirrors
Appraisal Service Available
   Directions: 22 Miles N of
   Atlanta; I-75N to Exit 116
   Roberts Rd; then 1 Mile N
   on Hwy 41

**WOODLIEF'S MILITARY
ANTIQUES**
   US Hwy 41   30144
   404 428-4262   Est: 1970
   Proprietor: H L Woodlief
   Hours: Tues-Sat, 9-5
Types & Periods: Military
Arms, Accouterments &
Aviation Items
Specialties: Civil War
Collectibles

La Grange

LEMON TREE
   Old Hutchinson Mill Rd
                        30240
   404 882-1795   Est: 1968
   Proprietor: Richard &
   Betty Daniel
   Hours: Mon-Sat, 10-5
Types & Periods: American &
English
Specialties: Primitives
   Directions: 1 blk N of
   I-85, La Grange Exit 2

OAK WOOD ANTIQUES
   Hamilton Rd
   US Hwy 27 S   30240
   404 882-8149
   Proprietor: Ellis & Jean
   Smith
   Hours: Mon, Wed-Fri,
   12:30-4:30; by
   Appointment, by Chance
Types & Periods: General
Line
Specialties: Furniture, Quilt
Rails, Porcelain, Mirrors
   Directions: 5 Miles S of
   La Grange on US 27

Lawrenceville

MARTIN'S ANTIQUES
   177 E Pike St   30245
   404 963-6728   Est: 1974
   Proprietor: Sam Martin
   Hours: Tues-Sat, 9-4
Types & Periods: General
Line
Specialties: Chair Caning

Leslie

**W MALCOLM PERRY
ANTIQUES**
   Commerce St   31764
   912 874-5570   Est: 1961
   Proprietor: W Malcolm
   Perry
   Hours: Mon-Fri; Sat by
   Appointment
Types & Periods: 18th &
19th Century Furniture &
Accessories
   Directions: 20 Miles W of
   Cordele; 1 Block Off
   US 280

Lumpkin

**BROWSE-A-BOUT
ANTIQUES**
   Box 685   31815
   912 838-6793   Est: 1954
   Proprietor: Edward G
   Holloway
   Hours: Mon-Sat
Types & Periods: European
Imports, American Primitives
Appraisal Service Available
   Directions: N Side,
   Courthouse Sq

Macon

MACON CLUSTER
   Directions: No Cluster; A
   Few Shops on Houston
   Ave & Vineville Ave
   (Restoration Area)

M P BOOKER ANTIQUES
   3256 Houston Ave   31206
                    Est: 1950
   Proprietor: M P Booker
   Hours: Daily, 9:30-5

Types & Periods: Oak &
Walnut Furniture, Glassware,
Collectibles

Marietta

THE EMPORIUM
1696 Cobb Parkway SE
                  30062
404 434-6465   Est: 1974
Proprietor: Geneva
Wallace
Hours: Mon-Sat, 10-6;
Sun, 1-6
Types & Periods: Complete
Line
Specialties: 19th Century
Furniture
Directions: I-75 Exit at
Windy Hill Rd; 1/4 Mile to
Cobb Parkway; R 1/4 Mile
to Emporium

Martinez

THE RED DOOR
Columbia Rd   30907
404 863-3608
Proprietor: Ann Spivey
Types & Periods: General
Line, Furniture

Midway

MILTON BRAUN ANTIQUES
Hwy 17   31320
912 884-2621   Est: 1957
Proprietor: Milton Braun
Hours: Mon-Sat
Types & Periods: Cut &
Pressed Glass, China,
Brass, Copper, Bottles,
Tools, Iron, RR & Ships'
Items, Jars, Crocks, Jugs
Specialties: Collectibles
Directions: Across from
Midway Museum; On US
Hwy 17, 2 Miles W of I-95;
1 Block from P O

Monticello

THE RED BARN
Rte 1   31064
404 468-8800   Est: 1970
Proprietor: Mrs Allan C
Brittain

Hours: Daily, 9-6
Types & Periods: Victorian &
Primitive Furniture
Directions: 1 1/4 Miles
from Monticello on Hwy
212 W

Moreland

MORELAND ANTIQUES
Hwy 29   30259
404 253-8335   Est: 1971
Proprietor: Charles R
Payne
Hours: Daily
Types & Periods: General
Line
Directions: 5 Miles S of
Newnan on Hwy 29;
Moreland Exit Off I-85

Morrow

THE TARA WORLD CO INC
6749 Green Ind Way
                  30260
404 471-5186   Est: 1972
Proprietor: Doug Hamrick
Hours: Mon-Sat, 9:30-5:30;
Auctions Wed & Sat, 7:30
Types & Periods: 17th, 18th
& 19th Century American,
English & Continental
Antiques
Directions: Across from
Southlake Mall Shopping
Center

Newnan

THE JEFFERSON HOUSE
51 Jefferson St   30263
404 253-6171   Est: 1970
Proprietor: Sally Wood &
Ann Knight
Hours: Daily
Types & Periods: General
Line, Brass & Porcelain
Appraisal Service Available
Directions: 2 Blocks N of
Court Sq on Hwy 29

Riverdale

AUNTIE'S ANTIQUES
7471 Hwy 85   30296
404 478-9084   Est: 1970

Proprietor: Nell Benefield
Hours: Daily
Types & Periods: All
Period, General Line, Cut
Glass, China, Carnival
Specialties: American Oak,
Primitives, Southern
Furniture, Pottery, Ironware
Directions: 5 Minutes S of
Atlanta Airport on Hwy 85

Rome

411 ANTIQUE SHOP
Rte Biddy Rd   30161
404 234-2551   Est: 1969
Proprietor: Etna Gaines &
Thelma B Braden
Hours: Mon-Sat, Sun by
Appointment
Types & Periods: General
Line
Specialties: 18th, 19th &
20th Century Oil Paintings
Directions: Off 411 Hwy N,
1 Mile on Biddy Rd

"SKELTON'S" RED BARN
ANTIQUES
Rte 8, Calhoun Rd   30161
404 295-2710   Est: 1968
Proprietor: Mr & Mrs W T
Skelton
Hours: Mon-Sat, 9-5:30
Types & Periods: From
Chippendale to Cabin; Some
Finished, Some in the
Rough
Specialties: Trunk Restoring
& Chair Caning
Directions: 1 Mile Outside
Rome City Limits on Hwy
53 going toward Calhoun

THOMAS ANTIQUES
Rte 5, Alabama Rd   30161
404 232-4878   Est: 1968
Proprietor: John W
Thomas
Hours: Daily
Types & Periods: Early
1900's Oak & Victorian,
Glass, Crockery
Directions: 8 Miles W of
Rome on Hwy 20

Rossville

BATTLEFIELD ANTIQUES
933 LaFayette Rd   30741
404 861-3690   Est: 1973
Proprietor: Ed & Reba
Bass
Hours: Daily
Types & Periods: Cut Glass,
Nippon, Tiffany, Signed
Glass, Furniture
Specialties: Tools
Appraisal Service Available
Directions: On Hwy 27, 2
Miles N of Ft Oglethorpe &
Chickamauga Battlefield

Roswell

MEETING HOUSE ANTIQUES
1158 Canton St   30075
404 993-5509   Est: 1974
Proprietor: Dorothy Coe &
Rose Sims
Hours: Daily
Types & Periods: Early
American Country Furniture
& Accessories
Specialties: Early Baskets,
Southern Pottery Folk Art,
Quilts & Tole
Directions: "Rte 19 from
Sandy Springs go N to
Roswell, Take Rte 140 on
Canton St in Roswell;
Small White House on Left
Side of Street"

ROSWELL CLOCK & ANTIQUE CO
955 Canton St   30075
404 992-5232   Est: 1976
Proprietor: Larry
Davenport
Hours: Mon-Sat
Types & Periods: Antique
Clocks of All Types,
Furniture, Primitives &
Nauticals
Specialties: Clocks, Sales &
Service
Appraisal Service Available
Directions: 15 Miles N of
Atlanta; 10 Miles N of 285,
Just Off 400

Savannah

SAVANNAH CLUSTER
Directions: Number of
Shops located on Bull St,
W Bay, W Liberty, W
Jones; Not Contiguous

THE ATTIC ANTIQUES
230 W Bay St   31401
912 234-4141   Est: 1971
Proprietor: Julian M Head
Hours: Daily
Types & Periods: Furniture,
Silver, Accessories
Appraisal Service Available
Directions: 2 Blocks W of
City Hall in Old Savannah

DAISS ANTIQUES AT ANTIQUE MALL
125 W Congress St 31401
912 234-4089   Est: 1974
Proprietor: Mrs Pat Daiss
Hours: Daily
Types & Periods: Furniture,
Depression Glass, Clocks,
Bric-a-Brac, Coca Cola
Items
Directions: Second Floor

THE HOOKERY
18 Bishops Court   31401
912 232-6015   Est: 1974
Proprietor: Rita Limpert
Hours: Mon-Fri, 11-3 &
6-9; Sat & Sun, 12-6
Types & Periods: General
Directions: E Broad & Bay
Sts, Across from the
Pirates' House Restaurant

LEVY JEWELERS
101 E Broughton St 31401
912 233-1163   Est: 1900
Proprietor: Jack M &
Aaron Levy
Hours: Daily, 9-6
Types & Periods: Jewelry,
Silver
Specialties: Same
Appraisal Service Available
Directions: Corner of
Broughton & Drayton Sts

THE MAN OF KENT INC
230 Bull St   31401
912 233-8434   Est: 1973
Proprietor: John C Karr
Hours: Daily, 9-6, Nights
by Appointment
Types & Periods: English &
American Furniture, Glass,

China, Bronzes, Silver, Fine
Oil Paintings
Specialties: Glass
Appraisal Service Available
Directions: Heart of
Savannah, 1 Block N of
DeSoto Hilton Hotel

CARL MEADOWS INC
315 Barnard St   31401
912 233-6377   Est: 1946
Proprietor: Carl L
Meadows
Hours: Daily, 9:30-5
Types & Periods: 18th
Century Furniture,
Porcelains, Silver, Brass
Specialties: Brass
Appraisal Service Available
Directions: On Pulaski Sq;
2 Blocks W of
DeSoto-Hilton Hotel

THE MULBERRY TREE
205 W River St   31401
912 236-4656   Est: 1973
Proprietor: Mrs William
Taylor
Hours: Daily
Types & Periods: Primitives
Directions: Located on the
Waterfront

OLD ARCH ANTIQUES
235 W Beverly St   31401
912 232-2922   Est: 1971
Proprietor: Julian M Head
Hours: Mon-Sat
Types & Periods: General
Line

ARTHUR G SMITH ANTIQUES
1 W Jones St   31401
912 236-9701   Est: 1962
Proprietor: Arthur G
Smith, Jr
Hours: Daily; By
Appointment
Types & Periods: 18th &
19th Century English,
American & Continental
Furniture, Porcelain, Rugs,
Fixtures
Specialties: Porcelain,
Lamps
Appraisal Service Available
Directions: 2 Blocks S of
DeSoto Hilton Hotel

STUFF 'N' SUCH ANTIQUES
125 W Congress 31401
912 232-9736 Est: 1974
Proprietor: Howard O
Sturgis, Jr
Hours: Daily
Types & Periods: Bottles,
Mechanical Music,
Stamps, Coins,
Turn-of-the-Century
Furniture
Specialties: Repair of
Mechanical Music
Appraisal Service Available
Directions: Between
Barnard & Whitacker Sts
on Ellis Sq

SYLVIA'S ANTIQUES
125 W Congress St 31401
912 232-9736 Est: 1975
Proprietor: Sylvia
Rosenberg
Hours: Daily
Types & Periods: China,
Silver, Cut & Art Glass,
Jewelry, Furniture, Umbrella
Stands, Wash Bowls,
Cigarette Boxes, Match
Safes
Directions: Between
Whitaker St & Darnard; It
is a one-way St; Turn R
on Barnard to Congress

TEMPTATIONS-UPSTAIRS-DOWNSTAIRS
230 W Bay St 31401
912 233-5500 Est: 1973
Proprietor: Marilyn S
Smith
Hours: Mon Sat, 11-5
Types & Periods: Victorian
Furniture, Glass, Dolls, Toys,
Bottles, Primitives
Specialties: Bottles, Toys,
Dolls
Appraisal Service Available
Directions: Located
Downstairs in Savannah
Flea Mkt; Entrance on
Factors Walk off River St

Scottsdale

BEE'S SHOPPE-HAWTHORNE VILLAGE
3032 N Decatur Rd 30033
404 292-2142 Est: 1964
Proprietor: Mrs W H
Wilder
Hours: Daily, 10-5

Types & Periods: Victorian,
Primitives, Wicker, Oak,
General Line
Directions: Between
Memorial Dr & Emory U, 2
Miles W of the University

Smyrna

A BIT O' THE PAST
2798 Atlanta St 30080
404 432-0267
Hours: Tues-Sat,
10:30-4:30; Sun, 2-5
Types & Periods: Furniture,
Lamps, China, General Line

ANTIQUE GALLERIA
2794 Atlanta St 30080
404 434-3727 Est: 1970
Proprietor: Helen B Spinks
Hours: Tues, Thurs & Sat
Types & Periods: Any-All
Specialties: Lamps, Hand
Painted China; Lamps Hand
Painted & Restored, Copied
Appraisal Service Available
Directions: Old Atlanta
Hwy, 5 Miles S of
Marietta; between Powder
Springs & Bank St

THE ANTIQUE INN
2788 Atlanta St SE 30080
404 432-5616 Est: 1971
Proprietor: B Perkins, M B
Fossett & B Malnoske
Hours: Tues-Thurs & Sat
Types & Periods: Furniture,
China, Glass, Jewelry
Specialties: Furniture,
Victorian & English
Directions: Hwy 5 off I-285

THE ART HACIENDA
3410 Atlanta Rd SE
30080
404 434-6920 Est: 1970
Proprietor: Mrs Doris G
Fondren
Hours: Sat & Sun;
Afternoons & Nights
during the week by
Appointment
Types & Periods: Some
Furniture & Bric-a-Brac;
Primarily Art of all Kinds:
from Modern or Abstract to
Antique, Oils, Watercolors,
Prints, Original Woodblocks
& Woodcuts, Etc
Specialties: Art
Directions: 2 Miles N of

I-285 on State Rte 2,
Smyrna Exit (Exit 11);
Large Spanish House on
R, Antiques sign by
driveway

ATTIC GALLERY
2728 Atlanta St 30082
404 435-3654 Est: 1971
Proprietor: Arline Hughes
Hours: Daily; By
Appointment
Types & Periods:
Collectibles

B-HIVE ANTIQUES
Atlanta Rd at Jane Lyle
30080
404 436-2758
Hours: Daily; By
Appointment
Types & Periods: General
Line

CARTER'S ANTIQUES
2806 Atlanta St 30080
404 435-9073
Hours: Mon-Sat, 10-4:30;
Sun, 1-4:30
Types & Periods: Furniture,
Bric-a-Brac

CONCORD ANTIQUES
1265 Sunset St 30080
404 434-1083
Hours: Mon-Fri,
10:30-4:30; Sat, 10:30-5;
Sun, 2-5
Types & Periods: General
Line, Primitives

CORNER COTTAGE
2756 Atlanta St 30080
404 434-8465
Hours: Mon & Tues,
Thurs-Sat, 11-4:30
Types & Periods: General
Line, Depression Glass

CREATWOOD COLONY
3216 Atlanta Rd SE 30080
404 432-1534
Hours: Mon-Sat, 10:30-5;
Sun, 1-5
Types & Periods: Potpourri
of European & American
Furniture; Wicker

Smyrna   **Cont'd**

DIXIE GALLERIES ANTIQUES
1270 Sunset St   30080
404 436-9605
Hours: Tues-Sat,
10:30-4:30; Sun, 2-5
Types & Periods: Furniture,
Cut Glass, Silver, Jewelry

KATHY'S KORNER
3604 Atlanta Rd SE 30080
404 435-7422
Hours: Tues-Sat, 11-5;
Sun, 2-5
Types & Periods: General
Line

OLD SMYRNA ANTIQUES
2796 Atlanta St   30080
404 432-2185
Hours: Mon-Sat, 10:30-5;
Sun, 1-5
Types & Periods: Primitive &
Oak Furniture

POLLIE'S PANTRY
3216 Atlanta Rd SE 30080
404 436-7095
Hours: Mon-Sat, 10:30-5;
Sun, 1-5
Types & Periods: Primitives,
Ice Boxes, Advertisements

STRICKLAND'S INTERIORS
2968 Atlanta St   30080
404 436-7522
Hours: Daily, by
appointment
Types & Periods: French,
English & American

Statesboro

ALLEN'S ANTIQUES
252 N Main St   30458
912 764-5530   Est: 1973
Proprietor: Francis W
Allen
Hours: Daily, 10-5
Types & Periods: Furniture
Directions: 3 Blocks from
Downtown on Hwy 301, 1
Block off Hwy 80

Sylvester

DREAM HOUSE ANTIQUES
                           31791
                    Est: 1964
Proprietor: Doris Cochran
Hours: By appointment, By
chance
Specialties: Cut Glass,
China

Talbotton

MADDOX ANTIQUES AT REBEL RIDGE
US Hwy 80   31827
404 665-8604   Est: 1972
Proprietor: Mr & Mrs Otis
N Maddox
Hours: Daily; By
Appointment
Types & Periods: General
Line
Directions: Rebel Ridge is
an ante-bellum home, built
in 1845 and located at the
city limits of Talbotton
which is on the US
highway between
Columbus & Macon, on
the E side of town

Talmo

PARDUE'S ANTIQUES
                           30575
404 693-2500   Est: 1963
Proprietor: Claud Pardue
Hours: Open Auction Days
Only; Auctions 1st & 3rd
Fri at 7
Types & Periods: General
Line
Appraisal Service Available
Directions: 55 Miles E of
Atlanta between I- 85
& Hwy 129 Gainesville,
on US Hwy 129

Thomasville

JAMES S MASON ANTIQUES
149 Lee   31792
912 226-4454   Est: 1970
Proprietor: James S
Mason
Hours: Daily, 8:30-5:30

Types & Periods: 18th
Century Period Furniture,
Porcelain, Oriental Rugs
Appraisal Service Available
Directions: 1 Block W of
Intersection of Madison &
Fletcher Sts

TOWN & COUNTRY ANTIQUES INC
119-121 S Madison St,
Box 797   31792
912 226-5863   Est: 1966
Proprietor: Vernon &
Martha Hall
Hours: Mon-Sat, 9:30-5
Types & Periods: General
Line
Specialties: Brass Fireplace
Equipment & Brass
Specialty Items
Appraisal Service Available
Directions: Downtown on
2 Main Business Rtes:
Hwys 19 & 84

Tifton

APPLE TREE ANTIQUES
1020 N Central   31794
912 382-0119
Proprietor: Micha E
Winder, Pat Doss
Hours: Tues-Sat and by
Appointment; Closed
during June
Types & Periods: China,
Glass, Silver, Jewelry, 19th
& 20th Century Furniture
Specialties: Silver
Appraisal Service Available
Directions: Old US 41
(12th St) at North Central

Toccoa

HOUSE OF ANTIQUES
228 E Currahee   30577
404 886-3226   Est: 1973
Proprietor: Mrs F J Heaton
& Mrs J R Free
Hours: Mon-Sat
Types & Periods: American
Furniture, China, Glassware
Appraisal Service Available
Directions: On Hwy 123,
Center of Town

Tucker

TOWNES TIFFANIES
3875 B Stephens Court
30084
404 934-1186   Est: 1974
Proprietor: Corporation
Hours: By Appointment
Types & Periods: Tiffany
Style Reproductions of
Lamps & Custom Windows
& Doors; Repair Work also
Done
   Directions: Located 1
   Block off Brockett Rd

Vidalia

**THE OLD HOUSE
ANTIQUES**
500 W 1st St   30474
912 537-7191   Est: 1970
Proprietor: Mrs H A
Burns Jr
Hours: Daily; By Chance
Types & Periods: Furniture,
China, Brass
Specialties: Lamps &
Shades
   Directions: Hwy 280 W;
   Next to Coca Cola Plant

Warner Robbins

HELEN BALLOU ANTIQUES
1001 Green St   31093
912 922-1923
Proprietor: Helen Ballou
Hours: Daily
Types & Periods:
Collectibles, Furniture,
China, Glass
Appraisal Service Available
   Directions: Corner of
   Green & Holly Sts in Rear
   of House

BARRY'S JUNKTION
603 S Davis Dr   31093
912 923-4868   Est: 1970
Proprietor: Howard T &
Eunice Barry
Hours: By Appointment;
By Chance
Types & Periods: American
& English Furniture, China
(including Flow Blue China),
Glass, Cut Glass, Primitives

Specialties: Furniture, Bow
Front China Cabinets, Flow
Blue China
   Directions: 7 Miles off
   I-75; Turn L on S Davis Dr

**GLISSON'S OLD
FURNITURE AND
ANTIQUES**
Rte 1 Box 742   31093
912 923-5241   Est: 1969
Proprietor: Paul & Eloise
Glisson
Hours: Mon & Tues,
Thurs-Sat; Flea Market
Every Saturday
Types & Periods: Furniture,
Bric-a-Brac, Primitives,
Caning
   Directions: 3 Miles N of
   Warner Robbins; Hwy 247
   & Elberta Rd

**WEATHERVANE ANTIQUE
SHOP**
903 McArthur Blvd   31093
912 923-9704   Est: 1971
Proprietor: Judd & Mildred
Stafford
Hours: By appointment, By
chance
Types & Periods: Glassware,
China, Silver, Brass, Copper,
Primitives, Furniture, Books,
Lamps
   Directions: Just off
   Watson Blvd

Williamson

H B CONNELL ANTIQUES
30292
404 227-4715   Est: 1948
Proprietor: H B Connell
Hours: Daily
Types & Periods: American
& English China, Bric-a-Brac
   Directions: Hwy 362, 6
   Miles W of Griffin

Winder

**BETTY'S VARIETY &
ANTIQUES**
407 Broad St   30680
404 867-2930   Est: 1958
Proprietor: D E & Betty
Stafford
Hours: Daily
Types & Periods: General
Line
Specialties: Glass
   Directions: S of May St

Woodbine

GRIFFIS ANTIQUES
Box 41   31569
912 576-5458   Est: 1973
Proprietor: Eugene & Dixie
Griffis
Hours: Mon-Sat, 10-5:30;
Telephone Anytime
Types & Periods: Country
Pine, Oak, Wicker, Glass
Specialties: Wicker
   Directions: Corner of Hwy
   17 & 3rd St

Georgian Side Chair.
Notice Queen Anne
cabriole with pad foot
and Chippendale back.

STATE OF HAWAII

Honolulu

HONOLULU CLUSTER
Directions: City Center has a number of Shops on Neighboring Streets, Ala Moana (I000 Block) South King St (1000 Block), Beretania St, Queen St, Kapahulu Ave (1000 Block)

ANCESTRAL ARTS
423 Nahua St   96815
808 923-8888   Est: 1975
Proprietor: Charles & Janice Mack
Hours: Mon-Sat 9:30-4:30
Types & Periods: Museum Quality "Primitive Art" Ethnographic, Archeological, Pre-Columbian, From Oceania, Africa, The Americas, Orient
Specialties: Ancient Polynesian, Indian Baskets
Appraisal Service Available
Directions: Directly behind Internat'l Market Pl, 1 Block Down on Right

ANSTETH LIMITED
1020 Auahi Ave   96814
808 531-0177   Est: 1948
Proprietor: George S Spencer
Hours: Daily, By Appointment, By Chance
Types & Periods: Furniture, Porcelain, Orientals
Specialties: Orientals
Appraisal Service Available
Directions: Corner of 1020 Auahi St & Kamakee St

ANTIQUES & OBJETS D'ART
1016-B Kapahulu Ave   96816
808 737-7815   Est: 1958
Proprietor: Ted Adameck
Hours: Tues Thru Sat I0-4
Types & Periods: Orientalia, Collectables
Specialties: Oriental
Directions: 5 Minutes from Waikiki at Mountain End of Kapahulu

ARIAN BAZAAR
International Market Place   96815
808 9233-3351   Est: 1972
Proprietor: Mohammad Akbar
Hours: Daily
Types & Periods: 19th Century Khyber Pass Hand Guns, Rugs, Plates
Directions: International Market Place in Waikiki

THE CARRIAGE HOUSE
I016 F Kapahulu Ave 96816
808 737-2622   Est: 1960
Proprietor: Connie Pickett
Hours: Daily 10:00-4:30, Closed Sunday
Types & Periods: American, European, Oriental
Specialties: China, Glass, Silver
Appraisal Service Available
Directions: Kilohana Square

CREATIVE DECORATING
1465 S King St   96814
808 947-1695   Est: 1963
Proprietor: Allison Holland
Hours: Daily 8-3
Types & Periods: Furniture, Accessories
Specialties: Boxes, Bird Cages, Wicker
Directions: Between Keeaumoku & Kalakaua, Several Blocks from Ala Moana Shopping Center

FABULOUS THINGS LTD
Kahala Mall   96816
808 732-7070
Proprietor: Harlan & Judith Koch
Hours: Daily, Weekends
Types & Periods: Korean Chests, Thai & Burmese Buddhas, Temple Carvings
Specialties: Oriental
Directions: Take Kiluea Exit From Kalanaimole Hwy

FAR EAST ANTIQUITIES
2005 Kalia Rd   96815
808 949-4321   Est: 1975
Proprietor: Sherwood Chock

Hours: Daily, Weekends
Types & Periods: Chinese, Thailand, Porcelain, Carvings, Netsuke, Ivory
Specialties: Oriental
Directions: Hilton Hawaiian Village, Rainbow Bazaar

PAULINE LAKE INC
2259 Kalakaua Ave 96816
808 923-5011   Est: 1949
Proprietor: Pauline Lake Miller
Hours: Daily 9-5, Closed Sun
Types & Periods: Oriental Chinese Coats, Snuff Bottles, Japanese Kimona, Obi, Netzukes, Thai Buddhas
Specialties: Clothing
Directions: In the Royal Hawaiian Hotel

THE LANTERN SHOP ANTIQUES
1030 Kapahulu Ave   96816
808 737-4771
Proprietor: B Stuhlmacher
Hours: Daily I0:00-4-30, Except Sun
Types & Periods: 16th, 17th & 18th Century Screens, Scroll Paintings, Lacquerware, Bronzes, Porcelains, Furniture
Specialties: Rare Japanese Screens, Bronzes, Rare Chinese Chests
Appraisal Service Available
Directions: From Waikiki Up Kalakaua Ave (Main St) to Kapahulu Ave (Past Zoo) to Kilohana Square

SPIRIT HOUSE ANTIQUES
4910 Kahala Ave 96816
808 732-6000   Est: 1972
Proprietor: Christopher Fahey Black
Hours: By Appointment
Types & Periods: SE Asian Antiques & Original Art, 12th & 20th Century, Buddhist Figurines & Art, Porcelains, 19th Century Wood Carved Temple Gables
Specialties: Dongsung Bronze Drums, Buddhas
Appraisal Service Available

Kaneohe

ANTIQUES & JUNQUE AT KAHALUU
47-659 Kamehameha Hwy
96744
808 239-7811 or Evenings
808 923-2240   Est: l958
Proprietor: Ted Adameck
& Dennis Marlow
Hours: By Appointment,
By Chance
Types & Periods: 90%
Oriental (Especially Netsuke
& Snuff Bottles)
Specialties: Netsuke, Snuff
Bottles, Bronzes, Stone
Pieces, General Orientalia,
and Seashells
Appraisal Service Available
Directions: 1 Mile North of
Valley of the Temples

Lahaina

THE GALLERY LTD
714 Front St   96761
808 661-0696   Est: l959
Proprietor: Tim Morrow
Hours: Daily 9.30 to 4.30,
Closed Sun
Types & Periods: Chinese &
Japanese, Antique and
Contemporary Works of Art
Specialties: Fine Jewelry
(Jade and Pearl Only) Ivory
Carvings
Directions: Center of Town
on Only Main St

The Georgian Period has been described as a mingling of various styles but that does not preclude a magnificent result.

This Georgian secretary, desk and bookcase, is Santo Domingan mahogany. The quadruple hooded top is William & Mary. The bookcase is Queen Anne. The brasses and applied bracket base are Chippendale.

STATE OF IDAHO

Bellevue

CHALET ANTIQUES
124 S Main   83313
208 788-2293   Est: 1971
Proprietor: Richard & Sally
Drake
Hours: Daily, By
Appointment
Types & Periods: General
Line 1860-1930's
Appraisal Service Available
Directions: Hwy 93 on
Road to Sun Valley

Boise

GLORIA'S ANTIQUES
3204 Overland   83705
208 343-3372   Est: 1968
Proprietor: Gloria
Showmaker
Hours: Mon-Sat, 10-5:30
Types & Periods: General
Line, Furniture, Clocks &
Glassware
Specialties: Clocks
Appraisal Service Available
Directions: Take Vista Exit
off Hwy 80; Turn L on
Overland Rd

HAPPYS ANTIQUES
2003 Vista   83705
208 344-9931   Est: 1970
Proprietor: Happy & Olie
Olsen
Hours: Mon-Sat
Types & Periods: Oak
Furniture, Primitives, Tools,
Tin Advertising
Specialties: Refinishing &
Brass
Directions: Vista Exit,
Corner of Vista & Palouse

HELEN S RIEBE
2910 Good St   83703
208 344-3745
Proprietor: Helen S Riebe
Hours: By Appointment,
By Chance
Types & Periods: General
Line

VICTORIA ONE
109 N 8th   83701
208 344-2541   Est: 1971
Proprietor: Jerry Hall &
Ken Uranga
Hours: Daily & Weekends
Types & Periods: Dolls,
Jewelery, Silver, China,
Victorian & Oak Furniture,
Copper, Brass, Oriental
Rugs, Linens, Stained
Glass Windows
Specialties: Glass
Appraisal Service Available
Directions: Downtown

VICTORIAN SHOP
108 N 10th   83701
208 344-2634   Est: 1968
Proprietor: Jerry Hall &
Ken Uranga
Hours: Daily & Weekends
Types & Periods: Jewelry,
Oriental Items, Art Glass,
Copper, Brass
Specialties: Jewelry &
Oriental Collectibles
Appraisal Service Available
Directions: Downtown

THE WHISTLE STOP
2406 W Idaho St   83706
208 344-6045   Est: 1975
Proprietor: Jay & Patty
Wadsworth
Hours: By Appointment,
By Chance
Types & Periods: 1890-1940
Collectibles, Toys,
Advertising, Radios,
Phonographs, Art Deco
Specialties: Copper & Brass;
Reproduciton Hardware
Appraisal Service Available
Directions: 1 Block off
Main St, Downtown Boise

Burley

A SIDE DOOR
2735 S Overland   83318
208 678-1145   Est: 1975
Proprietor: Larry & Sue
Stephenson
Hours: Mon-Fri, 10-5:30;
Sat, 10-5

Types & Periods: Furniture
& Glass Collectibles
Specialties: Stripping &
Refinishing
Appraisal Service Available

Garden City

RON'S EMPORIUM
204 E 36th   83704
208 343-6100   Est: 1959
Proprietor: Ron Lester
Hours: Daily
Types & Periods: Primitives
& Furniture
Specialties: Glass
Directions: 1 Block E of
Ranch Club off Chinden
Blvd in Big Red Barn

Idaho City

BLACK BARTS ANTIQUES
409 Montgomery   83631
208 392-4543   Est: 1973
Proprietor: Barton E
Lester
Hours: By Appointment,
By Chance
Types & Periods: Primitives
Specialties: Mining
Equipment
Directions: NE from Boise
to Idaho City on Hwy 21,
By PO & Library

Ketchum

HITCHING POST ANTIQUES
Box 656A River St 83340
208 726-5179
Proprietor: Mildred & Bert
Barlow
Hours: Daily 9-5, Also By
Appointment
Types & Periods: Furniture
& Glass, China, General
Line

Mullan

MULLAN HOTEL RELIC SHOP
204 Earl St   83846
208 744-1516   Est: 1972
Proprietor: Edgar T
DeShazo
Hours: By Appointment,
By Chance
Types & Periods: General
Line, Collectibles, Nostalgia
Specialties: Mining & Ghost
Town Relics
    Directions: Mullan Exit Off
    Ramp, I-90; Main Part of
    Town

Nampa

BICE ANTIQUES & GIFTS
824 Winther Blvd   83651
208 466-6232   Est: 1968
Proprietor: Mrs L R Bice
Hours: By Chance
Types & Periods: General
Line
Specialties: Dried & Pressed
Flower Pictures
Appraisal Service Available
    Directions: 4th Exit from
    Freeway W at City off
    Midland Blvd

Pocatello

THE ANTIQUE STUDIO
641 N Arthur   83201
208 232-8359
Types & Periods: General
Line, Furniture, Primitives

CRESTFALLEN MANOR ANTIQUES
N Main St   83201
208 233-5179   Est: 1970
Proprietor: Mrs Leon
Hapke
Hours: By Appointment,
10-5
Types & Periods: Glass,
China, Furniture, General
Line
Appraisal Service Available
    Directions: Downtown

THE FARM HOUSE ANTIQUES
1555 N Arthur   83201
208 232-6750
Hours: Daily, 10-5
Types & Periods: General
Line

HUBBY'S POCKET
204 N Main   83201
208 232-5448
Types & Periods: General
Line & Collectibles

THE JUNQUE SHOP
1525 N Arthur   83211
208 233-3093
Hours: Daily
Types & Periods: General
Line

LINCOLN ANTIQUES
317 N Lincoln   83201
208 232-3905
Hours: By Appointment,
By Chance
Types & Periods: Clocks,
Stringed Instruments,
Furniture

STAGE STOP
015 Yellowstone   83201
208 232-6705   Est:1963
Proprietor: Dan, Carolyn,
Myron, Dan Jr, Curtis
Hours: Daily

Types & Periods: Glass,
Tokens, Toys, Pottery,
Advertising Items, Bottles,
Silver
Specialties: Post Cards,
Trains, Bottles, Idaho
Items,Tokens
Appraisal Service Available
    Directions: Across from
    Alameda Shopping Center

Salmon

HOUSE OF BARGAINS
Box 70   83467
208 756-3705   Est: 1973
Proprietor: G C Dale
Baxter
Hours: Mon-Sat
Types & Periods: All
Appraisal Service Available
    Directions: 504 Main St;
    Corner of Shoup & N.
    Terrace

Twin Falls

SNAKE RIVER AUCTION
1979 Kimberly Rd   83301
208 733-7754
Proprietor: Ronald D
Pattee
Hours: Daily 9-7; Auction
Every Sat at 11

Swing Leg Table, Queen Anne, dropleaf. Notice
back-sloping rounded leg with pad foot.

STATE OF ILLINOIS

Aledo

THE OUTPOST
RR 3   61231
309 582-2550   Est: 1975
Proprietor: Mr & Mrs
Glenn Moffit
Hours: Tues-Sun
Types & Periods: "The
Outpost is an Antique Mall
with 18 dealers under one
roof; General Line"
  Directions: 5 miles N of
  Aledo on IL 94, just W of
  Perryton Church

Algonquin

THE BUSY BEE INC
301 S Main St   60102
312 658-4800   Est: 1974
Proprietor: Evelyn Peters
& Betty Blasy
Hours: Tues-Sat, 11-4
Types & Periods: Victorian
thru Turn of the Century
  Directions: On Rte 31

Alton

GENERAL ECLETRIC LTD
205-A E Broadway   62002
Hours: Sat-Sun
Types & Periods: Lamps,
Bric-A-Brac & Furniture

GENEVIEVE'S UPSTAIRS
ANTIQUES
205-A E Broadway   62002
Types & Periods: General
Line, Glass, China,
Primitives & Jewelry

THE GREAT AMERICAN
COVERUP
205-A E Broadway   62002
Hours: Sat-Sun
Types & Periods: Quilts &
Accessories

HOUSE OF THE HUNTER
31 E Broadway   62002
618 465-0086   Est: 1968
Proprietor: Samuel &
Harriet Hunter
Hours: Wed-Sun

Types & Periods: General
Line
Specialties: Refinished
Furniture

MINDY'S MEMORIES
301 E Broadway   62002
618 462-8381   Est: 1978
Proprietor: MeLinda Ward
Hours: Tues-Sun
Types & Periods: Primitives,
American Oak, Glassware &
Turn of the Century
Antiques
Specialties: Oak Clocks
  Directions: Mineral
  Springs Mall; take Rte 3 to
  Broadway, turn W

THE PINE DOOR
207 Broadway   62002
618 462-8945
Proprietor: M Boedeker &
D Hawkins
Hours: Thur-Sun & by
appt
Types & Periods: General
Line

RAINBOW TRADERS
216 E Broadway   62002
618 465-4910
Hours: Sat-Sun, 11-6 & by
appt
Types & Periods: Indian
Arts, Crafts, Jewelry &
General Line

SCARBOROUGH FAIR
208 E Broadway   62002
618 462-3240   Est: 1974
Proprietor: Toni
Scarborough
Hours: Thurs-Sun, 12-5 &
by appt
Types & Periods: Antique
Furniture & General Line

SLOAN'S ANTIQUES
217 E Broadway   62002
618 465-1091
Proprietor: Bill Sloan
Hours: Thurs-Mon, 12-5 &
by appt
Types & Periods: Stained
Glass Windows, Brass Light
Fixtures, Oriental Rugs,
Jewelry & General Line of
Furniture
  Directions: 15 minutes N
  of I-270, St Louis Missouri

STEVE'S ANTIQUES
13 E Broadway   62002
618 465-7407
Hours: Mon, Wed-Fri,
11-5; Sat, 10-5 & Sun 12-5
Types & Periods: Oak
Furniture, Lamps, Glass,
Clocks & Collectibles

SAM THAMES CO
205 E Broadway   62002
618 462-1337
Proprietor: Sam Thames
Hours: Mon-Sun, 9-5
Types & Periods: Stained
Glass, Furniture, Brass,
Metal & Chandeliers

TIME WORN TREASURES
16 E Broadway   62002
618 465-4282
Hours: Mon, Tues & Fri,
12-4; Sat & Sun, 12-5
Types & Periods: General
Line & Collectibles

TRADITION HOUSE
205-A E Broadway   62002
Hours: Weekends
Types & Periods: Furniture,
China, Glass, Collectibles

Antioch

THE COURTYARD
384½ Lake St   60002
312 395-2766
Proprietor: Jo Anna
Larson
Hours: Mon-Tues &
Thurs-Sat, 10-4; Also by
appt
Types & Periods: Furniture,
Metals, Cut Glass,
Porcelains

Arcola

ASHLEY'S
209 S Jacques   61910
217 268-3365
Hours: Mon-Sun
Types & Periods: General
Line

Augusta

THE CANNERY ANTIQUES
PO Box 42   62311
217 392-2111   Est: 1975
Proprietor: William
Goodrich
Hours: Mon-Sun
Types & Periods: Furniture,
Music Boxes, Primitives, Cut
Glass & Brass Beds
Directions: 1 block S of
Hwy 61

Belleville

ANTIQUES BY ELAINE
510 Freeburg Ave   62221
618 234-5122   Est: 1964
Proprietor: Elaine
Matthews
Hours: By appt or chance
Types & Periods: China,
Porcelain, Pattern Glass,
Children's Items & Misc
Appraisal Service Available

Belvidere

THE HOSPICE ANTIQUES
9633 Beaver Valley Rd
                        61008
815 547-5128
Proprietor: William
Durham & William
Galaway
Hours: By appt
Types & Periods: Tea Leaf
Ironstone, Glass, Oil Lamps
& General Line

Berwyn

**HELEN NEWSON
ANTIQUES**
3300 Grove Ave   60402
312 788-6694   Est: 1964
Proprietor: Helen Newson
Hours: Mon-Tues, Fri-Sat,
10:30-5; Thurs 10:30-9
Types & Periods: General
Line, No Furniture
Directions: 6700 W-3300 S
in Berwyn; 1/2 block S of
Burlington Northern
Station & 1 block W of
MacNeal Memorial
Hospital

RUSNAK'S ANTIQUES
6338 W 26th St   60402
312 788-4086
Proprietor: John & Edward
Rusnak
Types & Periods: Indian
Relics, Weapons, Pewter,
Art Glass, Orientals,
Furniture, Copper & Brass

SHADES OF TIME
1212 S Oak Park Ave
                        60402
312 484-9683   Est: 1970
Proprietor: W Lozeau
Hours: Mon-Sun
Types & Periods: Used
Furniture, Antiques,
Re-Manufactured Specialties
& General Line
Specialties: Wood Burning
Stoves & Old Gas Stoves
Appraisal Service Available
Directions: 1/4 block S of
Roosevelt Rd on Oak Park
Ave at alley

Bloomington

ANTIQUE MART
903 Eldorado   61701
309 827-9129   Est: 1964
Proprietor: Mrs Charles
Wood Williams
Hours: Mon-Sat, 10-5
Types & Periods: Silver,
Clocks, Jewelry, Furniture,
Dishes, Phonographs & Cars
in mint condition
Specialties: Oriental Rugs,
Brass & Copper
Directions: 10 shops in
Brick Bldgs, Old City, 66
at Lincoln

ANTIQUES-INTERIORS
709 E Taylor   61701
309 829-1594
Proprietor: Russel K
Young
Hours: By appt
Types & Periods: General
Line & Collectibles

MARY BELL ANTIQUES
2405 S Main St   61701
309 829-6497   Est: 1936
Proprietor: Marie Bishop
Hours: Mon-Sun, 1-5
Types & Periods: Fine
Furniture, Glass, China &
General Line

Appraisal Service Available
Directions: 1 mile N of
I-74 on Rte 51

FREEMAN'S RUINS
229 Robinhood Lane
                        61701
309 662-3032
Proprietor: Ruby &
Wendell Freeman
Hours: Mon-Sun; Also by
appt or chance
Types & Periods: General
Line, China, Cut & Art Glass

EDNA JAMES ANTIQUES
905 S Lee St   61701
309 829-5291
Proprietor: Edna M James
Hours: By appt or chance
Types & Periods: Art Glass,
China, Dolls & General Line

PRATHER'S
311 E Baker   61701
309 828-9257
Proprietor: Ethel Prather
Hours: Evenings, 6-9 by
appt only
Types & Periods: General
Line
Specialties: Danish
Christmas Plates

Bourbon

TOWN PUMP ANTIQUES
                        61953
217 268-4813
Proprietor: Wayne &
Thelma Jensen
Hours: By appt
Types & Periods: Carnival
Glass, China, Clocks &
Primitives
Directions: 3 miles N of
Rte 133 between Arcola &
Arthur IL

Burbank

REX'S GENERAL STORE
5940 N 87th St   60459
312 636-6262   Est: 1972
Proprietor: Lela Rex
Hours: Mon-Sat, 10-5 &
Sun by appt

REX'S GENERAL STORE
Cont'd
Types & Periods: General
Line
Directions: SW of
Chicago; Tri State Tollway
to Rte 12-20 at 95th St, E
to 6000 W & N to 87th St

Byron

BYRON COTTAGE
ANTIQUES
134 E Blackhawk Dr
61010
815 234-8608
Proprietor: Eleanor Dexter
& Ruth Clow
Hours: By appt & by
chance
Types & Periods: Primitives

Cairo

MICKEY'S FURNITURE
PLACE
1907 Commercial Ave
62914
618 734-0601   Est: 1971
Proprietor: Joseph L
Hessian
Hours: By appt
Types & Periods: General
Line
Directions: 2 blocks E, Rte
51 on 20th St, S to Court
House

Carbondale

CURTIS ANTIQUES
Rte 51 S   62901
618 549-1551   Est: 1974
Proprietor: Wm D Curtis
Hours: Mon-Sun
Types & Periods: General
Line
Appraisal Service Available
Directions: 1 mile S of
Carbondale on Rte 51

POLLYS ANTIQUES &
COUNTRY CRAFTS
RR 4 W Chautauqua St
62901
618 549-3547   Est: 1956
Proprietor: Polly & Marion
Mitchell
Hours: Mon-Sun

Types & Periods: General
Line
Directions: SW of
Carbondale

Carthage

GEISSLER'S ANTIQUES
510 Buchanan   62321
217 357-2632   Est: 1965
Proprietor: Carl Geissler
Hours: Mon-Sat, 10-5;
Sun 1-5
Types & Periods: Clocks,
Art, Carnival & Pattern
Glass, China & Furniture
Appraisal Service Available
Directions: On Hwy 136,
1/2 block E of 4 way stop

WAGON WHEEL ANTIQUES
708 Buchanan   62321
217 357-3056   Est: 1974
Proprietor: Leroy Morley &
Nita Johnson
Hours: Sat-Sun, by appt
or chance
Types & Periods: General
Line, Pine, Oak & Walnut
Furniture, Primitives &
Victorian & Golden Oak
Specialties: Furniture, Amity
Furniture Stripping
Appraisal Service Available
Directions: On Hwy 136, 2
blocks E of 4-way stop
sign

Cedarville

EARLY ATTIC ANTIQUES
Box 186   61013
815 563-4513 or 564-4947
Est: 1968
Proprietor: Ruth Stimpert
Hours: Mon, Wed-Sun,
10-5
Types & Periods: General
Line, Furniture & Primitives
Appraisal Service Available
Directions: 3 blocks W Rte
26, corner Cherry &
Mill St

Chadwick

DONS ATTIC
61014
815 684-5152   Est: 1970
Proprietor: D E Smith
Hours: Mon-Sun by appt
Types & Periods: General
Line, 3 Shops

Champaign

ANTIQUES, JEAN & ERNIE
MEHNERT
819 W Washington St
61820
217 352-3844
Proprietor: Jean Mehnert
Hours: By appt or chance
Types & Periods: Pattern
Glass, Heisey, China, Small
Furniture & Misc

HAYLOFT ANTIQUES
Rte 5   61820
217 352-2990   Est: 1969
Proprietor: Vernon H
Lewis
Hours: Sat-Sun by appt or
chance
Types & Periods: Country &
Victorian Furniture
Specialties: Player Pianos
Directions: S of
Champaign on Rte 45 to
Savory, W 1 mile

Channahon

GRIMES ANTIQUES
US 6 & I-55   60410
815 462-2672
Proprietor: Walter & Betty
Grimes
Hours: Mon-Fri, 10-4;
Sat-Sun, 1-5
Types & Periods: Art & Cut
Glass, Furniture & General
Line
Directions: At Treasure
Island

Chatham

WHITE FENCE ANTIQUES
506 E Locust   62629
217 483-2092   Est: 1976

Proprietor: Ernie & Joyce Christensen
Hours: Tues-Sat, 9-6; Sun 12-5 & Also by appt
Types & Periods: General Line, Clocks & Furniture
Specialties: Clocks & Clock Repair
Directions: Rte 4 & Walnut St

Chicago

CHICAGO CLUSTER
Directions: Concentration on the N side; N Wells St (500-800 blocks), N Michigan 900 block, N Clark, N Lincoln, others include W Belmont & S Western Ave

ADDIE'S ATTIC
2108 W Belmont Ave
60618
312 525-8497   Est: 1971
Proprietor: Addie Niemet
Hours: Fri-Wed, 11-7
Types & Periods: Cut Glass, Hand Painted China, Collectibles & Bric-A-Brac
Specialties: Primitives
Directions: Between Damen & Western

ALLEGRETTI ORIENTAL RUGS
7765 N Sheridan Rd
60626
312 743-7200   Est: 1973
Proprietor: Mark A Allegretti
Hours: Mon-Sun
Types & Periods: Oriental Rugs
Specialties: Rugs
Appraisal Service Available
Directions: Along the lake on border of Chicago & Evanston

ANTIQUES & COLLECTIBLES INC
8020 S Western Ave
60620
312 737-9195   Est: 1952
Proprietor: James E Wahl
Hours: Mon-Sat
Types & Periods: Glassware, Ivory, Bronze, Cut Glass, Furniture & General Line

ANTIQUES FORUM
1361 N Wells St   60610
312 664-7844   Est: 1963
Proprietor: H B Cohen
Hours: Mon-Sun
Types & Periods: General Line, Victorian Furniture & Accessories
Appraisal Service Available
Directions: 1 mile N of Chicago Loop

ANTIQUES LTD
1517 Merchandise Mart
60654
312 644-6530   Est: 1956
Proprietor: R M Warsaw
Hours: Mon-Sun
Types & Periods: European & Oriental Decorative Accessories, Restaurant Artifacts, Carvings, Nautical, Chandeliers & Lamps

ARTS & ANTIQUES
746 N Wells St   60610
312 337-6087   Est: 1934
Proprietor: Mr & Mrs H Jirousek
Hours: Mon-Fri, 10:30-4:30; Sat-Sun by appt
Types & Periods: General Line, American , English & Oriental
Directions: Corner of Wells & Chicago

BEHIND THE TIMES ANTIQUES
674 N Dearborn St   60610
312 440-1615   Est: 1974
Proprietor: C Carnot Fay
Hours: Mon-Sat, 12-5; Sun 1-5
Types & Periods: General Line, English & American
Specialties: English Imports
Directions: Between Erie & Huron, 4 blocks W of Michigan Ave

THE BELL JAR ANTIQUES
6981 N Clark   60626
312 743-1236   Est: 1974
Proprietor: Kate Ellingson
Hours: Mon-Sun, 1-6
Types & Periods: General Line
Specialties: Furniture, Jewelry & Erotica
Directions: N side, Rogers Park

BETSY'S ANTIQUES
11400 S Western Ave
60655
312 239-4360
Proprietor: Betsy & Tom Kauffman
Hours: Mon-Sun, 11-5
Types & Periods: China, Glass & Bronzes

BROWN BEAVER ANTIQUES
6836 N Sheridan Rd
60626
312 338-7372   Est: 1968
Proprietor: Wm R Brown
Hours: Tues-Sun, 12-5; Mon 12-8
Types & Periods: Brass Beds , Hall Trees & Bird Cages
Specialties: Brass Beds
Directions: From Downtown Chicago follow Outer Dr to Sheridan Rd & continue N

CAVALIER ANTIQUE STUDIOS
4412 N Ashland Ave
60640
312 561-5957   Est: 1953
Proprietor: Thomas L Bagby
Hours: Tues-Sat, 10-5; Sun 1-5
Types & Periods: Tiffany Lamps, Chandeliers, Furniture & General Line
Specialties: Furniture & Wall Sconces
Appraisal Service Available
Directions: Close to Lake Michigan, 4400 N, 1600 W

CRADLE ANTIQUES & COLLECTIBLES
2252 W Belmont   60618
312 528-4515   Est: 1975
Proprietor: Helen Walsh
Hours: Mon-Sun, 12-7
Types & Periods: Depression Glass, Furniture, Clothes from 20's, Comics & Dolls
Directions: 1 block E of Western Ave-14 Shops in area

DIRECT AUCTIONEERS
7232 N Western Ave
60645
312 465-3300   Est: 1962
Proprietor: Michael Modica
Hours: Mon-Sun

Chicago   Cont'd

DIRECT AUCTIONEERS
Cont'd
Types & Periods: General
Line
Appraisal Service Available

DONROSE GALLERIES INC
751 N Wells   60610
312 337-4052   Est: 1965
Proprietor: Don Rose
Hours: Mon-Sat, 10-5
Types & Periods: 18th &
19th Century French,
English & Oriental Furniture,
Objets d'Art, Paintings,
Bronzes, Porcelain &
Orientalia
Specialties: Bric-A-Brac,
17th-19th Century Paintings
Directions: Corner of
Chicago & Wells Sts

EDMUND'S DESIGN
SERVICE
2962 N Lincoln Ave 60657
312 477-3400   Est: 1972
Proprietor: Willard E
Soper
Hours: Mon-Sun by appt
Types & Periods: General
Line 1860-1930 Collectibles
& Glass
Appraisal Service Available
Directions: 2 blocks S
from Lincoln, Belmont &
Ashland Shopping Area

EDWARDIAN COLLECTION
2262 N Lincoln Ave 60614
312 549-6622   Est: 1970
Proprietor: Edward Katien
Hours: Mon-Tues, by appt
or chance; Wed-Thurs,
11-7; Fri 11-9; Sat 11-5;
Sun 1-4
Types & Periods: 20th
Century Design & Decorative
Art, Furniture, Textiles,
Sculpture (Ceramic, Metallic
& Glass), Graphics &
Lighting
Specialties: Art Nouveau, Art
Deco, Art Moderne
1900-1950 & 20's-40's
Women's Fashions
Appraisal Service Available
Directions: Midnorth area
near Lake Michigan & W
of main entrance to
Lincoln Park Zoo

JOSEPH W FELL LTD
3221 N Clark St   60657
312 549-6076   Est: 1970
Proprietor: Joseph W Fell
Hours: Tues-Sat, 10-5;
appt advisable
Types & Periods: Oriental
Rugs
Appraisal Service Available
Directions: 4 miles N of
the Loop, 1/2 mile W of
Lake Shore Dr, Belmont
exit

MARSHALL FIELD &
COMPANY
111 N State St   60690
Proprietor: Marshall Field
Hours: Mon-Sat
Types & Periods: Antique
Silver & Pewter, Jewelry,
Rare Books & Prints,
American, English &
Continental Furniture
Specialties: Silver, Pewter,
Jewelry, Books, Prints &
Furniture
Directions: Chicago Loop
Area

MARSHALL FIELD &
COMPANY
Water Tower Place,
835 N Michigan Ave 60611
Proprietor: Marshall Field
Hours: Mon-Sun
Types & Periods: Antique
Silver & Pewter, Jewelry,
Rare Books & Prints,
American, English &
Continental Furniture
Specialties: Silver, Pewter,
Jewelry, Books, Prints &
Furniture
Directions: Water Tower
Place

FISHER'S ANTIQUES
2569 N Clark St   60614
312 525-4999   Est: 1934
Proprietor: Shirley Clark
Hours: Mon-Sun
Types & Periods: Jewelry,
Bronzes, Glass, China, Art
Objects
Specialties: Watches &
Jewelry
Appraisal Service Available

FLY-BY-NITE GALLERY
714 N Wells St   60610
312 664-8136   Est: 1962
Proprietor: Thomas M
Tomc

Hours: Mon-Sat, 10-4:30
by appt or chance
Types & Periods: Art
Nouveau & Art Deco, Arts &
Crafts, Art Pottery, Bronzes,
Paintings, Graphics, Posters,
Copper, Pewter, Textiles,
Books, Rare Artifacts,
Furniture & Jugendstil
Specialties: World Non-Scott
Listed Revenue & Cinderella
Stamps & Rare Picture Post
Cards
Appraisal Service Available
Directions: Approx 6
blocks N of Merchandise
Mart or 1½ blocks S of
Chicago Ave, approx 6
blocks W of Michigan Ave

MALCOLM FRANKLIN INC
126 E Delaware Pl   60611
312 337-0202   Est: 1947
Proprietor: Paul, Mark,
Franklin & Mary Ann
Sullivan
Hours: Winter: Mon-Sun;
Summer: Mon-Fri & Sun
Types & Periods: 17th &
18th Century English
Furniture & Accessories
Specialties: Furniture
Appraisal Service Available
Directions: Off Michigan
Ave

GALLAI LTD INC
666 N Michigan Ave
60611
312 321-1360   Est: 1966
Proprietor: Rosalind Gallai
Hours: Mon-Sat; If
unknown to us, we require
appt
Types & Periods: Antique
Jewelry 18th & 19th Century
Specialties: English Antique
Rings
Directions: 3 blocks S of
John Hancock Bldg,
directly across from Saks
Fifth Ave on Michigan Ave

GRIGGS ANTIQUE-LAMPS
5406-08 N Clark   60640
312 561-8489   Est: 1962
Proprietor: Anthony &
Virginia Griggs
Hours: Mon-Tues,
Thurs-Fri, Sun 9-5; Sat
9-2; Closed all holidays
Types & Periods: Furniture,
General Line, Art Nouveau &
Art Deco

Specialties: Lamps, Fixtures & Shades
Directions: 5400 N, 3 blocks from Lake Shore Dr

MARK & LOIS JACOBS AMERICANA COLLECTIBLES-ANTIQUES
702 N Wells St   60610
312 787-8027   Est: 1974
Proprietor: Mark & Lois Jacobs
Hours: Mon-Fri, 10-5; Sat 10-4; Sun & Evenings by appt
Types & Periods: Political Items & Advertising, Breweriana, Sports Memorabilia, Radio Premiums, Comic Books, Character Items & Paper Americana
Specialties: Post Cards, Tin Containers & Pharmaceutical Items
Appraisal Service Available

JAN'S HIDDEN TREASURE HOUSE
4111 N Lincoln   60618
312 929-1411   Est: 1970
Proprietor: Jim & Jan Constantine
Hours: Mon-Sat, 10:30-6; Some Sun & Evenings by appt
Types & Periods: China, Oriental Jewelry, Crystal, Period Furniture, Depression Glass & Pictures
Directions: 3 other locations: 4103 N Lincoln, 1844 W Irving Park & 1950 W Irving Park; All in Chicago

LAKE SHORE FURNITURE
934 W Roscoe   60657
312 327-0972   Est: 1925
Proprietor: Robert Pierson
Hours: Daily
Types & Periods: American Oak, Victorian & French Furniture, Bric-A-Brac, Glassware, Dishes & Jewelry
Appraisal Service Available
Directions: 2 blocks S of Cubs Park at Clark St in New Town Area

LINCOLN AVE ANTIQUES
2954 N Lincoln   60657
312 477-6180   Est: 1969
Proprietor: Gary Gist

Hours: Daily 12:30-5 & also by appt
Types & Periods: General Line, American & Victorian Furniture, Late 18th Century China & Glass
Specialties: Furniture (Dining Room, Chairs & Bedroom Sets)
Appraisal Service Available
Directions: Exit I-94 at Addison E about 10 city blocks

LOST ERAS ANTIQUES
1517-19 W Howard St
        60626
312 764-7400   Est: 1970
Proprietor: R J Shick & C A Simmons
Hours: Mon-Tues, Thurs-Fri, 12-7; Sat 11-6
Types & Periods: Victorian Furniture, Light Fixtures, Stained Glass, Art Nouveau & Art Deco & Civil War Items
Specialties: Art Deco
Appraisal Service Available
Directions: Far N side of Chicago (7500 N); 1½ blocks W of Sheridan Rd

MAGIC LAMP
1545 North Wells   60610
312 787-0075   Est: 1974
Proprietor: Raymond Buralli
Hours: Daily
Types & Periods: Objets Vertu, Art Nouveau & Art Deco, 18th & 19th Century Glass & China & Political Collectibles
Specialties: Art Glass, Porte Bouquet & Early American Glass
Appraisal Service Available
Directions: Old Town near N side, 3 blocks W of Lincoln Park & North Ave; Lake Shore Dr to North Ave exit, 2 blocks W

MAX MAREK ANTIQUES
3800 N Sheffield Ave
        60613
312 549-1505   Est: 1959
Proprietor: Max Marek
Hours: Daily, 12-6
Types & Periods: Oak Furniture, Round Tables, Chairs, Pews & Stained Glass

MISCELLANIA
2659 N Racine   60614
312 525-9565   Est: 1972
Proprietor: Linda Mark
Hours: Mon, Wed-Fri & Sun, 2-6; Sat 12-6
Types & Periods: General Line from 20's, 30's & 40's
Directions: 1 block S of Lincoln & Diversey

M DAVID MORRIS & CO
70 E Watson   60611
312 944-4448   Est: 1966
Proprietor: M David Morris
Hours: Daily by appt or chance
Types & Periods: Jewelry & Objets d'Art
Appraisal Service Available

NAHIGIAN BROTHERS INC
645 N Michigan Ave
        60611
312 943-8300   Est: 1890
Proprietor: Haig S Nahigian
Hours: Mon-Fri & Sun 9-5, Sat 9-4
Types & Periods: Orientals & Aubussons
Appraisal Service Available
Directions: Entrance on Erie St

RICHARD NORTON, INC
612 Merchandise Mart
        60654
Proprietor: Richard F Norton
Hours: Mon-Fri
Types & Periods: French & English Antique Furniture & Decorative Accessories

OLD WORLD ANTIQUES
958 W Webster   60614
312 871-5500   Est: 1972
Proprietor: F Steven Barick
Hours: Tues-Fri 12-7, Sat-Sun 1-7
Types & Periods: English, American, Victorian, Art Nouveau & Bronze
Specialties: Art Nouveau
Appraisal Service Available
Directions: Corner of Webster & Sheffield

Chicago Cont'd

RUDEE ANTIQUE & MODERN JEWELRY
55 E Washington St
60602
312 332-0633
Proprietor: Miriam Rasnick
Hours: Mon-Sun
Types & Periods: Jewelry & Estate Pieces
Directions: Pittsfield Bldg across from Marshall Field

RUMMAGE 'ROUND ANTIQUES
435 North LaSalle St.
60610
312 642-8283   Est: 1956
Proprietor: Elaine M. Kay
Hours: By appointment
Types & Periods: Bric-A-Brac
Specialties: Wood

RUTH'S ANTIQUE UNLIMITED
5303 N Clark St   60640
312 271-4438   Est: 1973
Proprietor: Ruth Goranson Vosnos
Hours: Mon-Sun 11-5
Types & Periods:
Collectibles, China, Silver, Glass
Directions: In Andersonville Area, 6 miles N of the loop, 5300 N, 1500 W

STANLEY'S ANTIQUES
415 N Franklin St   60610
312 321-1900   Est: 1951
Proprietor: Stanley A Levine
Hours: Mon-Sun 8:30-5
Types & Periods: 18th & 19th Centuries European Only
Specialties: Wholesale Only
Directions: 1/2 block from Merchandise Mart

TUREEN & PLATTER ANTIQUES
2928 N Lincoln Ave 60657
312 472-1673   Est: 1969
Proprietor: Neil K Brown
Hours: Mon-Sat, 12-5; Sun by appt
Types & Periods: Glass, China, Furniture, Brass,

Copper & Silver
Specialties: Chandeliers & Lamps
Directions: 2900 N & 1300 W; Seven shops in our block

THE TURQUOISE BUTTERFLY SHOP
604 Barry Ave   60657
312 549-2245   Est: 1968
Proprietor: L B Earle
Hours: Tues, Thurs-Sat, 11-4
Types & Periods: Miscellaneous
Specialties: Books, China, Glass
Directions: Near Belmont & Broadway; N side of City

WEBBERLEY GALLERIES
202 S State St   60604
312 922-5278
Proprietor: Rosalind Mikesell
Hours: Mon-Sun by appt
Types & Periods: 19th & Early 20th Century European & American Paintings
Appraisal Service Available
Directions: "The Loop"

WELLINGTON INTERNATIONAL
3223-27 N Clark St 60657
312 549-4430
Proprietor: Louise Lane
Hours: Mon-Sun
Types & Periods:
Bric-A-Brac, American & European Furniture & Collectibles
Appraisal Service Available
Directions: Belmont Ave & Clark St

WHITE ROSE SALON
2262 N Lincoln Ave 60614
Proprietor: Adrienne & Mary Jvell
Hours: Mon-Thurs, 11-7; Fri 11-9; Sat 11-5; Sun 1-4
Types & Periods: Clothing: Mostly special occasion Dress & Sleepwear, one-of-a-kind Dresses, Hats, Scarves, Gloves, Purses & Jewelry
Specialties: Chicago Designers creating 20's, 30's & 40's styles out of vintage fabric with a contemporary flair

WORLD'S ANTIQUE MART
1006 S Michigan Ave
60605
312 922-1939   Est: 1949
Proprietor: 8 Dealers
Hours: Mon-Wed, Fri-Sun
Types & Periods:
Bric-A-Brac, China, Glass, Jewelry, Art Pottery, Afro & Columbian Art Pieces & Furniture
Specialties: Wholesale
Directions: 1½ blocks S of Conrad Hilton Hotel

Cicero

VILLAGE COLLECTIQUES
Box 244   60650
312 743-5522
Proprietor: Malcolm C Hart
Hours: By appt
Types & Periods: General Line

Clarendon Hills

YANKEE PEDDLER ANTIQUES
211 W Burlington   60514
312 654-9043   Est: 1970
Proprietor: Myrna Mohler & Susan Tanner
Hours: Tues-Sat 10-4
Types & Periods: Country Furniture, Pottery & Tin Toys
Appraisal Service Available
Directions: In an old Fire Station converted to Tea Room with 10 shops

Coal City

TIME TUNNEL
155 S Broadway   60416
815 634-4195
Proprietor: Joyce Vota & Janice Dell
Hours: Tues-Sun, 10-4
Types & Periods: Glass & General Line

Congerville

NORRIS ANTIQUES
1-74 Goodfield
Interchange   61729
309 448-2288
Proprietor: Buelah Norris
Hours: Mon-Sun
Types & Periods: Cut,
Pattern & Art Glass, China &
Primitives

Crete

JILL'S
1361 Main St   60417
312 672-6877   Est: 1976
Proprietor: Jill Baker
Hours: Tues-Sat, 10-5
Types & Periods: Wicker &
American Country Primitives
Specialties: Pine & Wicker
Furniture
Directions: In center of
Town

**THE MARKET PLACE
BAZAAR**
550 Exchange St   60417
312 672-5556   Est: 1967
Proprietor: Kathryn Daum
& Kathryn Fairchild
Hours: Mon-Sun
Types & Periods: Furniture,
Dolls, Glass, China,
Primitives, Toy Trains,
Coins, Jewelry & Collectibles
Directions: 4th road past
Rte 30, W on Exchange, 2
blocks past Stoplight; 15
Dealers under one roof

Crossville

NELLIE'S ANTIQUES
Box 18   62827
618 966-3601   Est: 1969
Proprietor: Nellie P
Edmunson
Hours: Mon-Sun, 9-5;
Evenings by appt
Types & Periods: Primitives,
China & Furniture
Directions: Main & 460, E

Crystal Lake

**ROYAL OAKS MUSEUM OF
ANTIQUES**
US Hwy 14 at 176   60014
815 459-4278   Est: 1960
Proprietor: Ernest C
Andreas
Hours: Mon-Sun, 10-4:30
Types & Periods: General
Line, Northern Illinois
History 1820-1930
Appraisal Service Available

De Kalb

SERENDIPITY ANTIQUES
522 Joanne Lane   60115
815 756-9359
Proprietor: Jo Boardman
Hours: By appt or chance
Types & Periods: Primitives
& Country Furniture

Decatur

THE BROWSE SHOP
Rock Springs Rd   62521
217 423-9884   Est: 1971
Proprietor: M & C
Meisenheimer & C Pribble
Hours: By appt or chance
Types & Periods: China,
Glass & Small Furniture

DE JANS ANTIQUES
1024 E Lincoln   62521
217 429-0123
Proprietor: Don & Jan
Deetz
Hours: By appt
Types & Periods: General
Line

HOUSE OF DECOR
Rte 7, Box 262   62521
217 864-4512   Est: 1973
Proprietor: Mrs Jay
Ball, Jr
Hours: Wed-Sun
Types & Periods: Country &
Victorian Furniture,
Primitives, Brass & Copper
& Clocks
Directions: Rte 36 E; 20
miles E of Airport

HELEN PRICE ANTIQUES
242 W Main St   62523
217 422-4442   Est: 1960
Proprietor: Helen E Price
Hours: Mon-Sun by appt
Types & Periods: China,
Glass, Orientals, Jewelry,
Sterling, Flatware &
Furniture
Directions: 2 blocks from
center of uptown

STRAW FLOWER, INC
801 W Eldorado   62522
217 428-7212   Est: 1972
Proprietor: Virginia
Cannon & M Jane Jurgens
Hours: Tues-Sat, 10-4:30
Types & Periods: General
Line of Antiques &
Collectibles, Primitives,
Stained Glass Windows,
Clocks & Haviland China
Specialties: Haviland China
Appraisal Service Available
Directions: Route 36 thru
Decatur

Deerfield

**TREASURE HOUSE
ANTIQUES**
827 Waukegan Rd   60015
312 945-0888   Est: 1960
Proprietor: Marge
Moroney
Hours: Mon-Tues,
Thurs-Sat, 10:30-4; Also
by appt
Types & Periods: Old Wicker
Furniture, Jewelry &
Miscellaneous Items
Appraisal Service Available
Directions: Edens Expwy
is 2 miles E of shop

Donnellson

**DONNELLSON FURNITURE
MART**
Rte 127   62019
217 537-3013   Est: 1974
Proprietor: H J Hallers
Hours: Tues-Sat, 10-4;
Also by appt
Types & Periods: Furniture,
Tools & Dishes & General
Line
Directions: Right hand
side of Rte 127, when
traveling S

Dover

VILLAGE ANTIQUES
Rte 34   61323
815 643-2550   Est: 1977
Proprietor: Laura
Prendergast
Hours: Mon-Sat, 11-4
Types & Periods: Primitives,
Oak & Walnut Furniture,
Fine China & Glassware &
Collectibles
Directions: 5 miles N of
Princeton, IL on Rte 34 at
Dover Homestead Farm

Downers Grove

**COLONEL DANHELKA'S
ANTIQUES, INC**
1804 Ogden Ave   60480
312 971-2522   Est: 1970
Proprietor: Colonel D
Danhelka
Hours: Mon-Sun
Types & Periods: Furniture,
Clocks, Barber Shop Pieces
& Cars
Specialties: Wooden Desks
Appraisal Service Available
Directions: 22 miles W of
Chicago

East Alton

HENRY THE III
111 Henry St   62024
618 259-2707
Hours: Wed-Sun, 12-6
Types & Periods: Furniture,
Glass & Collectibles

KEN'S COINS & ANTIQUES
106 W Main St   62024
618 259-5995
Hours: Mon-Sat, 9-8; Sun
by appt
Types & Periods: China,
Pottery, Coins, Stamps &
Supplies

East Dubuque

ANTIQUE CORNER
519 Sinsinawa   61025
815 742-6158   Est: 1975
Proprietor: Paul Henkel

Hours: By chance, owner
lives next door
Types & Periods: General
Line
Specialties: Clocks &
Watches
Directions: Hwy 20 at
corner of Sinsinawa Ave &
Hill St

East Moline

BARN ANTIQUES
17328 Hwy 5 & 92   61244
309 755-3717   Est: 1964
Proprietor: Marjorie
Gottman
Hours: May-Oct: Mon-Fri,
10-5
Types & Periods: General
Line, Victorian & Early 1900
Furniture
Specialties: Hanging Lamps
Directions: 2 miles off I-80

East Peoria

**HAND-E-CRAFT ANTIQUE
SHOP**
417 Arnold Rd   61611
309 699-2048
Proprietor: Wayne &
Louise Abercrombie
Hours: Mon-Sun
Types & Periods: China,
Glass, Furniture, Primitives
& Woodenware

Effingham

**NEVA'S ANTIQUES 'N
THINGS**
601 W Fayette   62401
217 342-4731
Proprietor: Neva Mahon
Hours: Tues-Sat by appt
or chance
Types & Periods: Glass,
China, Victorian Furniture &
Lamps, Art Nouveau
Specialties: Jewelry
Directions: E, first exit off
I-70; W, 3rd exit off I-70

Eldorado

**KENNEDY'S ANTIQUE
SHOP**
1701 Locust St   62930
618 273-6696   Est: 1969
Proprietor: Alex & Georgia
Kennedy
Hours: Mon-Sun, 10-5;
Also by appt
Types & Periods: Flow Blue
Dishes, Depression &
Glassware, Furniture, Oil
Lamps & Picture Frames
Specialties: Come hear
Charles & Alex play the
violins
Appraisal Service Available
Directions: 1 block off 142
N & 1/4 mile N on Rte 45

Elgin

ANTIQUE CENTER
475 Walnut Ave   60120
312 695-6616   Est: 1968
Proprietor: Frank M
Farwell
Hours: Mon-Sun
Types & Periods: General
Line
Appraisal Service Available
Directions: 6 blocks W of
Rte 31

BILL'S FURNITURE
801 Dundee Ave   60120
312 695-0055   Est: 1963
Proprietor: Bill Shelton
Hours: Mon-Sat, 10-7
Types & Periods: General
Line
Directions: Corner of
Lincoln & Dundee Ave at
N end of town

KAY FLORA'S ANTIQUES
125 N Weston Ave   60120
312 742-1027
Proprietor: Roy &
Kathleen Flora
Hours: By appt or chance
Types & Periods: China,
Glass, Primitives, Furniture,
Decorator Items & Prints

TRAILS & TREASURES
I Trout Park Blvd   60120
312 742-1454   Est: 1967
Proprietor: Inc
Hours: Tues-Sat, 11-3
Types & Periods: Tea Room,

Ginger Patch: Primitives,
Whistle Stop: Small &
Christmas Items, Butternut
House: Furniture & Misc
Directions: On the Fox
River, S of the NW
Tollroad

Elizabeth

**LITTLE BARN
ANTIQUES-CHURCH
STORE**
115 S Main   61028
815 858-2037   Est: 1965
Proprietor: Wm F
Boekhaus
Hours: Winter: Sat-Sun
only; Summer: Mon-Wed &
Fri-Sun
Types & Periods: 19th
Century Furniture, Lamps,
Pictures, Oriental Rugs,
Ivory, Cloisonne, Indian
Rugs & Primitives
Specialties: Art & Cut Glass;
Toys
Directions: 15 miles E of
Galena IL (NW IL area);
Rte 20 in town

Elliott

STEMBEL ANTIQUES
Box 8   60933
217 749-2236   Est: 1968
Proprietor: Doc Stembel
Hours: Sat-Mon by chance
or appt
Types & Periods: Primitives,
Silver, Glass, Tools & Oak,
Walnut & Cherry Furniture
Appraisal Service Available
Directions: I-57 to Paxton
IL, 8 minutes W on
IL Rte 9

Elmhurst

VICTORIA HOUSE
320 N York St   60126
312 833-1562
Proprietor: Rose Parish
Hours: Tues-Thurs & Sat,
9:30-5
Types & Periods: Victorian
Furniture & Primitives

Specialties: Rosemaling
Appraisal Service Available
Directions: 1st block N of
North Ave

WOOD 'N' WONDERS
110 W Second St   60126
312 832-6665   Est: 1972
Proprietor: Nancy Wells
Hours: Mon-Sat
Types & Periods:
Architectural Items: Mantels,
Pier Mirrors, Staircases,
Paneling, Custom Made
Furniture & New Fretwork
Made to Order
Specialties: Old Church
Pews (cut to size) & Stained
& Beveled Glass (made to
order)
Directions: Downtown, 2
blocks S of North Ave
(Rte 64); 1/2 block W of
York Rd

El Paso

**HELEN'S ANTIQUES &
RESALE SHOP**
546 Elmwood Court
                    61738
309 527-2445
Proprietor: Helen Scott
Types & Periods: General
Line, China, Furniture, &
Jewelry

Elwood

BILL'S TRADING POST
114 Mississippi Ave 60421
815 423-5170
Proprietor: Bill Reid
Hours: Sat 10-5; Also by
appt
Types & Periods: General
Line

Erie

CUBBYHOLE ANTIQUES
PO Box 58   61250
309 659-2977   Est: 1969
Proprietor: Bev Froeliger
Hours: By chance

Types & Periods: General
Line
Specialties: Primitives
Directions: Off I-5, 1 block
W of Phillips 66

Eureka

THE OLD SHOP
108 E Center   61530
309 467-3613   Est: 1966
Proprietor: R J Herschel
Hours: Mon-Sun, 9-11:30
& 1-4
Types & Periods: 18th &
19th Century Antiques
Specialties: Unusual &
Historical Items
Appraisal Service Available
Directions: Rte 24, across
from Court House

Evanston

**ALLEGRETTI ORIENTAL
RUGS**
815 Chicago Ave   60202
312 866-6668   Est: 1970
Proprietor: Mark A
Allegretti
Hours: Mon-Sat
Types & Periods: New, Old
& Antique Oriental Rugs &
Carpets
Specialties: Oriental Rugs
Appraisal Service Available
Directions: S of Main St in
Evanston

THE DYNASTY SHOP
2644 Green Bay Rd
                    60201
312 864-2495   Est: 1972
Proprietor: Major Gen T B
Evans
Hours: Mon-Sun
Types & Periods: Oriental
Circa 1300-1900
Appraisal Service Available
Directions: N Evanston
near Wilmette Village City
Limits, N of Central St

HALFPENCE HOUSE
1327 Greenleaf   60202
312 DA8-1818   Est: 1973
Proprietor: Jan Martin &
Joanne Sherry
Hours: Tues-Fri, 10-4;
Sat 10-5

Evanston   Cont'd

HALFPENCE HOUSE Cont'd
Types & Periods: 18th-20th
Century Furniture, China,
Glass & Silver
Appraisal Service Available

HARVEY ANTIQUES
1231 Chicago Ave   60202
312 866-6766
Proprietor: Harvey Pranian
Hours: Tues-Sat, 10-5
Types & Periods: 18th &
19th Century American
Furniture & Accessories &
Jewelry
Appraisal Service Available

KINGS 3 ANTIQUES
705-07 Washington 60202
312 491-6171   Est: 1972
Proprietor: Charles
Schultz & W L Jonke
Hours: Mon-Sun
Types & Periods:
Collectibles
Specialties: Silver
Appraisal Service Available

**KITCHEN KUPBOARD
ANTIQUES**
1919 Central   60201
312 864-6060   Est: 1972
Proprietor: John Kopplin
Hours: Mon-Fri & Sun,
10-6; Sat 10-5
Types & Periods: Victorian &
Turn of the Century Oak
Furniture
Directions: N Evanston on
Central, 1 block W of
Green Bay Rd

MIDWEST FOLK ART
1235 Chicago Ave   60202
312 475-2044   Est: 1976
Proprietor: Beverly
McTigue & Rosalyn
Praniom
Hours: Tues-Sat, 11-4
Types & Periods: Furniture,
Country Accessories &
General Line
Directions: SE Evanston,
Dempster & Chicago Ave

**ORIGINAL CROST
FURNITURE STORE INC**
1004-6 Emerson   60201
312 UN4-0189   Est: 1898
Proprietor: Albert Fink
Hours: Mon-Sun

Types & Periods: English
Imported Antiques
Specialties: Restoration of
Antiques
Appraisal Service Available
Directions: Near
Northwestern University &
Downtown

**WILD GOOSE CHASE
QUILT GALLERY**
526 Dempster   60202
312 328-1808   Est: 1973
Proprietor: Gail Struve &
Marilyn Packer
Hours: Tues-Sat, 1-5 or
by appt
Types & Periods: Quilts
1840-Now (95% of the quilts
are 1860-1930)
Specialties: Amish &
Graphic Quilts
Appraisal Service Available
Directions: 3 blocks E of
the lake

**KEN YOUNG ANTIQUE
JEWELRY**
703 Washington   60202
312 869-6670   Est: 1970
Proprietor: Ken Young
Hours: Mon-Sun
Types & Periods: Jewelry,
Watches & Clocks
Appraisal Service Available

Fieldon

A & B ANTIQUES
Rte 1   62031
618 576-2493   Est: 1966
Proprietor: Aubrey Bailey
Hours: By appt or chance
Types & Periods: General
Line, Primitives & Dishes
Directions: On Rte 16 W
end, 1 mile E of Hardin

Flossmoor

H L ENTERPRISES
1630 Holbrook Rd   60422
312 798-7066   Est: 1968
Proprietor: Henry B
Leopold
Hours: By chance
Types & Periods: Victorian &
French Furniture, H P China,
Glass & Silver
Specialties: New England
Peach Blow Glass

Appraisal Service Available
Directions: SW of
Chicago, 19300 S 1600 W,
using Chicago's street
numbering system

Forest Park

SOMETHING ELSE LTD
7501 Madison   60130
312 366-0599   Est: 1975
Proprietor: Marie V Gits
Hours: Tues-Fri, 12-8;
Sat 12-5
Types & Periods: 19th
Century Furniture &
Accessories, Collectibles,
China, Glass & Primitives
Specialties: Furniture &
Accessories
Directions: 1 block E of
Des Plaines Ave on
Madison, 3 blocks N of
Eisenhower Expwy (I-90)

Frankfort

ALLEN'S ANTIQUES
100 Kansas St   60423
815 469-5535
Proprietor: Faye Allen
Hours: Tues-Sun
Types & Periods: General
Line & Furniture
Specialties: China & Glass
Appraisal Service Available
Directions: 3 blocks from
Rte 30

DAYS GONE BY
20555 La Grange Rd
                   60423
815 469-9891   Est: 1972
Proprietor: Thomas &
Nancy Benda
Hours: Mon-Sun
Types & Periods: Furniture,
Primitives, China, Porcelains
& Accessories
Directions: Rte 45, 2 miles
from I-80, or 1/2 mile N of
Rte 30

**OLDE STUFF ANTIQUES &
OLDE TYME BOUTIQUE**
111 Ash St   60423
312 469-3394   Est: 1977
Proprietor: Barbara
Pillasch
Hours: Mon-Sun

Types & Periods: General
Line Antiques
Specialties: Vintage
Clothing, Household Textiles
& Accessories
Directions: Across From
Bank

Freeport

GALLOPING HORSE
ANTIQUES
220 Broadway   61032
815 232-2266
Proprietor: Marian Laible
Types & Periods: General
Line

Galena

HELENE'S COUNTRY
CUPBOARD
304 S Main   61036
815 777-1420
Proprietor: Helene Wirth
Hours: Mon-Sun, 10-4
during season; Also by
appt
Types & Periods: General
Line & Primitives

LLOYD
Spring & Prospect   61036
815 777-1000   Est: 1974
Proprietor: Lloyd Brett
Hours: Mon-Sun
Types & Periods:
Victorian-Early 1900's
Specialties: Clothing &
Linens
Directions: Hwy 20 near
the bridge

UNIQUE ANTIQUES
121 S Main St   61036
815 777-0179   Est: 1974
Proprietor: George &
Marilyn Lamb
Hours: Mon-Sun
Types & Periods: General
Line
Specialties: Victorian,
Walnut & Golden Oak
Furniture
Appraisal Service Available
Directions: Center of
restored Galena, Main St
historic area

Galesburg

ANTIQUES, AMERICANA
435 Kellogg St N   61401
309 342-4334
Proprietor: Ron & Nancy
Harms
Hours: By appt or chance
Types & Periods: General
Line
Specialties: Primitives

HICKORY HILL ANTIQUES
RR 2   61401
309 343-5828   Est: 1969
Proprietor: Pam
Quanstrom
Hours: Mon-Sun by appt
or chance
Types & Periods: Country
Furniture & Decorative
Accessories from 1800-1890
Specialties: Furniture
Directions: Rte 34 to
Cameron corner, N 2½
miles, turn right at stop
sign, 3rd house from
corner

Gardner

ITEMS FROM R E L &
OPERA HOUSE MUSEUM
212 W Division   60424
815 237-2171
Proprietor: Richard &
Betty Lee
Hours: June-Aug:
Mon-Wed, Fri-Sun, 1-5;
Sept-May: Sat-Sun, 1-4 or
by appt
Types & Periods: General
Line

Geneva

D GRUNWALD ANTIQUES
402 Anderson Blvd 60134
312 232-2862   Est: 1976
Proprietor: D Grunwald
Hours: Tues-Sat, 10-5;
Also by appt
Types & Periods: General
Line
Specialties: Silver, Jewelry,
Glass & Furniture
Directions: 3 blocks W of
center of town; 4 blocks N
of Rte 38

GRUNWALD GALLERY OF
ANTIQUES
315 W State St   60134
Proprietor: A F Grunwald
Hours: Mon-Sat
Types & Periods: China,
Glass, Jewelry, Silver,
Enamels, Paintings &
Oriental Rugs
Specialties: Silver & Jewelry
Appraisal Service Available
Directions: 30 miles W of
Chicago on Rte 38
(Roosevelt Rd); Located in
Theatre Bldg

HOUSE OF ANTIQUES
314 E State St   60134
312 232-9650
Proprietor: Jeanne &
Marvin Smith
Hours: Wed-Sat, 10-5;
Sun 12-5
Types & Periods: Flow Blue,
Tea Leaf, Primitives,
17th-19th Century American
Furniture

SHIRLEY MC GILL
ANTIQUES
717 E State St   60134
312 232-4196   Est: 1961
Proprietor: Chirley McGill
Hours: Tues-Sat, 10-4;
Sun 12-4
Types & Periods: Furniture,
Stonewear, Lithographs,
Textiles, Metals, Pattern
Glass & Folk Art
Specialties: American
Country Furniture
Appraisal Service Available
Directions: Rte 38 on east
edge of Geneva, N side of
street, 1st bldg W of
Franks Market

Genoa

THE SWAN HOUSE
122 N Sycamore   60135
815 784-5537   Est: 1969
Proprietor: Janice G
Campbell
Hours: Sat-Sun
Types & Periods: Country
Furniture, Treen & Tinware
Specialties: Tinware

Gilman

**SHIRLEY RYAN'S
ANTIQUES**
530 E 2nd St   60938
815 265-7256
Proprietor: Shirley Ryan.
Hours: Mon-Sun
Types & Periods: General
Line
Specialties: Jewelry

Glencoe

CARDAY ANTIQUES
348 Tudor Ct   60022
312 835-4776   Est: 1970
Hours: Tues-Sat, 10-4
Types & Periods: Jewelry,
General Line & Collectibles
Specialties: Jewelry
Directions: Middle of
Glencoe; W of Green Bay
Rd

IT'S ABOUT TIME
375 Park Ave   60022
                     Est: 1972
Proprietor: Fred Crane
Hours: Wed-Sat, 10-5
Types & Periods: Music
Boxes, Player Pianos
Specialties: Clocks
Appraisal Service Available
Directions: 20 minutes N
of Chicago Loop

Glen Ellyn

THE ANTIQUE GALLERY
482 Duane St   60137
312 469-3555   Est: 1969
Proprietor: H Gray
Hours: Tues-Fri, 1-4; Sat
10-4; Also by appt
Types & Periods: General
Line
Specialties: Paintings, Prints
& Oriental Porcelains
Appraisal Service Available
Directions: Rte 38 W to
Main St, proceed N, 4
stop signs to Duane St,
1 block W

CAPE COD HOUSE
439 Pennsylvania Ave
                     60137
312 858-0040
Proprietor: Marge Landies

Types & Periods: Pattern
Glass, Lamps, Primitives &
Furniture
Directions: At the sign of,
"The House in the Glen"

GALERIE DE PORCELAINE
520 Hillside   60137
312 858-9494   Est: 1969
Proprietor: Marian
Zickefoose
Hours: Wed-Sat, 12-4; By
appt; Mail order
Types & Periods: Old French
& American Haviland China
Specialties: Haviland China
Matching & Sets
Appraisal Service Available
Directions: 1st shop E of
Main St on Hillside

THE HOUSE IN THE GLEN
439 Pennsylvania   60137
312 858-0040   Est: 1975
Proprietor: Geraldine
Olson
Hours: Tues-Sun
Types & Periods: Victorian,
Ironstone, Brass, Copper &
Primitives
Specialties: Country Pine
Furniture
Appraisal Service Available
Directions: Downtown

**MARCY KING'S
STAGECOACH ANTIQUES**
526 Crescent   60137
312 469-0490
Proprietor: Marcy King
Hours: Mon-Sat
Types & Periods: Country
Primitives, Glass & China

**PATRICIA LACOCK
ANTIQUES**
526 Crescent Blvd   60137
312 858-2323
Hours: Mon-Sat, 10-4
Types & Periods: Furniture,
Art & Pattern Glass, China,
Jewelry, Copper, Brass &
Pewter

NADINE P MARTENS
522 Hillside   60137
312 858-9249   Est: 1968
Proprietor: Nadine
Martens
Hours: Tues-Sat, 11-4,
Also by appt
Types & Periods: 18th &
19th Century, English &
American, Country & Formal

Furniture & Accessories
Specialties: Furniture
Appraisal Service Available
Directions: 3 doors E of
Main St in Downtown,
approx 1 mile N of Rte 38
(Roosevelt Rd)

OLD PARR ANTIQUES
475 Duane St   60137
312 469-1519   Est: 1970
Proprietor: Virginia B Parr
Hours: Mon-Sat, 11-4
Types & Periods: Art Glass,
Handpainted China, Jewelry,
Collectibles, Dolls & Clocks
Directions: 1st street S of
N Western tracks; 1½
blocks W of Main St in
Apt Bldg

BETTY PITTS ANTIQUES
22 W 640 Burr Oak Dr
                     60137
312 469-3643
Proprietor: Betty Pitts
Hours: By appt
Types & Periods: General
Line
Specialties: Toys (Dolls)

POSITIVELY POSH
558 Crescent Blvd   60137
312 858-6886
Hours: Mon-Sat, 10-5
Types & Periods: Clocks &
General Line
Directions: Cluster of
shops

PRAIRIE HOUSE ANTIQUES
509 Main St   60137
312 858-2170
Proprietor: Diana & Jim
Eyre
Hours: Tues-Sat, 10-4
Types & Periods: Pine,
Walnut & Cherry Furniture,
Pressed Glass, Country
China, Primitives, Quilts,
Kerosene Lamps, Picture
Frames & Mirrors
Specialties: Custom Lamp
Shades in Old & New
Fabrics
Appraisal Service Available
Directions: Next door to
Post Office in downtown
Glen Ellyn

THE SHADY LADY
439 Pennsylvania Ave
                     60137
312 469-0245

Hours: Tues-Sat, 10-4;
Sun 1-4
Types & Periods: General
Line
Specialties: Lamps

THE WAY WE WERE
363 Hill Ave   60137
312 858-6147
Proprietor: Norma & Don
Burgeson
Hours: By appt
Types & Periods: Country
Furniture & Collectibles

WINDSOR MANOR
548 Crescent Blvd   60137
312 858-6460
Hours: Mon-Sat, 10-4
Types & Periods: Furniture,
Collectibles & Glass
Specialties: Stained Glass
Windows

Glenview

**A LITTLE BIT ANTIQUES
LTD**
1011 Harlem Ave   60025
312 724-7070   Est: 1060
Proprietor: James & Fern
Meehan
Hours: Mon-Sat, 10:30-5
Types & Periods: Period
Furniture, Art Glass, Cut
Glass, Porcelains, Jewelry,
Clocks & Dolls
Specialties: Flow Blue &
Historical
Appraisal Service Available
Directions: 20 minutes to
Loop, close to Tri-State &
O'Hare

Golconda

**SHAWNEE FURNITURE &
ANTIQUE**
Main St   62938
618 683-3176
Proprietor: Alvera Hobbs
Hours: By appt or chance
Types & Periods: Depression
& Pressed Glass, Jars,
Pottery, Primitives, Ironware,
Bottles & Furniture
Directions: 2nd block from
4-way stop sign

Grafton

JODENE ANTIQUES
Box 112   62037
618 786-3661   Est: 1946
Proprietor: Aldene
Leonard
Hours: Wed-Sun, 10-5;
Also by appt
Types & Periods: Oak &
Walnut American Furniture
& General Line
Specialties: Lamps
Appraisal Service Available
Directions: 3 miles W of
town on Illinois River

RIVER ROAD ANTIQUES
Box 158   62037
618 786-3358   Est: 1966
Proprietor: Gretchen
Maurer
Hours: Tues-Sun, 10-5
Types & Periods: Bronzes,
Silver, Cloisonne, Crystal,
China, Brass, Copper &
Furniture
Specialties: Lamps & Lamp
Parts
Appraisal Service Available
Directions: On Great River
Road, 13 miles N of Alton

Greenup

P & M ANTIQUES
509 E Cincinnati   62428
217 923-3325
Proprietor: Paul &
Margaret Wright
Hours: Mon-Sun
Types & Periods:
Collectibles, Glass,
Primitives, Furniture &
Clocks

Greenville

BROWN'S ANTIQUES
102 Latzer Dr   62044
618 664-0629   Est: 1973
Proprietor: Mr & Mrs
Raymond Brown Jr
Hours: By chance
Types & Periods: General
Line, Furniture, Dishes, Iron
& Granite Ware & Pictures
Directions: 50 miles E of
St Louis on I-70

HERRINGS ANTIQUES
R 3   62246
618 664-4211   Est: 1969
Proprietor: Charles &
Helen Herring
Hours: Mon-Sun, 10-5
Types & Periods: Oak
Furniture, General Line &
Collectibles
Specialties: Oak Furniture
Directions: 5 miles W of
Greenville on Rte 40
Frontage Rd

Gridley

MARY CAMPBELL
Center St   61744
Proprietor: Mrs Robert B
Campbell
Hours: Wed, Fri & Sat,
11-4
Types & Periods: Country,
Pine, Cherry & Walnut
Furniture & General Line

Hamilton

OAKWOOD ANTIQUES
1890 Keokuk St   62341
217 847-2648   Est: 1972
Proprietor: Robert &
Louise Allen
Hours: Mon-Sun, 8-5; Also
by chance or appt
Types & Periods: General
Line, Oak & Victorian
Furniture
Specialties: Refinishing &
Repairing
Appraisal Service Available
Directions: Rte US 136

Henry

NU-VALU
418 Park Row   61537
309 364-2580   Est: 1945
Proprietor: Marie Reimers
Hours: Thurs-Sat, 9-4
Types & Periods: Books,
Collectibles, Silver, Glass,
Primitives & Furniture
Directions: 35 miles N of
Peoria; Rte 29 to Rte 18

Highland

**M & M SCHNEIDER
ANTIQUES**
1705 Olive St   62249
618 654-8051
Proprietor: Melba &
Merton Schneider
Hours: By appt or chance
Types & Periods: Pattern &
Cut Glass, China &
Collectibles

Highland Park

**ALADDIN'S LAMP
ANTIQUES**
1913 Sheridan Rd   60035
312 432-0439   Est: 1960
Proprietor: Herman &
Rosemary Wren
Hours: Tues-Sat, 10-5
Types & Periods: General
Line, "Over 100,00 Items"
Specialties: Clocks
Directions: Downtown

ART BRONZES COMPANY
2118 Magnolia Lane
                          60035
312 831-3646   Est: 1970
Proprietor: A Harris
Hours: Mon-Sat by appt
Types & Periods: 18th &
19th Century, French &
Foreign Bronzes
Specialties: Full Figures:
Animals, Busts, etc
Directions: Northern
Suburb of Chicago

**FRANK & BARBARA
POLLACK**
1303 Lincoln Ave S 60035
312 433-2213
Proprietor: Frank &
Barbara Pollack
Hours: By appt
Types & Periods: Early
American Folk Art,
Paintings, Painted Tole &
18th & 19th Century Country
Furniture

**REBECCA ANNE
ANTIQUES**
1891 2nd St   60035
312 498-1312   Est: 1974
Proprietor: Michael D
Simon
Hours: By appt or chance

Types & Periods: Oak &
Wicker Furniture,
Collectibles & Primitives
Directions: 1 block E of
Green Bay, 1 block N of
Central Ave

Highwood

FREIDARICA LTD
257 Waukegan Ave 60040
312 433-4595   Est: 1970
Proprietor: Mimi Wilson &
Marjorie Reed
Hours: Tues, Thurs-Sun,
10-4
Types & Periods: 18th
Century English & French
Furniture, Pewter, Brass,
Copper Accessories & Dolls
Specialties: Furniture (Small
English)
Directions: Between
Highland Park & Lake
Forest on Lake Michigan

Hillsboro

FOXES TRADING POST
719 S Main St   62049
217 532-6059   Est: 1971
Proprietor: Doris Fox
Hours: Tues-Sat, 9-5; By
appt anytime
Types & Periods: Oak &
Walnut Furniture, China
Cabinets, Desks, Tables,
Glassware, Lamps, Clocks &
Primitives
Directions: On Rte 127;
9 miles E of Litch Field
off I-55

Hinsdale

**BARBARA CURTIS
ANTIQUES**
5900 S Grant St   60521
312 323-7914
Proprietor: George &
Barbara Curtis
Hours: Tues-Sat, 11-4
Types & Periods: Furniture,
Tin, Pewter, Copper, Oil
Paintings & Frames
Directions: 1 mile S of
Business District, near
I-194, Rte 83

THE LAIR
35 E First St   60521
312 323-7750   Est: 1969
Proprietor: Henry L
Soukup
Hours: Mon-Sat by appt
Types & Periods: English
18th & 19th Century Small
Furniture, Chairs, Brass,
Copper, China, Glass, Prints
& Pictures
Specialties: Chairs &
Pictures
Appraisal Service Available
Directions: Downtown

LONGLEYS OF ENGLAND
53 S Washington St
                          60521
312 887-1975   Est: 1973
Proprietor: John Longley
Hours: Mon-Sat, 9:30-5:30
Types & Periods: Furniture,
Brass, Copper, Clocks &
Accessories
Directions: NE corner of
1st St & Washington St

Homer

**MONROE SANDS
ANTIQUES**
308 S Ellen St   61849
217 896-2628
Proprietor: Monroe Sands
Hours: By appt or chance
Types & Periods: General
Line
Specialties: Phonographs &
Records
Directions: I-74 E to Rte
49; S 5 miles

Jacksonville

THE GENERAL STORE
224-226 E State   62650
217 243-5252   Est: 1972
Proprietor: George M
Stice
Hours: Tues-Sat, 9:30-5
Types & Periods: Oak &
Walnut Furniture, Primitives
& Clocks
Specialties: Jewelry
Directions: Block off Plaza
East

LA FAYETTE ANTIQUES
1320 W LaFayette Ave
                          62650
217 245-6934
Proprietor: Mrs Paul
Aufdenkamp
Hours: Mon-Sun
Types & Periods: General
Line

TAYMAN'S TIN TO TIFFANY
200 E Morton   62650
217 245-7971   Est: 1970
Proprietor: Watson &
Margaret Tayman
Hours: Mon-Sun, 10:30-5;
Closed Feb,part of March
Types & Periods: General
Line, Brass Beds, Trunks,
Toys, Dolls, Old Tin,
Advertising Signs, Vending
Machines
Specialties: Rolltop Desks,
Player Pianos, Old Saloon
Backcars & Music Boxes
Appraisal Service Available
Directions: Just before
Main St, coming in from N
on Hwy 35; just past Main
St coming from W

VICKIE'S ANTIQUES
1050 W College   62650
217 245-6706
Proprietor: Mrs William C
Ator
Hours: By appt
Types & Periods: Art, Cut &
Pressed Glass, China,
Jewelry, Primitives &
Furniture

Kenilworth

THE ANTIQUE EMPORIUM
640 Green Bay Rd   60043
312 251-6090
Proprietor: Susan &
Vincent Graham
Hours: Mon-Sat,
11:30-4:30; Closed Sat
July-Aug
Types & Periods: 17th, 18th
& 19th Century English
Furniture & Accessories
Specialties: Furniture
(Windsor Chairs & Welsh
Dressers)
Appraisal Service Available
Directions: 3rd Suburb N
of Chicago; 5 blocks W of
Lake Michigan

THE ELF SHOP
642 Green Bay   60043
312 251-6502   Est: 1971
Proprietor: Anne Juell
Hours: Tues-Sat, 10-5
Types & Periods: Primitives
& Country Antiques
Specialties: Tools
Appraisal Service Available
Directions: N Shore of
Chicago Area; on dividing
line between Kenilworth &
Winnetka

FEDERALIST ANTIQUES
523 Park Dr   60043
312 256-1791   Est: 1974
Proprietor: Michael
Corbett
Hours: Tues-Sat, 10-4:30
Types & Periods: American
Furniture of the Federal
Period & Related Decorative
Objects of the Period
1770-1830
Appraisal Service Available
Directions: Directly
opposite the Kenilworth
Station of the Chicago &
NW RR or E off the
Edens Expwy at Lake Ave,
E to Green Bay Rd, N of
Green Bay to Park Dr

MANOR HOUSE ANTIQUES
412 Green Bay Rd   60043
312 251-4294
Proprietor: Caroline T
O'Malley
Types & Periods: General
Line
Specialties: Silver (English &
American Sterling) & Oil
Paintings

THE SPARROW
515 Park Dr   60043
312 251-8001   Est: 1973
Proprietor: Floyd & Sybil
White
Hours: Mon-Sun, 11-5
Types & Periods: Direct
Importer of Country, English
& American Furniture &
Primitives
Specialties: Brass & Copper
Directions: Green Bay Rd
to Kenilworth RR Station;
1/2 block W off Green
Bay Rd

Lake Bluff

**GILBERT L HARVEY AND
COMPANY**
18 N Waukegan Rd 60044
312 295-1510   Est: 1952
Proprietor: G L Harvey
Hours: Mon-Thurs, Sat,
9:30-5:30; Fri 9:30-9
Types & Periods: Mostly
18th Century English, Some
American & European

**LYDIA'S SHOP OF MANY
THINGS**
41 Scranton Ave   60044
312 234-0651   Est: 1955
Proprietor: Lydia Hanson
Hours: Mon-Tues,
Thurs-Sat, 10-5
Types & Periods: General
Line
Directions: 1 block E of
NW Depot, next door to
Barber Shop

THE OLD POST SHOP
36 Center   60044
                  Est: 1964
Proprietor: Doree Debree
Hours: Mon-Sun
Types & Periods: General
Line

Lake Forest

CAT & FIDDLE INC
270 Market Square 60045
312 234-0160   Est: 1950
Proprietor: Annie May
McLucas
Hours: Mon-Sat
Types & Periods: 18th &
19th Century French,
Beidermeir, English & Italian
Specialties: Porcelain
Directions: N Shore
Suburb, 30 miles from
Chicago on Rte 94 or 294

THE COUNTRY HOUSE INC
280 E Deer Path   60045
312 234-0244   Est: 1936
Proprietor: Mrs William P
Boggess II
Hours: Mon-Sun
Types & Periods: English,
French & American
Porcelains
Appraisal Service Available
Directions: Main St

Lake Forest   Cont'd

SNOW-GATE ANTIQUES, INC
654 N Bank Lane   60045
312 234-0655   Est: 1964
Hours: Mon-Sat, 10-4:45
Types & Periods: General
Line, Jewelry & Collectibles
Specialties: Jewelry
  Directions: Middle of Lake
  Forest, off Market Square

SPRUCE ANTIQUES
188 E Westminister 60045
312 234-5334   Est: 1973
Proprietor: Jone R Gedge
Hours: Mon-Sun, 10-5
Types & Periods: 18th &
Early 19th Century Furniture,
Porcelain, Brass &
Accessories
Appraisal Service Available
  Directions: 1 block N of
  Town Square, 2 blocks E
  of Chicago-Northwestern
  Railroad Station

Lebanon

IDYL-A-WHYL
125 E St Louis St, Rte 50
                    62254
618 537-2398
Hours: Mon-Wed, Fri-Sat,
10-5; Sun 1-5 & Wed
Evenings until 8
Types & Periods: General
Line, Collectibles & Coins

OLDE TOWNE ANTIQUES
218-220 W St Louis St
                    62254
618 537-2217
Hours: Mon-Sun
Types & Periods: General
Line, Collectibles & Gifts

POVERTY HOLLOW ANTIQUES
Monroe St   62254
618 537-2243
  Proprietor: Georgia
  Halasey
  Hours: By appt or chance
Types & Periods: Furniture,
Glassware & Primitives
  Directions: 2 miles N of
  Lebanon

TIQUES 'N THINGS
225 W St Louis St   62254
Hours: Mon-Sun
Types & Periods: General
Line & Collectibles

TOWN 'N COUNTRY SHOP
205 W St Louis St   62254
618 537-6726
Hours: Mon-Sat, 10-5;
Sun 12-5
Types & Periods: General
Line & Collectibles

Lemont

LITTER BOX
310 Canal   60439
312 257-6149   Est: 1970
  Proprietor: Martha Miskus
  Hours: Mon-Sun, 10:30-4
Types & Periods: General
Line
Appraisal Service Available
  Directions: I-55 to Lemont
  Rd; S 2½ miles to
  Canal St

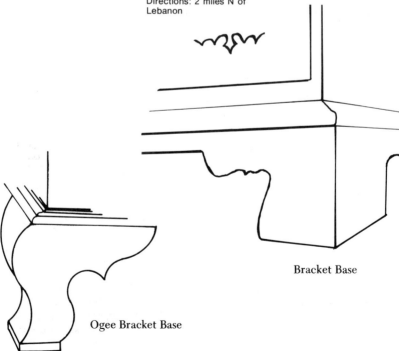

Bracket Base

Ogee Bracket Base

Lincolnwood

THE CONSORTIUM
6740 Nokomis   60646
312 677-5070
Proprietor: Norm & Elaine
Milin
Hours: By appt
Types & Periods: Jewelry,
Wedgwood & General Line

RSVP GALLERIES
3458 N Devon Ave   60645
312 679-5858   Est: 1906
Proprietor: Pat Shore
Hours: Mon-Sun, 10-5; By
chance
Types & Periods: Paintings,
Graphics, Silver, Furniture,
Oriental Rugs, Jewelry,
Porcelains, Crystal &
Bronzes
Appraisal Service Available
Directions: Suburb of
Chicago

Litchfield

L B ANTIQUES
222 Monroe   62056
217 324-4534   Est: 1974
Proprietor: Leone
Bergfield
Hours: By appt or chance
Types & Periods: General
Line
Specialties: Advertising
Items (1875-1975)
Appraisal Service Available
Directions: Rte 66 & 16,
turn E on Rte 16, 3rd stop
light, continue 1 block E,
2½ blocks S (across st
from Police & Fire Depts)

**OWENS COUNTRY
CORNER ANTIQUES**
62056
217 324-5662   Est: 1975
Proprietor: Ellen L Owens
Hours: Mon-Sun
Types & Periods: Victorian,
Walnut Furniture, Primitives
& General Line
Specialties: Furniture, Cut &
Art Glass & Hand Painted ·
China
Appraisal Service Available
Directions: 33 miles S
Springfield, Ill & 70 miles
N of St Louis

Lockport

**PILGRIM HALL ANTIQUE
MALL**
10th & Hamilton   60441
815 838-0435   Est: 1974
Proprietor: Richard K
Wiener
Hours: Mon-Sun
Types & Periods: General
Line
Specialties: Refinishing
Furniture
Appraisal Service Available

Lovington

NANA'S TREASURES
Rte 1   61937
217 873-4848   Est: 1973
Proprietor: Jane Foley
Hours: By chance
Types & Periods: General
Line
Appraisal Service Available
Directions: 1½ miles NW
of Lovington on Rte 32

Lyons

BARR ANTIQUE
4018 Joliet Ave   60534
312 442-9025   Est: 1973
Proprietor: Patricia Barr
Hours: Mon-Fri, 9:30-5:30
Types & Periods: General
Line
Directions: 1 block S of
US 34 W side of street

Macomb

FRIER'S ANTIQUES
234 E Carroll St   61455
309 837-3821   Est: 1970
Proprietor: David Frier
Hours: Mon-Sun
Types & Periods: Tools,
Pottery, Brass, Political
Items, Lamps, Primitives,
Furniture & Advertising
Specialties: Duck Decoys

**GENERAL STORE
ANTIQUES**
101½ W Carroll   61455
309 837-4000   Est: 1971

Proprietor: Bill & Janice
Van Dell
Hours: Mon-Sun, 12-5;
Also by appt or chance
Types & Periods: Primitives,
Country Furniture &
Depression Glass
Appraisal Service Available
Directions: Junction of
Rtes 67 & 136, downtown

**HALLIBURTON'S
ANTIQUES**
420 S McArthur   61455
309 837-1473
Hours: By appt
Types & Periods: General
Line & Dishes

THE HAYMOW
61455
309 837-3621
Hours: Mon-Sun
Types & Periods: Furniture,
Primitives & Collectibles
Directions: 3 miles E of
Macomb, Junction of Rtes
67 & 136; then 1 mile E &
1 mile N

JACOBSEN'S ANTIQUES
526 E Carroll St   61455
309 833-5360   Est: 1967
Proprietor: James II
Jacobsen
Hours: By appt or chance
Types & Periods: American,
Pine, Walnut & Cherry
Furniture & Clocks
Appraisal Service Available
Directions: 1 block N of
Rtes 67 & 136 on
Edwards St

STONE HOUSE ANTIQUES
614 W Murray   61455
309 833-5362
Proprietor: Verda Shake
Hours: Mon-Sun, 9-5
Types & Periods: Primitives,
Pine & Walnut Furniture

**SYL'S SECOND-TIME-
AROUND BOUTIQUES**
206 N Lafayette   61455
309 837-3603   Est: 1972
Proprietor: Sylvia Runkle
Hours: Mon-Fri, Sun, 12-5;
Sat 10-5
Types & Periods: Original
Deco, Nouveau Clothing &
Accessories 1800-1950
Specialties: Period Clothing
& Fur Coats
Directions: On Rte 67, 1
block N of Square

Macon

THE GOLD MINE LTD
Hwy 51   62544
217 764-5130   Est: 1974
Proprietor: 6 Decatur
Ladies
Hours: Tues-Sat, 11-4
Types & Periods: General
Line
Directions: 9 miles S of
Decatur on Hwy 51

Manhattan

POST HOUSE ANTIQUES
Box 199   60442
815 478-3805
Proprietor: Mr & Mrs F R
Beck
Hours: Mon-Sun, 10-5 &
Evenings by appt
Types & Periods: General
Line
Directions: 4 miles W of
US 45 on US 52

Manteno

**J DARTER'S ANTIQUE
INTERIORS**
143 S Locust (Rte 50)
                          60950
815 468-3675   Est: 1969
Proprietor: Joe R Darter
Hours: Sat-Sun by appt
Types & Periods: Furniture
Specialties: Lamps, Stained
Glass, Copper & Brass
Directions: On Rte 50

Marengo

ANTIQUES BY PEGGY LEE
219 W Grant Hwy   60152
815 568-7753
Proprietor: Earl Lee
Hours: By appt
Types & Periods: China,
Glass, Dolls & Furniture

CARLSON'S ANTIQUES
1002 E Grant Hwy   60152
815 568-7795
Proprietor: Martha J
Carlson
Hours: Mon-Sun

Types & Periods: Buttons,
Toys, Minatures, Primitives
& Furniture

Marseilles

CALLA'S
428 Main St   61341
815 795-2137   Est: 1975
Proprietor: R R Callahan
Hours: Mon-Sun, 1-5
Types & Periods: General
Furniture & Glass
Directions: 3 miles S of
I-80 between Joliet &
Ottawa on State Rd 6

GOLDEN DOOR ANTIQUES
442 Main   61341
815 795-5566   Est: 1973
Proprietor: Sylvia Feiltz
Hours: Tues-Sat
Types & Periods: General
Line
Directions: Downtown

Mattoon

BETTY'S ANTIQUES
601 N 19th   61938
217 235-1188   Est: 1968
Proprietor: Elizabeth &
Loran Owens
Hours: Mon-Sat, 10-6;
Sun 2-6
Types & Periods: General
Line
Appraisal Service Available
Directions: Rte 45 N

EARLY ATTIC ANTIQUES
508 S 8th   61938
217 235-3261   Est: 1974
Proprietor: T V Janes
Hours: Tues-Sat, 10-5
Types & Periods: Primitives,
Jewelry, Watches, Dishes &
Furniture
Specialties: Clocks &
Watches
Directions: 3 blocks S of
Pizza Hut on Rte 16

**NANCY & AL LANDON
ANTIQUES**
1305 S 9th St   61938
217 234-7308   Est: 1976
Proprietor: Nancy & Al
Landon
Hours: Mon-Sun by appt
or chance

Types & Periods: China,
Porcelains, Art Glass &
Furniture
Directions: SE part of
Mattoon

MARY'S RESALE SHOP
713 N 12th St   61938
217 234-4183
Hours: Tues-Sun, 9-6
Types & Periods: Furniture,
Jim Beam Bottles & General
Line

**GRACE L WALLACE
ANTIQUES**
509 S 14th St   61938
217 234-3545   Est: 1946
Proprietor: Grace L
Wallace
Hours: Mon-Sun
Types & Periods: 18th
Century Porcelain, Art Glass
& Furniture

McHenry

THE LITTLE CORNER, INC
c/o McHenry Depot Hotel,
3939 Main St   60050
815 385-6633   Est: 1966
Proprietor: Jim Hoekje
Hours: Tues-Sun, 10-4:30
Types & Periods: General
Line, American Furniture &
Original Posters
Specialties: Clock repair
Appraisal Service Available
Directions: E of the
Train Station

NOSTALGIA ANTIQUES
4304 W South St   60050
815 385-3560   Est: 1973
Proprietor: Charles
Hollenbach
Hours: By appt
Types & Periods: Oak
Furniture & Clocks
Specialties: Roll Top Desks
Directions: 3 blocks from
downtown

McLean

**PUFFABELLY STATION
ANTIQUES**
Rte 136   61754
309 874-2112   Est: 1969
Proprietor: Rebecca
Beeler

Hours: Wed-Sat, 10-5
Types & Periods: Oak, Pine,
Walnut Furniture, Tins,
China, Glass & Indian
Jewelry
Specialties: Primitives &
Railroad Items
    Directions: Halfway
    between Chicago & St
    Louis, McLean exit off
    I-55; directly N of Dixie
    Truck Stop on Rte 136

Melvin

WINDMILL ANTIQUES
    Box 1   60952
    217 388-7725
    Proprietor: Nancy &
    Arnold Brucker
    Hours: Mon 1-4 or by appt
Types & Periods: General
Line, Primitives &
Advertising

Midlothian

**RELIANCE UPHOLSTERY &
ANTIQUES**
    3356 W 147th St   60445
    312 385-5298   Est: 1965
    Proprietor: Louis Kalis
    Hours: Mon-Sun, 9-6
Specialties: Chinese Brass
    Directions: S leg of I-57,
    get off at 147th & Sibley
    Blvd, W to 147th &
    Homan Ave

Milan

**THE OLD TOLL GATE
ANTIQUES**
    Rte 5, Box 7X   61264
    309 787-2392   Est: 1948
    Proprietor: Marie Baker
    Hours: Mon-Sun
Types & Periods: General
Line
Specialties: Haviland China
    Directions: Hwy 67
    between Rock Island &
    Milan Bridges

Momence

CAL-JEAN SHOPS
    127 E Washington   60954
    815 472-2667   Est: 1972
    Proprietor: Calvin Brown
    Hours: Mon-Sat, 9-5;
    Sun 12-5
Types & Periods: General
Line
    Directions: E 1 block from
    stop light; SW corner from
    Post Office

Monroe Center

LAWRENCE E KING
    The Old Village Hotel
                        61052
    815 393-4735
    Proprietor: Lawrence E
    (Gene) King
    Hours: By appt or chance
Types & Periods: Art Glass,
Queen Anne Furniture &
General Line

Morton Grove

**CAROUSEL INDUSTRIES
INC**
    6288 Oakton St   60053
Types & Periods: Gumball
Machines

Mount Morris

**MIDDLEKAUFF'S
ANTIQUES**
    RR 1 North   61054
    815 734-4936
    Proprietor: Harold
    Middlekauff
    Hours: By appt or chance
Types & Periods: Currier &
Ives Prints, Furniture &
General Line

Naperville

BONNIE'S BYGONES
    530 White Oak Dr   60540
    312 355-2863   Est: 1970
    Proprietor: Bonnie &
    Howie Cosyns
    Hours: By appt or chance

Types & Periods: Country,
Primitive & Victorian
Furniture, General Line
Appraisal Service Available
    Directions: 30 miles W of
    Chicago; Naperville exit on
    East-West Tollway

**BLODWEN EVANS' 1850
HOUSE**
    509 W Aurora Ave   60540
    312 420-0675   Est: 1974
    Proprietor: Ruth & Warren
    Hirt
    Hours: Mon-Sat, 11-4
Types & Periods: Primitive &
Victorian Furniture, China &
Glass
Appraisal Service Available
    Directions: Rte 65, across
    from High School

THE SWAP SHOP
    Ogden at Columbia   60540
    312 355-8788   Est: 1953
    Hours: Mon-Sun
Types & Periods: Buffalo
Horn Chair Circa 1786,
Camelback Trunks Circa
1880, Oriental Rugs, Frames
& 17th Century Oak Chests
Appraisal Service Available
    Directions: EW Tollway to
    Naperville Rd, S to Ogden
    Ave (Rte 34), right on
    Ogden, then W to 1st
    Curve, on SW corner on
    Curve

Nauvoo

SANDERS ANTIQUE SHOP
    Hwy 96   62354
                    Est: 1968
    Proprietor: Mrs B D
    Sanders
    Hours: Tues-Sat, 10-5;
    Sun 1-6
Types & Periods: 1800-1840
General Line, Ironstone,
Flow Blue, Quilts & Toys
Appraisal Service Available
    Directions: On Hwy in
    restored 1839 brick house

Niota

GRACE OCHSNER DOLL HOUSE
RR 1   62358
217 755-4362   Est: 1950
Proprietor: Grace Ochsner
Hours: Mon-Wed, Fri &
Sat, 8-10
Types & Periods: Dolls &
Doll Furniture
Specialties: Costume
Antique Dolls
Appraisal Service Available
Directions: 3 miles S of
Dallas City on Rte 9, 2
miles W

North Riverside

THE TEST OF TIME ANTIQUE SHOP
3046 S Des Plaines Ave
                          60546
312 447-7766   Est: 1973
Proprietor: Carol Collier
Hours: Tues-Sat, 11-4:30
Types & Periods: General
Line
Directions: 12 miles W of
the Loop (3100 S, 6
blocks W of Harlem Ave)

Oak Park

ACORN ANTIQUES
35 Chicago Ave   60302
312 386-9694   Est: 1970
Proprietor: Eleanour
DeCamp
Hours: Tues 12-4; Wed
9:30-4 & Sat 10-4
Types & Periods: Furniture,
Glass, Primitives, Jewelry,
Brass & Copper
Specialties: Furniture &
Primitives
Appraisal Service Available
Directions: Expwy or
Chicago Ave; Oak Park
has 28 shops

ANTIQUE BOUTIQUE
1115 Chicago Ave   60402
312 386-6069   Est: 1969
Proprietor: Peggy Foster
Hours: Mon & Thurs, 1-9;
Tues, Wed & Fri, 1-5 &
Sat 10-5

Types & Periods: Oriental,
Beleek, Wedgwood, Royal
Vienna & Victorian Furniture
Appraisal Service Available

KERIN DEE ANTIQUES
522 Belleforte Ave   60302
312 386-6227
Proprietor: Kerin Dee
Hours: By appt
Types & Periods: General
Line
Specialties: American Glass

LITTLE RED CAR ANTIQUE SHOP
159 S Oak Park Ave
                          60302
312 383-4816   Est: 1969
Proprietor: Erwin & Gladys
Koehler
Hours: Tues-Wed & Fri,
1-6; Thurs 1-7:30; Sat 10-5
Types & Periods: 19th
Century American &
European Furniture, General
Line
Appraisal Service Available
Directions: Central Oak
Park

ST JAMES ANTIQUES
163 S Oak Park Ave
                          60302
312 386-5319   Est: 1973
Proprietor: Sue
Bohenstengel
Hours: Tues-Sat
Types & Periods: Refinished
18th & 19th Century Walnut,
Oak, Mahogany & Wicker
Furniture
Directions: 1½ blocks S of
Lake St; directly W of
Chicago Loop 10 miles

VILLAGE EMPORIUM ANTIQUE AND GIFT SHOPPE
183 S Oak Park Ave
                          60302
312 386-0641   Est: 1961
Proprietor: Nick Maffei
Hours: Mon-Tues,
Thurs-Sat
Types & Periods: Clocks,
Pocket Watches, Small
Furniture, Jewelry,
Primitives, Glassware,
Pewter & Collectibles
Specialties: Clocks
(Repairing)

Directions: 1st Suburb W
of Chicago, off I-90 on
Oak Park Ave, 2 blocks S
of Lake St

Oakley

BEV'S JUNTIQUES
                          62552
217 763-6206   Est: 1971
Proprietor: Everett &
Beverly Brown
Hours: Mon-Sun
Types & Periods: Walnut,
Oak & Victorian Furniture
Specialties: S Roll Top
Desks, Oak Ice Boxes &
Hoosier Kitchen Cabinets
Appraisal Service Available
Directions: 7 miles E
Decatur on 105, N 2 miles
on County 25

Odin

LINCOLN TRAIL ANTIQUES
US Hwy 50   62870
618 775-8255   Est: 1964
Proprietor: James A Soper
Hours: Mon-Sun
Types & Periods: General
Line
Directions: 5 miles W of
I-75 on US Hwy 50

OLDTOWN ANTIQUES
Main   62870
618 775-6360
Proprietor: Sam Davidson
Hours: Tues-Sun
Types & Periods: General
Line
Directions: 1 block E of
Hwy 50

Ohio

KATIE'S ATTIC
208 N Main St   61349
815 376-7591   Est: 1977
Proprietor: Kay Chase
Hours: Mon-Wed, 10-4:30
Types & Periods:
Needlework & Quilts,
Pottery, China, Glass,
Pictures, Furniture &
Accessories
Specialties: Birdcages &
Decorator Items

Directions: Right on Rte
26, N of Rte 92; 12 miles
N of Interstate 80 at
Princeton exit; 18 miles S
of Tollway 5 at Dixon exit

Orland Park

ANTIQUES OF ORLAND
9915 W 143rd Place
                    60462
312 349-0507   Est: 1974
Proprietor: Dorothy Lynch
& Arlene Meter
Hours: Mon-Sat, 11-4:30;
Sun 12-5
Types & Periods: General
Line
Specialties: Jewelry
Directions: 9900 W-14300
S, 1 block S Of Main St

Oswego

LENORE'S ANTIQUES
79 Main St   60543
312 554-3900   Est: 1952
Proprietor: Lenore
Schiewe
Hours: Mon-Sun, 1-5;
Evenings by appt
Types & Periods: General
Line
Specialties: Glass, Clocks &
Dolls
Directions: Corner of Rte
34 & Main St in downtown

**THE NEVER-NEW TWO
ANTIQUES**
20 Main St   60543
312 554-3333
Proprietor: Barbara
Corrigan & Sue Keyes
Hours: Tues-Sat, 10:30-5
Types & Periods: Primitives,
Country Furniture & General
Line

Ottawa

BETTY'S ANTIQUES
223 Bellevue Ave   61350
815 434-4606   Est: 1970
Proprietor: Betty & Wayne
Thomas
Hours: Mon-Sat, by appt

Types & Periods: General
Line
Directions: Rte 6 to Post
St; Post St to Bellevue
Ave

**RAY & BETH BURKE'S
ANTIQUES**
1323 W Lafayette   61350
815 443-2340
Proprietor: Raymond &
Elizabeth Burke
Hours: By appt or chance
Types & Periods: Lamps,
Furniture, Glass, China &
Primitives

**SCHERER'S TOWN &
COUNTRY ANTIQUE SHOP**
641 Gentleman Rd   61350
815 433-2495   Est: 1968
Proprietor: Willard &
Evelyn Scherer
Hours: Mon-Sun, best to
telephone first
Types & Periods: General
Line
Specialties: Restored
Antique Lamps
Directions: Shop 1/2 mile
E off Rte 23

TOWPATH HOUSE
700 E Superior   61350
815 434-0230   Est: 1972
Proprietor: Norville & Elois
Love
Hours: Mon-Wed, Fri-Sun,
10-4
Types & Periods: Furniture
Specialties: Oak Furniture
Directions: 1 block S of
Canal & 2 blocks W of
Aquaduct

Palatine

**MELONE'S GIFTS &
ANTIQUES**
Rte 3, Box 289   60067
312 358-5955   Est: 1970
Proprietor: Dan & Joan
Melone
Hours: Tues-Sun;Closed
Suns July 4th-Labor Day
Types & Periods: General
Line
Directions: E side of Rand
Rd (Rte 12); N of Lake
Cook Rd

Palestine

DILL'S ANTIQUES
West 33   62451
Proprietor: Wayne Dill
Hours: By chance
Types & Periods: General
Line
Directions: On Main Rd at
edge of town

Palmyra

ANTIQUE & CURIO SHOP
                    62674
217 436-2378   Est: 1970
Proprietor: Gilbert & Hilda
Pitchford
Hours: Wed, Thurs &
Sat, 10-5
Types & Periods: General
Line
Specialties: Glass
(Depression)
Directions: Rte 111

PETALS & KETTLES
E State & Mill   62674
217 436-2321   Est: 1972
Proprietor: Mr & Mrs
Carroll Woolfolk
Hours: Mon-Wed, Thurs
morning & Fri-Sat, 8:30-5
Types & Periods: Glassware
& Furniture
Appraisal Service Available
Directions: 1 block E of
Rte 111

Park Ridge

THE HALLWAY
145 Vine St   60068
312 696-2891
Proprietor: Dorothy
Hinkley
Hours: Tues & Thurs,
10-4; Sat 10-2
Types & Periods: Primitives,
Country Furniture, Pottery &
Wooden Ware

Pekin

ANDY'S ANTIQUE SHOP
1308 Willow St   61554
309 346-0173
Proprietor: Rex & Bernice
Andrews
Hours: By appt or chance
Types & Periods: China, Art
& Cut Glass, General Line

FRAN'S ANTIQUES
1217 State   61554
309 346-0703
Proprietor: Fran Mickle
Hours: Mon-Sun, 9-5
Types & Periods: Glass,
China, Primitives & Country
Furniture

Peoria

ALBERTA'S ANTIQUES
1708 S Arago St   61605
309 637-2156
Proprietor: Kurt & Alberta
Leucht
Types & Periods: China &
Glassware

B & M ANTIQUES
1600 W Kettelle St   61605
309 676-1000
Proprietor: Bernard E
Harding & E F McHugh
Hours: Mon-Sun
Types & Periods: General
Line

**BETTY GRISSOM
ANTIQUES**
602 W Maywood   61604
309 685-0841   Est: 1970
Proprietor: Betty Grissom
Hours: By appt
Types & Periods: Art Glass,
American & European
Pottery, Porcelain &
Primitives
Appraisal Service Available

**THE SPRUCE ACRES
ANTIQUES**
1514 E Gardner Lane
                61614
309 685-7315
Proprietor: Mildred & Fred
Birwin

Hours: Mon-Sun by
chance
Types & Periods: General
Line

Pittsfield

**BARRETT HOUSE
ANTIQUES**
332 W Washington St
                62363
217 285-6033   Est: 1945
Proprietor: Alta Claus
Hours: Mon-Sun & also by
appt
Types & Periods: Victorian &
Early American Furniture,
Primitives & General Line
Directions: On Hwy 36, 3
blocks W of Square

Pocahontas

**VILLAGE SQUARE
ANTIQUES**
Box 185   62275
618 669-2825   Est: 1968
Proprietor: Glen &
Theresa Nance
Hours: Mon-Wed, Fri-Sun,
10-5
Types & Periods: General
Line, Primarily American
Furniture, Primitives &
Lamps
Directions: 45 miles E of
St Louis; I-70 Pocahontas
exit, 2 blocks E, 1 block
right

Port Byron

CHURCHMOUSE ANTIQUES
111 Cherry St   61275
                Est: 1970
Proprietor: Marilyn L
Johnson
Hours: Tues-Sat, 10-5
Types & Periods: Early
American, Victorian
Furniture, Paintings &
Orientals
Appraisal Service Available
Directions: Hwy 84, 3
miles N of 180

Prospect Heights

**THE COLLECTOR'S
ANTIQUES**
9 N Pkwy   60070
312 255-0484
Proprietor: Joanne & Bill
Kuhns
Hours: By appt
Types & Periods: Country
Furniture, Farm Things,
Lamps & Primitives

GREEN GABLES
7 E Camp McDonald Rd
                60070
312 771-7867
Types & Periods: General
Line & Collectibles
Appraisal Service Available

MY HOUSE ANTIQUES
1003 E Camp McDonald
                60070
312 392-0383
Proprietor: June Johnson
Hours: Tues-Sun, 12-6
Types & Periods: General
Line
Specialties: Glass

Quincy

DEN OF ANTIQUITY
427 S Seventh St   62301
217 223-8929
Proprietor: Frances G
Castle
Hours: Mon-Sun, 11-4
Types & Periods: General
Line

FLEUR DE LIS ANTIQUES
126 S 24th   62301
217 222-6138   Est: 1964
Proprietor: Mary Tanner
Hours: By appt or chance
Types & Periods: 18th
Century Country Furniture,
Paintings, Copper, Brass,
Pewter, Crocks & Prints
Directions: In the Carriage
House in back of French
farm house

Rantoul

WEATHERVANE ANTIQUES
317 E Wabash   61866
217 893-9414

Proprietor: Charles &
Verla Hamilton
Hours: By appt or chance
Types & Periods: General
Line, Furniture, Primitives,
China & Glass

Richmond

ED'S ANTIQUES
10321 Main St   60071
312 634-9611 &
815 678-2911   Est: 1958
Proprietor: Edward N
Flynn
Hours: Mon-Sun
Types & Periods: Furniture,
Stained Glass & Dolls
Specialties: Furniture
Appraisal Service Available
Directions: 10321 Main St
Richmond; Another
Location in Long Grove

LITTLE BIT ANTIQUES
5603 Broadway   60071
815 678-4218   Est: 1970
Proprietor: Connie
Blanchette
Hours: Mon-Sun, 10:30-5
Types & Periods: Furniture,
Glass, Fine China & Silver
Appraisal Service Available
Directions: US Rte 12,
near Rte 173

OLD BANK ANTIQUES
5611 Broadway   60071
815-678-4331   Est: 1976
Proprietor: Connie
Blanchette
Hours: Mon-Sun, 10:30-5
Types & Periods: Period
Furniture, Cut Glass,
Jewelry, Beer Steins,
Cranberry Glass & Gas
Lamps
Appraisal Service Available
Directions: Rte 12 at 173,
near IL-Wisc line

ROOM 102
10331 Main St   60071
815 678-3211   Est: 1975
Proprietor: Marjorie
Johnson & Barbara
Krause
Hours: Mon-Sat, 10:30-5;
Sun 12-5
Types & Periods: General
Line, Large Book Shop, New
Books on Antiques &
Jewelry, Glass, China,

Furniture, Primitives & Music
Specialties: Book Shop
Appraisal Service Available
Directions: On Rte 12
(Main St), 2 miles S of
ILL-Wisc line

Riverdale

**SALLAY'S PAST &
PRESENT**
11 W 144th St   60627
312 841-1210   Est: 1975
Proprietor: Shirley Sallay
Hours: Tues-Sat, 10:30-4;
Evenings by appt
Types & Periods: General
Line
Directions: Calumet Expy
to Sibley Blvd (147th st),
W to Indiana Ave, N to 1st
stop light (147th St), W
five blocks

Rochelle

RAIL FENCE FARM
Rte 3   61068
815 562-6486
Proprietor: Mae A &
W F Baltman
Hours: By chance
Types & Periods: General
Line
Specialties: Glass before
1900
Appraisal Service Available
Directions: 2 miles S of
Rochelle on Hwy 51, first
house on Left after going
under tollroad, Hwy 5

Rochester

HELEN'S ANTIQUES
RR 2, Oak Hill Rd   62563
217 637-7416
Proprietor: Helen Cutler
Hours: By appt or chance
Types & Periods: General
Line, Pattern Glass,
Souvenir Spoons & Toys

Rockford

VI DIXSON ANTIQUES
1412 Scottswood Rd
61107
815 226-5383
Proprietor: Vi Dixson
Hours: By appt
Types & Periods: Glass,
China, Silver & Primitives

**THE EAGLE'S NEST
ANTIQUES**
7080 Old River Rd,
RR 6   61103
815 633-8410
Proprietor: C Richard
Franke
Hours: Mon-Sun, 10-6
Types & Periods: American
Furniture & Primitives
Directions: 3 miles N of
RKFD, 1/2 mile off Rte 2

**BARBARA A JOHNSON
ANTIQUES**
7801 E State   61125
815 397-6699   Est: 1961
Proprietor: Barbara & Fred
Johnson
Hours: Mon-Sun
Types & Periods: Primitives,
Period Furniture, Decoys,
Copper & Lamps
Directions: I-90 &
Rockford Business 20 at
Clock Tower Inn

**JOYCE'S SILVER &
ANTIQUES**
5207 Illini Ct   61107
815 226-8255
Proprietor: Joyce M
Stewart
Hours: By appt
Types & Periods: Silver
Plated Flatware &
Hollowware & General Line

**THE LOFT COUNTRY
STORES**
5859 N Main Rd   61103
815 877-1958   Est: 1947
Proprietor: Shirley Oler
Kowing
Hours: Mon-Sun, 10-5;
Evenings by appt
Types & Periods: Glass,
China, Furniture & Prints
Appraisal Service Available
Directions: Hwy 2, 2 miles
N of the city

STONER'S ANTIQUE & ESTATE ITEM
424 N Independence Ave
61103
Proprietor: Ralph W & Winifred A Stoner
Hours: By appt or chance
Types & Periods: General Line
Appraisal Service Available
Directions: 4 blocks N of US 20 (W State St)

Rock Island

HALFWAY HOUSE ANTIQUES LTD
1833-1st St   61201
309 788-3952   Est: 1960
Proprietor: Aline & Don Kruzan
Hours: Mon-Sat by appt
Types & Periods: Country Furniture, Coverlets & Folk Art
Specialties: Country Furniture
Appraisal Service Available
Directions: Off Rte 92 & 199 at 18th St exit

Rossville

WHISTLER'S ART & ANTIQUE SHOP
104 S Chicago   60963
217 748-6544
Proprietor: Joe Whistler
Hours: Mon-Sat, 8-5; Sun 12-5
Types & Periods: General Line
Specialties: Furniture

Sadorus

ANTIQUE & CURIOSITY SHOP
61872
217 598-2200
Proprietor: Gene & Jeannine Taylor
Hours: Tues-Sun, 12-5
Types & Periods: Furniture, Glassware, China, Bottles, Books & Collectibles
Specialties: Furniture (in the rough)
Directions: 1 mile S & 4½ miles W of Tokono

St Charles

CENTURIAL ANTIQUES
404 S 2nd St   60174
312 584-6363   Est: 1976
Proprietor: H F Abraham
Hours: Mon-Sun
Types & Periods: 19th Century Furniture
Directions: 2nd St (Rte 31); Located on W side of Fox River

FRITZ GALLERY
412 S 2nd St   60174
312 584-5131   Est: 1973
Proprietor: H Fritz Abraham
Hours: Mon-Sun
Types & Periods: 19th Century Antiques
Specialties: Chairs
Directions: 2nd St (Rte 31); Located on W side of Fox River

PARSONAGE ANTIQUES
22 N Fourth St   60174
312 584-3640   Est: 1973
Proprietor: Laurette Grove & June Cavins
Hours: Tues-Sun
Types & Periods: European & American Furniture, Oriental Rugs & Clothes
Directions: W of Fox River; 1 block N of Rte 64

Salem

LAWSON'S ANTIQUES
Rte 4   62881
618 548-2989   Est: 1969
Proprietor: O O Lawson
Hours: By appt or chance
Types & Periods: Primitives, Depression & Other Glass, Fruit Jars, Paper Americana & Tools
Directions: Off I-57 E side; 1st house N of Standard Service Station

Sandorus

BANK ANTIQUES
Market St   61872
217 598-2517   Est: 1970

Proprietor: E J Armurst & F A Maxheimer
Hours: Sat-Sun by appt
Types & Periods: Primitives, Country, Walnut, Cherry & Pine Furniture
Specialties: Refinishing Furniture
Appraisal Service Available
Directions: Downtown, Champaign County's oldest settlement

Shelbyville

HODGE PODGE LODGE
419 E Main St   62565
217 774-4960   Est: 1975
Proprietor: Amy Berger
Hours: Mon-Sun
Types & Periods: General Line
Specialties: Jewelry
Directions: 2 blocks E of the Historical Shelby Co Courthouse

Skokie

COUNTRY SHOP
10001 Harms Rd   60077
312 966-4144   Est: 1966
Proprietor: E Gasser
Hours: Tues-Sat
Types & Periods: Furniture, Brass, Copper & Primitives
Specialties: Country Pieces & Pine
Directions: W of old Orchard Shopping Center in Forest Preserve

Somonauk

HOUSE OF 7 FABLES
300 E Dale St   60552
815 498-2289
Proprietor: M A Shaw
Hours: Mon-Sun, 9-5; Also by appt or chance
Types & Periods: General Line

South Beloit

THE HOSPICE ANTIQUES
Rte 1, Box 309   61080
815 389-2198
Proprietor: William R
Durham & William J
Galaway
Hours: By appt or chance
Types & Periods: Tea Leaf
Ironstone, Glass Lamps &
General Line

Springfield

**AARDVARK CLOCKS &
ANTIQUES**
1406 S 5th St   62703
217 789-1129   Est: 1972
Proprietor: Estelle Booth
Hours: Mon-Sat, 10-5; Sun
12-5
Types & Periods: General
Line
Specialties: Clocks &
Furniture
Appraisal Service Available
Directions: 10 blocks S of
downtown

BLACK KETTLE
2429 Whittier   62704
217 523-7434
Proprietor: Nancy V
Goodall
Hours: Tues-Fri, 1-4:30;
Sat & Sun by appt
Types & Periods: Heirlooms
& Collector's Items

**BLUE MING ANTIQUE
SHOP**
17 Forest Ridge   62707
217 529-1197
Proprietor: Gerald Wm
Barnaby
Hours: By appt
Types & Periods: Ivory,
Jade, Cloisonne, Bronze,
Porcelain & Furniture
Specialties: Oriental Items
Appraisal Service Available

THE DISCOVERY SHOP
1500 W Washington
                      62702
217 546-4103   Est: 1967
Proprietor: Patricia Doyle
& John Booker
Hours: Mon-Sat

Types & Periods: General
Line
Appraisal Service Available

HOUSE OF ANTIQUES
202 N 5th St   62701
217 544-9677   Est: 1965
Proprietor: Joe Seigel &
Chas Kuhnline
Hours: By appt
Types & Periods: China,
Glass, Furniture & Sterling
Flatware
Specialties: Flatware
Matching service

**MURRAY'S OXBOW
ANTIQUES**
2509 Whittier   62704
217 528-8220
Proprietor: W Jerome &
Helen T Murray
Hours: By appt or chance
Types & Periods: China,
Glass, Primitives, Ironstone,
Copper, Brass & Collectibles

NOSTALGIA ANTIQUES
4201 Old Jacksonville Rd
                      62707
217 546-7946   Est: 1973
Proprietor: Lee F Winkler,
Jr
Hours: Tues-Sat, 10-5 &
by appt
Types & Periods: Early
American Furniture,
Stoneware, Primitives,
Copper & Brass
Specialties: Furniture &
Furniture Restoration; Floor
& Woodwork Restoration
Appraisal Service Available
Directions: 4 miles W of
Chatam Rd on Old
Jacksonville Rd

THE PACK RATS
2324 Huntington Rd
                      62703
217 529-5229   Est: 1972
Proprietor: Dorothy Worth
Hours: By appt or chance
Types & Periods: Sterling,
China, Glass, Primitives &
General Line
Specialties: Sterling (Serving
Pieces made before 1910)
Directions: SE end of
town; 4 blocks S of
Stevenson Dr

PRAIRIE ARCHIVES
641 W Monroe   62704
217 522-9742   Est: 1970
Proprietor: John R Paul &
P J Doyle
Hours: Mon-Sat, 11-5
Types & Periods: Books,
Prints, Posters, Paper Items
& Primitives
Specialties: Books, 19th
Century Prints & WW I
Posters
Appraisal Service Available

**SILENT WOMEN ANTIQUES
SHOP**
2760 W Jefferson   62207
217 787- 3253   Est: 1968
Proprietor: Helen
Schwette
Hours: Mon-Sat,
10:30-4:30
Types & Periods: General
Line
Directions: Rte 97-125; W
of Springfield

WATSON'S ANTIQUES
48 Cheyenne Dr   62704
217 546-0201
Proprietor: Walter & Eve
Watson
Hours: By appt or chance
Types & Periods: Out & Art
Glass, Sterling & Watches

**YE OLDEN DAYS
ANTIQUES**
2300 E Sangamon   62702
217 544-2691
Proprietor: John &
Barbara Bensi
Hours: By appt
Types & Periods: General
Line

Stillman Valley

**IRONSTONE INN
ANTIQUES**
108 E Main St   61084
815 645-2557
Proprietor: Bon & Bob
Stremmel
Hours: By appt or chance
Types & Periods: Ironstone,
Pine Furniture & Primitives

Streator

LORISDENE'S ANTIQUES
RR 4   61364
815 672-9509
Proprietor: Lorisdene
Finfgeld
Hours: By appt or chance
Types & Periods: Glass,
China, Metals & Furniture

Sullivan

**THE DEPOT ANTIQUES &
GIFTS**
RR 3   61951
217 797-6445   Est: 1968
Proprietor: Paul I
Harshman
Hours: Mon-Sat, 10-6; Sun
2-6 & by appt
Types & Periods: Primitives,
Furniture, Glass, Jewelry,
Dishes & General Line
Specialties: Limited Edition
Prints of Art & Duck Stamp
Prints
Appraisal Service Available
Directions: 6 miles W of
Sullivan, on Eden St Rd

Sycamore

STOREYBOOK ANTIQUES
Henderson Rd   60178
815 895-6336   Est: 1972
Proprietor: Jean A Larkin
Hours: April-Dec: By appt
or chance
Types & Periods: General
Line (pre 1900)
Specialties: Books, China
(Haviland & Staffordshire) &
Silver
Appraisal Service Available
Directions: 23 N out of
Sycamore, E on Mt
Hunger Rd to first cross
road which is Henderson,
turn left

Trenton

**GRANDA'S EARLY
AMERICANA**
Rte 50   62293
Types & Periods: Furniture,
Glass, Lamps, Books,
Collectibles & General Line

Specialties: Fruit Jars
Directions: 1 mile W of
Trenton on Rte 50

IRON GATE ANTIQUES
7 West Broadway   62293
618 244-7113   Est: 1972
Proprietor: Mr & Mrs
David Stepp
Hours: Mon-Sun by
chance
Types & Periods: Primitives,
Oak, Pine & Walnut
Furniture
Specialties: Graniteware,
Baskets, Crockery, Copper
& Brass Items
Appraisal Service Available
Directions: 7 miles N I-64;
Lebanon exit to Hwy 50; 7
miles from Lebanon, E in
Trenton

Tuscola

**CHRIS L HILL ANTIQUES
INC**
Rte 36E   61953
217 253-2653   Est: 1968
Proprietor: Chris L Hill
Hours: Tues-Sun
Types & Periods: General
Line, Furniture, Glassware,
Country Store & Advertising
Items
Specialties: Pattern Glass &
Walnut Furniture
Appraisal Service Available
Directions: Tuscola exit off
I-57; W on Rte 36

Urbana

WANTLAND'S ANTIQUES
604 W Vermont Ave
                        61801
217 344-5315
Proprietor: Ralph &
Virginia Wantland
Hours: By appt
Types & Periods: Glass,
Silver & General Line

Utica

**THE SECOND LOOK
STORE**
Rte 6 & 178   61373
                     Est: 1967

Proprietor: Frank &
Joanne Nordie
Hours: By appt or chance
Types & Periods: Furniture,
Glassware & Primitives
Directions: 1/2 mile S of
Rte 80

Vermont

THE DIP-IT SHOP
Main St   61484
309 784-5641   Est: 1972
Proprietor: J B & Helen
Carithers
Hours: Mon, Wed & Fri,
1-6; Sat 9-5 & Also by
appt
Types & Periods: General
Line & Country
Directions: 4 miles off 136;
6 miles off 24

Villa Park

VIOLETTA'S
128 W St Charles Rd
                        60181
312 834-4444   Est: 1969
Proprietor: Violetta R
Johnson
Hours: Tues-Thurs & Sat,
10:30-4:30; Sun 1-5;
Closed Mon & Fri, June &
Jan
Types & Periods: Furniture,
Dolls, Pattern Glass &
Primitives
Specialties: Pattern Glass,
Toys, Banks, Silver, Jewelry
& Furniture
Appraisal Service Available
Directions: 1 mile W of
Rte 83

Washington

**MARY RACHEL ANTIQUE
SHOP**
501 Walnut   61571
309 283-2911   Est: 1959
Proprietor: Mary Levery
Hours: Mon-Sat, 10-5; Sun
1-5
Types & Periods: China,
Pressed, Cut & Art Glass,
Silver, Jewelry, Clocks,
Lamps, 18th-Early 20th

Century Furniture & Drug
Store Items
Appraisal Service Available
Directions: 10 miles E of
Peoria on Rte 24, 4 blocks
E of square

Wauconda

ANTIQUE JUNCTION
760 Old Rand Rd   60084
312 526-8006   Est: 1977
Proprietor: Marilyn Becker
Hours: Tues-Sun, 10:30-5
Types & Periods: General
Line of Furniture, Glassware
& Collectibles
Specialties: Unusual
Decorator Pieces
Directions: On Rte 12, 1
mile S of Rte 176 in
Wauconda

THE BARN
760 S Old Rand Rd 60084
312 526-8000
Hours: Mon-Sun
Types & Periods: General
Line

COUNTRY CASUALS
370 W Liberty   60084
312 526-8000
Types & Periods: General
Line

GRANNY'S ANTIQUES
211 S Main St   60084
312 526-3030   Est: 1976
Proprietor: Betty Jean
Smith
Hours: Tues-Sat, 9-5; Sun
12-4
Types & Periods: General
Line, Country Furniture,
Primitives, Depression Glass,
Woodenware & Dishes
Specialties: Depression
Glass
Directions: 1½ blocks N of
Rte 176 on old Rte 12

HEMMED-IN HOLLOW
N Old Rand Rd   60084
312 526-7575   Est: 1955
Proprietor: Marguerite C &
Charles E Krupp
Hours: By appt
Types & Periods: General
Line, Country & Pine
Furniture & Primitives

Specialties: Early Lighting &
Butter Prints
Directions: 2 miles N of
Rte 176

THE LITTLE CORNER, INC
117 Bangs   60084
312 526-8452   Est: 1966
Proprietor: Lee Hoekje
Hours: Mon-Sat, 10-5; Sun
12-5
Types & Periods: General
Line & Midwest Antiques
Specialties: Jewelry, Dolls &
Doll Hospitals
Appraisal Service Available
Directions: 2 doors W of
The Village Hall

MARY'S DOLL HOSPITAL
211 Main St   60084
312 526-3030 or 587-5533
Est: 1975
Proprietor: Mary
Underwood
Hours: Tues-Sun
Types & Periods: Dolls,
Bisque, China Heads &
Wood
Specialties: Parts & All
Types of Repairs
Appraisal Service Available
Directions: 1½ blocks N of
Rte 176 on Old Rte 12

THE ROBIN'S NEST
Hwy 176 at 12   60084
312 526-5255
Proprietor: Dee Wenburg
Hours: Wed-Sun, 12-4
Types & Periods: American
Furniture & Accessories

ROBERT E SMITH
225 Skyhill   60084
312 526-2871 or 526-3030
Est: 1971
Proprietor: Robert E Smith
Hours: By appt or chance
Types & Periods: Tools &
Work Benches (Cobbler's
Items)
Specialties: Tools & Work
Benches, Furniture Stripping
& Repair
Directions: 100 yds off Rte
176, 3/4 mile E of center
of town, 1½ miles E of Rte
12

VILLAGE STORE ANTIQUES
211 S Main   60084
312 526-3030   Est: 1972
Proprietor: Mary B Smith

Hours: Tues-Sat, 12-5;
Sun 12-4; Also by appt
Types & Periods: General
Line of Furniture, Dishes &
Misc
Specialties: Chairs,
Depression Glass & Country
Furniture
Directions: 1½ blocks N of
Rte 176 on Old 12

WAUCONDA ORCHARDS
1201 Gossell Rd   60084
312 526-8553
Hours: Mon-Sun 10-5
Types & Periods: General
Line

Waukegan

HELLO DOLLY SHOPPE
21 N Genessee St   60085
312 623-4371   Est: 1967
Proprietor: Elizabeth Craig
Hours: Mon-Sat, 10-5:30
Types & Periods: Victorian,
English & American
Furniture & Decorative
Accessories
Specialties: Furniture &
Children's Miniatures
Directions: Downtown on
the Main St

THINGS IN GENERAL
611 North Ave   60085
312 623-0104   Est: 1971
Proprietor: Jean J Bailey
Hours: Mon-Sat, 12-5:30;
Also by chance
Types & Periods: Misc
Antiques & Collectibles
Specialties: Jewelry,
Glassware, Dolls & Furniture
Appraisal Service Available
Directions: In the heart of
"Old Waukegan"

Wenona

CANDELIGHT ANTIQUES
126 Chestunut St, Rte 17
61377
815 844-5645
Proprietor: Chuck &
Louise Young
Hours: By appt or chance
Types & Periods: Pattern
Glass, China, Dolls, Jewelry,
Furniture & General Line

HOGES ANTIQUES
128 Chestnut 61377
815 853-4686
Proprietor: Leroy & Jo Hoge
Hours: Mon-Sun, 12-5
Types & Periods: General Line, Furniture & Primitives

West Chicago

COL RALPH E BESIC ANTIQUE AUCTION GALLERY
160 W York Ave 60185
312 231-2222 Est: 1976
Proprietor: Col & Mrs Ralph T Besic
Hours: By appt or chance
Types & Periods: General Line
Appraisal Service Available
Directions: York is 2 blocks N of the center of old downtown

THE HOLLOW FINCH
136 Main 60185
312 293-0260 Est: 1975
Proprietor: Wayne & Nell Livezey
Hours: Tues-Sat by appt
Types & Periods: General Line (3 floors)
Appraisal Service Available
Directions: Off Rte 59 between Rtes 38 & 64, 30 miles due W of the Loop

Wilmette

BUGGY WHIP ANTIQUES
1143 Greenleaf 60091
312 215-2100
Proprietor: Mary & Gorin Caskey
Hours: Mon-Sun
Types & Periods: American & English Furniture & General Line
Appraisal Service Available

THE ROYAL PEACOCK
1515 Sheridan Rd 60091
312 256-6716 Est: 1975
Proprietor: Joan Mollner
Hours: Mon-Sat by appt

Types & Periods: European, Oriental & American Furniture, Jewelry & General Line
Directions: On N shore in "Plaza Del Lago"

Wilmington

BOB'S TRADING POST
624 S Water St 60481
815 476-9926 Est: 1971
Proprietor: Bob & Mary Ritter
Hours: Mon-Sun
Types & Periods: Oak & Walnut Furniture, Depression & Pattern Glass & Primitives
Directions: 1/2 block N of stoplight at intersection of Rtes 53 & 102

CENTURY BAZAAR
116 N Water St, PO Box 334 60481
815 476-9618 Est: 1975
Proprietor: L B Dixon
Hours: Tues-Sun, 12-5; Also by chance
Types & Periods: Antiques, Furniture, Primitives & Glass
Specialties: Primitives
Appraisal Service Available
Directions: 60 miles SW of Chicago on ILL Rte 53 between I-55 & I-57

COOKIE JAR ANTIQUES
104 S Water St 60481
815 476-9477
Proprietor: Hap & Jean Ludwig
Hours: Tues-Fri, 1-5; Sat & Sun, 10-5
Types & Periods: General Line

ET CETERA SHOPPE
219 N Water St 60481
815 476-9947 Est: 1972
Proprietor: Robert E Bass
Hours: Sat-Sun by appt
Types & Periods: General Line, Collectibles, Glass & Furniture
Directions: 2 blocks N of signal lights in downtown Wilmington

HANDY HANDS ANTIQUES
RR 3 60481
815 476-7697
Proprietor: Thelma & Bob Hand
Hours: By appt or chance
Types & Periods: General Line & Jewelry
Directions: In Symerton

HIDDEN TREASURES
109 S Water St 60481
815 476-9036
Proprietor: Donna Nowman
Hours: Mon-Sun, 10-6
Types & Periods: Glass, China, Collectibles & General Line

HOLIDAY BOUTIQUE
903 James St 60481
815 476-9088
Proprietor: Maurine Crawford
Hours: Tues-Sun, 1-5
Types & Periods: Glass & Crafts

HOPE CARROLL
202 N Water St 60481
815 476-2746 Est: 1970
Proprietor: Hope Rajala & Carol Lewis
Hours: Tues-Sun, 1-5
Types & Periods: Primitives, Country Furniture, Wood & Pattern Glass

MEYER & SONS COUNTRY ANTIQUES
RR 3, Box 129 60481
815 476-6072 1976
Proprietor: Gordon C Meyer
Hours: Mon-Sun by chance or appt
Types & Periods: Turn of the Century, Oak & Walnut Furniture
Directions: 5 miles E of Wilmington, look for sign

MOSTLY POTTERY
700 S Kankakee St 60481
815 476-6172
Proprietor: Mary & Terry Turan
Hours: By appt
Types & Periods: Pottery & Silverplate
Specialties: Flatware Matching Service

OLDIES BUT GOODIES
222 N Water St   60481
815 476-7320 or 458-2779
Proprietor: Karl & Mary
Schuster
Hours: Winter: Tues-Sun;
Summer: Mon-Sun
Types & Periods: English,
French & American
Furniture, English Pottery,
Art & Cut Glass, Heisey ,
Cambridge, Duncan & Glass
Grinding
Specialties: European
Furniture, Heisey,
Cambridge & Duncan Glass
(also other hand glass in
20-30-40 period)
Directions: 2 blocks N of
Rte 53 on Water St;
Wilmington is off I-55, take
Wilmington exit to Rte 53,
go to stop light and N 2
blocks

PARAPHERNALIA
112 N Water St   60481
815 476-9841
Proprietor: Chuck & Sue
Jeffries
Hours: Tues-Fri, 1-5; Sat
10-6; Sun 1-5
Types & Periods: General
Line

WAY OUT
HOUSE-ANTIQUES
Box 129, RR 3   60481
815 476-2904
Proprietor: Barbara & Jack
Bertino
Hours: June-Aug:
Mon-Sun; Sept-May.
Sat-Sun & by chance
Types & Periods: General
Line & Collectibles
Directions: In Symerton;
off Wilmington, Peotone
Rd

THE WAYSIDE SHOP
102 S Water St   60481
815 476-9449
Proprietor: Earline & Carl
Hurst
Hours: Tues-Fri, 1-5; Sat
10-5; Also by chance or
appt
Types & Periods: Oak,
Walnut, Cherry & Pine
Furniture, China, Glass & Art
Glass

WOOD 'N THINGS
111 S Water St   60481
815 476-2700
Proprietor: Gene Taylor &
Tom Robbins
Hours: Mon-Fri, by
chance; Sat 9-5; Sun 1-5
Types & Periods: General
Line & Records

Winfield

STONE APPLE FARM
ANTIQUES
118 Winfield Rd   60190
312 653-9719   Est: 1970
Proprietor: Helene
Ruecking
Hours: Tues-Thurs & Sat,
10-3; Sun 1-5
Types & Periods: Importers
European Oddities, Brass,
Furniture, Primitives
American & European
Specialties: Primitives
Directions: 2 miles W of
Wheaton, 34 miles W of
Chicago, off Roosevelt Rd

Winnebago

VIVIAN G HEFFRAN
ANTIQUES
2223 N Weldon Rd   61088
815 962-6223
Proprietor: Vivian G
Heffran
Hours: By appt
Types & Periods: Sterling
Silver Matching Service,
Fine China, Cloisonne & Art
Objects
Specialties: Sterling Silver
Directions: Business Hwy
20 W to Weldon Rd; N
1/4 mile

UTING'S ANTIQUES
Main St   61088
815 335-2348
Hours: By appt or chance
Types & Periods: Primitives
& Furniture

Winnetka

THE ANTQUARIAN
1050 Gage St   60093
312 441-6766   Est: 1974
Proprietor: William Gene
Bowers
Hours: Mon-Sat, 12-5;
Evenings by appt; Sun by
chance
Types & Periods: 1820 to
Later Victorian
Directions: 1 block N of
Tower & Green Bay Rds

CALEDONIAN
562 Lincoln Ave   60093
312 446-6566   Est: 1949
Proprietor: Ethel Harris,
Albert Heath & Barrie
Heath
Hours: Sept-May:
Tues-Sat, 9-5; June-Aug:
Tues-Fri, 9-5
Types & Periods: 18th &
Early 19th Century English
Furniture & Accessories
Specialties: Mahogany &
Oak Furniture
Directions: 45 minutes N
of Loop along Sheridan
Rd. adjacent to Lake
Michigan

DOMINIQUE ANTIQUES
899 Linden (Hubbard
Woods Section)   60093
312 446-0584   Est: 1967
Proprietor: Dominique
Del-Medico
Hours: Mon-Sun, 10-5
Types & Periods: Country &
French Furniture
Directions: Rte 94 to
Winnetka E exit, left on
Hibbard Rd, left on Tower
Rd & left on Linden

GEORGETTE ANTIQUES
897½ Linden   60093
312 446-5515   Est: 1972
Proprietor: Georgia B
Bernett
Hours: Mon-Sun by appt
Types & Periods: American
& English Country Furniture,
Porcelain & Needlework
Appraisal Service Available

Winnetka   Cont'd

H & D ANTIQUES
903 Linden Ave   60093
312 466-1660   Est: 1975
Proprietor: Harriet &
Donald Rosenaweig
Hours: Tues-Sat
Types & Periods: Jewelry,
European & American
Antiques
   Directions: 25 miles N of
   Chicago; I-94 to Dundee
   Rd, right to Green Bay Rd
   & right again approx 2
   miles

THE LION MARK
721 Elm St   60093
312 446-8448
Proprietor: Charles &
Virginia Packer
Hours: Sept-June:
Tues-Sat, 10-5; July-Aug:
Tues-Fri, 10-5
Types & Periods: British
Sterling Silver of 18th &
Early 19th Century
Specialties: Silver
Appraisal Service Available
   Directions: 20 miles N of
   Chicago, Willow Rd exit
   off I-94

THE MUSHROOM
559 Lincoln Ave   60093
312 446-1091   Est: 1972
Proprietor: Lorayne
Engstrom
Hours: Mon-Sun, 10-5
Types & Periods: 18th &
19th Century Copper, Brass,
China, American & English
Primitive Furniture

MARVIN SOKOLOW
990 Linden Ave, Hubbard
Woods   60093
312 446-6986
Proprietor: Marvin
Sokolow
Hours: Mon-Sat, 10-5
Types & Periods: Chinese &
Japanese Art

SUZANNE ANTIQUE
ACCESSORIES
384 Green Bay Rd   60093
312 446-4656   Est: 1974
Proprietor: Suzanne
McReynolds
Hours: Tues-Sat, 11-5;
Also by appt

Types & Periods:
Collectibles, 18th & 19th
Century, English, French,
American, Pottery,
Porcelain, Brass & Copper
Specialties: Furniture
(Minature Chests) & Boxes
   Directions: N of Willow Rd
   & S of Police Station

WEST END ANTIQUES LTD
1054 Gage St   60093
312 446-1665   Est: 1971
Proprietor: M A Banks
Hours: Mon-Sat, 10:30-5
Types & Periods: Oriental
Porcelains, Ivory, Jade,
Snuff Bottles, Netsuke,
Woodcuts from Japan,
Wood Carvings from
Indonesia & Celedon
Specialties: English
Furniture
Appraisal Service Available
   Directions: N Border in
   Hubbard Woods off Edens
   Expwy; Offices in Hong
   Kong, London & Dublin
   for special orders

Queen Anne styled Side chair

Chippendale styled Side chair

Demonstrates the change of mood when embellishments are added.

STATE OF INDIANA

Anderson

BEAL'S ANTIQUES SHOP
705 W 9th St   46016
317 644-4372   Est: 1962
Proprietor: Otis & Alice
Beal
Hours: Daily, also by
appointment or by chance
Types & Periods: Primitives,
Glass, China, General Line
Specialties: Furniture,
Primitives
Directions: 7 squares W of
town, corner of 9th &
John Sts

**FLO'S ANTIQUES-THE
HOUSE OF NIPPON**
5904 Pendleton Ave 46011
317 643-4541
Proprietor: Flo & Ray
Meyer
Hours: By appointment
Types & Periods: Nippon,
Silver, Clocks, General Line

JERRY'S JUNKATIQUE
2221 Meridian   46016
                    Est: 1968
Proprietor: Jerry Spradlin
Hours: Daily, Weekends by
appointment
Types & Periods: General
Country Store & Advertising,
Wicker, Paper Items
Specialties: Magazines &
Post Cards
Directions: On Meridian
St, one way S out of town

MUDD'S USED FURNITURE
1434 Main St   46016
317 644-1433   Est: 1962
Proprietor: Felix Mudd
Hours: Daily
Types & Periods: Wood
Directions: 3 blocks from
downtown

Atlanta

THE ATLANTA GALLERY
100 E Main St   46031
317 292-2202   Est: 1976
Proprietor: Mary Agnes
Mattingly

Hours: Tues-Sun, 11-6
Types & Periods: Paintings,
Furniture, China, Glass

Austin

**WHEEL & DEAL ANTIQUE
SHOP**
RR 1 Box 490   47102
812 794-2649   Est: 1964
Proprietor: Effie A Miller
Hours: Daily, by
appointment or by chance
Types & Periods: General
Line, "Something for
Everyone"
Directions: Hwy 31, 1 mile
S of Austin, 3 miles N of
Scottsburg

Bloomington

CLASSIC ERAS
424 E 4th St   47401
812 339-7799
Proprietor: David & Julie
Vezmar
Hours: Daily
Types & Periods: General
Line, Furniture, Stained
Glass, Bronzes

PEEK'S ANTIQUES
6767 E 3rd St   47401
812 330-5406   Est: 1968
Proprietor: Constance O
Krueger
Hours: By appointment, by
chance
Types & Periods: General
Line, Furniture, China,
Glassware
Directions: 4 miles E of
College Mall Shopping
Center, Hwy 46

TRASH & TREASURES
RR 14   47401
312 334-0091   Est: 1973
Proprietor: Claycomb &
Holmes
Hours: Daily
Types & Periods: Glassware,
Furniture
Directions: 3 miles W on
Hwy 45

**WILLIAM UPHOLSTERY
SHOP**
5101 E 3rd   47401
812 336-6148   Est: 1968
Proprietor: George W
Williams
Hours: Mon-Sat
Types & Periods: General
Line

Bluffton

ROY-L ANTIQUES
312 E South   46714
219 824-1390
Proprietor: Roy C Haab
Hours: By appointment, by
chance
Types & Periods: General
Line
Directions: 3 blocks S of
Courthouse, 2½ blocks E

TOLL GATE ANTIQUES
RR5   46714
219 824-0431   Est: 1970
Proprietor: Bill & Zella
Gilliom
Hours: By appointment or
by chance
Types & Periods: Primitives,
Pottery & Depression Glass,
Akro Agate
Directions: 1/4 mile W of
stop light, Road 1 & 116
W, N side of road

Bowling Green

**VILLAGE SQUARE
ANTIQUES**
Hwy 46   47833
812 986-2870   Est: 1968
Proprietor: June Clevenger
Hours: By appointment, by
chance
Types & Periods: General
Line
Directions: Hwy 46

Bristol

THE OLD STORE
110 Vistula St   46507
219 848-7241   Est: 1973
Hours: Tues-Sun, 12:30-5
Types & Periods: Furniture,
Primitives, China, Glass,
Collectibles
Directions: At the
crossroads of St Rds 15 &
120

SUGAR 'N' SPICE ANTIQUES
621 E Vistula   46507
219 848-4359   Est: 1970
Proprietor: Nancy H Van
Patten Clements
Hours: Appointments
during week, Sat 9-6
Types & Periods: General
Line
Specialties: Jewelry (Indian)
Appraisal Service Available
Directions: 6 blocks E of
light on St Rd 120

Brooklyn

WILLIAM G NEPTUNE ANTIQUES
PO Box 54   46111
Write for appointment
                Est: 1963
Proprietor: William G
Neptune
Hours: Appointment only
Types & Periods: Art Glass
(Steuben, Tiffany, Etc),
Lamps, Shades, China for
serious collectors, dealers

Brownsburg

EASTBURG LAMPLITER ANTIQUES
RR 1 Box 32A   46112
317 852-3584   Est: 1968
Proprietor: Eugene &
Lillian Miller
Hours: Daily, 11-6
Types & Periods: Furniture,
Cut Glass
Specialties: Collector Plates
Directions: Hwy 136, 1/4
mile E of Brownsburg, just
off I-74

Bryant

BRYANT ANTIQUES
234 E Main St   47326
219 997-6448   Est: 1975
Proprietor: John C Logan
Hours: Mon-Sat, 10-5
Types & Periods: Primitives,
Victorian, Oak, Ash
Directions: N Indiana, St
Rte 27 N, E 1 block in
center of town

Carmel

ACORN FARM ANTIQUES INC
15466 Oak Rd   46032
317 846-2383   Est: 1961
Proprietor: Herb, Dee &
Judee Sweet
Hours: Tues-Sat
Types & Periods: Furniture,
Paintings, Silver, Country
Specialties: Furniture
Appraisal Service Available
Directions: Comet Rd 31 N
& 151st St, follow signs

Carthage

BLUE DOOR ANTIQUES
3 N Main St   46115
317 565-6080   Est: 1970
Proprietor: Phyllis & Ralph
McClarnon
Hours: Wed-Thurs, 1-8;
Sat-Sun, 1-8
Types & Periods: General
Line, Furniture
Directions: 5 miles S of
Rd 40

Centerville

ALCORN ANTIQUES
214 W Main St   47330
317 855-3161
Types & Periods: General
Line
Specialties: Embroidery &
Needlework (Quilts &
Coverlets)

CUSTER HOUSE ANTIQUES
207 E Main   47374
317 855-3521   Est: 1974

Hours: Weekends and by
appointment
Types & Periods: Period
Furniture, Art Glass, Indiana
Glass, China, Ceramics,
Regional Paintings, Prints
Specialties: Period Furniture,
Art Glass, Indiana Glass,
Good China, Ceramics,
Regional Paintings, Prints
Directions: 1 block from
stop light, across from
Mansion House Inn

BOB DAFLER ANTIQUES
109 S Morton   47330
317 855-5532
Types & Periods: General
Line

DE BRULERS ANTIQUES
116 E Main   47330
317 855-3841   Est: 1968
Proprietor: Willard &
Velma DeBruler
Hours: Daily
Types & Periods: Primitives
& Books, General Line
Directions: On US 40, 5
miles W of Richmond, 60
miles E of Indianapolis

DOUGLAS AND JACQUELINE EICHHORN
208 W Main   47330
317 855-3398   Est: 1972
Proprietor: Douglas &
Jacqueline Eichhorn
Hours: By appointment, by
chance
Types & Periods: American
Furniture, Folk Art, Graphic
Quilts
Specialties: Wholesale to
dealers
Appraisal Service Available

HELEN'S ANTIQUES
102-104 W Main St   47330
317 855-5122
Proprietor: Helen Schaaf
Types & Periods: General
Line

JONES ANTIQUES
College Corner Rd   47330
317 855-3610
Proprietor: Stephen &
Betty Jones
Hours: Daily
Types & Periods: 18th &
19th Century & Period
Furniture
Directions: 1 mile from
Morton Ave

PINK PANTRY
305 E Main St   47330
317 855-2743
Proprietor: Alma Glisson
Types & Periods: China,
Glass
Specialties: Glass
(Depression)
Directions: Corner of 2nd
& Main

SUBURBAN ANTIQUES
134 W Main St   47330
                    Est: 1963
Proprietor: Betty
Hohenstein
Hours: Mon-Tues, Fri-Sat,
1-5
Types & Periods: Furniture,
Glass, China, Silver
Specialties: Cherry Furniture
Directions: 5 miles W of
Richmond on US 40, 65
miles E of Indianapolis, 3
miles S of I-70, Centerville
Exit

TOM'S CABIN ANTIQUES
129 E Main St   47374
317 962-3619   Est: 1977
Proprietor: Tom Kurtz
Hours: By appointment
only
Types & Periods: Fine
Lamps, Furniture, Toys

TWIN PINES
401 N Morton Ave   47330
Proprietor: Ken & Cathy
Musselman
Hours: Daily
Types & Periods: General
Line

VERLON WEBB AUCTIONS
311 N Spruce   47330
317 855-5542   Est: 1968
Proprietor: Verlon Webb
Hours: Monthly auctions
Types & Periods: General
Line
Specialties: Fine Victorian
Antiques
Appraisal Service Available
Directions: 1 block W of
Grain Elevator

WEBB'S ANTIQUES
311 E Main St   47330
317 855-2282   Est: 1951
Proprietor: Ellis Webb
Hours: Daily, 9-6
Types & Periods: General
Line

Specialties: Oak and
Victorian Primitive
Appraisal Service Available
Directions: On US 40

Chesterton

THE ANTIQUE SHOP
105 W Porter Ave   46304
219 926-1400   Est: 1973
Proprietor: Kathy Shutts &
Betty McNutt
Hours: Tues-Sun
Types & Periods: Victorian
Furniture, Walnuts & Oak,
Stained Glass, Primitives
Specialties: Furniture
Appraisal Service Available
Directions: Off St Rd 49 W
on Porter Ave

CAROL'S ANTIQUES
119 Broadway   46304
219 926-4757   Est: 1973
Proprietor: Carol R
Bratcher
Hours: Mon-Fri, 10-5;
Sat-Sun, 10-6; Also by
appointment
Types & Periods: 18th &
19th Century Furniture,
Porcelain, Glass
Specialties: Embroidery &
Needlework, Oriental Rugs,
Chinese Porcelain
Appraisal Service Available
Directions: Downtown,
corner of 2nd &
Broadway, across from
Centenial Park Bandstand

FIVE GABLES ANTIQUES
500 S Calument   46304
219 926-7411   Est: 1960
Proprietor: Freda & Bud
Rice
Hours: Mon-Sat, 10-5;
Sun, 12-6
Types & Periods: Dolls,
Country Furniture,
Primitives, General Line
Specialties: Furniture,
Country & Primitive
Appraisal Service Available
Directions: Exit S I-94 to
Chesterton, go to Porter
Ave, right 4 blocks

THE FREIGHT STATION
123 N 4th St   46304
219 926-6030   Est: 1975
Proprietor: Mimi Mitchell

Hours: Tues-Sun, by
appointment
Types & Periods: General
Line, Kitchen Pieces,
Accessories, Dolls
Specialties: Refinishing,
Four Dealers Under One
Roof
Directions: Downtown

TREE HOUSE ANTIQUES
M R Box 522   46304
219 926-4418   Est: 1968
Proprietor: Miriam Brinkley
Hours: Tues-Sun, 1-4:30
Types & Periods: General
Line, 19th Century Country
Pieces, Primitives
Specialties: Furniture
Appraisal Service Available
Directions: Rte 20, 3 miles
E of Junction 49 & 20,
between Chesterton &
Michigan City

Columbus

EDNA'S TREASURES
1695 Jonesville Rd   47201
812 376-6043   Est: 1967
Proprietor: Harlan
Ahlbrand
Hours: Sun-Mon, Wed-Sat,
by appointment or by
chance
Types & Periods: Furniture,
Primitives, China, Glassware
Specialties: Furniture
Directions: Located on S
31A about 1 1/2 miles S of
Columbus

**WOOD & STONE
ANTIQUES**
1116 Pear St   47201
812 376-8337   Est: 1975
Proprietor: Robert Brown
Hours: By appointment, by
chance
Types & Periods: Country
Furniture, Stoneware, Quilts,
Baskets, Coverlets
Specialties: Furniture
(Country), Quilts, Stoneware
Appraisal Service Available
Directions: 8 blocks N of
Courthouse

Connersville

SHANNONS ANTIQUES
119 E 3rd St   47331
317 825-6143   Est: 1973
Proprietor: Cecil T
Shannon
Hours: Daily
Types & Periods: Furniture,
Knives, Coins, Guns
Specialties: Glass
(Depression)
Directions: Midway
between Cincinnati &
Indianapolis on St Rd 44

Converse

LOUISE'S ANTIQUES
8360 Delphi Pike 27 46919
317 395-3579
Proprietor: Louise Boyd
Hours: Daily, by chance
Types & Periods: Fine
China, Art, Greentown,
Furniture
Specialties: Greentown
Directions: On Hwy 18, 8
miles W of Marion

Crawfordsville

BILL & FAYE'S ANTIQUES
RR 4, 500 W   47933
317 234-2345   Est: 1971
Proprietor: Faye Hemphill
Hours: Tues-Sat, 9:30-5
Types & Periods: Furniture
(All Periods)
Specialties: Chairs, Pedestal
Tables
Appraisal Service Available
Directions: 1 mile N of
Hwy 136 on Co Rd 500 W

P MICHELS JONES STUDIO
402 S John St   47933
317 362-8236   Est: 1961
Proprietor: Paul Jones, Jr
Hours: Sun-Tues,
Thurs-Fri, by appointment,
by chance
Types & Periods: Period
Antiques, English, French &
American (Nothing newer
than 1880 in furniture),
Chandeliers, Paintings,
Silver, Glassware

Specialties: Interior
Designing, Period Furniture
for the beginner & collector,
restorations
Appraisal Service Available
Directions: 7 blocks off S
Washington St (Hwy 231
or 43)

Dale

**LINCOLN HILLS GENERAL
STORE**
Brown St   47523
812 937-4039   Est: 1966
Proprietor: E Rosenblatt &
L Blemker
Hours: Tues-Sun
Types & Periods: Primitives,
Furniture, Glassware
Appraisal Service Available
Directions: 1/2 block off
US 231 in Dale

Darlington

CEDAR LANE ANTIQUES
RR 1   47940
317 794-4267
Proprietor: Madge Schoen
Hours: By appointment
Types & Periods: General
Line

Delphi

**LEONA G CROUCH
ANTIQUES & INTERIORS**
404 E Main St   46923
317 564-4195
Proprietor: Leona G
Crouch
Hours: Mon-Fri, 10-6
Sat & Sun, by
appointment or by chance
Types & Periods: Art Glass,
Porcelain, Jewelry

Dunreith

DANTE ANTIQUES
                  47337
317 987-7838   Est: 1960
Proprietor: May Linville
Hours: Mon-Fri; Weekends
by appointment

Types & Periods: Furniture,
Primitives, Glass, China,
Books, Post Cards
Directions: At Water &
Washington on Hwy 40

Eaton

HEIRLOOM ANTIQUE SHOP
301 N Hartford St   47338
317 396-3472   Est: 1955
Proprietor: Ina Loughmiller
Hours: Mon-Tues,
Thurs-Sat, 9-5
Types & Periods: General
Line
Specialties: Chandeliers,
Jewelry, Silver
Appraisal Service Available
Directions: 1/2 mile off St
Rd 3, between Muncie &
Hartford City

Elkhart

THE RED SHED ANTIQUES
300 Division St   46514
219 294-2834   Est: 1963
Proprietor: Jennet &
Walter Coveaugh
Hours: Daily, by chance
Types & Periods: General
Line
Appraisal Service Available
Directions: 2 blocks from
Main St

**STERLING AVENUE
ANTIQUES**
2334 Sterling Ave   46514
219 294-7006   Est: 1968
Proprietor: Josephine L
King
Hours: Mon-Sat, 8-5; Sun
by appointment
Types & Periods: General
Line
Appraisal Service Available
Directions: S Main to
Lusher, E to Sterling

Evansville

**MILDRED BOINK'S BRASS
BELL SHOP**
2705 Bellemeade   47714
812 476-0261   Est: 1944
Proprietor: Mildred Boink

Hours: Daily 9-5:30, or by chance
Types & Periods: English, Victorian, French
Specialties: Rugs (Oriental)
Appraisal Service Available
Directions: E of Hwy 41

FRONTIER TRADERS
1111 Diamond Ave Expwy   47717
812 425-7069   Est: 1972
Proprietor: John F Wright
Hours: Daily, by chance
Types & Periods: Guns, Muzzle Loaders, Black Powder Replicas
Appraisal Service Available
Directions: 2 blocks W of US Hwy 41

MARCHAND'S ANTIQUES
311 N Main   47711
812 426-0610   Est: 1968
Proprietor: Tom & Barbara Marchand
Hours: Mon-Sat
Types & Periods: American Art, Pottery, Jewelry, Orientalia, Art Glass, Silver & Gold Items, Books, Furniture
Specialties: Glass (Ctoubon & Cloisonne), Rookwood, Diamonds
Appraisal Service Available
Directions: Near downtown

ROWE'S IMPORT SHOP
204 Main St   47708
812 423-7415   Est: 1950
Proprietor: C Duncan Rowe
Hours: Mon-Sat, 10-5; Fri 'til 7:30
Types & Periods: French, Italian & British Furniture, 16th-19th Centuries
Directions: 2 blocks from Ohio River

Forest

ORIENTAL GARDEN ANTIQUES
RR 1   46039
317 249-2479   Est: 1974
Proprietor: Richard & Gertrude Hansen
Hours: By appointment or by chance

Types & Periods: Primitives, Art Glass, Cut Glass, Lamps, Dolls
Specialties: China, Oriental (Cloisonne)
Directions: 1½ miles E, 1/2 mile S of town

Fort Branch

BUGGY SHED ANTIQUES
RR 2   47648
812 753-4830   Est: 1965
Proprietor: Joe & Juanita Stone
Hours: Daily
Types & Periods: Early 18th Century American Country Furniture & Wooden Ware
Directions: County Rd 175 E, 4th house on right

Fort Wayne

ANNETTE'S ANTIQUES
6910 Lincoln Hwy E 46803
219 749-2745   Est: 1962
Proprietor: Mrs Abe Latker
Hours: Tues-Sun, by appointment
Types & Periods: General Line
Appraisal Service Available
Directions: On US 30 & 24 E of Fort Wayne, 5 miles

THE ANTIQUE GALLERY
4303 S Hanna   46806
219 744-2561   Est: 1971
Proprietor: Stanley & Janice Brown
Hours: Tues-Fri, 12-5; Sat, 10-5
Types & Periods: General Line, Clocks, Glass, Furniture
Specialties: Clocks, Also Repair
Directions: US 27 to McKinnie, E to next stop light

EVELYN'S ANTIQUES
2324 Brooklyn   46804
219 432-0135   Est: 1970
Proprietor: Ed Boltin
Hours: By appointment or by chance
Types & Periods: General Line, Glass, China

Specialties: Depression & Cambridge, Jewelry
Appraisal Service Available
Directions: Just off Rtes 1 & 3

GASKILL'S ANTIQUES & AUCTIONS
6340 Bass Rd   46818
219 432-1736   Est: 1958
Proprietor: Orlie & Shirley Gaskill
Hours: Daily, by chance
Types & Periods: Country Furniture, Oak, Glass, General Line
Specialties: Furniture
Appraisal Service Available
Directions: 2 miles off Hwy 30 W at Flaugh Rd

KIRKS FINE CLOCKS AND ANTIQUES
633 Riverside Ave   46805
219 422-7748   Est: 1968
Proprietor: Kenneth Kirkpatrick Sr
Hours: Daily, 9-9
Types & Periods: Clocks, Fireplace Equipment, Brass
Specialties: Clocks, Metalwork
Directions: Off Spy Run

RED CARPET ANTIQUES
4920 S Monroe St   46806
219 744-3298   Est: 1976
Proprietor: Iva Griffin, Glen & Bonnie Durnell
Hours: Mon, Tues & Thurs, 8-5; Wed & Fri, 8-8; Sat & Sun, 1-4
Types & Periods: Art Glass, Cut Glass, Lamps, Clocks, China Cabinets, Tables
Appraisal Service Available
Directions: 3 blocks E of Hwy 27 in rear of L I Griffin & Sons Inc

STATE STREET ANTIQUES
826 E State Blvd   46805
219 484-6324   Est: 1950
Proprietor: D D Long
Hours: Daily until 9
Types & Periods: Furniture, China, Jewelry, Primitives
Specialties: Furniture, Picture Frames
Appraisal Service Available
Directions: N central part of town on the main street

Fountaintown

MC CLURE ANTIQUES
Box 434   46130
317 861-5079   Est: 1948
Proprietor: Mary McClure
Hours: Tues-Sat, 10-4;
Sun, 12-5
Types & Periods: Glass,
China, Primitives, Collector's
Items
Appraisal Service Available
Directions: Hwy 52, 25
miles SE of Indianapolis

Frankfort

HEAVILON'S ANTIQUES
RR 7   46041
317 659-1026   Est: 1970
Proprietor: Nellie Heavilon
Hours: Daily, Weekends
Types & Periods: General
Line, Primitives, Dishes,
Glass, Furniture, Lamps,
Clocks, Brass, Copper
Specialties: Embroidery &
Needlework, Solid Brass
Lamps
Appraisal Service Available
Directions: 5 miles NW of
Frankfort, RD 250 N

MOZELLES ANTIQUES
265 E Clinton St   46041
317 659-3754   Est: 1954
Proprietor: Mozelle & Ray
Faring
Hours: Mon-Sat, 1-5
Types & Periods: Glass,
China
Specialties: Lamps
Appraisal Service Available
Directions: 1/2 block E of
Courthouse

Fremont

BARN STABLE ANTIQUES
RR 1 Box 201   46737
219 495-5875   Est: 1966
Proprietor: Madelene
Mundy
Hours: Sun-Tues;
Thurs-Sat; Winter by
chance
Types & Periods: General
Line, "Barn full of furniture
including primitives"
Directions: 3 miles W on
St Rd 120

French Lick

FERN'S ANTIQUES
Wells & Indiana Ave 47432
812 936-4385   Est: 1971
Proprietor: Fern Davis
Hours: Daily, Weekends
Types & Periods: General
Line, Glass, Toys, Primitives
Specialties: Toys (Dolls),
Persian Rugs, Furniture
Appraisal Service Available
Directions: On US Hwy 56

Garrett

**COUNTRY COUSIN
ANTIQUES**
110 W King   46738
219 357-5587
Proprietor: Eileen Daly
Hours: By appointment
Types & Periods: Country
Furniture, Lighting,
Primitives

Goodland

ALBERTS ANTIQUES
Rte 2 Box 21   47938
219 297-3293
Proprietor: Keith & Patti
Alberts
Hours: Daily 8-8, Closed
Thurs afternoons
Types & Periods: Art & Cut
Glass, Furniture, Lamps,
Clocks

Goshen

RAY'S ANTIQUES
1715 E Monroe   46526
219 533-1843
Proprietor: Ray Nisley
Hours: Mon-Fri, 7-5; Sat,
7-12, by appointment
Types & Periods: General
Line
Directions: Across Gate 1
of Elkhart Co Fair
Grounds

Greencastle

MC MILLAN ANTIQUES
13 Sunset Dr   46135
317 653-9512   Est: 1967
Proprietor: Catherine
McMillan
Hours: Daily, by
appointment, by chance
Types & Periods: General
Line
Appraisal Service Available
Directions: N of I-70,
halfway between
Indianapolis & Terre Haute

Greenfield

ROLLIN ACKERS ANTIKES
PO Box 205   46140
317 462-2451   Est: 1969
Proprietor: Russell &
Dorothy Conaway
Hours: Sun-Fri
Types & Periods: Furniture
Directions: St Rd 40 & 9
to Greenfield, S 1 mile,
turn left for 1¼ miles

Hardinsburg

MC NEELEY'S ANTIQUES
Rte 1   47125
812 472-3328   Est: 1945
Proprietor: Merrill &
Mildred McNeely
Hours: Daily, by
appointment or by chance
Types & Periods: Early
American Cherry, Walnut &
Pine Furniture
Specialties: Furniture (Rope
Beds, Corner Cupboards,
Chests)
Appraisal Service Available
Directions: On Hwy 150 W
from New Albany or
Louisville, Ky, 35 miles,
sign on Hwy, turn S, go
1½ miles

Hartford City

KENNETH BENNETT
1400 N Walnut   47348
317 348-1535   Est: 1944
Proprietor: Kenneth
Bennett

Hours: Daily
Types & Periods: General
Line
Specialties: Ivory,
Soapstone, Cloisonne
Carvings, Jewelry
Appraisal Service Available
Directions: Hwy 3

Holton

COUNTRY TREASURE SHOP

Rte 1 Box 168   47023
812 689-6899   Est: 1973
Proprietor: Bert & Betty
Naylor
Hours: Daily, Weekends by
chance
Types & Periods: General
Line
Directions: 2 miles S of
Hwy 50

Hope

HOPE ANTIQUE SHOP

624 Main St   47246
812 546-5187   Est: 1962
Proprietor: Carl Hatton &
Mae Hatton
Hours: Mon-Wed, Fri-Sun,
9-5
Types & Periods: General
Line, Primitives
Appraisal Service Available
Directions: Columbus 46
to 9, N to Hope

Huntington

MRS CAMELIA J LA PAGLIA ALLEN

33 W Market
219 356-6127   Est: 1970
Proprietor: Mrs Allen
Hours: Daily, by chance
Types & Periods: General
Line
Directions: Downtown

THE ATTIC

33 W Market   46750
219 356-6127   Est: 1970
Proprietor: Camelia J Allen
Hours: By appointment, by
chance
Types & Periods: General
Line

Appraisal Service Available
Directions: Just off the
mall

B'NADDIES JUNQUE SHOPPE

815 Poplar St   46750
219 356-0886
Hours: By appointment, by
chance
Types & Periods: General
Line

CARLETON HOUSE ANTIQUES

703 Oak St   46750
219 356-7072
Hours: By appointment, by
chance
Types & Periods: General
Line

CELLAR ANTIQUES

46750
219 356-7072
Types & Periods: General
Line
Directions: Downtown,
opposite Police Station

COUNTRY ANTIQUE SHOPPE

RR 1   46750
219 344-2858
Proprietor: Garr & Elsie
Kitt
Hours: By appointment, by
chance
Types & Periods: Art &
Colored Glass, China,
Lamps, Dolls

SMITH'S COPPER KETTLE

Hwy 224   46750
219 356-5058
Types & Periods: General
Line
Directions: 1 mile E on
Hwy 224

WELLS VARIETY BARN

St Rd 5 & 37   46750
219 468-2040
Hours: By appointment, by
chance
Types & Periods: General
Line
Directions: 5 miles S of
Huntington

Indianapolis

INDIANAPOLIS CLUSTER

10th, 2000-3000 Blocks
Directions: Many shops
scattered throughout city,
concentration on E

ABC GIFT SHOP

8849 McGaughey Rd
46239
317 862-4137   Est: 1970
Proprietor: Jeanette
Beidelachies
Hours: Daily
Types & Periods:
Collectibles
Directions: 1 block S of
I-74 at Post Rd

LARRY D ARNOLD

3454 E Fall Creek
Parkway N Dr   46205
317 926-7762   Est: 1967
Proprietor: Larry D Arnold
Hours: By appointment
Types & Periods: English,
Italian, French, 18th Century
Furniture, Chinese
Porcelains
Appraisal Service Available
Directions: I-465 to 38th
St, turn S

CARRIAGE TRADE STUDIOS

1451 N Delaware St 46202
317 636-9911   Est: 1948
Proprietor: Jack Holland
Hours: Mon-Fri, 9-5;
Weekends by appointment
Types & Periods: 18th &
19th Century Furniture, Oil
Paintings, Lamps
Specialties: Paintings &
Mirrors
Appraisal Service Available
Directions: "Old North
Side", 3 blocks E of
Meridian

DEN OF ANTIQUITY INC

1340 N Alabama   46202
317 632-6000   Est: 1969
Proprietor: Bob & Sue
Beauchamp
Hours: Mon-Sat, 10-5
Types & Periods: American
Victorian, Oak Furniture,
Gas & Electric Light
Fixtures, Brass Beds
Specialties: Victorianna

Indianapolis   Cont'd

DEN OF ANTIQUITY Cont'd
Appraisal Service Available
Directions: "In the historic
Old North Side", 1st exit
off I-65 N from I-70 W

GOLDEN RULE ANTIQUES
9600 E Washington 46229
317 898-8561   Est: 1955
Proprietor: Ronald Cox
Hours: Daily
Types & Periods: Victorian
Furniture, Glass, China,
Silver, Primitives, Oak,
Wicker
Specialties: Books on
Antiques
Directions: US 40, 2 miles
E of I-465

KENNINGTON'S ANTIQUES
4600 E 16th St   46218
317 359-8917   Est: 1966
Proprietor: Vi Kennington
Hours: Daily
Types & Periods: General
Line
Directions: I-70 to
Emerson & 16th

RED BARN GALLERIES
325 E 106th St   46280
317 846-8928   Est: 1969
Proprietor: Marion Lang
Hours: Wed-Sun, 12-6
Types & Periods: Primitives,
Country Items, Old Tools,
Ironstone, Victorian
Furniture, Art, Copper
Specialties: Primitives from
Indiana Farms
Directions: From I-465 &
US 31 Interchange, 3
blocks N on US 31, 3
blocks E on 106th St

**TRAYLOR'S ANTIQUE FLEA
MARKET**
7159 E 46th St   46226
317 545-0339   Est: 1970
Proprietor: Leo & Laura
Traylor
Hours: Weekends
Types & Periods: General
Line, 50 Permanent Dealers
Directions: Shadeland Ave
Exit off I-465

THE WEBER CLOCK SHOP
6354 N Guilford Ave 46220
317 259-8007   Est: 1968

Proprietor: Richard H
Weber
Hours: Mon-Sat, 10-6;
Sun, 1-6
Types & Periods: American,
German, English & French
Clocks
Specialties: Clock
Restoration & Repair
Appraisal Service Available
Directions: Where Guilford
crosses the canal in Old
Broadripple Village

**WHISPERING WINDS
ANTIQUES**
10622 Brookville Rd 46239
317 862-2782   Est: 1971
Proprietor: Denver &
Gladys Veteto
Hours: By appointment, by
chance
Types & Periods: General
Line
Specialties: Furniture
Directions: SE of
Indianapolis about 5 miles
E of I-465, 2 miles E of
Post Rd

WOODY'S ANTIQUES
6319 Rockville Rd   46224
317 241-5349   Est: 1970
Proprietor: Mary Woods
Hours: Mon-Sat, 9-5
Types & Periods: General
Line, Glassware
Directions: Rte 465 to Exit
13B or Rte 36, right off
465

Knightstown

**CANDLE CUPBOARD
ANTIQUES**
RR 2 Box 33   46148
317 345-2488
Proprietor: Tom & Teri
Barnes
Hours: Sun-Wed, Fri-Sat
Types & Periods: Furniture,
Country & Primitives, Tools,
Antique Car Parts & Tools
Specialties: Furniture,
Primitives, Car Parts & Tools
Appraisal Service Available
Directions: 1 mile W of
Knightstown on US 40

Kokomo

HILL'S ANTIQUE STUDIO
124 W Walnut St   46901
317 457-2972   Est: 1952
Proprietor: Joseph A
Michalski
Hours: Daily, by
appointment
Types & Periods: Toys,
Dishes, Furniture, Paintings,
Glass
Specialties: War Relics
Appraisal Service Available

KIRK ANTIQUES
RR 5 Box 2210   46901
317 452-6916   Est: 1964
Proprietor: Ruth & John
Kirk
Hours: By appointment, by
chance
Types & Periods: Early
American Pattern Glass,
Cut, Carnival, Art Glass;
China; Silver
Appraisal Service Available
Directions: 4 miles E on St
Rd 22

OPAL SALLEE
1600 S Armstrong   46901
317 457-0554   Est: 1940
Proprietor: Opal Sallee
Hours: By appointment
Types & Periods: 19th
Century Art Glass
Directions: 1 block W of
Business Hwy 31

THE WHITE ELEPHANT
513 N Buckeye St   46901
317 457-0700   Est: 1972
Proprietor: Glenn E Henry
Hours: Tues-Sat, 12-5:30
Types & Periods: General
Line
Directions: W side of
Courthouse, 5 blocks N

Lafayette

**THE AFTERYEARS-YORE
STORE**
625 N 4th St   47905
317 742-6012   Est: 1976
Proprietor: Jane Parsons
Hours: Mon-Sat, 10-5
Types & Periods: Primitives,
General Line, Furniture,
Advertising
Specialties: Kitchenware

Appraisal Service Available
Directions: 6 blocks N
from downtown
Courthouse

H & S SHOP
304 S 29th   47904
317 448-1291   Est: 1977
Proprietor: Homer & Suzie
Patrick
Hours: Tues-Thurs,
10-4:30; Fri 'til 8; Sun,
12-4
Types & Periods: Glass,
China, Primitives
Directions: Near Home
Hospital

LAHR HOUSE ANTIQUES
115 N 5th St   47901
317 742-2469   Est: 1976
Proprietor: Frank Simmons
Hours: Wed & Fri, 12-5;
Thurs, 12-9; Sat, 10-5, by
appointment or by chance
Types & Periods: Choice
Antique Furniture, all
periods & woods, restored &
refinished
Specialties: Home of famous
EM-CEE polish & restorer
Directions: 1½ block N of
St Rd 26 on N 5th,
downtown

LEONARD'S ANTIQUES
N 14th St   47904
317 742-8668   Est: 1972
Proprietor: Leonard &
ReJonnah Haley
Hours: Mon-Fri, 1-5 &
7-10; Sat, 10-5; Sun by
chance
Types & Periods: General
Line
Directions: 2 blocks N of
St Elizabeth Hospital

PACK RAT
424 Main   47905
                  Est: 1978
Proprietor: Mary Gene
Brock
Hours: Mon-Fri,
11:30-5:30; Sat, 10-5
Types & Periods: General
Line
Appraisal Service Available
Directions: Downtown

WULFF'S ANTIQUES
1731 Morton St   47904
317 742-2646   Est: 1964
Proprietor: Walter & Iona
Wulff

Hours: Daily, by chance
Types & Periods: China,
Glassware, Primitives,
Stamps, General Line
Directions: Corner of N
18th & Morton St

La Fontaine

TOLL HOUSE ANTIQUES
105 N Wabash Ave   46940
219 981-7931
Hours: By appointment, by
chance
Types & Periods: General
Line
Directions: 2nd house S of
School

La Grange

WHAT-NOT-SHOP
305 S Detroit St   46761
219 463-2005   Est: 1971
Proprietor: Virginia
Rundles
Hours: Daily
Types & Periods: General
Line, Furniture, China
Directions: Corner of Rte
9 & 20, opposite Post
Office

Lagro

LAWSON'S ANTIQUES
RR 1   46941
219 782-2200
Hours: By appointment, by
chance
Types & Periods: General
Line

La Porte

**FAR CORNERS IMPORTS &
ANTIQUES**
705 Lincolnway   46350
219 362-7720   Est: 1972
Proprietor: Stephen
Boardman
Hours: Daily
Types & Periods: 1800 &
1900 Furniture
Directions: Main St, 1
block E of Courthouse

Lewisville

DOT'S ANTIQUES
PO Box 251   47352
317 987-7753   Est: 1968
Proprietor: Dorothy
Minneman
Hours: By appointment, by
chance
Types & Periods: Furniture,
Pre 1900, Dolls, Primitives,
Glass
Directions: On old
National Rd 40E, between
Richmond & Indianapolis

Logansport

THIS & THAT SHOP
222 E Market   46947
219 753-9377   Est: 1968
Proprietor: L J Dennis
Hours: Mon-Sat; Also by
appointment
Types & Periods: General
Line
Appraisal Service Available
Directions: Junction 24,
35, 29 & 16

Madison

GOURLEY'S OLDE SHOPPE
2242 Cragmont   47250
                  Est: 1966
Proprietor: Mrs Helen
Gourley
Hours: Mon-Fri, 10-6;
Weekends by appointment
Types & Periods: Primitives,
General Line
Specialties: Chair Caning,
Furniture Restoration
Directions: Near Clifty
Plaza Shopping Center on
Hilltop

**SHREWSBURY HOUSE
MUSEUM & ANTIQUES**
301 W First St   47250
812 265-4481   Est: 1948
Proprietor: Mr & Mrs John
T Windle
Hours: Daily; Jan & Feb
by appointment
Types & Periods: 18th &
19th Century Furniture,
Porcelains, Silver, Glass,

**SHREWSBURY HOUSE
MUSEUM & ANTIQUES**
                    Cont'd
Domestic Artifacts,
Primitives, American,
English, Continental
    Directions: On the Ohio
    River between Louisville &
    Cincinnati

Marion

**M WILSON'S ANTIQUE
SHOP**
    211 W 3rd St   46952
    317 662-6250   Est: 1970
    Proprietor: Ted L Sroufe
    Hours: Mon & Tues; Thurs
    & Fri; Sat & Sun by
    appointment
Types & Periods: General
Line, Glass, China,
Furniture, Lamps
Appraisal Service Available
    Directions: 1½ blocks W
    of Courthouse

Martinsville

S & E ANTIQUES
    209 N Park Ave   46151
    317 342-2684   Est: 1968
    Proprietor: Samuel &
    Evelyn Denney
    Hours: Mon-Tues,
    Thurs-Sat, 12-5; Sun &
    Wed by appointment
Types & Periods: Furniture,
Collectibles
    Directions: S of
    Indianapolis on Rte 67, to
    Rte 39 Bypass, 1st
    entrance to Martinsville,
    turn left at 1st Street, 1
    block

McCordsville

**ALICE'S ANTIQUES &
STRIPPING UNLIMITED**
                        46055
    317 335-2452   Est: 1969
    Proprietor: J M & A R
    Turney
    Hours: Mon-Sat, 8-6
Types & Periods: General
Line, Period Furniture,
Collectibles

Specialties: Stripping,
Caning & Refinishing
    Directions: St Rd 234 off
    Hwy 67, 1/2 mile E of
    McCordsville, first house
    on N side

Mishawaka

CHASE'S ANTIQUE
    1234 W Sixth St   46544
    219 259-1788   Est: 1968
    Proprietor: Mr & Mrs
    Charles Chase
    Hours: Daily
Types & Periods: Furniture,
Paintings, Clocks, Wicker
    Directions: On US 33

Mongo

THE OLDE STORE
    Hwy 3   46771
    219 367-2206   Est: 1964
    Proprietor: Carroll Van
    Buskirk
    Hours: Tues-Sun
Types & Periods: Glass,
China, Furniture, Music
Items
Appraisal Service Available
    Directions: On Rte 3, 3
    miles N of Rte 20 W of
    Angola

Monticello

GRIFFIN'S ANTIQUE SHOP
    116 N Illinois St   47960
    219 583-5722   Est: 1941
    Proprietor: Mrs Vernece
    Griffin
    Hours: Daily
Types & Periods: General
Line
Appraisal Service Available
    Directions: Across street
    from Courthouse,
    downtown

Mooresville

KINNETT ANTIQUES
    5 E Harrison St   46158
    317 831-0346   Est: 1962
    Proprietor: Roy & Linda
    Kinnett

    Hours: Mon-Sat, 11-5;
    Other times by
    appointment
Types & Periods: Antiques,
Heirlooms, Collectibles
Specialties: Sterling & Silver
Plated Flatware, Haviland
China Matching, Early
American Pattern Glass
Appraisal Service Available
    Directions: 1 block S of
    the main intersection, on
    the corner opposite the
    Police & Fire Station

Morgantown

BROWN'S CLOCK SHOP
    RR 3 Box 153   46160
    812 697-5992
    Proprietor: Melvin Brown
    Hours: By appointment, by
    chance
Types & Periods: 19th &
Early 20th Century
American, French & German
Wall & Mantle Clocks
Specialties: Clocks
    Directions: 8 miles N of
    Nashville on St Rd 135

**FULLER POLISHING
COMPANY**
    Box 277   46160
    812 597-5839
    Proprietor: Donald &
    Teresa Fuller
    Hours: Daily, 10-6
Types & Periods: General
Line
Specialties: Brass Beds
    Directions: 6 miles N of
    Nashville on St Rd 135

Nashville

AGE OF ELEGANCE
    Main St   47448
    812 988-6141
    Proprietor: David & Julie
    Vezmar
    Hours: Daily, 11-5
Types & Periods:
Architectural Items;
Furniture
Specialties: Glass (Stained),
Bronzes

ALBERTS MALL
Box 618   47448
812 988-2397   Est: 1976
Proprietor: Keith & Patti
Alberts
Hours: Mon, Wed-Sun,
10-2
Types & Periods: Jewelry,
Furniture, Copper, Brass,
General
Directions: 1 mile S of
Nashville, across from
Opry

BETTY'S ANTIQUES
N Van Buren   47448
812 988-2542   Est: 1974
Proprietor: Mike & Betty
Sansone
Hours: Daily, 10-5:30
Types & Periods: China,
Glass, Furniture, Primitives
Specialties: China (Haviland)
Directions: 45 miles S of
Indianapolis

**JAY & ELLEN CARTER
ANTIQUES**
PO Box 252   47448
812 988-7904   Est: 1966
Proprietor: Jay & Ellen
Carter
Hours. By appointment
Types & Periods: 18th &
19th Century Country
Furniture & Accessories,
Shaker Items, Indian
Baskets & Rugs, Early
Lighting
Specialties: Painted Country
Furniture
Appraisal Service Available
Directions: 1 mile N of
center of Village on St Rd
135 N

FAY'S ANTIQUES
Main St   47448
812 988-2648
Proprietor: Fay McGahey
Hours: Daily, 11-5
Types & Periods: Victorian,
Silver, Copper, Brass, Coins,
19th & Early 20th Century
Dolls
Directions: Main St behind
Post Office

THE GARRET
Box 398   47448
812 988-6133   Est: 1973
Proprietor: Roger &
Genevieve Meshberger
Hours: Daily, 12-5

Types & Periods: General
Line
Specialties: Stained Glass,
Brass Beds
Appraisal Service Available
Directions: Above the Hob
Nob in the Miller Drug
Store Bldg on the Public
Square

GYPSY POT ANTIQUES
Van Buren   47448
812 988-2759
Proprietor: L D Percifield
Hours: Daily, 9-5
Types & Periods: China,
Glassware
Specialties: Oriental (Rugs)
Directions: Mailing: PO
Box 366

**HOB NOB CORNER
ANTIQUES**
Hob Nob Bldg   47448
812 988-6038
Proprietor: Bob & Lisanne
Hamilton
Hours: Daily, 11-5
Types & Periods: Country
Furniture, Primitives, Glass,
Bottles

JIM'S MILITARY RELICS
N Van Buren St   47448
Proprietor: Jim & Karen
Hazel
Hours: Daily
Types & Periods: Guns,
Swords, Military Antiques
from Civil War to Present

LEE'S ANTIQUES
Van Buren St   47448
                Est: 1954
Proprietor: Lee Howery
Hours: Daily
Types & Periods: Furniture,
Glass, Dolls, Jewelry,
General Line
Appraisal Service Available
Directions: Located on
main street of Nashville

MARTINS' ANTIQUES
RR 3 Box 30   47448
812 988-7349   Est: 1969
Proprietor: David &
Catherine Martin
Hours: By appointment, by
chance
Types & Periods: 19th
Century Furniture &
Accessories

Appraisal Service Available
Directions: 1 mile N of
stop light in Nashville on
St Rd 135 N

MARY'S ANTIQUES
Heritage Mall   47448
812 372-5301
Proprietor: Mary
Muellenberg
Hours: Sun-Mon, Wed-Sat,
11-5
Types & Periods: Art & Cut
Glass, Jewelry, Victorian
Furniture
Specialties: Toys (Dolls)

**MICHAEL'S ANTIQUES &
DRIED FLOWERS**
RR 4 Box 172   47448
812 988-2689
Proprietor: Mike & Syd
Nickels
Hours: Daily, 11-5
Types & Periods: Old Pie
Safes, Country Furniture,
Rough Primitives

THE RED ENGINE SHOP
E Main St   47448
812 988-7597
Proprietor: Richard &
Marcia Smith
Hours: Daily
Types & Periods: General
Line, Quilts, Collectibles

SCARCE O' FAT HOUSE
Box 669   47448
812 988-7266
Proprietor: R H Deer & J
R Whitten
Hours: Sun-Mon, Wed-Sat,
10-5
Types & Periods: General
Line, Quilts
Specialties: Furniture, Glass
(Stained & Beveled)
Directions: Corner of E
Main & Artist Dr

STONEHEAD STORE
RR 2 Box 134   47448
812 988-7627
Proprietor: Romuald &
Sonia Shultz
Hours: Daily
Types & Periods: General
Line, Cut Glass, Primitives

Nashville   Cont'd

WALKER'S ANTIQUES
Box 331   47448
812 988-7730
Proprietor: Edward T
Walker
Hours: Daily
Types & Periods: Country
Furniture, Cupboards, Tools,
General, Primitives
Directions: N Jefferson,
1/2 block N of Main St

WILLIAMSON'S ANTIQUES
RR 4   47448
812 988-7947
Proprietor: Jon Williamson
Hours: By chance
Types & Periods: General
Line of Furniture, Primitives

**YANKEE DOLLAR
ANTIQUES**
Box 508   47448
812 372-1498
Proprietor: Norval & Elaine
Fischvogt
Hours: By appointment
Types & Periods: Furniture,
Tools
Directions: 3 miles E on St
Rd 46

New Albany

ANTIQUE ART
509 W Market   47150
812 945-6081   Est: 1972
Proprietor: Virginia S
Rosenbarger
Hours: Wed, Thurs & Sun,
12:30-4; Fri & Sat, 10-4
Types & Periods: Furniture,
Glass, China, Tools
Specialties: Rugs (Hand
Loomed), Primitives
Directions: Across the
street from Holiday Inn

New Harmony

THE 'WAGGIN' WHEELER
Main St   47631
Proprietor: W Roger &
Rita A Wheeler
Hours: Mon-Fri
Types & Periods: General
Line
Specialties: 18th & 19th
Century Americana

Noblesville

BRUNSON SHOPPE
12611 Markay Dr   46060
317 849-3208
Proprietor: Keith & Estryl
Brunson
Hours: By appointment
Types & Periods: Primitives,
Furniture, China, Glass

North Vernon

OLE CORRAL ANTIQUES
RR 4   47265
812 346-6376   Est: 1956
Proprietor: Mrs Bernice A
Showers
Hours: By appointment, by
chance
Types & Periods: General
Line
Specialties: Pressed Glass,
Old Books
Directions: Hwy 50 W
edge of North Vernon

Oakford

**SLABAUGH'S FURNITURE
& ANTIQUES**
                  46965
317 453-0723   Est: 1975
Proprietor: Truman
Slabaugh
Hours: Daily, 10-5
Types & Periods: General
Line, Furniture, Glassware
Appraisal Service Available
Directions: 4 miles S of
Kokomo on US 31 to St
Rd 26 E 1 mile

STEVE'S TRADING POST
Box 72   46965
317 453-0900   Est: 1958
Proprietor: Owen M
Stevens
Hours: Mon-Sat, by
appointment, by chance
Types & Periods: Furniture,
Collectibles
Directions: 1¼ miles E of
Intersection US 31 & St
Rd 26

Osgood

**ANTIQUES BY
NEGANGARD**
148 N Buckeye St   47037
812 689-4962   Est: 1974
Proprietor: Charles F
Negangard
Hours: Weekday
Afternoons or by
appointment or by chance
Types & Periods: China, Cut
Glass, Victorian Silver Plate,
Sterling Silver Flat and
Hollow Ware, Victorian &
Early American Furniture
Appraisal Service Available
Directions: On main
thoroughfare

Owensburg

**GINGERBREAD HOUSE
ANTIQUES**
Box 31   47453
812 863-4436   Est: 1972
Proprietor: Patsy & Don
Foust
Hours: Tues-Thurs, 10-5;
Weekends by appointment
Types & Periods: Early
Country Furniture, Primitives
Directions: 23 miles SW of
Bloomington on St Rd 45

Plymouth

B J'S ANTIQUES
119 S Center   46563
219 936-7053   Est: 1973
Proprietor: Bonnie J
Frushour
Hours: Sat-Thurs, May-Dec
Types & Periods: Furniture,
Glass, Dishes, Books, Bottles
Specialties: Glass
Appraisal Service Available
Directions: Downtown,
1 blk W of Michigan St

GEORGIA C BOGGS
RR 1   46563
219 936-2619   Est: 1950
Proprietor: Georgia C
Boggs
Hours: Daily or by chance
Types & Periods: Glass,
China, Furniture

Appraisal Service Available
Directions: 1/2 mile N of
Holiday Inn on old US 31,
E side of road

CENTURY ANTIQUES
1011 W Jefferson St 46563
219 936-4783   Est: 1969
Proprietor: James
Manuwal
Hours: Daily
Types & Periods: Fine
American Furniture from
1800-1915
Directions: Old US 30 W

Portland

**HARTLEY BELL & WHISTLE
ANTIQUES**
1103 W Arch   47371
317 726-7440   Est: 1951
Proprietor: Alton H Hartley
Hours: Mon-Sat, 9-5; Sun
by chance
Types & Periods: General
Line
Specialties: Clocks
Directions: W on Hospital
St to Park St, on corner

MERIDIAN HILL ANTIQUES
RR 1   47371
317 726-7506   Est: 1948
Proprietor: Bereniece
Mattheus
Hours: Daily
Types & Periods: Glass,
China, Tin Ware, Paper
Items, Campaign
Directions: US 27, S edge
of Portland

THE TREASURE CHEST
114 N Meridian St   47371
317 726-4511   Est: 1969
Proprietor: James Burk
Hours: Daily, by chance
Types & Periods: China,
Glass, Furniture
Appraisal Service Available
Directions: Downtown

UPP'S ANTIQUES
1120 W Main St   47371
317 726-4700
Proprietor: Virlis Upp
Hours: By chance
Types & Periods: General
Line
Directions: Between
Richmond & Fort Wayne
on US 27

Poseyville

**KOPPER DOORS ANTIQUE
SHOP**
Hwy 68 & 165 W   47633
812 874-2816   Est: 1971
Proprietor: E Mott Wade
Hours: Mon-Fri, 8:30-5;
Weekends, 12-5
Types & Periods: Primitives,
Wooden articles, Glassware,
Furniture, Farm tools, Black-
smith tools, Fruit jars,
Iron Ware
Specialties: Light fixtures,
Farm tools, License Plates
Directions: 1½ miles S
of I-64

Prairieton

PRAIRIE HOUSE ANTIQUES
Box 48   47870
812 299-5552   Est: 1974
Proprietor: Beverly Cristee
Hours: Tues-Sat, 11-4
Types & Periods: Primitives,
Furniture
Specialties: Embroidery &
Needlework (Quilts &
Coverlets)
Directions: 5 miles S of
Terre Haute on St Rd 63

SHAKER TABLE ANTIQUES
Hwy 63   47870
812 299-4768   Est: 1972
Proprietor: Tim & Cindy
Weir
Hours: Daily
Types & Periods: Country
Furniture, Primitives, Paper
Americana, Dolls,
Stoneware, Baskets
Appraisal Service Available
Directions: Hwy 63 in
center of Prairieton, 6
miles S of Terre Haute

Princeton

THE WHITE BARN
RR 1   47570
812 385-2784   Est: 1971
Proprietor: Burnice Rogers
Hours: Mon-Sat, 9-5; Sun,
1-5

Types & Periods: General
Line
Directions: Rd 100 W, 1/4
mile off 41 Bypass

Richland

**CENTURY HOUSE
ANTIQUES**
Rte 1 Box 353   47634
812 359-4870   Est: 1968
Proprietor: Jean Fueger
Hours: By appointment, by
chance
Types & Periods: Furniture,
Primitives, Glass, China,
Lamps
Specialties: Round Tables,
Refurbishing Trunks
Directions: Off St Rd 161,
1 mile S of Midway

Roann

**CARMEN COLBERT
ANTIQUETS**
105 Arnold St   46974
219 833-4961   Est: 1958
Proprietor: Carmen
Colbert
Hours: By appointment, by
chance; phone evenings
for appointment
Types & Periods: 1850-1910
Furniture, Art Glass, Oriental
Rugs and Tapestries,
Hanging, Tiffany Type
Banquet Lamps
Appraisal Service Available
Directions: 2 miles W of St
Rd 15 on St Rd 16, turn S
1st, 1½ blocks, in front of
water tower

Roanoke

OLD CURIOSITY SHOP
373 Posey Hill   46783
219 672-2424
Hours: By appointment, By
chance
Types & Periods: General Line
Directions: W 4th St
extended

Salem

JEANIES ANTIQUES
47167
812 883-4777   Est: 1974
Proprietor: Regina Gilstrap
Hours: Daily, by
appointment or by chance
Types & Periods: General
Line
Specialties: Primitives
Directions: On Hwy 60 W
toward Mitchell, "Large
Sign on Left"

Shipshewana

HAARER'S ANTIQUES
Morton St   46565
219 768-4787   Est: 1972
Proprietor: Paul & Shirley
Haarer
Hours: Mon-Sat
Types & Periods: Primitives,
Early American Furniture,
Antique Amish Furniture
Appraisal Service Available
Directions: 2 blocks E of
Indiana St Rd 5

Solsberry

RICHARD-ANNE SIPE
Rt 1   47459
Est: 1961
Proprietor: R & A Sipe
Hours: Thurs-Sat, Also by
chance
Types & Periods: Primitives,
Wooden Items, Cupboard,
Quilts
Directions: Rt 45 W, 13
miles from Bloomington

Somerville

DEE'S ANTIQUES
Box 302   47683
812 795-2532   Est: 1975
Proprietor: Delores Sevier
Hours: Daily; Also
evenings by appointment
Types & Periods: General
Line
Specialties: Furniture, Bitters
Bottles, Fruit Jars

Appraisal Service Available
Directions: 1 block off
Hwy 57 at Somerville

South Bend

**ANTIQUE WORLD INC-A-W
AUCTION**
1116-1122 Mishawaka Ave
46615
219 288-0708   Est: 1971
Proprietor: Mary Ann
Melching,
Hours: Mon-Fri, 9-5; Sat,
10-12
Types & Periods: General
Line
Specialties: Auctions, Hand
Stripping, Refinishing,
Caning
Appraisal Service Available
Directions: Base of
Cooper Bridge, back of
store looks over at
Farmer's Market

PRIMROSE ANTIQUES
26950 Dunn Rd   46628
219 288-6764   Est: 1965
Proprietor: Barbara
Carbiener
Hours: Mon-Fri, 10-4,
Weekends by appointment
or by chance
Types & Periods: General
Line
Specialties: Furniture (Pine,
Cherry, Country, English)
Directions: 6 miles W of
South Bend off US 20

SCHUELL ANTIQUES
51027 Portage Rd   46628
219 272-9310   Est: 1934
Proprietor: Franklin
Schuell
Hours: By appointment
Types & Periods: French
Paperweights, Art Glass,
Porcelain, Oriental Rugs,
Paintings
Specialties: French
Paperweights
Directions: 6 miles NW on
Portage Rd at Adams Rd

Spencer

**CORNER CUPBOARD
ANTIQUES**
RR 2 Box 198A   47460
317 795-3155
Proprietor: Ray & Norma
Linneman
Hours: Wed-Sat, 9:30-5;
Sun, 12:30-5
Types & Periods: Glass,
Haviland China, Furniture
Specialties: China
Directions: Located at
Cataract, 12 miles NW of
Spencer, 8 miles SW of
Cloverdale

**VALLEY HAVEN WOOD
SHOP**
RR 1 Box 216   47460
812 829-2496   Est: 1961
Proprietor: Donna
Galimore
Hours: By appointment, by
chance, open most
Sundays
Types & Periods: Furniture
Specialties: Restoration
Directions: 5 miles S of
Spencer on Pottersville Rd

Terre Haute

**AARDVARK ALLEY
ANTIQUES**
639 S Ninth St   47807
812 234-2250   Est: 1971
Proprietor: Patricia & Jerry
Rollings
Hours: Mon-Sat, 10-7; Sun
by appointment
Types & Periods: Glass,
China, Primitives, Furniture
Appraisal Service Available
Directions: Corner of
Crawford & S 9th Sts

THE ATTIC
2511 S 3rd St   47802
812 232-8606   Est: 1969
Proprietor: Robert J
Lambert
Hours: Sun-Mon,
Thurs-Sat, 10-6; Tues-Wed
by chance

Types & Periods: Furniture, Collectibles
Specialties: Turn of the Century Furniture & Collectibles
Directions: 4 blocks N of I-70 on US 41

THE DOWNSTAIRS ANTIQUES
1714 Poplar St   47807
812 232-7125   Est: 1972
Proprietor: Samuel W Smith
Hours: "All year in the late afternoons & at night"
Types & Periods: Pattern, Cut & Art Glass, Brass, Pewter, Quilts
Specialties: Glass (By Gillinder & Sons)
Appraisal Service Available
Directions: Terre Haute Exit at US 41, then N to stop light at Montgomery Ward corner, then right

MARTIN'S ANTIQUES
1605 S 7th St   47802
812 232-8756   Est: 1968
Proprietor: Paul A & Helen Martin
Hours: Mon-Sat
Types & Periods: General Line
Specialties: Post Cards, Furniture, Glass
Appraisal Service Available
Directions: 73 miles SW of Indianapolis on I-70

ROST'S CARRIAGE HOUSE ANTIQUES
2950 S 7th St   47802
812 234-5223   Est: 1974
Proprietor: Robert E Rost II
Hours: Mon-Sat
Types & Periods: Victorian & Empire East Lake Bedroom, Dining Room & Living Room, Circa 1835
Specialties: Depression Glass, Pattern & Carnival Glass, Art Pottery
Appraisal Service Available
Directions: 1 block N of I-70, 5 blocks E, 1/2 block N of stop light

SWANK'S ANTIQUES
1119 N 8th St   47807
812 235-7734   Est: 1966
Proprietor: William & Gary Swank

Hours: By appointment, by chance
Types & Periods: Oak Furniture, Clocks
Specialties: Refinished Oak Furniture
Appraisal Service Available

Thorntown

BARBER'S ANTIQUES & COLLECTIBLES
504 N Pearl   46071
317 436-7715
Proprietor: Dorothy Barber
Hours: By appointment, by chance
Types & Periods: General Line
Specialties: Furniture, Glass, Primitives
Directions: 4 blocks N of 47

Tipton

BILL & MARGE SMITH ANTIQUES
RR 1   46072
317 758-5827
Proprietor: Bill & Marge Smith
Hours: By appointment, by chance
Types & Periods: Furniture, Primitives, Pottery

Vernon

THE BUTTERNUT TREE
On the Curve   47282
812 346-4880   Est: 1974
Proprietor: Lew & Millie Leathers
Hours: Mon-Wed, Fri-Sat, 10-5; Sun, 1-5
Types & Periods: Primitive & Early Furniture, Pressed Glass, Jewelry, Linens
Directions: Midway between Indianapolis, Louisville & Cincinnati, on Hwys 3 & 7, 1 mile off Hwy 50

DOLL WORLD
PO Box 264   47282
812 346-3450   Est: 1966
Proprietor: Virginia Amos

Hours: Mon, Wed-Sat, 10-5; Sun, 12-5
Types & Periods: Old & Modern Dolls, Porcelain Reproductions, Doll Houses & Related Items, Doll Hospital
Appraisal Service Available
Directions: Hwys 7 & 3, opposite Courthouse

VILLAGE SHOPPE
Pike St PO Box 278 47282
812 346-2044   Est: 1968
Proprietor: Roland S Wilson
Hours: Daily
Types & Periods: General Line, Glass, Furniture
Directions: Across from courthouse on Hwys 3 & 7

Versailles

VERSAILLES ANTIQUES
RR 1 Box 311A   47042
812 689-5488   Est: 1973
Proprietor: Edward Gibbs
Hours: Daily
Types & Periods: General Line, Furniture, Trains, Steam Engines
Specialties: Furniture
Directions: Hwy 50 next to State Park

Vevay

LOST CAUSE ANTIQUES GALLERY
Main at Main Cross 47043
812 427-2900   Est: 1969
Proprietor: Ann Farnsley
Hours: Daily
Types & Periods: General Line
Directions: On the Ohio River midway between Cincinnai & Louisville, 20 miles upstream from Madison, cross the Ohio River at Ghent, Ky to Vevay on the Martha A Graham ferryboat

Wabash

COPPOCK'S ANTIQUES
Baily Rd N   46992
219 563-6521
Hours: By appt or chance
Types & Periods: General
Line
Directions: Hwy 15 S to
500 S, then E 1¼ miles to
Baily Rd N, the first house

MAPLE LAWN ANTIQUES
1105 N Cass   46992
219 563-5738
Hours: By appt or chance
Types & Periods: General
Line
Directions: On St Rd 15
btwn US 24 & 24 Bypass

THOMPSON'S ANTIQUES
1306 Columbus   46992
219 563-1408
Hours: By appt or chance
Types & Periods: General
Line

**YE HERITAGE HOUSE
ANTIQUES**
Hwy 13   46992
219 563-1935
Hours: By appt or chance
Types & Periods: General
Line
Directions: RR 3 Rd 400
S, 1st crossroad off Hwy
13, turn R, 2nd house

Washington

**MIDWAY ANTIQUES &
COUNTRY STORE**
Rte 3, Box 297, Hwy 50 E
47501
812 254-3883   Est: 1966
Proprietor: Mrs Harold
Roberts
Hours: By appt or chance
Types & Periods: General
Line
Specialties: Ceramics
(Bowls), Plates & Quilts
Directions: 4 miles E of
Washington on Hwys 50 &
150, across from E 50
Drive-In

Waterloo

CURRY'S ANTIQUES
RR 2   46793
219 281-2349   Est: 1970
Proprietor: Wayne Curry
Hours: Daily
Types & Periods: Oak &
Walnut Furniture, Primitives
& Collectibles
Specialties: Furniture (Oak
Hi-Back Chairs, Round &
Square Oak Tables)
Appraisal Service Available
Directions: 2 miles W of
I-69 at Waterloo Exit

DOROTHY DUNN
530 S Washington   46793
219 837-4283   Est: 1969
Proprietor: Dorothy Dunn
Hours: Daily
Types & Periods: Pressed
Glass, R S Prussia, China,
Bisque & China Dolls &
Jewelry
Appraisal Service Available
Directions: 2 miles E of
I-69 & State Rd 6
Intersection

Waveland

VIVIAN'S ANTIQUES
218-220 Cross St   47989
Est: 1944
Proprietor: Vivian C
Stewart
Hours: Daily, 9:30-4
Types & Periods: Furniture,
all periods
Specialties: China & Glass
Appraisal Service Available
Directions: Downtown on
St Rd 59

Westfield

**HENRY & JANE ECKERT
ANTIQUES**
131 W Main St   46074
317 896-3776   Est: 1973
Proprietor: Henry & Jane
Eckert
Hours: Mon-Sun, 11-5 &
by chance

Types & Periods: Early
Country Furniture, Coverlets
& Paintings
Appraisal Service Available
Directions: 20 miles N of
Indianapolis on Hwy 31, at
the Intersection of Hwys
31 & 32 turn R & go 5
blocks

**MAX'S WATERTOWER
ANTIQUES**
211 N Union   46074
317 896-3515   Est: 1962
Proprietor: Max W Bender
Hours: Daily
Types & Periods: General
Line, Furniture, China, Glass
Specialties: Rugs (Oriental),
Stained Glass Windows
Directions: At the base of
town's old water tower

West Terre Haute

J & M SALES
1 W Paris Ave   47885
Est: 1963
Proprietor: John & Martha
Carpenter
Hours: Daily, 10-5:30
Types & Periods: Furniture,
Cut Glass, Carnival, R S
Prussia, Rose Medallion,
Late 1800 & Early 1900
Directions: Across the
Wabash Bridge W of Terre
Haute on Rte 40 to Y,
Keep left

Williamsport

ANTIQUES & THINGS
314 Lincoln   47993
317 762-3687   Est: 1954
Proprietor: Gerald Sanders
Hours: Daily, by
appointment or by chance
Types & Periods: China,
Glass, Silver, Furniture,
Sheet Music
Specialties: Magazines, Post
Cards, Advertising
Appraisal Service Available
Directions: Just off US 41,
12 miles N of I-74

Winslow

BARRETT ANTIQUES & FURNITURE
RR 1   47598
812 789-2180   Est: 1968
Proprietor: Ira H Barrett
Hours: Tues & Thurs
afternoons by
appointment; Sat, 10:30-6
Types & Periods: Primitives,
Early American, Depression
& Carnival Glass, General
Line
Appraisal Service Available
Directions: 300 yards N of
IN Hwy 64 & 61 Jct at
Arthur IN on W side

Zionsville

BROWN'S ANTIQUES
315 N 5th   46077
317 873-2284   Est: 1945
Proprietor: Marshall &
Mary Jane Brown & Son
Hours: Mon-Sat, 10-5;
Sun, 2-5
Types & Periods: General
Line
Specialties: Period Furniture
in "Williamsburg Setting"
Appraisal Service Available
Directions: NW of
Indianapolis

HELEN KOGAN ANTIQUES
195 S Main St   46077
317 873-4208   Est: 1965
Proprietor: Helen Kogan
Hours: Daily by
appointment; Tues-Sat,
10-5; Sun & Mon, by
chance
Types & Periods: Early
Country Furniture
Specialties: Lighting Fixtures
Appraisal Service Available
Directions: 8 miles N of
Indianapolis

TYPICAL LEGS OF THE FEDERAL PERIOD

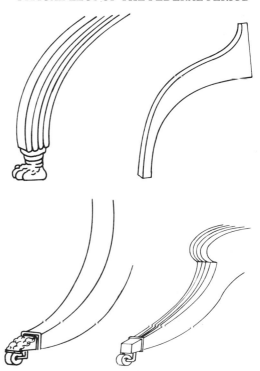

Sewing Table, wooden work basket, Duncan Phyfe. Notice the Federal styled legs.

STATE OF IOWA

Amana

ANTIQUE TOWER HAUS
Main St   52203
319 622-3888
Proprietor: Vivian Hergert
Hours: April-Dec, Sun-Mon
Types & Periods: Primitives,
Glassware, China,
Collectibles & Some
Furniture

Ames

THE PINES ANTIQUES
RR 4 Lincolnway W 50010
515 292-3742   Est: 1957
Proprietor: Margaret
McMahon
Hours: Mon-Sun, 1-5
Types & Periods: Furniture,
Glass, China, Silver, Art,
Oriental Rugs & Linens
Specialties: Furniture
restored or refinished
Appraisal Service Available
Directions: W edge of
Ames

Aurelia

ODDITY SHOP ANTIQUES
Main St   51005
712 434-5380   Est: 1970
Proprietor: Richard Vogt
Hours: April-Dec,
Mon-Sun; then by chance
Types & Periods: General
Line
Appraisal Service Available
Directions: Located on
Hwy 7; 17 miles W of
Storm Lake; 5 miles E of
Cherokee

Bellevue

CRAF-TIQUE CELLAR
Off Hwy 52 N   52031
319 872-4930   Est: 1971
Proprietor: Joan & Stu
Wagner
Hours: by appt & by
chance

Types & Periods: General
Line & Picture Frames
Directions: 2 miles S of St
Donatus & 1 1/4 miles on
Scenic Country Rd

Bloomfield

TREASURE HOUSE
103 E Franklin   52537
515 664 1817   Est: 1969
Proprietor: Lorraine D
Lofgren
Hours: Mon-Sat, 9-5
Types & Periods: General
Line

Boone

OAK OUT HOUSE
804 22nd St   50036
515 432-5991   Est: 1974
Proprietor: Gail & Patricia
Evans
Hours: by appt or by
chance
Types & Periods: Midwest
American Antiques
Specialties: Restored
Kitchen Cabinets
Directions: Last St N in
Boone

Burlington

ANTIE Q & UNCLE
JUNQUE
707 W Burlington Ave
                52601
319 753-1276
Hours: by appt
Types & Periods: General
Line

BENEDICT'S ANTIQUES
Hwy 99   52601
319 752-0419
Hours: by appt & by
chance
Types & Periods: Furniture,
Primitives, China & Art Glass
Directions: 1 1/4 mile N of
Case Company on Hwy 99

BIG JOHN ANTIQUES
219 S Main St   52601
319 754-4736   Est: 1975
Proprietor: John
Wagner, Jr
Types & Periods: China,
Glassware, Clocks, Lamps,
Primitives, Collectibles, Oak
Furniture & Walnut
Primitives
Specialties: Primitives &
Collectibles
Appraisal Service Available
Directions: Across the St
& 1 block N of RR & Bus
Depot; 1 block S of RR
track

MRS S L BROWER
ANTIQUES
2432 S 3rd   52601
319 752-3989
Hours: Mon-Sun, 9-5
Types & Periods: China &
Glassware

CHAMBERLAIN HOUSE
ANTIQUES
401 S Main   52601
Proprietor: Dolores
Kinneer
Hours: Mon-Sat, 12-4
Types & Periods: Cut Glass,
Handpainted China,
Furniture & Primitives

JUANITA CONGER
FURNITURE & ANTIQUES
900 Oak St   52601
319 753-2028
Hours: Mon-Sun
Types & Periods: General
Line

COUNTRY JUNQUE STORE
401 S Central   52601
319 752-5863
Proprietor: Wesley Cross
Hours: Mon-Sun
Types & Periods: General
Line
Directions: South Hill
Area; corner of Central &
Maple

HEDGEPETH ANTIQUES
115 S Main St   52601
319 752-8654   Est: 1965
Proprietor: William & Sally
Hedgepeth
Hours: Mon-Sat, 12-5

Types & Periods: General
Line & Collectibles
Specialties: Advertising,
Railroad & Pottery
Directions: Downtown
across the St from RR
Depot

JOHNSON'S ANTIQUES
918 Locust   52601
319 752-1597
Types & Periods: Oak
Furniture, Copper & Brass

**JUNKE 'N STUFFE
ANTIQUES**
213 S Main St   52601
319 752-8818   Est: 1969
Proprietor: Paul & Alyce
Aspengren
Hours: By appt & by
chance
Types & Periods: General
Line, Oak, Walnut & Pine
Furniture, Campaign
Buttons, Toys & Unusual
Items
Specialties: Hand stripping
of furniture, repairing &
refinishing antique furniture
Directions: Corner of S
0th Ct & Locust

LAMPLIGHT ANTIQUES
431 W Harrison   52601
319 752-1444
Hours: By appt & by
chance
Types & Periods: General
Line

**LUCY'S ANTIQUES &
UNIQUES**
410 Franklin   52601
Hours: Mon-Sun
Types & Periods: Furniture,
Depression Glass, Silver,
Jars & Bottles
Directions: 1 block N &
1/2 block W of Hwy 34 E

MAGGIE'S ANTIQUES
1221 Agency   52601
319 753-0897
Hours: Mon-Sat, 9-5
Types & Periods: General
Line, Collectibles & Furniture

MAUDE MARSH
Lincoln   52601
319 752-6741
Hours: Mon-Sun
Types & Periods: Avons &
Collectibles

MRS JOHN PAYTON
826 N 6th   52601
319 754-5922
Types & Periods: China,
Furniture, Glass & Primitives

**RIVER FRONT ANTIQUE
STUDIOS**
607 N 5th   52601
319 752-4465
Proprietor: Randy & Paul
Kingyon
Types & Periods: French &
Victorian Furniture,
Primitives, Copper, Brass,
Art Glass, Leaded Glass,
Windows, Lamps &
Paintings

TREASURE HOUSE
601 S Main   52601
Proprietor: A J Miller
Hours: Mon-Sun
Types & Periods: Furniture,
Art & Cut Glass
Appraisal Service Available
Directions: S on Main St
after entering Iowa from
bridge

WASSON'S ANTIQUES
217 Sweeney   52601
319 752-7217
Hours: by appt & by
chance
Types & Periods: Wooden
Furniture & Primitives

WILDWOOD ANTIQUES
W Ave Rd   52601
319 754-6864
Hours: Mon-Sun, 9-5 & by
appt
Types & Periods: Furniture,
Jewelry & Collectibles

Cedar Falls

ATTIC ANTIQUE SHOPPE
525 Lincoln   50613
319 268-0736   Est: 1968
Proprietor: Pat Koloc
Hours: Mon-Sat
Types & Periods: General
Line & Collectibles
Directions: 5 blocks off
Hwy 20 on old Hwy 20

**BRASS BUCKET ANTIQUE
SHOP**
1005 W. 19th St.   50613
319 266-4603   Est: 1973

Proprietor: Kay Glessner
Hours: Mon-Sun, 1-5:30
Types & Periods: Furniture,
Primitives & Decoratives
Appraisal Service Available
Directions: 3 Blocks from U
of northern Iowa Campus

CELLAR ANTIQUES
4912 University   50613
319 266-5091
Proprietor: Joe & DeEtta
Lisby
Hours: Sat-Thurs, anytime
when at home; Fri,
afternoons & Evenings by
appt
Types & Periods: Furniture,
Glass, Collectibles,
Primitives & Crocks
Specialties: Depression
Glass & Primitives
Directions: On Hwy 218, 4
houses W of Shakey's
Pizza, 1 block W of
Howard Johnsons

Cedar Rapids

CALICO CUPBOARD
1118 Second St SE 52401
319 366-4292   Est: 1974
Proprietor: Paula Agnew
Koza
Hours: Tues-Sat
Types & Periods: Furniture
& Primitives
Directions: Near Czech
Village Shopping Mall &
Community Theatre

CZECH COTTAGE
100-16th Ave SW   52404
319 366-4937   Est: 1975
Proprietor: Jitka Schaffer
Hours: Mon-Wed, Fri-Sat,
9:30-5; Thurs, 9:30-9; also
by appt & by chance
Types & Periods: Cut, Blown
& Hard Decorated Crystal,
Porcelain, Primitives, Wood,
Metal, Oil Paintings &
Weapons
Appraisal Service Available
Directions: On the corner
of 16th St & C St SW

GARDNER'S ANTIQUES
224 12th St NW   52405
319 362-8116   Est: 1965
Proprietor: Howard &
Janet Gardner

Cedar Rapids   Cont'd

GARDNER'S   Cont'd
Hours: by appt & by
chance
Types & Periods: Primitives,
Stoneware & Post Cards
Appraisal Service Available
Directions: 1st Ave W to
12th

HOUSE OF ANTIQUES LTD
221 23rd St NE   25402
319 365-1879
Proprietor: Marian Little &
Esther Lucore
Hours: by appt & by
chance
Types & Periods: General
Line, Furniture, Silver,
Oriental & Art Glass

J & E TRADING COMPANY
1028 12th Ave SE   52403
319 364-5047   Est: 1974
Proprietor: J Reineche
Hours: Mon-Fri, 10-4:30;
Sat 10-12
Types & Periods: General
Line
Directions: Corner of 15th
St & 12th Ave SE;
Numbers are goofy here

AGNES KOEHN ANTIQUES
5100 Johnson Ave SW
    52404
319 396-3836   Est: 1936
Proprietor: Donald C
Koehn
Hours: Mon-Sun, by
chance; If coming long
distance, call first
Types & Periods: Victorian
Art Glass, French Cameo &
French Dolls, Colored Glass
& Fine China
Specialties: Art Glass &
Dolls
Directions: 2 blocks from
Hwys 30 & 218 W

THE STABLE ON THE ALLEY
116 15th St   52403
319 365-2448   Est: 1969
Proprietor: Jo McGrath
Hours: Mon-Sat, 10-5
Types & Periods: Primitives,
Furniture & Antiques for
Decorating
Specialties: We conduct
household & estate sales

Appraisal Service Available
Directions: 1 1/2 block N
from First Ave on 15th St

Charles City

HOBERT'S ANTIQUES
603 N. Illinois   50616
515 228-3019   Est: 1966
Proprietor: Raymond &
Dorothy Hobert
Hours: Mon-Fri &
Sat-Sun by chance
Types & Periods: Oak &
Walnut Furniture, Pattern
& Carnival Glass &
Lamps
Specialties: Furniture &
Glass
Directions: 6 blocks W of
Main St

Clarence

J & M SHOPPE
611 Lombard St   52216
319 452-3808   Est: 1973
Proprietor: James C
Sawyer
Hours: Mon-Sat, 11-5; Sun
1-5 (usually)
Types & Periods: Early
1900's & Collectibles
Specialties: Primitives, Glass
& Furniture
Directions: Hwy 30, Main
St

Clear Lake

ARTICHOKE 11
204 S 4th St   50428
515 357-6060   Est: 1975
Hours: Mon-Sat
Types & Periods: Furniture,
Primitives, Pictures, Mirrors,
China, Glassware, Quilts,
Clocks & Collectibles
Directions: 1 block E of
Main St

Corydon

RED BARN ANTIQUES
205 E Jackson   50060
515 872-1478   Est: 1973

Proprietor: John & Mid
Bode
Hours: Mon-Sat, 9-4;
Closed noon hour
Types & Periods: General
Line, American Furniture &
Primitives
Specialties: Pattern Back
Chairs & Oak Furniture
Directions: Hwys 2 & 14;
Just off NE corner of
Town Square

Council Bluffs

D & D ANTIQUES
722 E Pierce St   51501
712 323-5233
Proprietor: Dennis &
Norma Devine
Hours: Mon-Sun
Types & Periods: Early
American Furniture, Brass
Beds & Clocks
Specialties: Antique
Phonographs, Brass Beds &
Wall Phones
Directions: 1 block S of E
Broadway; E end of town
by both hospitals

LEWIS TOWNSHIP ANTIQUES
1402 E S Omaha
Bridge Rd   51501
712 366-0551
Proprietor: James A
Neilsen
Hours: Mon-Sat; Sun,
Open in spring & fall
Types & Periods: Oak
Furniture, Collectibles,
Primitives & Dealer's
Discounts
Directions: SE of I-29 &
I-80 intersection S of
Council Bluffs; S at
stoplight of junction Hwys
275 & 92 for 1/2 mile; W
at dead end sign

SCOTTY'S SALES CO
720 W Broadway   51501
712 322-5662   Est: 1956
Proprietor: Hunter P Reid
Hours: Mon-Sun, 8-5
Types & Periods: General
Line
Appraisal Service Available
Directions: Center of town

Davenport

A & D ANTIQUES
3130 Hickory Grove Rd
52806
319 391-7099   Est: 1971
Proprietor: D F Giammetta
Hours: by appt & by
chance
Types & Periods: General
Line
Specialties: Furniture &
Glass
Directions: Bendix Area

ALADDINS' LAMP ANTIQUES
627 N Division   52802
319 323-4038   Est: 1971
Proprietor: Jim & Dorothy
Miles
Hours: Tues-Sat, 10-5 &
by appt
Types & Periods: General
Line, Furniture, Pottery,
Primitives & Depression
Glass
Specialties: Kewpie
Collectibles & Dolls
Directions: Corner of 7th
& Division; W end of
Davenport

ALLEN'S ANTIQUES
301 Perry St   52801
Proprietor: Albert W Siegel
Hours: Mon-Sun, 9:30-5
Types & Periods: China, Art
Glass, Watches & Jewelry
Specialties: Watches
Directions: Downtown;
Corner of Blackhawk Hotel
& 3rd St

PARLOR ANTIQUES INC
1107 Mound St   52803
319 323-1612   Est: 1975
Proprietor: Barbara A
Hunter
Hours: Tues-Sat, 11-4;
also by appt
Types & Periods: Furniture
& Glassware
Specialties: Gold & Silver
Jewelry
Appraisal Service Available
Directions: River Dr to
Mound St, 1 block over;
shop is on corner of
Mound St & 11th

RIVERBEND ANTIQUES, GIFTS & RESTORATION
425 Brady   52801
319 323-8622   Est: 1974
Proprietor: Ronald L
Bellomy
Hours: Tues-Fri, 11-6; Sat
10-5
Types & Periods: Primitives
to Funky, 1900-1935
Art Nouveau - Art Deco
Period Collectibles, Golden
Oak Furniture, Men's &
Women's Antique Clothing
Specialties: Stain Glass,
Golden Oak Furniture &
Antique Handmade gifts
Appraisal Service Available
Directions: Located at the
end of Brady St; A
wooden cigar store indian
marks the spot

Des Moines

DES MOINES CLUSTER
Directions: W Des Moines
at Valley Junction; 5th St
(100-300 blocks)

ANTIQUES FOR INTERIORS
4300 Lincoln Ave   50310
515 277-3174   Est: 1972
Proprietor: D Randolph
Tesdell
Hours: Mon-Sun by appt
Types & Periods: 17th &
18th Century American &
English Furniture, 16th-18th
Century Accessories,
Oriental Rugs, Early Prints &
Paintings
Appraisal Service Available
Directions: In N central
Des Moines, 1 block S of
Hickman Rd off 44th St

THE BOULEVARD MART
2718 Kingman Blvd   50311
515 279-4510   Est: 1965
Proprietor: Rosamond
Webster Bliss
Hours: Tues-Sat, 10-5 &
by appt
Types & Periods: General
Line & Consignment Shop
Appraisal Service Available
Directions: Corner of 28th
& Kingman; 2 blocks of
Drake University

ENGELBERT HOUSE
1910 Army Post Road
50315
515 285-3856   Est: 1975
Proprietor: C F Swenson
Hours: Tues-Sun, 11-5
Types & Periods: Large
building with 10 shops
containing mostly antiques,
but also includes a Frame
Shop, Stitchery Shop &
Light Shop; they carry large
quantities of late Victorian
Oak & Walnut Furniture,
Victorian Art Glass,
Depression Glass, Gas
Lightings, Aladdins & does
repairs on Lights & Frames
Appraisal Service Available
Directions: 1/2 block E of
the Des Moines Airport on
Army Post Rd; close to
Fleur & Army Post Rd &
across from the Hyatt
House

HOPE CHEST ANTIQUES
2539 Forest Ave   50311
515 274-1497   Est: 1962
Proprietor: Eugene &
Beverly Hope
Hours: Tues-Sat, 12-5
Types & Periods: General
Line
Specialties: Handling &
Arranging Estates & Moving
Sales
Appraisal Service Available
Directions: Corner of 25th
& Forest Ave, in the
vicinity of Drake University

MAXINES LIMITED
0570 University   50311
515 276-7204   Est: 1967
Proprietor: Helena
Rosenburg
Hours: Mon-Sat, 11-5
Types & Periods: General
Line
Specialties: Hummels,
Norman Rockwell & Kewpie
Dolls
Directions: I-235 to 63rd
Exit, go N to University
turn W, 3 blocks on N
side of St

McCARTHYS ANTIQUES
420 College Ave   50314
515 243-1081   Est: 1946
Hours: by appt & by
chance

Des Moines   Cont'd

McCARTHYS   Cont'd
Types & Periods: General
Line
  Directions: 6th Ave N to
  College, turn right 1½
  blocks

TURNER'S ANTIQUES
  6511 Elmcrest Dr   50311
  515 277-3890   Est: 1968
  Proprietor: C A Turner
  Hours: by chance
Types & Periods: China,
Glass, Primitives & Furniture
  Directions: 2 blocks N of
  University Ave off 66th St

Dexter

K G ANTIQUES
  I-80, exit 100   50070
  515 789-4406   Est: 1967
  Proprietor: Ken Gooch
  Hours: Mon-Sun by appt
Types & Periods: Victorian,
American, Walnut & Golden
Oak Furniture, Architectural
Items, Clocks, Art Glass &
Primitives
Specialties: Leaded &
Stained Glass Windows,
Doors & Lamps
Appraisal Service Available
  Directions: W of Des
  Moines, on I-80, exit 100

Dubuque

BURKART ANTIQUES
  908 Rhomberg Ave 52001
  319 582-2537
  Proprietor: Helen Burkart
  Hours: by appt
Types & Periods: General
Line
Appraisal Service Available
  Directions: Located on the
  way to Eagle Point Park &
  Wisconsin High Bridge

THE PRINCE OF PRUSSIA
  491 4th St W   52001
  319 556-8449   Est: 1973
  Proprietor: Dr George B
  Ehlhardt & R D Miller
  Hours: by appt & by
  chance

Types & Periods: Oriental,
Continental & English
Porcelain, Prints & Silver
Appraisal Service Available
  Directions: The Julien Inn,
  lobby level

SCHOEN'S ANTIQUES
  107-144 Locust   52001
  319 556-8942   Est: 1973
  Proprietor: Dulane Schoen
  Hours: Mon-Sun
Types & Periods: Wholesale
Furniture, Primitives &
Glassware
Specialties: over 4000 Sq Ft
of Furniture
Appraisal Service Available
  Directions: 2 blocks off
  Hwy 20 from Mississippi
  Bridge

Dysart

COLLECTORS PARADISE
  315 Main St   52224
  319 476-7700   Est: 1959
  Proprietor: Mr & Mrs
  Robert Schlotterback
  Hours: Mon-Fri, 10-12,
  1-5; Sat 10-12, afternoon
  by chance
Types & Periods: Antiques
dating back to 1870's
Appraisal Service Available
  Directions: Center of
  Business District

Eagle Grove

STOP AND STROLL
  402 S Commercial   50533
  515 448-3506   Est: 1974
  Proprietor: Edna Stoll
  Hours: Mon-Sun, 1-5
Types & Periods: Glass
Furniture & Primitives
  Directions: 2 blocks N of
  Village Restaurant on
  Hwy 17

HARGRAVE ANTIQUES
  Hwy 20 W   50595
  515 832-4070   Est: 1971
  Proprietor: Ann Gargrave
  Hours: Daily & by appt
Types & Periods: Pattern
Glass, Lamps, Walnut
Furniture, Stoneware, Dolls,
Jewelry & Wood Trunks

Specialties: Pattern Glass
  Directions: 10 miles from
  I-35 on Hwy 20 W of town

Fort Dodge

**HAMILTON HOUSE
ANTIQUES**
  209-211 S 12th St   50501
  515 576-2881   Est: 1971
  Proprietor: Howard
  Dreasler
  Hours: Mon-Sun, 10-5
Types & Periods: General
Line
Specialties: Merchandise
Characteristic of Iowa &
Midwest
  Directions: 2 blocks N of
  Hwy 20, 1 mile E of Ft
  Dodge interchange on
  Hwy 169

RUTH'S ANTIQUES
  703 S 30th   50501
  515 576-0097   Est: 1973
  Proprietor: Ruth Ely
  Hours: Mon-Fri by chance
Types & Periods: Dishes,
Primitives, Picture Frames,
Depression Glass &
Collectibles
Specialties: Refinish &
Repair Furniture
  Directions: 1½ block S off
  Exit 20, past Shopping
  Center

Fort Madison

COUNTRY LANE ANTIQUES
  RR2, Box 202   52627
  319 372-5908   Est: 1970
  Proprietor: Pat & Joe
  Tebbs
  Hours: Evenings &
  Weekends
Types & Periods: General
Line
Specialties: Furniture
  Directions: 3 miles NW of
  Fort Madison on Hwy 103

HEDGEPETH ANTIQUES
  617 Ave H   52627
  319 372-7548   Est: 1966
  Proprietor: Paul & Donna
  Hedgepeth
  Hours: Fri-Sun, evenings
  by appt or by chance

Types & Periods: Pottery,
Primitives, Advertising,
Tools, Locks, RR Items,
Copper, Brass & Furniture
Specialties: Iowa & Illinois
Pottery, Old Sleepy Eye
Pottery & Advertising
Appraisal Service Available
Directions: On Hwy 61
across from the Riverview
Park

**RED & WHITE ANTIQUE
SHOPPE**
1305 Ave H   52627
319 372-1496   Est: 1960
Proprietor: Ruby Mitchell
Hours: Mon-Sun by appt
Types & Periods: Furniture,
Glass, Pictures & Primitives
Specialties: Walnut Furniture
Directions: Hwy 61, (same
as 1305 Ave H)

Fremont

INA-MARY SHOP
Main St   52561
815 933-4597   Est: 1969
Proprietor: Mrs Inez
Albertson
Hours: Mon-Sat, 10:30-5
Types & Periods: Glass,
China, Small Furniture,
Primitives & Pottery
Specialties: Depression
Glass & Lamps
Directions: On Rte 163
between Ottumwa &
Oskaloosa

Gilmore City

PRESLER ANTIQUES
Main St   50541
515 373-6673   Est: 1974
Proprietor: Clayton &
Pansy Presler
Hours: Mon-Fri, 9-4:30;
Sat & Sun by appt or by
chance
Types & Periods: Walnut &
Oak Furniture, Clocks,
Alladin & Kerosene Lamps,
Pottery & Primitives
Specialties: Victorian &
Walnut Furniture & Wood
Items, Telephones,
Phonographs
Appraisal Service Available

Directions: NW IA Hwy 3,
20 miles NW of Fort
Dodge or between
Humboldt & Pocahontas
on Hwy 3

Goldfield

FIELD ANTIQUES
                        50542
515 825-3655   Est: 1960
Proprietor: Duane Field
Hours: Mon-Sat, 8:30-5;
Sun 1-5; also by appt
Types & Periods: General
Line, Primitives, Glass,
China, Furniture & Clocks
Directions: On Farm Rd
4½ miles NW of Town

Grant

JOE'S ANTIQUES
PO Box 155   50847
712 763-4333   Est: 1973
Proprietor: Joe Driver
Hours: Mon-Sun; After Hrs
by chance or by appt
Types & Periods: Furniture
& Primitives
Directions: Across the
street from the Post Office

Hazleton

STOFFER'S ANTIQUES
Main & Hayes   50641
319 636-2102   Est: 1968
Proprietor: Hank Stoffer
Hours: Tues-Sat, 8-5:30;
Sun 1-5 & Mon by chance
Types & Periods: Anything &
Everything except Guns,
Coins & Jewelry
Specialties: Oak Furniture
Primitives, Glass & Beer
Cans
Appraisal Service Available
Directions: Center of town
on Hwy 150

Hedrick

**HEDRICK DEPOT
ANTIQUES**
Main St   52563
515 653-2214   Est: 1976
Proprietor: Mary Faye
Clingman

Hours: Mon-Sun, 9-5
Types & Periods: General
Line, Glass, China,
Primitives & Furniture
Directions: Restored
Depot on Hwy 149 &
Main

HITCHING POST ANTIQUES
Box 185, Main St   52563
515 653-2416   Est: 1967
Proprietor: Mrs Norma
Newman
Hours: Mon-Sat & Sun
afternoons
Types & Periods: 1880-1925
Glass, China, Silver,
Jewelry, Linens & Primitives
Directions: 17 miles NE of
Ottumwa on 149, W side
of Main St

**WHITE SHUTTERS
ANTIQUES**
211-215 Main St   52563
515 653-2222   Est: 1967
Proprietor: Norman &
Betty Crow
Hours: Mon-Sat, 8-5; Sun
& Evenings by appt
Types & Periods: Victorian,
Walnut & Oak Furniture,
Primitives & Lamps
Directions: 15 miles N of
Ottumwa

Hinton

**FRANK'S FOLLY ANTIQUE
SHOP**
Floyd & Main   51024
712 947-4091   Est: 1961
Proprietor: Frank
Bogenrief
Hours: Mon-Fri, 2-5:30;
Sat 2-4
Types & Periods: General
Line
Specialties: Restored
Antique Brass Chandeliers
of the twenties & New
Beveled & Stained Glass
Windows made to order, any
size
Directions: 10 miles N of
Sioux City on Hwy 75

Imogene

THE EARLY ATTIC
Rte 1   51645
712 386-2118   Est: 1970
Proprietor: Harold & Jo
Ann Hinz
Hours: Mon-Sun by appt &
by chance
Types & Periods: General
Line
Specialties: Miniatures,
Paper Americana & Iowa
Primitives
Appraisal Service Available
  Directions: 6 miles S of
  Emerson on 59 or 12
  miles N of Shenandoah on
  59, then 1/4 mile W

Independence

COOK'S SWAP SHOP
RR2   50644
319 334-2359   Est: 1972
Proprietor: Ronald N Cook
Hours: Mon-Sun
Types & Periods: General
Line
  Directions: E of
  Independence on Hwy 20

Indianola

YOURS, THEIRS AND OURS
103 W Salem   50125
515 961-7755   Est: 1973
Proprietor: Mrs Jack
Bottoree
Hours: Mon-Sat, 10-5:30
Types & Periods: Pressed,
Depression & Cut Glass,
Oak & Walnut Furniture &
Primitives
  Directions: S side of
  Square

Iowa City

DAVE & MARY'S ANTIQUES
1214 Sheridan Ave 52240
319 338-6885   Est: 1964
Proprietor: Dave & Mary
Kral
Hours: by appt & by
chance

Types & Periods: General
Line
Specialties: Victorian Lamps
  Directions: "Call for
  directions"

MARY DAVIN'S ANTIQUES
1509 Muscatine Ave 52240
319 338-0891   Est: 1969
Proprietor: Mary Davin
Hours: Mon-Sun by
chance or appt
Types & Periods: Walnut,
Cherry, Maple, Oak & Pine
Furniture, Lamps, Clocks,
Copper, Brass & Primitives
Appraisal Service Available
  Directions: Burlington St E
  to Muscatine Ave

**IOWA CITY ANTIQUE
COMPANY**
20 S Van Buren   52240
319 351-6061   Est: 1972
Proprietor: William &
Donna Launspach
Hours: Mon-Sat, 12-5
Types & Periods: Primitives,
Brass, Copper, Pewter,
Quilts, Jewelry, Oak, Walnut
& Pine Furniture
Specialties: 3 rooms of
many unusual items with
room to browse and enjoy
the many antiques
  Directions: 4 blocks E of
  Old Capitol Bldg
  Downtown

Jefferson

COLLECTORS CORNER
506 S Wilson   50129
515 386-3946   Est: 1973
Proprietor: Pauline
Richardson
Hours: Mon-Sun by appt
Types & Periods: General
Line
  Directions: S from
  Carillion Tower to 506 S
  Wilson, across from City
  Park

Keokuk

COUNTRY TREASURES INC
Hwy 218-61
319 524-8141   Est: 1967
Proprietor: Doris & Dick
Thompson

Hours: Mon-Sat, 11-5; Sun
1-5; also by appt
Types & Periods: Glass,
China, American Walnut,
Cherry & Oak Furniture
Appraisal Service Available
  Directions: 4 miles N on
  Hwy 218-61

RICH'S COUNTRY STORE
Johnson St Rd   52632
319 524-5764   Est: 1971
Proprietor: Richard
Biddenstadt
Hours: Mon-Sun
Types & Periods: General
Line & Furniture
  Directions: 1/2 mile W on
  Johnson St Rd

Keosawqua

**VERNON SCHOOL
ANTIQUES**
RR 2   52565
319 592-3427   Est: 1972
Proprietor: Elizabeth Mohr
Hours: by appt or chance
Types & Periods: Pine
Furniture, Primitives, Early
Lighting & Textiles
  Directions: 5 miles E of
  Keosawqua or S side of
  Des Moines River in
  Bentonsport

La Porte City

THE LANTERN ANTIQUES
300 Main St   50651
                          Est: 1969
Proprietor: Ron & Laura
Fultz
Hours: Tues-Sat, 10-5;
Sun & Mon by appt
Types & Periods: Local
Furniture: Oak & Pine; Local
Primitive Items: Crocks &
Jugs
Specialties: Primitives &
Furniture
  Directions: Corner of Hwy
  218 & Main St

Lehigh

SWANSON'S FARMHOUSE ANTIQUES
RFD   50557
515 359-2358   Est: 1971
Proprietor: John & Maggie Swanson
Hours: Mon-Sun
Types & Periods: Dishes & Furniture before 1900
Specialties: Furniture & Primitives
Appraisal Service Available
Directions: 15 miles SE of Ft Dodge in Webster County

Le Mar

RED SHACK ANTIQUES
425 1st St   51031
Types & Periods: General Line

Maquoketa

BANOWETZ ANTIQUES
RR 1   52060
319 652-2359   Est: 1970
Proprietor: Virl & Kathleen Banowetz
Hours: Mon-Sat, 9-5; Sun 11-5
Types & Periods: Glassware, China, Brass Beds, Wicker, Hummels & Collectibles
Specialties: Clocks & Furniture
Appraisal Service Available
Directions: 1 mile N of Jct 64 & 61 on Hwy 61

Marengo

RED ROBIN FARM
Rte 3   52301
319 642-5450   Est: 1960
Proprietor: Mrs Kenneth McCune
Hours: By appt & by Chance
Types & Periods: Furniture: New England, Midwest Period, Country Pine & Painted , also accessories

Specialties: Redware, Lighting, Iron, Pewter & Hand Loomed Rugs
Appraisal Service Available
Directions: 5 miles W of Marengo on Hwy 212, red house

Marion

ANTIQUES BY THE BULLARDS
260 7th Ave   52302
319 377-6007   Est: 1960
Proprietor: Marjorie G Bullard
Hours: Mon-Sun by chance
Types & Periods: Glass, China, Primitives, Clocks & Furniture
Specialties: Furniture
Appraisal Service Available
Directions: 30 miles N of I-80 on Hwy 151

COPPER'S ANTIQUES
320 Isham Dr   52302
319 377-3995   Est: 1960
Proprietor: Jane Cooper
Hours: Mon-Sat, 10-5; also by appt or chance
Types & Periods: Primitives, Clocks, American Furniture, Decorative Accessories, Glass & China
Specialties: Primitives
Directions: Isham Dr off Alburnett Rd

LITTLE HOUSE ANTIQUES
1041 /th   52302
319 377-1342   Est: 1958
Proprietor: Alice E Dirks
Hours: Mon-Sat, 9-7; Sun PM
Types & Periods: General Line, Collectibles & Furniture & Picture Frames
Specialties: Clock Repairs
Appraisal Service Available
Directions: 2½ blocks off 7th Ave on 7th St, N

ORIGINAL ANTIQUE SHOP
933 8th Ave   52302
319 377-1130   Est: 1956
Proprietor: Mrs J J Monn
Hours: Mon-Sat by appt or chance
Types & Periods: Early American, French & Victorian China

Specialties: Haviland (Pre-World War I) & Victorian China
Appraisal Service Available
Directions: 1 block N & 1 Block W of City Park

Marshalltown

GRANNY'S ANTIQUE SHOP
1603 Hwy 30 W   50158
515 752-0614   Est: 1974
Proprietor: Marian F Harrison
Hours: Mon-Sun by chance
Types & Periods: Primitives, Pine, Oak & Walnut Furniture, Glassware & Quilts
Specialties: Primitives
Directions: Hwy 30 W of town in big red barn

Mason City

COBWEB CORNERS ANTIQUES
915 N Federal   50401
515 423-2100   Est: 1968
Proprietor: Shirley Pirkl
Hours: Tues-Sat, 1pm; Other Times by Chance or Appt
Types & Periods: Furniture, Primitives & Dishes
Specialties: We Buy Estates
Directions: On Hwy 65, 9 blocks from Downtown

McGregor

MIKE & BERTHA'S
312 Main St   52157
319 873-2257   Est: 1961
Proprietor: Mike & Bertha Davis
Hours: Mon-Sun
Types & Periods: General Line
Specialties: Dolls, Player Pianos & Music Boxes
Appraisal Service Available

**RUNNING WATERS
ANTIQUES**
326 Main St   52157
319 873-3520   Est: 1974
Proprietor: Gene & Liz
Waters
Hours: June-Oct 15:
Mon-Sun, 8-8; Oct
15-May: Mon-Sun, 9-5
Types & Periods: Wood,
Glassware, Lamps, Brass,
Primitives & Jewelry
Specialties: Jewelry, Player
Pianos, Gone with the Wind
Lamps
Appraisal Service Available
    Directions: Downtown

Mondamin

**COUNTRY STORE
ANTIQUES**
Main St   51557
712 646-2268   Est: 1970
Proprietor: Larry Stevens
Hours: By appt & by
chance
Types & Periods: 1860-1930
Furniture & Primitives
Specialties: Oak, Walnut &
Pine Furniture
    Directions: 40 miles N of
    Omaha on I-29

Mount Pleasant

WILBURN'S ANTIQUES
Rte 1   52641
319 385-2491   Est: 1960
Proprietor: Robert D
Wilburn
Hours: Daily
Types & Periods: Early
American Furniture &
Primitives
    Directions: E edge of Mt
    Pleasant on Hwy 34

Mount Union

KRIEGER'S ANTIQUES
Main St   52644
319 865-4641   Est: 1970
Proprietor: Mr & Mrs
Laurel Krieger
Hours: Mon-Fri & Sat AM

Types & Periods: General
Line, Primitives & Pottery,
Glassware & Furniture
    Directions: Henry County
    in SE Iowa

Mount Vernon

THE WOODEN HORSE
117 Main St   52314
                        Est: 1963
Proprietor: Daisy C
Beckhelm
Types & Periods: General
Line
Specialties: Unusual Items
    Directions: 11 miles E of
    Cedar Rapids & 19 miles
    of Iowa City

Nevada

WE TWO ANTIQUES
720 15th St Pl   50201
515 382-2613   Est: 1975
Proprietor: Alberta
Stansbury & Hazel
Coleman
Hours: by chance
Types & Periods: Glassware,
Dishes, Furniture &
Primitives

Ogden

LION'S DEN ANTIQUES
5 miles S Hwy 169   50212
515 275-4011   Est: 1968
Proprietor: Ted & Betty
Swanson
Hours: Mon-Sat, 9-11:30 &
1-5; Closed Holidays
Types & Periods: Furniture,
Light Fixtures, Chandeliers,
European Carved Art Glass
Specialties: Furniture &
Chandeliers
Appraisal Service Available
    Directions: 5 miles S of
    Ogden on Hwy 169; 45
    miles N of I-80 & 45 miles
    NE of Des Moines

Oskaloosa

MAXINE'S HEN HOUSE
Rte 1   52577
515 672-2922   Est: 1967
Proprietor: Mrs Joe Gray
Hours: Daily
Types & Periods: Furniture,
Primitives, Glass & China
Specialties: Frankoma &
Sleepy Eye Pottery
    Directions: 5 miles SE of
    Oskaloosa between Hwy
    92 E & 63 S

Ottumwa

ANOTHER STORY
1626 E Main St   52501
515 684-6026   Est: 1950
Proprietor: Rose Ernest
Hours: Mon-Sun by
chance or appt
Types & Periods:
Antiquarian Books, Canes,
Jewelry, Oriental Crystal &
WWI Brass Artillery Shells
    Directions: 2 blocks W of
    Hwy 34 E Turnoff

ANOTHER STORY
2455 N Court   52501
515 684-5788   Est: 1950
Proprietor: Rose Ernest
Hours: Mon-Sun by appt
Types & Periods: Books,
Coins, Jewelry, Crystal,
Oriental Pieces & WWI
Brass Artillery Shells

BROWN'S ANTIQUE SHOP
1626 E Main St   52501
515 684-6026   Est: 1954
Proprietor: William H
Brown
Hours: Daily
Types & Periods: Glass,
China, Brass, Silver, Copper
& Orientals, Jewelry &
Collectibles
Specialties: Glass
    Directions: 2 blocks W of
    Hwy 34, E Turnoff

Parkersburg

THE VICTORIAN HOUSE
211 Sixth St   50665
319 346-2511

Proprietor: Rose Brooks &
Ethel Meikle
Hours: By appt & by
chance
Types & Periods: Cut Glass,
Wavecrest, Pattern Glass,
Furniture & Dolls

Rockford

PHELP'S ANTIQUES
126 W Main   50468
515 756-3634   Est: 1968
Proprietor: Clarence E
Phelps
Hours: Tues-Sat, 9-5; Sun
1-5; also by appt
Types & Periods: Furniture,
Lamps, Clocks, China,
Primitives & Jewelry
(Turquoise & other types)
Directions: 14 miles W of
Charles City & 20 miles
SE of Mason City

Sabula

ISLAND CITY ANTIQUES
509 Pearl Ct   52070
319 687-2291   Est: 1969
Proprietor: Carl F Haynes
Hours: By appt
Types & Periods: Victorian,
Oak & Walnut Furniture
Specialties: Furniture
Appraisal Service Available
Directions: 42 miles N of
I-80 on US 67; 1st
interchange W of
Mississippi River

Salem

SALEM ANTIQUES
NW corner Main   52649
319 258-4231   Est: 1971
Proprietor: Mr & Mrs G R
Hast
Hours: Mon-Wed, Fri-Sat,
9-6; Sun 1-6
Types & Periods: Primitives,
Glass, Clocks, Dolls, Lamps,
Furniture, Tin, Brass,
Copper & Books
Appraisal Service Available
Directions: Rte 218 or the
Salem Black Top Rd from
Mt Pleasant; On the
corner of Town Square

Seymour

THE WEDGWOOD SHOP
North Side of Square
                    52590
515 898-7504   Est: 1969
Proprietor: Esther Marston
Hours: Mon-Sun
Types & Periods: General
Line
Appraisal Service Available
Directions: Hwy 55 S of
Hwy 2

Shenandoah

ELIZABETH'S ANTIQUES
Village Green at Sheridan
& Elm   51601
712 246-2833   Est: 1960
Proprietor: Elizabeth Neill
Hours: Mon-Sat, 1-5
Types & Periods: General
Line, Antique Spoons, Paper
Goods & Dolls
Specialties: Estate sales
Appraisal Service Available
Directions: Downtown
Shenandoah

THE TREASURE TRUNK
411 W Sheridan St   51601
712 246-3863   Est: 1970
Proprietor: Marlin L
Tillman
Hours: Mon-Fri, 9-5;
Sat-Sun by appt
Types & Periods: Early
American Furniture
Directions: On E end of
the main business street
by Safeway

Sioux City

GAS LIGHT ANTIQUES
1310 Jennings   51105
712 252-2166   Est: 1968
Proprietor: Elva G
Aronson
Hours: By appt & by
chance
Types & Periods: Victorian,
Early 20th Century &
Collectibles
Specialties: China,
Primitives, Pattern & Colored
Glass

Appraisal Service Available
Directions: 7 blocks N of
St Vincent's Hospital-on
Jennings St; near
downtown

HERITAGE HOUSE
ANTIQUES
3900 4th Ave   51105
712 276-3366
Proprietor: Lloyd & Ferne
Moravec
Hours: By appt or by
chance
Types & Periods: Furniture,
China, Glass & Primitives

PIPER'S ANTIQUE KELLER
1835 S Olive   51106
712 276-1801   Est: 1966
Proprietor: Mrs Emma
Piper
Hours: Afternoons &
Evenings by appt
Types & Periods: General
Line, Primitives, Victorian,
China, Glassware, Lamps &
Furniture
Appraisal Service Available
Directions: In Morningside
Area, 1½ blocks N of
Morningside Ave

RED WHEEL ANTIQUES
Rte 2   51106
712 276-3645   Est: 1956
Proprietor: Ken & Wilma
Coulson
Hours: Mon-Sat, 1-5 by
appt; No holidays
Types & Periods: Furniture
Specialties: Brass Beds,
Stained & Jeweled Windows
Appraisal Service Available
Directions: 1 mile past
City limits on Old Denison
Hwy

THE VICTORIAN ANTIQUE
SHOP
3720 6th Ave   51106
712 276-6141   Est: 1941
Proprietor: Bernice M
Kundert
Hours: By appt or chance
Types & Periods: General
Line, Dolls, Furniture, Cut
Glass, Pressed Glass &
Haviland Matching Service
Specialties: Haviland
Matching Service & Dolls

THE VICTORIAN   Cont'd

Appraisal Service Available
Directions: Morningside;
Hwy 20 to 75 off the
Viaduct to Transit, to St
Marys to 6th Ave

Slater

**NORTHERN LITE
ANTIQUES**
Main St   50244
515 685-3032   Est: 1969
Proprietor: Doris L Davis
Hours: Daily
Types & Periods: Primitives,
Glassware, Porcelain,
Furniture, Lamps, Clocks &
Radios
Directions: 12 miles S of
Ames off Hwy 69 & 5
miles W; 20 miles N of
Des Moines off Hwy 69 &
5 miles W

Spencer

THE COBWEB
122 W Second St   51301
712 262-4242   Est: 1974
Proprietor: Helen
Coughenour
Hours: Mon-Sun & Mon
evenings
Types & Periods: Primitives,
Furniture, Pressed & Choice
Glass, Stoneware & Stained
& Leaded Glass Windows
Specialties: "An interesting
8 room house featuring
homespun Americana"
Appraisal Service Available

Spirit Lake

**COTTAGE JUNCTION
MOTEL & ANTIQUE SHOP**
Jct Hwy 9 & 32   51360
712 336-1450   Est: 1972
Proprietor: Mr & Mrs Don
Morrison
Hours: Winter: Mon-Sun,
10-5; Summer: Mon-Sun,
9-6
Types & Periods: General
Line
Specialties: Primitives

Appraisal Service Available
Directions: 5 miles W of
Spirit Lake; SE corner of
Jct 9 & 32

Strawberry Point

YE OLDE VILLAGE SHOPPE
107 S Commercial   52076
319 933-4332   Est: 1972
Proprietor: Maxine Hansel
Hours: Mon-Wed &
Fri-Sun, 9-5; Closed
Sundays after Christmas
until April
Types & Periods: Furniture,
Primitives, China & Beer
Cans
Directions: "2nd door
down from world's largest
strawberry"

Sumner

**HEAVENLY DAZE
ANTIQUES**
122 E 1st St   50674
515 224-3227
Proprietor: Helen M Miller
Hours: Mon-Sun, 1:30-5
Types & Periods: General
Line

Wapello

TIQUES 'N' THINGS
222 Van Buren   52653
319 523-8230   Est: 1973
Proprietor: Lihs Family

Waterloo

ALLEN STREET ANTIQUES
720 Allen St   50702
319 233-4602   Est: 1974
Proprietor: Mildred M
Schmitt
Hours: Mon-Sat, 11-5
Types & Periods: Furniture,
Primitives, Quilts, Glass &
Lamps
Directions: 218 to W 5th,
W 5th to Allen, left 1/2
block

MRS B'S ANTIQUES
1319 Baltimore St   50702
319-232-1846   Est: 1962
Proprietor: Roger &
Delores Briner
Hours: Mon-Sun
Types & Periods: Wavecrest,
Art Glass, Cut Glass,
Handpainted China,
Primitives & Furniture
Specialties: Glass
Directions: Hwy 218 to
intersection of 5th St; 5th
St to Baltimore St; turn
left approx 7 blocks

**ELSIE FORNEY'S
TREASURES**
104 Berkshire Rd   50701
319 235-7490
Proprietor: Elsie Forney
Hours: By appt
Types & Periods: Glass,
China & Decorative
Accessories

**HOFREITER'S ANTIQUES
INC**
4025 University Ave 50701
319 233-3691
Proprietor: Dr, Mrs & Bob
Hofreiter
Hours: Mon-Tues,
Thurs-Fri & Sun, 10-5;
Sat, 10-4
Types & Periods: General
Line & Wholesale

PILOT HOUSE ANTIQUES
266 Falls Ave   50701
319 232-5414   Est: 1970
Proprietor: Lee D
Campbell
Hours: Mon-Sat, 9-5;
Sunday's & evenings by
chance
Types & Periods: Glass,
China, Furniture, Collectibles
& Primitives
Specialties: Stripping,
Repairing & Refinishing
Furniture
Directions: Hwy 63 S

THE RED PUMP
1438 Liberty Ave   50702
319 233-0610
Proprietor: Mary & Lyle
Graber
Hours: By appt
Types & Periods: General
Line

Waverly

EVELYN'S ANTIQUES
118 E Bremer Ave   50677
319 352-5826   Est: 1974
Proprietor: Evelyn
Minnaert
Hours: Mon-Sat, 9-5
Types & Periods: Furniture,
Glass & Primitives
Specialties: Dishes
Appraisal Service Available
Directions: Downtown

Wayland

**HIRSCHY'S USED
FURNITURE & ANTIQUES**
103 Washington   52654
319 256-2075   Est: 1973
Proprietor: J Duwaine
Hirschy
Hours: Sat by chance;
other times by appt
Types & Periods: General
Line
Specialties: Oak Furniture,
Lamps, Bottles & Jugs

Wellman

**BLOOM ANTIQUES &
COLLECTIBLES**
Box 128   52356
319 646-2650   Est: 1969
Proprietor: Mrs Rex T
Bloom
Hours: Mon-Sat, 9-5:30;
Sun by appt
Types & Periods: Art, Cut &
Depression Glass, Pottery,
Pine Walnut & Oak
Furniture, Primitives, Fruit
Jars, Crocks & Jugs
Appraisal Service Available
Directions: Downtown

West Branch

PUMP HOUSE ANTIQUES
111 E Main St   52358
319 643-2879   Est: 1971
Proprietor: Mrs Maxine
Montgomery
Hours: Summer: Mon-Sun,
10-5; Winter: closed on
Mon

Types & Periods: From
1850, General Line, Pressed,
Depression & Sandwich
Glass, China & Pickle
Castors
Specialties: Glass
Appraisal Service Available
Directions: Off I-80
½ mile into town

West Burlington

**HORN'S FURNITURE
STRIPPING & ANTIQUES**
RR 4, Hwy 34   52655
319 754-7012   Est: 1972
Proprietor: Dwight Horn
Hours: Thurs-Fri, 8-9; Sat
8-6; Sun-Wed by appt or
chance
Types & Periods: General
Line, Midwest Furniture,
Dishes, Farm Tools
Appraisal Service Available
Directions: On Hwy 34, 1
mile W of 406 Jct

West Des Moines

A B C ANTIQUE SHOPPE
120 5th St   50265
515 255-8216   Est: 1968
Proprietor: Mrs Ruth
Ankrom
Hours: Mon-Sun
Types & Periods: Primitives,
Furniture, Pressed Glass,
Flow Blue China & Clocks
Specialties: Furniture &
Kitchen Primitives
Directions: Near I-35 & 80,
Downtown

CENTURY SHOPPE LTD
114 5th St   50265
515 255-7373   Est: 1975
Proprietor: Jack Mendrys
& Ron Hoyt
Hours: Mon-Fri, 10-4; Sat
10-5
Types & Periods: Early
American Furniture, Kitchen
Tools & Decorator Items
Specialties: Furniture
Directions: Downtown

CRACKER BOX
225 5th St   50265
515 255-7088   Est: 1973
Proprietor: Fran Schiers &
Phyllis Boo
Hours: Mon-Sun
Types & Periods: General
Line
Directions: S off Grand on
5th St to Downtown

VIRGINIA'S ANTIQUES
138 5th St   50265
515 274-2158
Proprietor: Dean
Alexander
Hours: Mon-Sat, 10-5
Types & Periods: Walnut
Furniture, Art Glass &
Wedgwood

West Union

OLD MILL
211 E Maple   52175
319 422-5283   Est: 1970
Proprietor: D A Martin
Hours: Mon-Sun
Types & Periods: Toys, Pine
Furniture & Indian Artifacts
Specialties: Bottles
Appraisal Service Available
Directions: Hwy 18 E

Wever

**JOLLYVILLE HILL
ANTIQUES**
RR 1   52658
319 372-3600   Est: 1970
Proprietor: Nettie
Schroeder
Hours: Mon-Sun
Types & Periods: General
Line
Directions: 5 miles N of Ft
Madison or 2 miles S of
Wever on Hwy 61

STATE OF KANSAS

Abilene

THE WAY STATION
Old Abilene Town   67410
913 263-2379   Est: 1962
Proprietor: Mark
Goodenow
Hours: Daily, 9-6
Types & Periods: Rustic
Directions: 1 Block S of
Eisenhower Center

Atwood

**HORSE TRADERS
ANTIQUES**
503 Main   67730
913 626-9501   Est: 1972
Proprietor: Fred Downing
& Allen Riepl
Hours: Mon-Sat, 9-5
Types & Periods: Wholesale
refinished furniture & store
fixtures
Specialties: Oak
Appraisal Service Available
Directions: Intersection of
Hwys 36 & 25 in NW
corner of Kansas

**THE LITTLE ANTIQUE
SHOP**
411 Main   67730
913 626-3150   Est: 1966
Proprietor: Ed & Ruby
Downing
Hours: Mon-Sat; Sun by
appointment
Types & Periods: Everything
(Our motto is "If we don't
have it, you don't need it"),
also antique car parts
Appraisal Service Available
Directions: 5 Blocks S of
Hwy 36 on 5th St & Main

Auburn

**MEETINGHOUSE
ANTIQUES**
    66402
913 862-0917
Proprietor: Don & Donna
McEachern
Hours: Daily

Types & Periods: Country,
Primitives, Furniture,
Accessories
Directions: 5 Miles S on
Auburn Rd next to Village
Mall

Augusta

BUCKBOARD ANTIQUES
Rte 1 Box 269   67010
316 775-7029   Est: 1971
Proprietor: John & Marge
Kromka
Hours: Daily, 9-6
Types & Periods: General
Line, Furniture, Glass, Farm
Machinery
Directions: Hwy 54 2 1/2
miles W of Augusta, Hwy
54 10 miles E of Wichita

**HIME'S YESTERDAY'S
ANTIQUES**
RR2 Box 50A   67010
316 775-7000   Est: 1968
Proprietor: Ralph &
Dorothy Hime
Hours: Daily
Types & Periods: Pattern &
Depression Glass, Primitives,
Collectibles, Furniture
Specialties: Furniture
Directions: 2 Miles E of
Town on Hwys 54, 96 &
77

Beattie

LOMAX ANTIQUES
Box 214   66406
913 353-2318   Est: 1970
Proprietor: Virgil & Kate
Lomax
Hours: Daily
Types & Periods: General
Line
Directions: 1 1/2 miles N
of Hwy 99 & 36 junction

Belleville

SUNFLOWER ANTIQUES
1208 M St   66935
913 527-2661   Est: 1970
Proprietor: Shirley
Danielson

Hours: Daily, by chance
Types & Periods: General
Line
Specialties: American Oak
(1900)
Directions: N on M St

Clay Center

KEELER'S ANTIQUES
925 Clarke   67432
913 632-2286   Est: 1976
Proprietor: Dorothy Keeler
Hours: By chance
Types & Periods: Primitives,
Depression Glass, Jewel Tea
Linens, Some Furniture,
Collector Items
Directions: 1 Block S & 1
Block E of Cedar Court
Motel on Hwy 24

NEWELL ANTIQUES
527 Court St   67432
913 632-5955   Est: 1950
Proprietor: Loyall
Newell Jr
Hours: Seven days a week
Types & Periods: Art Glass,
Carnival Glass, Depression
Glass; Furniture; General
Line Novelty Items; Antique
Pool Tables
Specialties: Renovation of
Pool Tables, Antique Pool
Tables
Appraisal Service Available
Directions: On the square

Coffeyville

**THE OLD TELEPHONE
EXCHANGE**
RR 1 Box 305   67337
316 251-5605   Est: 1954
Proprietor: Oral & Malone
Watts
Hours: By appointment or
by chance
Types & Periods:
Telephones & Parts from
1800 to Present
Specialties: Telephones &
Parts
Appraisal Service Available
Directions: 2 miles W of
Hwy 169 on State Line Rd

Columbus

JORDEN'S ANTIQUES
403 S Kansas   66725
316 429-3275   Est: 1974
Proprietor: Marian Jorden
Hours: Seven days a week
Types & Periods: Walnut
Early American, Pine & Oak
Furniture, Art & Cut Glass,
Brass, Copper, Primitives,
Light Fixtures, Oriental Art
Objects
Specialties: Furniture
Restored & Refinished
Directions: 2 Blocks S of
stop light

Derby

**ANTIQUES & UNUSUALS
BY IMOGENE**
Fleming's GB Ranch
RR 1   67037
316 788-2525   Est: 1964
Proprietor: Imogene Gick
Fleming
Hours: By appointment, by
chance
Types & Periods: Art Glass,
Primitives, Furniture
Specialties: Collectibles
Directions: 1 1/2 mile S of
Town, "Big round yellow
barn"

**FURNITURE WORKSHOP
ANTIQUES**
325 N Baltimore   67037
316 788 2013   Est: 1965
Proprietor: Sue Herren
Hours: Daily
Types & Periods:
Americana, 18th & 19th
Centuries, Paper, Silver,
Collectibles
Specialties: Furniture
Directions: Main St of
town

El Dorado

**FISHER'S ANTIQUES &
FURNITURE STRIPPING**
630 N Taylor   67042
316 321-1598   Est: 1971
Proprietor: Mr & Mrs Olan
Fisher
Hours: By appointment, by
chance

Types & Periods: General
Line, Collectibles, Furniture
Specialties: Pottery,
Primitives
Directions: Corner of 6th
& Taylor on Truck Rte N
of town

THE WAGON WHEEL
112 W 4th St   67042
316 321-4998   Est: 1962
Proprietor: Ray & Doris
Siegrist
Hours: Daily
Types & Periods: General
Line
Specialties: Jewelry (Indian)
Appraisal Service Available
Directions: 4 Blocks N on
Main, turn left

Eureka

FRENCH'S
206 1/2 N Main   67045
316 583-6704   Est: 1972
Proprietor: Lois French
Hours: By chance
Types & Periods: Glass,
China, Primitives, Western
Art
Directions: 2 1/2 Blocks N
on Main

Fort Scott

APPLE HOUSE ANTIQUES
1248 Crawford   66701
316 223-5770   Est: 1974
Proprietor: Janice Allen
Hours: By chance
Types & Periods: Country
Pine, Primitives, Picture
Frames
Directions: City Rte 69 to
12th St, W 2 Blocks & S
1/2 Block

MOORE'S ANTIQUES
510 S Eddy St   66701
316 223-2113   Est: 1946
Proprietor: Mrs S P Moore
Hours: By appointment, by
chance
Types & Periods: China,
Glassware, Furniture,
Primitives
Directions: 3 Blocks W of
city, Rte 69 at 6th St

**MRS C D SAMPLE
ANTIQUES**
812 S National Ave 66701
316 223-1211   Est: 1963
Proprietor: Mrs C D
Sample
Hours: Daily
Types & Periods: Art Glass,
China, Primitives, Victorian
Furniture
Directions: City Rte 69

Gardner

YESTERYEAR ANTIQUES
Rte 1 Box 320   66030
913 884-7885   Est: 1969
Proprietor: Phyllis Shupert
Hours: Daily, by chance
Types & Periods: General
Line, Furniture
Directions: I-35 to
Gardner-Antiock Exit, then
1 Mile N

Great Bend

DETRICH ANTIQUES
10th & Harrison   67530
316 793-8039   Est: 1978
Proprietor: Alan Detrich
Hours: Mon-Sat; Sun by
appointment
Types & Periods: General
Line
Specialties: Furniture (Oak),
Paper Goods, Architectural
Items, Toys
Directions: Along the
Santa Fe Trail

Harper

**PLOWSHARE & POLKA
DOT CORNER ANTIQUES**
409 E Main St   67058
316 896-2997   Est: 1967
Proprietor: Mrs Graydon
Murray
Hours: Daily
Types & Periods: Pattern
Glass, Miniatures, Primitives,
Furniture, Hall Trees, Brass
Bells, Sleigh Bells
Specialties: Furniture,
Figurines, Round Ice Box,
Wooden Washers, Bentwood
Churn

**PLOWSHARE & POLKA
DOT CORNER** Cont'd
Directions: Plowshare, 3
Blocks E on Main St from
Polka Dot, which is 4
Blocks N of Hwy 160 on
Washington St

Holton

ERIN'S ANTIQUES
324 Lincoln 66436
913 364-2472 Est: 1972
Proprietor: C L Riley
Hours: Daily, by chance
Types & Periods: R S
Prussia, Pressed Glass, Oak
Furniture, Primitives
Specialties: R S Prussia
Appraisal Service Available
Directions: 3 Blocks E of
Hwy 75 & 16 intersection

Hoyt

VIRGINIA'S ANTIQUES
W 5th St 66440
913 986-6540 Est: 1965
Proprietor: Mrs George
Meeker
Hours: Daily; By
appointment, by chance
Types & Periods: Pine &
Walnut Furniture, Clocks,
19th Century Wedgwood,
French Peg Lamps,
Primitives
Specialties: Clocks,
Primitives
Appraisal Service Available
Directions: 1st house E of
Hwy 214

Hudson

TREASURE INN
Main St 67545
316 458-2205 Est: 1974
Proprietor: Duane & Trudy
Hanson
Hours: Daily, by
appointment
Types & Periods: General
Line
Specialties: Custom Made
Furniture, Antique Furniture
Repair & Refinishing

Directions: 7 Miles N of St
John on Hwy 281 to New
Hope Church & 5 Miles E
to Hudson Main St

Independence

**BARBARA'S GIFTS AND
ANTIQUES**
123 E Myrtle 67301
316 331-7960 Est: 1978
Proprietor: Barbara C
Clark
Hours: Tues-Sat, 10-5
Types & Periods: Primitives,
Pine, Cherry, Walnut,
Victorian, Oak, Iron, Wood,
Crockery
Directions: On Hwy 96,
corner of 6th & Myrtle in
downtown Independence

Kansas City

**DOT & JOE'S BROWSER'S
DELITE**
330 S 10th St 66102
913 371-3214 Est: 1960
Proprietor: Dot & Joe
Minghini
Hours: Mon-Wed, 9-5;
Fri-Sat, 9-5
Types & Periods: Dishes,
Lamps, Furniture

La Crosse

H-H ANTIQUES GALLERY
16th & Lincoln 67548
913 222-2845 Est: 1961
Proprietor: Howard N Yost
Hours: Weekends by
appointment; Advance
notice a must
Types & Periods: Primitives,
Country Furniture, Cast Iron,
Colored Glass, Collectibles
Specialties: Washing
Machines, Washboards,
Irons
Appraisal Service Available
Directions: 4 Blocks E on
Hwy 4

Lawrence

EMERALD CITY ANTIQUES
415 N 2nd 66044
913 842-1808 Est: 1971
Proprietor: William Fair
Hours: Daily, 11-5
Types & Periods: General
Line
Appraisal Service Available
Directions: N of the bridge

**QUANTRILL'S FLEA
MARKET**
811 New Hampshire 66044
913 842-6616 Est: 1971
Proprietor: Randolph S
Davis
Hours: Sat-Sun
Types & Periods: General
Line, 40 dealers with
collectibles from 1800's to
1900's
Specialties: Furniture
Appraisal Service Available
Directions: 1 Block E of
Massachusetts St

Lindsboro

VILLAGE BAZAAR
105 S Main 67456
913 227-2272 Est: 1972
Proprietor: Annamae J
Ahlstedt
Hours: Daily
Types & Periods: Primitives,
Glass
Specialties: Brass Lamps
Directions: 20 Miles S of
I-70, I-35 Interchange at
Salina

Manhattan

**HAVENSTEIN FUR
REFINISHING & ANTIQUE
SALES INC**
Rte 3 Box 308A 66502
913 776-5111 Est: 1969
Proprietor: Don
Havenstein
Hours: Mon-Sat, 8-5; Sun,
12-5

Types & Periods: Furniture,
China, Primitives
Specialties: Custom
Furniture Refinishing,
Custom Made Round Center
Pedestal Dining Table
Directions: 1 Mile S of
Manhattan on Hwy 177

**LEASURES TREASURE
CHEST**
523 S 17th   66502
913 537-2344   Est: 1966
Proprietor: Elden & Sylvia
Leasure
Hours: Mon-Sat, 10-5:30
Types & Periods: General
Line
Specialties: Coins, Stamps,
Military Relics, Guns,
Swords, Books &
Magazines, Political & Paper
Americana
Appraisal Service Available
Directions: I-70 onto 177,
N to Manhattan, S on 3rd
St to Yuma, W on Yuma
to Old Town Mall

**LEASURES TREASURE
CHEST**
1124 Moro   66502
913 537-2344   Est: 1966
Proprietor: Elden & Sylvia
Leasure
Hours: Mon-Sat, 10-6
Types & Periods: General
Line
Specialties: Coins, Stamps,
Military Relics, Guns,
Swords, Books &
Magazines, Political & Paper
Americana
Appraisal Service Available
Directions: I-70 onto 177,
N on 3rd St to Poyntz, W
to 11th St, N to Moro

Maple Hill

**CLARK'S STONE HOUSE
ANTIQUES**
                    66507
913 663-2408
Hours: By appointment
Types & Periods: General
Line
Directions: 3 Miles W of
town from I-70

Morganville

LOU'S LOT NO 2
Main St   67468
913 926-3594   Est: 1968
Proprietor: Lou & Ella
Allen
Hours: Daily, by
appointment
Types & Periods: General
Line Collectibles
Specialties: Furniture,
Dishes, Telephones, Tools,
Primitives, Sterling & Silver
Plates
Appraisal Service Available
Directions: 35 Ft left of
only stop light on Hwy 80

VILLAGE SHOP
203 Main St   67468
913 632-2183   Est: 1964
Proprietor: Walter W
Merten
Hours: Fri, Sat, Sun 1-5
Types & Periods: Cloisonne,
Gibson Girl Plates, Haviland,
Glass, General Line
Appraisal Service Available
Directions: 6 Miles N & 4
W of Clay Center, Hwy 15

Neodesha

FENNER'S ANTIQUES
1105 N 8th St   66757
316 325-2304   Est: 1967
Proprietor: Mr & Mrs Chas
B Fenner
Hours: Daily
Types & Periods: Primitives,
Turn-of-the-Century Oak
Furniture, Frames, Clocks
Specialties: Furniture (Roll
Top Desks, Round Tables,
Pattern Back Chairs)
Directions: SE Kansas,
100 Miles N of Tulsa, 100
Miles E of Wichita, 100
Miles NW of Joplin

Newton

WHARF ROAD
415 Main   67114
316 283-3579   Est: 1972
Proprietor: Roy & Vivian
Hedrick
Hours: Tues-Sat

Types & Periods: General
Line, Oak
Specialties: Copper & Brass
Stripping
Appraisal Service Available
Directions: Main St across
from depot

Norton

THE ROBBINS STORE
202 N 2nd   67654
913 927-3542   Est: 1974
Proprietor: Guy Robbins
Hours: Daily
Types & Periods: Advertising
Collectibles
Appraisal Service Available

Ottawa

CENTURY ANTIQUES
730 S Main   66067
913 242-3621
Proprietor: Dallas Turner
Types & Periods: Furniture,
Primitives, Books

COUNTRY ANTIQUES
E Wilson St   66067
913 242-2303   Est: 1960
Proprietor: Jack D Bennett
Hours: Mon-Fri, 10-5; Sat
& Sun, By Appointment or
By Chance
Types & Periods: General
Line, Furniture, Brass,
Copper
Directions: 1 1/2 Miles E
on Wilson

ERMEY'S ANTIQUES
743 S Main   66067
913 242-3928
Hours: Daily
Types & Periods: General
Line, Dolls
Specialties: Toys &
Automata

GEORGE HAAS ANTIQUES
206 E Wilson   66067
913 242-3752
Types & Periods: General
Line
Specialties: Furniture

IKE AND MIKE'S
222 E Logan   66067
913 242-2753
Types & Periods: General
Line

OLD & KLASSIC
508 N Main   66067
Hours: Daily
Types & Periods: General
Line, Furniture
Specialties: Furniture, Avon
Collection

OUT BACK
534 N Main St   66067
913 242-1178   Est: 1970
Proprietor: Gail Smith &
Jan Wallace
Hours: Daily, By Chance
Types & Periods: Primitives,
Advertising, Architectural
Items, Store Fixtures,
Furniture
Directions: Off I-35, 50
Miles SW Kansas City

PARK ANTIQUES
Tecumseh & Santa Fe
RR Tracks   66067
913 242-1914   Est: 1970
Proprietor: Jean & Ben
Park
Hours: Weekends; By
appointment, By chance
Types & Periods: Primitive
Country Furniture, Fireplace
Iron
Specialties: Tools, Fireplace
Iron, Lighting
Directions: Across from
"Old Depot Museum"

Overland Park

BRAND'S ANTIQUES
4804 Goodman   66203
913 722-3931
Proprietor: George &
Leona Brand
Hours: Daily, 12-5; Also by
appointment
Types & Periods: Glass,
China, Furniture, Primitives

CLEO MEANS ANTIQUES
7701 W 61st St   66202
913 432-3516
Proprietor: Cleo Means
Hours: Daily, 10-5
Types & Periods: General
Line

Paola

TRADING POST
18 E Peoria   66071
913 294-2146   Est: 1956
Proprietor: Gertrude M
McKain
Hours: Daily, 9-4:30
Types & Periods: General
Line
Appraisal Service Available
Directions: 1 Block E of
Miami Co Natl Bank

Parsons

DIVINES ANTIQUES
927 Main St   67357
                Est: 1975
Proprietor: Mrs Paul
Divine
Hours: Tues-Sat, 10-5
Types & Periods: General
Line, Furniture, Primitives,
China, Art, Cut, Pressed &
Depression Glass, Jewelry,
Collectibles
Specialties: Jewelry (Indian)
Directions: 1/2 Block E of
10th & Main on Hwy 160

**SALIBAS' ANTIQUES &
IMPORTS**
1808 1/2 Broadway 67357
316 421-6981   Est: 1964
Proprietor: Nehme Saliba
Hours: Mon-Sat, Sun by
appointment
Types & Periods: American,
European, Oriental,
Glassware, Primitives, Quilts,
Jewelry, Furniture
Appraisal Service Available
Directions: Downtown,
above Sears Co

Paxico

MILL CREEK ANTIQUES
                66526
913 636-2755   Est: 1973
Proprietor: Steve Hund Jr
Hours: Daily, Weekends,
By appointment, by
chance
Types & Periods: Furniture
Specialties: Lamps, Mirrors
Directions: 1 Mile off I-70
at Paxico Exit, 30 Miles W
of Topeka, next ot
General Store on Main St

Phillipsburg

THE YESTERDAY SHOP
Box 383   67661
                Est: 1965
Proprietor: Paul Hilbrink
Hours: Daily, weekends
Types & Periods:
Collectibles
Directions: 9 Blocks N Jct
US 36 & 183

Russell

**DUMLER'S HOUSE OF
DEPRESSION**
Rte 3   67665
913 483-2944   Est: 1971
Proprietor: Dean &
Marjorie Dumler
Hours: By chance
Types & Periods: Furniture,
Primitives, Glassware,
Lamps
Specialties: Glass
(Depression)
Directions: 8 Blocks E of
stop light on Hwy 281 &
Old 40, 1 Mile off I-70

Sabetha

HITCHING POST ANTIQUES
Sycamore Springs
Rte 1   66534
913 284-2436   Est: 1973
Proprietor: Dennis A
Dodson Jr
Hours: Daily, May thru
Sept 1-5; Other Times By
Appointment
Types & Periods: General
Line
Specialties: Post Cards,
Furniture, Glass
Directions: Hwy 75 to
Sycamore Springs, turn
off black top rd, go 3
Miles

Sedgwick

ELLA'S ANTIQUES
519 Commercial   67135
316 772-5261   Est: 1954
Proprietor: Ella Kater
Hours: Daily, also by
appointment

Types & Periods: Pressed,
Cut & Depression Glass,
Opalescent, China, Furniture
Directions: 20 Miles N of
Wichita

Stockton

BOUCHEY'S ANTIQUES
514 Main St   67669
913 425-6157   Est: 1973
Proprietor: Russell & Leta
Bouchey
Hours: Daily
Types & Periods: Primitives,
Glass, Furniture, Bottles,
China, Clocks
Directions: 1 1/2 Block E
of stop light at
intersection of Hwys 24 &
183

Topeka

ANDERSON ANTIQUES
4409 W 17th St   66604
913 272-6454   Est: 1950
Proprietor: Leila B
Anderson
Hours: Daily
Types & Periods: China,
Glassware, Brass, Copper,
Jewelry, Lamps, Furniture

BACK DOOR ANTIQUES
1275 Garfield   66604
913 233-4788
Proprietor: Evelyn Dinkel
Hours: Daily, 10-5
Types & Periods: Furniture,
Collectibles

GEORGE BENGE SR
1017 Kansas Ave   66612
913 233-5823   Est: 1960
Proprietor: Mr George
Benge Sr
Hours: Mon-Fri, 10-5; Sat
& Sun, 10-2; Also by
appointment
Types & Periods: General
Line
Specialties: Lamps,
Primitives
Appraisal Service Available
Directions: Downtown

BISHOP ANTIQUES
4849 W 17th   66604
913 272-3471
Hours: Daily, 10-5
Types & Periods:
Collectibles, Furniture
Specialties: China
(Wedgwood)

BROWN'S
3703 Burlingame Rd 66609
913 266-9516
Hours: Sat-Thurs, 9-5
Types & Periods: General
Line

THE CENTURY HOUSE
2100 Maryland   66605
913 354-1776   Est: 1974
Proprietor: Don E & Freda
N Tilton
Hours: Daily
Types & Periods: General
Line From 1850

THE COBWEB
2508 W 15th St   66604
913 357-7498   Est: 1971
Proprietor: Bill & Elaine
Bowen
Hours: Daily, Weekends,
12-5
Types & Periods: General
Line
Specialties: Glass, Pottery
Appraisal Service Available
Directions: In SW Topeka
near University

COMPTON'S HOMESTEAD
1257 Fillmon   66604
913 233-3388
Proprietor: Howard &
Florence Compton
Hours: By Appointment
Types & Periods: China,
Pattern Glass, Books

ETZEL'S ANTIQUES
720 Green St   66616
913 234-9085
Hours: By Appointment
Types & Periods: Art Glass,
China, Lamp, Paintings

NELSON'S ANTIQUES
2801 Fairlawn Rd   66614
913 272-6870
Hours: Sun-Mon, 10-5;
Wed-Fri, 10-5; Tues, 10-7;
Sat, 10-3
Types & Periods: General
Line

Specialties: Furniture (Oak)
Appraisal Service Available
Directions: 29th &
Fairlawn off Interstate

PENDLETON ANTIQUES
Rte 8   66604
913 663-2335
Hours: By Appointment
Types & Periods: General
Line
Directions: W on I-70 to
Willard Exit, 3 Miles N

PIN OAK ANTIQUES
1001 E Hwy 24   66608
913 234-2268
Proprietor: Sara Yingling
Hours: Daily, 12-5
Types & Periods: General
Line
Specialties: Clocks,
Miniatures

**RADENZ RED HOUSE
ANTIQUES**
2922 Munson   66604
913 233-0914
Hours: By Appointment
Types & Periods: Early
American Furniture,
Collectibles
Directions: 1 Block N of W
12th St

THE RELIC
1300 Boswell   66604
913 232-0670
Proprietor: Jack Hamilton
Hours: Mon-Thurs, 9-5;
Sat, 9-5
Types & Periods: General
Line

SENNES' OLD STABLE
2520 SE 45th   66619
913 266-3111
Hours: Thurs-Sun, 1-5;
Also by appointment;
closed Jan & Feb
Types & Periods: Furniture,
Farm Relics, Collectibles

**SPENCER
ANTIQUES-ODDTIQUES
INC**
1930 Gage Blvd   66604
913 272-8450   Est: 1964
Proprietor: Betty D
Spencer
Hours: Mon-Sat
Types & Periods: General
Line, Decorative Small
Items, Furniture

Topeka   Cont'd

SPENCER   Cont'd
Specialties: Antique Dolls,
Haviland
Appraisal Service Available
Directions: Centrally
located between Hwys
I-70 & I-470

TERRY'S ANTIQUES
4206 Burlingame Rd 66609
913 266-6497
Hours: By Appointment
Types & Periods: Glass,
Furniture

WOODS SHED ANTIQUES
913 233-3068   Est: 1968
Proprietor: Frank & Chloe
Woods
Hours: Daily, 10-5:30
Types & Periods: General
Line Furniture
Specialties: Furniture
(Primitive Pine)
Appraisal Service Available

Towanda

DENNETT'S ANTIQUES
408 Main   67144
316 536-2329   Est: 1967
Proprietor: Mrs Barbara E
Dennett
Hours: Sun-Tues;
Thurs-Sat; By
appointment, by chance
Types & Periods: Early
Turn-of-the-Century, Golden
Oak, Walnut Furniture,
Primitives, Depression Glass
Specialties: Glass,
Collectibles of the 50's
Directions: On Hwy 254
between Wichita & El
Dorado

Valley Center

LUCILLA ANTIQUES
123 S Meridan   67147
316 755-1622   Est: 1967
Proprietor: Lucilla Slinkard
Hours: Daily, 10-6; Also by
appointment
Types & Periods: Furniture,
Kerosene Lamps, Glass
Specialties: Furniture
Directions: 2 Miles W of
Hwy 81, Valley Center Exit

Wamego

COLONEL'S CORNER
510 Elm   66547
913 456-7472   Est: 1970
Proprietor: Glenn & Cleo
Applegate
Hours: Sat afternoon, Sun
evenings, by chance
Types & Periods: General
Line, Primitives, Furniture,
Pottery, Glassware, Prints,
Roll-Top Desks
Appraisal Service Available
Directions: Hwy 99 thru
Wamego, 1 Block W on
6th, 1/2 Block S

Washington

CELLAR ANTIQUES
308 E 6th St   66968
913 325-2104   Est: 1969
Proprietor: Josie
Lundblade
Hours: Daily; By
appointment, by chance
Types & Periods: Art Pattern
& Depression Glass, China,
Primitives
Specialties: Old Pattern
Glass
Directions: SE edge of
Washington, 1 Block N of
Hwy 36

Wellington

MARY COWELL ANTIQUES
1213 S Washington 67152
316 326-2347   Est: 1957
Proprietor: Mary Cowell
Hours: Tues-Sun
Types & Periods: General
Line
Specialties: Painting &
restoring lamps; restoration
and repair of old dolls
Appraisal Service Available
Directions: S End of Main
St, Hwy 81, 3 Miles W of
I-35

Wichita

WICHITA CLUSTER
Directions: Shops on
Broadway (running N-E);
heavier concentration on
S Broadway (1000-5000
Blocks); N Broadway
(1000-2000 Blocks);
Intersecting streets have
shops, especially E
Douglas Ave (3000-4000
Blocks)

AAA ANTIQUES
311 E Murdock   67214
316 267-3190   Est: 1975
Proprietor: Grace Bishop
Hours: Tues-Sat, 11-5:30
Types & Periods: General
Line
Directions: Between
Broadway & Topeka Sts

ANTIQUE CORNER
3820 E Lewis   67211
316 263-9762   Est: 1970
Proprietor: Katy Mills
Hours: Daily
Types & Periods: General
Line, Collectibles
Directions: S on Hwy 81

THE ANTIQUE SHOP
1356 N Topeka   67214
316 267-8627   Est: 1959
Proprietor: Harold Yeager
Hours: Tues-Fri, 12-5;
Sat-Mon, by appointment
Types & Periods: 18th &
19th Century Furniture,
Paintings, Chandeliers
Directions: 10 short blocks
W of 13th St Exit off I-35

COUNTRY ANTIQUES
201 E Kechi Rd   67067
316 744-0932   Est: 1966
Proprietor: Jan & Steve
LeDou
Hours: Daily, by
appointment
Types & Periods: Country
Furniture & Accessories,
Primitives
Specialties: Country
Furniture & Accessories,
Primitives
Directions: 1 Block E of
Oliver on 61st St N

COUNTRY STORE
5500 W Central   67212
316 942-5874   Est: 1971
Proprietor: Ralph & Betty
Glass
Hours: Daily, 12-5

Types & Periods: American
Furniture, Primitives,
Pottery, Glass, Collectibles
  Directions: Central & I-235
  By-Pass W

LAND M SHOPPE
  16082 E Kellog   67230
  316 733-1701   Est: 1973
  Proprietor: Muriel
  Leimkuhl & Louise Walker
  Hours: Mon-Sat, 9-4
Types & Periods: Glass,
Furniture, Collectibles
Specialties: Quilts
  Directions: Hwy US 54 &
  Andover-Rosehill Rd

**MADLINE'S ANTIQUES &
COLLECTIBLES**
  1808 S Broadway   67211
  316 262-8981
  Proprietor: Mrs Earl C
  Tramell
  Hours: Daily, Weekends
Types & Periods: Primitives,
American Oak Furniture, Art
Glass, Prints, Early
American

NORTH END FLEA MARKET
  2759 N Broadway   67219
  310 830-5001   Est: 1971
  Proprietor: Mr & Mrs
  Ralph H Vanderpool
  Hours: Daily, 10-6
Types & Periods: Glass,
Collectibles, Pottery, Tins
Specialties: Glass
(Depression)
  Directions: 31 Blocks N of
  US 54 on Broadway

**TROY'S SECOND HAND
STORE**
  501 N Anna   67212
  316 942-7461   Est: 1974
  Proprietor: Troy Griffin
  Hours: Tues-Sat, 10-6
Types & Periods: "Super
Market of Used Things"
  Directions: 2 Blocks S of
  Central

WHITE EAGLE ANTIQUES
  1215 Franklin   67203
  316 262-1514   Est: 1971
  Proprietor: Onnallee &
  Ron Slade
  Hours: Daily, by
  appointment
Types & Periods: Furniture,
Dishes, Sterling, Silver,
Copper, Brass, Clocks

Appraisal Service Available
  Directions: 3 Blocks N of
  Mid American Indian
  Center

Winfield

**A BACKWARD GLANCE IN
THE WINFIELD MARKET**
  119 W 9th   67156
              Est: 1974
  Proprietor: Tom Williams
  Hours: Sun-Fri, 9-5
Types & Periods: 7 Shops
under one roof, General
Line
Specialties: Wood Carving
  Directions: 1 Block off
  Main

ESTHER'S JUNQUE
  416 Bliss St   67156
  316 221-0763   Est: 1970
  Proprietor: Esther A Wilt
  Hours: Daily
Types & Periods: General
Line, Collectibles
Specialties: Glass
(Depression)

LITTLE SHOP ANTIQUES
  7th & Main   67156
  316 221-1732
  Proprietor: Virginia M
  Jarvis
  Hours: By appointment
Types & Periods: Furniture,
Clocks, Lamps, China,
Glass, Jewelry, Frames,
Copper, Brass, Silver, Iron,
Pewter, Toys, Primitives,
Trunks
Appraisal Service Available
  Directions: Hwys 77 & 15,
  2 Blocks N of Hwy 160

Hepplewhite pedestal ta-
ble with tripod legs and
spade feet.

Sheraton side chair with
Prince of Wales plumed
back and plainly turned
front legs.

212

(From page 112).   he was influenced by Oriental styles. His designs assumed a Chinese manner utilizing square legs sometimes being moulded on both outside faces, and also fretback and ladderback chairs. His upholsteries were of the most elegant fabrics including brocades, needlepoints and leathers. Drawer fronts were adorned with the beautiful Chippendale "butterfly" pulls made of finely worked brass.

In 1788, George Hepplewhite, also an Englishman, published his book of designs. Its title was *Cabinet-maker and Upholsterer's Guide*. The Hepplewhite leg is square and tapers toward the bottom. It may also be embellished with the so-called spade foot which, as with the garden tool, has shoulders on it. (See page 125). His furniture is characterized by its delicate lines, and his chairs by their shield-shaped backs. His cased pieces can have both concave as well as bowed fronts. Many of his pieces were ornamented by inlaying satinwood or the wood of the holly to create designs of Prince of Wales plumes, husks, bellflowers, etc. The dining tables frequently had a pair of slender legs at each corner, rather than one heavy leg, creating the illusion of lightness. Formal furniture was made of solid or veneered imported mahoganies, satinwoods and rosewoods. Upholstery of the finest fabrics as well as leathers and hair cloth were used. His drawer pulls were usually stamped oval plates embossed with many varied designs and bail handles.

Thomas Sheraton followed the well established practice of publishing his designs in *Cabinet-maker and Upholsterer's Drawing Book* of 1793. It was filled with delicate, simple styles. His work may be charcterized by the leg being rounded on a lathe, either being very plainly turned or else reeded or fluted. (See page 104). His chair backs were square lattice work or open work with a narrow top rail and central panels. Ornamentation of his furniture consisted of turnings, reeding, inlays or being painted. His designs also incorporated tambour doors for cabinets and secretaries. Like others, he used both solids and veneer of mahogany, satinwood and other exotic woods. His upholsteries were plain or patterned silks, brocades and other then current fabrics. Sheraton's drawer pulls were either oval or round, stamped brass plates with fancy brass knobs such as rings passing through a lion's mouth.

The end of the 18th Century and beginning of the 19th Century in America is called the Federal Period. It is referred to as the Regency Period in England. With the advent in this country of the townhouse, more elegant living, and somewhat scaled-down architecture for city dwelling, furniture of this period is ideally suited to our houses of today. Its reduction in scale brought about a more pleasing proportion to the eye. (See page 191). Styles were influenced by Hepplewhite, Sheraton and the French. After the American Revolution we were responsive to the influences of France. Mahogany was the popular wood, both solid and veneered. Incorporated into the designs were the very popular reeding, lyre motif and carvings. Since we were a new nation, a decorative eagle was occasionally to be seen on various pieces of furniture. Upholstery reflecting the elegance of the age was the finest brocades, satins, damasks and silks which appeared frequently in striped patterns. Hair cloth was also used. Federal drawer pulls were brass with bails, or rings on fancy stamped plates and also knobs of brass, glass and wood. America's foremost cabinetmaker of this period was Duncan Phyfe (1768-1854) of New York. His was an extremely long career which spanned the time from handcrafting into the rudimentary furniture factory. The later years of this period gave way to the vogues of the French Empire under Napoleon Bonaparte.

All of the above periods produced some of the finest examples of the cabinetmaker's art which endure with us today. Remember, we find these not only in exotic woods but in the native woods available to local cabinetmakers. In New England it would have been maple, sugar pine and birch. In other areas it might have been woods native to the region in which the cabinetmaker worked. As a result, you find examples of the finest designs skillfully executed in many varied woods. To help in determining the broad regions of manufacture for a piece of furniture, you may wish to become knowledgeable about where particular types of secondary wood were used. Since the outside wood was very costly, the unseen or secondary woods were of something less expensive. Secondary woods were used for the insides of drawers, the back boards of chests, etc. They can help you determine if it was made in New England, Pennsylvania, the Southern States or even England.

From France, in a roundabout manner, America received the Empire Period. It may be attributed to the rise of Napoleon and his demand for grandeur. Design in this period was influenced by his conquests. He brought back classical ideas from Egypt, the ruins of Herculaneum, Pompeii and elsewhere. In the creation of the new Empire Period, buildings, homes and other structures were designed and constructed in a grander manner. Consequently, furniture was scaled to larger proportions to correspond to the more impressive buildings. Furniture came to be designed with columns, pilasters and other forms of architectural (Continued, page 278).

THE EVOLVING CHAIR

Jacobean, English Oak.

Queen Anne with turned legs and
Spanish (Brush) feet,
New England.

Late Chippendale, Cherry.

Federal with Sheraton legs.
Notice the stretchers.

STATE OF KENTUCKY

Ashland

MINER'S COINS & ANTIQUES
700 29th St   41101
606 325-9425   Est: 1970
Proprietor: Miner & June
Kirk
Hours: Daily, Weekends
II-5, Closed Sun & Mon
Types & Periods: General
Line
Specialties: Coins
Appraisal Service Available
Directions: 29th St &
Lexington Ave

Bardstown

WHIMSY HOUSE
114 E Stephen Foster Ave
                        40004
502 348-5203   Est: 1972
Proprietor: Robert Walker
Hours: Daily, "A Call
Ahead is Advisable"
Types & Periods: 18th
Century & American
Furniture, Coins, Pottery,
Porcelain
Directions: 1/2 block from
Court Sq, 2 Miles from
Blue Grass Pkwy

Bedford

SURREY SHED ANTIQUE SALES
West St   40006
502 255-7544   Est: 1972
Proprietor: Kenneth I
Foree
Hours: By Appointment,
By Chance
Types & Periods: General
Line, Estate Dispersals,
"Regular Auction Sales
Conducted"
Appraisal Service Available
Directions: 36 Miles NE
Louisville, I block from
Intersection US 42 & 421,
1/2 block from Court Sq

Bowling Green

FULLER'S CEDAR HOUSE
Rte 4, 31 W South   42101
502 842-7695   Est: 1965
Proprietor: Ray & Evelyn
Fuller
Hours: Daily, Weekends,
By Appointment
Types & Periods: Furniture,
China, Glass, Primitives
Directions: 8 Miles S of
Bowling Green on Hwy 31
W

GARY'S BRASS BELL ANTIQUES
1022 31 W By-Pass 42101
502 842-8256   Est: 1974
Proprietor: Billy Joe &
Barbara Gary
Hours: Daily 10-5, Closed
Sun, By Appointment
Types & Periods: Early
Kentucky Pieces of Cherry,
Walnut, Pine, Poplar,
Victorian Walnut, China,
Silver, Glassware, Quilts,
Linens

RIVER BEND ANTIQUE MALL
Beech Bend Rd   42101
502 781-5773   Est: 1972
Proprietor: Juanita Runner
Hours: Daily 10-5, Sun 1-5
Types & Periods: Collections
of 42 Dealers
Directions: Beech Bend
Rd 1 Mile before entering
Beech Bend Park

Campbellsville

SAPP BROTHERS ANTIQUES
1109 Lebanon Ave   42718
502 789-1089   Est: 1975
Proprietor: Tommy &
Michael Sapp
Hours: Daily 9am-10pm
Types & Periods: Victorian
Furniture, Primitives,
Glassware, Silver
Directions: Hwy 68 N

Danville

RIFFEMOOR
Lexington Rd   40422
606 236-6582   Est: 1927
Proprietor: Nancibel &
Don Williams
Hours: Daily, Closed Sun
Types & Periods: 18th &
19th Centuries Furniture &
Accessories, Oriental Rugs,
Paintings, Silver, Brass,
Pewter, Garden Ornaments
Appraisal Service Available
Directions: Hwy 34 Across
from Danville Country
Club

TRASH TO TREASURES ANTIQUES
1310 Hustonville Rd 40422
606 236-5447   Est: 1962
Proprietor: Wm Stearman
Hours: Daily
Types & Periods: General
Line, Furniture, China,
Clocks, Brass, Empire &
Victorian, Primitives
Appraisal Service Available
Directions: Hwy 127 S of
Danville, 1/2 Mile inside
Bypass

Elizabethtown

THE OLE HOUSE GIFTS
127 N Main St   42701
502 765-6525   Est: 1972
Proprietor: Mr & Mrs John
R Gardner
Hours: Mon-Sat 9-5
Types & Periods: Rayo &
Aladdin Lamps, Furniture,
Pictures, Glass
Specialties: Lamps
Directions: 1 block from
Courthouse on N Main St
across from Brown-Pusey
House

Farmington

LORA'S TREASURE HUT
Rte 1   42040
502 345-2724   Est: 1974
Proprietor: Lora N Barton

LORA'S
TREASURE HUT   Cont'd
Hours: Sun-Fri 10-5,
Closed Sat
Types & Periods: Primitives,
Furniture, Glassware, China,
Quilts, Collectibles
Specialties: Kitchen
Cabinets, American Oak,
Handmade Quilts
Directions: Hwy 121 btwn
Mayfield & Murray, 1 Mile
E of Farmington

Frankfort

BURCH INTERIORS
4 Fountain Place   40601
502 875-2240   Est: 1971
Proprietor: Ruby Evelyn
Burch
Hours: Mon-Fri 10-4,
Weekends-By Chance, By
Appointment
Types & Periods: Empire,
Federal, Early & Mid
Victorian (Brass, Glass &
Bisque), Primitives
Specialties: Oriental (Rugs)
Appraisal Service Available
Directions: Center of
Downtown under the
Plaza Tower

Franklin

COLONY SHOP
714 N Main St   42134
Est: 1971
Proprietor: Charles West
Hours: Daily, Weekends
Types & Periods: General
Line
Directions: On 31 W, N 1
Mile from Courthouse

KENTUCKY ANTIQUE MALL
42134
502 586-3759   Est: 1971
Proprietor: Norma Ghent
& Evelyn Carnwell
Hours: Daily 9-6, Sun 1-6,
Winter 9-5, Sun 1-5
Types & Periods: Furniture,
Primitives, Glassware, China,
Pictures
Specialties: 22 Permanent
Dealers Under One Roof
Directions: 3 Miles N of
Franklin on US 31 W

Glasgow

SADLER'S HERITAGE
ANTIQUES
N Bypass 31 E   42141
502 651-8522   Est: 1965
Proprietor: Moena E
Sadler
Hours: By Appointment
Types & Periods: General
Line
Directions: N of Jerry's
Restaurant, Next door to
Glasgow Coca Cola Plant

THE WHAT'ZIT SHOP
123 St Mary's Ct   42141
502 651-3218
Proprietor: James &
Frauline Wilkinson
Hours: "If We Are Home,
We Are Open"
Types & Periods: General
Line, Lamps
Directions: 1 block off S
Green on Leslie Ave to St
Mary's Ct

Greenville

ROBERTSON'S TREASURE
HOUSE
Rte 1 Hwy 62W   42345
502 338-5860   Est: 1971
Proprietor: Paul &
Margaret Robertson
Hours: Daily
Types & Periods: General
Line
Directions: Hwy 62 W at
City Limits

Henderson

OLD CLARK HOUSE
1002 S Green St   42420
502 826-8541   Est: 1965
Proprietor: H H Farmer, Jr
& Lucretia Y Farmer
Hours: Mon-Sat 10-5,
Closed Sun
Types & Periods: 18th &
19th Centuries European
Antiques, Furniture,
Accessories, Jewelry
Specialties: Jewelry, Copper
& Brass
Appraisal Service Available

Directions: S Side of Town
on US 41A & 60, 7 Miles
from Evansville, Indiana

Lebanon

TRASH & TREASURE SHOP
Rte 2, Box 92   40033
502 692-4865   Est: 1971
Proprietor: Joyce & Tom
Wheatley
Hours: Daily
Types & Periods: General
Line
Specialties: Furniture
Directions: 1 Mile N of
Lebanon on Hwy 49 at
Hwy 84

Lexington

LEXINGTON CLUSTER
Directions: Along N
Broadway (300-900
Blocks) & Adjacent Sts of
High, Euclid, N Limestone,
Also on Main St (E-W)

ANTIQUITIES
636 W Main   40508
606 255-5912   Est: 1970
Proprietor: Frank J
Cutadean
Hours: Daily, Weekends,
10-5
Types & Periods: Period
Country Furniture &
Accessories from Queen
Anne, Sheraton, Early
Victorian, Glass
Specialties: Brass, Brass &
Copper Accessories
Appraisal Service Available
Directions: Take Newtown
Pike Exit off I-75, Left on
Main St 1 block

THE APPLE TREE
113 Walton Ave   40508
606 252-1309   Est: 1967
Proprietor: Zeef Wile and
Sue Clay Moloney
Hours: Daily 10-4, Closed
Sun
Types & Periods: 17th &
18th Centuries English,
American Furniture, Oriental
Rugs
Directions: 1/2 block right
off E Main St

BOONE'S ANTIQUES OF KENTUCKY INC
4996 Old Versailles Rd
40504
606 254-5335
Proprietor: Boone's
Antiques of Wilson NC
Hours: Mon-Sat 8:30-5:30
Types & Periods: Furniture,
Oriental Rugs, Bric-A-Brac,
Clocks, Paintings, 75%
Imported & 25% American
Specialties: English &
American 18th & 19th
Centuries Furniture, Glass,
Brass, Porcelains, Oriental
Rugs and Paintings
Appraisal Service Available
Directions: Located on Old
Section of US 60 I Mile W
of Keeneland Race Track

BOULTINGHOUSE & HALL ANTIQUES
900 N Broadway   40505
606 254-4911   Est: 1970
Hours: Mon-Sat 10-4:30,
other times by
appointment
Types & Periods: American,
English Furniture &
Accessories Prior to 1850
Specialties: American &
Kentucky Silver
Appraisal Service Available

DOME ANTIQUES & BOOKS
191 N Limestone   40507
606 255-6955
Proprietor: Mary
Hazelwood Baumstark
Hours: By appointment, By
Chance 11:30-4:00
Types & Periods: General
Line, China, Brass, Glass,
Cut and Pressed, Small
Furniture.
Appraisal Service Available
Directions: 3 blocks N of
Main St

THE FONTAINE SHOP
732 E High St   40502
606 266-5211   Est: 1949
Proprietor: B B Fontaine
Hours: Daily
Types & Periods: General
Line

HEINSMITH GALLERIES
866 E High St   40502
Proprietor: Mr & Mrs E
Stephen Hein & Mr & Mrs
Clifton Smith

Hours: Mon-Fri 10-6, Sat
10-5:30
Types & Periods: 18th &
19th Centuries Antiques &
Accessories
Appraisal Service Available
Directions: Just off Euclid

HERITAGE ANTIQUE GALLERIES
377 E Main St   40507
606 253-1035   Est: 1970
Proprietor: Nelson
Maloney
Hours: Daily 10-5, Closed
Wed & Sun
Types & Periods: General
Line
Appraisal Service Available
Directions: Downtown

RUSSELL LUTES ANTIQUES
807 Euclid Ave   40502
606 266-1109   Est: 1946
Proprietor: Russell Lutes
Hours: Daily 10-5, Closed
Sun
Types & Periods: English
Mahogany, Colonial Silver,
Oriental Rugs
Appraisal Service Available
Directions: Chevy Chase

DONALD MC GURK INC
Kentucky & Central Aves
40502
606 253-0137   Est: 1969
Proprietor: Donald McGurk
Hours: Daily, Weekends
10-5, Closed Sun, Also by
Appointment
Types & Periods: 18th
Century English & American
Furniture, English & Chinese
Porcelain, Oriental Rugs,
Lamps, Brass
Specialties: Furniture
Directions: 1 block S of E
Main St, US 25 E

STRAWBERRY HILL ANTIQUES
2640 Richmond Rd 40502
606 266-2029   Est: 1918
Proprietor: Elwood
Elizabeth Coleman
Hours: Daily, Weekends
10-5, Closed Sun
Types & Periods: General
Line
Specialties: Toys
Appraisal Service Available

Louisville

LOUISVILLE CLUSTER
Directions: Butchertown &
Bakery Square, Bardstown
Rd btwn Grinstead Dr &
Eastern Pkwy

ARCHITECTURAL ARCHIVES
618 Baxter Ave   40204
502 582-1925   Est: 1974
Proprietor: Wm S Vatter
Hours: Mon-Sat 10-5
Types & Periods: Primitive
to Art Nouveau
Specialties: "Anything
architectural including log
cabins, iron fencing,
gingerbread, & the unusual"
Appraisal Service Available
Directions: Centrally
located 2 blocks from
Intersection of Broadway
& Cherokee Rd on
Phoenix Hill

BITTNERS
731 E Main St   40299
502 584-6349   Est: 1854
Proprietor: William B
Schneider
Hours: Daily
Types & Periods: 17th, 18th
& Early 19th Centuries
English, American & French
Furniture
Specialties: Furniture
(English)
Appraisal Service Available
Directions: Btwn Shelby &
Clay on E Main St

MAURICE L BROWN ANTIQUES
507 S 3rd St   40202
502 585-2912   Est: 1965
Proprietor: Maurice L
Brown
Hours: By Appointment,
By Chance, Daily
Types & Periods: Furniture,
Oil Paintings, Silver, Oriental
Rugs, Clocks, Porcelain
Appraisal Service Available
Directions: Downtown

THE CENTURY SHOP
1703 Bardstown Rd 40205
502 451-7692   Est: 1958
Proprietor: Howard
Wagner
Hours: Daily 10-4, Sat 1-4

Louisville   Cont'd

CENTURY SHOP   Cont'd
Types & Periods: 17th &
18th Centuries English &
Continental Furniture &
Accessories
Specialties: Furniture (18th
Century English &
Continental), Porcelain,
Pottery
Appraisal Service Available
    Directions: On Main Artery
    into City

**CORONADO ANTIQUES
MALL & AUCTION
GALLERY**
    6407 Preston Hwy   40219
    502 968-0866   Est: 1975
    Proprietor: Larry
    Baumgardner
    Hours: Daily
Types & Periods: Furniture,
Collectibles, Glass, Clocks
Appraisal Service Available
    Directions: 1½ Miles off
    I-65, Fern Valley Rd Exit

**THE LITTLE MUSTARD
HOUSE**
    13210 Shelbyville Rd
                        40223
    502 245-9917   Est: 1974
    Proprietor: Doreen
    Peterson
    Hours: Sun, Thurs, Sat
    11:30-5, By Chance
Types & Periods: General
Line, Flow Blue China
    Directions: 1 Mile E of
    Middletown on US 60 E

B A MAHANEY CO
    925 Baxter   40204
    502 458-8629   Est: 1946
    Proprietor: B A Mahaney
    Hours: Mon-Sat
Types & Periods: Country
Furniture
Specialties: Cherry & Walnut
Appraisal Service Available

KEVIN SCOTT ANTIQUES
    1040 Bardstown Rd 40204
    502 583-0033   Est: 1968
    Proprietor: Ronnie
    Doggott
    Hours: Mon-Sat 10:30-5,
    Closed Sun
Types & Periods: English &
American 18th & 19th
Centuries Furniture,
Accessories

    Directions: Broadway to
    Bardstown Rd, Right to
    1040

THE STRASSEL CO
    1000 Hamilton Ave   40204
    502 587-6611   Est: 1845
    Proprietor: Charles Mendel
    Hours: Daily 9-5, Sat 10-1
Types & Periods: 18th &
19th Centuries English,
French & some Italian
Specialties: Porcelains
    Directions: Eastern part of
    Downtown,Located at very
    end of Lexington Rd after
    you cross Baxter Ave

E S TICHENOR COMPANY
    122 N Adams St   40206
    502 583-6271   Est: 1968
    Proprietor: Scott & Leslie
    Tichenor
    Hours: Mon-Fri 9-5, Sat
    During Nov-Dec Only
Types & Periods: All Types,
English, Continental,
American, Folk, 17th
Century to Turn of the
Century
Specialties: Snuff &
Tobacco Boxes, Painted
Furniture, Lamps, "Livable"
Furniture Pieces, Rugs,
Pictures
    Directions: In Butchertown
    Area, Take Story Ave Exit
    off I-64 E, or Mellwood
    Ave Exit off I-64 W, Turn
    Right on Adams St

**TREASURE TROVE
ANTIQUES**
    1416 Bardstown Rd 40204
    502 458-2009   Est: 1973
    Proprietor: Maxine
    Johnson
    Hours: Daily, Weekends
    10:30-5, Sun by Chance
Types & Periods: Art Glass,
Jewelry, Furniture,
Glassware
    Directions: 1½ blocks N of
    Eastern Pkwy on
    Bardstown Rd across from
    Edinside Church

Marion

**COLONIAL HOUSE
ANTIQUES & MARION
AUCTION BARN**
    343 E Belleville   42064
    502 965-2934   Est: 1970
    Proprietor: Clinton Easley
    Hours: Daily
Types & Periods: Primitives,
Furniture
Appraisal Service Available
    Directions: E on Belleville
    St

Maysville

**HENDRICKSON'S
ANTIQUES**
    2nd & Sutton Sts   41056
    606 564-5734   Est: 1908
    Proprietor: Bill B
    Hendrickson
    Hours: Daily 9-5, Closed
    Sun
Types & Periods: Complete
Line
Specialties: Furniture
(Regional)
Appraisal Service Available
    Directions: Downtown 3
    blocks from Ohio River
    Bridge, 60 Miles E of
    Cincinnati, 60 Miles N of
    Lexington

Paducah

CHOATE'S ANTIQUE SHOP
    1623 Broadway   42001
    502 442-1776   Est: 1948
    Proprietor: Mrs Martha
    Choate
    Hours: Mon-Sat 9:30-5
Types & Periods: European
Antiques, Lamps, Gifts &
Accessories
    Directions: On Broadway
    across from Sears parking
    lot

**THOMPSON'S ANTIQUES &
GIFT SHOP**
    3831 Clark's River Rd
                        42001
    502 442-3040   Est: 1945
    Proprietor: Mrs Harley
    Thompson
    Hours: Daily, Weekends,
    By Appointment

Types & Periods: Furniture,
China, Clocks, Art, Pattern
& Depression Glass
Specialties: China, Lamps
Directions: Hwys 60, 62 &
68 E of Paducah

**WOOD WHITTLERS
ANTIQUE SHOP**
2504 Bridge St   42001
502 443-7408   Est: 1970
Proprietor: David A Nelson
& Philip Hocker
Hours: Mon-Fri
Types & Periods: Walnut
Furniture & Oak Furniture
Specialties: Repairing &
refinishing (Custom
Woodturning Hardware)
Appraisal Service Available

Paris

BRENT'S ANTIQUE SHOP
2001 S Main St   40361
606 987-4360   Est: 1957
Proprietor: Elizabeth K &
Hugh I Brent Jr
Hours: Daily, Weekends
9:30-6, Closed Sun
Types & Periods: General
Line
Specialties: Furniture
(American Country)
Directions: US 68 & 27

Pendleton

LONG BRANCH ANTIQUES
I-71 & Ky 153   40055
502 743-5133   Est: 1972
Proprietor: Doris M
Coleman
Hours: Daily, By
Appointment, By Chance
Types & Periods: Primitives,
Rough Furniture,
Collectibles, Glassware
Specialties: Oak in the
Rough, Kerosene Lamps
Directions: 28 Miles NE of
Louisville

Prospect

LITTLE GABLE ANTIQUES
Hwy 42   40059
502 228-1519   Est: 1965
Proprietor: Ellen W Sell

Hours: Tues-Sat,
11:30-4:30, Sun 1-5,
Closed Mon
Types & Periods: Furniture,
Cut Glass, Silver, Objet d'Art
Appraisal Service Available
Directions: Hwy 42 at
Prospect, Right outside
Louisville going E toward
Cincinnati

Richmond

LENA'S ANTIQUES
Rte 2   40475
606 623-4325   Est: 1954
Proprietor: Lena B
Pennington
Hours: Daily
Types & Periods: General
Line
Specialties: Flo Blue, R S
Prussia, R S Germany
Directions: 5 Miles S
Richmond on US 25

THE SUMMIT SHOP
223 Summit   46475
606 623-3040   Est: 1960
Proprietor: S E & E S
Bagley
Hours: Weekends, By
Chance
Types & Periods: General
Line, Fabrics, Prints
Appraisal Service Available
Directions: S on Madison,
2 blocks off E Main St,
Dead-end Intersection at
Summit & Richmond

Rockfield

**ROCKFIELD ANTIQUE
MALL**
Rte 1   42274
502 842-8923, 781-2440
Est: 1973
Proprietor: Curtis &
Martyne Peay
Hours: Mon, Tues,
Thurs-Sat 10-5, Sun 1-5,
Closed Wed
Types & Periods: Walnut &
Cherry Furniture, Primitives,
Glassware, Oak Furniture,
"Largest Selection of
Choice Antiques in
Kentucky"

Appraisal Service Available
Directions: 6 Miles W of
Bowling Green on US 68

Russellville

CALICO INN
671 S Nashville   42276
502 726-3570   Est: 1969
Proprietor: Mrs Dorothy
Estes
Hours: Daily
Types & Periods: Country
Furniture, Primitives

COLONY HOUSE
187 S Main   42276
502 726-9635   Est: 1975
Proprietor: Carol Dyche
Hours: Mon-Sat, Closed
Sun
Types & Periods: English,
American, Some Victorian
Specialties: Custom made
Cherry & Walnut
Reproductions, Georgian
Style, Gifts & Interiors
Directions: 1/2 block S of
Square on Main St

DIXIE ANTIQUES
149-53 E 4th St   42276
502 726-7577
Proprietor: Mrs P M
Winston
Hours: Daily, Weekends
10-5, Closed Sun
Types & Periods: Furniture,
Cut & Pattern Glass,
Oriental Porcelain
Specialties: Wood Block
Prints

LOG HOUSE ANTIQUES
9th St   42276
502 726-7222   Est: 1975
Proprietor: Nancy & Les
Newberry
Hours: Daily, Weekends
8-4:30, Sun 1-4:30
Types & Periods: Early
American, Primitives
Specialties: Primitives
Directions: Jct US
79-68-80-100

RUSSELLVILLE ANTIQUE MALL
205 W 4th St   42276
502 726-6900   Est: 1975
Proprietor: Lloyd & Betty Allen
Hours: Daily 9:30-5,
Closed Tues, Sun 1-5
Types & Periods: Furniture, Wicker, Glass, China, Silver, Lamps
Specialties: Wicker, Primitives, Trunks
    Directions: In Front of Courthouse

RUSSELLVILLE FLOWER SHOP & ANTIQUE GALLERY
104 Bowling Green Rd
                            42276
502 726-7608
Proprietor: Roy Gill
Hours: Daily
Types & Periods: English, American, Period, Victorian, Centennial
Specialties: Gold Leaf Mirrors
    Directions: Opposite Hospital on Hwy 68 E

Shelbyville

BANICKMAN ANTIQUES
Rte 6   40065
502 633-4425   Est: 1956
Proprietor: Gilbert Banickman
Hours: Daily 9-4:30
Types & Periods: General Line
Appraisal Service Available
    Directions: US 66 E 1 Mile off I-64

CHATHAM STATION
220 N 7th St   40065
502 633-6397   Est: 1974
Proprietor: Betty & Don Chatham
Hours: Daily 9-5
Types & Periods: General Line
    Directions: Corner of 7th & College Sts

Somerset

CURIOSITY SHOPPE
522 Ogden St   42501
606 678-4596   Est: 1976
Proprietor: Richard & Janice Simpson
Hours: Mon-Sat 10-5
Types & Periods: General Line
Appraisal Service Available
    Directions: 1 block from Intersection Hwy 27 & Cumberland Bypass Hwy 80

Springfield

DAVISON HOUSE
209 E Main St   40069
606 336-7985   Est: 1973
Proprietor: Ben Simms Haydon
Hours: Daily, By Appointment
Types & Periods: General Line
Appraisal Service Available

Versailles

CORNER ANTIQUE SHOP
229 Lexington St   40383
606 873-4214   Est: 1959
Proprietor: Christine Sheets
Hours: Daily 9-9
Types & Periods: Lightwood Country & Primitive Furniture
Specialties: Furniture (lightwood)
    Directions: Rte 60 1½ blocks E of Courthouse

MASON ANTIQUES
Lexington Rd   40383
606 873-4792   Est: 1956
Proprietor: Katherine Mason
Hours: Daily
Types & Periods: English & American, Period & General Line
    Directions: 11 Miles from Lexington, Btwn Lexington & Frankfort

Empire Chest of Drawers, small scale.
Notice overhanging top drawer and pilaster.

STATE OF LOUISIANA

Alexandria

CENLA AUCTION CO
Box 1934   71301
318 448-1783   Est: 1970
Proprietor: Paul Moreau
Hours: Daily 8-5, By
Appointment
Types & Periods: Furniture,
Bric-A-Brac
Appraisal Service Available
Directions: Hwy 9 N 7
Miles

THE FIELD HOUSE
ANTIQUES
1241 Texas Ave   71301
318 445-6921   Est: 1964
Proprietor: Mrs J H Field
Hours: Tues-Sat 10-5, Sun
& Mon By Appointment
Types & Periods: Glass,
China, Art Nouveau, Imari,
Furniture, Boxes, Circa
1840-1939
Specialties: Toys (Dolls)
Appraisal Service Available
Directions: Jackson &
Texas, 1 block off Main
Hwy, Exit at A&P or K
Mart on 4 Lane Hwy

GERAMI FURNITURE &
ANTIQUES
6524 Masonic Dr   71301
318 445-2668   Est: 1966
Proprietor: Tom Gerami
Hours: Daily
Types & Periods: General
Line
Directions: 2 Miles S of S
Traffic Circle on Hwy 165

THE OLD TIME SHOP
105 Bolton Ave   71301
318 445-8693   Est: 1965
Proprietor: J Ben Carter
Hours: Daily 9-5, Sat 9-1,
Closed Sun
Types & Periods: Clocks

Amite

MORSES' ANTIQUES ETC
106 E Mulberry   70422
504 748-6793   Est: 1974
Proprietor: Aubrey E
Morse

Hours: Mon-Sat 10-5
Types & Periods: Victorian,
Empire & Primitive Furniture,
Chandeliers, Lamps, Coin &
Sterling, Clocks, Frames,
China, Glassware, Old Light
Fixtures, Bric-A-Brac
Directions: 2 Miles off I-55
btwn McComb, Miss &
Hammond, La

Arabi

NOEL WISE ANTIQUES
6503 St Claude Ave 70032
504 279-6896   Est: 1971
Proprietor: Noel G Wise
Hours: Daily 9-5, Sat 10-5,
Closed Sun
Types & Periods: China,
Glass, Oil Paintings,
Furniture
Specialties: Chair Cane,
Brass Hardware, Veneers
Appraisal Service Available
Directions: 35 Feet
Outside City Limits of New
Orleans on St Claude Ave

Bastrop

NELL GIBSON ANTIQUES
Rte 4, Box 196   71220
Est: 1950
Proprietor: Nell Gibson
Gee
Hours: Mon-Tues,
Thurs-Sat
Types & Periods: Furniture,
China, Press Glass, Cut
Glass, Glass, Primitives,
Books & Prints
Appraisal Service Available
Directions: 4 Miles N of
Bastrop at Log Cabin on
Shelton Rd

R L MAYBERRY
GALLERIES
Hwy 165 E   71220
318 281-8558   Est: 1966
Proprietor: R L Mayberry
Hours: Daily
Types & Periods: French &
American Furniture,
Glassware, Art Objects

Specialties: Rugs (Oriental)
Appraisal Service Available
Directions: Mer Rouge Rd,
just outside City Limits

Baton Rouge

BATON ROUGE CLUSTER
Directions: Heavy
concentration on
Government St (2000-4000
Blocks), Other Shops
scattered throughout City

THE ANTIQUE
WAREHOUSE
16329 George O'Neil Rd
70816
504 293-5269   Est: 1974
Proprietor: Mrs Jo
Bordelon
Hours: Sun 2-6, Thurs-Sat
10-6
Types & Periods: Victorian,
Country, Louisiana,
European China, Glass,
Silver, Brass, Jewelry, Old &
New Gift Items
Specialties: Tester Beds,
Armoire's Marble Top Tables
Appraisal Service Available
Directions: No 7 Exit off
I-12, Right to Harrell's
Ferry Rd, 4 blocks Left on
Jones Creek Rd, 1 Mile to
George O'Neil Rd, 7/10
Mile

BARKERS COUNTRY
ANTIQUES
7565 Jefferson Hwy 70806
504 927-4406   Est: 1968
Proprietor: Wayne & Linda
Barker
Hours: Mon-Sat
Types & Periods: 18th &
19th Centuries American
Country Furniture &
Accessories
Directions: Btwn Lobdell &
Old Hammond Hwy

CRACKER BARREL
ANTIQUES
11611 Plank Rd   70811
504 775-7855   Est: 1973
Proprietor: J C Brown
Hours: Daily 10-6

Baton Rouge   Cont'd

CRACKER BARRELL Cont'd
Types & Periods: General
Line
Specialties: Furniture,
Lamps, Chandeliers
Appraisal Service Available
Directions: 1 Mile Past
City Limits & Airport

NELL FETZER INTERIORS
711 Jefferson Hwy   70896
504 927-7420   Est: 1954
Proprietor: Nell Fetzer
Hours: Daily 9-5, Closed
Sat & Sun
Types & Periods: English &
European Oil Paintings,
Oriental Rugs, Furniture
Directions: 1 block off
Government St btwn
Government &
Goodwoods, 1 Mile from
I-10

LAGNIAPPE ANTIQUES
2165 Dallas Dr   70806
504 927-053l
Proprietor: Joan B Guillory
Hours: Daily, Weekends
9-5, Closed Sun
Types & Periods: General
Line
Appraisal Service Available

**MANY MANSIONS
ANTIQUES & GIFTS**
7856 Airline Hwy   70815
504 925-5542   Est: 1941
Proprietor: D F Many
Hours: Daily 9-5, Closed
Sun & Mon
Types & Periods: General
Line
Specialties: Jewelry, Dolls,
Miniatures
Directions: Hwy Bypass 61
& 190, btwn Greenwell
Sprgs Rd & Florida St
Overpass, 2½ Miles N of
I-12

**OLD HOMESTEAD
ANTIQUES & COUNTRY
THINGS**
3748 Government St
70806
504 343-3185   Est: 1966
Proprietor: Sue & Homer
Spaht
Hours: Tues-Sat 10-5

Types & Periods: Paintings,
China, Pressed Glass,
Brass, Graniteware
Specialties: Wicker

**PECQUET'S BROCANTURE
ANTIQUE SHOPPE**
1735 Plank Rd   70802
504 344-6979   Est: 1966
Proprietor: Urline Pecquet
Hours: Daily
Types & Periods: English,
French & Early American
Furniture, Brass, Copper,
China, Bric-A-Brac
Specialties: China, Furniture
Directions: W on I-10, off
on Scenic Hwy, N on
Plank Rd for 6 blocks

WOMACK'S ANTIQUES
1502 Convention   70802
504 348-4427
Proprietor: Robert
Womack & Earnest Gatlin
Hours: Daily, Weekends
9-5, Closed Sun
Types & Periods: Furniture,
Jewelry, China

YESTERDAY & TODAY'S
3457 Government   70806
504 344-6376   Est: 1975
Proprietor: Virginia Peters
& Sharon Loup
Hours: Daily, Weekends,
Closed Fri & Sun, By
Appointment
Types & Periods: General
Line, Collectibles
Directions: Centrally
located on Main E-W
Thoroughfares, Also Exit
off I-10 at S Acadian N to
Government

Belle Chasse

SCHLIEF'S ANTIQUES
201 Schlief Dr   70037
504 394-3087
Hours: Daily, Weekends
9-5, Closed Sun
Types & Periods: Furniture,
Bric-A-Brac, Art Glass,
Porcelains
Directions: Suburb of New
Orleans

Benton

**COUNTRY CABIN
ANTIQUES**
Rte 1, Box 229   71006
318 746-7852   Est: 1970
Proprietor: R E McMillian
Hours: Daily, Closed Sun
Types & Periods: European
& American Furniture,
China, Glassware
Specialties: English China
Wash Bowl & Pitcher Sets
Directions: Hwy 3, 8 Miles
N of Bossier City

Bernice

MARSH ANTIQUES
206 6th St   71222
318 285-7373   Est: 1970
Proprietor: Fred Marsh
Hours: Daily, Weekends
9-5, Sun 1-5, Closed Sat
Types & Periods: Oak
Furniture, Pressed, Pattern
& Depression Glass
Directions: 1 block off US
Hwy 167 & State 2

Bossier

CAIN'S INC
455 Riverside Dr   71010
318 222-2497   Est: 1950
Proprietor: J H & Leila
Cain & Martha Cain Hill
Hours: Daily 8:30-5
Types & Periods: English
Period Furniture, English &
Oriental Porcelain &
Accessories
Specialties: Porcelain
Directions: Hamilton Rd
Exit off I-20, 4 blocks S

Chalmette

**AUTOMOTIVE ANTIQUE
SPECIALTY**
303 E Prosper   70043
504 277-5110   Est: 1975
Proprietor: Al Tinney
Hours: Mon-Sat 9:30-5:30
Types & Periods: Auto
Parts, New from 1900-1959
Appraisal Service Available

Convent

TEZCUCO PLANTATION
Rte 1, Box 157   70723
504 473-4250   Est: 1966
Proprietor: Mrs Robert H
Potts Jr
Hours: Daily, Weekends
10-4, Sun 1-4
Types & Periods: Art Glass,
Porcelain, China, Primitives,
Jewelry, Silver
Directions: 6 Miles off I-10
on River Rd Near
Sunshine Bridge

Duson

**SUNCO-SUN TRADING
COMPANY**
Rte 2, Box 272-A   70529
318 873-6954   Est: 1972
Proprietor: Fred dela
Houssaye
Hours: Daily
Types & Periods: European,
American
Specialties: Furniture (Curio
Cabinets, Vitrines)
Directions: Off I-10 at
Duson Exit S, 1st Left on
Hwy 95

Franklin

FRANCES PLANTATION
Hwy 90 E, PO Box 557
70538
318 828-5472   Est: 1965
Proprietor: Mrs F F Sutter
Hours: Tues-Sat 9-5
Types & Periods: Georgian,
Queen Anne, Chippendale,
Victorian & American
Plantation Furniture, Silver,
Oil Paintings, Objet d'Art
Directions: 3 Miles E of
Franklin on Hwy 90

Frierson

**FRIERSON COUNTRY
STORE**
Box 105, Hwy 175   71027
318 861-2047   Est: 1975
Proprietor: George M &
Barbara Camp
Hours: Tues-Sat 9:30-5,
Sun 1-5

Types & Periods: Americana
& Primitives
Directions: Hwy 1 S from
Shreveport, Right on Hwy
175, Cross RR Tracks at
Frierson, Left about 1 Mile
on Left, 9.9 Miles from
Hwy 1 to Store

Gretna

**ANTIQUES & DISCOVERIES
OF GRETNA INC**
839 Franklin St   70053
504 361-4833   Est: 1975
Proprietor: Vivian Dulcich
Hours: Weekends, By
Appointment
Types & Periods: English &
American
Appraisal Service Available
Directions: W Bank
Expwy, Right on Franklin

Hammond

DEC'S ANTIQUES
Rte 1, Box 5A   70401
504 345 1960   Est: 1968
Proprietor: Oneil G
Decoteau
Hours: Mon-Sat, Sun
2-5:30
Types & Periods: Furniture,
Glass, Clocks, Miscellaneous
Appraisal Service Available
Directions: Exit I-55 to 190
E, Take Right at Internat'l
Harvester, Go 3 blocks

Harahan

ANTIQUE HAVEN
6495 Jefferson Hwy 70123
504 738-2380   Est: 1977
Proprietor: John H Henson
Hours: Mon-Sat 10-5
Types & Periods:
American-1900 & Back to
Primitives, Furniture
Specialties: Furniture
Stripping, Repairing,
Restoration & Refinishing
Appraisal Service Available
Directions: Past Huey
Long Bridge coming from
New Orleans

**BACK PORCH ANTIQUES
INC**
920 Hickory Ave   70123
504 738-1903   Est: 1978
Proprietor: Rita Winter,
Herbert & Nathalie Winter
Willig
Hours: Mon-Sat 10-5
Types & Periods: Primitives,
Oak Pieces, Bric-A-Brac,
Jewelry, Early Louisiana &
English, Late 1800's to Early
1900's
Directions: Jefferson
Parish-btwn Airline Hwy &
Jefferson Hwy in City of
Harahan, In Hickory Hall

**BEL'S ANTIQUES & GIFTS
INC**
924 Hickory Ave   70123
Est: 1975
Proprietor: Mrs Bel
Swartzfager
Hours: Mon, Wed, Fri
12-6, Sat, Sun, Tues,
Thurs By Chance, By
Appointment
Types & Periods: American
18th & Early 19th Centuries
Depression Glass & Gifts
Specialties: Old & Special
Edition Plates
Directions: In Jefferson
Parish-btwn Airline Hwy &
Jefferson Hwy, 7 Miles
from the Heart of New
Orleans

BROWSER DOWSER
920 Hickory Ave   70123
504 738-1903   Est: 1978
Proprietor: Lynn Courrege
& Louise McCarthy
Hours: Mon-Sat 10-5, Sun
By Appointment
Types & Periods: English &
American, French, Brass
Specialties: Depression
Glass, Brass
Directions: I-10 to
Clearview Pkwy S, Exit at
Earhart Expwy to Dickory,
Dickory becomes Hickory

THE KEEPSAKE INC
920 Hickory Ave   70123
504 738-1903   Est: 1970
Proprietor: Shirley
Sollenberger & Grace Hale
Hours: Mon-Sat 10-5

THE KEEPSAKE   Cont'd

Types & Periods: All Types
of Furniture, Emphasis on
Turn-of-the-Century Oak,
Bric-A-Brac, Junque
   Directions: Btwn Airline &
   Jefferson Hwys

Homer

AUNT MIRIAM'S ANTIQUES
   402 N Main   71040
   318 927-6745   Est: 1961
   Proprietor: Miriam B
   Johnson
   Hours: Daily, Mon-Sat,
   Sun By Appointment
Types & Periods: Victorian,
French, English & American
Oak, Walnut & Mahogany
Pieces
Appraisal Service Available
   Directions: 2 blocks off
   Square on Hwy 9

LILLIAN'S ANTIQUE SHOP
   309 N Main St   71040
   318 927-3918   Est: 1938
   Proprietor: Lillian Bellizio
   Hudson
   Hours: Daily 10-5, By
   Appointment
Types & Periods: Victorian
Furniture, Art & Cut Glass,
China
Specialties: Art Glass
Appraisal Service Available
   Directions: 17 Miles from
   I-20 Arcadia-Homer Exit,
   Hwy 9, 3 blocks from
   Square toward El Dorado,
   Large White House

Houma

THE ATTIC
   2744 W Main   70360
   504 873-7854   Est: 1973
   Proprietor: Bonnie Burns
   Hours: Daily 9:30-4:30, Sat
   1-5, Closed Sun
Types & Periods: 19th
Century American &
European Furniture,
Bric-A-Brac Decorator
Lamps, Furnishings, Imports

Directions: Across Bayou
Terrebonne from
Southland Mall on the
Houma Couplet

J J'S ANTIQUES
   2506 W Main St   70360
   504 879-1085   Est: 1971
   Proprietor: James Wilson
   Hours: Daily
Types & Periods: General
Line, 1830-1930
Specialties: Refinishing &
Repair Shop
Appraisal Service Available

Jefferson

**AAA ANTIQUE &
RESTORATION**
   4617 Jefferson   70121
   504 733-4511   Est: 1977
   Proprietor: Sidney or
   Dugarden
   Hours: Mon-Sat, By
   Appointment
Types & Periods: Early
American, Primitives,
Reproductions
Specialties: Repairs &
Refinishing, Woodturning
   Directions: Suburb of New
   Orleans

Jonesboro

BRINSON'S ANTIQUES
   310 Main St   71251
   318 259-7527   Est: 1958
   Proprietor: Mrs Charles
   Brinson
   Hours: Daily
Types & Periods: English
Furniture, Glass, Picture
Frames
   Directions: In front of
   Jackson Parish
   Courthouse

Lafayette

ABSHIRE'S ANTIQUES
   210 N Magnolia St   70501
   318 232-6441   Est: 1974
   Proprietor: Kenneth J
   Abshire
   Hours: Daily 10-6, Closed
   Sun & Mon

Types & Periods: Louisiana
Colonial, Country French,
English & American
Furniture, Decorations,
Accessories
Appraisal Service Available
   Directions: US Hwy 167 or
   US Hwy 90 at Simcoe St

**ANDERSON'S ANTIQUE
CLOCKS**
   108 W Vermilion St   70501
   318 235-3028   Est: 1974
   Proprietor: June A & Joe
   N Anderson
   Hours: Tues-Sat 9:30-5
Types & Periods: American,
French, German & English
Antique Clocks
   Directions: Downtown
   across from Lafayette
   Bldg Assoc

ANTIQUES & INTERIORS
   616 Gen Mouton   70501
   318 234-4776   Est: 1967
   Proprietor: Jane Fleniken
   Hours: Thurs-Sat 10-4
Types & Periods: Country
French, English, American
Specialties: Country French
   Directions: New U of SW
   La Campus

THE BROWN HOUSE
   624 Garfield   70502
   318 234-6579   Est: 1974
   Proprietor: Mrs Jane
   Collins
   Hours: Mon-Fri 9-5, Sat
   9-3, Closed Sun
Types & Periods: General
Line, American Art Pottery,
Furniture, China, Cut Glass
Specialties: American Art
Pottery, Cut Glass
   Directions: Exit Johnston
   St from 167, Left at 1st
   Traffic Light, 2nd block

**COLLAGE ANTIQUES AND
COLLECTIBLES**
   117 SW Evangeline
   Thruway   70501
   318 234-5321   Est: 1975
   Proprietor: Kathy Norman
   & Judi Cole
   Hours: Mon-Sat 9-5, Sat
   10-3, By Appointment
Types & Periods: 1800-Early
1900's American Antiques &
Collectibles, Some Imports,
Architectural, Cypress
Doors, Mantels & Shutters,
Stained & Beveled Glass

Specialties: Refinishing
Directions: 1 block S of
Jefferson St, Corner of
SW Evangeline Thruway &
5th St on 167 S

LAFITTE'S TREASURE ATTIC
110 Olivier St   70501
318 234-1568   Est: 1966
Proprietor: Mrs Agnes
Voorhies
Hours: Daily 9-5, Closed
Sun & Mon
Types & Periods: American
& English Import Furniture,
Glassware, Crystal,
Porcelain, China
Specialties: Queen Anne &
Chippendale Dining Chairs,
Banquet Tables
Directions: 6 Corners Next
to Lafayette Lumber Co

LEBLANC'S ANTIQUES
618 St John   70501
318 234-2000
Proprietor: Marty L
LeBlanc
Hours: Tues-Sat 9:30-5
Types & Periods: Early
Louisiana, French &
American Walnut &
Mahogany
Specialties: Beds & Brass
Light Fixtures
Directions: Off Thru-Way
onto Mudd, to St John,
Corner Congress & St
John

Lake Charles

BARBARA'S ANTIQUES
2140 Kirkman St   70601
318 436-2103   Est: 1971
Proprietor: George &
Barbara Woolman
Hours: Thurs-Sat 10-5, By
Appointment
Types & Periods:
Specialized in Restored
Furniture, French, American,
English
Specialties: French Furniture
Directions: Corner of 14th
St, on Kirkman btwn I-10
& Bypass 210

THE BRASS BELL
3311 Ernest St   70601
318 477-8447   Est: 1974
Proprietor: Emily Coleman

Hours: Mon 1-5:30,
Tues-Sat 9:30-5:30,
Closed Sun
Types & Periods: European
& American Furniture &
Accessories
Specialties: Native Baskets,
Nostalgic Kitchen Pieces
Directions: 1/2 block off
I-20, Exit Lake or Ryan St

LAUGHLIN'S ANTIQUES
3433 Patrick St   70601
318 477-2564   Est: 1973
Proprietor: Albert Jr &
Vergia Laughlin
Hours: Daily 9-5, Closed
Sun
Types & Periods: Handmade
Primitives, Furniture,
Pressed & Depression
Glass, Pottery
Directions: Ryan St Exit
off I-210, S I block, Turn E
on E La Grange I block

Mandeville

WIND HAVEN ANTIQUES
2143 Lake Shore Dr
                      70448
504 626-3374   Est: 1952
Proprietor: Dale M Gale
Hours: Daily
Types & Periods: English
1790-1900, Country Oak &
Pine, Regency Mahogany,
Chinese Teakwood,
Coromandel Screen,
Cloisonne
Specialties: Books,
Paintings, Bottles, Louisiana
Cypress Furniture,
Cloisonne, Bronze, Porcelain
Appraisal Service Available
Directions: Directly across
the Causeway on Lake
Pontchartrain from New
Orleans

Metairie

B & F UPHOLSTERY
3210 Metairie Rd   70001
504 831-1955   Est: 1972
Proprietor: Floyd J Holmes
Hours: Mon-Sat 8-4:30, By
Appointment, By Chance
Types & Periods: Oaks,
Mahoganies, Walnuts,
Teakwoods & Ebonies, Buy
& Sell

Specialties: " Love to Deal
in Hand-Carved & Diamond
Tufted Upholstered
Furniture"
Appraisal Service Available
Directions: Exit I-10 at
Causeway Blvd S to
Metairie Rd, Corner of
Metairie & Causeway

CASTLE & COTTAGE ANTIQUES
204 Stella St   70005
504 834-9005   Est: 1972
Proprietor: R D Mackie
Hours: By Appointment
Types & Periods: English
18th & Early 19th Century
Mahogany and Early Oak
Pieces

Monroe

HOUSE OF EUROPE
1019 N 6th St   71201
318 322-3401   Est: 1974
Proprietor: Barry
Bernhardt & Walter Krauss
Hours: Daily 10-5, No
Weekends
Types & Periods: European,
English, American
Specialties: Furniture
(Restoration)
Directions: 3rd block N of
Hwy 80

JIMBEE ANTIQUES
903 N Second St   71201
318 323-9416
Proprietor: Bee & Jim
Balluff
Hours: Daily, Weekends
9:30-5, Closed Sun
Types & Periods: Glass,
China, Jewelry, Furniture,
Sabino

KLOCK KRAFTS
2311 S Grand   71201
318 387-8090   Est: 1972
Proprietor: Charles E
Wilkins
Hours: Daily
Types & Periods: Furniture,
Clocks
Specialties: Clocks

New Orleans

A-ANTIQUES
5423 Magazine St 70115
504 899-3001 Est: 1958
Proprietor: Roy A Slocum
Hours: Tues-Sat, 1/2 Day
Mon
Types & Periods:
Furniture-17th, 18th & 19th
Centuries, Bric-A-Brac
Specialties: Glass,
Porcelains
Appraisal Service Available
Directions: In the Garden
District btwn Jefferson &
Octavia

ANTIQUES UNLIMITED
2855 Magazine St 70115
504 891-9948 Est: 1972
Proprietor: G A Guidroz &
M Charbonnet
Hours: Daily 9-5, Closed
Sun
Types & Periods: 18th
Century to Edwardian,
American, French, English
Specialties: Wholesale &
Retail
Appraisal Service Available
Directions: At Corner of
6th St

ANTOINETTE'S
237 Royal 70130
504 523-6952 Est: 1938
Proprietor: Ezra Feldman
Hours: Sept-May 9-5,
Mon-Sat; June, July,
Aug-Weekdays 9-5, Sat
9-1
Types & Periods: French &
English 18th & 19th
Centuries Furniture,
Porcelain, Glass, Sculpture,
General Line & Decorative
Pieces, Jewelry
Directions: Across St from
Monteleone Hotel

AS YOU LIKE IT
3929 Magazine St 70115
504 897-6915 Est: 1969
Proprietor: Helen Cox
Hours: Mon-Sat 12-5
Types & Periods:
Silver-Sterling & Silverplate,
Unusual Holloware
Directions: In the Heart of
the Antique District

**THE BANK
ARCHITECTURALS**
5435 Magazine St 70115
504 891-4523 Est: 1971
Proprietor: Mike Wilkerson
Hours: Mon-Sat
Types & Periods: Early
American & Victorian
Architectural
Specialties: Beveled &
Stained Glass, Doors,
Mantels, Shutters
Appraisal Service Available
Directions: Uptown New
Orleans

BEP'S ANTIQUES INC
3921 & 3923 Magazine St
70115
504 891-3468 Est: 1975
Proprietor: Bep De Jonge
Hours: Daily 10-5
Types & Periods: English &
Scottish-Import Containers,
Furniture, China, Cut & Art
Glass, Copper, Brass,
Clocks, Jewelry,
Bric-A-Brac, Bottles &
Crocks
Appraisal Service Available
Directions: "Get on the
Interstate that goes into
Town, Exit at St Charles,
Follow St Charles away
from the Central City,
Take a Left on Louisiana,
Take a Right on
Magazine, It's a few
blocks down"

**BLACKAMOOR ANTIQUES
INC**
3433 Magazine St 70115
504 897-2711 Est: 1965
Proprietor: A F Masters &
D T Ballard
Hours: Tues-Sat 10-5
Types & Periods: 18th
Century English & French,
Chinese Porcelain

BRASS & COPPER SHOP
518 Chartres St 70130
504 522-2031
Proprietor: I A I, Inc
Hours: Daily 10-5:30
Types & Periods: Brass,
Copper, Bronze Pieces of
Various Types & Dates
Specialties: Antiques &
Reproductions, Chandeliers,
Vases, Statuary, Specialty
Items

Directions: In the French
Quarter, Across the St
from Royal Orleans Hotel
Parking Garage

**CARROLLTON LUMBER
AND WRECKING CO, INC**
2940 Leonidas St 70118
504 861-3681/3682
Est: 1929
Proprietor: Henry G
DeFraites, Jr
Hours: Mon-Fri 8-5,
Closed at Noon, Sat 1-5
Types & Periods: Early
American & French
Provincial
Specialties: Building
Materials, Interior & Exterior
Directions: 8600 Block
Earhart Blvd

CASEY & CASEY, INC
621 Toulouse St 70130
504 525-8390 Est: 1935
Hours: Mon-Sat
Types & Periods: English,
18th & 19th Centuries
Directions: French Quarter

CASS-GARR COMPANY
235-37 Chartres St 70130
504 522-8298 Est: 1975
Proprietor: Angelo A
Cassimus
Types & Periods: 18th &
19th Centuries Bric-A-Brac,
Porcelain, Cloisonne,
Bronzes & Gift Items
Specialties: Cloisonne &
Bronzes
Directions: Vieux Carre
(French Quarter)

COLLECTOR ANTIQUES
2900 Magazine St 70115
504 897-0904, 899-0230
Est: 1976
Proprietor: Emmarie M
Mayer
Hours: Mon-Sat 10-5
Types & Periods: English &
American 18th & 19th
Centuries
Specialties: Linens, Clothes,
Furniture, Silver, Jewelry,
Bric-A-Brac, Primitives,
Quilts
Appraisal Service Available
Directions: Magazine St at
6th St

THE COLONY LTD
3424 Magazine St   70115
504 891-2643   Est: 1966
Proprietor: Dr Robert B
Smythe
Hours: Daily 11:30-4:15,
Closed Sun
Types & Periods: English &
French Furniture, English &
Chinese Export Porcelains,
Paintings
Specialties: Oriental
Directions: '' Magazine St
Bus from Canal St''

DIXON ANTIQUE & GIFT
641 Royal   70130
504 523-6308   Est: 1974
Proprietor: Mary & Dave
Dixon
Hours: Mon-Sat 10-5:30,
Closed Sun
Types & Periods: English,
French, Oriental Furniture,
Porcelains, Cut Glass,
Objets d'Art, Jade & Ivories,
Silver, Jewelry, China,
Paintings, Oriental Rugs
Directions: In the Heart of
the French Quarter

ENGLISH ANTIQUES
5533 Magazine St   70115
504 891-3803   Est: 1068
Proprietor: William C
Maute
Hours: Tues-Sat, By
Appointment
Types & Periods: 18th &
Early 19th Centuries English
Furniture imported directly
from England

FINDERS KEEPERS
3150 Calhoun St   70125
504 866-7903   Est: 1968
Proprietor: Coleman &
Treleaven
Hours: Mon-Sat
Types & Periods: English
1800's
Directions: Near University

FLAIR INC
1423 Joseph St   70115
504 899-5777   Est: 1961
Proprietor: Dooley
Chalaron, Bitsy Duggins,
Mimi Stamps
Hours: Daily, Closed Sun
Types & Periods: 18th &
19th Centuries Furniture,
China, Lap Desks, Chests,
Tables, Chairs, Mirrors,
Pictures, Silver, Crystal

Appraisal Service Available
Directions: Uptown, 2
blocks off St Charles Ave
btwn Nashville Ave &
Jefferson Ave

FLEUR DE LIS ANTIQUES
3912 Magazine St   70115
504 899-4104   Est: 1976
Proprietor: Mr & Mrs A P
Claverie
Hours: Tues, Thurs-Sat
10:30-4, Closed Sun, Mon
& Wed, By Appointment
Types & Periods: English
18th & 19th Centuries, Early
1900's American & French
Furniture, China, Brass
Specialties: Furniture, Queen
Anne Chairs, Gate Leg
Tables, Chest of Drawers
Directions: Center of
Town, One of 75 Shops,
On Premises Parking

GARGOYLE
5725 Magazine St   70115
504 895-6928   Est: 1974
Proprietor: Alicia Grande
Hours: Mon-Sat
Types & Periods: American,
English
Directions: Corner
Nashville & Magazine

GRANNY HAD ONE
3717 Magazine   70115
504 899-0014   Est: 1974
Proprietor: R Breaux & K
Bondurant
Hours: Mon-Sat, Sun by
Appointment
Types & Periods: General,
American, English,
European, Oriental,
Furniture, Bric-A-Brac,
Silver, China, "From 17th
Century thru Art Deco"
Appraisal Service Available
Directions: Across Canal
St from the French
Quarter

THE HABERSHAM SHOP
434 Barracks St   70116
504 522-7048   Est: 1973
Proprietor: Jerry L Dixon
Hours: Daily, Weekends,
Closed Tues & Wed
Types & Periods: Furniture,
Porcelain, Glassware,
Decorative Accessories,
Crystal

Directions: Corner
Barracks at Decatur, Just
Behind Old US Mint, In
French Quarter

**HAMILTON HOUSE
ANTIQUES**
422 Chartres St   70130
504 581-4960   Est: 1973
Proprietor: Corporation
Hours: Mon-Sat 9:30-5
Types & Periods: Early
English Primitives, Furniture
Specialties: China, Brass,
Copper
Directions: Center of
Vieux Carre

**HERITAGE GALLERIES
ANTIQUES**
8216 Oak St   70118
504 861-4492   Est: 1972
Proprietor: C Craig
Babylon
Hours: Daily, Weekends,
By Appointment
Types & Periods: Stained
Glass, Beveled Glass,
Entrance Sets, Architectural
Items, Iron Fencing, Brass
Hardware, Brass Light
Fixtures, Furniture
Specialties: Glass (Stained &
Beveled)
Appraisal Service Available
Directions: 2 blocks off
Carrollton Ave

KNIGHT'S ANTIQUES
3927 Magazine St   70115
504 895-3927   Est: 1973
Proprietor: James S
Knight
Hours: Daily, Closed Sun
& Mon Except by
Appointment
Types & Periods: Victorian,
English, American, 19th
Century, Country &
Primitives
Specialties: Old Tools, Iron
Items
Appraisal Service Available
Directions: Parallel to St
Charles

**LAMPE'S ANTIQUE &
GOURMET SHOPPE**
3918 Old Gentilly Rd
70126
· Est: 1975
Proprietor: Mr & Mrs Fred
Lampe

New Orleans   Cont'd

LAMPE'S   Cont'd
Hours: Mon-Tues,
Thurs-Sat 10-5:30, Closed
Sun & Wed
Types & Periods: Victorian,
English, Early American
Specialties: In Conjunction
with Art Gallery, Sell &
Display American Primitive
Art
Directions: E New
Orleans, Across from
Baptist Theological
Seminary

STAN LEVY IMPORTS
3128 Magazine St   70115
504 482-8536
Proprietor: Stanley G Levy
Hours: Daily 8:30-6
Types & Periods: English
Imports, Furniture, China,
Glass

MAGAZINE ARCADE
3017 Magazine St   70115
504 899-9144   Est: 1976
Proprietor: M Deane &
Eight Other Dealers
Hours: Mon-Sat 10-4
Types & Periods: Furniture,
Bric-A-Brac, American
Paper, Nostalgia,
Collectibles, Books, Stock
Varies
Specialties: Several Dealers
Under One Roof
Directions: Magazine St
btwn 7th & 8th Sts

CAMILLE MAHER
ANTIQUES & GIFTS
5408 Magazine St   70115
504 897-6849   Est: 1973
Proprietor: Camille Maher
Hours: Mon-Sat 10-4, Sat
10-5
Types & Periods: European
& American Antiques &
Collectibles, Neo-Antiques
Specialties: Dolls,
Miniatures, Work of Local &
Regional Artists & Craftsmen
Directions: Magazine St
Bus from Central Business
District (Canal St) &
Central Hotel Locations

MANHEIM GALLERIES
403-409 Royal St   70130
504 568-1901   Est: 1918
Proprietor: A G Manheim
Hours: Mon-Sat 9-5,
Closed Sat June-Aug
Types & Periods: English,
French, Continental,
Oriental, Furniture,
Porcelain, Painting,
Chandeliers, Mantels,
Boehm & Cybis Porcelains
Specialties: Large Jade
Collection, Oriental Objets
d'Art, Handmade Furniture
Appraisal Service Available
Directions: Corner of Conti
and Royal Sts in French
Quarter

THE MARINER INC
622 Saint Peter St   70116
504 523-6375   Est: 1966
Proprietor: F H Sellars.
Hours: Daily 9-5, Closed
Sun
Types & Periods: Marine &
Nautical Artifacts Only
Appraisal Service Available
Directions: French
Quarter, 1/2 block from
Jackson Square

MORTON'S AUCTION AND
SALES CO
643 Magazine St   70130
Proprietor: Morton
Goldberg
Hours: Mon-Sat 8:30-5:30
Types & Periods: Early
English, French & American,
Oriental Antiques & Rugs,
Silver, Paintings, China &
Porcelain, Cut Glass &
Crystal, Victorian, Edwardian
Antiques
Specialties: Furniture &
Paintings Native to the
South
Appraisal Service Available
Directions: Downtown New
Orleans near New Hilton
Hotel

NEARING'S ANTIQUES
526 Royal St   70130
504 525-2767   Est: 1948
Proprietor: Mrs Lois S
Vales
Hours: Mon-Sat 10-4:30
Types & Periods: Antique
Jewelry & Sterling Silver
Flatware

Specialties: Historical Maps
(US & World), Antique Prints
Directions: In the Heart of
the French Quarter

NEW ORLEANS ANTIQUE
MALL
511 North Solomon St
70124
504 488-0918   Est: 1977
Proprietor: Joseph F
Wegman
Hours: Mon-Sat 8:30-5:30
Types & Periods: All
Periods-All Types, Anything
Antique and is in Good
Condition
Specialties: The Rare-The
Unusual
Appraisal Service Available
Directions: Off 4100 Block
of Famous Canal St

THE OLD MINT RUMMAGE
SHOP
1305 Decatur   70116
504 524-9967   Est: 1970
Proprietor: Marie Williams
Hours: Weekends
Types & Periods: General
Line
Specialties: Toys (Dolls)
Directions: Across from
the Old New Orleans Mint

THE OLD OAKEN BUCKET
4537 Magazine St   70115
504 895-0889   Est: 1968
Proprietor: Fran
McCracken & Juliana
Robert
Hours: Daily, Weekends,
By Appointment
Types & Periods: Early
American Country &
Primitives, All Period
American
Specialties: Early American
Country

OLDE TOWN
ANTIQUE SHOPPE
323 Opelousas Ave
70114
504 366-1939   Est: 1977
Proprietor: Jewel L
Salathe
Hours: Tues-Sat
Types & Periods: Victorian,
Empire, Early American, Oak
Furniture, Bric A-Brac
Specialties: Victorian

Directions: At Algiers Point, W Bank of New Orleans, Across Mississippi River Bridge

THE OPERA-TUNITY SHOP
3933 Magazine St   70115
504 897-3505   Est: 1974
Proprietor: Women's Guild of the New Orleans Opera Assoc
Hours: Daily 10-4, Closed Sun, Mon 1-4
Types & Periods: 18th Century English thru Victorian, Glassware, Silver, Collectibles
Directions: Uptown New Orleans on Magazine Bus Rte

PETERS' TRADING POST
1530 Magazine St   70130
504 524-0057   Est: 1977
Proprietor: David & Judy Peters
Hours: Tues-Sat, By Chance
Types & Periods: A Little of Everything
Specialties: Bottles, Silver, Collectibles
Directions: Close to Coliseum Square

M S RAU, INC
630 Royal St   70130
504 522-4120, 523-5660
    Est: 1912
Proprietor: M S Rau, Inc
Hours: Mon-Sat 8:15-5, Sun 9-Noon, By Appointment
Types & Periods: Victorian, Americana, English, French, Oriental, Cut Glass, China, Iron, Silver, Brass, Copper, Bronze, Chandeliers, Mirrors, Furniture & Decorative Accessories
Specialties: Ornamental Iron, Garden Accessories, Victorian Furniture, Cut Glass
Appraisal Service Available
Directions: In the Heart of the Vieux Carre (French Quarter)

THE RENAISSANCE INC
1101 First St   70130
504 529-2286   Est: 1968
Proprietor: Jean Diaz
Hours: Daily

Types & Periods: 18th & 19th Century English, American, French, Chinese & Japanese Furniture, Porcelain, Bric-A-Brac
Directions: Corner of First St & Magazine St in the Garden District

CHARLES F RUSSO-ANTIQUES
3112 Magazine St   70115
504 899-6237   Est: 1954
Proprietor: Charles F Russo
Hours: Mon-Sat
Types & Periods: American, Victorian & Empire, Some 1900-1920, Some English Imports, Brass, Copper Gift Items, Reproduction of Bakers Racks
Specialties: American, Victorian & Empire, Reproduction Gift Items in Brass & Copper, Reproduction of Bakers Racks
Directions: Located in Heart of Antiques Section of the city on world famous Magazine St. Everyone knows where Magazine St is

ST CHARLES ANTIQUES LTD
2125 St Charles Ave
    70130
504 524-0243   Est: 1973
Proprietor: Frank Rizza MD
Hours: Mon-Sat
Types & Periods: 18th & 19th Centuries Furniture, Paintings, Porcelain
Specialties: Furniture, English, Oriental Porcelain
Appraisal Service Available
Directions: In Old Garden District Mansion Above Lee Circle

SAROUK SHOP
3033 Magazine St   70115
504 891-9574   Est: 1973
Proprietor: Bob Rue
Hours: Mon-Sat
Types & Periods: Antique Oriental Carpets
Specialties: Repair & Cleaning

Appraisal Service Available
Directions: Corner 8th & Magazine in the Garden District

SHIRLEY'S ANTIQUES
3956 Magazine St   70115
504 899-2478   Est: 1971
Proprietor: Tom Althans
Hours: Daily
Types & Periods: Early American & English Furniture & Glassware
Specialties: Furniture, (Victorian), Bric-A-Brac
Appraisal Service Available
Directions: Btwn Napoleon & Louisiana Aves

SIXPENCE INC
4904 Magazine St   70115
504 895-1267   Est: 1972
Proprietor: Doris Cerise, Glen Eagan, Betty Fowler
Hours: Mon-Sat 10-4
Types & Periods: English, American, 18th & 19th Centuries Furniture, Objets d'Art
Appraisal Service Available

NINA SLOSS ANTIQUES & INTERIORS
6008 Magazine St   70118
504 895-8088, 895-7668
    Est: 1962
Proprietor: Mrs Fred Maclin Sloss
Hours: Mon-Sat
Types & Periods: 18th Century English, Some 19th Century, 18th & 19th Centuries French, Oriental Porcelains, Ironstone, Accessories
Specialties: Chairs, Oriental (Mostly 18th Century) Vases
Appraisal Service Available
Directions: Uptown, Corner of State & Magazine

TOMATO WAREHOUSE
430 Barracks St   70116
504 522-2645   Est: 1972
Proprietor: Jake R Grilletta
Hours: Daily 10-6, Closed Tues & Wed
Types & Periods: Nostalgia, Art Nouveau, Art Deco, Primitive, Victorian, Glass, Wood, Bric-A-Brac
Directions: Back of Old US Mint, 1 block from Community Flea Market

New Orleans   Cont'd

THE UPTOWNER ANTIQUES
1305 Dublin St   70118
504 866-3520   Est: 1973
Proprietor: James M
Schneider
Hours: Daily, Tues-Sat
10-5
Types & Periods: 18th &
19th Centuries French &
English Furniture, Chinese
Export & English Porcelain,
Lamps, Coffee Tables, Lap
Desks, Cuttery Trays
  Directions: One block off
  Carrollton Ave, Uptown
  New Orleans

THE VILLAGE OLDE
3943 Magazine St   70115
504 895-7071   Est: 1965
Proprietor: Marvin E
Bennett
Hours: Daily 10-6, Sun
1-5, Wed 'til 9
Types & Periods: 18th
Century English,
Turn-of-the-Century,
American, Oriental,
Primitives, "Very Eclectic"

WALDHORN COMPANY INC
343 Royal St   70130
504 581-6379   Est: 1881
Proprietor: Stephen A
Moses
Hours: Mon-Sat
Types & Periods: 18th &
19th Centuries English
Furniture, Porcelain, Silver &
Plate, English & American
Jewelry
  Directions: French
  Quarter, Corner of Royal
  & Conti Sts

WHISNANT GALLERIES
319 Rue Chartres   70130
504 524-9766   Est: 1968
Proprietor: Pete Whisnant
& Felix Landry III
Hours: Mon-Sat 10-5:30
Types & Periods: Unusual
Collectibles, Decorator
Pieces, Oil Paintings,
Jewelry, Furniture,
Porcelain, Hardstone
Carvings, Ivory, Bronzes
Specialties: French Furniture
& Oriental

Directions: 2½ blocks from
Canal St opposite the Dela
Poste Hotel

WHITE PILLARS EMPORIUM
8238 Oak St   70118
504 861-7113   Est: 1969
Proprietor: Angelo Ricca &
Kelvin Delaney
Hours: Mon-Sat 10-5
Types & Periods: Leaded
Stained & Beveled Glass
Windows, Victorian
Architectural Embellishments
Specialties: Ceiling Fans,
Bar Furnishings, Nostalgic
Advertising
  Directions: Follow St
  Charles St Car Tracks to
  Carrollton Ave & Oak St,
  About 5 blocks from
  Corner of Charles &
  Carrollton, 2 blocks off
  Carrollton Ave on Oak St

Ponchatoula

ARNETT'S ANTIQUES
135 SW Railroad Ave
                    70454
504 386-2007   Est: 1976
Proprietor: Mrs Shirley G
Arnett
Hours: Daily, Weekends,
Closed Mon
Types & Periods: Primitive,
English Formal, Country
English, Early American, Cut
Glass, Crystal, Bric-A-Brac,
Books
Specialties: (Chinese Stack
Tables), Stamps, Meissen
China
  Directions: Diagonally
  across from "Country
  Market", Across from
  Bicentennial Museum, 1/2
  block off Hwy 51 or 1 Mile
  off Interstate to New
  Orleans

THE CARRIAGE HOUSE ANTIQUES
PO Box 308   70454
504 386-2449   Est: 1976
Proprietor: Mrs Shirley C
Jackson
Hours: Mon-Sat, By
Appointment
Types & Periods: General
Line
  Directions: Hwy 22, W 1½
  Miles from I-55 Overpass

THE PIONEER SHOPPE
101 W Pine St   70454
504 386-3002   Est: 1976
Proprietor: Mr & Mrs L C
Larrieu
Hours: Daily
Types & Periods: Early
American Furniture
  Directions: Corner of W
  Pine St & Railroad Ave

St Francisville

CABIN CRAFTS
Rte 5, Box 438   70775
504 635-6312   Est: 1975
Proprietor: Mrs Anne B
Poindexter
Hours: Tues-Sat 10-4
Types & Periods: Primitives,
General Line
Specialties: Needlework
(Quilts), White Oak Baskets
  Directions: US Hwy 61, 2
  Miles N of Town

MYRTLES ANTIQUES & GIFTS
Hwy 61   70775
504 635-6277   Est: 1975
Proprietor: Arlin K Dease,
Robert S Ward & Stephen
M Saunders
Hours: Daily
Types & Periods: 18th &
19th Century English,
French & American
Specialties: Architectural,
Primitives
Appraisal Service Available
  Directions: 1 Mile N of
  I-10 & Hwy 61

OLD KITCHEN SHOP
Cottage Plantation,
Hwy 61   70775
504 635-3674   Est: 1952
Proprietor: Mrs Eudora S
Brown
Hours: Daily
Types & Periods: General
Line, Cut Glass, Silver,
Pressed Glass, China,
Brass, Iron, Botfles
  Directions: 6 Miles N of St
  Francisville on Hwy 61

SHADETREE ANTIQUES
Royal at Ferdinand 70775
504 635-6116   Est: 1974
Proprietor: Kenneth Wood
Kennon

Hours: Mon, Wed-Sat
10-5, Sun 12-5, Closed
Tues
Types & Periods: Tables,
Cypress Benches, Chairs,
Hall Trees, Old Hardware,
Brass
Specialties: Rainbow Crystal,
Quilts, Jewelry, Pottery,
Corn Shuck Weavings
Directions: Royal at
Ferdinand, W End of Town
on Hill across the Street
from Catholic Church

**TROY ANTIQUES & GIFT
SHOP**
Hwy 956   70775
504 635-3662
Proprietor: Mary Alice
Lambert
Hours: Daily, Weekends
10-5, Closed Sun & Mon
Types & Periods: General
Line, Furniture

St Joseph

IDLE ISLE ANTIQUES
River Rd   71366
318 766-3902
Proprietor: Lou & Howard
Jones
Hours: Daily 10-5, Closed
Noon Hour
Types & Periods: Furniture,
Cut Glass, R S Prussia,
Silver, China

Shreveport

SHREVEPORT CLUSTER
Directions: Scattered
Shops throughout City,
Some concentration on
the Adjacent Sts of
Fairfield Ave (1000-2000
Blocks), Texas Ave &
Youree Dr

ALEXANDER ANTIQUES
3106 Centenary Blvd
                      71104
318 868-0459   Est: 1962
Proprietor: Lura G
Alexander
Hours: Mon-Sat 9-5

Types & Periods: Period
Furniture, China, Brass,
Copper, Silver
Directions: Corner of
Kings Hwy

ANTIQUEDADES SHOP
201-207 E Stoner   71101
318 221-3717   Est: 1966
Proprietor: Hi Lawrence
Hours: Tues-Sat 10-5
Types & Periods: American
Furniture
Directions: Stoner btwn
Youree Dr & Centenary
Blvd

EMILY ZUM BRUNNEN INC
635 Stoner   71101
318 221-5540   Est: 1973
Proprietor: Emily Zum
Brunnen
Hours: Mon-Sat 9-5
Types & Periods: 18th
Century English Furniture &
Oriental Rugs & Accessories
Specialties: English Period
Furniture
Directions: Exit Off I-20,
Left on Stoner

MANNING'S ANTIQUES
6235 Greenwood Rd
                      71119
318 635-0911
Proprietor: R M Manning
Hours: Daily, Weekends
9-5, Closed Sun
Types & Periods: Furniture,
American Cut Glass
Specialties: American Cut
Glass
Directions: I-20, Exit 10

MAY'S ANTIQUES
2713 Fairfield Ave   71104
318 422-6297
Proprietor: Elizabeth &
Joe May
Hours: Daily, Weekends
9-5, Closed Sun
Types & Periods: Period,
English & Dutch Furniture,
General Line

STANLEY J SADLER CO
1905 Fairfield Ave   71101
318 221-3571   Est: 1960
Proprietor: Mr & Mrs
Stanton Dossett & Stanley
J Sadler
Hours: Daily, By
Appointment

Types & Periods: Furniture,
Oriental Rugs, English &
Oriental Porcelains
Specialties: Paintings
Appraisal Service Available

T S STATION CABOOSE
750 Shreveport-Barksdale
Hwy   71105
318 865-3594
Hours: Daily 11-4
Types & Periods: English
Victorian Pieces, Hall Trees,
Wash Stands, Lap Desks,
Hutches, Tea Caddies
Directions: Line Ave S Off
I-20, Left at Kings Hwy, 3
Miles to Shop

Sulphur

GRANNY'S FLEA MARKET
1278 Napoleon   70663
318 527-9333   Est: 1972
Proprietor: Faye & Eddie
Ward
Hours: Weekends, By
Chance
Types & Periods: Glassware,
Furniture, Jewelry
Directions: E Hwy 90
Across from VFW Hall

Ville Platte

RAGIN' CAJUN ANTIQUES
105 W Cotton St   70586

Zwolle

THE LEPRECHAUN
Box 467E   71486
713 645-6672   Est: 1976
Proprietor: Peggy O'Neill
Hours: Daily, Weekends,
By Appointment

The above Federal Couch is a transitional piece. It has the smaller size of the earlier Federal Period, but is beginning to exhibit such Empire characteristics as the Lion's Paw feet. The lower couch has made the complete transition to Empire with larger scale and greater visual mass.

STATE OF MAINE

Alfred

BEEHIVE ANTIQUES
Oak St   04002
207 324-0990   Est: 1971
Proprietor: J Morningstar
& D Smoot
Hours: By Appointment
Types & Periods: 19th
Century
Specialties: Musical
Instruments, Reed Organs,
Repair, Restoration
  Directions: Rte 202 & 4,
  Across from Country
  Store, Center of Town

RENEE BOWEN ANTIQUES
Alfred Square   04002
207 324-4446   Est: 1974
Proprietor: Renee Bowen
& Jim Hastrich
Hours: Mon-Fri, Closed
Tues
Types & Periods: American
& Continental

**SOMEPLACE ELSE
ANTIQUES & BOOKS**
Oak St   04002
207 324-6292   Est: 1971
Proprietor: Connie & Bob
Canney
Hours: By Appointment,
By Chance
Types & Periods: General
Line, Furniture, Glass,
China, Woodenware,
Baskets, Quilts
Specialties: Books, Furniture
  Directions: Across from
  Village Green on Hwy
  202 & 4

Ashville

BEDFORD'S BARN
PO Box 386   04607
207 963-7715   Est: 1964
Proprietor: David & Holly
Colton-Manheim
Hours: Mon-Sun
Types & Periods: General
Line, Primitives, Glass,
Books
  Directions: Rte 1 at 186 in
  W Gouldsboro

Augusta

CAMPBELL'S ANTIQUES
405 Western Ave   04330
207 622-5414   Est: 1959
Proprietor: Gloria
Campbell
Hours: Mon-Sun, Spring
thru Late Fall, Also By
Chance
Types & Periods: Victorian
Glass & China, Lamps,
Furniture, Primitives,
General Line
Specialties: China, Lamps &
Parts
Appraisal Service Available
  Directions: 2 Miles from W
  Side Augusta Rotary, 1/4
  Mile from I-95, W Exit US
  Rte 202, Near Holiday Inn

**CHARLES ANTIQUES &
BOOKS**
RFD 6   04330
207 445-2245   Est: 1968
Proprietor: Mabel Charles
Hours: By Chance
Types & Periods: General
Line, Collectibles
Specialties: Books,
Primitives
Appraisal Service Available
  Directions: 10 Miles E of
  Town on Rtes 202, 3 & 9

CUSHNOC SHOP
151 Sewall St   04330
207 622-5132   Est: 1972
Proprietor: Thelma Swain
& Mary Wells
Hours: Mon-Sat 11-5,
Closed Sun
Types & Periods: China,
Glass, Furniture, Primitives,
Silver, Jewelry
Specialties: Pressed Glass
  Directions: 2 Blocks S of
  State House

WHITE BARN ANTIQUES
Riverside Dr   04330
207 622-6096   Est: 1969
Proprietor: Eleanor N
Merrill
Hours: Mon-Sun 'til Labor
Day, Winter By
Appointment
Types & Periods: General
Line, Books

Appraisal Service Available
  Directions: 8 Miles from
  Augusta Exit off I-95, E
  Side of Augusta on Rte
  201 Going N to Waterville

Belfast

GOLD COAST ANTIQUES
RFD 1   04915
207 548-2939   Est: 1971
Proprietor: Vasco &
Marguerite Baldacci
Hours: Mon-Fri
Types & Periods: Victorian
Furniture, Lamps, Art Glass,
China, Bisque Dolls, Oil
Paintings
Specialties: China, Ivory,
China from Silesia
Appraisal Service Available
  Directions: US Rte 1 on
  Belfast Searsport

AVIS HOWELLS ANTIQUES
21 Pearl St   04915
207 338-3302
Proprietor: Avis & William
Howells
Hours: Daily By Chance,
By Appointment
Types & Periods: Furniture,
Shaker, Canton China,
Accessories
  Directions: Belfast
  Business Exit

Biddeford

OLD MILL ANTIQUES
59 Main St   04090
207 282-5358   Est: 1966
Proprietor: Robert F
Melanson
Hours: Mon-Sat, Sun By
Appointment, By Chance
Types & Periods: General
Line, Collectibles
Appraisal Service Available
  Directions: At Intersection
  of US 1 & Main St Turn
  Right, (When Traveling N)
  Go 4 Blocks

ROLAND'S ANTIQUES
167 Elm St   04005
207 284-6997
Proprietor: Roland
Sylvestre
Hours: Daily April to Jan
10-5, Closed Sun
Types & Periods: Glass,
China, Orientals, Pewter,
Paintings

Boothbay Harbor

THE LITTLE BARN
86 Commercial St   04538
207 882-7742
Proprietor: Shirley
Andrews
Hours: Mon-Sat July 1 to
Sept 15, Closed Sun
Types & Periods: 18th &
19th Century Furniture,
Porcelain, Pewter, Copper,
Brass
Directions: Next to Maine
Trading Post

Bowdoinham

OLD GLASS SHOP
Upper Main St   04008
207 666-8805
Proprietor: Norman &
Daisy Nye
Hours: Mon-Fri
Types & Periods: General
Line, Glass, China, Linens

Brewer

**THE CHAMBERLAIN
CARRIAGE HOUSE
ANTIQUES & NOT**
350 N Main St   04412
207 989-7412   Est: 1977
Proprietor: Rose E
Demaso
Hours: Tues-Sat, Also By
Appointment, By Chance
Types & Periods: Early to
Late 19th Century, Furniture,
Glass, China, Silver
Specialties: Collection of
Dogs Belonging to a 100
Year Old Woman,
Papier-Mache, Iron,
Celluloid, Chalk, China
Directions: Across from
Cox's Lodge

**KENNETH L TAYLOR
ANTIQUES GALLERIES**
990 Wilson St   04412
207 989-3794   Est: 1948
Proprietor: Kenneth L
Taylor
Hours: Mon-Fri
Types & Periods: Queen
Anne Period Pieces,
Victorian Furniture, Hanging
Lamps, Leaded Shades,
Clocks, Watches
Specialties: Paintings, Prints,
Classic Cars
Appraisal Service Available
Directions: Rte 1A

Bridgton

BLUE MOOSE ANTIQUES
89 Main St   04009
                Est: 1969
Proprietor: Ivy L Carlson
Hours: Mon-Fri in
Summer, Winters By
Appointment
Types & Periods: General
Line, Furniture, Glass
Directions: Center of
Village

**THE BROWSING HOUSE
ANTIQUES**
55 N High St   04009
207 647-2432   Est: 1963
Proprietor: Jenifer Johns
Hours: Mon-Sat May-Nov,
By Appointment in Winter
Types & Periods: Furniture,
Dishes, Books, Bric-a-brac,
General Line
Directions: Rte 302

Bristol

MARY & GENE KLEBE
Rte 130   04539
207 677-2633   Est: 1951
Proprietor: Mary & Gene
Klebe
Hours: Mon-Sat 10-5,
Closed Sun
Types & Periods: Glass,
China, Wood, Metals,
Victorian Period
Directions: On Rte 130
Out Of Damariscotta, 8
Miles from US Rte 1 on
Road to Pemaquid Point

Brunswick

**BRUNSWICK ANTIQUE
MALL**
341 Bath Rd   04011
207 725-6262
Proprietor: Eugene J
Lussier Jr, Mgr
Hours: Oct-May Wed-Sun
9-5, June-Sept Tues-Sun
9-5
Types & Periods: General
Line, 20 Dealers
Directions: 1 Mile N of
Cook's Corner

**OLD BARN ANNEX
ANTIQUES**
RFD 2 Gurnet Rd   04011
207 729-8975   Est: 1967
Proprietor: Emery Goff
Hours: By Appointment,
By Chance
Types & Periods: Pine
Furniture, Primitives,
Country Items, Carousel
Horses
Appraisal Service Available
Directions: 3.9 Miles S on
Rte 24 from Cooks Corner

Bryant Pond

DELFT BOWL ANTIQUES
Lower Main St   04219
                Est: 1967
Proprietor: Arthur E Lien
Hours: Daily 10-5, Closed
Wed May-Nov, Off Season
By Appointment
Types & Periods: General
Line, 18th & 19th Century,
Collectibles
Specialties: Glass, Pottery,
Porcelain
Appraisal Service Available
Directions: On Rte 26 in
Center of Village, Phone
207 Bryant Pond 58, "Still
have crank phones,
Operator assistance is
needed"

MOLL OCKETT ANTIQUES
Lower Main St   04219
Proprietor: Starr D Seguin
Hours: Thur-Sun 11-5,
Mar-Dec
Types & Periods: General
Line, Tin
Specialties: Books
Directions: Phone 80

Buckfield

**THE BRIDGE HOUSE &
RED BARN**
By The Bridge   04220
207 336-2604   Est: 1959
Proprietor: David & Ruth
Winslow-Field
Hours: Tues-Sat
Types & Periods: Furniture,
Glass, China
Specialties: Antique Houses
& Building Materials
Directions: Rte 117, In
Middle of the Square, 9
Miles from Paris, 17 Miles
from Lewiston

Camden

RUFUS FOSHEE ANTIQUES
Belfast Rd   04843
207 236-2838
Proprietor: Rufus & Joan
Foshee
Hours: Mon-Fri, By
Appointment June-Oct
Types & Periods:
Spongeware, Spatterware,
Ironstone, 10th & Early 19th
Century English Pottery &
Porcelain, Yelloware,
Ceramics
Directions: 3½ Miles N on
Rte 1

THE RICHARDS ANTIQUES
93 Elm St   04843
207 236-2152   Est: 1957
Proprietor: Barbara &
Chad Richards
Hours: Daily 9-5,
June-Oct, Closed Wed &
Sun, Appointment
Advisable
Types & Periods: Furniture,
Decorative Accessories,
Primitives
Specialties: Lamps
Directions: On US Rte I, S
Side of Village

A SHOP IN THE GARDEN
25 Mountain St   04843
207 236-3906   Est: 1970
Proprietor: Mrs Eleonor D
Hodson
Hours: Mon-Fri 10-4,
June-Oct
Types & Periods: Early 19th
Century Furniture, China,
Glassware, Collectibles

Directions: N of Camden
on Rte 52 (Mountain St),
One Minute Drive from
Town

SUFFOLK GALLERY
47 Bay View   04843
207 236-8868   Est: 1972
Proprietor: Richard &
Marjorie Jones
Hours: Mon-Sun
Summer Only
Types & Periods: 18th &
19th Century English China,
19th Century European &
American Paintings, English
Furniture
Directions: Located on
Waterfront

SUFFOLK GALLERY
13 Elm St   04843
207 236-8868   Est: 1972
Proprietor: Richard &
Majorie Jones
Hours: Mon-Sat Open
All Year
Types & Periods: 18th &
19th Century English China,
19th Century European &
American Paintings, English
Furniture
Directions: Center of Town

TEN PLEASANT STREET
10 Pleasant St   04843
207 236-4352
Proprietor: Nicholas & Ann
Kuhn
Hours: Tues-Sat 10-4
Summer, Winter By
Appointment
Types & Periods: American
Quilts, Country Furniture,
Folk Art

RUTH TROIANI ANTIQUES
Rte 1 & Bay View St
                    04843
207 236-2745
Proprietor: Ruth Troiani
Hours: Mon-Fri 9-6,
June-Sept
Types & Periods: 18th &
19th Century American &
English Paintings, Furniture,
Pottery, Porcelain, Glass,
Lighting, Primitives

Canaan

ROBERTS ANTIQUES
Rt 2 PO Box 104   04924
207 474-3209
Proprietor: Charles
Roberts
Hours: Mon-Sat, Closed
Sun, By Appointment in
Winter
Types & Periods: General
Line, Furniture, China,
Glass, Silver, Books

Cape Elizabeth

PILLSBURY'S
Two Lights Rd   04107
207 799-0638
Proprietor: Mary Alice
Pillsbury
Hours: Mon-Sun, Also By
Appointment, By Chance
Types & Periods: Country
Pine & Oak Furniture,
Wooden & Tinware, Glass,
China
Directions: Located on
Road to Two Lights State
Park, Rte 77 from
Portland or Scarboro

THE PRIMITIVE PAST
300 Ocean House Rd
                    04843
207 799-4270
Proprietor: Jack &
Michelle Boyce
Hours: Tues-Fri 10-5,
Oct-March By
Appointment Only
Types & Periods: Country
Furniture & Accessories

Cape Neddick

ESTELLE'S ANTIQUES
Rte 1 Box 89   03902
207 363-4841   Est: 1965
Proprietor: Estelle V
Roberge
Hours: Mon-Fri 9-6, Also
By Appointment
Types & Periods: Cut Glass,
Nippon, Lamps, Sterling
Collectibles & Flatware,
Jewelry, Limoge, Collectibles
Specialties: Jewelry, Silver
Directions: 12 Miles N on
Rte 1 from NH Border

Cape Porpoise

PADDY'S COVE ANTIQUES
Ward Rd   04014
207 967-4842
Proprietor: Priscilla
Flannery
Hours: Mon-Fri 10-5,
Closed Tues May-Nov, By
Appointment, By Chance
in Winter
Types & Periods: Country
Furniture, Primitives,
General Line
Specialties: Furniture
(Cupboards)
Directions: 2 Miles from
Kennebunkport off Rte 9

Damariscotta

BRANNON-BUNKER INN
Rte 129   04543
207 563-5941   Est: 1978
Proprietor: David &
Charlene Bunker
Hours: Mon-Sun 9-5
May-Sept, Winter By
Chance
Types & Periods: General
Line, Country Antiques
Directions: 4 Miles S of
Damariscotta on Rte 129

THE DITTY BOX
Rte 1   04543
207 644-8390
Proprietor: Mrs George E
Lewis
Hours: Mon-Sat 10-5,
June 20-Sept 20
Types & Periods: Country
Furniture, American Folk Art
Directions: Adjacent to
Clarissa Illsley Tavern

PINE CHESTS & THINGS
Bristol Rd   04543
207 563-3267
Proprietor: Richard Else
Hours: Mon-Fri May
15th-Oct 1st, Winter By
Appointment or By
Chance
Types & Periods: General
Line

Deer Isle

JEFFERSON BORDEN 5th
Pressey Village Rd   04627
207 348-6015   Est: 1965
Proprietor: Jefferson
Borden 5th
Hours: By Appointment
Types & Periods: European,
Early American Porcelains,
Pottery, Books
Specialties: Books, Porcelain
Appraisal Service Available
Directions: Pressey
Village Rd

Douglass Hill

GLASS BASKET ANTIQUES
Rte 107   04024
207 787-3527
Proprietor: Dorothy-Lee
Jones
Hours: Mon-Sat
June 21-Sept 30
Types & Periods: 18th, 19th
& Early 20th Century Glass,
English, Continental & Far
Eastern Ceramics

Dover-Foxcroft

JENKINS ANTIQUES
56 W Main St   04426
207 564-2765
Proprietor: Grace L
Jenkins
Hours: Mon-Sat, Sun By
Appointment
Types & Periods: Glass,
Primitives, Furniture
Appraisal Service Available

**ROBERT G HALL-JOHN E
VIGUE**
9 Essex St   04426
207 564-3383
Proprietor: Robert G Hall
& John E Vigue
Hours: By Appointment
Types & Periods: American
Furniture & Accessories
Appraisal Service Available

Eliot

ARDELLE TAYLOR
173 Main St   03903
207 439-0422
Proprietor: Ardelle Taylor
Hours: By Appointment,
By Chance
Types & Periods: Colored
Glass, Small Furniture,
Primitives, China, Toys,
Paintings, Prints
Directions: On Rte 103,
About 1½ Miles Past
Marina on Left

Ellsworth

**CALISTA STERLING
ANTIQUES**
Bayside Rd Rte 230
04605
207 667-8991   Est: 1953
Proprietor: Calista Sterling
Hours: Mon-Sat
June-Sept, By
Appointment Oct-May
Types & Periods: Early
Period Furniture, Porcelain,
Soft Paste
Directions: From
Ellsworth, Rte 230,
Alternate Rte to Bar
Harbor

CINDY'S ANTIQUES
Box 244 Bucksport Rd
04605
207 667-4476
Proprietor: Lawrence
Clough
Hours: Mon-Fri
Types & Periods: General
Line
Directions: US Rtes 1 & 3

Farmington

**COUNTRY ANTIQUES &
FOLK ART**
94 High St   04938
207 778-3719
Proprietor: Tom & Sandy
Veillecex
Hours: Wed 9-5, Or By
Chance
Types & Periods: General
Line

DAVIS ANTIQUES
90 Perhman St   04938
207 778-4868
Joe & Jackie Davis
Hours: By Appointment,
By Chance
Types & Periods: Paper,
Stoneware, Tinware
Specialties: Country
Furniture

FROST'S ANTIQUES
RFD 3 Rte 4   04938
207 778-3761   Est: 1966
Proprietor: Donald &
Brenda Frost
Hours: Wed 11-5, Also By
Appointment, By Chance
Types & Periods: Furniture,
Primitives & Victorian
Specialties: Furniture,
Primitive Accessories
Directions: Rte 4, 5 Miles
N of Farmington

MAPLE AVENUE ANTIQUES
23 Maple Ave   04938
207 778-4850
Proprietor: Frank P
Dingley
Hours: Tues & Wed
July-Aug Other Times By
Appointment, By Chance
Types & Periods: Country
Furniture, Folk Art, General
Line

**STANWOOD PARK
AUCTION**
RFD 1 Box 224   04938
207 778-2168   Est: 1970
Proprietor: Larry & Jean
Dubord
Hours: Auctions
Types & Periods: Early
Americana Victorian, Oak
Appraisal Service Available
Directions: US Rte 2, 2
Miles SE of Farmington

THE STONE WALL SHOP
Rte 27 New Vineyard Rd
04938
207 778-3131
Proprietor: John M
Lippman
Hours: Mon-Sun 9-5
Types & Periods: Country
Furniture, Primitives,
Collectibles
Directions: 4 Miles N of
Farmington on Rte 27

Farmington Falls

THE BARN SALE
Box 58 Main St   04940
207 778-3429   Est: 1973
Proprietor: Ethel Emerson
Hours: Mon-Sun, Also By
Chance
Types & Periods: Table Top
Antiques, Collectibles, Old
Pictures, Good Used Items,
Books
Specialties: Good Browsing
Shop
Directions: 0.1 Mile on
Loop, Off Rte 2 on W end
of Rtes 41 & 156

THE COUNTRY MOUSE
04940
207 778-2030   Est: 1974
Proprietor: Corabel
McEntee
Hours: By Appointment,
By Chance
Types & Periods: Early
Country Furniture &
Accessories
Specialties: Furniture
Restoration
Directions: About 5 Miles
SE of Farmington on Rte
41, Just off Rte 2

Fort Fairfield

COUNTRY LANE ANTIQUES
Lincoln   04742
207 472-2141
Proprietor: Marie
Christensen
Hours: April to Dec By
Appointment, By Chance
Types & Periods: Pine
Primitives, Glass, China
Directions: Corner of
Lincoln & Park

Frankfort

MARY IRENE BIRMINGHAM
Rte 1 A   04438
207 223-4406   Est: 1973
Proprietor: Mary Irene
Birmingham
Hours: Open Daily
Year-Round, Also By
Appointment, By Chance
Types & Periods: General
Line, Collectibles

Specialties: China, Glass
Directions: Halfway btwn
Belfast & Bangor

Gardiner

MORRELL'S ANTIQUES
106 Highland Ave   04345
207 582-4797   Est: 1959
Proprietor: Hazel I Morrell
Hours: By Appointment,
By Chance
Types & Periods: Art, Cut &
Pattern Glass, Victorian
Glass, Lamps & Collectibles
Directions: From Rte 201,
Turn at Quickstop Store,
Go 1/3 Miles

PHIPPS OF PITTSTON
PO Box 841   04345
207 582-3555
Proprietor: Maggi Phipps
Hours: Mon-Sat 10-5
Types & Periods: Pine
Furniture, Glass, China,
Metals
Specialties: Spongeware,
Ironstone
Directions: On Rte 27
Btwn Wiscasset &
Gardiner

**KEN & PAULETTE TUTTLE
ANTIQUES**
Jct Rts 194 & 27
PO Box 841   04345
207 582-4496
Proprietor: Ken & Paulette
Tuttle
Hours: By Chance
Types & Periods: Furniture,
Cupboards, Slant Front
Desks
Directions: Btwn
Wiscasset & Gardiner

Gorham

**HANSON'S CARRIAGE
HOUSE**
Lower Main St   04038
207 839-6092
Proprietor: Jean & Arn
Hanson
Hours: Mon-Fri 9-9
Types & Periods: Country
Furniture, Quilts, Stoneware,
Redware, Shaker, Maine
Indian Items
Directions: Rte 25 at
Moshers Corner

Greene

WILBUR'S ANTIQUES
Rte 202   04236
207 946-5711   Est: 1960
Proprietor: Rena & Philip
Wilbur
Hours: By Appointment,
By Chance Year Round
Types & Periods: General
Line, Late 1700's Furniture
Specialties: Country Items
Appraisal Service Available
Directions: 7 Miles N of
Lewiston off Exit 13 of
Maine Trpk Heading
Toward Augusta on
Rte 202

Hallowell

BERDAN'S ANTIQUES
151 Water   04347
207 622-0151   Est: 1964
Proprietor: Charles M
Berdan, III
Hours: Mon-Sat, Closed
Sun & Holidays
Types & Periods: Country
Furniture, Primitives,
Stoneware, Redware, Quilts,
Coverlets & Country Store
Advertising
Specialties: Maine Country
Antiques
Appraisal Service Available
Directions: Rte 201, 2
Miles S of Augusta

JOHNSON'S ANTIQUES
202 Water St   04347
207 622-9081   Est: 1972
Proprietor: Max & Will
Johnson
Hours: Mon-Sat 9:30-5,
Sun By Chance
Types & Periods: General
Line, Collectibles
Directions: 2 Miles S of
Augusta on Rte 201

**JORGENSENS OF
HALLOWELL**
173 Water St   04347
207 622-1104   Est: 1973
Proprietor: Helene & David
Jorgensen
Hours: Mon-Sat
Types & Periods: New
Country Primitives,
Reference Books on
Antiques

Specialties: Decoys, Quilts,
Baskets
Directions: Main St, 2
Miles S of State Capitol at
Augusta

MAXWELL'S ANTIQUES
172 Water St   04347
207 623-3441   Est: 1960
Proprietor: Mrs Gilbert
Maxwell
Types & Periods: General
Line

MCLEAN'S ANTIQUES
124 Water St   04347
Proprietor: Majorie
McLean
Hours: Mon-Sat
Types & Periods: Primitives,
Glass, China, Furniture, Doll
Houses & Related Miniatures

OLDE VALUES HOUSE
200 Water St   04347
207 622-9797   Est: 1973
Proprietor: Stephen N
Goldman
Hours: Mon-Sun, Days &
Evenings
Types & Periods: Early
Period Furniture, Glass,
China, Wood Stoves, Tools,
Baskets, Silver, Nautical
Items
Directions: S of Augusta,
2 Miles on Rte 201

Hanover

LYON'S DEN
Rte 2 Box 57   04237
207 364-8634
Proprietor: Elmer Lyons Jr
Hours: Mon-Fri
Types & Periods: China,
Glass, Furniture, Bric-A-Brac

**OXFORD COUNTY
ANTIQUES**
Rte 2   04237
207 364-8321   Est: 1971
Proprietor: Albert Bouffard
Hours: Mon-Sun 9-5
Types & Periods: Glass,
Furniture, Tools, Primitives
Directions: 12 Miles from
Rumford

Houlton

YOUNG'S ANTIQUES
10 Alfred St   04730
207 532-6774   Est: 1951
Proprietor: L D Young, Jr
Hours: Mon-Sun, Also By
Appointment, By Chance
Types & Periods: Art,
Colored, Cameo & Cut
Glass, Oriental & European
Porcelains, Pewter,
Paintings, Prints, Clocks,
Sterling Silver, Collectibles
Appraisal Service Available
Directions: Turn Off
Columbia St to Brooks St

Jonesport

JONESPORT WOOD CO
PO 295   04649
207 497-2322
Proprietor: Cooperative
Hours: Mon-Sun
Types & Periods: Tools,
Primitives, General Line
Appraisal Service Available
Directions: Rte 187 at
Bridge

Kennebunk

THE BIG E ANTIQUES
Rte 1   04043
207 985-3276   Est: 1962
Proprietor: Richard &
Joanne Brown
Hours: Tues-Sat 9-5
Types & Periods: General
Line
Directions: Exit 3 Off I-95,
S on Rte 35, 1½ Miles to
Rte 1, S on Rte 1 for
1 1/2 Miles

**CRIMSON CRICKET
ANTIQUES**
Alewive Rd   04043
207 985-4867   Est: 1971
Proprietor: Nancy Libby
Hours: Tues-Sun in
Summer, Winter By
Appointment, By Chance
Types & Periods: Early
American Furniture, Pine
Primitives
Specialties: Furniture
(Cupboards)
Directions: Rte 35, 5 Miles
N of Town

J J KEATING ANTIQUES
70 Portland Rd   04043
207 985-2097   Est: 1956
Proprietor: James J
Keating
Hours: Mon-Sun May-Oct,
Nov-April Fri & Sat, Also
By Appointment
Types & Periods: Furniture,
Glass, China, Silver,
Paintings, Victorian,
Reproduction Accessories,
Lamp Parts
Appraisal Service Available
Directions: Portland Rd
Rte 1, 1 Mile N of
Kennebunk Ctr

KENNEBUNK ANTIQUES
105 Main St   04043
207 985-4808   Est: 1975
Proprietor: Nancy McC
Glendenning
Hours: Mon-Sat 10-5,
April-Nov
Types & Periods: 19th
Century, China, Glass,
Silverplate, Tin, Iron, Wood,
Lighting, Country & Formal
Furniture
Specialties: 19th Century
China, Staffordshire, Wash
Pitchers & Bowls, Castor
Sets
Directions: Adjacent to
Brick Store Museum at
Junction of Rte 1 & Rte
35, 2 Miles from Exit 3 on
Maine Trpk

Kennebunkport

BONNEY'S ANTIQUES
Western Ave   04046
207 967-4828
Proprietor: Mrs Bernard
Noyes
Hours: Daily
Types & Periods: Furniture,
Glass, China, Victorian
Specialties: Bottles, Buttons
Directions: Turn Right at
Blinker at 35 & 9, Go
about 1 Mile W of
Kennebunkport

GEM ANTIQUES
Ocean Ave   04046
207 967-2089
Proprietor: Geraldine G
Wolf
Hours: Mon-Sat,
June-Labor Day

Types & Periods: Jewelry
Directions: Near the
Colony Hotel

GOLDEN WHALE
Wharf Lane   04046
207 967-3151   Est: 1963
Proprietor: Mary Fisher
Hours: Mon-Sat, Sun By
Appointment
Types & Periods: General
Line
Directions: Off Ocean Ave

THE GOOSE HANGS HIGH
Pearl St   04046
207 967-5717
Proprietor: Jean Pineo
Hours: Mon-Sat April-Nov,
Winter By Appointment,
By Chance
Types & Periods: Primitives,
Small Items, Wood, Tin,
Glass
Directions: "Look for
Goose Over Barn
Entrance"

NAUTICAL ANTIQUES
Dock Sq   04046
207 967-3218   Est: 1972
Proprietor: John Rinaldi
Hours: By Appointment
Types & Periods: Marine
Antiques
Appraisal Service Available
Directions: Center of
Village

**OLD FORT SHOPPE &
GALLERY**
Old Fort Ave   04046
207 967-2700   Est: 1967
Proprietor: Marjorie Brass
Hours: Open May-Nov, Sat
& Sun By Appointment
Types & Periods: China,
Glassware, Furniture, Quilts,
Fabrics, Primitives,
Decorative Items, Paintings,
Graphics
Specialties: Paintings &
Graphics
Appraisal Service Available
Directions: Express Hwys
to Maine Trpk, Exit 3 at
Kennebunk, Left on Rte
35, Follow Signs

THE PIG & SADDLE LTD
Ocean Ave   04046
207 967-3022   Est: 1959
Proprietor: Henry W Swain

Hours: Mon-Sat 10-5
June-Sept, Sun & Mon
April-Dec
Types & Periods: Oriental
Objets d'Art, Chinese Snuff
Bottles, English & American
Furniture, Rose Medallion &
Canton China, Brass,
Pewter, Prints, Ship Models
Directions: Dock Sq

PREBLE ANTIQUES
PO Box 471A   04046
207 967-5980   Est: 1976
Proprietor: Hetty Preble
Archer
Hours: Tues-Sun
Types & Periods: General
Line
Directions: Corner of Rte
9 & Maine St

RAND'S ANTIQUES
Western Ave Rte 9 04046
207 967-3353
Proprietor: Florence Rand
& Gloria Rand Sundin
Hours: Daily Summer 9-5,
Winter 10-4
Types & Periods: China,
Glass, Primitives
Specialties: Pine Furniture

SIMPSONS ANTIQUES
Ocean Ave   04046
207 967-4625   Est: 1967
Proprietor: Louise M
Simpson
Hours: Daily 10-4:30,
Closed Thur & Sun,
June 1-Oct 1
Types & Periods: China,
Glass, Chinese Export,
Staffordshire, Canton,
Fitzhugh, Flow Blue
Specialties: Watches
Directions: Near Colony
Hotel

THE STONES ANTIQUES
Maine St   04046
207 967-5916
Proprietor: Edward &
Honey Lou Stone
Hours: Tues-Sun
Types & Periods: 18th &
19th Century Furniture,
Paintings, Glass, China,
Silver
Directions: Corner of
Maine & Pearl Sts

Kennebunkport   Cont'd

TIMBERLEE ANTIQUES
Ocean Ave   04046
207 967-2647   Est: 1968
Proprietor: Bertha E
Timson
Hours: Open All Year By
Appointment, By Chance
Types & Periods: Early
American Silverplate
1845-1898
Specialties: Figurals
Appraisal Service Available
Directions: Opposite
Chick's Marina, House in
Rear

WINDFALL ANTIQUES
Ocean Ave   04046
207 967-2089 or 967-4710
                Est: 1969
Proprietor: Anne S
Kornetsky
Hours: Mon-Sat June-Sept
Types & Periods: China,
American & European Silver,
Orientals, 19th Century Art
Appraisal Service Available
Directions: Ocean Ave
Near Colony Hotel

Kezar Falls

OLD FARM ANTIQUES
21 New Rd   04047
207 839-3067
Proprietor: Mrs Martin
McIntyre
Hours: Mon-Sat, By
Appointment
Types & Periods: Glass,
China, Small Furniture
Specialties: Portland Glass

Kittery

POST ROAD ASSOCIATES
Rte 1   03904
207 439-0578   Est: 1977
Proprietor: Multiple
Hours: Mon-Sun, Also By
Appointment
Types & Periods: All Periods
of American & English
Furniture, Ceramics,
Paintings, Prints, Oriental
Rugs, Decorative
Accessories, Trade &
Advertising Signs
Appraisal Service Available
Directions: Take Exit 3A
(Coastal Rte 1 N) Off I-95

Liberty

HIGH-RIDGE FARM ANTIQUES
Rte 3   04949
207 589-4351
Proprietor: Dave Olson
Hours: By Appointment,
By Chance
Types & Periods: Victorian
Era Featuring the Wares of
C F Monroe, Stevens &
Williams, Boston &
Sandwich Glass Co, Thomas
Webb, Mt Washington &
New England Glass Co
Directions: 13 Miles from
Belfast Towards Augusta

Limerick

AT THE SHADE OF THE ELM INN
Main St   04048
207 793-8026
Proprietor: Blanche M
Kingsbury
Hours: Wed-Sun 10-5
June-Oct
Types & Periods: Furniture,
Glass, Primitives, China,
Paintings, Dolls
Directions: Corner of Main
& Elm

J & L LORMAN
Main   04048
207 793-2089   Est: 1962
Proprietor: J & L Lorman
Hours: Mon-Fri, Also By
Appointment
Types & Periods: Glass,
China, Silver, Collectibles
Directions: On Double Rte
Maine 5 & 11

Lincolnville

BETTY'S TRADING POST
Rte 1   04849
207 789-5300
Proprietor: Betty Smith
Hours: Mon-Fri
Types & Periods: Furniture,
Glass, China, Jewelry, Dolls,
Coins

DUCK TRAP ANTIQUES
RFD 2   04849
207 789-5575
Proprietor: Natalie
MacInnis
Hours: By Appointment
Spring thru Fall
Types & Periods: Glass,
China, Decorative
Accessories, Small Furniture
Specialties: Flow Blue,
China
Directions: 7 Miles N of
Camden

THAR SHE BLOWS
Rte 1   04849
207 789-5671
Proprietor: J Daniel Fartin
Hours: Mon-Fri
Types & Periods: Ship's
Wheels, Lights, Bridge
Telegraphs, Long Glasses,
Marine Gear & Paintings,
Whaling Tools, Scrimshaw
Directions: 1/4 Mile N of
Lincolnville Beach

Litchfield

THE COUNTRY HOUSE
Upper Pond Rd   04350
207 737-2870   Est: 1962
Proprietor: Helen B &
Allan B Smith
Hours: By Appointment
Types & Periods: Open
Salts, Salt Spoons, Books
on Salt

Mexico

J & J ANTIQUES OF MAINE
35 Main St   04257
207 364-2702   Est: 1960
Proprietor: J E Martin &
Sons
Hours: By Appointment
Types & Periods: General
Line of Furniture, Nautical
Items
Specialties: Furniture
Appraisal Service Available
Directions: US Rte 2, 70
Minutes from Portland

Newcastle

MARY & FRED HODES ANTIQUES
Mills Rd   04553
207 563-5151   Est: 1952
Proprietor: Mary Hodes
Hours: Mon-Sun April-Oct,
Winter By Appointment,
By Chance
Types & Periods: Furniture,
China, Art, Pressed &
Colored Glass, Lamps,
Mettlach Steins, Primitives,
Tools, Toys, Pewter, Brass,
Copper, Bronzes, Tin
   Directions: Mills Rd is Also
   Rte 215, Rte 215 Runs
   Btwn Rte 1 & Business
   Rte 1

PATRICIA ANNE REED
5 Pump St   04553
207 563-5633   Est: 1969
Proprietor: Patricia Anne
Reed
Hours: Mon-Sat, Sun By
Appointment, By Chance
Types & Periods: 18th &
Early 19th Century American
Furniture & Accessories,
Folk Art, Toys, Doll Houses,
Miniatures, Paintings, Prints,
Oriental & Hooked Rugs
Appraisal Service Available
   Directions: Turn off
   Business Rte 1 at the
   Chevron Station

THE SAIL LOFT
Box 278   04553
               Est: 1934
Proprietor: Wallace &
Harriet William
Hours: By Appointment,
By Chance June-Oct
Types & Periods:
Staffordshire, Pewter,
Continental & Early
American, Flint Glass,
Canes, Rare Books
(Illustrated & Childrens)
Specialties: China, Glass,
Pewter, Books
   Directions: On
   Damariscotta River,
   Business Rte 1, Behind
   PO in Newcastle

Nobleboro

OLIVER'S ANTIQUES
Old Rt 1 Village Rd 04555
207 563-3760
Proprietor: George W
Oliver
Hours: Mon-Fri
Types & Periods: Glass,
China, Furniture, Primitives

North Berwick

HILTON'S ANTIQUES
RFD   03906
207 676-5570   Est: 1950
Proprietor: Gordon E
Hilton
Hours: Mon-Fri
Types & Periods: Primitive
Furniture & Accessories
Specialties: Tools
Appraisal Service Available
   Directions: 2 Miles off Rte
   4 Btwn N Berwick &
   Sanford

STONE WALL ANTIQUES
Rts 4 & 9   03906
207 676-4429
Proprietor: Lois Tucker
Hours: By Appointment
Types & Periods: Flow Blue,
Staffordshire, Mocha,
Spatterware, Canton,
Furniture

North Edgecomb

JACK PARTRIDGE
Rte 1   04556
207 882-7745   Est: 1939
Proprietor: Jack Partridge
Hours: Mon-Sat May-Oct
Types & Periods: 18th
Century English, American &
Continental Furniture, 19th
Century Paintings
Specialties: Furniture,
Paintings
Appraisal Service Available
   Directions: Rte 1 Btwn
   Wiscasset & Damariscotta

Northeast Harbor

HILL ANTIQUE GALLERIES
Main St   04662
207 276-3929   Est: 1904
Proprietor: Charles H
Jones
Hours: Mon-Fri 9-5
Types & Periods: Period
Furnishings from William &
Mary thru Queen Anne
Chippendale, Hepplewhite,
Sheraton, Empire &
Victorian of American &
English Origin
Specialties: Clocks, Mirrors
Appraisal Service Available
   Directions: Rte 1 to
   Ellsworth, Rte 198 to
   Northeast Harbor

WILLIAM D HOCKER INC
Main St Box 148   04662
207 276-5131   Est: 1968
Proprietor: William D
Hocker
Hours: Mon-Sat June-Sept
Types & Periods: Marine
Antiques, 18th Century
Copper & Brass, Georgian
Furniture
   Directions: Main St,
   Northeast Harbor

Ogunquit

FOXHOLE ANTIQUES
39 Main St   03907
207 646-8437   Est: 1973
Proprietor: Jocelyn C
Searles
Hours: Mon-Fri May-Oct,
Winter By Appointment,
619 862-2931
Types & Periods: China,
Glass, Silver, Jewelry,
Pocket Watches, Clocks,
Paintings, Prints, Furniture,
Stationery, Quilts
Specialties: Watches,
Jewelry, Oriental
Appraisal Service Available
   Directions: Leavitt Theatre
   Bldg on Rte 1 in Center of
   Town

THE MATHEWS ANTIQUES
112 Shore Rd   03907
207 646-2537   Est: 1956
Proprietor: Mrs George D
Mathews

THE MATHEWS ANTIQUES Cont'd
Hours: Tues-Fri June-Oct,
Also By Appointment
Types & Periods: American
& English Pewter, Pattern
Glass, Primitives, Porcelain,
Fans, Pewter Ice Cream
Molds
Specialties: Pewter, Pattern
Glass

MINI-TIQUES
43 Main St   03907
207 646-9380   Est: 1972
Proprietor: Hilda Cori
Hours: Mon-Fri May-Oct,
Nov-April By Appointment,
By Chance
Types & Periods: Miniatures
of Silver, Copper, Brass,
Pewter, China, Glass,
Porcelains, 19th Century
"The Heirloom Miniatures of
Tomorrow"
Directions: Rte 1 N of the
Village at Shedio East

POTPOURRI ANTIQUES
Rte 1   03907
207 646-3529   Est: 1961
Proprietor: Thomas N
Zankowich
Hours: Mon-Sun
Types & Periods: Jewelry
Specialties: Jewelry
Appraisal Service Available
Directions: 1½ Miles N of
Ogunquit Ctr, E Side of
Rte 1

SCOTCH HILL ANTIQUES
43 Main St   03907
207 646-9380   Est: 1972
Proprietor: Will & Hilda
Cori
Hours: Mon-Fri May-Oct,
Nov-April By Appointment,
By Chance
Types & Periods: China,
Glass, Furniture, Silver,
Brass, General Line
Specialties: Coins, Stamps,
Medals, Pocket Watches
Directions: At Shedio E,
Rte 1 N of the Village

Orrington

JACKS ANTIQUES
RFD 2   04474
207 825-4086   Est: 1969
Proprietor: Harold Jack

Hours: Mon-Sun 10-5,
Also By Appointment
Types & Periods: General
Line, Collectibles
Directions: Rte 15, On
Bangor to Bucksport Rd,
Situated 1/2 Way Btwn,
On Main Rd, On Sharp
Curve

THE 1782 HOUSE
Rte 15   04474
207 825-4922
Proprietor: John & Delores
Reglin
Hours: Mon-Fri In
Summer, Winter By
Appointment
Types & Periods: Country &
Primitive Furniture
Directions: Btwn
Bucksport & Bangor

Pemaquid Harbor

THE CHATFIELDS ANTIQUES
US Rte 1   04560
                Est: 1971
Proprietor: Donald &
Dorothy Chatfield
Hours: Mon-Fri, Sat & Sun
By Appointment, By
Chance, Open All Year
Types & Periods: 19th
Century Country Furniture &
Furnishings, Primitives
Specialties: Stoneware,
Country Furniture
Appraisal Service Available
Directions: 12 Miles S Off
Rte 130 From
Damariscotta

Perry

TRADING POST
Rte 1   04667
207 853-2507   Est: 1975
Proprietor: Robert J
Marran
Hours: Mon-Fri 9-5
May-Oct
Types & Periods: General
Line
Directions: Down Coast

Pittsfield

KENNISTON'S ANTIQUES
Rte 2 Box 343   04967
207 487-5032
Proprietor: Barbara
Kenniston
Hours: April 10-Nov 15,
Also By Appointment
Types & Periods: Primitives,
Glass, China, Furniture,
Paintings, Jewelry, Baskets,
Silver, Books

Portland

PORTLAND CLUSTER
Directions: No Real
Cluster, Old Portland
Exchange Area, Congress
St to Fore St & Adjacent
Streets Of Pleasant,
Exchange & Middle

F O BAILEY COMPANY INC
141 Middle St   04104
207 774-1479
Proprietor: Franklin B
Allen
Hours: Mon-Sat 9-5,
Closed Sun & Holidays
Types & Periods: Glass,
China, Furniture, Paintings,
Oriental Rugs

BARRIDOFF GALLERIES
242 Middle St   04101
207 772-5011   Est: 1977
Proprietor: Annette & Rob
Elowitch
Hours: Mon-Sat 10-5, Sun
& Evenings By
Appointment
Types & Periods: 19th &
Early 20th Century American
Paintings, Contemporary
Prints, Watercolors, Oils &
Acrylics, Custom Framing
Appraisal Service Available
Directions: I-295, Franklin
Arterial Exit, to Congress
St, In the Heart of
Downtown Portland

VENTURE IN THE MARKETPLACE
107 Exchange St   04112
207 773-6064   Est: 1978
Proprietor: Isabel F
Thacher
Hours: Mon-Sat 10-5

Types & Periods: General
Line
  Directions: In Old Port
  Exchange Area, Corner
  Federal St & Exchange St

VOSE-SMITH ANTIQUES
  652 Congress St   04101
  207 773-6436
  Proprietor: Donald W
  Harford
  Hours: Mon-Sat
  Types & Periods: Copper,
  Brass, Bronze

Pownal

THE MAIN-E-ACK TRADER
  Rte 9   04069
  207 829-3442   Est: 1965
  Proprietor: Betty Stowell
  Hours: Mon-Thurs By
  Appointment, Fri, Sat &
  Sun Always Open
Types & Periods: Furniture,
Primitives, Baskets, Books,
General Line
Appraisal Service Available
  Directions: Rte 9, On N
  Yarmouth-Pownal Town
  Lines

Presque Isle

ANN'S ANTIQUE SHOP
  160 State St   04769
  207 764-0626
  Hours: Mon-Sat 9:30-4:30
Types & Periods: General
Line

Rangeley

**BLUEBERRY HILL FARM
ANTIQUES**
  Saddleback Rd   04970
  207 864-3431
  Proprietor: Monett
  Robbins
  Hours: Mon-Sat 1-5, Or By
  Appointment, June 15-
  Oct 15
Types & Periods: General
Line
  Directions: 3 Miles E Off
  Rte 4

Richmond

THE LOFT
  9 Gardiner St   04357
  207 737-2056
  Proprietor: Kay Pierce
  Hours: Mon-Sat 10-4,
  Summer, Also By
  Appointment, By Chance
Types & Periods: Early
Decorative Accessories
Specialties: 19th Century
Clothing, Early Textiles &
Sewing Tools
  Directions: I- 95, Exit 197
  to Richmond, 3 Blocks S
  of Main St

Robinhood Cove

**ROBINHOOD COVE
ANTIQUES**
  Robinhood Marina   04530
  207 371-2339
  Proprietor: Bathena
  Deermont
  Hours: Mon-Fri June-Nov
Types & Periods: Furniture,
China, Brass, Hooked Rugs,
Collectibles
  Directions: 10 Miles from
  Bath

Rockland

TRUMAN HILT
  202 Camden St   04841
  207 594-8293   Est: 1963
  Proprietor: Truman Hilt
  Hours: By Appointment
Types & Periods:
Turn-Of-The-Century Oak &
Victorian Furniture
  Directions: 1/2 Mile N of
  MacDonalds on Rte 1

Rockport

**EDWARD AND JOAN
ELLIS-ANTIQUE PRINTS**
  19 High St   04856
  207 236-4524   Est: 1941
  Proprietor: Edward & Joan
  Ellis
  Hours: By Appointment,
  By Chance

Types & Periods: Prints,
18th & 19th Century
Woodcuts, Engravings,
Lithographs
  Directions: S End of
  Goose River Bridge

TOWN SHOP ANTIQUES
  Union St   04856
  207 236-8280   Est: 1970
  Proprietor: Kitty Jenkins
  Hours: Mon-Fri Summer,
  Winter By Chance, By
  Appointment
Types & Periods: General
Line, Primitives, Quilts,
Period Furniture, Decorative
Objects
Specialties: Embroidery &
Needlework, Quilts, Hooked
Rugs
Appraisal Service Available
  Directions: Next to Post
  Office

Round Pond

GRANITE HALL STORE
                   04564
  207 529-5414   Est: 1972
  Proprietor: Charles F
  Holme
  Hours: Daily, Closed Wed
  Summer, Early Spring &
  Fall By Appointment
  Directions: Rte 32, 10
  Miles from Damariscotta,
  Center of Town

Roxbury

YANKEE GEM CORP
  Rte 17   04275
  207 364-8551
  Proprietor: Dean McCrillis
  Hours: Sun-Fri, May 1-Nov
  1, Winter, By Appointment
Types & Periods: Furniture,
Glass, China, Pewter,
Primitives, Guns, Coins

Rumford

CONNIE'S ANTIQUES
  190 Lincoln Ave   04276
  207 364-8886
  Proprietor: Constance P
  Gaudreau

CONNIE'S Cont'd
Hours: By Appointment,
By Chance
Types & Periods: Dolls,
Paintings, Furniture, Glass,
China, Books, Stuffed Birds,
Postcards, Jewelry

Rumford Center

**RUMFORD CENTER
ANTIQUES**
US Rte 2 04278
207 364-2073 Est: 1961
Proprietor: Mr & Mrs
Albert H Brown
Hours: Mon-Sat 9-5
Types & Periods: Glass,
China, Clocks, Prints,
Paintings, Primitives, Early
Furniture, Oriental
Porcelains, Tools
Appraisal Service Available
Directions: On US Rte 2

Scarboro

THE MULBERRY HOUSE
Rte 1 04047
207 883-2802
Proprietor: Mary Alice
Pillsbury
Hours: Daily 12-9, May to
Oct, Closed Sun & Mon,
Spring & Fall
Types & Periods: Furniture,
Glass, China, Primitives
Directions: Near
Intersection of Rte 9

Searsport

BAYBERRY ANTIQUES
W Main St Rte 1 04974
207 548-6647
Hours: Mon-Sun 9-5,
April 1-Dec 1
Types & Periods: Marine Art,
Primitives, Books, Furniture

**THE CAPTAIN'S HOUSE
ANTIQUES**
Rte 1 04974
207 548-6047
Hours: Mon-Sat, Also By
Appointment

Types & Periods: General
Line, Collectibles
Directions: 2½ Miles E of
Town

GOLD COAST ANTIQUES
US Rte 3 04974
Hours: Mon-Sun
Types & Periods: General
Line, Collectibles, China,
Furniture
Specialties: Glass, Lamps,
Dolls
Directions: 3 Miles S of
Village

**MORSE & APPLEBEE
ANTIQUES**
Rte 1 04974
207 548-6314 Est: 1969
Proprietor: Sylvia & Curtis
Morse
Hours: Mon-Sat in
Summer, By Appointment,
By Chance in Winter
Types & Periods: Bottles,
Tools, Glass, Jewelry, Art
Glass, Collectibles
Appraisal Service Available

PEASLEE PARK ANTIQUES
Main St 04974
207 548-2864 Est: 1970
Proprietor: Elizabeth T
Palmer
Hours: Mon-Fri June-Oct,
By Appointment Nov-May
Types & Periods: General
Line, Everything from
Primitives to Fine Silver
Specialties: Individual Salts
Directions: Corner of Main
& Leach in the historic
Merithew Block

RED KETTLE ANTIQUES
Rte 1 04974
207 548-2978 Est: 1967
Proprietor: Dennis & Patti
Middleswart
Hours: By Appointment,
By Chance
Types & Periods: Oak &
Walnut Victorian Furniture,
General Line
Specialties: Dolls
Appraisal Service Available
Directions: 3 Miles N of
Searsport Village on US
Rte 1

**TREASURES AND TRASH
BARN**
E Main 04974
207 548-2787 Est: 1962
Proprietor: Earl Merry
Hours: Mon-Fri
Types & Periods: China,
Glass, Tools, Books,
Furniture
Directions: 3/4 Mile E of
Searsport on US 1

Skowhegan

THE OLD MILL SHOP
Notch Rd 04976
207 474-9429 Est: 1966
Proprietor: Emma Sanders
Hours: Wed & Sat
Types & Periods: General
Line
Specialties: Buttons, Tools
Directions: 2 Miles E of
US 2

Stockton Springs

BRICK HOUSE ANTIQUES
Rte 1 04981
207 567-3173
Proprietor: Violet K
Pakkock
Hours: Mon-Fri May-Oct
Types & Periods: New
England & French Furniture,
Primitives, Art Glass, China,
Iron, Tools, Copper, Brass,
Bronzes, Lamps, Paintings
Directions: Rte 1 at Sandy
Point

OLD LAMP BARN
Rte 1 04981
207 567-3348 Est: 1955
Proprietor: Arline
Blanchard
Hours: Mon-Fri
Types & Periods: Lamps,
Hanging Fixtures, Country
Furniture
Specialties: Lamps
Directions: Rte 1

Tempe

SAVAGE'S ANTIQUES
Rte 43 W 04984
207 778-4806 Est: 1969

Proprietor: Glennys &
Martin Savage
Hours: Daily, By Chance
Types & Periods: Primitives,
Glass, Furniture
Directions: From W
Farmington, 3 Miles, 1st
House on Left, Varnum
Pond Rd

Tenants Harbor

MARY BECKON'S SHOP
Rte 131   04860
207 372-8862
Proprietor: Mary B Holmes
Hours: Mon-Fri April-Nov
Types & Periods: General
Line, Furniture, Glass, China
Directions: Martinsville Rd

Trenton

MERRILL'S ANTIQUES
Bar Habor Rd   04605
207 667-8273
Proprietor: Ada Merrill
Goodwin
Hours: May-Oct
Types & Periods: General
Line

Union

**AMANDA'S HOUSE
ANTIQUES**
                         04862
207 785-3273
Proprietor: C Cates & F
Bessey
Hours: By Appointment,
By Chance
Types & Periods: General
Line
Directions: Old Rte 17
Near Fairgrounds btwn
Rockland & Augusta

DEACON'S LOT ANTIQUES
RFD 2   04862
207 785-4239   Est: 1972
Proprietor: U Gillis & C
Larner
Hours: Daily 9-5, Closed
Thurs March-Sept, Sat
9-5, Also By Appointment,
By Chance Oct-Feb

Types & Periods: Glass,
China, Primitives,
Collectibles
Specialties: China, Soft
Paste
Appraisal Service Available
Directions: Off Rte 17 to
Augusta, 8 Miles from
Rockland

**THE EBENEZER ALDEN
HOUSE ANTIQUES**
                         04862
207 785-2881
Proprietor: Hazel Marcus
Hours: By Appointment
Types & Periods: 18th &
19th Century Furniture,
Paintings, Oriental
Porcelains, Primitives
Directions: Next to
Firehouse

Wells

**THE EDITH E COOKE
SHOP**
Rte 1 Box 200   04090
207 646-2524
Proprietor: Robert R
James
Hours: April-Nov
Types & Periods:
Bric-A-Brac, Sandwich
Glass, Figurines, Chinese
Items, Staffordshire,
Wedgwood, Lustre

THE COUNTRY MOUSE
Sanford Rd   04090
207 646-7334   Est: 1971
Proprietor: Hazel &
Maynard Sandler
Hours: Daily
Types & Periods: Primitives,
Dolls, Miniatures, Country
Furniture, General Line
Appraisal Service Available
Directions: On Rte 109,
3½ Miles N & W of Exit 2,
Maine Turnpike

EASTMOOR ANTIQUES
Rte 1   04090
207 646-2663   Est: 1969
Proprietor: Russell &
Georgia Grethe
Hours: Daily
Types & Periods: General
Line & Military Items
Specialties: Ivory Piano
Keyboards

Appraisal Service Available
Directions: Rte 1 N, 7/10
Mile N of Wells Corner

THE FARM
Mildram Rd   04090
207 985-2656   Est: 1967
Proprietor: Thomas &
Jeannette Hackett
Hours: Mon-Sun 10-4
Types & Periods: Period
Antiques, Furniture, Brass,
Copper, Lamps, Paintings, &
Prints, Oriental Rugs
Directions: Maine Trpk to
Exit 2, Follow Signs About
4 Miles, Or Signs on Rte 1
in Wells Through Woods
2½ Miles

**MAC DOUGALL-GIONET
ANTIQUES GALLERIES**
Rte 1 Box 278 RFD 2
                         04090
207 646-3531   Est: 1961
Proprietor: R G
MacDougall & A J Gionet
Hours: Mon-Fri 10-6, Also
By Appointment
Types & Periods: American
Formal & Country Furniture,
Pewter, Glass, Rugs,
Paintings, Chinese Porcelain
Specialties: Furniture
Appraisal Service Available
Directions: Exit 2 From
Maine Trpk, N on Rte 1,
One Mile

1685 MILL HOUSE
Rte 1 Box 193   04090
207 646-9444
Proprietor: Robert N
Jorgensen
Hours: Daily, In Summer,
Winter By Appointment
Types & Periods: 18th &
19th Century Furniture,
Oriental Rugs, Clocks,
Copper, Iron, Brass
Directions: Btwn Wells &
Ogunquit on Rte 1
(Post Rd)

**ARTHUR L PAGE
ANTIQUES**
Rt 1   04090
207 646 3320   Est: 1954
Proprietor: Arthur L Page
Hours: Mon-Fri April-Oct
Types & Periods: General
Line of Furniture & Glass

Wells Cont'd

GLADYS M SISSON
Rte 109   04090
207 646-7554
Proprietor: Gladys M
Sisson
Hours: Mon-Sun
Afternoons
Types & Periods: China, Art
Glass, Furniture, Primitives,
Paintings, Toleware, Decoys
Directions: Btwn Rte 1 &
Maine Trpk

WELLS FARGO HOUSE
Post Rd   04090
207 646-3997   Est: 1968
Proprietor: Mario J &
Charlotte Grasso
Hours: Mon-Fri
Types & Periods: Early
Americana, Nostalgic
Potpourri
Directions: Rte US 1, 7/10
Mile N of Jct Rte 109 on
Left

West Bath

WITCH SPRING ANTIQUES
Witch Spring Hill   04530
207 443-3180   Est: 1971
Proprietor: Barbara
Gallagher
Hours: By Appointment,
By Chance Evenings
Types & Periods: General
Line, Primitives
Specialties: Primitives
Directions: Rte 95, Exit
Bath-Brunswick, From this
Hwy take 1st Bath Exit,
Turn Left up the hill

West Brooklin

OLD FRIENDS BARN
04616
207 359-8949
Proprietor: Louisa R
Goodyear
Hours: Mon-Fri in
Summer, Winter By
Appointment
Types & Periods: Furniture,
Primitives, Collectibles,
Quilts, Bric-a-Brac, Country
Items
Directions: 1 Mile from
Sedgwick Church, 5 Miles
from Deer Isle Bridge

West Farmington

GARY & DALE GUYETTE
Box 662   04992
207 778-6266   Est: 1973
Proprietor: Gary & Dale
Guyette
Hours: By Appointment,
By Chance
Types & Periods: Country
Furniture & Accessories,
Mostly Pre 1830
Specialties: Duck, Geese,
Shorebird Decoys
Directions: Rte 4, 3½
Miles N of Farmington,
Large Gold House on Left

West Leanon

**LITTLE HORSE ANTIQUE
SHOP**
Rte 16   04027
207 658-4543
Proprietor: Bill Howell
Hours: Daily, Closed Thur
May-Nov, Dec-April By
Appointment
Types & Periods: General
Line
Specialties: Lamps
Directions: Off Rte 16 at
Milton, NH

Westbrook

RONALD L MEYER
1399 Bridgton Rd   04092
207 854-8008   Est: 1928
Proprietor: Ronald L
Meyer
Hours: Mon-Fri 8-5, Sat
9-4
Types & Periods: Early
Chippendale, Hepplewhite,
Sheridan
Specialties: 1700 & Early
1800 Furniture
Appraisal Service Available
Directions: Rte 302

Winterport

BROADLAWN ANTIQUES
Box 184   04496
207 223-4821
Proprietor: Dorothy Jean
Horr
Hours: Mon-Sat May-Nov,
Also By Appointment
Types & Periods: General
Line, Collectibles
Directions: Main Rd

RIVERSIDE ANTIQUES
Rte 1A   04496
207 223-5536
Proprietor: Richard &
Patricia Bean
Hours: Mon-Sat, Winter By
Appointment
Types & Periods: 18th &
19th Century American
Furniture, Porcelains,
Primitives
Directions: Main Rd

WAYSIDE ANTIQUES
Main   04496
207 223-4813   Est: 1972
Proprietor: Kenneth &
Marcia Opdyke
Hours: Mon-Sat 9-6, Also
By Chance
Types & Periods: Period
Primitive Furniture,
Cupboards, Blanket Chests,
Drop Leaf Tables, Glass
Specialties: Paintings
Appraisal Service Available
Directions: Rte 1A Off
Main Rte 1 & Rte 495

Wiscasset

THE COACH HOUSE
Pleasant St   04578
207 882-7833   Est: 1966
Proprietor: William
Glennon
Hours: Mon-Sat in
Summer, Winter By
Appointment
Types & Periods: Country
Furniture, Primitives,
Decorative Accessories
Directions: 1 Block off
Main St

LILAC COTTAGE
Rte 1   04578
207 882-7059
Proprietor: Shirley
Andrews
Hours: Mon-Sat
June 1-Oct 1
Types & Periods: 18th &
19th Century Furniture,
Porcelain, Pewter, Glass,
Decorative Items
Directions: On the Green

MARINE ANTIQUES OF AMERICANA
Main St   04578
207 882-7208   Est: 1968
Proprietor: John & Patricia Newton
Hours: Mon-Fri, By Appointment
Types & Periods: Marine, Americana, 18th & 19th Century, Furniture, Primitives, Scrimshaw, Marine Paintings, Models, Instruments
Appraisal Service Available
Directions: Rte 1 N

TWO AT WISCASSET ANTIQUES
Main St   04578
207 882-5286
Proprietor: Doris Stauble
Hours: Mon-Fri In Summer, By Appointment In Winter
Types & Periods: Americana, Primitives, Period Furniture, Paintings, Folk Art, Nautical Items, Quilts

Yarmouth

THE RED SHED
12 Pleasant St   04096
207 846-3128
Proprietor: Joy Piscopo
Hours: Mon-Fri
Types & Periods: Americana Furniture, Folk Art, Paintings

W M SCHWIND JR ANTIQUES
17 E Main St   04096
207 846-9458
Proprietor: W M Schwind Jr & Elizabeth B Schwind
Hours: Mon-Fri 10-5 in Summer, Winter By Appointment, By Chance
Types & Periods: Period Furniture, Paintings, Prints, Oriental Porcelains, Rugs, Americana, Paper, Valentines
Directions: Rte 88

York

GORGEANA ANTIQUES
Southside Rd   03909
207 363-3842
Proprietor: Norman C & Julie Upham
Hours: By Appointment, By Chance
Types & Periods: Glass, China, Collectibles
Directions: 1/2 Mile E of Rte 1

MARITIME ANTIQUES
US Rte 1   03909
207 363-4247   Est: 1975
Proprietor: Chuck DeLuca
Hours: Daily
Types & Periods: Nautical & Military Antiques
Specialties: Nautical, Collector Weapons
Appraisal Service Available
Directions: US Rte 1

The Empire Style was accommodated to all price ranges. The turned four-poster of solid wood would have been much more costly than the hollow, plain four-poster.

STATE OF MARYLAND

Annapolis

ANNAPOLIS CLUSTER
Directions: Maryland Ave

ANNE ARUNDEL ANTIQUES
713 Giddings Ave   21401
301 268-3429   Est: 1960
Proprietor: Vivien W Smith
Hours: Mon-Sun by appt
or chance
Types & Periods: 18th
Century Furniture, Silver,
English, American, Crystal,
Porcelains, Chinese Rose
Medallion
Specialties: Russian
Enamels
Appraisal Service Available
Directions: Near US Naval
Academy

**THE HOLLY & THE IVY
ANTIQUES**
57 Maryland Ave   21401
301 268-8151   Est: 1975
Proprietor: Lydia Griscom
Daffer
Hours: Mon-Sat & some
Sundays by appt
Types & Periods: Furniture,
Glass, Porcelain, Quilts,
Lace, Embroideries, Jewelry,
Rugs & Lamps
Specialties: Paintings, Prints,
Etchings & Pastels
Directions: Middle of first
block Maryland Ave; right
hand side going toward
the Naval Academy

TREASURE CHEST
47 Maryland Ave   21401
301 268-8900   Est: 1967
Proprietor: Helen & Jim
Opsata
Hours: Tues-Sat, 11:30-5
Types & Periods: Glass,
Tools, Small Furniture, Keys,
Copper & Brass
Directions: 1/2 block from
State Capitol Bldg

Baldwin

**CAROL T TRELA,
ANTIQUES**
2950 Baldwin Mill Rd
21013
301 557-9827   Est: 1972
Proprietor: James & Carol
Trela
Hours: Mon-Sun by appt
or chance
Types & Periods: 18th &
19th Century American
Furniture & Accessories
Specialties: Fine Furniture of
the 18th & 19th Century
Appraisal Service Available
Directions: Exit 24 N
Baltimore Beltway; Rte 83
N to Exit 20A; right on Rte
45 (York Rd); 1/2 mile left
to Rte 145 (Papermill Rd);
7 miles to Rte 165; left
1/2 mile to house

Baltimore

BALTIMORE CLUSTER
Directions: N Howard St
(700-800 block); N Charles
St

ANTIQUE CENTER
8231 Woodmont Ave
20014
301 652-4522   Est: 1962
Proprietor: Irene Iskander
Hours: Mon-Sun, 11-5:30
Types & Periods: Chinese,
Victorian, Oak, Collectibles
& Coins & Stamps
Specialties: Furniture, Glass
& Silver
Appraisal Service Available
Directions: Exit 19
(Wisconsin Ave) on 495
Beltway by the Ramada
Inn

**ANTIQUE TRAIN & TOY
WORLD**
3626 Falls Rd   21211
301 889-9544   Est: 1976
Proprietor: Ralph Baeverle
Hours: Mon-Tues,
Thurs-Sun, 9-6

Types & Periods: Toys,
Trains, Bottles, Guns &
Advertising Items
Appraisal Service Available
Directions: From
downtown Baltimore, take
Jones Falls Expwy & exit
on Jones Falls, 50 yds on
left past 1st light

BRASS TOWNE
219 W Mulberry St   21201
301 539-8284   Est: 1946
Proprietor: Hyman Levy
Hours: Mon-Sat, 10-5
Types & Periods: Glass,
China, Brass, Copper &
Garden Furniture
Specialties: Fireplace
equipment
Directions: Downtown
Baltimore

CHARLES VILLAGE SHOP
414 E 31st St   21218
301 889-1444   Est: 1972
Proprietor: Philip &
Margaret Cuomo
Hours: Wed-Sun, 11-5
Types & Periods: China,
Crystal, Objets d'Art,
Oriental Rugs, Mahogany,
Chippendale & Queen Anne
Furniture
Directions: 1 block off
Greenmount or 3 blocks
off St Paul

THE COLLECTOR'S ITEM
209 W 25th St   21211
301 243-5072   Est: 1969
Proprietor: Frank & Carol
Bianca
Hours: Mon-Sat, 10-5
Types & Periods: Antique
Trains, Toys & Dolls
Specialties: Toys
Appraisal Service Available
Directions: Off of the 28th
St exit of Jones Falls
Expwy

CREST ANTIQUES
817 N Howard St   21201
301 669-8120   Est: 1950
Proprietor: Mr S Pleet
Hours: Mon-Sat, 12-5:30;
other by appt

Types & Periods: Early
American & Country
Furniture, Primitives, Folk
Art, Porcelain, China &
Glass
Specialties: Old Iron & Tools
Directions: Downtown
Baltimore; 4 doors from
Madison Ave on Howard
St

DAVANNA'S ANTIQUES
3612 Putty Hill Ave   21236
301 661-0794
Proprietor: Mildred A
Baumgardner
Types & Periods: Pattern
Glass, Lamps, China & Dolls

**DEAN'S USED FURNITURE-
ANTIQUES-GLASS**
2115 W Pratt St   21223
301 947-9684   Est: 1976
Proprietor: Dean Martin
Hours: Mon-Sat, 9-5
Types & Periods: General
Line, Oak Furniture & Art
Deco

THE DUSTY ATTIC
9411 Harford Rd   21234
301 668-2343   Est: 1972
Proprietor: Doris E Shirey
Hours: Wed-Sat, 11-4; Sun
12-5
Types & Periods: General
Antiques & Collectibles
Specialties: Oak Furniture
Directions: Exit 31 N off
Baltimore Expwy

CHRIS EVANS ANTIQUES
1026 E 36th St   21218
301 366-4078   Est: 1970
Proprietor: Chris Evans
Hours: Shows Only By
appt

HORNE'S ANTIQUES
1330 Smith Ave   21209
301 435-4635
Proprietor: Richard Horne
Hours: Wed-Sat by appt
Types & Periods: General
Line of Strange Things
Specialties: Toys, Trains &
Neon Signs
Directions: N Baltimore; 5
min from I-83

IMPERIAL HALF BUSHEL
831 N Howard St   21201
301 462-1192   Est: 1976
Proprietor: Nancy S &
Fredrick F Duggan, Jr.

Hours: Tues-Sat, 10-4
Types & Periods: Antique
Silver, Brass, Copper &
Pewter & some misc
Specialties: Maryland Silver
Appraisal Service Available
Directions: On Baltimore's
"Antique Row"; 800 block
of N Howard near State
Office Bldgs & Armory

JE VONS CURIOSITY SHOP
2336 E Monument St
                    21205
301 675-5874   Est: 1964
Proprietor: Jeanette Grant
Hours: Mon-Sat, mornings
Types & Periods: General
Line, Jewelry, Dolls & Good
Collectibles
Directions: 3 blocks N of
Rte 40 & 4 blocks E of
John Hopkins Hospital in
E Baltimore

HAZEL H JORDAN
4401 Ridge Rd   21236
301 665-7276
Proprietor: Hazel H Jordan
Types & Periods: General
Line

THE LONDON SHOP
1500 Bolton St   21217
301 669-5400   Est: 1959
Proprietor: William Tarum
Fehsenfeld
Hours: Mon-Fri by appt
Types & Periods: Furniture,
China, Porcelain, Paintings,
Prints, Silver & Glass
Appraisal Service Available
Directions: Downtown off
Howard St at 6th Reg
Armory

MARGOLET ANTIQUES
833 N Howard St   21201
301 728-3969   Est: 1940
Proprietor: Bernice
Margolet
Hours: Mon-Sat
Types & Periods: European
& American Furniture,
Paintings, Bronzes,
Porcelain & Silver

PEACOCK & PARRETT
1330 Smith Ave   21209
301 323-2149   Est: 1975
Proprietor: Carol Peacock
Kinre
Hours: Wed-Sat, 10-5;
other days by appt

Types & Periods: 19th
Century Country Furniture
Specialties: Quilts, Hooked
Rugs & Kitchen Antiques
Directions: In the
Baltimore Antique
Warehouse just N of the
Northern Pkwy exit of I-83,
from Northern Pkwy, left
on Falls Rd, 1/2 mile left
on Smith Ave

**THE J S PEARSON
COMPANY**
16 W Hamilton St   21201
                    Est: 1977
Proprietor: John S
Pearson
Hours: Tues-Fri; Sat-Mon
by appt
Types & Periods: 1850
American Furniture, Oriental
Rugs, Coin, Silver &
American Paintings
Specialties: American
Printed & Decorated
Furniture
Appraisal Service Available
Directions: On Hamilton St
between Charles &
Cathedral St; 1 block S of
Walters Art Gallery

THE PLACE
1948 W Pratt St   21223
301 233-9650   Est: 1967
Proprietor: Irma Albert
Hours: Mon, Thurs & Sat,
12-3
Types & Periods: General
Line
Directions: 1½ miles from
downtown

NANCY SCOTT ANTIQUES
7625 Bellona Ave   21204
301 296-0008
Proprietor: Nancy Scott
Hours: Mon-Fri, 10-5; Sat
10-2
Types & Periods: 18th
Century Furniture, Chinese
Export Porcelains, English &
French Porcelains,
Staffordshire Animals,
Paintings & Prints
Directions: Ruxton
Suburb, 3 miles from City
Limits

SECOND HAND ROSE
5748 Falls Rd   21209
301 433-3077   Est: 1971
Proprietor: Sandra C
Fendell

Baltimore   Cont'd

ROSE   Cont'd
Hours: Thurs-Sun
Types & Periods: Turn of
the Century Oak & Walnut
Furniture, Victorian Lamps,
China, Glassware &
Paintings
Directions: Jones Falls
Expwy, exit Northern
Parkway E, left at first
light to Falls Rd

MYRTLE SEIDEL ANTIQUES
1015 N Charles St   21201
301 685-8851   Est: 1943
Proprietor: Myrtle Hellman
Hours: Mon-Sun
Types & Periods: Jewelry,
Glass, China & Furniture
Directions: S of Jones
Falls Expwy

THINK 'N THINGS ANTIQUES
1330 Smith Ave   21209
301 433-2500   Est: 1968
Proprietor: Lawrence M
Kloze
Hours: Thurs-Sat, 12-5;
also by appt
Types & Periods: Victorian,
Oak, Mission, Deco
Furnishings, Country Store
Fixtures & Advertising &
Office Furniture
Specialties: Leaded Glass,
Lamps & Windows,
Instruments, Vending
Machines, Neon Signs &
Cash Registers
Directions: 83 S to
Northern Pkwy E, left 1
block on Falls Rd & left
first street past light

THE TWO WORLDS
819 S Broadway   21231
301 732-2121   Est: 1967
Proprietor: John Herndon
Hours: Sept-June: Sat by
appt or chance
Types & Periods: General
Collectibles, Bottles, Glass &
Aviation Items
Directions: Rte 40 crosses
Broadway; go S to the
end of Harbor; located at
the foot of S Broadway

Barnsville

THE NEW AND OLD SHOP
20703
301 349-9850   Est: 1968
Proprietor: John A
Anderson
Hours: Fri evenings, Sat &
Sun
Types & Periods: Furniture,
Glassware, Tools, Books,
Musical Instruments,
Pictures, Lights, Frames &
Clocks
Specialties: Refinishing
Furniture
Directions: Rte 117 & 109
Barnsville Rd

Benson

NANA'S ATTIC ANTIQUE SHOP
1807 N Harford Rd   21018
301 879-0733   Est: 1966
Proprietor: William Donald
Long, Jr
Hours: Mon-Sat, 10-4; Sun
12-5
Types & Periods: Furniture,
Glass, China & Silver
Specialties: Refinishing
Furniture
Appraisal Service Available
Directions: Rte 147, 12
miles N 695, exit 31 off
Beltway

SOMETHING OLD
1807 Harford Rd   21018
301 879-0587   Est: 1966
Proprietor: Mary K Davis
Hours: By appt or chance
Types & Periods: Country
Furniture, Primitives, Silver,
Brass & Jewelry
Appraisal Service Available
Directions: Hartford Rd
1/2 mile W of Rte 1;
Bypass of Belaire

Bethesda

JANE ALPER ANTIQUES
5309 Edgemoor Lane
20014
301 652-2942
Hours: By appt

Types & Periods: 17th, 18th
& 19th Century English
Furniture & Objets D'Art
Specialties: English
Furniture

ANTIQUES BY WALLACE INC
4912 Cordell Ave   20014
301 652-6613   Est: 1969
Proprietor: Wallace Berch
Hours: Tues-Sat by appt
Types & Periods: General
Line of Fine Quality
Merchandise, Porcelain, Art
Glass, Furniture, Bronzes &
Pottery
Specialties: Russian
Enamels: stone carvings in
Faberge manner
Appraisal Service Available
Directions: 1 block from
main street of Wisconsin
Ave

WM BLAIR LTD., INC
4839 Del Ray Ave   20014
301 654-6665   Est: 1953
Proprietor: Wm B Blair
Hours: Tues-Sat, 10-5 or
by appt
Types & Periods: 17th &
18th Century English
Furniture & Marine Art
Specialties: Wm & Mary &
Queen Anne & Georgian
Walnut Furniture
Appraisal Service Available
Directions: 1½ blocks in
from Old Georgetown Rd
on Del Ray Ave

BROMWELL'S
7215 Wisconsin Ave 20314
301 654-6515   Est: 1873
Proprietor: D L Bromwell
Hours: Mon-Sun
Types & Periods: Silver,
Brass, Copper & French,
English, Early American
Furniture & Victorian
Furniture
Directions: Suburb of
Washington D C

PHYLLIS CUPIT ANTIQUES
7946 Norfolk Ave   20014
301 656-4611   Est: 1973
Proprietor: Phyllis M Cupit
Hours: Mon-Sun
Types & Periods: 18th &
19th Century Country
American Furniture

Directions: "Woodmont Triangle" between Wisconsin Ave & Old Georgetown Rd

EVELETH AND SUMMERFORD
4865 Cordell Ave 20014
301 652-4999 Est: 1970
Proprietor: Sarah Hansen Ben Summerford & Assoc
Hours: Tues-Sat, 11-4
Types & Periods: Pre-1840 American & English Furniture, Early English Ceramics, Chinese Exports, Paintings & other suitable accessories of 18th & early 19th centuries
Specialties: American Furniture, English Ceramics & Chinese Exports
Directions: From the Washington Beltway, exit either Old Georgetown Rd or to Wisconsin Ave, in the direction of Bethesda; turn respectively left or right on to Cordell

FLEUR-de-LIS ANTIQUES INC
7921 Norfolk Ave 20015
301 652-1500 Est: 1957
Proprietor: Donothea M Beers
Hours: Tues-Sat
Types & Periods: Chinese & Continental Porcelain & French and English Furniture
Specialties: Meissen & Sevres Porcelain
Appraisal Service Available
Directions: 3 miles S, Beltway 495, Bethesda exit "Old Georgetown Rd" (30 minutes from WHITE HOUSE, DC)

Bowie

OLD BOWIE ANTIQUE MARKET
Rte 197,
8604 Chesnut Ave 20715
301 262-9844 Est: 1973
Proprietor: Abbie Banks
Hours: Tues-Sun

Types & Periods: Oak & Primitive Country Furniture, Advertising Items, Memorabilia, Kitchen Paraphenalia & Country Store Items
Specialties: Oak Furniture & Advertising Items
Directions: 7 miles Washington Beltway, exit 30 E, 5 miles Rte 50 W

TREASURE HOUSE ANTIQUES
13012 9th St 20715
301 262-2878 Est: 1966
Proprietor: Mildred & Al Jacobs
Hours: Tues-Fri, 11-4; Sat 11-5 & Sun 12-5
Types & Periods: 18th & 19th Century English & American Antiques
Specialties: Copper, Brass, Stained Glass & Primitives
Appraisal Service Available
On MD Rte 564, 1 block from MD Rte 197

Braddock Hts

FIN-COR
21714
301 371-7676 Est: 1954
Proprietor: Marian F Corey
Hours: By appt or chance
Types & Periods: Primitives, Country Furniture & Tools
Specialties: Tools
Directions: 50 miles W from Washington or Baltimore Via I-270 or 170, 4 blocks off 40 Alt W at the Hts

Cambridge

THE ANVIL SHOP
Route 50 21613
301 228-5044
Proprietor: Beulah & Joe Brocato
Hours: Tues-Sat, 11-5; Sun 1-5
Types & Periods: Furniture, Glass, China & Brass
Directions: 1½ Miles E of Town

CAMBRIDGETOWNE ANTIQUES
411 Muse St 21613
301 228-5467
Proprietor: Edna B Pattison
Hours: Tues-Sat, 11-5
Types & Periods: Furniture, Glass, China, Brass, Woodenware & Collectibles
Directions: Across from Fire House

JONES' ANTIQUES
520 High St 21613
301 228-1752 Est: 1956
Proprietor: Mrs Gertrude Jones
Hours: "Almost Anytime"
Types & Periods: Victorian Periods & Others; Glass, Brass, Silver & China
Specialties: China
Directions: US 50 Eastern Shore into Cambridge MD

MARSHY HOPE NAUTICAL ANTIQUES
Box 18, Rte 50 21613
301 228-6330 Est: 1970
Proprietor: Bev & Roger Pfost
Hours: Mon-Sun, 11-5
Types & Periods: Nautical Antiques including Waterfowling Items
Appraisal Service Available
Directions: On major Rte 50

Charlotte Hall

SCOSHIE'S ANTIQUES
Rte 5 20622
301 884-4734 Est: 1972
Proprietor: Scoshie Yerkie
Hours: Wed & Sat or by appt
Types & Periods: Furniture, Glass, China, Bisque Figurines & Dolls
Directions: 301 to Waldorf, left on Rte 5 past Hughesville to Charlotte Hall

Chestertown

BAYSIDE ANTIQUES
High St   21620
301 728-5050   Est: 1973
Proprietor: A Thomas &
Edgar H Legg
Hours: Mon-Sat, 10-5
Types & Periods: Primitives,
Oak
Directions: State Rte 20 at
the Bay

BIG DIPPER, INC
851 High St   21620
301 778-4876   Est: 1975
Proprietor: Bertram E
Wilson, Jr
Hours: Mon-Fri &
Weekends by appt
Types & Periods: American
Country Furniture
Specialties: Antique
Furniture Restoration,
Refinishing & Repairs
Directions: N end High St;
45 miles N of Bay Bridge
& 50 miles S of
Wilmington, Del

**RIVER COUNTRY
ANTIQUES**
Rte 213 Kings Town 21620
301 778-0653   Est: 1973
Proprietor: M Douglas
Gates
Hours: Mon-Sun
Types & Periods: Early
American 19th Century
Country Furniture
Appraisal Service Available
Directions: S of Chester
River Bridge

Chevy Chase

JAMSHID ANTIQUE RUGS
5416 Wisconsin Ave 20015
301 657-2725   Est: 1976
Proprietor: Jamshid
Aghamolla
Hours: Mon-Sat, 10-6
Types & Periods: 19th &
20th Century Antiques &
Oriental (Chinese,
Caucasian & Persian) Rugs
Specialties: Rugs
Appraisal Service Available
Directions: Corner of
Willard & Wisconsin Ave;
near Neiman-Marcus &
Saks Fifth Ave

MENDELSOHN GALLERIES
6826 Wisconsin Ave 20015
301 656-2766   Est: 1898
Proprietor: Wilton B
Mendelsohn
Hours: Mon-Fri, 9-6; Sat
9-5:30
Types & Periods: 18th &
19th Century French &
English Furniture, Paintings
& Bric-A-Brac
Specialties: Baccarat
Crystal, Chandeliers &
Sconces

Churchville

**END OF THE LINE
ANTIQUES**
3056 Churchville Rd 21028
301 734-6393   Est: 1973
Proprietor: G Hays
Hours: Tues, Thurs-Sun
Types & Periods: General
Line
Specialties: Glass
Appraisal Service Available
Directions: Rte 22
between Aberdeen & Bel
Air; Shop in a Caboose

HATT-IN-HAND ANTIQUES
3100 Aldino Rd (Rte 22)
                             21028
301 734-4254   Est: 1970
Proprietor: Jan & Jack
Scott
Hours: Tues-Sat by appt
or chance
Types & Periods: 18th &
19th Century English
Metalware & Pottery &
American & English Country
Furniture
Specialties: Restoration of
Brass, Copper & Pewter
Appraisal Service Available
Directions: 3 miles W on
Rte 22 at exit 5
(Aberdeen) off I-95

Clinton

COYNE'S CORNER
5824 Kirby Rd   20735
301 297-4848   Est: 1973
Proprietor: J R Coyne
Hours: Mon-Sun, 10-5 by
appt

Types & Periods:
Continental, European &
American
Appraisal Service Available
Directions: Rte 495 to exit
36 (Rte 5) Waldorf, 5
miles, 3rd traffic light turn
right to Kirby

Cockeysville

**BILL BENTLEY'S ANTIQUE
SHOW MART**
10854 York Rd   21030
301 667-9184   Est: 1967
Proprietor: William R
Bentley
Hours: Mon, Wed-Sat
10-5; Sun 12-6
Types & Periods: A Great
Variety of Everything, Early
Oriental China, Glass,
Porcelain & Collectibles
Specialties: Linens &
Oriental Porcelain
Appraisal Service Available
Directions: Exit 17 off Rte
83, turn left on York Rd,
two miles & stop at
underpass

**THE KEY & PENDULUM
CLOCK SHOP**
10744 York Rd   21030
                        Est: 1976
Proprietor: Fred C Vieck
Sr
Hours: Mon-Sun
Types & Periods: Pocket
Watches & Clocks of the
19th Century
Appraisal Service Available
Directions: 15 miles N of
Baltimore

College Park

**GASLIGHT LANE
ANTIQUES**
5000 Berwyn Rd   20747
301 474-2720   Est: 1973
Proprietor: Mary Margaret
Camus
Hours: Tues-Sat, 11-5
Types & Periods: Country
Items & New & Old
Decorating Accessories
Directions: Off US Rte 1, 1
mile N of University of MD

LEN'S COUNTRY BARN ANTIQUES
9929 Rhode Island Ave
20740
301 441-2545   Est: 1970
Proprietor: Len Ferber,
Len's Inc
Hours: Mon-Tues &
Thurs-Fri: 9-5; Wed 9-8;
Sat 9-4
Types & Periods: Oak &
Walnut Furniture, Brass
Beds & Round Tables
Specialties: Wicker, Chair
Cane & Upholstery Supplies
& Refinishing Supplies
Appraisal Service Available
    Directions: Exit 27 on 495,
    N 1 mile, right on
    Sunnyside Rd, right at
    Rhode Island & proceed S
    under Beltway to Len's on
    Left

Cordova

GRANNY'S WORKSHOP
Rte 1, Box 66   21625
301 822-6178   Est: 1975
Proprietor: Carl & Ethel H
Asche
Hours: Mon-Sun
Types & Periods: Glassware,
China, Early American &
Victorian Furniture &
Collectibles
Specialties: All Types of
Furniture, Refinished,
Repaired & Built &
Everything Hand Stripped
    Directions: Off Rte 50 to
    309, Asche Acres Rd; look
    for Saw Blade at the end
    of the road

Creagerstown

REBEL YELL ANTIQUES
Main St   21798
301 898-7766   Est: 1970
Proprietor: James R
Beachley
Hours: Mon-Sat, 9-5
Types & Periods: 18th
Century Country Furniture,
Ironware, Old Tools, Quilts,
Country Store Items, Civil
War Items & Baskets
Specialties: Restoration
Services & Handmade
Reproductions
Appraisal Service Available

Directions: From
Frederick, MD; Rte 15 N
to Old Frederick Rd, take
left, follow 4 miles to
Creagerstown

Denton

THE COUNTRY STORE
Rte 404   21629
301 479-2766
Proprietor: Paul & Jean
Hurst
Hours: Mon-Tues &
Thurs-Sat, 10-5; Sun 1-5
Types & Periods: General
Line
Appraisal Service Available
    Directions: 4 miles E of
    Town

STOCKLEY'S ANTIQUES
708 Market St   21629
301 749-1750
Proprietor: Carol D
Stockley
Types & Periods: Country &
Formal Furniture with
Accessories

Dunkirk

PENWICK SQUARE
Rte 4   20754
301 257-2738   Est: 1966
Proprietor: Donald &
Audrey Davenport
Hours: Tues-Sat, 10-5;
Sun 1-5
Types & Periods: Victorian,
Empire, Primitives &
Collectibles
    Directions: Rte 4 at Ferry
    Landing Rd, 18 miles E of
    495 (Washington Beltway),
    exit 34 E

Easton

YEARDLY D ELDER CO
15 N Harrison St   21601
301 822-2686   Est: 1940
Proprietor: Mary P Coulby
Hours: Mon-Sat, 9:30-5
Types & Periods: 17th &
18th Century Furniture &
Accessories
    Directions: Across from
    the Goldroom Entrance to
    the Tidewater Inn

Elkton

CHEYNEY HOUSE ANTIQUES
Rte 7, Box 402   21921
301 398-6484   Est: 1968
Proprietor: Martha Adams
Hours: Mon-Sun
Types & Periods: Pine
Country Antiques, Lamps &
Furniture
Appraisal Service Available
    Directions: Rte 40, 3½
    miles W of Elkton across
    from YMCA

McINTYRE'S ANTIQUES
517 North St   21921
301 398-4176
Types & Periods: Silver, Cut
Glass, China, Toys & Dolls

Ellicott City

ALADDIN'S LAMP ANTIQUES
10141 Century Dr   21043
301 465-5432   Est: 1973
Proprietor: Donald L &
Mildred L Shields
Hours: By appt
Types & Periods: Victorian
Lighting & Accessories
    Directions: 2 miles from
    Enchanted Forest
    Children's Park

RAG & BONE ANTIQUES
8145 Main St   21043
301 465-5823   Est: 1970
Proprietor: Ms Brenda
Fenster
Hours: Wed-Fri, 11-4:30;
Sat-Sun, 12-5:30
Types & Periods: Primitives,
Turn of the Century
Furniture & Jewelry

REBEL TRADING POST
8181 Main St   21043
301 465-9595   Est: 1976
Proprietor: Vernon R
Scoone
Hours: Mon-Sun, 11-5
Types & Periods: Military &
War Antiques, Furniture,
Collectibles, Books & Beer
Cans

REBEL TRADING   Cont'd

Specialties: Civil War Relics
Appraisal Service Available
Directions: Take exit 13
off of Baltimore Beltway,
go W 5 miles on Fredrick
Rd to Ellicott City, half
way up the hill, shop is on
the left

REGAN'S ROOST

8344 Main St   21043
301 747-6513   Est: 1975
Proprietor: Mrs E Melva
Regan
Hours: By appt
Types & Periods: China,
Bisque, Staffordshire,
Mettlach, Satsuma, Weller,
Cranberry, Old Pattern
Glassware, Vaseline & Cut
Glass, Nippon, Pictures,
Collectibles & Small pieces
of Furniture
Directions: 3 doors from
the Fire House

WAGON WHEEL ANTIQUES

8061 Tiber Alley   21043
301 465-7910 or
747-7911   Est: 1967
Proprietor: Ed Crowl
Hours: Sat & Sun by appt;
Summer: Mon-Sun by appt
Types & Periods: Furniture,
Glassware & Clocks
Specialties: All types of
repairs & refinishing
Directions: 200 feet from
the Historic B & O
Railroad Terminal

Fork

KENDALL'S ANTIQUES

12548 Harford Rd   21051
301 592-8074   Est: 1978
Proprietor: Dennis & Kathy
Kendall
Hours: Tues-Sun, 10-5
Types & Periods: Oak,
Walnut, Mahogany & Pine
Furniture, Collectibles &
Glassware
Specialties: Oriental Rugs
Directions: Beltway 695 to
Harford Rd, 8 miles N

Frederick

ANTIQUE IMPORTS

125 East St   21701
301 662-6200   Est: 1967
Proprietor: William B
Anderson
Hours: Mon-Sun
Types & Periods: General
Line of 17th, 18th & 19th
Century British Furniture, Art
& Clocks; Wholesale only

COLONIAL JEWELERS

9 W Patrick St   21701
301 663-9252   Est: 1900
Proprietor: Will Hurwitz
Hours: Mon-Sun
Types & Periods: Jewelry &
Pocket Watches
Appraisal Service Available
Directions: Downtown

ODDS & END SHOP

Carroll & South Sts 21701
301 662-5388   Est: 1972
Proprietor: Dennis J
Dugan
Hours: Fri-Sun, 9-6
Types & Periods: General
Line
Specialties: Paper
Americana, "Breweriana"
Directions: Short distance
from Rtes 40 & 270 (70)

FRANKLIN RAPPOLD, INC

10 W College Terrace
                     21701
301 898-5533 or 663-6102
Proprietor: Franklin &
Eleanor Rappold
Hours: Wed-Sat, 11-4;
other times by appt
Types & Periods: 18th
Century American Furniture
Directions: 1/2 mile E
Rtes 15 & 40 at exit 6

Funkstown

FUNKSTOWN ANTIQUE MART

G West-Side Ave   21734
301 797-6246   Est: 1971
Proprietor: Gary &
Barbara Hovermill
Hours: Thurs-Sat, 11-5;
Sun 1-5
Types & Periods: Furniture,
Quilts, Frames, Glassware,

Jewelry, Collectors Books,
Linens, Coins, Silver &
Pottery
Specialties: Arms & Armor
(WW I & II, German Items)
Directions: 1/2 mile E of
Hagerstown on Alt 40

RUTH'S ANTIQUE SHOP INC

41 E Baltimore St   21734
301 739-0311   Est: 1937
Proprietor: Beckley &
Shobe
Hours: Mon-Sat by appt
Types & Periods: 18th &
19th Century Furniture &
Accessories from America,
England, Ireland & Far East
Specialties: Furniture
Appraisal Service Available
Directions: Take Rte 40
W, Hagerstown exit, turn
left at first traffic light,
then turn right at first stop
sign

Galena

CROSSROADS ANTIQUES

Rte 213   21635
301 755-6831   Est: 1967
Proprietor: James D Quinn
Hours: By appt or by
chance
Types & Periods: 18th
Century Irish & American
Furniture & Furnishings,
Oriental Export Porcelain,
Glassware, Silver & Queen
Anne Style Candlesticks
Specialties: Fireplace
Fenders, Fire Tools &
Andirons
Directions: At the
Crossroads of Rtes 213,
313 & 290, 3 miles off
Rte 301

Galesville

PINK DOMAIN ANTIQUES

                     20765
301 867-1482   Est: 1957
Proprietor: Champ & Bob
Watson
Hours: Fri-Sun or by appt
Types & Periods: General
Line, 18th & 19th Century
Furniture
Specialties: Furniture

Appraisal Service Available
Directions: 12 miles S of
Annapolis, S on Rte 2 & E
on Rte 255

Glen Burnie

THE LIGHTHOUSE
311 Crain Hwy SE   21061
301 761-6119   Est: 1963
Proprietor: Joanna
Weigman
Hours: Tues-Sat
Types & Periods: Lamps, Oil
Lamps, Oak & Turn of the
Century Furniture & Misc
Specialties: Lamp Creation
& Repair
Directions: S of Baltimore,
on Rte 2 (Crain Hwy, SE)

Goldsboro

WAYSIDE ANTIQUES
PO Box 155   21636
301 482-8701   Est: 1968
Proprietor: Matt Walsh
Hours: By chance
Types & Periods: General
Line
Specialties: Decoys, Games
& Bird Scenes
Appraisal Service Available
Directions: Rte 313

Hyattsville

OLD MILL ANTIQUES
6522 Sligo Pkwy   20782
301 422-2400   Est: 1960
Proprietor: Ben & Jean
Lemen
Hours: Fri-Sun, 12-5 or By
appt
Types & Periods: 19th
Century Paintings, Bronzes,
Art Glass & General Line
Specialties: Restoration of
Paintings
Appraisal Service Available
Directions: Intersection of
E-W Hwy (Rte 410) &
Riggs Rd; approx 1 mile
from Washington DC line

Joppa

STAGE COACH STOP
516 A Philadelphia Rd
21085
301 676-2555
Proprietor: Joyce &
Jacque Anderson
Hours: Mon-Sun by appt
Types & Periods: Walnut,
Oak & Victorian Furniture,
Brass, Copper, Stained
Glass, Bowed Glass China
Closets, Crystal & Lamps
Specialties: Furniture
(Walnut Plantation Desk,
circa 1876)
Directions: 19 miles E of
Baltimore, 1/2 mile from
Pulaski Hwy E

Kensington

ANTIQUES ANONYMOUS
10421 Fawcett St   20795
301 949-1124   Est: 1972
Proprietor: Robbin Mullin
Hours: Tues-Sun
Types & Periods: General
Line, Jewelry, Paintings, Art
Nouveau & Deco, Dolls &
Furniture
Specialties: Jewelry & Deco
Directions: 2 miles N of
Beltway 495 Connecticut
Ave exit N, right on
Howard Ave & 2 blocks
right on Fawcett St

ANTIQUES BOUTIQUE
3760 Howard Ave   20795
301 933-8823   Est: 1975
Proprietor: Ann R
Mahassel
Hours: Tues-Sun, 10-6
Types & Periods:
Continental Porcelain &
English & American
Furniture
Specialties: Arms & Armor
Directions: In the heart of
Kensington Antique
Center

**ANTIQUES OF CHEVY
CHASE**
10419 Armory Ave   21795
301 933-6077
Proprietor: John & Edith
Chappelear
Hours: Mon-Sat,
10:30-4:30; Sun 1-5

Types & Periods: Chinese
Export Porcelain, Jewelry,
17th, 18th & 19th Century
Silver, Glass, Tools, Small
Furniture, Early Lighting
Devices & Staffordshire
Directions: Capital
Beltway, exit 20 N, 2 miles

**ANTIQUE WHOLESALERS
INC**
4233 Howard Ave   20795
301 933-1035   Est: 1970
Proprietor: Mark Broosky
Hours: Mon-Sun, 10-5
Types & Periods: British
Furniture, Bric-A-Brac &
Oriental Porcelain
Specialties: Clocks
Appraisal Service Available
Directions: Near
Washington DC, exit 20
CT Ave, Kensington on
Capital Beltway, Howard
Ave is 1st St after 3rd
stop light

KRAMER & SCOTT INC
3774 Howard Ave   21157
301 949-9188 or 946-1291
Hours: Mon-Sat,
10:30-5:30; Sun 12-5:30
Types & Periods: Late 19th
Century French Furniture &
Accessories, Japanese &
Chinese Cloisonne
Specialties: French Furniture
Appraisal Service Available
Directions: Connecticutt
Ave, exit N off Capital
Beltway (I-495) to
Kensington, right on
Howard Ave

**THE OLD PRINTED WORD
INC**
3808 Howard Ave   20795
301 933-7253   Est: 1968
Proprietor: Dr Dean Des
Roches
Hours: Mon-Sun, 10-5:30
Types & Periods:
Antiquarian & Rare Books,
Prints, Documents,
Pamphlets & Maps
Appraisal Service Available
Directions: Rte 495 (DC
Beltway) to Connecticutt
Ave, exit to Kensington,
1.6 miles to Howard Ave,
turn right, 1st Shop on
right

Kensington   Cont'd

POTOMAC TRADING POST
3610 University Blvd 20795
301 949-5656   Est: 1957
Proprietor: Bill Printz
Hours: By appt
Types & Periods: Arms,
Guns, Swords, Toys &
Trains
Specialties: Arms & Armor
(Civil War & US Military prior
to 1880)
Appraisal Service Available
Directions: 2 miles N of
Washington Capitol
Beltway (I-495) at exit 20
N

**RICE'S PLATING &
ANTIQUES**
4212 Howard Ave   20760
301 949-4460   Est: 1971
Proprietor: Ted Rice
Hours: Tues-Sun
Types & Periods: Furniture,
Brass Beds & Lamps
Directions: Off
Connecticutt Ave, 2 lights
& 1 block N of Beltway
I-495

THIS 'N' THAT SHOP
4216 Howard Ave   20795
301 942-9532   Est: 1972
Proprietor: Michael L Plant
Hours: Mon-Sun
Types & Periods: Paper
Americana, China, Glass &
Victorian Furniture
Specialties: Post Cards,
Stereo Cards & Out of Print
Books
Appraisal Service Available
Directions: W of
Connecticutt Ave, 2 miles
N of Capital Beltway (US
495), exit 21N

**PHYLLIS VAN AUKEN
ANTIQUES**
10425 Fawcett St   20795
301 933-3772   Est: 1970
Proprietor: Phyllis Van
Auken
Hours: Mon-Sat,
10:30-4:30; Sun 12-5 & by
appt
Types & Periods: 18th &
19th Century Antiques:
Furniture, Lighting, Brass,
Copper, Tin, Kitchen Items
& Primitives; 20th Century
Collectibles

Specialties: American
Primitives & Quilts
Directions: 2 miles from
495 Beltway, exit 20N;
Howard & Fawcett Ave
(Antique Row)

THE VICTORIAN PARLOR
4229 Howard Ave
Rear   20795
301 942-9741   Est: 1974
Proprietor: Barbara Rassin
& Phyllis Friedlander
Hours: Thurs-Sun, 12-5
Types & Periods: General
Line & Furniture
Specialties: Furniture,
Mirrors & Frames
Directions: Capital
Beltway, exit 20 N to
Howard Ave, W to 4229
Rear; on Antique Row

Keymar

L & S ANTIQUES
840 Francis Scott
Key Hwy   21757
301 775-2946   Est: 1968
Proprietor: Leakins &
Soper
Hours: Mon-Sun, 12-5
Types & Periods: Pattern
Glass, China, Lamps & Misc
Directions: Along Rte 194

**THE LOOKING GLASS
ANTIQUES**
950 Francis Scott
Key Hwy   21757
301 775-2589   Est: 1970
Proprietor: Joan & Lee
Cox
Hours: By appt or chance
Types & Periods: American
Pattern Glass, Heisey &
Carnival, China &
Collectibles
Specialties: Glass (Goblets)
& Post Cards
Appraisal Service Available
Directions: MD Rte 194;
just 50 minutes from
Washington or Baltimore
& 15 minutes from I-70

McGINNIS MILL ANTIQUES
610 Francis Scott
Key Hwy   21757
301 775-2545   Est: 1973
Proprietor: Beverly Norris
Hours: By appt or chance

Types & Periods: Furniture
in rough, Tins, Clocks &
Collectibles
Directions: N of Fredrick
on Rte 194, 1/2 mile S of
Keymar

Kingsville

PETE'S PICKINS
Bradshaw Rd   21156
301 592-6884   Est: 1958
Proprietor: Louise H
Clarke
Hours: Mon-Sat, 10-5
Types & Periods: Country &
Period Furniture, Glass,
China, Silver, Jewelry,
Primitives, Hardware, Lamps
& Lamp Parts
Specialties: Primitives
Appraisal Service Available
Directions: 1½ mile E of
Rte 1, Kingsville, 8 miles S
of Bel Air & 16 miles N of
Baltimore

Laurel

LAUREL ANTIQUE SHOP
99 Main St   20810
301 498-2004   Est: 1966
Proprietor: Mazie C Frank
Hours: Thurs-Sun, 11-6; or
by appt
Types & Periods: General
Line
Directions: 1 block E of
Rte 1, N in Laurel at Main
St across from B&O
Railroad Station

Laurel Grove

FAMILY FLOUR ANTIQUES
Mt Zion Church Rd 20659
301 373-8160   Est: 1973
Proprietor: Ronald Lee
Stone
Hours: Sun, Wed & Sat,
12-5
Types & Periods: Primitives,
Victorian & Turn of the
Century Furniture, Glass,
China, Curios & Collectibles
Specialties: Restoration &
Seat Caning

Directions: Rte 5 S to Rte 235, 2 miles S & left onto Mt Zion Church Rd, then right still on Mt Zion Church Rd

Laytonsville

OAK TREE ANTIQUES & COLLECTIBLES
21517 Laytonsville Rd
20760
301 253-5572   Est: 1975
Proprietor: A C Bennethum
Hours: Tues-Sun, 11-5
Types & Periods: American & English Furniture & Decorative Accessories
Directions: Rte 108, Village of Laytonville, Main St

YESTERYEAR FARMS
7420 Hawkins Creamery Rd
20760
301 948-3979   Est: 1965
Proprietor: Earl & Elizabeth Marshall
Hours: Sat-Thurs, 12-6
Types & Periods: General Line, Glassware, Country Store Items, Primitives & Pine
Appraisal Service Available
Directions: Approx 1 hour from Downtown Washington DC

Leonardtown

RICHARDSON'S ANTIQUES
21 Fenwick St   20650
301 475-5610   Est: 1957
Proprietor: Vera C Richardson
Hours: Wed-Sat, 10-4:30
Types & Periods: General Line, Glass, China, Silver & Furniture
Directions: Rte 5, from Washington DC to Leonardtown MD

Lutherville

THE WOOD BUTCHER LTD
506 W Seminary Ave
21093
301 821-8767   Est: 1952
Proprietor: Mr Robert E Vogle
Hours: By appt or chance
Types & Periods: 18th & 19th Century Furniture
Directions: Exit 26 N off Baltimore Beltway to 2nd light, left 2 miles on Seminary Ave

Mardela Springs

C U ANTIQUES
US 50   21837
301 749-0373
Proprietor: Charles & Irene Upham
Hours: Mon-Sun, 10-5
Types & Periods: Art, Carnival & Cut Glass, Tiffany Lamps, Dolls, Jewelry, Silver & Furniture

Middlesburg

KLIPP'S BOOKS & BRIC-A-BRAC
PO Box 101   21768
301 775-2966
Proprietor: Robert H Klipp
Hours: Mon-Sun
Types & Periods: Books & Collectibles

Mount Rainier

BOBBS TRADING CO
3310 Rhode Island Ave
20822
301 643-5815   Est: 1926
Proprietor: Robert L Haislip
Hours: Mon-Sun
Types & Periods: General Line
Specialties: Jewelry
Appraisal Service Available
Directions: Rte 1 between Baltimore & Washington DC

New Market

COMUS ANTIQUES
1 N Federal St   21774
301 831-6464   Est: 1964
Proprietor: The William Armstrongs
Hours: Tues-Sun, 12-5
Types & Periods: Country Furniture & Accessories, Copper, Brass, Tools, Toys & Tin
Specialties: Brass & Copper
Directions: 7 miles from Frederick, off I-70; Federal St is on the E side of town & off the main st

COUNTRY SQUIRE ANTIQUES
4 W Main St   21774
301 865-3217
Proprietor: L Schimpff
Hours: Tues-Sun, 11-5
Types & Periods: Primitives & Country Furniture

CYNTHIA FEHR
51 W Main St   21774
310 865-5909   Est: 1964
Proprietor: Henry Schiess
Hours: By appt
Types & Periods: Furniture, Paintings & Netsuke
Directions: 7 miles E of Frederick on I-70

MARIA'S CHALET
2 E Main St   21774
301 865-5225   Est: 1972
Proprietor: Maria T Brown
Hours: Tues-Sun & Mon by chance
Types & Periods: Rugs, German Steins, Clocks & Collectibles
Appraisal Service Available
Directions: Corner 8th & Main

SUE W'MSON-MICHAELS, ANTIQUES
20 W Main St   21774
301 865-5355   Est: 1966
Proprietor: Sue W Michaels
Hours: Sat-Sun, 11-5; Mon-Fri by chance or appt
Types & Periods: 18th & 19th Century Furniture, Glass & China
Specialties: Sandwich Glass
Appraisal Service Available

FRANKLIN RAPPOLD INC
5 W Main St   21774
301 865-5111
Proprietor: Franklin
Rappold
Hours: By appt or chance
Types & Periods: 18th
Century American Furniture

Newburg

**CATHEY'S COUNTRY
STORE**
                     20664
301 259-2727   Est: 1952
Proprietor: Troy J Cathey
Hours: Mon-Tues &
Fri-Sat, 10-5; Sun & Wed,
11-6:30
Types & Periods: Dolls,
China, Cut Glass & Furniture
Directions: 1 mile N of
Patomac River Bridge on
Hwy 301

Ocean City

DRAGON RETREAT
72nd St- Bayside   21842
301 289-3273
Proprietor: Mrs Cleo
Warriner
Hours: Summer: Mon-Sun,
10-5; Evenings by appt;
Winter: by chance
Types & Periods: General
Line, Jewelry & Frames
Directions: Green Bldg
behind Bowling Alley

**LEE GRAHAM'S JEWELRY
& ANTIQUES**
311 S Baltimore Ave
                     21842
301 289-4171
Proprietor: Lee Graham
Hours: Summer: Mon-Tues
& Thurs-Sun, 10-10;
Winter: Mon-Tues &
Thurs-Sun, 10-6
Types & Periods: Diamonds,
Gold, Indian Jewelry,
Handcrafted Silver, China,
Glass, Limoges &
Collectibles
Directions: At Somerset St

**MOFFETT COTTAGE
ANTIQUES**
8006 Coastal Hwy   21842
301 524-9555

Proprietor: Jessie M
Moffett
Hours: Summer:Mon-Tues
& Thurs-Sun, 10-6; Winter:
Fri-Sun, 10-6
Types & Periods: China,
Glass, Hummels &
Collectibles

**THE PAZZAZZ ANTIQUES
SHOP**
6303 Ocean Hwy   21111
301 472-4094
Proprietor: Paul & Betty
Phillips
Hours: Summer Only:
Mon-Sun, 9-9
Types & Periods: General
Line

Olney

CARL'S ANTIQUES
16650 Georgia Ave 20832
301 774-6900
Proprietor: Edmund D
Carl, Jr
Hours: Thurs-Sat, 11-5 &
Sun 1-5
Types & Periods: Victorian &
Empire Furniture, China &
Glass
Specialties: Glass
Directions: 7 miles N of
Washington Beltway

Owings Mills

PICK & POKE
10624 Reisterstown Rd
                     21117
301 542-1760   Est: 1976
Hours: Miss Harriet L
Kahn
Hours: By appt or chance
Types & Periods: General
Line, All Periods,
Collectibles, Second Hand
Antiques, Furniture,
Glassware, Jewelry, Silver,
Gold, Rare Books &
Phonograph Records
Specialties: Rare Books &
Phonograph Records
Directions: Reisterstown
Rd (US 140) out to
Owings Mills MD

Parkton

COUNTRY TRADER
                     21120
                  Est: 1972
Proprietor: Eleanor
Kaufman
Hours: By appt
Types & Periods: General
Line, Jewelry, Prints,
Primitives & Art Nouveau
Appraisal Service Available
Directions: N on Hwy 83
to Parkton second exit,
then S on York Rd 1/2
mile to School House

Pikesville

THE ELEGANT TABLE
1500 Reisterstown Rd
                     21208
301 486-5310   Est: 1975
Proprietor: Debra Krome
Hours: Tues-Fri,
10:30-3:30 & Sat by appt
Types & Periods: Furniture
Specialties: Everything for
Elegant Dining
Directions: 1 mile S
Baltimore Beltway, exit 20

Reisterstown

E J CANTON ANTIQUES
319-321 Main St   21136
301 883-7274
Proprietor: Eugene A
Shaw
Hours: Mon-Sun
Types & Periods: Oriental
Rugs, American & English
Silver & 19th Century
Decorative Arts
Specialties: Jewelry
Appraisal Service Available
Directions: Exit 20 on
Baltimore Beltway, 8
minutes N to Reisterstown

**MARGIE'S ANTIQUES,
COLLECTIBLES & DOLLS**
239 Main St   21136
301 526-5656   Est: 1974
Proprietor: Marjorie
Schapiro
Hours: Mon-Sun, 11-5
Types & Periods: Large
Variety of Dolls, also

Furniture, Glassware &
Collectibles
Specialties: Dolls
Directions: Baltimore, exit
20 (Reisterstown),
continue for almost 10
miles; Store is on right
side of Reisterstown Rd
(becomes Main St when it
enters community of
Reisterstown), Antique
Row

NETTIE PENN ANTIQUES
234 Main St   21136
301 833-5558   Est: 1969
Proprietor: Nettie Penn
Hours: Sat-Sun by appt
Types & Periods: Period
Furniture, China, Glass,
Gifts, Primitives, Decorator
Pieces & Collectibles
Directions: N of the
Beltway, Reisterstown exit;
Main St of Antique Center

THE SHUTTER DOOR
222 Main St   21136
301 833-7288
Proprietor: Virginia & Jim
Smith
Hours: By appt or chance
Types & Periods: General
Line
Specialties: 18th & 19th
Century Collectibles
Directions: N off 695, exit
21

TRELA ANTIQUES
501 Sunbrook Rd   21136
301 833-2449   Est: 1972
Proprietor: Carol & Jim
Trela
Hours: By appt or chance
Types & Periods: 18th &
19th Century American
Furniture & Accessories
Specialties: 18th & 19th
Century Furniture
Appraisal Service Available
Directions: Exit 20
Baltimore Beltway, N 7
miles, left on Berryman's
Lane, 3 miles, left on
Church, turn right on
Sunnydale Way, 1 mile to
Dead End

Rhodesdale

CLOVERDALE ANTIQUES
Rte 1, Box 235 Cloverdale
Rd   21659
301 943-4220
Proprietor: Hedy Messick
Hours: Mon-Sat, 11-5 &
Sun by appt
Types & Periods: Country &
Victorian Furniture

Rock Hall

BAYSIDE ANTIQUES
Rte 2, Box 139   21661
301 639-7274   Est: 1973
Proprietor: A Thomas &
Edgar H Legg
Hours: Sat-Sun &
Evenings
Types & Periods: Primitives,
Duck & Goose Decoys
Directions: State Rte 20 at
the Bay

Rockville

THE LOFT
304 N Stonestreet Ave
              20850
301 762-3676   Est: 1973
Proprietor: Roy Lambert
Hours: Tues-Sat, 9-4
Types & Periods: Turn-of-
the-Century Oak & Other
Furniture
Specialties: Furniture
Stripping
Directions: I-495 Beltway
to Rte 355 about 5 miles
to Park St, turn right &
go 1 block

**ROGER'S AUCTION
GALLERY**
12101 Nebel St   20852
301 881-5544   Est: 1975
Hours: Mon-Sat
Types & Periods: Estate
Liquidation, Furniture, Glass,
Porcelain, Art & Jewelry
Specialties: Fri Night
Auction, 7:30
Appraisal Service Available
Directions: 1 block N of
Rockville Pike off Randolf
Rd

Royal Oak

OAK CREEK SALES
              21662
              Est: 1970
Proprietor: Charles E
Kilmon
Hours: Mon-Sun
Types & Periods: Furniture
& Collectibles
Appraisal Service Available
Directions: From Easton,
Rte 33 to Rte 329, next to
Post Office

Ruxton

RUXTON IMPORTS
7623 Bellona Ave   21204
301 828-8110   Est: 1961
Proprietor: Anne J Shriver
Hours: Mon-Sat, 10-5
Types & Periods: Furniture
& China
Specialties: Boxes
Directions: About 2 miles
W of N Charles St

Salisbury

HOLLY RIDGE ANTIQUES
Morris Leonard Rd 21801
301 742-4392
Proprietor: Viola Timmons
Hours: Wed-Sun, 10-5
Types & Periods: Primitives
to Formal, Victorian Queen
Anne Furniture
Specialties: Furniture
Directions: E on Rte 50
from Salisbury to Phillip
Morris Dr, opposite flag
pole turn left, continue
straight 1½ miles, take
right on Morris Leonard
Rd, 3rd house on left

THE ROCKING HORSE
412 Lincoln Ave   21801
301 742-3789
Proprietor: Ruth S Burnet
Hours: Mon-Sun, 11-7 &
also by appt
Types & Periods: Formal &
Country Furniture, Brass,
Copper, Silver, Lamps,
Glass, China, Primitives,
Dolls, Toys & Miniatures
Directions: Between S
Division St & Spring Ave

SPINNING WHEEL ANTIQUES
Rte 12   21801
301 749-3806   Est: 1969
Proprietor: Barbara &
Franklin Evans
Hours: By appt or chance
Types & Periods: Furniture,
Glass, Lamps & Primitives
Directions: 4 miles from
Salisbury on right

Savage

THE ANTIQUE GALLERY LTD
Foundry St   20863
301 953-7850   Est: 1973
Proprietor: Ed Grant &
George Ray
Hours: Mon-Sun
Types & Periods: Furniture
& Grandfather Clocks
Appraisal Service Available
Directions: Rte 32, exit off
I-95 towards Rte 1 E, right
at Rte 1, right at next
light, left at 1st stop sign
into Old Mill

CELE'S OLD MILL ANTIQUES & INTERIORS
Savage Industrial Ctr
                    20863
301 792-0211   Est: 1972
Proprietor: Cecelia Winer
Hours: Mon-Fri, 11-5 &
Sat-Sun, 12-5
Types & Periods: Furniture,
Jewelry, Glass & Dolls
Specialties: Art Glass
Directions: 3 blocks off
Hwy 1, 1½ miles N of
Laurel, midway between
Baltimore & Washington
DC

Severna Park

MOUSE HOUSE ANTIQUES
Ritchie Hwy   21146
301 647-9303   Est: 1972
Proprietor: Charlene
Fowler
Hours: Mon-Sun
Types & Periods: American
19th Century Oak, Walnut &
Pine Furniture, China, Glass,
Primitives & Collectibles
Directions: Intersection of
Ritchie Hwy & Earleigh
Heights Rd, 59

Silver Spring

BREEZEWOOD FARMS ANTIQUES
Box 1111 Blair St   20910
301 897-8784
Proprietor: E Lee Glover &
Richard A Gibson
Hours: By appt
Types & Periods: Art & Cut
Glass & Orientals

South Chesapeake City

BLUE MAX ANTIQUES
3rd & Bohemia Ave 21915
301 287-2077   Est: 1974
Proprietor: Shirley Hunter
Hours: Wed, Fri & Sat,
10:30-4
Types & Periods: American
Primitives to English
Victorian, General Line
Directions: Turn right just
S of C&D Canal Bridge off
Rte 213

CHESAPEAKE ANTIQUES
Rte 213   21915
301 885-5952
Proprietor: Betty R Moor
Hours: Mon-Sat, 9-5
Types & Periods: General
Line
Directions: S of
Chesapeake Canal Bridge,
on the right at the Manor
Shopping Area in the
Complete Coin Corp Bldg
on 2nd floor

Sparks

GLENCOE GARDENS
15900 York Rd   21152
301 472-2300   Est: 1954
Proprietor: Mrs Roger W
Carroll
Hours: Mon-Sun
Types & Periods: General
Line & Country Pine
Furniture
Directions: York Rd (Rte
45), Shop is located
between Baltimore City &
York, Pa

Stevenson

HEIRLOOM JEWELS
Stevenson Village Center
                    21153
301 486-1923
Proprietor: Susan F
Garten
Hours: Mon-Sun
Types & Periods: Antique
Jewelry, Watches, Slide
Chains, Silver, Napkin Rings,
Plates, Mirrors, Netsukes &
More
Specialties: Jewelry
Appraisal Service Available
Directions: 1½ miles N of
Beltway, exit 21

Stevensville

LOOKAWAY ANTIQUES
Box 65   21666
301 643-2292   Est: 1974
Proprietor: Mary Paul
Hours: Tues-Sun, 12-5
Types & Periods: General
Line & Collectibles
Directions: Rte 8 & 18, 2
blocks N of Rtes 50 & 301
(Kent Island)

Taneytown

CAROUSEL ANTIQUES
202 E Baltimore St 21787
301 756-2480   Est: 1967
Proprietor: Margaret J
Maas
Hours: Mon-Sun
Types & Periods:
Hepplewhite, Chippendale,
Victorian, Primitive Pine &
Oak (1890-1900) Furniture,
China & Collectibles
Specialties: Refinished
Furniture
Directions: On Rte 97, 12
miles W of Westminister

Thurmont

MOLLY GATES ANTIQUES
Rte 2, Box 330   21738
301 271-7370
Hours: Mon-Sun, 12-6
Types & Periods: Silver,
Primitives, Pattern Glass,
Country Furniture, B & G &
RC Christmas Plates

Trappe

ADAM'S EMPORIUM
Maple & Main   21673
301 476-3992   Est: 1971
Proprietor: Kurt & Natalie
Adam
Hours: Tues-Sun
Types & Periods: General
Line, Americana, Primitives,
Decoys, Porcelain &
Decorative Accessories
  Directions: 8 miles below
  Easton on US 50, turn
  right onto Maple & watch
  for Hwy signs

**CARTER'S ANTIQUES &
INTEREST**
35N Main St   21673
301 476-3474
Proprietor: Evelyn &
Emory T Carter
Hours: Wed-Fri & Sun,
10:30-5; Other days by
chance
Types & Periods: General
Line

YE OLE MILL ANTIQUES
3 Maple Ave   21673
001 476 3191
Proprietor: Triffinia Wyatt
Hours: Mon-Sun, 8:30-8:30
Types & Periods: Oriental
Porcelains, Collectibles &
American Country Furniture
Specialties: Colored Glass
Appraisal Service Available

Union Bridge

RED'S ANTIQUES
Maryland Rte 75   21791
301 775-2505   Est: 1967
Proprietor: David H &
Ruth R Morrow
Hours: Thurs-Sun, 11-6 &
by appt
Types & Periods: Victorian
American Furniture, Cut &
Pattern Glass, Heisey,
China, Silver & Collectibles
Specialties: Victorian
Furniture & Cut Glass
  Directions: On Maryland
  Rte 75, 7 miles N of
  Libertytown

Upperco

ECHO FARM BARN
4300 Mt Carmel Rd 21155
301 239-8833   Est: 1966
Proprietor: Elizabeth
Gorman
Hours: Sat-Sun by appt or
chance
Types & Periods: Country
Furniture, Early
Phonographs, Records &
Sound Equipment
  Directions: 3 miles E of
  Hampstead

THE SNOOPERY
3921 Mount Carmel Rd
21155
301 239-7454   Est: 1973
Proprietor: Mrs Betty
Mason & Mrs Heather
Dilkes
Hours: Sat-Sun by appt
Types & Periods: Period
Early Country & Oak
Furniture, Collectibles &
Accessories
Appraisal Service Available
  Directions: N of Baltimore
  on Rte 83 approx 22 miles
  to Mt Carmel Rd, turn W
  0½ miles to Shop

Walkersville

CREATIVE CORNER
1 W Frederick St   21793
301 845-8182   Est: 1969
Proprietor: Frances Lynch
Hours: Mon-Sat, 10-5
Types & Periods: General
Line, Primitives &
Collectibles
Specialties: Needlework
19th Century Textiles,
Coverlets, Quilts & Many
Original Creations
  Directions: Rte 194, 6
  miles from Frederick,
  located in a General Store
  in continuous operation
  since 1884

Westminister

ARCHER'S ANTIQUES
1758 Baltimore Blvd
21157
301 876-1215
Proprietor: Joe & Mary
Archer
Types & Periods: General
Line, Furniture, Glass &
China

THE LOAFING BARN INC
521 Old Westminister Pike
21157
301 848-8111   Est: 1972
Proprietor: Byrd N
Roadcap
Hours: May-Dec:
Tues-Thurs & Sat-Sun,
12-5; also by appt
Types & Periods: General
Line, English & American
Antiques, Fabrics &
Decorator Items
  Directions: 521 Old
  Westminister Pike (Main
  St extended), 100 yds
  beyond Rte 97

**TREASURE CHEST
ANTIQUES**
164 166 W Main St 21157
301 848-3783   Est: 1968
Proprietor: Doris A &
Carolyn A Kutilek
Hours: Mon, Wed-Sat,
11-3; Sun 11-4
Types & Periods: Restored
Antique Wicker Furniture,
Oak & Country Furniture,
Haviland & Other China,
Crystal, Primitives, Quilts &
Linens, Antique Clothing,
Prints, Braided Rugs & A
Fine Assortment of Baskets
Specialties: Restored
Antique Wicker Furniture
(largest selection in the
Mid-Atlantic) & Antique
Clothing
  Directions: Near Western
  Maryland College in
  Westiminster on MD Rte
  32 thru town at Western
  End

OLIVE TROXELL & B & B ASSOCIATES

412 Washington Rd 21157
301 848-6707   Est: 1940
Proprietor: Troxell Family
Hours: Dealers: Mon-Fri,
8-5; Retail Sales: By appt
only
Types & Periods: Period &
Country Furniture
Appraisal Service Available
    Directions: On Rte 32, 1
    mile from center of town

Wheaton

ANTIQUES 'N THINGS

11214 Grandview Ave
                            20902
301 933-7244   Est: 1967
Proprietor: Doris Ely
Hours: Mon-Sat, 11-4
Types & Periods: General
Line
Specialties: Leaded Glass
    Directions: Across from
    Wheaton Plaza Shopping
    Center, between Georgia
    Ave & Viers Mill Rd

White Marsh

FOLEY'S ANTIQUES

10807 Railroad Ave 21162
301 335-3313   Est: 1965
Proprietor: Inez & William
Foley
Hours: Tues-Sun, 12-5
Types & Periods: General
Line & Collectibles
Specialties: Oak Furniture
    Directions: Rte 40, off
    I-95, exit 3

Woodbine

DAISY TRADING POST

15948 Union Chapel Rd
                            21797
301 489-7610   Est: 1969
Proprietor: Ellen & Carl
Dingman
Hours: Mon-Sun, 12-5
Types & Periods: General
Line , Furniture Restoration
& 20th Century Dolls
Specialties: Collectible Dolls
(1930-1960)
    Directions: Corner of of
    Union Chapel Rd & Daisy
    Rd, Howard County, MD;
    Daisy, 3 miles from Lisbon

Woodsboro

CIRCUIT RIDER SHOP

Rt 550   21798
301 898-5555   Est: 1973
Proprietor: Gorden L
Wilson
Hours: Mon-Sun
Types & Periods: Chairs,
Rockers, Country Furniture,
Primitives, Tinware,
Enamelware & Collectibles
    Directions: On Rte 550,
    between Thurmont &
    Libertytown or just off Rte
    194, between Frederick &
    Taneytown, "In an old
    grain mill"

MARTIN'S FURNITURE
                            21798
301 845-6108
Types & Periods: General
Line

SHOP OF OLDE THINGS
                            21798
Hours: Mon-Sat, 10-5; Sun
12-5
Types & Periods: Furniture

Empire Peer Table with mirror
and marble top.

Empire Game Table

STATE OF MASSACHUSETTS

Acton

RICHARD W SHAW ANTIQUES
584 Massachusetts Ave
01720
617 263-0133
Proprietor: Richard W
Shaw
Hours: Mon-Sat, 10-5;
Sun, 12-6
Types & Periods: Country
Furniture, Primitives
Directions: Rte 111

Allston

ALLSTON ANTIQUES
171 Brighton Ave   02134
617 782-5108
Proprietor: Stephen
Franklin
Hours: Mon-Sat, 9-5
Types & Periods: Furniture,
Bric-A-Brac, Estate
Clearings
Specialties: Pianos, Antique
Clothes, Jewelry
Appraisal Service Available
Directions: Major Boston
street

ZEKE'S FURNITURE EMPORIUM
169 A Harvard Ave 02134
617 254-3856   Est: 1970
Proprietor: John W
Broome
Hours: Mon-Sat, 9-6
Types & Periods: Furniture,
Bric-A-Brac, Art, Rugs
Directions: Between
Commonwealth Ave &
Brighton Ave

Amherst

ABRAHAMS ANTIQUES & ACCESSORIES
266 Pelham Rd   01002
413 253-7646   Est: 1976
Proprietor: Rich & Flo
Newman
Hours: By appointment, by
chance

Types & Periods: Furniture,
From 1800 to 1920,
Collectibles
Specialties: Musical
Instruments
Appraisal Service Available
Directions: 2 miles from
center of town on main
street

R & R FRENCH ANTIQUES
657 S Pleasant St   01002
413 253-2269
Proprietor: Rachel French
Hours: Daily, 9-5
Types & Periods: Pewter,
Furniture, General Line

THE WOOD-SHED
156 Montague Rd   01002
413 549-1720   Est: 1952
Proprietor: Bea & Harlan
Wood Jr
Hours: Mon-Fri; Sat by
appointment
Types & Periods: Primitives
Directions: Rte 63 off 116
of I-91

THE WOOD SHED
150-156 Montague Rd
01002
413 549-1691
Proprietor: The Woods
Hours: Daily, by
appointment or by chance
Types & Periods: Books,
Bottles, Primitives, Prints,
Tin, Woodenware

Arlington

MILL BROOK ANTIQUES
81 Mystic St   02174
617 648-4600   Est: 1971
Proprietor: Paul Berberian
Hours: Tues-Sat; Sun &
Mon by appointment
Types & Periods: 18th &
19th Century Furniture,
Oriental Accessories,
American Accessories,
Paintings & Prints, Oriental
Rugs
Appraisal Service Available
Directions: Rte 3, just
outside Arlington

Ashfield

APPLEDORE ANTIQUES
Smith Rd   01330
413 628-3252
Proprietor: Helen G Stein
Hours: Daily, by chance
Types & Periods: New
England Furniture &
Accessories
Directions: Smith Rd &
Rte 112

M & L ANTIQUES
Box 102   01330
413 628-3241
Proprietor: Mark Suozzi
Hours: By appointment
Types & Periods: Political
Buttons, Mechanical 1-Cent
Banks, Toys, Photographs,
Americana

Ashland

AT THE SIGN OF THE THREE LAMBS
83 Cordaville Rd   01721
617 881-2267
Proprietor: Rae E
Lammerding
Hours: Mon-Wed, 1-5:30;
Also by appointment
Types & Periods: Country
Furniture, Primitives,
Collectibles

BRYNA CURLEY
01721
617 881-3251
Proprietor: Bryna Curley
Hours: Daily
Types & Periods: China,
Glass, Furniture,
Accessories

PECULIAR PEDDLER'S SHOP
80 Fountain St   01721
617 881-2953
Proprietor: Barbara
Camille
Hours: Wed-Sat, 1-5
Types & Periods: New,
Used, Renewed & Abused
Furniture, Glass, China
Directions: "In country
barn"

Ashley Falls

ASHLEY FALLS ANTIQUES SHOP
Rte 7A   01222
413 229-8759
Proprietor: Dina & Harry Weiss
Hours: Sun-Mon, Wed-Sat, 9:30-5:30
Types & Periods: 18th & 19th Century Furniture, Paintings, Clocks, China, Glass

JOHN E BIHLER/HENRY S COGER
Rte 7A   01222
413 229-8495   Est: 1950
Proprietor: J E Bihler & H S Coger
Hours: By appointment
Types & Periods: 18th Century English & American Furniture, American & English Paintings, Folk Art, China, Glass, Metals
Appraisal Service Available

LEWIS & WILSON
Rte 7A   01222
413 229-3330
Proprietor: Don Lewis & Tom Wilson
Hours: Daily, 10-5
Types & Periods: 18th & 19th Century Furniture, English, Continental & Chinese Accessories

Athol

BURNHAM'S ANTIQUE SHOP
958 S Main St   01331
617 249-4452
Proprietor: George & Marion Wonsey
Hours: Mon-Tues, Thurs-Sat; Sun & Wed by appointment
Types & Periods: Furniture, Glass, China

DON FRENCH ANTIQUES
1755 Main St   01331
617 249-8830
Proprietor: Helen & Benjamin Tighe
Hours: Weekends; Weekdays by appointment

Types & Periods: Dolls, Toys, Books, Pamphlets, Documents, Posters
Specialties: Glass, China

HACKETT'S ANTIQUES
37 Starrett Ave   01331
617 249-4865
Proprietor: Clarissa Hackett
Hours: By appointment
Types & Periods: Pine Furniture, Primitives, Glass, China, Buttons, Small Items

HOUSE OF BURGESS ANTIQUES
62 Summer St   01331
617 249-4625   Est: 1968
Proprietor: May Burgess
Hours: Daily, by appointment or by chance
Types & Periods: General Line, China, Glass, Primitives, Furniture
Specialties: Ruby Stained Pattern Glass
Directions: Directly off Rtes 2A & 32

MARGE'S NOOK ANTIQUES
284 S Main St   01331
617 249-7488   Est: 1976
Proprietor: Mrs Chas A Brauchle (Marge)
Hours: By appointment or by chance
Types & Periods: General Line, Primitives, Wood, Brass, Iron, Tin, Stoneware, Silver, China, Small Furniture
Specialties: Early Oil Lamps
Appraisal Service Available
Directions: Rtes 202 & 2A

Attleboro

THE CHARBBONEAUS
464 Newport Ave   02703
617 761-5063
Hours: By appt or chance
Types & Periods: Country Furniture, Cupboards & Accessories
Directions: Rte 123, 2 miles off Rte 95; At the Ebenezer Guild House

EBENEZER GUILD HOUSE
464 Newport   02703
617 761-5063   Est: 1961
Proprietor: Joyce Harpin Charbormeau
Hours: Daily
Types & Periods: Country Furniture, Cupboards, Accessories, Early 19th Century New England
Appraisal Service Available
Directions: Rte 123, 1 mile off Rtes 95, 1 & 1A

Barnstable

CHERRY & WATSON
Rte 6A   02630
617 362-6823   Est: 1965
Proprietor: James W Cherry & R O Watson
Hours: Daily, 9-6, May thru Nov
Types & Periods: 17th Early 19th Centuries, Mostly American, General Line
Specialties: Glass (Early Colored Sandwich)
Appraisal Service Available
Directions: 1 mile W of town

Belchertown

THE LOVING CUP ANTIQUES
17 Main   01007
413 323-7482   Est: 1956
Proprietor: Bill & Alice Ridenour
Hours: By appointment, by chance, "Always open on Sun afternoons"
Types & Periods: 18th & 19th Century Furniture, Glass, China, Primitives, Toys
Specialties: Pottery, Porcelain
Appraisal Service Available
Directions: On Rte 202 near Amherst

Belmont

CROSS & GRIFFIN
468 Trapelo Rd   02178
617 484-2837   Est: 1961

Proprietor: Robert Cross &
James Griffin
Hours: Mon-Sat; also by
appointment
Types & Periods: General
Line
Specialties: China, Glass,
Toys
Directions: Waverly
Square section near
Rte 60

Beverly

**FISH FLAKE HILL
ANTIQUES**
1 Front St   01915
617 922-9426
Proprietor: Eddie Talbot
Hours: Daily
Types & Periods: General
Line

OLDE TREASURE SHOPPE
93 Cabot St   01915
617 922-3236   Est: 1966
Proprietor: I Miller
Hours: Daily
Types & Periods: Furniture,
Glass, China, Primitives,
Frames
Directions: Downtown in
main shopping center

Boston

BOSTON CLUSTER
Directions: Charles St,
Newbury St

ALBERTS-LANGDON INC
126 Charles St   02114
617 523-5954   Est: 1960
Proprietor: Laura Langdon
& Russell Alberts
Hours: Sun-Fri, 9:30-5;
Sat, 10-2; Closed July &
Aug
Types & Periods: Oriental
Art
Specialties: Porcelains
Appraisal Service Available
Directions: At foot of
Beacon Hill

ARTICLES
270 Newbury St   02176
617 536-0474
Proprietor: David Rowell

Hours: Mon-Sat, 11-5
Types & Periods: Paper,
Quilts

**BEACON HILL
COLLECTIBLES**
23 River St   02108
617 523-0593   Est: 1973
Proprietor: Ruth Buskirk &
Liz Donahue
Hours: Daily
Types & Periods: General
Line
Appraisal Service Available
Directions: On Beacon Hill

**THE BOSTON ANTIQUE
SHOP INC**
63A Charles St   02114
617 227-3120   Est: 1890
Proprietor: Frederick A
Stainforth
Hours: Daily
Types & Periods: Metals,
Brass, Copper, Pewter,
Silver
Specialties: Pewter

BRODNEY ART GALLERY
811 Boylston St   02116
617 536-0500   Est: 1949
Proprietor: Edward
Brodney
Hours: Daily
Types & Periods: Paintings,
Sculpture, Jewelry
Specialties: Jewelry,
Paintings, Sculpture
Directions: Uptown

CHESTNUT GALERIE INC
85 Chestnut St   02108
617 523-8319   Est: 1971
Proprietor: Jeanne Colony
Hours: By Chance
Types & Periods: Paintings,
Drawings, Furniture, Mirrors,
French 17th, 18th & 19th
Century Kilim Carpets
Directions: Bottom of
Beacon Hill

H CLAYMAN & SON INC
16 Lomasney Way   02114
617 742-0404   Est: 1930
Proprietor: Samuel
Clayman
Hours: Mon-Fri, 1:30-6;
Sat, 11-5

Types & Periods: Victorian
Furniture, Old & Antique
Copper & Brass Fireplace
Items
Specialties: Copper & Brass
Appraisal Service Available
Directions: North Station
area

FIRESTONE & PARSON
Ritz Carlton Hotel   02117
617 266-1858   Est: 1946
Proprietor: Edwin I
Firestone & David
Firestone
Hours: Mon-Sat, 9:30-5
Types & Periods: Early
English & American Silver,
Antique Jewelry
Appraisal Service Available

FOREVER FLAMINGO
285 Newbury St   02115
617 267-2547   Est: 1974
Proprietor: Barry Swartz
Hours: Mon-Sat
Types & Periods: Nostalgia
& Collectibles From Art
Deco Period (1920 thru
1950), Furniture, Lamps,
Clothing, Jewelry,
Fiestaware
Specialties: Fiestaware &
Vintage Clothing,
Accessories for Men &
Women
Directions: Back bay area,
parallel to the Prudential
Center

**GEBELEIN SILVERSMITHS
INC**
286 Newbury St   02115
617 266-3876   Est: 1904
Proprietor: Herbert
Gebelein
Hours: Mon-Fri, by
appointment or chance
Types & Periods: Silverware,
American, English,
Continental (European), Old
Sheffield Plate
Specialties: Reproductions
Directions: "Uptown" near
Prudential Center

LEBLANC NUMISMATICS
36 Province St   02108
617 482-1921   Est: 1976
Proprietor: R C LeBlanc
Hours: Mon-Sat, 9-4
Types & Periods: Silver &
Bronze

Boston   Cont'd

LEBLANC   Cont'd
Specialties: Rare Coins
Directions: Downtown,
from Jordan Marsh &
Filene's, turn left on
Bromfield St, turn R on
Province

LION RAMPANT
3 River St   02108
617 227-4938   Est: 1974
Proprietor: Ruth G Buskirk
Hours: Mon-Sat, by
appointment or by chance
Types & Periods: 17th, 18th
& 19th Century French
Country Furniture, Moorish
Inlaid & Painted Furniture,
Decorative Accessories,
Brass Canopied Beds,
Mother-of-Pearl Inlaid
Furniture
Appraisal Service Available
Directions: River St at
Beacon St, at Public
Gardens

**SAMUEL L LOWE JR
ANTIQUES INC**
80 Charles St   02114
617 742-0845   Est: 1964
Proprietor: Samuel L
Lowe Jr
Hours: Mon-Fri, 10:30-5;
Sat, 10:30-4; Closed Sat
during summer
Types & Periods: Americana
Shop, Paintings, Prints,
Models, Scrimshaw, Whaling
Gear, Chinese Export
Porcelain
Specialties: American
Marine Art & Antiques
Appraisal Service Available
Directions: "Charles St is
a one-way street between
the Boston Common &
Public Garden & is long
famous for antiques"

MARCOZ ANTIQUES
281-B Newbury St   02115
617 262-0780   Est: 1971
Proprietor: Marc S
Glasberg
Hours: Daily
Types & Periods: Furniture,
Accessories, Jewelry,
Porcelains

Specialties: Jewelry, Oriental
Appraisal Service Available
Directions: One block from
Boston's Prudential Center

MARIKA'S ANTIQUE SHOP
130 Charles St   02114
617 523-4520
Proprietor: Marie G Raisz
(Mrs Erwin)
Hours: Mon-Sat; Closed
Sat during summer
Types & Periods: General
Line, Jewelry
Directions: At corner of
Charles & Revere Sts

PHOEBE
214 Newbury   02116
           Est: 1975
Proprietor: Samuel
Feinstein
Hours: Mon-Sat
Specialties: Antiques &
Objets d'Art, American,
European, Oriental

**PINCKNEY HOUSE
ANTIQUES**
106 Charles St   02114
617 227-1580
Proprietor: Lloyd A
Hathaway
Hours: Daily, 10:30-5
Types & Periods: General
Line

LOUIS D PRINCE
73 Chestnut St   02801
617 227-9192
Proprietor: Louis D Prince
Hours: Daily
Types & Periods: French &
English Lighting, Hurricane
Sconces & Chandeliers

**ERNEST J REPETTI III
ANTIQUES**
88 Charles St   02114
617 523-6090
Proprietor: Jack Repetti
Hours: Mon-Sat, 12-5:30
Types & Periods:
Collectibles, General Line,
No Furniture
Specialties: Glass, Jewelry,
Silver

ROACH & CRAVEN INC
21 River St   02108
617 742-2080   Est: 1918
Proprietor: Charles H
Willauer

Hours: Mon-Fri, 9-4:30;
also by appointment
Types & Periods: French
18th Century
Directions: Beacon Hill
section of Boston, off
Charles St

FAITH D RUBIN ANTIQUES
107 Pinckney St
Beacon Hill   02114
617 227-1158   Est: 1971
Proprietor: Faith D Rubin
Hours: By appointment
Types & Periods: English
Medical, Nautical, English
Household Pieces
Appraisal Service Available

**ELEANOR RUSKIN
ANTIQUES**
140 Charles St   02114
617 742-1147   Est: 1958
Proprietor: A Ruskin
Hours: Mon-Sat
Types & Periods: 18th &
Early 19th Century English
Furniture

SHELL'S OF ENGLAND
. 84 Chestnut St   02108
617 523-0373   Est: 1973
Proprietor: Douglas
Grandgeorge
Hours: Mon-Sat,
10:30-5:30; also by
appointment
Types & Periods: English
Antiques, Fine Glass &
China, Pocket Watches,
Clocks, Unique Items
Specialties: Finding Service
for any Antique of English
Origin
Appraisal Service Available
Directions: Corner of
Chestnut & River Sts on
Beacon Hill, 1 block from
Charles St

SHER-MORR ANTIQUES
103B Charles St   02114
617 227-4780   Est: 1965
Proprietor: John A
Sherman & Ernest J
Morrell
Hours: Daily, 10-5
Types & Periods: Oriental
Art, Books on Dance

**VOSE GALLERIES OF
BOSTON INC**
238 Newbury St   02116
Proprietor: Robert J Vost
Jr, President

Hours: Mon-Sat; Eves by appointment
Types & Periods: Paintings Only, 18th, 19th & First half 20th Century American, 18th & 19th Century English & French
Specialties: Early American Portraits, 19th Century American Landscapes, 19th Century American Marines, American Impressionists
Appraisal Service Available
Directions: Back Bay Boston, 2 blocks from Prudential Center, 5 blocks up Newbury St from the Ritz

WEINER'S ANTIQUE SHOP
11 Park St   02108
617 227-2894   Est: 1896
Proprietor: Paul A Weiner
Hours: Mon-Fri, 10-4
Types & Periods: General Line, Furniture, China, Glass, Paintings, Pewter
Specialties: Clocks
Appraisal Service Available
Directions: Opposite State House

Bourne

BOURNEDALE COUNTRY STORE
26 Herring Pond Rd 02532
617 888-4400   Est: 1974
Proprietor: Jude & Joan Flynn
Hours: Daily
Types & Periods: Antique Toys, Banks, Country Store Products, General Line
Appraisal Service Available
Directions: Between the Bourne & Sagamore Bridges at the Cape Cod Canal

Boylston

THE FRENCHS'
4 Carol Dr   01505
617 869-2554
Proprietor: Bill & Marion French
Hours: By appointment, by chance

Types & Periods: Clocks, Paintings, Primitives, Furniture, Lamps
Specialties: Clocks
Directions: Off Rtes 140 & 170

Brewster

WILLIAM M BAXTER ANTIQUES
Box 778   02631
617 896-3998   Est: 1960
Proprietor: William M Baxter
Hours: Mon-Sat, 10-5, June thru Oct
Types & Periods: Period American, European & Oriental Furnishings, Paintings, Accessories
Directions: On King's Hwy (Rte 6A) in Brewster opposite Nickerson State Park

DONALD B HOWES ANTIQUES
Rte 6A W   02631
                          Est: 1952
Proprietor: Don Howes
Hours: By appointment, by chance
Types & Periods: General Line, Books
Specialties: Books, Paintings
Directions: Rte 6A

KEEPSAKE HOUSE ANTIQUES
Rte 6A   02631
017 255-5036   Est: 1972
Proprietor: Patti A Smith
Hours: Mon-Sat during season; by chance or appointment other times
Types & Periods: Early Country Antiques & Accessories
Directions: Rte 6A near the Brewster-Orleans line (Mailing: PO Box 1016, Orleans, Mass 02653)

MARSHLANDS ANTIQUES
Main St, Rte 6A   02631
617 385-9919   Est: 1961
Proprietor: Mrs Helen A Kevorkian
Types & Periods: Primitives, Woodworking Tools, Flint Glass, 18th & 19th Century, Some Early 1900's

Specialties: Tools, Primitives
Directions: Rte 6A, from Rte 6 take Exit 9, left on Rte 134, right on 6A, 1 mile to shop

CAPTAIN FREEMAN PERRY HOUSE
Rte 6A   02631
617 896-5323
Proprietor: Sarah & Victor Cohen
Hours: Daily, 9-5
Types & Periods: Brass, Copper, Primitives, Oak Furniture, Silver

SUNSMITH HOUSE ANTIQUES
Rte 6A   02631
617 896-7024   Est: 1978
Proprietor: Wendell & Muriel Smith
Hours: Daily, April-Oct; off-season by chance or appointment
Types & Periods: Country Furniture, Primitives, China, Glass, Collectibles, Toys, Miniatures
Specialties: Primitives & Toys
Directions: Diagonally across from LaSalette

TOWN-HO ANTIQUES & NEEDLEWORKS
1912 Main St   02631
617 896-3000   Est: 1960
Proprietor: Mr Barry C Barnes
Hours: Mon-Sat, 10-5
Types & Periods: 18th & 19th Century

YANKEE TRADER
2071 Rte 6A   02631
617 896-7822   Est: 1960
Proprietor: Stephen & Sheilah Rosen
Hours: Daily, all year
Types & Periods: "Always the unusual"
Directions: 1/4 mile E of The Brewster General Store in Historic Brewster

Bridgewater

BIX FURNITURE RESTORATION
552 Bedford St   02324
617 697-4717   Est: 1964
Proprietor: Ron Peterson
Hours: Mon-Tues,
Thurs-Sat, 9:30-5
Types & Periods: Complete
Stripping & Furniture
Restoration Service
Appraisal Service Available
Directions: Rtes 18 & 28,
1 mile S of Bridgewater
Center

DAM' YANKEE ANTIQUE SHOPPE
36 Central Square   02324
617 697-2934   Est: 1972
Proprietor: Taffy & Jim
Hours: Mon-Sat, 9-5; Eves
by appointment
Types & Periods: Refinished
Oak Furniture & Country
Kitchen Utensils
Specialties: Complete
Bedroom, Dining Room &
Kitchen Furnishings (Oak)
Appraisal Service Available
Directions: Junction of
Rtes 104, 28 & 18, on the
common

HARVEST HILL ANTIQUES
450 Plymouth St   02324
617 697-7160   Est: 1972
Proprietor: Phyllis & Pete
Pike
Hours: Daily, 10-7
Types & Periods: Pine,
Period, Country Furniture,
Decorative Accessories
Specialties: Cupboards
Directions: 1 mile out of
Bridgewater Center on Rte
104

RECOLLECTIONS ANTIQUES
1001 Pleasant   02324
617 697-8519   Est: 1974
Proprietor: Elinor Peabody
Hours: Daily
Types & Periods: Primitives,
Stoneware, Pine Furniture
Directions: Rte 104, 1 mile
E of Rte 104

Brighton

PILGRIM ANTIQUE SHOPPE
54 Leo M Birmingham
Pkwy   02135
617 738-7933   Est: 1937
Proprietor: Samuel
Blumenthal
Hours: By appointment, by
chance
Types & Periods: Victorian,
Empire & Period
Reproductions
Appraisal Service Available
Directions: Take a left at
Black & Decker Tools on
Western Ave

Brimfield

THE BENNETTS
Warren Rd   01010
413 245-7263
Proprietor: Roger & Bee
Bennett
Hours: By appointment, by
chance
Types & Periods: Pressed
Glass, Cup Plates, Sandwich
Glass, Furniture, Primitives
Appraisal Service Available
Directions: 8 miles from
Old Sturbridge Village,
beside church in center

BRIMFIELD ANTIQUES
Main St   01010
413 245-3350
Proprietor: Susan &
Richard Raymond
Hours: By appointment, by
chance; call ahead
appreciated
Types & Periods: American
Period Furniture Prior to
1830, Decorative
Accessories
Specialties: Country Formal
& Federal Furniture
Appraisal Service Available
Directions: On Rte 20, 8
miles W of Old Sturbridge
Village

YELLOW HOUSE ANTIQUES
Rte 20   01010
413 245-9271
Proprietor: Laura P May
Hours: By appointment, by
chance

Types & Periods: General
Line, Jewelry
Directions: 6 miles W of
Old Sturbridge Village

Brockton

BILL'S PLACE
240 Warren Ave   02401
617 588-9615   Est: 1975
Proprietor: William F
Baumann
Hours: Daily
Types & Periods: General
Line
Appraisal Service Available
Directions: Between
Pleasant & Belmont Aves,
Rte 123

BEN GERBER & SON INC
1285 Belmont St   02401
617 586-2547   Est: 1947
Proprietor: Ben Gerber
Hours: Daily, 9-5
Types & Periods: Early
American, Victorian
Furniture, Glass, China,
Silver, Jewelry, Clocks, Dolls
Appraisal Service Available
Directions: Rte 123
(Easton Exit off Exp 24),
1/2 mile down the road

RAY'S FURNITURE
79 Pleasant St   02401
617 583-9532   Est: 1951
Proprietor: Guerino Rea
Hours: Daily
Types & Periods: Furniture,
Glass, China, Jewelry, Silver
Appraisal Service Available
Directions: Rte 27, about
1 block W from Main St

Brookfield

RUGGLES FARM ANTIQUES
                    01506
617 867-3658
Hours: By appointment
Types & Periods: Sandwich,
Art, Cut & Other American
Glass, Victorian &
Centennial Furniture
Directions: 1 mile W on
Rte 9

Brookline

ANTIQUES III
171 A Harvard St 02146
617 738-6718 Est: 1968
Proprietor: Corey Warn &
Mark Feldman
Hours: Sun-Mon, Wed-Sat
Types & Periods: General
Line, Art Pottery
Specialties: Glass (Heisey,
Cambridge, Duncan-Miller)

BARSOM ANTIQUES
1392A Beacon St 02146
617 277-7000 Est: 1974
Proprietor: Barsom J
Kashish
Hours: Daily, also by
appointment
Types & Periods: Meissen,
Dresden, Limoge, Rose
Medallion, Satsuma, Oil
Paintings, Sterling, Jewelry,
Furniture
Directions: At corner of
Winchester in Coolidge
Corner

**BROOKLINE ANTIQUE
GALLERIES**
1684 Beacon St 02146
617 566-3666 Est: 1977
Proprietor: Florence Lee &
Donna Klein
Hours: Tues-Sat, also by
appointment
Types & Periods: 18th &
19th Century American &
Continental Furniture,
Paintings, Oriental Rugs,
Objets d'Art & Distinctive
Accessories
Appraisal Service Available
Directions: Between
Coolidge Corner &
Cleveland Circle, 12
minutes from downtown-
Boston

BROOKLINE VILLAGER
12 Cypress St 02147
617 731-2773 Est: 1974
Proprietor: Richard Childs
Hours: Daily, 12-6· also by
chance
Types & Periods: Oak,
Walnut, Marble Tops, Silver,
Tools
Specialties: Oriental
Appraisal Service Available
Directions: Corner of
Cypress & Washington St

**HORSE IN THE ATTIC
BOOKSHOP**
52 Boylston St 02146
617 566-6070
Proprietor: Margo
Lockwood
Hours: Daily, 10:30-5
Types & Periods: Books,
Prints, Bindings, Children's
Books

PUNCH BOWL ANTIQUES
52 Boylston St 02146
617 566-6070
Proprietor: L Kohn
Hours: Daily, 10:30-5; also
by appointment; Closed
Aug
Types & Periods: China,
Oriental Rugs, Furniture
Directions: Rte 9 in
Brookline Village

RAHAVI GALLERY
1622 Beacon St 02146
617 731-5150 Est: 1970
Proprietor: Iraj Rahavi
Hours: Mon-Sat
Types & Periods: Fine
General Line, Chinese &
Japanese Cloisonne,
Porcelain, Bronzes,
Paintings, Objet d'Art &
Fine Oriental Rugs (Old &
new)
Appraisal Service Available

Brookline Village

TOWNE ANTIQUES INC
256 Washington St 02146
617 731-3326 Est: 1970
Proprietor: Francis
O'Boy Jr
Hours: Daily, 9-6
Types & Periods: Furniture,
Hepplewhite, Sheraton,
Chippendale
Appraisal Service Available
Directions: Downtown 2
blocks from Rte 9

Buzzards Bay

ANTIQUE MART
61 Main St 02532
617 759-5013 Est: 1973
Proprietor: James B
Potts Jr
Hours: Sun-Mon,
Thurs-Sat in summer;

Year Round: Sat-Mon
Types & Periods: Furniture,
Frames, Lamps, Glass,
Paperweights, Hummels
Specialties: Jewelry, Lamps,
Shades & Parts
Directions: Rtes 6 & 28,
opposite RR station next
to Post Office

**GOLDEN AGE ANTIQUE
SHOP**
Sawyer Rd 02532
617 759-4500 Est: 1970
Proprietor: Muriel M Ellis
Hours: Daily; closed
occasionally
Types & Periods: General
Line
Appraisal Service Available

Cambridge

ACADIA SHOP
1700A Massachusetts Ave
02138
617 492-4142 Est: 1973
Proprietor: Germaine
Carbury-Breau
Hours: Mon-Sat
Types & Periods: Oriental
Rugs, Chinese & Other
Oriental Pottery, Violins
Specialties: Oriental Rugs,
Oriental Objets d'Art, Violins
Appraisal Service Available
Directions: Between
Harvard Square & Porter
Square

**BERNHEIMERS' ANTIQUE
ARTS**
52C Brattle St 02138
617 547-1177 Est: 1963
Proprietor: P Bernheimer
Hours: Mon-Sat
Types & Periods: Antiquities,
European Art, Asiatic Art,
Primitive Art, Antique
Jewelry
Specialties: European,
Asiatic & Primitive Art,
Antique Jewelry
Appraisal Service Available
Directions: 2 blocks from
the center of Harvard
Square

**THE CAMBRIDGE
ANTIQUARIAN**
4 Brattle St 0213·
617 876-1200 Est: 19·
Proprietor: Fred Meyer

Cambridge   Cont'd

ANTIQUARIANA   Cont'd
Hours: By appointment
Types & Periods: We Buy
Glass, China, Jewelry, Toys,
Silver, Paintings, Etc
Specialties: Purchase only,
no sales
Appraisal Service Available

THE GAMES PEOPLE PLAY
1105 Massachusetts Ave
        02138
617 492-0711   Est: 1974
Proprietor: C Monica
Hours: Mon-Sat, 10-6
Types & Periods: Adult
Games, Game Boards &
Antique Toys
Directions: Just outside
Harvard Square

GOLD DIGGERS OF 1933
143 Pearl St   02139
617 868-1933   Est: 1972
Proprietor: William Sarill
Hours: By appointment
Types & Periods:
Memorabilia from the 20's
thru the 40's
Specialties: Toys, Books
(Comics)
Appraisal Service Available
Directions: 6 blocks down
Pearl St from Central
Square

HARVARD ANTIQUES
1654 Massachusetts Ave
        02138
617 354-5544   Est: 1957
Proprietor: Mrs Fred Flett
Hours: Daily
Types & Periods: Early
American Furniture, China,
Glass, Brass, Pewter
Specialties: Furniture
Directions: Just outside
Harvard Square going N

**THE MUSIC EMPORIUM
INC**
2018 Massachusetts Ave
        02140
617 661-2099   Est: 1975
Proprietor: James F
Bollman
Hours: Mon-Sat
Types & Periods: Buy, Sell
or Trade Antique Stringed
Musical Instruments
(Guitars, Banjos, Mandolins)

Appraisal Service Available
Directions: Porter Square

Cape Cod

THE GOLDEN OAR
Rte 28 N Chatham   02650
617 945-1111   Est: 1973
Proprietor: Eleanor S
Mower
Hours: Daily, June-Oct;
Weekends thru
Thanksgiving
Types & Periods: Country &
Nautical Antiques,
Collectibles in Glass, Tin &
Wood, Furniture
Specialties: Folk Art Prints &
Paintings
Directions: 1¼ miles N
from Center Chatham
Rotary on Rte 28 on road
to Orleans S of Northport

Charlemont

**CHARLEMONT HOUSE
GALLERY**
Maple Terrace   01339
413 339-6642   Est: 1973
Proprietor: Claire Roth &
Janice Weisblat
Hours: Daily, July & Aug;
Weekends only, June,
Sept & Oct
Types & Periods: General
Line, China, Glass,
Furniture, Quilts, Victoriana
Specialties: Rugs (Oriental)
Directions: On Rte 2

Chatham

**MARINE FINE ARTS &
ANTIQUES**
262 Chipping Stone Rd
        02633
617 945-0880
Proprietor: The Kittredges
Hours: By appointment
Types & Periods: General
Line

SUITSUS II
1369 Main St   02633
617 945-0683   Est: 1974
Hours: Tues-Sun, 11-5
May thru Oct; Weekends

by appointment or by
chance, Nov thru April
Types & Periods: Early
American Furniture thru
Victorian, Historical China,
Oriental Objects
Specialties: Pattern &
Sandwich Glass
Directions: Rte 28

TALE OF THE COD
450 Main St   02633
617 945-0347   Est: 1960
Proprietor: Frank T Weinz
Hours: Mon-Sat, 9-5
Types & Periods: Oriental,
Early American

**TREASURE CHEST
ANTIQUES**
Main St   02633
617 945-9476   Est: 1970
Proprietor: Mrs Helen J
Proctor
Hours: Daily, 10-5; also by
appointment
Types & Periods: Early
American, Empire &
Victorian Furniture, Jewelry,
Primitives, China, Glass,
Clocks, Collectibles
Specialties: Clocks, Glass
Directions: Beside Triangle
with Memorial Monument

YANKEE INGENUITY
525 Main St   02633
617 945-1288   Est: 1971
Proprietor: Jon & Lynne
Vaughan
Hours: Mon-Sat, 10-5,
summer; Weekends 10-5,
winter
Types & Periods: Nautical,
Railroad, Automobile,
Chests, Tables, Lamps,
Clocks
Specialties: Nautical
Directions: Downtown next
to Town Hall parking lot

Chatham Port

JOHN WALLACE WHELAN
1082 Orleans Rd   02650
617 945-2600   Est: 1964
Proprietor: John Wallace
Whelan
Hours: Mon-Sat, 10-5
Types & Periods: American,
European, Oriental

Directions: Rte 28 (Or
Crows Pond Rd &
Orleans Rd)

Cheshire

**CHESHIRE VILLAGE
ANTIQUES**
South St., Rt 8   01225
413 743-4385
Proprietor: June & Gus
Nelson
Hours: Wed-Sun, 10-5,
May thru Oct
Types & Periods: General
Line, Antiques, Country
Furniture, Shaker & Oak
Specialties: Furniture
(Country & Shaker)
Directions: Rte 8, just N of
Pittsfield

Chester

CHESTER GALLERY
Rte 20   01011
413 354-6378
Proprietor: Will
Fredericksen
Hours: Daily, 9-5
Types & Periods: Oriental
Art, 18th & 19th Centuries,
Tea Caddies, Incense
Burners, Vases
Specialties: Japanese
Woodblock Prints

Chestnut Hill

HOUSE OF ORIENT
1216 Boylston St   02167
617 277-1187   Est: 1974
Proprietor: S C Fong
Hours: Tues-Sat, 10-6
Types & Periods: Ching
Dynasty of Chinese
Porcelain, Approximately
150-300 years old
Specialties: Oriental (Jade,
Ivory, Furniture)
Appraisal Service Available
Directions: Across from
Longwood Cricket Club in
Brookline

J & C ANTIQUES
PO Box 121   02167
617 232-4468
Proprietor: Jack &

Charlotte Cashman
Hours: By appointment
Types & Periods: Art Glass,
China, Silver, Lamps

**SONIA PAINE ANTIQUES
GALLERY**
616A Hammond St   02167
617 566-9669
Proprietor: Sonia Paine
Hours: Tues-Sat, 12-4,
also by appointment
Types & Periods: French &
Oriental Antiques, KPM
Porcelains, Art Glass,
General Line
Specialties: French &
Oriental Antiques, KPM
Porcelains, Art Glass,
Accessoring Estates, Interior
Decorating
Appraisal Service Available
Directions: Adjacent to
Boston, intersection of Rte
9 & Hammond St

REDCOATS LTD
1216 Boylston St   02167
617 738-7060   Est: 1978
Proprietor: Jonathan
Saunders
Hours: Mon-Sat, 10-5:30
Types & Periods: Brass,
Copper, China, Glass,
Furniture, Antique
Decorative Accessories,
Antique Prints & Paintings,
Art Nouveau & Art Deco
Periods
Specialties: English
Furniture & Brass, English &
Continental Antique
Accessories & Pictures
Directions: Rte 9 on side
approaching Boston
opposite Star Market

SUMNER ROSS ANTIQUES
The Mall at Chestnut Hill
02167
617 965-0080   Est: 1945
Proprietor: Sumner Ross
Hours: Daily
Types & Periods: Porcelain,
Brass, Jewelry
Appraisal Service Available
Directions: 5 miles W of
Boston on Rte 9

Cochituate

THE ANDERSONS
Box 195   01778
617 653-5154
Proprietor: Caroline &
Arthur Anderson
Hours: By appointment
Types & Periods: Trains,
Stamps, Children's Glass
Dishes & Sets, Heisey Glass
Specialties: Glass (Heisey)

Cohasset

**THE CORNER LIGHT
HOUSE**
19 Elm St   02025
617 383-6512   Est: 1975
Proprietor: Ann M
Hamilton
Hours: Daily
Types & Periods: Early Pine
Furniture, Victorian
Specialties: Lamps
Directions: Cohasset
Center

**CREATION ANTIQUES &
INTERIORS**
8 Depot Ct   02025
617 383-1451   Est: 1968
Proprietor: Philip H Smith
Hours: Sun-Fri, 10-5; Sat
by chance or appointment
Types & Periods: Oriental,
18th & 19th Century
Furniture
Specialties: Furniture
Directions: Rte 128 to Rte
228, from Boston Expwy

Concord

DEPOT GALLERIES
86 Thoreau St   01742
617 369-8876
Proprietor: Ernest &
Sandy Verrill
Hours: Mon-Sat, 9:30-5:30;
Sun by chance
Types & Periods: Country
Furniture, Primitives, Tools,
General Line
Directions: In RR station

**DIAMOND IN THE WINDOW
ANTIQUES**
148 Walden St   0174
617 369-6096

DIAMOND IN Cont'd
Proprietor: Charlene
Pappas
Hours: Tues-Sat, 11-4;
Sun & Mon by chance or
appointment
Types & Periods: General
Line, Furniture &
Accessories
Directions: Rte 126

Conway

CONWAY HOUSE
Rte 116 01341
413 369-4660
Proprietor: Jack & Ray
Van Gelder
Hours: Daily, by
appointment, by chance
Types & Periods: 18th &
19th Century Furniture &
Accessories, Glass, China,
Furniture, Iron, Copper,
Brass, Mocha, Coverlets &
Quilts, Samplers, Early
Lighting Devices, Paintings
& Silhouettes
Specialties: 17th, 18th &
19th Century Lighting
Devices, Samplers,
Paintings, Silhouettes,
Coverlets & Quilts, Mocha
Appraisal Service Available
Directions: Near old
Deerfield village, on Rte
116, 1½ miles from center
of town

Cummaquid

CUMMAQUID ANTIQUES
Rte 6A 02637
617 362-2492 Est: 1955
Proprietor: Kathryn Arkus
Hours: Daily, phone call
advisable after Nov 15
Types & Periods: Furniture,
Chinese Export, Soft Paste,
Rugs
Specialties: Clocks,
Weathervanes
Directions: Near Hyannis
on N Shore, exit 7 from
Mid Cape Hwy

**THE OWL'S NEST
ANTIQUES**
Rte 6A, Main St 02637
617 362-4054 Est: 1973

Proprietor: Nancy & Dave
Galloni
Hours: Daily, all year
Types & Periods: Country
Furniture, Unusual
Decorator Pieces, Oak,
Victorian, Glass, Silver,
China, Dolls, Children's
Items, Woodenware,
Primitives
Specialties: Furniture
Refinishing
Appraisal Service Available
Directions: Rte 6A, 4th
house E of Post Office

Cummington

**STEELE'S TINY OLD NEW
ENGLAND**
Main St 01026
413 634-5406
Proprietor: Alice Steele
Hours: By appointment
Types & Periods: Doll House
Furniture
Specialties: Toys (Dolls)

Danvers

**GIDEON PUTNAM
"TAVERN ANTIQUES"**
Corner Park & Elm Sts
01923
617 774-2323 Est: 1973
Proprietor: Irene & Gordon
Kent
Hours: By appointment or
by chance
Types & Periods: Early
American & General
Antiques of New England,
Furniture, Glass, Fine China
Specialties: Clocks
Appraisal Service Available
Directions: Off Rtes 1 &
95, Rte 128, Rte 114,
opposite Town Hall

Dedham

THE CENTURY SHOP
626 High St 02026
617 326-1717
Proprietor: Henry Meagher
Hours: Mon-Sat, 10-5

Types & Periods: Furniture,
China, Glass, Oriental Rugs,
Pottery
Directions: Exit 58 off Rte
128

DEDHAM ANTIQUE SHOP
622 High St 02026
617 329-1114 Est: 1910
Proprietor: Simon Nager
Hours: Mon-Sat, 12-4
Types & Periods: 18th &
19th Century Furniture &
Furnishings

**LYNN HUIDEKOPER
ANTIQUES**
18 School St 02026
617 326-7218
Proprietor: Lynn
Huidekoper
Hours: Mon-Sat, 10-5
Types & Periods: General
Line

Deerfield

GRAY COTTAGE ANTIQUES
Rtes 5 & 10 01342
413 773-8404 Est: 1940
Proprietor: Norman &
Margaret Carey
Hours: By appointment, by
chance
Types & Periods: 18th &
19th Century Furniture &
Accessories
Specialties: Early Iron
Appraisal Service Available
Directions: Rtes 5 & 10

Dennis

SYLVIA H HOSLEY
1170 Main St 02638
617 385-3690 Est: 1967
Proprietor: Sylvia H Hosley
Hours: Daily, by
appointment, June-Sept,
mail order
Types & Periods: 18th &
19th Century Staffordshire,
Porcelains, Furniture
Specialties: Staffordshire
Directions: On Rte 6A 1
mile beyond Dennis Post
Office

SIGN OF THE CLOCK
593 Rte 6A 06238
617 385-2123

Proprietor: Ruth & Charles Lydecker
Hours: Sun-Tues, Thurs-Sat, 9-5
Types & Periods: American Clocks

LOIS SKLAR ANTIQUES
838 Main St   02638
617 385-2921   Est: 1974
Proprietor: Lois & Bob Sklar
Hours: Daily
Types & Periods: Early Wicker, Primitives, Faience, Tin, Country Furniture, Baskets
Specialties: Wicker
Directions: Rte 6A, near Cape Playhouse, corner Corporation Rd

Dover

DOVER COUNTRY STORE INC
14 Dedham St   02030
617 785-0287   Est: 1945
Proprietor: Michael H Dowd
Hours: Mon-Wed, Sat, 9-5; Thurs & Fri, 9-9; Sun, 1-4; also by appointment
Types & Periods: General Line
Appraisal Service Available
Directions: Old RR station, Dover Centre, direct off Exit 56 W on Rte 128, 9 miles thru Needham to Dover

Duxbury

GORDON AND GENEVIEVE DEMING
125 Wadsworth Rd   02332
617 934-5259   Est: 1965
Proprietor: Gordon & Genevieve Deming
Hours: By appointment, by chance
Types & Periods: 18th & 19th Century Furniture, Early Pewter, Fireplace Equipment, Quilts, Oil Paintings, Baskets, Woodworking, Tools, Stoneware

Specialties: Pewter
Appraisal Service Available
Directions: Exit 34 off Rte 3, 1 mile N on right

DUXBURY GALLERIES
590 Washington St   02332
617 934-5529
Proprietor: Corn & Lynch
Hours: Tues-Sat, 12-5
Types & Periods: Furniture, Paintings, Accessories

East Bridgewater

"ANTIQUES" AT FORGE POND
35 N Bedford St   02333
617 378-3057   Est: 1976
Proprietor: Barbara, Edna, Mabel & Marie (4 shops in 1)
Hours: Mon-Fri, 9-4; Sat & Sun, 12-5
Types & Periods: General Line, Primitives, Paper, Dolls, Toys, Tools, Jewelry, Furniture
Appraisal Service Available
Directions: Rte 18, 20 chops within 5 mile radius

ELMWOOD BOOKSHOP AND GALLERY
55 N Bedford St   02333
617 378-7587   Est: 1965
Proprietor: M Fruzzetti
Hours: Mon, other times by appointment or chance
Types & Periods: Period American & Victorian Furniture, Books
Specialties: Oriental Rugs, Prints, Paintings
Appraisal Service Available
Directions: On Forge Pond, Rte 18

ELIOT'S JOPPA GALLERY
590 Bedford St   02333
617 378-7800   Est: 1938
Proprietor: Eliot Rosen
Hours: Tues-Sun, 8-5
Types & Periods: Turn-of-the-Century Furniture, American Antiques & Collectibles
Appraisal Service Available
Directions: Rte 18 (Bedford St) at junction of Rte 106

1750 HOUSE ANTIQUES
142 South St   02333
617 378-4710   Est: 1966
Proprietor: Ann L Prosper
Hours: Mon-Fri, by chance
Types & Periods: General Line, Furniture, Dolls, Jewelry, China, Primitives
Directions: 1 mile S of E Bridgewater Center, off Rte 106

YE OLDE TYME SHOPPE
280 N Bedford St   02333
617 378-3222   Est: 1973
Proprietor: Edward C Patt
Hours: Daily
Types & Periods: General Line
Specialties: Clocks, Grandfather Clocks (Sales, Repairs)
Directions: On Rte 18, 1/2 mile N from center of town

Eastham

COLLECTOR'S WORLD
Rte 6   02642
617 255-3616   Est: 1970
Proprietor: Chris & Maria Alex
Hours: Daily, by chance
Types & Periods: General Line
Specialties: Marine Items
Directions: 1 mile N of Cape Cod National Park Salt Pond Visitor's Center

Easthampton

GLASKOWSKY & COMPANY
180 Main St   01027
413 527-2410   Est: 1946
Proprietor: Nicholas A Glaskowsky
Hours: Daily, evenings by appointment
Types & Periods: American Chests, Desks, Tables, Chairs, Andirons, Fenders, Fireplace Tools, Paintings, Prints, Maps, Art Pottery, Art Glass, Quilts, Coverlets, Clocks, Toys, Bronzes, Silver, Copper, Brass, Mechanical & Still Banks, Mettlach Steins, Baccarat's Paperweights

GLASKOWSKY Cont'd
Specialties: American 18th &
19th Century Furniture
Appraisal Service Available
Directions: Rte 10

East Longmeadow

STEBBINS ANTIQUES
30 N Circle Dr   01028
413 525-3554
Hours: By appointment
Types & Periods: Primitives,
Pine Furniture

East Sandwich

**THE HOUSE OF THE
CLIPPER SHIP**
600 Hwy 6A   02537
617 888-3068   Est: 1932
Proprietor: Polly & Charles
Gaupp
Hours: Daily, by
appointment or by chance
Types & Periods: 18th &
19th Century American &
British, Oriental Pottery &
Porcelains
Specialties: Pewter, Pottery,
Porcelain
Appraisal Service Available

East Walpole

DANOM FORGE ANTIQUES
123 Washington St 02032
617 668-0494   Est: 1974
Proprietor: William J &
Patricia W Collins
Hours: Daily, or by
appointment
Types & Periods: General
Line, located in blacksmith
shop, items in keeping with
the atmosphere
Directions: S of Boston 1
mile from Exit 9 S,
Rte I-95 & Rte 1

Elmwood

ELMWOOD ANTIQUES
734 Bedford St   02337
617 378-3179   Est: 1974

Proprietor: Walter Myers
Hours: Mon-Sat, 8-5:30;
Sun by chance
Types & Periods: General
Line, Furniture, Glassware
Specialties: Tools
Directions: Intersection
Rtes 18 & 106

POLLY'S ANTIQUES
741 Bedford   02337
617 378-3856   Est: 1976
Proprietor: Polly Long
Hours: Daily, 8-5:30
Types & Periods: General
Line, Furniture
Specialties: Prints,
Watercolors, Oils
Appraisal Service Available
Directions: Corner Rte 18
& Rte 106

Essex

THE ANNEX ANTIQUES
Main St   01929
617 768-6071   Est: 1968
Proprietor: Marion Potter
& Barbara Dyer
Hours: Daily, May 1-Oct
20
Types & Periods: General
Line

BELL, BOOK, & CANDLE
166 Eastern Ave   01929
617 768-7510
Types & Periods: General
Line, Collectibles
Directions: Rte 133

**CHRISTIAN MOLLY
ANTIQUES**
167 Main St   01929
617 768-6079
Hours: Daily
Types & Periods: 18th &
19th Century Furniture,
Glass, China, Silver,
Paintings

**COLONIAL HOUSE
ANTIQUES**
26 Martin St   01929
617 768-7195
Types & Periods: Furniture,
Iron, Treenware
Directions: Opposite Fire
Station

HOWARD'S ANTIQUES
165 Eastern Ave   01929
617 768-6844   Est: 1978

Proprietor: Ann Herrick &
Ed Howard
Hours: Daily, except
Thanksgiving & Christmas
Types & Periods: General
Line
Specialties: Glass, Furniture
Appraisal Service Available
Directions: Rte 133, 1½
miles off Rte 128 towards
Essex, red house on left

**HOWARD'S FLYING
DRAGON**
136 Main St   01929
617 768-7282   Est: 1974
Proprietor: Laura & Ed
Howard
Hours: Daily, 10:30-dark,
except Thanksgiving &
Christmas
Types & Periods: General
Line
Specialties: Glass, Furniture,
Nautical
Appraisal Service Available
Directions: Rte 133 off Rte
128 Main St is Rte 133,
near Gloucester &
Rockport

WHITE ELEPHANT SHOP
32 Main St   01929
617 768-6901
Types & Periods: Glassware,
China, Furniture, Collectibles
Directions: Rte 133

Fairhaven

ANTIQUES AND INTERIORS
115 Green St   02719
617 992-1389   Est: 1972
Proprietor: James &
Martha Crowley
Hours: Daily, 12-5, by
appointment
Types & Periods: Fine
Period & Custom Mahogany
Furniture & Accessories,
Brass, Silver, Crystal, China,
Old Rugs
Specialties: Restoration of
Fine Furniture
Appraisal Service Available
Directions: E on Rte 195,
Exit 240 to Rte 6, turn
right to Fairhaven Center
to 115 Green St

FANTASY HOUSE ANTIQUES
32 Cedar St   02719
617 993-8558
Proprietor: Kenneth L Tobergta Sr
Hours: By appointment
Types & Periods: Glass, China, Silverplate & Silver, Lamps
Specialties: Mt Washington, Pairpoint & Gundersen
Appraisal Service Available
Directions: Rte 6 at F H High School, take Green St S 1 mile, then Cedar St 2 blocks E

Fall River

RED VELVET ANTIQUES
187 Rock St   02720
617 673-4769
Proprietor: J Robert Mello
Hours: Daily, 1-5, also by appointment
Types & Periods: General Line
Directions: In the rear

Falmouth

GRAIN MILL ANTIQUES
Depot Ave   02540
617 548-0241   Est: 1890
Proprietor: Fera D Eldridge
Hours: Mon-Sat; Sun by appointment
Types & Periods: Country Pine, Cupboards
Specialties: Country Pine, Cupboards
Appraisal Service Available
Directions: Depot Ave, center of Falmouth, ask anyone

SOPHISTICATED JUNK & ANTIQUE SHOP
108 King St Box 645
                        02541
617 548-1250   Est: 1974
Proprietor: Manuel R & Eva Lopes
Hours: Mon & Thurs Sat, 10-5; Sun, 1-5; Summer; Fri & Sat, 10-5, Sun, 1-5 during Spring & Fall
Types & Periods: General Line

Specialties: Furniture
Directions: Center of Falmouth, behind the Fire Station

Florence

BERNARD PLATING WORKS
660 Riverside Dr   01060
413 584-0659   Est: 1928
Proprietor: Marshall C Warner
Hours: Mon-Fri, 8-12, 12:30-4:30; Sat, 8-12
Specialties: Plating-Gold, Silver, Copper, Nickel, Hand Wiped Tinning, Pewter Repair & Restoration, Stripping, Polishing & Repair of most Antiques
Directions: N on Rte 9, 3 miles from Northampton center, take left at lights onto Maple St, turn right at bottom of hill, then immediate left

Foxboro

THE FOXVALE BARN
310 Center St   02035
617 543-2315
Proprietor: Marge & Joe Paza
Hours: Daily
Types & Periods: Furniture, General Line
Directions: Off Rte 140

Framingham

FAINI'S ANTIQUES
35 Shawmut Terrace
                        01701
617 875-5402
Proprietor: Arthur E Faini Jr
Hours: By appointment
Types & Periods: Victorian Glass, General Line

Franklin

JOHNSTON'S ANTIQUES
789 W Central St   02038
617 528-0942   Est: 1964

Proprietor: J Johnston
Hours: Daily, 10-10, by appointment or by chance; call first advisable
Types & Periods: Pewter, Rare Books, Period Furniture, Early Glass, General Line
Specialties: Pewter, Rare Books, Period Furniture, Early Glass, General Line
Appraisal Service Available
Directions: Directly off Exit 17, Rte 495 W

MARIE RISTAINO
148 Washington St   02038
617 528-4779
Proprietor: Marie Ristaino
Hours: By appointment
Types & Periods: General Line

THE TRADING POST
3 Summer St   02038
617 528-4460
Proprietor: Vera A Ledbury
Hours: Mon-Tues, Thurs-Sat, 10-6; Wed, 10-12; Evenings by appointment
Types & Periods: Glass, Dolls, Furniture
Directions: Cinema parking lot

Gardner

ANTIQUES AT THE YELLOW HOUSE
21 Green St   01440
617 632-1738
Proprietor: Aileen A Howe
Hours: By appointment, by chance
Types & Periods: General Line
Directions: On Rte 140 N

Georgetown

GEORGETOWN ANTIQUE CENTER
1 E Main St   01921
617 352-6404   Est: 1970
Proprietor: Fred D Newell
Hours: Daily, 10-5
Types & Periods: General Line

GEORGETOWN ANTIQUE CENTER   Cont'd
Appraisal Service Available
Directions: 25 miles N of
Boston off Rte 95, get off
at Rte 133, go W 2 miles,
in center of town, 10
shops in bldg

THE ROMAN EMPIRE
1 E Main St   01833
617 352-6006
Hours: Wed, Thurs & Sat,
11:30-4; Sun, 9-5;
Evenings by appointment
Types & Periods: General
Line

SEDLER'S ANTIQUE VILLAGE
51 W Main St   01833
617 352-8282   Est: 1977
Proprietor: Robert &
Patricia Sedler
Hours: Tues-Sun, 10-5
Types & Periods: Early &
Victorian Furniture, China,
Miniatures, Dolls, Jewelry,
Kitchen Tools, Wooden
Tools
Appraisal Service Available
Directions: 25 miles N
from Boston, Rte 95 to
Rte 97 into Georgetown
Center, 30 shops in large
Victorian house

Gloucester

BURKE'S BAZAAR
512 Essex Ave   01930
617 283-4538   Est: 1949
Proprietor: Mrs Peggy
Pynn
Hours: Daily
Types & Periods: General
Line
Appraisal Service Available
Directions: On Rte 133, 5
minutes off Rte I-28

THE GRANGE GALLERY
457 Washington St 01930
617 283-4021   Est: 1973
Proprietor: Jon E
Steinberg
Hours: Fri, Sat & Sun
Types & Periods: General
Line, Interior Design
Appraisal Service Available
Directions: Rte 127 N,
Riverdale

DONNA & JOE MELLO
23 Marble Rd   01930
617 283-6916   Est: 1971
Proprietor: Donna Mello
Hours: By appointment
Types & Periods: Cut Glass,
Art Glass, China, Lamps
Specialties: Cut Glass,
Nippon China
Appraisal Service Available

RICHARD J SOUZA
561 Essex Ave   01930
617 281-2236
Hours: By appointment
Types & Periods:
Craftsmen's Tools,
Primitives

Grafton

ATTIC TUCKAWAY
Moroney Rd   01519
617 839-6563
Proprietor: Barbara
Hazzard
Hours: Daily, 1-6,
March-Dec; Mornings by
chance
Types & Periods: Primitive &
Country Things, Furniture,
Folk, Shaker, Country Store
Items
Directions: Off Rte 140 at
Upton Line

Granby

P T DARR ANTIQUES
507 E State St   01033
413 467-6726
Proprietor: The Darrs
Hours: Daily, 9-5
Types & Periods: Art Glass,
General Line
Appraisal Service Available

Great Barrington

BARNBROOK ANTIQUES
72 Stockbridge Rd   01230
413 528-4423   Est: 1964
Proprietor: Lila & Ed
Landy
Hours: Sun-Mon, Wed-Sat,
9-5
Types & Periods: 18th &
19th Century American
Furniture

Appraisal Service Available
Directions: Rte 7, N of
Great Barrington

CORASHIRE ANTIQUES
Rtes 7 & 23
Belcher Square   01230
413 528-0014
Proprietor: John & Nancy
Dinan
Hours: Sun-Mon, Wed-Sat,
10-5
Types & Periods: Country
Furniture, General Line

NORTH FAMILY JOINERS
Rte 23   01230
Est: 1971
Proprietor: Charles &
Nancy Caffall
Hours: Sun-Wed, Fri-Sat
Types & Periods: Antique
Tools, Shaker Reproductions
& Restorations
Specialties: Shaker
Reproductions &
Restorations
Directions: On Rte 23, 100
yards E of Rte 7

Greenfield

RED BARN OF GREENFIELD
95 River St   01301
413 773-7225
Proprietor: Howard Arkush
& Samuel Weiss
Hours: Daily
Types & Periods: Glassware,
Copper, Brass, Toleware,
Paintings, Furniture

Groton

1810 HOUSE ANTIQUES
PO Box 276   01450
617 448-6046   Est: 1973
Proprietor: Helen L Friot
Hours: By appointment;
Shows
Types & Periods: Country
Furniture, Pottery, Paintings
& Accessories
Specialties: Children's Items
Directions: Call for
directions

Groveland

ELM PARK ANTIQUES
35 Elm Park   01834
617 372-8004
Proprietor: Bob & Jan
Hamilton
Hours: Mon-Sat, 10-5;
Evenings by appointment
Types & Periods: General
Line, Collectibles, China,
Glass, Primitives
Directions: Rte 977

Hadley

**ANTIQUES-A JOINT
VENTURE**
206 Russell St   01035
413 586-1633   Est: 1975
Proprietor: Meg & Bruce
Cummings
Hours: Most days 12-4:30
Types & Periods: Oak &
Victorian Furniture, Wicker,
Clocks, Silver, Fine
Accessories
Specialties: Victorian Marble
Top Furniture
Appraisal Service Available
Directions: Rte 9, just 2½
miles E of I-91

21ST CENTURY ANTIQUES
01035
413 549-6678
Proprietor: Peter
Rakelbusch
Types & Periods: The Arts
Nouveau & Deco; Mail
Catalogue Available

Halifax

LEMMENS ANTIQUES
394 Plymouth St   02338
617 293-2292
Proprietor: Willem H
Lemmens
Hours: Sun-Fri; a call
ahead advisable
Types & Periods: American
Furniture & Accessories
Directions: Rte 106

Hamilton

BAY ROAD ANTIQUES
587 Bay Rd   01936
617 468-1563   Est: 1945
Proprietor: Chester N
Twiss
Hours: Daily, 12-5
Types & Periods: General
Line, Furniture, Paintings,
Glass, China, Silver,
Jewelry, Primitives,
Collectibles
Appraisal Service Available
Directions: Exit 20 N at
Beverly, 4½ miles on 1-A,
next to Hamilton Town
Hall

**YE OLDE LANTERN
ANTIQUES**
164 Bay Rd   01936
617 283-6837
Hours: Wed-Sat, 1-5
Types & Periods: Glass,
Furniture, Clocks, Jewelry,
Lamps, Silver, Paintings,
China, Dolls, Collectibles
Directions: Rte 97

Hampden

THE MAPLES ANTIQUES
180 Glendale Rd   01036
413 566-8711
Proprietor: Anne & Jack
Loder
Hours: Daily
Types & Periods: China,
Glass, Brass, Prints, Silver,
Tin, Woodenware, Clocks,
Furniture

Hanson

THE ATTIC DWELLERS
341 E Washington St
02341
617 447-3650   Est: 1966
Proprietor: Rita Marshall
Hours: By appointment
Types & Periods: Primitives,
Glass, Furniture, Silver,
Advertising
Appraisal Service Available
Directions: Off Rte 58

PHILIP P STELLA
30 E Washington St 02341
617 447-9057   Est: 1960

Proprietor: Philip P Stella
Types & Periods: General
Line, Furniture
Appraisal Service Available
Directions: Rte 58

Hardwick

THE WINDLE SHOPPE
Ridge Rd   01037
413 477-8714
Proprietor: Anna M
Warburton
Hours: By appointment
Types & Periods: Period
Furniture, Pewter, Brass,
Copper, Tin, Woodenware,
Quilts, Coverlets, Coin Silver
Specialties: Ironware,
Pewter
Appraisal Service Available
Directions: 2 miles off Rte
32

Harwich Center

HARWICH HOUSE
510 Main St   02645
617 432-1660
Proprietor: Joseph Walsh
Hours: Daily
Types & Periods: 17th &
18th Century Furniture
Appraisal Service Available
Directions: Rte 28,
Harwich Port, take Bank
St to Harwich Center

Harwich Port

**MARSH-ACKERMAN
ANTIQUES, LTD**
7 South St   02646
617 432-4366   Est: 1973
Proprietor: Lawrence
Marsh & Laurie Ackerman
Hours: Summer Only, Daily,
10-6
Types & Periods: Specializing
in Silver & Jewelry, Late 19th
& Early 20th Century
Decorative Arts, Silver
Collectibles
Directions: First House Off
Main St, Rte 28

Haverhill

LYNCH & GRAHAM ANTIQUES
420 Water St   01830
617 374-8031
Hours: Mon, Fri & Sat, 12-6 during winter; Mon-Tues, Thur-Sat, 10-5 during summer
Types & Periods: Glassware, Pattern Glass, China, Bottles, Country Furniture, Silver, Lamps, Guns
Directions: Rte 97

Haydenville

GOOD TIME STOVE COMPANY
Rte 9   01039
                Est: 1973
Proprietor: Richard "Stoveblack" Richardson
Hours: Tues-Sat, 10-5, by appointment;open more hours in fall
Types & Periods: Antique Wood Kitchen Ranges & Parlor Stoves from Early 1800's thru 1940's, Gas/Wood Combos, Restored for Use
Specialties: Restore Woodstoves, Sell Old Tubs, Sinks, Stained Glass Windows, Old Architectural Details
Appraisal Service Available
Directions: Right on Rte 9 in Western Mass on the Northampton-Williamsburg town line

Hingham

CATHARINE SCHOFIELD DELARGY
312 High St   02189
617 749-9873   Est: 1939
Proprietor: Catharine DeLargy
Hours: Weekends
Types & Periods: Furniture, Silver, General Line
Appraisal Service Available
Directions: Off Rte 228, Hingham to High St

UNICORN ANTIQUES
66 South St   02043
617 749-6767   Est: 1969
Proprietor: Ann Brandon
Hours: Tues-Sat, 10-5
Types & Periods: Furniture, Paintings, Clocks, Pewter, China, Glass
Appraisal Service Available
Directions: Hingham Square off Rte 228, near old Ship Church

Hinsdale

DON & EDNA TENCH
Curtis St   01235
413 655-2740
Proprietor: Don & Edna Tench
Hours: By appointment
Types & Periods: Shaker, American Furniture, Primitives, Glass, China

Holliston

CANDLEGLOW
                      01746
617 429-5868
Proprietor: Barbara Gentiluomo
Hours: By appointment
Types & Periods: Country Furniture, Clocks, General Line

CENTURY ANTIQUES
18 Concord St   01746
617 429-2300
Proprietor: Charles & Celia Shurtleff
Hours: Daily
Types & Periods: General Line
Directions: Junction of Rtes 126 & 16

FARR'S FARM
268 Fiske St   01746
617 429-5804
Hours: By appointment, by chance
Types & Periods: Country Furniture, Primitives, General Line

LADIES EXCHANGE
400 Washington St   01746
617 429-4991   Est: 1969
Proprietor: Mary M Lee

Hours: Mon-Sat, 10-4
Types & Periods: China, Orientals, Furniture, Paintings
Directions: Junction 16 & 126

Hopedale

ANTIQUE DECORAMA
PO Box 433   01747
617 473-9250
Proprietor: The McKnights
Hours: By appointment
Types & Periods: Art Glass, Oil Paintings, Prints, Bronzes

BEVERLY'S BARN SHOPPE
370 S Main St   01747
617 473-9250
Proprietor: Beverly Demers
Hours: Daily, 10-6; Evenings by chance or appointment
Types & Periods: General Line, Oak & Walnut Furniture, Tin Primitives, Glass, Collectibles
Directions: On Rte 140

Hopkinton

HERITAGE ANTIQUES
216 Wood St   01748
617 435-4031
Proprietor: Clifton L Gilson
Hours: Daily, 9-7
Types & Periods: Furniture, Accessories, Rugs, Objets d'Art
Directions: Rte 135

LAURAL ANTIQUES
255 Wood St   01784
617 435-3906   Est: 1966
Proprietor: Al & Laurie Los
Hours: Mon-Fri, 1:30-5; Sat, 10-5
Types & Periods: Country & Period Furniture with Accessories
Directions: Rte 135, Woodville section

OLD BOOKS & ANTIQUES
228 Hayden Rowe   01748
617 435-3558
Proprietor: Ruth J Berg
Hours: By appointment

Types & Periods: Paper,
Primitives, Collectibles,
Oddments
Directions: Rte 85

THE WELCHES
16 Hayden Rowe   01748
617 435-4039
Proprietor: David &
Eleanor Welch
Hours: By appointment
Types & Periods: General
Line, Miniature Paintings

**THE WORKSHOPS OF FAIR
ACRES FARM**
152 Hayden Rowe   01748
617 435-3523
Proprietor: Wm H &
Marcia W Preston
Hours: Sun-Mon, Wed-Sat,
12-5
Types & Periods:
Collectibles, Furniture

Hyannis

CARROUSEL ANTIQUES
25 Sherman Square 02601
617 771-4060   Est: 1977
Proprietor: Felippa Garrity
Hours: Mon-Sat, 10-5
Types & Periods: Art,
Collectibles, Jewelry,
Furniture, Primitives
Specialties: Carrousel
Horses
Directions: W junction
Main & South Sts

**STONE'S ANTIQUE
SHOPPE**
659 Main St   02601
617 775-3913   Est: 1919
Proprietor: E Stone
Hours: Daily
Types & Periods: Furniture,
China, Glass, Brass, Copper,
Pewter
Specialties: Glass
(Sandwich), Weathervanes
Appraisal Service Available
Directions: Rte 6 to Rte
132 to Main St

Hyannis Port

**RICHARD A BOURNE CO
INC**
Box 141   02647
617 775-0797   Est: 1958

Proprietor: Richard A
Bourne Co
Hours: Daily, by
appointment
Types & Periods: European
& Continental, Paintings,
Decoys, Dolls, Marine Glass
Appraisal Service Available
Directions: Rte 28 &
Corporation St, 7/10 mile
from airport

Ipswich

**HILDA KNOWLES
ANTIQUES AND
COLLECTABLES**
207 High St   01938
617 356-4561   Est: 1969
Proprietor: Hilda Knowles
Hours: Mon, Wed, Fri-Sat,
11-5; other days by
chance
Types & Periods: China,
Glass, Dolls, Jewelry,
Furniture, Collectibles
Specialties: Glass (Pattern,
Cut, Heisey & Art)
Directions: Rte 1A

**LAURA'S ANTIQUES &
COLLECTABLES**
115 High St   01938
617 356-2325
Hours: Daily; evenings by
appointment
Types & Periods: Furniture,
Glass, China
Directions: Rte 1A

**OLD POST OFFICE CLOCK
SHOP**
7 Market Square   01938
617 356-5756
Proprietor: R Ziebell
Hours: Tues-Thurs, 2-5;
also by appointment
Types & Periods: Period,
English, French & Other
European & American
Clocks, American & High
Grade Foreign Watches
Specialties: Clocks &
Watches
Appraisal Service Available
Directions: On Rte 1A,
center of town

THE TUTTLES
40 High St   01938
617 356-3780
Hours: By appointment, by
chance

Types & Periods: Tools,
Country Primitives

**WHATS NEW? NOTHING
ANTIQUES**
3 Elm St   01938
617 356-4382
Proprietor: Jan Moffett &
Lee Peacock
Types & Periods: Dolls,
Toys, Primitives, General
Line

Kingston

**VICTORIAN HOUSE
ANTIQUES**
204 Main St   02364
617 585-2300   Est: 1958
Proprietor: Isabel
McAndrews
Hours: Daily
Types & Periods: Victorian &
Early China & Glass,
Furniture, Lamps
Specialties: Ceramics,
Lamps
Appraisal Service Available
Directions: On Rte 106 off
3A in Kingston

Lakeville

**DOUBLE AUCTION
GALLERY**
Bedford St   02346
617 947-0283   Est: 1957
Proprietor: Florence
Cornell
Hours: Sun, 12-5
Types & Periods: General
Line, Auction every Sat nite
at 7
Appraisal Service Available
Directions: Rte 105

Lancaster

WHOLESALE ANTIQUES
Ballard Hill   01523
617 537-8691   Est: 1968
Proprietor: Jeffrey Dana
Hours: Daily
Types & Periods: Country &
Formal Furniture
Specialties: Furniture
Restoration
Appraisal Service Available
Directions: Off Rte 2 to
Pennerburg Rd, S to Rte
117, right 1½ miles

(From page 212A) treatment, such as large plain sur-faces, large legs and brackets. They can be very elaborate and may also have much carving. Pilasters of either columns or scrolls were incorporated under overhanging drawers. (See page 218). There were a few marble tops. The chief woods used were mahogany and various veneers. Decoration included stenciling and also the paint-ing of designs. Development of an early automatic lathe allowed the use of turnings for such things as spool beds and the front legs of fancy chairs among which was the Hitchcock chair. Massive chests of drawers, heavy pedestal tables, scroll sofas and sleigh beds are characteristically Empire. (See pages 230 and 297).

Initially much of this furniture was handcrafted in a very meticulous manner showing evidence of the use of fine woods, inlaid brass designs, ormolu castings and elaborately matched veneers. All in all, quite acceptable craftsmanship and design. The invention of the steam engine provided more inexpensive power for machinery than the world had previously known. In the later Empire Period much of the furniture was being made by machinery with a lessening of fine detail and craftsmanship. This is not meant to imply that handcrafted items suddenly ceased to be made. On our frontiers and in less developed towns, cabinetmakers continued on with the old processes they had always used. The transition was made very slowly.

In a search for antiques today, one finds reasonable quantities of Empire furniture. It is well made of the finest woods and may still be purchased at reasonable prices. However, it must be remembered that most of this furniture was designed for the large houses with the high ceilings of the period. It is sometimes hard to work into today's modern houses. It is often good judgment before buying a piece of Empire to try it in your home to see if the proportions will be correct. Not too long ago I had a customer telephone and rather aloofly ask me to stop by. Upon my arrival things had changed. Tearfully she said she wanted my advice on how to use a piece of furniture she had just purchased. I didn't truly understand, so I asked to see it. She opened the door to her bedroom and there stood "four telephone poles". She had bought an Empire poster bed and had been trying to assemble it in a modern bedroom with an eight foot ceiling. It would literally have pushed itself out of the room. After telling her I did not know of anything that might help, I asked what had induced her to purchase the bed. With that her eyes lit up and she smiled for the first time. "Oh, I just couldn't pass it up. It was such a good bargain!" You, yourself, (Continued, page 322)

Lanesboro

AMBER SPRINGS ANTIQUES
Rte 7   01237
413 442-1237   Est: 1957
Proprietor: Gae & Larry Elfenbein
Hours: Daily
Types & Periods: American Country Furniture, Pottery, Coin Silver, Tools
Directions: 5 miles N of Pittsfield

WALDEN'S ANTIQUES
Main St   01237
413 499-0312
Proprietor: William C Walden
Hours: Daily by appointment, May thru Oct; also by chance
Types & Periods: General Line, Books
Appraisal Service Available

Lawrence

BROADWAY SECOND HAND SHOP
242 Broadway   01841
617 682-2443   Est: 1923
Proprietor: Harold Landy
Hours: Mon-Sat
Types & Periods: General Line
Appraisal Service Available
Directions: Rte 28

Lee

PINEWOOD SHOP
Rte 102   01238
413 243-0905
Proprietor: Lillian & Russell King
Hours: Daily, by appointment or by chance
Types & Periods: Pine Furniture, Rockers, Blanket Chests, Quilts

Lenox

COLONIAL HOUSE
463 Pittsfield-Lenox Rd
                      01238

413 637-0429
Proprietor: Molly & Lawrence Hamilton
Hours: Sun-Wed, Fri-Sat, 10-4:30
Types & Periods: Shaker, Early American, General Line

CRAZY HORSE ANTIQUES & INTERIOR DESIGN
Box 88 Main St   01240
413 637-1634   Est: 1966
Proprietor: Charles L Flint
Hours: Daily, by appointment or by chance
Types & Periods: Shaker, Folk Art, General Line
Specialties: Shaker
Directions: Main St, Rte 7A

HAMLET ANTIQUES
90 Church St   01240
413 637-2309
Proprietor: F Brooks Butler
Hours: June thru Sept, 10-4
Types & Periods: American & English Furniture

Leverett

PAUL WEISS ANTIQUES
184 N Leverett Rd   01054
413 367-9952   Est: 1973
Proprietor: Paul Weiss
Hours: By appointment only
Types & Periods: Country & Formal Early American Furniture, 19th Century American Paintings, American Folk Art
Specialties: 18th Century New England Furniture
Appraisal Service Available
Directions: 3 miles E of the junction of Rtes 47 & 63 on N Leverett Rd about 25 minutes from Historic Old Deerfield & Hwy 91

Lexington

THE BACK ROOM AT THE TOADSTOOL
1632 Massachusetts Ave
                      02173
617 861-6096   Est: 1977

Proprietor: Harriet Bridges & Madelyn Wejman
Hours: Mon-Sat, 10-5
Types & Periods: White Clothing, Linens, Laces, Fabrics, Quilts, Bedspreads, Kimonos, Textiles, Paisleys
Appraisal Service Available
Directions: Diagonally across from Post Office

Lincoln

STAGECOACH ANTIQUES
S Great Rd   01773
617 259-9563   Est: 1978
Proprietor: Jane & Lee Young
Hours: By appointment
Types & Periods: Early American Furniture & Accessories (Country Furniture of late 18th & Early 19th Centuries)
Specialties: Early Windsor Chairs, Country Chippendale Chairs, Chinese Porcelain

Littleton

ANTIQUES AT THE SIGN OF THE BLUEBIRD
287 Great Rd   01460
617 486-3067   Est: 1972
Proprietor: Carol W & James Baird
Hours: Wed-Sun, 12-5; also by appointment
Types & Periods: General Line, Furniture, Glass, Pottery, China & Primitives
Specialties: Pattern Glass
Appraisal Service Available
Directions: Center of Littleton on Rte 119-2A opposite Harvard Trust Bank, 1/2 mile from intersection of Rte 119 & I-495

BLUE CAPE ANTIQUES
Rte 119   01460
617 486-4709   Est: 1964
Proprietor: Normand Caron
Hours: Wed-Sat, by appointment or by chance
Types & Periods: General Line, Collectibles
Appraisal Service Available
Directions: On Rte 119, 1 mile W of Rte 495

Ludlow

ADIRONDACK ANTIQUE BARN
345 West St   01056
413 583-4430   Est: 1974
Proprietor: Edward Bardon
Hours: Mon-Fri, 9-5; Sat,
9-4; Sun by chance
Types & Periods: General
Line, Collectibles
Directions: 2 miles E off
Exit 6 of MA Trnpk

Lynn

THE BERGENDAHLS
57 Newhall St   01902
617 599-5836
Proprietor: Peter & Nancy
Bergendahl
Hours: By appointment
Types & Periods: Early
Americana, Furniture

DENNIS ANTIQUES
54 Union St   01902
617 599-8000   Est: 1952
Proprietor: Stephen &
Marcia Dennis
Hours: Daily
Types & Periods: 18th &
19th Century Items,
Depression Glass
Specialties: Glass
(Depression), Primitives
Appraisal Service Available

Magnolia

HESPERUS BOTTLE HOUSE
38 Lexington Ave   01930
617 525-3775
Hours: Daily
Types & Periods: Bottles &
Collectibles

Mansfield

THE VILLAGE BARN
62 Pratt St   02048
617 339-9450   Est: 1973
Proprietor: R Mei, R
Scialoia & A Viscardi
Hours: Wed-Fri, 5:30-9;
Sat & Sun, 9:30-5

Types & Periods: Oak,
Brass, Wicker, Primitives,
Victorian, General Line
Specialties: Wicker, Brass
Directions: Mansfield Exit
off Hwy 95, 1 mile to Rte
106, left 1½ miles

Marblehead

THE GOOD BUY
120 Pleasant St   01945
617 631-7555
Hours: Mon-Sat, 10-5:30
Types & Periods: General
Line, Collectibles
Directions: Opposite
Warwick Theater

MARBLE HARBOUR ANTIQUES
84 Washington St   01945
617 631-4591
Hours: Daily
Types & Periods: Country
Pine, Wicker, Ironware,
Pottery, Glass, Nostalgia
Directions: Old Town
House Square

MARBLEHEAD ANTIQUE COOPERATIVE
118 Pleasant St   01945
617 631-9791
Types & Periods: Victorian
Furniture, Prints, Clocks,
Brass, Copper, Books,
Primitives

SACKS ANTIQUES
38 State & Front Sts
                     01945
617 631-0770   Est: 1912
Proprietor: Stanley &
Judith Sacks
Hours: Mon-Tues,
Thurs-Sat, 10:30 5; Wed,
1-5; also by appointment
Types & Periods: English &
American Mahogany
Furniture, Fine China, Silver
& Silver Plate, 18th & 19th
Centuries
Directions: Across from
Marblehead Harbor & The
Towne Landing

CHRISTINE VINING ANTIQUES
9 Pleasant St   01945
617 631-8224   Est: 1972
Proprietor: Christine
Vining

Hours: Tues-Sat
Types & Periods: Fine
American 18th & Early 19th
Century Furniture, Coin
Silver, English & Continental
Ceramics
Specialties: Fire
Memorabilia, China Trade
Porcelains
Appraisal Service Available
Directions: "Old Town"
Marblehead, corner of
Washington & Pleasant
Sts

JACK WEIL
202 Pleasant St   01945
617 631-3031   Est: 1960
Proprietor: Jack Weil
Hours: By appointment
Types & Periods: General
Line
Specialties: Americana
Appraisal Service Available
Directions: On main Rte

Marion

HEIRLOOMS UNLIMITED
369 Wareham Rd, Rte 6
                     02738
617 748-1663   Est: 1964
Proprietor: Albert F Ford II
Hours: Sun-Mon, Wed-Sat
Types & Periods: Fine
Period Furniture, Silver,
Chinese Porcelain, Bronzes,
Paintings, Gold & Jewelry,
Oriental Rugs
Appraisal Service Available
Directions: Rte 195 to Rte
105 to Rte 6, left 200
yards on the left

THE HOBBY HORSE
339 Front St   02738
617 748-0763   Est: 1962
Proprietor: Robert E
Mower
Hours: Fri-Sun
Types & Periods: 17th, 18th
& 19th Century Furniture,
Accessories, Fine Arts,
Collectibles
Specialties: Furniture,
Andirons, Graphics
Appraisal Service Available
Directions: Exit 26, I-95

Marlborough

THE CELLAR SHOP
643 Stevens St   01752
617 485-7891
Proprietor: Phyllis & John
Auricchio
Hours: Mon-Fri, 2:30-5;
Sat & Sun by chance or
by appointment
Types & Periods: General
Line, Furniture, Glass
Directions: Rte 20 to
Hosmer

**ROBERT CLEAVES &
LILIAN SLINGER**
121 Pleasant St   01752
617 481-1374
Proprietor: Robert Cleaves
& Lilian Slinger
Hours: Daily, 10-5
Types & Periods: Furniture,
Glass, China, Silver, Oriental
& Hooked Rugs, Dolls,
Jewelry
Directions: Rte 20 to
Marlboro

Marshfield

**1690 EMBANKMENT
HOUSE**
530 Summer St   02050
617 834-9848
Proprietor: Henry & Helen
Ryan
Hours: Daily
Types & Periods: Country
Furniture, Brass, Copper,
Mirrors
Directions: Shore Rd to
Humarock off 3A

SOUTH RIVER PRIMITIVES
22 Main St   02050
617 834-7774   Est: 1971
Proprietor: Willis & Karel
Henry
Hours: By appointment or
by chance
Types & Periods: 18th &
19th Century American
Furniture & Accessories
Specialties: Furniture,
Textiles, Quilts, Baskets,
Iron, Woodenware, Period
Accessories
Appraisal Service Available

Directions: Junction of
Rtes 3A & 139, take the
SE Expwy from Boston,
Exit at Marshfield, Rte
139, turn left at the 1st
traffic light onto 3A

Marstons Mills

TREASURE HIGHLAND
Falmouth Ave   02648
617 428-6380   Est: 1936
Proprietor: Robert Hayden
Hours: Daily
Types & Periods:
Collectibles, Architectural
Items, Pictures, Prints,
Furniture
Specialties: Opaque &
Stained Leaded Glass
Windows
Appraisal Service Available

Mattapoisett

**1812 HOUSE FULL OF
ANTIQUES**
Bolles Corner   02739
617 758-6267   Est: 1967
Proprietor: Arlene C
Dexter
Hours: Daily, 10:30-5; also
by appointment
Types & Periods: Primitives,
Country Furniture, General
Line
Appraisal Service Available
Directions: 150 yards off
Rte 6

VALLADOA'S ANTIQUES
Rte 6   02739
617 758-3381   Est: 1954
Proprietor: Edmond R
Valladoa
Hours: Mon-Sat, 9-4, by
chance
Types & Periods: Post
Cards, Furniture, Historical,
Souvenir Items, Paper
Goods, General Line,
Textiles, Books
Specialties: Post Cards,
Historial & Souvenir Items
Appraisal Service Available
Directions: Between New
Bedford & Wareham on
Rte 7, just E of
Mattapoisett Pharmacy

Medfield

**COPPERFIELD'S ANTIQUES
& COLLECTIBLES**
447 Main St   02052
617 359-7400
Hours: Tues-Sat, 10:30-5
Types & Periods: Victorian,
Turn-of-the-Century,
Furniture, Accessories,
Brass Beds, Oriental Rugs,
China, Glass, Advertising,
Country Store Items
Directions: Rte 109

**RUDISILL'S ALT PRINT
HAUS**
3 Lakewood Dr   02052
617 359-2261   Est: 1970
Proprietor: John &
Barbara Rudisill
Hours: By appointment
Types & Periods: Currier &
Ives & Other Early American
Prints & Trade Cards
Appraisal Service Available
Directions: Call for
directions

Medway

ERIC'S ANTIQUES
PO Box F   02053
617 884-7520
Proprietor: Eric Sidman
Hours: By appointment
Types & Periods: Art
Pottery, Carnival & Cut
Glass, China

J B & SON ANTIQUES
163 Holliston St   02053
617 533-7148
Hours: Daily, 10-4; also by
chance
Types & Periods: Oak &
Pine Furniture, Glass,
General Line

TINKERBELL ANTIQUES
50 Main St   02053
617 533-7102
Proprietor: Barby Horowitz
& Len Kronman
Hours: Daily
Types & Periods: Period
Country Furniture, Redware,
Stoneware, American
Paintings, Accessories
Directions: Rte 109

WEST STREET ANTIQUES
102 West St   02053
617 533-7811
Hours: Daily
Types & Periods: Heisey
Glass, Pottery, Oak &
Victorian Furniture
Directions: Off Rte 109

Middleboro

ACORN HILL ANTIQUES
W Grove St   02346
617 947-0982   Est: 1946
Proprietor: Arnold W Shaw
Hours: Daily
Types & Periods: General
Line
Appraisal Service Available
Directions: Rte 28,
beginning of Cranberry
Hwy

Milford

**THE HOUSE THAT JACK
BUILT**
482 E Main St   01757
617 473-8595
Proprietor: Jack Garfield &
Les Hudson
Hours: By appointment
Types & Periods:
Collectibles, General Line
Directions: Rte 16

Millbury

JOY P YOUNG
PO Box 108   01527
617 865-6600
Hours: Daily
Types & Periods: Dolls &
Accessories

Millers Falls

BLUE LAMP ANTIQUES
35 Forest St   01349
413 659-3808
Proprietor: Julia M
Constance
Hours: Mon-Sat; Sun by
appointment

Types & Periods: Silver,
Brass, China
Specialties: Glass (Art)
Directions: Rtes 2 & 63

Millis

BIRCHKNOLL ANTIQUES
Box 94   02054
617 376-8808
Proprietor: Carole M
Greco
Hours: By appointment
Types & Periods: Clocks,
Pewter, Brass, Copper, Early
Furniture

BLYTHEBROOK GALLERY
80 Island Rd   02054
617 376-2712
Proprietor: Bob & Carol
Geraghty
Hours: Mon-Sat, 10-6;
Sun, 1-5
Types & Periods: General
Line
Directions: Off Rte 115, 1
mile from Rte 109

THE HOME SHOP
323 Exchange St   02054
617 376-2209
Proprietor: Eleanor
Woodard
Hours: Mon-Fri, 11-4;
weekends by chance or
by appointment
Types & Periods: General
Line

THE POLE & CAP
183 Main St   02054
617 376-5555   Est: 1966
Proprietor: Mat & Phyllis
Tavares
Hours: By appointment
Types & Periods: American
Folk Art
Specialties: Decoys,
Scrimshaw, Cigar Store
Figures, Carrousel Animals
Appraisal Service Available
Directions: Rte 109

Mill River

LOST CREEK ANTIQUES
Hayes Hill Rd   01244
413 229-2644   Est: 1952
Proprietor: Hazel B Kuhns

Hours: Daily
Types & Periods: General
Line

Nantucket

VAL MAITINO ANTIQUES
31 N Liberty St   02554
617 228-2747   Est: 1950
Proprietor: Michael J
Maitino
Hours: Mon-Sat; Sun by
appointment
Types & Periods: Furniture,
Marine Items, Light Fixtures,
Old Hooked Rugs
Directions: Opposite
Franklin St

**UPSTAIRS DOWNSTAIRS
LTD**
21 Main St   02554
617 228-4250   Est: 1975
Proprietor: Adelaide P
Chuckrow
Hours: Daily; weekend
nites during summer
Types & Periods: Georgian
Pieces, Rustic Irish Country
Cupboards, Copper, Pewter,
Staffordshire, Wedgwood,
Irish Ships in Bottles
Specialties: Irish Pieces

Natick

**CARRIAGE HOUSE
ANTIQUE SHOP**
314 N Main St   01760
617 653-8861
Hours: Daily, open 1 pm
Types & Periods: Furniture,
Glass, China, Jewelry,
Oddities
Directions: Rte 27

**GEORGE A GILBOY
ANTIQUES**
17 Pleasant St   01760
617 655-1433   Est: 1935
Proprietor: George A
Gilboy
Hours: Tues-Sat, 10-5
Types & Periods: Furniture,
Accessories
Directions: Off Rte 16 at
center of S Natick, 1st
house on right

WM SYDNEY MICHAEL
39 Wellesley Rd   01760
617 653-8861
Hours: By appointment
Types & Periods: Early
American Furniture, Mocha,
Spatterware, China, Glass,
Shaker Items, Toys, Dolls,
Folk Art, Samplers, Oriental
Rugs

MUSHROOM ANTIQUES
95 E Central St   01760
617 655-5454   Est: 1966
Proprietor: Eleanor
Steinfeid
Hours: Mon-Sat, 10-4:30
Types & Periods: Furniture,
Oriental Rugs, Jewelry
Specialties: Wicker, Oak,
Copper
Appraisal Service Available
Directions: Rte 135 next to
Amory, 1 mile from
Wellesley

**THE PINK SPINNING
WHEEL ANTIQUES**
728 Worcester St   01760
617 655-1856
Proprietor: Ida & Max
Goldberg
Hours: Daily; also by
appointment
Types & Periods: Oriental
Items, Objets d'Art
Directions: Rte 9

H G SHORE CO INC
49 Eliot St   01760
617 235-6160
Proprietor: Harry G Shore
Hours: Mon-Sat, 11-5
Types & Periods: Furniture,
China, Glass, Lamps,
Shades, Andirons, Fenders,
Fire Tools
Appraisal Service Available
Directions: Rte 16

Needham

ABC SHOP
34 Central Ave   02192
617 235-5138
Proprietor: Alice Bob
Cassidy
Hours: Mon-Sat, 11-5;
Sun, 1-5

Types & Periods: Paper
Americana, Postcards,
Music Boxes, General Line
Directions: Over Echo
Bridge Country Store

**ECHO BRIDGE COUNTRY
STORE**
34 Central Ave   02194
617 444-9528   Est: 1972
Proprietor: Gary & Jackie
Wallace
Hours: Mon-Sat, 10-4;
Sun, 1-4
Types & Periods: Furniture,
Bric-A-Brac
Appraisal Service Available
Directions: Close to Rte 9
& 128

**GOLDEN FLEECE
ANTIQUES**
PO Box 29   02192
617 444-8767   Est: 1969
Proprietor: Margery A
Bailit
Hours: By appointment
Types & Periods: Early
Country Furniture & Fine
Decorative Accessories
Appraisal Service Available
Directions: Off Rte 135

NELSON-LEWIS ANTIQUES
908 Great Plain Ave 02192
617 449-0717
Proprietor: John N Lewis
Hours: Tues-Sat, 10-5
Types & Periods: General
Line, Collectibles, Furniture,
China, Glass, Silver,
Victoriana

**THE STEWARTS OF
NEEDHAM**
190 Nehoiden St   02192
617 444-0124   Est: 1927
Proprietor: Mrs Sidney
Stewart & James A
Turbayne
Hours: By appointment
Types & Periods: "Antiques
for Amateur & Expert"
Directions: Off Rte 135

New Bedford

NEW BEDFORD CLUSTER
Directions: Water St

HOUSE OF BRASS
1280 Ashley Blvd   02745

617 998-1751   Est: 1972
Proprietor: Arthur Teves
Hours: Mon-Sat, 12-4;
Sun, 1-4; evenings by
chance or by appointment
Types & Periods: General
Line, Victorian, Late 19th to
Early 20th Century Furniture,
Victorian Chandeliers,
Sconces, Brass Accessories
Specialties: Brass & Copper,
Oak Furniture
Directions: Rte 195 to Rte
140 N, Exit 4 to Ashley
Blvd

**NEW BEDFORD ARTS AND
ANTIQUES**
297 Coggeshall St   02746
617 999-1660   Est: 1963
Proprietor: Mary V Quintall
Hours: Mon-Sat, 10-5
Types & Periods: Art Glass,
Paintings, Objets d'Art,
Victorian Furniture
Specialties: Glass (Art)
Directions: Exit 16 E or 23
W from Rte I-195

Newbury

**ROGER WILLIAMS AT THE
OLD CURIOSITY SHOP**
313 High Rd RIA   01950
617 462-2072   Est: 1971
Proprietor: Roger Williams
Hours: By chance
Types & Periods: Formal &
Federal Period Furniture,
Oriental Rugs, Paintings,
Chinese & Period
Accessories
Specialties: Furniture
Appraisal Service Available
Directions: From I-95 or
Rte 1, take Rte 133 Exit or
Rte 113 Exit to Rte 1A

Newburyport

**CHANDLER'S LANE
ANTIQUES**
82 State St   01950
617 465-8240
Hours: Daily
Types & Periods: Country
Furniture, Tools

THE RANSHAW'S
344 Merrimac St   01950
617 465-5404
Types & Periods: Glass,
China, Canadian Eskimo Art

KENNETH & STEPHEN SNOW
12 Auburn St   01950
617 462-2882   Est: 1946
Hours: Mon-Sat, by chance
Types & Periods: Marine & Primitive Paintings, Liverpool & Canton China, Large Lustre Collection, General Line, Collectibles
Appraisal Service Available

SUMMIT SHOP ANTIQUES
117 Water St   01950
617 462-7298   Est: 1974
Proprietor: Thomas & June Powers
Hours: Wed-Fri, 10-4:30; Sat, 10-5; also by appointment
Types & Periods: Furniture, Accessories
Appraisal Service Available
Directions: Rte 95 to Newburyport Rte 113 Exit, follow High St to Lime St, at the foot of Lime St

Newton

ANY OLD THING
28 York Rd   02168
617 332-6747
Hours: By appointment
Types & Periods: Dedham Pottery Primitives, Baskets, Mocha & Spongeware
Directions: Waban

EDWARDS ANTIQUES
301 Watertown St   02158
617 244-2927   Est: 1964
Proprietor: Edward Getman
Hours: Sun-Fri; Sat by appointment
Types & Periods: Paintings, Jewelry, Clocks, Watches, Oak & Walnut Furniture
Directions: On Rte 16

MARILYN KOLKENBECK
14 Leslie Rd   02166
617 527-5996
Proprietor: Marilyn Kolkenbeck
Hours: By appointment
Types & Periods: General Line
Directions: Off Rte 16, Auburndale

Newton Centre

NOVACK GALLERY
424 Langley Rd   02159
617 527-1147   Est: 1967
Hours: Mon-Fri, by appointment or by chance
Types & Periods: 18th & 19th Century Furniture, Primitives, Brass, Copper, Wood, Paintings, Prints, Jewelry
Specialties: Early 19th Century Boxes, Samplers, Lighting Devices & Decorative Accessories
Appraisal Service Available
Directions: Rte 9

Newton Upper Falls

CHESTNUT ST ANTIQUES MARKETPLACE
1005-9 Chestnut St 02164
617 527-0286
Proprietor: Many Dealers
Hours: Daily, 10-5; Sun, Oct-May
Types & Periods: Furniture, Jewelry, Wicker, China, Glassware, Brass, Clocks, Paintings
Directions: 1005-9 Chestnut St, near junction of Rtes 9 and 128

SHIRLEY VAN ANTIQUES
381 Elliot St   02164
617 969-1846   Est: 1965
Proprietor: Shirley Van
Hours: Sun-Thurs, Sat
Types & Periods: Fine China & Glass, Sterling Silver, Flow Blue
Specialties: Mail Order, Silver Matching
Appraisal Service Available
Directions: Mall at Echo Bridge next to Mills Fall Rest

Newtonville

AROUND THE CORNER ANTIQUES
10 Austin St   02160
617 964-1149   Est: 1974
Proprietor: N Storm
Hours: Mon-Sat
Types & Periods: Victorian Furniture & Accessories, Antique Jewelry
Directions: Off Mass Tpke, or take Walnut St (off Commonwealth Ave) to Austin

Norfolk

CHEZ MARGOT
31 North St   02056
617 528-4334
Hours: By appointment
Types & Periods: Jewelry, Silver, Lamps, Stoves, Dolls, China, Glass
Directions: Rte 115

North Adams

NEW ENGLANDIANA
Box 787, 48 Ashland St
01247
413 664-9417   Est: 1961
Proprietor: Roger D Harris
Hours: Sun, 12-5
Types & Periods: Used Books
Directions: Near North Adams Post Office

North Andover

NOSTALGIC NOOK ANTIQUES
Rte 114 Jct 125   01810
Hours: Tues Thurs, opens at 11; Sun opens at 12
Types & Periods: Music, Furniture, Books, General Line
Directions: At Kent Movers

Northboro

IRON KETTLE ANTIQUES
113 Whitney St   01532
617 393-2431
Proprietor: Alise Lindberg
Hours: Daily, by chance
Types & Periods: General
Line, Collectibles,   Pine
Furniture, Primitives
Directions: 1/2 mile from
center

Northbridge

**HOUSE OF JAMES
ANTIQUES**
163 Sutton St   01534
617 234-2756
Proprietor: James A Prece
Hours: Sun & Mon, 10-10;
Evenings 5-10; also by
appointment
Types & Periods: Furniture,
Lamps, Oil Paintings

North Dartmouth

GEORGE CONSIDINE
632 Faunce Corner Rd
        02747
617 995-9425   Est: 1944
Proprietor: George
Considine
Hours: Daily, 9-4:30
Types & Periods: Early
American Furniture &
Accessories
Directions: 1½ mile N of
Faunce Corner, Exit Rte
I-95

North Falmouth

**UNCLE BILL'S COUNTRY
STORE**
28A   02556
617 564-4355   Est: 1973
Proprietor: Willard Weaner
Hours: Daily
Types & Periods: Furniture,
Primitives, Country Store
Items
Directions: Cross Bourne
Bridge, follow Rte 28 S to
Rte 151 Exit, left to red
light, then left 1/2 mile on
Rte 28A

Northfield

THE CARRIAGE STOP
166 Main St   03160
617 544-3885   Est: 1956
Proprietor: Dot & Gil
Gillmore
Hours: Sun-Wed & Sat in
the summer, Sun-Mon,
Wed, Fri-Sat in the winter
Types & Periods: General
Line
Specialties: Furniture
(Country), Lamps
Directions: Right on Rte
10 in center of town

**OLDE LIBERTY BELL
SHOPPE**
Rte 10   01360
413 498-2832   Est: 1962
Proprietor: L J Paparazzi
Hours: Sat, Sun & Mon,
11-5; Tues-Fri by chance
Types & Periods: Pine
Furniture, Fabric, Parch &
Glass Lampshades, Lamps,
Lamp Parts
Directions: On Rte 10
(outside Northfield) and on
the road to Winchester NH

North Hatfield

**RED BRICK SCHOOL
HOUSE**
PO Box 14   01066
413 249-5761   Est: 1925
Proprietor: W B Mew
Hours: Mon-Fri, 8-5; also
by appointment or chance
Types & Periods: Early
American Furniture
Appraisal Service Available
Directions: N Exit 22 off
91, S Exit 23

Norton

BLANCHE'S OLD HOUSE
9 Smith St   02766
617 285-4747
Proprietor: Blanche &
Herbert DuBois
Hours: Daily
Types & Periods: Furniture,
Primitives, Paintings, Prints,

China, Glass, Pottery,
Books, Tools
Directions: Rte 140 at
Reservoir

YE COUNTRY CAPE
1 Dean Rtes 123 & 140

Norwood

**TOWN & COUNTRY
ANTIQUES**
        02062
617 769-3080
Proprietor: Genevieve
Clampa
Hours: By appointment
Types & Periods: Porcelains,
Art Glass, Primitives,
Pottery, Orientals

Orange

MARY A BAKER
36 E Main St   01364
617 544-3155
Hours: By appointment
Types & Periods: Painting,
China, Glass, Primitives

EDGAR STOCKWELL
Rte 2A   01364
617 249-6541
Hours: Mon-Tues,
Thurs-Sat; Wed & Sun by
appointment
Types & Periods: Art Glass,
Oriental Art, Porcelains,
General Line
Directions: Rte 2A E of
Orange

Orleans

THE BUTCHER BLOCK
Rte 6A   02653
617 255-5160   Est: 1974
Proprietor: Jerrie Butcher
Hours: Daily, May-Oct
Types & Periods: Primitives,
Signed Handel & Tiffany
Lamps, Early Americana,
Advertising Pieces

BUTCHER BLOCK Cont'd
Specialties: Silver, Ceramics,
Weatherwares
   Directions: Rte 6A
   (Cranberry Hwy), near the
   Rotary of Rte 6, which is
   Mid-Cape Hwy to
   Provincetown or Boston

CAPE COD ANTIQUES EXPOSITION
   Nauset Regional Middle
   School, Rte 28   02653
   617 255-9726   Est: 1970
   Proprietor: Robert Mower
   Hours: 1st weekend in
   August
Types & Periods: 53
Room-like Settings of
Furniture, Silver, Fine Arts,
Porcelains, Jewelry, Prints,
Maps & Period Accessories
Specialties: Furniture
   Directions: Exit 12 from
   Mid-Cape Hwy opposite
   Orleans Police Station

JUDITH CRONIN-ANTIQUES
   Monument Rd   02653
   617 255-1792   Est: 1967
   Proprietor: Judith Cronin
   Hours: By appointment or
   by chance
Types & Periods: 19th
Century American Glass
Specialties: Early American
Pattern Glass (Early Flint to
Victorian Era Patterns), Rare
Sandwich, Colored Flint &
Ruby Stained Glass,
Opalesent, Historical, Cup
Plates & Books
   Directions: On Cape Cod

Oxford

BLACK LANTERN ANTIQUES
   Sutton Ave   01540
   617 987-2610   Est: 1943
   Proprietor: Florence E
   Whipple
   Hours: Daily, by
   appointment
Types & Periods: General
Line
Specialties: Art Glass
Appraisal Service Available
   Directions: E of stop light
   on Rte 12 in center of
   town, 9/10 mile to colonial
   house on corner of Lovett
   Rd & Sutton Ave

Peabody

LEGRO
                          01960
   617 595-7823
   Hours: By appointment
Types & Periods: China,
Glass, Furniture, Centennial
Items

Phillipston

COUNTRY ANTIQUES
                          01331
   617 249-9693
   Proprietor: Louis Chandler
   Hours: By appointment
Types & Periods: General
Line, Country Furniture,
Primitives
Specialties: Arms & Armor
(Guns)
   Directions: 1½ miles S of
   Rtes 2, 2A & 202, turn at
   King Philip Motel

PETER & DIANE NELSON
   Rte 101   01331
   617 939-5656
   Hours: By appointment, by
   chance
Types & Periods: Period,
Country & Formal Furniture,
Lighting, Andirons,
Paintings, Quilts, Hooked
Rugs, Silver, Brass
   Directions: 2 miles W of
   Templeton Common

Plainville

RED FARM OF BLAKE'S HILL
   Hancock St   02762
   617 695-5167
   Proprietor: Chevers
   Associates
   Hours: By appointment, by
   chance
Types & Periods: Primitives,
Related Items
Appraisal Service Available
   Directions: Off Rtes 121 &
   1A

Plymouth

ANTIQUE HOUSE
   174 Court St   02360
   617 746-8885   Est: 1972
   Proprietor: Mark & Elinor
   Marbet
   Hours: Daily, 10-6
Types & Periods: Antiques
from Early Plymouth Homes,
Clocks, Art Glass, Pottery
Specialties: Jewelry (Indian),
Indian Artifacts
Appraisal Service Available
   Directions: On Rte 3A,
   across from Plymouth
   Plaza, "Shop is restored
   home built before 1630 &
   is oldest structure in
   Plymouth"

Prides Crossing

ENGLISH MANOR ANTIQUES
   357 Hale St   01965
   617 927-3869   Est: 1961
   Proprietor: Mrs Joseph M
   Williams (Carol)
   Hours: By appointment
Types & Periods: English
Period Furniture of 16th,
17th & 18th Periods
Specialties: Furniture, Oak,
Walnut, Mahogany,
Satinwood
   Directions: Rte 127 (part
   of Beverly) right on the
   water

Provincetown

SEPTEMBER MORN ANTIQUE ORIENTAL ART
   350 Commercial St 02657
   617 487-9092   Est: 1971
   Proprietor: Dennis &
   Ronnie Szeszler
   Hours: Daily, 11-6 & 8-10
   pm, late May thru late
   Sept
Types & Periods: Antique
Netsuke, Snuff Bottles,
Ivories, Bronzes, Pottery,
Porcelain, Tsuba, Jade,
Lacquer & Enamels,
Satsuma, Kutani, Cloisonne
Appraisal Service Available
   Directions: Main street of
   Provincetown

MASSACHUSETTS   287

SMALL PLEASURES LTD
373 Commercial St   02657
617 487-3712   Est: 1970
Proprietor: Stephen Clover
& Darryl Moore
Hours: Daily, April-Oct
Types & Periods: Decorative
Arts & Jewelry, 1880-1940
Specialties: Fine Antique
Jewelry
  Directions: E end of
  Commercial St by
  Johnson St parking lot

Quincy

LANNAN NAUTIQUES
259 Harvard St   02170
617 479-5091   Est: 1969
Proprietor: Joe Lannan
Hours: Daily, by
appointment
Types & Periods: Fine
Nautical Artifacts & Ship
Models
Appraisal Service Available
  Directions: Just off Rte 3

Randolph

THE ANTIQUE LADY
8 Highland Ave   02368
617 961-1320   Est: 1960
Proprietor: Taffy Landy
Hours: Daily, 10-5
Types & Periods: Victorian
Specialties: China, Jewelry
  Directions: Rte 139 &
  Highland Ave

MACDONALDS BARN
233 S Main St   02368
617 963-9857   Est: 1973
Proprietor: Donald J
Macdonald
Hours: Daily, 12-5
Types & Periods: Glass,
China, Furniture
  Directions: Rte 128 to Rte
  28 near Avon Line

Reading

CARROLL-HARTSHORN
HOUSE
572 Haverhill St   01867
617 944-2952   Est: 1949
Proprietor: Shirley Carroll

Hours: Mon-Sat, 9:30-4:30
Types & Periods: 1690 Early
American Furniture,
Primitives, General Line
Appraisal Service Available
  Directions: Exit 34 N off
  Rte 128

COBWEB CORNER
ANTIQUES
44th St   01867
617 944-6039   Est: 1972
Proprietor: Angela
Babaian
Hours: Mon-Sat, 10-5
Types & Periods: Victorian &
Oak Furniture, Brass Beds,
Clocks, Oriental Rugs
Specialties: Furniture (late
1800 & Early 1900)
  Directions: Off Reading
  Square opposite American
  Legion

CARL W STINSON INC
AUCTIONEERS-APPRAISERS
01867
617 944-6488   Est: 1960
Proprietor: Carl W Stinson
Hours: By appointment
Types & Periods: General
Line
Specialties: NE Antiques
Appraisal Service Available

Rehoboth

ELEPHANT WALKS
ANTIQUES
462 Winthrop St   02769
401 438-6985   Est: 1972
Proprietor: Paul & Nancy
Rose
Hours: Tues, Thurs & Sat
& Sun, evenings
Types & Periods: Art Glass,
Toys, Dolls, Orientals
Specialties: Orientalia
Appraisal Service Available
  Directions: Rte 44

REHOBOTH ANTIQUE
VILLAGE
183 Winthrop St   02769
617 252-9367
Proprietor: Dennis A
Dubue
Hours: Daily, 7-6
Types & Periods: Furniture,
Jewelry, Bric-A-Brac, Gold,
Silver, Brass, Pewter

Appraisal Service Available
  Directions: Between
  Providence, Plymouth &
  Cape Cod on Rte 44

Rockport

BAYBERRY HILL ANTIQUES
26 South St   01966
617 546-2723
Hours: May-Nov
Types & Periods: General
Line

FIVE CORNERS ANTIQUES
5 Corners   01966
617 546-7063
Types & Periods: General
Line, Collectibles

GALLERY ONE
SEVENTEEN ANTIQUES
117 Main St   01966
Est: 1964
Proprietor: Roger W Clark
& Thomas C Schwab
Hours: Tues-Sat, by
appointment, May-Sept
Types & Periods: General
Line, Oriental, Paintings,
Books
Specialties: Paintings, Books
Appraisal Service Available
  Directions: Main St in
  center of village, 1 block
  from Five Corners

PENDLETON ANTIQUE
SHOP
55 Broadway   01966
617 546-3935
Hours: Daily, May to Nov;
other times by
appointment
Types & Periods: China,
Glass, Furniture, General
Line

PINXIT
55 Broadway   01966
617 546-2173   Est: 1965
Proprietor: Aldora R
Guarnera
Hours: Daily in the
summer; by appointment
or chance in the winter
Types & Periods: Orientals
(Chinese & Japanese),
17th-19th Centuries, General
Line

PINXIT   **Cont'd**
Specialties: Satsuma &
Kutani (19th Century)
Appraisal Service Available
  Directions: Center of town
  of Rockport

RO-DAN ANTIQUES
  Bearskin Neck   01966
  617 546-7152
  Hours: Daily, April thru
  Oct; also by appointment
Types & Periods: General
Line, Bronze
Specialties: Oriental
(Porcelain)

Rowley

GINNY'S FLEA MARKET
  Jct Rtes 1A & 133   01969
  617 948-2591   Est: 1966
  Proprietor: Virginia
  Douglas
  Hours: Sunday, holidays &
  special group
  accommodations during
  week
Types & Periods: General
Line

**TODD FARM ANTIQUES &
FLEA MARKET**
  Rte 1A   01969
  617 948-2217
  Hours: Thurs-Sun, 10-5
Types & Periods: Furniture,
China, Glass, Bric-A-Brac

Salem

**GAINSBORO STUDIO
ANTIQUES**
  317 Essex St   01970
  617 744-1055
  Hours: Tues-Sat, 10-5
Types & Periods: General
Line
  Directions: Opposite Witch
  House

HAWTHORNE ANTIQUES
  Hawthorne Blvd   01970
  617 745-5497
  Proprietor: Anne Carteris
  & Richard DiFillipo
  Hours: Daily
Types & Periods: Period
Antiques

MOLLY WALDO ANTIQUES
  5 S Pine St   01970
  617 744-2771
  Hours: By appointment, by
  chance
Types & Periods: General
Line, Collectibles

Sandwich

**CORNER HOUSE
ANTIQUES**
  172 Rte 6A   02563
  617 888-3662
  Proprietor: Dennis P
  Samson & David B
  Shermon
  Hours: Tues-Sun, 9-6; also
  by appointment
Types & Periods: Glass,
Porcelain, Furniture

**DILLINGHAM HOUSE
ANTIQUES**
  71 Main St   02563
  617 888-0999   Est: 1967
  Proprietor: Mr Jesse
  Leatherwood
  Hours: By chance, call
  ahead advisable
Types & Periods: 18th &
19th Century Furniture,
Paintings, Oriental Rugs,
Sandwich Glass,
Accessories
Specialties: Glass
(Sandwich)
Appraisal Service Available
  Directions: 1 mile from
  Sandwich Glass Museum
  heading W on Rte 130

CLIFFORD D HANSON
  Town Hall Sq   02563
  617 888-3230   Est: 1940
  Proprietor: Clifford D
  Hanson
  Hours: Daily
Types & Periods: Furniture,
Glass, China, Silver,
Paintings, Rugs
Specialties: Lamps
Appraisal Service Available
  Directions: Opposite
  Famous Sandwich Glass
  Museum

THE HAWKES
  24 Rte 6A   02563
  617 888-0378   Est: 1955
  Proprietor: Mrs E A
  Hawkes
  Hours: Daily, 10-6

Types & Periods: Glass,
China, Primitives, Early
Lighting, General Line
Specialties: Glass (Sandwich
& American), Cup Plates,
Primitives
  Directions: NW end of Rte
  6A, just entering town,
  about 2 miles from the
  Cape Cod Canal

Seekonk

**ANTIQUES AT
HEARTHSTONE HOUSE**
  15 Fall River Ave   02771
  617 336-6273   Est: 1938
  Proprietor: Lillian, Robert
  & Anne Wood
  Hours: Daily, 10-4:30, by
  appointment
Types & Periods: 18th &
19th Century Country &
Formal Furniture,
Decoratives & Collectibles,
Pewter & Brass
Appraisal Service Available
  Directions: Rte 195, Exit 1,
  go left on 114A thru 2
  traffic lights, shop on left

**RUTH FALKINBURG
ANTIQUES**
  208 Taunton Ave   02771
               Est: 1958
  Proprietor: Mrs Ruth
  Falkinburg
  Hours: Daily, by chance;
  call first advisable
Types & Periods: Antique
Dolls
Specialties: Antique Dolls
Appraisal Service Available
  Directions: Off 195, Exit 1,
  right on 114A to Taunton
  Ave (Rte 44), right again 1
  block, across from
  Hearthstone Motor Inn

LEONARD'S ANTIQUES INC
  600 Taunton Ave   02771
  617 336-8585   Est: 1933
  Proprietor: Robert L
  Jenkins
  Hours: Mon-Sat, 8-5; Sun,
  1-5
Types & Periods: Early
American thru Victorian
Furniture
Specialties: Restoring Rope
Beds
  Directions: 5 miles E of
  Providence on Rte 44

Sheffield

ANTIQUES OF RIVERSIDE INC
Rte 7 Box 284   01257
413 229-2598   Est: 1965
Proprietor: Max & Esther
Rosenberg
Hours: Daily, May-Oct 12
Types & Periods: China,
Glass, Orientals, Bronze,
European Porcelain, Art
Glass
Specialties: Ceramics, Royal
Worcester Crown Derby
English Porcelain
Directions: Rte 7, main
N-S road, located midway
between Sheffield & Great
Barrington

DOVETAIL ANTIQUES
Rte 7   01257
413 229-2628
Proprietor: David & Judith
Steindler
Hours: Daily, 10-5; also by
appointment
Types & Periods: Clocks,
American Furniture

LAWRENCE GOLDSMITH ANTIQUES
S Main St, Rte 7   01257
413 229-6660
Proprietor: Lawrence
Goldsmith
Hours: Daily, 10-5
Types & Periods: American
Furniture, Country & Formal,
Rough & Finished Primitives,
Folk Art, Pewter
Appraisal Service Available

GOOD & HUTCHINSON ASSOCIATES
Main St   01257
413 258-4555
Proprietor: David Good &
Robert Hutchinson
Hours: Daily, 10-5
Types & Periods: American
Furniture, 18th & 19th
Century Accessories, Suka
Needlework
Directions: "On the
Green"

CHARLES REICHARDT ANTIQUES
Box 254 S Main St   01257
413 229-8624   Est: 1975
Proprietor: Charles
Reichardt

Hours: Sun-Mon, Wed-Sat,
10-5
Types & Periods: Country
Furniture, Accessories
Directions: Rte 7

LOIS W SPRING
Ashley Falls Rd   01257
413 299-2542
Proprietor: Lois Spring
Hours: Daily, 10-5
Types & Periods: American
Furniture, Quilts, Oriental
Rugs, Paintings, Silver
Directions: Rte 7A

TWIN FIRES ANTIQUES
Undermountain Rd   01257
413 229-8307   Est: 1973
Proprietor: Joseph
Schwartzman
Hours: Daily, 10-4
Types & Periods: Stripped
Pine English Furniture
(Period Georgian-Victorian),
Linen Press, Accessories
Specialties: Brass, Copper,
Iron
Directions: 3 miles out on
Berkshire School Rd

Sherborn

BERESFORD ANTIQUES
86 N Main St   01770
617 655-2582
Proprietor: Carl & Dorothy
Beresford
Hours: By appointment, by
chance
Types & Periods: Glass,
Pewter, Clocks, Furniture
Directions: Rte 27

LO LU ANTIQUES
12 Washington St   01770
617 653-6261
Proprietor: Bob & Louise
Luther
Hours: Daily
Types & Periods: American
Art Pottery, General Line,
Collectibles
Directions: Rte 16

Somerset

CLEVELAND'S ANTIQUES
672 Lees River Ave 02725
                Est: 1946

Proprietor: Anne & Mason
Cleveland
Hours: Mon-Tues & Thurs-
Sat
Types & Periods: General Line
Specialties: Art Glass &
Scrimshaw
Appraisal Service Available
Directions: Between Rtes
195 & 6, 2 miles E of Fall
River

Somerville

DALE'S BARN
577 Somerville Ave 02143
617 628-0250   Est: 1973
Proprietor: Dale F
Consalvi
Hours: Mon-Sat
Types & Periods: General
Line
Appraisal Service Available
Directions: Between Union
Square & Davis Square

TO EACH THEIR OWN
75 Park St   02143
                Est: 1976
Proprietor: Nadine
Penniston
Hours: Daily
Types & Periods:
Turn-of-the-Century
Furniture, Collectibles
Specialties: Furniture
(Students)
Directions: Corner of
Beacon & Park Sts

TYMES PAST ANTIQUES
678 Broadway   02144
617 623-9553   Est: 1971
Proprietor: Tony Greist
Hours: Mon-Sat, 10-6
Types & Periods: Victorian
Furniture, Oak & Walnut
Marble Top, Custom
Mahogany Furniture, Brass
& Iron Beds
Appraisal Service Available
Directions: 1 mile W of
I-93, 6 miles E of Rte 128,
5 minutes from Harvard
Square

South Attleboro

THE CHARBONNEAUS'
464 Newport Ave   02703
617 761-5063

CHARBONNEAUS' Cont'd
Hours: By appointment or
chance
Types & Periods: Country
Furniture, Cupboards,
Accessories
  Directions: Rte 123, 2
  miles off Rte 95, at the
  Ebenezer Guild House

**GEORGE LEONARD
ANTIQUES**
707 Washington St   02703
617 761-5063
Proprietor: Irene & George
Leonard
Hours: Mon-Wed, Sat-Sun,
2-5; Thurs & Fri, 2-8:30;
also by appointment
Types & Periods: General
Line

Southboro

THE GOLDEN PARROT
22 E Main St   01772
617 485-5780
Proprietor: Glen & Gladys
Urquhart
Hours: Mon-Tues,
Thurs-Fri, 1-5; Sat & Sun
by chance or appointment
Types & Periods: General
Line, Furniture, Glass,
Collectibles

OUR PLACE ANTIQUES
116 Framingham Rd 01772
617 481-0256
Hours: Tues-Sun, 9-5
Types & Periods: Furniture,
General Line
  Directions: Off Rte 30 next
  to Buffalo Farm

**TOOMEY'S HAVEN
ANTIQUES**
89 Framingham Rd 01772
617 485-6910   Est: 1970
Proprietor: Helen L
Toomey
Hours: Tues-Sun, 1-5
Types & Periods: General
Line, Collectibles
Specialties: Furniture
  Directions: Down by
  Willow Brook Farm

Southbridge

**CHEZ CASAVANT
ANTIQUES**
27 Brook Rd   01550
617 761-2134
Proprietor: Louise H
Casavant
Hours: By appointment
Types & Periods: General
Line
  Directions: Rte 178 to
  Elm, 3rd left

South Dartmouth

THE WOODHOUSE SHOP
312 Elm   02748
617 993-5014   Est: 1970
Proprietor: Bill & Marcelle
Woodhouse
Hours: Daily, 10-5
Types & Periods: General
Line, Collectibles
  Directions: 5 minutes from
  Rte 195 in the center of
  Padanaram Village

ZABETH ANTIQUES
330 Elm St   02748
617 997-6832   Est: 1978
Proprietor: Gina Funicella
Hours: Mon-Fri, 12-4; Sat,
10-4; evenings by
appointment
Types & Periods: Victorian
Furniture, Paintings, General
Line of Collectibles
  Directions: 5 minutes from
  Rte 195 in center of
  Padanaram Village

South Deerfield

LIGHTHOUSE ANTIQUES
Rte 5-10   01373
413 665-2488
Proprietor: Ed & Helene
Petrovic
Hours: Daily
Types & Periods: American
& Victorian Furniture, Art,
Cut & Pattern Glass, Clocks,
Bronzes
Specialties: Lighting

South Easton

THE JOE'S ANTIQUES
688 Washington St   02375
617 238-7516   Est: 1967
Proprietor: Jos L Miskinis
Hours: By appointment
only
Types & Periods: Art & Cut
Glass, China, Lamps &
Lighting
Specialties: Wanted: Cut
Glass Lamps & Antique
Glass Shades
  Directions: On Rte 138

**ROBERT E RICHARDS
ANTIQUES**
24 Meeting House Ln
                   02375
617 238-4758
Hours: Daily
Types & Periods: General
Line, Primitives

South Egremont

ATTIC ANTIQUES
Box 306 Main St   01258
413 528-9550   Est: 1973
Proprietor: Steve & Nancy
Kahn
Hours: Sun-Mon, Wed-Sat,
10-6; during winter please
call
Types & Periods: Antique
Jewelry, Estate Jewelry
Appraisal Service Available
  Directions: Heart of village
  on Rte 23

BIRD CAGE ANTIQUES
Main St, Rte 23   01258
413 528-3556   Est: 1957
Proprietor: Marilyn &
Arnold Baseman
Hours: Daily, 9:30-5:30;
other hours by
appointment
Types & Periods: Primitive
Furnishings & Accessories,
Objets d'Art, Dolls, Toys
Appraisal Service Available
  Directions: Between Rte
  22 in NY & Rte 7 in Mass

South Hadley

HERITAGE GALLERY
01075
413 534-7056
Proprietor: Mr & Mrs Peter
Urbon
Hours: By appointment
Types & Periods: General
Line
Specialties: Art

South Harwich

THE SLIDING DOOR
820 Main St   02661
617 423-2182   Est: 1970
Proprietor: Harold &
Martha Clark
Hours: Daily, Mid-May thru
Mid-Oct
Types & Periods: Art & Cut
Glass, Silver, Paintings,
China, Orientals, Clocks,
Furniture, Iron, Brass,
Copper, Jewelry
    Directions: On Rte 28,
    about 15 miles E of
    Hyannis

Springfield

**WILLIAM & NANCY
BAKEMAN**
81 Woodlawn St   01108
413 736-3947   Est: 1970
Proprietor: William &
Nancy Bakeman
Hours: By appointment
Types & Periods: 18th &
19th Century Furniture
Specialties: Fabrics
Appraisal Service Available

BLUEBIRD ANTIQUES
55 Blake St   01108
413 739-5572
Proprietor: H P Vogt & R
E MacBrian
Hours: By appointment
Types & Periods: Oriental,
Porcelains, Glass, General
Line

**ARTHUR COOLEY
JEWELERS**
1210 Main St   01103
413 736-6850   Est: 1929
Proprietor: Phil Thompson

Hours: Mon-Fri, 9:30-5;
Sat at times
Types & Periods: Estate &
Antique Jewelry
Appraisal Service Available
Directions: State St &
Main St downtown, 1
block E off I-91

INTERIORS & ANTIQUES
210 Maple St   01105
413 734-4975   Est: 1970
Proprietor: Harry E Childs
Hours: By appointment
Types & Periods: American,
English, Pewter, Chinese,
Brass, Copper
Appraisal Service Available
Directions: Downtown

Stockbridge

**ANTIQUES AT TOM
CAREY'S PLACE**
Sergeant St   01262
413 298-3589   Est: 1972
Proprietor: Lucille
Nickerson
Hours: Sun-Mon, Wed-Sat,
by appointment
Types & Periods: Country
Furniture of 18th & 19th
Centuries, Lamps &
Accessories
Specialties: Clocks
    Directions: 1 block from
    Red Lion Inn, directly
    behind Mission House

FETICH
Pine St   01262
413 232-4475
Proprietor: William Ellery
Channing
Hours: May 15 thru Oct,
also by appointment
Types & Periods: N
American Indian Art of
1840's-1940's, Basketry,
Pottery, Weavings, Jewelry,
Beadwork
    Directions: House of
    Shops

Stow

ELIZABETH C FREED
PO Box 221   01775
617 897-8849

Hours: By appointment
Types & Periods: General
Line

Sudbury

GALLERIE DES JARDINS
738 Boston Post Rd 01776
617 443-6393   Est: 1958
Proprietor: Robert
Desjardin
Hours: Tues-Sat, 10-4
Types & Periods: 18th &
19th Century French
Furniture & Accessories
Specialties: 18th & 19th
Century French Furniture &
Accessories
Appraisal Service Available
Directions: Rte 20

WOODVINE ANTIQUES
254 Old Sudbury Rd 01776
617 443-2374
Hours: Tues & Thurs, 1-5;
Sat, 10-5; other times by
appointment
Types & Periods: American
18th & 19th Centuries

Sunderland

SUNDERLAND GALLERIES
N Main St   01375
413 665-3461
Proprietor: Robert T Duby
Hours: Daily 1-5, June to
Sept, Sun year round, 1-5;
also by appointment or
chance
Types & Periods: Furniture,
General Line
Directions: Rte 47 N

Sutton Center

POLLY'S ANTIQUES
Boston & Singletary Ave
01527
617 865-2654
Proprietor: Polly Shaw
Hours: Tues-Sun, 10-5
Types & Periods: General
Line
Directions: Near Rte 146

Swansea

FAN-TAS-TIQUES
2305 GAR Hwy Rte 6
02777
617 379-0015   Est: 1973
Proprietor: E Kotler
Hours: Sun-Mon, Wed-Sat
Types & Periods: General
Line, Collectibles
Directions: I-195 to
Massachusetts Exit 2, to
Rte 6, left on Rte 6

Templeton

**THE BLACK LANTERS
ANTIQUES**
Rtes 2A & 202 Athol Rd
01468
617 939-5066
Proprietor: Bernard T Cote
Hours: Daily
Types & Periods: Oriental
Rugs, Furniture, Victorian,
Primitives, China

Tolland

**MARIE WHITNEY
ANTIQUES**
Rte 57   01034
413 258-4538
Hours: Daily by
appointment; Mon-Sat,
April-Dec
Types & Periods: General
Line, 18th & 19th Century,
Pottery, Porcelain, Furniture,
Clocks
Specialties: Primitive Art of
New Guinea
Directions: On Rte 57, 25
miles W of Springfield

Topsfield

COURTYARD ANTIQUES
Rte 1 at Parsons Corner
01983
617 887-9363   Est: 1974
Proprietor: 6 Dealers
Hours: Mon-Sat
Types & Periods:
Collectibles
Specialties: Primitives
Appraisal Service Available
Directions: 5 minutes N of
Topsfield fair grounds

FOUR WINDS ANTIQUES
37 Main St   01983
617 887-5327
Types & Periods:
Collectibles, Furniture,
General Line

Townsend Harbor

**PETER & JILL LUKESH
ANTIQUES**
01469
617 597-8155
Proprietor: Peter & Jill
Lukesh
Hours: By appointment
Types & Periods: Pattern
Glass, Furniture

Upton

BOULDER FARM ANTIQUES
Grove & Mendon Sts
01568
617 529-3948
Proprietor: George & Nan
Haven
Hours: Daily, 1-5; also by
appointment
Types & Periods: General
Line
Directions: Off Rte 140

COUNTRY COTTAGE
6 Pearl St   01568
617 529-3417
Proprietor: Mrs Maude E
Ledoux
Hours: Daily
Types & Periods: General
Line
Directions: Take Elm St
off Rte 140, then Christian
Hill Rd to Pearl

**ELM STREET BARN
ANTIQUES**
7 Elm St   01568
617 529-3133
Proprietor: Rose Family
Hours: Daily; wholesale by
appointment or chance
Types & Periods: Victorian
Oak, Walnut, Wicker &
Mahogany Furniture &
Accessories
Appraisal Service Available
Directions: Exit 11 off
Massachusetts Trnpk, take
Rte 122 S to Rte 140 to
Elm St; from Rte 495 Exit

21B, go straight
approximately 6 miles to
Rte 140, turn left, Elm St
approximately 1½ miles

**OLDE TOWN ROAD
ANTIQUES**
270 Mendon St   01568
617 520-3163
Hours: Mon-Fri, 1-6; Sat &
Sun, 12-6
Types & Periods: General
Line, Furniture
Directions: Off Rte 140

TRASK FARM ANTIQUES
Mendon St   01568
617 529-3000
Hours: Weekdays by
chance or appointment;
Sun, 1-5
Types & Periods: General
Line

Uxbridge

**BIX FURNITURE STRIPPING
SERVICE**
Elmdale Rd   01569
617 278-5660   Est: 1973
Proprietor: John W Deiana
Jr
Hours: Tues-Sat
Types & Periods: Furniture,
Stripping
Specialties: Furniture
Stripping, Refinishing &
Antique Restoration

WILDACRES ANTIQUES
Henry St   01569
617 473-0068
Hours: By appointment, by
chance
Types & Periods: General
Line
Directions: Off Rte 16

Vineyard Haven

THE ANTIQUE POST
Union St   02568
617 693-3109   Est: 1974
Proprietor: Robert & Linda
Post
Hours: Daily, Weekends by
appointment

Types & Periods: General
Line, Early American
Furniture
    Directions: On Island of
    Martha's Vineyard, up the
    street from Steamship
    Authority

Wakefield

GIBSON GIRL CURIO
SHOPPE
    111 Albion St   01880
                     Est: 1976
    Proprietor: Judith E
    Esposito
    Hours: Tues-Sat
Types & Periods:
Collectibles, General Line
    Directions: Rte 128 to
    Wakefield Rte 129, follow
    Main St to center, right on
    Albion St

RANDY'S ANTIQUES
    935 Main St   01880
    617 245-3106   Est: 1969
    Proprietor: Ralph T
    Randell
    Hours: Mon-Sat
Types & Periods:
Turn-of-the-Century
Specialties: Paintings &
Statuatory
Appraisal Service Available
    Directions: Exit 34 off Rte
    128, Main St thru
    Greenwood section of
    Wakefield

WAKEFIELD ANTIQUES
    67 Albion St   01880
    617 245-4550   Est: 1950
    Proprietor: Barbara &
    Warren Wright
    Hours: Sun-Thurs, by
    chance; Fri & Sat, 10-5 or
    by appointment
Types & Periods: Clocks,
Lamps, General Line
Specialties: Clock Repair &
Antique Lamp Parts &
Repair
Appraisal Service Available

Wales

MEMORY LANE ANTIQUES
    1733 House   01081
    413 245-7006

Proprietor: Pearl & Ron
Medhurst
Hours: Daily
Types & Periods: Porcelain,
Pottery, Art Glass, Cut
Glass, Primitives
    Directions: Main street

Walpole

THE SCUTTLE SHOP
    536 High Plain St   02081
    617 668-3280
    Proprietor: Helen Shea
    Wolf
    Hours: Daily, 9-5
Types & Periods: General
Line
    Directions: Rte 27

Waltham

ANTIQUES 'N ODDITIES
    461A Main St   02154
    617 891-9456   Est: 1965
    Proprietor: Edith & Irving
    Newman
    Hours: Mon-Sat, 9-5
Types & Periods: Antiques,
Collectibles, Custom
Furniture
Specialties: Slag Glass
Lamps, Sterling, Jewelry
Appraisal Service Available
    Directions: Rte 20, 2¼
    miles from Rte 128

HOLLY HILL ANTIQUES
    48 Weston St   02154
    617 891 0300   Est: 1966
    Proprietor: Mr & Mrs M
    Beckwith
    Hours: Mon-Sat; Sat by
    chance during July & Aug
Types & Periods: American
Pewter, Silver, Furniture,
19th Century Paintings, Art,
Pattern & Sandwich Glass,
Pottery, Toys
Specialties: Glass
Appraisal Service Available
    Directions: On Rte 20, Exit
    49 on Rte 128, E 3/4 mile

Waquoit

WAQUOIT EMPORIUM
    Next to Post Office   02536
    617 540-4475   Est: 1976
    Proprietor: C R Savery

Hours: Mon-Sat, 9-4, June-
Sept; Sat, 9-4, Sept-June;
Also by Appointment
Types & Periods: Old Cape
Cod Items.

Watertown

PANDORA'S BOX
    117 Galen St   02172
    617 923-8987   Est: 1976
    Proprietor: Joy Pindo
    Hours: Tues-Sat, 11-6
Types & Periods: General
Line
    Directions: Midway
    between Watertown
    Square & Newton Corner,
    Exit 13 off Massachusetts
    Trnpk

Wayland

REMINISCE ANTIQUES
    33 Main St   01778
    617 655-7163
    Proprietor: Elizabeth L
    Moody
    Hours: Daily
Types & Periods: Primitives,
Victorian, Collectibles

Webster

TRINKET TO TREASURE
SHOPPE
    6 & 8 Lake St   01570
    617 943-0653
    Proprietor: Philla M
    DuPont
    Hours: By appointment, by
    chance
Types & Periods: Art Glass,
Pattern Glass, Orientals

Wellesley

THE BLUE LADY ANTIQUES
    283 Linden St   02181
    617 237-3442   Est: 1967
    Proprietor: Mrs Ann Tallen
    Hours: Mon-Sat
Types & Periods: Cut Glass,
Pottery, Art Glass, Bronzes,
General Line
Specialties: Oriental

THE BLUE LADY   Cont'd

Appraisal Service Available
   Directions: Massachusetts
Trnpk to Rte 128, S to
Exit 54, Rte 16
(Washington St) to
Wellesley, turn right at
Mobil station to 1st left

DEN OF ANTIQUITY

552 Washington St   02181
617 235-3240   Est: 1945
Proprietor: Leslie F Slavid
& Sons
Hours: Daily, 9-5
Types & Periods: General
Line of 18th & 19th Century
English & Oriental
Specialties: English &
Oriental Pottery & Porcelain
Appraisal Service Available
   Directions: Junctions Rtes
16 & 135 in Wellesley
Square, 15 minutes W of
Boston

PROCTOR GALLERIES

572 Washington St   02181
617 235-9163   Est: 1977
Proprietor: Robert & Karin
Proctor
Hours: Mon-Sat,
10:30-4:30
Types & Periods: Oriental &
European Objets d'Art,
Paintings, Early Furniture,
Oriental Rugs, Antique
Jewelry
Appraisal Service Available
   Directions: In Wellesley
Square, next to American
Express office & Treadway
Inn

SPIVACK BROS ANTIQUES

54 Washington St   02181
617 235-1700   Est: 1929
Proprietor: Max, Benjamin
& Jerome Spivack
Hours: Daily, 8:30-5:30
Types & Periods: 18th &
19th Century Furniture,
Porcelain, Glass, Bronzes,
Clocks, Lamps, Copper,
Brass, Paintings
Specialties: European
Imports
Appraisal Service Available
   Directions: Rte 128 to Exit
54W, then Rte 16 for 1/2
mile

THE WOMEN'S EXCHANGE

868 Worcester St   02181
617 235-8365
Proprietor: Rachel
Steinberg & Evelyn Lourie
Hours: Daily, 10-4
Types & Periods: General
Line
   Directions: Rte 9

West Acton

THE BAZAAR

566 Massachusetts Ave
                    01720
617 263-8154
Proprietor: Bradford E &
Grace M Johnson
Hours: Tues-Sat,
10:30-4:30
Types & Periods: Furniture
& Accessories
   Directions: Rte 111

RICHARD W SHAW ANTIQUES

584 Massachusetts Ave
                    01720
617 263-0133   Est: 1967
Proprietor: Richard W
Shaw
Hours: Daily
Types & Periods: 18th
Century Country Furniture &
Accessories
Specialties: Wrought Iron,
Lighting
Appraisal Service Available
   Directions: 25 miles NE of
Boston on Rte 111

Westborough

KNIGHT'S ANTIQUES

10 Walker St   01581
617 366-2720
Proprietor: Dick & Peg
Knight
Hours: By appointment
Types & Periods: General
Line, Collectibles
   Directions: Off Rte 30

THE MAYNARD HOUSE

11 Maynard St   01581
617 366-2073
Proprietor: Lloyd & Betty
Urquhart

Hours: Weekends April
thru Christmas; also by
appointment or chance
Types & Periods: Country,
"Displayed in our early
barn"

West Boylston

OLDE ROSE COTTAGE

24 Worcester St   01583
617 835-4864
Proprietor: Julie & Johnnie
Zalansky
Hours: Daily
Types & Periods:
Collectibles, Coins, Jewelry,
Silver, Clocks, Cut Glass,
Furniture, Lamps, Paintings,
Primitives
   Directions: On Rtes 12,
110 & 140 N of center

West Brewster

KINGSLAND MANOR ANTIQUES

Rte 6A   02631
617 385-9741
Proprietor: Norman &
Doris Schepps
Hours: Daily, 10-6
Types & Periods: General
Line

THE PACKET ANTIQUES

Stony Brook Rd   02631
617 385-3189   Est: 1923
Proprietor: Mr & Mrs Lloyd
S Godwin Sr
Hours: Mon-Fri, June 15
thru Sept 15; also by
chance or appointment
Types & Periods: General
Line
Appraisal Service Available
   Directions: Off Rte 6A on
Main Rd

West Bridgewater

ARMEN AMERIGIAN ANTIQUES

240 W Center St   02379
617 586-7563   Est: 1965
Proprietor: Armen
Amerigian
Hours: Sun-Mon,
Thurs-Sat, by appointment

Types & Periods: Sterling Silver, Glass, China, Furniture & Prints
Specialties: Art Glass
Appraisal Service Available
Directions: Rte 106 at Elm Square

VIRGINIA ENSLTER ANTIQUES
175 Lincoln St   02379
617 588-6463
Hours: Daily
Types & Periods: China, Primitives, Oriental Rugs, Furniture, General Line
Directions: Just off Rte 106 near Rte 24 Expwy

THE LAMPLITE SHOP
426 E Center St   02379
617 586-7104   Est: 1958
Proprietor: Helen & Donald Wood
Hours: Daily, 10-8 during summer; Daily, 10-6 during winter
Types & Periods: General Line, "Antiques to Elegante Junque"
Directions: Rte 106 E

West Dennis

BASS RIVER COUNTRY STORE
191 Main St   02670
                    Est: 1976
Proprietor: Marion & Joe Krawczyk
Hours: Daily
Types & Periods: Primitives, Oak, Glassware, China, Collectibles
Directions: Rte 28 just over the Bass River Bridge

West Falmouth

CALAB'S ANTIQUES
606 Old Main Rd   02574
617 548-9812   Est: 1977
Proprietor: Karan Hannigan
Hours: Mon-Sun, 10-5
Types & Periods: Victorian, Country Pine, Primitives, Baskets, Crocks, Quilts & Glassware

Directions: Rte 28A, West Falmouth Village, between Jenkins Funeral Home & W Falmouth Market

THE RED BARN ANTIQUES
681 W Falmouth Hwy
Rte 28A   02574
617 548-4440   Est: 1940
Proprietor: Frank & Joyce Clark
Hours: Daily, May 15-Oct 15; winter by appointment
Types & Periods: Early American, Glass, China, Furniture, Jewelry, Silver

UNCLE BILL'S COUNTRY STORE
606 Rte 28A   02574
Proprietor: Willard Weaner
Types & Periods: Furniture, Primitives, Country Store Items

Westfield

SOPHIE R ADZIMA
69 E Silver St   01085
413 568-1191
Proprietor: Sophie R Adzima
Hours: By appointment
Types & Periods: Collectibles, China, Copper, Furniture, Glass, Pewter, Silver
Directions: Off Rte 20

West Newton

ANTIQUE CORNER
209 A River St   02165
617 969-6446   Est: 1962
Proprietor: Ruth Sones
Hours: Mon-Sat, by chance
Types & Periods: General Line
Specialties: Victorian Furniture & Accessories, Cut Glass, Leaded Shades
Appraisal Service Available
Directions: Near Rte 30, 128 & Massachusetts Trnpk

JOSEPH CONWAY ANTIQUES
130 River St   02165
617 244-0066   Est: 1973
Proprietor: Joseph Conway
Hours: Daily, by appointment
Types & Periods: Pocket Watches, Clocks, Mechanical Curiosities
Specialties: Watches (Pocket)
Appraisal Service Available
Directions: Off W Newton Centre by W Newton Exit of Massachusetts Trnpk

Weston

WESTON ANTIQUE EXCHANGE
584 Boston Rd   02193
617 893-4337   Est: 1971
Proprietor: Caroline Stone
Hours: Tues-Sat, 10-4
Types & Periods: General Line
Directions: Off Rte 128, Rte 20 W 1 mile

Westport

YANKEE ANTIQUE SHOP
1128 Main Rd   02790
617 636-4498   Est: 1958
Proprietor: Janice L Field
Hours: Wed-Sat, 1-4
Types & Periods: Country Furniture & Accessories
Specialties: Dolls & Miniatures
Appraisal Service Available
Directions: I-95 S to Rte 88, at 4th set of lights bear right on Hix Bridge Rd, left on Main 1/4 mile

West Springfield

ANTIQUE CENTER
988 Riverdale St   01089
Proprietor: Frances McDonald
Hours: Mon-Sat, 10-4
Types & Periods: General Line
Directions: Rte 5

Westwood

PEG WILLS ANTIQUES
117 Oak St   02090
617 762-6684
Hours: By appointment, by
chance
Types & Periods: Early
American Furniture, Dedham
Pottery, Tin, Woodenware,
Marine, Baskets, Folk Art
  Directions: Turn off Rte
109 at Pont St, then 1
mile to Oak St

Weymouth

MARSHALL 1700 HOUSE
231 Washington St   02188
617 331-1700   Est: 1962
Proprietor: William C
Marshall
Hours: 6 Days a Week,
9-5
Types & Periods: Period,
Country, Formal & Oriental
Furniture & Accessories
  Directions: Rte 53, off Rte
3 Exit Weymouth Landing,
Rte 18, 2 miles

Whately

RED BRICK SCHOOL HOUSE
Box 14   01093
413 247-5761
Proprietor: W B Mew
Hours: Mon-Fri, 8-5; Sat,
8-12
Types & Periods: General
Line

Williamsburg

EARL B OSBORN
Old Goshen Rd   01096
413 268-7513   Est: 1940
Proprietor: E B Osborn
Hours: By appointment
Types & Periods: 18th
Century Furniture &
Accessories
Appraisal Service Available
  Directions: 1½ miles off
Rte 9

THE SMITH SHOP
Buttonshop Rd   01096
413 268-7335
Proprietor: Michael
Sissman-Blacksmith
Hours: By appointment
Types & Periods: Hardware,
Fireplace Accessories

Williamstown

BREWSTER ANTIQUES
                           01267
413 458-3221
Types & Periods: Jewelry

THE VICTORIAN SHOP
610 Main St   01267
413 458-3037
Proprietor: Mary L
Dempsey
Hours: Daily, 9-5:30;
evenings by appointment
Types & Periods: Early
American Furniture, Glass,
China, Quilts

WILLIAMSTOWN ANTIQUES
63 North St   01267
413 458-3162
Proprietor: Elsie &
Lorence Moore
Hours: Fri & Sat, 12-5;
also by appointment
Types & Periods:
Collectibles, Decorator Items
  Directions: Rte 7

Winthrop

RENEE'S ANTIQUE SHOPPE
PO Box 274   02152
617 846-0750   Est: 1963
Proprietor: Sherman &
Renee Altshuler
Hours: By appointment
Types & Periods: Art Glass
Lamps, Cut Glass, Pottery,
Porcelain, Clocks, Jewelry
(Turn-of-the-Century)
Specialties: Lamps, Art
Glass
Appraisal Service Available

Woburn

KELLEY'S
553 Main St Box 125
                           01801
617 935-3389   Est: 1950
Proprietor: Harold Kelley
Hours: Mon-Sat
Types & Periods: Antique &
Used Furniture, Military
Equipment Auctions
Specialties: Military Medals,
Swords, Uniforms, Helmets,
from 1750 to present
Appraisal Service Available
  Directions: Take Exit 39
from Rte 128, 2 miles on
left

Worcester

BUTLER ANTIQUES
299 Plantation St   01604
617 799-4994
Proprietor: Lucille &
Wayne Butler
Hours: By appointment
Types & Periods: General
Line
Specialties: Glass (Art)

LORRAINE HOGAN ANTIQUES
7 Denmark St   01605
617 757-1604
Proprietor: Lorraine B
Hogan
Hours: Daily
Types & Periods: Pewter,
Primitives, Pottery, Early
American Brass, Copper,
Iron, Tin

MARJORIE L HUMES
12 Birch Hill Rd   01604
617 853-1198
Hours: By appointment
Types & Periods: Early
American Furniture, Glass,
Brass

Wrentham

KING PHILLIP ANTIQUES
234 South St   02093
617 384-3857
Hours: Weekends, by
appointment
Types & Periods: 17th, 18th,
19th & 20th Century
Furniture, Paintings,
Collectibles
Specialties: Furniture
(Shaker)
   Directions: Rte 1A

Yarmouth Port

LIL-BUD ANTIQUES
142 Main St   02675
617 362-6675   Est: 1968
Proprietor: Walter L &
Lillian E Marchant
Hours: By Appointment or
By Chance
Types & Periods: Early
American Pattern Glass,
Some China & Silver
Specialties: Early American
Pattern Glass
Appraisal Service Available,
Glass Only
   Directions: Main St is
   Rte 6-A

**MOUSE HOUSE FARM
ANTIQUES**
28 Lookout Rd   02675
617 362-4957   Est: 1972
Proprietor: Ada & Walter
Slifer
Hours: By appointment
Types & Periods: Antique
Toys
Specialties: Early Rag Dolls,
Doll Houses, Doll House
Furniture, Miniatures
Appraisal Service Available
   Directions: Call for
   appointment & directions

This Empire Secretary was "Top of the Line" Mahogany. The Dresser with its marble top was of very good quality. Both are more than 7 feet.

298

STATE OF MICHIGAN

Albion

ALBION ANTIQUES
105 W Porter 49224
Est: 1973
Proprietor: Joan W McGee
Hours: Daily
Types & Periods: Art Glass,
Furniture, Pictures
Directions: Downtown, E
of Charlies

Algonac

YANKE POTTERY
5055 Pte Tremble Rd
(M-29) 48001
313 794-4840 Est: 1964
Proprietor: Norman &
Barbara Yanke
Hours: Mon-Fri, 10-5:30;
Sat, 10-6; Sun, 11-7
Types & Periods: Primitives,
Nautical Mechanical Music,
General Line
Specialties: Candles
Directions: I-94 E to New
Baltimore Exit, turn right &
follow M-29 for 15 miles,
right hand side of road

Allen

ANDY'S ANTIQUES
118 W Chicago 49227
517 869-2182 Est: 1972
Proprietor: Andy &
Rosemary Bailey
Hours: Sun-Tues,
Thurs-Sat, 10-5
Types & Periods: General
Line
Specialties: Furniture, Glass
(Depression)
Directions: Downtown, N
side of US 12

Ann Arbor

THE FINISHING TOUCH
10 Nickels Arcade 48108
313 994-3433 Est: 1974
Proprietor: Siegel, Grimes
& Power

Hours: Daily, 12-5
Types & Periods: Brass,
Copper, Victoriana, Small
Furniture
Directions: Between State
St & Maynard on Campus
of U of M

**SALLY THOMAS &
COMPANY**
220 N Fifth Ave 48104
313 663-5232
Proprietor: P Mangrum
Hours: Mon-Sat
Directions: 1 block N of
city hall

THE TREASURE MART
529 Detroit St 48104
313 662-9887 Est: 1960
Proprietor: Demaris E
Cash
Hours: Mon-Sat
Appraisal Service Available
Directions: Downtown

Atlas

MAURICE E REID
8470 Perry Rd 48411
313 636-2240 Est: 1946
Proprietor: Maurice E Reid
Hours: Daily
Types & Periods: American
Furniture, 18th & 19th
Centuries
Appraisal Service Available
Directions: 5 miles E of
Grand Blanc

Battle Creek

DEMPSEY'S ANTIQUES
1423 E Michigan 49017
616 964-7466
Proprietor: Rosalyn &
Charles Dempsey
Hours: Daily, 9-7
Types & Periods: General
Line

Bay City

NANCIES' FANCIES
1400 Center Ave 48706
517 892-7347 Est: 1971
Proprietor: Nancy Lettrup
Hours: By appointment, by
chance
Types & Periods: General
Line
Appraisal Service Available

VARADI'S ANTIQUE SHOP
503 E Midland 48706
517 892-9721 Est: 1966
Proprietor: Alex & Lottie
Varadi
Hours: Tues-Sat, 10-5;
also by appointment
Types & Periods: Objets
d'Art, Clocks, Furniture,
Glass, China
Specialties: Clocks,
Furniture
Directions: Westside, off
Euclid, 1 block from
Henry, same street as
Sage Library

Berkley

**DOUBLE L ANTIQUES,
COLLECTORS DIVISION
LTD**
2631 N Woodward Ave
48072
313 548-4144 Est: 1971
Proprietor: Lieselotte H
Harris
Hours: Tues-Sat
Types & Periods: Glassware,
Figurines (Rosenthal &
Hutschenreuther), European
China, Dresden Items
Specialties: Collector's
Plates, China, Hummel
Figurines
Appraisal Service Available
Directions: N of Detroit on
Woodward Ave at 11½
Mile Rd

Bessemer

ANTIQUES UNLIMITED
E US 2   49911
906 667-1491   Est: 1973
Proprietor: Ron & Marilou
Vincent
Hours: Daily, 11-5
Types & Periods: Oak
Furniture, Brass, Primitives,
Collectibles
Specialties: Tiffany &
Stained Glass
Appraisal Service Available
Directions: E US 2, across
from school

COLLECTOR'S CORNER
301 E Mary St   49911
906 663-4003
Hours: Daily, 11-4 during
summer; afternoons
during winter
Types & Periods: China,
Glass, Furniture
Directions: S of US 2, 1
block

Big Rapids

THE OLD PIONEER STORE
118 N Michigan   49307
616 796-2502   Est: 1971
Proprietor: Jack & Nancy
Batdorff
Hours: Mon-Thurs, Sat,
9-5; Fri, 9-9
Types & Periods: Primitives,
Country, Currier & Ives
Specialties: Blacksmith
Bellows, Tables, Pine Items
Appraisal Service Available
Directions: Downtown

RED PUMP
S Northland Dr
Rte 2 Box 97   49307
616 796-2339   Est: 1973
Proprietor: Tom Kutzli
Hours: Daily, 9-6
Types & Periods: General
Line
Appraisal Service Available
Directions: 1 mile S of
Ferris State College on
Hwy 131

Birmingham

AQUARIAN BOOK SERVICE
Box 57   48012
313 645-1225   Est: 1976
Proprietor: Ruth S
Kennedy
Hours: By appointment
Types & Periods: Rare &
Scarce Books, First Editions,
Illustrated Books,
Americana, Western
Americana & Mormon
Specialties: Free search
service for any book for
anyone
Appraisal Service Available

**H GEORGE BICKELMANN
ANTIQUES**
1020 N Hunter Blvd 48011
313 642-2400   Est: 1969
Proprietor: H George
Bickelmann
Hours: Mon-Sat
Types & Periods: Pre-1830
American Furniture,
Paintings
Appraisal Service Available
Directions: N end of town
near junction of
Woodward & Hunter

**MADELINE'S ANTIQUE
SHOPPE**
1034 N Hunter   48011
313 644-2493   Est: 1962
Proprietor: Madeline
Harshaw
Hours: Daily, 11-4
Types & Periods: Furniture,
China, Art Glass
Specialties: Oriental (Rugs)
Appraisal Service Available
Directions: Woodward
Ave, N between Oak & Big
Beaver, or I-75 to Big
Beaver to Woodward S,
1/2 block

**MAZE POTTINGER
ANTIQUES**
726 N Woodward   48009
313 646-1996
Proprietor: Maze Pottinger
Hours: Daily, 10:30-5:30
Types & Periods: 18th &
19th Century American &
English Country Items

**THE UNDERGROUND
COLLECTOR**
790 N Woodward   48011
313 644-3982   Est: 1973
Proprietor: Barbara K
Book
Hours: Mon-Sat, 9:30-5
Types & Periods: Primitives,
China, Silver
Appraisal Service Available
Directions: 5 blocks N of
Birmingham's main street

Brighton

**POOR RICHARD'S
ANTIQUES**
114 E Main   48116
313 229-9120   Est: 1969
Proprietor: Lois & Dick
Waskin
Hours: Daily, 11-5
Types & Periods: General
Line, Furniture
Directions: Downtown

**SALLY THOMAS &
COMPANY**
8480 Hyne Rd   48116
313 227-3828
Proprietor: P Mangrum
Hours: By appointment
Types & Periods: Country &
Period Furniture
Specialties: Stoneware,
Treenware
Appraisal Service Available
Directions: Between
Hacker & Old US 23

Cedar Springs

GRANNY'S ROLLING PIN
13543 Pine Lake Rd
                     49319
616 696-2962   Est: 1968
Proprietor: Lois M Weaver
Hours: By chance; Shows
Only
Types & Periods: Primitives,
Furniture
Directions: 131 to Cedar
Springs Exit, E to end, S
on Pine Lake, 1st large
farm house

Chassell

THE EAGLE SHOP ANTIQUES
148 N Willson Dr   49916
906 523-4423   Est: 1964
Proprietor: Mrs Hattie Vial
Hours: Daily during summer; by appointment or chance during winter
Types & Periods: Lamps, Clocks, Primitives, Furniture, China, Glass, Books, General Line
Specialties: Signed Tools, Oil Lamps
Directions: On Hwy 41 in N part of upper peninsula of Michigan, 265 miles N of Mackinaw Bridge

THE EINERLEI SHOP
Hwy 41   49916
906 523-4612   Est: 1975
Proprietor: Bill & Nancy Leonard
Hours: Daily during summer; other times by chance or by appointment
Types & Periods: American Country Furniture, Primitives
Directions: Hwy 41, in Michigan's upper peninsula

PINE CONE SHOP
308 Willson Memorial Dr
49916
906 523-4709   Est: 1953
Proprietor: Frances & Paul Anderson
Hours: Mon-Sat, June 1-Nov 1
Types & Periods: China, Glass, Furniture, General Line
Appraisal Service Available
Directions: On US 41, main street in town

Clarkston

CLARKSTON MAIN STREET ANTIQUES
21 N Main St   48016
313 625-3122   Est: 1963
Proprietor: Daisy Dowling & Virginia Schultz
Hours: Mon-Sat, 11-5; Sun, 2-5

Types & Periods: General Line, Primitive, Early Victorian
Specialties: Baskets, Toleware, Cupboards, Chairs, Quilts, Pictures, Mirrors, Lamps, Custom Lampshades, China, Glass, Flamstead Clothes
Appraisal Service Available
Directions: 5 minutes from I-75 between Pontiac, Troy & Flint

Coldwater

ABBOTT'S ANTIQUES
315 Fiske Rd   49036
517 278-6729   Est: 1966
Proprietor: Bud & Betty Abbott
Hours: Sun-Wed, Sat, 9-5
Types & Periods: Primitives, Glass, Furniture
Appraisal Service Available

Coloma

MILLSTONS ANTIQUE SHOP
6162 Martin Rd   49038
616 468-6667   Est: 1958
Proprietor: Marlin & Jean Marguart
Hours: Daily, 10-5, except Jan-March, Sun-Tues & Sat
Types & Periods: General Line
Specialties: Furniture
Directions: Exit 7 (I-196), 1 mile E to Martin Rd

Corunna

LAWSON'S ANTIQUES
111 N Shiawassee   48817
517 743-3180   Est: 1951
Proprietor: Bill & Jeanne Lawson
Hours: Daily, by appointment
Types & Periods: General Line, Glass, China
Appraisal Service Available
Directions: Main St of Corunna

Davison

PLANTATION GALLERIES
6400 Davison Rd   48423
313 743-5258   Est: 1960
Proprietor: Diana Peters
Hours: By appointment
Types & Periods: Oak Furniture, Art Glass, Tiffany Lamps, Clocks
Appraisal Service Available
Directions: Off I-69 outside Flint, 1 hour from Detroit

Detroit

DETROIT CLUSTER
Directions: No Cluster, few shops on W McNichols (20000 Block), Mack (14000 Block), Hamilton Hill Pk (16000 Block)

CENTURY HOUSE ANTIQUES
24550 W McNichols
48219
313 538-6550
Proprietor: Frank Bezenah
Hours: By appointment
Types & Periods: General Line
Appraisal Service Available
Directions: A few blocks W of Telegraph (US 24)

DROVERS EAST ANTIQUES
48219
313 532-9677
Proprietor: Rae Choma
Hours: By appointment
Types & Periods: Jewelry, Dolls, Silver, Porcelains
Specialties: Jewelry, Dolls, Silver, Porcelains
Appraisal Service Available

UNICORNS
1723 Iroquois Ave   48214
313 924-2222
Proprietor: Stuart Wilber & Dale Jamros
Hours: By appointment
Types & Periods: Porcelain, Oriental, General Line

De Witt

DE WITT MANOR ANTIQUES
303 N Bridge St   48820
517 669-3116
Proprietor: Frances J
Schrader
Hours: By appointment
Types & Periods: Cloisonne,
Decorative Accessories,
General Line

Dorr

BACK DORR ANTIQUES
4219 18th St   49323
616 681-9415   Est: 1967
Proprietor: Anthony
Rakowski
Hours: Weekends, by
appointment
Types & Periods: Furniture,
Primitives, Glass, China,
Victorian, Mission Oak
Appraisal Service Available
Directions: 2 miles W of
Hwy 131, 1 block N

Eastport

**THE HINTER HAUS
ANTIQUE & GIFT SHOP**
US 31, PO Box 62   49627
616 599-2311   Est: 1970
Proprietor: Mrs Margery R
Burrill
Hours: Mon-Sat, 10-5; also
by appointment
Types & Periods: Furniture
(Pre 1925 Victorian, Early
American 1800 & Oak)
Specialties: Glass, China,
Restored Furniture
Directions: US 31, just S
of M88

Eaton Rapids

CHINA CUPBOARD
4885 West St   48827
517 663-4231   Est: 1968
Proprietor: Vida M Fernold
Hours: Mon-Sat, 9-5
Types & Periods: From
1800, Furniture, General
Line

Specialties: China, Glass
Directions: S of downtown
to Williams St, W to end
of street to West St, 2nd
place S of new part of
cemetery

SILHOUETTE ANTIQUES
315 S Main   48827
517 663-4777
Proprietor: Dorothy C
Hemans
Hours: By appointment, by
chance
Types & Periods: Dolls, Art
Glass

Escanaba

TRASH & TREASURES
906 Ludington   49829
906 786-0492   Est: 1961
Proprietor: Melba B Coan
Hours: Daily
Types & Periods: Primitives,
Glassware, China, Silver,
Furniture, From Victorian to
Collectibles
Specialties: Silver
Directions: On main street

Farmington

MARK FISCHER GALLERY
32732 Northwestern Hwy
48018
313 851-6166   Est: 1960
Proprietor: Mark Fischer
Hours: Mon-Sat, 11-5
Typou & Periods: English &
American Furniture, Glass,
Brass, Clocks, Lamps, Light
Fixtures
Specialties: Restoration &
Refinishing, Picture Framing
Appraisal Service Available
Directions: Between
Middlebelt & 14 Mile Rd

**DOROTHY THOMPSON
ANTIQUES**
24117 Twin Valley Court
48024
313 476-6224   Est: 1972
Proprietor: Dorothy & Jack
Thompson
Hours: By appointment
Types & Periods: 18th &
19th Century English Accent
& Decorator Items in Brass

& Copper, Wood Boxes,
Barometers, Small Furniture
Specialties: Brass & Copper
Decorator Items

Fenton

SILVER STAR ANTIQUES
5900 Green Rd   48430
517 546-9587   Est: 1964
Proprietor: Mr & Mrs
Andrew J Kardos
Hours: Wed-Sat, 9-6; Sun,
11-6
Types & Periods: Victorian
Furniture, Clocks, Brass,
Copper, Ironware, China,
Cut Glass, Primitives
Specialties: Clocks,
Furniture
Directions: 1 mile N of
Clyde Rd

Ferndale

**ANTIQUES BY SALLIE
WRIGHT**
22446 Woodward Ave
48220
313 399-0339   Est: 1971
Proprietor: Sallie Wright
Hours: Mon, Thurs, Fri &
Sat, 10:30-5
Types & Periods: Stained
Glass Windows, Doors,
Lamps, Furniture, Jewelry
Appraisal Service Available
Directions: Between 8 & 9
Mile Rd, 3 blocks S of 9
Mile Rd

Flint

ERMA'S ANTIQUE SHOP
G 5393 S Saginaw   48507
313 694-0270   Est: 1972
Proprietor: Erma Nolan
Hours: Thurs-Sat, 11-5;
also by appointment
Types & Periods: Victorian &
Oak Furniture, Lamps,
Dishes
Specialties: Lamps

**FLORENCE PINES
ANTIQUES**
1224 W Court   48503
313 235-4582   Est: 1961
Proprietor: Florence Pines

FLORENCE PINES   Cont'd
Hours: Daily, 12-6
Types & Periods: General Line
Appraisal Service Available
Directions: On M56 W, across from Michigan School for Deaf, on corner of Hoylton

Flushing

1866 HOUSE ANTIQUES
G 5279 Flushing Rd
48433
313 732-2400
Proprietor: Richard H Morrish
Hours: Sun-Fri, 11-5
Types & Periods: Primitives, Fruit Jars, Tools, Paper, China

Franklin

CURIOSITY SHOPPE LTD
32800 Franklin Rd   48025
313 626-2554   Est: 1956
Proprietor: M M Michaels
Hours: Tues-Sat, 9:30-5:30; also by appointment or by chance
Types & Periods: Country French, English & American Colonial, Continental Jacobean, Paintings & Bronzes, Oriental
Specialties: Crystal, Porcelains, Nautical
Appraisal Service Available
Directions: Corner of Franklin Rd & 14 Mile Rd, diagonally across from the Franklin Cider Mill

Galesburg

SWAP SHOPPE INC
8418 Michigan Ave   49053
616 345-1752   Est: 1962
Hours: Mon-Sat, 10-5
Types & Periods: Primitives, Glassware, Clocks, European & American
Specialties: WHOLESALE ONLY
Directions: 8 miles E of Kalamazoo

Grand Ledge

THE SIGN OF THE PEACOCK
202 S Bridge   48837
517 627-7722   Est: 1965
Proprietor: Angus B Cory
Hours: Tues-Sat, 10-5
Types & Periods: General Line
Specialties: Furniture, Jewelry, Oriental
Appraisal Service Available
Directions: 1 block N of M100 & M43 in downtown

Grand Rapids

GRAND RAPIDS CLUSTER
Directions: Wealthy St SE section crisscrossed by side streets & intersecting streets

BRASS SMITH SHOP
1450 Wealthy SE   49505
616 454-0493   Est: 1974
Proprietor: Gary Hampton
Hours: Mon-Sat, 11-6
Types & Periods: Brass Beds, Brass & Copper Items, Restoration Work
Specialties: Brass Beds, Brass & Copper Items, Restoration Work
Appraisal Service Available

Greenville

HAY-RAKE ANTIQUES
10368 Leland Dr   48838
Proprietor: Mildred Fisher (Mrs Robert Fisher)
Types & Periods: SHOWS ONLY

Harrison

JUNQUE SHOP
2020 E Cranberry   48625
313 539-7223   Est: 1961
Proprietor: Richard & Faith Foutch
Hours: Daily
Types & Periods: General Line, Furniture, Glass, Books, Postcards, Tools
Specialties: Auctions

Appraisal Service Available
Directions: 1 mile N of Wilson State Park, corner of Old US 27 & Cranberry Lake Rd

Hartland

SALLY THOMAS & COMPANY
3568 Avon   48029
Est: 1970
Proprietor: Sally Thomas
Hours: By appointment & By chance
Types & Periods: Furniture
Specialties: Stoneware
Appraisal Service Available
Directions: 1 blk from US 23 N downtown

Holland

ANTIQUES ETC
383 Central   49423
616 396-4045   Est: 1968
Proprietor: Ruth C Athey
Hours: Tues-Sat, afternoons; Fri evenings
Types & Periods: Glassware, Dishes, Advertising, Books, Furniture
Appraisal Service Available
Directions: Off Gerald Ford Hwy at 16th St Exit

THE DUTCH BARN
1200 Ottawa Beach Rd
49423
616 335-5548   Est: 1971
Proprietor: Mr & Mrs Jay Van Wieren
Hours: Mon-Sat, 11-5 May thru Dec 24; Mon-Sat, 11-9, June 21 thru Aug 3
Types & Periods: Furniture, Primitives, Empire, Victorian, Mission Oak, English Imports
Specialties: Furniture, Jugs, Crocks
Directions: 8 miles from Hwy 31 & I-96

Holly

BATTLE ALLEY ANTIQUES
108 Battle Alley   48442
313 634-7711   Est: 1974

Proprietor: Ellen Hilty &
Evelyn Raskin
Hours: Tues-Sat, 10-5;
Sun, 12-5
Types & Periods: 19th
Century Furniture,
Collectibles, Jewelry,
Paintings
Specialties: Picture Framing
Appraisal Service Available
Directions: Downtown, 5
minutes off I-75, Holly Exit

GOOD-OL-DAYS ANTIQUES
108 S Saginaw St   48442
313 634-5291   Est: 1965
Proprietor: Dorothy
Schneider
Hours: By appointment, by
chance
Types & Periods: Primitives,
Victorian, China, Glass,
Tools
Specialties: Cut Glass,
Beveled Glass Doors &
Windows, Tin & Bottles
Appraisal Service Available
Directions: 15 miles S of
Flint between I-75 & US
23

O & B ANTIQUES
107 Battle Alley   48442
313 634-9053   Est: 1973
Proprietor: Mona Ormiston
& Sophie Bridgett
Hours: Daily, 11-5
Types & Periods: Furniture,
Glass, China, Collectibles,
Primitives
Specialties: Furniture
(Victorian)
Directions: E of US 23 &
W of I-75, between
Pontiac & Flint

Iron Mountain

BLUE ROOM ANTIQUES
205 E Flesheim St   49801
906 774-0166   Est: 1972
Proprietor: Margaret &
Paul Campbell
Hours: Mon-Sat, 12-4:30
Types & Periods: Glass,
Porcelain, Furniture,
Primitives, Collectibles
Directions: 2 blocks off
Hwy 2 E

THE COBWEB ANTIQUES
N Hwy 2   49801
906 774-6560   Est: 1968

Proprietor: Richard &
Virginia Williams
Hours: Mon-Sat
Types & Periods: Furniture,
China, Glass, Copper, Brass,
Brass & Iron Beds, Oak &
Pine Primitives
Directions: 3 miles N of
Iron Mountain at the Y of
M95 & Hwy 2

NORA K SHOP ANTIQUES
837 E B St   49801
906 744-4545
Proprietor: Norm & Nora
Flemington
Hours: Daily, 9-5
Types & Periods: General
Line

Ironwood

**BROTTLUND'S ROCK &
ANTIQUE SHOP**
North Lake Rd   49938
906 932-5797
Types & Periods: Primitives,
Collectibles, Local Mineral
Crystals

DOREEN'S ANTIQUES
313 Lake St   49938
906 932-4310   Est: 1977
Proprietor: William &
Doreen Heilig
Hours: Mon-Sat; Sun by
chance or by appointment
Types & Periods: Furniture,
Glassware, Lamps, Clocks,
Watches, General Line,
Collectibles
Appraisal Service Available
Directions: 2 blocks S of
US 2, turn S at Holiday
Station

KORNWOLF'S ANTIQUES
631 E McLeod Ave   49938
906 932-3124   Est: 1971
Proprietor: Anita Kornwolf
Hours: Daily, 8-8; also by
chance or by appointment
Types & Periods: Furniture,
Lamps, Clocks, Primitives
Specialties: Furniture,
Primitives
Directions: 4 blocks E of
Police Station

THE NET LOFT
Black River Harbor   49938
906 932-3660
Proprietor: Lorraine Allen

Hours: Daily
Types & Periods: Primitives,
Oak Furniture, Rock &
Agate Jewelry

**THE VILLAGE STORE
ANTIQUES**
655 E McLeod Ave   49938
906 932-5394
Proprietor: Orene Reinikka
Hours: Mon-Sat, 9-5; by
appointment
Types & Periods: General
Line
Specialties: Glassware &
China, Primitives
Appraisal Service Available
Directions: 1/2 mile S of
US 2, 2 miles E of Rte 51

Ishpeming

41 ANTIQUES
Box 220   49849
906 339-2117   Est: 1967
Proprietor: Eleanore A
Salmi & George E Salmi
Hours: Daily, 9-5, June
thru Sept
Types & Periods: General
Line
Specialties: Store Items,
Automotive, Glass, Pottery,
Furniture, Primitives
Appraisal Service Available
Directions: 12 miles W of
Ishpeming on US 41

Jackson

HINKLEY'S ATTIC
955 Floyd   49203
517 784-2318   Est: 1973
Proprietor: Robert & C
Marie Hinkley
Hours: Tues-Sat; Sun &
Mon by appointment
Types & Periods: General
Small Line
Specialties: Mustache Cups,
Horse Weights, Depression
Glass
Appraisal Service Available
Directions: Vander Cook
Lake, 4 miles out of
Jackson near Townsend
School

MARY MIDDLEBROOK
7516 E Michigan Ave
49201
517 764-3635   Est: 1960
Proprietor: Mary
Middlebrook
Hours: By appointment, by
chance
Types & Periods: General
Line, Primitives, Stoneware,
Silver, Jewelry
Appraisal Service Available
Directions: Halfway
between Jackson & Grass
Lake on Old East
Michigan Ave

Jonesville

**SOUVENIRS OF
YESTERYEARS**
211 Maumee   49250
517 849-9153
Proprietor: William Gamble
Hours: By appointment, by
chance
Types & Periods: Victorian
Pattern Glass, Furniture,
Lamps

Kalamazoo

RED WAGON ANTIQUES
5348 N Riverview Dr
49004
616 382-5461   Est: 1974
Proprietor: Dale D
Schiedel
Hours: Mon-Sat, 10-6;
Wed 'til 7
Types & Periods: General
Line
Directions: Just N of
Parchment

Kent City

OLSON'S ANTIQUES
7 Muskegon St   49330
616 678-7611
Proprietor: Olive & Walter
Olson
Hours: Tues-Sat, 9-5:30
Types & Periods: General
Line

Lake Linden

NOW & THEN-ANTIQUES
310 Calumet   49945
906 296-9401   Est: 1977
Proprietor: Randy &
Charlotte Ophaug
Hours: Mon-Sat, 10-5
Types & Periods: General
Line
Specialties: Handcrafted gift
items
Directions: Hwy M-26

Lake Orion

**BETSY'S CORNER
ANTIQUES**
59 S Broadway St   48035
313 693-6071   Est: 1976
Proprietor: Betsy J
Roetzel
Hours: Mon-Fri, 9-3; Sat &
Sun, 9-5
Types & Periods: Victorian
Primitives, Colonial, French,
Chippendale, Queen Anne
Directions: N of Pontiac,
M-24 N, downtown

**THE GINGERBREAD
HOUSE BY ROHAMA**
302 S Broadway   48035
313 693-9283
Proprietor: Ruhama E
Beinke
Hours: By chance
Types & Periods: Dolls &
Accessories, Children's
Collectibles
Specialties: Dolls
Directions: 3rd light N of
I-75

Lansing

ADA'S TREASURE VAULT
2500 E Mt Hope   48910
517 372-6023   Est: 1964
Proprietor: Mr & Mrs Harry
Bridge
Hours: Tues-Sun, 10:30-6;
by chance
Types & Periods: Orientals,
Netsukes, Snuff Bottles,
Pekin, Bronzes
Specialties: Dr Wall-1st
Period Worcester, Tiffany,
Steuben, Cameo

Appraisal Service Available
Directions: 5 minutes from
Lansing, 5 minutes from
MSU, E end of Arboretum
Park

Lawton

IRENE'S ANTIQUES
112 Main St   49065
616 624-6184
Proprietor: Irene Newland
Hours: Wed-Sun, 1-5
Types & Periods: Glassware,
China, Furniture
Directions: 3 miles S of
I-94 at Pau Pau & Lawton
Exit, on M-40

Lowell

ANN BATTISTELLA
1019 E Main St   49331
616 897-9374
Proprietor: Ann Battistella
Hours: By appointment
Types & Periods: Art Glass,
General Line

**CRANBERRY URN
ANTIQUES-BORGERSON**
208 E Main St   49331
616 897-9890   Est: 1939
Proprietor: Violet C Murray
Hours: Mon-Sat, 10-5
Types & Periods: General
Line
Specialties: Toys
Directions: 18 miles E of
Grand Rapids on Hwy 21

Macatawa

HARBOR HILLS ANTIQUES
2301 S Shore Dr   49434
616 335-5368   Est: 1960
Proprietor: Bonnie Van
Regenmorter
Hours: Tues-Sun, 10-6,
May thru Oct
Types & Periods: Glass,
China, Oriental, Furniture,
Prints, Primitives, Museum
Pieces
Specialties: Silver, Ceramics,
Furniture, Oriental

Appraisal Service Available
Directions: 5 miles on S
Shore from Holland, 16th
St to S Shore

Marquette

RED KETTLE AUCTION BARN
6595 US 41 S   49855
906 249-3159   Est: 1968
Proprietor: Alton F Conrad
Hours: Auction every
other weekend
Types & Periods: Furniture,
China, Glass, Guns, Coins,
Tools
Appraisal Service Available
Directions: 8 miles S of
Marquette on US 41

Marshall

DEMPSEY'S ANTIQUES
1423 E Michigan Ave
49068
616 963-2521
Hours: Sun-Mon, Wed-Sat
Types & Periods: General
Line
Directions: 8 miles from
Battle Creek

HEATH'S OLDE PUMP HOUSE
17880 H Dr S   49068
616 781-8728   Est: 1967
Proprietor: Agnes Heath
Hours: Daily
Types & Periods: General
Line
Appraisal Service Available

HOUSE OF WALTMAN
314 N Marshall   49068
616 781-2584
Proprietor: Steve &
Ernestine Trupiano
Hours: By appointment
Types & Periods: Furniture,
Glass

J & J ANTIQUES
18025 Division Dr   49068
616 781-5581   Est: 1966
Proprietor: Joyce Tolan
Hours: Daily
Types & Periods: General
Line, Dolls, Clocks, China,
Furniture, Jewelry, Primitives

Appraisal Service Available
Directions: Left off Homer
Rd, 2nd house on left

MCKEE MEMORIAL WORKS
201 Exchange St   49068
616 781-8921   Est: 1946
Proprietor: Wm J McKee
Hours: Mon-Wed, Fri-Sat,
12-6
Types & Periods: General
Line
Specialties: Books
Directions: Business Rte
I-94, 3rd stop light going
E, right 1 block, 1st stop
light going W, left 1 block

MORTON'S
227 W Michigan Ave
49068
616 781-9977
Types & Periods: General
Line

THE UNDERGROUND RAILROAD
102 S Eagle   49068
616 781-2214   Est: 1972
Proprietor: Mrs Wm R
Biggs
Hours: Tues-Thurs,
10-5:30; Fri-Sat, 10-9;
Sun, 11:30-5:30
Types & Periods: Empire
Mirrors, Tables, Primitives,
Farm Implements

Mason

MASON FLEA MARKET
208 N Mason St   48854
517 676-9753   Est: 1972
Proprietor: George R
Parish
Hours: Sun & Wed, 10-6
Types & Periods: Primitives,
Oak, Depression Glass,
Clocks, Collectibles, Dishes
Appraisal Service Available
Directions: 1 block from
old railroad depot

Negaunee

MR & MRS LUDWIG HYTINEN
Teal Lake Ave   49866
906 475-7552   Est: 1965
Proprietor: Inez Hytinen

Hours: Daily, 9-5
Types & Periods: General
Line
Specialties: Primitives
Appraisal Service Available
Directions: Hwy 41 across
from city waterworks

Niles

ROBERT & CYNTHIA BAKER
PO Box 32   49120
616 683-4545
Proprietor: Robert &
Cynthia Baker
Hours: By appointment
Types & Periods: 18th &
Early 19th Century American
Antiques, Furniture &
Accessories
Appraisal Service Available
Directions: Call or write
for directions

Northville

SUNFLOWER SHOP
116 E Main   48167
313 349-1425   Est: 1970
Proprietor: M Bonamici
Hours: Daily, Fri evening
'til 9
Types & Periods: Jewelry,
Collectibles, American
Indian Items
Specialties: Books, Jewelry
Directions: 1st block E of
Sheldon Rd

Okemos

1849 HOUSE ANTIQUES
4662 Okemos Rd   48864
517 349-2313   Est: 1969
Proprietor: Dr & Mrs I J
Breckenfeld
Hours: Daily, 2-5
Types & Periods: General
Line, Collectibles
Specialties: Glass (Pattern)
Directions: 3 miles N of
I-96, Okemos Mason Exit

HOWARD SHAPIRO ANTIQUES
4245 Okemos Rd 48864
517 349-4648 Est: 1972
Proprietor: Howard A Shapiro
Hours: Tues-Sat, 10-4
Types & Periods: General Line
Specialties: Postcards, Souvenir Spoons
Appraisal Service Available

WOODEN SKATE ANTIQUES
1259 W Grand River 48864
517 349-1515 Est: 1973
Proprietor: Gary & Diane Durow
Hours: Mon-Fri, 10-5:30; Sat, 10-6
Types & Periods: Glass, Toys, Primitives, Watches, Jewelry, Furniture
Specialties: Watches, Jewelry, Furniture
Appraisal Service Available
Directions: 1 mile E of Meridian Mall

Owosso

MARR'S
1544 E Main 48867
517 723-5436 Est: 1960
Proprietor: Richard Marr
Hours: Mon-Sat, 9:30-6; by chance
Types & Periods: General Line
Directions: 5 blocks W of intersection of M-52 & M-21

MARR'S
900 W Main 48867
517 723-5436 Est: 1960
Proprietor: Richard Marr
Hours: Mon-Sat, 9:30-6; by chance
Types & Periods: General Line
Directions: 1½ miles E of intersection of M-52 & M-21

Paris

ILENE'S SECOND HAND STORE
22886 US 131 49338
616 832-2941 Est: 1964
Proprietor: Ilene Hooker
Hours: Mon-Sat
Types & Periods: Primitives, Glass, China, Furniture, Tools

Petoskey

LONGTON HALL GALLERIES
401 Bay 49770
616 347-9672 Est: 1969
Proprietor: Edith E Littler
Hours: Mon-Sat, 9:30-5:30
Types & Periods: General Line
Specialties: Chinese, Japanese, English Porcelain
Directions: Downtown, 35 miles S of Mackinac Bridge

Plainwell

PLAINWELL FLEA MARKET
585 N 10th St 49080
616 685-5443 Est: 1969
Proprietor: Mrs Roy Wood
Hours: Weekends
Types & Periods: General Line
Directions: 1½ miles N of stoplight, between Kalamazoo & Grand Rapids

Plymouth

DEE MORGAN ANTIQUES
149 W Liberty St 48107
313 455-7155 Est: 1973
Proprietor: Dolores Morgan
Hours: Mon-Sat, 12-5; Sun, 1-5
Types & Periods: General Line
Directions: In old village off Mill St

Pontiac

C B CHARLES GALLERIES INC
825 Woodward Ave 48053
313 338-9203 Est: 1959
Proprietor: C B Charles
Hours: Mon-Sat, 9-5
Types & Periods: General Line
Appraisal Service Available
Directions: Opposite St Joseph Hospital, approximately 1 mile N of Square Lake Rd

JOHN A MCGUIRE
120 S Telegraph 48053
313 681-3906
Proprietor: John A McGuire
Hours: Daily, 8-6
Types & Periods: 18th & Early 19th Century American Furniture
Specialties: Furniture (New England Country)

Reed City

BISBEE ANTIQUE & GIFT SHOPPE
101 E Upton Ave 49677
616 832-6611 Est: 1975
Proprietor: Kenneth & Evelyn Bisbee
Hours: Mon-Sat, 9-5
Types & Periods: General Line
Appraisal Service Available
Directions: Main corner of city

Rochester

COUNTRY COUSIN COINS & ANTIQUES
415 Walnut Blvd Box 219 48063
313 652-4790 Est: 1974
Proprietor: Mr & Mrs John C Bigham
Hours: Mon-Sat, 10-5; also by appointment
Types & Periods: Early N American Indian Baskets, Pine, Small Furniture, Coins, Clothes before 1900

Specialties: Baskets
Appraisal Service Available
Directions: Downtown
across from Post Office

Royal Oak

BAZZAR ANTIQUES
301 S Center   48067
313 543-3766   Est: 1962
Proprietor: Selma Sofferin
Hours: Mon-Tues,
Thurs-Sat
Types & Periods: General
Line Antiques & Collectibles
Appraisal Service Available
Directions: Downtown, 2
blocks S 11 Mile Rd, 1
block W Main St

THE BLOOMIN' ATTIC
123 S Third St   48067
313 545-5363
Hours: Mon-Sat, 10-5:30
Types & Periods: General
Line

JOHN BRYANT ANTIQUES
209 S Main   48067
313 548-0412
Hours: Daily, 11-5, 2nd
Sun
Types & Periods: Furniture,
Stained Glass, Primitives

EVE & BRIAN BUNCE
722 S Main   48067
313 545-6083   Est: 1973
Proprietor: Brian Bunce
Hours: Tues-Sat
Types & Periods: Dolls,
English Imports
Appraisal Service Available
Directions: S Main, N of
Lincoln

THE COLLECTION
315 S Washington   48067
313 545-2159
Hours: Daily, 11-5; 2nd
Sun
Types & Periods: General
Line

THE DANDELION SHOP
114 W 4th St   48067
313 547-6288   Est: 1962
Proprietor: Inez Frost
Hours: Daily, 12:30-5
Types & Periods: American
& English Antiques,
Furniture, Accessories, Light

Fixtures, Art Glass, Art
Pottery, Oriental Artifacts
Appraisal Service Available
Directions: S of 11 Mile
Rd Between Main &
Washington

ORIENTAL RUG GALLERY
321 S Main   48067
313 545-4483
Hours: Daily, 10-7; Wed &
Fri 'til 9; 2nd Sun
Types & Periods: Oriental
Rugs

RARE OLD PRINTS
520 S Washington   48067
313 548-5588   Est: 1969
Proprietor: Jorgen K
Andersen & Robert D
Logsdon
Hours: Daily, 11-5
Types & Periods: 18th &
19th Century Prints, Oil
Paintings, Accessories
Directions: Corner of
Washington & 6th Sts

**THE WHITE ELEPHANT
SHOP**
724 W 11 Mile Rd   48067
313 543-5140   Est: 1945
Proprietor: Gary Austin
Rea
Hours: Tues-Sat, 10-4;
2nd Sun
Types & Periods: Furniture,
Silver, Glassware, China,
Bric-A-Brac, Paintings,
Chandeliers, Oriental
Screens, Rugs
Appraisal Service Available
Directions: 4 blocks E of
Woodward Ave, corner of
Maple Ave on 11 Mile Rd

Saginaw

HIDDEN TREASURES
1316 Court St   48602
517 799-5980   Est: 1973
Proprietor: Sally Draper
Hours: Mon-Fri
Types & Periods:
Consignment Shop, China,
Glass, Furniture, Pictures &
Collectibles
Appraisal Service Available
Directions: About 5 blocks
W of Court House
between the 2 one-way
streets (Woodbridge &
Mason)

**MARY MARGRATH'S
ANTIQUE SHOP**
216 N Webster   48602
517 793-6331
Proprietor: Mary Margrath
Hours: Weekends
Types & Periods: General
Line
Appraisal Service Available
Directions: 3 blocks from
Court House

Saint Ignace

RIVER REST ANTIQUES
550 Chambers St   49781
906 643-8009   Est: 1963
Proprietor: Ola G
Touchstone
Hours: By chance, daily
during July & Aug
Types & Periods: Colonial
Lamps, Furniture, General
Line, China, Art Glass
Specialties: Clocks, Musical
Instruments, Silver
Appraisal Service Available
Directions: N from Collins
Motel

St Johns

**BANNER ANTIQUES &
SISTERS SHOPPE**
3293 Banner Rd   48879
517 224-7247   Est: 1965
Proprietor: Larry & Peg
Rasey
Hours: Daily
Types & Periods: General
Line
Directions: N US 27 to
Kinley Rd, left on black
top to school, W on
Banner

St Joseph

CURIOSITY SHOP
3720 Red Arrow Hwy
                         49085
616 429-5321
Types & Periods: Books,
Glassware

Saugatuck

MAIN STREET ANTIQUES
119 Butler St   49453
616 857-5351
Proprietor: Frank Van
Antelek
Hours: Daily, 10:30-5:30
Types & Periods: Jewelry,
Furniture, Silver, Glass,
China

Spring Lake

TRADING POST ANTIQUES
Rte 1   49456
Est: 1953
Proprietor: Evelyn Vickers
Hours: Mon-Sat, 11-6
Types & Periods: Furniture,
China, Glass
Directions: 1½ miles N of
Ferrisburg on 174th Ave
(Old US 31), or 8 miles S
of Muskegon on Grand
Haven Rd

Standish

**MR & MRS VICTOR
BISSONNETTE**
RD 2 Box 296   48658
517 846-6700   Est: 1958
Proprietor: Mr & Mrs
Victor Bissonnette
Hours: Daily, by
appointment or by chance
Types & Periods: Glassware,
Dolls, Postcards, Lamps,
Victorian Furniture
Specialties: Clocks
Appraisal Service Available
Directions: On M-13, 5
miles N of Pinconning or 4
miles S of Standish

Stevensville

J'S BIT OF EVERYTHING
4173 Red Arrow   49127
616 429-1577   Est: 1972
Proprietor: J Wenzlaff
Hours: Daily, 12-6
Types & Periods: General
Line
Appraisal Service Available
Directions: 300 feet S of
Glenlord Rd

Sturgis

OTIS COCHRAN ANTIQUES
PO Box 365   49091
616 651-2794
Proprietor: Otis Cochran
Hours: By appointment
Types & Periods: Art &
Pattern Glass, China,
Pottery

Taylor

**TED & NELL INGHAM
ANTIQUES**
20135 Eureka   48180
313 282-3496
Proprietor: Ted & Nell
Ingham
Hours: By appointment
Types & Periods: Signed
Tiffany Lamps, Handels,
Pairpoints, Art Glass,
Collectibles, Hummels
Appraisal Service Available

Watervliet

OPAL LYONS
RR2 Box 268   49098
616 463-5650
Hours: Sun-Tues,
Thurs-Sat
Types & Periods: General
Line

Z'S
Red Arrow Hwy   49098
616 463-5487
Hours: Daily, 12-6
Types & Periods: General
Line
Directions: Between
Colome & Watervliet

West Bloomfield

BOB HARRIS ANTIQUES
6821 W Dartmoor   48033
313 626-6329
Proprietor: Bob Harris
Hours: By chance

Types & Periods: Bronze
Sculpture, American &
European Paintings, Indian
Beadwork, Baskets,
Weapons
Specialties: Arms & Armor,
Bronze Sculpture
Appraisal Service Available

Whitehall

THE PACK RATS
116 W Slocum   49461
616 893-6885   Est: 1970
Proprietor: Cal & Katey
Halberg
Hours: Tues-Sun, 10-6
Types & Periods: 18th &
19th Century Pine &
Victorian Furniture,
Primitives, Clocks, Lamps,
Dolls, Glass, Porcelain,
Pottery, General Line
Appraisal Service Available
Directions: 2 blocks S on
Mears from stop light, 1
block W on Slocum

THE WHIPPOORWILL
2962 W Lakewood Rd
49461
616 894-4306   Est: 1972
Proprietor: William L
Suder & Rita M Suder
Hours: Sun-Mon, Wed-Sat,
10-6
Types & Periods: Country
Furniture, Accessories,
Primitives
Specialties: Fine Country
Furniture
Directions: From traffic
light in Whitehall, 2½ miles
S on Mears-Zellar Rd, 1½
miles E on Lakewood

Ypsilanti

SCHMIDT'S ANTIQUES
5138 W Michigan Ave
48197
Proprietor: N T & J J
Schmidt
Hours: Mon-Sat, 9-5; Sun,
11-5; closed holidays
Types & Periods: General
Line

STATE OF MINNESOTA

Afton

AFTON ANTIQUE SHOP
16040 32nd St S   55001
612-436-7798
Proprietor: The Cooleys
Hours: Daily, 9:30-5
Types & Periods: Art &
Colored Glass, General Line

Aitkin

**SCHMITT'S ANTIQUES
FURNITURE & JEWELRY**
218 1st Ave NE   56431
218 927-3217   Est: 1950
Proprietor: Mark & Martha
Schmitt
Hours: Daily
Types & Periods: Glassware,
Dishes, Furniture, Dolls,
Tools
Specialties: Watches, Toys
   Directions: First place N of
   Ford Motor Co

Albert Lea

**THE HEART OF THE
ARTICHOKE**
222 E Clark St   56007
507 373-4258   Est: 1968
Proprietor: Gwen Hanson,
President
Hours: Mon-Sat, 10-5
Types & Periods: General
Line
Appraisal Service Available
   Directions: 1 1/2 blocks E
   of Broadway

Alden

THE KALICO KORNER
101 S Broadway   56009
507 874-3274   Est: 1974
Proprietor: Lucy Stiehl,
Lois Hemmingsen &
Shirley Phinney
Types & Periods: General
Line, Furniture, Glassware
Specialties: Primitives
Appraisal Service Available
   Directions: 2 blocks off
   I-90

Anoka

PINE HUTCH ANTIQUES
848 E River Rd   55303
612 427-9040   Est: 1969
Proprietor: Junne Link
Hours: Tues-Sat, 12:30-5
Types & Periods: General
Line
   Directions: 2 blocks W of
   city limits on old Hwy 10

**POOR RICHARD'S
ANTIQUES**
1047 North St   55303
612 427-8672   Est: 1973
Proprietor: Richard
Gourley
Hours: By appointment, by
chance
Types & Periods: Victorian
Walnut, Oak, Lamps, Clocks
Specialties: Furniture
Stripping
   Directions: Just off Hwy
   10 N frontage road

Arden Hills

**ARDEN HILLS ANTIQUE
SHOP**
1660 W Hwy 96   55112
612 636-1233   Est: 1976
Proprietor: Margaret & Bill
Reeves
Hours: Mon-Sat, by
chance
Types & Periods: Glass,
China, Furniture, Primitives,
Art Glass, Pattern Glass, Cut
Glass
Specialties: Glass & China
   Directions: E of Hwy 35
   1/2 mile

**SEXTON'S LAKE JOHANNA
ANTIQUES**
3300 Lake Johanna 55112
612 633-4786   Est: 1960
Proprietor: Marcella
Sexton
Hours: Mon-Fri, 1-6; Sat &
Sun, by appointment, by
chance

Types & Periods: Navajo
Rugs, Beadwork, Lamps,
Nautical, Brass, Silver
   Directions: S on Hwy 35W
   from I-694, 2 miles to
   County Rd D exit, right on
   D to second stop sign, left
   1 block

Austin

DEWEY ANTIQUES
1400 9th St NW   55912
507 433-6879   Est: 1961
Proprietor: Lawrence M
Dewey
Hours: By appointment, by
chance
Types & Periods: China,
Glassware, Primitives, Silver,
Pottery, Furniture,
Miscellaneous
   Directions: Exit I-90, 4th
   St NW, turn S to 13th Ave
   NW, W to 9th St

Bemidji

**ISHNALA HOUSE OF
ANTIQUES & CURIOS**
Rt 1 Box 314   56601
218 243-2241   Est: 1968
Proprietor: Bonnie Jean
Steinicke
Hours: May thru Dec,
9 - Dark
Types & Periods: Primitives,
China, Glass, Jewelry, Dolls
& Toys
Appraisal Service Available
   Directions: Hwy 2 W to
   Irvine Ave (County Rd 15)
   & N 11 miles; watch for
   sign

STAN'S ANTIQUES
56601
218 751-6345   Est: 1976
Proprietor: Stan Ulrich
Hours: Weekends, by
appointment, by chance
Types & Periods: Hand
Painted China, Cut Glass,
Cast Toys, Coins, Lamps,
Furniture
Specialties: Ceramics, R S
Prussia

Bethel

ANTIQUES AMERICANA
Rt 1   55005
612 434-9701
Proprietor: Gerry & Sue
Czulewicz
Hours: Daily, 10-6, or by
chance
Types & Periods: Nautical,
Books, Art, Western,
Documents

Blomkest

C T S ANTIQUES
Hwy 7   56216
612 995-5126
Hours: By appointment
Types & Periods: Glass,
Furniture, Watches, Guns
Directions: Red house 1
block W of Mobil station

Blue Earth

MILT'S ANTIQUES
209 S Main   56013
507 526-8814   Est: 1960
Proprietor: Milton W
Weber
Hours: Mon-Sat, by
appointment
Types & Periods: Furniture,
Primitives, Glass, Clocks
Specialties: Gun Shop
Appraisal Service Available
Directions: S on Main

Brownsdale

DOVI ANTIQUES
103 S Mill   55918
507 567-2595   Est: 1957
Proprietor: Mrs Don Ames
Hours: By appointment, by
chance
Types & Periods: Glass,
China, Books, Primitives,
parts for lamps, Furniture
Directions: Hwy 56 in town

Cottage Grove

TIN CUP
8155 Belden Blvd   55016
612 459-5132
Hours: Mon-Fri, 4-9; Sat &
Sun, 10-5
Types & Periods: "Things of
yesteryear"
Directions: Behind
shopping center

Crosby

**BITS OF YESTERYEAR
ANTIQUES**
4 3rd Ave SW   56441
218 546-6639   Est: 1971
Proprietor: Mattie S
Broden
Hours: Daily
Types & Periods: General
Line
Directions: Hwy 210 & 6

Dakota

**APPLE COUNTRY
ANTIQUES**
RFD 1   55925
Proprietor: Connie Kubista
Hours: Daily, 9-5, May thru
Oct
Types & Periods: General
Line

RESALE & ANTIQUES
Box 155   55925
507 643-6716   Est: 1961
Proprietor: Charlotte
Uehling
Hours: Sat-Thurs, 10-6; Fri
by appointments
Types & Periods:
Kitchenware, Tools, Wood,
Copper, Metals, Books,
Glass, China, Laces,
Tapestries, Quilts
Specialties: Frames
Appraisal Service Available
Directions: On Mississippi
River & Hwys I-90 14 & 61

Dodge Center

CHARLOTTE'S ANTIQUES
11 2nd St NE   55927
507 374-6648

Proprietor: Charlotte J
Cooper
Hours: By appointment, by
chance
Types & Periods: General
Line, Pine, Walnut, Oak
Furniture
Specialties: Collectibles,
Sabino Figurines
Directions: Hwy 15,
Lutheran Church,
2 blocks S

ELSA'S ANTIQUES
Hwy 14   55927
507 374-6522   Est: 1969
Proprietor: Elsa Snyder
Hours: Mon & Wed-Sat,
9-12, 1-5; Sun & Tues by
appointment
Types & Periods: Victorian
Furniture & Glass,
Primitives, Decorative Items,
Depression Glass
Specialties: Fine China, Cut
Glass
Appraisal Service Available
Directions: 20 miles W of
Rochester on Hwy 14

WENDELL'S ANTIQUES
18 E Main St   55927
507 374-2140   Est: 1958
Proprietor: Wendell R
Nelson
Hours: Mon-Sat, 10-5;
Sun, 2-5
Types & Periods: General
Line, Select Merchandise
Appraisal Service Available
Directions: 18 miles W of
Rochester on Hwy 14, 4
blocks S on Main St

Duluth

APPLETREE ANTIQUES
1902 London Rd   55812
218 724-5024   Est: 1974
Proprietor: Michael
Letourneau
Hours: Daily
Types & Periods: General
Line
Specialties: Clocks,
Watches, Also Repair
Appraisal Service Available
Directions: Hwy 61

WILSON ANTIQUES
2332 W Third St   55806
218 722-0700
Proprietor: H Earleen
Wilson
Types & Periods: General
Line

Edina

BOOTS CORNER
3907 W 50th St   55424
612 926-3379
Proprietor: Jean Boots
Sigler
Hours: By appointment
Types & Periods:
Lampshades for Candlestick
Jug Lamps, Coverlets,
Primitives

THE HERITAGE SHOP
3903 Sunnyside Rd 55424
Proprietor: Norma Dorsey
& Mary Scanlon
Hours: Tues-Sat, 10:30 -5
Types & Periods: General
Line, Antiques & Collectibles
Appraisal Service Available

Elgin

MIKES ANTIQUES
RR   55932
507 876-2740   Est: 1971
Proprietor: Mike Sveen
Hours: Weekends, by
appointment
Types & Periods: Oak
Walnut, Pine, Primitives,
Dishes, Clocks, Lamps,
Stained Windows, Brass
Beds
Appraisal Service Available

Excelsior

**FURY'S ANTIQUES &
COLLECTABLES**
2821 Washta Bay Rd
55331
612 474-6850
Proprietor: Ann Fury
Types & Periods: Pattern
Glass, Depression Glass,
Memorabilia, Furniture

Faribault

CURIOSITY SHOP
Rt 3 Box 245   55021
507 334-5959   Est: 1971
Proprietor: Delmer
Schafhuck
Hours: Daily
Types & Periods: Furniture,
Lamps, Marble Top
Furniture
Specialties: Furniture
(Victorian, Walnut)
Directions: W of Faribault
3 miles on County Rd 38,
call for instructions

**STOECKEL'S ANTIQUE
CLOCKS & DOLLS**
615 NW 3rd St   55021
507 334-7772   Est: 1960
Proprietor: Fritz & Pat
Stoeckel
Hours: By appointment, by
chance
Types & Periods: Clocks,
Dolls, Watches & Jewelry
Specialties: Clocks, Dolls
Appraisal Service Available
Directions: 6 blocks W of
Main St

Fergus Falls

HEIRLOOM GALLERIES
213 E Summit Ave   56537
218 736-7634   Est: 1951
Proprietor: Elyn Oyloe
Hours: Daily, Weekends,
By appointment
Types & Periods: General
Line in Art Gallery as well as
Museum Qualifications
Specialties: Educational
Hours for Small Groups
Appraisal Service Available
Directions: 1 block off
Main Ave

Geneva

MILO CRAFT
103 2nd St SE   56035
507 256-7694   Est: 1968
Proprietor: Mrs Miles
Bedker & Paul Bedker
Hours: Daily, Weekends
Types & Periods: General
Line, Pressed Glass, Lamps,
Jewelry, Bottles, Furniture

Specialties: Lamps & Lamp
Parts, Restored Furniture
Appraisal Service Available
Directions: 1 mile E of
I-35, turn right at stop, 2
blocks, turn left, 1/2 block
on left

Grand Meadow

HATTIE'S ANTIQUES
55936
507 754-5635   Est: 1960
Proprietor: Hattie
Bremseth
Hours: Mon-Sat, 9-5
Types & Periods: General
Line
Directions: Across from
Telephone Office

Granite Falls

VALLEY VIEW ANTIQUES
Rte 2   56241
612 564-3214
Proprietor: Herb &
Vernette Nelson
Hours: Mon-Sat, 10-6, or
by appointment or by
chance
Types & Periods: General
Line, Furniture, Primitives,
Glassware
Directions: 3/4 mile S on
Hwy 67

Hamel

BUTTERMILK CORNER
342 Hamel Rd   55340
612 478-6500
Proprietor: Dorothy Moir
Hours: By appointment
Types & Periods: Country
Furniture, Primitives

Harmony

**DEBORAH LEE'S
ANTIQUES**
Hwy 52   55939
507 886-6411   Est: 1977
Proprietor: Kim & Deborah
Embretson

DEBORAH LEE'S Cont'd

Hours: Thur-Sun, June thru Aug; By appointment, by chance, Sept thru May
Types & Periods: Local Primitive, Furniture, Art Glass, Collectibles, General Line
Directions: At the bend of Hwy 52 in Harmony, 48 miles SE of Rochester

Hastings

LAMBTIQUES
117 E 5th St   55033
612 437-9697   Est: 1972
Proprietor: Sally Lamb
Hours: Daily, Weekends
Types & Periods: Furniture, Glassware, China, Collectibles
Directions: E 5th St off Hwy 61

Hokah

YE OLDE ANTIQUE SHOPPE
R 1   55941
507 894-4270   Est: 1970
Proprietor: Arlene M Kaatz
Hours: Sun-Tues, Thurs-Sat
Types & Periods: China, Glassware, Crockery, Hull, Roseville & Sleepy Eye Pottery, Leaded Shade Lamps
Specialties: Glass (Carnival)
Directions: On Hwy 44 1 block S of Comm St Bank, 9 miles W of La Crosse WI on US 16

Homer

THE LION
Homer Rd   55942
507 452-3739
Proprietor: Edith & Marilyn Dragowick
Types & Periods: General Line, Collectibles
Directions: 3 miles E of Winona, 1 block above Hwy 61-14

Hopkins

BRUDA COLLECTABLES
6 Suburban Sq   55343
Est: 1969
Proprietor: B Wilkinson & D Bowler
Hours: Mon-Sat
Types & Periods: Oriental Items, Jewelry, Furniture, China, Glass, Silver
Specialties: Oriental Items, Jewelry
Appraisal Service Available
Directions: Excelsior Ave W at Shady Oak Rd

Houston

WITTS ANTIQUES
RFD 2   55943
507 896-3794
Proprietor: Marion J Witt
Hours: By appointment, by chance
Types & Periods: Collectibles, General Line

Hutchinson

SUNNY'S ANTIQUES
228 N Main   55350
612 879-2602   Est: 1970
Proprietor: Harold & Sunny Odegaard
Hours: Mon-Sat, 11-5
Types & Periods: Furniture, Glass
Appraisal Service Available
Directions: By Crow River Dam on Main St

Kennedy

OLDE TYME SHOPPE
56733
218 674-4119   Est: 1974
Proprietor: Barbara Swenson
Hours: Wed-Sat, 10-5; Sun, 1-5
Types & Periods: Furniture, Glass, Primitives, Dolls
Specialties: Furniture (Oak)
Directions: Main St on Hwy 75, 30 miles from Canadian border

Lake Benton

BURK ANTIQUES
106 S Fremont   56149
507 368-9343
Proprietor: Jack Burk & Mrs Alvina Burk
Hours: Mon-Sat, 9-5; Sun by chance or by appointment
Types & Periods: American Color Pattern Glass, Pattern Glass, Walnut Furniture

Lake City

FUHRMAN ANTIQUES & HOBBY
513 N 6th St   55041
612 345-3705   Est: 1972
Proprietor: Leslie & Dorothy Fuhrman
Hours: Daily
Types & Periods: Furniture, Stoneware, Primitives, General Line
Directions: Across from baseball field

LONGHORN ANTIQUES
403 N High St   55041
612 345-5260   Est: 1975
Proprietor: Dennis C Simanski
Hours: By chance
Types & Periods: Primitive, Glassware, Furniture
Appraisal Service Available
Directions: 1 block off Hwys 63 & 61

SUMMER KITCHEN ANTIQUES
522 N Lakeshore Dr 55041
612 345-2883   Est: 1965
Proprietor: Ber & Milt Scholer
Hours: Daily, by chance
Types & Periods: General Line
Specialties: Early Red Wing Stoneware, Flo Blue
Appraisal Service Available
Directions: Hwy 61

Lake Park

STAN'S ANTIQUES
                  56554
218 238-5900   Est: 1974
Proprietor: Stan Ulrich
Hours: Daily, by
appointment
Types & Periods: General
Line, Coins
Specialties: Ceramics (R S
Prussia), Cast Toys & Banks
Directions: Downtown

Lanesboro

OLD VILLAGE SHOP
106 Parkway N   55949
507 467-3773   Est: 1961
Proprietor: Catherine St
Mane
Hours: Tues-Sat, 10-4:30;
other times by
appointment
Types & Periods: General
Line of Antiques &
Collectibles
Specialties: Paper
Americana, Postcards,
Books
    Directions: Downtown on
    Hwy 250 just off Hwy 16

Lindstrom

THE OLD COUNTRY STORE
                  55045
612 257-2946   Est: 1972
Proprietor: Ethel E Corey
Hours: Mon-Sat, 9-5;
Fri, 9-7:30
Types & Periods: Dishes,
Furniture
    Directions: On Hwy 8 in
    Lindstrom

Litchfield

JEANNIE'S PLACE
329 E Hwy 12   55355
612 693-2170
Hours: M-F, May to Sept,
12:30-4:30; Sat & Sun by
appointment
Types & Periods: General
Line, Collectibles
Specialties: Jewelry (Indian
Turquoise)

Long Lake

BEEHIVE ANTIQUES
1844 Wayzata Blvd 55356
612 473-4883
Proprietor: Harlan
Stockton
Hours: Mon-Sat, 10-5;
Sun, 1-5
Types & Periods: General
Line
Specialties: Furniture, Glass

Mabel

VICTORIANA
Cedar Ave   55954
507 493-5696
Proprietor: Dwayne &
Diane Houdek
Hours: By appointment or
by chance
Types & Periods: General
Line, Early Walnut &
Victorian Furniture, Oriental
Rugs
    Directions: On Iowa state
    line

Mankato

BARGAIN CENTER
731 S Front   56001
507 388-1834   Est: 1954
Proprietor: Ila Bergien
Hours: Daily, 8-5
Types & Periods: Depression
Glass, Post Cards, General
Line
Specialties: Furniture,
Books, Pictures
    Directions: Toward
    downtown from West High
    School

STUTZMAN'S ANTIQUES
403 N Broad St   56001
507 388-5294
Proprietor: Florence &
Paul Stutzman
Hours: By appointment or
by chance
Types & Periods: Art,
Colored & Pattern Glass,
China

**WILLARD'S COLONIAL
HOUSE ANTIQUES**
20 Skyline Dr   56001
507 387-2400   Est: 1969

Proprietor: Hugh & Eileen
Willard
Hours: By appointment or
by chance
Types & Periods: Pattern,
Cut & Art Glass, China,
Furniture, Silver, Toys,
Watches, Postcards, Tin,
Iron

Maple Plain

THE WAGGIN' WHEELER
Rt 1 Box 132   55359
612 479-2521   Est: 1963
Proprietor: Rita Alice
Wheeler & W Roger
Wheeler
Hours: Tues-Sat, By
appointment or by chance
(Call first)
Types & Periods: 18th &
19th Americana, General
Antiques & Collectibles
Specialties: Treen, Tin,
Lighting
Appraisal Service Available
    Directions: Hwy 12,
    approximately 20 miles W
    of Minneapolis

Marshall

**"THE ORPHANAGE"
ANTIQUES**
Hwy 59   56258
507 532-3998   Est: 1973
Proprietor: Mary Lou
Peterson
Hours: Tues-Sat, 1-5;
Other times by
appointment or by chance
Types & Periods: Fine
China, Glassware, Furniture,
Primitives, Toys, Lamps
Specialties: Architectural,
Indian, Country Store Pieces
Appraisal Service Available
    Directions: 1 mile S of
    Marshall on Hwy 59

Minneapolis

MINNEAPOLIS CLUSTER
Directions: SW section of
city especially W 40's to
W 50's, Frances Ave to
Nicollet Ave

ABE'S ANTIQUES
1711 University Ave NE
55413
612 780-2486   Est: 1974
Proprietor: James Bailey
Hours: Tues-Sat, 11-5
Types & Periods: Clocks,
Furniture, Glassware,
General Line
Appraisal Service Available
Directions: 17 blocks N of
Hennepin

**ALBATROSS ANTIQUES
AND RESTORATION
WORKSHOP**
4311 Upton Ave S   55410
612 926-4024   Est: 1974
Hours: Mon-Fri, 12-5:30;
Sat, 10:30-5:30
Types & Periods:
Americana, Country
Furniture, Folk Art,
Norwegian Antiques,
Stoneware
Specialties: Furniture
Stripping, Repair,
Refinishing; Metal Repair;
Clock Repair; Caning; Seat
Weaving-Splint, Reed, Rush;
Wicker Repair
Appraisal Service Available
Directions: 8 blocks E of
France Ave S

AMERICAN CLASSICS
4944 Xerxes S   55410
612 926-2509   Est: 1972
Proprietor: Jeffrey &
Marge Drogue
Hours: Tues-Sat,
10:30-4:30; Evenings by
appointment
Types & Periods: Country
Furniture
Specialties: Quilts, Crocks,
Early Advertising
Appraisal Service Available
Directions: Corner 50th &
Xerxes in SW Minneapolis

ANTIQUE FINDS
1758 Hennepin Ave 55403
612 374-1553
Proprietor: Edith Lubov
Hours: Tues-Sun

Types & Periods: Oriental,
Art, Furniture
Specialties: Jewelry
Appraisal Service Available
Directions: Near Guthrie
Theatre & Walker Art
Center

ATTIC TREASURES
2813 W 43rd St   55410
612 929-4282   Est: 1973
Proprietor: Nancy Lewan
& Claire Gilbert
Hours: Mon-Sat, 10-4:30
Types & Periods:
Consignment Shop, General
Line
Appraisal Service Available
Directions: Shop faces
parking lot

**THE BEARD ART
GALLERIES**
1006 Nicollet Mall   55403
612 332-7802   Est: 1886
Proprietor: J E Walton &
G W Steep
Hours: Daily
Types & Periods: European
& Oriental Antiques
Specialties: Etchings,
Engravings
Appraisal Service Available
Directions: On the mall

**BLACK SWAN COUNTRY
STORE**
3020 W 50th St   55410
612 926-9134
Proprietor: Kerrie Drogue
Hours: Mon-Sat, 10:30-5;
Sun, 12-5
Types & Periods: Small
Primitives, Prints, Post
Cards & Trade Cards,
Advertising, Beer Trays,
Quilts, Tin Signs
Specialties: Quilts, Paper
Goods, Christmas Plates
Appraisal Service Available
Directions: 50th & Xerxes
in SW Minneapolis

COBBLESTONE ANTIQUES
3018 W 50th St.   55410
612 922-6222   Est: 1976
Proprietor: Wm J Brantner
& Gary Lindberg
Hours: Mon-Sat, 10-5; Sun
by chance
Types & Periods: Victorian
to Deco Furniture, Stained
Glass Window, Lamps,
Lighting Fixtures, Oriental
Carpets

Specialties: Furniture,
Antique Carpets, Windows
Appraisal Service Available
Directions: Corner of W
50th St & Xerxes Ave S,
12 blocks N of County
Hwy 62

**DUANE'S ANTIQUES &
THINGS INC**
1705 Arthur St NE   55413
612 788-3543   Est: 1972
Proprietor: Duane
Brodersen
Hours: By appointment
Types & Periods: European
& American Furniture,
Clocks, Bronzes
Specialties: Bronzes & Wood
Carvings
Appraisal Service Available
Directions: 10 blocks E of
Hwy 65, S on Arthur

EICHHORN INTERIORS INC
66 S 10th St   55403
612 335-8709
Proprietor: Warren Moen,
Lorraine Strickland
Hours: Mon-Fri, 10-4; Sat
by appointment
Types & Periods: 18th &
19th Century Furniture,
Crystal, Pewter, Silver,
Porcelain
Specialties: Full Range of
Reproductions, Complete
Interior Design Service
Directions: Downtown
Minneapolis, between
Nicollett Mall & LaSalle on
S 10th

**FJELDE & COMPANY
ANTIQUES**
3022 W 50th St   55410
612 922-7022   Est: 1971
Proprietor: Ralph Popehn
Hours: Mon-Sat, 10-5;
Sun, 12-5
Types & Periods: Primitives,
Furniture, Collectibles
Directions: Corner of 50th
St & Xerxes

GOSSE'S ANTIQUES
3803 Grand Ave S 55409
612 823-3337   Est: 1974
Proprietor: Loretta Gosse
Hours: Mon-Sat, 11-5
Types & Periods: Fine China
& Glass, Victorian Furniture,
General Line

Specialties: Hand Painted
China, Restoration of China
& Pottery
Appraisal Service Available

HANSEN'S ANTIQUES
6945 Park Ave   55423
612 869-5774
Proprietor: Robert Hansen
Hours: By appointment
Types & Periods: Art &
Colored Glass

LITTLE GREENWICH
4318 Upton Ave S   55410
612 920-5169   Est: 1966
Proprietor: Pat & Fran
Arland
Hours: Tues-Sat, Evenings
by appointment
Types & Periods: Silver,
China, Glassware, Jewelry,
Furniture, Oriental Rugs,
Collectibles, Primitives,
Pictures, Paintings, Prints,
General Line
Appraisal Service Available
Directions: SW
Minneapolis, just W of
Lake Harriet

MINNEHAHA ANTIQUES
3700 E 34th St   55406
612 721-7196   Est: 1960
Proprietor: C A & Iola
Near
Hours: Tues-Sat
Types & Periods: General
Line
Specialties: Refinished
Furniture, Primitives,
Glassware
Appraisal Service Available
Directions: E Minneapolis
4 blocks S Lake St &
toward Mississippi River

**POTPOURRI ANTIQUES
INC**
7750 Normandale Blvd
                    55435
612 835-3430
Proprietor: Helen LeGrand
Hours: Mon & Sat,
9:30-5:30; Sun and
evenings by appointment
only
Types & Periods: Furniture,
Paintings, Glass, Silver
Directions: In Radisson S
Shopping Village, across
from lobby of Radisson S
Hotel, Junction 100 & 494

RATHBUN STUDIO INC
2100 Pillsbury   55404
612 871-1060   Est: 1946
Proprietor: Jeanne B
Mullen
Hours: Tues-Sat, 9-4:30
Types & Periods: General
Line, Furniture, Estate Sales
Appraisal Service Available
Directions: S on Lyndale
to Franklin, E on Franklin
for 5 blocks, turn S onto
Pillsbury, 4th mansion on
right

THE STUDIO
3015 W 50th St   55410
612 922-6120
Proprietor: Gary Lindberg
Hours: Tues-Sat, 11-5;
Sun & Mon by chance
Types & Periods: General
Line
Specialties: Jewelry

J A SUNDBERG ANTIQUES
113 N 1st St   55401
612 332-5993
Proprietor: Jack Sundberg
Hours: Daily, 10-5
Types & Periods: General
Line

SWITCHING POST
2015 Aldrich Ave S 55405
612 870-1485   Est: 1963
Proprietor: Minneapolis
League of Catholic
Women
Hours: Thurs-Sat, 10-4:30;
Closed during summer
Types & Periods: General
Line of Antiques on
Consignment
Appraisal Service Available

**WHITE ELEPHANT
CONSIGNERY**
13728 Nicollet Ave   55337
612 894-1777   Est: 1975
Hours: Mon-Sat, 10-5
Types & Periods: Pressed &
Cut Glass, Furniture,
Primitives, Lamps,
Miniatures, Books, Linens,
Collectibles, Collector's
Plates
Directions: 15 miles S of
Minneapolis, 35-W to Hwy
13 to Nicollet

WICKERWORKS
4405 France Ave   55410
612 922-3032   Est: 1973
Hours: Mon-Sat, 10-5;
Thurs evening 'til 7;
Sun, 1-5
Types & Periods: Antique
Wicker Furniture
Specialties: Furniture
(Wicker)
Directions: 10 minutes
from downtown, close to
35-W

YANKEE PEDDLER
5008 Xerxes Ave S 55410
612 926-1732
Proprietor: Mary Ann
Pensz
Hours: Tues-Sat, 10:30-4
Types & Periods: General
Line
Specialties: Furniture
(Country)

Monticello

**MONTICELLO FLORAL
GRANNY'S ATTIC**
107 W Broadway   55362
612 295-3900   Est: 1974
Proprietor: Phyllis Johnson
& Sally Martie
Hours: Daily
Types & Periods: Dining
Room, Bedroom &
Occasional Tables
Directions: Exit 193 from
Freeway 94, turn N to
Monticello, proceed to
main intersection of Hwy
25 & City Rd 75, located
on NW corner

Nevis

**THE GEORGIA CRACKER
ANTIQUES**
Rte 2   56467
218 652-3550
Proprietor: Rob & Carolyn
Zimmerman
Hours: Mon-Sat, Sun by
chance, May to Oct
Types & Periods: Glass,
China, Primitives, Jewelry
Appraisal Service Available
Directions: 9 miles E of
Park Rapids on Lake Belle
Taine Rd

LOG CABIN ANTIQUES
RR 2   56467
218 732-9863
Proprietor: D Hunter
Hours: June thru Sept,
10-5
Types & Periods: Small
Items
Directions: 7 miles E on
Hwy 34 from Park Rapids,
County 80, halfway
between Nevis & Park
Rapids on Lake Belletaine

Northfield

THREE ACRES ANTIQUES
302 S Division   55057
507 645-4997   Est: 1963
Proprietor: Mr & Mrs
Donovan Parker
Hours: Mon-Sat
Types & Periods: General
Line, 18th & 19th Century
English & American
Furniture, Glass, Silver,
China
Appraisal Service Available
Directions: Main St
downtown

Olivia

ANTIQUE NOOK
301 9th St   56277
612 523-2435
Hours: Daily, closed 2
months in winter
Types & Periods: Glass,
China, Primitives

Osseo

ED'S TRADIN SHOP
311 Central Ave   55369
612 425-6556   Est: 1973
Proprietor: Edward Stieg
Hours: Mon-Thurs, 9-5:30;
Fri, 9-7; Sat, 9-5
Types & Periods: China
Hutches, Sideboard, 1800 &
Early 1900's
Directions: 2 doors down
from bank on Central Ave

Owatonna

ROBERT'S ANTIQUES
236 Plainview   55060
507 451-4649   Est: 1970
Proprietor: Robert G
Huber
Hours: Daily, by chance
Types & Periods: Primitives,
"Hard to Find" Pottery,
General Line
Specialties: Red Wing Jugs,
Crocks, Covers, Maps of
Dealers (Local &
Surrounding Towns)
Appraisal Service Available
Directions: Any exit off
I-35 to Oak St, follow to
Plainview

Park Rapids

JOHN'S ANTIQUES
105 E 1st St   56470
218 732-9281   Est: 1970
Proprietor: John Goplerud
Hours: Daily, 10-5 during
summer; by appointment
or by chance
Types & Periods: General
Line
Appraisal Service Available

Paynesville

COUNTRY TRADING POST
Hwy 124   56362
612 243-4027
Hours: Mon-Fri, 12-7; Sat,
9-5; Also by appointment
Types & Periods: Country
Primitives, Collectibles,
Furniture, General Line
Directions: 2½ miles S of
Paynesville on Hwy 124

Pennock

OLSON'S ANTIQUES
                      56279
612 599-4215   Est: 1962
Proprietor: Cliff & Mayvis
Olson
Hours: Summer, Daily
9:30-5; Winter by
appointment

Types & Periods: Early
Norwegian Primitives, Art,
Cut & Depression Glass
Specialties: Needlework
(Quilts), Brass, Copper
Appraisal Service Available
Directions: Hwy 12, 100
miles W of Minneapolis

Pequot Lakes

**HARDESTYS COINS &
ANTIQUE SHOP**
                      56472
218 568-4052   Est: 1957
Proprietor: Elmer &
Thelma Hardesty
Hours: Mon-Sat, 9-5
Types & Periods: General
Line
Directions: 3 blocks W of
Mobil station in Pequot
Lake

Plainview

RED HORSE INN
420 First Ave NW   55964
507 534-3511
Proprietor: Jerry Gallagher
Hours: Daily, 11-4; Also by
appointment
Types & Periods: General
Line, Paper, Early Heisey

Racine

PATIO PLACE ANTIQUES
                      55967
507 378-2386   Est: 1971
Proprietor: Evelyn Mayer
Hours: By appointment, by
chance anytime
Types & Periods: Glass,
China, Primitives, Small
Furniture, Crocks, Antique
Pottery
Specialties: Pottery
Directions: 1 mile S of
Racine on Hwy 63, 2 miles
W on Township Rd

Red Wing

**GEORGE ENZ
ANTIQUES-HISTORIC
GRAHAM HOUSE**
625 W 5th   55066
612 388-2650   Est: 1947
Proprietor: Edna Enz
Hours: Mon-Sat, 10-5, Sun
by appointment
Types & Periods: Fine
Furniture, Country Primitive,
Collectors Items,
Accessories
Specialties: Victorian
Furniture, Ironstone China
Directions: 5th & Dakota
Sts

**GRAHAM HOUSE
ANTIQUES**
625 W 5th St   55066
612 388-2650
Proprietor: George Enz
Hours: Mon-Sat, 11-5;
Sun, 1-5; Also by
appointment
Types & Periods: Furniture,
Accessories, Collectibles,
General Line

STRUCKS' ANTIQUE SHOP
Rte 2   55066
612 388-6875   Est: 1970
Proprietor: Aaron & Ethel
Struck
Hours: Daily
Types & Periods: General
Line
Specialties: Victorian
Furniture, Bing & Grondahl
Christmas & Mothers Day
Plates, Pine & Oak Furniture
Directions: 6 miles W of
Red Wing on Hwy 61, 1
mile S on Hwy 19

TEAHOUSE ANTIQUES
927 W 3rd   55066
612 388-3669   Est: 1965
Proprietor: Morris &
Delores Callstrom
Hours: Mon-Sat, 11-5
Types & Periods: China,
Glass, Silver, Linens, Picture
Frames, Furniture, Primitives
Directions: 1 block off
Hwy 61 at corner of 3rd &
Hill Sts in "Octagon"
House

Renville

**EVIE'S TREASURES &
TRASH**
222 E. Park   56277
612 329-3579
Hours: By appointment, by
chance
Types & Periods: Furniture,
Dishes, Tools
Directions: On Hwy 212,
across from Catholic
Church

Robbinsdale

JE DON'S
4164 W Broadway 55422
612 537-4461   Est: 1973
Proprietor: Don & Dean
Carpenter
Hours: Mon-Sat; Sun by
appointment
Types & Periods: Antiques,
Collectibles, New Gift Items,
Furniture
Specialties: Furniture
Refinishing, Upholstering
Appraisal Service Available
Directions: Right off Hwy
52 & Co Rd 9, Main street
in Robbinsdale, W of
Minneapolis

Rochester

THE ANTIQUERY
501 4th Ave NW   55901
507 289-0520   Est: 1976
Proprietor: Mary Lou
Brady & Barb Feidt
Hours: Wed-Sat, 10-4
Types & Periods: Victorian &
Country Furniture, China,
Glass, Primitives, General
Line
Directions: 6 blocks N of
Mayo Clinic

ARTS OF ASIA
5 SW 1st Ave   55901
507 289-6532   Est: 1972
Proprietor: Barbara
Callaway
Hours: Mon-Sat; Mon &
Thurs evenings until 9
Types & Periods: Oriental
Antiques

Specialties: Oriental
(Japanese Woodblock
Prints)
Directions: Downtown
Rochester, Kahler Hotel
block, street level, E
Arcade

BLONDELL ANTIQUES
1406 2nd St SW   55901
507 282-1872   Est: 1965
Proprietor: R C Blondell
Hours: Daily, 8-8
Types & Periods: 18th &
19th Century American &
Norwegian Primitives & Folk
Art
Appraisal Service Available
Directions: Next to St
Mary's Hospital

**DAVID M CAFFES
ANTIQUES**
1901 Bamber Valley
Rd SW   55901
507 282-8497   Est: 1969
Proprietor: David M Caffes
Hours: Daily, Weekends
Types & Periods: American
Country Furniture, Folk Art,
Norwegian Items
Appraisal Service Available
Directions: 1 1/2 miles W
on County Rd 8, off
Hwy 52

A CELLAR ANTIQUE SHOP
505 10th St SE   55901
507 282-3322   Est: 1955
Proprietor: Clifford & Ruth
Kendall
Hours: By appointment, by
chance
Types & Periods: Silver,
China, Glass, Copper, Brass,
Lamps
Appraisal Service Available
Directions: SE Rochester,
3 blocks from K-Mart

THE GALLERY
113 First Ave SW 55901
507 289-4238   Est: 1964
Proprietor: Ross T
Husband
Hours: Daily
Types & Periods: Traditional,
English, French, Oriental

Rochester Cont'd

THE IRIDESCENT HOUSE
215 1st Ave SW   55901
507 288-0320   Est: 1960
Proprietor: Richard R
Townsend
Hours: Daily
Types & Periods: Art Glass,
General Line Antiques,
Jewelry
Specialties: Art Glass
  Directions: Two blocks
  from Mayo Clinic

MAYOWOOD GALLERIES
Kahler Hotel   55901
507 288-2695
Proprietor: Rita H Mayo
Hours: Daily, 10:30-5:30
Types & Periods: 18th &
Early 19th Century English &
Continental Furniture,
General Line

GLENN MILLER INTERIORS
1102 7th Ave SW   55901
507 289-4566   Est: 1970
Proprietor: June & Glenn
E Miller
Hours: Mon-Fri, 10-5
Types & Periods:
Collectibles
  Directions: Across from
  Mayo Clinic in main hotel

POTPOURRI
16 3rd St SW   55901
507 288-2523   Est: 1970
Proprietor: May Morman,
Rachel Maus & Lorraine
Bridwell.
Hours: Mon-Sat, 10-5
Types & Periods: Primitives,
Collectibles, Furniture

TOMKINS ANTIQUE CLOCKS
1205 14th Ave NE   55901
507 289-9038   Est: 1969
Proprietor: H Tompkins
Hours: By appointment, by
chance
Types & Periods: Clocks

Rockville

IHS ANTIQUES
Hwy 23   56369
612 252-4543   Est: 1968
Proprietor: Inge H Seelen

Hours: Daily
Types & Periods: Furniture,
Primitives, Oriental Rugs,
Frames, Paintings, Lighting
Fixtures, Glass, Brass,
Bronzes
Specialties: Objets d'Art
Appraisal Service Available
  Directions: Hwy 23 W out
  of St Cloud 8 miles,
  Rockville General Store

Rosemount

COUNTRY STORE
120th St & Hwy 3   55068
612 423-1242
Hours: By appointment
Types & Periods: Clocks,
Lamps, Shades

Royalton

LEBLANC ROCK & ANTIQUE SHOP
Box 163   56373
612 584-5774   Est: 1968
Proprietor: Dorothy
LeBlanc
Hours: Daily, by
appointment, by chance
Types & Periods: China,
Clocks, Silver, Art Glass,
Furniture
Specialties: Hand Cut &
Polished Gem Stones
  Directions: 2nd block E off
  Hwy 10, large white &
  blue house

St Cloud

THE ANTIQUE STORE
2600 3rd St N   56301
612 252-5651
Proprietor: Susan &
Eugene Petersen
Hours: Daily, 9-5, Summer
hours; By appointment
Types & Periods: General
Line, Calendar Plates, Old
Wedgwood, Coca Cola
Specialties: Art Glass to
Depression
Appraisal Service Available
  Directions: 3 blocks N of
  Hwy 23, turn at the Dairy
  Queen

FIFTH AVENUE ANTIQUE HOUSE
314 6th Ave S   56301
612 253-2680   Est: 1969
Proprietor: Doris &
Chester Otto
Hours: Mon, Wed-Sat,
10-4:30, by appointment
Types & Periods: Old
Wedgwood, Glass, China,
General Line
Specialties: Calendar Plates
Appraisal Service Available
  Directions: 1½ blocks S of
  Hwys 23 & 52

St. James

313 ANTIQUES
313 Armstrong Blvd 56081
507 375-3869   Est: 1974
Proprietor: Brian Mays
Hours: By appointment, by
chance
Types & Periods: General
Line, Jim Beam Bottles
Specialties: Glass (Art &
Depression)
  Directions: 1 block N of
  Main

St Paul

ST PAUL CLUSTER
Directions: Cluster of
shops on two avenues,
Payne (800-1000 Blocks)
& Grand Ave (800-1000
Blocks), a number on W
7th St (100-200 Blocks)

THE ANTIQUE MART
872 Payne Ave   55101
612 771-0860   Est: 1974
Proprietor: Thomas
Benedum
Hours: Daily
Types & Periods: General
Line, Glassware, Collectible
Furniture
Specialties: Military
Collectibles
Appraisal Service Available
  Directions: E side of town

CHIMNEY HOUSE ANTIQUES
1472 Grand Ave   55105
612 698-3036   Est: 1973
Proprietor: Lorraine E
O'Malley

Hours: Tues-Sat, 11-5
Types & Periods: Antique
Clothing, Rental & Sales;
Furniture, Glassware; China
Primitives
Specialties: Clock Repair
Appraisal Service Available
Directions: 10 blocks S of
I-94 on Snelling Ave,
1½ blocks E on Grand Ave

CORNER DOOR
1112 Grand Ave   55105
612 298-0913
Proprietor: Margaret
McCarty
Hours: Daily; Weekends &
by appointment
Types & Periods:
Collectibles, Furniture,
General Line
Appraisal Service Available
Directions: Grand &
Lexington "European Flea
Market Atmosphere"

GRAND HOUSE ANTIQUES
889 Grand Ave   55105
612 222-6520   Est: 1974
Proprietor: James E
Kroschel
Hours: Tues-Sat, 10-5
Fri nite until 7
Types & Periods: American
& European Furniture,
Victorian, Primitives
Specialties: Stained Glass
Windows, Art Glass, Lamp
Shades & Lamps,
Chandeliers
Appraisal Service Available
Directions: 2 miles W of
downtown

HUDGINS GALLERY
250 W 7th St   55102
612 222-4388   Est: 1970
Proprietor: Charles J
Hudgins
Hours: Tues-Sat
Types & Periods: 18th &
19th Century Furnishings,
Oriental Porcelains, Glass,
China, Bronze, Paintings
Appraisal Service Available
Directions: 2 blocks W on
7th St from St Paul Civic
Center, within walking
distance of downtown

J & E ANTIQUES
1000 Arcade   55106
612 771-9654   Est: 1970
Proprietor: Elon J Piche
Hours: Fri-Sun, 9-5;
Mon-Thurs, by
appointment
Types & Periods: Victorian
Pieces
Specialties: Electric Trains,
Victorian Furniture, Brewery
Items
Directions: Hwy 61 thru
town, 1 mile N of I-94,
1 mile E of 35E

**JOHNSON'S COUNTRY
STORE ANTIQUES**
1738 Grand Ave   55105
612 698-4886   Est: 1973
Proprietor: Ruby & Gerald
Johnson
Hours: Mon-Sat
Types & Periods: General
Line
Appraisal Service Available
Directions: Grand &
Wheeler Aves

KRAMER GALLERY
229 E 6th St   55101
612 225-0863   Est: 1972
Proprietor: Leon & Wes
Kramer
Hours: Mon-Fri, 9-5; Sat,
10-3
Types & Periods: 19th &
20th Century Paints &
Prints, Furniture, Clocks,
American Indian Art,
Oriental Art, Japanese Prints
Specialties: American Indian
Art
Appraisal Service Available
Directions: Off I-94 & 7th
St Exit

NAKASHIAN O'NEIL
23 W 6th St   55102
612 224-5465   Est: 1905
Proprietor: Mr Daniel F
O'Neil
Hours: Daily
Types & Periods: 18th &
19th Century French &
English Furniture, Chinese
Porcelains & Textiles,
Meissen, Paintings, Bronzes,
Silver
Directions: Downtown

ROBERT J RIESBERG
1349 Delaware Ave 55118
612 457-1772   Est: 1970
Proprietor: Robert J
Riesberg
Hours: By appointment
Types & Periods: American
18th and Early 19th
Centuries
Specialties: American
Pewter, Windsor Chairs,
Country Furniture &
Accessories
Appraisal Service Available

ANN WAGNER ON GRAND
1050 Grand Ave   55105
612 222-0575   Est: 1976
Proprietor: Salken & Linoff
Hours: Mon-Sat, 10-4:30
Types & Periods: 18th &
19th Century Furniture,
Jewelry
Specialties: Architectural
Appraisal Service Available
Directions: Between
Lexington & Oxford, 6 blks
off I-94

Shorewood

FARR'S LAMP SHOP
27175 Beverly Dr   55331
612 474-8220
Proprietor: Roy & Grace
Farr
Hours: By appointment
Types & Periods: Coal Oil
Burning Lamps
Specialties: Red Wing
Pottery
Appraisal Service Available

Spicer

**CURIOSITY SHOPPE &
MUSEUM**
Hwy 23   56288
612 796-2622
Proprietor: Frances
Hillman
Hours: Daily, 10-5, May
thru Oct
Types & Periods: "This &
that", "Junque"
Directions: On Hwy 23 S 1
block of town

320 MINNESOTA

Spring Valley

CHASE'S ANTIQUES
508 Huron Ave   55975
507 346-2850   Est: 1971
Proprietor: Bob &
Jeannine Chase
Hours: Daily
Types & Periods: Refinishing
Furniture

IRIDESCENT HOUSE
520 N Section Ave   55975
507 346-2121   Est: 1958
Proprietor: Mrs R E
Townsend
Hours: Daily, by chance
Types & Periods: General
Line
Specialties: Glass (Cut &
Heisey), Hand Painted China
Directions: On Hwy 74 N
of Intersection 16 & 63

WHITE HOUSE ANTIQUES
305 S Broadway   55975
507 346-2052
Proprietor: Wayne & Rita
Fenske
Hours: By appointment, by
chance
Types & Periods: Furniture
Appraisal Service Available
Directions: End of
business district

Stanchfield

ARTIFACTS LTD
PO Box 16   55080
612 396-2378   Est: 1973
Proprietor: Wm & Mary
Danneman
Hours: Thurs-Sun; Also by
appointment
Types & Periods: Depression
Glass, Dishes, Early
Phonographs, Radios,
Clocks, Collectibles, Frames,
Prints
Specialties: Clock Repair,
Radios, Phonographs

Stillwater

**THE BARN WITH THE RED
DOOR**
1030 4th Ave S   55082
612 439-2115   Est: 1972

Proprietor: Mrs Barbara
Charlsen
Hours: Fri-Sat, 10-5; Also
by appointment
Types & Periods: Furniture,
Glass, China, Brass, Clocks,
Jewelry, Primitives,
Furniture, Wood
Specialties: Furniture
(Victorian, Walnut, Wicker),
Primitives
Directions: On the hill
above St Croix River, from
town Chestnut to Third St,
S 9 blocks to Burlington,
E on Burlington 5 blocks
to 4th Ave

THE BELFRY
500 S 4th St   55082
612 439-9105   Est: 1975
Proprietor: Mrs Carol
Strandberg
Hours: Weekends, by
appointment
Types & Periods: Glass,
Furniture
Directions: Across from
Courthouse on S hill of
Stillwater

COURT YARD ANTIQUES
220 E Myrtle   55082
612 439-7530
Proprietor: Mrs Lucille
Holm
Hours: Mon-Sat, 11-5
Types & Periods: Jewelry,
China, Glass, Silver, General
Line

Wayzata

ATHENA ANTIQUES
307 Manitoba Ave S 55391
612 473-2500
Proprietor: Bob & Elaine
Luartes
Hours: Daily, or by chance
Types & Periods:
"Mini-Mall" of Antiques
Specialties: Jewelry
Appraisal Service Available
Directions: Downtown
Wayzata

THE CORNER DOOR INC
1250 E Wayzata Blvd
55391
612 473-2274   Est: 1968
Proprietor: Dee Dee
Savage
Hours: Mon-Sat, 10-4:30

Types & Periods: General
Line
Specialties: Estate Sales
Appraisal Service Available
Directions: In the Wayzata
Home Center on the lower
level

GOLD MINE ANTIQUES
332 S Broadway   55391
612 473-7719   Est: 1960
Proprietor: Jane Atwood
Hours: Mon-Sat
Types & Periods: Silver,
China, Oriental Objects,
Furniture, Oils, Prints,
Primitives
Appraisal Service Available
Directions: On the shores
of Lake Minnetonka in
Wayzata, 12 miles W of
downtown Minneapolis on
Hwy 12

THE PLUSH HORSE
18246 Minnetonka Blvd
55391
612 473-3242   Est: 1968
Proprietor: Lynn Luber
Hours: Wed-Sat,
10:30-4:30 or by
appointment
Types & Periods: 18th &
19th Century Furniture,
Accessories
Appraisal Service Available
Directions: 3 miles W of
I-494

Welch

**CANNON VALLEY
ANTIQUES**
RR 2 Box 40   55089
612 388-7346   Est: 1971
Proprietor: Bob & Jewell
Peterson
Hours: Daily, by chance
Types & Periods: Primitives,
Stoneware, Copper, Brass,
Tin, Glassware
Specialties: Stoneware
Appraisal Service Available
Directions: 6 miles N of
Red Wing on County Rd
46, just off Hwy 61

Willmar

GENETTE'S ANTIQUES
302 Becker Ave E   56201
612 235-0229   Est: 1967
Proprietor: Genette Nelson
Hours: By appointment or
by chance
Types & Periods: China,
Glass, Collector Books,
General Line
Specialties: Art Glass, Salt &
Pepper Shaker Collection
Directions: 1 block S, 2
blocks E of Hwy 12 & 71
Intersection

THE TURNING POINT
309 W 3rd St   56201
612 235-5650   Est: 1974
Proprietor: Peter W
Hanson & David Berglund
Hours: Mon-Sat, 10-5 or
by chance
Types & Periods: Furniture
(Oak, Walnut Primitives),
Collectibles, Paper Products
Specialties: Oak Furniture
Directions: Downtown
Willmar

Winona

MARY TWYCE ANTIQUES & BOOKS
601 E 5th St   55987
507 454-4412   Est: 1970
Proprietor: Mary E
Pendleton
Hours: Mon-Sat, 10-5;
shorter winter hours
Types & Periods: General
Line, Furniture, Glass,
China, Jewelry, Pictures,
Crocks, Interesting
Oddments
Specialties: Old Postcards,
Rare & Out-of-Print Books
Directions: On E 5th 4
blocks W of Mankatao
Ave, across from St Stans
Church

Worthington

STUBS COUNTRY STORE
1924 Dover St   56187
507 376-4718   Est: 1963
Proprietor: Evelyn Seeberg
Hours: Mon-Sat by
appointment, most
afternoons in summer
Types & Periods: General
Line, Furniture, Primitives,
Glass, China
Directions: 1st place S of
Best Western Motel on NE
corner of city, on Hwys
59, 60 & old 16

Zumbro Falls

BREMERS' ANTIQUES & COLLECTIBLES
55991
507 753-2515   Est: 1968
Proprietor: Mrs Carl
Bremer
Hours: Mon-Sat; Sun by
chance or by appointment
Types & Periods: Clocks,
Furniture, Lamps, Dishes,
Glassware, Primitives
Specialties: Furniture
Directions: 3 miles E of
town on Hwy 60 to
Antique Sign, 1 mile N,
1/2 mile E

BUSY "B" ANTIQUES
Ryans Bay
RR 1 Box 99   55991
507 753-2087   Est: 1975
Proprietor: Margaret M
Benike
Hours: By appointment, by
chance
Types & Periods: Dolls,
Toys, Dishes, Jewelry,
Primitives, Furniture
Specialties: Dolls
Directions: 10 miles N of
Rochester on Hwy 63,
then 2 miles W on City 12,
then follow signs 3 miles

THE TIN CUP
Hwy 63 Box 293   55991
507 753-2957   Est: 1973
Proprietor: Cecil &
Rachael Morris
Hours: Wed-Thurs,
Sat-Sun, 10-5
Types & Periods: General
Line, Collectibles
Specialties: Country Items
Directions: Hwy 63 in
Zumbro Falls

ZUMBRO VALLEY
RFD   55991
507 753-2398   Est: 1970
Proprietor: Mr & Mrs Allen
Graves
Hours: Wed-Sun, 10-5
Types & Periods: Pine, Oak,
Walnut Furniture, Glassware,
Postcards, Primitives,
Collectibles
Specialties: Furniture
Directions: 13 miles N on
Hwy 63 from Rochester to
South Troy Church 1
mile W

Gothic side chair
with quatrefoil.

322

(From page 278)   can judge the quality of that bargain.

Queen Victoria came to the English throne as a young woman in her teens in 1837. She was to reign during a most remarkable period in history until her death in 1901. The facade of orderliness in this presentation of the Victorian Era will become fairly strained because 64 years of fleeting vogues defy pigeonholes.

It was an age of prospering nations, expanding trade throughout the world, and rapidly expanding industrialization in America. We were a nation with perhaps 17 million people who had moved only a bit west of the Mississippi River when Victoria came to the throne. We had only touched the borders of the new Republic of Texas lightly with very few settlers and had not established ourselves on the Great Plains. At the end of her reign, we were 76 million people who had long before reached the Pacific Ocean. We possibly had the most explosively growing national economy in the world, despite a few very serious hiccups along the way. It was a time of a rapidly increasing middle class who were becoming rapidly more affluent. This expanding middle class desired something new in architecture and in furniture, and was able to afford it. Circumstances were such that designers could dream up styles and receive an audience. The new styles were being influenced by virtually anything and everything from the milleniums that had gone before. With an abundance of hardwoods at hand and an evolving mechanization, the new furniture factories could produce the quantities of goods needed for an expanding population. The ever popular walnut, mahogany and rosewood were to be used, but ebony became more prevalent.

In studying the furniture of the Victorian Era, dividing it into three periods will simplify circumstances somewhat. A concensus about names for these periods does not yet seem to exist. I will use Early Victorian Period for the time approximating 1837 through perhaps 1855. The Middle Victorian Period will encompass the years 1855 through 1875. Then the Late Victorian Period will run from 1875 through 1901. These are not wholly suitable but they should accomplish our purpose.

The first pattern for a coiled steel spring to be used in upholstery was made in 1828, and then came into use in the following years. Comfort was coming at last. This invention changed the proportion of the chair by shortening its legs. When later used in the back of a chair, the first "overstuffed" furniture came into existence.

The Early Victorian Period, 1837-1855, was influenced by a multiplicity of styles,   (Continued, page 322B).

Left: Early Victorian side chair of French influence with carving and finger roll.

Right: Rococo lady's chair.

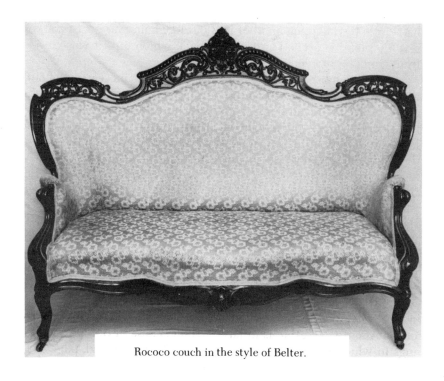

Rococo couch in the style of Belter.

(From page 322). all interpretations of the past. The Greek Revival influence was on the wane. Tradition was seemingly no longer able to provide either guidance to or restraint upon design. This might well be called a transitional period from Empire into the Victorian. Designers were hard pressed to come up with new ideas, so they reverted to old ones. This might also be called Historical or Classical Revivalism, and it was to prevail for the balance of the century. A principal problem for the designer was that of adapting both the surviving Empire period and the new designs to production by machinery. In 1840, a Baltimore architect, John Hall, published a book of designs intended for furniture. There were about 200 designs making use of single and double "S" scrolls and the "C" scroll. In order to reduce carving, all were to be cut on the band saw with the intent of producing inexpensive furniture.

From ancient Greece and Rome two chair forms were redis-covered, the "klismos" and the "curule". The klismos had curved legs resembling sabre blades. The front and rear legs curved in and then away from each other in a very pleasing effect. The curule chair had both front and rear legs made of a very large "S" shape. On each side the front leg crossed over the rear leg. This produced either the appearance of an "X" shape or the appearance of a half circle resting upon another half circle. Chairs were occasionally given a pleasing arched and curved back which, in fact, was copied from gondolas or even chariots.

An inclination toward romanticism was to increasingly flour-ish. A new rationale was coming into fashion which stated that the decor of one's surroundings could contribute to particular traits for the people who lived among it. It was said that Gothic designs facilitated contemplation upon the metaphysical and intellectual development in general. A. J. Downing and an architect, A. J. Davis, worked together to promote the revival of interest in Gothic during the 1840's. Of course, it was a design which incorporated into furni-ture the architectural forms found in medieval English Gothic ca-thedrals. It never attained much popularity in the United States, but it was much more successful in England. American Gothic furniture was used mostly in churches as chairs, benches and podiums. The possible motifs used were limited, but principal among them were the pointed arch, trefoil and quatrefoil. The arch was often applied on a solid background repetitively. All motifs might be pierced into splats, skirts or anywhere with remarkable effect on occasion. Most of the American Gothic is in large scale because of the large build-ings in which it was used. (Continued, page 344).

STATE OF MISSISSIPPI

Belzoni

THE COCKY CROW
101 Pecan   39038
601 247-2817   Est: 1969
Proprietor: Lola D Serpas
Hours: By Appointment,
By Chance
Types & Periods: Country,
Primitives, General Line
Specialties: Quilts &
Coverlets
Directions: Downtown By
City Hall

Biloxi

HOBBY HOUSE ANTIQUES
4850 Southern Ave 39531
601 388-3063
Proprietor: Verta Lee
Swetman
Hours: Weekends, By
Appointment After 6
Types & Periods: General
Line
Specialties: Furniture, Glass
Directions: "Turn at
Sun-N-Sand Light, Go 1
Block to White Picket
Fence"

**MARION'S ANTIQUE
HOUSE**
Magnolia   39530
601 436-3229
Proprietor: Mrs Lola
Marion
Hours: Daily
Types & Periods: General
Line
Directions: Magnolia &
Water Streets

RUSSENE'S ANTIQUES
128 Porter Ave   39530
601 432-0903   Est: 1949
Proprietor: Bill & Russene
Shingleton
Hours: Mon-Sat 9-5
Types & Periods: General
Line
Appraisal Service Available
Directions: 1/2 Block off
Beach at Biloxi Lighthouse

Booneville

**THE GRAY HORSE
ANTIQUES & STITCHERY**
Box 392   38829
601 728-9321   Est: 1966
Proprietor: Mr & Mrs W T
Barnett Jr
Hours: By Appointment,
By Chance
Types & Periods: 18th &
19th Century Furniture,
Bric-a-brac
Directions: Front St on
Square near Princess
Theatre

Brookhaven

LA COMBE'S ANTIQUES
502 N Railroad   39601
601 833-4191
Proprietor: Mr & Mrs Tom
C Lofton
Hours: Fri & Sat, Other
Days By Appointment
Types & Periods: General
Line

Canton

**FRANCES PARKE
ANTIQUES**
336 S Liberty St   39046
601 859-3646   Est. 1970
Proprietor: Kay
Oilschlager
Hours: Tues-Sun, Closed
Mon
Types & Periods: American
& English Victorian
Furniture, Art Glass, Cut
Glass, & Collectibles
Specialties: 78 RPM
Records, Carnival Glass
Appraisal Service Available
Directions: 2 1/2 Blocks
S of the Square on Old
Hwy 51

Cleveland

THE FIRESIDE SHOP
109 N St   38732
601 843-3311   Est: 1960
Proprietor: Clemmie Griffin
Hours: Mon-Sat, By
Chance
Types & Periods: English
Antiques, 18th & 19th
Century Country Oak
(English)
Appraisal Service Available
Directions: Just Off Main
Street

Clinton

OUIDA'S ANTIQUES
303 Jefferson   39056
601 924-6407   Est: 1976
Proprietor: Ouida Borham
Hours: Tues-Sat
Types & Periods: Furniture,
China, Bronze, Silver,
Jewelry, Cloisonne,
Ironstone China, Clocks,
Brass, Copper
Specialties: Oriental
Porcelain, Ivory Boxes,
Plates, Japanese Figures,
Silks, Wood Block Prints
Directions: 2 Blocks From
The MS College, Across
the Street From City Hall

Columbus

ARTIQUE ARCADE
616 Military   39701
601 327-1593   Est: 1977
Proprietor: Margaret R
Lancaster
Hours: Mon-Sat
Types & Periods: American
Antiques, Furniture,
Glassware, Collectibles, Art
Directions: Turn N off Hwy
82 Onto 9th St For Approx
6 Blocks, Military Rd is
the same as Hwy 12

JEAN BROWN ANTIQUES
315 College   39701
601 327-1812   Est: 1974
Proprietor: Jean Heath &
Brown Jones
Hours: Daily 10-4, Closed
Mon, By Chance
Types & Periods: English &
American 18th & 19th
Century Furniture,
Accessories
Specialties: Porcelains,
Brass, Paintings
Appraisal Service Available
Directions: Across St from
St Paul's Episcopal
Church

Corinth

LEROY FLOYD ANTIQUES
Hwy 72 E   38834
601 287-2625
Proprietor: Mr & Mrs
Leroy Floyd
Hours: Mon-Sat, Also By
Appointment
Types & Periods: Walnut,
Victorian, Oak, Primitives,
China, Glass

Florence

BAGWELL'S ANTIQUES
Rte 4 Box 475A   39073
601 939-1243
Hours: Daily, Weekends
10-5:30
Types & Periods: General
Line
Directions: On Hwy 49 S

Forest

THE HOMEPLACE INC
Hwy 80 E   39074
601 469-1761   Est: 1970
Proprietor: J V Lackey & T
H Shelton
Hours: Daily 9-5, Closed
Mon
Types & Periods: 18th &
19th Century English
Imports

MC MULLAN ANTIQUES
210 E Fourth St   39074
601 469-1354   Est: 1976

Proprietor: Mary E
McMullan
Hours: Tues-Sat
Types & Periods: English &
American Furniture,
Primitives, Bric-A-Brac
Directions: Downtown
Behind Gulf Service
Center of 80 E

ROBYS ANTIQUE BARN
Old Hwy 35 N   39074
601 469-4866   Est: 1968
Proprietor: A O Roby
Hours: Daily 9-5,
Weekends By Appointment
Types & Periods: American,
Primitive
Directions: 2 1/2 Miles N
of I-20 Exit 27 on
Townsend Rd

Greenville

**TOWN & COUNTRY
ANTIQUE BARN**
Hwy 82 W   38701
601 335-2436   Est: 1972
Proprietor: Mrs Hilman
Logan
Hours: Daily
Types & Periods: Primitives,
Early American, Glass,
China, Furniture, Baskets
Appraisal Service Available
Directions: 1 Mile W on
Hwy 82

**WELLS JUNK-TIQUE &
WOODWORK**
Rt 3 Box 135   38701
601 335-7525   Est: 1972
Proprietor: J A Wells
Hours: Daily 9-5, Closed
Sun & Mon
Types & Periods: Oak,
Walnut & Primitive Furniture
Directions: 3 Miles from
City Hwy 82 E

Greenwood

FINCHER'S ANTIQUES
514 W Park Ave   38930
601 455-4961   Est: 1978
Proprietor: Mrs Gene
Fincher
Hours: Mon-Sat 10-5:30,
Nites & Sun By
Appointment

Types & Periods: General
Line of American & English
Furniture & Accessories,
Some Oriental Rugs
Directions: 1 Block Past
Ramada Inn Off Hwy
49-82 Bypass Yellow
House 2 Story Brown
Shutters

GENE'S ANTIQUES
1703 1/2 A Carrollton Ave
38930
601 453-4921   Est: 1966
Proprietor: Mrs Jesse
Murphree
Hours: Tue-Sat, By
Appointment
Types & Periods: American,
English, Victorian, 18th
Century, Empire, French, &
Oriental Furniture, Silver,
Clocks, China, Glass
Specialties: Beds, Dressers,
Clocks, (Seth
Grandfather-Perfect Shape,
Running Now, Restored
Complete)
Appraisal Service Available
Directions: Hwy 82 Onto
Bowie Ln proceed to
Carrollton Ave Turn Right,
Located In 2nd Block on
the Right

**WALKER MCINTYRE
ANTIQUES**
216 W Claiborne-Rear
38930
601 455-3390   Est: 1977
Proprietor: Walker
McIntyre
Hours: Mon-Sat
Types & Periods: English
Antiques
Specialties: Oriental Rugs,
Decorative Accessories,
Silver, Mahogany, Walnut,
Oak Furniture

RUSSELL'S ANTIQUES
802 South Blvd   38930
601 453-4017
Proprietor: Mr & Mrs H R
Cohron
Hours: Daily, Weekends
9-5, Closed Sun
Types & Periods: General
Line, Jewelry, Silver
Flatware

Gulfport

ADAMS LORAINE ANTIQUES
2009 25th Ave   39501
601 863-3758   Est: 1967
Proprietor: Mrs Bill Adams
Hours: Mon-Sat
Types & Periods: Good Country Primatives, Victorian Furniture, Bric-A-Brac
Directions: Hwy 49, 7 Blocks From the Beach

ANTIQUES & COLLECTABLES
2905 7th Ave & Pass Rd
        39501
601 863-1868
Hours: By Appointment
Types & Periods: Depression Glass, Collectibles, Furniture

BETTY'S TREASURE SHOP
2300 25th Ave   39501
601 863-4280   Est: 1971
Proprietor: Mrs Betty J Roberts
Hours: Daily
Types & Periods: General Line, Mostly Glassware
Specialties: Glass
Directions: Hwy 49

THE DEN OF ANTIQUITY
229 Courthouse Rd 39501
601 896-4164   Est: 1971
Proprietor: Roman Garriga
Hours: Mon-Sat 10-5, Sun 1-5
Types & Periods: Orientals, Stained Glass, Clocks, Jewelry, Oil Paintings, Silver, Glass, China, Rare Books, Chandeliers, General Line
Specialties: Oriental, Art Glass, Metal Restoration
Appraisal Service Available
Directions: 2 Blocks N of Hwy 90

EARLY TIMES ANTIQUES
01217 Pass Rd   39501
601 896-7133   Est: 1976
Proprietor: Anne Smith
Hours: Mon-Sat 9-5
Types & Periods: Antiques, Collectibles, Gift Items
Specialties: Oak Furniture
Directions: Corner of Pass Rd & Cowan, Just Off Beach

HANDSBORO TRADING POST
504 Pass Rd   39501
601 896-6787
Hours: Daily
Types & Periods:
Bric-a-Brac, General Line
Specialties: Glass (French)

MARTIN MIAZZA
1208 Pass Rd   39501
601 863-1252
Proprietor: Martin Miazza
Hours: Daily 9:30-4:30
Types & Periods:
Wedgewood, Spode, Baccarat, Stieff, English Pieces 1775-1825

PORT O'CALL ANTIQUES
1416 20th Ave   39501
601 863-4073   Est: 1972
Proprietor: B C Fant
Hours: Mon-Sat, Closed Sun, Also By Appointment
Types & Periods: Furniture, Glassware, Pottery, Silver, Bric-A-Brac

ROSE'S RELIC ROOMS
804 36th Ave   39501
601 863-7508
Proprietor: Vella E Rose
Hours: By Appointment
Types & Periods: General Line, Collectibles
Specialties: Furniture, Glass (Depression & Carnival)
Directions: Intersection of Hwy 90 at 36th Ave

Handsboro

HALEY'S COLLECTABLES
1217 Pass Rd   39501
601 896-8172   Est: 1974
Proprietor: Fred & Lynn Haley Jr
Hours: Sat 10-5, Sun to Fri 8-8, Also By Appointment
Types & Periods: Furniture
Specialties: Furniture (Caning & Refinishing)
Appraisal Service Available
Directions: E on Hwy 90 to Cowan Rd, Turn Left to 1st Stop Light, Left to 2nd Shop

Hattiesburg

AUSTIN TIKI HOUSE
601 Adeline St   39401
601 582-1475   Est: 1966
Proprietor: Mrs Mary Lou Austin
Hours: Mon-Fri 10-5, By Appointment (601 582-2845)
Types & Periods: Oriental Antiques Only
Specialties: Oriental
Directions: Corner of Hardy & Adeline Across From Old City Cemetery

DOWNTOWN ALLEY ANTIQUES
116 1/2 Front St   39401
601 545-7869   Est: 1977
Proprietor: F M Morris
Hours: Tue-Sat, By Appointment
Types & Periods: All Periods Furniture, General Line
Appraisal Service Available
Directions: Old Downtown Hattiesburg In Alley Rear UniFirst Federal

MC NEASE ANTIQUE'S
1319 N Main St   39401
601 582-0081   Est: 1973
Proprietor: Shelton & Rose McNease
Hours: Mon-Sat 9-5
Types & Periods: All Types French, Victorian, American, Primitives, Country English, English
Appraisal Service Available
Directions: Hwy 40 Business Rte

VADA'S ANTIQUE SHOP
Box 35 Rte 6   39401
601 582-5805   Est: 1965
Proprietor: Lavada Burleson
Hours: Daily, By Appointment, At Night
Types & Periods: Furniture, Clocks, Lamps, China, Primitives
Specialties: Furniture (Victorian & Oak)
Appraisal Service Available
Directions: US Hwy 49 S Between N & S Gate of Camp Shelby

Itta Bena

AD-MIXTURE
123 Front St   38941
601 254-7961   Est: 1975
Proprietor: Mrs Joe
Pritchard, Mrs Jack
Williams, Mrs Rogers
Haydon
Hours: Tue-Fri, By
Appointment
Types & Periods: A Mixture
of the Old & the New, All
Periods
Specialties: Antique &
Semi-Antique, Oriental Rugs

Jackson

ANTIQUE BROWSE SHOP
737 N State St   39201
601 355-1158   Est: 1969
Proprietor: Mrs Charlotte
McKinnon
Hours: Daily 10-5, Closed
Sun
Types & Periods: 18th &
19th Century Furniture, prior
to 1840, Oriental Rugs To
Pine Furniture, Quilts,
Lamps, English & Oriental
Porcelain & Accessories. We
Are Direct Importers From
England & Scotland,
Selecting Every Piece
Personally, As Well As
Bringing In Merchandise
From Various Points In The
U S
Specialties: Oriental &
English Porcelain &
Ironstone
Appraisal Service Available
Directions: Across From
Hilton Hotel In
Mid-Jackson, 7 Blocks N
Of Old Capitol, 4 Blocks N
Of New Capitol, Or 6
Blocks W Of I-55 (High St
Exit) To North St

ANTIQUES ET CETERA
160 Highland Village
                    39211
601 981-3666   Est: 1975
Proprietor: John E
Buchanan
Hours: Mon-Sat
Types & Periods: Direct
Importers Of Fine 18th &
19th Century English
Antique Furniture

ANTIQUES GALLERY
831 N President St   39206
601 355-6895
Hours: Mon-Sat 10-5,
Closed Sun
Types & Periods: China,
Silver, Collectibles, Orientals
Specialties: Furniture
(American, Country)

COBWEB SHOPPE
186 Shepperd Rd   39206
601 982-1416
Hours: Daily, Weekends
l0-5:30
Types & Periods: Furniture,
Collectibles

DRAGONWYCK ANTIQUES
RFD 9 Box 164   39212
601 372-6691   Est: 1974
Proprietor: Barbara L
Therrell
Hours: By Appointment
Types & Periods: Orientals,
Art Glass, Fine Porcelains,
American Crystal
Specialties: Cameo, Tiffany,
Steuben, Art Glass, Webb,
Stevens & Williams,
Sandwich, Cambridge,
Heisey
Appraisal Service Available

HERITAGE ANTIQUES
2939 Old Canton Rd
                    39216
601 366-6000   Est: 1976
Proprietor: Shirley Abney
& Lisa Kilgore
Hours: Mon-Sat 10-5
Types & Periods: 18th &
19th Century Furniture &
Accessories, Oriental Rugs
Appraisal Service Available

JACKSON COIN SHOP
4471 N State St   39206
601 362-4987   Est: 1973
Proprietor: John C
McIntyre
Hours: Mon-Sat 10:00-5:30
Types & Periods: Glassware,
Pottery, Small Antiques
Specialties: American Art
Pottery, Royal Doulton
Directions: Northwood
Shopping Center N
State St

JO'S ANTIQUES
5234 Robinson Rd Ext
                    39204
                Est: 1973
Proprietor: Jo Lippincott

Hours: Mon-Sat 8:30-5:30
Types & Periods: American
& English Antiques (Direct
Import) 17th, 18th & 19th
Century Furniture
Specialties: Maintaining A
Complete Hand Selected
Inventory At All Times To
Re-furbish Antebellum
Homes
Appraisal Service Available
Directions: Metro-Center
Vicinity (Corner Raymond
Rd & Robinson Rd Ext)

OLD SOUTH ANTIQUES
324 E Pascagoula St
                    39206
601 856-4327
Hours: By Appointment,
By Chance
Types & Periods: Glass,
China, Indian Jewelry

SUZANTIQUES
4390 Hwy 80 W   39206
601 922-1313
Hours: Daily 9-4:30, Sat
12-4:30
Types & Periods: General
Line

LUCIE VANN ANTIQUES
146 E Griffith St   39309
601 969-3311
Proprietor: Lucie Vann
Fleming
Hours: By Appointment,
By Chance
Types & Periods: General
Line

YOUR BARGAIN SHOP
4743 South Dr   39206
601 922-1415
Proprietor: Pearl Wade
Jones
Hours: Daily 10-5
Types & Periods: General
Line
Specialties: Furniture,
Clocks

Kosciusko

THE CABIN ANTIQUES
206 E Adams   39090
601 289-6853   Est: 1942
Proprietor: Mrs George
Thornton
Hours: Daily, Closed Sun

Types & Periods: 18th
Century Furniture, 19th
Century Items, Country
Furniture
Specialties: Silver, Jewelry
Appraisal Service Available
Directions: Between N
Huntington & Natchez

Leland

CEDAR HILL ANTIQUES
202 Deer Creek Dr SW
38756
601 686-4836
Proprietor: Anne McGee
Hours: Mon-Sat, Closed
Sun, By Chance
Types & Periods: English
Silver, Porcelain, Furniture
Of The 18th & 19th Century
Directions: Located In The
Small Guest House Behind
My House

Louisville

THE HOBBY SHOP
528 E Main St   39339
601 773-5111   Est: 1970
Proprietor: Catherine
Smyth
Hours: Daily
Types & Periods: General
Line
Directions: Located in E
Plaza Shopping Ctr on
Hwy 14 E

Lyon

**CAPTAIN KIDD'S
TREASURE HOUSE**
105 Main St   38645
601 627-7002   Est: 1965
Proprietor: Mrs Harold D
Kidd
Hours: Mon-Fri 9:30-5, Sat
1:30-4:30, Closed Sun &
Wed
Types & Periods: Furniture,
Primitives, Victorian,
Oriental, Collectibles, Brass,
Iron, Lamps, Imports
Directions: 2 Miles N of
Clarksdale, 3 Blocks off
Hwy 61 Along RR Track

Madison

MARY'S FUTURE ANTIQUES
Main St   39110
601 856-4327
Hours: Mon-Sat, 10-5; also
By Appt & By chance
Types & Periods: Turn-of-
the-Century pieces
Specialties: Victorian
furniture

RED BARN ANTIQUES
Old Hwy 51 S   39110
601 856-4407
Proprietor: Edith & Gene
Hamil
Hours: Daily, By
Appointment
Types & Periods: General
Line

Meridian

**THE A & I PLACE
ANTIQUES & INTERIORS**
2021 24th Ave   39301
601 483-9281   Est: 1971
Proprietor: Mrs Ann Cook
Hours: Daily, By
Appointment
Types & Periods: Imports,
American & Country
Furniture, Oriental Rugs,
Porcelain, Accessories
Appraisal Service Available

C H MAPP ANTIQUES
Hwy 39 N Box 5335
39301
601 483-9341   Est: 1920
Proprietor: W V McElwee
Hours: Daily
Types & Periods: American
& Primitive
Appraisal Service Available
Directions: 1 Mile from US
45, N on Hwy 39

Monticello

ANTIQUE CORNER
2 Oak Park   39654
601 587-2572   Est: 1970
Proprietor: Mrs Brantley
Pace
Hours: Daily 9-5

Types & Periods: General
Line
Directions: Located on
Hwy 27 & 84, 60 Miles S
of Jackson, 120 Miles N of
New Orleans

Moss Point

WHITE HOUSE ANTIQUES
3509 Grierson St   37563
601 475-4533   Est: 1963
Proprietor: Bernard Clark
Hours: By Appointment,
By Chance, Eves After 6
Types & Periods: Art
Nouveau, Wicker, Glass,
Marble Topped Furniture,
General Line
Appraisal Service Available

Natchez

**HELEN B FIGURA
ANTIQUES**
326 Main St   39120
601 445-5431   Est: 1966
Proprietor: Helen B Figura
Hours: Mon-Sat, Sun By
Appointment
Types & Periods: American
Primitives thru Empire
Victorian, Paintings, Cut
Glass, China, Audubon
Prints, Art Glass, Rugs,
Dolls
Specialties: Furniture
Appraisal Service Available
Directions: Main St
Between Pearl & Wall
Across from the Eola
Hotel Bldg

HARPER'S ANTIQUES
205 N Canal St   39120
601 445-8147   Est: 1974
Proprietor: Buzz Harper Jr
Hours: Mon-Sat 9-5
Types & Periods: 18th &
19th Century
Specialties: Jewelry
Appraisal Service Available
Directions: Next to
Connelly's Tavern

**MOLASSES FLATS
ANTIQUES**
200 Main St   39120
601 445-4591   Est: 1971
Proprietor: Mrs J Wesley
Cooper

**MOLASSES FLATS
ANTIQUES** Cont'd
Hours: Daily
Types & Periods: English &
American
Specialties: Southern
Americana
Appraisal Service Available
Directions: 1 Block from
MS River at Main & Canal
St

OLD NATCHEZ ANTIQUES
300 N Canal St   39120
601 442-1331
Proprietor: John
Lombardo
Hours: Mon-Sat 9-5:30,
Sun By Appointment
Types & Periods: Glass,
China, Silver, Accessories
Appraisal Service Available
Directions: Next Door to
Post Office

THIEVE'S MARKET
Corner Canal at State
39120
601 445-4034   Est: 1976
Proprietor: Reynolds
Atkins
Hours: Sat & Sun Only
Types & Periods: Flea
Market, Antique Furniture,
Collectibles
Directions: Covers 1/2
City Block in Old RR
Station

Ocean Springs

THE ANTIQUE SHOPPE
Hwy 90 W   39564
601 875-8418   Est: 1969
Proprietor: Ann German
Hours: Mon-Sat 9:30-5
Types & Periods: Furniture
& Bric-A-Brac
Directions: 1 Mile E of
Biloxi-Ocean Springs
Bridge, Look for Lavender
Colored Shop

BARGAIN BARN
Hwy 90 E   39564
601 875-2845   Est: 1976
Proprietor: Mrs A E Speed
Hours: Tues-Sun, Closed
Mon
Types & Periods: Furniture,
Glassware, Primitives, China,
Collectibles

Specialties: Depression
Glass (Flea Market Sat &
Sun)
Directions: 1 Mile from 57
& 90 Intersection

THE CURIOSITY SHOP
1508 Government St
39564
601 875-8654   Est: 1973
Proprietor: Jim & Birdie
Evans
Hours: Daily
Types & Periods: General
Line
Specialties: Furniture
Stripping

**SILVER KNIGHT
ANTIQUE'S**
831 Porter St   39564
601 875-7410 or 875-8318
Est: 1967
Proprietor: Kay W Casson
Hours: Mon-Sat
Types & Periods: Antique
Toys, Collectors Books,
Linens, China, Glass
Specialties: Miniatures,
Paper Americana
Directions: On Gulf Coast
Between New Orleans &
Mobile, Across Bridge
from Biloxi

Oxford

**COUNTRY STORE
ANTIQUES**
1402 Jackson Ave   38655
601 234-4721   Est: 1969
Proprietor: Mrs Loren
Young
Hours: Mon-Sat 8:30-5:30
Types & Periods: Furniture,
Glass, Pictures & Prints,
Primitives, Collectibles
Specialties: Stained Glass
Appraisal Service Available
Directions: NE Corner of
Square Behind City Hall in
Country Village Mall

Pascagoula

IRMA FELTS ANTIQUES
1763 S Market St   39567
601 769-6401   Est: 1969
Proprietor: Irma K Felts
Hours: Daily, Closed Mon,
Also By Appointment

Types & Periods: American
Furniture, Primitives,
Glassware, China, Cut
Glass, Silver, Lamps,
Pictures, Mirrors
Specialties: Oriental
Appraisal Service Available
Directions: S Off Hwy 90

LILL'S ANTIQUES
2519 Telephone Rd
Hwy 63   39567
601 937-8336   Est: 1972
Proprietor: Lillian Moorer
Hansen
Hours: Mon-Sun 10-6
Types & Periods: Furniture,
Primitives, Bottles, Linens,
Flow Blue, Limoge,
Depression Glass, Oil
Paintings, Jewelry from 1840
to Present
Specialties: Bottles & Flow
Blue
Directions: Gold Gulf
Coast of MS, Hwy 63

**PORTHOLE ANTIQUES &
GIFTS**
1349 1/2 Market St 39567
601 769-2429   Est: 1976
Proprietor: Mrs C T
Torgusen
Hours: Tues-Sat 10-5,
Also By Appointment
Types & Periods: American
Furniture, Glassware, China
Appraisal Service Available

Pass Christian

HILLYER HOUSE INC
207 E Scenic Dr   39571
601 452-4810   Est: 1970
Proprietor: Katherine B
Reed
Hours: Mon-Sat
Types & Periods: English &
Southern
Appraisal Service Available
Directions: "In the Heart
of the Oldest City on the
Riveria of the Gulf Coast"

Pearl

M & S ANTIQUES INC
105 Pruitt St   39208
601 939-8330   Est: 1972
Proprietor: George
Sandifer

Hours: Mon-Sat 10-6
Types & Periods: General
Line of European Antiques
Appraisal Service Available
Directions: Off Hwy 80

Perkinston

**PERKINSTON TRADING
POST**
Hwy 49   39573
601 928-4371   Est: 1972
Proprietor: Lora Johnson
& Maxine Cuevas
Hours: Daily
Types & Periods: General
Line

Picayune

**THE BLUE WILLOW
SHOPPE**
614 E Canal St   39466
601 798-1684   Est: 1974
Proprietor: Mrs Freda
Schwenker
Hours: Tues-Sat 10-5
Types & Periods: General
Line
Directions: Located Off
Hwy I-59, Approx Midway
Btwn Hattiesburg & New
Orleans

Potts Camp

**OLD SOUTH ANTIQUES
INC**
Hwy 78 E   38659
601 333-7616   Est: 1976
Proprietor: Richard Jung
& David Douglas
Hours: Daily
Types & Periods: General
Line, Glass, Furniture
Directions: 7 Miles E of
Holly Springs on Hwy 78

Ripley

C S A AUCTION CO
1805 Hwy 15 N   38663
601 837-8148
Proprietor: Conny Dixon
Hours: Auction Days

Types & Periods: Victorian,
Period, French Furniture, All
Types Of Fine Bric-A-Brac

HOWAT ANTIQUES
106 Siddal   38663
601 837-9425   Est: 1955
Proprietor: W M Howat
Hours: Mon-Sat 9-5
Types & Periods: Victorian,
Early American
Specialties: China, Glass
(Cut)
Directions: Next to
Peoples Bank, Hwy 15

Starkville

MOSLEY INC
Industrial Park Rd   39759
601 323-5215   Est: 1972
Proprietor: Joe Thomas
Mosley
Hours: Daily, Weekends,
By Appointment
Types & Periods: 18th &
19th Century American
Furniture,
Turn-of-the-Century Oak
Specialties: Primitives
Appraisal Service Available
Directions: S on Hwy 12
to Industrial Park Rd, 1/2
Mile from Hwy on Left

Tupelo

B & E ANTIQUES
111 S Highland   38801
601 842-5522   Est: 1971
Proprietor: Mrs Earline
Brooks
Hours: Mon-Sat 10-5
Types & Periods: Furniture,
Glassware, Collectibles,
Antiques
Directions: Hwy 6 W, 1/2
Block South, 5 Lights from
Crowtown Intersection

**BROOKS SPINNING WHEEL
ANTIQUES**
354 N Gloster   38801
601 842-0685 or 842-0647
Est: 1969
Proprietor: Susan Brooks
Hours: By Appointment
Types & Periods: American
& English Furniture,
(Primitives & Period Pieces)
Glass (Cut, Pressed, Blown,

Carnival & Depression)
Dolls, Sterling, Porcelain,
Jewelry, Oil Ptgs, 100's Of
Picture Frames, Clocks, Doll
House Miniatures, Wicker,
Iron, Pottery, Lamps, Brass,
Copper
Directions: 2 Blocks N of
Center of Town on Hwy
45 N (Gloster St)

MURPHEY ANTIQUES LTD
1120 W Main St   38801
601 844-3245   Est: 1976
Proprietor: Mrs Eugene
Murphey III
Hours: Mon-Sat
Types & Periods: English,
19th Century
Specialties: Furniture,
Chests, Sideboards, Odd
Chairs, Porcelain, Silver,
Lamps
Directions: Mini Plaza,
West Main St (Hwy 6)
Appro 3 Blocks W of
Hwy 45

NOSTALGIA ALLEY
1604 1/2 W Main   38801
601 842-2757   Est: 1969
Proprietor: Mrs Walter
Fleishhacker
Hours: Mon-Sat, By
Chance
Types & Periods:
Advertising, Glass, Toys,
Furniture, Oddities, Paper
Directions: Hwy 6 Behind
Todds Big Star

**SUNNYCROS ANTIQUES
FLOWERS & GIFTS**
415 N Gloster   38801
601 844-6235   Est: 1953
Proprietor: Faye & Joe
Bishop
Hours: Daily 8-5
Types & Periods: Primitives,
Victorian, Glass, Bedroom,
Living & Dining Room
Furniture in Room Settings
Directions: N of Hwy 45,
4th Block N of Hwy 6 & 45
& Frisco RR Crossing

Vicksburg

**MCNUTT HOUSE
ANTIQUES**
815 First E St   39180
601 638-9192 or 636-6612
Est: 1975

MCNUTT HOUSE   **Cont'd**

Proprietor: Juanita H
Whitaker
Hours: Mon-Sat
Types & Periods: 18th &
Early 19th Century Furniture,
Oriental Rugs, Paintings,
Prints, Decorative
Accessories
Specialties: Quality
American Country Furniture
Appraisal Service Available
Directions: Corner of
Monroe & First E St, 1
Block N of City
Auditorium, In Antebellum
Home on Tourist Route In
Historic Zone

West Point

**HELEN BUCK ANTIQUES
GIFTS JEWELRY**
201 Commerce St   39773
601 494-3521   Est: 1974
Proprietor: Helen Buck
Hours: Mon-Sat 10-5
Types & Periods: 18th &
19th Century Antiques
Directions: Downtown

Yazoo City

**STEWARTS ANTIQUES &
GIFTS**
644 15th St   39194
601 746-7497   Est: 1974
Proprietor: Mrs C L
Stewart
Hours: Daily, By
Appointment
Types & Periods: 18th
Century & Primitives
Specialties: Musical
Instruments
Directions: 3 Blocks Off
Hwy 49 E

YESTERYEAR ANTIQUES
212 Main St   39194
601 746-6528   Est: 1970
Proprietor: Ernest &
Gertrude Galyerr
Hours: Daily 8-5, Sun 1-5
Types & Periods: 18th
Century Antiques
Specialties: Furniture, Glass
Appraisal Service Available
Directions: Downtown

Gothic pedestal table, marble topped.

Spool Crib with posts for mosquito netting.

STATE OF MISSOURI

Ballwin

LARSONS ANTIQUES
950 Clayton Rd   63011
314 227-5600
Proprietor: Roger & Barb
Larson
Hours: Mon-Sat 9-5, Eve &
Sun By Appointment
Specialties: Cut Glass

Barnett

MORGAN'S ANTIQUES
65011
314 392-4154
Types & Periods: General
Line, Lamps
Specialties: Lamps
Directions: Next Door to
Post Office

Blue Springs

CENTURY HOUSE ANTIQUES
111 South 8th   64015
816 229-7141   Est: 1974
Proprietor: Barbara A
Dowell
Hours: Mon-Sun
Types & Periods: Cut &
Press Glass, Tables,
Postcards, Chairs, Dressers,
Clocks, Pictures, Pianos,
Wiokor
Specialties: Furniture
Appraisal Service Available
Directions: Located
Downtown, Largest House
In Area (100 Years Old)

Boonville

GINNIE'S ANTIQUE SHOP
1001 Ashley Rd   65233
816 882-2139   Est: 1966
Proprietor: Mrs Laura
Virginia Olebeare
Hours: Daily
Types & Periods: Furniture,
Glassware, China, Primitives,
Victorian
Directions: Hwy 40,
Business Loop 70, Hwy 5
& Ashley Rd

THE LITTLE HOUSE
313 Spring   65233
816 882-2298
Proprietor: Eleanor Penick
Hours: Daily
Types & Periods: Furniture,
Glass, China, Primitives,
Jewelry, Empire Country
Furniture, 18th Century
Victorian
Directions: Off I-70, 1 1/2
Blocks Off Main St

Bridgetown

ANNE'STIQUE SHOPPE
3153 Fee Fee Rd   63044
314 291-4586   Est: 1973
Proprietor: Anne C Krelo
Hours: Daily 9:30-5:30
Types & Periods: General
Line
Directions: I-70 to
Lindburg Blvd, S to Old St
Charles, Turn W 1 Block
to Fee Fee Rd

Camdenton

ALLIETT'S ANTIQUES
Hwy 54 West   65020
314 346-5438
Types & Periods: Primitives,
General Line

BETHEL'S ANTIQUES
448 West Hwy 54   65052
314 346-7651
Types & Periods: Glass,
China, Collectibles
Specialties: Dolls

GRANNY'S COUNTRY STORE
65020
Types & Periods: Country
store items, Primitives

MASHBURN'S ANTIQUES
65020
314 346-5425
Types & Periods: General
Line, Furniture, Glassware,
Clocks, Primitives
Directions: 4 Miles S of
Town on Hwy 5

OLD TRAIL HOUSE ANTIQUES INC
Star Rte C Box 112B
65020
314 873-5323   Est: 1955
Proprietor: V & V T Zanitis
Hours: Mon-Sun April I-
Nov 15, By Appointment,
By Chance Nov 15-March
Types & Periods: Early Pine,
Victorian & Walnut
Furniture, Also Oak, Pattern
Glass, Lamps, Copper,
Brass, Primitives & Iron,
Some Art
Specialties: Cut Glass
Appraisal Service Available
Directions: 6 Miles N of
Town on Hwy 5

Cape Girardeau

GEORGE'S ANTIQUES
1106 S Kings Hwy   63701
314 334-3331   Est: 1970
Proprietor: George
Semonis
Hours: Mon-Thur By
Appointment, By Chance,
Fri-Sat 10-5, Sun 1-5
Types & Periods: Primitives,
Art Pottery, Art Glass,
Advertising, Bottles, Pattern
Glass, Porcelains, Limited
Furniture, RR Collectibles,
Jewelry
Specialties: Art Pottery,
Porcelain Plates, Primitives
Directions: I/4 Mile Off
I-55 at 1st Southern Exit-
Kings Hwy is Also US Rte
61 & Business I-55

MOTHER EARTH PLANTS & ANTIQUES
826 Themis   63701
314 335-1552
Proprietor: Debbie Martin
Hours: Mon-Sat 10-5, Also
By Appointment
Types & Periods: Victorian,
Primitive, Art Nouveau, Art
Deco, Advertising Items,
Curios
Directions: Off I-55 Rte K
Exit, East to Pacific, N 3
Blocks to Themis on
Corner

Carrollton

FAR MEADOW ANTIQUES
W 7th St   64633
816 542-2971   Est: 1955
Proprietor: Mrs Magna
O'Dell
Hours: Open Daily, By
Appointment, By Chance
Types & Periods: Country
Furniture & Accessories
Appraisal Service Available
Directions: 1½ Miles W on
Rte E from Carrollton
Town Square, 1/4 Mile N

Centralia

**COUNTRY ROAD
ANTIQUES**
Rte 1   65240
314 682-3192   Est: 1975
Proprietor: Lee Hardin &
Tish Soucy
Hours: Mon-Sun, Also By
Appointment, By Chance
Types & Periods: Country,
Victorian, Primitives, Glass,
Copper, Brass, General Line
Specialties: Tea Leaf
Ironstone China
Appraisal Service Available
Directions: Columbia Area,
Hwy 70 E to Z, North on Z
10 Miles to D, Take D 1
Mile to 1st Gravel Rd on
Right 2½ Miles (7 Shops
in 10 Mile Radius)

Clayton

STAIRCASE ANTIQUES
4 S Central Ave   63105
314 725-6412   Est: 1969
Proprietor: Rosa Lee
Holcomb
Hours: Daily 10-4, Closed
Sun & Mon
Types & Periods: Country &
Victorian Furniture
Directions: Across From
County Court House

Columbia

DEN OF ANTIQUITY
810 Rangeline   65201
314 449-1601   Est: 1970
Proprietor: Ellen Exon
Hours: By Appointment,
By Chance
Types & Periods: Glass,
China, Silver, Brass, Copper,
Furniture, Primitives
Specialties: Quilts, Silver
Matching Service, Oddball
Items
Appraisal Service Available
Directions: Corner of
Rangeline & Wilkes, 1/4
Mile S of I-70 at N 63 Exit,
1 Block S of College

Eldon

CATLIN'S ANTIQUES
Hwy 54 & 52 S   65026
314 392-4426   Est: 1951
Proprietor: S Hale Catlin
Hours: Daily, Closed Wed
Types & Periods: Clocks,
Music Boxes, Furniture,
Jewelry, General Line
Directions: Hwy 54 & 52 S
in Town

FAYE'S ANTIQUES
                          65026
314 392-4432
Types & Periods: Glass,
Clocks, Primitives, Dolls,
China, General Line
Directions: Hwy 52 W of
Town

Eureka

THE PIE SAFE
219 S Central   63025
314 938-5600   Est: l975
Proprietor: Sunny Saladin
Hours: Daily, Mon By
Appointment, By Chance
Types & Periods: American
Country Furniture, Tools,
Wood Stoves & Primitives,
Late 1800 Early 1900
Specialties: Pie Safes
Directions: I-44 to Eureka
Exit Over Viaduct S on
Central 1/2 Mile

Faucett

LITTLE OLE SHOPPE
                          64448
417 238-1598
Hours: Tues-Fri & By appt
Types & Periods: Primitives,
Glassware, Tole, General
Line
Directions: 10 miles S,
½ mile W of I-29

Frontenac

FRONTENAC ANTIQUES
801 S Lindbergh Blvd
                          6313l
314 997-6197   Est: 1972
Proprietor: Dorothy E
Spanogle
Hours: Mon-Sat 10-5,
Closed Sun
Types & Periods: 18th &
19th Century, English &
American Furniture,
Oriental Porcelains,
Collectibles
Appraisal Service Available

Gower

**PLATTE PURCHASE
ANTIQUES**
DD   64454
816 424-6493   Est: 1970
Proprietor: Harriet & Fred
Schuster
Hours: Wed-Sun 11-4
Types & Periods: Country,
Early American, English,
French, Spanish Furniture
Specialties: Glass, Porcelain,
Crystal

Grandview

ANTIQUE BARN
13012 Grandview Rd
                          64030
816 763-7470   Est: 1958
Proprietor: Merilyn J
McQuerry
Hours: Weekends, By
Appointment
Types & Periods: General
Line, Primitives, Glassware,
Bottles
Specialties: Toys
Appraisal Service Available
Directions: 1 Block S off
Hwy 71 in Grandview at
Main St Exit

Grovois Mills

**SPRING LAKE LODGE
ANTIQUES**
              65037
Hours: Thur thru Tues, May-
Oct, 10-5:30
Types & Periods: Furniture,
Porcelains, Paintings, Glass,
Primitives
   Directions: On the lake &
   Hwy 5

Halltown

CAMERON'S ANTIQUES
Box 65   65664
417 749-2227   Est: 1956
Proprietor: R H Cameron
Hours: Daily
Types & Periods: General
Line
Specialties: Furniture
   Directions: 16 Miles W of
   Springfield on I-44

Hamilton

**MARTIN'S HARDWARE &
FURNITURE STORE CO**
207-9 N Davis   64644
816 583-2114   Est: 1883
Proprietor: Kirk Martin
Hours: Daily, Weekends,
By Appointment, By
Chance
Types & Periods: General
Line
   Directions: 1½ Blocks N of
   Railroad Tracks

Hannibal

KOPPER KETTLE
220 S Main   63401
314 221-3534   Est: 1970
Proprietor: James & John
Lyng
Hours: Daily, Weekends
Types & Periods: General
Line
Specialties: Brass & Copper

Hermann

**WHITE HOUSE HOTEL
ANTIQUES & GIFTS**
232 Wharf St   65041
314 486-3200 or 486-3493
              Est: 1973
Proprietor: Bob & Judi
Plummer
Hours: Mon-Sat 10-5, Sun
After 2, By Appointment,
By Chance
Types & Periods: General
Line
   Directions: Rtes 19 & 100,
   On the Missouri River

Higginsville

LONG'S ANTIQUES
1711 Main St   64037
              Est: 1971
Proprietor: Mrs Donald
Long
Hours: Daily 10-5, Sun 1-5
Types & Periods: General
Line
Specialties: Furniture
(Walnut), Pattern Glass,
China
Appraisal Service Available
   Directions: 5 Miles N of
   I-70

Independence

**BLACK FLAG ANTIQUES
INC**
101 N Main   64050
816 833-1134   Est: 1972
Proprietor: Jeanie White
Hours: Mon-Sat 10-5
Types & Periods: Primitives,
Furniture, China, Depression
Glass, Pottery, Advertising,
Political Buttons, Miniatures
Specialties: Books About
Antiques
   Directions: SE Corner of
   Historic Independence
   Square

LASATER'S ANTIQUES
10620 E 23rd   64052
816 836-3574   Est: 1970
Proprietor: George & Larry
Lasater
Hours: By Appointment,
By Chance

Types & Periods: Furniture,
Clocks, Lamps, Dishes
Specialties: Victorian
Furniture
   Directions: 2 Miles E of
   435

**LIBERTY HOUSE
ANTIQUES**
206 N Liberty   64050
816 254-4494   Est: 1974
Proprietor: Ann Kuhn
Hours: Mon-Sat 10-4:30
Types & Periods: Walnut,
Pine Primitives, Oak,
Stoneware, Glass, Baskets,
Quilts, Toys, Silver
   Directions: 1/2 Block S of
   Truman Rd on Liberty

**MARY & MONTY'S
ANTIQUES**
9302 E Hwy 40   64152
816 737-1427   Est: 1973
Proprietor: Monty
Kimbraugh & Mary
Smallwood
Hours: Daily, Closed Sun
Types & Periods: Furniture,
Glass, China
Specialties: Oak Furniture
   Directions: Blue Ridge Exit
   Off I-70 Interstate N to
   Hwy 40 1 Block E

SERENDIPITY
211 N Main   64050
816 252-6161   Est: 1971
Proprietor: Susan Walter
Hours: Mon-Sat 10-5, Sun
1-5
Types & Periods: General
Line, Glassware, Dishes,
Primitives, Some Furniture
Specialties: Miniatures,
Dollhouse Furniture
   Directions: 3 Doors S of
   Old Jail Museum on Indep
   Square

Kansas City

KANSAS CITY CLUSTER
   Directions: Shops
   throughout City especially
   on Stateline (4000-7000
   Blocks), Troost (3000-6000
   Blocks), Truman Rd, E &
   W (800-11000 Blocks),
   Westport Rd (400-1000
   Blocks) W 45 (1000 Block)

Kansas City   Cont'd

ANTIQUE WORLD
Union Station   64108
816 421-1787   Est: 1976
Proprietor: James Russell
Hours: Daily, Weekends
10-6, Fri 10-9
Types & Periods: Imported
Antiques from 27 Countries
Plus Fine Home Furnishings,
19th & 20th Century
European & Oriental
Furniture & Accessories, .
Architectural Pieces, Prints,
Rugs, Paintings, Jewelry,
China, Pewter, Copper,
Brass, Stained Glass
Specialties: Largest Antique
Store in the Country, Brass
Beds, Quantities of Stained
Glass, Oriental, Unusual
Items, Dishes, Wardrobes,
Bedroom & Dining Room
Suites
    Directions: Main at
    Pershing Across From the
    Crown Center

**BETTY'S BOTTLE
BOUTIQUE**
823 Westport Rd   64111
816 753-0028   Est: 1972
Proprietor: Betty Waldon
Hours: Thurs-Sun 10-5
Specialties: Limited Edition
Collectors Plates, Hummel
Figurines

BLUE VALLEY ANTIQUES
4609 E 50 Hwy   64130
816 923-3521   Est: 1973
Proprietor: Wash & Willie
Mae Powell
Hours: Daily
Types & Periods: General
Line
Specialties: Furniture

BROOKSIDE ANTIQUES
6219 Oak St   64113
816 444-4774   Est: 1963
Proprietor: "The Zoglin
Family"
Hours: Mon-Sat 10-5
Types & Periods: 18th &
19th Century English,
French, Oriental & American
Glass, Porcelain, Bronze,
Paintings, Furniture
Specialties: Bronze,
Mosaics, Art Glass
Appraisal Service Available
    Directions: N of
    Intersection of 63rd & Oak

COLLECTORS HARVEST
Crown Ctr Hotel
1 Pershing Rd   64108
816 474-3424   Est: 1973
Proprietor: C T & Marie
Falk
Hours: Mon-Sat 10-5
Types & Periods: Jewelry,
Art Glass, Objets d'Art

CORBIN & SON
6122 Troost   64110
816 361-1545   Est: 1960
Proprietor: James E
Corbin
Hours: Daily
Types & Periods: Cut Glass,
Silver, Brass Beds
Specialties: Silver
Appraisal Service Available

**GENERAL STORE
ANTIQUES**
4200 Genessee   64111
816 531-7888   Est: 1962
Proprietor: Mrs James
Currens
Hours: Tue-Sat 11-4:30,
Sun & Mon By
Appointment
Types & Periods: Furniture
Directions: 2 Blocks E of
State Line, 1 Block N of
Westport Rd

**ROBERT HOFFMANN
ANTIQUES**
5909 Main St   64113
816 363-4103
Proprietor: Robert
Hoffmann
Hours: Daily 10-5
Types & Periods: English
Furniture & Accessories

KARGO ANTIQUES
1110 Grand Ave   64106
816 421-5695   Est: 1965
Proprietor: Della & Frank
Gooddem
Hours: Daily 8-6,
Weekends 8-3
Types & Periods: Jewelry
Specialties: Jewelry
Restoration
Appraisal Service Available
    Directions: Downtown

OLD WORLD ANTIQUES
1806-12 W 45th St   64111
816 561-8242
Proprietor: Art & June
Dimsdle
Hours: Mon-Sat 9:30-5,
Closed Sun

Types & Periods: Furniture
Decoratives, Jewelry,
General Line

STARK OBJECTS AS ART
1714 W 45th St   64111
816 561-1842   Est: 1970
Proprietor: Gordon A
Stark
Hours: Mon-Sun 11-5
Types & Periods: American
Antiques, Folk Art, Rare Old
Advertising, Walnut, Cherry
& Pine Furniture Before 1900

THINGS UNLIMITED INC
817 Westport Rd   64111
816 753-9789   Est: 1968
Proprietor: Guy Bell
Hours: Weekends 10-5
Types & Periods:
Collectibles, 100 Dealers,
Oldest & Largest Indoor Flea
Market in Midwest
Appraisal Service Available
    Directions: 8 blocks N of
    Plaza, 1 block E of SW
    Trafficway

MRS CHARLES B WHEELER
804 E 109th St   64131
816 942-5356   Est: 1946
Proprietor: Mrs Charles B
Wheeler
Hours: By Appointment
Types & Periods: French
Haviland China from
1842-1940
Appraisal Service Available
    Directions: S Kansas City
    off Holmes Rd

YESTERDAYS
Suite 311
2450 Grand Ave   64108
816 274-8425
Proprietor: Crown Center
Assoc Stores
Hours: Thurs 10-6, Fri
10-9
Types & Periods: English &
French Furniture, Silver,
Jewelry

Kennett

**COTTON BOLL GIFT SHOP
& ANTIQUES**
325 1st St   63857
314 888-9880   Est: 1973
Proprietor: Vinda Sherrill

Hours: Daily, By
Appointment
Types & Periods: General
Line
Specialties: Primitives
Directions: Hwy 84
Becomes 1st St

Kirksville

ANTIQUES BY WELTE
1006 S Baltimore   63501
816 665-6495   Est: 1967
Proprietor: Loyd Welte
Hours: Daily 9-6
Types & Periods: General
Line,Telephones, Dolls,
Glass, Silver
Specialties: Dolls
Appraisal Service Available
Directions: Hwy 63 SE
Section of Town
(Baltimore St is Hwy 63
thru E part of Town)

HUSTED'S ANTIQUES
915 N Osteopathy Ave
63501
816 665-2392
Proprietor: Rena & Wayne
Husted
Hours: Daily, Weekends
8-6
Types & Periods: China,
Pottery, Brass, General Line

Kirkwood

KISSLING'S ANTIQUES
610 Bedford Oaks Dr
63122
314 821-3573
Proprietor: Irma & Les
Kissling
Hours: By Appointment
Types & Periods: Cut Glass,
China, Lamps, General Line

Knob Noster

WHAT NOT SHOP
101 E McPherson   65336
816 563-2195   Est: 1974
Proprietor: Darryl Swaim
Hours: Daily 9-5
Types & Periods: Primitives,
Furniture, Brass, Copper
Directions: 80 Miles E of
Kansas City on Hwy 50

Laclede

STREET'S ANTIQUES
Main & Cushman   64651
816 963-2382   Est: 1966
Proprietor: Hiram C Street
Hours: Mon-Sat, Closed
Sun
Types & Periods: General
Line of Local Items
Specialties: Country
Furniture, Primitives
Directions: In City Limits,
1 Block W of Methodist
Church

TREASURE CHEST
Hwy 36   64651
816 963-2650   Est: 1972
Proprietor: Darlene Rogers
Hours: Mon-Sat 9-5, Sun
& Evenings By
Appointment, By Chance
Types & Periods: Oak &
Walnut Furniture, Glass,
China, Lamps, Dolls,
Primitives, Misc
Directions: Hwy 36 18
Miles E of Chillicothe or 6
Miles W of Brookfield

La Grange

THE TWINS ANTIQUES
Main St   63448
314 655-4320   Est: 1968
Proprietor: Shelby Dent &
Shirley Shouse
Hours: Mon-Fri 10-5,
Closed Sat & Sun
Types & Periods: China,
Glass, Silver, Furniture
Directions: Exit Rte B off
Hwy 61

Lamar

PANSY'S FLEA MARKET
604 E 12th   64759
417 682-5721   Est: 1972
Proprietor: Pansy Johnson
Hours: Mon-Sun
Types & Periods: All Types
Of Antiques & Collectibles &
Good Junque
Directions: 1 Block S & 1
Block E of Harry S
Truman's Birthplace

La Plata

RUMMERFIELDS ANTIQUES
Box 187 W Side Sq 63549
Est: 1971
Proprietor: Lee & Dorothy
Rummerfield
Hours: By Appointment,
By Chance
Types & Periods: General
Line, Toys, Depression
Glass, Aladdin Lamps
Specialties: Toys,
Depression Glass, Aladdin
Lamps

Linn

**THE HAVILANDS'
ANTIQUES**
Hwy 50 Box W   65051
314 455-2630   Est: 1969
Proprietor: Van B Haviland
Hours: Weekdays By
Chance & By Appointment
Types & Periods: Bronzes,
Glassware, Porcelains,
Victoriana, Collectibles
Directions: Across from
Linn High School

Linn Creek

**COL BOB'S COUNTRY
FLEA MKT**
Hwy 54   65052
314 346-5033   Est: 1975
Proprietor: Willard Jones
Hours: Mon-Sun
Types & Periods:
Collectibles, Primitives,
Glass, Furniture, Lionel
Trains
Directions: 1 Mile N of
Linn Creek

THE BOTTLE HOUSE
65052
314 346-5890
Types & Periods: Avons,
Bottles, Fruit Jars,
Insulators, Medicines
Directions: Jct of Hwy 54
& St Rd A, 1 Mile N of
Town

LINNCREEK AUCTION
Main St 65052
314 346-5622 Est: 1969
Proprietor: Col Roy
Hansen
Hours: Mon-Sat 1-5,
Closed Sun
Types & Periods: General
Line
Specialties: Antique Auction
Always 7 PM First Sat Night
of Month
Appraisal Service Available
Directions: 3 Miles NE of
Camdenton County Seat
on Hwy 54

Macon

EDNAMAY'S ANTIQUES
203 Jackson 63552
816 385-3021 Est: 1965
Proprietor: Ednamay E
Arnold
Hours: Daily, Closed 1st
Sun Each Month
Types & Periods: General
Line, Collectors Plates,
Furniture
Specialties: Glass, Ceramics,
Collectors Plates

Manchester

CYRIL'S ANTIQUES
730 Manchester Rd 63011
314 227-7617 Est: 1967
Proprietor: Rosemary
Mueller
Hours: Mon-Sat 9:30-5
Types & Periods: General
Line of Furniture, Canopy
Beds, Walnut, Oak, Cherry,
Mahogany
Specialties: China, Silver,
Cut Glass, Art Objects,
Primitives
Directions: Hwy I-270 W
on Manchester Rd, 4 1/2
Miles, Municipality of St
Louis

Marceline

SEEK & FIND ANTIQUES
624 S Chestnut 64658
816 376-3601 Est: 1972
Proprietor: Marjorie
Leopold

Hours: Daily "Live Next
Door, Ring & Wait"
Types & Periods: General
Line, Glassware, Pictures,
Primitives
Specialties: Depression
Glass
Directions: 3 Miles S of
Hwy 36 on Hwy 5, Last
Bldg on St

Mexico

HAN-MAR'S ODD SHOP
Box 291 65265
314 581-5056 Est: 1969
Proprietor: Hanley &
Margaret Jennings
Hours: Daily, By
Appointment, By Chance
Types & Periods: General
Line
Appraisal Service Available
Directions: 2 Miles W of
Mexico on Hwy 22, Turn S
across RR Tracks to 1st
Place on W

**SILVER DOLLAR TRADING
CO**
314 W Love 65265
314 581-0473 Est: 1973
Proprietor: Jim
Stubblefield
Hours: By Appointment
Types & Periods: General
Line
Specialties: Primitive
Furniture
Directions: 1 1/2 Blocks
NW of City Square

Moberly

**ROBINWOOD INN
ANTIQUES & CRAFTS**
Rt 3 Box 232A 65270
816 263-6507 Est: 1974
Proprietor: Dorothy A
Robb
Hours: Wed-Sat 10-5
Types & Periods: Primitives,
Art Glass, Country &
Victorian Furniture
Specialties: Embroidery,
Handmade Quilts
Appraisal Service Available
Directions: 3 1/2 Miles E
of Moberly on Hwy 24, 1
Mile S & 1 Mile E on
Gravel

Montgomery City

FAIRWAY ANTIQUES
Hwy 19 S Box 29 63361
314 564-2247 Est: 1974
Proprietor: Phyllis Bermat
Hours: Daily, By
Appointment, By Chance
Types & Periods: Cut & Art
Glass, Walnut Furniture,
Jewelry, China
Appraisal Service Available
Directions: 6 Miles NW off
I-70 at New Florence
Junction

Mt Vernon

**MELTON'S ANTIQUES &
GIFTS**
Rte 1 Box 59 65712
417 466-3355 Est: 1972
Proprietor: Mrs C W
"Dottie" Melton
Hours: Daily, Weekends,
By Appointment
Types & Periods: Furniture,
Glass, China
Directions: Take Outter Rd
on S Side of I-44 at Hwy
39 1/4 Mile, then S 1/4
Mile

Neosho

**STEVES FURNITURE &
ANTIQUES**
1022 N College 64850
417 451-3287 Est: 1945
Proprietor: Leo H Stueve
Hours: Daily
Types & Periods: Primitives,
Early American
Directions: Hwy 71 & 60,
N Edge of Town

New Franklin

BUSY BEE ANTIQUES
107 E Broadway 65274
816 848-2922 Est: 1970
Proprietor: Robert E
Wingate
Hours: Daily 9-5, Sun 12-4
Types & Periods: General
Line, Wood, Glass,
Primitives
Specialties: Arms & Armor
(Guns)

Appraisal Service Available
Directions: Rte 70 to
Boonville to Rte 5 to
Downtown

Olean

LOLA'S ANTIQUES
65064
314 392-6617
Types & Periods: Glassware,
China, Furniture, Primitives
Directions: 1 Mile Off Hwy
87, 6 Miles from Town

Osage

FRANKLIN'S ANTIQUES
65065
314 348-2611
Hours: April-Nov
Types & Periods: Furniture,
Primitives, Stoneware,
General Line

MALIBU BEACH RESORT
Lake Rd 54-49   65065
314 348-2233   Est: 1965
Proprietor: Phil Tryon
Hours: Mon-Sun
Types & Periods: Kerosene
& Alladin Lamps
Directions: 1/2 Mile off
Hwy 54

Osage Beach

**POVERTY FLATS TRADIN'
POST**
65065
314 348-2202
Hours: By Chance
Types & Periods: General
Line, Primitives, Guns,
Coins, Lamp Parts
Directions: 1 Mile W of
Grand Glaize Bridge in
Poverty Flats Village

Ozark

MAXINES ANTIQUES
Rt 1 Box 165-4   65721
417 587-3795   Est: 1975
Proprietor: Mrs Wilbur
Wilson

Hours: By Appointment,
By Chance
Types & Periods: Oak &
Walnut Furniture, Pressed &
Pattern Glass, Lamps
Specialties: Lamps
Directions: 6 Miles S of
Ozark on Hwy 65

NORMAN'S ANTIQUES
Rte 4 Box 110   65721
417 485-7826   Est: 1970
Proprietor: Norman F
Hicks
Hours: Mon-Sat
Types & Periods: Furniture
(Antiques) Also Manufacture
Reproduction Furniture,
Resilver Mirrors, Refinish
Furniture
Directions: Hwy 65

TIMELESS TREASURES
1601 S 3rd   65721
417 485-7205   Est: 1974
Proprietor: Mary Nell Pruitt
Hours: Daily 10-5, Closed
Sun & Mon
Types & Periods: General
Line of Furniture, Stained
Glass, Brass Beds, Brass,
Copper, Depression Glass,
Primitivoo
Appraisal Service Available
Directions: Jct Bus Rte
65, Hwys F & 14

Pacific

IRON GATE ANTIQUES
129 W St Louis St   63069
314 257-5130   Est: 1970
Proprietor: Ron &
Charlene Sansone
Hours: Tues-Sat 9-4
Types & Periods: Primitives,
Glassware, Furniture,
Advertising
Specialties: Bottles
Directions: 3 Miles W of
Six Flags

Palmyra

RULE'S ROOST
112 E Olive St   63461
314 769-4550   Est: 1968
Proprietor: Mrs Griffin
Rule
Hours: Mon-Sat 10-5, Sun
1-5

Types & Periods: Furniture,
Glass, China, Brass, Copper,
Wood, Tin, Iron
Specialties: Primitives
Directions: Off Hwy 61, 10
Miles N of Hannibal, 125
Miles N of St Louis

Phillipsburg

THE J L RANCH ANTIQUES
Box 664   65722
417 589-6269   Est: 1969
Proprietor: Johnnie A &
Lucille Jones
Hours: Mon-Sun
Types & Periods: American
Oak & Walnut Stoneware
Specialties: Wholesale &
Retail
Directions: 35 Miles E of
Springfield, 9 Miles W of
Lebanon on I-44

Platte City

WELLS B ROOKE
500 Main Box 2366 64079
816 431 6306   Est: 1974
Proprietor: Mary Ann &
Dave Brook
Hours: Wed-Sun, Closed
Mon & Tue
Types & Periods: General
Line, Furniture, Primitives
Appraisal Service Available
Directions: 1 Block E of
Court House & Square

Pleasant Hill

**COUNTRY PEDDLER
ANTIQUES**
Rte 4   64080
816 987-2911   Est: 1968
Proprietor: Mrs Irmgard
Brisendine
Hours: Wed & Sat All Day,
Sun After 1
Types & Periods: Furniture,
Frames, Clocks, China, Cut
& Pressed Glass, Primitives,
Trunks
Directions: Between
Harrisonville & Lee's
Summit, From Hwy 291
Take 58E 3 Miles to "BB",
1½ Miles N

Riverside

THE OLD N' YOU ANTIQUE MART
PO Box 9222   64168
          Est: 1970
Proprietor: Sam Mundorff
Hours: Daily, Weekends
Types & Periods: General
Line, Collectibles
Specialties: Furniture, Glass
Appraisal Service Available
Directions: N of Kansas
City W of 129

Roach

KIRBY'S CLOUD NINE
          65787
314 346-7112
Types & Periods: Lamps,
Miniatures, Glassware,
Pictures, Collectibles
Directions: 5 Miles N of
Town

ROBBIE MORGAN'S ANTIQUES & GIFTS
          65787
314 346-7577
Types & Periods: General
Line
Specialties: Glass, (Pressed
& Carnival)
Directions: 1st Right Turn
Past Niangua Bridge on
Old Hwy 54

Robertsville

WOOD'N THINGS SHOPPE
Rt 1   63072
314 257-2711   Est: 1972
Proprietor: Carole
Holtwick
Hours: By Appointment,
By Chance
Types & Periods: Furniture,
Primitives
Specialties: Refinishing,
Caning, Weaving
Directions: 20 Miles SW of
Six Flags, I-44 to Pacific
Hwy F to Hwy O to
Robertsville, 9 Miles Hwy
N, 3 Miles to House
Across from Mt Olive
Church, Or 5 Miles N of
Lone Dell on N

Rogersville

CURIO SHOP
Rt 2   65742
          Est: 1968
Proprietor: Mrs Charlene
White
Hours: Mon-Sat, Also By
Appointment
Types & Periods: Primitive
Oak, Walnut & Pine
Furniture
Directions: Hwy 60 E from
Springfield to J Hwy, Left
1 Mile then Right 1 Mile

St Charles

AUNT HEIDI'S CORNER
600 S Main   63301
314 946-7494   Est: 1974
Proprietor: Sue & Eric
Herrmann
Hours: Daily, Weekends
9:30-6
Types & Periods: Furniture,
Toys, Quilts, Primitives
Specialties: Glass, (Stained),
Miniatures, Printers Type &
Drawers
Appraisal Service Available
Directions: St Charles
Antique Dist, Old Main St
on the Missouri River

ROUND ROBIN ANTIQUES
714 S Main St   63301
816 724-2284   Est: 1969
Proprietor: Josephine
Laskwitz
Hours: Daily
Types & Periods: Glass,
Silver, Oriental Rugs,
Paintings, Primitives,
Furniture
Appraisal Service Available
Directions: Main St off
Hwy 70

ST CHARLES LIVERY CO
709 S Main   63301
314 723-3901   Est: 1972
Proprietor: Karen
Satterfield
Hours: Tues-Sat 11-4
Types & Periods:
Turn-of-the-Century
Furniture
Directions: Main St
Historic District

St Clair

TOWN & COUNTRY AUCTION
Hwy 30 E   63077
314 629-9951   Est: 1970
Proprietor: Nelle Gibson
Hours: Mon-Sat
Types & Periods: American
Antiques, Glass, Primitives

St Joseph

CREVERLINGS ANTIQUES & TREASURES BOUTIQUE
1125 Charles   64501
816 232-9298   Est: 1969
Proprietor: Dorothy
Creverling Sigears &
Elmer Sigears
Hours: Daily, By
Appointment, By Chance
Types & Periods: Room
Sets, Paintings, China,
Bedroom Sets, Books,
Postcards
Specialties: House Tours
Showing 1st Prize Winner in
1893 World Fair, Victorian
Bedroom Set
Appraisal Service Available
Directions: Across St on N
Side of St Joseph
Museum

DALSING'S
2717 Pear   64503
816 279-9816   Est: 1967
Proprietor: Fred & Mary
Ellen Dalsing
Hours: Mon-Sat, Flea
Market 1st Sun of Month
Types & Periods: American
& English Furniture, Glass,
Lamps, Postcards, Clocks,
Phones, Record Players,
Dolls, Books
Specialties: Depression &
Other Glass, China Cabinets
Appraisal Service Available
Directions: On Hwy 169 E
of 22nd & W of Belt Hwy

GRAY BARN ANTIQUES
6109 N 71 Hwy   64506
816 232-6036   Est: 1969
Proprietor: Helen & Ray
Roberts
Hours: Daily 9-6, Closed
Sun

Types & Periods: Furniture, Glass, Stoneware, Lamps
Specialties: Primitives
Appraisal Service Available

HELEN'S ANTIQUES
1001 N 10th St   64501
816 232-5338   Est: 1972
Proprietor: Helen & Loren Tanner
Hours: Tues-Sat 11-3, By Appointment
Types & Periods: General Line
Specialties: Pattern & Depression Glass, Pottery
Directions: 6 Blocks N of Fredrick Ave

HERYFORD'S ANTIQUES
1201 Penn St   64506
816 279-9347
Hours: By Appointment
Types & Periods: Cut Glass, China, Furniture

IRENE'S ANTIQUES
5304 Frederick Ave 64506
816 232-4526
Hours: Daily
Types & Periods: General Line
Specialties: Primitives
Directions: 1 Mile E of Holiday Inn & I-29

MARTS ANTIQUES
1520 Mitchell Ave   64506
816 232-9566
Hours: Daily
Types & Periods: Collectibles, Furniture, Dishes

PARKER'S HOUSE OF TREASURES
1314 N 4th   64501
816 232-8343
Hours: Tues-Sat 10-4
Types & Periods: Glass, China, Pottery, Primitives, Furniture, Collectibles

TURNER'S ANTIQUES
302 Illinois Ave   64504
816 238-2970
Types & Periods: Oak Furniture, Walnut Dressers, Oak Commodes, Roll Top Desks, Wardrobes, Kitchen Safes, Cabinets

WHITTINGTON'S ANTIQUES
1501 N 3rd St   64505
816 232-7224
Hours: Daily Closed Mon
Types & Periods: General Line

St Louis

ST LOUIS CLUSTER
Directions: Maryland Plaza, St Charles (Outskirts of City)

AARDVARK ANTIQUES
387 N Euclid   63108
314 361-1725   Est: 1972
Proprietor: Candy McCandliss
Hours: Daily 10:30-4:30, Closed Tues
Types & Periods: General Line, Orientals, Bric-a-brac
Directions: St Louis's Central W End, 2 Blocks N of Chase Hotel

BRAUN GALLERIES
10315 Clayton Rd   63131
314 991-1798   Est: 1960
Proprietor: Arthur Braun
Hours: Mon-Sat 10-5
Types & Periods: 19th Century Victorian, English, French, American, Cut Glass, China, Silver, Furniture, Oriental Rugs
Specialties: Jewelry
Appraisal Service Available
Directions: Hwy 40 to Lindberg S to Clayton, W 1/4 Block

DRAPER ANTIQUES
4749 McPherson   63108
314 361-7584   Est: 1973
Proprietor: Mrs Richard Draper
Hours: Daily, Weekends 11-5, Closed Mon
Types & Periods: Oriental, Silver, General Line
Specialties: Oriental
Appraisal Service Available
Directions: 1 Mile NE of Chase Park Plaza Hotel & Forest Park

CLARK GRAVES ANTIQUES
132 N Meramec Ave
                    63105
314 725-2695   Est: 1940
Proprietor: Clark V Graves
Hours: Tues-Fri 9:30-5, Sat 10-4, Closed Sun & Mon
Types & Periods: 18th & 19th Century English & French Furniture, Accessories
Directions: Clayton is Suburb of St Louis to the W

GRAVOIS-ANTIQUES & FLEA MARKET
8003 Gravois   63123
314 353-9818   Est: 1973
Proprietor: Don Underwood
Hours: By Appointment, By Chance, Fri-Mon 10-5
Types & Periods: General Line
Specialties: Furniture
Appraisal Service Available
Directions: From 270 Straight Down Gravois N Hwy 30

THE HAWKEN SHOP
3028 N Lindbergh   63074
314 739-7300
Proprietor: Arthur Ressel
Hours: Mon, Tues, Thurs 10-6, Wed & Fri 10-9, Sat 9-5, Closed Sun
Types & Periods: Military Accoutrements, Weapons, Beer Cans, Guns, Swords
Appraisal Service Available
Directions: N of Page Blvd, S of St Charles Rock Rd

HOMEMAKER FURNITURE & ANTIQUE SHOP
2124 Cherokee St   63118
314 776-4267   Est: 1945
Proprietor: The Heffners
Hours: Daily, Weekends
Types & Periods: "From Finest to Primitive Collectibles"
Appraisal Service Available
Directions: Corner of Cherokee & Missouri Ave S St Louis

St Louis   Cont'd

KINGS ROW GALLERY
13472 Clayton Rd   63131
314 434-7510   Est: 1972
Proprietor: Mrs Walter W
King
Hours: Daily 9:30-5
Types & Periods: Century
English Furniture &
Accessories
Appraisal Service Available
Directions: Clayton at
Mason Rd, W of St Louis,
Mason Rd Exit from US
40, 1 Block S

REGENT PARADE
7731 Clayton Rd   63117
314 727-4959   Est: 1973
Proprietor: Mary Lou
Crockett
Hours: Tues-Sat, Closed
Sun & Mon
Types & Periods: Antique
Furniture, Porcelain, Silver,
Crystal, Jewelry
Appraisal Service Available
Directions: Rte 40 to
Hanley Rd N Exit, First
Major Intersection is
Clayton Rd, Turn Left

**ROTHSCHILD-WOOD
ANTIQUES**
398 N Euclid   63108
314 361-4870   Est: 1969
Proprietor: Peter
Rothschild
Hours: Mon-Sat 9:30-6,
Also By Appointment
Types & Periods: Stained
Glass, Brass Light Fixtures,
Furniture, Jewelry,
Memorabillia
Specialties: Stained Glass
Appraisal Service Available
Directions: Hwy 40 E to N
King Hwy, Left to
McPherson, Right on
Euclid 1 Block to SE
Corner of Euclid &
McPherson

ZIERN GALLERIES INC
10333 Clayton Rd   63131
314 993-0809   Est: 1925
Proprietor: A Ziern
Hours: Tues-Sat, Closed
Sun & Mon
Types & Periods: 18th &
19th Century French,
Englsih & American
Furniture

Sainte Genevieve

MAISON MEMORIES
222 N Main   63670
314 883-7000   Est: 1973
Proprietor: Marjorie Marts
Hours: Daily, Weekends
10-5, Other Hours Call
883-2375
Types & Periods: Furniture,
Pressed & Cut Glass, Hand
Painted China, Bottles,
Primitives, Collectibles, Farm
Tools, Drugstore &
Apothecary Cabinets
Directions: 5 Miles off I-55
in St Genevieve, 2 Blocks
E & 3 Blocks N of Town
Square in Restored 100
Year Old House

**MARY JANE'S ANTIQUES &
GIFTS**
73 N Main St   63670
314 883-5838   Est: 1970
Proprietor: Mary Jane
Jorgensen
Hours: Mon-Sun
Types & Periods: All Types,
Glass, Silver, Dolls, Dolls
Repaired, Lamps & Lamps
Repaired, Chairs Caned,
Old Paintings, Prints,
Primitives
Appraisal Service Available
Directions: 65 Miles S of
St Louis, I -55 to O or
Hwy 32 to St Genevieve
Exit

Salem

KEY ANTIQUES
516 N Main St   65560
314 729-5005   Est: 1968
Hours: Daily, Summer
Closed Sun, Winter By
Chance
Types & Periods: General
Line
Directions: 1/2 Block N of
Square on Hwy 19

Sedalia

**DOROTHY'S ANTIQUES
INC**
1842 S Barrett Ave 65301
816 826-7911   Est: 1964

Proprietor: Dorothy
Lippard
Hours: Daily, Weekends,
By Chance
Types & Periods: General
Line
Specialties: Glass, China,
Crystal, Jewelry
Appraisal Service Available
Directions: S on Hwy 65
to Sambo's, Turn Left go
3 Blocks

Sikeston

LOGAN'S ANTIQUES
Hwy 60 E   63801
314 472-0600   Est: 1971
Proprietor: B L Crenshaw
Hours: Daily
Types & Periods: Furniture,
Primitives, Glassware
Appraisal Service Available

Springfield

SPRINGFIELD CLUSTER
Directions: Scenic Dr to
By-Pass 65, Grand to
Chestnut Expy, Adjacent
Streets College, Elm,
Boonville & Cherry

**BONNIE'S BARGAIN
BRIC-A-BRAC**
800 W Locust   65803
314 862-3373   Est: 1970
Proprietor: Bonnie Mecum
Hours: Wed & Sat Only
Types & Periods: General
Line

CAROUSEL ANTIQUES
4055 W Sunshine   65807
417 866-9130   Est: 1973
Proprietor: Gary Runge
Hours: Daily 10-5
Types & Periods: American
Oak Furniture, Primitives,
Glassware
Specialties: Furniture
Directions: Hwy 60 W

PATCHWORK CORNER
702 E Commercial   65803
417 866-6160   Est: 1974
Proprietor: Jacque & Dale
Wimmer
Hours: Mon-Fri 10-5:30,
Sat 10-4, Closed Sun

Types & Periods: General
Line of Antique Furniture,
Glass, Dolls, Crocks, Jugs
Specialties: Primitives, Iron
& Wooden
Directions: In N Central
Springfield, From I-44, S
on Bus Hwy 65 (Glenstone
Ave) to Commercial St,
Right (W) Approx 10
Blocks

Stover

MAXINE'S ANTIQUES
65078
314 377-4103
Types & Periods: Furniture,
Glass, China, Primitives,
Clocks, Collectibles

Sunrise Beach

GLASS KNOB ANTIQUES
65069
314 374-7666
Types & Periods: Glass,
China, Plates, Pictures,
Stoneware, Brass, Iron,
Primitives, Furniture
Directions: 1/2 Mile S of
Town on Hwy 5 at Lake
Rd 5-37

Sweet Springs

**BROWNSVILLE STATION
ANTIQUES**
226 Main   65351
816 335-6713   Est: 1974
Proprietor: J D & Mary
Robins
Hours: Weekends
Types & Periods: Empire,
Victorian & Early Pine,
Glass, China, Books
Specialties: Furniture
Appraisal Service Available
Directions: 67 Miles E of
Kansas City, I-70

Unionville

DAVIS ANTIQUES
Rte 3   63565
816 344-2351   Est: 1961
Proprietor: Dana D Davis
Hours: Daily
Types & Periods: General
Line
Directions: 1 Mile S of
Lemon, on Gravel Rd

Versailles

BASHORE'S ANTIQUES
Rt 2 Box 119   65084
314 372-6536   Est: 1964
Proprietor: Harvey
Bashore
Types & Periods: Primitives,
Clocks, Glass, China,
Collectibles, General Line
Directions: Off Hwy 5 on
Rte TT, 1/2 Mile S of
Jacob's Cave

Warrensburg

HOHN'S ANTIQUES
213 E Market St   64093
816 747-8258   Est: 1950
Proprietor: Isla M Hohn
Hours: Mon-Sun, By
Appointment, By Chance
Types & Periods: Country
Pine Furniture, Victorian
Walnut, Oak, American,
Brass, Copper, China, Glass,
All Guaranteed Old, No
Reproductions
Specialties: Primitives &
Country Furniture
Appraisal Service Available
Directions: W on Hwy 13
at Market St, Shop is 1/2
Block on Right

Warrenton

RED DOOR ANTIQUE SHOP
714 Steinberger Rd 63383
314 456-8854   Est: 1963
Proprietor: Homer L
Nistendick
Hours: Daily
Types & Periods: Walnut
Furniture, Hanging Lamps,
Dishes
Specialties: Furniture,
(Refinished)
Directions: 1 Block Off
I-70 S Behind Skelly
Station

Washington

**TOWN & COUNTRY
AUCTION**
215 Oak St   63090
314 239-0911   Est: 1970
Proprietor: Nelle Gibson
Hours: Daily 10-4, Closed
Wed
Types & Periods: Furniture,
Glass, General Line
Directions: Downtown, 1/2
Block from Banks

Windsor

LINDA'S LOFT ANTIQUES
108 W Benton   65360
816 647-2822   Est: 1968
Proprietor: Linda Garrison
Hours: Mon-Sat 10-4,
Closed Sun, By
Appointment
Types & Periods: China,
Furniture, Post Cards, Silver,
Jewelry, Primitives
Specialties: Post Cards,
Toothpick Holders
Appraisal Service Available
Directions: Hwys 2 & 52,
Next to City Hall, Across
From Bank

STATE OF MONTANA

Billings

A B'S ANTIQUES
901 Terry Ave   59102
406 252-1706   Est: 1972
Proprietor: Annabelle
Turner
Hours: Daily 12-5, Also By
Appointment
Types & Periods: Furniture,
Glass, Pottery, Primitives
Directions: W on
Broadwater Ave to 9th St,
2 Blocks S

FLEA MARKET
2503 Montana Ave   59101
406 259-0913   Est: 1970
Proprietor: Helyn Neiss &
Harold Hanson
Hours: Tues-Sat 11-5
Types & Periods: Primitives,
Cut Glass, Cans, Books,
Furniture
Specialties: Indian Beadwork
Appraisal Service Available
Directions: Downtown by
Railroad Depot

THE HERITAGE HOUSE
2513 Montana Ave   59101
406 259-6246   Est: 1970
Proprietor: Carney &
Gloria Tod & Esther
Sackman
Hours: Mon-Sat
10:00-4:30, Also By
Appointment
Types & Periods: Glass,
Pottery, China, Furniture,
Toys, Collectibles
Appraisal Service Available
Directions: Right Off 27th
St Exit 1 1/2 Block

LEFLER'S ANTIQUES
1404 Main   59101
406 252-1198   Est: 1966
Proprietor: Gertrude Lefler
Hours: Daily, Also By
Appointment
Types & Periods: Furniture,
Jewelry, General Line
Specialties: Glass (Cut &
Art)
Appraisal Service Available
Directions: Located in
Billings Height's Main St
on Hwy 87, N of Fair
Grounds

Butte

THE ANTIQUE SHOP
108 S Montana   59701
406 792-9008   Est: 1975
Proprietor: Carolyn Lewis
Hours: Mon-Sat 10-5:30
Types & Periods: Victorian,
Walnut, Pine, Oak,
Primitives, Cookstoves,
Heating Stoves
Specialties: Stoves, Heating
& Cooking
Directions: Uptown Butte,
Across the Street from the
Elks

EICHERS ANTIQUES
1926 Texas Ave   59701
406 723-6991
Proprietor: M A & Martha
L Eicher
Hours: By Appointment
Types & Periods: General
Line

GOLDEN LEAF ANTIQUES
19 W Broadway   59701
406 792-5976   Est: 1969
Proprietor: Maxine King
Hours: Mon-Sat 9:30-5:30
Types & Periods: Furniture,
General Line
Specialties: China, Glass
Directions: Uptown

TONYS ANTIQUE STORE
209 E Park St   59701
406 723-9656   Est: 1936
Hours: Daily 8-6
Types & Periods: General
Line
Appraisal Service Available

Galata

THE GENERAL STORE &
ANTIQUE SHOP
                   59444
406 432-2687   Est: 1966
Proprietor: Christabel
Matteson
Hours: Mon-Sat 8:30-5
Types & Periods: General
Line
Directions: Hwy 2 Between
Chester & Shelby, Take
Galata Exit Approx 1/2
Mile N across RR Tracks

Glasgow

DAVE'S USED MART
Hwy 2 W   59230
406 228-8152   Est: 1960
Proprietor: Lovetta J
Prather
Hours: Mon-Sat 9-5
Types & Periods: General
Line
Directions: 3 Miles W of
Glasgow on Hwy 2

Great Falls

THE BET ANTIQUE SHOP
116 Central Ave   59401
406 453-1151   Est: 1957
Proprietor: Gene Bowden
& Doug Carter
Hours: Daily, Weekends
Types & Periods: Art Glass,
Primitives, Jewelry, Clocks,
Furniture, Cut Glass,
Oriental Items, Books, Prints
Appraisal Service Available
Directions: Civic Center
Block, Downtown Main
Street

MONTANA OUTFITTERS
308 Riverview Dr E 59404
406 761-0859   Est: 1965
Proprietor: Lewis E
Yearout
Hours: By Appointment
Types & Periods: Firearms,
Accessories &
Accoutrements
Specialties: Arms
(Winchester & Colt)
Appraisal Service Available

THE TIME SHOP
1524 10th Ave S   59401
406 761-5695   Est: 1970
Proprietor: Theodor
Mroehej
Hours: Daily 9-6
Types & Periods: Clocks,
American, European,
General Line
Specialties: Clocks
(European Grandfather)
Appraisal Service Available
Directions: Main
Thoroughfare N & S

Hamilton

BITTERROOT TRADING POST
910 N 1st 59840
406 363-5950 Est: 1974
Proprietor: Will Neustrom
Hours: Daily
Types & Periods: Oak Furniture, Firearms, Western Americana
Specialties: Western Art, Indian Artifacts, Old West Items
Appraisal Service Available
Directions: Hwy 93 N

Harden

LAMMERS TRADING POST
17 E 4th St 59034
406 665-2605 Est: 1912
Proprietor: Gayle Lammers
Hours: Daily
Types & Periods: Indian Beadwork, Collectors Curios

Helena

BERYL B KAISERMAN
628 Dearborn Ave 59601
406 442-6487
Proprietor: Beryl Kaiserman
Hours: By Appointment
Types & Periods: Silver, Porcelain, Glass, Enamels, Decorative Accessories

Livingston

YELLOWSTONE FLORAL & ANTIQUE SHOP
120 N Main St 59047
406 222-1626 Est: 1959
Proprietor: Jennie Hallowell
Hours: Daily, Closed Sun
Types & Periods: China, Glass, Furniture, Primitives
Directions: On Main St I Block off Hwy

Missoula

A ABLE CO
223 W Railroad 59801
406 721-2999
Proprietor: David Burnhan & Robert Oakley
Hours: Daily 9-5
Types & Periods: General Line, Art, Primitives, Collectibles

AAA MOTIQUES
332 E Broadway 59201
406 543-3193 Est: 1973
Proprietor: Emmett J Burns
Hours: Daily
Types & Periods: Lamps, Clocks, Stoneware, Copper
Directions: 4 Blocks W of Van Buren St Interchange in City Center Motel

GUNS N STUFF
9 Hammond Arcade 59801
406 543-4089 Est: 1972
Proprietor: John E Fox
Hours: Daily
Types & Periods: Firearms & Accessories
Appraisal Service Available
Directions: Downtown

HORSE TRADER ANTIQUES
1920 Russell 59801
Est: 1976
Proprietor: Lew Dacts
Hours: Daily 10-5:30
Types & Periods: Furniture, Glassware, Collectibles

JEAN'S ANTIQUES
1359 W Broadway 59801
406 543-7003 Est: 1969
Proprietor: Lois Jean & Jodie R Walker
Hours: Mon-Sat
Types & Periods: General Line
Specialties: Art Cut Enameled & Cameo Glass, Sterling Silver
Appraisal Service Available
Directions: 13 Blocks W of Higgins Ave

Polson

CAROL'S COUNTRY CORNER
Rte 1 Box 26B 59860
406 883-2940 Est: 1975
Proprietor: Carol Dubay Pastos
Hours: Daily
Types & Periods: Primitives, Glassware, European & American Furniture, Tools, Hardware, Art, Artifacts
Directions: Just Past the "Y" of Hwy 35 & 93, Before the Polson Golf Course

THE MISER MART
505 Main 59860
406 883-4849 Est: 1974
Proprietor: W A Maughan
Hours: Daily 10-5, Closed Suns
Types & Periods: General Line
Directions: 3 1/2 Blocks S of Hwy 93 on Main

Ronan

TRAILS END ANTIQUES
US Hwy 93 59864
406 676-8242 Est: 1976
Proprietor: Karen Vanden Bosch
Hours: Daily, Weekends 10-6, Also By Appointment
Types & Periods: American, Glass
Specialties: Glass, Oak & Primitive Pine
Directions: Next to Lynn's Drive Inn

St Regie

PLACE OF ANTIQUES
Box 2 Hwy 10 59866
406 649-2397 Est: 1974
Proprietor: Rose Gotcher
Hours: Daily, Weekends 10-5
Types & Periods: Oak Furniture, Clocks, Stoves, Depression Glass, Art Glass, Primitives, Collectibles
Directions: Hwy 10 Downtown

PUYEAR'S ANTIQUES
Box 7   59870
406 777-5803
Proprietor: Donald L
Puyear
Hours: Tue-Sat 10-5,
 Also By Appointment
Types & Periods: Furniture
Primitives, Glass,
Collectibles, General Line
Specialties: Furniture,
Primitives

A gentleman's chair, Middle Victorian.

(From page 322B).   Chairs, beds and large cabinets are the most frequently seen pieces of Gothic Revival for use in households.

Elizabethan was revived because of its presumed association with chivalry. This style was shown primarily by use of the spiral twist form, or cork screw shape, so often found on Elizabethan tables and chairs. That spiral is called a "barley twist" today. Although otherwise mentioned, we may attribute the beginning of Victorian turned spool furniture to this period. The various spool turnings may be identified as button, sausage and knob turnings. Spool turnings, a simpler form, were much better suited to machine manufacture than were the barley twists. This revival was not particularly successful in the United States, but spool beds became popular.

The French influence was pronounced during the Early Victorian period. Both the Baroque and Rococo styles were revived in a modified form. French styles were said to promote good conversation. At first the plainer Louis XIV styles were favored but quickly gave way to those of Louis XV. The styles of all three Kings Louis were intermingled in the furniture produced at that time. Development of modern machinery permitted the reproduction of the curves and beautiful lines of the Louis XV which was nicely styled and proportioned. It may well be   (Continued, page 356).

STATE OF NEBRASKA

Ainsworth

JO'S JUNQUE
341 N Pine   69210
402 387-2647
Proprietor: Lyle Irwins
Hours: By Appointment;
By Chance
Types & Periods: Glassware,
Furniture, Primitives,
Collectibles

Ansley

PRICE'S ANTIQUES
RR 2, Box 81   68814
308 935-3510   Est: 1968
Proprietor: Jim & Darlene
Price
Hours: By Appointment;
By Chance
Types & Periods: Furniture,
Oak, Pine, Walnut,
Primitives, Store Fixtures,
Small Items, Farm Items,
Cook Stoves, Heaters
Directions: 2½ Miles S of
Ansley on Hwy 183; Old
Hotel Bldg, Main St of
Ansley

Auburn

IRON KETTLE ANTIQUES
1015 Central Ave   68305
402 274-4212   Est: 1970
Proprietor: Raymond &
Dona Wheeler
Hours: Daily, By
Appointment, Closed Sun
& Mon
Types & Periods: Glass,
China, Lamps, Primitives,
Furniture
Specialties: Furniture
(Refinished)

Beatrice

THE ANTIQUE HUT
916 Herbert St   68310
402 223-3975
Hours: Daily

Types & Periods: China
Glass, Lamps, Primitives
Directions: "Four blocks
W & 2 blocks S of Bike's
Burger Bar on Hwy 77"

CEDAR HILLS ANTIQUES
RFD 4   68310
    Est: 1966
Proprietor: Katherine
Maiwald
Hours: Daily
Types & Periods: Oak, Pine
& Walnut Furniture, Lamps,
Dishes, Mirrors
Specialties: Furniture
Directions: E of Beatrice
Country Club

Bennington

THE ANTIQUE SHOP LTD
17400 State St, RR l
    68007
402 238-2732
Proprietor: Mrs Robert C
Holcombe
Hours: Sun, Wed-Sat, l0-3
Types & Periods: 18th &
19th Centuries English
Country Furniture, Pewter,
Brass, Copper, Soft &
Medium Paste Porcelain,
Primitives
Specialties: Pine
Directions: NW of Omaha
at 174th and State St

Blair

KALICO KEEPING ROOM
ANTIQUE SHOP
1660 Lincoln St   68008
402 426-9691   Est: 1975
Proprietor: Sandra
Simmons
Hours: Mon-Sat l0-4; By
Appointment
Types & Periods: Fine
Antique Furniture, American
Oak, Glass, Jewelry, Printers
Type & Typetrays,
Primitives, Decorating Items
Appraisal Service Available
Directions: One block S of
Main St, Across from the
Library & Safeway Store

Bloomington

MUCKEL'S ANTIQUES
Hwy 136, Main St   68929
308 775-2702   Est: 1958
Proprietor: Barbara E
Muckel
Hours: By Appointment;
By Chance
Types & Periods: Pressed
Glass, Cut Glass, China,
Primitives, Furniture, Musical
Instruments, Player Pianos,
Guns, Tools, Silver, Dolls
Directions: Main Street

Broken Bow

THE ANTIQUE ATTIC
335½ S 10th Ave   68822
308 872-5835
Types & Periods: Glass,
Primitives, Collectibles,
Junque

BITS & PIECES
1240 South E St   68822
308 872-2110
Hours: By Appointment
Types & Periods: General
Line
Specialties: Glass

Brownville

VILLAGE FOLK SHOPPE
Main St   68321
Proprietor: Ruth McCauley
Hours: Sun, Tues-Sat;
Summer Only
Types & Periods: Early
Country Quilts, Hand
Carved Birds
Specialties: Our Original
Calico Fashions

Columbus

EL-BI-GON ANTIQUES
3811 17th St   68601
402 564-8033
Proprietor: Bill & Eleanor
Gonka
Hours: Daily

EL-BI-GON Cont'd
Types & Periods:
Turn-of-the-Century
Specialties: Furniture
  Directions: Hwy 81 or 5
  blocks W of Hwy 30

SUNSET ANTIQUES
  Rte 3, Box 612   68601.
  402 564-2662
Types & Periods: General
Line, "Treasures of
Yesteryear"
  Directions: 4 Miles NW on
  Hwy 81

Cozad

YEUTTER'S ANTIQUES
                    69130
  308 784-2052
  Hours: By Chance
Types & Periods: Furniture,
Glass, Primitives
Specialties: Glass
(Depression)
  Directions: 1½ Miles S, 4½
  Miles W of I-80

Elm Creek

**RAILROAD DEPOT
ANTIQUES**
                    68836
  308 856-4437
Types & Periods: Furniture,
Glass, Primitives, Railroad
Items, General Line
  Directions: One block S of
  Post Office just off Hwy
  30

Fairbury

SINGLETON'S ANTIQUES
  Hwy 136   68352
  402 729-3090
Types & Periods: General
Line, China, Pressed Glass,
Primitives

Fremont

**ANTIQUE SHOP & THIS &
THAT**
  650 E 5th   68025

  502 721-3516   Est: 1968
  Proprietor: Martha Connor
  Hours: Daily
Types & Periods: General
Line, Glass, China,
Primitives, Books, Pictures
  Directions: Corner of 5th
  & Irving Sts

JOHNSON ANTIQUES
  348 N Main St   68025
  402 721-4022   Est: 1976
  Proprietor: Elden & Marge
  Johnson
  Hours: Mon-Sat l0-5:30
Types & Periods: Glass,
China, Furniture, Jewelry,
Primitives
Appraisal Service Available
  Directions: Downtown

**PLAIN & FANCY ANTIQUES
IMPORTS**
  649 N Park   68025
  402 721-0130   Est: 1961
  Proprietor: Lola Mueller
  Hours: Daily 1-7
Types & Periods: American
Furniture, Glassware,
Primitives, Dolls
Specialties: Toys (Dolls)
Appraisal Service Available
  Directions: One block E of
  Hwy 77 on Military St

Goehner

KNISLEY'S ANTIQUES
  Box 85   68364
  402 523-4010
  Hours: Mon-Sat
Types & Periods: Refinished
Furniture, American (No
Imports)
Specialties: Furniture
  Directions: 25 Miles W of
  Lincoln

Grand Island

B & G COLLECTIBLES
  505 N Pine   68801
  308 384-8277   Est: 1977
  Proprietor: Gary W
  Falldorf
  Hours: Mon-Sat 9-5; By
  Appointment; By Chance
Types & Periods: Golden
Oak Era Furniture,
Depression Glass, Pottery,
Primitives,

Turn-of-the-Century to
1950's Collectibles, Beer
Cans
  Directions: 4 blocks N of
  Hwy 30 on Pine St

THE EARLY ATTIC
  380-376 N Walnut St
                    68801
  308 382-3382   Est: 1971
  Proprietor: Bob Miller &
  Glen Vogt
  Hours: Mon-Sat; Closed
  Noon Hour & Sun
Types & Periods: 1880 Oak,
Architectural, Wicker, Store
Display Items, Heirloom
Collectibles
Specialties: Architectural &
General Store Items
Appraisal Service Available
  Directions: 3 Blocks N of
  Hwy 30, N of Railroad
  Tracks

**KEITH'S RED LAMP
ANTIQUES**
  1503 W 4th St   68801
  308 384-7577   Est: 1964
  Proprietor: Roger L Keith
  Hours: Mon-Sat 9-5
Types & Periods: China,
Glassware, Victorian Lamps
Specialties: Lamps
Appraisal Service Available
  Directions: 2 blocks E of
  Broadwell Ave on 4th St

KNUDSEN ANTIQUE SHOP
  920 W 3rd   68801
  308 384-1841
Types & Periods: Glass,
China, Lamps, Primitives
  Directions: One block N of
  Hwy 30

RUTH'S ANTIQUES
  1309 W 3rd St   68801
  308 382-0818   Est: 1964
  Proprietor: Ruth Whitmore
  Hours: Daily
Types & Periods: Dolls,
Furniture, Dishes, Primitives

TED'S ARTISTIQUES
  Valentine's Motel   68801
  308 384-1740
Types & Periods: Art Glass,
China, Furniture
  Directions: One block S of
  Hwy 34 & S Locust

VILLAGE FOLK SHOPPES & STUDIO
1402 W 3rd   68881
308 381-0534   Est: 1960
Proprietor: Ruth McCauley
Hours: Daily, Weekends,
8-4:30
Types & Periods: Country
Primitives

Hastings

BERDINA'S TREASURE TROVE
406 S Maple   68901
402 462-6596   Est: 1974
Proprietor: Berdina A
Dunham
Hours: Daily; By
Appointment; By Chance
Types & Periods: Glassware,
Collectibles
Specialties: Depression
Glass
Directions: Straight W of
Burger King, S Burlington
Ave & 'B' St

CASSELL'S ANTIQUES
227 W 9th   68901
402 462-6451   Est: 1973
Proprietor: Gary P Cassell
Hours: Mon-Sat ll:30-5; By
Appointment
Types & Periods: 1900 Farm
House, General Line,
Watches, Razors, Clocks,
Indian Rugs, Baskets
Appraisal Service Available

FRAN'S ANTIQUES
3019 W 7th   68901
402 462-2877
Hours: After 1 pm
Types & Periods: ''Lovely
things of the past'',
Collectibles & General Line

Holdrege

ANDERSON'S ANTIQUES
136 W 8th Ave   68949
308 995-8148   Est: 1977
Proprietor: Ruth & Glen
Anderson
Hours: Daily
Types & Periods: 1850-1935
General Line
Specialties: Clocks & Dishes
Directions: 3/4 block W of
Hwy 183 on 8th Ave

HUDSON'S ANTIQUES
1422 East Ave   68949
308 995-8774
Hours: Daily; After 5pm or
By Appointment
Types & Periods: ''A little bit
of everything''
Directions: 10 blocks N of
Hotel Dale

LITTRELL'S ANTIQUES
208 Blaine   68949
308 995-5117
Hours: Daily
Types & Periods: General
Line, Glass, China, Clocks,
Iron
Directions: One block W
of Water Tower

LOAR'S ANTIQUES
718 Sherman   68949
308 995-8247
Proprietor: Neil & Hazel
Loar
Hours: Daily; By
Appointment; By Chance
Types & Periods: China,
Glass, Furniture, Primitives
Appraisal Service Available
Directions: 4 blocks N of
Skelly Station

Kearney

BETTY'S ANTIQUES
1310 5th Ave   68847
308 234-3048
Types & Periods: General
Line
Directions: 3 blocks W on
14th St & half block S of
I-80

OLSEN'S ANTIQUES
924 S Central   68847
308 237-5284
Types & Periods: General
Line, Collectibles
Directions: 2 blocks E & l
block S of I-80 Access

Lexington

BARGAIN JOHN'S ANTIQUES
707 S Washington   68850
308 324-4576   Est: 1961
Proprietor: John H Ostrom
Hours: Daily, By
Appointment, By Chance

Types & Periods: Victorian
Furniture
Specialties: Unusual Oak
Furniture
Directions: N from I-80
into Lexington, Left at Y,
3rd Business on Right

WM B FELLENZ ANTIQUES
E Hwy 30   68850
308 324-3024
Types & Periods: General
Line, Collectibles
Directions: ''Next to
Villager''

HANNA'S ANTIQUES
Rte 2 Box 90A   68850
308 324-4719
Types & Periods: General
Line, Furniture
Directions: 6 Miles S of
Town on Hwy 283 or 4
Miles N of Johnson Lake

HAUGH'S ANTIQUES
1610 N Taylor St   68850
308 324-4130   Est: 1962
Proprietor: Rodney Haugh
Hours: By Chance
Types & Periods: Furniture
Specialties: Furniture (Oak)
Directions: NW Part of
Town, N on Hwy 21 to
17th St, l block E

Lincoln

BUNKER HILL ANTIQUES
2345 N Cotner Blvd 68507
402 464-2230
Hours: By Appointment,
Also Wed, Thurs & Sat
12-4:30
Types & Periods: Furniture,
Primitives, Glass,
Advertising, Collectibles

CITY CLOCK COMPANY, INC
210 Gateway North,
PO Box 5187   68505
402 466-8148   Est: 1946
Proprietor: Wayne M
Burkey
Hours: Mon, Tues, Wed &
Fri 8-6, Thurs 8-9, Sat 8-5
Types & Periods: Antique
Clocks, Watches
Specialties: Clock & Watch
Repair

Lincoln Cont'd

CITY CLOCK Cont'd
Appraisal Service Available
Directions: Just E of
Gateway Hinky Dinky
Store, White House with
Black Roof

COACH HOUSE ANTIQUES, INC
135 N 26th   68503
402 475-0429   Est: 1972
Proprietor: Brad Binning
Hours: Mon-Sat; Sun By
Appointment; Eves By
Appointment
Types & Periods: 18th &
19th Centuries Primitives,
American, European
Furniture
Specialties: Brass, Copper,
Art (Oils, Watercolor, Prints),
Art Glass, China
Appraisal Service Available
Directions: 26th & P

THE COUNTRY STORE
2156 S 7th   68502
402 432-2254   Est: 1971
Proprietor: Wayne
Carpenter
Hours: Mon-Sat I0:30-4:30;
Sun 1-4
Types & Periods: Glassware,
Furniture, Primitives,
Postcards
Specialties: Glass
(Depression) & Heisey
Directions: One block S of
South St

FRINGE & TASSEL
722 N 27th   68503
402 475-9861
Hours: Wed-Sun 12-5,
Mon-Thurs Eves 6-8
Types & Periods: General
Line, Carpets, Furniture,
Nostalgia from the 40's &
Earlier
Specialties: Caning, Rockers
Recovered

THE HERITAGE HOUSE
2764 South St   68502
402 475-7281   Est: 1970
Proprietor: Cyvil D Sterner
Hours: Wed-Sat I0-5
Types & Periods: Victorian
Furniture, China, Glass,
Clocks
Specialties: Furniture,
Stained Glass Windows

JO-EM'S NOOK
2710 Vine St   68503
492 477-2993
Hours: Most
Weekends-Sat & Sun I-6
Types & Periods: Books,
Paperbacks, Dishes, Glass,
Miniatures, Jewelry,
Figurines, Linens, Pictures,
Pottery, Prints

KNIGHTS' ANTIQUES & GIFTS
47II Huntington   68504
402 466-2645
Proprietor: Bus & Jo
Knight
Hours: Wed-Sat 11-5; By
Appointment
Types & Periods: General
Line, Collectibles, Primitives,
Stained Glass Windows
Directions: In Plainsman
Center

MARTIN ANTIQUES & ESTATE SERVICES
2125 Winthrop Rd   68502
402 488-5058   Est: 1974
Proprietor: Bruce & Diane
Martin
Hours: Mon-Sat 10-5; By
Appointment
Types & Periods: Art Glass,
Victorian & Early American
Furniture, Fine China,
Primitives, Dolls, Collectibles
Appraisal Service Available
Directions: Rathbone
Village at 32nd & South
Sts, 20 blocks S of 'O'
Street; 10 Min from
Downtown

MILLER JEWELRY
6127 Havelock Ave   68507
402 464-7929
Hours: Daily, Weekends
I0-5:30, Wed Till 8:30,
Closed Sun
Types & Periods: Art & Cut
Glass, Pressed Glass, China,
Jewelry, Watches,
Collectibles

MILLER'S USED FURNITURE, ANTIQUES & DOLLS
2713 N 48th   68502
402 464-2128   Est: 1976
Proprietor: Karl & Karen
Miller
Hours: Mon-Sat 10:30-5:30

Types & Periods: Victorian,
Used Furniture, Knic-Knacs
Specialties: Dolls, Plates,
Sometimes Hummels
Directions: University
Place of Lincoln, near
Nebraska Wesleyan Univ,
'O' St Center of Town 27
blocks N on N 48th St

KEN MITZNER'S RARE COIN CO
6106 Havelock Ave   68507
402 464-3814   Est: 1964
Proprietor: Ken Mitzner
Hours: Daily II-5:30, Sat
9-1, Closed Sun
Types & Periods: Coins &
Supplies, Stamps &
Supplies, Art Glass,
Collectibles, Art, Limited
Editions
Specialties: Refinish all
Metals
Appraisal Service Available
Directions: Next to Jayo
Theater on 61st &
Havelock Ave

KELLY PETERSON'S ANTIQUES
5820 Morrill Ave   68507
402 464-4988
Hours: Daily, Weekends
1-4:30, Closed Sun
Types & Periods: Primitives,
Furniture, Collectibles

PIEDMONT ANTIQUES-PAINT BAR
1265 S Cotner Blvd 68510
402 488-8004
Hours: Daily, Weekends
9:30-5:30, Closed Sun
Types & Periods: General
Line, Victorian, Silver,
China, Pottery
Directions: Piedmont
Shopping Center

PIONEER PEDDLER
127 S 27th   68510
402 435-8153   Est: 1974
Proprietor: Shirley
Haberlan
Hours: Daily I0-4:30,
Closed Sun & Mon
Types & Periods: Pine,
Primitives, Pressed Glass,
Nippon, Art Glass
Directions: 2 Doors S of
27th & 'O' St on W Side
of Street

RAGGEDY ANN'S ANTIQUE & GIFT SHOPPE
1527 N Cotner   68505
402 464-0456   Est: 1970
Proprietor: Anna Mary York
Hours: Mon-Sat, Closed Sun, By Appointment
Types & Periods: Furniture, Primitives, Pine, Full Country Line, Walnut Furniture
Specialties: Miniatures, Doll Houses, Country Style Handmade Gifts
Directions: 10 Blocks N of Gateway Shopping Center

SHIRLEY'S ANTIQUES & THINGS
3903 S 48th   68506
402 483-2166   Est: 1975
Proprietor: Shirley Foster
Hours: Sun, Wed-Fri 1-5, Closed Mon, Tues & Sat; By Appointment
Types & Periods: Victorian Furniture
Directions: Across Street from Union College

SWAPPERS PARADISE
1016 P St   68508
402 477-5580   Est: 1958
Proprietor: Murrell B Johnson
Hours: Daily, Mon-Fri 1:30-4
Types & Periods: General Line
Specialties: Toys & Automata, Marbles
Appraisal Service Available
Directions: Off US 80 Across from Bus Depot

THE VILLAGE STORE
710 'B' St   68502
402 432-8422
Proprietor: Eleanor I Bailey
Hours: Mon-Sat
Types & Periods: General Line, China, Glass, Silver, Furniture, Primitives

WAGON WHEEL ANTIQUES
1541 N Cotner   68505
402 464-6023   Est: 1974
Proprietor: Sheara A Rowden
Hours: Tues-Thurs, Sat
Types & Periods: China, Glassware, Primitives, Pictures, Wicker, Furniture, Collectibles

Specialties: Primitives, Wicker, Fiesta Ware, Depression Glass, Pictures
Directions: 15 blocks N of 'O' St & 66th St in Bethany

YE OLDE CORNER SHOPPE
2350 Sumner   68502
402 477-1664   Est: 1974
Proprietor: Betty Browning & Sally Lee
Hours: Daily, l0-5, Closed Sun
Types & Periods: Furniture, Glassware, Primitives, Pictures, Collectibles
Directions: 24th & Sumner, 4 blocks N of South St

Lisco

THE WEATHERVANE ANTIQUES
          69148
308 772-3329   Est: 1973
Proprietor: Ione Hublou
Hours: By Appointment, By Chance
Types & Periods: General Line, Oak Furniture, Primitives, Collectibles
Directions: On Hwy 26 1 block W of Main St

McCook

HOMESTEAD ANTIQUES
306 W 7th   69001
308 314-3536   Est: 1973
Proprietor: Imogene Moore
Hours: Daily
Types & Periods: General Line
Specialties: Furniture (Primitives & Old Pine)
Directions: First block N of Hwys 6 & 34

RAY'S COINS & ANTIQUES
106 W C St   69001
308 345-6836
Proprietor: Ray & Ardyce Rose
Hours: Daily, 11:30-5:30, Closed Sun
Types & Periods: China, General Line

Melbeta

CAMPBELL'S ANTIQUES
Box 46, Main St   69355
308 783-1518   Est: 1972
Proprietor: Orland or Edna Campbell
Hours: Daily 9-5, Closed Sun
Types & Periods: Furniture, Glass, China, Brass, Iron, Crockery, Wood, Indian Items
Specialties: Unique Items, Old Items before 1900
Directions: Located on Hwy 92, 8 Miles E of Gering

Minden

THE HOUSE OF ANTIQUES
          68959
308 832-2200
Hours: Daily 10-10
Types & Periods: "Yesterday's heirlooms-Today's Treasures"
Directions: 1/2 Mile N of Pioneer Village

Nebraska City

PHILLIPS ANTIQUES
218 S 11th   68410
402 873-7050   Est: 1961
Proprietor: Bernice M Phillips
Hours: Daily 9-5, During Summer Sun 1-5, By Appointment
Types & Periods: Pressed, Cut, Depression, Carnival & Art Glass, Wedgwood, Haviland, Bavarian China, Primitives, Furniture
Specialties: China, Glass
Appraisal Service Available
Directions: 2 blocks S of Main St on Hwy 73-75

YE OLDE JUNQUE SHOPPE
S 11th St   68410
402 873-5336   Est: 1965
Proprietor: Ronald Chapin
Hours: 10-5, Closed Mon

YE OLDE JUNQUE SHOPPE   Cont'd
Types & Periods: General Line, Old Car Parts
Specialties: Furniture & Metal Stripping
  Directions: S Hwy 73-75

Norfolk

BENTZ ANTIQUES
  830 S 9th St   68701
  402 371-1516
  Hours: After 5, Weekends, Also by Appointment
Types & Periods: China, Pattern Glass, Lamps, Furniture
  Directions: 4 blocks E & 2 N of Holiday Inn

North Bend

RAND'S ANTIQUES
  Hwy 30   68649
  402 652-3384
  Hours: Daily
Types & Periods: General Line, Furniture, China, Pattern Glass, Gadgets
  Directions: 2 miles E of Town

North Platte

POTTS ANTIQUES
  419 West 4th   69101
  308 532-0900   Est: 1969
  Proprietor: Jim & June Potts
  Hours: By Appointment, By Chance
Types & Periods: General Line
Appraisal Service Available
  Directions: 4 blocks W of Courthouse

THIS OLE HOUSE ANTIQUES
  2019 W Rodeo Rd 69101
  308 532-1815
Types & Periods: General Line
  Directions: Rodeo Rd & Hwy 30

WEITZEL'S ANTIQUES
  2903 W 9th   69101
  308 532-9479
Types & Periods: General Line, China, Pattern & Cut Glass, Brass, Copper, Furniture
  Directions: "Watch for signs on W Hwy 30, then 1 block S"

THE YESTERDAY SHOPPE
  320 William   69101
  308 534-3601
  Proprietor: Murena Howard
  Hours: Daily
Types & Periods: General Line
Specialties: Glass (Goblets)
  Directions: 3 blocks W of Hwy 83

Omaha

ANTIQUARIUM ANTIQUES
  1215 Harney St   68102
  402 341-8077   Est: 1975
  Proprietor: Jan Sanford
  Hours: Mon-Sat 10:30-8, lst Sun of Month 2-8
Types & Periods: General Line
  Directions: 2nd Floor just around corner from Omaha's Old Market

THE ANTIQUE BROKERAGE
  8320 Blondo   68134
  402 392-2324   Est: 1975
  Proprietor: John & Colleen Sullivan
  Hours: Sun, Wed-Sat; Closed Mon & Tues
Types & Periods: American Furniture, Oak, Walnut, Pine, 1850-1930, European Furniture
Specialties: Salvage Architectural Items & Reproduction Brass Hafdware Fittings
  Directions: Call for specific location of personal interests

BEAUTY & THE BEAST
  5011 Leavenworth St
                        68106
  402 551-6155   Est: 1972
  Proprietor: John & Joyce Petkosek

  Hours: Tues-Fri 10-4, Sat 12-4, Closed Sun & Mon
Types & Periods: Turn-ofthe-Century American Oak, 18th, 19th & 20th Centuries Clocks, Architectural Items
Specialties: Stained Glass Windows
Appraisal Service Available
  Directions: 60th St Exit off I-80 N to Leavenworth

COSGROVE AUCTION
  3805 Leavenworth 68105
  402 342-5254   Est: 1934
  Proprietor: Leila M Cosgrove
  Hours: By Appointment, By Chance
Types & Periods: General Line
Specialties: Estate Auctions
Appraisal Service Available
  Directions: 8 blocks S of Dodge St

DREW'S ANTIQUES & ART OBJECTS INC
  400 S 39th St   68131
  402 342-8464   Est: 1928
  Proprietor: Jack & Louis Drew
  Hours: Daily 8-5, Closed Sun
Types & Periods: General Line, Imports, American
Appraisal Service Available
  Directions: Corner 39th & Harney

FROSTED LION ANTIQUES
  2204 S 13th St   68108
  402 342-4711   Est: 1965
  Proprietor: Dick & Shirley Bombard
  Hours: Sun 1-4, Wed-Sat 10-4, Eves Call 291-0344
Types & Periods: Victorian Walnut & Oak Furniture, Glass
Specialties: Art Glass, Tiffany & Galle
  Directions: 13th St Exit off I-80 W; 13th St N Exit off I-80 E, 1/2 Mile from exit

GINGER JAR ANTIQUES
  8604 N 30th St   68112
  402 455-2529   Est: 1973
  Proprietor: Ginger Johnson
  Hours: Mon-Sat 11-4
Types & Periods: 1890-1910 Glass, China, Dolls, Bottles,

Postcards, Prints, Some
Furniture, Small Collectibles
Appraisal Service Available
  Directions: 3 blocks S of
  Mormon Bridge

**HONEST JOHN'S
EMPORIUM**
  1210 Howard   68102
  402 345-5078   Est: 1966
Proprietor: John Ruggiero
Hours: Daily, Weekends,
  By Appointment
Types & Periods: General
Line
Appraisal Service Available
  Directions: "Old Market
  Area" near Downtown

**JOELLA'S
HOUSE-ANTIQUES &
HEIRLOOMS**
  512 N 40th St   68131
  402 553-2399   Est: 1974
Proprietor: Joella Cohen
Hours: Fri-Sun 1-5, By
  Appointment
Types & Periods: Art Glass,
China, Furniture, Beer
Steins
Specialties: Clocks,
Watches, Beer Steins
Appraisal Service Available
  Directions: 5 blocks N of
  Dodge, Take Dodge St
  Exit off 480, W to 40th,
  then N; Area's only Dinner
  Auction, Held Second
  Tues of Feb, April, June,
  Aug, Oct & Dec at Omaha
  Elks Club, 75th & Hickory

KATELMAN COMPANY, INC
  144 S 30th St   68131
  402 551-4388   Est: 1972
Proprietor: Rick & Jenelle
  Katelman
Hours: Daily, By
  Appointment Eves
Types & Periods: European
& American Antiques
Specialties: Furniture,
Lamps, Chandeliers, Custom
Built Stained Glass
(Windows & Lamps)
  Directions: NW Corner of
  39th & Farnam Sts

**KIRKNER JEWELRY &
ANTIQUES**
  4805 S 24th   68107
  402 731-7475   Est: 1968
Proprietor: Clifford &
Lorraine Kirkner
Hours: Daily

Types & Periods: General
Line, Glass, Furniture,
Jewelry
Appraisal Service Available
  Directions: 24th St Exit S
  to M St from I-80

MOORE'S OF OMAHA
  5220 Ames Ave   68104
               Est: 1962
Proprietor: Al Moore
Hours: Daily, Closed Sun
Types & Periods: General
Line
Specialties: Coins
Appraisal Service Available

NEW CITY CAMP GROUND
  4095 S 84th St   68127
  402 339-0800   Est: 1971
Proprietor: Bill Barnard
Hours: Daily, Weekends,
  By Chance
Types & Periods: General
Line
Specialties: Farm Primitives
  Directions: I-80

PATHFINDER ANTIQUES
  1008 Howard   68102
  402 344-4949.   Est: 1973
Proprietor: Virgil & Faye
  Patterson
Hours: Daily, Also Eves
Types & Periods: Furniture,
Primitives, Glass, China
  Directions: Omaha's Old
  Market, 10th & Howard

THINGS GALORE
  3907 Leavenworth St
                  68105
  402 346-1500,
  346-1503   Est: 1965
Proprietor: W E Cady
Hours: Daily 12-4, except
  Sun, By Appointment
Types & Periods: General
Line, Small Collectibles,
Political Buttons, Postcards
  Directions: 8 blocks S of
  main thoroughfare at
  39th St

WAREHOUSE ANTIQUES
  3508 South 168th St
                  68130
  402 330-3947   Est: 1974
Proprietor: Larry & Judy
  Brown
Hours: By Chance
Types & Periods:
Turn-of-the-Century Oak
Furniture, Some Original,

Some Refinished, Stock
Pine and Walnut Furniture
Specialties: Furniture,
Primitives, Collectibles
  Directions: Located
  Western edge of Omaha
  1/2 Mile S of 168 &
  Center Streets

**WOODEN WAYS & OLDEN
DAYS**
  2823 S 87th   68124
  402 393-2607   Est: 1974
Proprietor: Robert &
Jeanne Smith
Hours: Daily, Weekends
Types & Periods: Clocks,
Furniture
Specialties: Furniture,
(Refinishing & Repair)
  Directions: S of Center St

O'Neill

ETOYLE'S ANTIQUES
  117 S 9th   68763
  402 336-2285
Types & Periods: Furniture,
Glass, Primitives

ROONEY'S ANTIQUES
  119 N 6th Apt 6   68763
  402 336-2751
Hours: By Appointment
Types & Periods: General
Line

Ord

**CEDARCREST FARM
ANTIQUES & AUCTIONS**
  204 S 14th St   68862
  308 728-3026   Est: 1971
Proprietor: Mr & Mrs
Eldon C Buoy
Hours: Daily 9:30-5:30
Types & Periods: Furniture,
Primitives, Collectibles,
China, Glass
Appraisal Service Available
  Directions: Hwy 11 in
  Downtown

Pawnee City

THE DUGOUT ANTIQUES
 600 G St   68420
 402 852-2203
 Proprietor: Bill Edwards
 Hours: By Appointment
Types & Periods: Complete
Line of Collectibles
Specialties: Primitives
Appraisal Service Available
 Directions: On Main St

Pierce

ANTIQUES MARTELLE
 222 W Main   68767
 402 329-6351
 Proprietor: L D Martelle
 Hours: Daily
Types & Periods: General
Line, Pattern Glass, Lamps,
Primitives
Specialties: Pattern Glass,
Lamps, Primitives
Appraisal Service Available
 Directions: NE Nebr 5
 miles W of US 81, NW of
 Norfolk, W on State 13 (W
 of Chevrolet)

Plattsmouth

BETTY'S BIT OF ANTIQUES
 648 Main St   68048
 402 296-3860   Est: 1971
 Proprietor: Betty Lindquist
 Hours: Daily 10-6 Closed
 Sun
Types & Periods: Lamps,
Furniture, Leaded Windows,
Glassware, Primitives, Brass,
Copper, Toys, Frames
 Directions: S of Omaha,
 18 miles on Hwy 73 & 75

St Paul

DOT'S ANTIQUES
 613 Howard   68873
 308 754-5201
Types & Periods: Glass,
Primitives, Furniture, "The
shop of Country
Collectibles"

Seward

BIVIN'S ANTIQUES
 8 N First St   68434
 402 643-4610
 Hours: By Chance
Types & Periods: General
Line, Glass, China,
Primitives, Dolls

Superior

TREASURE HOUSE
 Hwy 14 N   68978
 402 879-4125   Est: 1966
 Proprietor: Ray & Barbara
 Norris
 Hours: Daily 9-5, Closed
 Sun
Types & Periods: Glass,
China, Primitives, Furniture
Appraisal Service Available
 Directions: E of Hwy 14, N
 Edge of Town

Sutton

ALLES ALT ANTIQUES
 Hwy 6   68979
 402 773-4242
 Hours: Daily, By
 Appointment
Types & Periods: General
Line, Collectibles
 Directions: 2 blocks N of
 Cafe

York

**MRS W ARNOLD
REFSHAUGE**
 503 Thompson Ave 68467
 402 362-3502
Types & Periods: Glass,
China, Dolls, Primitives,
Clocks, Collectibles
 Directions: 6 blocks E
 from NE Corner of
 Courthouse Sq

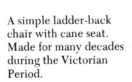

A simple ladder-back
chair with cane seat.
Made for many decades
during the Victorian
Period.

STATE OF NEVADA

East Las Vegas

MOM'S ANTIQUES
5902 Boulder Hwy   89122
Types & Periods: General
Line, Collectibles

VILLAGE ANTIQUES
5947 Boulder Hwy   89122
702 451-5258
Hours: Daily
Types & Periods: Chairs,
Clocks, Scales, Furniture

Elko

SUNSHINE HOUSE
1033 Idaho St   89801
702 738-7418   Est: 1972
Proprietor: Robert W
Millard
Hours: Tues-Sat, 1-5;
Closed Sun & Mon
Types & Periods: Primitives,
Oak, Collectibles
Directions: I-80 or U S 40
Main St

Fallon

COLLECTOR'S CORNER
E Center   89406
702 423-2706   Est: 1969
Proprietor: Ethel Lucille
Clayton
Hours: Mon-Sat
Types & Periods: Antiques &
Collectibles
Directions: Two Blocks
from Hwy 50, South Two
Blocks From South Main,
East

Gardnerville

**PURPLE BOTTLE
ANTIQUES**
1400 S Hwy 395   89410
702 782-3054   Est: 1967
Proprietor: Bill & Betty
Evans
Hours: Mon-Sat, 9-5; Sun
& Holidays By
Appointment

Types & Periods: 1800 to
present Furniture, China,
Glass, Bottles, Insulators,
Collector's Items, Jewelry
Primitives, Lamps, Records,
Books
Specialties: Primitives, Lamp
Parts
Appraisal Service Available
Directions: South End of
Main Street, Hwy 395

Henderson

**U-NAMIT ANTIQUE &
COLLECTOR'S SHOP**
334 Water   89015
702 564-2157   Est: 1969
Proprietor: Mr & Mrs L E
Steiger
Hours: Mon, Tues, Wed,
Fri, Sat, 11-5; Sun 1-5;
Closed Thurs & 1st Sun of
each Month
Types & Periods: Furniture,
China, Glass, Collectibles
Specialties: Turn-of-the
Century Americana
Directions: 15 Minutes
From Las Vegas or
Hoover Dam; Center of
Town

Incline Village

VILLAGE ANTIQUES
754 Mays Blvd   89450
702 831-1288   Est: 1973
Proprietor: Mr & Mrs
Thomas R Zellers
Hours: Tues-Sat, 12-5;
Sun & Mon By
Appointment
Types & Periods: American &
European Furniture, Jewelry,
Art Glass, Indian & Persian
Turquoise Jewelry
Appraisal Service Available
Directions: Village
Shopping Center

Las Vegas

LAS VEGAS CLUSTER
Directions: Along E
Charleston Blvd
(1000-2000 Blocks)
Intersected By Main St
(N-S) & Fremont St; Also
Adjacent Streets of
Carson, Bridger, Clark,
Las Vegas Blvd

A TO Z MART
1223 South Main   89104
702 382-5047   Est: 1966
Proprietor: Al Steward
Hours: Mon-Sat
Types & Periods: Furniture
in Oak, Mahogany & Walnut
Specialties: Largest
Selection of Furniture in Las
Vegas in Antiques &
Collector's Period
Directions: Between The
Strip and Downtown

ABBOT'S ANTIQUES
1661 C E Charleston
                    89104
702 386-5952
Types & Periods: General
Line

ANTIQUES UNLIMITED, INC
212-214 W Sahara   89102
702 384-2338   Est: 1976
Proprietor: Sheila
Goodman
Hours: Mon-Sat, 10-7; Sun
12-5
Types & Periods: Primitives,
Victorian, Furniture, Oriental,
Collectibles, Glass, Jewelry
Appraisal Service Available
Directions: One Block W
of the Sahara Hotel; Next
Door to the Library
Restaurant in Enchanted
Village

**AULD COUNTRY CORNER,
INC**
1626 E Charleston Blvd
                    89104
702 382-3716   Est: 1974
Proprietor: Gail Dixon &
Jean Williams
Hours: Mon-Sat
Types & Periods: General
Line, Collectibles, Primitives

Las Vegas   Cont'd

AULD COUNTRY   Cont'd
Appraisal Service Available
Directions: On South Side
of Charleston Blvd
Between Maryland
Parkway and Boulder
Highway

**BUZZ AND COMPANY FINE
ANTIQUES**
2026 East Charleston
     89104
702 382-2777   Est: 1974
Proprietor: Dave C Wells
Hours: Mon-Sat,
10:30-5:30; By
Appointment
Types & Periods: 18th &
19th Century Fine
Porcelains, 1890-1920
Lighting Lamps,
Chandeliers, Fine French
Furniture, Continental Line
in General
Appraisal Service Available
Directions: In Antique
Square, Only One in Las
Vegas; Las Vegas Strip to
Charleston, Go East for 15
Blocks

DREAM FACTORY
806 Las Vegas Blvd S
     89101
702 386-2963
Types & Periods: General
Line, Furniture

THE GLASS SHACK
1626 E Charleston   89104
702 382-3716   Est: 1978
Proprietor: Violet Henze
Hours: Mon-Sat
Types & Periods: Antique
Glass
Specialties: Heisey and
Collectible Glass

**THE GRAND ANTIQUE
SHOP**
3645 Las Vegas Blvd S
     89109
702 736-2682   Est: 1974
Proprietor: Gallery Shops,
Inc
Hours: Daily, 10 am to 12
pm
Types & Periods: Clocks,
Furniture, Jewelry, Art Work,
Brass Beds, Pianos,
Chandeliers, Crystal

Appraisal Service Available
Directions: In Arcade of
MGM Grand Hotel

GRANDMA'S ANTIQUES
217 E Bridger Ave   89101
702 382-1501   Est: 1973
Proprietor: Barbara H Kent
Hours: Daily, 12-5:30
Types & Periods: Furniture,
China, Glass, Collectibles
Directions: Downtown,
Across from County
Courthouse

HABITAT'R
1626 E Charleston   89101
702 382-3716
Types & Periods: Framed &
Unframed Paper,
Collectibles, Prints

HOUSE OF ANTIQUES
1334 Las Vegas Blvd S
     89104
702 382-1520   Est: 1974
Proprietor: Joseph
Piersanti
Hours: Mon-Sat, 10-6
Types & Periods: Furniture,
Glass, China, Clocks
Appraisal Service Available
Directions: On the Strip
Between Sahara Ave &
Charleston Blvd

**MARY'S DEN OF
ANTIQUITY**
1701 East Charleston
     89104
70 2 384-9053   Est: 1976
Proprietor: Mary Malin
Hours: Mon-Sat, 10-5:30;
Closed Sun
Types & Periods: Jewelry,
Art Glass, Porcelains,
Miniatures, Furniture,
Primitives to Period Pieces
Specialties: The Difficult to
Find Antique's
Appraisal Service Available
Directions: 17th and East
Charleston Blvd

ODD SHOP ANTIQUES
57 E Hacienda Road
     89109
702 736-2724   Est: 1948
Proprietor: Edith Giles
Barcus
Hours: Mon-Sun, By
Chance

Types & Periods: Oriental,
Brass, Porcelain, Glass,
China, Lamps, Dishes,
Furniture, Jewelry
Appraisal Service Available
Directions: Hacienda &
Giles Ave; Across from
Hotel Hacienda

PARKINS, LTD
2028 E Charleston   89104
702 382-2080
Types & Periods: Oriental
Appraisal Service Available

POW WOW TRADING POST
2211 S Maryland Parkway
     89104
702 732-9393   Est: 1974
Proprietor: Margaret &
Derry Parker
Hours: Mon-Sat, 9-6;
Types & Periods: Relics of
Southwestern Mining Towns;
Indian Jewelry
Specialties: Jewelry
Appraisal Service Available
Directions: One Block N
Off Sahara Ave

Minden

IRON FENCE ANTIQUES
1495 Hwy 395   89423
702 782-2813   Est: 1966
Proprietor: Jean
Millholland
Hours: Mon, Tues, Wed,
Fri, 11-5:30; Closed Thurs
Types & Periods: China,
Glass, Furniture, Pottery
Specialties: Glass,
(American Pattern)
Appraisal Service Available
Directions: Main St thru
Town

Reno

DEN OF ANTIQUITY
77 S Wells   89509
702 322-5213   Est: 1972
Proprietor: Neva M
Gardner
Hours: Open Tues thru
Sat
Types & Periods: Small
Furniture, Primitives,
Glassware, Collectibles,

Specialties: Cut and Pressed
Glass
Directions: Corner of Mills
St & Wells Ave

**FAUST'S ANYTHING
COLLECTABLE**
265 Golden Lane   89502
702 322-4644   Est: 1974
Proprietor: Bob & Bonnie
Faust
Hours: Daily, Weekends;
By Chance
Types & Periods: General
Line
Specialties: Glass, Small
Collectibles
Directions: Two Blocks
East of Kietzke; N off Mill;
Last Bldg on Left

ICE HOUSE ANTIQUES
310 Spokane Street 89512
702 322-6116   Est: 1972
Proprietor: Sam & Beebe
Savini
Hours: Mon-Sat, 10-5
Types & Periods: Restored
Furniture, Mostly American,
Selected European, Oriental,
Indian Baskets
Specialties: Custom
Restoring
Appraisal Service Available
Directions: Off East 4th,
Two Blocks East of Wells
Overpass

THOMSON'S ANTIQUES
76 Court St   89501
702 323-3341   Est: 1970
Proprietor: Charles
Thomson
Hours: Mon-Sat, 11-6;
Also By Appointment
Types & Periods: Antique
Furniture, Both Domestic
and Imported, principally
from England; China,
Clocks, Dressing Tables,
Chests of Drawers
Specialties: Marble Top
Wash Stands, Hall Trees,
Wardrobes, Brass Beds, Iron
Beds, Desks, Bookcases,
Dining Tables, Chairs
Appraisal Service Available
Directions: Across Court
Street South From Heart
East Downtown Reno;
(Washoe County
Courthouse, Corner
Virginia & Court Street)

TREASURES ET CETERA
3434 Lakeside Dr   89509
702 825-0514   Est: 1973
Proprietor: Cornelia
Rhodes & Emma Petersen
Hours: Mon-Sat, 10-5:30
Types & Periods: 'Little Bit
of Everything'
Specialties: Silver, Copper,
Brass
Directions: Moana W
Shopping Center;
Lakeside Drive & Moana

Tonopah

THE ODD SHOP
Box 1086   89049
702 482-3548   Est: 1969
Proprietor: Mary Ann
Risley
Hours: Mon-Fri; By
Appointment
Types & Periods: China,
Pressed Glass, Collectibles,
American Furniture
Directions: Downtown

Virginia City

COMSTOCK ANTIQUES
N End A St   89440
702 847-0626
Proprietor: Aileen
Jacobsen
Hours: By Appointment;
By Chance
Types & Periods: Primitives,
Furniture, China, Glass,
Jewelry, Paintings

**HERITAGE HOUSE
ANTIQUES**
48 S B St   89440
702 847-0255   Est: 1965
Proprietor: Lorraine Gipe
Hours: Daily, Most
Weekends
Types & Periods: Furniture,
Lamps, Glass, China,
Jewelry, General Line
Specialties: Signed Tiffany
Webb & Acron; Signed
Tiffany 12 Shade Tulip Lamp
Directions: One Block
From Main St in Old
Virginia City; Water
Company Bldg.

**SILVER STOPE ANTIQUE
SHOP**
25 North 'C'   89440
702 847-0255   Est: 1965
Proprietor: Lorraine Gipe
Hours: Sun, Tues, Wed,
Thurs, Sat
Types & Periods: China, Cut
Glass, Pressed Glass,
Furniture, Jewelry,
Collectibles
Appraisal Service Available
Specialties: Tiffany Lamp
(Webb & Acron), Pairpoint
Puffy Lamp, Hummel
Collectibles
Directions: Main Street
'C'; Right on the Highway
through Virginia City

**VIRGINIA CITY TRADING
POST**
23 C St   89440
702 847-0676   Est: 1970
Proprietor: Bill & Dona
Epperson
Hours: Daily; Closed Nov
thru April
Types & Periods: General
Line

Wadsworth

WADSWORTH ANTIQUES
Box 38   89442
702 329-7047   Est: 1943
Proprietor: Evelyn Kubler
Hours: By Appointment;
By Chance
Specialties: Indian Artifacts
Directions: 30 Miles E of
Reno (I-00)

Zephyr Cove

HAAS ANTIQUES, LTD
Box 209   89448
702 588-2520   Est: 1973
Proprietor: Otto & Eileen
Haas
Hours: Mon-Sat, 10-5:30;
Sun By Appointment
Types & Periods: English
Silver, Victorian Sterling,
Bronzes, Art Objects
Specialties: Waterford
Crystal

HAAS ANTIQUES   Cont'd
Appraisal Service Available
  Directions: Inside Round
  Hill Village Shopping Mall,
  Two Miles from
  Southshore Stateline
  Hwy 50

**STONE'S ANTIQUES &
COLLECTIBLES**
  Box 1525   89448
  702 588-4292   Est: 1971
  Proprietor: Patricia &
  George Stone
  Hours: Mon-Sat 11-5
Types & Periods: Cut Glass,
Silver, Jewelry, Oriental
Objects, Tiffany Style
Lamps, Bronzes
  Directions: 1 1/2 Miles E
  of State Line; S Shore of
  Lake Tahoe, In Round Hill
  Village Mall

A lady's chair, Middle
Victorian.

(From page 344).   the most beautiful of Victorian furniture. It is characterized by elaborate hand carvings crisply and
deeply done in the wood. Chairs and sofas were beautifully curved
and the "finger roll" design was very popular on parlor pieces.
Primary woods used in this furniture were the beautiful rosewoods,
mahoganies and walnuts. However, birds-eye maple, zebra, chest-
nuts and many others were also used. The proper parlor of the
Victorian time might consist of the marble topped table placed in
the center of the room, a three-seat sofa, a gentleman's chair, a lady's
chair and several side chairs.

Between 1844 and 1863, an immigrant to New York, John
Henry Belter, became a very famous cabinetmaker. He began his
business about the time Duncan Phyfe retired. Belter formed curved
backs and arms for his furniture by laminating together thin layers
of rosewood and then steam warping them. This was something
brand new, and it anticipated our plywood of today. His elaborately
carved open fretwork is very ornate and was made possible by the
strength created in his process. His pieces were both strong and
lightweight. His designs were of the most elegant proportions. The
high, curved, balloon backed sofas   (Continued, page 404).

STATE OF NEW HAMPSHIRE

Alexander

COLE HILL FARM ANTIQUES
03222
603 744-8768   Est: 1961
Proprietor: Harold &
Harriet Bennett
Hours: Daily, 10-5 During
July & Aug; Other Times
By Appointment
Types & Periods: English
Period Furniture, Pewter,
English Paintings & Prints
Specialties: Pewter
    Directions: 7 Miles From
    Bristol

Alton

FLEUR DE LIS ANTIQUES
Rte 11   03809
603 875-6555   Est: 1956
Proprietor: Audrey S
Ritchie
Hours: 7 Days a Week
Types & Periods: Pattern &
Art Glass, China, Primitives,
Jewelry, Clocks
Specialties: Clock Repair
    Directions: Rte 11
    Between Alton & Alton
    Bay

S & D ANTIQUES
Box 146 Ave   03809
603 875-2180   Est: 1973
Proprietor: Dorothy Rollins
Hours: Daily, 'Open All
Year'
Types & Periods: Glass,
China, Clocks, Coins,
Jewelry, Furniture, Primitives
    Directions: 1/4 Mile N of
    Rotary, Rte 11 Next to
    Cemetery

Amherst

BLUE SPRUCE ANTIQUES
Rte 101   03031
603 673-2752
Proprietor: The
Halverson's
Hours: Daily, 10-5; By
Appointment or By
Chance
Types & Periods: General
Line

THE CARRIAGE SHED
Walnut Hill Road,
Rte 2   03031
603 673-2944   Est: 1954
Hours: Daily, Weekends,
10-5; Closed Wed; Winter
Thurs-Sun, 1-5
Types & Periods: Primitives,
Country, General Line
Specialties: Clocks,
Primitives
    Directions: Rte 101 1st
    Road on Rt After Horace
    Greeley Rst

CRICKET FARM ANTIQUES
Boston Post Road   03031
603 673-4154   Est: 1968
Proprietor: Lyna Mueller
Hours: Sun-Sat, By
Appointment or By
Chance
Types & Periods: Period
Furniture, Glass and China
Specialties: English
Porcelain and Pottery,
1750-1850
Appraisal Service Available
    Directions: 2 Miles South
    of the Village Big Red
    Barn

THE HALVERSON'S
Rte 101   03031
603 673-2752   Est: 1964
Proprietor: Dick & Fran
Cherry
Hours: Sun-Sat, By
Appointment or By
Chance
Types & Periods: Primitives,
Country Funiture,
Accessories
Appraisal Service Available
    Directions: Between
    Milford and Manchester

OUTDOOR ANTIQUES MARKET
Rte 122   03031
603 673-2093
Proprietor: Dick Douglas
Hours: Sun, May Thru Oct
& Holidays, 9-4
Types & Periods: 100
Exhibitors, Antique Auto
Swap Last Sun of the
Month; Indoor & Outdoor
Displays

THERESA AND ARTHUR GREENBLATT
Box 276   03031
603 673-4401   Est: 1965
Proprietor: Theresa &
Arthur Greenblatt
Hours: Open Year Round,
Prior Phone Call
Advisable; By Chance
Types & Periods: Glass,
Paperweights, Silver,
Needlework
Appraisal Service Available

Andover

THE BARN
Meadowlark Lane   03216
603 735-5449
Proprietor: Alycia Lyons
Types & Periods: 'This,
That, and the Other Thing'
    Directions: Rear of
    Andover Meadow Motor
    Inn, Rtes 4 & 11

Ashland

FERN ROCK ANTIQUES
Common Man Restaurant
Main St   03217
603 536-2131
Proprietor: Gloria Searles
Hours: Sun-Sat,
11:30-10:00, Year Round
Types & Periods: New
Hampshire Furniture From
Primitive Through
Semi-Formal. Circa
1760-1900, Also Copper &
Brass, Tin & Ironware,
Baskets, Quilts, Paintings,
Prints; Good inventory of
Country Pine Furniture
Specialties: Country
Furniture & Accessories
    Directions: At Common
    Man Restaurant

Barrington

THE RED SHED ANTIQUES
Rte 125 & 9   03825
603 664-2825
Proprietor: Dick & Ruth
Rowell
Hours: May Thru Nov
Types & Periods: General
Line, Furniture, Wood, Tin,
Iron, Bottles
Directions: Across From
Calef's Country Store

Bedford

BELL HILL ANTIQUES
Rt 101   03102
603 472-5580   Est: 1973
Proprietor: 17 Dealers In
One Large Shop
Hours: Sun-Sat, 10-5:30,
By Appointment
Types & Periods: Country
Furniture & Furnishings, Tin,
Toys, Quilts, Folk Art, Silver,
Paintings, Advertising,
Clocks, Rugs
Appraisal Service Available
Directions: Corner of Bell
Hill Road in Houck
Realtor's Bldg

Bethlehem

CHURCHILL'S ANTIQUES
Main St   03574
608 869-2074   Est: 1968
Proprietor: William &
Margery Churchill
Hours: Summer, Daily 1-5;
All Year By Appointment
Types & Periods: General
Line
Appraisal Service Available
Directions: Rte 302,
Downtown

Boscawen

BETTY'S OLD BARN SHOP
Rtes 3 & 4   03301
603 796-2171
Proprietor: Betty Blake
Types & Periods: General
Line, Collectibles

Bristol

**CRAWFORD CORNER
ANTIQUES**
Box 83   03222
603 744-8717   Est: 1976
Proprietor: Joseph W
Walker
Hours: By appointment,
May 31-Oct 12
Types & Periods: General
Line, American Indian
Weaving
Specialties: Furniture
(English & American)
Directions: On Mt
Cardigan Rd in Alexandria

Campton

FERN ROCK ANTIQUES
Rte 49   03223
603 536-2131
Proprietor: Gloria Searles
Hours: Daily, 9-10:30
Types & Periods: New
Hampshire Furniture from
Primitive thru Semi-Formal,
Circa 1760-1900, Copper,
Brass, Tin, Ironware,
Baskets, Quilts, Paintings &
Prints, Country Pine
Furniture
Specialties: Country
Furniture & Accessories
Directions: At Snowy Owl
Inn, Waterville Valley Ski
Area

Candia

SILENT WOMEN ANTIQUES
Rte 101B   03034
Est: 1960
Proprietor: Helen Kendall
Hours: Daily, May-Sept; By
appointment, Sept-Dec
Types & Periods: Dolls,
Primitives, Art Glass
Specialties: Dolls
Directions: Rte 101B next
to Museum

Center Conway

MILL FARM ANTIQUES
03813
Hours: Mon-Sat, 12-5,
June 15-Oct 15; also by
appointment
Types & Periods: General
Line
Directions: 1 mile off Rte
302 at Conway Lake

Center Harbor

**HOLIDAY HOUSE
ANTIQUES**
Bean Rd   03226
603 253-6891
Proprietor: The Windsor
Murphy's
Hours: Daily
Types & Periods: General
Line, Furniture, China, Glass
Directions: Off Rte 25

Center Ossipee

SWITAJ'S ANTIQUES
Main St   03814
603 539-6043   Est: 1971
Proprietor: Pat & Frank
Switaj
Hours: By appointment, by
chance
Types & Periods: Primitives,
Jewelry, General Line
Specialties: Wood Carvings,
Carved Birds
Directions: Mile off Rte 16,
30 miles S of N Conway

Chester

OLDE CHESTER ANTIQUES
Raymond Rd, Rte 102
03036
603 887-4778   Est: 1972
Proprietor: Barney &
Elizabeth Priest
Hours: Daily
Types & Periods: Country
18th & 19th Century
Furniture & Accessories
Specialties: Country
Furniture & Accessories
Appraisal Service Available
Directions: 3.6 miles from
Chester Center towards
Raymond on Rte 102

Chesterfield

HELEN C BURLEY
Main St   03443
603 363-4791   Est: 1942
Proprietor: Helen C.
Burley
Hours: By appointment, by
chance
Types & Periods: General
Line
Specialties: American
Primitives
Directions: 1½ miles S of
Rte 9 on Rte 63

Chichester

**BLACKEYED SUSAN
ANTIQUES**
Pleasant St   03263
603 435-6628   Est: 1973
Proprietor: Bill & Polly
McCown
Hours: Daily
Types & Periods: Primitives,
Country Furniture &
Accessories
Directions: Turn N off Rte
128 at Grain Stone Sign
between Epson & Pittsfield

Claremont

ELDERBERRY ANTIQUES
95 Winter St   03743
603 542-2111   Est: 1975
Proprietor: John M
Meloney
Hours: Daily, by chance
Types & Periods: General
Line, Country Items
Specialties: Post Cards,
Tools, Primitives
Directions: 2 blocks N of
Rte 11 from Claremont
toward Newport, next door
to National Guard Armory

LADEAU'S FURNITURE
127 Main St   03743
603 542-6762   Est: 1948
Proprietor: Leon &
Lawrence Wight
Hours: Mon-Thurs, 9-5:30;
Fri, 9-9
Types & Periods: Furniture,
Pine, Primitives, Victorian,
Glassware, Lamps

Appraisal Service Available
Directions: Take the
Aschutney Exit off I-91
just after crossing Sugar
R Bridge, 5 miles off the
Interstate

LEVARN'S ANTIQUES
RFD 1 Newport Rd   03743
603 863-1411   Est: 1962
Proprietor: Doc & Carolyn
LeVarn
Hours: Daily, by
appointment or by chance
Types & Periods: All Periods
Specialties: Victorian
Appraisal Service Available
Directions: Rte 11-103,
halfway between
Claremont & Newport

Concord

CARR BOOKS
51 N Spring St   03301
603 225-3109   Est: 1970
Proprietor: Roberta M Carr
Hours: By appointment, by
chance
Types & Periods: Books,
Prints, Paintings, Post
Cards, Valentines, Paper
Americana
Appraisal Service Available
Directions: Cross Main
Street at the Bridge Street
lights, 3rd street to the left

F E HAMEL ANTIQUES
150 Loudon   03301
603 224-7949   Est: 1972
Proprietor: Florian E
Hamel
Hours: Daily
Types & Periods: General
Line
Appraisal Service Available
Directions: 2 miles E of
City & I-93 on Rtes 202, 4
& 9

VERNA H MORRILL
River Rd   03036
603 224-0163
Proprietor: Verna H Morrill
Hours: Mon-Sat, Sun by
appointment
Types & Periods: General
Line, Collectibles
Directions: 4 miles S
Concord, Rte 3A, across
from entrance to Mary
Eddy Birthplace

ROOSER ANTIQUES
RFD 4   03301
603 798-5912   Est: 1966
Proprietor: Doug & Connie
Hamel
Hours: Daily
Types & Periods: 18th &
19th Century Country
Furniture, Shaker, Folk Art
Specialties: Shaker
Appraisal Service Available
Directions: Rtes 202, 4 &
9, 7 miles E of town

Danbury

PAT ROBIE-ANTIQUES
Rte 104   03230
603 768-3443
Proprietor: Pat Robie
Types & Periods: General
Line, Glass, Tin, China

Derry

**CRYSTAL ANTIQUE
SHOPPE**
32 Crystal Ave   03038
603 432-2783   Est: 1973
Proprietor: Olga S
Downing
Hours: By appointment, by
chance
Types & Periods: General
Line, Early 1800-1900 Glass
& China
Directions: Center of town
on Rte 28

THE OLD EMERY PLACE
27 S Main St   03038
603 432-9640   Est: 1956
Proprietor: Julian C Hayes
Hours: Mon-Sat, 10-4;
Sun, 11-4
Types & Periods: General
Line
Specialties: Post Cards,
Wood & Iron Primitives
Appraisal Service Available
Directions: On Rte 28
By-Pass, 8th place S of
rotary where Rte 102
crosses By-Pass

Dover

CAROLINE FRENCH PERRY
202 Mast Rd   03820
603 742-6250
Proprietor: Caroline
French Perry
Hours: Daily
Types & Periods: Samplers,
Quilts, Primitives, Country
Furniture, Jewelry
Directions: Corner of Mast
& Black River Rds

**STEPPINGSTONE
ANTIQUES**
Rte 2 Box 124   03820
603 868-5239   Est: 1969
Proprietor: Stanley D
Hettinger
Hours: Tues-Sat, 9-4; Sun,
2-5
Types & Periods: General
Line
Appraisal Service Available
Directions: From 95 N,
take 4 W to 125 S, 1/4
mile on right

East Kingston

**KENSINGTON HISTORICAL
COMPANY**
Box 87   03827
603 778-0686   Est: 1972
Proprietor: Peter & Doris
Atwood
Hours: By appointment
Types & Periods: 18th
Century American Building
Materials
Specialties: Doors,
Hardware, Barn Siding
Appraisal Service Available
Directions: 4½ miles W of
Exit 1 on I-95

1680 HOUSE ANTIQUES
Rte 108   03827
603 642-3153   Est: 1965
Proprietor: Evelyn
Edwards
Hours: Sun, Mon, Wed &
Fri, 12-5; Sat by
appointment
Types & Periods: Country
Furniture & Primitives,
Glass, Bric-A-Brac
Specialties: Dropleaf Tables,
Candle Molds, Baskets,
Windsor Chairs, Country Tin

Appraisal Service Available
Directions: About 3 miles
E of Rte 125 and about 6
or 7 miles W off Rte 95

Epping

LATCHSTRING ANTIQUES
Old Rte 101 W   03042
603 679-8720   Est: 1966
Proprietor: Louise M
Dorsch
Hours: Daily, by
appointment, by chance
Types & Periods: Country,
Primitives, Accessories,
Furniture
Directions: 3 miles W of
Rte 125, just beyond
Lamprey Bridge

Epson

E WILSON ANTIQUES
03234
603 736-9077   Est: 1968
Proprietor: Ernestine F
Wilson
Hours: By appointment, by
chance
Types & Periods: Tin,
Woodenware, Textiles
Appraisal Service Available

Exeter

THE CHURCH ANTIQUES
4 Elm   03833
603 778-8633
Proprietor: Herschel B
Burt
Hours: Mon-Sat, 10-5
Types & Periods: Clocks,
Fine Antiques
Specialties: Clocks
Appraisal Service Available
Directions: Corner Elm &
Maple Sts, facing Exeter
Academy Green

**OCTOBER STONE
ANTIQUES**
Jady Hill   03833
603 772-2024   Est: 1970
Proprietor: Linda J Rogers
Hours: Daily, 10-5
Types & Periods: Country
Furniture & Accessories,
General Line

Specialties: Clocks, Lamps
Directions: Next to Exeter
Country Club, 2 minutes
from Exeter Center

Fitzwilliam

**THE BENCHMARK
ANTIQUES**
General James Reed
Hwy E   03447
603 585-2273   Est: 1969
Proprietor: Louise W
Hamilton
Hours: Daily
Types & Periods: General
Line, China, Glass, Silver,
Ironware, Furniture,
Primitives
Appraisal Service Available
Directions: Next to Post
Office

**WILLIAM LEWAN
ANTIQUES**
Old Troy Rd   03447
603 585-3365   Est: 1972
Proprietor: William Lewan
& Deborah Stoesser
Hours: Daily, 9-5
Types & Periods: Country
Furniture & Accessories
Appraisal Service Available
Directions: Follow Rte 119
from Fitzwilliam 4½ miles
to Old Troy Rd, turn right
for 3/4 mile

ALICIA F MURPHY
Lower Troy Rd   03447
603 585-7719
Proprietor: Alicia F
Murphy
Hours: By appointment, by
chance
Types & Periods: General
Line

**THE OLD VILLAGE
SCHOOLHOUSE**
Rte 119   03447
603 585-6645   Est: 1948
Proprietor: Fran & Tom
Yasvin
Hours: Open April-Nov;
Dec-March by
appointment or by chance
Types & Periods: Primitives,
Woodenware, China, Cut &
Pattern Glass, Sterling
Crocks, Clocks, Furniture
Appraisal Service Available
Directions: Fitzwilliam
Village

SERENDIPITY ANTIQUES
Jaffrey Rd   03447
603 585-6822   Est: 1969
Proprietor: Mr Dudley P
Housman
Hours: Mon-Fri, Weekends
by appointment or by
chance
Types & Periods: General
Line, Country Furniture,
Primitives, Accessories
Specialties: Furniture
(Restoration)
Directions: 1st right off
Rte 12 N of junction of
Rte 119 & 12

Franklin

BRADBURY M PRESCOTT
232 S Main St   03235
603 934-4136   Est: 1942
Proprietor: Bradbury M
Prescott
Hours: Daily, by
appointment or by chance
Types & Periods: 18th &
19th Century Furniture
Appraisal Service Available
Directions: 18 miles N of
Concord on US 3

Fremont

JUST ANTIQUES
RR 1 Box 443   03044
603 895-2395   Est: 1973
Proprietor: Barbara & Ed
Millman
Hours: Daily, 10-6
Types & Periods: Country
Furniture, Accessories
Directions: Rte 111A, 1
mile S of Rte 107

George Mills

MILL POND ANTIQUES
                          03751
603 763-2905   Est: 1967
Proprietor: Betty Chase
Hours: Weekends, by
appointment
Types & Periods: General
Line, Tools
Directions: Off Rte 89 to
Exit 12 toward Sunofee

Gilford

FERN ROCK ANTIQUES
Rtes 3 & 11   03264
603 536-2131
Proprietor: Gloria Searles
Hours: Daily, 5-10:30 pm
Types & Periods: New
Hampshire Furniture from
Primitive thru Semi-Formal,
Circa 1760-1900, Copper,
Brass, Tin & Ironware,
Baskets, Quilts, Paintings &
Prints, Country Pine
Furniture
Specialties: Country
Furniture & Accessories
Directions: At B Mae
Denny's Restaurant &
Lounge

Goffstown

MAYFIELD
7 High St   03045
603 497-4666   Est: 1974
Proprietor: Allen & Joan
Beddoe
Hours: Daily during
summer; nights &
weekends during winter;
also by appointment
Types & Periods: Furniture,
Glass, China, Silver, Doll
Accessories, Books,
Jewelry, Clocks, Watches
Specialties: Books, Clocks &
Watches, Kitchen Primitives
Appraisal Service Available
Directions: Take Exit 10
from Hwy 3 or I-93 to Rte
101 to 114 through to
Goffstown Center, shop
faces Center Square

Grafton

ARLENE'S ANTIQUES
Rte 4   03240
603 523-4437
Proprietor: Arlene Niel
Types & Periods: General
Line, Glass, Primitives

**OLD STUFF
BARN-OBSOLETE SHOP**
E Grafton Rd   03240
603 523-9960

Proprietor: Al & Dot
Dadmun
Types & Periods: General
Line, Paraphernalia

Grantham

PEDERSEN ANTIQUES
Main St   03753
603 863-3086   Est: 1976
Proprietor: Andrea P
Pedersen
Hours: Daily
Types & Periods: 18th
Century Furniture, Oriental
Rugs, Quimper Pottery
Specialties: 18th Century
Furniture, Oriental Rugs,
Quimper Pottery
Directions: 1 mile off Exit
13, I-89, next to Town Hall

Hampton

**TO HAVE & TO HOLD
SHOPE**
760 Lafayette Rd   03842
603 926-2139
Proprietor: James &
Eleanor Burnley
Hours: Daily, 9-5:30
Types & Periods: China,
Glass, Furniture

H G WEBBER ANTIQUES
495 Lafayette Rd   03842
603 926-3349   Est: 1930
Proprietor: R S Webber
Hours: Tues-Sun
Types & Periods: General
Line, Music Boxes
Specialties: Clocks
Appraisal Service Available
Directions: Across from
Sheraton Motel, Rte 1

Hancock

THE COBBS
Old Dublin Rd   03449
603 525-4053   Est: 1970
Proprietor: Charles M
Cobb
Hours: Daily, by
appointment or by chance
Types & Periods: American
17th, 18th & Early 19th
Century Furniture &
Accessories

THE COBBS   Cont'd
Specialties: Furniture,
Fireplace Iron
Appraisal Service Available
   Directions: 1¼ miles SW
   of town

HARDINGS OF HANCOCK
   Depot   03449
   603 525-3518   Est: 1965
   Proprietor: Mrs Vincent
   Harding
   Hours: Daily, by chance or
   by appointment
   Types & Periods: Country
   Furniture, Brass, copper,
   Early Woodenware, Hand
   Forged Ironware, Lighting,
   Tin, Primitive Accents
   Specialties: Lighting, Iron,
   Brass & Copper
   Directions: Red house on
   the point overlooking
   Norway Pond on Rte 123,
   2 minutes from the center
   of village W

Henniker

FELSEN'S ANTIQUES
   Main St   03242
   603 428-7512   Est: 1961
   Proprietor: Rita Felsen
   Parmenter
   Hours: By appointment, by
   chance
   Types & Periods: Early
   American Country & Formal
   Furniture, Glass, Paintings,
   Oriental Rugs, Rarities
   Specialties: Furniture
   (Queen Anne, Chippendale,
   Hepplewhite)
   Directions: 1 mile from
   202 & 9 on Main St

Hill

THE GOLDEN EAGLE
ANTIQUES
   Mountain View Dr   03243
   603 934-3429
   Proprietor: Wen & Sue
   Ackerman
   Hours: By appointment, by
   chance
   Types & Periods: General
   Line, Guns, Collectibles
   Directions: New Hill Village

Hillsboro

KNOLLCROFT ANTIQUES
   Rte 2   03244
   603 478-5771   Est: 1970
   Proprietor: Helen H
   Andersen
   Hours: By chance or
   appointment all year
   Types & Periods: Furniture,
   Primitives, General Line
   Directions: Take E
   Washington Rd off Rte 31,
   go 4 miles

OLD DUNBAR HOUSE
   Centre Rd   03244
   603 464-3937   Est: 1952
   Proprietor: Ralph C Stuart
   Hours: By appointment, by
   chance
   Types & Periods: Early Local
   Furniture, American &
   English Pewter
   Directions: Take School
   St, 3½ miles straight
   ahead

THE SHADOW SHOP
   Preston St   03244
   603 464-5413   Est: 1969
   Proprietor: Barbara A
   Meredith
   Hours: Mon-Sat, Sun by
   appointment or by chance
   Types & Periods: General
   Line
   Specialties: Post Cards,
   Paper Americana
   Appraisal Service Available
   Directions: 3rd house on
   right from Henniker St

Hillsboro Centre

WELL SWEEP ANTIQUES
                      03244
   603 464-3218   Est: 1977
   Proprietor: Carol &
   Richard Withington Jr
   Hours: By appointment or
   by chance all year
   Types & Periods: Country
   Furniture & Accessories
   Directions: In Historic
   Hillsboro Centre, 3 miles
   from Hillsboro Village

Holderness

GORDON'S ANTIQUES
   Rtes 3 & 25   03245
   603 968-4441   Est: 1944
   Proprietor: Gladys &
   Richard Gordon
   Hours: By chance
   Types & Periods: Early
   American, Paintings
   Appraisal Service Available
   Directions: In central New
   Hampshire on Squam
   Lake

Hollis

JETTE'S COUNTRY STORE
& FLEA MARKET
   436 Silver Lake Rd   03049
   603 465-7813   Est: 1969
   Proprietor: Louis &
   Frances Jette
   Hours: Weekends, by
   appointment
   Types & Periods: General
   Line
   Directions: On Rte 122

Hooksett

HARRINGTON'S ANTIQUES
   Rte 3   03106
   603 485-3092
   Hours: Mon-Sat
   Types & Periods: General
   Line
   Directions: Between Indian
   Cliff & China Dragon

Hopkinton

MEADOW HEARTH
ANTIQUES
   Briar Hill Rd   03301
   603 746-3947   Est: 1965
   Proprietor: John H Howe
   Hours: Daily, by
   appointment or by chance
   Types & Periods: Early
   American Furniture &
   Paintings, Decorative
   Accessories
   Specialties: Furniture &
   Paintings
   Directions: Briar Hill Rd
   from center of Hopkinton,
   1/2 mile

MITCHELL'S ANTIQUES
Rollins Rd   03301
603 746-5056   Est: 1960
Proprietor: C J Mitchell
Hours: By appointment, by
chance
Types & Periods: Primitives,
Country Furniture, Tools,
Tin, Iron, Wood, Redware,
Early Lighting
Specialties: Tools
Directions: 1/2 mile from
Village Square, off Briar
Hill Rd

THE OLD PARSONAGE
Concord-Hopkinton Rd
                 03301
603 228-0217   Est: 1967
Proprietor: Stanley & Clara
Jean Davis
Hours: Daily, weekends by
appointment
Types & Periods: Iron, Tin,
Wood Accessories of 17th &
18th Centuries, Country
Furniture, Fabrics, Samplers
Directions: Sign on
Concord-Hopkinton Rd
which is 202 & 9

SUGAR HILL ANTIQUES
Sugar Hill Rd   03301
603 746-3065   Est: 1972
Proprietor: A L & M E
Price
Hours: By appointment, by
chance
Types & Periods: 18th &
19th Century Country &
Formal Furniture,
Accessories
Directions: I-89 Exit 5, 202
W 1½ miles, left on
Stumpfield Rd 1½ miles

**WHEAT & CHAFF
ANTIQUES**
Hopkinton Rd   03301
603 746-3313   Est: 1972
Proprietor: Peg & Wayne
Woodard
Hours: By chance or by
appointment all year
Types & Periods: 18th &
19th Century Furniture, Early
American Pattern Glass, Art
Glass
Specialties: Furniture, Glass
Appraisal Service Available
Directions: 8 miles W of
Concord, 1 mile N of I-89
on Hwy 103

Hudson

**GEORGE H LABARRE
GALLERIES**
111 Ferry St   03051
603 882-2411
Proprietor: George H
LaBarre
Hours: By appointment, by
chance
Types & Periods: American
Collectibles including
Political, Medals, World's
Fair, Early Photographs,
Paper Americana,
Autographs, Books,
Advertising Items, Sports
Related Items
Specialties: Political, Lincoln
& Early Photographs,
Autographs
Appraisal Service Available

Jackson

RED SHED ANTIQUES
PO Box 364   03864
603 383-9267
Proprietor: Bernice E
Berman
Hours: Tues-Sun, May
30-Oct 12
Types & Periods: General
Line, Furniture, Primitives,
China, Clocks, Glass
Directions: Rte 16 above
N Conway

Keene

BEECH HILL GALLERY
Old Concord Rd   03431
603 352-2194   Est: 1969
Proprietor: Harold &
Miriam Goder
Hours: Daily, by
appointment or by chance
Types & Periods: 18th
Century Furniture, 19th
Century American Paintings,
Quilts, Silver, Samplers
Appraisal Service Available
Directions: N on Rte 9 to
Airflite Station, turn right
to Old Concord Rd

PREGENT'S ANTIQUES
142 Marboro St   03431
603 352-6736
Hours: By appointment, by
chance
Types & Periods: Country
Furniture, Primitives

Kingston

VILLAGE BARN ANTIQUES
Main St   03848
603 642-5278   Est: 1962
Proprietor: A H Reynolds
Hours: By chance
Types & Periods: General
Line, Furniture, Glass,
China, Primitives
Directions: Off Rte 125 on
Rte 111 W

THE WOODEN INDIAN
Little River Rd   03848
603 642-8365   Est: 1972
Proprietor: Mr & Mrs
William Rent
Hours: By appointment or
by chance, call ahead
Types & Periods: General
Line (No Furniture)
Specialties: Paper
Americana
Directions: End of Little
River Rd, close to
intersection of 125 & 111

Laconia

FERN ROCK
Bean Hill Rd   03246
603 536-2131
Proprietor: Gloria Searles
Hours: Tues-Sun, 11:30-9,
May 31-Oct 12
Types & Periods: New
Hampshire Furniture from
Primitive thru Semi-Formal
Circa 1760-1900, Copper,
Brass, Tin, Ironware,
Baskets, Quilts, Paintings &
Prints
Specialties: Country
Furniture & Accessories
Directions: At Hickory
Stick Farm Restaurant, off
Rte 3

KAY MC GOWAN
91 Province St   03246
603 524-4211   Est: 1969
Proprietor: Kay McGowan
Hours: Mon-Thurs, Sat &
Sun, by appointment or by
chance, May 1-Sept 30
Types & Periods: Country
Antiques, Tin, Paper, Dolls
Specialties: Dolls, Tin, Paper
Appraisal Service Available
Directions: 1/4 mile from
business district on old
Rte 107

Lancaster

LOFT ANTIQUES
North Rd   03584
603 788-4455   Est: 1972
Proprietor: Barbara W
Bartow
Hours: Daily, by chance,
May 30-Oct 12
Types & Periods: Country
Furniture, Doll Houses &
Furniture, Rookwood Pottery
Specialties: Scottish Pebble
Jewelry, Early American
Silver (Coin) Before 1850
Appraisal Service Available
Directions: Exactly 3 miles
from Lancaster National
Bank, Middle St turns into
North Rd

THE SHOP IN THE BARN
Prospect St   03584
603 788-2313
Proprietor: Marguerite
Monahan & Rosalie
McGraw
Hours: Daily, June-Nov
Types & Periods: Furniture,
China, Glass, Books,
Jewelry, Lamps,
Lampshades
Directions: Rte 3 S

Lebanon

HAYWARD'S ANTIQUES
Dartmouth College Hwy
                        03766
603 448-2052   Est: 1965
Proprietor: Clifton A
Hayward
Hours: By appointment, by
chance

Types & Periods: Country
Furniture, Guns & Related
Items
Specialties: Furniture
Restoration
Appraisal Service Available
Directions: Rte 4 E from
center of town, 1 mile on
right, or take Exit 17 off
I-89 & go 1 mile on 4 W

Lisbon

RIVER BEND ANTIQUES
RFD 1 Box 29A   03585
603 838-5929   Est: 1952
Proprietor: William
Marshall
Hours: Daily, by
appointment
Types & Periods: 18th &
19th Century Furniture,
Lamps, Porcelain, Glass
Appraisal Service Available
Directions: 6 miles S of
Exit 42 on Rte 93

Littleton

BEAL HOUSE INN &
ANTIQUES
247 Main St   03561
603 444-2661   Est: 1955
Proprietor: Mrs Marjorie
Beal Grady
Hours: Daily, 9-5
Types & Periods: Furniture,
General Line
Specialties: Canopy Beds
Directions: From Boston
on I-93 to Exit 42, 1 mile
N of Exit

BROOKSIDE ANTIQUES
Bethlehem Rd   03561
603 444-2986   Est: 1944
Proprietor: A M Wright
Hours: Daily, 10-5:30
Types & Periods: General
Line of Collectors Items
Specialties: Primitives
Appraisal Service Available
Directions: Rte 302,
between Littleton &
Bethlehem

THE CUPOLA
187 Main St   03561
603 444-5870   Est: 1973
Proprietor: Littleton Motel

Hours: Daily, 9-6 by
appointment, May 6-Oct
Types & Periods: General
Line
Directions: In barn at rear
of Littleton Motel

Lyme

CONSTANCE
BERGENDOFF ANTIQUES
On the Common   03768
603 795-2672   Est: 1970
Proprietor: Constance
Bergendoff
Hours: Daily
Types & Periods: Fine
Country Furniture, Samplers,
Stoneware, Quilts, Hooked
Rugs
Specialties: Country
Furniture, Samplers,
Stoneware, Quilts, Hooked
Rugs
Directions: At the Claflin
House on the Common,
Rte 10

Manchester

END OF THE TRAIL
ANTIQUES
420 Chestnut St   03101
603 669-1238   Est: 1964
Proprietor: June Kos
Hours: Mon-Sat
Types & Periods: Victorian &
Pine Furniture, General Line
Appraisal Service Available
Directions: Across from
the Post Office

SANDI'S ANTIQUES
426 Chestnut St   03105
603 624-1069   Est: 1958
Proprietor: Sandra
Gersten
Hours: Mon-Fri, 10-5,
Thurs 'til 8; Sat, 10-4
Types & Periods: Copper,
Brass, Jewelry, Silver
Specialties: Jewelry, Silver
Appraisal Service Available
Directions: Across from
the Post Office

Marlborough

ELIZABETH H THOMAS
McKinley Circle   03455
603 876-3765   Est: 1967
Proprietor: Elizabeth H
Thomas
Hours: Daily, May-Nov;
also by chance
Types & Periods: China,
Glassware, Furniture, Iron,
Baskets
Directions: Turn off Rte
101 on to Rte 124, take
right on McKinley Circle

WOODWARD'S ANTIQUES
130 Main   03455
603 876-3360   Est: 1971
Proprietor: Terry & Gene
Woodward
Hours: Daily, by
appointment, by chance
Types & Periods: Country
Furniture & Accessories
Specialties: Refinished
Furniture
Appraisal Service Available
Directions: On Rte 101,
sign out front

Marlow

**SAND POND GUN &
ANTIQUE SHOP**
Sand Pond Rd   03456
603 446-3460   Est: 1961
Proprietor: James C
Tillinghast
Hours: Sun-Mon, Wed-Sat
Types & Periods: Tools,
Bottles, Tobacco Tins,
Paintings, Books, Country
Store Items, Tinware, Guns,
Obsolete Ammunition, Paper
Items
Appraisal Service Available
Directions: Rte 10 N of
Marlow 3 miles, turn right
on Sand Pond Rd, go 3/4
mile

Meredith

**BURLWOOD ANTIQUE
MARKET**
Rte 3   03253
603 279-6387   Est: 1964
Proprietor: Tom & Nan
Lindsey

Hours: Daily,
April-Christmas, By
appointment, Jan-March;
35 Dealer Market, Fri-Sun,
June-Oct
Types & Periods: General
Line
Specialties: Furniture, China,
Primitives
Appraisal Service Available
Directions: Rte 3, between
Meredith & Weirs Beach

Merrimack

B'S ANTIQUES
D W Hwy   03054
603 424-9224   Est: 1974
Proprietor: Barbara &
Russell Scheider
Hours: By appointment
Types & Periods: Furniture
& Oriental Export
Directions: Rte 3 next to
Indian Head Bank

Milford

PINE SHED ANTIQUES
Upper Elm St   03055
603 673-2167   Est: 1950
Proprietor: Cynthia & Jim
Forsyth
Hours: Daily, by chance
Types & Periods: General
Line, Victorian, Early
American Primitives, China,
Glass
Specialties: Jewelry
Directions: Between
shopping center &
Hayward Farms

YANKEE STOREKEEPER
20 Clinton St   03055
603 673-7800   Est: 1970
Proprietor: E Boulton
Hours: Daily
Types & Periods: General
Line
Specialties: Post Cards, Tin,
Country Store Items
Directions: Off Rte 13 S

Moultonboro

**R & B ANTIQUE AUCTION
COMPANY**
Box 147   03254
603 476-9770   Est: 1973
Proprietor: Lawrence W
Porter
Hours: Daily, by
appointment
Types & Periods: Early
American, Oak, Victorian,
Primitives
Appraisal Service Available
Directions: 10 miles right
on Rte 25

New Ipswich

ESTELLE M GLAVEY INC
Rte 124   03071
603 878-1200
Proprietor: Estelle M
Glavey
Hours: Tues-Sun, July &
Aug; Weekends, spring &
fall
Types & Periods: Early
American Furniture

New London

**LAURIDS
LAURIDSEN-ANTIQUES**
Knights Hill Rd   03257
603 526-6407
Types & Periods: Early
Country Furniture, Artifacts

**THE MAD EAGLE
ANTIQUES INC**
RFD 2 Rte 11   03257
603 526-4880   Est: 1961
Proprietor: M S & P H
Lash
Hours: Daily, 10-5,
May-Oct
Types & Periods: Early
American Furniture (Before
1840)
Appraisal Service Available
Directions: 2 miles E of
New London on Rte 11,
also 2 miles E of Exit 11,
I-89 on Rte 11

Newton Junction

PETER H EATON ANTIQUES INC
Thornell Rd   03859
603 382-6838   Est: 1970
Proprietor: Peter Eaton
Hours: By appointment, by chance
Types & Periods: 18th Century American Country Furniture
Specialties: Original or as found condition
Appraisal Service Available
Directions: 4 miles from Merrimac Mass Exit of Rte 495

North Conway

GRALYN ANTIQUES INC
S Main St   03860
603 356-5546   Est: 1920
Proprietor: Robert A Goldberg
Hours: By appointment, by chance
Types & Periods: Early American, General Line
Specialties: White Mountain Art
Directions: Rte 16, S Main St

THE LOG CABIN ANTIQUES
Main St   03860
603 356-3333   Est: 1976
Proprietor: Richard M Plusch
Hours: Daily, June-Oct; Weekends, Nov-May; also by appointment
Types & Periods: Period Furnishings, China, Glass, Silver, Rugs, Paintings, Clocks
Specialties: American Country Furniture & Blown, Pattern, Art & Cut Glass
Appraisal Service Available
Directions: On the W side of Main St, 2 blocks S of the traffic light in N Conway

Northhampton

BLUE BOAR ANTIQUES
Rte 1   03862
               Est: 1978
Proprietor: Ronald Gagne & Linda Rogers
Hours: Daily, 10-5
Types & Periods: General Line, Refinished & Stuff in the Rough, China, Glass
Specialties: Country Furniture, Lamps
Directions: 2-1/5 miles N of Hampton Center on Rte 1, on the left side of the road in a small white building

PAUL MC INNIS ANTIQUE CENTER
1 Lafayette Rd Rte 1
               03862
603 964-6596   Est: 1971
Proprietor: Paul McInnis
Hours: Daily, 9-5
Types & Periods: General Line, Collectibles, Early American, Victorian, Turn-of-the-Century
Appraisal Service Available
Directions: On Rte 1 on the Hampton-N Hampton line

Northwood

THE FIANDERS
Rtes 4, 9 & 202   03261
603 942-8114   Est: 1972
Proprietor: Ginger & Walter Fiander
Hours: Daily, 9-6
Types & Periods: General Line, Collectibles
Directions: Between Concord & Portsmouth

THE OLD BARN
Rte 4   03261
603 942-8615   Est: 1969
Proprietor: Virginia & Watson Baker
Hours: Daily
Types & Periods: General Line, Primitives
Appraisal Service Available
Directions: US 4, 1/2 way between Concord & Portsmouth

Ossipee

HOOPER'S FARM ANTIQUE SHOP
Rte 16   03864
603 539-6834   Est: 1955
Proprietor: Ed & Eleanor Hooper
Hours: By appointment, by chance
Types & Periods: Primitives, Furniture, Folk Art, American Indian Items, Flint Glass, Photographs, Collectibles
Specialties: White Mountain Art, Period Costumes
Appraisal Service Available
Directions: 1 mile S of Rte 28, on the road to Crawford Notch White Mountains

Pelham

HARTLEY'S BARN
Rte 128   03076
603 883-3269   Est: 1940
Proprietor: Mrs Winston J Hartley
Hours: By appointment, by chance
Types & Periods: General Line
Specialties: Jewelry, Silver Registry
Appraisal Service Available
Directions: 10 miles (On Rte 128) N of Lowell, 7 miles E of Nashua, 7 miles W of Rte 93, off Rte 111

Penacook

ARTHUR HENDERSON
Box 98   03301
603 796-2488   Est: 1967
Proprietor: Arthur Henderson
Hours: Daily
Types & Periods: Primitives, Advertising, Bottles
Directions: Exit 17 on I-93, 10 miles N of Concord, 3 & 4 in Boscawen

WILLOW HOLLOW ANTIQUES
185 S Main St   03301
603 753-4281   Est: 1952

Proprietor: Al & Nancy
Schlegel
Hours: Daily, 10-6
Types & Periods: Porcelain,
Primitives, Paper Americana,
Tools, Tin, Wood, Jewelry,
Toys, Advertising, Furniture
Specialties: Paper
Americana, Tools, Primitives
Directions: Hwy 3 & 4, 4
miles N of Concord, 70
miles N of Boston

Pequaket

**THE SLOP CHEST
ANTIQUES**
Rte 16   03875
603 367-4715   Est: 1955
Proprietor: Ralph Raabe
Hours: Daily
Types & Periods: General
Line
Specialties: Copper
Appraisal Service Available
Directions: On Rte 16, 8
miles S of Conway

Peterborough

MARY WARNER HOFFMAN
Wilton Rd   03458
603 924-6836   Est: 1965
Proprietor: Mary Warner
Hoffman
Hours: Daily
Types & Periods: General
Line
Specialties: New England
Primitives
Directions: Rte 101, 1/2
mile E of Peterborough
from intersection of Rtes
101 & 202

**STRAWBERRY HILL
ANTIQUES**
3 Elm St   03458
603 924-6443
Proprietor: Richard & Eva
Day
Hours: Daily, 10-4
Types & Periods: Oriental
Items, Dolls, Miniatures,
China, Glass, Paintings,
Silver, Toys
Directions: Off Rte 101

Pittsfield

COUNTRY ANTIQUES
RFD 2   03263
603 435-6615   Est: 1959
Proprietor: Joann & Fred
Cadarette
Hours: Daily, by
appointment, by chance
Types & Periods: Early
Country Furniture, Paintings,
Primitives
Specialties: Furniture, Folk
Art
Directions: 15 minutes
from Concord on Rte 129

Plaistow

KAY'S ANTIQUE SHOP
Box 33 Main St   03865
603 382-8305   Est: 1963
Proprietor: Grace Kay
Hours: Mon, Wed & Fri,
10-5; Sat, 2:30-5
Types & Periods: Country
Furniture
Specialties: Primitives, Early
Pattern Glass
Directions: Rte 125 to
121A

Plymouth

RED GATE FARM
160 Highland St   03264
603 536-2476
Proprietor: Joy Prichard
Types & Periods: Victoriana,
Furniture, Clocks, Decorator
Items, Glass, Silver, China
Directions: 1¼ miles W of
Green

Portsmouth

ANTIQUES 19 SHEAFE
19 Sheafe St   03801
603 431-5496   Est: 1974
Hours: Daily, by
appointment, by chance
Types & Periods: 18th &
Early 19th Century, English
Pottery, Porcelain
Appraisal Service Available

**MARGARET SCOTT
CARTER INC**
175 Market St   03801
603 436-1781   Est: 1958
Proprietor: Margaret Scott
Carter
Hours: Mon-Sat, 10-5
Types & Periods: 18th &
19th Century Country
Furniture & Accessories,
Pewter, Decoys, Tools,
Books on Antiques &
Traditional Crafts
Specialties: Tools
Directions: Exit 7 off Rte
95N to Market St, first
antique shop on left

HARBOR VIEW ANTIQUES
117 Market St   03801
603 436-3623   Est: 1972
Proprietor: T J Towey, L G
Sochia & C E Litchfield
Hours: Mon-Sat, 10-5;
Sun, 12-4
Types & Periods: 18th &
19th Century Furniture,
Rugs, Paintings
Specialties: Watches
(Pocket)
Directions: Last
Portsmouth Exit going N
of Rte 95, Market St Exit,
take right to top of hill

**WHERE THE RAINBOW
ENDS**
89 Market St   03801
603 431-5050   Est: 1975
Proprietor: Betsy Gimbel &
Robin Sanborn
Hours: Mon-Sat; also Fri &
Sat evenings; also by
appointment
Types & Periods:
Advertising, Collectibles,
Art Noveau & Deco, Carousel
Horses, Toys, Rolltop Desks,
Wooden Cigar Store Indian,
Miniatures, Oriental Rugs
Specialties: Old Advertising,
Toys, Mugs
Directions: Exit 7 off I-95
N (Market St & downtown
Portsmouth), 1 mile, next
to Theater By the Sea

Raymond

**COZY CORNER ANTIQUE
SHOPPE**
Rte 101 & 156   03077
603 895-2875   Est: 1967

COZY CORNER   Cont'd

Proprietor: John Peoples
Hours: Daily
Types & Periods: General
Line
Directions: On main road
(101) & 156 at corner, 18
miles from Manchester &
Derry

Rindge

THE SETH DEAN HOUSE ANTIQUES

Rte 202   03461
603 899-5618
Proprietor: Louella & Ray
Racicot
Hours: Daily
Types & Periods: General
Line

Rollinsford

PICKET FENCE ANTIQUES

Clement Rd   03820
603 742-5037   Est: 1939
Proprietor: Evelyn L
Norton
Hours: Daily, "At Home"
Types & Periods: Pattern
Glass, China, Primitives,
Early American Furniture
Appraisal Service Available
Directions: 2 miles out
Broadway from Dover,
turn right on Rollins Rd,
Clement Rd next left

Rumney

MILL ROAD ANTIQUES

Mill Rd   03266
603 786-2101   Est: 1970
Proprietor: The
Munkittricks
Hours: Daily, by
appointment or by chance
Types & Periods: Early Flo
Blue, Marked Bennington in
Flint Enamel, Rockingham,
Porcelain Glaze, Rare
Decorated Stoneware with
Cobalt
Specialties: Flo Blue,
Stoneware
Directions: 1/4 mile on
dirt street from village
Post Office

NELSON'S ANTIQUES

Stinson Lake Rd   03266
603 786-3421   Est: 1951
Proprietor: John & Kay
Nelson
Hours: By appointment, by
chance
Types & Periods: General
Line, Collectibles
Specialties: Furniture,
Primitives
Directions: Off Rte 25 at
Rumney Depot Blinker,
1/2 mile on road to
Stinson Lake

Rumney Village

STINSON HOUSE BOOKS & ANTIQUES

Quincy Rd   03266
603 786-3412   Est: 1963
Proprietor: George & Ann
Kent
Hours: Daily during
summer; winter by
appointment or by chance
Types & Periods: General
Line, Books
Appraisal Service Available
Directions: Right turn from
village common to 2nd
large white house

Salem

ANN'S ANTIQUE SHOP

84 Main   03079
603 898-4547   Est: 1967
Proprietor: Johanna G
Bourque
Hours: By appointment, by
chance
Types & Periods: Art Glass,
General Line
Specialties: Akro Agate
Glass & Marbles, Auctioneer
Appraisal Service Available
Directions: I-93 Exit 2, 1/4
mile E just before 1st light

Salisbury Heights

BARKERS OF SALISBURY HEIGHTS

Rte 4   03268
603 648-2488
Proprietor: Eileen & Dana
Barker

Hours: Daily
Types & Periods: Furniture,
General Line

FALES' SUMMER BOOK SHOP

Rte 4   03268
603 648-2484
Proprietor: Edward &
Hazel Fales
Types & Periods: Books,
Manuscripts

Sanbornville

ALADDIN ANTIQUES

Governor's Rd   03872
603 522-8503
Hours: Daily
Types & Periods: Iron Toys
& Banks, Mechanical & Still
Dolls, Doll Stuff, Country
Store Items, Primitives,
Tools, China, Glass, Bottles
Directions: On the
Brookfield Line

Seabrook

DONALD J MC INNIS

LaFayette Rd   03874
603 474-9263   Est: 1969
Proprietor: Donald J
McInnis
Hours: Daily
Types & Periods: General
Line, Victorian
Appraisal Service Available
Directions: Exit last stop
in Salisbury on Rte 95 N,
1st shop on Rte 1

Somersworth

CHAMBERLAIN ANTIQUES

240 Rte 16   03878
603 749-2565   Est: 1966
Proprietor: Dorothy
Chamberlain
Hours: Daily
Types & Periods: General
Line
Directions: 5 miles from
Dover or Rochester on
Rte 16, Exit 9 from
Spaulding Trnpk

South Weare

HARRISON HOUSE ANTIQUES
Rte 77   03281
603 529-7174   Est: 1972
Proprietor: Barbe Harrison
Hours: Daily, 9-6
Types & Periods: Early Pine
Country Furniture &
Accessories
Specialties: Furniture
(Kitchen), Utensils, Wood
Advertising
Directions: 20 minutes N
of Milford

Spofford

FINE ANTIQUES
                    03462
603 363-4363
Proprietor: William W
Lewis
Hours: By appointment,
May 15-Nov 15
Types & Periods: Furniture,
Oil Paintings, Glass, Copper
Lustre, Silver

THE STONE HOUSE
Rtes 9 & 63   03462
603 363-4616   Est: 1950
Proprietor: Gordon A
Chamberlin
Hours: Daily, by
appointment, by chance
Types & Periods: Glass,
China, Furniture
Specialties: New England &
New York Stoneware
Directions. Corner of Rtes
9 & 63

Stratham

THE OLDE TANNERY ANTIQUES
249 Portsmouth Ave
                    03885
603 772-4997
Proprietor: Pat & Esther
Flanagan
Hours: Daily
Types & Periods: Country
Furniture of the 18th & 19th
Centuries
Specialties: Furniture (Early
New England) & Accessories
Directions: Rte 101
between Portsmouth &
Exeter

THE TIN DRUM ANTIQUES
23 Portsmouth Ave 03885
603 772-6395   Est: 1972
Proprietor: Ruth Anne
Rhodes
Hours: Daily
Types & Periods: 18th &
19th Century Country
Furniture, Formal Pieces,
Accessories, Primitives
Specialties: Furniture (Pine
Country)
Directions: On Rte 101
just N of Exeter, about 8
miles SW of Portsmouth,
10 minutes from Rte 95

Sugar Hill

ELEANOR M LYNN & ELIZABETH A MONAHAN
Rte 117   03585
603 823-5550
Proprietor: Eleanor M
Lynn & Elizabeth A
Monahan
Hours: By appointment
Types & Periods: Quality
American Period Furniture &
Decorative Accessories,
Oriental Rugs, Paintings
Appraisal Service Available
Directions: Rte 117, near
museum

Sunapee

PRISCILLA DRAKE ANTIQUES
Rte 11   03782
603 763-5546   Est: 1972
Proprietor: Priscilla Drake
Hours: Daily, Memorial
Day to Christmas; Closed
Jan-March; also by
appointment
Types & Periods: 17th
Century Furniture, Glass,
China, Pewter, Toys,
Jewelry, Tools, Guns
Appraisal Service Available
Directions: 5 miles W of
Exit 12 on Rte 89

Tilton

HIGH HOPE FARM
Rte 3   03276
603 286-8050
Proprietor: Bird & Elliott

Types & Periods: Early NH
Furniture including large
stock of Beds, Flower Print
Lamp Shades, Hand
Weaving
Directions: 2 miles N of
junction 93 & 3 on Rte 3

HOPKINSON'S ANTIQUES
RFD 1   03276
603 524-3206
Hours: Daily
Types & Periods: General
Line, Furniture, Glass, China
Appraisal Service Available
Directions: US Rte 3, 2
miles N of I-93

SHAW'S ANTIQUES
Clark Rd   03276
603 286-4220   Est: 1950
Proprietor: Herbert E
Shaw
Hours: Daily
Types & Periods: Early
American Furniture
Appraisal Service Available
Directions: Near Soldiers'
Home

Tuftonboro Corner

DOW'S CORNER SHOP
                    03864
603 539-4790   Est: 1948
Proprietor: Albert H Dow
Jr
Hours: Daily, 9-5;
Mon-Sat, Nov 1-May 1
Types & Periods: General
Line
Specialties: Furniture, Rugs,
Primitives
Appraisal Service Available
Directions: Rte 171
between Rtes 16 & 25

Wakefield

GAGE HILL ANTIQUES
Gage Hill Rd   03872
603 522-3496   Est: 1957
Proprietor: Elsie M
Johnson
Hours: Daily
Types & Periods: China,
Glass, Primitives, Pine
Furniture
Appraisal Service Available
Directions: 22 miles N of
Rochester on Rte 16, just
off Rte 16 by Palmer's
Motel

Walpole

ANDREWS' ANTIQUES
Old Keene Rd   03608
603 756-3795   Est: 1973
Proprietor: Dan & Elsie
Andrews
Hours: By appointment, by
chance
Types & Periods: Country,
Primitives, Folk Art, Country
Accessories
Appraisal Service Available
Directions: S of Walpole
on Rte 12, look for sign
"Antiques Next Left"

LANTERN SHOP
Old Keene Rd   03608
603 756-9810   Est: 1965
Proprietor: Ruth S
Brennan
Hours: By appointment, by
chance
Types & Periods: Early
Lighting, Miniatures,
Primitive & Country
Accessories, Furniture
Directions: Off Rte 12, 12
miles N of Keene, 6 miles
from I-91 Exit 5 N & then
S to 123 & 12

Warrier

MARY PAGE
Burnt Hill Rd   03278
603 456-3351
Proprietor: Mary Page
Hours: By chance
Types & Periods: 18th &
Early 19th Century Furniture,
Accessories
Appraisal Service Available
Directions: 20 minutes N
of Concord, Hwy 89,
Exit 8

Washington

HALF-MOON ANTIQUES
Half-Moon Pond Rd
                          03280
603 495-3663   Est: 1972
Proprietor: Steve Davis &
Jim Pratt
Hours: Daily, 8-5
Types & Periods: New
England Antiques &
Accessories

Specialties: Furniture (Pine)
Appraisal Service Available
Directions: 1st road past
Historic town buildings

TINTAGEL ANTIQUES
Box 21   03280
                    Est: 1973
Proprietor: Sally Krone
Hours: Sun-Wed, Fri-Sat;
open late spring thru fall
Types & Periods: Country &
Primitive Items,
Woodenware, Tin, Copper,
Tools, Kitchenware, Frames,
Small Furniture, Collectibles
Directions: 1 mile N of
Washington village on
Rte 31

Weare

**THE ONE FIFTH GROUP
INC**
Mulberry House   03281
603 529-2936   Est: 1973
Proprietor: Murray &
Carole Wigsten
Hours: By appointment
only
Types & Periods: Period
Furniture, Accessories,
Kitchen Hearth Things,
Tools
Specialties: Antique Tools
Appraisal Service Available
Directions: Rtes 114 & 77

ELIZABETH STOKES
Sugar Hill Rd   03281
603 398-2363
Hours: Daily
Types & Periods: Furniture,
Accessories, Hooked Rugs
Directions: S 1 mile off
Rte 77

Wentworth

BERNIER STUDIO
Rte 25   03282
603 764-5720
Proprietor: Mrs Carol Ann
Bernier
Hours: Daily, May-Oct
Types & Periods: Glass,
Silver, Old Books, China
Directions: Take Exit 26
off I-93, follow Rte 25
approximately 16 miles,

follow the signs, take left
at sign that says Bernier
Studio, big white house
with pillar porch

West Franklin

**THE DUTCHESS ANTIQUE
SHOP**
605 S Main St   03235
603 934-4573   Est: 1955
Proprietor: Verna R Rowell
Hours: "Dawn to 5"
Types & Periods: Primitives,
General Line
Directions: N of Concord,
18 miles on Rte 3, Old
blue Haywagon on lawn

**SIGN OF THE GOLDEN
WOLF**
1200 S Main   03235
603 934-2226   Est: 1950
Proprietor: Stephen &
Harriet Wilson
Hours: Tues-Sun
Types & Periods: Art Glass,
China, Furniture
Appraisal Service Available
Directions: Exit 17 US 93
N 9 miles on Rte 3

West Nottingham

**THE UNICORN ANTIQUE
SHOP**
Rte 132   03291
603 942-7084   Est: 1968
Proprietor: Ray & Jean
Farrell
Hours: Daily
Types & Periods: Primitives,
Victorian, Brass, Copper
Specialties: Rugs (Hand
Braided)
Directions: Rte 152, 1 mile
off Rte 4

West Ossipee

PEPPERSAUCE ANTIQUES
Box 52 Rte 16   03890
603 539-7707   Est: 1974
Proprietor: Judyth M Allen
Hours: By Chance or
appointment
Types & Periods: Early
American Primitives, New
England Furniture, Folk Art,

Samplers, Quilts, Wooden
Ware, Crocks
Specialties: Early
Stoneware, Spongeware,
Redware, Painted Furniture
Appraisal Service Available
    Directions: On Rte 16 on
    the way to the White
    Mountains, by Mt Whittier
    Ski Area

Wilmot

CENTER BROOK FARM ANTIQUES
    Rte 4A   03278
    603 526-4657   Est: 1974
    Proprietor: Lee & Bob
    Burgess
    Hours: By appointment, by
    chance
Types & Periods: Early
American Furniture, Crocks,
Jugs, Decoys, Primitives,
Baskets, Boxes, Quilts, Rugs
Specialties: Baskets,
Decoys, Jugs
    Directions: 2.2 miles on
    Rte 4A, N of Rte 11, just
    N of New London

THE SUGARPLUM
    Rte 4   03230
    603 768-3925   Est: 1974
    Proprietor: Anne & Nick
    Rowe
    Hours: Daily, by chance
Types & Periods: Early
Country Furniture, Pressed
Pattern & Flint Glass, China,
Pottery

Specialties: Primitives
    Directions: 3 miles W of
    Rte 11 on Rte 4

Wilton

BROOKSMEET ANTIQUE SHOP
    Abbot Hill Rd   03086
    603 654-6237   Est: 1950
    Proprietor: Leslie Frye
    Hours: Daily, by chance
Types & Periods: General
Line
Specialties: Primitives, Old
Tools
    Directions: Abbot Hill Rd
    at end of Gage Rd E

Wolfeboro

BIRCH ROAD ANTIQUES
    Birch Rd   03894
    603 569-2674   Est: 1955
    Proprietor: Mrs E H Swift
    Hours: By chance,
    April-Oct 15
Types & Periods: China,
Glass, Country Style
Furniture
    Directions: Off 28 at
    Wolfeboro Falls, 1 mile
    from center of town

HAINES HILLTOP ANTIQUES
    Haines Hill Rd   03894
    603 569-3697   Est: 1967

Proprietor: Mrs Donald A
McBeth
Hours: Sun-Mon, Wed-Sat,
July-Sept
Types & Periods: Pattern
Glass, Primitives, China
Specialties: Old Goblets
    Directions: Look for sign
    on Rte 28 at N Wolfeboro
    Rd between Wolfeboro &
    Ossipee

RALPH K REED
    Pleasant Valley Rd   03894
    603 569-1897   Est: 1965
    Proprietor: Ralph K Reed
    Hours: Mon-Sat, 10-5, July
    1-Sept 1; other times by
    chance or appointment
Types & Periods: Furniture,
Marine Items
Specialties: Military Chests,
Camphorwood Boxes
    Directions: 3 miles off Rte
    28, S of Wolfeboro

TOUCHMARK ANTIQUES
    S Main St   03894
    603 569-2572   Est: 1974
    Proprietor: Helen Bradley
    & Anne Roome
    Hours: Daily, June 1-Oct
    15
Types & Periods: Primitives,
Country Furnishings,
Kitchenware, Tools,
Decorative Items
Appraisal Service Available
    Directions: Rte 28 S
    Wolfeboro, across from
    the Baptist Church

Couch, Middle
Victorian.

STATE OF NEW JERSEY

Alpine

E B HILLE
Closter Dock Rd   07620
201 768-0026   Est: 1940
Proprietor: E B Hille
Hours: Daily, 1-5
Types & Periods: General
Line
Appraisal Service Available

Andover

**FROGMORE COUNTRY
STORE & ANTIQUES**
Rte 206 Cranbury Lake
07821
201 347-6259   Est: 1968
Proprietor: E Haddad & D
Thompson
Hours: Daily
Types & Periods: General
Line
Directions: Rte 80 to
Newton Exit, 3 miles N of
Exit on Rte 206

Atlantic City

REESE PALLEY
1911 The Boardwalk
08401
609 344-1128   Est: 1958
Proprietor: Reese Palley
Hours: Daily; Mon-Sat
during July & Aug
Types & Periods: Boehm
Birds
Specialties: American
Collector's Porcelains
Appraisal Service Available

**PRINCETON ANTIQUES &
BOOKSHOP**
2915-17-31 Atlantic 08401
609 344-1943   Est: 1927
Proprietor: Robert E
Ruffolo II
Hours: By appointment, by
chance
Types & Periods: Art Glass,
Books, Furniture
Specialties: International
Search Service
Appraisal Service Available
Directions: Main
Business St

**YELLOW HOUSE OF
ANTIQUES**
451 N Maryland Ave
08401
609 927-6356   Est: 1961
Proprietor: Johanna Grist
Roberts
Hours: Sun, 12-3
Types & Periods: General
Line
Directions: Hwy 559, NE
corner Jeffreys Landing
Rd, Scullville

Barnegat

**AUDRAY'S BEST OF THE
WEST**
360 N Main St   08005
609 698-2415
Proprietor: Audray & Neil
Lindstrom
Hours: Daily
Types & Periods: Arcade &
Amusement Machines,
Furniture, Indian Jewelry,
Guns, Swords, Military
Items, Move Photos
Specialties: Posters, Swords,
Photos, Lobby Cards,
Baseball Memorabilia
Appraisal Service Available
Directions: Garden State
Pkwy to Exit 67 S, left ot
light, 3rd bldg on right

Beach Haven

HOUSE OF 7 WONDERS
7600 Long Beach Blvd
08008
609 494-9673   Est: 1966
Proprietor: John & Lucy
Arakelian
Hours: Daily during
summer season;
Weekends during May,
Oct & Nov
Types & Periods: General
Line, Furniture
Specialties: Restoration,
Refinishing, Caning
Appraisal Service Available
Directions: Garden State
Pkwy to Exit 63, E on 72

to the Blvd on Long
Beach Island, right turn on
Blvd, go S approximately
3 miles

Belleville

ANTIQUE SHOPPE
506 Washington Ave
07109
201 759-7369
Proprietor: Ruth Mowen
Hours: Tues-Sat
Types & Periods: China,
Glass, Silver, Dolls,
Furniture
Appraisal Service Available

Belvidere

**FIVE ACRES AUCTION
GALLERY**
Rte 46   07823
201 475-2572   Est: 1947
Proprietor: Jim Bishop &
Dot Phillips
Hours: Weekends by
appointment, closed
holidays
Types & Periods: Period
Furniture, Art Glass,
Paintings, Jewelry
Appraisal Service Available
Directions: 1 mile from Rte
31, 12 miles from
Delaware Watercap, 7
miles from I-80, 70 miles
W of NYC, 80 miles from
Philadelphia

Bernardsville

ANTIQUE CORNER
41 Olcott Square   07924
201 766-3915   Est: 1971
Proprietor: Dolores
Sheppard & Claryse Doerr
Hours: Wed-Sat, 10-4
Types & Periods: Refinished
Furniture, Lamps, Copper,
Brass, Mirrors, General Line
Specialties: Refinished
Furniture, Mirrors, Lamp
Shades & Parts

Appraisal Service Available
Directions: Center of town,
across from Bernardsville
Cinema

Boonton

DISCOVERY HOUSE
811 Main St   07005
201 335-5670   Est: 1967
Proprietor: Jeanne
Marsden
Hours: Tues-Sat, by
appointment
Types & Periods: Victorian,
English, European,
Primitives
Specialties: Gifts, Jewelry
Appraisal Service Available
Directions: Rtes 46, 287 &
80, center of town

THE OLDE TYME MUSIC SCENE
915 Main St   07005
201 335-5040   Est: 1975
Proprietor: Don Donahue
& Lou DeCicco
Hours: Wed-Sun
Types & Periods:
Phonographs, Cylinders,
Diamond Discs, Records,
Sheet Music, Piano Rolls,
Music Cases
Appraisal Service Available
Directions: Exit 40A off
Rte 287N

Bound Brook

GRANDMOTHER'S TRUNK
114 E Union Ave   08805
201 356-3166   Est: 1968
Proprietor: Diane Zepp
Hours: Daily, by
appointment, by chance
Types & Periods: Small
Furniture (Mostly 1850 &
Earlier), Primitives, Pine,
Walnut, Cherry Pieces
Specialties: Early Kitchen
Utensils & Tools
Directions: 50 miles E of
NYC, 3 blocks off Rte 22
on Rte 28, near traffic
light at Mountain Ave

THE TIMEPIECE SHOP
132 W Franklin St   08805
201 356-6920
Proprietor: Thomas J
Stratford
Types & Periods: Clocks

Bridgeton

THE HITCHING POST ANTIQUES
81 N Pearl St   08302
609 451-2481   Est: 1952
Proprietor: S F McKinnie
Hours: Mon-Sat, 2-8; other
times by appointment
Types & Periods: General
Line
Directions: On Rte 77
which runs thru city

Buttzville

TRIFLES & TREASURES
Rte 46 Box 106   07829
201 453-2918   Est: 1961
Proprietor: M J Gustafson
Hours: Daily, 11-5
Types & Periods: Furniture,
Glass, China, Paintings,
Jewelry, '20-'50 Clothing
Specialties: Collectible China
& Depression Glass
Directions: 1000 ft W of
intersection of Hwys 31
& 46

Cape May

CAPE MAY COUNTRY STORE
Jefferson & Columbia Aves
08204
609 884-8658   Est: 1940
Proprietor: Jane & Kathie
Kurtz
Hours: Daily, May-Oct;
Weekends, Nov-April
Types & Periods: General
Line, Oak Furniture, Country
Store Items
Specialties: Hand-Dipped
Candles, Pewter, Doll House
Miniatures, Decoys, Food
Items
Directions: Lafayette St,
turn left 1 mile onto
Jefferson St

THE ROADRUNNER
609-611 Jefferson St
08204
609 884-4563   Est: 1956
Proprietor: Carol & Bob
Gomm
Hours: Daily during
season, Weekends
year-round
Types & Periods: Furniture,
China, Glass, Nautical Items
Specialties: Tiffany Style
Shades
Directions: At end of NJ
Pkwy, go straight on
LaFayette St to Jefferson
St, turn left

Centertown

CROWN & FEATHER ANTIQUES
Moorestown-Centertown Rd
08054
609 234-0432
Proprietor: Mrs May E
Wright
Hours: Daily, 12-5
Types & Periods: Pattern
Glass, Country Furniture,
Accessories, General Line

Cherry Hill

MARY'S MEMORIES
08003
609 429-5931   Est: 1970
Proprietor: Mary & John
Kane
Hours: By appointment
only
Types & Periods: Antique &
Collectible Jewelry
Specialties: Maintain Full
Gemology Lab for ID &
Grading of Gemstones
Appraisal Service Available
Directions: Call for
directions

Cinnaminson

WEB & ASSOCIATES
1101 E Broad St   08077
609 829-2033   Est: 1958
Proprietor: Wm & Robert
Barron
Hours: By appointment

WEB & ASSOC   Cont'd

Types & Periods: Antiques, Jewelry, Art, Furniture
Appraisal Service Available

Clifton

ANTIQUERY
430 Lexington Ave   07011
201 546-5952   Est: 1974
Proprietor: Judd Berkey
Hours: Mon-Sat, or by appointment or chance
Types & Periods: Furniture & Furnishings, Pre 1970
Specialties: Furniture, Oak, Walnut in the Victorian Era
Appraisal Service Available
Directions: From W Rte 80 E to Exit 57, Market St, Paterson to Lakeview, left to Clifton Ave, right to Lexington, left

GRANNY'S ATTIC
1080 Main Ave   07011
201 772-1929   Est: 1966
Proprietor: Maury Lubman
Hours: Daily
Types & Periods: General Line, Furniture, Bric-A-Brac, Collectibles
Appraisal Service Available

ROWE-MANSE EMPORIUM INC
1065 Bloomfield Ave
    07012
201 472-8170   Est: 1957
Proprietor: Carmen J Maggio, President
Hours: Mon & Wed, 10-6; Tues, 10-9; Sun by appointment or chance
Types & Periods: General Line
Appraisal Service Available
Directions: 1/3 mile E of Garden State Pkwy, adjacent to Rte 3 in Styertowne Shopping Center

MR WIPPLES CHARMING COUNTRY STORE
1076 Main Ave   07011
201 772-1929
Proprietor: Maury Lubman
Hours: Daily
Types & Periods: Country Primitives, Oak, Pine, Walnut Furniture, Country Store

Items, Advertising Items, Stained Glass, Candy Cases with Penny Candy for the kids
Appraisal Service Available

Cranbury

COBWEB ANTIQUES
115 N Main St   08512
609 655-1875   Est: 1970
Proprietor: Anne Ostergaard
Hours: By appointment
Types & Periods: Small Furniture, Cut & Pressed Glass, China
Directions: 8 miles E of Princeton

FRITZ'S ANTIQUE
149 Old Trenton Rd
    08512
609 448-5682
Proprietor: Fritz Wospil
Hours: By appointment, by chance
Types & Periods: Victorian, Oak & Fancy Furniture, Clocks, Lamps, Brass Items
Appraisal Service Available
Directions: 2 miles from Exit 8, NJ Trnpk at intersection of 1 mile road & Old Trenton Rd

THE LANTERN ANTIQUES
S Main St   08512
609 395-0762   Est: 1967
Proprietor: Dorothy S Titzeh
Hours: By appointment
Types & Periods: Tin, Iron, Wood, Collectibles
Directions: Next to Hagerty the Florist

Cranford

GOOD FAIRY DOLL MUSEUM & HOSPITAL
205 Walnut Ave   07016
201 276-3815   Est: 1967
Proprietor: Mr & Mrs James Connors
Hours: By appointment, by chance
Types & Periods: Antique Dolls, Portrait Dolls, Comics Dolls, Advertising, Bottles,

Banks, Fairytale Dolls Houses, Animation Bears Museum
Appraisal Service Available
Directions: Exit 137 Garden State Pkwy, go 5 traffic lights & turn left

Creiskill

GENERAL STORE
18 Union Ave   07626
201 568-2652   Est: 1965
Proprietor: Derna Wehmann
Hours: Mon-Fri, 1-5; Sat, 11-5
Types & Periods: General Line
Directions: 7 miles N of George Washington Bridge, Rte 9W to Creiskill

Dover

BERMAN'S AUCTION BARN
4 Dewey St   07801
201 361-3110   Est: 1965
Proprietor: Ed & Millie Berman
Hours: Auctions held 2nd & 4th Sat of each month & middle Wed
Types & Periods: Cut Glass, Art Glass, Art, Porcelain, Pottery, Furniture
Specialties: Coins, Steins, Guns
Appraisal Service Available
Directions: On Bassett Hwy in Dover, 5 minutes off Rte 80 & 10, & 1 minutes off Rte 46, 50 minutes from NY

Elizabeth

FRAN'S ANTIQUE SHOP
1002 Elizabeth Ave   07201
201 352-0155   Est: 1960
Proprietor: Frances Girgus
Hours: Mon-Sat, 10-5
Types & Periods: General Line, Bric-A-Brac, Curios, Jewelry
Directions: Near Rte 1 & 9 overpass

Englewood

LEONARD BALISH
124A Engle St   07631
201 871-3454   Est: 1966
Proprietor: Leonard Balish
Hours: By chance
Types & Periods: American
Graphics, Indian Material,
Instruments, Folk Art,
Redware, Quilts, Toys
Specialties: Needlework,
Toys, Graphic Americana

COLONY ANTIQUE SHOP
1 E Palisade Ave   07631
201 568-5357   Est: 1958
Proprietor: Sylvia Franklin
Hours: Mon-Sat,
10:30-5:30
Types & Periods: Jewelry,
Fixtures, China, Glass,
Furniture, Silver, Lamps
Specialties: Jewelry
Appraisal Service Available
Directions: George
Washington Bridge to
Palisades Pkwy, 1st Exit

Far Hills

**BROWNSTONE BARN
ANTIQUES**
RD 1 Box 129   07931
Proprietor: Mrs Bertalan
De Nemethy
Hours: Daily, by
appointment
Types & Periods: English
Antique Furniture, Early
English Oak
Directions: Call for
appointment & directions

Fort Lee

**ANTIQUES &
TEMPTATIONS**
136 Main St   07024
201 944-1692   Est: 1974
Proprietor: Blanche
Jacobson
Hours: Daily, by
appointment
Types & Periods: Porcelain,
Crystal, Silver, Chandeliers,
Cranberry & Ruby Glass,
Bronze, Primitives, Furniture
Directions: 3 blocks S of
George Washington
Bridge

APROPOS INC
249 Main St   07024
201 461-7775   Est: 1973
Proprietor: Arlene Wahl
Forziati & Rhea Adler
Hours: Mon-Wed, Fri-Sat,
10-6; Thurs, 10-8
Types & Periods: Miniatures,
Furniture, Glassware,
Fixtures, Jewelry, Frames
Directions: Corner of
Center & Main

Garfield

THE COLLECTOR
85 Passaic St   07026
201 473-1377   Est: 1971
Proprietor: Joan Corry
Hours: Tues-Sat, 2-9
Types & Periods: Furniture,
Glass, Crystal, China, Silver,
Cameras, Jewelry, Clocks,
Bronzes, Paintings, Trunks,
Dolls, Appliances, Cars
Specialties: Firearms,
Military Clothing, Books,
Musical Instruments, Toys &
Automata, Dolls, Glass, Art
Deco, Paintings, Rugs,
Clocks, Silver, Jewelry
Appraisal Service Available
Directions: 5 minutes from
Rte 80, left on River Rd
Exit

FUSCO
101 Westminister Pl
                        07436
201 546-0308   Est: 1970
Proprietor: Ralph J Fusco
Hours: Thurs, Fri & Sat,
also by appointment
Types & Periods: Country
Store Items
Directions: Off Rte 46

Greenwich

SCHOOL HOUSE SHOP
                        08302
609 455-1944
Proprietor: Mrs Gertrude
Hallman
Hours: Sun-Mon, Wed-Sat,
2-6
Types & Periods: Glass,
China, Dolls, 19th Century
Buttons
Directions: Rte 2
Bridgeton

Hackensack

THE GOLD MAN
183 Main St   07601
201 342-6110   Est: 1971
Proprietor: Enid Goldman
Hours: Mon-Tues,
Thurs-Sat; also by
appointment
Types & Periods: Jewelry,
Small Objets d'Art,
Collectibles
Specialties: Watches
Appraisal Service Available
Directions: From Rte 80, N
on Hudson St onto
Main St

HONORE INC
256 Riverside Square
                        07601
203 489-2212
Proprietor: Ronald &
Honore Kaplan
Hours: Daily
Types & Periods: Jewelry,
Artifacts

Highland Park

**RUTGERS GUN AND BOAT
CENTER**
127 Raritan Ave   08904
201 545-4344   Est: 1961
Proprietor: Mark Aziz
Hours: Mon-Tues, 10-6;
Thurs-Fri, 10-9; Sat, 9-5
Types & Periods: Firearms &
Books
Appraisal Service Available

Hopewell

COX'S COBWEB ANTIQUES
21 E Broad St   08525
609 466-1614   Est: 1953
Proprietor: Ruth E Cox
Hours: Fri, Sat & Sun,
11-4, by appointment
Types & Periods: Country
Furniture, China, Glass,
Stoneware, Pottery

**HOPEWELL ANTIQUE
CENTER AT THE TOMATO
FACTORY**
Hamilton Ave   08525
609 466-2990
Proprietor: 8 Dealers
Hours: Daily, 10:30-5

HOPEWELL ANTIQUE CENTER   Cont'd
Types & Periods: Country Furniture, Primitives, Copper, Brass, Early Iron Pottery, Treen, Toleware, Glass, China

Irvington

HOUSE OF 7 WONDERS
759 Springfield Ave 07111
201 373-5618   Est: 1962
Proprietor: John & Lucy Arakelian
Hours: Tues-Sun
Types & Periods: General Line, Furniture
Specialties: China Repairs, Refinishing & Repairing Furniture, Caning
Appraisal Service Available
Directions: Garden State Pkwy to Exit 143 to Springfield Ave, go E 5 or 6 blocks

Jersey City

CHEZ JON INC
PO Box 1780   07307
201 963-0712
Proprietor: John Wilkins
Hours: Mon & Fri, by appointment
Types & Periods: Glass, Jewelry, Bric-A-Brac, Records
Specialties: Repair Stain Glass
Appraisal Service Available
Directions: Corner of Poplar & Summit

Lafayette

PUMLEYE'S ANTIQUES SHOP
Rte 15   07419
201 383-2114   Est: 1948
Proprietor: John Pumleye
Hours: Sun, 12-5; Mon & Fri, 1-5; other days by chance
Types & Periods: Chippendale, Queen Anne, Hepplewhite, Early Empire Primitives

Specialties: Clocks, Corner Cupboards
Directions: 20 miles from Rte 80 E, then N on Rte 15

Lakewood

EDITH REILLY
1985 Lanes Mill Rd 08701
201 363-2675
Proprietor: Edith Reilly
Types & Periods: Paintings, Export Porcelain, Items of the China Trade

Lambertville

GOLDEN NUGGET ANTIQUE FLEA MARKET
Rte 29   08530
609 397-0811   Est: 1964
Proprietor: Daniel R Brenna & Angelo R Peluso
Hours: Weekends
Types & Periods: Period Furniture, Americana, Coins, Stamps, China, Glass, Silver, Pictures, Prints, Jewelry
Directions: 1½ miles S of town on US 29

GOVERNORS ANTIQUE MARKET AND OUTDOOR FLEA MARKET
Rte 179   08530
609 397-2010   Est: 1976
Proprietor: E M Cad
Hours: Tues, Sat & Sun, 8-5
Types & Periods: Dolls, Furniture, Clocks, Glass, Bric-A-Brac, Early & Collectible Paper (Postal Cards), Jewelry, Weapons, Coins
Specialties: Furniture, Jewelry, Pocket Watches
Appraisal Service Available
Directions: 1½ miles N of Lambertville on Rte 179, S on Rte 202 to Lambertville Exit

Lawrenceville

WILLIAM R PAQUIN ANTIQUES
10 Rydal Dr   08648
609 883-0569
Proprietor: William R Paquin
Hours: By appointment
Types & Periods: American Furniture & Paintings of the 18th-20th Centuries, Decoys, Redware, Quilts, Coverlets, Oriental Rugs, American Indian Rugs

Marlboro

GRANDMA'S TREASURES
35 N Main St   07746
201 462-2381   Est: 1960
Proprietor: Jack & Alida Hendrickson
Hours: Mon-Tues, Thurs-Sat, 11-5; Sun, 1-5
Types & Periods: China, Glassware, Primitives, Silver, Jewelry, Oriental, Furniture, Lighting Devices
Appraisal Service Available
Directions: 4 miles N of Historic Freehold on Hwy 79

Martinsville

THE MOUNTAIN HOUSE INC
                   08836
201 469-2195   Est: 1971
Proprietor: Carl & Jane Tonero
Hours: Daily, by appointment only
Types & Periods: Signed Art Glass, Oriental & European Porcelains, 18th & 19th Century Clocks, 18th & 19th Century Furniture
Specialties: Expert Clock Reconstruction & Repair
Appraisal Service Available
Directions: 1 mile N of Rte 22 near Somerville

Masonville

CROWN & FEATHER ANTIQUES
163 E Moorestown-
Centerton Rd   08054
609 234-0432
Proprietor: Mrs May E
Wright
Hours: Daily, 12-5
Types & Periods: Pattern
Glass, Country Furniture,
Accessories, General Line

Matawan

THE COLLECTOR'S INC
83 Main St   07747
201 583-3222   Est: 1971
Proprietor: Corporation
Hours: Mon-Sat, 12-5
Types & Periods: General
Line, Furniture, Collectibles,
Bric-A-Brac, Dolls,
Miniatures
Appraisal Service Available
Directions: Between Rte
34 & Rte 35 on Main St,
Exit 117A on Garden State
Pkwy, in 150 year old
house

Merchantville

**ANTIQUES-DOROTHY R
BLINDENBACHER**
10 S Centre St   08109
609 662-6318   Est: 1960
Proprietor: Dorothy R
Blindenbacher
Hours: Mon-Sat, 12-5
Types & Periods: Furniture,
China, Art Glass, Sterling,
Clocks, Jewelry, Civil War
Items
Appraisal Service Available
Directions: 4 miles from
Camden

Milltown

GARAGE SALE CORNER
60 N Main St   08850
201 846-8181   Est: 1973
Proprietor: Irene Pardun
Hours: Tues-Sat, 10-4

Types & Periods: Cut Glass,
Furniture, Lamps, Clocks,
Depression Glass, Pressed
Glass, Primitives, Stoneware
Directions: Off Rte 1
between Princeton &
Newark

Montclair

CLAIRMONT LTD
51 Church St   07042
201 746-3641   Est: 1954
Proprietor: Philip Schwartz
Hours: Daily
Types & Periods: Cut Glass,
China, Paintings, Silver,
Jewelry, Clocks, Dolls,
Coins, Records, Bric-A-Brac
Appraisal Service Available
Directions: Church &
Parks, 1 block above
Bloomfield Ave, across
from Hahnes Dept Store

Moorestown

**AULD LANG SYNE
ANTIQUES**
111 E Main St   08057
609 234-5014   Est: 1971
Proprietor: Janet B Uzzell
Hours: Tues-Thurs, Sat;
also by appointment
Types & Periods: General
Line
Specialties: Paintings
Appraisal Service Available
Directions: 20 minutes
from Philadelphia via Rte
38 across from Friends
School

Mount Holly

**THE BROWSE AROUND
SHOP INC**
Rte 38 RD 2   08060
609 261-0274   Est: 1964
Proprietor: Chuck &
Charlie Johnson
Hours: Wed-Sun
Types & Periods: General
Line, Furniture
Directions: Hwy 38, 7
miles E of Moorestown

Mullica Hill

**ANTHONY & ELLEN
BARRETT ANTIQUES**
S Main St   08062
609 478-4120   Est: 1973
Proprietor: Anthony &
Ellen Barrett
Hours: By appointment, by
chance
Types & Periods: American
Painted Furniture, Folk Art,
Antiques for the Country
Home
Specialties: Penna Furniture
& Folk Arts
Appraisal Service Available
Directions: Rte 322 to Rte
45, 3 miles from Exit 2 of
NJ Trnpk

EAGLES NEST ANTIQUES
38 S Main St   08062
609 478-6351   Est: 1974
Proprietor: Bea & Richard
Murray
Hours: Daily, 11-5
Types & Periods: China,
Glass, Furniture, Tinware,
Coins, Jewelry, Primitives
Specialties: Depression
Glass
Directions: 6 miles S of
Woodbury on Rte 45, 3
miles E of Exit 2, NJ
Trnpk

**FURNISHINGS FOR THE
CONNOISSEUR**
13 N Main St   08062
609 478-4848   Est: 1975
Proprietor: Peter R
Kressler
Hours: Fri, Sat & Sun, 1-5;
also by appointment
Types & Periods:
Chippendale, Hepplewhite,
Sheraton, Empire, Brass
Beds
Directions: Center of town
on Rtes 322 & 45

**KINGS ROW OF MULLICA
HILL**
44 N Main St   08062
609 478-4361   Est: 1969
Proprietor: 7 Dealers
Hours: Daily, 11-5
Types & Periods: General
Line, Collectibles
Directions: 3 miles E of
Exit 2, NJ Trnpk

KATE & STAN LAMBORNE ANTIQUES
34-36 S Main   08062
609 478-2484
Proprietor: Kate & Stan
Lamborne
Hours: Tues-Sun
Types & Periods: Country
Furniture, Accessories
Directions: Exit 2 from NJ
Trnpk, follow signs to
Mullica Hill, about 2 miles

ROBERT & ANN SCHUMANN ANTIQUES
74 N Main St   08062
609 478-2553   Est: 1973
Proprietor: Robert & Ann
Schumann
Hours: By appointment, by
chance
Types & Periods: American,
Country, Period Furniture &
Accessories
Specialties: Furniture, Folk
Art, 18th & 19th Centuries
Directions: Rte 322,
Mullica Hill, 3 miles E of
NJ Trnpk, Exit 2

THE SIGN OF ST GEORGE
56 S Main St   08062
609 478-6101   Est: 1963
Proprietor: Edmund P &
Jean V Cordery
Hours: Wed, Thurs, Sat &
Sun; other times by
appointment
Types & Periods: 17th, 18th
& Early 19th Century
Country Furniture, Ironware,
Stoneware, Pewter, Tinware,
Period Furniture
Appraisal Service Available
Directions: Southern NJ,
Gloucester County,
approximately 4 miles
from Exit 2 of NJ Trnpk,
thru village to S end, 16
shops in this village

Neshanic Station

BRANCHBURG ANTIQUES CENTER
RD 2 Rte 202   08853
201 369-9811   Est: 1975
Proprietor: Janet
Rosenthal
Hours: Sun-Mon,
Thurs-Sat
Types & Periods: General
Line

Appraisal Service Available
Directions: On Rte 202,
midway between
Flemington & Somerville

Newark

HALO
268 Washington St   07102
201 643-9533   Est: 1938
Proprietor: Paul Halo
Hours: Mon, Wed & Fri,
11-3; also by appointment
Types & Periods: Jewelry
Specialties: Jewelry
Appraisal Service Available

GEORGE SCHEINER & SON
429 Broad St   07102
201 621-8311   Est: 1897
Proprietor: Augustus
Scheiner
Hours: Daily, 12-5; also by
appointment
Types & Periods: American
Furniture, Paintings, Art
Appraisal Service Available

New Egypt

THE BARRACKS
Brindletown Rd   08533
609 758-8384   Est: 1976
Proprietor: Carol Reed
Hours: Daily, 10-10
Types & Periods:
Turn-of-the-Century
Furniture, Collectibles
Specialties: Restoring &
Refinishing
Directions: 1/4 mile off
Main St

THE HOBBY HORSE
New Egypt Market Rte 537
                      08533
609 758-2082   Est: 1974
Proprietor: Fritz Davis
Hours: Wed & Sun, 10-4;
also by appointment
Types & Periods: General
Line, Collectibles, Furniture
Appraisal Service Available
Directions: Between
intersection of Rtes 528 &
539

Newton

GRAYCE I LENGA ANTIQUES
RD 6 Box 125   07860
201 383-6796   Est: 1956
Proprietor: Grayce I Lenga
Hours: By appointment
Types & Periods: Pine &
Cherry Furniture, Pressed
Glass, Primitives,
Appraisal Service Available
Directions: Rte 94 to
Anderson Hill Rd to Circle
Dr

Ocean City

ORA'S POTPOURRI SHOP
306 55th St   08226
609 398-0296   Est: 1975
Proprietor: Mrs William
Gardiner
Hours: Daily, June-Oct
Types & Periods: Pine,
Colonial, Victorian,
Glassware
Directions: Ocean Dr

Ocean View

STAGE COACH INN ANTIQUES
140 Shore Rd   08230
609 263-3594   Est: 1969
Proprietor: Mat & M G
Vance
Hours: Daily
Types & Periods: General
Line
Specialties: China
Directions: W side of Rte
9, between Woodbine &
Sea Isle Rds

Passaic

JAN JILL & JON
170 Main Ave   07055
201 777-4670   Est: 1949
Proprietor: Rhoda &
Seymour Zucker
Hours: Tues-Sat, 10-6
Types & Periods: Orientalia,
Victorian, Art Noveau, Art
Deco, Antique Jewelry,
Silver, Crystal, Art Glass,
Porcelains, Paintings,
Bronzes

Appraisal Service Available
Directions: 15 minutes
from NYC, Lincoln Tunnel
to Rte 3, Main Ave
Passaic Exit, right on Main
Ave, less than 1 mile

Pemberton

STONE HEARTH ANTIQUES VILLAGE
Arney's Mt,
Birmingham Rd   08068
609 267-6919   Est: 1962
Proprietor: Mrs Ruth Isgro
Hours: Tues-Sun, by
appointment
Types & Periods: Country
Period or Primitive Furniture,
China, Glass, Dolls, Paper
Items, Tin, Iron, Crockery,
Lighting, Kitchen Items &
Other Bric-A-Brac, Colquitts
Specialties: Furniture, Period
Country & Primitive
Appraisal Service Available
Directions: From Rte 205,
take Woodlane Rd E
(Slumberland Motel on
corner), to Arney's Mt,
Birmingham, turn left, 3/4
mile to drive

Perth Amboy

THE CRYSTAL SHOPPE
289 High St   08861
201 442-2704   Est: 1941
Proprietor: Lena B
Gincborg
Hours: Mon-Fri, 10-5;
weekends & evenings by
appointment
Types & Periods: Furniture,
Glass, Rugs, Paintings,
Prints, Documents, Chinese
Porcelains, Cloisonne,
Ivories
Specialties: Glass,
Porcelains
Appraisal Service Available
Directions: Garden State &
NJ Trnpk, "Police Officers
will give directions"

Pine Brook

DUTCH GABLES
58 Maple Ave   07058
201 227-2803

Proprietor: Betsy D
Demarest & Marion C
Douglass
Hours: By appointment, by
chance
Types & Periods: Early
American Primitives
Directions: Corner of Hook
Mt Rd & Maple Ave

Pluckemin

COUNTRY ANTIQUES SHOP
Rte 202-206   07978
201 658-3759   Est: 1950
Proprietor: Ellie & Bob
Haines
Hours: Wed-Fri, 10-5; Sat
& Sun, 10-6
Types & Periods: Large
stock of Refinished Antique
Furnishings
Directions: 7 miles N
Somerville Circle, 9 miles
S Morristown

Port Murray

PORT MURRAY EMPORIUM ANTIQUES
Main St   07865
201 689-1760   Est: 1967
Proprietor: Vivienne
Opdyke
Hours: Wed-Sat, 1-5
Types & Periods: General
Line
Specialties: Toys (Dolls &
Accessories)
Directions: Off Rte 57
between Washington &
Hackettstown, 65 miles
from NYC

Princeton

HOUSE OF TREASURES
Rte 1   08540
609 452-1234   Est: 1960
Proprietor: Elizabeth
Benedik
Hours: Tues-Sat, 11-5
Types & Periods: Furniture,
Primitives
Appraisal Service Available
Directions: At Princeton
Circle, 2 blocks from
Harrison on S side of
Rte 1

JOSEPH'S COAT ANTIQUES
RD 4 Box 575   08540
201 821-9447
Proprietor: Frank & Helen
Schumacher
Types & Periods: Primitives,
China, Pottery, Tin, Copper,
Brass
Directions: Little Rocky
Hill, Rte 27, 5 miles N of
Princeton

ROSE H MINTZ, ANTIQUAIRE
35 Forester Dr   08540
609 921-8660
Proprietor: Rose H Mintz
Hours: By appointment
Types & Periods: 17th, 18th
& 19th Century
Staffordshire, Chinese
Exports, Enamels,
Porcelains
Appraisal Service Available

Quakertown

OLD VILLAGE STORE
Main St   08868
201 735-8043
Proprietor: George J Miller
& Wm E Fretz
Types & Periods: General
Line

Raritan

GERALD STERLING "STERLING AUCTION GALLERY"
62 N 2nd Ave   08869
201 685-9565   Est: 1959
Proprietor: Gerald Sterling
Hours: Daily, by
appointment, by chance
Types & Periods: Period to
Turn-of-the-Century
Furnishings, Bric-A-Brac,
Sold at Auction
Specialties: Auctions
Appraisal Service Available
Directions: From
Somerville, take Rte 202
S, 1/4 mile to 1st U-Turn,
complete, go N on 202,
1/2 block to 2nd Ave, on
right

Red Bank

THE HUDSON SHOP INC
511 Broad St   07701
201 747-2003   Est: 1940
Proprietor: C Alan Hudson
Jr
Hours: Wed-Sat, by
appointment

**INTERNATIONAL
GALLERIES**
10 Riverside Ave   07701
201 747-6200
Proprietor: Frank Martelli
Hours: Daily
Types & Periods: 16th, 17th,
18th & 19th Century
American, English &
Continental Furniture
Appraisal Service Available
Directions: Exit 109,
Garden State Pkwy

**THE RED BANK ANTIQUE
CENTER**
217 W Front St   07701
201 741-5331   Est: 1964
Proprietor: Nan Johnson
Hours: Daily
Types & Periods: Glassware,
Silver, Jewelry, Primitives,
Deco
Appraisal Service Available
Directions: Exit 11 NJ
Trnpk to Rte 35 S, Exit
109 Garden State Pkwy,
W Front St at Bridge Ave

River Edge

EDWARD MALAKOFF
276 Princeton Dr   07661
201 487-1989   Est: 1947
Proprietor: Edward
Malakoff
Hours: By appointment
Types & Periods: Pairpoint
Lamps
Appraisal Service Available

Rosemont

RALEIGH ANTIQUES
At Cane Farm   08556
609 397-2700   Est: 1965
Proprietor: Lee Kolarsey
Hours: Daily, by telephone
call

Types & Periods: Country &
Formal Furniture, Porcelain,
Glass, Silver, Wood
Specialties: 18th & 19th
Century Antiques
Directions: 6 miles from
New Hope PA, on NJ
Rte 519

Saddle River

**RICHARD C KYLLO
ANTIQUES**
210 W Saddle River Rd
07458
201 327-7343
Proprietor: Richard C
Kyllo
Hours: Thurs, Fri & Sat,
1-4:30; also by
appointment
Types & Periods: 18th
Century American Furniture
& Accessories

Sergeantsville

LEE DAVIS ANTIQUES
Rte 523   08557
Proprietor: Mrs Lee Davis
Hours: Mon-Sat, 10-5; Sun
by appointment
Types & Periods: 17th-19th
Century Oriental Porcelain &
Furniture, Canton & Imari
Export, American & English
Formal Furniture
Specialties: Porcelains
Appraisal Service Available
Directions: "Just above
the blinker lights", Rte
523, 6 miles from
Flemington, 6 miles from
New Hope Pa

**HAWTHORN & GRAY
DESIGN STUDIO**
Rte 523   08557
609 397-2359   Est: 1975
Proprietor: Edward P
Bailey Jr
Hours: Mon-Sat; Sun by
appointment or by chance
Types & Periods: Small or
Scaled Down Pieces of
Furniture
Specialties: Tables, Brass,
Candlesticks, Bric-A-Brac
Directions: In the heart of
Sergeantsville, two floors

of a newly renovated barn
beside the newly
renovated stone house
which is over 100 years
old, S from Flemington on
Rte 523 & N from Trenton
on Rte 29 N to Rte 523
towards Flemington

Shrewsbury

THE HUDSON SHOP INC
511 Broad St   07701
Proprietor: C Alan Hudson
Jr
Hours: Wed-Sat
Types & Periods: American,
17th & 18th Century
Furniture & Accessories
Specialties: New Jersey
Country Pieces
Appraisal Service Available
Directions: 1½ miles from
Garden State Pkwy, Exit
109, Rte 35, Grey house
with red shutters, opposite
Shop Rite Super Market

Sicklerville

**CRAWFORD'S CORNER
ANTIQUES**
08081
609 728-2263
Proprietor: Vernon & Anna
Crawford
Hours: By appointment
Types & Periods: General
Line

Somers Point

**SOMERS POINT
CURIOSITY SHOP**
816 Shore Rd   08244
609 927-0805   Est: 1973
Proprietor: John & Sue
Conroy
Hours: Wed-Sun, 11-5
Types & Periods: Furniture,
Cut Glass, China, Flow Blue
Pottery, Ironstone
Specialties: Wicker Furniture
Appraisal Service Available
Directions: Close to
Causeway into Ocean
City, on main street in
town

Sparta

COBWEB CORNER INC
34 Layton Lane RD 2
                     07871
201 383-1952   Est: 1957
Proprietor: Betty Grosch
Hours: Daily
Types & Periods: General
Line
Appraisal Service Available
    Directions: Rte 15 in NW
    New Jersey

Stillwater

**BUDD'S COUNTRY STORE
ANTIQUES**
Box 17   07875
301 383-5610   Est: 1973
Proprietor: Charles R
Budd
Hours: By chance
Types & Periods: Early
American Furniture
Directions: On Rte 610

Summit

A CENTER OF ANTIQUES
488 Springfield Ave 07901
201 273-0307   Est: 1975
Proprietor: Sophie Weill
Hours: Daily, 11-5, also by
appointment
Types & Periods: Victorian,
American, French & English
Furniture, China, Silver,
Glass, Brass, Copper,
Bronze
    Directions: Rte 78

**MURIAL'S ANTIQUE
GALLERY LTD**
451 Springfield Ave 07901
201 277-0959   Est: 1968
Proprietor: Muriel K
Goldberg
Hours: Daily
Types & Periods: General
Line
Specialties: Jewelry, Oriental
(Porcelain)
Appraisal Service Available
    Directions: 25 miles from
    NYC, Path Train to
    Hoboken

Toms River

THE BENNETT'S
16 Sutton Place   08753
201 349-5114   Est: 1963
Proprietor: Betsy Bennett
Hours: By chance
Types & Periods: Paintings,
Folk Art, Early Tools,
Country Furniture, Primitives
Appraisal Service Available
    Directions: Exit 81,
    Garden State Pkwy

CEDAR HOUSE ANTIQUES
                     08753
201 244-3356
Proprietor: Bob & Doris
Haug
Hours: By appointment
Types & Periods: Quality
Country & Period Furniture,
Folk Art, Decoys, Tools,
Canton
Appraisal Service Available
    Directions: Please call for
    directions

Trenton

BEVERLY ANTIQUES
2516 Pennington Rd
                     08638
609 737-0073   Est: 1975
Proprietor: Harry R McKim
Hours: Tues-Sat, by
appointment or by chance;
best to call first
Types & Periods: General
Line, Glass, Furniture, Silver,
China, Dolls
    Directions: State Rte 31, N
    on I-95 & I-295, Exit Rte
    31 off I-95

CASTAWAYS
215 Woodside Ave 08618
609 393-6103   Est: 1970
Proprietor: Clarence J
Haney
Hours: Daily, by
appointment
Types & Periods: Oak &
Walnut Furniture
    Directions: Cadwalader
    Park area

**CONTI REALTY & AUCTION
SERVICE**
116 Youngs Rd   08619
Proprietor: Richard Conti

Types & Periods: Antiques
at Auction
Specialties: Boehm, Lybis &
Ispanky Porcelains Bought &
Sold
Appraisal Service Available

S & S COLLECTIBLES
1520 Princeton Ave 08638
609 599-1520   Est: 1974
Proprietor: Stanley T
Sredinski Jr
Hours: Daily, by
appointment
Types & Periods: General
Line, Furniture
    Directions: Princeton Ave
    at N Olden Ave

Washington

THE RED BARN
49 Broad St   07882
201 689-6665   Est: 1975
Proprietor: Gloria
Matthews
Hours: Tues-Sun, 10:30-5
Types & Periods: General
Furniture, Glass, China,
Steins, Some Jewelry
    Directions: 1 block S of
    traffic light at center of
    town, which is Rte 57

Wayne

ANTIQUE ASSOCIATES
Box 783   07470
201 839-1212   Est: 1907
Proprietor: Bruce
Hertzberg
Hours: By appointment
Types & Periods: Hummels
Early American Furniture,
Oriental Rugs, Jewelry,
Silver
Specialties: Hummels Early
American Furniture, Oriental
Rugs, Jewelry, Silver
Appraisal Service Available

Wenonah

FURNISHINGS FOR THE CONNOISSEUR
7 N Jackson Ave   08090
609 478-4848
Proprietor: P R Kressler
Hours: Fri, Sat & Sun, 1-5;
also by appointment
Types & Periods: Period
Furniture, Brass Beds,
General Line

Westfield

EILEEN'S ANTIQUES
27 E Broad St   07090
201 232-2281   Est: 1977
Proprietor: Eileen Nott
Hours: Mon-Sat
Types & Periods: China,
Glass, Silver, Furniture,
Jewelry, Collectibles
Directions: Main business
district

THE WHIPPLETREE
522 Central Ave   07090
201 233-6644   Est: 1973
Proprietor: Dick & Joyce
Smythe
Hours: Mon-Wed, Fri-Sat,
10-5:30; Thurs, 10-9
Types & Periods: Primitive,
Victorian Furniture,
Bric-A-Brac, Glass,
Crockery, Paintings,
Hardware, Woodware,
Tinware, Collectibles
Appraisal Service Available
Directions: Garden State
Pkwy Exit 135 is Central
Ave, 4 traffic lights
(approximately 2 miles)
into Westfield or 1 short
block off South Ave
toward Pkwy on Central
Ave

Westwood

GARDNER'S II ANTIQUES
333 Broadway   07675
201 664-0612
Proprietor: Walter &
Gertrude Gardner
Hours: Daily, 9-6
Types & Periods: General
Line, Furniture

Whitehouse

YESTERYEAR TREASURES
Rte 22 at Ryland Inn
08888
201 534-4017   Est: 1960
Proprietor: Dorothy & Fred
Saalfield
Hours: Wed, Sat & Sun
Types & Periods: American
Lighting & Primitives
Specialties: Kerosene & Gas
Lamps, Country Furniture
Directions: Large antique
barn on grounds of
Historic Ryland Inn,
Rte 22

Yardville

THE CELLAR SHELF
4217 S Broad St   08620
609 585-6778   Est: 1970
Proprietor: Gena D
Hawthorne
Hours: Tues-Sun, 1-4:30
Types & Periods: Pressed
Glass, Oil Lamps, Doll
Furniture, Picture Frames,
China Plates
Specialties: Early Pressed
Glass
Appraisal Service Available
Directions: E from White
House Circle 1 mile

Side Table, marble
topped, Middle
Victorian.

STATE OF NEW MEXICO

Alamogordo

THE DEPOT ANTIQUES
3127 N White Sands Blvd
88310
505 437-5199   Est: 1974
Proprietor: Nolan & Cis
Conner
Hours: Daily 9-5
Types & Periods: General
Line
Specialties: Furniture
Appraisal Service Available
Directions: North Side of
City, On Hwys 70,54,82

R & B TRASH & TREASURE
3005 N White Sands Blvd
88310
505 437-5110   Est: 1970
Proprietor: Bessie Robling
Hours: Daily, Suns by
Appointment, By Chance
Types & Periods: Furniture,
American & English, Glass,
Primitives, Indian Artifacts,
Pottery, Rugs, Paintings
Specialties: Jewelry (Indian)
Appraisal Service Available
Directions: N on Hwys
70-54 about 1½ Miles from
Chamber of Commerce
Bldg

Albuquerque

ALBUQUERQUE CLUSTER
Directions: NW Section of
City & Old Town Area
especially 4th St NW, Area
of Plaza S-N, Romero &
Central Ave

THE ANTIQUE PARLOR
243 Wyoming NE   87123
505 266-0171   Est: 1970
Proprietor: Mary Loring
Hours: Daily, By
Appointment
Types & Periods: Cut & Art
Glass, Silver, Dolls (50
Years or Older), Doll
Furniture, Doll House
Miniatures, Furniture,
General Line
Specialties: Antique Doll
Repair

Appraisal Service Available
Directions: 2 blocks N of
Central btwn Central &
Lomas NE

ANTIQUE WORKSHOP
7322-4th St NW   87107
505 898-0348   Est: 1964
Proprietor: Bob & Harvey
Jean Byers
Hours: Mon-Sat 10-5
Types & Periods: Furniture
(All Periods), Antique &
Collectible Glass
(Depression, Heisey,
Cambridge, Stems), China,
Pottery, Lamps, Silver
Appraisal Service Available

A TO Z FURNITURE
1441 N San Mateo 87110
505 268-4976   Est: 1912
Proprietor: Bill Maupin
Hours: Mon-Sat 9-6, Sun
12-5
Types & Periods: Wood
Furniture, Some Nic-Nac
Items
Appraisal Service Available
Directions: Approx 6
blocks S of I-40 and San
Mateo Exit, 1 block S
Constitution & San Mateo

KEN DAVIS INTERIORS
1504 Candelaria Rd NW
87107
505 344-4283   Est: 1960
Proprietor: Ken Davis
Hours: Daily 12-4:30
Types & Periods: Asia Arts,
Bronze, Jade, Porcelains,
Screens, Scrolls, Sculpture,
Prints
Appraisal Service Available
Directions: 4th St N to
Candelaria Rd (From
Central Ave), Turn Left on
Candelaria Rd W to 1504

JACKSON'S EMPORIUM
416 Romero NW   87104
505 843-6768   Est: 1973
Proprietor: Darleen
Jackson
Hours: Mon-Sat
11:30-4:30, By
Appointment
Types & Periods: Furniture
& Small Items
Directions: In Old Town

JAMIL ORIENTAL CARPETS
3105 Central NE   87106
505 255-1179   Est: 1977
Proprietor: Zainab &
Abdul Hadi Miller
Hours: Daily
Types & Periods: New, Used
and Antique Handmade
Oriental Rugs from Iran,
Afghanistan, India, China,
Romania, Pakistan & Turkey
Specialties: Restore Old
Oriental Rugs & Hand wash
them, Free Estimates
Appraisal Service Available
Directions: E of the Univ
of New Mexico

MELIDONES ANTIQUES,
CLOCKS & COLLECTIBLES
203 Wellesley SE   87108
Est: 1976
Proprietor: Joyce
Melidones
Hours: Mon-Sat
Types & Periods: General
Line
Appraisal Service Available
Directions: 1 block S of
the 3300 block of E
Central (Hwy 66)

OZARK COUNTRY
ANTIQUES
9450 Candelaria NE
87112
505 293-3607   Est: 1975
Proprietor: Catherine
Bushey
Hours: Mon-Sat
Types & Periods: Country
Furniture & American
Primitives, Early Stoneware,
Baskets, Vintage Quilts
Specialties: Shaker & Amish
Furniture of New England
Appraisal Service Available
Directions: In E Dale
Shopping Ctr, just W of
Eubank Blvd

PACKARDS OF
ALBUQUERQUE
7120 Menaul NE   87110
505 883-6964   Est: 1975
Proprietor: Frank O
Packard, Jr
Hours: Tues-Sat
Types & Periods: German,
English, American, French,
Oriental, American Indian
Relics, Early 1800's-1920's

Albuquerque   Cont'd

PACKARDS   Cont'd

Specialties: American Indian
Old Navajo Rugs, Pots,
Baskets, Kachinas, Other
Relics from Packard Private
Collection (Been in Indian
Business for over 40 years)
    Directions: Btwn Louisiana
    Blvd and Pennsylvania
    Blvd, in Sun Square
    Shopping Ctr, S Side of
    Street

GRACE PIERCE ANTIQUES AT MACFIELD'S INTERIORS
1705 San Pedro NE
                       87110
505 268-3806   Est: 1977
Proprietor: Grace Pierce
Hours: Tues-Sat
Types & Periods: General
Line, 18th, 19th Centuries &
Fine Reproductions
Appraisal Service Available
    Directions: Corner of San
    Pedro & Constitution

SEDDON'S RANCHO CHICO ANTIQUES
6923 4th NW   87107
505 344-5201   Est: 1960
Proprietor: Betty Seddon
Hours: Daily
Types & Periods: European
& American Period
Furniture, Clocks, Brass,
Copper, Southwestern
Artifacts
Specialties: Clocks, (Repair)
Appraisal Service Available
    Directions: On N Hwy 85

THE SILVER SUNBEAM GALLERY
3409 Central NE   87106
505 256-7103   Est: 1974
Proprietor: Richard Levy
Hours: Tues-Sat 11-5:30
Types & Periods: Prints,
Posters, Photographs,
Postcards
Specialties: Postcards &
Photographs
Appraisal Service Available
    Directions: 8 blocks E of
    Univ of New Mexico, 2
    blocks W of Carlisle

Belen

ARTHUR & THELMA ATKINS
106 Howard St   87002
505 864-4565   Est: 1970
Proprietor: Arthur &
Thelma Atkins
Hours: By Appointment,
By Chance
Types & Periods: General
Line, Furniture, China
Specialties: Coins
    Directions: I-25 to Rte 6 E

Clovis

ADA'S HOUSE OF DEPRESSION
713 Connelly   88108
505 763-6201   Est: 1976
Proprietor: Mrs A O Netzel
Hours: Sun 1-4, Mon
6-9PM, Tues & Thurs-Fri
8-9, Wed & Sat 8-4, Will
Open any of these hours if
home
Types & Periods: Depression
Glass, Fiesta, Small
Antiques, Primitives
    Directions: First House W
    of Payless Shoe Store

LEE & MAVIS BRICKER
1614 N Main   88101
505 784-3213   Est: 1978
Proprietor: Lee & Mavis
Bricker
Hours: Daily 9-6
Types & Periods: All Types
& Period from 1900
Specialties: Depression
Glass
    Directions: Across from
    Marshall School

THE LEGACY COLLECTION
1424 Pile St   88101
505 763-6402   Est: 1977
Proprietor: Betsy Threet
Hours: Mon-Fri, By
Appointment
Types & Periods: Furniture,
Glass, Decorator Items,
Light Fixtures, Stained &
Leaded Windows & Doors

SECOND HAND ROSE
614 W 7th St   88101
505 784-3040   Est: 1977
Proprietor: Susan L Evans
Hours: Mon-Sat 12-4

Types & Periods: Antique
Clothing, Records, Radios,
Depression Glass, Furniture,
Baskets, Books, Wicker
    Directions: On Hwy 60/84

Deming

ARMSTRONG'S ANTIQUES
712 Gold   88030
505 546-9194   Est: 1972
Proprietor: Joyce
Armstrong
Hours: Daily 9-5, By
Appointment
Types & Periods: General
Line
Specialties: Glass (Pressed),
Lamps, Primitives
Appraisal Service Available
    Directions: Off Frwy at
    Gold St

Hillsboro

BELL'S ANTIQUES
Box 502   88042
505 895-5270   Est: 1971
Proprietor: Ross Bell
Hours: Daily 9-5
Types & Periods: 18th
Century-Early 20's,
Furniture, Glass
    Directions: 18 Miles from
    St Hwy 90 Exit Off I-25

SUE'S ANTIQUES
Star Rte 2, Box 88   88042
505 895-5328
Proprietor: Sue Bason
Hours: Daily 10:30-5
Types & Periods: 1800 to
1976 Collectibles, General
Line
Specialties: 1860 Walnut
Burl Dental Cabinet
    Directions: Hwy 90 btwn
    Silver City & Truth or
    Consequences

Hobbs

BEA'S DOLL SHOP
Star Rte H, Box 603
                       88240
505 392-5784   Est: 1972
Proprietor: Bea Whinery
Hours: Daily

Types & Periods: Dolls
Directions: Humble City,
btwn Hobbs & Lovington
in same bldg as Bea's Pet
Shop

Las Cruces

**CATES ANTIQUES &
SELECT USED FURNITURE**
570 W Griggs Ave   88001
505 526-8325   Est: 1969
Proprietor: Robert V Cates
Hours: Daily
Types & Periods: General
Line
Specialties: China, Furniture,
Glass
Appraisal Service Available
Directions: Central Area
across from 1st Baptist
Church, 4 blocks W of
Main St

THE 1860 HOUSE
266 W Court Ave   88001
505 524-2934   Est: 1960
Proprietor: Ms L F Babey
Hours: By Appointment,
By Chance
Types & Periods: General
Line
Specialties: New Mexican &
Mexican Iconographic Art
Directions: 1½ blocks off
Downtown Mall

**OLHAUSEN POOL TABLE
MANUFACTURING**
1145 Lenox Ave   88001
505 524 4337   Est: 1962
Proprietor: G E Olhausen
Hours: Daily, By Chance
Types & Periods: Antique
Pool Tables-1845 to Present

Las Vegas

ATTIC ANTIQUES
1027 8th St   87701
505 425-3124   Est: 1963
Proprietor: Mrs Ralph D
McWilliams
Hours: By Chance
Types & Periods: General
Line
Specialties: China, Glass

Portales

**NORTH MAIN TRADING
POST**
1115 N Main   88130
505 356-6017   Est: 1976
Proprietor: Edwin &
Martha Tobias

Roswell

HOUSE OF ANTIQUES
824½ N Main   88201
505 623-1751   Est: 1963
Proprietor: Alice Moratzka
Hours: Daily 12-5, By
Appointment
Types & Periods: General
Line
Directions: Face 9th St at
Main

LAS LOMAS ANTIQUES
4506 W 2nd   88201
505 622-5218   Est: 1958
Proprietor: Edward C
Kruse
Hours: Mon-Sat, By
Appointment
Types & Periods: Primitivoo,
Victorian, Oak, General Line,
Iron
Specialties: Cut Glass,
Silver, The Unusual, Auction
Service
Appraisal Service Available
Directions: W Hwy 70 to
Ruidoso

REID'S ANTIQUES
807 W 2nd·   88201
505 623-6292   Est: 1967
Proprietor: Mamie Reid
Hours: Daily 8:30-5
Types & Periods: General
Line & Furniture
Specialties: China, Glass
Directions: Hwys 70 &
380 W

WINGFIELD'S ANTIQUES
3109 N Main   88201
505 622-8069   Est: 1971
Proprietor: William R
Wingfield
Hours: Daily
Types & Periods: General
Line
Directions: Hwy 285 & 70

Ruidoso

NANA'S ANTIQUES
Sudderth Dr   88345
505 257-7257   Est: 1973
Proprietor: Marilyn O'Hara
Hours: Daily 10-5 May thru
Aug, By Appointment
Types & Periods: General
Line
Directions: E of Pizza Hut

Santa Fe

ESTATES BOUTIQUE
803 Camino Atalaya
   87501
505 988-1915   Est: 1970
Proprietor: Diana Skouras
Fowler
Hours: By Appointment
Types & Periods: Paintings,
Indian Arts & Artifacts

ADELENE B MC LAUGHLIN
Rte 1, Box 204F   87501
505 455-2544   Est: 1976
Proprietor: Adelene B
McLaughlin
Hours: By Appointment,
By Chance
Types & Periods: New
Mexican Colonial & other
Primitive & Country
Furniture
Specialties: Blue Willow
China, Hispanic Religious
Art, Indian Artifacts, Cobalt
Glass
Directions: Approx 2
blocks off Taos Hwy at
Pojoaque, or 16 Miles N of
Santa Fe

**TRAILS END TRADING
POST**
402 Old Santa Fe Trail
   87501
505 982-8141   Est: 1960
Proprietor: Richard H
Canon
Hours: Daily 9:30-5
Types & Periods:
Southwestern & Spanish
Colonial Items
Specialties: Jewelry, Pottery
(Pre-Columbian)
Directions: Across from
"The Oldest Church"

TURQUOISE TRADING COMPANY
72 E San Francisco
87501
505 983-8443   Est: 1972
Proprietor: Yvonne Dravo
Hours: Daily

CHRISTOPHER WEBSTER ANTIQUES/INTERIOR DESIGN
54½ Lincoln Ave, Suite 202; Box 3438
Pojoaque Station   87501
505 988-2533   Est: 1974
Proprietor: Christopher Webster
Hours: Mon-Sat, By Appointment, By Chance
Types & Periods: Old American Indian Artifacts, Spanish Colonial Furniture
Appraisal Service Available
Directions: W Side of Plaza in Downtown, Upstairs in Batts Bldg above Plaza Bar and Liquor Store

WILSON GALLERIES
143 Lincoln Ave   87501
505 982-8911   Est: 1936
Proprietor: David H Wilson
Hours: Mon-Sat, By Appointment
Types & Periods: 17th, 18th & Early 19th Centuries English Furniture & Accessories
Specialties: Early Georgian & Queen Anne Walnut & Mahogany
Appraisal Service Available
Directions: Corner of Lincoln & Marcy Sts, 1 block N of Plaza

Texico

BORDERTOWN ANTIQUES
Hwys 60-70-84   88135
505 482-9238   Est: 1929
Proprietor: James D Blake
Hours: Daily
Types & Periods: General line of American antiques
Specialties: Depression Glass & Obsolete Ammunition
Appraisal Service Available
Directions: Center of town

Dresser with mirror, Burl veneer applied on drawer fronts, Middle Victorian.

Wash Stand with marble splash back.

STATE OF NEW YORK

Aberdeen

RILEY'S ROADSIDE ANTIQUES
Rte 1   28315
919 944-1131   Est: 1947
Proprietor: Mr & Mrs Fred
W Riley
Hours: Daily, 9-7, by
chance
Types & Periods: Primitive
Tools & Relics, Clocks,
China, Cut Carnival &
Depression Glass, Coins,
Bottles
Specialties: Glass (Carnival),
Primitive Tools
    Directions: Hwy 211, 5
    miles E of Aberdeen

Acra

LITTLE BROWN JUG
Old Rte 23   12405
518 622-9288   Est: 1962
Proprietor: Shirley Selzner
Hours: Daily from July
1-Labor Day, then by
appointment
Types & Periods: Furniture,
Glass, China, Lamps
Specialties: Furniture
Primitives
    Directions: Across from
    Acra Manor, N Y S
    Thruway Exit 21, W on
    Rte 23

Albany

ALBANY CLUSTER
Directions: Lark St
(100-300 Blocks)

FOUR CENTURIES
247 Lark   12209
518 463-7888   Est: 1974
Proprietor: Leslie Zeller
Hours: Mon-Sat, 10-5
Types & Periods: Coins,
Stamps, Militaria, Books &
Prints, Silver, Rugs, Jewelry
Specialties: Off-beat Relics,
Documents, Memorabilia
Appraisal Service Available

Directions: N Y S Thruway
Exit 24, up Delaware Ave
to Lark St

JOSEPH PREISS INC
545 Broadway   12207
518 463-5931   Est: 1933
Proprietor: A L Preiss
Hours: Sun-Fri, 9:30-5:30;
Sat, 9:30-1; Closed July &
August
Types & Periods: Jewelry,
Watches, Cameras, Musical
Instruments
    Directions: Downtown,
    next to Union Station

Amherst

THE ANTIQUERY
309 A Hartford Rd   14226
716 837-2096   Est: 1970
Proprietor: Robert Krefta
Hours: By appointment
Types & Periods: General
Line
Specialties: Stained &
Beveled Glass Windows
Appraisal Service Available
    Directions: 1 block N of
    Sheridan Dr off Millersport
    Hwy

Andes

**FLYALONG FARMS ARTS &
TREASURES INC**
Rte 28   13731
914 676-4446   Est: 1971
Proprietor: Anne Geiger
Hours: Daily
Types & Periods: Glass,
China, Antique Novelties,
Lighting Fixtures, Furniture,
Art, Jewelry, Primitives
    Directions: From N Y S
    Thruway at Kingston,
    proceed W on Rte 28 to
    Andes (about 1 hour), on
    Rte 28 two doors W of
    hotel

THE PATINA SHOP
Rte 28   13731
914 676-4630
Proprietor: Arline Legis

Hours: By appointment, by
chance, summer only
Types & Periods:
Americana, Country
Furniture, Copper, Tinware,
Iron, Lamps

Angola

DUMINUCO'S ANTIQUES
8488 Erie Rd   14006
716 549-3543   Est: 1960
Proprietor: Louis
Duminuco
Hours: Mon-Sat, 10-5
Types & Periods: All Periods
up to 1935, Furniture, Glass,
China, Oak, Lamps, Guns,
Toys, Coins
Appraisal Service Available
    Directions: Rte 5, five
    minutes from US 90 Exit
    57A

Ardsley

JIM'S BOTTLE SHOP
609 Saw Mill River Rd
                       10502
914 693-3660
Proprietor: Jim Whetzel
Hours: Sat & Sun, 12-5;
also by appointment
Types & Periods: Antique
Bottles, Historical Flasks &
Bottle Reference Books
Specialties: Antique Bottles
& Historical Flasks
Appraisal Service Available

Armonk

STROMAK'S GALLERY
37 Maple Ave   10504
914 273-3429
Proprietor: John C
Stromak
Hours: Daily, 10-5
Types & Periods: American
& English

Ashville

MEADOWOOD SHOP
Randolph Rd Box 100
14710
716 782-3045   Est: 1968
Proprietor: Helen Shelters
Hours: Mon-Sat, 10-5, May
thru Sept
Types & Periods: Primitives,
Early American
Specialties: Boxes (Tole),
Folk Art Items
Directions: Off Rte 474
between Ashville &
Panama

Attica

CREEKSIDE ANTIQUES
23 High   14011
Est: 1965
Proprietor: Andy & Barb
Snyder
Hours: Daily
Types & Periods: Primitives,
Glass, Oak, & Walnut
Furniture, Tinware, Crocks,
Jugs, Brass, Copperware
Specialties: Primitives
Appraisal Service Available
Directions: Rte 98 from
Batavia, Rte 354 from
Buffalo

Auburn

**GRANDMA'S DUSTED
TREASURES**
37 E Genesee St   13021
315 253-4040   Est: 1971
Proprietor: Dwaine
Durniah
Hours: Mon-Sat, 10:30-5;
Sun, 1-3; also by
appointment
Types & Periods: Primitives,
Furniture, Glass
Specialties: Furniture, Movie
Items, Magazines
Appraisal Service Available
Directions: Rte 20 to
center of city

WARD'S ANTIQUES
56 E Genesee St   13021
315 252-7703   Est: 1951
Proprietor: Wallace Ward

Hours: Mon-Sat, 9-9; Sun,
1-5, anytime by
appointment
Types & Periods: General
Line & Period Furniture
Specialties: Wholesale &
Retail
Appraisal Service Available
Directions: Rte 20 in
Auburn

Aurora

TEASEL RUN
Dublin Hill Rd   13026
315 364-3289   Est: 1972
Proprietor: Linn Hopkins
Hours: Daily
Types & Periods: General
Line, Primitives
Specialties: Restoration &
Refinishing
Directions: 1½ miles E of
Aurora, Rte 90 to Dublin
Hill Rd

Austerlitz

**ROBERT HERRON
ANTIQUES**
Rte 22   12017
518 392-5478
Proprietor: Robert Herron
Hours: Daily, by
appointment; Auctions
Types & Periods: Americana
Appraisal Service Available

Baldwin

**ALTHEA'S ANTIQUE
JEWELRY**
592 Merrick Rd   11510
516 379-8080   Est: 1960
Proprietor: Althea
Pechenik
Hours: Tues-Sat,
12:30-4:30
Types & Periods: Jewelry,
Georgian, Victorian,
Bric-A-Brac, Furniture
Specialties: Jewelry
Directions: Merrick Rd
opposite Loft Lake

ANTIQUE QUEST
871 Merrick Rd   11510
516 623-8351   Est: 1971
Proprietor: Muriel Forray &
Lorraine Chipetine
Hours: Daily
Types & Periods: Cut,
Pressed, Colored & Art
Glass, Jewelry, Silver,
Porcelain, Post Cards,
Pictures, Furniture
Directions: Southern State
Pkwy to Exit 20, S to
Merrick Rd, left for 2
blocks

**BALDWIN ANTIQUES
CENTRE**
906 Merrick Rd   11510
516 223-9842   Est: 1969
Proprietor: 10 Dealers
Hours: Sat & Sun,
Tues-Thurs
Types & Periods: General
Line
Directions: Corner Merrick
Rd & Harrison Ave

**THE DECORATORS DEN
INC**
97 Merrick Rd   11510
516 223-1789   Est: 1966
Proprietor: Phyllis Barrett
Hours: Sun, 12-5; Wed-
Sat, 11-5
Types & Periods: English,
French, Oriental, 18th &
19th Centuries, Bronzes,
Porcelains, Clocks, Pressed
Glass, Crystal, Ivories
Specialties: Professional Art
Cleaning & Restoration
Appraisal Service Available
Directions: Southern State
Pkwy to Grand Ave S Exit,
right to Merrick Rd, turn
left for 200 ft

THE ODDITY
831 Merrick Rd   11510
516 223-0455   Est: 1967
Proprietor: Ms Lue
Harriton Witt
Hours: Mon-Sat; Sun by
chance
Types & Periods: Decorative
Accessories, Fixtures,
Furniture, Bric-A-Brac, 19th
& 20th Centuries, Primitives
Appraisal Service Available
Directions: 1 block E of
Grand Ave which is S of
Exit 20 on Southern State
Pkwy

Baldwin Place

MORMARK ENTERPRISES INC
Rte 6, PO Box 241   10505
914 628-0362   Est: 1970
Proprietor: Mark Lifschitz
Hours: Wed-Sun, 10:30-5, or by appointment
Types & Periods: Oak, Victorian, Glassware, 19th Century, Collectibles
Specialties: Clocks
Appraisal Service Available
Directions: 2 miles from Mahopac Lake, next to lumber yard, "In the yellow shed"

Baldwinsville

THE OLDE HICKORY ANTIQUES
29 Artillery Ln   13027
315 635-5816   Est: 1972
Proprietor: Frank & Jean Loveless
Hours: By appointment, by chance
Types & Periods: General Line
Appraisal Service Available
Directions: W Genesee St from Main Village Square to Artillery Lane

Barryville

LILLIAN'S LITTLE SHOPPE
Rte 97   12719
914 557-6125
Proprietor: Lillian Wolff
Hours: Mon-Fri, 1-6; Sat & Sun, 10-6
Types & Periods: General Line

SHADOWFAX RESTORATIONS & ANTIQUES
12719
914 557-9382
Proprietor: Verna & Rob Jones
Hours: Mon-Sat, 10-4:30
Types & Periods: General Line, Furniture Restored
Directions: 1/2 mile N of Rtes 55 & 97

WHITE BARN ANTIQUES
Rte 97   12719
914 557-8084
Proprietor: August B Kaelin
Hours: Sat & Sun, 11-6
Jun-Aug; off season by appointment
Types & Periods: Furniture, Woodcrafts

Bath

ABBEY'S ANTIQUES
12 Gansevoort   14810
607 776-6719   Est: 1967
Proprietor: Frances P Abbey
Hours: By appointment, by chance
Types & Periods: Silver, Glass, Furniture, Porcelain, Clocks, Lamps, Cut Glass, Art Deco
Specialties: Jewelry, Paintings
Appraisal Service Available
Directions: Exit 40 on Rte 15, two blocks

DONNA'S ANTIQUES
105 Maple Hgts   14810
607 776-3003   Est: 1961
Proprietor: Walter Zydanowicz
Hours: Daily, by chance
Types & Periods: General Line, Furniture, China, Glass, Clocks, Lamps
Specialties: Clocks, Cut Glass, Lamps
Directions: Exit 38, 2nd left hand turn on Rte 54 past red light

Bay Shore

PAST TIMES
183 E Main St   11718
516 665-8993   Est: 1968
Proprietor: Jim Anderson & Ruth Reich
Hours: Daily
Types & Periods: 19th Century Toys, Jewelry, 19th Century Cut Glass & China, American Paintings
Specialties: Clocks
Appraisal Service Available
Directions: On the S side of Long Island, Rte 27A

Bayside

THE HEIRLOOM SHOP
212-10 48th Ave   11364
212 463-6220   Est: 1971
Proprietor: Edie & Bernie Steinberg
Hours: Tues-Sat, 10-5:30
Types & Periods: Furniture, Ceramics, Objets d'Art, Lamps
Specialties: Repair & Restoration of Antiques, Furniture, Ceramics, Objets D'Art, Lamps, Caning, Stripping
Appraisal Service Available
Directions: Bayside Hills section, corner 212 St, N of LI Expy, S of Northern Blvd, E of Clearview or "Call for directions"

Bearsville

BEARSVILLE ANTIQUES
Wittenberg Rd   12409
914 679-7398   Est: 1973
Proprietor: Phyllis Kislin
Hours: Tues-Sun
Types & Periods: Collectibles, Glass, Furniture, Watches, Clocks, US Coins, Jewelry
Specialties: China (Nippon), Lamps
Appraisal Service Available

Bedford Hills

AMERICAN QUILT ART
237 Cantitoe St   10507
914 234-7291
Proprietor: Lynne Berger
Hours: By appointment
Types & Periods: Patchwork Quilts, Quilt Tops

BEDFORD GALLERY
307 Railroad Ave   10507
914 241-2262   Est: 1969
Proprietor: John Clifton
Hours: Weekends, by appointment
Types & Periods: Period American & European Furniture, Turn-of-the-Century Oak, Victorian Walnut, Glass, Dolls

BEDFORD GALLERY Cont'd

Appraisal Service Available
Directions: Parallel to
Sawmill River Pkwy, 1½
miles from I-684

GOLDEN SPUR ANTIQUES
5 Haines Rd   10507
914 666-2643
Proprietor: Betty Ann &
Robert H Cronk
Hours: Tues-Sat
Types & Periods: 18th &
19th Century American &
English Furniture, Porcelain,
Silver & Accessories
Appraisal Service Available
Directions: At the Bedford
Hills exit of the Saw Mill
River Pkwy

Bellmore

ANTIQUE ALLEY INC
2972A Merrick Rd   11710
516 221-6256   Est: 1967
Proprietor: Norma & Dan
Sands
Hours: Daily
Types & Periods: General
Line Collectibles, Furniture,
Jewelry, Toys (Dealers
Welcome)
Appraisal Service Available
Directions: LI Expwy to
Northern State to
Wantagh Pkwy, to
Merrick Rd W, 3 blocks on
S side of Merrick Rd

**BERNARD'S ANTIQUES
LTD**
2928 Merrick Rd   11710
516 221-5260   Est: 1970
Proprietor: Bernard Karyo
Hours: Tues-Thurs, Sat &
Sun, 11-4
Types & Periods:
Turn-of-the-Century French
& American
Specialties: Glass (Stained)
Directions: Off Wantagh
State Pkwy to Merrick Rd,
opposite pond

COLLECTOR'S CORNER
2560 Sunrise Hwy   11710
516 826-2112   Est: 1964
Proprietor: Henry Ubinas
Hours: Mon-Sat, 9:30-5:30

Types & Periods: Shelf Size
Items, Trains, Toys, Banks,
Coins, Stamps, Edged
Weapons, Firearms
Specialties: Coins, Stamps,
Banks, Toys
Appraisal Service Available
Directions: S side of Hwy
between Meadowbrook &
Wantagh Pkwys

EXQUISITE ANTIQUES LTD
2938 Merrick Rd   11710
516 781-7305   Est: 1972
Proprietor: Ethel & Paul
Kampf
Hours: Tues-Sun, 11:30-5;
by appointment
Types & Periods: Art Glass
& French Cameo Glass,
European Porcelains,
Satsuma, Fine Japanese
Cloisonne, Ivory, 18th-Early
20th Centuries
Specialties: French Cameo
Glass & European
Porcelains
Appraisal Service Available
Directions: On S shore of
Long Island, on Merrick
Rd

**JOAN'S ANTIQUE
UNLIMITED**
2900 Merrick Rd   11570
516 826-8267   Est: 1966
Proprietor: Joan Stadt
Hours: Tues-Sun, also by
appointment
Types & Periods: European
Furniture, Lighting Fixtures
& Accessories
Specialties: Lighting Fixtures
Appraisal Service Available
Directions: Off
Meadowbrook Pkwy, S
shore of LI

**IRIS MARNELL ANTIQUE
JEWELRY LTD**
2970 Merrick Rd   11710
516 221-6220   Est: 1970
Proprietor: Iris Marnell
Hours: Wed-Sun
Types & Periods: Victorian
Jewelry, Gold, Gold-Filled
Sterling, Beaded Bags,
Miniatures, Shoes, Salt
Spoons, Thimbles
Specialties: Jewelry,
Miniatures
Appraisal Service Available

Directions: Between
Meadowbrook & Wantagh
Pkwys, LI, in the heart of
Antique Row in the
Antique Pavilion

RAY'S ANTIQUES
2974 Merrick Rd   11710
516 826-7129   Est: 1971
Proprietor: Ray & Roseann
Warren
Hours: Mon-Fri, 12-4:30;
Sat & Sun, 12-5:30
Types & Periods: General
Line, Victorian Furniture,
Clocks, Jewelry
Specialties: Clocks &
Watches, Military Furniture
Directions: Merrick Rd E

Binghamton

BRINKER'S ANTIQUES
4653 Vestal Parkway E
              13903
607 729-3128   Est: 1945
Proprietor: H S Brinker
Hours: Daily, by
appointment or by chance
Types & Periods: Pattern &
Cut Glass, Furniture, Lamps,
Primitives, Paintings
Specialties: Glass (Pattern)
Appraisal Service Available
Directions: Rte 424 W of
city, opposite Vestal Plaza

CONE HOUSE ANTIQUES
9 Church St   13901
607 722-5445   Est: 1945
Proprietor: Tracy &
Dorothy Cone
Hours: Mon-Sat, 9-5;
Appointment suggested
Types & Periods: Period &
Country Furniture, Paintings,
Primitives, Quilts &
Coverlets, Prior 1850
Specialties: Furniture
Directions: Just N of
Binghamton in Port
Dickinson

E & R GIFTS & ANTIQUES
52 Main St   13902
607 722-1917   Est: 1968
Proprietor: E Eloise &
Mark D Bowers
Hours: Mon-Fri, Weekends
by chance
Types & Periods: General
Line

EBASHAE INC
122 State St   13902
607 723-4862   Est: 1967
Proprietor: D Shurtteff & C
Bonefede
Hours: Daily
Types & Periods: Furniture,
Cut Glass, Mirrors, Brass,
Jewelry
Directions: Downtown

IRONSTONE ANTIQUES
666 Chenango St   13901
607 722-9593   Est: 1966
Proprietor: Bob & Sallie
Connelly
Hours: Daily, phone call
advisable
Types & Periods: Country &
Period Furniture, Clocks,
Watches, Jewelry, Lamps,
Advertising Tins, Tools,
Silver, Accessories
Specialties: Clocks,
Ironstone
Appraisal Service Available
Directions: From Rtes I-81
& NY 17, take exit 4N
north to first traffic light,
turn left, go 3 blocks, turn
left to 2nd building on left

LALLEY'S ANTIQUES
Rte 7 N   13901
607 724-9461   Est: 1948
Proprietor: Doris A Lalley
Hours: Sun, 2-5; Mon, 9-6;
by appointment or by
chance
Types & Periods: Glass,
China, Furniture, Primitives
Directions: 1/2 mile on
Rte 7 *Little Oak*

**DAVID W MAPES
ANTIQUES**
82 Front St   13905
607 724-6741   Est: 1972
Proprietor: David W
Mapes
Hours: Daily
Types & Periods: General
Line, Period Furniture,
Collectibles
Appraisal Service Available
Directions: Downtown,
opposite Ramada Inn

MARGUERITES ANTIQUES
128 Main St   13905
607 724-7869
Proprietor: Fred &
Marguerite Goughary
Hours: Daily, 12-5:30

Types & Periods: Furniture,
Glass, China, Oils, Primitives
Appraisal Service Available
Directions: Between Front
St & Oakdale Dr

NANCY'S ANTIQUES
29 Mulberry St   13901
607 722-6815
Proprietor: Nancy Booth
Hours: By appointment
Types & Periods: Furniture,
Glass, Collectibles
Directions: N on
Chenango St, then E on
Mulberry St

OXEN HILL ANTIQUES
35 Andrews Ave   13904
607 723-0841
Proprietor: Emmory &
Gerry Prior
Hours: Daily
Types & Periods: Furniture,
Folk Art, Woodenware,
Primitives
Directions: E on Robinson
St, N on Andrews Ave

POLLY'S PARLOR
14 John St   13903
607 724-3309
Proprietor: Art & Polly
Barber
Hours: Mon-Sat, by
chance, also by
appointment
Types & Periods: General
Line, Collectibles
Directions: E on Conklin
Ave, S on John St

**THE SECOND STORY
SHOP**
11 Court St   13901
607 722-1822
Hours: Daily, 10-5, or by
appointment
Types & Periods: Primitives,
Collectibles, Paintings
Directions: Main & Court
St

1776 HOUSE
81 State St   13901
607 722-0297   Est: 1973
Proprietor: Robert &
Penny Regni
Hours: Tues, Wed, Fri &
Sat, 9-5, Mon & Thurs, 9-9
Types & Periods: Paintings,
Folk Art

Specialties: American Prints
Directions: 1 block from
Treadway Inn, accessible
from Rte 81 N & S, also
Rte 17 E & W

Bloomingburg

**RIVER LANE ANTIQUE
SHOP**
Box 161   12721
914 733-4840
Hours: Daily
Types & Periods: China,
Clocks, Furniture, Primitives,
Country Store Items
Directions: Turn at light
between Bank & Post
Office

ROBERT WHITE ANTIQUES
Main St   12721
914 733-1109
Hours: By appointment
Types & Periods: Furniture,
Folk Art, Lighting, Pottery &
Porcelain

Bouckville

OLD BOTTLE SHOPPE
Canal St   13310
315 893-5361   Est: 1968
Proprietor: Stewart &
Maxine Barber
Hours: Mon-Fri, 4-9; Sat,
all day
Types & Periods: Bottles,
Avon, Old Telephones,
Furniture
Directions: Canal St N, off
Rte 20

THE VALLEY PEDDLER
Rte 20   13310
315 893-4461   Est: 1972
Proprietor: Barbara Martel
Hours: Daily, April-Dec;
Weekends, Jan-March; By
appointment or by chance
Types & Periods: Early
Country Furniture &
Accessories
Directions: Rte 20,
approximately 90 miles W
of Albany

Briarcliff Manor

ICHABOD FARM ANTIQUES INC
540 Sleepy Hollow Rd
10510
914 762-2270
Proprietor: Richard &
Cynthia Stammers
Hours: By appointment
Types & Periods: Early
American Furniture &
Accessories

YELLOWPLUSH ANTIQUE CENTER
1192 Pleasantville Rd
10510
914 762-0594
Proprietor: 5 Dealers
Hours: Daily, 11-4
Types & Periods: Furniture
& Accessories

Bridgehampton

BIRD IN HAND ANTIQUES
Main St   11932
516 537-3838
Proprietor: David V
Hermann
Hours: Sun-Tues,
Thurs-Sat, 10-5:30
Types & Periods: Primitive
Americana, Country
Furniture

HAYGROUND ANTIQUES
Montauk Hwy   11932
516 537-0578
Proprietor: Sally T Reigler
Hours: Daily, Jan-April;
weekends by appointment
Types & Periods: Early
American Country Furniture,
Quilts, General Line
Directions: Montauk Hwy
& Hayground Rd

STERLING & HUNT
Box 300   11932
516 537-1096
Proprietor: Aileen Hunt &
Florence Sterling
Hours: By appointment
Types & Periods: American
Folk Art, Paintings,
Sculpture, Weathervanes,
Early Signs

Brocton

SAXTON ANTIQUES
6 Lake Ave   14716
716 792-4472   Est: 1968
Proprietor: Gladys A
Saxton
Hours: Daily
Types & Periods: General
Line, Clocks
Specialties: Antique Clocks,
Clock Parts (American &
Imported)
Appraisal Service Available
Directions: 100 feet N of
Rte US 20 on Rte 380
between Fredonia &
Westfield, N of Big Rd
arch

Bronx

WESTCHESTER TRADING CO
2478 Arthur Ave   10458
212 933-3230   Est: 1957
Proprietor: John J Genito
Hours: Tues-Sat, 11-6
Types & Periods: Firearms &
Edged Weapons
Appraisal Service Available
Directions: 1 block S of
Fordham Rd between
Fordham U & Bronx Zoo

Bronxville

ON CONSIGNMENT
95 Pondfield Rd   10708
914 337-7172   Est: 1978
Proprietor: Patricia Silleck
& Jane MacNeil
Hours: Mon-Sat
Types & Periods: All Periods
Appraisal Service Available
Directions: Next to
Citibank, middle of
Bronxville, 1/4 mile from
Bronx River Exit

BOB SHEPARD ANTIQUES
81 Pondfield Rd   10708
914 779-8700   Est: 1967
Proprietor: Bob Shepard
Hours: Tues-Sat, 10-5;
Also by appointment
Types & Periods: 18th
Century Furniture, French,
English & American;
Paintings, Porcelains

Appraisal Service Available
Directions: N Y Thruway
to Exit 5, Palmer Rd, E to
Bronxville

Brooklyn

ANTIQUES IN A BROWNSTONE
190 Bergen St   11217
212 624-5647   Est: 1975
Proprietor: Marna Brill
Anderson
Hours: By appointment
only
Types & Periods: American
Folk Art
Specialties: Weathervanes

ATTIC TREASURES
1114 Cortelyon Rd   11218
212 287-5069   Est: 1966
Proprietor: Rose
Friedlander
Hours: Daily
Types & Periods:
Bric-A-Brac, Small Furniture,
Mirrors
Specialties: Frames
Directions: BMT to
Cortelyon Rd

BEA'S AS IS
3004 Ave J   11210
Est: 1965
Proprietor: Bea & Paul
Adelman
Hours: Mon-Wed, Fri-Sat,
10-6; Thurs 'til 8
Types & Periods: General
Line, Prints, Frames
Specialties: Harrison Fischer
Pictures
Directions: Corner of
Nostrand Ave & Ave J

BROWNER ANTIQUES & GALLERY INC
783 Coney Island Ave
11218
212 856-0554   Est: 1946
Proprietor: Arthur P
Browner
Hours: By appointment or
by chance
Types & Periods: Art
Nouveau, Art Deco, Tiffany
Lamps & Glass, Russian &
French Enamels, Cameo &
Art Glass, Bronzes,
Chandeliers

Specialties: Furniture,
Paintings on Porcelain,
Leaded Glass Windows &
Lamps, Graphics
Appraisal Service Available

IMRE CSATARI
20-44 21st Dr   11214
212 755-7180
Proprietor: Imre Csatari
Hours: Daily, 8-6
Types & Periods: Boxes,
Furniture

D S W ANTIQUES
8304 Third Ave   11209
212 238-3493   Est: 1970
Proprietor: Walter &
Danuta Sobczynski
Hours: Tues-Sat
Types & Periods: Oil 18th &
19th Century Paintings,
Listed Artist, Bronze
Statues, Grandfather & Wall
Clocks, 19th Century Oak &
Walnut European Furniture
Directions: Bay Ridge, not
too far from the
Verrezanno Bridge and
Brooklyn Queens Expwy

DANTONE ANTIQUES
789 Coney Island   11218
212 693-4831   Est: 1970
Proprietor: Dinah Dantone
Hours: Tues-Thurs, Sat,
1-5
Types & Periods: Furniture,
Bronzes, Ivories, Porcelains,
Bric-A-Brac, Clocks,
Paintings
Specialties: Bronzes, Ivories
Directions: Between
Dorchester & Cortelyou
Rds

DEJA VU ANTIQUES
803 Coney Island Ave
                      11218
212 856-7714   Est: 1974
Proprietor: R DeFalco &
Joe Darienzo
Hours: Mon-Fri, 12-5;
Sat-Sun, 12-6; also by
chance
Types & Periods:
Turn-of-the-Century Oak,
Telephones, Toys of Early
1900's
Specialties: Glass, Toys &
Automata, Telephones

GENYA'S FINE ANTIQUES
1057 Coney Island Ave
                      11230
212 434-4172   Est: 1967
Proprietor: Helen
Schreiber
Hours: Daily, 1:30-5;
Sun-Fri, 1:30-5 during July
& Aug
Types & Periods: Paintings,
Victorian, French,English &
American Furniture,
Porcelain, Chandeliers,
Bronzes, Lamps, Jewelry,
Bric-A-Brac
  Directions: Between Ave H
  & Glenwood Rd

**THE HARRY MARK
ANTIQUARY AND ART
GALLERY OF BROOKLYN**
753 Fulton St   11217
212 522-3610   Est: 1903
Proprietor: Mr D Arthur
Mark
Hours: By appointment
Types & Periods: 17th, 18th
& 19th Century English,
American, French &
German, Rugs, China,
Glass, Silver
Appraisal Service Available
  Directions: At corner of
  the LaFayette Ave Subway
  Station & near the
  Brooklyn Bridge

HERITAGE GALLERIES
1010 Coney Island Ave
                      11230
212 859-4939   Est: 1960
Proprietor: Al Lerman &
Rudy Farano
Hours: By appointment or
by chance at time of
auction & exhibition
Types & Periods: General
Line
Appraisal Service Available
  Directions: Belt Pkwy to
  Coney Island Ave Exit to
  1010, near Foster Ave

KELLOGG ANTIQUES
309 Henry St   11201
212 852-8390   Est: 1966
Proprietor: Paul Kellogg
Hours: Weekends by
appointment
Types & Periods: Furniture,
Paintings, Early 19th
Century American
Specialties: "Antiques to live
with"

  Directions: Across
  Brooklyn Bridge from
  Manhattan in a
  neighborhood of landmark
  houses

KRAKEN ANTIQUES
373 Atlantic Ave   11217
212 875-8646   Est: 1972
Proprietor: Stephen Koch
Hours: Weekends by
appointment
Types & Periods:
Turn-of-the-Century
Imported & American Oak
Furniture
  Directions: Downtown, 10
  minutes from Manhattan,
  easy access to Brooklyn &
  Manhattan Bridges,
  Atlantic Ave is a main
  artery connecting
  Brooklyn with Kennedy
  Airport

MAVOLINE'S MUSE INC
349 Atlantic Ave   11217
212 855-6447   Est: 1974
Proprietor: Mavoline Liben
Hours: Weekends by
appointment
Types & Periods: Oak
Furniture, Americana,
Bric-A-Brac
  Directions: Between Hoyt
  & Bond Sts, near
  downtown

OAK 'N STUFF
786-788 Coney Island Ave
                      11218
212 941-1727   Est: 1969
Proprietor: Norman &
Mildred Rubin
Hours: Daily, by
appointment
Types & Periods: Furniture,
Collectibles

OLD WORLD CURIO SHOP
1634 Coney Island Ave
                      11230
212 951-9239
Proprietor: Louise & Fred
Vinciguerra
Hours: Mon-Sat, 1-4:30
Types & Periods: Furniture,
Chandeliers, Bric-A-Brac,
Paintings
  Directions: At the corner
  of Ave M

Brooklyn Cont'd

A TIME TO REMEMBER ANTIQUES
369 Atlantic Ave   11218
212 237-1732   Est: 1975
Proprietor: Phil Berger
Hours: Tues-Sun, 11-4:30
Types & Periods:
Turn-of-the-Century
American Oak Furniture
Specialties:
Turn-of-the-Century
American Oak Furniture
  Directions: 2 minutes from
  Brooklyn & Manhattan
  Bridges

TROPPER ENTERPRISES
524 Brighton Beach Ave
    11235
212 648-0036   Est: 1972
Proprietor: Gary Tropper
Hours: By appointment
Types & Periods: English
Ceramics

TESS AND ALLEN USATIN
3389 Bedford Ave   11210
212 258-1222   Est: 1947
Proprietor: Tess & Allen
Usatin
Hours: By appointment
Types & Periods: China,
Glass, Antique Jewelry
Specialties: Jewelry, China,
Inkwells, Frames
  Directions: Antique
  Shows, Dealers come only
  by appointment

Buffalo

BUFFALO CLUSTER
Directions: Major cluster
of shops are along Allen
(Beginning thru 100
block), Genesee (200-1000
Blocks), scattered shops
along Broadway, Franklin
St & other side streets in
downtown area

THE CRACKED POT
2152 Genesee St   14211
716 897-2611   Est: 1973
Proprietor: Robert Sevier
& Charles Scaglione
Hours: By appointment
Types & Periods: WWI & II
Military Items
Appraisal Service Available

DELL'S COIN CORNER
2207 Broadway   14212
716 897-3460   Est: 1971
Proprietor: Dell Reitz
Hours: Mon & Tues, Thurs
& Fri, 10-2 & 6-9; Sat,
10-4
Types & Periods: Coins,
Stamps, Supplies
Appraisal Service Available
  Directions: Between Bailey
  & Harlem Rd in Sloan

EATON GALLERIES
115 Elmwood Ave   14201
716 882-7823   Est: 1973
Proprietor: Wm J Eaton
Hours: Mon-Sat, 11-5
Types & Periods: General
Line
Specialties: Oriental Rugs,
Stained Glass Windows
Appraisal Service Available
  Directions: Allentown
  section of Buffalo

GOOD EARTH ANTIQUES
299 Kenmore Ave   14223
716 837-1110   Est: 1971
Proprietor: S Korman
Hours: Mon-Sat
Types & Periods:
Collectibles, Furniture,
Glass, China, Primitives
Appraisal Service Available
  Directions: Near State U
  of NY

SABINE LAW
4415 Main St   14226
716 839-1961   Est: 1935
Proprietor: Sabine Law
Hours: By appointment
Types & Periods: Gold
Jewelry up to 150 years old
Specialties: Jewelry

PAULINE'S ANTIQUES
567 Elmwood Ave   14222
716 882-3173   Est: 1969
Proprietor: Pauline Fedele
Hours: Daily, 10-3:30
Types & Periods:
Turn-of-the-Century
Furniture, Art Glass, Silver,
Early Lighting
  Directions: In the heart of
  Elmwood Village, 6 blocks
  N of Allentown

Caledonia

THE OLD STONE HOUSE
2 & 23 Spring St   14423
716 538-4780
Proprietor: George D
Feeley
Hours: Daily, 1:30-6, by
appointment
Types & Periods: General
Line
Appraisal Service Available
  Directions: Rte 5, 45 miles
  E of Buffalo

Callicoon

GRAY BARN ANTIQUES
    12723
914 887-5005
Proprietor: Mary Eisner
Hours: "Open all year, off
season by appointment"
Types & Periods: Primitives,
Furniture, Glassware, China,
Copper
  Directions: 2 miles past
  center of town, right turn
  off Rte 97 onto dirt road,
  proceed 1 mile

PALMER'S ANTIQUE SHOP
River Road   12723
Hours: April-Dec,
Weekends only
Types & Periods: General
Line
Specialties: Railroad
Collectibles
  Directions: 2 miles up
  River Rd from town

PLATTS HOUSE OF ANTIQUES
RFD 1   12723
914 887-5349   Est: 1956
Proprietor: Mr & Mrs
David Platt
Hours: Daily, by chance
Types & Periods: General
Line, Furniture, Glass,
Collectors Items, Museum
Pieces
  Directions: 18 miles from
  Monticello

Campbell Hall

SOPHIE LANDTHALER
Rte 207   10916
914 427-2409

Types & Periods: General
Line, Dolls
Directions: At the Mobil
station

TORY KNOLL ANTIQUES
Sarah Wells Trail   10916
914 496-6106
Proprietor: Bob & Ginny
Oeder
Hours: By appointment, by
chance, 10-5
Types & Periods: General
Line
Directions: Between Shea
& Ridge Rd

Canaan

IRIS COTTAGE
Rte 295   12029
518 781-4379   Est: 1966
Proprietor: Andrea & Alan
Koppel
Hours: Wed-Sat, April-Oct;
Other times by
appointment
Types & Periods: Pattern
Glass, General Line, Mail
Orders on Glass
Specialties: Pattern Glass
Directions: Rte 295 & City
Rte 5, in the center of
town at blinking light, near
N Y S Thruway & Taconic
Pkwy

Canandaigua

**EDWARD E DAVIS
ANTIQUES**
Rte 5 & 20,
Geneva Trnpk   14424
716 394-6429
Proprietor: Ed Davis &
Charlotte Baker
Hours: Mon-Sat, 10-6;
Sun, 2-5; Nov 1-May 1 by
appointment only
Types & Periods: 18th &
19th Century Furniture, Oil
Paintings, Oriental Rugs,
Period Accessories
Specialties: 18th & 19th
Century Furniture & Oil
Paintings, Queen Anne,
Hepplewhite & Chippendale
Appraisal Service Available
Directions: Rtes 5 & 20,
Geneva Trnpk, 4 miles E
of Canandaigua

HARVEST MILL
40 Parrish St   14424
716 394-5907   Est: 1961
Proprietor: J Gardner
Hours: Tues-Sun,
June-Jan; Weekends,
Feb-May
Types & Periods: Period &
Country Furniture, Glass,
China, Tin, Woodenware
Specialties: Furniture
Directions: Off Hwy 20 on
W Lake Rd

HEIRLOOM GALLERY
Rtes 5 & 20,
Geneva Rd   14424
315 596-6220
Proprietor: Ed Davis &
Charlotte Baker
Hours: Mon-Sat, 10-6;
Sun, 2-5; Nov 1-May 1 by
appointment only
Types & Periods: 18th &
19th Century Furniture, Oil
Paintings, Oriental Rugs,
Period Accessories
Specialties: 18th & 19th
Century Furniture & Oil
Paintings, Queen Anne,
Hepplewhite & Chippendale
Appraisal Service Available
Directions: Rte 5 & 20, 6
miles from Canandaigua
and 12 miles from Geneva

Carmel

**KENT CLIFFS ANTIQUE
SUPER MARKET**
Peekskill Hollow Rd &
Rte 301   10512
914 225-6991   Est: 1966
Proprietor: Bernard
Feldman
Hours: Wed-Sun, 11-6;
Also holidays
Types & Periods: Oak &
Victorian Furniture, Antique
Jewelry, China, Bric-A-Brac,
Paintings, General Line
Directions: Taconic Pkwy
to Peekskill Hollow Rd

MURIEL W JUST
RD 2   10512
914 225-3075
Proprietor: Muriel W Just
Hours: By appointment
Types & Periods: China,
Glass, Pictures, Mirrors

Catskill

OPEN GATES ANTIQUES
Rte 23A   12414
518 943-3806
Proprietor: Renee Zwickel
Hours: By appointment
Types & Periods: General
Line

Cazenovia

ENDERS ANTIQUES
2363 Rte 20 E   13035
315 655-8323   Est: 1967
Proprietor: Richard &
Janet Enders
Hours: Daily, by
appointment or by chance
Types & Periods: Painted
Country Furniture thru
Refinished Victorian
Furniture & Related
Accessories
Appraisal Service Available
Directions: 100 yards E of
village of Cazenovia on
US Rte 20

Champlain

THE WOODSHED
53 Church St   12919
518 298-8165
Types & Periods: Country
Directions: Off Rte 11

Chappaqua

**PLEASANT VALLEY
ANTIQUES**
Briarcliff Rd   10514
914 238-3074
Proprietor: A Washbum
Hours: By appointment
Types & Periods: Early
American Furniture, Glass,
China

RED CARPET ANTIQUES
142 King St   10514
914 238-4918
Proprietor: Vincent
Fulgenzi & Donald Brock
Hours: Mon-Sat

RED CARPET Cont'd

Types & Periods: Furniture, Paintings, Prints, Glass, China, Collectibles, Picture Framing, Lamps, Lamp Shades
Appraisal Service Available

Chatham

LANDES ANTIQUES

161 Hudson Ave   12037
518 392-3738   Est: 1972
Proprietor: Mark Feder
Hours: Mon-Fri, 10-5; Weekends, 1-5; By chance or appointment
Types & Periods: Oak, Walnut, Marble Top Victorian, China, Glass, Jewelry, Restored Gaslite Fixtures & Lamps
Specialties: Expert Refinishing & Lamp Restoration
Appraisal Service Available
Directions: Rte 66, 1 block S junction Rtes 66 & 203

Chazy

ALAN & JEAN SMITH

Chazy Landing   12921
518 846-7192   Est: 1966
Proprietor: Alan & Jean Smith
Hours: By appointment, by chance
Types & Periods: Colonial, Victoriana, Bric-A-Brac, Memorabilia, Woodenware, Tinware
Specialties: Clocks, Furniture
Appraisal Service Available
Directions: Exit 41, Adirondack Northway (Rte 87), take Rte 191 E, thru Chazy to Lake Champlain, 2nd house to right

Chenango Forks

THE TREASURE CHEST

Main St   13746
607 648-8923   Est: 1972
Proprietor: Marlene & Kermit Kirby
Hours: Tues-Sat, 10:30-5

Types & Periods:
1840-1920's Furniture
Directions: 7 miles N of Exit 6 off 81

Cherry Valley

OLD STORY TAVERN ANTIQUES

171 Main St   13320
607 264-3354   Est: 1969
Proprietor: Sherry & David Fink
Hours: Daily, 9-6
Types & Periods: General Line, Furniture
Specialties: Furniture
Appraisal Service Available
Directions: On Rte 166 off Rte 20, 50 miles W of Albany

Chester

SCHOOL HOUSE ANTIQUE SHOP

Maple Ave   10918
914 469-2307
Proprietor: Helen J Hulse
Hours: Sun-Tues, Thurs-Sat
Types & Periods: Glassware, Copper, Lamps, Clocks, Furniture
Directions: Off Rte 94

Circleville

THE ODD SHOP

        10919
914 361-4781
Proprietor: Silvia Jordan
Hours: Sun-Mon, Thurs-Sat, 10-7
Types & Periods: Art Nouveau, Clocks, Furniture, Fixtures, China
Directions: Quickway Exit 119 to Rte 302

WINDWARD ANTIQUES

        10919
914 361-2681
Proprietor: Lillian Zakrzeski
Hours: Daily, 9:30 -6

Types & Periods: Furniture, Lamps, Glass, China, Collectibles
Directions: Rte 302 N 1/2 mile from Rte 17, Exit 119

Clarence

BAUMER ANTIQUES

10548 Main, Rte 5   14031
716 759-6468   Est: 1958
Proprietor: Elmer & Hildegarde Baumer
Hours: Tues-Sat, by appointment
Types & Periods: General Line
Appraisal Service Available
Directions: NY Rte 5, 12 miles E of Buffalo

VI & SI'S ANTIQUES

8970 Main St   14031
716 634-4488   Est: 1956
Proprietor: Vi & Si Altman
Hours: Daily
Types & Periods: General Line
Specialties: Buffalo Pottery, Mechanical Music Items
Appraisal Service Available
Directions: 5 miles N of Buffalo on Rte 5, 2 miles from N Y S Thruway Exit 49

Claryville

ARGONAUT BOOK SEARCH SERVICE

        12725
914 985-2474
Hours: By appointment
Types & Periods: Books

Clyde

THE DOLL SHOP

16 Mill St   14433
315 923-7134   Est: 1960
Proprietor: Margaretta Rebeor
Hours: Daily, by chance
Types & Periods: Dolls, Glass, China, Children's Furniture, Doll Accessories
Specialties: Toys (Dolls)

Cobleskill

THE FISHER'S
62 E Main St   12043
518 234-3374   Est: 1960
Proprietor: Clifford Fisher
Hours: By appointment or
by chance
Types & Periods: Early
American Furniture,
Paintings, Primitives, Tools,
Prints, Books, Maps

EARL TINKLEPAUGH
14 Park Lane   12043
518 234-3374
Proprietor: Earl
Tinklepaugh
Hours: By appointment
Types & Periods: General
Line, Furniture, Glass, Silver,
Copper, China

Cochecton

SUNSET HILL ANTIQUES
County Rd 114   12726
914 932-8395
Proprietor: Alice & Robb
Guss
Hours: Daily, 1-6
Types & Periods: Furniture,
Stoneware, Collectibles
Directions: 3.6 miles from
Fosterdale

WILLOW FARM ANTIQUES
County Rd 114   12726
Proprietor: J R McKinney,
N G Hadley, G L Dorresen
Hours: Weekends,
June-Labor Day, 12-6; off
season by appointment
Types & Periods:
Americana, Folk Art,
Paintings, General Line
Directions: Halfway
between Fosterdale &
Cochecton

Cold Spring

**ROUND MOUNTAIN
ANTIQUES**
Rte 9D   10516
914 896-9351   Est: 1978
Proprietor: Jane & Jim
Apuzzo
Hours: Wed-Sun

Types & Periods: 18th &
19th Century Country
Furniture, Primitives,
Stoneware
Specialties: Cupboards in
old or original paint
Directions: 1/4 mile N of
Boscobel Restoration

Congers

**DOROTHY KNAPP
ASSOCIATES**
Mayo's Hotel   10920
914 623-5710
Proprietor: Dorothy Knapp
Hours: Tues
Types & Periods: General
Line, Auctions
Appraisal Service Available
Directions: W of Rtes 303
& 9W, opposite railroad
station

Conwango Valley

**BERTHA'S WHAT NOT
SHOP**
Rte 62   14726
716 287-2633   Est: 1972
Proprietor: Percy & Bertha
Annis
Hours: Tues-Sun
Types & Periods: General
Line
Appraisal Service Available
Directions: Rte 62 midway
between Clear Creek &
Conewango Valley

Cooperstown

JUNE BIGGAR ANTIQUES
Box 138, RD 3   13326
607 547-8847   Est: 1976
Proprietor: Mrs R William
Furman
Hours: By appointment, by
chance; mostly shows
Types & Periods: General
Line Antiques, Collectibles,
Glass, China
Specialties: Glass, China
Directions: Cooperstown,
1 mile on Rte 33 from
Bowerstown Bridge

BOB COOK
Brookwood   13326
Est: 1968
Hours: Daily
Types & Periods: General
Line
Appraisal Service Available
Directions: 1 mile N of
Fenimore House on Rte
80

**COOPERSTOWN COUNTRY
STORE & ANTIQUES**
10 Hoffman Ln   13326
607 547-8955   Est: 1970
Proprietor: Eileen Damon
Hours: Daily
Types & Periods: 18th &
19th Century Country
Furniture & Accessories
Specialties: Furniture (Pine
& Cherry Cupboards)
Appraisal Service Available
Directions: Hoffman Lane
off Main St, across from
Baseball Hall of Fame

THE FROG HOLLOW SHOP
92 Pioneer St   13326
607 547-8631
Proprietor: Jean T Knapp
Types & Periods: Country,
Primitives, China, Glass,
Jugs, Crocks

THE LEDGES
139 Main St   13326
607 547-9546   Est: 1973
Proprietor: Howard &
Doris Reiss
Hours: Mon-Sat; Sun &
evenings, by chance or by
appointment
Types & Periods: Clocks,
Furniture, Glassware
Specialties: Clocks,
Furniture, Glassware (From
Pilgrim Century thru the
Turn-of-the-Century
Directions: 1 block from
the Baseball Hall of Fame,
next door to the theatre
marquis

**STAGE COACH LANE
ANTIQUES**
14 Chestnut St   13326
607 547-2473
Proprietor: Mrs Helen
Shafer
Types & Periods: General
Line
Specialties: Lamps & Silver
Appraisal Service Available

Corning

MARGARET S KING
10 E 1st St   14830
607 962-0876
Proprietor: Margaret S
King
Hours: By appointment
Types & Periods: 18th &
19th Centuries

Cornwall

THE EAGLE GLASS BARN
482 Quaker Ave   12518
914 534-9047   Est: 1967
Proprietor: Edna M Brown
Hours: Tues-Sun, 10-5;
Evenings by appointment
Types & Periods: Art Glass,
Patter Glass, General Line
Specialties: Glass
Directions: Rte 307 at 9W

FRIENDLY ACRES
Otterkill Rd   12518
914 534-2943
Proprietor: Bill & Ann
Siegler
Hours: Fri-Sun, 1-7; Also
by appointment and by
chance
Types & Periods: Flow Blue,
Salt Spoons, General Line
Directions: Off Orrs Mill
Rd

Cornwall-on-Hudson

**BUTTER HILL ANTIQUE
SHOP**
211 Hudson St   12520
914 534-2361   Est: 1972
Proprietor: Thomas R
Trainor
Hours: Thurs-Sun, 1-5
Types & Periods: General
Line
Specialties: Furniture,
Clocks, Watches, Flow Blue
China, Paintings, Bronzes,
Oriental Items, Jewelry
Appraisal Service Available
Directions: 50 miles N of
NY City, 5 miles N of West
Point on Rte 218, 5 miles
S of I-84, Rte 9W to Hwy
218 to village of Cornwall,
5 miles S of Newburgh off
N Y S Thruway

Cortland

PHEASANT HILL ANTIQUES
4030 Kinney Gulf Rd
                     13045
607 756-8142   Est: 1964
Proprietor: Lydia Doug
Warfield
Hours: Daily
Types & Periods: Country &
Period Furniture
Directions: Exit 12 off I-81,
2 miles S on Rte 281

Cuba

COUNTRY ANTIQUES
8 Spring St   14727
716 968-2371   Est: 1960
Proprietor: Jim & Erna
Underwood
Hours: Daily, Call ahead
adviseable
Types & Periods: General
Line
Appraisal Service Available
Directions: "Find the only
laundromat in Cuba and
you have found us"

**MY GRANDMOTHER'S
ATTIC**
58 South St   14727
716 968-1650   Est: 1977
Proprietor: Kay Lee
Bradley & Linda C Eckert
Hours: Daily
Types & Periods: General
Line
Appraisal Service Available

Davenport

STEWART'S ANTIQUES
100 Mill Rd   13750
607 278-9962
Proprietor: Rosemary A
Stewart
Hours: By appointment or
by chance, May thru Dec
Types & Periods: General
Line, China, Art Glass,
Pottery, Primitives, Lamps,
Furniture, Tinware, Post
Cards
Directions: 1/4 mile off
Rte 23, turn at Texaco
station

Delhi

ACKERLY AUCTION BARN
Main St   13753
607 746-3895
Proprietor: Tom Ackerly Jr
Hours: Tues-Sun
Types & Periods: Furniture,
Old Country Items, Crocks,
Churns, Tools, Glass
Specialties: Furniture (Oak,
Pine)
Directions: W on Rte 28
into Delhi, make left at
light in village, mile on
right

DAVISON ANTIQUES
94 Main St   13753
607 746-3850   Est: 1976
Proprietor: Richard
Davison
Hours: Mon-Sat, 10:30-5
Types & Periods:
Americana, Country,
Primitive
Specialties: Furniture
(Country), Quilts

HELEN WALLIS ANTIQUES
PO Delhi   13753
607 832-4251
Proprietor: Helen Wallis
Hours: By appointment,
May thru Oct
Types & Periods: China,
Glass, Paintings, Tables
Directions: Rte 28 Lake
Delaware

Deposit

AXTELL ANTIQUES
1 River St   13754
607 467-2353   Est: 1968
Proprietor: Richard S
Axtell
Hours: Daily, 10-5
Types & Periods: Early
American Country Furniture,
Lighting Devices,
Accessories, Folk Art,
Paintings, Iron & Wood
Rarities
Appraisal Service Available
Directions: Off NY Rte 17,
Exit 84, at Rtes 8 & 10

Downsville

TEAZEL ANTIQUES
Rte 2, Box 72   13755
607 363-2298   Est: 1966
Proprietor: Ted & Hazel
Eiben
Hours: By appointment or
by chance
Types & Periods: Art Glass,
Furniture, Primitives
  Directions: Rte 17, Exit 90,
  Rte 30 to Shinhopple,
  cross river, 2½ miles

East Amherst

OLD IRONSIDES
11500 Transit Rd   14051
716 625-8125   Est: 1971
Proprietor: J Lawrence
Hayden
Hours: Mon-Sat, 9-5
Types & Periods: General
Line
  Directions: Intersection of
  Rtes 78 & 263,
  approximately 7 miles NE
  of Buffalo

East Aurora

**FIRE HOUSE ANTIQUES
CO-OP**
82 Elm St   14052
716 655-1035   Est: 1974
Proprietor: S Bray, M
Apgar, R Cary
Hours: Wed-Sun,
12:30-4:30, by
appointment
Types & Periods: Period
Furniture, Lamps, Silver,
General Line
Specialties: Lamps, Early
China
Appraisal Service Available
  Directions: N Y S Thruway
  (Rte 90) to Expwy 400,
  Exit at 20A to East
  Aurora, W 2 blocks to Rte
  16, left 1 block to
  Oakwood, 1 block, corner
  Oakwood & Elm

**GLENN & JOANNE HAGER
ANTIQUES**
Grover Rd   14052
716 652-1334   Est: 1968
Proprietor: Joanne Hager
Hours: Daily

Types & Periods: Country
Furniture, Lamps, General
Line
Appraisal Service Available
  Directions: 1 block from
  Rte 20A, 1 mile from
  circle in E Aurora

SHAKER HOUSE ANTIQUES
502 Main St   14052
716 652-2088
Proprietor: Nancy A Hurd
Hours: Daily, 9-5; also by
appointment
Types & Periods: Period
Furniture, Shaker, Pewter
Appraisal Service Available

THE STRABELS
165 Buffalo Rd   14052
716 652-5936   Est: 1969
Proprietor: Eunice Strabel
Hours: Sun-Fri, By
appointment or by chance
Types & Periods: Early
Period Furniture (Birch,
Cherry Walnut & Mahogany)
Specialties: Furniture
(Swing-Leg Tables, Period
Chests & Windsor Chairs)
  Directions: Rtes 78 & 16,
  NW end of village almost
  across from Girard Ave,
  Buffalo Rd is a
  continuation of Seneca St
  from Buffalo (Sign just
  says "The Strabels")

East Bloomfield

**AUDREE AND BRYCE
CHASE'S COLLECTORS
CORNER**
62 Main St   14443
Proprietor: Audree &
Bryce Chase
Hours: By appointment or
by chance
Types & Periods: Furniture,
Paintings & Accessories
from before 1840,
Americana, Dealers
Welcome
Appraisal Service Available
  Directions: NY Rte 20C,
  one block N of Rtes 5 &
  20, turn at the village
  green, 10 minutes from N
  Y S Thruway Exit 45,
  located at the rear of the
  house at the basement
  level

East Moriches

**JEAN LAUER-WILLIAM
FOOTE ANTIQUES**
E Main St   11940
516 878-2172
Proprietor: Jean Lauer &
William Foote
Hours: Weekends, 1-5;
also by appointment
Types & Periods: American
Furniture, Stoneware,
Pattern Glass
  Directions: On Long Island

Elbridge

**FIELDMOUSE MANOR
ANTIQUES**
116 W Main St   13060
315 698-6469   Est: 1966
Proprietor: Patricia Conroy
Hours: Daily
Types & Periods: 18th &
19th Century Furniture,
Paintings, Silver, Oriental
Rugs
Appraisal Service Available
  Directions: Between
  Syracuse & Auburn

Ellenville

**STATUS SYMBOL
ANTIQUES**
Rte 52 W   12428
914 647-6312   Est: 1951
Proprietor: The Hirsch
Family
Hours: Daily, spring,
summer & fall; Weekends
& holidays during winter
Types & Periods: Victorian,
Oak, China, Glass
Appraisal Service Available
  Directions: Rte 17 to Exit
  113, Rte 209 N to
  Rte 52 W

Ellington

**LOCK STOCK & BARREL
COUNTRY STORE**
            14732
716 287-3675   Est: 1967
Proprietor: Clara Green
Hours: Mon-Sat, 10-6;
Sun, 1-6; open weekends
Jan-March

LOCK STOCK &   Cont'd

Types & Periods: Tools,
Toys, Dolls, Furniture,
Primitives
   Directions: 12 miles E of
   Jamestown, Rte 62

Endicott

JONES' LAMP SHOP
   909 W Main St   13760
   607 748-7741
   Hours: By appointment
Types & Periods: Lamps,
Chimneys, Shades

REINING ANTIQUES
   303 River Terr   13760
   607 785-3453
   Hours: By chance
Types & Periods: Glass,
China, Coins, Cherry,
Walnut & Pine Furniture
   Directions: Near Ideal
   Hospital

**STEDMAN'S USED
FURNITURE & ANTIQUES**
   123 W Main   13760
   607 754-1335
   Hours: Mon-Wed, Fri-Sat,
   10-9:30; Thurs, 10-9
Types & Periods: Furniture,
Glass, China
   Directions: Between
   Badger Ave & Nanticoke
   Ave

Esperance

**HERITAGE HOUSE
ANTIQUES**
   Box 290 Rte 20   12066
   518 875-6357
   Proprietor: Ruth J Nielsen
   Hours: Daily
Types & Periods: General
Line
   Directions: Red log cabin
   1/2 mile E of town on Rte
   20

Fairport

DE LAP'S ANTIQUES
   32 Parce Ave   14450
   716 223-0155   Est: 1966
   Proprietor: Dave & Lee
   De Lap

   Hours: Daily, 12-6
Types & Periods: Glass,
Collectibles, Oak, Cherry,
Walnut, Mahogany, Pine,
Primitive 1920 & Older
Furniture
Specialties: Furniture
Appraisal Service Available
   Directions: Off Rte 250 (N
   Main St) in center of town,
   2 blocks N of Barge
   Canal, 2nd house off N
   Main

Falconer

**EVELYN NORBERG
ANTIQUES**
   RD 1   14733
   715 665-3105   Est: 1962
   Proprietor: Evelyn Norberg
   Hours: Daily
Types & Periods: General
Line
Specialties: Furniture
   Directions: Rte 394, Exit
   13, 1 mile E of town

Fishers Island

RUTH WOOLFE
   PO Box 577   06390
   516 788-7533
   Proprietor: Ruth Woolfe
   Hours: By appointment
Types & Periods: General
Line, Dolls

Fishkill

**FISHKILL TRADING POST
INC**
   Rte 9 S   12524
   914 896-8310   Est: 1973
   Proprietor: Jessie G
   Grabowsky
   Hours: Thurs-Sun, 10-5
Types & Periods: Furniture,
Clocks
Specialties: Hand Carved
Eagles, Rocking Horses
Appraisal Service Available
   Directions: 1 mile S of
   Hwy 84 on Rte 9

Floral Park

EASTLAKE ANTIQUES
   270 Jericho Trnpk   11001
   516 437-5151   Est: 1971
   Proprietor: Art Castellano
   & Tom Russo
   Hours: Mon-Sat, 11-4
Types & Periods: Glass,
China, Silver, Bric-A-Brac,
Lamps, Oak Furniture,
Steins, Mugs
Specialties: Caning, Rush
Seats Replaced
Appraisal Service Available
   Directions: Just E of Floral
   Theatre, half mile W of
   Lakeville Rd

WILLIAM C FRICKER
   40 Tulip Ave   11001
   516 775-8296   Est: 1940
   Proprietor: William C
   Fricker
   Hours: By appointment
Types & Periods: General
Line
Appraisal Service Available
   Directions: Off Long Island
   Expwy, S of Jericho Trnpk

**REMEMBER WHEN?
ANTIQUES**
   56 Cherry Lane   11001
   516 354-8223   Est: 1968
   Proprietor: Otto R Bade
   Hours: Tues-Sat, 1-5, Oct
   thru April; Tues-Fri, 1-5,
   May thru Sept
Types & Periods: Bronzes,
Jewelry, Porcelains
Specialties: Clocks,
Watches, Silver
Appraisal Service Available
   Directions: LI Expwy to
   Exit 33, S to Hillside Ave,
   turn right, 8 blocks to
   Cherry Ln, turn left to 1st
   traffic light (3 blocks), on
   corner of Cherry Lane &
   Lowell Ave

Flushing

LILLIAN ASCH ANTIQUES
   162-19 Depot Rd   11358
   212 961-2630   Est: 1966
   Proprietor: Lillian Asch
   Hours: Tues, Thurs-Sat
Types & Periods: General
Line

Specialties: Clocks, Silver,
Porcelain
Directions: Queens
County, just off Northern
Blvd at 162nd St, where
Depot Rd branches N

DAWN ANTIQUES
29-06 172nd St   11358
212 353-7511   Est: 1969
Proprietor: Dawn Hantman
Hours: Wed-Sat, 11-5;
Alternate Suns
Types & Periods: Wall,
Mantle & Grandfather
Clocks, French, English,
Belgian & Oak Furniture,
Decorative Accessories
Specialties: Clocks
Directions: Northern Blvd
to Francis Lewis & 29th
Ave

HANSENS ANTIQUE
42-17 162nd St   11358
212 353-1654   Est: 1965
Proprietor: Mary Hansen
Hours: Mon-Sat, 11-6;
Sun, 1-6
Types & Periods: Furniture,
Lamps, Rugs, Glass,
Jewelry, Oak
Appraisal Service Available
Directions: 2 blocks S of
Northern Blvd

J LAFFAN
135-11 Roosevelt Ave
                      11354
212 359-2499   Est: 1933
Proprietor: James Laffan
Hours: Daily; By
appointment or by chance
July & Aug
Types & Periods: General
Line, Art Objects
Appraisal Service Available
Directions: End of subway
line, corner of Main St &
Roosevelt

THE RAGAZZI GALLERY
162-03 Northern Blvd
                      11358
212 539-4711   Est: 1964
Proprietor: Virginia &
Joseph Ragazzi
Hours: Daily, by
appointment
Types & Periods: 18th &
19th Centuries, General
Line, Art Glass, Lamps,
Oriental Rugs, Silver,
Paintings

Specialties: Member
Appraisers Association of
America
Appraisal Service Available
Directions: 59th St Bridge
to Northern Blvd & 162nd
St

THE TYLERS ANTIQUES
181-32 Union Trnpk 11366
212 380-4636   Est: 1947
Proprietor: Lou & Rosalind
Tyler
Hours: Mon-Wed, Sat;
Closed July & August
Types & Periods: 18th, 19th
& 20th Century Paintings,
Bronzes, Mosaics,
Porcelains, Furniture
Appraisal Service Available
Directions: Grand Central
or LI Expwy to Utopia
Pkwy Exit

Fly Creek

**MOHICAN CRAFTSMEN'S
SHOP**
Rtes 28 & 80   13337
607 547-9212
Proprietor: Paul Michaelo
Hours: Daily
Types & Periods: Furniture,
China, Glass, General Line

Forest Hills

LITTLE NEMO SHOP
100 30 Ascan Ave   11375
212 263-5296   Est: 1969
Proprietor: Joseph
Parente
Hours: Mon, Wed-Sat,
11-6
Types & Periods:
Collectibles, Paper Items
Specialties: Original Comic
Art, Political Art
Appraisal Service Available
Directions: 1 block S of
Queens Blvd, between
72nd & 73rd Ave

Forestburgh

BLACKBROOK BARN
Rte 42   12701
914 794-8778

Proprietor: John & Kay
Doty
Hours: Daily, 10-10, April
thru Oct
Types & Periods: Glassware,
Frames, General Line

MERRIWOLD ANTIQUES
Rte 42-Port Jervis Rd
                      12701
914 794-0290   Est: 1972
Proprietor: Jack Sonbert
Hours: Daily, June 15-Sept
15
Types & Periods: Oriental,
Victorian, French Cameo
Glass, European Paintings,
Bric-A-Brac, Americana
Specialties: Mettlach Steins,
Art Glass
Directions: 6 miles S of
Monticello on Rte 42

Franklin

THE ART GALLERY
123 Main St   13775
607 829-5552
Proprietor: Ruth Payne
Hours: By appointment
Types & Periods: General
Line
Specialties: Paintings

**MARC & MARY
HILDERBRAND**
54 Center St   13775
607 829-5866   Est: 1970
Proprietor: Marc & Mary
Hilderbrand
Hours: Daily, by
appointment
Types & Periods: Early
Blown & Pressed Glass,
Sandwich Glass
Specialties: Early Blown &
Pressed Glass, Sandwich
Glass

Fredonia

**FREDONIA WOODS &
WARES**
161 Liberty St   14063
716 672-4451   Est: 1972
Proprietor: Stanley B
Jakiel
Hours: Daily, by chance
Types & Periods: Victorian,
Oak Furniture, Clocks,
Lamps, Primitives,

WOODS & WARES Cont'd
Glassware, Jewelry,
Collectibles
Specialties: Clocks, Post
Cards, Refinished Furniture
Appraisal Service Available
Directions: 1/2 mile off
Rte 20

THE LUWEIBDEH SHOP
4587 W Main Rd   14063
716 673-1915   Est: 1974
Proprietor: Boo Rowland
Hours: Wed-Sun, 11-6; by
chance or by appointment
Types & Periods: General
Line
Directions: Shop in tenant
house & barn, located on
4 acres overlooking Lake
Erie N, 20 acres of grapes
to S

POTTERS ANTIQUES
12 Liberty St   14603
716 672-8171   Est: 1965
Proprietor: Everett L
Potter
Hours: Daily, by chance
Types & Periods:
Collectibles
Appraisal Service Available

Freeport

KRON JEWELERS
30 W Merrick Rd   11520
516 868-7818   Est: 1971
Hours: Mon, Wed-Sat; Fri
nite 'til 9
Types & Periods: Rings,
Jewelry, Pocket Watches,
Sterling Silver
Appraisal Service Available
Directions: Southern State
Pkwy to Meadowbrook S
Exit, M9 W to Freeport,
stay on Merrick Rd, 1/2
block W of Freeport Mall

THE OLD OYSTER WHARF
265 S Main St   11520
516 378-1926   Est: 1956
Proprietor: Dorothea E
Miller
Hours: Sun-Mon, Wed-Sat,
1-4:30
Types & Periods: Early
American Furniture, Flint,
Sandwich & Pattern Glass,
Staffordshire, Rockingham,
Basalt

Specialties: Glass
Directions: On Freeport
River

Garden City

WHITNEY ANTIQUES
60 First St   11530
516 741-0781   Est: 1970
Proprietor: Helen & Bob
Stenard
Hours: By appointment
Types & Periods: 18th &
Early 19th Century American
Furniture, Sandwich Glass,
18th & 19th Century Clocks
& Barometers
Specialties: French Carriage
Clocks
Appraisal Service Available

Geneseo

CRAIG ADAMSON
4419 Adamson Rd   14454
716 243-0220   Est: 1972
Proprietor: Craig Adamson
Hours: Daily, by
appointment
Types & Periods: Primitives,
Stoneware, Period Furniture
Specialties: Arms
Appraisal Service Available
Directions: 4 miles S of
town

Geneva

**MAH JONG ORIENTAL
ANTIQUES**
391 S Main St   14456
315 789-4684   Est: 1965
Proprietor: Dr Donald K
Ourecky & Richard Callard
Hours: Daily, 10-5; also by
appointment
Types & Periods: Oriental
(Ming to 19th Century),
Collectibles, Rugs,
Paintings, Porcelain
Specialties: Oriental
Appraisal Service Available
Directions: Located 1/2
block from Business
District (Rte 14)

Ghent

ALMSHOUSE ANTIQUES
Rte 66   12075
518 392-5242
Proprietor: Ghent
Almshouse Ltd
Hours: Tues-Sun, 10-5
Types & Periods: General
Line, English & American
Furniture & Accessories

Gilbertsville

ANTIQUES & OLD STUFF
Rte 51   13776
607 783-2323
Proprietor: John
Newhouse & Family
Hours: Eves or weekends
by appointment or chance
Types & Periods: China,
Glass, Furniture,
Collectibles, General Line

VALLEY VIEW ANTIQUES
Commercial St   13776
607 783-2436
Proprietor: Marga
Albanese & Helen
Cleinman
Types & Periods: General
Line

Gilboa

BRANDOW'S ANTIQUES
W Conesville   12076
607 588-7577
Proprietor: Florence
Brandow
Hours: By appointment or
by chance
Types & Periods: General
Line, Furniture, China,
Lamps
Directions: 1 mile E of
Gilboa

Glen Cove

**MUSKETOE COVE
ANTIQUES**
147 Glen St   11542
516 671-8393
Proprietor: Mr & Mrs P
Carucci
Hours: Mon-Sat

Types & Periods: American,
Primitives, English,
Porcelains, Paintings
Specialties: Restorations of
old Paintings
Appraisal Service Available
Directions: Opposite
Police Dept in old home
built in 1810

Glen Wild

BARN FULL ANTIQUES
Church Rd   12738
914 434-4094
Hours: Daily, April-Oct; off
season by appointment
Types & Periods: Framed
Prints, Books, Old Things
Directions: 1/4 mile off
Glen Wild Rd

THE BROWSERY
Glen Wild Rd PO Bldg
                     12738
914 434-6252
Hours: Daily, 9-5,
June-Oct; off season by
appointment
Types & Periods: General
Line

Glens Falls

ANTIQUE MART
5 Davis St   12801
518 793-3130   Est: 1972
Proprietor: Six Dealers
Hours: Mon-Sat, 10-4;
Sun, 1-4
Types & Periods: Furniture,
China, Glass, Primitives,
Silver, Paper, Collectibles
Appraisal Service Available
Directions: 1 block W of
Glen St (Rte 9), between
Grant Ave & Grove Ave

BAILEY'S ANTIQUES
W Mountain Rd   12801
518 792-6776   Est: 1961
Proprietor: Richard Bailey
Hours: Daily, 9-5
Types & Periods: Furniture,
Lamps, Clocks, Dolls, Coins,
China, Cut Glass, General
Line
Directions: Exit 19 off
Adirondack Northway Rte
87, left on Aviation Rd to
W Mountain Rd, left about
1000 ft

BAY ANTIQUES
72 Bay St   12801
518 793-9223
Proprietor: Irene D
Einstein
Hours: Daily, 11-7
Types & Periods: General
Line, Art Glass, Bronzes,
Oriental Objects

Gloversville

BRICKWOOD ANTIQUES
RD 1   12078
518 725-0230   Est: 1969
Proprietor: Mr & Mrs G R
Frisbie
Hours: By appointment;
mail inquiries
Types & Periods: Pottery,
Porcelains, Glass,
Miniatures, Silver, Brass,
Objets d'Art
Specialties: Ceramics,
Staffordshire, Oriental
Porcelains, Georgian,
Sheffield Plated Silver
Appraisal Service Available
Directions: Write or
telephone for directions

Goshen

MARION LEWIS COBB
RD 1, Scotchtown Rd
                     10924
914 294-7049
Proprietor: Marion Lewis
Cobb
Hours: By appointment or
by chance
Types & Periods: Furniture,
Glass, China, Tinware
Specialties: Primitive Items
Appraisal Service Available
Directions: From Village,
pass county complex, turn
left on Scotchtown Ave,
continue about 1½ miles,
house on left just past
horse farm

GREAT HOUSE ANTIQUES
262 Greenwich Ave 10924
914 294-6655
Proprietor: June Wiegert
Hours: Tues-Sun, 11-5; by
appointment

Types & Periods: General
Line, 18th & 19th Century
Furniture, Glass, China,
Silver, Jewelry
Appraisal Service Available
Directions: Rte 207, Exit
124B at Rte 17

**RED WHEELBARROW
ANTIQUES**
Maple Ave   10924
914 294-5872
Proprietor: Lyle Wagner
Hours: By appointment or
by chance
Types & Periods: Dolls,
Toys, General Line
Directions: 17M, 3/4 mile
W of Goshen Quickway

Grahamsville

ALFRED W COOK
Brown Rd   12740
914 647-5762
Proprietor: Alfred W Cook
Hours: Sun-Wed, Fri-Sat
Types & Periods: Brass,
Copper, Lamps, Crocks,
Roseville Pottery
Directions: Off Rte 55 & S
Hill Rd

COPPER POT ANTIQUES
Forest Rd   12740
914 985-2866
Hours: Daily
Types & Periods: 4 shops in
1 location: Furniture, Glass,
Bric-A-Brac, China, Rocks,
Bottles, Model T & A Parts,
Collectors' Items
Directions: Off Rte 42

**HORSESHOE BARN
ANTIQUES**
S Hill Rd   12740
914 985-2452   Est: 1960
Proprietor: Carol Jones
Smythe
Hours: By appointment
Types & Periods: Country
Antiques

(From page 356). and chairs were delicately carved with grapes, roses, leaves and scrolls of foliage in crisp detail. The Rococo style became almost synonymous with the name Belter in America. There were many imitators, and a lot of elegant Victorian furniture is attributed to him. If it isn't signed Belter, it is not his. This writer has a 1949 book which says, "A living room in good Belter today might demand as much as two or three thousand dollars." A recent auction house report, Spring 1979, says they just sold a circa 1850, three-piece, carved rosewood parlor suite by J. H. Belter for $42,000. That is appreciation! (See page 322A).

In the 1850's there appeared the Renaissance Revival which is hard to discern from those styles leading into it. Whereas, the baroque and rococo styles were filled with flowing lines, this style tends to be large and heavy. It has straight lines with rounded ends, oval panels filled with applied carvings, pediments, cartouches and applied medallions. This furniture was designed to go into the large, high ceilinged rooms of huge houses. Often it had to be large in scale to fit the architecture. Walnut was the popular wood, and there was an abundance of marble tops. It is well made and of good quality, but one must be aware of its scale in terms of modern houses.

In 1850, the previously mentioned Andrew J. Downing published a book entitled *Architecture of Country Houses*. He still showed the revival styles and still retained the look of the ancient Roman and Greek furniture. However, in London in 1853, J. K. Lowden put out a book entitled *Encyclopedia of Cottage, Farm and Villa Architecture and Furniture*. That book indicated a continuation of the revival styles in which chairs were still the same design, but the front legs had been replaced by a turned leg rather than the previously curved leg. His designs were widely circulated and noted in this country.

It was during the Early Victorian that marble topped furniture came into popularity. The early pieces of this period had black onyx, but white marble came to dominate. There came to be more and more marble used upon furniture tops throughout all three Victorian periods. The use of steam-powered machinery made the grinding and polishing of the marble possible. It came to be used on parlor tables, dressers and washstands with elaborate splashboards on their backs. It was not present on the least expensive product lines. (See page 386).

Prior to the Early Victorian, furniture was not ordered in sets as we know it, but was an assemblage of individual pieces made by cabinetmakers. With the establishment (Continued, page 424).

Great Neck

ARLINE INTERIORS INC
587 Middle Neck Rd 11023
516 466-0024   Est: 1971
Proprietor: Arline R
Stanton, NHFL
Hours: Mon-Sat, 11-5;
Eves by appointment
Types & Periods: Antique
Oriental, French, English,
Lamps, Art, Decorative
Accessories
Specialties: Oriental Antique
Artifacts
Appraisal Service Available
    Directions: Northern Blvd
    to S Middle Neck Rd,
    across from St Aloysius
    Church

JOAN DAVID
83 Middle Neck Rd 11023
516 482-0575
Proprietor: Fay Tanner
Hours: Daily
Types & Periods: French &
English Porcelains, Silver,
Furniture, Paintings,
Bric-A-Brac
    Directions: Northern Blvd
    to Lakeville Rd to Middle
    Neck Rd

ANN L HOLZER INC
446 E Shore Rd   11024
516 482-4556
Proprietor: Ann L & Philip
Holzer
Hours: By appointment
Types & Periods: Jewelry,
Collectibles

**L & J KNIGHT ANTIQUE
JEWELRY LTD**
78 Middle Neck Rd 11023
516 487-5250   Est: 1961
Proprietor: Leonard &
Jessie Knight
Hours: Mon-Wed, Fri-Sat,
11-4
Types & Periods: Victorian &
English Jewelry, Estate
Jewelry, Collectibles
Specialties: Jewelry
Appraisal Service Available
    Directions: LI Expwy,
    Northern State Pkwy, or
    Northern Blvd to Lakeville
    Rd, which becomes
    Middle Neck Rd, corner of
    Middle Neck & Elm St

**THE SHOWCASE
ANTIQUES**
113 Middle Neck Rd 11021
516 487-7815   Est: 1956
Proprietor: Lila & Bob
Bodkin
Hours: Mon-Sat, 10-5:30
Types & Periods: French,
English, 19th & 20th
Centuries, Accessories,
Mirrors, Occasional
Furniture
Specialties: Chandeliers
Appraisal Service Available
    Directions: Center of
    Great Neck on the main
    street next to Squire
    Theater

THEN ANTIQUES
9 Bond St   11021
516 466-8592   Est: 1971
Proprietor: Marge
Messenger
Hours: Tues-Sat, by
chance
Types & Periods:
Bric-A-Brac, Mercury, Art
Glass, Oak Furniture,
Collectibles
Appraisal Service Available
    Directions: 1 block E of
    Middle Neck Rd at Great
    Neck Railroad Station

**THE TOWN SHOP
ANTIQUES**
20 Maple Dr   11021
516 487-6461   Est: 1946
Proprietor: Alex Spano &
John I Reid
Hours: Daily
Types & Periods: French &
English Furniture, Lamps,
Glass, China, Silver
    Directions: Middle Neck
    Rd (near theatres) to
    Maple Dr

Greene

SUGAR KNOLL ANTIQUES
Rte 12   13778
607 656-8036   Est: 1965
Proprietor: William
Whitaker
Hours: By chance
Types & Periods: Primitives,
Lamps, Wood, Tin, Picture
Frames
    Directions: 1 mile N of
    Greene on Rte 12

Greenport

HUGHES ANTIQUES
210 Main St   11944
516 477-1160
Proprietor: Robert &
Eleanor Hughes
Hours: Mon-Sat, 9:30-5
Types & Periods: American
& English Furniture, China,
Brass

Groton

**ELIZABETH SEAGERS
ANTIQUES**
201 E Cortland   13073
607 898-3227   Est: 1951
Proprietor: Elizabeth
Seagers
Hours: By appointment
Types & Periods: 18th &
19th Century Americana,
Formal & Country Furniture
& Accessories
Specialties: Glass, Primitives
Appraisal Service Available
    Directions: On Rte 222, 10
    miles W of Cortland Exit
    on Rte 81, 55 minutes S
    of N Y S Thruway Exit at
    Syracuse

Guilderland

KENESTON ANTIQUES
Rte 20   12303
518 356-1777   Est: 1960
Hours: By appointment
Types & Periods: Oak &
Walnut Furniture
Appraisal Service Available
    Directions: Exit 25 N Y S
    Thruway

Hammond

CHAPMAN'S ANTIQUES
Main St   13646
315 324-5515   Est: 1964
Proprietor: Harold L
Chapman
Hours: Mon-Sat, 9-5; Sun,
2-5
Types & Periods: General
Line

CHAPMAN'S   Cont'd

Appraisal Service Available
Directions: Just off Scenic
Rte 12 on Parallel Rd
Between Alexandria Bay &
Morristown

HOUSE OF RAY'S ANTIQUES

Main St Rte 37   13646
315 324-5519   Est: 1973
Proprietor: Raymond W
Chapman
Hours: Daily
Types & Periods: Primitives
& Glassware, Early
American, Oak & Victorian
Furniture
   Directions: On Rte 37 near
   school

TLC ANTIQUES

Rte 37   13646
315 324-5383
Proprietor: Tom & Betty
Chapman
Hours: Daily
Types & Periods: Furniture,
Glass, Crocks, Decoys
   Directions: 15 miles from
   Alexandria Bay on Rte 12

Hampton Bays

ADA'S ATTIC

116 W Montauk Hwy
                    11946
516 728-2141   Est: 1971
Proprietor: Robert Jones
& George Tetzel
Hours: Daily
Types & Periods: Victorian
Oak, Paintings, Glassware,
Collectibles
Specialties: Restoration
Appraisal Service Available

Harriman

BLAINE A HILL

1A Rake St   10926
914 783-7297   Est: 1968
Proprietor: Blaine A Hill
Hours: By appointment
Types & Periods: Antique
Dolls, Children's Books,
Miniatures
Specialties: Antique Dolls,
Children's Books, Miniatures
   Directions: Old stone
   schoolhouse 2 blocks E of
   Rte 17M

Hartwick

THE VICTORIAN HOUSE

RD 1 Box 168   13348
607 293-6644   Est: 1974
Proprietor: Edna &
Richard Fletcher
Hours: Sun-Mon, Wed-Sat,
10-5; Eves by appointment
Types & Periods: Country,
Victorian & Period Furniture,
Lighting Devices, Decorative
Objects
Specialties: Fine Furniture &
Furnishings
   Directions: Rte 205, 19
   miles N of I-88 or 3 miles
   S of Rte 80, 10 miles W of
   Cooperstown

Herkimer

ANDY'S ANTIQUES

105 Mohawk St   13350
315 866-0288   Est: 1971
Proprietor: Andrew
Scialdo
Hours: Mon-Thurs, 9:30-6;
Fri, 9-9; Sat, 9-6; also by
appointment
Types & Periods: Oak &
Victorian Furniture, Glass,
China, Jewelry, Paintings,
Frames, Quilts, Clocks,
Music Makers, Oriental
Rugs, Old Banks, Brass
Beds
Specialties: Old Instruments,
Cast Iron Stoves
   Directions: Off N Y S
   Thruway Exit 30, 1st right
   directly to Mohawk St for
   3 blocks, located on
   corner of Mohawk & Main

CANASTAR'S ANTIQUES

357 Eureka Ave   13350
315 866-2476   Est: 1968
Proprietor: Frank &
Matilda Canastar
Hours: Mon-Fri; Weekends
by chance
Types & Periods: Furniture,
Pressed, Cut & Art Glass,
Primitives & Collectibles,
Mail Order
Specialties: Old Jewelry,
Sterling Silverware, Ceiling
Domes & Lamps

Appraisal Service Available
   Directions: Thruway Exit
   30, Rte 5 E, first right
   after last stop light, 3
   blocks, on corner

Hewlett

DECOR-TIQUES

1160 A Broadway   11557
516 374-4919
Proprietor: Lillian Lesser
Hours: Mon-Sat, 12-4:30
Types & Periods: Desk
Accessories, Wall Decor,
Furniture, Accent Country
Pieces, Bric-A-Brac, Art
Glass, Miniatures
Specialties: English Leather
Binding Sets
   Directions: "Five towns
   location"

PAST & PRESENT

1165 Broadway   11557
Proprietor: Barbara Sinkin
Hours: Mon-Sat
Types & Periods:
Bric-A-Brac, Small Furniture,
Primitives
   Directions: Sunrise Hwy to
   Broadway

YESTERDAY'S CHARM ANTIQUES

1152-A Broadway   11557
516 374-2926
Proprietor: Joan & Bob
Karan
Hours: Mon-Sat, 11-5
Types & Periods: Clocks,
Oak Furniture, Country
Store Items
   Directions: On Long Island

Hillsdale

JOHN LEE KAPNER ANTIQUES

Main St   12529
518 325-4811
Proprietor: John Lee
Kapner
Hours: Tues-Sat, 10-6;
Sun, 12-6; also by
appointment
Types & Periods: American
Country & Formal 18th &
Early 19th & Empire
Furniture, Tools
   Directions: Rte 23

Himrod

GA-NUN-DA-SA-GA ANTIQUE SHOP
269 Severne Rd   14842
607 243-8349   Est: 1970
Proprietor: Donald &
Sylvia Fisher
Hours: Daily, 8-5
Types & Periods: General
Line, Furniture, Glass,
China, Pottery
Specialties: Glass (Carnival)
Appraisal Service Available
  Directions: 15 miles N of
  Watkins Glen, 1/4 mile E
  of Rte 14

Holmes

THE COUNTRY CARRIAGE HOUSE
Rte 52   12531
914 878-6240
Proprietor: Nicki Huebbe
Hours: Weekends, also by
appointment
Types & Periods: Victorian
Oak, Early American Tools,
Pot Belly Stoves, Crocks

RUTH COATES ANTIQUES
Rte 52   12531
914 878-9707
Proprietor: Ruth Coates
Hours: By appointment, by
chance
Types & Periods:
Bric-A-Brac, Furniture

Hopewell Junction

ROUND MOUNTAIN ANTIQUES
W Hook Rd   12533
914 896-9351
Proprietor: J Apuzzo
Hours: By appointment, by
chance
Types & Periods: Primitives,
Country Furniture, Tin,
Treen, Stoneware

Horseheads

STONEY KNOLL
E Franklin St   14845
607 739-4108

Proprietor: Leah B
Woloson
Hours: By appointment
Types & Periods: 18th
Century Accessories, Early
Lighting, Folk Art, Toys,
Tools, Treen

Hubbardsville

ANITA & ANDREW SWATKOVSKY
Poolville   13355
315 691-4028
Proprietor: Anita &
Andrew Swatkovsky
Hours: By appointment, by
chance
Types & Periods: Country
Furniture, Primitives, Tole,
Woodenware, Toys, Iron,
Pottery, Textiles
Specialties: Soft Paste
  Directions: 9 miles S of
  Rte 20

Hudson

HOUSE OF ANTIQUES
430 Warren St   12534
518 828-1319   Est: 1970
Proprietor: Ronald Moore
Hours: Mon-Sat, 9-5; Sun
by appointment
Types & Periods: Oak,
Walnut, Clocks
Specialties: Clocks
  Directions: Rte 9 on Main
  St

TOWNHOUSE ANTIQUES
306 Warren St   12534
518 828-7490   Est: 1967
Proprietor: George
Jurgsatis & Al Michels
Hours: Tues-Sat, 12-5
Types & Periods: General
Line
  Directions: Located
  downtown by corner of
  3rd St (Rte 9G)

Huguenot

AMBER SPRINGS ANTIQUES
Peenpack Trail   12746
914 856-2650
Proprietor: Elsie Elfenbein

Hours: Sun-Mon, Wed-Sat,
11-6
Types & Periods: Furniture,
China, Glassware, Victorian,
Kitchenware, Primitives
  Directions: 5 miles N of
  Port Jervis

Huntington

THE CARROUSEL
Box 736   11743
516 423-1757   Est: 1965
Hours: By appointment
Types & Periods: 17th, 18th
& 19th Century Furniture,
Silver, Pewter, Brass, Glass,
China, Paintings
Specialties: Furniture
Appraisal Service Available

CRACKER BARREL GALLERIES INC
17 Green St   11746
516 421-1400   Est: 1951
Proprietor: Ernest Fried
Hours: Mon-Sat
Types & Periods: Furniture
Appraisal Service Available
  Directions: 1 block S of
  Main St (25A), 2 blocks E
  of Rte 110 or New York
  Ave

NORTH SHORE ANTIQUE
417 New York Ave   11743
516 673-8995   Est: 1974
Proprietor: Mary Bregas
Hours: Tues-Sat
Appraisal Service Available
  Directions: E on Long
  Island Expwy to Rte 110,
  N to 417

YANKEE PEDDLER ANTIQUES INC
1038 New York Ave 11746
516 271-5817   Est: 1972
Proprietor: Gloria Smith
Hours: Daily, 9-5
Types & Periods: 18 Rooms,
14 Dealers; Early American,
European, Primitives,
Clocks, Tools, Art,
Miniatures, China
  Directions: Long Island
  Expwy to Rte 110 N (New
  York Ave), 3 miles

Huntington Station

HAYSEED ANTIQUES
195 W Hills Rd   11746
516 421-4369
Proprietor: Allan Coombs
Hours: Tues-Sun, 11-5:30
Types & Periods: Primitives,
Stoneware

POINT-IN-TIME ANTIQUES
616 E Jericho Tpke 11746
516 423-0099
Proprietor: Anne & Marty
Ellman
Hours: Tues-Sat, 10-6;
Sun, 12-6
Types & Periods: Folk Arts,
Oak, Pine

Hurley

VAN DEUSEN HOUSE
11 Main St   12443
914 331-8852   Est: 1959
Proprietor: Jonathan & Iris
Oseas
Hours: By appointment or
by chance; always open
on Tues & Thurs
Types & Periods: American,
Oriental & European
Porcelains, China, Silver,
Glass, Furniture, Tools,
Paper Memorabilia
Specialties: Oriental, Tools,
Paper
Directions: 2 blocks off
Rte 209 on the main street
of Hurley

Hurleyville

ACE TRADING CO
Main St   12747
914 434-4553
Proprietor: Hal Wexler
Hours: Daily
Types & Periods: Furniture,
Bric-A-Brac, "Bargain
Hunter's Paradise"

BRAMBLEDOWN ANTIQUES
& BRIC-A-BRAC
Brophy Rd   12747
914 434-5579
Proprietor: Joy Searl Davis
Hours: Daily, 9-6
Types & Periods: General
Line, Collectibles

BYGONES OF
YESTERYEAR
Brophy Rd   12747
914 434-5190
Hours: Tues-Sun,
10:30-4:30, July & August
Types & Periods: General
Line, Bric-A-Brac,
Collectibles, Jewelry,
Pressed Glass

THE PAST TENSE
ANTIQUES
Main St   12747
914 434-7575
Hours: Daily, May-Nov
Types & Periods: China, Art,
Glass, Coins, Furniture,
Jewelry, Bottles

Hyde Park

A COLLECTOR'S CORNER
Rte 9 Box 294   12538
914 889-3140   Est: 1941
Proprietor: Mildred &
Harry Calhoun
Hours: Sun-Mon, Wed-Sat,
1-4:30
Types & Periods:
Chandeliers, Jewelry, Glass,
China, General Line
Specialties: Paper Items
Appraisal Service Available
Directions: 2 miles N of
Hyde Park on Rte 9
between New York &
Albany

EDWARD J HOLDEN
Mill Rd   12538
914 229-2940
Proprietor: Edward J
Holden
Hours: Mon-Sat, 10-5
Types & Periods: General
Line

Ilion

HERKIMER FAMILY
TREASURE HOUSE
Upper Ostego   13357
315 895-7832   Est: 1970
Proprietor: Norma S
Basloe
Hours: Mon-Fri, 9-5; Sat,
11-3; Sun by chance
Types & Periods: Victorian,
Art Nouveau, Deco, Fina
Glass, China, Silver

Flatware, Picture Frames,
Lamps, Jardineres, Jewelry,
Artworks, Small Items (Pen
Knives, Pens & Pencils,
Hatpins)
Specialties: Ruby Glass,
Cobalt Blue Souvenier
Items, Custard Glass,
Jewelry
Appraisal Service Available
Directions: On Rte 51, just
S of Ilion, take Rte 5, 5 S
or 20 to 51

MAIN STREET EXCHANGE
124 E Main St   13357
315 895-7181   Est: 1947
Proprietor: Geraldine J &
W H Williams
Hours: Sun-Tues,
Thurs-Sat; Wed & Sun by
appointment
Types & Periods: Furniture,
Dishes, Glassware
Specialties: Arms
Appraisal Service Available
Directions: Located on
Rte 5 S

Island Park

SEYMOUR & FAYE'S
ANTIQUES & JUNKTIQUES
INC
4090 Austin Blvd   11558
516 432-9712   Est: 1966
Proprietor: Seymour &
Faye Berch
Hours: Mon-Tues,
Thurs-Fri, 12-5; Weekends
by appointment
Types & Periods: Statuary,
Marble, Bronze, Porcelain,
Furniture (Oak), Ivory,
Oriental Jewelry
Specialties: Statues
Directions: Between
Alabama Ave & Saratoga
Ave

Islip

ISLIP ANTIQUES AND
DOLL HOSPITAL
469 Main St   11751
516 581-9568   Est: 1966
Proprietor: Richard Antos
Hours: Mon-Wed, Fri-Sat,
12-4

Types & Periods: Victorian, Early American, Toys, Antique Dolls
Specialties: Antique Doll Repairs
Appraisal Service Available
Directions: On Montauk Hwy 27A, Southern State Pkwy Islip Ave S Exit to Main

Ithaca

ANTIQUE HOUSE
111 N Cayuga St   14850
607 273-2531   Est: 1956
Proprietor: Rose L Ocello
Hours: Tues-Sat
Types & Periods: Furniture, China, Glass, Lamps & Shades, General Line
Directions: Downtown

ASIA HOUSE GALLERY & MUSEUM
118 S Meadow St   14850
607 272-8850   Est: 1969
Proprietor: Dr von Reinhold Jamesson
Hours: Tues-Sat, 11-5
Types & Periods: Asian Art, 10th to 19th Century Asian Artifacts, Oriental Rugs, Tapestries
Specialties: Tibetan & Nepalese Art
Appraisal Service Available
Directions: Downtown, 1 block from State St

HOUSE OF HOFFMAN
17 Bush Ln   14850
607 257-0943   Est: 1970
Proprietor: Frederick & Marilyn Hoffman
Hours: By appointment
Types & Periods: American 18th & Early 19th Century Furniture & Accessories
Specialties: Empire Furniture
Appraisal Service Available

OLD THINGS
604 E Buffalo St   14850
607 277-0276   Est: 1970
Proprietor: Jody Pitari
Hours: Tues-Sat, 10-5:30
Types & Periods: Jewelry, Clothing, Nostalgia
Directions: E hill area on fringe of Cornell University, Buffalo St runs parallel with Rte 79

PERRY'S TRASH & TREASURES
615 W Green St   14850
607 272-2699   Est: 1971
Proprietor: Ralph & Lois Perry
Hours: Mon-Sat, 10-4:3-
Types & Periods: General Line, Furniture, Glassware, Collectibles
Directions: E off Rte 13 on Rte 79, "Huge red barn"

YESTERDAYS
430 N Cayuga St   14850
607 273-4712   Est: 1975
Proprietor: T Clongen & T Long
Hours: Daily, by appointment
Types & Periods: Early American Primitives, Furniture
Specialties: Restoration
Directions: Rte 13 or 79 to W State St, N Cayuga off State St

Jamaica

YE OLDE TREASURE SHOP
106-20 New York Blvd   11433
212 523-5765   Est: 1956
Proprietor: S R Newberry
Hours: Tues-Sat, also by appointment or chance
Types & Periods: Art Glass, Cut Glass, Silver, Furniture, General Line

Jamesville

ELVIRA BERARDI ANTIQUES
5195 Jamesville Rd   13078
315 446-2935
Proprietor: Elvira Berardi
Hours: By appointment
Types & Periods: Collectibles, General Line

Jeffersonville

BERVIE BRAE ANTIQUES
Gain Bldg   12791
914 482-4540
Proprietor: Eleanor Dubinbaum

Hours: Mon-Tues, Thurs-Sat, 11:30-4:30; by appointment or by chance
Types & Periods: China, Bric-A-Brac, Silver, Early American & Victorian Furniture, Frames
Appraisal Service Available
Directions: Main St, in rear of Gain Bldg

GAIN HOUSE ANTIQUES
Main St   12748
914 482-4464
Hours: Daily, by appointment, July & August
Types & Periods: Early American Glass

MALMAISON ANTIQUES
Box 354 Rte 52   12748
914 482-5753
Hours: Daily, July-Sept
Types & Periods: Furniture, Glass, Porcelain & Paintings of Louis XV & XVI Period, Jewelry, Silver

Jewett

TOWER MOUNTAIN ANTIQUES
Merwin St   12444
518 734-3782
Proprietor: Geraldine D Kirkman
Hours: By appointment, by chance
Types & Periods: Primitives, General Line

Johnson City

BARTLETT ANTIQUES
110 Main St   13790
607 729-9651
Proprietor: Betty S Bartlett
Hours: Tues-Sat, 11-5
Types & Periods: Period Furniture, Sterling Silver, Cut Glass, Flo Blue, Limoges, Staffordshire, Paintings, Copper, Brass, Clocks
Specialties: Sterling Silver Matching Service
Appraisal Service Available
Directions: Rte 17C, Exit 70S from N Y 17, right on 17C thru village

COUNTRY HOUSE ANTIQUES
1466 Oakdale Rd   13790
607 797-7263
Hours: Daily
Types & Periods: General Line, Collectibles
Diréctions: E side of N Oakdale Rd

COUNTRY HOUSE ANTIQUES
Harry L Dr   13790
607 797-7263
Hours: Weekends, 9-5, or by appointment
Types & Periods: General Line
Directions: Corner of Harry L Dr & Oakdale Rd

Johnstown

GINNY'S ANTIQUES
Block 500 N Perry St
        12095
518 762-7545   Est: 1951
Proprietor: Virginia Griffin
Hours: Daily, by appointment or chance
Types & Periods: General Line, Furniture, China, Glass, Ironware, Brass
Directions: Between Gloversville & Johnstown

SHULER & DUROSS
230 N Perry   12095
518 762-8116   Est: 1944
Proprietor: Ella Mae & Dick Oxford
Hours: Mon-Sat, 8-5
Types & Periods: General Line, Furniture, Metals, Lamps, Silver, Jewelry
Appraisal Service Available
Directions: 5 miles, Rte 30A from Exit 28 N Y S Thruway

Keeseville

BOSWORTH TAVERN ANTIQUES
Rte 1 Box 116   12944
518 834-7736   Est: 1969
Proprietor: Fritz & Marilyn Knight
Hours: Mon-Sat, Summer; Winter by chance

Types & Periods: Primitive Pine, Furniture, General Line
Specialties: Restoration
Directions: 3 miles S of Keeseville on Rte 9, or I-87 Exit 33, 1 mile N on Rte 9

Kenmore

VILLAGE ANTIQUES
2798 Delaware   14217
716 877-6981   Est: 1973
Proprietor: Concetta & George Capuano
Hours: Mon-Sat
Types & Periods: Glass
Specialties: Glass (Flow Blue)
Appraisal Service Available
Directions: From Main St to Delaware Ave, N of Buffalo

Kerhonkson

EVELYN BERNSTEIN ANTIQUES
        12446
914 626-7672
Proprietor: Evelyn Bernstein
Hours: Daily
Types & Periods: "A Little Bit of Everything"
Directions: 1 mile N of Kerhonkson, intersection on Rte 209 just 200 ft off hwy

Kinderhook

MILROSS ANTIQUES
5 Kinderhook St   12106
518 758-6412
Proprietor: Ross & Mildred Pigott
Hours: Tues-Sat, 12:30-5; also by appointment
Types & Periods: Blown Glass, Folk Art, Furniture, General Line
Directions: Rte 9

Kingston

ARTIE'S ANTIQUE SHOP
64 Crown St   12401
914 331-9639   Est: 1970
Proprietor: Arthur Elting
Hours: Daily, 8:30-5:30
Types & Periods: Furniture, Stoves, Lamps, Tools, Frames
Directions: 1/4 mile from N Y S Thruway Exit 19

FRED J JOHNSTON
Main & Wall St   12401
Proprietor: Fred J Johnston
Hours: Mon-Sat, by appointment
Types & Periods: Rare American 17th & 18th Century Antiques
Specialties: 18th Century Furniture
Appraisal Service Available
Directions: 4 minutes from N Y S Thruway Exit 19

JAY MARTIN
55 N Front St   12401
914 331-4848   Est: 1936
Proprietor: Jay Martin
Hours: Mon-Fri, 10-4; or by chance
Types & Periods: China, Glass, Furniture
Appraisal Service Available

OUTBACK ANTIQUES
72 Hurley Ave   12401
914 331-4481
Proprietor: Ann Knowles
Hours: Mon-Sat, 10-5; Sun by appointment or chance
Types & Periods: General Line, Clothing, Victorian & Art Deco, Laces & Doilies
Directions: 3 blocks from N Y S Thruway Exit 19

POSNERS ANTIQUES & JUNKTIQUES
277 Millers Lane Ext 12401
914 331-4228   Est: 1974
Proprietor: Miriam S Posner
Hours: Tues & Thurs, or by appointment or chance
Types & Periods: General Line, Collectibles, Paper Americana & Post Cards

Directions: N Y S Thruway
Exit 19, to Washington
Ave, right turn on Lucas
Ave, 4th block on left

TRI-CYCLE ANTIQUES
292 E Chester St   12401
914 331-5827
Proprietor: Marina Gille
Hours: Daily, 11-5:30
Types & Periods: General
Line

VIN-DICK ANTIQUES
RD 3 Box 117   12401
914 338-7113   Est: 1969
Proprietor: R Goshin & V
Mogavero
Hours: Tues-Sun, by
appointment
Types & Periods: American
Empire, Victorian, Primitive
& Accessories
Directions: 5 miles S of
Kingston, on Rte 209

**JACK & MARYELLEN
WHISTANCE**
RD 2 Box 232   12401
914 338-4397   Est: 1954
Proprietor: Jack &
Maryellen Whistance
Hours: By appointment or
by chance
Types & Periods: 18th &
Early 19th Century American
Country Furniture, Paintings,
Glass, Folk Art, Collectibles
Specialties: Historical Flasks,
American Paintings
Appraisal Service Available
Directions: 1 mile N of
Exit 19 on N Y S Thruway,
on Rte 28

Lake Katrine

R & R ASSOCIATES
Old Kings Hwy   12249
914 331-9753   Est: 1971
Proprietor: V Riwaldi
Hours: Daily
Types & Periods: Victorian
Furniture, Art Glass, Lamps
Appraisal Service Available
Directions: Exit 20
Thruway, Saugerties Old
King's Hwy to Lake
Katrine

Lake Peekskill

**THE FOXY LADY ANTIQUE
JEWELRY**
Box 431   10537
914 528-1799
Proprietor: Joyce & Harold
Weitzberg
Hours: By appointment
Types & Periods: Victorian &
Art Nouveau Jewelry,
Georgian Art Deco

Larchmont

COLDSTREAM ANTIQUES
2076 Boston Post Rd
   10538
914 834-3030   Est: 1969
Proprietor: R & H Wexler
Hours: Tues-Sat, 10:30-5;
also by appointment
Types & Periods: Early
American & English
Furniture & Accessories
(Porcelain, Paintings)
Specialties: Early American
& English Furniture, 18th &
Early 19th Centuries
Appraisal Service Available

**MONT VERT ANTIQUE
FURNITURE**
15 York Rd   10538
914 834-2957   Est: 1964
Proprietor: W Parkman
Rankin
Hours: By appointment
Types & Periods: Early
American Antique Furniture
Specialties: Small Tables,
Chairs, Mirrors, Yarn
Winders
Directions: Off Fenimore
Rd, near Winged Foot Golf
Club in Mamroneck

Laurens

**DIANTHA & WALTER
SCHULL**
Box 201 Rte 205   13796
607 432-8954
Proprietor: Diantha &
Walter Schull
Hours: By appointment
Types & Periods: Country
Furniture, Fabrics,
Stoneware, Paintings
Directions: 1 mile N of
Laurens on Rte 205

Lew Beach

ABA DABA ANTIQUES
   12753
914 439-4590
Hours: Daily, June-Oct
Types & Periods: "Spunk &
Junk"

Liberty

**AROUND THE CORNER
ANTIQUES**
16 School St   12754
914 292-5080   Est: 1975
Proprietor: Alton & Diana
Reeves
Hours: Mon-Tues,
Thurs-Sat
Types & Periods: Victorian &
Turn-of-the-Century Country
Oak Furniture
Specialties: Jewelry
Directions: Off Main St,
middle of block

BELLE'S ELEGANT JUNK
Loomis Rd   12754
914 292-6647
Hours: Daily, April-Nov, off
season by appointment
Types & Periods:
Collectibles, Glassware,
Lanterns, Small Furniture,
Pictures, Lamps

DIPSEY DOODLE
22 S Main St   12754
Hours: Daily, 10-5;
Mon-Sat in wintor
Types & Periods:
Wedgwood, Art Glass,
Satsuma, Small Furniture,
Deco, Books, First Editions,
Pictures, Jewelry, Coins

**EDDIE ANTIQUE
JEWELERS**
13 S Main St   12754
914 292-5411   Est: 1925
Proprietor: Eddie Spitz
Hours: Daily, 10-5
Types & Periods: Georgian,
Victorian, French
Specialties: Watches
Appraisal Service Available
Directions: 100 miles from
NYC on Rte 17 W, in the
Catskills

Liberty   Cont'd

PAMELA MOORE EPSTEIN'S MY MOTHER'S PLACE
20 School St   12754
Proprietor: Dena Davidson
Hours: Daily, 10-5
Types & Periods: General Line

PAMELA MOORE'S AUCTION CENTER
Rte 55 Box 708   12740
914 292-8655
Proprietor: Pamela Moore Epstein
Hours: Sat night, auctions at 7pm
Types & Periods: Complete Estates, "The Lady Auctioneer"
Directions: Opposite Banta's Mill

POND IN THE MEADOW
Old Loomis Rd   12754
914 292-8635
Hours: By appointment, April-Oct
Types & Periods: General Line, Furniture, Bottles
Directions: Old Loomis & M T Morris Rds off Rte 52

STONE HILL CHAPEL ANTIQUES
Buckley St   12754
914 292-8635
Hours: Daily, 12-6
Types & Periods: Glass, China, Furniture, Woodenware, Collectibles, Bric-A-Brac
Directions: 1.3 miles from Main St "Historic Area"

Lima

LIMA ANTIQUES
7348 Main St   14485
716 624-4700
Proprietor: Tecla Benson
Hours: Daily
Types & Periods: Oak Furniture, Victorian, Primitives, Glass, China
Specialties: Glass (Depression)
Directions: Rte 5 & 20 near Rtes 15 & 15A

THOMAS E TREMER
6489 Avon Lima Rd 14485
716 624-1200   Est: 1969
Proprietor: Thomas E Tremer
Hours: Weekends, by appointment or by chance
Types & Periods: General Line, Collectibles, Furniture, Glass
Specialties: Furniture (Refinished)
Appraisal Service Available
Directions: Rte 5 & 20 midway between Lima & E Avon

Loch Sheldrake

BECKER'S ANTIQUES
PO Box 303 Hurleyville Rd
                     12759
914 434-6719
Hours: Daily, 9-7 summer months, off season by chance
Types & Periods: General Line, Furniture, China, Glass, Bottles, Bric-A-Brac, Lamps, Tins, Collector Items
Directions: 200 ft from Rte 52 intersection

THE BOTTLE BIN
Box 24   12759
914 434-4757
Hours: By appointment
Types & Periods: Bottles(including Sodas), Beers, Medicines, Whiskeys, Household Bitters
Directions: 1/4 mile toward Woodbourne off Rte 52

Lockport

M BANCROFT & SONS
400 S Niagara St   14094
716 433-4334   Est: 1959
Proprietor: M Bancroft
Hours: Daily, by chance
Types & Periods: "Mostly old horsedrawn equipment", Wooden Wagons, Buggies, Sleighs, Wooden Wagon Wheels, Old Cars & Trucks of Yesteryear

Appraisal Service Available
Directions: 1 block N off Rte 31 W at City Line

DOT'S ANTIQUES AND UPHOLSTERY SHOP
185 S Transit   14094
716 433-3793   Est: 1972
Proprietor: Gary L & Dorothy A Lawton
Hours: Mon-Fri, 9:30-6; Sat, 10-5; evenings by appointment
Types & Periods: Upholstered Victoriana, Tobacco Collectibles, Paintings & Prints
Specialties: Tobacco, Pipes, Upholstered Furniture Restoration
Appraisal Service Available
Directions: Rte 78 N of N Y S Thruway Depew Exit, 12 miles to Lockport

HAVEN HOUSE
4864 Ridge Rd   14094
716 434-5450   Est: 1962
Proprietor: Mrs G Haven Thompson
Hours: Daily
Types & Periods: Early American
Specialties: Furniture
Appraisal Service Available
Directions: 5 miles W of junction Rtes 78 & 104

Locust Valley

RAYMOND B KNIGHT CORPORATION
113 Birch Hill Rd   11560
516 671-7046
Proprietor: Raymond B Knight
Hours: Mon-Sat, 8:30-5:30; also by appointment
Types & Periods: English & American 18th & 19th Century Furniture

LOCUST VALLEY ANTIQUES
15 Forest Ave   11560
516 671-7710   Est: 1964
Proprietor: Carol Prisant
Hours: Mon, Wed-Sat
Types & Periods: English, American & European Furniture, Objects & Paintings, Collectibles

Appraisal Service Available
Directions: LI Expwy to
Glen Cove Rd, N about 4
miles to School St, right
to Forest

Long Eddy

THE VILLAGE SHOP
Rte 97 & Acid Factory Rd
12760
914 887-5138
Hours: By appointment
Types & Periods: General
Line
Specialties: Lamps

Long Island City

OLD CHINA CUPBOARD
45-08 41st St   11104
212 937-0749   Est: 1971
Proprietor: Ruth Waldman
Hours: Mon-Fri, Weekends
by appointment
Types & Periods: China,
Glass, Pictures, Bric-A-Brac
Directions: 1 mile E of
59th St Bridge off Queens
Blvd, Sunnyside

Loudonville

**LOUDONVILLE ANTIQUE
EXCHANGE**
423 Loudonville Rd 12211
518 434-2631
Hours: Mon-Fri
Types & Periods: General
Line
Specialties: 18th Century
English & American
Appraisal Service Available
Directions: Rte 9 N from
Albany, approximately 3
miles

Lynbrook

**VICTOR AND SONIA
FARBER**
163 Atlantic Ave   11563
516 593-1696   Est: 1955
Proprietor: Victor & Sonia
Farber
Hours: Tues-Fri, 10-5; Sat
by appointment

Types & Periods: General
Line, Furniture, Glass,
China, Metals, All Periods
Directions: 2 blocks S of
Sunrise Hwy on Atlantic
Ave, which crosses Hwy in
center of Lynbrook

Lyons

PARKER'S ANTIQUES
29 Butternut St   14489
315 946-4684   Est: 1972
Proprietor: Gordon & Lila
Parker
Hours: Daily
Types & Periods: Silver,
Glass, Kerosene Lamps,
Picture Frames
Specialties: Silver Replating,
Brass Stripping & Buffing
Appraisal Service Available
Directions: 3 houses N of
Wayne County Museum

Macedon

THE GOLDEN PAST
401 Penfield Rd   14502
716 377-5385   Est: 1972
Proprietor: Thelma
Trynoski
Hours: By appointment
Types & Periods: Victorian
Furniture, Dolls, Lamps,
Silver, Jewelry, Prints
Specialties: Glass, Heisey,
Duncan
Directions: 4½ miles E of
Rte 250, 3½ miles W of
Rte 350

Madison

**COYNE'S ANTIQUES
GALLERY**
Main St Rte 20   13402
315 893-7174   Est: 1969
Proprietor: Bernard & M
June Coyne
Hours: Mon-Sat, Sun by
appointment
Types & Periods: Country
Furniture & Accessories,
Framing & Prints, Paintings,
Bronzes, Orientals, Art
Glass, Folk Art
Directions: Rte 20, in
center of village in
business block

J & R FERRIS
Rte 20   13402
315 893-7006   Est: 1970
Hours: By appointment or
by chance
Types & Periods: Country
Primitives, Furniture, Wood,
Tin and Iron
Specialties: Toys, Tools,
Military Items
Appraisal Service Available
Directions: 2 doors W of
the Post Office, center of
town

Malden Bridge

LUCIE VINE CLERK
Columbia County   12115
518 766-2516
Proprietor: Lucie Vine Clerk
Hours: Daily, 10-5; also by
appointment
Types & Periods: Shaker,
Early Country Furniture, Tin,
Primitives, Paintings

COREY DANIELS
Star Rte   12024
518 766-4662   Est: 1969
Proprietor: Corey Daniels
Hours: Tues, by appt or
by chance
Types & Periods: Period
American Furniture,
Paintings, Folk Art, American
& European Accessories
Directions: 1 mile N of
Malden Bridge on Rte 66

**JOHN & JACQUELINE
SIDEZI**
Rte 66   12024
518 766-3547
Proprietor: Jacqueline &
John Sidezi
Hours: By appointment or
By chance
Types & Periods: Country
Furniture, Folk Art, Quilts

Malone

BONNER'S BARN
25 Washington St   12953
518 403-4001
Proprietor: Bob & Jimmie
Bonner
Hours: Daily

BONNER'S BARN   Cont'd
Types & Periods: Furniture,
Paintings, Iron, Tin, Brass,
Rugs, Quilts
   Directions: 3rd house in
   back of Post Office

Malvern

BEA GOLD ANTIQUES
   131 Franklin Ave   11565
   516 593-6730   Est: 1966
   Proprietor: Beatrice Gold
   Hours: Mon-Tues, Thurs-
Sat, 1:-4:30
Types & Periods: General
Line, Glass, China, Bronze,
Oriental
   Directions: ½ mile S of
   Southern State Pkwy

Mamaroneck

RITA BARG ANTIQUES
   125 E Prospect Ave 10543
   914 472-4047   Est: 1970
   Proprietor: Rita Barg
   Hours; Mon, Tues, Thurs
   & Sat; By appointment
Types & Periods: Wicker, Oak,
Graphics, Collectibles, Eng-
lish Bamboo, English Country
Furniture
   Directions: 1 block N of
   Post Rd, US 1, turn right
   "Down the Hill"

CORTLANDT ANTIQUES INC
   116 Mamaroneck Ave
                    10534
   914 698-4395   Est: 1972
   Proprietor: Beatrice G &
   Jules Spiegel
   Hours: Tues-Sun, 11-5
Types & Periods: Tiffany,
Bronzes, Art Glass, Silver,
19th Century American &
English Furniture,
Miniatures, Ivories,
Cloisonne &
Decorative Items, Benezit
Listed Paintings
   Directions: Off New
   England Thruway, Off
   Rte 1

GROSSMAN ANTIQUES
   616 Munro Ave   10543
   914 698-8489
   Proprietor: Mrs R E
   Grossman
   Hours: By appointment
Types & Periods: "You
name it, I'll find it"

GARY P GUARNO
   125 E Pospect Ave 10543
   914 381-2440
   Proprietor: Gary P Guarno
   Hours: Mon-Sat, 9:30-5:30
Types & Periods: Victorian,
Oak, Good Quality
Mahogany
Specialties: Furniture of All
Periods
   Directions: Just 2 shops E
   of Mamaroneck Ave, 1
   block N of US 1

LYMAN'S ANTIQUES
   157 Mamaroneck Ave
                    10543
   914 698-2373
   Proprietor: Edward H
   Lyman
   Hours: Daily, 11-5
Types & Periods: Furniture,
Cameo Glass, Netsuke,
Bronzes

**THE WOLFE'S LAIR
ANTIQUES**
   587 E Boston Post Rd
                    10543
   914 698-5340
   Proprietor: Mrs Jane
   Wolfe
   Hours: Mon-Sat, 11-5
Types & Periods: 18th &
19th Century International,
Jewelry

YESTERDAYS
   135 Mamaroneck Ave
                    10543
   914 698-4369   Est: 1973
   Proprietor: Norma Hauser
   Hours: Wed-Sat,
   11:30-4:30
Types & Periods: Wicker,
Decorative Accessories &
Collectibles, Victorian, Oak
   Directions: 15 miles S of
   Greenwich, CT & 30 miles
   N of NYC

Manlius

THE FANLIGHT INC
   4574 Meadowridge Rd
                    13104
   315 682-6551   Est: 1974
   Proprietor: J S Caldwell III
   Hours: By appointment
Types & Periods: Paintings,
18th Century Furniture,
Porcelains, Silver, Firearms
Appraisal Service Available
   Directions: 8 miles SE of
   Syracuse off Rte 173

Marcellus

**CUMMINGS ANTIQUE &
CANDY SHOP**
   31 North St   13108
   315 673-3285   Est: 1922
   Proprietor: Jack
   Cummings
   Hours: Daily
Types & Periods: General
Line
Specialties: Paintings &
Reprints by Ruth Reed
Appraisal Service Available

THE NEW IMAGE
   40 E Main St   13224
   315 673-4665   Est: 1978
   Proprietor: Douglas Low
   Hours: Mon-Sat, by
   appointment
Types & Periods: Mirrors
Specialties: Re-silvering
Antique Mirrors
   Directions: Downtown

Margaretville

LIBERTY BELL ANTIQUES
                    12455
   914 586-4805 Est: 1958
   Proprietor: Dorothy C
   Fairbairn
   Hours: Daily May-Oct;
   Nov-April by chance
Types & Periods: Primitives,
Furniture, Lamps, Indian
Jewelry
Specialties: Glass (Art &
Cut)
   Directions: "Up hill off Rte
   28 & 30"

Marlboro

BLACKBERRY HILL ANTIQUES
Old Marlboro Rd   12542
914 561-4388
Proprietor: Sibyl Rigas
Types & Periods:
Collectibles, Glass, China, Lamps, Furniture, Primitives

Maryland

PICK & POKE ANTIQUES
PO Box 1   12116
607 286-9045   Est: 1952
Proprietor: Iris & Walter Wilson
Hours: By appointment or by chance
Types & Periods: Dolls, Primitives, General Line
Specialties: Dolls
Directions: From Rte 7, turn on Co Rte 35 to Westville, turn right, 1/2 mile, shop on right, sign in front of house

Maybrook

RONALD V DECKER ANTIQUES
102 Main St   12543
914 427-2338
Proprietor: Ronald V Decker
Hours: Tues-Sun, 9-5, also by appointment
Types & Periods:
Americana, Collectibles, Clocks, Glass, China, General Line
Directions: Off Rte 84, Exit 5

Mayville

DAZE OF YORE
5073 W Lake Rd   14757
716 753-7933   Est: 1971
Proprietor: Harriet C Michael
Hours: Daily, May-Sept; Oct-April by chance
Types & Periods: General Line, Collectibles

Appraisal Service Available
Directions: Rte 394, 1 mile S of Mayville, on Chautauqua Lake

Middlehope

EAGLES ROOST ANTIQUES
RD 1 Old Maryboro Trnpk
12542
914 562-2362
Proprietor: Jeanne De Santis
Hours: Daily, 10-8
Types & Periods: Clocks, Glass, General Line, Collectibles, Furniture

Middletown

BETTY-JANE ANTIQUES
280 Highland Ave   10940
914 343-6274
Proprietor: Betty Gibson & Jane Cole
Hours: Mon-Fri, 4-8; Sat & Sun all day
Types & Periods: General Line

KIT & CABOODLE
RFD 3 Union School Rd
10940
914 361-1744
Proprietor: Barbara Meier
Hours: Daily
Types & Periods: General Line, Copper, Brass, Hearth Accessories
Directions: Off Collabar Rd, 1 mile from Rte 17K

OXBOW ANTIQUE SHOP
542 North St   10940
914 342-3427
Proprietor: Pat & Garth Smith
Hours: Daily
Types & Periods: Furniture, Primitives, Tools, RR Items, Collectibles

PETERSEN'S EXCHANGE
48 Mill St   10940
914 343-5717
Proprietor: Marion Petersen Suway
Hours: Mon-Fri, by appointment

Types & Periods:
Collectibles, General Line
Furniture
Specialties: Glass (Depression Era)
Appraisal Service Available
Directions: 68 miles N of NYC, Harriman Exit N Y S Thruway, Rte 17 to Middletown

PINNACLE ANTIQUE SHOP
684 North St   10940
914 343-2690
Proprietor: Jeanette Trautman
Types & Periods: Carnival Glass, Furniture, Quilts, General Line

SEELY'S OLD LAMP SHOP
36 Woodlawn Ave   10940
914 343-6008   Est: 1947
Proprietor: Frieda & Cal Seely
Hours: By appointment
Types & Periods: China, Glass, Lamps, General Line
Specialties: Old Oil Lamps
Directions: Just outside city of Middletown, off NY Rte 17, Exit 122

STEPPING STONE INN ANTIQUES
RD 3 Box 354   10940
914 361-2261   Est: 1973
Proprietor: Leona Trimmer
Hours: Mon-Sat, 10-6; other times by appointment
Types & Periods: Flow Blue China, Tuthill Cut Glass, Primitives, 10th Century Furnishings, Hearth Items, Kitchen Collectibles
Directions: Rte 17 Exit 119 to Rte 302, right on Goshen Tpk, 1 mile from Circleville

Millbrook

MILLBROOK ANTIQUE CENTER
12545
914 677-3921
Proprietor: Bette & Chub Wicker
Hours: Mon-Sat, 10-5
Sun, 1-5

MILLBROOK ANTIQUE CENTER   Cont'd

Types & Periods: 18 Dealers Under One Roof
Appraisal Service Available
Directions: Rte 44, in the heart of the village

WICKER'S ANTIQUES
12545
914 677-3906
Proprietor: Bette & Chub Wicker
Hours: By appointment only
Specialties: Early American Pattern Glass

Millwood

RUSEY ART & ANTIQUES
Box 456   10546
914 941-0920   Est: 1974
Proprietor: Ruth Geringer
Hours: By appointment
Types & Periods: Pottery, Cameo Glass

Mineola

EASTLAKE ANTIQUES
307 Willis Ave   11501
516 746-5544   Est: 1971
Proprietor: A Castellano
Hours: Tues-Sat,
11:30-4:30; Mon by chance
Types & Periods: Glass, China, Silver, Jewelry, Pocket Watches, Oil Lamps, Post Cards, Paintings, Oak & Period Furniture
Specialties: Oriental
Appraisal Service Available
Directions: S Exit 37 LI Expwy, approximately 2 miles, between Hillside & Jericho Tpk

LAVENDER & OLD LACE ANTIQUES
317 Willis Ave   11501
516 747-0941   Est: 1968
Proprietor: Dae C Bade
Hours: Daily, 1-5, May-Sept; Tues-Sat, 1-5, Oct-April
Types & Periods: Orientalia, English & German Porcelain, Bronzes, Furniture, Paintings

Appraisal Service Available
Directions: LI Expwy to Exit 37 S, approximately 2-4/10 miles S of Willis Ave, on corner of Linden Rd & Willis Ave

MERE PITTANCE
299 Willis Ave   11501
516 294-0358   Est: 1967
Proprietor: Lucille Walkowski
Hours: Tues-Sat, 11-4:30
Types & Periods: Glassware, Furniture, Jewelry, Prints, Oils
Specialties: Glass (Cut & Pressed)
Directions: 1 block N of Jericho Turnpike

ORPHANS OF THE ATTIC
313 Willis Ave   11501
516 741-0477   Est: 1972
Proprietor: Rosalyn Rudin & Morton Rudin
Hours: Tues-Sat, 11:30-4:30; Tues-Fri June-August
Types & Periods: Porcelain, Jewelry, Glass, Furniture, Collectibles
Directions: 1 block N of Jericho Trnpk

PICKWICK DECORATORS INC
111 Jericho Turnpike
11501
516 248-1699   Est: 1952
Proprietor: Mark Brown
Hours: Mon-Sat, also by appointment or by chance
Types & Periods: French & English Furniture
Appraisal Service Available

TIME WAS ANTIQUES
315 Willis Ave   11501
516 742-0195   Est: 1971
Proprietor: Laura & Nat Lipkin
Hours: Mon-Sat, 2-4, July & August, also by appointment
Types & Periods: Early American Clocks, Cut Glass, General Line
Specialties: Clocks
Appraisal Service Available
Directions: Long Island Expwy to Exit 37 Willis Ave

Mohawk

YE OLDE SHOPPE ANTIQUES
11-E Main St   13407
315 866-0943   Est: 1942
Proprietor: John & Edna Mayton
Hours: Daily, by chance
Types & Periods: General Line, Art & Fancy Glass, Oak & Barn Furniture
Specialties: Furniture, Lamps
Appraisal Service Available
Directions: N Y S Thruway Exit 30 & W on Rte 5 S & Rte 28

Monroe

MONROE ANTIQUES
163 Stage Rd   10950
914 783-6347   Est: 1970
Proprietor: Jean & Sidney White
Hours: Sun-Mon, Wed-Sat; Phone call advisable
Types & Periods: 18th & Early 19th Century Americana, Oriental Items, Miniature Paintings on Ivory
Specialties: Federal and Country Furniture
Appraisal Service Available
Directions: N Y S Thruway Exit 16, then Quickway to Monroe Exit, turn left on Lake St, then turn on to Stage Rd

Monsey

ROCKLAND INDOOR-OUTDOOR FLEA MARKET
88 Rte 59   10952
914 352-2637   Est: 1975
Proprietor: Mrs Baron
Hours: Weekends
Types & Periods: Over 90 Dealers, All Types of Antiques
Directions: Tappanzee Bridge to Thruway Exit 14 or Palisades Pkwy to Thruway to Exit 14

Montgomery

**MARTY & ANNE ELLMAN
ANTIQUES**
RD 2 River Rd   12549
914 457-3847
Proprietor: Marty & Anne
Ellman
Hours: By appointment or
by chance
Types & Periods: Oak,
Wicker, Folk Art, American
Indian & Eskimo Artifacts
Appraisal Service Available
Directions: River Rd

Monticello

CAYLEE CURIOS
Rubin Rd   12701
914 794-7493   Est: 1967
Proprietor: C Rubin
Hours: Summer every day;
Winter by chance or
appointment
Types & Periods: China,
Lamps, Paintings, Furniture,
Frames, Statues, General
Line
Directions: On Rubin Rd
off Rte 42 S

DINGLE DAISY ANTIQUES
Dingle Daisy Rd   12701
914 794-5939   Est: 1968
Proprietor: Evelyn Moss
Hours: By chance
Types & Periods: Jewelry,
China, Deco, Oak Furniture,
Sterling, Americana, General
Line
Specialties: Jewelry
Directions: 30 ft off
Forestburgh Rd (Rte 42 S)

ELEGANTE SHOPPE
266 Broadway   12701
914 794-2656
Hours: Daily in summer;
Mon-Sat rest of the year
Types & Periods: Jades,
Ivories, Art, Art Glass

GUSTAVE ANTIQUES
Port Jarvis Rd   12701
914 794-1611
Hours: Daily

Types & Periods: 19th
Century Oil Paintings,
Original Art Deco Paintings,
Framed Prints, Chandeliers,
General Line
Directions: 1 mile S of
town on Rte 42

JA-CO ANTIQUES
41 Jefferson St   12701
914 794-7060
Proprietor: J E Ross
Hours: Fri-Sun, by
appointment or by chance
Types & Periods: General
Line
Specialties: Lighting
Fixtures, Furniture in ruff
Directions: Off Exit 104,
Rte 17 Quickway, 1/4 mile
on street into Monticello

LINNEA'S ANTIQUES
199 Broadway   12701
914 794-7299   Est: 1969
Proprietor: Linnea
Salomon
Hours: Daily, closed in
cold weather
Types & Periods: Dolls (Old
& Repairs), Lamps,
Paintings, Old Post Cards,
Primitive Furniture to 1900
Appraisal Service Available
Directions: Just off N Y S
Rte 17, Monticello Exit on
Rte 42, in the rear of Miss
Monticello Diner &
Restaurant

NOB HILL ANTIQUES
Old Liberty Rd   12701
914 794-7089
Proprietor: Ethel Garrelick
Hours: Daily, 10-5 in
summer, after Sept by
appointment
Types & Periods: Glass,
China, Porcelain, Silver,
Frames, Pictures, General
Line
Directions: Near Kutshers

SOUTHWOODS ANTIQUES
Southwoods Dr   12701
914 794-7517
Hours: Daily
Types & Periods: Furniture,
Glass, Clocks, Paintings,
Dolls, Country Items
Directions: Exit 107 from
Quickway

Moores

BARCOMB'S ANTIQUES
Main St   12958
518 236-5851
Proprietor: Roland &
Bernice Barcomb
Hours: Daily
Types & Periods: Glass,
China, Furniture, Primitives
Directions: Corner of Rtes
11 & 22

Morris

BEEHIVE ANTIQUES
                       13808
607 263-5249
Proprietor: Corinne &
Arthur Colvin
Hours: By appointment, by
chance
Types & Periods: General
Line, Lamps, Cherry
Furniture
Directions: Turn S at
Morris & go 2 miles, turn
right at Red Schoolhouse
Antiques

Morrisville

BURY FARM ANTIQUES
                       13408
315 684-3208
Proprietor: Richard &
Norma Bury
Hours: Mon-Sat, 9-5; also
by appointment
Types & Periods: Country
Furniture, American Folk
Art, Pencil Post Beds,
Country Sofas

Mountainville

RUTH KRANZ ROSNER
Taylor Rd   10953
914 534-2011   Est: 1948
Proprietor: Ruth Kranz
Rosner
Hours: By appointment
Types & Periods: Porcelains,
English, French, American
Furniture, Quality Selections
Appraisal Service Available
Directions: 1 mile W of
Rte 32 (Cornwall)

Mount Morris

MYRTLE'S WHAT NOT SHOP
84 Chapel St   14510
            Est: 1960
Proprietor: Myrtle Croston
Hours: Daily
Types & Periods: General
Line
Specialties: Furniture (Early
American)
Appraisal Service Available
Directions: Hwy 408

Mount Vernon

CONTINENTAL CRAFTS
1 West Broad St   10552
914 668-5342   Est: 1958
Proprietor: William
Margulis
Hours: Tues-Sat, 10-5:30;
closed July & Aug
Types & Periods:
Bric-A-Brac, Bronzes, Silver
Specialties: Jewelry (Also
Repair)
Appraisal Service Available
Directions: Cross Country
Pkwy Exit 4 off N Y S
Thruway

Narrowburg

BRICK HOUSE ANTIQUES
Delaware Dr   12764
914 252-7148
Proprietor: David &
Jeanette Barnes
Hours: Daily, June to Oct
Types & Periods: China,
Glass, Country Store Items,
Bottles, Insulators

Newark

THE AUCTION HOUSE
Rte 31 E Box 24C   14513
315 331-1365   Est: 1973
Hours: Daily
Types & Periods: "Anything
& Everything"
Directions: 1 mile E of
Newark on State Rte 31

BEMAN'S ANTIQUES
2168 Welcher Rd   14513
315 331-3463   Est: 1973
Proprietor: Phil & Erma
Beman
Hours: By appointment, by
chance
Types & Periods: General
Line
Specialties: Repairs &
Refinishing
Directions: 3 miles from N
Y 88 N, 4 miles from
downtown

**CHRISTOPHER'S
COLLECTABLES**
309 Peirson Ave   14513
315 331-4078   Est: 1973
Proprietor: Christopher T
Davis
Hours: Fri-Sun, 10-10; also
by appointment or by
chance
Types & Periods: Old
Bottles, Jars, Stoneware,
Flasks, Good Glass, China,
Hotchkiss Peppermint
Bottles (Lyons), General
Line
Specialties: Old Bottles,
Glass
Appraisal Service Available
Directions: Near plaza

**TOWN & COUNTRY
ANTIQUES**
Vienna Rd   14513
315 331-4532   Est: 1961
Proprietor: Irene Ridley
Hours: By appointment, by
chance
Types & Periods: General
Line, Furniture, Glass,
Paintings, China
Appraisal Service Available
Directions: 1 mile outside
Phelps on Rte 88 N,
connects Rte 88 to Rte 31

Newburgh

BALMVILLE ANTIQUES
24 Balmville Rd   12550
914 561-2710
Hours: Thurs-Sat, also by
appointment
Types & Periods: Furniture
Decorations
Directions: 1/2 mile from
bridge

IDA F BESSO ANTIQUES
164 West St   12550
914 561-3377
Proprietor: Ida F Besso
Hours: Daily, 9-5; also by
appointment
Types & Periods:
Collectibles, China, Glass,
Paintings, Silver, Bronze,
Jewelry

CORNELL JEWELERS
Mid Valley Mall   12550
914 561-2566   Est: 1901
Proprietor: Thos F
Kavanagh
Hours: Mon-Fri, 10-9, Sat,
10-6
Types & Periods: Jewelry,
Watches, Diamonds, Sterling
Flatware
Appraisal Service Available
Directions: From
intersection of Rte 9W &
I-84, 4 miles E of N Y S
Thruway, Newburgh
Interchange

SLEIGH HILL ANTIQUES
36 Rte 17K   12550
914 562-6960
Proprietor: Eleanor Dill
Types & Periods: Period &
Country Furniture, Paintings,
Primitives, Grandfather
Clocks
Directions: 1/4 mile left of
Thruway Entrance

New City

THE VILLAGE WORKSHOP
60 S Main St   10956
914 634-9384   Est: 1971
Proprietor: Phyllis G
Neumeyer
Hours: Tues-Fri, 10-4; Sat,
10-1
Types & Periods: 18th &
Early 19th Century Furniture
Specialties: English &
American Teapots
Appraisal Service Available
Directions: Diagonally
across street from Post
Office

New Lebanon

CHARLIE & CAROL PUTNAM-AMERICANA
Rte 20 Box 356   12125
518 794-7295
Proprietor: Charlie & Carol Putnam
Hours: By appointment
Types & Periods: Weathervanes, Folk Art, Stoneware

New Paltz

CORINNE BURKE
                    12561
914 255-1078
Proprietor: Corinne Burke
Hours: By appointment
Types & Periods: Country Furniture & Accessories

JAMES PUGLIESE
39 N Chestnut St   12561
914 255-7055   Est: 1955
Proprietor: James Pugliese
Hours: Daily, 11-5:30
Types & Periods: General Line
Specialties: Books
Directions: 1 mile N from New Paltz Exit on N Y S Thruway, Rte 32

Newport

JEAN GREELEY ANTIQUITIES
PO Box 1   03773
603 863-1133   Est: 1970
Proprietor: Bill & Jean Greeley
Hours: By appointment
Types & Periods: Military, Paper Americana, Autographs, Aviation & Automotive Memorabilita, Collectibles

New Rochelle

ANTIQUAIRE
310 North Ave   10801
914 576-2383
Proprietor: Luce A Klein
Hours: Tues-Sat, 11-6

Types & Periods: Furniture, Paintings, Objets d'Art, 17th Century, Art Deco

New Windsor

THE YESTERDAY SHOP
RD 2 Temple Hill Rd
                    12550
914 565-5354
Proprietor: Shirley Marano
Types & Periods: Furniture, Primitives
Directions: Near Rte 207

New York City

NEW YORK CITY CLUSTER
Directions: In Manhattan, 57th St between Madison & Park Aves, Madison Ave between 57th & 79th Sts, 3rd Ave between 45th & 70th Sts, Bleecher St, 2nd Ave to 26th St & S Houston St Soho

BRIAN ALBERT
415 E 53rd St   10022
212 486-0941
Hours: Tues-Sat, 10:30-5:30; Sun, 12-6
Types & Periods: Jewelry, General Line
Directions: "The Antiques Center of American Inc"

ALDIN-ELLIS LTD
415 E 53rd St   10022
212 486-0841
Proprietor: Bruce Aldin & Richard Becker
Hours: Tues-Sat, 10:30-5:30; Sun, 12-6
Types & Periods: English Porcelains, Napoleonic Memorabilia
Directions: "The Antiques Center of American Inc"

AMBERGRIS
415 E 53rd St   10022
212 624-6292   Est: 1974
Proprietor: Andrew Heimer
Hours: By appointment
Types & Periods: Colonial To Deco Silver, Gold & Silver Jewelry, Objets d'Art, American Impression Paintings

Specialties: Early American Silver
Directions: "The Antiques Center of America Inc"

AMERICA HURRAH ANTIQUES
316 E 70th St   10021
Proprietor: Joel & Kate Kopp
Hours: Mon-Sat, 12-7
Types & Periods: Specialists in American Patchwork Quilts (19th & Early 20th Century Folk Art & Graphic Quilts, Amish), Folk Art Paintings & Carvings, 19th Century Photographs
Specialties: Quilts
Appraisal Service Available
Directions: Between 1st and 2nd Aves

AMERICAN BRILLIANT CUT GLASS CO
415 E 53rd St   10022
212 486-0841
Proprietor: Harry Kraut
Hours: Tues-Sat, 10:30-5:30; Sun, 12-6
Types & Periods: American Cut Glass
Directions: "The Antiques Center of America Inc"

AMPERSAND
415 E 53rd St   10022
212 486-0941
Proprietor: David Newton & Berle Weinstein
Hours: Tues-Sat, 10:30-5:30; Sun, 12-6
Types & Periods: Porcelains, Glass, Scientific Instruments
Directions: "The Antiques Center of America Inc"

ANNTIKS
415 E 53rd St   10022
212 535-5375
Proprietor: Olivia Starman
Hours: Tues-Sat, 1-5:30; Sun, 12-6
Types & Periods: Crystal, China, Art Work
Directions: "The Antiques Center of America Inc"

ANTIQUE ARTS & ENDS
1122 Madison Ave   10028
212 861-6777
Proprietor: Fred Silberman
Hours: Mon-Sat, 10-6

New York City   Cont'd

ARTS & ENDS   Cont'd
Types & Periods: Art
Nouveau, Porcelain,
Bronzes, Art Deco, Glass

ANTIQUE BUYERS OF AMERICA INC
790 Madison Ave   10021
212 861-6700   Est: 1962
Proprietor: Parviz Nemati
Hours: Daily, 10-6
Types & Periods: 16th to
19th Century Oriental Rugs,
Tapestries, Paintings
Specialties: Carpets & Rugs
(Oriental such as Kazak,
Khila)
Appraisal Service Available
Directions: Corner of 67th
St & Madison Ave

ANTIQUE CACHE
415 E 53rd St   10022
212 486-0841
Proprietor: Tillie Steinberg
Hours: Tues-Sat,
10:30-5:30; Sun, 12-6
Types & Periods: English
Boxes
Directions: ''The Antiques
Center of America Inc''

THE ANTIQUES CENTER OF AMERICA INC
415 E 53rd St   10022
212 486-0941   Est: 1970
Proprietor: Wendy K Nadel
Hours: Tues-Sat,
10:30-5:30; Sun, 12-6
Types & Periods: General
Line
Appraisal Service Available
Directions: Between 1st
Ave & Sutton Pl, 106
shops under one roof

ATIKOTH INC
415 E 53rd St   10022
212 755-2634   Est: 1975
Proprietor: Gloria Abrams
Hours: Tues-Sat,
10:30-5:30, Sun, 12-6
Types & Periods: Judaica
Hebraica, Antiquity Ancient
Jewelry & Art of all
Religions, Europe, Near &
Far East
Directions: ''The Antiques
Center of America Inc''

ANTHONY BARTELUCCI
415 E 53rd St   10022
212 486-0941
Hours: Tues-Sat,
10:30-5:30, Sun 12-6
Types & Periods: Paintings,
Porcelains
Directions: ''The Antiques
Center of America Inc''

TEINA BAUMSTONE
17 E 64th St   10021
212 734-8360   Est: 1940
Proprietor: Teina
Baumstone
Hours: Mon-Sat, 10-5
Types & Periods: 18th
Century American Furniture

J BEER
415 E 53rd St   10022
212 486-0841
Hours: Tues-Sat,
10:30-5:30; Sun, 12-6
Types & Periods:
Bric-A-Brac
Directions: ''The Antiques
Center of America Inc''

DORIS LESLIE BLAU INC
15 E 57th St   10021
Proprietor: Doris Blau
Hours: Mon-Sat, by
appointment
Types & Periods: Antique
Rugs & Carpets, Some
Tapestries
Appraisal Service Available
Directions: Between 5th
Ave & Madison Ave, N
side of 57th St, 5th floor

JO-ANNE BLUM INC
415 E 53rd St   10022
212 688-0690
Proprietor: Anne Blum
Hours: Tues-Sat,
10:30-5:30; Sun, 1-6
Specialties: China
(Wedgwood)

ROBERT L BROOKS
415 E 53rd St   10022
212 486-0841
Hours: Tues-Sat,
10:30-5:30; Sun, 12-6
Types & Periods: Arms,
Armor
Specialties: Antique Arms &
Armor
Appraisal Service Available
Directions: The Antiques
Center of America

IRIS BROWN ANTIQUES
253 E 57th St   10022
212 593-2882
Proprietor: Iris Brown
Hours: Mon-Sat,
11:30-6:30; Sun by
appointment
Types & Periods: Dolls, Doll
Houses, Miniatures

BUTTONS & BOWS
415 E 53rd St   10022
212 486-0941
Proprietor: Irene Levitt
Hours: Tues-Sat,
10:30-5:30; Sun, 12-6
Types & Periods: Dolls,
Buttons, Jade, Paintings
Directions: ''The Antiques
Center of America Inc''

GLORIA CANTOR ANTIQUES
127 W 96th St   10025
212 865-9643
Proprietor: Gloria Cantor
Hours: By appointment
Types & Periods: American
& English Ceramics, Brass,
Pottery, Primitive Paintings

FRANK CARO CO
41 E 57th St   10022
212 753-2166   Est: 1920
Proprietor: Francis J Caro
Hours: Tues-Sat, 9-4:30
Types & Periods: Chinese &
Arts of Southeast Asia
Specialties: Oriental
Appraisal Service Available
Directions: Madison Ave &
57th

CLINTON GALLERY
415 E 53rd St   10022
212 486-0941
Proprietor: George Kurtz
Hours: Tues-Sat,
10:30-5:30; Sun, 12-6
Types & Periods: Prints,
Porcelains, Oils
Directions: ''The Antiques
Center of America Inc''

COLLECTORS ANTIQUES
415 E 53rd St   10022
212 980-3158
Proprietor: Jean
Feigenbaum
Hours: Tues-Sat,
10:30-5:30; Sun, 12-6
Types & Periods: Russian
Enamels, Jewelry, Books
Directions: ''The Antiques
Center of America Inc''

SARAH POTTER CONOVER INC
17 E 64th St   10021
Hours: Mon-Sat, 10-5;
Closed Sat during July &
Aug
Types & Periods: 18th &
Early 19th Porcelain, 18th &
19th Century Furniture
Specialties: Chinese Export
Porcelain
    Directions: 1/2 block from
    Central Park

THE COPPER MINE INC
1242 Madison Ave   10028
212 289-1212
Proprietor: Greg Sund &
Al Panarello
Hours: Tues-Sun, 10-6;
also by appointment
Types & Periods: Copper,
Brass, Artifacts,
Accessories, Kitchenware,
Fireplace, Candlesticks
    Directions: Madison &
    89th

NORMAN CRIDER
415 E 53rd St   10022
212 486-0841
Hours: Tues-Sat,
10:30-5:30; Sun, 12-6
Types & Periods: Ballet,
Opera, Theatre, Circus
    Directions: "The Antiques
    Center of America Inc"

CHICK DARROW'S FUN ANTIQUES
1174 E 62nd St   10021
212 838-0730   Est: 1964
Proprietor: Chick Darrow
Hours: Mon-Sat, 11-5
Types & Periods: Cast Iron
Toys, Tin Wind-Up Toys,
Vending Machines, Comic
Watches, Radio Premiums
Specialties: Memorabilia
Appraisal Service Available
    Directions: 3 blocks N
    from 59th St Bridge

DORAL ANTIQUES
415 E 53rd St   10022
212 486-0841
Proprietor: Doris Garwood
Hours: Tues-Sat,
10:30-5:30; Sun, 12-6
Types & Periods: Bronzes,
Glass, Silver
    Directions: "The Antiques
    Center of America Inc"

JOHN DWYER ANTIQUES & ACCENTS
415 E 53rd St   10022
212 486-0841
Proprietor: John Dwyer
Hours: Tues-Sat,
10:30-5:30; Sun, 12-6
Types & Periods: Clocks,
Lamps, Music Boxes
    Directions: "The Antiques
    Center of America Inc"

R H ELLSWORTH LTD
163 E 64th St   10021
212 753-4661   Est: 1960
Proprietor: Robert H
Ellsworth
Hours: By appointment
Types & Periods: Oriental
Fine Arts, Furniture,
Ceramics, Sculpture,
Paintings from India, SE
Asia, China & Japan
Specialties: Oriental
(Furniture)
Appraisal Service Available

ISI FISCHZANG
29 W 47th St   10036
Proprietor: Isi Fischzang
Hours: Mon-Fri
Types & Periods: Antique &
Art Deco Jewelry, Snuff
Boxes, Old Mine Diamonds
Specialties: Antique Jewelry,
Pocket Watches, Snuff
Boxes
    Directions: In the heart of
    the wholesale jewelry
    district

FORTIES & BEFORE
415 E 53rd St   10022
212 486 0841
Proprietor: Richard
Greene
Hours: Tues-Sat,
10:30-5:30; Sun, 12-6
Types & Periods: Pottery,
Glassware, Prints
    Directions: "The Antiques
    Center of America Inc"

E & J FRANKEL LTD
25 E 77th St   10021
212 879-5733
Proprietor: Edith & Joel H
Frankel
Hours: Mon-Sat, 10-5:30
Types & Periods: Chinese &
Japanese Art (Ceramics,
Jade, Netsuke, Lacquer)

Appraisal Service Available
    Directions: At the Hyde
    Park Hotel off Madison
    Ave

FRIVOLITE
415 E 53rd St   10022
212 486-0941
Proprietor: Sally Lee
Hours: Tues-Sat,
10:30-5:30; Sun, 12-6
Types & Periods: Collectors
Plates, European & Oriental
Porcelains
    Directions: "The Antiques
    Center of America Inc"

GEM ANTIQUES
415 E 53rd St   10022
212 826-0918
Proprietor: Jack Feingold
Hours: Tues-Sun, 10:30-5
Types & Periods:
Paperweights, American &
English Pottery & Porcelain,
Books on Antiques
Appraisal Service Available

GOOD'S ANTIQUES
415 E 53rd St   10022
212 486-0841
Proprietor: Phyllis Good
Hours: Tues-Sat,
10:30-5:30; Sun, 12-6
Types & Periods: Oriental
Jewelry, Pottery
    Directions: "The Antiques
    Center of America Inc"

JOHN GORDON GALLERY
37 W 57th St   10019
212 832-2255
Proprietor: John Gordon
Hours: Daily, 10-6
Types & Periods: Americana

JOSEPH GOURDJI
415 E 53rd St   10022
212 486-0841
Hours: Tues-Sat,
10:30-5:30; Sun, 12-6
Types & Periods: Silver,
Jewelry, Bronzes
    Directions: "The Antiques
    Center of America Inc"

GRAHAM GALLERY
1014 Madison Ave   10021
212 535-5566   Est: 1857
Proprietor: James &
Robert Graham, Robert Jr
& Michael Graham
Hours: Mon-Sat, 10-5

New York City   Cont'd

GRAHAM GALLERY   Cont'd
Types & Periods: 18th, 19th & 20th Century Paintings, Sculpture, Silver
Specialties: 19th Century American Paintings, French Anamalier Bronzes
Appraisal Service Available
Directions: Madison Ave & 78th St

GRAMERCY GALLERIES LTD
52 E 13th St   10003
212 477-5656   Est: 1942
Proprietor: Arnold Feingold
Hours: Daily
Types & Periods: French & English Furniture (18th & 19th Centuries), Marble Statuary, Accessories
Specialties: Bronze Statuary
Appraisal Service Available
Directions: 1 block S of Union Square between Broadway & University Pl

HIGGINS ART
415 E 53rd St   10022
212 486-0841
Proprietor: Henrietta Higgins
Hours: Tues-Sat, 10:30-5:30; Sun, 12-6
Types & Periods: Oriental Rugs, Paintings, General Line
Directions: "The Antiques Center of America Inc"

RONALD HOFFMAN
415 E 53rd St   10022
212 758-1252
Hours: Tues-Sat, 10:30-5:30; Sun, 12-6
Types & Periods: Silver, China, Jewelry, Paintings
Directions: "The Antiques Center of America Inc"

THE INCURABLE COLLECTOR
36 E 57th St   10022
Proprietor: Mr Alastair A Stair
Hours: Mon-Fri, 9:30-5:30; Sat, 10-4
Types & Periods: 18th & Early 19th Century English & Chinese Furniture, 18th &

Early 19th Century Chandeliers, 19th Century English & Chinese Paintings
Directions: Between Park Ave & Madison Ave

JAMES II GALLERIES LTD
12 E 57th St   10022
Proprietor: Edward Munves Jr
Hours: Mon-Sat; Closed Sat during July & Aug
Types & Periods: Porcelains, Glass, Brass, Papier Mache, Wood, Silver Plate, Silver Jewelry
Directions: Between 5th & Madison Aves

KALARSON
415 E 53rd St   10022
212 486-0841
Proprietor: Ira Yellen
Hours: Tues-Sat, 10:30-5:30; Sun, 12-6
Types & Periods: Graphics, Paintings, Framing
Directions: "The Antiques Center of America Inc"

LEO KAPLAN LTD
910 Madison Ave   10021
Hours: Mon-Sat, 10 5:30
Types & Periods: Modern & Antique Paperweights, Russian Enamel & Porcelain, 18th Century English Pottery & Porcelain (Wedgwood), French & English Cameo Glass
Specialties: Paperweights, Porcelain, Pottery, Glass
Appraisal Service Available
Directions: Corner of Madison Ave & 73rd St

KATHERINE JOYCE
415 E 53rd St   10022
212 486-0841
Hours: Tues-Sat, 10:30-5:30; Sun, 12-6
Types & Periods: Jewelry, Collectibles
Directions: "The Antiques Center of America Inc"

KHAN EL-KHALILI BAZAAR
415 E 53rd St   10022
212 486-0841
Proprietor: Sion Khadre
Hours: Tues-Sat, 10:30-5:30; Sun, 12-6

Types & Periods: Objets d'Art, Argenterie, Rugs, Crystal
Directions: "The Antiques Center of America Inc"

HINDA KOHN
415 E 53rd St   10022
212 486-0841
Hours: Tues-Sat, 10:30-5:30; Sun, 12-6
Types & Periods: Silver
Directions: "The Antiques Center of America Inc"

L'ANTIQUE FREAQUE
415 E 53rd St   10022
212 486-0841
Proprietor: Maurie Welsh
Hours: Tues-Sat, 10:30-5:30; Sun, 12-6
Types & Periods: Period Fashions
Directions: "The Antiques Center of America Inc"

LA BARAQUE
415 E 53rd St   10022
212 486-0841
Proprietor: Louise Schwartz
Hours: Tues-Sat, 10:30-5:30; Sun, 12-6
Types & Periods: Bronzes, Porcelains, Bric-A-Brac
Directions: "The Antiques Center of America Inc"

LANDRIGAN & STAIR
17 E 71st St   10021
212 794-0393
Hours: Mon-Sat, 10-5
Types & Periods: 17th, 18th & Early 19th Century English Furniture, Paintings, Works of Art
Specialties: Furniture (English)
Appraisal Service Available

THE LAST TOTAL STYLE
415 E 53rd St   10022
212 486-0841
Proprietor: Judith Brigagliano
Hours: Tues-Sat, 10:30-5:30; Sun, 12-6
Types & Periods: Art Deco
Directions: "The Antiques Center of America Inc"

LENARD'S GALLERIES LTD
1050 2nd Ave   10022
Proprietor: Leonard
Dukeman
Hours: Daily
Types & Periods: General
Line
Appraisal Service Available
Directions: Corner of 56th
St, located on first
concourse, shop 51

LET'S CALL IT QUILTS
7 Park Ave Apt 173 10016
212 686-2633
Proprietor: Mitchell & Ellen
Silver
Hours: By appointment
Types & Periods: Quilts,
Quilt Pillows

BERNARD & S DEAN LEVY
981 Madison Ave   10021
Proprietor: Bernard Levy &
S Dean Levy
Hours: Tues-Sat
Types & Periods: American
Furniture, Silver, Pottery,
Paintings, English Porcelains
& Pottery, 18th & 19th
Centuries
Appraisal Service Available
Directions: 76th St &
Madison Ave, second floor
of Carlyle Hotel

LUBIN GALLERIES INC
72 E 13th St   10003
212 254-1080   Est: 1957
Proprietor: Irwin Lubin
Hours: Auctions on
alternate Sat, exhibits
Thur & Fri before sale
Types & Periods: Fine Arts,
Silver, Porcelain, Bronzes,
Rugs, Furniture
Appraisal Service Available
Directions: 13th St
between 4th Ave &
Broadway

MANHATTAN ART &
ANTIQUES CENTER
1050 2nd Ave   10022
212 355-4400
Proprietor: 92 Dealers
Hours: Daily
Types & Periods: Furniture,
Silver, Jewelry, China,
Porcelain, Bibelot
Directions: 2nd Ave at
56th St

MAN-TIQUES
415 E 53rd St   10022
212 758-7599
Proprietor: Eleanor Zelin &
Margaret Weiss
Hours: Tues-Sun, 11-5:30
Types & Periods:
Collectibles, Medical,
Historical, Political, Unusual
Walking Sticks, Inkwells,
Bronzes, Paper Americana
Specialties: Collectibles,
Medical, Historical, Political,
Unusual Walking Sticks,
Inkwells, Bronzes, Paper
Americana
Directions: "The Antiques
Center of America Inc"

MANYA
415 E 53rd St   10022
212 486-0941
Proprietor: Manya G
Futterman
Hours: Tues-Sat,
10:30-5:30; Sun, 12-6
Types & Periods: Furniture,
Minton, KPM
Directions: "The Antiques
Center of America Inc"

MEMORABILIA ANTIQUES
384 Second Ave   10010
212 674-3624   Est: 1967
Proprietor: John & Elissa
Montana
Hours: Mon-Fri, 12-7, Sat
& Sun, 12-5:30
Types & Periods:
Turn-of-the-Century Oak &
Walnut Furniture
Directions: Corner of 2nd
Ave & E 22nd St in
Manhattan

ELINOR MERRELL
18 E 69th St   10021
212 288-4986
Proprietor: Elinor Merrell
Hours: Daily, 9-6
Types & Periods: Fabrics

HELEN & MICKY MIKITEN
ANTIQUES
415 E 53rd St   10022
212 486-0841
Proprietor: Helen Mikiten
Hours: Tues-Sat,
10:30-5:30; Sun, 12-6
Types & Periods: General
Line, Collectibles
Directions: "The Antiques
Center of America Inc"

MILNE MINIATURES
106 Prince St   10012
212 226-5361
Proprietor: Robert S Milne
Hours: By appointment
Types & Periods: All Types
& Periods Miniature
Furniture, Accessories, Doll
Houses, Doll House Dolls
Specialties: Miniature
Furniture & Accessories,
Doll Houses, Doll House
Dolls
Appraisal Service Available
Directions: Historic SoHo
District S of Washington
Square

THE NAGA
415 E 53rd St   10022
212 486-0841
Proprietor: Marilyn
Marinacio
Hours: Tues-Sat,
10:30-5:30; Sun, 12-6
Types & Periods: Oriental &
Primitive Art
Directions: "The Antiques
Center of America Inc"

NOW & THEN
982 2nd Ave   10022
212 755-0722
Proprietor: Gene Murphy
& Barbara Duffy
Hours: Mon-Sat, 12-7; also
by appointment
Types & Periods: Furniture,
Lamps, General Line
Directions: At 52nd St

ANN PHILLIPS ANTIQUES
899 Madison Ave   10021
212 535-0415
Proprietor: Ann Phillips
Hours: Daily
Types & Periods:
Staffordshire, Lustreware,
Brass, Stoneware, Glass,
Samplers
Specialties: English &
American Commemorative
Directions: Between 72nd
& 73rd Sts

PIERRE DEUX ANTIQUES
INC
369 Bleecker St   10014
212 243-7740   Est: 1967
Proprietor: Pierre Moulin &
Pierre LeVec
Hours: Mon-Sat, 10-6;
Closed Sat during July &
Aug

424

(From page 404).   during this time of the evolving and rudimentary furniture factories, standardized designs began providing a more abundant flow of parlor, dining and bedroom sets which might be purchased from the newly conceived "furniture store". Such stores would be dependent upon a transportation system. The new railroads were expanding rapidly but not as rapidly as our early people were able to move westward.

It seems appropriate to comment upon the fact that I have been writing of furniture intended mostly for cities and mostly for members of the affluent middle class. I have not mentioned furniture designed for the less prosperous city homes, nor for the rural areas. By the 1850's there was coming to be a well developed line of furniture designed for the less pretentious city, small town and rural home. It came to be known as "Cottage Furniture". It was of a simpler design and made of less costly woods such as pine, maple, hickory, chestnut, cherry and other native woods. Decoration was machine carving and mouldings with some applied split turnings. Spool furniture, easily made on a simple lathe, was very popular in the Cottage style. It was often painted rather than varnished or shellacked. A bedroom suite might be painted in pastel blue outlined with a darker blue. Panels were being decorated with bouquets of pastel flowers in immitation of the elaborate carvings found upon its city counterparts. The fancy Hitchcock chairs with their paint and gilt finishes best fit here.

There was throughout the entire Victorian Era a very unusual furniture being designed and executed in accordance with a set of religious precepts. It was well executed. Its design was so simple as to resemble what could appear to be modern. This Shaker furniture would have appeared wildly different throughout Victorian times. The Shakers held to many old hand crafting techniques, but they did utilize some of the newer tools. It can almost be classified as Early American and is often represented to be of the 18th Century. One must check for toolmarks.

Now, let me mention those Americans who not only outran the rapidly expanding railroads but also began getting out of reach of any of the more economically developed areas of this country. Where water transport was available, they may very well have had access to factory made furniture. However, the vast majority simply reverted to the older system of hand crafting by cabinetmakers in their area. The frontier cabinetmaker used the materials at hand, the styles and techniques he had always known and had otherwise been known for a century.   (Continued, page 442).

New York City   Cont'd

PIERRE DEUX   Cont'd

Types & Periods: Country
French, 18th & 19th
Centuries
Specialties: Furniture
Appraisal Service Available
Directions: Greenwich
Village, W of 7th Ave,
between 10th & 11th Sts

THE PILLOWRY
929 Madison   10021
212 535-2604
Proprietor: Marjorie J
Lawrence
Hours: Mon-Sat; Closed
Sat during July-Sept
Types & Periods: Oriental
Rugs, Pillows & Furnishings,
Panache Clothing &
Trappings
Specialties: Kilims & Durries
Appraisal Service Available
Directions: Madison Ave
between 73rd & 74th, one
flight up

ROSA POYNER ANTIQUES
912 Madison Ave   10021
212 681-1268   Est: 1975
Proprietor: Rosa Batt
Poyner
Hours: Tues-Sat, 10-4
Types & Periods: Silver,
Pressed Glass & Crystal

JAMES ROBINSON INC
15 E 57th St   10022
212 752-6166   Est: 1915
Proprietor: Edward
Munves
Hours: Mon-Sat, 10-5;
Closed Sat during July &
Aug
Types & Periods: Silver,
Jewelry, Porcelains, Glass
from Elizabethan thru
Victorian Periods
Specialties: Georgian Period
Silver, Georgian & Victorian
Period Glass
Directions: Between 5th &
Madison Ave

VINCENT ROCCO
415 E 53rd St   10022
212 486-0941
Hours: Tues-Sat,
10:30-5:30; Sun, 12-6

Types & Periods: Art Glass,
Pottery, Bronzes, Lamps
Directions: "The Antiques
Center of America Inc"

**RITA SACKS-LIMITED
ADDITIONS INC**
415 E 53rd St   10022
212 486-0841
Hours: Tues-Sat,
10:30-5:30; Sun, 12-6
Types & Periods: Jewelry,
Orientalia, Art
Deco-Nouveau
Directions: "The Antiques
Center of America Inc"

MARIA SANDI
415 E 53rd St   10022
212 486-0841
Hours: Tues-Sat,
10:30-5:30; Sun, 12-6
Types & Periods: Table
Cloths, Bedspreads,
Fashions
Directions: "The Antiques
Center of America Inc"

SHERBERT ANTIQUES
415 E 53rd St   10022
212 486-0841
Proprietor: Shirley Artin
Hours: Tues-Sat,
10:30-5:30; Sun, 12-6
Types & Periods: Art Glass,
Crystal
Directions: "The Antiques
Center of America Inc"

S J SHRUBSOLE CORP
104 E 57th St   10022
Proprietor: Eric N
Shrubsole
Hours: Mon-Fri
Types & Periods: Fine
Antique English & American
Silver, Antique Jewelry
Appraisal Service Available
Directions: On E 57th St
between Park Ave &
Lexington Ave

SMITH'S EMPORIUM
415 E 53rd St   10022
212 486-0841
Proprietor: Ethel
Ackerman
Hours: Tues-Sat,
10:30-5:30; Sun, 12-6
Types & Periods: Paintings,
Collectibles, Trinkets, Toys
Directions: "The Antiques
Center of America Inc"

STAIR & COMPANY INC
59 E 57th St   10022
Proprietor: Alastair A Stair
Hours: Mon-Fri, 9:30 to
5:30; Closed July &
August
Types & Periods: English
18th & Early 19th Century
Antiques Only, English
Sporting & Landscape
Paintings (19th Century)
Directions: Central New
York City

SAMUEL STRAUS
415 E 53rd St   10022
212 486-0941
Proprietor: Samuel Straus
Hours: Tues-Sat,
10:30-5:30; Sun, 12-6
Types & Periods: Silver,
Jewelry
Directions: "The Antiques
Center of America Inc"

THEN & NOW
415 E 53rd St   10022
212 755-1357
Proprietor: Gloria
Boscardin
Hours: Tues-Sat,
10:30-5:30; Sun, 12-6
Types & Periods: Miniatures,
Paintings, Art Deco
Directions: "The Antiques
Center of America Inc"

**ERNEST TROGANOWAN
INC**
306 E 61st St   10021
212 755-1050   Est: 1917
Hours: Mon-Fri; Sat & Sun
by appointment or chance
Types & Periods: All Types
of Persian, Chinese &
European Rugs & Carpets,
Antique, Semi-Antique &
New
Specialties: English
Needlepoint Designs
Appraisal Service Available
Directions: between 1st &
2nd Aves

TUDOR ROSE
415 E 53rd St   10022
212 486-0841
Proprietor: Myra & Howard
Donowitz
Hours: Tues-Sat,
10:30-5:30; Sun, 12-6
Types & Periods: Furniture,
Clocks
Directions: "The Antiques
Center of America Inc"

New York City   Cont'd

VICAI'S ANTIQUE CLOCKS
415 E 53rd St   10022
212 486-0841
Proprietor: Thomas Vicai
Hours: Tues-Sat,
10:30-5:30; Sun, 12-6
Types & Periods: French
Clocks
Directions: "The Antiques
Center of America Inc"

DUANE VOTH
415 E 53rd St   10022
212 371-1240
Hours: Tues-Sat, 12-5:30;
Sun, 1-6
Types & Periods: Fine
Objects for Collectors
Directions: "The Antiques
Center of America Inc"

WILLIAM H WOLFF INC
22 E 76th St   10021
212 988-7411   Est: 1959
Proprietor: William H Wolf
Hours: Daily, 10-5; Closed
July & Aug
Types & Periods: Far
Eastern Antiquities
Specialties: Sculpture
Appraisal Service Available
Directions: Off Madison
Ave toward 5th St

**THOMAS K WOODARD,
AMERICAN ANTIQUES &
QUILTS**
1022 Lexington Ave 10021
212 988-2906
Proprietor: Thomas K
Woodard
Hours: Mon-Sat, 11-6
Types & Periods: Patchwork
& Applique Quilts, Hooked
Rugs, Rag Carpet, Painted
Furniture, Baskets, Folk Art
Specialties: Quilts & Textiles
Appraisal Service Available
Directions: Corner of 73rd
St & Lexington, second
floor

YORK ANTIQUES LTD
12 E 12th St   10003
212 893-7588   Est: 1961
Proprietor: Fred Rotondo
Hours: Daily, 8-5; Monthly
Auctions
Types & Periods: General
Line
Directions: Between 5th
Ave & University Place

Nineveh

**DAILEY'S DEN OF
ANTIQUITY**
E River Rd   13813
607 693-1800   Est: 1957
Proprietor: W T Dailey
Hours: Daily
Types & Periods: Primitives,
Tools, Country Furniture,
China, Glass
Appraisal Service Available
Directions: 1 mile E of
town

Norwood

STELLA'S ANTIQUES
14 Main St   13668
315 353-6606
Proprietor: Mrs Norma
Malek
Hours: Daily
Types & Periods: Glass,
China, Furniture

Nyack

ARLENE'S ANTIQUES
65 S Broadway   10960
914 358-5889
Proprietor: Arlene Schrier
Hours: Wed, Thurs, Sat &
Sun
Types & Periods: Victorian,
Copper, Oak, Brass, Mirrors

CHRISTOPHER'S
71 S Broadway   10960
914 358-9574   Est: 1970
Proprietor: Job
Christopher
Hours: Daily
Types & Periods:
Turn-of-the-Century
Furniture
Directions: Next to Tappan
Zee Bridge, 25 miles N of
NYC on Hudson River

ERE 'N AFT
290 Main St   10960
914 358-8934   Est: 1974
Proprietor: Lewis
Gutterman
Hours: Tues-Sun, 11-5
Types & Periods: Porcelain
Specialties: Hummel,
Collectors Plate

Appraisal Service Available
Directions: 9W & Rte 59

**THE GABEL'S ANTIQUE
CENTER**
292 Main St   10960
914 358-9151   Est: 1960
Proprietor: Paul Gabel
Hours: Tues-Sat, 11-6;
Sun, 12-6
Types & Periods: 9 Dealers,
"Antiques from all over the
world"
Appraisal Service Available
Directions: Exit 11 off N Y
S Thruway at corner of
Rtes 59 & 9W

GOOSE HILL ANTIQUES
298 N Rte 9 W   10960
914 358-1874   Est: 1942
Proprietor: James R
Jackson
Hours: By appointment
Types & Periods: Early
American Furniture & Books
Specialties: Books
Appraisal Service Available
Directions: George
Washington N on 9 W,
Tappan Zee Bridge to Exit
11 on N Y S Thruway, N
on Rte 9 W, 298 & 300

HORSEFEATHERS
81 S Broadway   10960
914 358-8880   Est: 1973
Proprietor: Linda &
Gordon Rauer
Hours: Tues-Sat, 12-6
Types & Periods: Primitives,
Tools, Kitchen Equipment,
Farm Implements, Oddities
Directions: N Y S Thruway
N across Tappan Zee
Bridge, 1st Exit off (Exit
11), follow signs to S
Nyack, right turn at stop
sign to Clinton Ave, 2
blocks to Broadway, left
on to S Broadway

PAST TENSE INC
75 S Broadway   10960
914 358-4131   Est: 1968
Proprietor: Florence Gross
Hours: Tues-Sat, 11-5;
Sun, 12-5
Types & Periods: Furniture,
Clocks, Copper, Brass,
Wicker, Lamps, Fixtures
Specialties: Doll House &
Furniture, Miniatures

Appraisal Service Available
Directions: From
Westchester over Tappan
Zee Bridge Nyack Exit,
from N Y over Geo
Washington Bridge Exit 9
W, No 4 to Broadway

Oceanside

EDITH WEBER
125 Atlantic Ave   11572
516 764-8733   Est: 1961
Proprietor: Edith Weber
Hours: Tues-Sat, by
appointment
Types & Periods: General
Line, Jewelry
Specialties: 18th Century
Rings, Necklaces
Appraisal Service Available
Directions: On the way to
Long Beach

Odessa

TRUCKER'S TREASURES
203 Main St   14869
Est: 1976
Proprietor: Robert T Perry
Hours: Mon-Sat, 12-8
Types & Periods: General
Line, Furniture, Glassware,
Collectibles
Directions: Rte 224 in
center of town

Ogdensburg

HOLLY'S ANTIQUES
506 New York Ave   13669
315 393-3853   Est: 1959
Proprietor: Evelyn
Hollomon
Hours: Daily
Types & Periods: Small
Period Furniture
Specialties: Glass (Art &
Signed), China (Haviland,
Limoges, Noritake, Azela)
Directions: Rte 37, N or S
to New York Ave

Oneonta

ANITA'S ANTIQUES
Rte 205 RD 3   13820
607 432-8529
Proprietor: Anita Koenke
Hours: Daily
Types & Periods: Primitives,
Country Furniture,
Woodenware, Iron

CAROL'S ANTIQUES
Rte 23 Box 377   13820
607 432-6820
Proprietor: Carol A
DeSilva
Hours: Daily
Types & Periods: Lamps,
Jewelry, Glassware,
Furniture, Art Glass
Appraisal Service Available
Directions: 5 miles E of
Oneonta on Rte 23

SCAMMON SEINE
48 W End St   13820
607 432-4862
Proprietor: Lucy Scammon
Hours: Daily, by
appointment or by chance
Types & Periods: Walnut
Frames, China, Glass, Tin,
Toys, Primitives

Orangeburg

VERNA'S PLACE
Rte 303   10962
914 359-8185   Est: 1976
Proprietor: Verna Boersma
Hours: Wed-Sun, 1-5:30
Types & Periods: General
Line, Furniture, Dolls,
Primitives, Collectibles,
Paintings, Pottery, China,
Crystal
Directions: Rear of
Hogan's Diner, 1/4 mile N
of Palisades Interstate
Pkwy, Exit 5

Oswego

**RICHARD
PURVIS-ANTIQUES &
APPRAISAL SERVICE**
99 Ellen   13126
315 342-1623   Est: 1966
Proprietor: Richard Purvis
Hours: By appointment

Types & Periods: Furniture,
Bronzes, Oriental Rugs,
Clocks, Objets d'Art
Appraisal Service Available
Directions: 40 minutes N
of Syracuse on Rte 104

Otego

**OLD PARSONAGE
ANTIQUES**
RD Otsdawa Ave   13825
607 988-6390
Proprietor: Alma W Davis
Hours: By appointment, by
chance
Types & Periods: Primitives,
Country Furniture, Tinware,
Baskets, Woodenware

SHOPKEEPER ANTIQUES
41 Main St   13825
607 988-6322
Proprietor: Buzz & Jackie
Hesse
Hours: By appointment, by
chance
Types & Periods: General
Line
Specialties: Furniture
(Country American)
Directions: At the sign of
the Cruse

Oyster Bay

ELLEN FALES LOMASNEY
W Shore Rd   11771
516 922-0770
Proprietor: Mr & Mrs
Anderson F Hewitt
Hours: By appointment
Types & Periods: English &
American 18th & 19th
Century Furniture &
Accessories
Directions: Long Island

**THE NORTH COUNTRY
EXCHANGE INC**
104 W Main St   11771
516 922-6522   Est: 1949
Proprietor: For benefit of
Community Hospital at
Glen Cove
Hours: Mon-Fri, 9:30-5;
Sat, 9:30-12
Types & Periods: General
Line, Glassware, Silver,
China, Bric-A-Brac

Palisades

THE BAZAAR
Closter Rd   10964
914 359-5070   Est: 1965
Proprietor: Dossi Thayer
Hours: Wed-Sat, 2-5
Types & Periods: General
Line
Directions: 600 ft W of Rte
9 W

YONDERHILL DWELLERS
9 W & Closter Rd   10964
914 359-0456   Est: 1931
Proprietor: Wm (Tippy)
O'Neil
Hours: Tues-Sat, 10-5
Types & Periods: 18th &
Early 19th Century Furniture
& Accessories
Directions: 12½ miles N of
George Washington
Bridge

Palmyra

THE RED BARREL
FURNITURE STRIPPING
60 Canandaigua Rd 14522
315 597-5421   Est: 1970
Proprietor: Betty Briggs
Hours: Weekends, by
appointment
Types & Periods: Country
Furniture, Glass
Directions: On Rte 21, 1
mile S of Palmyra

Parksville

ANTIQUE CELLAR
Rte 17 Quickway   12768
914 292-8612   Est: 1968
Proprietor: Dawne Norris
Hours: Daily, by chance
Types & Periods: General
Line, Furniture, Glassware,
Primitives, Tools, Dolls
Directions: 1 mile W of
traffic light

HILLIG'S CASTLE
ANTIQUES
Novaselski Rd   12768
914 292-6370
Proprietor: Jan Blair
Hours: Tues-Sun 11-5,
March-Nov; Off season by
appointment

Types & Periods: Furniture,
Glass, China, Gifts,
Collectibles, Clocks, Tools
Directions: Off Cold
Spring Rd from Liberty

LIBERTY ANTIQUE
WAREHOUSE
Rte 17   12768
914 292-7450
Hours: Tues-Sat, 9-5; Sun,
10-4
Types & Periods: Furniture,
Clocks, Glass, China
Specialties: "Specializing to
auctioneers & high volume
buyers"

QUICKWAY ANTIQUES
Rte 17 Box 267   12768
914 292-3947   Est: 1970
Proprietor: Thomas Immel,
Manager
Hours: Daily, 11-5
Types & Periods: "Largest
quantity of quality American
Oak Furniture in Sullivan
County. Dealers Welcome"
Directions: Rte 17, 500 ft
W of Parksville traffic light

Patterson

ADORN'S
Rte 22   12563
914 878-3191   Est: 1960
Proprietor: Joseph Grossi
Hours: Daily
Types & Periods: General
Line
Directions: N of New York
City

Pearl River

ANNABEGH ANTIQUE &
GIFT SHOP
1 Railroad Place   10965
914 735-9570   Est: 1971
Proprietor: Anne M &
Agnes Sarah Fallon
Hours: Mon-Sat,
10:30-4:30
Types & Periods: Victorian
Furniture, Bric-A-Brac, Wall
Hangings
Specialties: Porcelains,
Spelter Figurines
Directions: In RR Station

BLUE HILL ANTIQUES
Blue Hill Rd W   10965
914 735-3385   Est: 1963
Proprietor: Wm Seth Jr
Hours: Daily, By
appointment
Types & Periods: Furniture,
Accessories, 18th & 19th
Century Pieces, Glass
Paperweights
Appraisal Service Available
Directions: SE of Pearl
River in Early Dutch
Colonial, off Blue Hill Rd
facing Lake Tappan

BURNS GLASS COMPANY
11 N John St   10965
914 735-2539   Est: 1946
Proprietor: Jack Burns
Hours: Daily, 8:30-5:30
Types & Periods: Cameo
Glass, Glass Paperweights

Peekskill

THE WESTCHESTER
COMMISSION MART
115-117 N Division St
                     10566
914 737-8880
Proprietor: Cornelia T
Black
Hours: Sun-Tues,
Thurs-Sat, 10-3
Types & Periods: General
Line

Pine Bush

BOXWOOD COTTAGE
ANTIQUES
RD 2 Box 110   12566
914 744-5285
Proprietor: J & J Pullin
Hours: Daily, by
appointment or by chance
Types & Periods: 18th &
19th Century Country
Furniture, Accessories &
Lighting
Specialties: Lighting
Directions: Rte 52 W of
bridge at entrance to Pine
Bush Trade Mkt

Pittsford

BARBARA N COHEN
13 E Park Rd   14534
716 586-4744   Est: 1962
Proprietor: Barbara N
Cohen
Hours: By appointment, by
chance
Types & Periods: Paintings,
Rugs (Oriental), Russian Art
& Enamels
Specialties: Paintings, Rugs
(Oriental), Russian Art &
Enamel
Appraisal Service Available
Directions: Outside of
Rochester

Plattsburgh

ANTIQUES ET CAETERA
9 S Peru St   12901
518 561-6240   Est: 1972
Proprietor: Madeline
Broderick
Hours: Mon-Fri, by chance
Types & Periods: Jewelry,
Art, Glass, China, Primitive
Furniture
Specialties: Hanging Shades
& Lamps
Directions: Exit 36 I-87 N,
2 miles

CHERRY HILL ANTIQUES
69 Court St   12901
518 563-1773   Est: 1970
Proprietor: Lois W Walker
Hours: By appointment,
June-Nov; also by chance
Types & Periods: Primitives,
Period & Country Furniture,
Glass, China, Sterling Silver
Specialties: Primitives
Directions: Cumberland
Head, 2 house N of Ferry
Dock

**PHILIP & SHIRLEY
GORDON ANTIQUES**
41 Prospect Ave   12901
518 561-3383
Proprietor: Philip & Shirley
Gordon
Hours: By appointment, by
chance
Types & Periods: China,
Glass, Silver, Jewelry,
Lamps
Specialties: Fine Art Glass,
Tiffany, Sterling, Jewelry,
China, Lamps

Pleasant Valley

KENPORT ANTIQUES
Main St   12569
914 635-9962   Est: 1966
Proprietor: Ginlio
Portabello
Hours: Daily
Types & Periods: General
Line
Directions: Located on Rte
44 downtown

Port Chester

HOUSE OF WELTZ
26 Poningo St   10573
914 939-6513   Est: 1963
Proprietor: Robert Weltz
Hours: Mon-Sat, 12-5
Types & Periods: Furniture,
Bric-A-Brac, Paintings, Rugs
Specialties: Silver, American
Furniture, Paintings
Appraisal Service Available
Directions: Near New
England Thruway & 684 in
Westchester, off King St,
Rte 120 & Westchester
Ave

Port Jefferson

**CAPT AHAB'S ANTIQUES
INC**
450 Main St   11777
516 473-1526   Est: 1973
Proprietor: Don Smith
Hours: Daily, 8.30-5
Types & Periods: Nautical,
Military, Early American
Appraisal Service Available
Directions: LI Expwy Exit
64, N on Rte 112

SUWASSET ANTIQUES
105 Tuthill St   11776
516 473-2153
Proprietor: Harvey &
Barbara Dolloff
Hours: Daily, 1-5
Types & Periods: Early
Country Furniture &
Accessories
Directions: On Long Island

Portlandville

BLUE BONNET ANTIQUES
Rte 28   13834
607 286-7568
Proprietor: S Damon
Hours: May thru Oct
Types & Periods: Primitives,
18th & 19th Century
Furniture, China, Glass

Port Washington

**THE MEATING PLACE
ANTIQUES**
279 Main St   11050
516 883-9659   Est: 1972
Proprietor: Jean
Sinenberg
Hours: Mon-Sat, by
appointment or by chance
Types & Periods: Furniture,
Porcelain, Pottery, Silver,
Lamps, Fixtures, Baskets,
Quilts
Specialties: Quilts, Baskets,
Furniture, Lamps
Appraisal Service Available
Directions: Harbor area,
Exit 36 Searington Rd to
Port Washington Blvd to
Main St, turn left &
continue to harbor area

N K B ANTIQUES
3 Carlton Ave   11050
516 883-4184   Est: 1953
Proprietor: Nancy K
Banker
Hours: Tues-Sat, by
appointment
Types & Periods: Glass,
China, Silver, Brass, Copper,
Occasional Furniture,
Decorative Antiques
Directions: N shore of
Long Island, 30 minutes
from midtown NYC

**SANDS POINT ANTIQUE
SHOP**
287 Main St   11050
516 883-0045   Est: 1973
Proprietor: Leo Manolis
Hours: Tues-Sat, also by
appointment
Types & Periods: English,
American, European &
Oriental, "Eclectic"
Directions: On the N shore
of Long Island (Nassau
County)

VILLAGE INTERIORS & ANTIQUES
  207 Main St   11050
  516 883-7804
  Proprietor: Pearl Straus
  Hours: Daily, 10-5
Types & Periods: General
Line, Furniture
Specialties: Furniture
(Wicker, Oak)
Appraisal Service Available
  Directions: Long Island
  Expwy to Searington Rd
  Exit, left to Main

Poughkeepsie

ANCHORAGE ANTIQUES
  33 Collegview Ave   12603
  914 471-7210   Est: 1964
  Proprietor: George E
  Marsh
  Hours: Tues-Sat, 11-5
Types & Periods: Jewelry,
China, Glass, Bronzes,
Clocks, Furniture, Toys
Specialties: Watches,
Jewelry, Coins
Appraisal Service Available
  Directions: Corner of
  Fairmont across
  Collegeview Ave from
  Vassar College campus

APOLLO
  391 South Rd   12601
  914 462-6342
  Proprietor: Glenn Opitz
  Hours: By appointment
Types & Periods: General
Line, Art
  Directions: US Rte 9

Pound Ridge

ALAN Y ROBERTS INC
  Scotts Corners   10576
  914 764-5427
  Proprietor: Alan Y Roberts
  Hours: Mon-Sat, 9:30-5
Types & Periods: English
Furniture of Walnut &
Mahogany

**SCOTTS CORNERS
ANTIQUES GALLERY**
  Westchester Ave   10576
  914 764-4953
  Hours: Tues-Sun, 11-5

Types & Periods: Furniture,
Clocks, Early American
Glass, Civil War Items,
Indian Artifacts,
Phonographs, Dolls

RUTH TROIANI ANTIQUES
  Old Stone Hill Rd   10576
  914 764-5512
  Hours: Daily, 9-6, Oct-May
Types & Periods: 18th &
19th Century American &
English Paintings, Furniture,
Pottery, Porcelain, Glass,
Lighting, Primitives
  Directions: Off Rtes 124 &
  137 near Rte 35

Prattsville

GRANDMA'S TRUNK
  Wright St   12468
  518 299-3184   Est: 1972
  Proprietor: Virginia
  Gutierrez
  Hours: Daily, by chance
Types & Periods: Furniture,
Rockers, Clocks, Lamps,
Glassware, Primitives
  Directions: Rte 23 & 23A
  to Main, 1 block from Post
  Office, turn on Wright St,
  300 ft on left

Putnam Valley

ALLEN'S ANTIQUITIES
  RD 1   10579
  914 528-8989
  Proprietor: Mark &
  Marjorie Allen
  Hours: By appointment
Types & Periods: 18th &
Early 19th Century Furniture
& Accessories

Ransomville

OLD ROCKING CHAIR
  2568 Youngstown-
  Lockport Rd   14131
  716 791-4409   Est: 1971
  Proprietor: Jack & Anita
  Jacobs
  Hours: Daily
Types & Periods: Furniture,
Glass, Ceramics, Collectibles

Specialties: Repair &
Refinish Furniture
Appraisal Service Available
  Directions: Hamlet of
  Ransomville in town of
  Porter on Rte 93 between
  Lockport & Fort Niagara, 4
  miles from Lake Ontario

Red Hook

ROCK CITY ANTIQUES
  7 N Broadway   12571
  914 758-5354   Est: 1968
  Proprietor: Rose
  Borromeo
  Hours: Daily, 11-4, by
  appointment
Types & Periods:
Collectibles
Specialties: Toys (Trains)
  Directions: Downtown

Rego Park

CELE SHAPIRO
  6541 Saunders St   11374
  212 896-2490
  Proprietor: Cele Shapiro
  Hours: By appointment
Types & Periods: Jewelry,
Papier Mache, Porcelains,
Glass

WEEDY'S ANTIQUES
  6384 Fitchett St   11374
  212 459-5152
  Proprietor: Samuel
  Wiederhorn
  Hours: Daily, 10-6
Types & Periods: Paintings,
Chandeliers, Furniture,
General Line

Rhinebeck

**DUTCHESS VALLEY
ANTIQUE GALLERY**
  Rte 9   12572
  914 876-2121   Est: 1974
  Proprietor: George Elk
  Hours: Daily, 11-5:30
Types & Periods: General
Line, Furniture, Porcelain,
Paintings, Jewelry, Rugs,
Bronzes

Appraisal Service Available
Directions: 1 mile N of
Rhinebeck traffic light on
Rte 9, located opposite
main entrance to
fairgrounds

**WM & MARIAN HODGES
ANTIQUES**
71 E Market St   12572
914 876-4962   Est: 1951
Proprietor: Wm Hodges
Hours: Mon-Sat, 10-5:15
Types & Periods: General
Line, Silver, Period
Appraisal Service Available
Directions: On Rte 308 in
the village

**LITTLE RED
SCHOOLHOUSE ANTIQUES**
Rte 2 Box 236   12572
914 876-3145   Est: 1967
Proprietor: John Donner
Hours: Daily
Types & Periods:
Contemporary
Directions: On Rte 9G, 3
miles S of Rtes 9 & 9G
intersection, on W side of
Rd

OLD MILL ANTIQUES
RD 1 Box 74   12572
914 758-5260   Est: 1968
Proprietor: Leila Gordon
Hours: Daily, Afternoons &
weekends by chance
Types & Periods: Home
Furniture, Lamps,
Bric-A-Brac, General Line
Directions: Rte 9, 1 mile N
or 9 & 9G intersection
from Kingoton Bridgo

Richmond Hill

KEW HILL ANTIQUES
85-50 118th St   11418
212 846-8337
Proprietor: Loretta Salerno
Hours: Daily, 12-5
Types & Periods: Victorian
Furniture, China
Specialties: Paintings
Restored
Directions: 1 block off
Hillside Ave, between
Hillside & 85th Ave

Ripley

ODELL'S ANTIQUES
E Main Rd   14775
          Est: 1936
Proprietor: Richard V
Odell
Hours: By appointment or
by chance
Types & Periods: General
Line
Directions: Rte 20 3 miles
E of Ripley, 5 miles W of
Westfield

Rochester

THE ANTIQUE CUPBOARD
597 Stone Rd   14616
716 865-7020   Est: 1974
Proprietor: Mr & Mrs
Charles Meagher
Hours: Sun-Mon, Fri-Sat,
11-4; Tues & Thurs, 6-9
Types & Periods: Furniture,
Lamps, Silver, Jewelry,
Quilts, China, Brass, Cut
Glass, Miniatures, "Old Time
Photo Studio"
Appraisal Service Available
Directions: Off Rte 104

BURKE JEWELERS INC
Midtown Plaza Arcade
          14604
716 325-5420   Est: 1903
Proprietor: Irving
Weisbuch
Hours: Mon-Sat, 10-5;
Thurs 'til 8
Types & Periods: Jewelry,
Watches
Appraisal Service Available
Directions: Downtown

COLLECTOR'S CASTLE
219 Monroe Ave   14607
716 454-6598   Est: 1971
Proprietor: M Boyle
Hours: Mon-Sat, 1-6
Types & Periods: Furniture
Appraisal Service Available

THE GLASS CORNER
PO Box 7130   14616
716 621-5060   Est: 1973
Proprietor: Paul H Preo
Hours: By appointment
Types & Periods: American
Brilliant Cut Glass

JACK GRECO
1611 Scottsville Rd   14623
716 328-9150
Proprietor: Jack Greco
Hours: Daily, 11-9; closed
holidays
Types & Periods: General
Line
Specialties: Furniture (Oak &
Walnut), Brass Beds
Appraisal Service Available
Directions: 2 miles S of
Rochester

JOHN B HENDRICK
128 Chili Ave   14611
716 436-9411   Est: 1962
Proprietor: John B
Hendrick
Hours: Thurs-Sat, 1-6;
anytime by appointment
Types & Periods: General
Line
Specialties: Books, Bottles,
Old Banks, Paperweights
Appraisal Service Available
Directions: Rte 33A at
Bull's Head, just inside
city, near St Mary's
Hospital

THE INTERIORS PLACE
2485 Dewey Ave   14616
716 663 3360   Eot: 1076
Proprietor: Susan
Winegard
Hours: Tues-Sat, 10-4:30
Types & Periods: American,
Primitive, Victorian Oak
Specialties: Ironware,
Utensils, Tools
Directions: Off Rte 104 N
to RR tracks, turn left
after crossing tracks

**MONROE ANTIQUE
CENTER**
733 Monroe Ave   14607
716 271-9550   Est: 1975
Proprietor: Carol Crissy &
Michel Dolan
Hours: Weekends, 9-5;
Thurs, 11-9
Types & Periods: General
Line, Collectibles
Specialties: Furniture, Doll
House Miniatures,
Gramophones
Appraisal Service Available
Directions: Off Rte 490

Rochester   Cont'd

E A SCONFITTO
1421 Clifford Ave   14621
716 454-1975   Est: 1973
Proprietor: Estella Ann
Sconfitto
Hours: By appointment
Types & Periods: General
Line

Rock City Falls

**SARATOGA COUNTY
ANTIQUE CENTER**
Rte 29   12863
518 885-7645
Proprietor: H & C Beyer
Hours: Daily; closed Mon
& Tues, Jan-March;
Closed Mon, April-June
Types & Periods: 15 Dealers
in 22 room Victorian
Mansion, General Line
Directions: 7 miles W of
Saratoga Springs

Rockville Centre

FISHMAN JEWELERS
29 S Park Ave   11570
516 678-4717   Est: 1960
Proprietor: Hazel & Martin
Fishman
Hours: Daily, by chance
Types & Periods: Jewelry,
Georgian, Victorian, Estate,
Modern
Specialties: Watch & Clock
Repair
Appraisal Service Available
Directions: S Park Ave,
between Merrick Rd &
Lincoln Ave

MOLLIES FOLLY
144 N Park Ave   11570
516 536-4382   Est: 1971
Proprietor: Mollie Miller
Hours: Tues-Sat, 1-4:30
Types & Periods: 19th &
20th Century Collectibles
Directions: Merrick Rd to
Rockville Centre, N on
N Park Ave

Roscoe

CAIN'S ANTIQUES
Rockland Rd   12776
607 498-4303   Est: 1946
Proprietor: Mr & Mrs
James Cain
Hours: Sun-Mon, Wed-Sat
Types & Periods: General
Line, Furniture
Directions: 1 mile off
Hwy 17

Roxbury

THE GRAY MILL
Bridge St   12474
607 326-7181   Est: 1972
Proprietor: Edward
Snegoski
Hours: Daily
Types & Periods: Glass,
Tools, Furniture from 1850
to early 1900's
Directions: 1 block from
square on Bridge St

Rye

AGE OF INNOCENCE
14 Purchase St   10580
914 967-2778   Est: 1970
Proprietor: Elaine Dillof
Hours: Mon-Sat, 1-4
Types & Periods: Furniture,
Quilts, Hooked Rugs,
Accessories
Specialties: Victoriana,
Costumes
Directions: On Main St
downtown

TWIG ANTIQUES
15 Purchase St   10580
914 967-4518
Hours: Mon-Fri, 10-4; Sat,
10-1
Types & Periods: Furniture
& Accessories

Sag Harbor

LITTLE BARN ANTIQUES
Sage St   11963
                Est: 1972
Proprietor: Hal McKusick
Hours: Daily, 11-5 by
appointment

Types & Periods: Furniture,
Folk Art, Accessories
Specialties: American
Primitives
Appraisal Service Available
Directions: 1 block S from
village

St James

ANTIQUE VILLAGE INC
555 Rte 25A   11780
516 862-9131   Est: 1975
Proprietor: M Adams
Hours: Wed-Sun, 10-5
Types & Periods: Victorian,
Primitives, Oak, Jewelry,
Books
Specialties: Lamps (Leaded)
Appraisal Service Available
Directions: N on Rte 111
to 25A, next to
Hitherbrook Nursery

St Johnsville

**DORIS E WALKER &
JAMES A WALKER**
RD 1 Box 130   13452
518 762-1168   Est: 1973
Proprietor: Doris & Jim
Walker
Hours: Daily, by
appointment or by chance
Types & Periods: Primitives
(Pine, Cherry, 18th & 19th
Centuries), Paintings, Currier
& Ives Prints, White
Ironstone China, Quilts
Specialties: White Ironstone
Directions: Rte 10,
approximately 11 miles N
of Canajoharie Exit from
N Y S Thruway, 1 mile N
of village of Ephratah on
Rte 10

Salem

EDEN GALLERIES
                     12865
518 854-7844
Proprietor: The Zweigs
Hours: By appointment
Types & Periods:
Americana, Paintings, Silver,
China
Appraisal Service Available
Directions: At the traffic
light

Sangerfield

**STAGECOACH STOP
ANTIQUES SHOP**
Box 73   13455
315 841-4741   Est: 1938
Proprietor: Mrs Ruth
Allison
Hours: Mon-Sat
Types & Periods: General
Line, Furniture, Glass,
China, Books
Directions: Corner of
Hwys 20 & 12

Saranac Lake

**TRADE WINDS EAST
ANTIQUES**
116 Main St   12983
518 891-0317   Est: 1971
Proprietor: Olive D Forth
Hours: Tues-Fri, 10-5; Mon
& Sat, 10-2
Types & Periods: General
Line
Specialties: Furniture
Appraisal Service Available
Directions: 2 houses past
Church & Main St
intersection

Saratoga Springs

LITTLE ANTIQUE SHOP
Gideon Putnam Hotel
                              12866
518 584-4335   Est: 1956
Proprietor: Mrs Edward
Delmore
Hours: Tues-Sat, 11-5;
Sun-Mon by appointment
Types & Periods: Porcelains,
Jewelry, Prints, General Line
Directions: Hotel located
in Spa, Exit 13 N off N Y
Northway, Rte 9 N
approximately 5 minutes
to entrance of Spa

THE MANSION
Rte 29   12866
518 885-7645
Proprietor: H & C Beyer
Hours: Daily
Types & Periods: General
Line

Directions: Saratoga
Country Antique Center,
multiple dealers, 10
minutes W of Saratoga
Springs on Rte 29 in Rock
City Falls

**YANKEE PEDDLER
ANTIQUE SHOP**
Smith Bridge Rd
RD 2   12866
518 584-9732   Est: 1967
Proprietor: George Green
Hours: Weekends,
Evenings also
Types & Periods: Furniture,
Primitives, Stoneware,
Military Items, Americana,
Coins, Oil Paintings
Specialties: Colonial,
Flintlock Firearms & Swords
Appraisal Service Available
Directions: 1½ miles N of
city on Rte 9

Savannah

WESCOTT'S ANTIQUES
Rtes 31 & 89   13146
315 365-3211   Est: 1970
Proprietor: Art & Ken
Wescott
Hours: Mon-Fri; Sat, 8-12;
Also by appointment
Types & Periods: Furniture
Specialties: Repair &
Refinish Furniture
Directions: Off N Y S
Thruway Weedsport or
Waterloo Exits,
approximately 30 miles
from Syracuse, 60 miles
from Rochester, 9 miles
from Seneca Falls, 17
miles from Auburn

Sayville

CROWN ANTIQUES
PO Box 266   11782
516 589-8038
Proprietor: Muriel S Hoost
Hours: By appointment
Types & Periods: General
Line, Collectibles

MILL POND ANTIQUES
45 Mill Pond Rd   11782
516 567-2537
Proprietor: Marilyn Pakis

Hours: By appointment
Types & Periods: Primitives,
Tools, Decoys, Quilts

BARBARA PETER
24 Center St   11782
516 589-3466
Proprietor: Barbara Peter
Hours: By appointment, by
chance
Types & Periods: American
Primitives, Textiles, Decoys,
Folk Art

Scarsdale

**BURTON & HELAINE
FENDELMAN**
1248 Post Rd   10583
914 725-0292
Proprietor: Burton &
Helaine Fendelman
Hours: By appointment
Types & Periods: American,
18th, 19th & 20th Century
Folk Art, Paintings, Rugs,
Sculpture, Furniture
Specialties: Painted &
Decorated Furniture
Appraisal Service Available
Directions: On Rte 22, 2
miles S of I-287, Exit 20
off Bronx River Parkway,
30 minutes from NYC

WINDSOR ANTIQUES
                              10583
914 723-3993
Proprietor: D & J Kemp
Hours: By appointment
Types & Periods: Small
American & English
Furniture
Directions: Mailing: Box
93, Bronxville, NY 10708

Schenectady

THE CLOCK WORKS
1726 State St   12304
518 393-6360   Est: 1974
Proprietor: Paul Major
Hours: Mon-Fri, 10-8; Sat,
10-7
Types & Periods: Variety of
Clocks
Directions: Rte 5, 2 blocks
E of Rte 7

ONA CURRAN ANTIQUES
3512 Rosendale Rd 12305
518 783-5788
Proprietor: Ona Curran
Hours: By appointment
Types & Periods: 18th &
19th Century American
Furniture & Accessories

BELL HAGAR ANTIQUES
1608 Union St   12309
518 346-3646   Est: 1956
Proprietor: Isabel A Hagar
Hours: Sun-Thurs, 9-5:30;
Fri & Sat, 9-9
Types & Periods: General
Line, Jewelry, Furniture
Specialties: Jewelry
Directions: Union St off
Rte 7, take 7 E from Exit
25 Thruway, Exit off at
Balltown Rd, left to Union
St

**MARY FRANCES
ANTIQUES**
302 Front St   12305
518 382-9006   Est: 1966
Proprietor: Mrs Mary
VanDenburgh
Hours: Mon, Wed-Fri,
11-3; Sat, 11-4, by
appointment
Types & Periods: General
Line, Furniture, Glass
Advertisements, Gas Lamps
Appraisal Service Available
Directions: Located in
historic stockade area of
downtown

Schoharie

GINNY'S HUTCH
Rte 30   12157
                Est: 1968
Proprietor: Virginia J Kintz
Hours: Daily
Types & Periods: Primitives,
Art Glass, Tiffany, Furniture,
Art Deco, Lamps
Specialties: Jewelry, Glass
(Art)
Directions: 1/2 mile S of
Schoharie on Rte 30

Sea Cliff

ARTIFACTS
318 Sea Cliff Ave   11579
516 671-3521   Est: 1973

Proprietor: Arthur Lambert
Jr
Hours: Thurs-Sun, also
holidays
Types & Periods: Objets
d'Art, China, Glass, Silver,
Americana
Specialties: Glass (Sandwich
& Cut)
Directions: Exit 39 N off LI
Expwy, follow signs to Sea
Cliff, approximately 7
miles off Expwy N

Shokan

THE BRASS EAGLE BARN
Rte 28   12481
914 657-8462   Est: 1975
Proprietor: Bonnie
Giacalone
Hours: Weekends, by
appointment or by chance
Types & Periods: General
Line, Furniture, Pictures,
Pottery, Frames, Country
Store Items, Porcelain,
Glass, Stoneware, Copper,
Brass, Tools
Specialties: Glass
(Depression & Pressed)
Directions: Exit 19
Kingston on N Y S
Thruway, 20 miles on Rte
28 N, located on Rte 28
on right side of road

COUNTRY ANTIQUES
41 A   12481
914 657-8195   Est: 1972
Proprietor: Philip Spinelli
Hours: Daily, by
appointment
Types & Periods: Furniture,
Lamps, Clocks, Paintings,
Jewelry
Appraisal Service Available
Directions: 2 miles past
Post Office going W on
Rte 28

Sidney

HUNTS ANTIQUES
34 River St   13838
607 563-1993   Est: 1962
Proprietor: Wm Hunt
Hours: Daily
Types & Periods: General
Line

Appraisal Service Available
Directions: At red light in
Sidney from Rte 7, turn
right onto River St

WHAT NOT SHOP
45 Pleasant St   13838
607 563-1623
Proprietor: Mrs Ernest
Loomis
Types & Periods: General
Line
Specialties: Glass (Pattern &
Majolica)

Sidney Center

**DOROTHY MERSCHROD
ANTIQUES**
Trout Creek Rd 27   13839
607 369-4989
Proprietor: Dorothy
Merschrod
Hours: By appointment, by
chance
Types & Periods: General
Line, Cut Glass, Furniture

Skaneateles

WHITE'S ANTIQUES
Fisher Rd   13152
                Est: 1972
Proprietor: Marjorie White
Hours: Daily, by
appointment
Types & Periods: Furniture
Specialties: Clocks, Toys,
Mechanical Banks, Old
Phonographs
Directions: 1 mile E of
Skaneateles, 1st left
off 175

Somers

**PEGGY'S COUNTRY STORE
ANTIQUES**
Rte 202   10589
914 277-3791
Proprietor: Margaret Arra
Hours: Daily, 10:30-5
Types & Periods: General
Line, Glass, Furniture

Southampton

HAKIM'S
234 Hampton Rd   11968
516 283-0647   Est: 1950
Proprietor: Nordam
Trading Corp
Hours: Daily
Types & Periods: Egyptian,
Mideast, European
Directions: LI Expwy to
Exit 70, then Sunrise Hwy
to Southampton

TIBBITS ANTIQUES
77 Meetinghouse Ln 11968
516 283-9084   Est: 1960
Proprietor: M L Tibbits
Hours: Daily, by
appointment
Types & Periods: Oriental
Furniture
Specialties: Oriental
(Furniture)
Appraisal Service Available
Directions: 2 blocks from
Main

South Durham

THE GRACE SHOPPE
Old Rte 23 Acra PO 12405
518 622-3391   Est: 1959
Proprietor: Grace Maletta
Hours: Daily
Types & Periods: China,
Glass
Specialties: Art Glass,
Furniture, Fixtures & Lamps
Directions: N Y S Thruway
to Exit 21, W on Rte 23

South Nyack

RED SETTER ANTIQUES
323 S Broadway   10960
914 358-0667   Est: 1968
Proprietor: B Backer & V
Osterndorf
Hours: By appointment
Types & Periods: American
Late 18th to Early 19th
Furniture, Decorative
Objects, Paintings
Specialties: Local Country,
Primitives
Directions: N Y S Thruway
to Nyack Exits 10 & 11

South Salem

**ANTIQUES ON PEACEABLE
STREET**
10509
914 533-2735
Proprietor: Gretchen
Sharp
Hours: Daily, 10-5:30
Types & Periods: American
18th & Early 19th Century
Furniture, Folk Art,
Accessories
Directions: Off corner of
Rtes 35 & 123

Stamford

**MONTGOMERY-EKLUND
ANTIQUES**
3 Railroad Ave   12167
607 652-3125
Proprietor: Bonnie & David
Montgomery & Carl
Eklund
Hours: Tues & Thurs,
10-5; Also by appointment
Types & Periods: Country
Furniture, Primitives, Oil
Paintings, Tools, Folk Art
Directions: 100 yards E of
Post Office

Stanfordville

COUNTRY FARE ANTIQUES
Rte 82   12581
914 868-7107
Proprietor: Anne & Arnold
Schack
Hours: Weekends, 1-6;
also holidays
Types & Periods: Jewelry,
Collectibles, Doll House &
Miniatures, General Line

Stanley

BALL TAVERN ANTIQUES
Box 106-2512   14561
Rtes 5 & 20
315 526-6298   Est: 1978
Proprietor: Skip & Shirley
Horwath
Hours: By appointment, by
chance

Types & Periods: General
Line, Furniture, Primitives,
Period, Lamps, Glass
Specialties: Furniture,
Trunks, Small Stands
Appraisal Service Available
Directions: 1/8 mile W of
Flint on Rtes 5 & 20, large
house E of Bob's
Equipment Farm
Implements

Staten Island

ARDEN ANTIQUES
4555 Amboy Rd   10312
212 984-4020   Est: 1953
Proprietor: Virginia Sloan
Hours: Weekends, by
appointment
Types & Periods: 18th &
19th Century Furniture,
China, Glass, Silver,
Bric-A-Brac, Paintings,
Clocks
Directions: Near Richmond
Ave

AS YOU WERE
7349 Amboy Rd   10307
212 356-0981   Est: 1972
Proprietor: Maryann
Wright
Hours: Wed-Fri, Sun, 12-5
Types & Periods:
Turn-of-the-Century
Furniture

DURFEY-CHALON
26 Cornish St   10308
212 984-6960
Proprietor: Frank
Durfey-Chalon
Hours: By appointment
Types & Periods: Pictures,
Silhouettes, Small Water
Colors, Painted & Period
Furniture, Boxes, Mirrors,
Folk Art
Directions: Staten Island
Great Kills off Hylau
Boulevard, 4 miles from
Verranzano Bridge

**JACQUES NOEL
JACOBSEN JR**
60 Manor Rd   10310
212 981-0973   Est: 1954
Proprietor: Jacques N
Jacobsen Jr
Hours: By appointment

JACQUES NOEL
JACOBSEN JR   Cont'd
Types & Periods: American
Military Antiques, Fire &
Police Antiques 1776-1945
Specialties: Photographs,
Eskimo Indian Items
Appraisal Service Available
 Directions: Manor Rd near
 Forest Ave

WALKER-MURPHY INC
 796 Castleton Ave   10310
 212 273-8585   Est: 1971
 Proprietor: John Murphy
 Hours: Mon-Sat, 11-5
Types & Periods: Formal &
Country Furniture
Specialties: American
Furniture of the Federal
Period
 Directions: N Shore,
 Staten Island

Stone Ridge

ATWOOD TREASURE COVE
 Rte 209   12484
 914 687-7078   Est: 1954
 Proprietor: Robert & Harry
 C Newell
 Hours: Wed-Sun, 10-4
Types & Periods: General
Line
Specialties: Furniture, Store
Decorator Items
 Directions: 4 miles W of
 Rte 209 at Stone Ridge,
 on Rte 213

THUMBPRINT ANTIQUES
 Tongore Rd   12484
 914 687-9318   Est: 1966
 Proprietor: R H Palmatier
 & F N Misner
 Hours: Tues-Sun, 12-5
Types & Periods: General
Line
Specialties: Silver, Glass
(Pressed)
Appraisal Service Available

Stony Point

WILLIAM J JURGENSEN
 W Main St   10980
 914 786-2174
 Proprietor: Wm J
 Jurgensen
 Hours: By appointment

Types & Periods: Antique
Arms, Americana
Specialties: Arms (Military &
American Long Circa
1795-1895)
Appraisal Service Available
 Directions: Old Rte 210

Suffern

ANTIQUE PEDDLER
 51 Lafayette Ave   10901
 914 357-3381   Est: 1970
 Proprietor: Gary Paulsen
 Hours: Mon-Fri, 9:30-5;
 Sat, 10-4
Types & Periods: General
Line, Depression Glass,
Furniture
 Directions: 1/2 hour from
 New York, At NY-NJ
 border on Rte 59

JAMES S DAMON
ASSOCIATES
 24 Viola Rd   10901
 914 357-6146
 Proprietor: James S
 Damon
 Hours: By appointment
Types & Periods: Formal &
Country Furniture,
Accessories

Syracuse

ANTIQUE CENTER
 1460 Burnet Ave   13206
 315 476-8270   Est: 1972
 Proprietor: R C McLean
 Hours: Daily, by
 appointment
Types & Periods: Oak,
Walnut, Pine & Cherry
Furniture, Glass
Appraisal Service Available
 Directions: Downtown
 area, within 2 blocks of
 Teal Ave, Exit off Rte 690

JEAN BRONNER ANTIQUES
 101 E Wells Ave N   13212
 315 458-8193   Est: 1965
 Proprietor: Jean Bronner
 Hours: By chance
Types & Periods: Primitive
Furniture, Pattern Glass,
General Line
Appraisal Service Available

COLELLA'S GALLERIES
 123 E Willow St   13202
 315 474-6950   Est: 1971
 Proprietor: Nicholas E
 Colella
 Hours: Daily, 9-5
Types & Periods: 18th &
19th Century Continental
Furniture & Porcelains,
16th-19th Century Oils,
Oriental Furniture Ivories &
Porcelains, Louis XV, Louis
XVI, Marquetry
Appraisal Service Available
 Directions: Close stop N Y
 S Thruway & I-690 &
 Rte 81

DOVER HOUSE LTD
 612 Lodi St   13203
 315 474-1604   Est: 1958
 Proprietor: C C Bradley III
 Hours: Sat & Sun, by
 appointment
Types & Periods: English,
French & European
Furniture, Porcelain, Silver &
Art Objects
Appraisal Service Available

CHARLES W JACOBSEN
INC
 401 S Salina St   13202
 Hours: Mon-Sat
Types & Periods: Oriental
Rugs
Appraisal Service Available

MCGANN ANTIQUES
 719 S Geddes St   13206
 315 476-4756   Est: 1973
 Proprietor: D McGann
 Hours: Mon-Fri, 9-5
Types & Periods: Oak &
Walnut Furniture, Brass
Beds, 1870-1920
 Directions: Rte 690 off N
 Geddes S to 719 S
 Geddes St

SWIFT'S CORNER
ANTIQUES
 201 Whittier Ave   13204
 315 475-5542   Est: 1968
 Proprietor: Mary Lou Swift
 Hours: Tues-Sun, 11-5
Types & Periods: Furniture,
Sterling, Post Cards,
Antique Clothing &
Memorabilia
Appraisal Service Available

Tannersville

SUDDEN WHIM ANTIQUES ETC
Main St   12485
518 589-5380   Est: 1970
Proprietor: V Harry
Nahabedian
Hours: "6 days a week
during the summer"
Types & Periods: Furniture,
Lamps, Handwork,
Collectibles, General Line
Appraisal Service Available
Directions: Rte 23A

Tappan

SCHOOLMASTER ANTIQUES
14 Conklin Ave   10983
914 359-7170   Est: 1969
Proprietor: Ron Johnson
Hours: Daily, 12-5:30; Sat
reopens 8-12
Types & Periods: Colonial to
Collectibles, 1750-1930,
Furniture, Silver, Porcelain,
Good Glass, Politicals,
General Line
Specialties: Furniture,
Political Items
Appraisal Service Available
Directions: Behind Gulio's
Restaurant, 1 block from
Main St and the firehouse

Theresa

BEASOR'S RED BARNS
Box 178   13691
315 628-4465   Est: 1967
Proprietor: Bruce Beasor
Hours: Weekends by
appointment
Types & Periods: Primitives,
Furniture
Directions: Rte 81 N,
Theresa Exit, 4 miles

Tomkins Cove

ANTIQUES AT THE ICE HOUSE OF BOULDERBERG MANOR
                   10986
914 786-5687
Proprietor: Margaret H
Carruthers

Hours: Tues-Sun, 12-4:30;
Sat evenings, 6:30-10:30
Types & Periods: Country
Furniture, Primitives, Brass,
Glass, China

Tuxedo

THE COUNTRY COLLECTOR
Rte 17   10987
914 351-2500   Est: 1972
Proprietor: Florence
Goldblatt, ASID
Hours: Sun-Mon, Wed-Sat,
10:30-5
Types & Periods: Furniture,
Accessories, Antique
Jewelry
Specialties: Antique Jewelry
& 19th Century Furniture &
Accessories for the home
Appraisal Service Available
Directions: On Rte 17
between the village of
Tuxedo and Sterling
Forest in the Tuxedo
Junction Bldg

GALERIE OBJECTS D'ART
Rte 17   10987
014 351-4466   Est: 1968
Proprietor: Vera Peterkin
Johnson
Hours: Tues-Sun, 10:30-5
Types & Periods: General
Line, 19th Century, Cut
Glass, Furniture, Lamps,
China & Silver (Mostly
American), Oriental Art
Specialties: Antique & Estate
Jewelry
Directions: 1 mile N of
Tuxedo Park, 1 mile S of
Sterling Forest

Unadilla

GALLOW'S ANTIQUES
12 River St   13849
607 369-9494
Proprietor: John & Nancy
Gallo
Hours: By appointment
Types & Periods: Country
Furnishings
Specialties: Stoneware &
Folk Art
Directions: 1/4 mile from
Main over RR tracks on
Clifton St

Utica

THE INKWELL
519 Columbia St   13502
315 732-2600   Est: 1970
Proprietor: Gale A Lytle Sr
Hours: Mon-Sat, 10-5
Types & Periods: China,
Glass, Victorian Flow Blue,
Signed Pieces
Specialties: Inkwells
Appraisal Service Available
Directions: Downtown

KIRKLAND GALLERIES
Box 153 Rte 1   13502
315 735-8469   Est: 1970
Proprietor: Philip Card
Hours: By appointment, by
chance
Types & Periods: General
Line
Specialties: Oriental, Special
Interest Autos, Art
Appraisal Service Available

Valley Cottage

DUTCH HOUSE ANTIQUES
381 Kings Hwy   10080
914 268-7080   Est: 1959
Proprietor: H & K Landolt
Hours: Daily
Types & Periods: 18th &
Early 19th Century American
Furniture & Accessories,
Formal & Country Period
Furniture, Copper, Brass,
Silver
Appraisal Service Available
Directions: 1½ miles N of
N Y S Thruway Exit 12
near Tappan Zee Bridge

Valley Stream

GRANNY'S ATTIC
381 Rockaway Ave   11581
516 872-9555   Est: 1971
Proprietor: Marie Pisano
Hours: Mon-Sat
Types & Periods: General
Line
Specialties: Doll Houses,
Miniatures
Directions: S shore of
Long Island, from Belt
Pkwy take Sunrise Hwy
Exit to Rockaway Ave

HORSES HEAD ANTIQUES
   109 N Central Ave   11580
   516 825-5588   Est: 1965
   Proprietor: Harriet Blank
   Hours: Tues-Sat
Types & Periods: Oak,
Fixtures, Jewelry, Silver,
Collectibles
Appraisal Service Available
   Directions: Southern State
   Pkwy Exit 13, Central Ave
   S approximately 2 miles

SIDNEY WISTON
   1052 Wright St N   11580
   516 825-8390   Est: 1946
   Proprietor: Sidney Wiston
   Hours: By appointment
Types & Periods: Suits of
Armor, Helmets, Shields,
Weapons
Appraisal Service Available
   Directions: Off Exit 15
   Southern State Pkwy,
   pass Franklyn General
   Hospital on right side of
   Franklyn Ave about 3
   blocks from Pkwy, left
   turn on Wright St, next to
   last building on corner
   with Coat of Arms on top

Vestal

COUNTRY COUSINS
   477 Echo Rd   13850
   607 785-6285   Est: 1973
   Proprietor: Russ & Kay
   Erwin
   Hours: Daily, by chance
Types & Periods: Country,
Primitives, 18th & 19th
Centuries
   Directions: Rte 434, S on
   Main St, right on
   Glenwood, first right on
   Echo Rd

Victor

EAST WEST SHOP
   27 Main St   14564
   716 924-5830   Est: 1970
   Proprietor: Merlin & Mary
   Ann Dailey
   Hours: Tues-Sat, 10-4; by
   appointment
Types & Periods: Arts of
Japan, China, Korea, India,
SE Asia, Africa, New

Guinea, Variety of Antique
European Prints
Specialties: Japanese Prints
& Paintings, Asian Works of
Art
Appraisal Service Available
   Directions: Rte 96
   E of Rochester

Walden

THE SPARROW HOUSE
   St Andrews Rd   12586
   914 778-7775   Est: 1966
   Proprietor: Jim Sparrow
   Hours: Daily, 12-5
Types & Periods: General
Line
Appraisal Service Available
   Directions: Off Rte 52, E
   of Walden on County
   Rte 85

Wallkill

HARTMANN'S ANTIQUES
   Hoagburg Hill Rd   12589
   914 895-3806   Est: 1954
   Proprietor: Harriet & Fred
   Hartmann
   Hours: By appointment, by
   chance
Types & Periods: Country
Furniture, Early Stoneware,
Early Iron & Tinware, Toys,
Woodenware, Country
Kitchenware
   Directions: 1/2 mile N of
   the Blue Chip Farms, up
   out of village of Wallkill

Walton

BLUE SPRUCE ANTIQUES
   138 Delaware St   13856
   607 865-5246
   Proprietor: Ada G
   Washburn
   Hours: Mon-Sat, 10:30-5
Types & Periods: General
Line, Lamps, Roseville,
Weller, Rockwood, Pottery,
Depression Glass

PAT'S ANTIQUES
   81 Liberty St   13856
   607 865-5177
   Proprietor: Bea Patterson
   Hours: Mon-Sat, 10-5

Types & Periods: Furniture,
China, Glass, Primitives,
Lamps

Wantagh

MY MOTHER'S PLACE
   3034 Merrick Rd   11793
   516 826-8883   Est: 1961
   Proprietor: Estelle Hall
   Hours: Tues, Thurs-Sun,
   1-5; also by appointment
   or chance
Types & Periods: Primitives,
Turn-of-the-Century,
Potpourri
Specialties: Jewelry,
Redesigning Heirloom
Pieces
Appraisal Service Available
   Directions: 2 blocks W of
   Wantagh Ave, "Out of
   towners, call for
   directions"

Warners

PANCHRONIA ANTIQUES
   2559 Brickyard Rd   13164
   Est: 1973
   Proprietor: Nancy & Mark
   Fratti
   Hours: By appointment
Types & Periods: General
Line
Specialties: Clocks, Oriental
(Rugs), Music Boxes
Appraisal Service Available
   Directions: 4 miles from
   Exit 39 of N Y S Thruway,
   11 miles NW of Syracuse

Warrensburg

FRANCES ANTIQUE SHOP
   27 Main St   12885
   518 623-6341   Est: 1942
   Proprietor: Frances M
   Carlucci
   Hours: Daily, 9-5
Types & Periods: Antique
Jewelry, China, Porcelain
Specialties: Ceramics,
Jewelry
   Directions: Exit 23 N to
   Rte 9, to Cut Stone Bldg

CHARLES E HASTINGS BOOKS & ANTIQUES
11 Horicon Ave   12885
518 623-2940
Proprietor: Charles E Hastings Jr
Hours: Tues-Sat, 11-4; also by appointment
Types & Periods: American Folk Art, Country Furniture, Books, Prints

KENNEDY'S ANTIQUES UNIQUE
179 Main Barn   12885
518 623-9678   Est: 1975
Proprietor: Walter & Ellen Kennedy
Hours: Daily, 12-5; also by appointment
Types & Periods: Tools, Scales & Measuring Devices, Musical Instruments, Ivory, Scientific Items
Specialties: Men's Collectibles
Directions: Heart of Warrensburg, Rte 9, Exit 23 N Y S Northway, 60 miles N of Albany

ROBERTS' ANTIQUES
179 Main St   12885
518 623-9404   Est: 1952
Proprietor: Ethel C Roberts
Hours: Daily, May-Oct
Types & Periods: General Line
Directions: On Rte 9 in N part of town

Washingtonville

BREWSTER BOARD
West Main St   10992
914 496-3712   Est: 1941
Hours: By appointment
Types & Periods: 17th, 18th & Early 19th Century Furniture
Specialties: Restoration
Appraisal Service Available
Directions: N Y S Thruway Exit 16 W on Rte 6-17 to Rte 208

Watkins Glen

EDWARD & CAROL PETERS
113 S Madison Ave   14891
607 535-4390   Est: 1967
Proprietor: Edward & Carol Peters
Hours: By chance
Types & Periods: General Line
Specialties: Furniture (Turn-of-the-Century Oak)
Directions: Corner of 2nd & Madison Ave

Wayland

PFEIFFER'S ANTIQUES
113 Main St   14572
716 728-2240   Est: 1963
Proprietor: E J Pfeiffer
Hours: Daily, 9-12; Sun-Tues, Thurs-Sat afternoons 1-5
Types & Periods: General Line

Webster

JUNE & CAROL AMES ANTIQUES
10 Lincolnshire Rd   14580
716 872-1651   Est: 1974
Proprietor: June & Carol Ames
Hours: By appointment
Types & Periods: General Line
Specialties: Glass (Heisey)
Directions: Near 4 corners Webster village, off Rtes 250 & 104

ANTIQUE GOLD & SILVER SHOPPE
75 W Main St   14580
716 872-1440   Est: 1936
Proprietor: Herman Wanderman
Hours: Tues-Sun, by appointment
Types & Periods: Jewelry, Watches, Stick Pins, Cameos
Specialties: Jewelry
Appraisal Service Available
Directions: Business section of town

CHICKEN COOP ANTIQUES
613 Ridge Rd   14580
716 671-2121   Est: 1973
Proprietor: Curt & Lee Davis
Hours: Daily
Types & Periods: China, Glass, Furniture, Oriental Rugs & Clocks & Lamps
Specialties: Oak Furniture, Prints, Frames (No Reproductions)
Directions: Off Bay Rd Exit Rte 104

Westbrookville

DERBY ANTIQUES
Rte 209   12785
914 745-8096   Est: 1973
Proprietor: Miles Moore
Hours: Mon-Fri; Sat & Sun by chance
Types & Periods: Collectibles, Custom Upholstering
Specialties: Restoring Period Furniture
Directions: Located on Rte 209, 7 miles from Wurstboro Exit 113 on Rte 17, or 12 miles from Port Jervis

VAN DYKE'S ANTIQUES
Rte 209   12785
914 754-8647   Est: 1961
Proprietor: Alma & Lyle Van Dyke
Hours: Sun, by appointment, by chance
Types & Periods: General Line
Appraisal Service Available
Directions: Rte 209, 12 miles from Port Jervis, 7 miles from Wurstboro, Exit Rte 17, Exit 113

Westbury

FORTUNOFF
1300 Old Country Rd   11590
516 334-9000
Hours: Mon-Sat, 10-9:30; Sun, 12-5
Types & Periods: Bronze Figurines

West Falls

WEST FALLS ANTIQUES
1894 Davis Rd   14170
716 652-7096   Est: 1967
Proprietor: Geraldine
Jackson
Hours: Daily, 1-5; also by
appointment
Types & Periods: General
Line
Specialties: Lamps
Appraisal Service Available
Directions: Davis Rd is
also Rte 240,
approximately 15 miles S
of Buffalo

Westfield

ANTIQUES BY TRIPPY
Rte 20 E   14787
716 326-3483   Est: 1972
Proprietor: Helen Trippy
Hours: Daily
Types & Periods: Primitive,
Glassware, Lamps, China,
Furniture, Collectibles
Directions: 2 miles E from
intersection of Rtes
20 & 17

DOROTHEA F BERTRAM
53 S Portage St   14787
716 326-2551   Est: 1915
Proprietor: Dorothea F
Bertram
Hours: Daily, by chance
Types & Periods: Victorian,
Empire, Primitive
Specialties: Pattern Glass,
China, Frames, Furniture,
Post Cards, Magazines,
Books
Appraisal Service Available
Directions: 1 block S of
Rte 20 on Rte 17

**THE COLLECTORS' SHELF
OF BOOKS**
PO Box 6   14787
716 326-3676
Proprietor: Mary E Militello
Hours: Mail Order Only
Types & Periods: Over 2000
current titles of Books about
Antiques, Lamps,
Chandeliers

THE LEONARDS ANTIQUES
E Main Rd   14787
716 326-2210
Proprietor: Len &
Jacqueline Leonards
Hours: Daily, 1:30-6
Types & Periods: French &
American, General Line

MILITELLO ANTIQUES
31 Jefferson   14787
716 326-2587   Est: 1922
Proprietor: Julia G Militello
Hours: Daily, 10-4
Types & Periods:
Americana, Glass, China,
Furniture, Prints, Dolls, 18th
& 19th Century
Directions: 1 block E of
Rte 17, 1 mile from Exit
60, I-90

**YANKEE TRADER ANTIQUE
SHOPPE**
Rte 20 Box 115   14787
716 326-2179   Est: 1961
Proprietor: Peg Sidaway
Hours: Sun-Wed, Fri-Sat,
10-6; better to call
Types & Periods: Furniture,
Americana, Dolls, Children's
Things, Primitives
Specialties: American
Furniture from Early
Turn-of-the-Century
Appraisal Service Available
Directions: Rte 20 is the
main street in Westfield,
we are on 20E

West Hempstead

GIFT HORSE ANTIQUES
715 Woodfield Rd   11552
516 586-8866   Est: 1959
Proprietor: Ruth Greenhut
Hours: Daily, by
appointment or by chance
Types & Periods: Early
American, Victorian, Civil
War Items
Specialties: Restored &
Refinished Work done on
premises
Directions: Lakeview Exit
18, Southern State Pkwy

West Hurley

NANCY & TED BROOKS
6 Fieldstone Rd   12491
914 679-2039
Proprietor: Nancy & Ted
Brooks
Hours: By appointment, by
chance
Types & Periods: Country
Furniture, Tools,
Kitchenware, Woodware

West Islip

THE FRIENDLY ATTIC
463 Montauk Hwy   11795
516 669-1038
Proprietor: Lena Ramsey
Hours: By appointment
Types & Periods: Export
Ware, Period Furniture,
Silver, Glass
Directions: Rte 27A

West Sayville

SHORE BIRDS ANTIQUES
156 Rollstone Ave   11796
516 589-6187
Proprietor: Bill Besemer
Hours: By appointment, by
chance
Types & Periods: Primitives,
Decoys, Crocks, Baskets
Directions: Box 23

West Winfield

**THE SIGN OF THE BLUE
BIRD**
RD 2   13491
315 855-4274   Est: 1965
Proprietor: Carmen &
Jerry Davis
Hours: Daily, by chance;
call first advisable
Types & Periods: All Periods
Furniture, Oak & Wicker,
Accessories, Lighting
Specialties: Textiles,
Lighting
Appraisal Service Available
Directions: Hamlet of
Unadilla Forks, 2 miles S
of Rte 20, between West
Winfield & Bridgewater

Whitehall

SKENESBOROUGH FLEA MARKET
Broadway   12887
518 499-2896   Est: 1975
Proprietor: Charles Rawitz
Hours: Daily, 11 'til dark
Types & Periods: Primitives,
Old Records, Bottles,
Clocks, Jug Crocks
Directions: Rtes 4 & 22,
Exit from Adarondack
Northway

White Plains

VICKI GLASGOW MUSIC BOXES
147 E Post Rd   10601
914 761-5225   Est: 1970
Proprietor: Vicki Glasgow
Hours: Daily, 10-5
Types & Periods: Music
Boxes, Antique & New
Appraisal Service Available
Directions: Center of
shopping area, 5 minutes
from Rte 287 on Rte 22

VOGUE DECORATONS INC
120 E Post Rd   10601
914 949-5277
Proprietor: Herbert I Ratet
Hours: Daily, 9-5
Types & Periods: Porcelains
Specialties: Imari

Whitestone

BERNAL ANTIQUES INC
12-55 150th St   11357
212 746-5064   Est: 1973
Proprietor: Bernice E
Berman
Hours: Daily
Types & Periods: General
Line, Victorian, Americana,
Primitives, China, Wall
Decors
Specialties: China, Wall
Decors

JOAN & LARRY KINDLER ANTIQUES INC
14-35 150th St   11357
212 767-2260   Est: 1964
Proprietor: Joan & Larry
Kindler

Hours: Tues, Thur & Sat,
11-4; also by appointment
Types & Periods: 18th &
19th Century American, Folk
Art, Dolls
Specialties: Toys (Dolls)
Appraisal Service Available
Directions: Between
Whitestone & Throg's
Neck Bridges

Windsor

MINER J COOPER
41 Main St Box 227 13865
607 655-2192   Est: 1943
Proprietor: Mr & Mrs
Miner J Cooper
Hours: Daily, by chance
Types & Periods: "Devices
from the old-time farm,
home & workshop", General
Line
Appraisal Service Available
Directions: 15 miles E of
Binghamton

Woodbury

BOB & BETSY'S ANTIQUE NOOK
500 Woodbury Rd   11797
516 692-4165
Proprietor: Betty Babcock
Hours: By appointment
only
Types & Periods: 18th
Century American Furniture
& Folk Art

Woodstock

VIRTU ANTIQUES & ART
54A Tinker St   12498
914 679-8300   Est: 1960
Proprietor: Lillian F Klein
Hours: Tues-Sun; Fri &
Sat during winter; also by
appointment
Types & Periods: Furniture,
Glass, China, Silver,
Jewelry, Brass, Copper,
Iron, Clocks, Lamps, Linens,
Clothing, Paintings, Prints,
Tools
Specialties: Books,
Magazines
Directions: Main St of
village which is St Rd 212

Worcester

FOREMAN'S FOLLY
RD 2   12197
607 397-8946
Proprietor: E & A Foreman
Hours: By appointment
Types & Periods: Stoves,
Primitives, General Line
Directions: 5 miles N of
Rte 7

THE TREASURE CHEST
Box 7 Main St   12197
607 397-8137
Proprietor: Emile
Schoutith
Types & Periods: General
Line
Specialties: Furniture, Glass
(Pattern)

Wurtsboro

WURTSBORO WHOLESALE ANTIQUES INC
Sullivan St   12790
914 888-4411   Est: 1961
Proprietor: Leo Wilensky
Hours: Mon-Sat, 9:30-5:30;
Sun by appointment
Types & Periods: "Huge
Inventory of Primitives",
American & European,
Wholesale Only
Appraisal Service Available
Directions: 70 miles N
of NY

Yonkers

MURIEL ENSLEIN ANTIQUES
432 Riverdale Ave   10705
914 423-5519
Proprietor: Muriel Enslein
Hours: Thur, Fri & Sat,
10-5
Types & Periods: General
Line

Yorktown Heights

THE ANNEX
334 Underhill Ave   10598
914 962-4931
Proprietor: Mary & Don
Palmer
Hours: Tues-Sat, 10-5;
Sun, 12-5
Types & Periods: General Line

(From page 424). The pieces were made in a simpler manner and were usually without the frills of city furniture. Plank bottomed chairs continued and chests were made of solid woods without the use of veneers. Tables were made more for usefulness than for decorative purposes. The natural result is that a lot of this Victorian furniture is sometimes dated much earlier than it really is. There is a tendency on the part of so many people to date things much earlier than they really are. Be alert for mechanical marks as well as hand toolmarks on furniture of this period. The usual finishes were varnish, shellac and paint. In the hope of making it appear more expensive, artificially grained wood may sometimes be found.

Furniture styles ebbed and flowed with periods of existence showing evidence of their origin sometimes decades earlier. It was a chaotic Era. Even those living in the time of the Middle Victorian Period, 1855-1875, were aware that this was true.

A great exhibit in England in the 1850's, the Crystal Palace, caused some to become aware of the abuses and excesses coming about in design. It was fashionable that things should not necessarily be that which they seemed. To illustrate, canvas covered walls were caused to appear as cut stone masonry. A table would be so hidden by heavy fabric that it could not be seen. Mantels and even flower pots were concealed with fabric or needlework. Marble statues of the classic human form came to be draped to conceal their bareness. All of this was justified by the subjective concept of "refinement". It persisted for decades, but voices rose against it. An English architect, William Morris, inventor of the famous chair and a designer spoke for change. His plea was essentially to possess nothing which was without use, and only those things that were felt to be beautiful. It did not prevail, but it was heard. The windows padded with voluminous draperies, so that air could not enter through them, persisted.

Only recently forced to trade with the Western world, Japan pursued that trade with determination. By the 1860's, Oriental art values were being widely displayed in the Western nations. That spare and austere elegance was a breath of fresh air in a world rapidly becoming stuffy. A very strong impact was made by an Englishman named Charles Locke Eastlake. It was not that his ideas were new, but that his book which reached this country in 1872 received a very wide audience. His plea was primarily for the adoption of simpler styles. He suggested lighter washable textiles for draperies and commented upon most everything.

The industrial revolution in furniture manufacture was accelerating throughout this interval, so that toward its conclusion the factory came to exist in a recognizably modern form. Grand Rapids, Michigan, was assuming the status of furniture capitol of the United States. Spool beds, Cottage and Rococo furnitures were still made. Throughout these years the Shakers went right along making their handmade furniture. What occurred was that furniture became heavier than that which prevailed under the earlier French influences. It was becoming just a tiny bit pompous along with its elegance, as is seen in our photograph of the Gentleman's chair. As contrary as the period may have been, it clearly came to possess a character that was all its own, a clear identity. (See page 344).

Eastlake and the trickle of Oriental goods shook the world of the Late Victorian Period, 1875-1901. His idea of design was essentially that function should be accented rather than hidden. He utilized straight lines on rectangular forms. The accents were of bandsaw scrollwork, turned spindles, applied medallions, incised carvings and heavy legs. Much of the carving was mechanically done in a tracery fashion. He thought in terms of machine manufacture and hoped inexpensive furniture in good taste would be achieved. A wood prevalently used in many of the "Eastlake" pieces was walnut with applied burl walnut panels. Oak, ash and chestnut may also be found. Furniture in the style of Eastlake is found in all grades of excellence. Excellence in this case refers both to overall design as well as craftsmanship. Although he included a few sketches of his ideas in his book, there were not enough to prevent their corruption by manufacturers attempting to supply the demand for furniture in the "style of Eastlake". It was occasionally abusively executed as well as occasionally executed in remarkable quality. His designs were completely at the mercies of the manufacturers.

Other familiar forms continued in manufacture. The Empire Period never lost its ability to influence Victorian furniture. Gothic persisted at a low level. Marble tops remained, but were being replaced by wooden tops. New things continued to appear at a very rapid rate. Oriental influence became stronger and again introduced a less elaborate approach to design. By the 1880's it was said that Bamboo furniture, a Chinese import, was always in demand by people of "artistic taste". Flat surfaces were often done in birds-eye maple to contrast with its light color. Much of that furniture even then was being made of turned wood in imitation of bamboo. During the same interval, both Rattan and Wicker furniture were being used widely. Today, Wicker has again become popular and reproductions may be easily found. (Continued, page 455).

Center Table, marble topped, Middle Victorian.

Small Buffet, marble topped, Middle Victorian.

STATE OF NORTH CAROLINA

Aberdeen

RILEY'S ROADSIDE ANTIQUES
Rte 1   28315
919 944-1131   Est: 1947
Proprietor: Mr & Mrs Fred
W Riley
Hours: Daily 9-7, By
Chance
Types & Periods: Primitive
Tools, Relics, Clocks, China,
Cut Carnival & Depression
Glass, Coins, Bottles
Specialties: Glass (Carnival),
Primitive Tools
Directions: Hwy 211, 5
Miles E of Aberdeen

Asheville

COLLECTOR'S CORNER ANTIQUES
68 N Market St   28801
704 252-2015   Est: 1973
Proprietor: Polly S
Hickling
Hours: Mon-Sat 11-5
Types & Periods: Complete
Antiques & Collectibles,
Period & Primitive Furniture,
Glass, Pottery, Dolls,
Jewelry, Iron, Tools,
Postcards, Prints, Paintings,
Rugs
Directions: 1 block off US
25, 1 block from Sheraton
Motel, Inn on the Plaza &
Thomas Wolfe Home

OLIVER'S ANTIQUES
27 Biltmore Ave   28801
704 252-2532, 254-8905
Est: 1970
Proprietor: Oliver V
Pressley, Jr
Hours: Mon-Sat 10-5
Types & Periods: "All Types
When Available"
Specialties: "We Purchase
Entire Estates-Any Size"
Appraisal Service Available
Directions: 1 block off
Central Square S

R S V P INC
640 Merrimon Ave   28804
704 254-0936   Est: 1977
Proprietor: Corporation

Hours: Tues-Sat
Types & Periods: Estate
Liquidations, All Periods, Oil
Paintings, China, Cut Glass
Specialties: Interior Design
Directions: US Hwy 25 N
at Serendipity Square, 2
Miles off Crosstown
Expwy, Merrimon Exit

Beaufort

FRONT ANTIQUES
301 Front St   28516
919 728-3669
Proprietor: Copeland &
Jean B Kell
Hours: By Appointment,
By Chance
Types & Periods: Furniture,
Primitives, Porcelain, Glass
Appraisal Service Available

TIMELY TREASURES
Rte 1, Box 40   28315
919 944-1154   Est: 1970
Proprietor: Mr & Mrs B E
Maxwell Sr
Hours: Daily 9-5:30, Sat
9-3:30, Sun 2-5:30
Types & Periods: Wicker,
China, Glassware, Furniture,
Bric-A-Brac, Collectibles

Beulaville

BEULAVILLE ANTIQUES & FURNITURE CO
Hwy 24 East   28518
919 298-3476   Est: 1972
Proprietor: O S Thigpen
Hours: Daily 9:30-5:30,
Sun 1:30-5:30
Types & Periods: "All Types
of Oak & Walnut", Pressed
Glass
Specialties: Furniture, Glass
Appraisal Service Available
Directions: 1 Mile E of
Town

Black Creek

BARDIN'S ANTIQUES
Center St   27813
919 237-8752

Hours: Sat 9-6, Sun 1-6,
By Appointment
Types & Periods: American
& Imported 18th & 19th
Centuries, Accessories

Blowing Rock

THE VAGABOND SHOP
Main St   28605
704 295-7722   Est: 1962
Proprietor: Mrs Virginia S
Wilson
Hours: Daily, May thru Oct
Types & Periods: 18th &
19th Centuries Furniture,
Porcelain, Brass
Specialties: Jewelry
Directions: On the Crest
of the Blue Ridge Mts, 38
Miles N of Hickory, 8 Miles
S of Boone

Broadway

VERA'S ANTIQUES
Beecharne Ave   27505
919 258-6603   Est: 1971
Hours: Weekends, By
Chance
Types & Periods: Victorian,
Chippendale, Queen Anne
Directions: US 421 E

Burnsville

THE PENDULUM SHOP
E Main St   28714
704 682-2463   Est: 1964
Proprietor: Margaret
Turner & Annie Hassell
Hours: Daily 10-5
Types & Periods: Mountain
Primitives, Country Pieces,
Clocks, Country Victorian
Specialties: Collages
Appraisal Service Available
Directions: On 19E
Business, N of Asheville,
Just off Square in
Burnsville

YANCEY COUNTY COUNTRY STORE
Town Square   28714
704 682-3779   Est: 1966

**YANCEY COUNTY
COUNTRY STORE**   Cont'd
Proprietor: Capt George A
Downing USCG Ret & Mrs
Downing
Hours: Daily
Types & Periods: Tools,
Primitives, Old Washing
Machines, Reproductions,
Books, Gourmet Foods, Art
Supplies, Maps
Directions: 37 Miles NE of
Asheville on 19E, 30
Minutes from Blue Ridge
Pkwy via Rte 80 or Spruce
Pine

Chapel Hill

ELIZABETH R DANIEL
2 Gooseneck Rd   27514
Proprietor: Elizabeth R
Daniel
Hours: Daily,
Appointment
Types & Periods: Fine
American Antiques of 18th &
Early 19th Centuries,
Decorative Items, Fine
Collection of Brass
Candlesticks
Directions: Off 15-501
Bypass

WHITEHALL SHOP INC
1215 E Franklin St   27514
919 942-3179   Est: 1930
Proprietor: Mrs Geo Bason
& Mrs J K Wilkins
Hours: Mon-Sat 9:30-5
Types & Periods: 18th &
19th Centuries Furniture,
Silver, Porcelain, Objets
d'Art, Paintings, Fireplace
Equipment
Directions: Hwy 15-501, E
Edge of Town

Charlotte

CHARLOTTE CLUSTER
Directions: Shops
scattered, Some
concentration in
Downtown Area btwn
Brookside Expwy & E
Independence Blvd,
Adjacent Sts of S Mint,
College, Brevard &
Elizabeth Ave,
Neighboring on
Providence Rd (600-1000
Blocks) & Fenton Place

**CHARLOTTE THIEVES
MARKET**
8501 N Tryon St   28206
704 596-9107   Est: 1948
Proprietor: Phillip A
Viviano
Hours: Daily
Types & Periods: General
Line
Specialties: Auction 1st Sat
of Month
Appraisal Service Available
Directions: Exit I-85 to
Hwy 29 N, Go 1 Mile

CLARA'S ANTIQUES
1525 E Independence Blvd
28205
704 376-6946   Est: 1971
Proprietor: Clara H. Gault
Hours: Mon-Sat, 10-5
Types & Periods: Furniture,
Wicker, Silver, Gold, Oriental
Items, Flow Blue China,
Paintings circa 1842,
Pictures
Specialties: Porcelain,
Crystal, Wicker
Directions: Downtown
Hwy 74 E at the Plaza

**COLONY FURNITURE
SHOPS INC**
811 Providence Rd   28217
704 333-8871   Est: 1950
Proprietor: Incorporated
Hours: Daily
Types & Periods: 18th
Century English Wood
Furniture, Accessories

THE COUNTRY STORE
8000 Park Rd   28210
704 554-5828   Est: 1965
Proprietor: Fletcher L
Honeycutt
Hours: Daily 8:30-5:30, By
Appointment
Types & Periods: Early
American, Primitives,
Tinware, Silver, Pattern
Glass, Pottery, Dolls,
Furniture
Specialties: Dolls
Appraisal Service Available
Directions: SE Section of
Charlotte

DEAN'S ANTIQUES
Rte 6, Box 747H   28208
704 399-5897   Est: 1970
Proprietor: Louis M &
Frances Dean
Hours: By Appointment

Types & Periods: Primitives,
Oak Furniture
Directions: 1 Mile S of
Shuffletown, Right on
Harwood Ln

**EM'S LOOK-A-NOOK
ANTIQUES**
3100 Little Rock Rd
28214
704 394-4426   Est: 1974
Proprietor: Emily Ingram
Hours: Daily, Weekends
10-5, Closed Sun & Mon
Types & Periods: Victorian,
Federal, Early Primitive,
English
Specialties: Glass
(Depression), China
Collectibles
Appraisal Service Available
Directions: I-85 (Little
Rock Rd Exit), Douglas
Airport, Back of Robert
Hall Clothing

GLORY BE!
1529 E Independence Blvd
28205
704 376-1213   Est: 1974
Proprietor: Elise Lyerly
Hours: Mon-Sat 10:30-4:30
Types & Periods: Furniture,
China, Glass, Jewelry
Specialties: Furniture
(Country)
Directions: Independence
Blvd on Hwy 74

G S MC KENNA GALLERY
1524 Providence Rd
28012
704 365-0788   Est: 1966
Proprietor: Kitty Gaston,
Alice Smyth & Anne
McKenna
Hours: Mon-Fri 10-4, By
Appointment
Types & Periods: 18th &
Early 19th Centuries English
and American
Specialties: Antique Oriental
Rugs
Directions: 1500 Block
btwn Beverly Dr &
Hanson Dr

THE SQUIRREL'S NEST
739 Providence Rd   28207
704 332-1655   Est: 1962
Proprietor: Mrs Carle R
Walton
Hours: Mon-Wed, Fri 10-4,
Sat 10-2

Types & Periods: Furniture,
Bric-A-Brac, Crystal, Silver,
Art Glass, Paintings,
Engravings
Appraisal Service Available
Directions: From
Downtown 3rd St Runs
into Providence Rd

THOMPSON ANTIQUE CO
8500 Wilkinson Blvd
28208
704 399-1405   Est: 1921
Proprietor: O O Thompson
Hours: Mon-Fri 8:30-5:30,
By Appointment
Types & Periods: Southern
American Period Antiques,
Walnut, Cherry, Mahogany,
Pine
Specialties: Cupboards,
Chest, Sideboards, Slant
Top Desks
Appraisal Service Available
Directions: Gastonia Hwy

Clinton

THE VARIETY SHOP
Rte 3, Box 383A   28328
919 564-4207   Est: 1972
Proprietor: Marie & James
R Blackmon
Hours: Daily 1-6
Types & Periods: Oak &
Mahogany Furniture, Chest,
Desks, "Many Old Things"
Appraisal Service Available
Directions: 3½ Miles N of
Clinton on Hwy 421

THE PEWTER MUG LTD
500 College St   28328
919 592-4743   Est: 1962
Proprietor: Nan Woodside
Hours: Tues-Sat
Types & Periods: Jacobean,
Queen Anne, Chippendale,
Accessories
Directions: Hwy 403, In
Town by First Baptist
Church

Durham

**AMERICAN
INTERNATIONAL
FURNITURE & ANTIQUES**
301 Duke St   27701
919 682-3694   Est: 1970
Proprietor: Tully & Phillip
Fletcher
Hours: Daily, Weekends,
Closed Sun
Types & Periods: Walnut,
Oak, Victorian, Late 1800
Furniture
Specialties: Furniture
Directions: Downtown

THE CORNER CUPBOARD
1640 Cole Mill Rd   27705
919 383-1426   Est: 1966
Proprietor: Mr & Mrs
Robert D Hughes Jr
Hours: Daily, Weekends,
Closed Sun & Mon
Types & Periods: General
Line, Furniture, Pictures,
Orientals, Brass
Specialties: Mirrors, Glass
Directions: "1/4 Mile
outside city limits"

QUALITY FURNITURE CO
308 Rigsbee   27701
Est: 1963
Proprietor: Larry G
Stewart
Hours: Daily 9-5:30
Types & Periods: American
& Primitives
Appraisal Service Available
Directions: Downtown,
Warehouse District

Elm City

**THE CRACKER BARREL
ANTIQUES**
27822
919 236-4000
Hours: Daily 11-5, Sun
2-5, Closed Mon
Types & Periods: Early
Southern Country Furniture
& Primitive Accessories
Directions: Off US Hwy
301 & I-95 at Elm City, 1½
Miles from the N & S Elm
City Exit on US 301
Business

Etowah

HELENE'S ANTIQUES
Box 297   28729
704 891-7743   Est: 1971
Proprietor: Helene Rogers
Hours: Daily, By Chance
Types & Periods: Furniture,
Oak, Walnut, Period &
Primitive, "A Very Wide
Variety of Everything"
Specialties: Art Glass,
Furniture
Directions: Off 64 W from
Hendersonville at RR
Tracks, Turn Right, Follow
Signs 1/4 Mile, Go Left

Fayetteville

CLOCK BOUTIQUE
142 Westwood Shopping
Ctr   28304
919 867-6061   Est: 1973
Proprietor: Dale Meyer
Hours: Mon-Fri 10-9, Sat
10-6, Sun 1/2 Day
Types & Periods: Clocks,
Dolls, Furniture
Specialties: Clocks,
Restoration
Appraisal Service Available

HAYMOUNT ANTIQUES
1205 Hay St   28305
919 484-4931   Est: 1974
Proprietor: Mrs Carra
Glass
Hours: Mon-Sat 10-5
Types & Periods: Early
American & Primitive
Specialties: Glass
Appraisal Service Available
Directions: Top of
Haymount Hill Next Door
to Fayetteville Little
Theater

THE PILGRIM
160 Westwood Shopping
Ctr   28304
919 867-9750   Est: 1971
Proprietor: Doris McPhail
& Carolyn Naylor
Hours: Daily 10-9
Types & Periods: 18th &
19th Centuries Country
Furniture & Accessories,
Primitives

THE PILGRIM   Cont'd
Appraisal Service Available
  Directions: Corner
  Morganton Rd &
  McPherson Church Rd
  near Cross Creek Mall

Greensboro

**ADAMS ANTIQUES-THE
CAROLINIANS**
  403 N Elm St   27401
  Proprietor: Harry & Anne
  Adams
  Hours: Mon-Fri, By
  Appointment On
  Weekends
Types & Periods: 18th &
19th Centuries English &
American Furniture, Oriental
Accessories
Specialties: 18th Century
Furniture
Appraisal Service Available
  Directions: Elm St Exit
  from I-85 & I-70

**AMERICAN
INTERNATIONAL
FURNITURE & ANTIQUES**
  1435 E Cone Blvd   27405
  919 621-3564   Est: 1970
  Proprietor: Tully & Phillip
  Fletcher
  Hours: Daily, Weekends
  10-7, Closed Sun
Types & Periods: Victorian,
Walnut, Oak, Late 1800
Furniture
Specialties: Furniture
  Directions: O'Henry
  Shopping Ctr off Hwy 29

B & B TREASURES
  627 S Elm   27406
  919 273-3771   Est: 1975
  Proprietor: Brad Moore
  Hours: Daily, Weekends,
  By Appointment
Types & Periods: General
Line
Specialties: Glass, Furniture
  Directions: I-85 to
  Greensboro, Take Lee St
  Exit (Rte 6) to Elm St, On
  Corner of Elm & Lee Sts

THELM B HARRISON
  518 N Elm St   27401
  919 272-5511   Est: 1957
  Proprietor: Thelma B
  Harrison
  Hours: Daily

Types & Periods: English
Formal Pieces, Chests,
Tables, Secretary Lamps,
Brass, Silver, Bronze
Specialties: Furniture (Brass
Beds)
Appraisal Service Available
  Directions: Downtown

THE MUSTARD SEED
  608 N Elm St   27401
  919 272-2040   Est: 1975
  Proprietor: Clarence &
  Jeannine Thompson
  Hours: Daily, Weekends
  10-4, Closed Sun
Types & Periods: Furniture,
Porcelain, Cloisonne,
Glassware, Silver, Brass,
Primitives
Appraisal Service Available
  Directions: 6 blocks N
  from Center of Town on
  the Main St

OTTO ZENKE INC
  220 S Eugene St   27401
  919 275-8487   Est: 1950
  Proprietor: Otto G Zenke
  Hours: Mon-Fri 9-5:30, By
  Appointment
Specialties: 18th Century
English
  Directions: Corner of S
  Eugene & Washington Sts,
  "Ring Bell at Double
  Black Doors"

**RHYNE'S CORNER
CUPBOARD ANTIQUES INC**
  603 S Elm St   27406
  919 272-7695   Est: 1972
  Proprietor: Mary M Rhyne
  Hours: Daily 10-4, Closed
  Sun, Mon Nites 5-9
Types & Periods: General
Line, Country, Oak,
Sheraton, French,
Chippendale
Specialties: Country Store,
Music Boxes, Back Bars,
Wheel Riding Items
Appraisal Service Available
  Directions: 3 blocks from
  Downtown

STYLE CRAFT ANTIQUES
  3806 High Point Rd 27407
  919 292-4640   Est: 1963
  Proprietor: Betty G Allred
  Hours: Mon-Sat 10-5:30
Types & Periods: Small
Antiques, Tables, Chairs,
Glass, Brass, Lamp Parts,
Shades (New & Used)

Specialties: Lamps
  Directions: Off Hwy I-85 &
  I-40 on old Hwy 70

TYLER-SMITH ANTIQUES
  501 Simpson St   27401
  919 274-6498   Est: 1970
  Proprietor: James E &
  Ridley Tyler Smith
  Hours: Mon-Sat 10-5, By
  Appointment
Types & Periods: 18th &
19th Centuries English &
American Furniture &
Accessories, Orientalia
Specialties: Porcelain,
Pottery, Prints
Appraisal Service Available
  Directions: Btwn Elm &
  Eugene Sts on the Corner
  of Smith & Simpson Sts

Greenville

JOHNSEN'S ANTIQUES
  1318-20 Evans St   27834
  919 758-4839   Est: 1963
  Proprietor: Elliott R
  Johnsen
  Hours: Daily
Types & Periods: 18th &
19th Centuries Furniture,
Glass, China, Silver, Jewelry
Specialties: Lamps & Lamp
Repair
  Directions: Corner of
  Evans & 14th

Grover

**OVERCASH & SON
ANTIQUES**
  Rte 1   28073
  704 739-3568   Est: 1968
  Proprietor: G W Overcash
  Sr
  Hours: Daily 10-6, Sun
  12-6
Types & Periods: Victorian,
Walnut, Primitives,
Chippendale, American Oak,
Clocks, Stained Glass
Windows
Specialties: Restoration
Appraisal Service Available
  Directions: Hwy 74 7½
  Miles W of Kings Mtn

Hendersonville

BROWNINGS
1st & Main   28739
704 693-6776   Est: 1975
Proprietor: Albert S
Browning III
Hours: Tues-Sat 10-6
Types & Periods: English &
American Period Pieces,
Oriental Art
Directions: Across from
the County Courthouse

**THE CENTURY SHOP OF
HERITAGE SQUARE**
121 Barnwell St   28739
704 692-4160   Est: 1973
Proprietor: Mrs Carol
Eicholtz
Hours: Mon-Sat
Types & Periods: General
Line, 18th & 19th Centuries
Furniture, Brass, Rugs,
Glass, China
Directions: Downtown 1
block off Main St at
Corner of Church &
Barnwell Sts

KENSINSER GALLERY
121 Barnwell St   28739
704 693-5383   Est: 1976
Proprietor: Jeannot
Kensinger
Hours: Mon-Sat
Types & Periods: Art Glass,
Paintings, 17th & 18th
Centuries Prints
Specialties: Restoration (25
Years Experience),
Preservation of Paintings
Appraisal Service Available
Directions: Off Main St,
Downtown

LEE'S ANTIQUES
346 7th Ave E   28739
704 693-1957   Est: 1972
Proprietor: Thomas R Lee
Hours: Mon-Sat 10-5
Types & Periods: Furniture,
Primitives, Copper, Brass,
Glassware
Specialties: Cast Iron Bells
Directions: Off I-26 to
Second Red Light, Turn
Right on 7th Ave 1/2
block on Right

RHODY'S ANTIQUES
Spartanburg Hwy   28739
704 693-6548   Est: 1950
Proprietor: C P Rhody

Hours: By Appointment,
By Chance
Types & Periods: General
Line
Specialties: Clocks
Appraisal Service Available
Directions: Rte 176 1½
Miles S of Town

**YE OLDE TREASURE
SHOPPE**
116 N Main St   28739
704 692-5154   Est: 1976
Proprietor: G Bailey & A
Cairnes
Hours: Mon-Sat
Types & Periods: Furniture,
Glassware, Collectibles
Directions: Directly Across
St from Henderson County
Courthouse, Downtown

Highlands

ANTIQUES BY LEE
"On the Hill"   28741
704 526-2330   Est: 1963
Proprietor: Lee Todd
Hours: Daily 10-5, Closed
Sun, Open May 1 to
Nov 15
Types & Periods: Jewelry,
China, Glass, Primitives,
Bric-A-Brac, Paintings
Directions: US Hwy 64 &
NC 28, Western NC

SCUDDER'S GALLERY
Main St   28741
704 526-5355   Est: 1976
Proprietor: F A Scudder
Hours: Daily 10-2, 7-10,
Closed Sun
Types & Periods: 18th
Century French, English,
American
Specialties: Jewelry
Appraisal Service Available
Directions: Downtown

Hillsborough

CLINTON LINDLEY LTD
220 S Churton St   27278
919 732-4300
Proprietor: Clinton Lindley
Hours: Daily 10-5, Closed
Mon
Types & Periods: Art,
American Primitives, Indian
& Pre-Columbian

Lattimore

BELL'S ANTIQUES
Box 98   28089
704 434-2254   Est: 1940
Proprietor: Steve Bell
Hours: Mon-Fri 8-5
Types & Periods: American
& European, Clocks, Glass,
Furniture
Directions: 7 Miles W of
Shelby, 2 Miles N of Hwy
74 btwn Charlotte &
Asheville

Lenoir

RUSSELL'S ANTIQUES
North Blvd & Hwy 321
                     28645
704 754-4932   Est: 1942
Proprietor: Mrs J C
Russell
Hours: Daily
Types & Periods: Pattern &
Cut Glass, Furniture, Clocks,
Lamps, Primitives

Lexington

**BAILEY'S ANTIQUES &
THINGS**
110 W Fifth Ave   27292
704 731-6019   Est: 1968
Proprietor: Ethel Bailey
Hours: Daily, Weekends
Types & Periods: Furniture,
China, Crystal
Appraisal Service Available
Directions: Hwy 52, 2
Miles N of Lexington

LINK'S ANTIQUE SHOP
2204 S Main St   27292
704 249-9590   Est: 1941
Proprietor: James Link
Hours: Daily 8-5
Types & Periods: Early
American, Corner
Cupboards, Chests, Dry
Sinks, Victorian & Oak
Furniture
Specialties: Furniture

Lumberton

ANTIQUES LTD
215 N Elm   28358
919 738-4607   Est: 1971
Proprietor: I P Sealey Jr
Hours: Daily
Types & Periods: General
Line
Directions: In Downtown
Plaza

PEMBEE ANTIQUES
Old Hwy 74 E   28358
919 738-7520   Est: 1974
Proprietor: Davis B Pillet
Hours: Tues-Sat 11-5:30
Types & Periods: General
Line, New England
Collectibles, Country,
Primitives, Victorian
Specialties: Jewelry,
Embroidery & Needlework
(Quilts)
Directions: Across Tracks
on Left Next to the Big
Blue Tower in Back of the
Pembee Manufacturing
Bldg, Entrance on Far
Side

Mocksville

FARMSTEAD ANTIQUES
Rte 2, Box 132A   27028
919 998-3139   Est: 1968
Proprietor: Mrs George C
Haire
Hours: Tues-Sat 10-5
Types & Periods: 18th &
19th Centuries Furniture,
Oriental Rugs, Accessories,
Primitives
Directions: I-40 at
Farmington Exit, Btwn
Winston-Salem &
Mocksville

Nashville

**JEAN SLEDGE'S COUNTRY
ANTIQUES**
Rte 3, Box 89   27856
919 459-2594   Est: 1974
Proprietor: Jean J Sledge
Hours: Weekends, By
Appointment
Types & Periods: Primitives,
Furniture

Directions: S on Alston St,
Proceed out of Town to
Elm Grove Bicentennial
Sign, Left for 1.3 Miles,
On Right

New Bern

ANTIQUE VILLAGE
Rte 6, Box 190   28560
919 633-300l   Est: 1973
Proprietor: Kenneth &
Louise Slade
Hours: Daily, Weekends
10-5, Closed Sun
Types & Periods: Furniture,
Glass, Frames, Clocks,
Tools, Primitives, Silver,
Pewter, Oriental, Lamps,
Tole
Appraisal Service Available
Directions: 3 Miles N of
New Bern, In Front of
Neuse River Campground

North Wilkesboro

BARE-NILLER ANTIQUES
307 10th St   28659
919 838-8821   Est: 1930
Proprietor: Mr & Mrs Trent
Crawford
Hours: Daily
Types & Periods: 18th
Century Victorian & English
Furniture
Appraisal Service Available
Directions: In the Heart of
Downtown

Old Fort

THE EMPORIUM
Old Fort Exit I-40   28762
704 668-4905   Est: 1977
Proprietor: Jane N
Thomason
Hours: Daily
Types & Periods: Antiques &
Collectibles
Specialties: Hand-Painted
Nippon, China Brass
Directions: At the Old Fort
Exit off I-40

Pinehurst

GARNIER ANTIQUES INC
Box 30   28374
919 295-6560   Est: 1950
Proprietor: Louise Garnier
Hours: Daily 10-12, 2-4:30
Types & Periods: General
Line, Silver
Specialties: China, Jewelry,
Paintings
Directions: Midland Rd
btwn Southern Pines &
Pinehurst

Raleigh

ADAMS ANTIQUES
2 Dixie Trail   27607
919 833-6322   Est: 1960
Proprietor: Dewey C
Adams
Hours: Daily, Closed Sun,
Nites by Appointment
Types & Periods: Early
American & Victorian
Furniture, Cut Glass, Hand
Painted China, Frames,
Bric-A-Brac
Specialties: Glass (Cut)
Appraisal Service Available
Directions: 2 blocks from
NC State Univ W Campus

**AMERICAN
INTERNATIONAL
FURNITURE & ANTIQUES**
2315 Essex Circle   27608
919 787-6625   Est: 1970
Proprietor: Tully & Phillip
Fletcher
Hours: Daily, Weekends
10-7, Closed Sun, Fri 'til 9
Types & Periods: Victorian
Walnut Furniture, Late
1800's Oak
Specialties: Furniture
(English Oak)
Directions: Glenwood
Village Shopping Ctr

CRAIG & TARLTON INC
122 Glenwood Ave   27603
919 828-2559   Est: 1964
Proprietor: J H Craig & W
S Tarlton
Hours: Daily 10-5, Closed
Sun, Closed Sat During
Summer
Types & Periods: Furniture,
Paintings
Appraisal Service Available

DB'S COUNTRY STORE INC
5815 Hillsborough St
27606
919 851-1697   Est: 1970
Proprietor: Dorothy H Broadwell
Hours: Daily, Weekends
Types & Periods: Country Items, Primitives, Early 19th Century American
Specialties: Country Items
Appraisal Service Available
Directions: Beyond NC State Fairgrounds on Cary-Raleigh Hwy

ARTHUR H DANIELSON ANTIQUES LTD
1101 Wake Forest Rd
27604
919 828-7739   Est: 1972
Proprietor: Arthur H Danielson & Leonida Fantini
Hours: Daily 12-6, By Appointment
Types & Periods: 17th, 18th & Early 19th Century Furniture, Fine Art & Accessories, Carpets, English, American, Italian, Oriental
Specialties: English & Oriental Ceramics of 18th & 19th Centuries, 18th Century Toby Jugs
Appraisal Service Available
Directions: Next to Downtown Historic Park, Pres Andrew Johnson Birthplace

ELLINGTON'S ANTIQUES
3050 Medlin Dr   27607
919 781-2383   Est: 1965
Proprietor: Mrs Jessie E Ellington
Hours: Mon-Thurs & Sat 10-5
Types & Periods: 18th & 19th Centuries Furniture & Accessories, American Primitives
Appraisal Service Available

SARA GREENE ART & ANTIQUES
530 N Person St   27608
919 833-3428   Est: 1959
Proprietor: Corporation
Hours: Daily 1-5, By Appointment, By Chance

Types & Periods: 18th & 19th Centuries American & English Furniture & Accessories
Specialties: Oriental
Appraisal Service Available
Directions: Historic Oakwood Section Near Governor's Mansion

MRS R B STOKES
927 S Saunders St   27603
919 833-2758   Est: 1969
Proprietor: Mr Stokes
Hours: Daily
Types & Periods: General Line
Directions: Near 401 S

WILLIAM-KEITH ANTIQUES
2511 Fairview Rd   27608
919 834-5708
Proprietor: Wm F McLawhorn
Hours: Daily 10-5, Sat 11-2
Types & Periods: 18th & Early 19th Centuries American & English Furniture
Specialties: Oriental (Rugs)
Directions: On Fairview Rd btwn Oberlin Rd & St Mary's St

Reidsville

L & S ANTIQUES
Hwy 29   27320
919 342-1800   Est: 1963
Proprietor: Clarence & Mary Suddreth
Hours: Mon-Sat 10-5:30
Types & Periods: 18th Century Furniture, Art Glass
Specialties: Furniture (French), China
Appraisal Service Available
Directions: 4 Miles S of Reidsville on Hwy 29

Roanoke Rapids

THE COLONIAL HOUSE
130 W 9th St   27870
919 537-1355   Est: 1971
Proprietor: Mrs Anne Hearth-Gregory
Hours: Daily, Weekends, 10:30-4, Closed Sun & Wed

Types & Periods: Early American, 18th & 19th Centuries English
Specialties: Lamps
Appraisal Service Available
Directions: 5 Miles off I-95 at Roanoke Rapids Exit

ESTELLE'S
53 Holiday Dr   27870
919 537-1110   Est: 1976
Proprietor: Estelle & Ira Dickens
Hours: Mon-Sat
Types & Periods: Victorian, Oak Furniture, Pitcher & Bowls, Glass, Clocks, Bric-A-Brac
Specialties: Pictures
Directions: Exit 173 I-95 Access Rd, Next to Holiday Inn

Rocky Mount

P A MOORE'S ANTIQUE SHOP
2800 Sunset Ave   27801
919 443-1298   Est: 1921
Proprietor: P A Moore
Hours: Mon-Fri, Closed Sun
Types & Periods: English & American Furniture, Handmade Beds
Appraisal Service Available
Directions: 5 Minutes from Hwy 64 & I-95 Interchange

THAT PLACE
107 Highland Ave   27801
919 446-1278   Est: 1972
Proprietor: Jerry & Elizabeth Jerome
Hours: Daily 9-6, Closed Sun & Mon
Types & Periods: General Line, Primitives, Collectibles
Specialties: Primitives
Appraisal Service Available
Directions: On Business 301

Roxobel

JOHN E TYLER
27401
919 344-5241   Est: 1954
Proprietor: John E Tyler
Hours: By Appointment
Types & Periods: 18th &
19th Centuries English &
American
Specialties: Oriental
(Porcelain)

Salisbury

THE HOUSE OF ANTIQUITY
1428 N Main St   28144
704 636-2647   Est: 1968
Proprietor: Loretta L
Butner
Hours: By Appointment
Types & Periods: American,
Victorian, Primitives, Crystal,
Pottery, China
Specialties: Lids for Teapots
& Sugar Bowls
Directions: I-88 Exit
Spencer

Shelby

MC SWAIN'S ANTIQUE SHOP
Rte 4   28150
704 434-6308
Proprietor: Max D
McSwain
Hours: Mon-Fri 8-5, By
Appointment
Types & Periods: Primitives,
Early American, General
Line
Appraisal Service Available
Directions: 5 Miles W of
Shelby on Hwy 74

Statesville

HOUSE OF ANTIQUES & COLLECTABLES
920 Carolina Ave N 28677
Proprietor: Mamie Lenker
Hours: Daily, Weekends
11-6, Fri & Sat 'til 8,
Closed Sun & Mon
Types & Periods: Furniture,
China, Glass, Clocks
Directions: I-40 & Hwy 21
Across from Holiday Inn

Summerfield

CARLSON FARMS ANTIQUES
Pleasant Ridge Rd   27358
919 643-5070   Est: 1973
Proprietor: Anne Carlson,
Holly Lucas, Millie Lucas
Hours: Tues-Sat 10-4
Types & Periods: "Carefully
Selected Furniture &
Accessories in a variety of
Styles & Periods"
Specialties: Direct Imports of
British Antiques
Directions: From US 220
take Hamburg Mill Rd to
Pleasant Ridge Rd, Right
for 1 Mile, Restored Log
Cabin on Right

Sylva

SYLVA ANTIQUES
Box 636   28779
704 586-4115
Proprietor: F L Rhoads
Hours: By Appointment
Types & Periods: Art Glass,
General Line

Tarboro

MIRIAM'S ORIENTAL RUGS
905 Main St   27886
919 823-4964   Est: 1970
Proprietor: Miriam Owen
Hours: By Appointment
Types & Periods: Oriental
Rugs
Appraisal Service Available
Directions: 16 Miles E of
I-95 at Rocky Mount, 64 E
is Main St

Wallace

RIVENBARK'S DISCOUNT & ANTIQUES
Rte 3   28466
919 285-3504   Est: 1972
Proprietor: Eugene
Rivenback
Hours: Daily
Types & Periods: Oak &
Walnut Furniture
Directions: 4½ Miles NE of
Wallace on 11, Right 1/2
Mile at Sign

Warrenton

SCOTT'S ANTIQUES
Rte 1, Box 165   27589
919 257-3980   Est: 1945
Proprietor: David J Scott
Hours: Mon-Sat 8-5:30,
Sun 2:30-5:30
Types & Periods: General
Line, Queen Anne,
Sheraton, Empire, Victorian,
Glass, China, Oriental
Specialties: Picture Frames
Appraisal Service Available
Directions: Btwn Norling &
Warrenton on State Rds
158 & 401

Waxhaw

BYRUM'S ANTIQUES
Main St   28173
704 843-2154   Est: 1955
Proprietor: Sara Lynn
Byrum
Hours: Daily, By
Appointment
Types & Periods: General
Line, Victorian, Primitives,
Pictures, Glassware
Appraisal Service Available
Directions: From Charlotte
Hwy 16, From Monroe
Hwy 75, From Lancaster
Hwy 521 & 75

DING A LING ANTIQUES
Main St   28173
704 843-2181   Est: 1975
Proprietor: Robert Worrall
Hours: Daily 10-5
Types & Periods: Victorian &
Colonial Tables & Chairs,
Oak Pieces, Wicker
Directions: Rte 16 S from
Charlotte, Left on Main

TRADER'S PATH ANTIQUES
28173
704 843-2628   Est: 1976
Proprietor: Elinor
McLaughlin & Euladia
Tyson
Hours: By Appointment,
Thurs, Fri & Sat 10-5
Types & Periods: Primitives,
Country, Early American,
Victorian
Specialties: "Sugar Hill
Reproductions"

Directions: Off Hwy 75, 11
Miles from Monroe, 22
Miles from Charlotte

Wilmington

**VIRGINIA N JENNEWEIN,
ANTIQUES**
318 S Front St   28401
919 763-3703   Est: 1950
Proprietor: Virginia N
Jennewein
Hours: Mon-Sat 9-12, 1-5
Sun
Types & Periods: Glass,
China, Furniture
Appraisal Service Available
Directions: Downtown,
Overlooking the Cape Fear
River

Wilson

THE ANTIQUE BARN
Forest Hills Rd   27893
919 237-6778   Est: 1966
Proprietor: Wayne E
Sidelinger
Hours: Daily 9-5:30, Sun
1-6
Types & Periods: Period,
Victorian, Oak, Brass Beds
Directions: Forest Hills Rd
& Downing St, 1 Mile off
Hwy 301

**BATTS LAMP & SHADE CO
INC**
US 301 S   27893
919 243-5931
Hours: Daily 9-5, Sat 10-5,
Closed Sun
Types & Periods: Lamps,
Lighting Fixtures, General
Line
Directions: US 301 S &
I-95

**NORWOOD BARNES
ANTIQUES**
507 Raleigh Rd   27893
919 291-5429
Hours: Daily, Weekends
10-5, Closed Sun, By
Appointment
Types & Periods: 18th &
19th Centuries American &
English Furniture &
Accessories, Oriental
Porcelain, Canton, Pewter,
Brass

BOONE'S ANTIQUES INC
Hwy 301 S, P O Box 3796
        27893
Proprietor: Edgar J Boone
Hours: Mon-Sat
Types & Periods: American
& English Furniture,
Wholesale & Retail,
Porcelain, Oriental Rugs,
Reproductions
Specialties: American &
English Period Furniture
Appraisal Service Available

**COLONIAL HOUSE OF
ANTIQUES**
108 S Jackson   27893
919 291-2543   Est: 1969
Proprietor: Edward E
Fulford
Hours: Daily 8-6, Closed
Sun, By Appointment
Anytime
Specialties: Furniture,
Corner Cupboards,
American Chests
Appraisal Service Available
Directions: 2 Miles off
Hwy 301

**GRANNY'S ANTIQUES &
REPRODUCTIONS**
1601 S Goldsboro St
        27893
919 291-2373
Proprietor: Blanche &
Rainey Wilkerson & Lucille
& Harry Wilkerson
Hours: Mon-Thurs 2-5, Sat
10-5, By Appointment
Types & Periods: English &
American Furniture, Brass,
Pewter, Tinware, Handmade
Pine Shelves, Pipe Boxes,
Candle Boxes, Benches

**RACKLEY-BARNES
ANTIQUES INC**
100 W Vance St   27893
919 237-0408   Est: 1946
Proprietor: Lucinda
Rackley & Norwood & Gail
Barnes
Hours: Daily 10-5
Types & Periods: Queen
Anne, Chippendale, Early
American, Pine, Maple &
Cherry, Oriental Porcelains,
Rose Medallion & Canton,
Brass, Pewter, China & Cut
Glass
Appraisal Service Available
Directions: 2 blocks off
Nash St (Main St Uptown)

Wingate

**TREASURES'-TRASH
ANTIQUES & GIFTS**
Hwy 74 E   28174
704 233-4872   Est: 1969
Proprietor: Lessie Trull
Hours: Daily, By
Appointment
Types & Periods: Glass,
China, Furniture
Specialties: Furniture, Glass
Directions: 1 Mile from
Wingate Stop Light, Left
side of Rd

Winston-Salem

**JAY ANDERSON ANTIQUES
INC**
120 Reynolds Village
        27106
919 724-3041   Est: 1971
Proprietor: June S Rhea &
Jay Anderson
Hours: Daily, By
Appointment
Types & Periods: 18th &
19th Centuries English,
American, Oriental Furniture
& Accessories
Directions: On Grounds of
the R J Reynolds Estate

BOOK SHOP
858 W 4th St   27101
        Est: 1970
Proprietor: J W Tatum
Hours: Daily
Specialties: Books
Appraisal Service Available
Directions: Basement

DAN'S ANTIQUE SHOP
626 S Main St   27108
919 722-6413   Est: 1934
Proprietor: Mrs A L Googe
Sr
Hours: Daily 10-4, Closed
Sun
Types & Periods: Primitives,
Early American, 18th
Century
Directions: Salem Square,
Old Salem

**SHEPHERD-LAMBETH INC;
HARRY'S ATTIC**
451 W End Blvd   27101
919 723-5343   Est: 1956
Proprietor: H L Lambeth
Jr

SHEPHERD-LAMBETH INC; HARRY'S ATTIC   Cont'd

Hours: Daily, Weekends 10-5, Sat 10-4, By Appointment
Types & Periods: Duncan Phyfe, Primitives, Queen Anne, Porcelain, China, Vases, Lamps, Oil Paintings, Books
Appraisal Service Available
Directions: Off I-40 at Broad St Exit

HOMESTEAD ANTIQUES

P O Box 1254   27102
919 765-6813   Est: 1967
Proprietor: Don & Yvonne Corbett
Hours: By Appointment
Types & Periods: Early Country Furniture & Accessories
Specialties: Early Lighting Devices
Appraisal Service Available
Directions: Btwn I-40 & US Hwy 21 Off Jonestown Rd

SUMMIT ANTIQUES

848 W 5th St   27101
919 723-6028   Est: 1972
Proprietor: Joseph R Hutchins
Hours: Mon-Sat 10-5, By Appointment
Types & Periods: Victorian Furniture, Glassware, Lamps, Collectibles
Specialties: Furniture
Appraisal Service Available
Directions: Downtown Winston-Salem, 3 blocks W of Hyatt House & Convention Center

TRASH & TREASURES ANTIQUES

914 S Stratford Rd 27103
919 768-3865   Est: 1968
Proprietor: Bob Costner Family
Hours: Tues-Sat 10-6, By Appointment
Types & Periods: General Line, Furniture, Glassware, Brass, Copper

Corner Cabinet, Middle Victorian. More than six feet tall.

STATE OF NORTH DAKOTA

Belfield

**FORT HOUSTON MUSEUM
& ANTIQUES**
58622
.701 575-4329
Hours: Daily 7-9
Types & Periods: General
Line
Directions: Downtown

Bismark

HERITAGE ANTIQUES
200 N 3rd St   58501
701 258-4349   Est: 1974
Proprietor: Robert &
Martin Thompson
Hours: Mon-Sat, 10-5
Types & Periods: Oak
Furniture, Brass & Nickel
Cash Registers, Depression
Glass, Early Farm Tools
Appraisal Service Available
Directions: Downtown,
Corner of 3rd St &
Broadway, in Basement

**WILMA'S ANTIQUES &
COLLECTIBLES**
Rte 2   58501
701 223-6592
Proprietor: Wilma Giardini
Hours: By Appointment
Types & Periods: Antiques &
Collectibles
Directions: 7 Miles S of
Bismarck, Call for
directions

Bottineau

THE KAMRUD ANTIQUES
Metigoshe Rd   58318
701 263-4653
Proprietor: Irvin Estella &
Earl Kamrud
Hours: Daily
Types & Periods: General
Line
Directions: 7½ Miles N of
Bottineau

Bowbells

MAC'S PLACE ANTIQUES
5th & Washington   58721
701 377-2910
Proprietor: Russ & Mary
McIntyre
Hours: By Appointment,
By Chance
Types & Periods: Furniture,
Glass, General Line
Specialties: Furniture, Glass

Carbury

**ANTIQUES BY FRANCIS
OLSON**
58724
Proprietor: Francis Olson
Types & Periods: Furniture,
General Line
Directions: 1 Mile W, 5
Miles N of Bottineau

Carrington

DIAMOND H ANTIQUES
58421
701 652-3219
Types & Periods: Furniture,
Glass, Silver, China
Directions: 2 Miles N on
281 & 3 Miles E of
Carrington

Devils Lake

**SIX R'S ANTIQUES &
CURIOS**
1113 N 4th Ave   58301
701 662-4530
Proprietor: R R Reynen &
Son
Hours: Daily
Types & Periods: General
Line

Dickinson

**ADE TORGERSONS'
ANTIQUES**
478 S Main   58601
701 225-3582
Proprietor: Ade Torgerson
Hours: By Appointment
Types & Periods: General
Line
Directions: Hwy 22 S

Fargo

GRANDPA'S GRANARY
Rte 1, Box 178   58103
701 232-6521   Est: 1969
Proprietor: Joyce Cossett
Hours: Mon-Sat,
Types & Periods: Depression
Glass, General Line,
Collectibles
Specialties: Depression
Glass
Appraisal Service Available
Directions: 6 Miles S of
Fargo on Old Hwy 81

Fessenden

NEUMANN SHOP
58438
701 547-3755
Proprietor: Judy Neumann
Hours: Daily
Types & Periods: General
Line

Flasher

**CHANTAPETA VALLEY
RANCH**
58535
701 597-3575
Proprietor: Mr & Mrs John
W Allen
Hours: Daily
Types & Periods: General
Line

Jamestown

A TO B ANTIQUES
323 1st Ave N   58401
701 252-3531
Hours: Daily
Types & Periods: General
Line
Specialties: Stripping &
Refinishing Furniture

Kenmare

JIM'S ANTIQUES
111 NE 2nd St   58746
701 385-4351   Est: 1955
Proprietor: Jim & Sylvia
Hillestad
Hours: Daily, Weekends,
By Appointment
Types & Periods: Furniture,
Stoves, Primitives
   Directions: 2 blocks E of
   Dutch Mill

La Moure

S & S ANTIQUES
                     58458
701 883-6211
Proprietor: Cathy & Claire
Scheibe
Types & Periods: General
Line, Collectibles
Specialties: Glass (Carnival),
Collectors Plates, Indian
Artifacts
Appraisal Service Available

Mandan

ANTIQUE BOTTLE SHOP
102 9th Ave NW   58554
701 663-6317
Proprietor: Bob & Jan
Barr
Hours: Daily
Types & Periods: Bottles

Minot

DECOUTEAU ANTIQUES
823 4th Ave SE   58701
701 839-6595   Est: 1973
Proprietor: Richard W
Timboe

Hours: Daily
Types & Periods: Stained
Glass, Oak Furniture,
Trunks, Turn-of-theCentury
Appraisal Service Available
   Directions: Near Roosevelt
   Park on Business Hwy 2
   thru City

KNOT HOLE ANTIQUES
807 42nd St SE   58701
701 838-5725   Est: 1973
Proprietor: Norm Hoiland
Hours: Daily, By
Appointment, By Chance
Types & Periods: Oak
Furniture, Primitives, Heaters
& Cook Stoves
   Directions: 2 Miles E of
   State Fairgrounds on Hwy
   2 East

Napoleon

YE OLDE SHOPPE
                     58561
701 754-2243
Proprietor: Helen & Nudge
Mueller
Hours: By Appointment,
By Chance
Types & Periods: General
Line

Valley City

DON MAR ANTIQUES
424 8th St NW   58072
701 845-2591
Types & Periods: General
Line, Collectibles, Furniture
Specialties: Furniture
Stripping

GENO'S ANTIQUES
                     58072
701 845-1560
Proprietor: Gene Loendorf
Hours: Daily
Types & Periods: General
Line
   Directions: In Char Mac
   Motor Hotel

MARTY'S SECONDHAND
509 Second St NW   58072
701 845-4690
Hours: Daily
Types & Periods: General
Line, Collectibles

Wahpeton

WYONA'S ANTIQUES
11th St & Hwy 81   58075
701 642-6098
Types & Periods: Curios,
General Line, Collectibles

Watford City

MARY BET ANTIQUES &
THRIFT SHOP
                     58854
701 842-2347
Proprietor: Mary Bet
Hours: Mon-Sat,
11:30-6:30
Types & Periods: General
Line, Collectibles
Appraisal Service Available

Westhope

HUBER'S ANTIQUES
                     58793
701 268-4465
Proprietor: Jerry Huber
Types & Periods: General
Line, Autos, Curios
   Directions: 6 Miles S & 6
   Miles W & I Mile S of
   Westhope on 83 or 35
   Miles N & 7 Miles E & 3
   Miles N of Minot on
   Hwy 83

Williston

ALADDIN'S TREASURES
12½ Second St W   58801
701 572-3489
Proprietor: Jeanne Lee
Dodd
Hours: Mon-Sat, 2-5:30
Types & Periods: General
Line

THE ORIGINAL FLEA
MARKET
PO Box 1152   58801
Hours: 1st Sun Each
Month 12-5, May thru Sept
Types & Periods: General
Line
   Directions: "In the Heart
   of Beautiful Downtown
   Williston at Red Owl"

THE PACK RATS

58801

701 572-7523
Proprietor: Grant Archer &
Larry Lynne
Hours: After 5 By
Appointment
Types & Periods: Primitives,
Collectibles

A lady's chair, Late
Victorian.

(From page 442A).

Another style of furniture, Bentwood, came to be in great favor during the 1880's and 1890's. It was produced in large quantities in this country. It had existed for nearly forty years but only then became truly popular. An Austrian, Thonet, developed a process for steam warping wood about 1840. Upon this process was formed a company to manufacture his designs. His staple product came to be the Vienna Cafe Chair which became ubiquitous. It was Thonet's process which provided Belter with the idea of bending his laminations. (See page 545).

In 1876 this nation celebrated its first Centennial. It caused a reawakening of interest in America's Colonial past. Furniture manufacturers returned to the styles of the 1700's and began reproducing the Queen Anne, Chippendale, Hepplewhite, Sheraton and other periods. Today, this phenomenon is identified by the names "Centennial Period" or "Of the Second Period". In 1884, the publication "Cabinet Making and Upholstery" reported that the manufacture of antiques had become a modern industry. Excellent cabinet woods were then available as well as many skilled men to do the intricate carving and joining. These pieces now legitimately qualify as antiques in their own right. (Continued, page 576).

STATE OF OHIO

Akron

AKRON CLUSTER
Directions: No real
Cluster; Some shops on W
Market (400-1000 blocks)
& on Cleveland NW
(9000-13000 blocks)

ANNELLE'S CURIOSITY SHOPPE
843 N Cleve-Mass Rd
44313
216 666-5151   Est: 1973
Proprietor: Ann J Lydic
Hours: Tues-Sat, 11-4:30
Types & Periods: General
Line
Appraisal Service Available

ATTIC ANTIQUES
443 W Market   44303
216 762-8281   Est: 1960
Proprietor: Kay Warren
Hours: Mon-Sat, 10:30-4
Types & Periods: General
Line & Collectibles
Directions: 4 blocks from
Main & Market going W

GOLDEN HORSE ANTIQUES
449 W Market St   44303
216 762-0381   Est: 1972
Proprietor: Barbara Austin
Hours: Mon-Sun
Types & Periods: Primitives
& Victorian Furniture (thru
1920's)
Directions: On a Main
Artery running E & W

MAD MONEY
1650 W Market St   44313
216 836-9442   Est: 1964
Proprietor: Ron Scnieger
Hours: Mon-Sat
Types & Periods: Coins,
Stamps & Currier & Ives
Specialties: Pre 1920
Papercana
Appraisal Service Available
Directions: Corner of W
Market Exchange &
Hawkins

JOAN MARIE ANTIQUES
121 Rhodes Ave   44302
216 376-1500   Est: 1969

Proprietor: Joan Marie
Chevrier
Hours: Mon-Sat, 10-4
Types & Periods: China,
Glass, Primitives, Oriental
Rugs, Sterling, Lamps,
Quilts, Furniture, Clocks &
Statues
Appraisal Service Available
Directions: 1 block off W
Market St

TRADING POST ANTIQUES
1353 Canton Rd   44312
216 733-1192   Est: 1962
Proprietor: D N Brown
Hours: Mon-Sat; Sun &
Evenings by appt
Types & Periods: General
Line, Clocks, Glassware,
China, Primitives & Furniture
Specialties: American &
European Clocks
Directions: Canton Rd is
old Rte 8; S of Rte 224 &
91

Amlin

RED BARN ANTIQUES
6077 Avery Rd   43002
614 889-2667   Est: 1971
Proprietor: Robert Anglin
Hours: Tues-Sat, 10-5
Types & Periods: Cherry,
Oak, Pine & Walnut
Furniture
Specialties: Furniture
(Chairs)
Directions: 2 miles W of
Dublin on Rte 161, 1/2
mile S

Archbold

WANDA'S ANTIQUES
RR 1   43502
419 267-3809   Est: 1969
Proprietor: Wanda Garmyn
Hours: Mon-Sun; By appt
Types & Periods: Dishes,
Furniture & Primitives
Appraisal Service Available
Directions: 3½ miles S of
Town, then W 1/2 mile

Ashland

JOHNNY CAKE ANTIQUE HOUSE
802 E Main   44805
Est: 1962
Proprietor: Betty Deever
Hours: Mon-Sun by
chance
Types & Periods: Toys,
Books, Postcards, Indian
Artifacts, Primitives, Pottery
Jewelry, Pattern Glass &
Political Items
Appraisal Service Available
Directions: Beside Red
Barn Restaurant, edge of
Town, Rte 250

Ashtabula

YESTERYEAR ANTIQUES
4226 Main Ave   44004
216 993-3866   Est: 1971
Proprietor: Hazel Snitcher
Hours: Mon-Sun, 1-5; Also
by appt
Types & Periods: General
Line
Specialties: Lamps &
Collectibles
Appraisal Service Available
Directions: Downtown; 2
blocks from Rte 20, 1 mile
from Rte 11, turn W

Athens

SIGNS OF THE TIMES
143 N Lancaster St 45701
614 592-2795   Est: 1973
Proprietor: Judith E Jones
Hours: Thurs-Sun, 12-5;
Also by appt
Types & Periods: Antique
Advertising Items, Country
Store Items, Decorator
Items, Furniture, Glassware,
Iron, Copper, Brass, Tools,
Tinware, Watches
Specialties: Advertising,
Country Store Items &
Furniture Restoration
Appraisal Service Available
Directions: Business Rte
33 Bypass, Columbus Rd
exit, 2 miles

Barberton

DEPENDABLE ANTIQUES
947 Wooster Rd W   44203
216 825-4806   Est: 1966
Proprietor: Felix Tanski, Jr
Hours: Tues-Sat, 9-5
Types & Periods: General
Line
Directions: Exit off I-76 &
I-80, S to Barberton exit,
off Hwy 21 & I-77, off I-70
N to Barberton

Bedford

VICARS ANTIQUES
772 Broadway   44146
216 232-3685   Est: 1954
Proprietor: Clayton &
Martha Vicars
Hours: Mon-Sun, 1-5; Also
by appt
Types & Periods: General
Line
Appraisal Service Available
Directions: Rte 14, 2nd
house from square

Bolivar

ANTIQUE EMPORIUM
Center Ave   44622
216 874-2553   Est: 1973
Proprietor: Tom & Jeanne
Graef
Hours: Tues-Sun, 12:30-5
Types & Periods: Victorian
Furniture, Primitives, Clocks,
China, Glass, Pottery &
Complete Line
Directions: Exit 83, I-77, S
of Canton

Bucyrus

V & R ANTIQUES
2254 SR 19   44820
419 562-4682   Est: 1970
Proprietor: Raymond R
Roberts
Hours: Mon-Fri, 3:15-9;
Sat 9-9; Sun by appt
Types & Periods: General
Line
Specialties: Clock Repair

**WALNUT HOUSE
ANTIQUES**
3342 Parcher Rd   44820
419 562-3369   Est: 1967
Proprietor: Jerry & Karen
Volkmer
Hours: By chance
Types & Periods: Victorian
Colored Pattern Glass,
Victorian & Country Walnut
Commodes, Lamps, Tables
& Desks
Specialties: American
Custard Glass
Appraisal Service Available
Directions: 1st cross rd E
of Bucyrus on 30 N,
turn N

Cambridge

**BLACK ROOSTER
ANTIQUES**
1018 Clark St   43725
614 432-3202   Est: 1972
Proprietor: Mrs Mickey
Sipe
Hours: Mon-Sun by
chance or appt
Types & Periods: General
Line, China, Glass,
Primitives & Wicker
Furniture
Specialties: Cambridge
Glass
Appraisal Service Available
Directions: Rte 40
(Wheeling Ave), turn N on
N 11th St which joins
Clark after 2 blocks,
proceed on Clark approx
8 blocks

**HAROLD & JUDY'S
ANTIQUES**
437 N 8th St   43725
614 432-5855
Proprietor: Judy Bennett
Hours: Mon-Sun by appt
Types & Periods: General
Line
Specialties: Cambridge
Glass
Appraisal Service Available
Directions: 4 blocks N of
Courthouse

HERITAGE ANTIQUES
7443 Sarchets Run Rd,
RD 5   43725
614 439-3241   Est: 1973
Proprietor: Roy & Doris
Isaacs

Hours: By appt or chance
(when home)
Types & Periods: China,
Cambridge & Heisey Glass,
Primitives, Furniture, Prints
& Tools
Specialties: Cambridge
Glass
Directions: 8th St N from
court house, 3½ miles to
the RR track

Camden

ANTIQUES AMERICA
RR 2   45311
513 796-3183   Est: 1970
Proprietor: Raiburn
Stanley & Lawrence King
Hours: By appt or chance
Types & Periods: 18th &
19th Century American
Furniture & Accessories,
Pewter & Early Iron
Directions: 10 miles N of
Oxford on 177 in Village
of Fairhaven

DAVIDSON'S ANTIQUES
RR2   45311
513 700-0101   Est: 1968
Proprietor: Bill Davidson
Hours: Sun; Mon-Fri by
chance or appt
Types & Periods: 19th
Century Furniture, Tools,
China, Iron, Tin, Fabrics &
Early American Items
Directions: On State Rd
177 in the village of
Fairhaven, 16 miles SE of
Richmond, 10 miles NW of
Oxford, Ohio

Canfield

DAVIS ANTIQUES
7580 Akron Canfield Rd
                44406
216 533-4977   Est: 1970
Proprietor: Jack & Freida
Davis
Hours: Mon-Sun, 11-5
Types & Periods: Furniture,
Glass, Primitives & General
Line
Directions: 1½ miles W of
Canfield on Rte 224

Canton

CANTON CLUSTER
Shops scattered
throughout city, some on
Cleveland Ave NW
(1000-9000 blocks)

THE BARN ANTIQUES
1310 E Tuscarawas 44707
216 452-0015 Est: 1966
Proprietor: Frances Kerns
Hours: By appt or chance
Types & Periods: General
Line, Oak Furniture,
Glassware & Primitives
Specialties: Lamp Shades &
Paperweights
Directions: 2 miles E of
Rte 77 on Rte 30

CAPESTRAIN ANTIQUES
503 High Ave NW 44703
216 456-4443 Est: 1957
Proprietor: Robert A
Capestrain
Hours: Mon-Sun, 9-5
Types & Periods: Jewelry,
Pocket Watches & Clocks
Directions: Near
downtown

MARIE'S ANTIQUES
807 Raff Rd SW 44710
216 477-3988
Types & Periods: General
Line & Furniture

**MC CULLOUGH'S
ANTIQUES**
624 18th St NW 44703
216 456-5534
Types & Periods: General
Line & Furniture

**JAMES H WELCH & SONS
TRADING CO**
325 McKinley Ave NW
44702
216 453-0800 Est: 1969
Proprietor: James H
Welch
Hours: By appt or chance,
generally afternoons
Types & Periods: Paintings,
Drawings, Bronzes &
Oriental Rugs
Specialties: Oriental Rugs &
American Paintings
Appraisal Service Available

WELDEN'S ANTIQUES
1009 McKinley NW 44707
216 455-5609
Types & Periods: General
Line

Centerville

**LINCOLN STUDIO OF
CENTERVILLE**
27 W Franklin St 45459
513 433-5424 Est: 1974
Proprietor: Bob Griep
Hours: Mon 9-4:30;
Tues-Fri, 9-5:30; Sat 10-1
& by appt; Sun by appt
Types & Periods: Furniture,
Brass & Copper
Specialties: Amity Paint &
Varnish Removers
Directions: Ohio Rte 725
at Rte 48 E of I-75 in
downtown Centerville

Chillicothe

THE BRASS BELL
331 N High St 45601
614 773-1500 Est: 1974
Proprietor: John O Hayes
Hours: Mon-Sun, 9-5
Types & Periods: General
Line
Directions: State Rte
104 N

TYGERT HOUSE ANTIQUES
245 Arch St 45601
614 775-0222 Est: 1967
Proprietor: John & Ivy
Yerian
Hours: Mon-Sun, 9-6
Types & Periods: General
Line, Pottery, China,
Glassware, Lamps, Jugs &
Furniture
Specialties: Oak Furniture
Appraisal Service Available
Directions: 1/2 block off
High St, Rte 104-35

Cincinnati

CINCINNATI CLUSTER
Directions: Montgomery
Rd (500-9000 blocks)

ABBOTTS
1204 Main St 45210
513 621-3000 Est: 1930
Proprietor: Becky Golding
Hours: Mon-Sat
Types & Periods:
Bric-A-Brac, Lamps, Dishes
& Collectibles
Appraisal Service Available
Directions: City Basin;
approx 12 blocks from
heart of city

ANTIQUE WORLD LTD
1752 Seymour 45237
513 631-7600 Est: 1972
Proprietor: Ira A Selevan
Hours: Mon-Sun
Types & Periods: Period
American, Oriental, English
& Continental Furniture,
Decorations, Objects of Art,
Clocks, Watches, &
Reproductions
Specialties: Clocks &
Furniture
Appraisal Service Available
Directions: 1 block E of
I-75 at Exit 9

ARONOFF GALLERIES INC
15 E 8th St 45202
513 241-3230 Est: 1930
Proprietor: Joseph M
Kaplan
Hours: Mon-Fri, 10-4:30;
Sat 10-4; July-Aug: until 1
Types & Periods: General
Line
Appraisal Service Available
Directions: Downtown
across from the Public
Library; 1 minute from I-75
& 1 minute from I-71

THE ATTIC
2727 Erie Ave 45208
513 321-2077 Est: 1971
Proprietor: Kate Mountjoy
& Jeanne Franz
Hours: Mon-Sun by appt
Types & Periods: General
Line
Appraisal Service Available
Directions: Hyde Park
Square, approx 1 mile off
I-71 at Edwards Rd exit

BRIARPATCH
3161 Linwood Ave 45208
513 321-0308 Est: 1974
Proprietor: Frances P
Slater
Hours: Mon-Sun, 10-2

Types & Periods: Decorator
Items, Primitives, Oak &
Kitchen Furniture, Baskets,
Brass & Copper
Directions: On Mt Lookout
Square

**CHRISTOPHER HOUSE
ANTIQUES**
2344 Ashland Ave 45206
513 281-6348 Est: 1970
Proprietor: Robert W
Christopher
Hours: By appt or chance
Types & Periods: Centennial
Furniture, Plate & Sterling
Silver & Oriental Items
Specialties: English &
American Tea Services, Art
Deco & Candelabra
Appraisal Service Available
Directions: In E Walnut
Hills, 2 blocks from
Victory Pkwy & E
McMillan

A B CLOSSON JR CO
401 Race St 45202
513 621-1536 Est: 1866
Proprietor: A B Closson,Jr
Hours: Tues-Sat,
9:30-5:30; Mon 9:30-8
Types & Periods: 18th &
19th Century Furniture,
Silver, China, Oriental Rugs
& Far Eastern African Art
Specialties: Silver, China,
Gifts, Oriental Rugs & Art
Appraisal Service Available
Directions: Corner of 4th
& Race Sts, downtown

THE COTTAGE
8419 Reading Rd 45215
513 761-6082 Est. 1972
Proprietor: C A Bell
Hours: Tues-Sat, 10-6;
Also by appt
Types & Periods: General
Line
Directions: 3 blocks E of
I-75 at Galbraith Rd exit

COUNTRY PEDLAR
3872 Round Bottom Rd
45244
513 561-8874 Est: 1973
Proprietor: Marie Lewis
Hours: Mon-Sun
Types & Periods: Primitives,
Country Furniture, Farm &
Victorian Items

Directions: 1 mile N of
Newtown, off Rte 32
between Mariemont &
Melford

HIDDEN HERITAGE
5663 Delhi Pike 45238
513 451-6337 Est: 1974
Proprietor: Mrs Robert
Hater
Hours: Mon-Fri, 10-5; Sat
10-4
Types & Periods: 18th &
19th Century Furniture,
China, Pewter, Crystal,
Silver, Toys, Childrens
Furniture, Wicker, Gifts &
Floral Shop
Specialties: Wicker Furniture
Appraisal Service Available
Directions: River Rd to
Delhi Pike, right on Delhi
Pike, located on left near
Mt St Joseph College

HOUSE OF YORE
3069 Madison Rd 45209
513 871-0172 Est: 1973
Proprietor: Hal Oiler
Hours: Mon-Fri, 11-7; Sat
11-6; Sun by appt
Types & Periods: Oak
Furniture & Period
Collectibles
Specialties: Caning Rush,
Refinishing & Repair
Directions: I-71 to exit 6,
cross Edwards Rd,
continue straight to
Madison Rd, turn left
Oakley Square

INDIAN MOUND ANTIQUES
5224 Montgomery Rd
45212
513 631-8111 Est: 1973
Proprietor: Peter J
Cholkas
Hours: Mon-Sun, 10-6;
Also by appt
Types & Periods: General
Line & Collectibles
Specialties: Clocks,
Furniture & Glass
Appraisal Service Available
Directions: The heart of
the town

JEANNE'S ANTIQUES
4352 River Rd 45204
513 451-5621 Est: 1961
Proprietor: Howard Poe
Hours: Sat-Sun, by appt
or chance

Types & Periods: General
Line
Appraisal Service Available
Directions: Rte 50 W at
Anderson Ferry, next to
Trolley Tavern Restaurant

**FRANK FARMER LOOMIS
IV ANTIQUES**
1981 Madison Rd 45208
513 871-4112 Est: 1975
Proprietor: Frank Farmer
Loomis IV
Hours: Mon-Sat
Types & Periods: Quality
Furniture from 1800 up
Appraisal Service Available
Directions: O'Bryonville W
of Torrence & Madison
Rds

**MADISON HOUSE
ANTIQUES**
6500 Madison Rd 45227
513 561-9805 Est: 1971
Proprietor: Elinor
Sternberg
Hours: Mon-Sat, 11:30-5;
Also by appt or chance
Types & Periods: Primitives,
Victorian, Empire & General
Line

**MAIN AUCTION GALLERIES
INC**
137 W 4th St 45202
513 621-1280 Est: 1871
Proprietor: Corp
Hours: Auctions every
Tues at 10:30 A.M.
Types & Periods: Rugs,
Paintings, Silver, Jewelry,
Pianos, China, Glassware,
Bric-A-Brac & Objets D'Art
Appraisal Service Available
Directions: Downtown,
take 5th St exit off I-75

MT WASHINGTON
2204 Beechmont Ave
45230
513 231-8358 Est: 1960
Proprietor: Jeannie & Paul
Peters
Hours: Mon-Sat, 10-5:30
Types & Periods: Pressed &
Cut Glass, China, Pottery,
Furniture, Coins, Medals,
Jewelry, Toys & Postcards
Specialties: Military Medals,
Daggers, Swords, Headgear,
Coins & Supplies, New
Lamp Parts & Postcards

Cincinnati   Cont'd

MT WASHINGTON   Cont'd
Appraisal Service Available
Directions: Rte 125,
corner of Beechmont &
Corbly

STAN NELSON ANTIQUES
2740 Atlantic Ave   45209
513 731-2215
Proprietor: Stanley F
Nelson
Hours: By appt
Types & Periods: 18th
Century Porcelain, Glass,
China, Enamels & Silver

PLAIN 'N' FANCY ANTIQUES WEEKEND SHOP
2100 Losantiville Ave
45237
513 631-1558   Est: 1970
Proprietor: Max Palm III
Hours: Sat & Sun, 11-6;
Also by appt
Types & Periods: General
Line, Table Items &
Furniture
Specialties: Gas & Electric
Light Fixutres, Shades,
Stained & Beveled Glass,
Hardware & Fiesta
Appraisal Service Available
Directions: I-75 N to
Seymour to Reading Rd,
Reading Rd N to
Losantiville Ave

PLEASANT RUN ANTIQUE SHOP
1980 W Kemper Rd 45240
513 825-7051   Est: 1960
Proprietor: James W Duwe
Hours: Mon-Sun by
chance
Types & Periods: General
Line, Old Used Furniture &
Collectibles
Appraisal Service Available
Directions: 1 mile N off
Hamilton Ave cross from
275 Interstate

RIDGE ANTIQUES
6102 Montgomery Rd
45213
513 731-2897   Est: 1970
Proprietor: Robert S
Valerius
Hours: Mon-Fri, 10-5; Sat
10-3

Types & Periods: American
Furniture, Collectibles,
Heisey Glass, Clocks,
Jewelry & Rookwood
Directions: Corner of
Ridge & Montgomery Rds,
Ridge Rd N exit off I-71,
about 1 mile N to
Montgomery, turn right

WEE SCOT ANTIQUES
6960 Harrison Pike   45239
513 941-1466   Est: 1971
Proprietor: Mary Parry
Hours: Mon-Sun, by
chance
Types & Periods: General
Line
Specialties: Books
Directions: Close to the
Rybolt Rd exit off I-74

WILMAR ANTIQUES
3318 Erie   45208
513 961-6358   Est: 1966
Proprietor: W J Baude &
M E Oshry
Types & Periods: Furniture,
Paintings, American &
English
Appraisal Service Available
Directions: 1 mile from
Hyde Park

YORK'S OLDE THING
6924 Plainfield Rd   45236
513 891-2232   Est: 1970
Proprietor: Mrs Jewel York
Hours: Tues-Fri, 11-5; Sat
12-4
Types & Periods: Furniture
Specialties: Furniture
Directions: Off
Montgomery Rd NW at US
Rte 22

Circleville

LITTLE TREASURE SHOP
163 W Franklin St   43113
614 474-5995   Est: 1971
Proprietor: Norman A
Osborne
Hours: Mon-Sun, 9-9
Types & Periods: General
Line
Directions: Guest House
Motel, Downtown

Cleveland

CLEVELAND CLUSTER
Directions: Lorain Ave
(3000-12000 blocks);
Cleveland W Side Ave of
Antiques

BERGMAN'S ANTIQUES
12401 Woodland Ave
44120
216 791-6418
Proprietor: W Bergman
Hours: Mon-Sun, 10-5:15
Types & Periods: European
& Oriental

BOBBY-LYNN ANTIQUES
15408 Madison Ave 44107
216 228-8900   Est: 1960
Proprietor: Robert Samide
& John Glynn
Hours: Mon-Sun by appt
Types & Periods: Brass
Beds, Cut Glass, Porcelains,
Objets d'Art, Furniture,
Decorator Items & General
Line
Directions: In suburb W of
Cleveland, 2 blocks S of
business section in
Lakewood

PAPPABELLO ANTIQUES
12119-23 Lorain Ave
44111
216 226-0355
Proprietor: James Pappas
& Robert Ciancibello
Hours: Mon-Sun, 10-5
Types & Periods: Art & Cut
Glass, Wedgwood & Objets
d'Art

Cleveland Heights

JUNE GREENWALD
3096 Mayfield Rd   44118
216 932-5535
Proprietor: June
Greenwald
Hours: Mon-Sat, 10-5; Sun
by appt
Types & Periods: Leaded
Domes, Glass, China &
Furniture

Columbus

COLUMBUS CLUSTER
Directions: Heavy
concentration on High St
(running N-S), 7 E Main St
(50 blocks); other shops &
streets throughout city

A-R-M APPRAISAL
SERVICE
4445 Indianola   43214
614 267-4636   Est: 1960
Proprietor: D G Smith
Hours: Mon-Fri, 9-5; Also
by appt
Types & Periods: General
Line
Specialties: Paintings, Art
Glass, Prints & Furniture,
appraisal
Appraisal Service Available
Directions: Between Cook
Rd & Morse Rd

ANTIQUE GALLERIES
1408 Oakland Park Ave
43224
614 263-3800   Est: 1966
Proprietor: Ellen &
Leonard Finelli
Hours: Sat & Sun by appt
Types & Periods: Furniture,
Glass, China & Autos
Appraisal Service Available
Directions: 1 mile E of
I-71, exit off E N
Broadway

BACK IN TIME
555 City Park Ave   43215
614 221-3529   Est: 1975
Hours: Mon-Sun
Types & Periods: General
Line, Mid 1800's to 1930's
Furniture, Glass, China,
Jewelry & Primitives
Directions: S of downtown
near Freeway, 2 blocks S
of Livingston Ave in
German Village

BUSY BEE ANTIQUES
1044 Dublin Rd   43215
614 486-8320   Est: 1969
Proprietor: William
Fredeuchs
Hours: Mon-Sun
Types & Periods: Glass,
Furniture, Prussian & Art
Glass & Primitives
Specialties: Cut Glass
Directions: Rte 33 N 1/2
mile from downtown

CHURCH ON THE LANE
ANTIQUES INC
1251 Grandview Ave
43212
614 488-3606   Est: 1948
Proprietor: Virginia C
Stoltz
Hours: Mon-Sun, 9-4
Types & Periods: Furniture,
Objects of Art, China, Glass
& Jewelry
Appraisal Service Available
Directions: In Old
Grandview Theatre Bldg,
4 blocks N of Rte 33

CLUFFS ANTIQUE SHOP
102 E Whitterg St   43206
Est: 1919
Proprietor: Bernard &
Ruth Cluff
Hours: Tues & Wed 10-4
Types & Periods: Furniture,
China, Glassware & Rugs
Appraisal Service Available
Directions: In German
Village

GERMAN VILLAGE
FURNITURE SHOP
129 E Columbus St 43206
614 444-0071   Est: 1964
Proprietor: Robert L
Pusecker
Hours: Mon-Sun 10-4;
Also by appt
Types & Periods: 18th &
19th Century Victorian &
Oak Furniture
Appraisal Service Available
Directions: In heart of
German Village off I-70, S
of downtown

KELLYS STUFF STORE &
FLEA MARKET
557 S High St   43215
614 221-2426   Est: 1970
Proprietor: Dave Kelly
Hours: Tues-Sun
Types & Periods: 20
Dealers; Coins, Glass,
China, Furniture,
Collectibles, Primitives &
General Line
Specialties: Nostalgia
Appraisal Service Available
Directions: In German
Village, 4 blocks S of I-70

MIRAN ARTS & BOOKS
700 Bryden Rd   43215
614 224-0600   Est: 1974
Proprietor: Ivan Gilbert
Hours: By appt or chance

Types & Periods: Books,
Posters, Pictures &
Magazines
Appraisal Service Available
Directions: 3 blocks off
Broad St exit of I-71

SELECTIONS
2353 East Main St   43209
614 236-0007   Est: 1972
Proprietor: Browne Paney
Hours: Mon-Sat, 9:30-5:30
Types & Periods: Decorative
Objects of 18th & 19th
Century, Continental &
Oriental Items
Appraisal Service Available
Directions: In Bexley; first
corner E of Capital
University

TREASURE TROVE
ANTIQUES
2893 N High St   43202
614 261-8886   Est: 1972
Proprietor: Toni Alexander
Hours: Tues-Sat, 11-6;
Sun 1-5
Types & Periods: 18th &
19th Century Furniture &
Accessories, Formal &
Country, Late 19th & Early
20th Century Collectibles
Appraisal Service Available
Directions: Weber Rd exit
off I-71 N, W to High St,
left to Shop

UNCLE SAM'S ANTIQUES
3169 N High St   43202
614 261-8549   Est: 1974
Proprietor: Don Williams
Hours: Wed-Sat, 11-6; Sun
12-5; Also by appt or
chance
Types & Periods: General
Line, American, Victorian &
Primitive Furniture
Specialties: Complete
Refinishing & Restoration
Service
Directions: I-71 Weber Ave
exit W to High St; 4
blocks N at High &
Pacemont

THE VILLAGE JEWEL
632 City Park   43206
614 224-1211   Est: 1972
Proprietor: Niels Keiper
Hours: Mon-Sat, 11-5; Sun
1-6
Types & Periods: Jewelry,
Watches & Related Items
Specialties: Indian Jewelry

Columbus Cont'd

VILLAGE JEWEL Cont'd
Appraisal Service Available
Directions: Located in
Original Refurbished
Village, off I-71

Covington

TROJAN ANTIQUES
8190 Covington-
Bradford Rd   45318
513 473-3834   Est: 1972
Proprietor: Dorothy &
Elmer Caskey
Hours: By appt or chance
Types & Periods: 19th
Century Country Furniture,
Primitives, Lamps, Art Glass
& China
Directions: 1/2 mile N of
Covington, 1st road to left,
2 blocks off St Rte 48

Dayton

DAYTON CLUSTER
Directions: Main Ave
(running N-S) Fair number
of Shops on this major
artery, Rte 48; 3rd
(running E-W) changes its
name to Linden, has many
Shops

AARON'S ANTIQUES
1301 E 2nd St   45403
513 222-9217   Est: 1970
Proprietor: James Davis
Hours: By appt or chance
Types & Periods: Paintings,
Rugs, Primitives, Postal
Cards, Jewelry & Furniture
Specialties: Picture Frames;
"Decorator Items appealing
to younger generation"
Directions: 2nd & Terry, 1
mile E of heart of Dayton

ANTIQUES AT OLD
IRONSTONE
8705 N Main   45415
513 890-2852   Est: 1947
Proprietor: Beulah D Bell
Hours: Mon-Sat, 12 noon;
Also by appt

Types & Periods: General
Line & Collector's Items &
Early American Furniture
from the 1700's
Specialties: Ironstone & Fine
China & Glass & Primitives
Appraisal Service Available
Directions: 8 miles N
Dayton on Main St which
is Rte 48 N 1 mile S I-70
at Englewood

THE CELLAR DOOR
41 E 1st St   45402
513 223-3825   Est: 1973
Proprietor: Paul Kandell
Hours: Mon-Sat, 10-5
Types & Periods: Glass,
Ceramics, Furniture,
Textiles, Paintings, Prints,
Art Deco & Nouveau &
Collectibles
Specialties: Oriental Art
Appraisal Service Available
Directions: Corner of 1st &
Jefferson

THE CLOCKS & WATCHES
4311 N Main St   45405
513 276-3708   Est: 1974
Proprietor: Tedford R
White
Hours: Mon-Sat, 10-8
Types & Periods: Clocks &
Watches
Specialties: Antique Clock &
Watch Repair
Appraisal Service Available
Directions: Forest Park
Shopping Plaza

Dover

WARTHER'S " THE
QUEEN'S ATTIC"
ANTIQUES
2740 N Wooster Ave
44622
216 343-5443
Proprietor: Mary S
Warther
Hours: By appt or chance
Types & Periods: Jewelry &
Orientals

Dublin

DUBLIN BARN ANTIQUES
8511 Dublin Rd   43017
614 889-1466   Est: 1960

Proprietor: Jim LaBadie &
Jay Suiter
Hours: Mon-Sun,
10:30-4:30
Types & Periods: General
Line, European & American
Items, Cut Glass & Silver
Specialties: Chandeliers
Appraisal Service Available
Directions: 3 miles N of
stop light in center of
Dublin on Rte 745, Dublin
is a suburb of Columbus

East Liverpool

MC DONALD'S ANTIQUES
1865 Dresden Ave   43920
216 385-5666   Est: 1939
Proprietor: Helen F
McDonald
Hours: Mon-Tues,
Thurs-Sun, by appt or
chance
Types & Periods: General
Line
Specialties: Ceramics,
Haviland China & Pottery
Appraisal Service Available
Directions: 1 mile N of
Pearl China off E
Palestine exit of Rte 11

Fairborn

BACK ROW BOOK SHOP
411 W Main St   45324
513 879-2131
Proprietor: Jerry Merkel
Hours: Mon & Tues, 10-8;
Wed-Sat, 10-6
Types & Periods: Second
Hand, Out-of-Print & Rare
Books
Appraisal Service Available
Directions: I-70 to Rte 235
S to Main St

Fairhaven

MARGE PIPER ET CETERA
ANTIQUES
410 Dollar Federal Bldg
45011
513 523-6591   Est: 1968
Proprietor: Marge Piper
Hours: Sun only
Types & Periods: 18th &
19th Century Country &

Painted Furniture, Paintings, Folk Art & Quality Accessories
Specialties: American Furniture & Folk Art
Appraisal Service Available
Directions: Rte 177 in Fairhaven, 25 miles S of Dayton

Findlay

GREENFIELD ACRES ANTIQUES
1539 Greenfield Dr   45840
419 423-0399   Est: 1972
Proprietor: Earl & Iris Shaffer
Hours: By appt or chance
Types & Periods: Pattern Glass, China, Furniture
Specialties: Findlay Pattern Glass 1888-1901
Directions: S end of Town, off 6th St

THE SIGN OF THE BELL
214 W Front St   45840
419 423-4525   Est: 1970
Proprietor: Marge Bell & Kay Bell Chesebro
Hours: Mon 12:30-5:30; Tues-Sat, 9:30-5:30
Types & Periods: General Line, Primitives & Gifts
Directions: Downtown, 1 block N of Rte 12

Fredericktown

THE JOHNNY APPLESEED SHOP
39 N Main   43019
614 694-3431   Est: 1974
Proprietor: Joe & Mary Cooper
Hours: Mon-Wed, 9-5; Sun 12-5; Also by appt or chance
Types & Periods: General Line & Furniture
Appraisal Service Available
Directions: W side of Rte 95

Fremont

OLDE STUFF
410 Justice St   43420
419 332-7191   Est: 1945
Proprietor: Harry Hoaser
Hours: By appt or chance
Types & Periods: Collectibles
Specialties: Beer Cans
Appraisal Service Available
Directions: 2 blocks N of Post Office

Granville

CONNELLY & CONNELLY
230 E Broadway   43023
614 587-2874   Est: 1974
Proprietor: Mr & Mrs Craig Connelly
Hours: Sat & Sun & by chance
Types & Periods: American Furniture, Tools, Crocks & Quilts
Specialties: 10 Dealers Shops in Granville Area with Variety
Appraisal Service Available,
Auction Service Available
Directions: 25 miles E of Columbus off I-70

TOLE HOUSE
126 N Prospect St   43023
614 587-2200   Est: 1968
Proprietor: Marjorie E Gibney
Hours: Mon-Sat
Types & Periods; 18th Century Furniture

WEE ANTIQUE GALLERY
1630 Columbus Rd   43023
614 587-2270   Est: 1971
Proprietor: Ruth Styche
Hours: Mon-Fri & Sun
Types & Periods: Maple, Cherry, Walnut & Mahogany Furniture
Specialties: Decorative Items
Directions: Rte 16, 1 mile SW of Town

Greentown

NOW & THEN SHOP
9636 Cleveland Ave N   44630
216 494-4049   Est: 1965
Proprietor: Stewart & Anne Pendleton
Hours: Mon-Sun, 9:30-4; Also by appt or chance
Types & Periods: General Line
Specialties: Dolls
Appraisal Service Available
Directions: 3 miles from I-77 at Canton-Akron Airport exit

Greenville

HOUSE & BARN ANTIQUES
Rte 3   45331
513 548-7002   Est: 1962
Proprietor: Robert & Edna Miller
Hours: Mon-Fri & Sun 1-10
Types & Periods: General Line Appraisal Service Available
Directions: 3 miles W of Greenville, off Rte 502 on Greenville-Palestine Rds

RED BARN ANTIQUES
140 13th St   45331
513 548-4292   Est: 1952
Proprietor: Florence Magoto
Hours: Tues-Sun, 12:30-5:30
Types & Periods: China, Glass, Lamps & Furniture
Directions: 3 blocks S of downtown

THE SHOE STRING
1526 E Main   45331
513 548-7174   Est: 1972
Proprietor: Isabel Eyler
Hours: Tues-Sat, 11-5
Types & Periods: General Line
Specialties: Antique Wicker Furniture
Directions: On E Main before 127 Overpass

**MAXINE THOMAS
ANTIQUES**
747 Garden Wood Dr
45331
513 548-9644
Proprietor: Maxine
Thomas
Hours: Mon-Sun by appt
Types & Periods: Art &
Colored Glass

Hamilton

GARRETT'S ANTIQUES
105 Gordon Ave   45013
513 892-2683
Proprietor: Viola Garrett
Hours: Mon-Sat 9-6
Types & Periods: Victorian
Furniture, China, Cut &
Pressed Glass, Clocks,
Lamps & Jewelry
Specialties: Furniture
Directions: W from Butler
Country Courthouse to B
St N, on B St to Gordon
Ave

THE SHED
5110 Hamilton Middletown
Rd   45011
513 863-3363   Est: 1974
Proprietor: Nancy Roth
Hours: Mon-Fri, 10-5; Sat
10-5:30
Types & Periods: General
Line
Directions: I-75 take Rte
63 W to Rte 4, S on Rte 4
approx 2 miles

Hillsboro

WAGON TRAIN ANTIQUES
Rte 1   45133
513 393-2727   Est: 1932
Proprietor: Mary Layman
Hours: Summer: Mon-Sun,
by appt
Types & Periods: Victorian,
Primitives, 20 Wagons,
Buggies, Sleighs & Steam
Engine 3/4 size
Specialties: Hand Made
Vehicles
Appraisal Service Available
Directions: Located at
large Lake Resort

Hudson

ROBIN HILL, LTD
15 S College St   44236
216 653-6300   Est: 1964
Proprietor: Jane Farrell
Fitch
Hours: Sept-May: Mon-Fri,
10-5
Types & Periods: 18th &
19th Century American,
English & French
Furnishings
Specialties: Hand Made
European Silk Flowers
Directions: Rte 91 & 303 E
on Rte 303 to 1st street
on right

VILLAGE CLOCK SHOP
178 N Main St   44236
216 653-5719   Est: 1971
Proprietor: Helen Bee
Hours: Mon-Sat, 9-5 or by
appt
Types & Periods: General
Line
Specialties: Clocks
Directions: On Rte 91

Huntsville

ROCK CHIMNEY
5562 RR   43324
513 686-2584   Est: 1952
Proprietor: L B Hord
Hours: Mon-Sun by appt
Specialties: Elder Brewster
1620 Chair & 1800 Child's
Carriage
Directions: Rte 366
between Huntsville &
Russells Pointe

Huron

THE ATTIC
132 N Main St   44839
419 433-2076   Est: 1973
Proprietor: Margaret A
Denslow
Hours: Oct-May: Mon-Sat,
11-8; June-Sept: Mon-Sun,
11-8
Types & Periods: Furniture,
Glass, Vases & Pictures
Directions: Next to Huron
River above Twine House
Restaurant

CROSBY'S ANTIQUES
517 Huron St   44839
419 433-2641   Est: 1968
Proprietor: Sally & Pam
Crosby
Hours: Sept-June:
Mon-Fri, 1-3 by appt or
chance, Sat & Sun;
July-Aug: Mon-Sun, 11-5
Types & Periods: Victorian
Furniture, Primitives, Glass,
Porcelain, Silver, Dolls,
Lamps, Paintings & Frames
Appraisal Service Available
Directions: Behind the
Wileswood Country Store
on Rtes 6 & 2; center of
town

Jamestown

**COUNTRY ROADS TRIVIA
SHOPPE**
16 E Washington St
45335
513 675-6177   Est: 1974
Proprietor: Robert A &
Diana M Johnson
Hours: Mon-Sat & Sun by
appt
Types & Periods: General
Line
Appraisal Service Available
Directions: US Rte 35 "In
big victorian house" in
center of town

Kent

SEVEN ACRES
5840 Horning Rd   44240
216 678-2224   Est: 1955
Proprietor: D A Philabaum
Hours: By appt
Appraisal Service Available
Directions: 1 block off Rte
59, S from light at
Murphy's Plaza to stop
sign, right to 2nd house

Lancaster

**FARMER'S COUNTRY
STORE**
6th & High St   43130
614 654-4853   Est: 1973
Proprietor: Mrs James
Jadwin

Hours: Tues-Sat, 10-5;
Extra hrs during Dec
Types & Periods: Furniture
Directions: On Rte 37

Lima

THE VELVET BOW
1077 Shawnee Rd   45805
419 222-7148   Est: 1969
Proprietor: Janet Coeling
& Mary Ann Myers
Hours: Mon-Tues & Thurs,
7-9; Wed, Fri & Sat, 10-4
Types & Periods: Wood, Tin
& Granite Primitives
Directions: Shawnee Rd at
Rte 117, W side of Lima

Lockland

TRIVIA TREASURES
106 N Cooper Ave   45215
513 821-4876   Est: 1973
Proprietor: Gladys Smith
Hours: Mon-Sat, 12-6
Types & Periods: General
Line
Specialties: Nostalgia
Collectibles
Directions: Next to I-75,
across from Lockland
Police Station

Lucas

GYPSY MOTH ANTIQUES
18 E Main St   44843
419 892 2697   Est: 1970
Proprietor: Marianne
Schulte
Hours: Mon, Wed, Fri-Sun;
Also by appt or chance
Types & Periods: General
Line, Hand Painted China,
Primitives & Furniture
Specialties: Amphora &
Painted China
Appraisal Service Available
Directions: 7 miles from
Mansfield on Rte 39

**THE LUCAS COUNTRY
STORE**
6 E Main St   44843
419 892-2200   Est: 1968
Proprietor: Gloria Evers
Hours: Mon-Sat, 11-5; Sun
12-6

Types & Periods: American
Furniture, Toys, Advertising,
Lamps, Primitives & RR
Lanterns
Specialties: Lanterns, Toys
& Advertising
Appraisal Service Available
Directions: Exit 169 from
I-71 to State Rte 39, 6
miles SE Mansfield

Lucasville

HENSON'S ANTIQUES
Main St   45648
614 259-4651   Est: 1945
Proprietor: Paul & Virginia
Henson
Hours: Tues-Sun
Types & Periods: General
Line
Appraisal Service Available
Directions: 10 miles N of
Portsmouth on US 23

Madison

HERITAGE SHOP
13 Main St   44057
216 428-4049   Est: 1966
Proprietor: Sibylla Linden
& Sherry Smith
Hours: Mon-Sun
Types & Periods: General
Line & Collectibles
Directions: I-90 to
Madison exit, 1 mile N on
Rte 528, 1 block E on Rte
84

QUAINT CORNERS
109 N Lake St   44057
216 428-1812   Est: 1961
Proprietor: Doris L
McIntosh
Hours: Mon-Sat, 10-12,
1-5
Types & Periods: General
Line

Mansfield

ROGERS & CO
248 W Park Ave, Box 1665
44902
419 522-1561   Est: 1922
Proprietor: J B Morris
Hours: Mon-Fri, 9-5
Types & Periods: General
Line

Specialties: Sterling Silver
Flatware
Directions: 2 min from
downtown Mansfield on
Main St

YESTER YEAR MART
1191 Park Ave W   44906
419 529-6212   Est: 1974
Proprietor: W Dennis
Crawford
Hours: Mon-Sat, 10-9; Sun
1-5
Types & Periods:
1800-Present Furniture,
Pottery, Primitives & Glass
Specialties: Lamp Parts
Appraisal Service Available
Directions: Located on W
Park Shopping Center;
From Columbus & S I-71:
exit at Rte 13 into
Mansfield, W on Cook Rd,
N on Trimble Rd & W on
Park Ave W to Shopping
Center on Left

Marietta

**DUTCHMAN'S 2nd
ANTIQUES**
221 Greene St   45750
614 374-5446   Est: 1970
Proprietor: Dutch Heiney
Hours: Mon-Sat, 8-7; Sun
by appt
Types & Periods: General
Line
Specialties: Furniture
Appraisal Service Available

MRS FRANK HALE
804 Seventh St   45750
614 373-5854   Est: 1960
Proprietor: Mrs Frank Hale
Hours: By appt or chance
Types & Periods: Primitives
& Country Items
Directions: Downtown

RIVERVIEW ANTIQUES
102 Front St   45750
614 373-4068   Est: 1964
Proprietor: Wm P Dorsey
Hours: Mon-Sun
Types & Periods: General
Line
Appraisal Service Available
Directions: Across from
Lafayette Motor Hotel

Marion

BLUESTONE MANOR
467 Mt Vernon Ave 43302
614 382-8671
Proprietor: Virginia Spohn
Hours: By appt
Types & Periods: Art,
Colored, Cut & Cambridge
Glass & China

Marysville

**AMERICAN GENERAL
STORE CO**
335-425 S Main St 43040
513 642-6901 Est: 1965
Proprietor: Glenn
Scheiderer Family
Hours: Tues-Sat, 10-6
Specialties: Furniture
(1840-1945), Hardware
Replacements, Lamp &
Lighting Fixtures,
Replacement Shades & Over
1200 Parts for Repair
Directions: 30 NW of
Columbus on State
Rte 33 W

**THE HEIRLOOM ANTIQUE
SHOP**
125 N Main St 43040
513 644-4464 Est: 1966
Proprietor: Edna & C P
Wagner
Hours: Tues-Sun, 9-5:30
Types & Periods: China,
Glassware, Lamps, Clocks &
Furniture

THE OLE VILLAGE
755 Milford Ave 43040
513 642-8916 Est: 1964
Proprietor: E L Ohnsman
Hours: Mon-Sat, 9-5; Sun
by chance
Types & Periods: General
Line
Specialties: Antique
Furniture Restoring &
Restored Log Cabin Village
Appraisal Service Available
Directions: 35 miles NW of
Columbus, Rte 4 & US 36

Massillon

**DANBAR'S DISTANT VIEW
FARM ANTIQUES**
6405 Arlington Ave NW
44646
216 832-6032 Est: 1967
Proprietor: Daniel &
Barbara Hoover
Hours: Fri-Sat, 10-5; Sun
1-6; Otherwise by appt
Types & Periods: Art & Cut
Glass & American Furniture
Specialties: Art Glass
Appraisal Service Available
Directions: 1-77; exit N
Canton-Canal Fulton, turn
W 3½ miles

GIBSON ANTIQUES
906 16th St SE 44646
216 832-0403 Est: 1960
Proprietor: Cleme Gibson
Hours: Mon-Sun by
chance
Types & Periods: Art Glass
& Collectibles
Specialties: Art Glass
Directions: Rte 77 to
Walnut Rd, E on 16th St &
turn N

**ANNE GROH'S ANTIQUE
GALLERY**
320 Lincoln Way E 44646
216 837-4700 Est: 1961
Proprietor: Anne Groh
Hours: Mon-Sun
Types & Periods: General
Line
Specialties: Oriental
Furniture
Appraisal Service Available
Directions: Rte 30

MARKHAM'S ANTIQUES
12441 Lincoln St NW
44646
216 832-5071
Proprietor: Ed Markham
Hours: Sat 1-5; Sun 1-6 or
by appt
Types & Periods: Furniture
& General Line
Specialties: Art, Colored &
Cut Glass & Clocks
Appraisal Service Available
Directions: 3 miles W on
State Rte 172

TIME CONTINUIM
6405 Arlington Ave NW
44646
216 832-6032

Types & Periods: General
Line
Specialties: Clocks

Maumee

ANTIQUES SS WARNER
219 W Wayne 43537
419 893-0470
Hours: Tues-Sun
Types & Periods: General
Line
Appraisal Service Available

MAD ANTHONY ANTIQUES
702 W Wayne 43537
419 893-5404 Est: 1974
Proprietor: Don
Stonestreet
Hours: Tues-Sat by appt
Types & Periods: American
Country Furniture
Directions: Corner of W
Wayne & Ford

**MAIL POUCH ANTIQUES IN
THE BROOM FACTORY**
311 Cass St 43537
419 893-2708 Est: 1974
Proprietor: Mrs Keith B
Knight
Hours: Tues-Sun; 12-5
Types & Periods: Clocks,
Collectibles, Primitives,
Photographica, Post Cards
& General Line
Specialties: Stained &
Beveled Glass Windows
Directions: 2 blocks W of
the Main St Conant
between W Dudley & W
Waynes

McConnelsville

**HANWOOD HOUSE
ANTIQUES**
168-172 E Main 43756
614 962-2166 Est: 1972
Proprietor: Betty Hanson
Hours: Mon-Sun,
7am-11pm
Types & Periods: General
Line
Directions: On State
Rte 60

Medina

BONNIE ROWLANDS
531 E Liberty St   44256
216 725-5982   Est: 1971
Proprietor: Bonnie
Rowlands
Hours: By appt or chance
Types & Periods: Primitive &
Country Accessories &
Country Furniture
Specialties: Toys &
Automata, Butter Molds,
Stoneware & Pottery
Directions: St Rte 3, N 4
blocks out from Town
Square

**THE SARGENT HOUSE
ANTIQUES**
329 W Liberty St   44256
216 725-5657   Est: 1971
Proprietor: Jim & Ellie
Hicks
Hours: Mon-Sat, 1-5;
Mornings by chance &
Evenings by appt
Types & Periods: Furniture,
Primitives, Jewelry, Railroad,
Civil War, Advertising &
Lighting Fixtures
Specialties: Country
Furniture & Primitives
Appraisal Service Available
Directions: St Rte 18, 2½
blocks W of City Square

MARJORIE STAUFER
2244 Remsen Rd   44256
216 239-1443   Est: 1968
Proprietor: Marjorie
Staufer
Hours: Mon-Sun by appt
or chance
Types & Periods: Early
Country Furniture &
Accessories
Directions: 7 miles NE of
Medina, close to I-71 &
I-271

Mentor

HILO FARM ANTIQUES
Little Mountain Rd   44060
216 255-9530   Est: 1952
Proprietor: Marjorie
Wearsch
Hours: By appt
Types & Periods: Primitives,
China, Glassware &
Furniture at times

Specialties: Books & Paper
Goods
Appraisal Service Available
Directions: Mentor Post
Office but located in
Kirtland Hills, so call
necessary for directions

Miamitown

ANTIQUES & THINGS
6756 St Rte 128   45041
513 921-8493   Est: 1974
Proprietor: Thompson &
Verna Carrier
Hours: Sat & Sun by appt
or chance
Types & Periods: Small
Antiques, Collectibles &
Victorian Era Furniture
Directions: 20 miles W of
Cincinnati, "Easy access
off I-74"

**THE E CHRISTOPHER
FIREARMS COMPANY**
6818 St Rd 128   45041
513 353-1321   Est: 1969
Proprietor: A W Bram
Hours: Tues & Sat, 11-7;
Wed & Fri, 11-9; Sun 12-5
Types & Periods: Firearms &
Accessories
Specialties: Arms
Appraisal Service Available
Directions: Downtown off
I-74

Middletown

LONG'S ANTIQUES
3809 Central Ave   45042
513 422-6672
Proprietor: E O Florence
Hours: By appt or chance
Types & Periods: Art & Cut
Glass, China, Lamps &
Furniture

Milan

**JOAN R COULTER
ANTIQUES**
123 Center St   44846
419 499-4061
Proprietor: Joan Coulter
Hours: By appt or chance
Types & Periods: 18th &
19th Century American

**SAMAHA ANTIQUES-BETTY
DOROW ANTIQUES**
Public Square   44846
419 499-4044
Proprietor: G W
Samaha-Betty Dorrow
Hours: Tues-Sat, 11-4;
Also by appt
Types & Periods: Country &
Formal Americana

Montgomery

**DUPRIEST HOUSE OF
ANTIQUES**
7872 Cooper Ave   45242
513 984-8810   Est: 1971
Proprietor: Michael
DuPriest
Hours: Tues-Wed, Fri &
Sat, 11-5; Sun by chance
Types & Periods: General
Line & Furniture
Directions: Corner of
Cooper & Main, 1 block E
of Montgomery Rd

New Philadelphia

**TRADER JO'S BOOKS &
ANTIQUES**
159 W High St   44663
216 364-5012   Est: 1969
Proprietor: Emily Dietz
Hours: Mon-Sat, 10-5:30
Types & Periods: Chairs,
Tables, Stands, Glassware &
Books
Directions: Off I-77,
Downtown

Newark

BERT'S BUDGET SHOP
403 W Main St   43055
614 349-8045   Est: 1963
Proprietor: Bertha R
Hoffman
Hours: Mon, Wed-Sat,
10-5
Types & Periods: Glass,
China, Furniture &
Collectibles
Specialties: Heisey Glass
Appraisal Service Available
Directions: Rte 79 S
towards center of City

1810 HOUSE
2341 Newark-Granville Rd
43055
614 344-3206   Est: 1970
Hours: Jan-Aug:
Tues-Sun, 1-4; Sept-Dec
11-4
Types & Periods: General
Line
Specialties: Profits go to
Miller Ranch for Boys
Directions: Across from
Garden Center

OHIO VALLEY ANTIQUES & GIFT SHOP
104 W Locust St   43055
614 345-7485   Est: 1963
Proprietor: Marguerite
Hiener
Hours: By appt or chance
Types & Periods: 1880
Wooden Articles, Ice Boxes,
Telephones, Dishes, Glass &
Heisey Collectibles
Appraisal Service Available
Directions: Off 16 E
Expwy at 4th St &
downtown, go to light,
turn right, go 1 block

North Canton

ANGELA'S ANTIQUES
201 Parkview Dr   44720
216 499-2138
Hours: By appt
Types & Periods: General
Line & Clocks

DORNHECKER'S CURIOSITY SHOP
Bonnet St SW   44720
216 499-7001
Hours: Mon-Sun
Types & Periods: General
Line

WIDEMAN'S ANTIQUE LOFT
525 N Main St   44720
216 499-7666
Types & Periods: General
Line & Furniture

Northfield Center

COOPER'S GENERAL STORE & AUCTION GALLERY
7868 Olde 8 Rd   44067
216 467-0086   Est: 1973
Proprietor: Floyd & June
Cooper
Hours: Wed-Thurs, 10-5;
Fri 10-9; Sun 12-5
Types & Periods: General
Line
Specialties: Handcrafted
Amish Furniture
Directions: N of exit 12
(Ohio Turnpike), 3 miles S
of Rte 82

North Lima

MARY WIRE
11657 Market St   44452
Proprietor: Mary Wire
Hours: Mon-Sun, 11-5
Types & Periods: Queen Anne,
Victorian, Empire & Primitives
Directions: 10 miles from
Youngstown

Norwalk

IRVING M ROTH ANTIQUES
89 Whittlesey Ave (Rte
250 N)   44857
419 668-2893   Est: 1945
Proprietor: Irving M Roth
Hours: Mon-Sun, 12-5; By
chance
Types & Periods: Glass,
China, Pottery, Iron, Tin,
Furniture, Indian Articles,
Weapons, Books, Paper
Items
Specialties: Books & Post
Cards
Appraisal Service Available
Directions: 2 blocks N of
Court House

Norwich

KEMBLE'S ANTIQUES
Sundale Rd   43767
614 872-3507   Est: 1967
Proprietor: Roland &
Marilyn Kemble
Hours: Mon-Sat

Types & Periods:
Chippendale, Sheraton &
Hepplewhite Furniture
Specialties: Corner & Wall
Cupboards & Rope Beds
Appraisal Service Available
Directions: Rte 40 off I-70,
1½ miles

STAGE COACH ANTIQUES
RR 1   43767
614 872-3720   Est: 1966
Proprietor: Herbert & Betty
Ward
Hours: Mon-Sun
Types & Periods: General
Line
Appraisal Service Available
Directions: I-70, Norwich
exit

Ontario

ONTARIO ANTIQUE & COIN SHOP
3644 Park Ave W   44862
419 529-6034   Est: 1969
Proprietor: Sis & Glenn
DeWeese
Hours: Mon-Wed, Fri-Sun,
1-7
Types & Periods: Coins,
Stamps, Post Cards,
Furniture, Glassware,
Primitives & Books
Specialties: Coins & Post
Cards
Appraisal Service Available
Directions: 2 miles S of
Rte 30 N in the center of
the Village

Oxford

THE BIRD HOUSE ANTIQUES
211 W Spring St   45056
513 523-3111   Est: 1973
Proprietor: Bertie
Wespiser
Hours: Mon-Sun,
11:30-5:30; by appt or
chance
Types & Periods: Sheraton,
Empire, Victorian & Golden
Oak Furniture, Pressed
Glass, Primitives, Quilts,
Clothing & Collectibles
Specialties: Quilts, Clothing,
Country Store & Advertising
Collectibles

Appraisal Service Available
Directions: 40 minutes N
of Cincinnati; located on
Spring St by the tracks,
Spring St intersects Rte
27 & 73 & is 3 blocks off
732

**MARGE PIPER ET CETERA
ANTIQUES**
45056
513 523-6591   Est: 1968
Proprietor: Marge Piper
Hours: By appt, Dealers
only
Types & Periods: 18th &
19th Century Country &
Painted Furniture, Paintings,
Folk Art & Quality
Accessories
Specialties: American
Furniture & Folk Art

Peninsula

JOHNNYCAKE SHOP
Riverview at Everett
44264
216 657-2275   Est: 1963
Proprietor: James J
Gifford
Hours: Mon-Sun, 12-5 or
by appt
Types & Periods: General
Line
Specialties: Country Store
Items & Advertiques

SHAFER'S ANTIQUES
6446 Stanford Rd   44264
216 657-2002   Est: 1960
Proprietor: Marshall &
Dorothy Shafer
Hours: Tues-Sun
Types & Periods: Carnival
Glass, Early American
Furniture & Primitives
Directions: Near exits 11 &
13 off Ohio Turnpike

Plain City

**PLAIN CITY AUCTION
SERVICE**
145 E Main St   43064
614 873-5622   Est: 1962
Proprietor: J Robert
Sweeney
Hours: By appt, Auction
Sale the last Fri of each
month

Types & Periods: China,
Glassware, Lamps, Dolls,
Oak Furniture, Brass, China
& Cabinets
Directions: 10 miles N of
I-70, 20 miles NW of
Columbus

Pleasant Hill

KRUG ANTIQUES
504 N Main St   45359
513 676-3373   Est: 1975
Proprietor: Joan Krug
Hours: Mon-Wed, Fri &
Sun, 12-5
Types & Periods: Furniture,
Primitives, Glass & General
Line
Directions: 20 miles N of
Dayton on I-75, W on Rte
55 to Rte 48, N 4 miles to
Pleasant Hill

Port Clinton

FLORAL ARTS & ANTIQUES
400 West 3rd St   43452
419 734-2901   Est: 1967
Proprietor: Delores M
Stevens
Types & Periods: Leaded
Stained Glass Windows,
Walnut, Oak & Pine
American Furniture, Art
Glass, Collectibles &
Primitives
Specialties: Leaded Stained
Glass Windows
Directions: Ohio Turnpike
exit 6, N on Rte 53 to Port
Clinton, brings you to the
front door

**WIGHT'S BUSY BEE
ANTIQUE SHOPPE**
117 W 3rd St   43452
419 734-4084   Est: 1968
Proprietor: Johanne Wight
Hours: Mon-Fri & Sun,
10-4; Sat Mornings by
appt
Types & Periods: Furniture,
Lamps, Clocks, Primitives,
Dishes & General Line
Appraisal Service Available
Directions: Rte 53 runs
into W 3rd, on Rte 2 S on
Madison or Monroe, shop
in middle of 3rd block
between these streets

Portsmouth

BOULEVARD ANTIQUES
1053 Coles Blvd   45662
614 353-3337   Est: 1973
Proprietor: Judith Bauer
Hours: Mon-Sun
Types & Periods: China, Cut
Glass & Carnival Glass
Directions: Rte 23 N, turn
right at Coles Blvd

Powell

POWELLPOURRI
14 W Olentangy St   43065
614 885-2556   Est: 1972
Proprietor: Caryl Snide
Hours: Sat-Sun by appt or
chance
Types & Periods: General
Line
Directions: 6 miles N of
Columbus, Rte 315 N to
Rte 750, Rte 750 into
Powell

Ravenna

THE ANTIQUE SHOWCASE
5941 State Rte 14-5
44266
216 296-5565   Est: 1965
Proprietor: Lois Hansen
Hours: By appt or chance
Types & Periods: Early &
Victorian Furniture
Specialties: Glass, China &
Porcelain
Appraisal Service Available
Directions: 1/2 mile S of
the cross roads of St Rte
14 and St Rte 59 on the
left side in long low yellow
bldg

THE HITCHING POST
7467 St Rte 88   44266
216 296-3686   Est: 1970
Proprietor: Doris McDaniel
Hours: By appt or chance
Types & Periods: Furniture,
Primitives, Glass, China,
Jewelry & Miniatures
Directions: 2 miles NE of
Rte 14 or 3 miles from
town on Rte 88

Reading

THE COTTAGE
219 Reading Rd   45215
513 761-6082   Est: 1972
Proprietor: C A Bell
Hours: Tues-Sat, 10-6;
Also by appt
Types & Periods: General
Line
Directions: 3 blocks E of
I-75 at Galbraith Road exit

Ridgeville Corners

REMEMBER WHEN
Box 2   43555
419 267-3428   Est: 1970
Proprietor: Lawrence
Ruffir
Hours: Mon-Fri, 8-5;
Sat-Sun by appt
Types & Periods: Empire,
Victorian, Early American &
Golden Oak Furniture
Directions: On Rte 6 in
town

Rootstown

CURIOSITY CORNER
4236 St Rte 44   44272
216 325-9471   Est: 1971
Proprietor: Dee Stefansic
Hours: Mon-Sun
Types & Periods: General
Line, Glass, China,
Primitives & Furniture
Directions: Exit Rte 44 S
off I-76

Salem

SHIMER'S ANTIQUES
8129 West Rd   44460
216 337-6388   Est: 1974
Proprietor: Mary & Fred
Shimer
Hours: Sat-Sun, 5-7 or by
chance
Types & Periods: General
Line, Glassware & Primtives
Specialties: Restoration
Directions: Rte 14A, 2
miles E of town

Sandusky

HEIRLOOMS ETCETERA
1222 Milan Rd   44870
419 625-8733 or 625-1821
Est: 1975
Proprietor: Judee Hill
Hours: Mon-Tues,
Thurs-Fri, 11-5; Wed 1-5;
Sat 12-3 & Some Suns
during season; Also by
appt or chance
Types & Periods: General
Line, Primitives, Country
Store Items, Clocks &
Victorian Furnishings
Specialties: Furniture &
Depression Glass
Appraisal Service Available
Directions: 4¼ miles N of
Rte 2 bypass exit Rte 250

Sharon Center

TWIN MAPLES ANTIQUES
1242 Sharon Copley Rd
44274
216 239-1627   Est: 1955
Proprietor: Mr & Mrs
Charles Bush
Hours: Mon-Sun, 9 until
dark
Types & Periods: General
Line & Furniture
Specialties: Lamps &
Lighting
Appraisal Service Available
Directions: On Rte 162, 12
miles W of Akron

Smithville

ALBRIGHT ANTIQUE SHOP
44677
216 669-5941   Est: 1971
Proprietor: Mr & Mrs John
Albright
Hours: Mon-Sat by chance
Types & Periods: Early
American & Country
Furniture, Glass & China
Appraisal Service Available
Directions: On Rte 585 on
Akron-Wooster Rd

Springfield

B & M JUNTIQUES
414 Selma Rd   45505
513 325-5668 or 323-9656
Est: 1970
Proprietor: Mike
Thompson
Hours: Tues & Sat, 10-5;
Also by appt or chance
Types & Periods: Post Cards
to Autos
Appraisal Service Available
Directions: 2 blocks E of
Rte 72

BACK ROW BOOK SHOP
11 E High St   45502
513 325-8861   Est: 1978
Proprietor: Jerry Merkel
Hours: Mon-Sat, 10-6
Types & Periods: Second
Hand, Out-of-Print & Rare
Books, LP & 78 RPM
Records
Appraisal Service Available
Directions: Downtown, at
the arcade

NOW N' THEN SHOP
1803 W Main St   45504
513 325-4821   Est: 1972
Proprietor: Mrs Doris S
Husted
Hours: Tues-Sat, 11:30-4
Types & Periods: General
Line & Victorian
Specialties: Clocks, Lamps
& Lamp Parts
Appraisal Service Available
Directions: I-70 by pass W
edge of town

Stony Ridge

**STONY RIDGE ANTIQUE
SHOP**
5535 Fremont Pike   43463
419 837-5164   Est: 1953
Proprietor: Roger L
Hillabrand
Hours: Sat-Thurs, 12-5
Types & Periods: Glassware,
Refinished Furniture,
Furniture in the Rough,
Pictures, Lamps, Linens,
Books, Victorian & Pre 1920
Furniture, Primitives &
Anything of Antique Value

Appraisal Service Available
Directions: In Stony Ridge,
8 miles from I-75 at
Perrysburg, E or W 280
on Rte 20 & 23

Sylvania

**ST JOSEPH ANTIQUE
ANNEX**
5404 S Main St   43560
419 882-4633
Proprietor: Cleo Smilo
Hours: Tues Only, 10-5
Types & Periods: General
Line

**SIDDENS & VALENTINE
ANTIQUES**
5270 W Alexis Rd   43560
419 882-1557   Est: 1952
Proprietor: Wayne Siddens
& Bob Valentine
Hours: Mon-Sat
Types & Periods: 18th
Century American Formal &
Country Furniture, Cut & Art
Glass & Oriental Rugs
Appraisal Service Available
Directions: 1 mile off I-475
& 23 on St Rte 184

Tiffin

RED SHED ANTIQUES
183 W Perry St   44883
419 447-7105   Est: 1974
Proprietor: Mrs Dorothy
Bero
Hours: Mon-Sun by appt
or chance
Types & Periods: General
Line, Curios & Art Glass
Appraisal Service Available
Directions: Corner of
Sandusky & Perry

SENECA SALES
94 N Washington St
                    44883
419 447-3262   Est: 1973
Proprietor: Patricia, Agnes
& Norbert Hohman
Hours: By appt or chance
& Sat, 9-5
Types & Periods: Furniture,
Glass, Clocks, Books &
Tools
Specialties: Books
Directions: On St at 2nd
light N of Sandusky River

Toledo

TOLEDO CLUSTER
Directions: Lagrange
(900-2000 blocks) & Main
(300-5000 blocks) have
many Shops, others
scattered throughout City

ANCESTOR HOUSE
3148 Tremainsville Rd
                    43616
419 472-7897
Hours: Tues, Wed, Fri &
Sat, 12-6
Types & Periods: General
Line

ARBOR HOUSE ANTIQUES
2503 N Reynolds Rd
                    43615
419 531-6263
Proprietor: Shirley M
Burnheimer
Hours: Tues-Sat, 1-5
Types & Periods: Cut & Art
Glass, Lamps & General
Line

THE CHESHIRE CAT
2215 Collingwood   43620
419 241-9553
Types & Periods:
Collectibles & Bric-A-Brac
Specialties: Art Glass

**CUSTER ANTIQUE
INVESTMENT COMPANY**
4139 Monroe St   43606
419 472-0050   Est: 1969
Proprietor: R A Bohl
Hours: Mon-Sun, 10-5:30
or by appt
Types & Periods: General
Line, Tiffany, Paintings,
Bronzes & Museum Quality
Antiques

**GEM ANTIQUES &
COLLECTIBLES**
4545 Westway   43612
419 478-6305   Est: 1973
Proprietor: David Lehner
Hours: By appt
Types & Periods: Dolls &
General Line
Specialties: Old Cameras,
Lamps, Lighting Fixtures &
Dolls
Appraisal Service Available
Directions: Miracle Mile
Area

DEE GOWEN ANTIQUES
3527 Indian Rd   43606
419 536-7460
Proprietor: Mrs George H
Gowen, Jr
Hours: By appt
Types & Periods: Art & Cut
Glass, Early Staffordshire &
Orientals

KING 50
2215 Collingwood   43620
419 246-4201   Est: 1940
Proprietor: Tom Yore
Hours: Sat & Sun by appt
Types & Periods: General
Line
Specialties: Furniture
Appraisal Service Available
Directions: Next to Toledo
Red Cross

LOOMIS ANTIQUES
2760 Lagrange St   43608
419 241-2662
Hours: Tues-Sat, 1-5
Types & Periods: General
Line

MECCA FOR COLLECTORS
2024 Collingwood Blvd
                    43620
419 241-9214   Est: 1971
Proprietor: Walter
Bollinger
Hours: Thurs-Sun, 12-5;
Also by appt
Types & Periods: General
Line
Specialties: Glass & Silver,
No Furniture
Appraisal Service Available
Directions: US 24, 1/4
mile N off I-475; 1/2 mile
from Toledo Art Museum

OLD WESTEND ANTIQUES
2360 Scottwood Ave
                    43620
419 255-2620   Est: 1973
Proprietor: Thomas Fisher
& Michael Teachout
Hours: By appt; Tues-Sun,
1-6
Types & Periods: Period
Furniture, Orientals, Art
Glass, Lamps, Cut Crystal &
Silver
Specialties: Furniture
Restoration
Directions: Old W end
historical area

Toledo   Cont'd

ROBERT'S ANTIQUES
2144 W Alexis Rd   43613
Hours: Sat-Sun, 2-5;
Tues-Thurs Evenings,
7-8:30
Types & Periods: General
Line

**TREASE TREASURERS
ANTIQUES**
11 Bronson Pl   43608
419 241-1710
Hours: By appt
Types & Periods: General
Line

WATERFRONT ANTIQUES
131 Water St   43604
419 241-4324   Est: 1923
Proprietor: Victor J
DePrisco
Hours: Mon-Sun by appt
Appraisal Service Available
Directions: Downtown,
across street from Holiday
Inn

Trotwood

APPLETREE ANTIQUES
100 E Main St   45426
513 837-5278   Est: 1968
Proprietor: Patricia Moss
Hours: Mon-Tues,
Thurs-Sun, 1-6
Types & Periods: Glassware,
Pressed, Cut, Art &
Depression Glass,
Cloisonne, Brass, Jewelry,
Trunks, Clocks & Furniture
Specialties: Glass & Jewelry
Appraisal Service Available
Directions: NW suburb of
Dayton

Union

GREEN TREE VILLAGE
7882 S Rte 48   45322
Est: 1974
Hours: Mon-Fri; Sat-Sun
by appt
Types & Periods: Primitives
& General Line
Appraisal Service Available
Directions: Across from
The Water Wheel Farm

Unionville

AL'S ANTIQUES
Rte 84, Box 67   44088
216 428-1316
Proprietor: Allan Brink &
Richard Curry
Hours: Mon-Sun, 8-11
Types & Periods: Furniture
& General Line

Urbana

**COPPER KETTLE
ANTIQUES**
116 Scioto St   43078
513 653-6896   Est: 1970
Proprietor: Dick & Peggy
Kline
Hours: Tues-Sat, 10-4;
Also by appt
Types & Periods: Cut Glass,
China, Lamps, Dolls,
Furniture & Art Glass
Specialties: Heisey Glass
Appraisal Service Available
Directions: Downtown

Vienna

TARA ANTIQUES
4340 Warren Sharon Rd
44473
216 856-2301   Est: 1964
Proprietor: M Shaffer
Hours: By appt or chance,
advisable to phone ahead
Types & Periods: Period
Primitive, Country Furniture
& Accessories
Directions: At traffic light
(Intersection of Rtes 193
& Warren Sharon Rd), 10
miles each way from
Warren, Youngstown &
Sharon

Wadsworth

**SHARON CENTER
ANTIQUES**
725 Sharon Copley Rd
44281
216 239-1525
Proprietor: Don & Judith
Cranmer
Hours: Mon-Tues,
Thurs-Sun

Types & Periods: Oak,
Victorian & Country
Furniture & Small Decorator
Items
Specialties: Toys, Books &
Country Store Items
Appraisal Service Available
Directions: 1 mile E of
Sharon Center on Rte 162
between Akron & Medina

**WALDEN HILL COUNTRY
STORE**
2175 Blake Rd   44281
216 334-1897   Est: 1969
Proprietor: Robert P &
Beverly June Secrist
Hours: By appt or chance
Types & Periods: Advertising
Signs, Tins, Posters &
Country Store Items
Appraisal Service Available
Directions: 1 mile N of
I-76 off Rte 57 E 1/4 mile

Waldo

BUGGY WHEEL ANTIQUES
135 St Rte 229 E   43356
614 726-2706   Est: 1971
Proprietor: Walt & Vi
Eaton
Hours: Mon-Sun, most
times & appt
Types & Periods: 19th
Century Country Furniture &
Primitives
Specialties: Cupboards,
Stoneware, Tools &
Kerosine Lamps (1870-1920)
Directions: US 23, 8 miles
N of Delaware, then E on
St Rte 229, 900 Ft

Warren

BUCKEYE ANTIQUES
1722 Mahoning Ave
44483
216 395-2786   Est: 1971
Proprietor: J F Vansant
Hours: Mon-Sun
Types & Periods: Glass,
China, Porcelain, Pottery,
Lamps & Statues
Directions: Opposite Music
Hall

Washington Court House

THE IDEA SHOP
309 W Temple St   43160
614 335-4910   Est: 1969
Proprietor: L N & Janet
Baer
Hours: Mon-Fri, 9-12 &
2-5; Sat & Sun by appt
Types & Periods: Primitives,
Furniture, Quilts, Toys,
Lamps, China, Glass &
General Line
Specialties: Old Light
Fixtures
Directions: By RR tracks
on old Rte 35 coming into
town

**MAE THOMPSON
ANTIQUES**
640 Perdue Plaza   43160
614 335-1845   Est: 1959
Proprietor: Mae Thompson
Hours: Mon-Sun
Types & Periods: China,
Glass, Primitives, Small
Furniture & Dolls
Specialties: Pattern Glass
Directions: 1st house off
St Rte 41 S

Waterville

SAGIT-TAURUS ANTIQUES
430 Overlook Dr   43566
419 878-9536
Hours: By appt after 6 &
on Sat & Sun
Types & Periods: General
Line

West Carrollton

THE COWEB SHOPPE
456 E Dixie Dr   45449
317 859-3440   Est: 1972
Proprietor: Martha Miller
Hours: Mon-Sat, 10-5
Types & Periods: General
Line, Furniture, Clocks,
Lamps, Primitives, China &
Glass
Directions: S of Dayton,
I-75 to exit 47

West Salem

KEENER'S KINGDOM
RD 3, Rte 175   44090
419 945-2539   Est: 1970
Proprietor: Alvin & Phylis
Keener
Hours: Mon-Sun by appt
or chance
Types & Periods: General
Line, Lamps, Furniture,
Bric-A-Brac & Primitives
Appraisal Service Available
Directions: Rte 42
between Ashland & W
Salem, on divided Hwy,
Church on corner in
direction to turn about 1½
miles N on Country Rd
175

West Unity

**WEEPING WILLOW
ANTIQUE SHOP**
Cty Rd K, Rd 2   43570
419 924-2988   Est: 1968
Proprietor: Dick & Helen
Hachtel
Hours: Mon-Sat, 9-6
Types & Periods: General
Line, Glass, China, Dolls,
Toys, Furniture, Primitives &
Collectibles
Specialties: Lamps, Repairs
& Chimneys
Directions: 7 miles from
exit 2 Ohio Turnpike, 3
miles S on Rte 15, 4 miles
E on Cty Rd K, 1 mile S
of West Unity on Hwy 127,
1 mile W on Cty Rd K

Westerville

**LOEFFLERS LAMPS &
ANTIQUES**
8708 N State Rd   43081
614 882-7664   Est: 1948
Proprietor: Mrs Wm E
Loeffler
Hours: By appt or chance
Types & Periods: General
Line & Furniture
Specialties: Lamps, Parts &
Service
Directions: 1/2 mile N of
Westerville on St Rte 3

WESTERVILLE
34 E College   43081
614 882-3004   Est: 1973
Proprietor: C R Volkmar
Hours: Tues-Sun, 12-5;
also by appt
Types & Periods: General
Line
Specialties: Clocks, Lamps
Directions: 1/2 block off
State St in Old Westerville

Worthington

SNOW HOUSE
41 W New England Ave
43085
614 846-7630   Est: 1972
Proprietor: Helen Heintz
Hours: Tues-Thurs, Sat,
10-5; Sun 1-5
Types & Periods: General
Line
Appraisal Service Available
Directions: 1 block S of St
Rte 161, 1/2 block W of
St Rte 23

Youngstown

**GLUCK'S GIFT & ANTIQUE
SHOP INC**
564 Gypsy Lane   44505
216 744-1788   Est: 1942
Proprietor: Theresa Gluck
& Paul Gluck
Hours: Mon-Sat
Types & Periods: China,
Furniture, Christmas Plates,
Jewelry, Copper & Glass
Specialties: Furniture, China,
Copper & Brass & Christmas
Plates
Appraisal Service Available

PROKOP'S ANTIQUES
2325 Mahoning Ave
44509
216 792-3670   Est: 1966
Proprietor: Dave & Kathy
Cicozi
Hours: By chance
Types & Periods: General
Line
Specialties: Lamps
Directions: W side of town

Zanesville

THE CURIOSITY SHOP
135 N 6th St　　43701
614 453-6259　Est: 1970
Proprietor: Mrs Jack
Bennett
Hours: Mon-Sat
Types & Periods: Furniture,
Heisey, Cambridge, Pressed
& Cut Glass, China,
Primitives & Pictures
　Directions: 1 block S I-70
　(Downtown), 5th or 7th St
　exit

QUONSET ANTIQUES
1360 W Main St　　43701
614 452-1971　Est: 1973
Proprietor: Phyllis Davis
Hours: Tues-Sat
Types & Periods: General
Line
　Directions: Rte 40 W side
　of town

WAYSIDE ANTIQUES
2290 E Pike　　43701
614 453-4776　Est: 1971
Hours: Wed-Thurs,
Sat-Sun, by appt or
chance
Types & Periods: Turn of
the Century Oak, Middle
Period (1850-1870)
Victorian, Pine & Maple
Furniture, Primitives,
Children's Furniture & Glass
Specialties: Oak Kitchen
Items, Books & Post Cards,
Ohio Pottery
Appraisal Service Available
　Directions: On Rtes 22, 40
　& 93; E of Zanesville (2
　milesfrom City limits), first
　shop on right going E

Pedestal Dining Table.

Although Late Victorian, it is a modified Empire design.

STATE OF OKLAHOMA

Altus

DUVALL'S CLOCKS & ANTIQUES
612 E Walnut   73521
405 482-4328   Est: 1970
Proprietor: Lowell & Lois Duvall
Hours: Tues-Fri 9-5, Closed Sat-Mon
Types & Periods: Furniture, Clocks, Glass, China, Lamps
Specialties: Clocks, Repaired
Appraisal Service Available
Directions: 1 block S of Broadway & Navajoe, Right on Walnut, Store behind House

Ardmore

FLEA MARKET
1 W Broadway   73401
405 223-1230   Est: 1965
Proprietor: Harry Stockdale
Hours: Daily
Types & Periods: General Line
Directions: Corner of Broadway & Washington, Off Hwy 70 E

HOBBY HORSE ANTIQUES
15 N Washington   73401
405 223-6678   Est: 1969
Proprietor: Mrs Frances James
Hours: Daily
Types & Periods: Furniture, Glass, China, Dolls, Clocks, General Line
Specialties: Glass, Dolls
Directions: Downtown, Few Doors N off Main St

LOVE'S HEIRLOOM ANTIQUES
1704 McLish   73401
405 223-0578   Est: 1950
Proprietor: Mr & Mrs Gordon Love
Hours: Tues-Thurs, By Appointment
Types & Periods: Jewelry, Silver, China, Glass, Furniture, Books

Appraisal Service Available
Directions: E of Hwy I-35 on Service Lane on Hwy 70 within City Limits

Bache

SMITH'S ANTIQUES
Box 26   74526
918 423-3210   Est: 1967
Proprietor: Alba Smith
Hours: Daily, Closed Jan & Feb
Types & Periods: Glass, China, Pottery, Lamps, Primitives, Furniture
Specialties: Violins, German, French, Italian
Directions: Hwy 270, 7 miles E of McAlester

Bartlesville

THE GALLERY
519 E 3rd St   74003
918 336 3200   Est: 1973
Proprietor: Mary Scullion & Ferol Rogers
Hours: Daily, By Appointment, 10-3, Wed, Thurs, Fri
Types & Periods: General Line
Appraisal Service Available

Bethany

PAULINE'S ANTIQUES
3707 N College   73008
405 787-5821   Est: 1970
Proprietor: Pauline B Wood
Hours: Daily, Weekends 10-5, Sun 1-5
Types & Periods: Pattern Glass, Black Glass, Primitives, Tables
Specialties: Pottery
Directions: 2 blocks S of Hwy 66

Canton

THE CRANBERRY SHOPPE
Box 606   73724
405 886-2890   Est: 1969
Proprietor: Lahoma Edsel
Hours: By Appointment
Types & Periods: Bronzes, 18th & 19th Centuries Porcelain, Cranberry Items, 18th & 19th Centuries French & English Furniture, Accessories
Specialties: Porcelain Figurines, Urns & Vases

Chickasha

FRAN'S ANTIQUES
1328 S 14th   73018
405 224-7111   Est: 1955
Proprietor: Frances Carter
Hours: Daily 9-5, Sun 1-6, Other Times By Appointment
Types & Periods: General Line, Pressed Glass, Art Glass, Cut Glass, China, Silver, Primitives, Furniture
Specialties: Glass (Pressed), Primitives
Appraisal Service Available
Directions: From Intersection of Hwy 81 S & Grand, 10 blocks W to S 14, Turn Right 6 blocks N on 14

LAWSON'S PAWN & ANTIQUES
211 S 5th St   73018
405 224-1733   Est: 1949
Proprietor: Elmer Lawson
Hours: Daily, Weekends 8-5, Also by Appointment
Types & Periods: General Line
Directions: 5th & Kansas Ave

Claremore

FRONTIER ANTIQUES
1140 S Lynn Riggs 74017
918 341-3442   Est: 1969
Proprietor: Betty Smith
Hours: Tues-Sat, By
Appointment, By Chance
Types & Periods: Primitives,
Collectibles
Specialties: Depression
Glass
Appraisal Service Available
Directions: 1/2 Mile S of
Claremore on Hwy 66

**LACY'S ANTIQUES GIFTS &
JEWELRY**
123 N Lynn Riggs Blvd
74017
918 341-9789   Est: 1960
Proprietor: E E & Dorothy
Lacy
Hours: Daily
Types & Periods: General
Line
Specialties: Furniture,
Jewelry
Appraisal Service Available
Directions: On Hwy 66, 1
block N of Will Rogers
Blvd

VENTRIS ANTIQUES
407 E Will Rogers 74017
918 341-8106   Est: 1964
Proprietor: E Q Ventris
Hours: Daily, Closed Sat,
By Appointment, By
Chance, Open when
Home
Types & Periods:
Turn-of-the-Century Oak &
Early Primitive Furniture,
General Line, Glass, China,
Lamps, Framed Antique
Prints
Specialties: Unusual Pieces
of Furniture
Appraisal Service Available
Directions: Main St E-W

**WARDEN'S ANTIQUES &
CLOCKS**
103 N Boling   74017
918 341-1770   Est: 1969
Proprietor: Bill F Warden
Hours: Daily, Weekends,
Closed Sun
Types & Periods: Clocks,
Furniture, Bric-A-Brac
Specialties: Clocks
Directions: 1 mile W of
Town, At the foot of Will
Rogers Memorial

Clinton

STUFF-N-THINGS
700 Frisco   73601
405 323-1350   Est: 1975
Proprietor: John & Judy
Peter
Hours: Mon-Sat 9-5,
Evenings & Sun by
Appointment
Types & Periods: Furniture,
Depression Glass, Crystal,
Silver, Primitives
Appraisal Service Available
Directions: 1 block S of
I-40 Business Rte at
Corner of 7th & Frisco

Cushing

**GWEN HARRISON
ANTIQUES**
810 S Harrison St   74023
918 225-1390   Est: 1968
Proprietor: Gwen Harrison
Hours: Daily 10-8, Sun 1-6
Types & Periods: General
Line, Primitives, Country
Store & Kitchen Items,
Advertising Bottles, Glass,
Furniture, Pottery, Farm
Items
Specialties: Antique &
Collector's Dolls & Related
Items
Appraisal Service Available
Directions: 7 blocks S of
Main St, Cushing halfway
btwn Tulsa & Okla City

VINSON & SON ANTIQUES
74023
918 225-5420   Est: 1974
Proprietor: Mae Vinson
Hours: Daily, Weekends,
11-'til Dark, Closed Sun
Except by Appointment
Types & Periods: Glassware,
Primitives, Furniture

Del City

**SEATON'S HOUSE OF
ANTIQUES**
4415 E Reno   73117
405 677-3565   Est: 1973
Proprietor: Marilyn Seaton
Hours: Daily 10-5, Closed
Sun & Mon

Types & Periods: General
Line, Furniture, Glass,
Collector's Items
Directions: Exit I-40 at
Reno (E of I-40 & I-35)
Intersection on E Side of
N Canadian River, E on
Reno Approx 1½ Miles

Durant

A H & PAULINE GREEN
202 W Evergreen   74701
405 924-9923   Est: 1958
Proprietor: Mr & Mrs
Green
Hours: Daily
Types & Periods: Furniture,
Primitives, Glassware
Specialties: Glass
(Depression), China
Cabinets
Directions: 2½ Miles E of
City on Hwy 70

Edmond

MOMMIE'S ANTIQUES
11 Burton Pl   73034
405 341-0699
Proprietor: Lothar &
Louise Smith
Hours: Daily, Weekends
10-5, Closed Sun
Types & Periods: China,
Glass, Furniture, General
Line

THIMBLEFIELD ANTIQUES
Box 324   73034
405 341-1275
Proprietor: Doris Blair
Hours: By Appointment,
By Chance
Types & Periods: Primitive &
Pine Furniture

Elk City

BEVERLY'S ANTIQUES
301 S Randall   73644
405 225-3637   Est: 1972
Proprietor: Beverly Ann
Jones
Hours: By Appointment
1-5:30
Types & Periods: China,
Glass, Jewelry

Directions: "From W Exit
of I-40, turn right at first
stop light, Go 3 blocks S"

MARTIN'S ANTIQUES
2424 W 3rd   73644
405 225-1497   Est: 1970
Proprietor: Leroy &
Bernice Martin
Hours: Mon-Sat 9-5:30,
Sun 1-6
Types & Periods: American
1920 Round Oak Tables,
Wooden Oak Ice Boxes,
Kitchen Cabinets, Church
Pews
Specialties: Spurs & Bits, All
Kinds Glassware, Carnival &
Depression
Directions: W Hwy 66

Grove

DON'S SWAP SHOP
                 74344
918 786-9590   Est: 1957
Proprietor: Don Davis
Hours: Daily, Weekends,
Closed Tues
Types & Periods: Furniture,
Glass, Metal, "Old Junk
Bought-Rare Antiques Sold"
Specialties: Primitives
Appraisal Service Available
Directions: 2 Miles NW on
Hwy 59

**YE OLDE ANTIQUE
SHOPPE**
                 74344
918 786-3359   Est: 1970
Proprietor: Esther V
O'Daniel
Hours: Daily, Weekends,
Closed Sat
Types & Periods: Porcelain,
Glassware, 18th & 19th
Centuries Furniture
Specialties: Glass (Signed
Cut Glass)
Appraisal Service Available
Directions: Near Sailboat
Bridge on US Hwy 59, 4
Miles W of Town

Hobart

**GRIESER BARGAIN
CORNER**
                 73651
405 726-2426   Est: 1965
Proprietor: Mrs Julius H
Grieser
Hours: Daily, Weekends,
Closed Sun
Types & Periods: Furniture,
Pictures, Bottles, China,
Brass, Copper, Iron,
Silverware
Specialties: Late 1800
Surrey
Directions: 2 Miles E of
Town on Hwy 9-183 E

Holdenville

TRADING BARN
P O Box 901   74848
405 379-2262   Est: 1974
Proprietor: Jesse M Booth
Hours: Thurs-Sat 10-6, By
Chance
Types & Periods: Primitives,
Collectibles, Wheels,
Directions: 2 Miles S of
Town on Hwy 48

Hugo

BROWSER SHOP
1009 W Jackson   74743
                 Est: 1974
Proprietor: Adelaide V
Davidson
Hours: Mon-Sat 9-4:30,
Closed Sun & Thurs
Types & Periods: Pattern
Glass, China, Depression
Glass, Furniture, Primitives,
Bottles
Directions: On Hwy 70 W

Kingfisher

VIRGINIA'S ANTIQUES
214 N Main St   73750
405 375-4246   Est: 1971
Proprietor: Virginia Shutler
Hours: By Appointment,
By Chance
Types & Periods: Furniture,
Primitives, Brass, Copper,

Glass, China, Orientals,
Pictures, Light Fixtures
Specialties: Household Items
Appraisal Service Available
Directions: Downtown,
Next Door to T G & Y,
Above Lawrence's Dept
Store

Lawton

AMBER BOTTLE
Box 5207   73501
405 355-4324
Proprietor: Leora B
Freeman
Hours: Daily, Sun & Eves
by Appointment
Types & Periods: General
Line, Paintings

Marlow

**CARRIAGE HOUSE
ANTIQUES**
Rte 2   73055
405 658-3594   Est: 1970
Proprietor: Benson's Inc
Hours: By Appointment,
By Chance
Types & Periods: Art & Cut
Glass, Lamps, Furniture
Directions: 1 Mile S of
Marlow on E Side

**LINAM WHOLESALE
ANTIQUES**
Rte 2   73055
405 658-3739   Est: 1968
Proprietor: Tom Linam
Hours: Daily
Types & Periods: Period thru
Collectors Items, Furniture,
Clocks, Stained Glass,
Brass, Silver, Pewter, China
Specialties: Clocks
Appraisal Service Available

McAlester

FRANCES ANTIQUES
1002 E Seneca   74501
918 423-1584   Est: 1967
Proprietor: Frances I
Bennett
Hours: Daily

FRANCES Cont'd

Types & Periods: Glass, China, Victorian, Depression Age
Specialties: Furniture, Oriental, Lamps, Pottery
   Directions: N of Hwy 69 Bypass

Miami

DAVE'S NEW & USED FURNITURE
   118 S Main   74354
   918 542-9373   Est: 1971
Proprietor: David Roberson
Hours: Daily, By Chance, Closed Sun
Types & Periods: General Line
Specialties: Furniture

Midwest City

MARGIE'S ANTIQUES
   200 W Mimosa Dr   73110
   405 732-5386   Est: 1961
Proprietor: Mrs Walter J Baum
Hours: Mon, Wed-Sat
Types & Periods: American Cut & Pattern Glass, Lamps, Clocks, China Primitives, Furniture
Appraisal Service Available
   Directions: 3 blocks S of 15th & Lockheed

Muskogee

ANTIQUES INC
   2215 W Shawnee   74401
   918 687-4447   Est: 1970
Proprietor: Mrs Mary Beckman
Hours: Daily, Weekends
Types & Periods: General Line
Specialties: English Antiques of the 17th, 18th & 19th Centuries

ISOM'S ANTIQUES & COLLECTABLES
   230 N 2nd   74401
   918 683-2181   Est: 1969
Proprietor: Howard Neal Isom
Hours: Daily, Weekends 9-6, Closed Sun, By Appointment
Types & Periods: Glass, Light Fixtures, French Furniture, Pictures, Primitives, Figurines, Oak, Brass
Specialties: Glass (Cut & Carnival), Jewelry
   Directions: Downtown

Nash

OKLAHOMA TERRITORY ANTIQUES
   106 S Main   73761
   405 839-2429   Est: 1974
Proprietor: Ron & Robbin Sheerill
Hours: Tues-Sat 9-6, Sun 1-6
Types & Periods: Oak, Walnut, Pine & Primitive Furniture, Dishes
Appraisal Service Available
   Directions: Across Street from Post Office

Ninnekah

KUNTRY KORNER
                     73067
   405 224-0539   Est: 1972
Proprietor: C D & Ruth Parks
Hours: Daily
Types & Periods: General Line
Specialties: Glass (Depression)
   Directions: 6 Miles S of Chickasha, at 81 & 277 Hwy Intersection

Norman

BETTE'S ANTIQUE CORNER
   330 S Porter   73069
   405 329-8311
Proprietor: Bette Crewson
Hours: Daily, Weekends 9-4:30

Types & Periods: Glass, Copper, Silver, Brass, All Types
   Directions: 2 blocks S of Main St

THE BUGGY WHIP ANTIQUE SHOP
   1414 24th Ave SW   73069
   405 364-4451   Est: 1975
Proprietor: Helen & Dale Stephens
Hours: Tues-Sat
Types & Periods: General Line, Furniture, Primitives, Glassware, Collectibles
Appraisal Service Available
   Directions: Exit I-35 on Lindsey, E to 1st Traffic Light, S 1½ blocks on the W Side of Street

KAYLAINE'S TREASURES
   205 W Main   73069
   405 364-5616   Est: 1976
Proprietor: Elaine Fore
Hours: Daily, Weekends 10-5, Closed Sun & Mon
Types & Periods: Glassware, Primitives, Furniture, "Little Bit of Everything"
   Directions: E of I-35 in Antique Mall

KING'S ANTIQUES
   215 W Main   73069
   405 360-0732   Est: 1973
Proprietor: Donna B King
Hours: Daily
Types & Periods: Furniture, Primitives, Glass, Collectibles
Specialties: Furniture, Oak, Turn-of-the-Century
   Directions: Downtown

THE OLD OAK TREE ANTIQUES
   1313 24th Ave SW   73069
   405 329-4206   Est: 1974
Proprietor: J & B Stout
Hours: Daily, 10-5, Closed Sun & Mon
Types & Periods: Oak & Victorian Furniture, Clocks, Watches, Primitives, Collectibles
Appraisal Service Available
   Directions: Off I-35, 1 block S of Ramada Inn

SIM'S COFFEE GRINDER
205 W Main   73069
405 364-1324   Est: 1975
Proprietor: Regena &
Simeon Friedman
Hours: Daily, Weekends
10-5, Sat 10-5, Closed
Sun & Mon
Types & Periods: Glass,
China, Furniture, Jewelry,
German Clocks, Oil
Paintings, Lithographs,
Manuscripts, Stamps, Coins
Directions: Main St Exit
Off I-35, in Antique Mall

Oklahoma City

OKLAHOMA CITY CLUSTER
Directions: N Broadway
(2000 Block) to Classen
Blvd (3000-9000 Blocks)
E-W including Adjacent
Street, N Western
(4000-9000) & smaller
Side Streets, Also S Klein
(300 Block), W Reno
(400-600 Blocks), NW 10th
(1000-3000 Blocks)

**ANDERSON ANTIQUES &
ART GALLERIES**
5101-11 Classen   73118
405 848-0944   Est: 1939
Proprietor: Phil Anderson
Hours: Mon-Sat, Sun 1-5
For New Shipments
Types & Periods: Furniture,
China, Glass, Iron, Brass,
Bronze, Sculpture, Stained
& Beveled Glass, Light
Fixtures, Western & Indian
Art, Jewelry
Specialties: Furniture, Cut
Glass
Appraisal Service Available
Directions: US 66 &
Classen Circle or I-240 &
Classen

ANTIQUE HOUSE
4409 N Meridian   73112
405 495-2221, 946-4292
Est: 1973
Proprietor: La June Ellis
Hours: Mon-Sat 9-5:30,
Sun 1-5:30, Eves by
Appointment
Types & Periods: Cut Glass,
Art Glass, Decorator Items,

Fine Furniture, "3 Houses
Full to Choose From"
Specialties: Lamps
Appraisal Service Available
Directions: I-40 to N
Meridian

**ARNOLA SCHRODER
ANTIQUES &
DECORATIVES**
2401 N Classen Blvd
73106
405 528-0461   Est: 1978
Proprietor: Ed & Marian
Cooksey, Denise Belden
Hours: Tues-Sat 10-6,
Thurs 'til 9, Sun 1-6,
Closed Mon
Types & Periods: European
& American Furniture,
Decoratives, Glassware
Specialties: French
Furniture, Clocks & Statuary
Directions: NW Corner of
Classen Blvd & NW 23rd,
Off I-35 Exit to Hwy 66 W
to Classen Circle, S to NW
23rd or Take Classen Exit
off I-40 W N to NW 23rd

ARTHUR-GRAHAM
6602 N Western   73116
405 843-4431   Est: 1977
Proprietor: Bill Hays
Hours: Mon-Sat
Types & Periods: English
Imports, Furniture, Small
Items, Collectibles
Specialties: English Imports
Directions: 3 blocks N of
NW 63rd on N Western

BLACK GOLD ANTIQUES
9501 NE Expwy   73111
405 478-0306   Est: 1972
Proprietor: Joseph N Bell
Hours: Daily
Types & Periods:
Americana, Primitives,
Country Furniture, Oak,
Wicker, Victorian, China,
Glass
Appraisal Service Available
Directions: I-35, 3 Miles
NE of Okla City

**BUCKBOARD ANTIQUES &
GIFTS**
1411 N May   73107
405 943-7020   Est: 1977
Proprietor: Judy Howard
Hours: Tues-Sat 10-4:30
Types & Periods:
Turn-of-the-Century Oak,
Walnut, Country Furniture,
Primitives, Baskets, Quilts &
Quilted Gift Items
Specialties: Free Antique
Guides to Okla City,
Handmade Gift Items &
Quilts
Directions: 4 blocks N of
the Fairgrounds (30 blocks
W & 14 blocks N of
Downtown)

CONNELY'S ANTIQUES
4920 S Western   73109
405 632-5042
Proprietor: Mrs Cea Willo
Connely
Hours: Daily 10-4
Types & Periods: Glass,
China, Objets d'Art

THE CONNOISSEUR SHOP
3317 N Villa   73112
405 946-6159   Est: 1976
Proprietor: Dess F Clay &
Laureta E Prince
Hours: Daily, Weekends,
Sun by Appointment
Types & Periods: General
Line
Specialties: Furniture, Silver

COTTAGE ANTIQUES
3815 NW 10th St   73107
405 943-1439   Est: 1968
Proprietor: Jacqueline
Whitwell
Hours: Daily 1-5:30,
Closed Tues
Types & Periods: Furniture,
Clocks, Copper, Brass,
China, Glassware
Specialties: Furniture
(Victorian,
Turn-of-the-Century)
Directions: I-240 to
Westbound NW 10th St
Exit

DOLPHA JUSTICE ANTIQUES
2121 SW 64th   73159
405 685-8498
Proprietor: Mrs Dave Justice
Hours: By Appointment, By Chance
Types & Periods: China, Glass

DON JUAN ANTIQUARIES
4401 NE 36th St   73111
405 424-3795
Proprietor: Juanita C Brown
Hours: By Appointment
Types & Periods: English & American Furniture, Oriental Objets d'Art

FAYE'S ANTIQUES ART & STUFF
3633 NW 19th St   73107
405 947-2116, 946-4240
    Est: 1969
Proprietor: Faye N Jones
Hours: Mon-Sat, Sun 2-4:30, By Appointment, By Chance
Types & Periods: Art Glass, Oriental Objets d'Art, China, Silver, Depression Glass, Primitives, Jewelry, Furniture, Dolls & Miniatures
Specialties: Antique Photo Restoration & Copy
Appraisal Service Available
    Directions: Corner NW 19th & N Portland Ave, Accessible from I-40, I-240 or Rte 66 Exit on N Portland Ave

FERRIS ANTIQUES
2323 N Indiana   73106
405 524-4052
Proprietor: Esther L Ferris
Hours: By Appointment, By Chance
Types & Periods: Art Glass, Oils, Bronzes, Porcelain, Orientals

FOXFORD GALLERIES
129 SW 29th   73109
405 239-9432
Proprietor: Clara M Moates
Hours: Daily 10-5
Types & Periods: General Line

THE HALL TREE
9915 Mashburn Blvd
    73127
405 722-1705
Proprietor: Joan & James Hall
Hours: By Appointment
Types & Periods: Primitives, Pine Furniture

HERITAGE GIFTS & ANTIQUES
420 W Reno   73102
405 235-2098   Est: 1968
Proprietor: Naomi A Woody
Hours: Daily 1-4
Types & Periods: General Line, China, Glassware

VERNITA KING INC
6480 Avondale   73116
405 843-5664   Est: 1963
Proprietor: Vernita King
Hours: Mon-Sat, By Appointment
Types & Periods: Bronzes, Porcelains, Chinese Embroideries, Oriental Art
Appraisal Service Available
    Directions: N of 63rd St btwn Western & Grand

LAMPLIGHTERS ANTIQUES & GIFTS
9225 N Western   73114
405 842-9136   Est: 1971
Proprietor: Reta Barber
Hours: Thurs-Sat 12-5, By Appointment
Types & Periods: Primitives, Art, Depression, Pressed Glass, China, General Line
Appraisal Service Available

LAURA'S ANTIQUES & GIFTS
2625 W Britton Rd   73120
405 755-0582   Est: 1971
Proprietor: Laura Lou Medley
Hours: Daily, Weekends 11-5, Sun by Appointment
Types & Periods: Furniture, Art & Cut Glass, Orientals
Specialties: China, Glass (Crystal)
Appraisal Service Available
    Directions: W of I-35

MEMORIES MALL
7210 Western N   73116
405 848-0408   Est: 1978
Proprietor: Don & Marcella Fleet
Hours: Mon, Wed, Fri 10-6, Tues, Thurs 10-9, Sun 1-5
Types & Periods: Furniture, Primitives, Glass, Art, Paper, "Six Different Shops"
Specialties: Oak
Appraisal Service Available

THE RUSHLIGHT
6612 N Western   73116
405 842-2266   Est: 1972
Proprietor: Shirley Robinson & Colleen Easter
Hours: Daily 11-4, Closed Sun, By Appointment
Types & Periods: Pre-1850 Furniture, Country, American, English Porcelain
Specialties: Furniture
Appraisal Service Available
    Directions: N off Rte 66 on E Side of City

SILHOUETTE SHOP
3623 N Shartel   73118
    Est: 1927
Proprietor: L Jane Brooks
Hours: Daily 10-5
Types & Periods: Silver, Orientals, Enamels, Porcelains, Furniture
Specialties: Enamels
Appraisal Service Available
    Directions: Corner of 36th & Shartel

THE WHAT NOT SHELF ANTIQUES
1116 NW 51st   73118
405 843-6040   Est: 1970
Proprietor: Daniel P & Jean I Thompson
Hours: Daily 11-4, Closed Sun & Mon
Types & Periods: General Line
Specialties: Glass
Appraisal Service Available
    Directions: 51st & N Western in "The Colonies"

ZIGLER ANTIQUES & DOLL STUDIO
3108 Classen   73118
405 524-2726   Est: 195l
Proprietor: Gertrude Zigler
Hours: Daily 9-6, Sun 1-6
Types & Periods: Furniture, Art & Cut Glass, Dolls, Lamps
Specialties: Toys
Appraisal Service Available
Directions: W on NW 23rd St

Oologah

JANKEYS' ANTIQUES
Box 16   74053
918 443-2328   Est: 1970
Proprietor: Bill & Ruby Jankey
Hours: Sun-Fri
Types & Periods: General Line
Specialties: Glass
Directions: 4 blocks W of Hwy 169

Rush Springs

GERTRUDE SWEANY ANTIQUES
Rte 2   73082
405 476-3012   Est: 1972
Proprietor: Gertrude Sweany
Hours: Sunday
Types & Periods: Primitives, Glassware, Pictures & Frames, Lamps, Books
Specialties: Telephones, Trunks

Sulphur

WIMPY'S ANTIQUES
1109 W Broadway   73086
405 622-5834   Est: 1951
Proprietor: Rick Patterson
Hours: Daily 9-5, Closed Sun
Types & Periods: 19th & 20th Centuries Oak & Walnut, Primitive Furniture, Glassware, Clocks

Specialties: Aladdin Lamp Parts
Appraisal Service Available
Directions: On Hwy 7 in Sulphur

Tahlequah

THE GALLERY
206 S Muskogee Ave
                  74464
918 456-2471   Est: 1971
Proprietor: Robt E Pullen
Hours: Mon-Sat 9:30-5:30, Usually Closed Sept-Oct
Types & Periods: Furniture, Glass, Firearms, Jewelry, General Line
Specialties: Indian Art
Appraisal Service Available
Directions: Downtown on Main St, 200 Ft from Courthouse Square

THE PINK HOUSE ANTIQUES
Rte 3, Box 43   74464
918 456-8152   Est: 1959
Proprietor: Edna Brace
Hours: Daily
Types & Periods: Primitives, Furniture, Lamps, Cut & Art Glass
Appraisal Service Available
Directions: 3 Miles E of Tahlequah to 'Y' at Foot of Illinois River Bridge, Turn Right at Sign

Tonkawa

MC WILLIAMS ANTIQUES
108 N 5th St   74653
405 628-3254
Proprietor: Lucile McWilliams
Hours: Daily 9-5, Closed Wed, Sun 9-5
Types & Periods: General Line, Pattern Glass, Lamp Parts

Tulsa

TULSA CLUSTER
Directions: Shops on E 3rd St (2000 Block), E 11th St (1000-9000 Blocks), E 15th St

(1000-3000 Blocks), E Admiral Place (3000 Block) which are crisscrossed by Streets with smaller number of Shops (Running N-S) i.e. Peoria, Harvard, Utica

AMIR'S PERSIAN IMPORTS
2204 E 15th   74104
918 939-6464   Est: 1964
Proprietor: Amir K Adib-Yazdi
Hours: Tues-Sat 10-5:30, Sun & Mon by Appointment
Types & Periods: Old Persian Rugs, Copper, Brass, Pottery, Inlaid, Enamel, Mini-Painting on Ivory, Jewelry
Specialties: Antique, Semi-Antique Persian Rugs, Metals, Jewelry
Appraisal Service Available
Directions: Btwn Lewis & Utica Ave, 3 blocks W off Broken Arrow Expwy, 15th St Exit

BARBER ANTIQUES
8948 E 11th St   74112
918 838-3690   Est: 1930
Proprietor: Alva L Barber
Hours: Daily, Closed Sun & Mon
Types & Periods: Furniture, Bronze, Glass, China, Chandeliers, Fireplace Pieces, Paintings, Porcelain
Specialties: Bronze
Appraisal Service Available
Directions: Near I-44 & 244

MRS HOWARD CONHAIM INC-DBA CARLIN SHOP
1579 E 21st St   74114
918 742-0066/2598
Proprietor: Mrs Howard Conhaim
Hours: Mon-Fri, Closed Sun & Sat
Types & Periods: 18th & 19th Centuries Furniture, China, Crystal, Prints, Light Fixtures
Directions: Helmerick & Payne Bldg, Across Utica from St John's Hospital

Tulsa   Cont'd

CHELSEA GALLERY
1809 E 15th   74104
918 939-6109   Est: 1973
Proprietor: Gary Quiggle
Hours: Daily 10-5:30, Sat
10-4, Closed Sun
Types & Periods: 19th &
20th Centuries European &
American Prints, Oils,
Watercolors
Specialties: English Prints,
Military Prints
   Directions: Btwn Utica &
   Lewis Aves

DOWELL ANTIQUE SHOP
1628 S Cheyenne   74119
918 583-7674   Est: 1940
Proprietor: Vern Dowell
Hours: By Appointment,
By Chance
Types & Periods: General
Line
Specialties: Glass (Colored
& Cut), Music Boxes
Appraisal Service Available
   Directions: 11 blocks from
   Downtown, 2nd St W of
   Main St, 1 block W, 1½
   blocks S of Skelly Oil Co
   Bldg

FANNING ANTIQUES
800 N Country Club Dr
                74127
918 587-5600   Est: 1944
Proprietor: Minnie & Bill
Fanning
Hours: Daily 9-6, By
Appointment, Owner Lives
on Premises
Types & Periods: Furniture,
China, Lamps, Orientals, Art
& Pattern Glass, Primitives
Appraisal Service Available
   Directions: N on Denver to
   400 Block, 2 blocks W on
   Edison, 2 blocks N on
   Country Club

THE GOLDEN EAGLE
3844 S Atlanta Place
                74105
918 743-1805
Proprietor: Florise W
Edwards
Hours: By Appointment,
By Chance
Types & Periods: General
Line

JOHNIE'S ANTIQUES
809 S St Louis   74120
918 587-3703   Est: 1969
Proprietor: Johnie Fakes
Hours: Daily 10-5
Types & Periods: Victorian,
English, French & American
Period Furniture, Metals,
Glass & China
Specialties: Furniture
Appraisal Service Available
   Directions: Downtown

**THE LAMPOST ANTIQUES
& SILVER CO**
8312 E 11th St   74112
918 835-3686   Est: 1963
Proprietor: Mrs Toni
Garrett
Hours: Mon-Sat 9-5:30
Types & Periods: General
Line, Matching Sterling
Flatware Service at
Discounts Ranging from
50%-75%, Rare Exceptions
Specialties: Sterling, Jewelry
   Directions: Btwn Memorial
   & Garnet, 1½ blocks E of
   Memorial

MRS W O MC DANIEL
3211 E Admiral Pl   74110
918 936-3975   Est: 1956
Proprietor: Sarah
McDaniel
Hours: Daily, By Chance
Types & Periods: General
Line, Furniture
   Directions: Hwy 33, 1
   block W from Harvard,
   From W Exit from Expwy
   at Delaware

SCHMIDT'S ANTIQUES
2701 E 7th St   74104
918 939-1169
Proprietor: W J Schmidt
Hours: Daily, Weekends
9-5, Closed Sun
Types & Periods: American
& European Furniture,
Bronzes, Accessories

SHARP'S 1860 ANTIQUES
1860 E 15th St   74104
918 939-1121   Est: 1964
Proprietor: Richard G
Sharp
Hours: Daily

Types & Periods: Art & Cut
Glass, 18th & Early 19th
Centuries Furniture, Early
Lighting, Primitives, Pewter
Appraisal Service Available
   Directions: 15th St Exit
   from Hwy 64 & Okla Hwy
   51

TOM'S ANTIQUES
1846 E 15th St   74104
918 932-4806   Est: 1963
Proprietor: Tom E Foster
Hours: Daily
Types & Periods: Orientals,
Circa-1780 Export Porcelain,
Glassware, Furniture
Specialties: China, Glass
Appraisal Service Available
   Directions: Btwn Lewis
   Ave & Utica Ave

Vinita

MILLER'S ANTIQUES
223 W South Ave   74301
918 256-2540 & 256-7292
              Est: 1970
Proprietor: Wayne & Jean
Miller
Hours: Mon-Fri, & By appt
Types & Periods: 18th & 19th
Centuries Art Glass, old
period Cut Glass, General
Line & Hard to find Objects
Specialties: Art Glass
Appraisal Service Available
   Directions: 2 blocks off US
   66 going W. Directional signs
   in town & outside town

Washington

DIAMOND "H" ANTIQUES
                73093
405 288-2490
Proprietor: Mrs K S
Holland
Hours: Daily, Weekends
9-6, Sun 1-5
Types & Periods: Cut Glass,
General Line
   Directions: 8 Miles S of
   Norman, I-35 & Ladd Rd,
   1 Mile W

Waurika

NANCY'S ANTIQUES
Hwy 70   73573
405 228-2575   Est: 1966
Proprietor: Jimmie &
Nancy Way
Hours: Mon-Sat 10-5, Sun
Afternoons, By
Appointment
Types & Periods: 19th &
20th Centuries Victorian &
Golden Oak, American &
European Furniture, General
Line
Specialties: Furniture
Refinishing

Appraisal Service Available
Directions: Located S
Edge of Town on Hwy 70,
"Large two-story
railroadrooming house"

Weatherford

THE HUTCH
320 E Main   73096
405 772-3801   Est: 1973
Proprietor: Jim & Wanda
Hutchinson
Hours: Mon-Sat

Types & Periods: Primitives,
American Oak
Directions: 70 Miles W of
Oklahoma City on I-40

THE JUNKTIQUE
400 N State   73096
405 772-3121   Est: 1971
Proprietor: E D Smith
Hours: By Appointment,
By Chance
Types & Periods: General
Line
Appraisal Service Available
Directions: "3 blocks N of
Main St at the old dead
tree"

This organ manufactured by the Sterling Company is of the Late Victorian Period. Its design is strongly influenced by Eastlake ideas. By the way, it still plays.

STATE OF OREGON

Albany

OLDIE ANTIQUES
222 S Ellsworth   97321
503 928-3439   Est: 1973
Proprietor: Ruth Black
Hours: Mon-Sat
Types & Periods: General
Line, Oak
Directions: Hwy 20 thru S
on Ellsworth St

Arch Cape

COLD COMFORT FARM ANTIQUES
Box 116 Leech Ave 97102
503 436-2751
Proprietor: Irene & Travis
Tyrrell
Hours: Thurs-Sun, 1-5; by
appointment or by chance
Types & Periods: 18th &
19th American Furniture &
Accessories, Pewter,
Copper, Brass,
Woodenware, Ironstone
China
Specialties: Samplers, Indian
Baskets & Pots, Decoys, Old
Tools
Directions: 1 block W of
Hwy 101 on Leech Ave

Ashland

AS YOU LIKE IT ANTIQUES
151 N Pioneer   97520
503 482-1652   Est: 1960
Proprietor: Sandra Berman
Hours: Daily
Types & Periods: Glass,
Bronze, Statues, Furniture
Appraisal Service Available
Directions: Slightly off
Main St or Siskiyou Blvd

HEIRLOOM ANTIQUES
Main St   97520
503 482-2496
Proprietor: Betty Hampton
& Reba Whittle
Hours: Daily, 9-5; also by
appointment
Types & Periods: Furniture,
Glass, General Line
Directions: Downtown

Aurora

TAYLORS TREASURES
2nd & Main   97002
503 678-5579   Est: 1966
Proprietor: Max & Vergie
Taylor
Hours: Daily
Types & Periods: Furniture,
Glass, Stoves, Lamps,
Chandeliers, General Line
Directions: Hwy 99E
between Salem & Portland

Bay City

ELAINE'S OLD BARN ANTIQUES
Rte 1 Box 960   97107
503 322-3683   Est: 1972
Proprietor: Elaine S
Galbreath
Hours: Daily, also by
appointment
Types & Periods: Furniture,
1800 & Early 1900,
Porcelain, Glass, Jewelry,
Prints, Oils
Directions: 8 miles N of
Tillamook, right on Ekroth
Rd just before Miami River
Bridge

Beaverton

ANTIQUE ANNEX
3340 SW Cedar Hills Blvd
                       97005
503 643-1176
Proprietor: Towner Brown
& Kay Scott
Hours: Mon-Sat
Types & Periods: Glass,
China, Furniture, General
Line
Directions: Across from
Beaverton Mall on Cedar
Hills Blvd

DROWSEY DONKEY ANTIQUES
2755 SW Cedar Hills Blvd
                       97005
503 646-9496   Est: 1970
Proprietor: Barbara A
Long
Hours: Mon-Sat, 11-5
Types & Periods:
Collectibles, Primitives,
Jewelry, Furniture
Directions: 1 block N of
Beaverton Mall

KEELER'S ANTIQUES
3340 SW Cedar Hills Blvd
                       97005
503 646-2746
Proprietor: Shari & Ken
Keeler
Hours: Daily, 11-4
Types & Periods: Art Glass,
Furniture, Dolls, Primitives,
Jewelry

Bend

BENOIT'S WOODWORKING
63220 O B Riley Rd
                       97701
503 382-0557   Est: 1972
Proprietor: Bud Benoit
Hours: Daily
Types & Periods: Furniture
Directions: 1 block N
Sambo's Restaurant on O
B Riley Rd, N of city

Brooks

WAY STATION ANTIQUES
9130 Portland Rd   97305
503 393-7262   Est: 1975
Proprietor: Dora Gower
Hours: Daily, 9-5; also by
appointment
Types & Periods: Art Glass,
Lamps, Furniture, Oak
Primitives
Specialties: Glass (Carnival,
Depression)
Directions: Hwy 99
between Salem & Oregon
City

Brownsville

SETTLEMENT ANTIQUES
104 Spaulding   97327
503 466-5707   Est: 1970

Proprietor: Joseph
DeZurney & Robbie
Robertson
Hours: Fri-Mon, 11-5; also
by appointment
Types & Periods: American
Furniture & Accessories
Directions: 4 miles E of I-5
in the Mid Willamette
Valley

Cannon Beach

WAYSIDE ANTIQUES
2nd St   97110
503 436-2825
Proprietor: Ellen M Peters
Hours: Daily, 10-5
Types & Periods: Middle
East & Early American
Directions: 2nd & Larch
Sts

Clackamas

WOOD PILE ANTIQUES
15665 S 82nd Dr   97015
503 655-2830   Est: 1972
Proprietor: Helen Handy
Hours: Daily, 10-5
Types & Periods: 1600 to
1880 Early American
Furniture
Specialties: Refinishing,
Caning, Rushing, Tole
Painting
Directions: Off I-205 at
Estacada Exit, turn left, at
light turn left, N about 2
blocks

Coburg

**DOTSON'S COBURG
ANTIQUES**
Main St   97401
503 342-2732   Est: 1955
Proprietor: Loy Dotson
Hours: Tues-Sat, 11-5
Types & Periods: Furniture,
Glassware, Jewelry,
Primitives, Silver, Copper,
Brass, Tools
Specialties: Ship Brass
Appraisal Service Available
Directions: 5 miles N of
Eugene, 3/4 miles off I-5

Corvallis

CENTURY ANTIQUES
6145 NW Ponderosa
                    97330
503 752-2624
Proprietor: Leota Wood
Hours: By appointment, by
chance
Types & Periods: American
Furniture & Accessories

The Dalles

FORT DALLES ANTIQUES
1314 E 10th St   97058
503 296-5122   Est: 1965
Proprietor: Milton &
Nadine Dunn
Hours: Daily, 9-7
Types & Periods: Early
Primitives of the 1720 to
1840 Era, Jewelry,
Glassware, Folk Art,
Textiles, General Line
Specialties: Furniture,
Fireplace Cooking Utensils,
Kitchenware
Appraisal Service Available
Directions: From
downtown, take Union St
to 10th & turn left

Dundee

DOD'S ANTIQUES
PO Box 129   97115
503 538-9524
Proprietor: Georgene N
Fraser
Hours: Daily, 10-6
Types & Periods: Art Glass,
Silver, Furniture

Eugene

BIG WHEEL ANTIQUES
1091 Coburg Rd   97401
503 344-7300   Est: 1969
Proprietor: Gilbert R &
Virginia Scott
Hours: Mon-Sat, 10-5
Types & Periods: Furniture,
Glassware, Primitives
Specialties: Furniture
Restoration & Repair
Appraisal Service Available
Directions: 1 mile N of
Thunderbird Motel

CARRIES ANTIQUES
34769 Hwy 58   97405
503 746-3411   Est: 1968
Proprietor: Bob & Carrie
Rieck
Hours: Tues-Sat, 11-5
Types & Periods: Furniture,
Jewelry, Glassware
Directions: 1 mile E of I-5
on Hwy 58

GRANDTOUR GALLERY
2055 Broadview St 97405
503 345-6459   Est: 1968
Proprietor: Beverly Strong
Hours: Daily, 12-5
Types & Periods: Oriental,
American, Indian, African
Specialties: Folk Art,
Primitives
Appraisal Service Available

LAKE'S ANTIQUES
32235 Coburg   97401
503 345-4931   Est: 1974
Proprietor: James &
Cecilia Lake
Hours: Daily, by
appointment, by chance
Types & Periods: Primitives,
American & European Oak,
Collectibles
Specialties: Furniture
(Hardware)
Directions: 1 mile from
downtown on Bottom
Loop Rd

SILAS MESSER
22 Oakway Mall   97401
503 343-2505   Est: 1972
Proprietor: Silas Messer
Hours: By appointment
Types & Periods: Guns,
Swords, Uniforms, Coins,
Sculpture, Indian Artifacts,
Scrimshaw, Western Art,
Medals, Vintage Cars
Specialties: Arms (Guns &
Swords)
Directions: Rear of
Oakway Mall

OAKWAY ANTIQUES
16 E Oakway Mall W
                    97401
503 484-1622   Est: 1970
Proprietor: Wes Armstrong
Hours: Daily
Types & Periods: General
Line

PURPLE LAMP ANTIQUES
89765 Green Hill Rd
97402
503 689-0285   Est: 1966
Proprietor: Don & Clara
Freeman
Hours: Mon-Tues, Fri-Sat,
10-5
Types & Periods: Early 1900
Oak Furniture, General Line
Specialties: Kerosene Lamps
& Parts
Appraisal Service Available
Directions: 1½ miles S of
Municipal Airport

Florence

RONALD W HOGELAND
1312 Bay St   97439
503 997-2002   Est: 1975
Proprietor: Ron Hogeland
Hours: Sun-Mon, Wed-Sat
Types & Periods: Primitives,
Oak Furniture
Specialties: Picture Frames
Directions: 2 blocks off
Hwy 101 in "Old Town"

Grants Pass

STIX & STONZ ANTIQUES
753 NE 7th St   97526
503 476-9031   Est: 1975
Proprietor: Elmer & Leslee
Jueden
Hours: Daily, 10-6;
evenings by appointment
Types & Periods: American
Pieces, Glassware
Specialties: Glass, Wood
Appraisal Service Available
Directions: Downtown

Hillsboro

**HILLSBORO NOSTALGIA
CENTER**
343 E Main   97123
503 640-2313   Est: 1973
Proprietor: Ruth Murphy
Hours: Mon-Sat, 10-5:30
Types & Periods: Furniture,
Collectibles
Specialties: Books
(Reference Books for
Collectors & Dealers)
Appraisal Service Available
Directions: Downtown

Hood River

ANTIQUES FROM DORCAS
Westcliff Dr   97031
503 386-3659
Proprietor: Dorcas Ross
Hours: Daily, 9-6
Types & Periods: China,
Crystal, Art Glass

Hubbard

B LOWD AND SON
Rte 1 Box 40   97032
503 982-5086   Est: 1958
Proprietor: Robert &
Pauline Lowd
Hours: Tues-Sat, 10-4:30;
Sun, 1-4
Types & Periods: General
Line, Pine, Oak, Walnut,
Mahogany
Specialties: China Cabinets
Directions: 1 mile N of
Hubbard on 99 E

MY MASTERS ANTIQUES
97032
503 981-3410   Est: 1974
Proprietor: Dave & Ruth
Hosley
Hours: Daily
Types & Periods:
Collectibles
Directions: On Old 99 E,
20 miles N of Salem

ROTAY'S ANTIQUES
97032
503 981-5886   Est: 1969
Proprietor: Flora M Rotay
Hours: Wed-Sun, 10-5;
also by appointment
Types & Periods: Art Glass,
China, Silver, Jewelry
Specialties: China, Glass
(Art), Sterling Souvenir
Spoons
Appraisal Service Available
Directions: On Hwy 99 E,
S of Aurora between
Portland & Salem

Independence

**THE OLD GRANARY
ANTIQUES**
Rte 1 Box 332A   97351
503 838-0359

Proprietor: Betty
Greenwade
Hours: Tues-Sat, 11-5
Types & Periods: General
Line, American Indian Arts &
Crafts

Jacksonville

DORMAN'S ANTIQUES
130 4th   97530
503 899-7045   Est: 1969
Proprietor: Robert Dorman
Hours: Daily, May 15-Sept
15; other times by chance
Types & Periods: Furniture,
Clocks
Specialties: Clocks
Directions: 6 miles W of
Medford on Hwy 238

SCHEFFEL'S ANTIQUES
180 W California   97530
503 899-7421   Est: 1953
Proprietor: Mr & Mrs W J
Scheffel
Hours: Daily, closed Oct
Types & Periods: 18th, 19th
& Early 20th Century
Furniture, Glass, China,
Silver, Primitives
Directions: 5 miles W of
Medford on Hwy 238

Monmouth

AGING TREASURE SHOPPE
410 E Main   97361
503 838-1195
Hours: Tues-Sat, 11-5
Types & Periods: General
Line, Collectibles

Oakland

**TOLLEFSON'S ANTIQUES
(TOLLYS)**
115 Locust   97462
501 459-3796   Est: 1962
Proprietor: Terry & Carol
Tollefson
Hours: Daily
Types & Periods: Furniture,
Art Glass, Silver, China,
Pressed & Cut Glass,
Primitives
Specialties: Furniture

Appraisal Service Available
Directions: Exit 138 on
I-15, 16 miles N of
Roseburg & 54 miles S of
Eugene, 1/4 mile off Hwy

Ontario

CLASSIQUE ANTIQUES
45 NW 9th St   97914
503 889-3528   Est: 1971
Hours: Tues-Sat
Types & Periods: Furniture,
Glassware, Primitives,
Collectibles
Appraisal Service Available
Directions: Corner of
Idaho & 9th, N of Hospital

Oregon City

CAST IRON & CAST OFFS
14941 S Henrici Rd 97045
503 656-0193   Est: 1960
Proprietor: Mary Lawrence
& Walter Youree
Hours: Tues-Sat, 1-5
Types & Periods: American
Country Furniture,
Advertising, Old Country
Store Cases & Fixtures,
Brass Cash Registers,
Primitives
Specialties: Hand Carved
Carousel Horses
Directions: In an old barn
2½ miles S of Oregon
City, just off Hwy 213 S

Portland

PORTLAND CLUSTER
Directions: NE Broadway,
SE Hawthorne, SE 13th,
NW Glison St to
Carruthers St (N-S), SW
1st Ave to SW 12th Ave,
especially on SW Adler St

**ACCUARDI'S ANTIQUE
WHOLESALE**
135 NW 5th Ave   97209
503 228-0578   Est: 1977
Proprietor: Nicholas
Accuardi
Hours: Mon-Sat, by
appointment

Types & Periods: French,
English, Georgian, Victorian,
Edwardian, American Oak,
Late Victorian to 1930's
Specialties: Restaurant
Furnishings
Directions: 5th & NW
Davis in Portland's Old
Town

ALBERT'S ANTIQUES
21 SW 2nd Ave   97204
503 222-7440   Est: 1970
Proprietor: Feivel Albert
Hours: Daily
Types & Periods: Art
Objects, Paintings, Rugs,
Jewelry, Furniture, Clocks
Directions: 1 block S of
Burnside St in Old Town

ANDREW'S ANTIQUES
916 SE 20th Ave   97214
503 234-9378   Est: 1914
Hours: Mon-Fri, 9-4:30;
Sat, 9-1
Types & Periods: American
& European Furniture,
Brass, Copper, Pewter,
Porcelain, Oriental Pieces
Specialties: Restored
Furniture
Directions: S of
Belmont St

ANTIQUES & HAS BEENS
9661 SW Canyon Rd
                    97225
503 292-1797   Est: 1954
Proprietor: Aden &
Catharine Jones
Hours: Fri-Mon, 12-5
Types & Periods: Glass,
China, Metals, Country
Furniture, Primitives, Paper
Specialties: Primitives &
Kitchen Items
Directions: 3½ miles from
downtown, past zoo on
Hwy 8

ANTIQUES FOR INTERIORS
81 NW Flanders   97210
503 223-7834   Est: 1948
Proprietor: Geo Root &
Byron Glenn
Hours: Daily, by
appointment
Types & Periods: 16th, 17th
& 18th Century European &
Oriental Furniture &
Accessories
Specialties: Watches, China,
Trade Porcelain

Directions: Approximately
1 mile from downtown, 3
blocks N of 23rd & W
Burnside

BEAVER TRADING POST
3713 SE Hawthorne
                    97214
503 232-8482   Est: 1958
Proprietor: Kenneth L
Isbell
Hours: Mon-Sat, 10:30-6
Types & Periods: Late
1800's & Early 1900's Oak
Furniture, Glassware
Specialties: Restoration &
Refinishing
Directions: Across
Hawthorne Bridge E to
37th St

**THE BLUE DAHLIA
ANTIQUES**
8301 SE 13th   97202
503 238-1695
Hours: Tues-Sat, 10:30-5
Types & Periods: Flow Blue,
Furniture, Clocks

**THE CAPTAIN & THE
COWBOY**
8309 SE 13th   97202
503 235-2652
Proprietor: Douglas E
Sabin
Hours: Tues-Sat, 11:30-5
Types & Periods: Nautical,
Western Antiques, Tools
Directions: Old Sellwood's
Antique Row

CATHY'S ANTIQUE SHOP
2425 NW Lovejoy   97210
                 Est: 1956
Proprietor: Cathy Bloch
Hours: Wed-Sat
Types & Periods: Cut Glass,
Art Glass, Silver, China,
Orientals
Specialties: French Cameo
Glass
Directions: About 10
minutes from downtown,
shop in a house in
residential block

CHOWN SHOWCASE
1643 Jantzen Beach
Center   97217
503 243-6501   Est: 1970
Proprietor: Mrs Frank
Chown
Hours: Mon-Fri, 10-9; Sat,
10-6; Sun, 12-4

Portland   **Cont'd**

CHOWN   **Cont'd**
Types & Periods: Chinese
Porcelain & Furniture
(European), Cut Glass,
Porcelain
Specialties: Chinese
Porcelain Antiques
  Directions: Jantzen Beach
  center on Hayden Island
  on way to Vancouver,
  Washington

CHOWN SHOWCASE
5331 SW Macadam Ave
                 97201
503 243-6503
Proprietor: Mrs Frank D
Chown
Hours: Mon-Fri, 10-9; Sat,
10-6; Sun, 12-5
Types & Periods: American
& European Furniture, Cut &
Stained Glass, Orientals
  Directions: John's Landing
  on the road to Lake
  Oswego

CHOWN SHOWCASE
921 SW Morrison   97205
503 243-6501   Est: 1970
Proprietor: Mrs Frank D
Chown
Hours: Mon-Fri, 10-9; Sat,
10-6; Sun, 12-5
Types & Periods: European
Furniture, Cut Glass,
Chinese Porcelain
Specialties: Chinese
Porcelain Antiques
  Directions: Downtown,
  10th & Morrison

CONKLIN'S ANTIQUES
10835 NE Sandy Blvd
                 97220
503 253-6064   Est: 1934
Proprietor: Vivan B
Conklin
Hours: Tues-Sun
Types & Periods: China,
Glass, Small Furniture,
Silverware
Specialties. China (Haviland)
  Directions: In general area
  of airport, E of city

THE CORNER HOUSE
8003 SE 13th   97202
503 232-8700
Hours: Tues-Sat, 10-4
Types & Periods: General
Line

DEN OF ANTIQUITY
8012 SE 13th   97202
503 233-7334   Est: 1972
Proprietor: Jim & Leslie
Goldsmith
Hours: Tues-Sat, 10-4:30;
also by appointment
Types & Periods: American
Golden Oak & Primitive
Furniture, Kitchen Primitives
Specialties: Furniture
Refinishing
  Directions: "Sellwood's
  Antique Row", near E end
  of the Sellwood Bridge

EVILO EATON ANTIQUES
7825 SE 13th   97202
503 235-6414
Proprietor: Evilo & R S
Eaton
Hours: Mon-Sat, 1-6
Types & Periods: Dolls,
Jewelry, Silver

ECLECTIC ARTS
630 SW 12th   97205
503 227-4710   Est: 1974
Proprietor: Arthur
Erickson
Hours: Tues-Sat,
11:30-5:30
Types & Periods: Primitives,
Arts, Baskets, Blankets,
Rugs, Pottery
Appraisal Service Available
  Directions: Downtown at
  12th & Morrison Sts

1874 HOUSE
8070 SE 13th Ave   97202
503 233-1874   Est: 1962
Proprietor: Liz Fowler
Hours: Mon-Sat, 10-4
Types & Periods:
Architectural Fragments,
Stained Glass, Hardware,
Lighting, Plumbing
  Directions: Near E end of
  Sellwood Bridge

ETC ANTIQUES
7908 SE 13th   97202
503 236-9092   Est: 1969
Proprietor: C Darwin Otto
& Carol Kelly
Hours: Tues-Sat, 12-5;
Sun, 12-4
Types & Periods: Country
Furniture & Accessories
  Directions: Cross Sellwood
  Bridge on Tacoma St, to
  13th St, right on 13th to
  Lexington (4 blocks)

**EVELYN'S FURNITURE
TREE**
2601 SE Clinton   97202
503 238-7165   Est: 1966
Proprietor: Evelyn Trevor
Hours: Daily
Types & Periods: Wicker,
Oak, Victorian thru 1920's
  Directions: On NE corner
  of SE 26th & Clinton

FABRILLE STUDIOS
8028 SE 13th   97202
503 235-6852
Hours: Daily, 8-5
Types & Periods: Leaded
Glass, Ornamental Brass,
Bronze Casting

LEE FARR ORIENTAL RUGS
2134 NW Hoyt   97210
503 223-8830   Est: 1974
Proprietor: Lee Farr
Hours: Wed-Sat, 1-4; by
appointment or by chance
Types & Periods: Oriental
Rugs
Specialties: Tribal & Village
Rugs
Appraisal Service Available
  Directions: Burnside to
  NW 21st to NW Hoyt St,
  located in a large Italian
  style house

THE FOUND OBJECT
8215 SE 13th   97202
503 234-1100
Hours: Tues-Sat, 12-5
Types & Periods: Primitives,
Collectibles, General Line

THE GENERAL STORE
7987 SE 13th   97202
503 233-1321   Est: 1972
Proprietor: Margie Waite
Hours: Tues-Sat, 11-4
Types & Periods: Oak
Furniture, Primitives, Kitchen
& Other Collectibles
Specialties: Oak Iceboxes
Appraisal Service Available
  Directions: "Old
  Sellwood", 25 antique
  shops in 12 blocks

GENERATION III ANTIQUES
6511 SW Beaverton Hwy
                 97225
503 297-3866   Est: 1965
Proprietor: Alison Abell
Hours: Mon-Fri, 10:30-4;
Sat, 10:30-2; also by
appointment or by chance

Types & Periods: English
Furniture, Country Maple &
Pine Furniture, Silver,
Pewter, Brass, Copper
Specialties: Oriental
Porcelain, Snuff Bottles &
Netsuke
Appraisal Service Available
Directions: "5 minutes
from downtown; call and
we'll pick you up"

**GREAT EXPECTATION
ANTIQUES**
7919 SE 13th   97202
503 233-9213
Hours: Tues-Sat, 10-6
Types & Periods: American
& European, Collectibles

HILBY'S ANTIQUES
1923 NE Broadway 97232
503 288-2273   Est: 1946
Proprietor: Alvin G & Ethel
A Hilby
Hours: Tues-Sat, 12-5;
also by appointment
Types & Periods: Art & Cut
Glass, Toys, China,
Furniture, Jewelry, Silver
Appraisal Service Available
Directions: Near Lloyd
Center

**HOLLYHOCK COTTAGE
ANTIQUES**
2914 NE 50th Ave   97213
503 287-1300
Proprietor: Emil & Esther
Tschanz
Hours: Daily
Types & Periods: General
Line, China, Glass, Pictures,
Silver

**HOT ICE ENTERPRISES
INC**
520 SE 73rd Ave   97215
503 254-0470
Proprietor: Larry & Karen
Potter
Hours: Mon-Fri, by
appointment; also mail
order
Types & Periods: Jewelry
Specialties: Engraving name
badges & signs for dealers
who do shows
Appraisal Service Available
Directions: On Mt Tabor in
Portland, up Yamhill St N
on 73rd

MAGGIE'S MANOR
7858 SE 13th   97202
503 234-3988
Hours: Tues-Sat, 10:30-5
Types & Periods: General
Line, Collectibles

**MC DUFFEE-MONGEON
GALLERIES**
115 SW Ash St   97204
503 223-9093   Est: 1963
Proprietor: Mr & Mrs J P
Mongeon
Hours: Tues & Wed, 12-4;
Thurs-Sat, 12-9
Types & Periods: Paintings,
Furniture, Silver, Pocelains,
Objets d'Art
Appraisal Service Available
Directions: 2 blocks S of
Burnside

**MIKE'S GOLD ANVIL
ANTIQUES**
5901 SE Foster Rd   97206
503 771-1066   Est: 1973
Proprietor: Mike Losli
Hours: Tues-Sat, call first
Types & Periods: Furniture
(Oak), Old Toys,
Promotional Cars, Old
Radios, General Line
Specialties: Old Toys,
Promotional Cars, Old
Radios (Battery Types,
Cathedral Types)

MILLIE'S DUSTY CORNER
8301 SE 13th   97202
503 238-1695
Hours: Tues-Sat, 10:30-5
Types & Periods: General
Line

**MORE OR LESS
COLLECTIBLES**
6744 SW Capitol Hwy
                          97219
503 244-9534   Est: 1974
Proprietor: Leslie Kelinson
& Lillian Zidell
Hours: Wed-Sat, 10-3; also
by appointment
Types & Periods: Art Glass,
Cut Glass, Orientalia,
Collectibles
Specialties: Steuben &
Tiffany
Directions: 10 minutes
from town at Vermont

**MOTHER GOOSE
ANTIQUES**
1219 SW 19th   97205
503 223-4493   Est: 1974

Proprietor: Sigrid Clark
Hours: Daily
Types & Periods: Toys,
Sewing Items, Jewelry,
Silver, Trinkets, Glass,
Curios, Oriental
Directions: Off of SW
Jefferson on 19th

NINA'S ANTIQUES
8301 SE 13th   97202
503 238-1695
Hours: Tues-Sat,
10:30-4:30
Types & Periods: China,
Glassware, Furniture,
Primitives

OAK TREE ANTIQUES
7783 SW Capitol Hwy
                          97219
503 244-4536   Est: 1972
Proprietor: John Haff
Hours: Tues-Sat, 8:30-5:30
Types & Periods: Late 19th
Century Country &
Turn-of-the-Century
Furniture
Specialties: Stained Glass
Windows, Wood Blade
Ceiling Fans
Directions: SW Portland,
Multnomah Blvd Exit off
I-5 heading S, right at SW
35th for 2 blocks

OLD MANTEL ANTIQUES
8624 SE 13th   97202
503 232-6789   Est: 1967
Proprietor: William
Lorenzana
Hours: Mon-Sat, 12-5
Types & Periods: Furniture,
Porcelains, Cut Glass
Directions: Across
Sellwood Bridge to SE
13th

THE OLD TIMERS
4759 NE Fremont St
                          97213
503 281-5184   Est: 1973
Proprietor: Paul & Ginny
Kowalk
Hours: Tues-Sat, 12-5:30
Types & Periods: Furniture,
Glassware, Collectibles
Directions: NE Portland

OLD WEIRD HERALD'S
6804 NE Broadway 97213
503 254-4942   Est: 1970
Proprietor: Hazel Herald &
Daughters

Portland   Cont'd

WEIRD HERALD'S   Cont'd
Hours: Tues-Sat, 12-6;
summer 12-9
Types & Periods: Paper
Americana & Nostalgia,
Books, Post Cards, Comics
for Collectors, Toys,
Magazines, Photos, Disney
Appraisal Service Available
Directions: Banfield Frwy
to 68th & Halsey Exit, left
to 67th, right 1 block to
Broadway, right to 6804

P M C ANTIQUE MART & FLEA MARKET
Memorial Coliseum 1408 N
Wheeler   97208
503 282-6467   Est: 1969
Proprietor: Stadelman
Production Inc
Hours: Every Sun 10-5
except holiday weekends
Types & Periods: 17th
Century Furniture, Buttons
to Baseball Cards
Appraisal Service Available
Directions: Centrally
located

POWELL'S BOOKSTORE
1207 W Burnside   97209
503 228-4651   Est: 1972
Proprietor: Walter W
Powell
Hours: Mon-Sat, 10-9;
Sun, 12-6
Types & Periods: Books
Directions: Corner of NW
12th & W Burnside

RITA'S ANTIQUE & NOSTALGIA STORE
7116 SE Foster Rd   97206
503 774-5331   Est: 1974
Proprietor: Rita K Chubin
Hours: Tues-Sat, 12-6
Types & Periods: General
Line, Photos, Indian Pictures

SECOND HAND ROSE
2168 W Burnside   97210
503 227-5282   Est: 1971
Proprietor: P Berg, D
Harper & B Nielsen
Hours: Mon-Fri, 10-4; Sat,
12-4
Types & Periods: General
Line, Collectibles

THE SELLWOOD PEDDLER
8535 SE 13th   97202
503 235-0946
Hours: Daily, 11-5
Types & Periods: Attic
Goodies

STUFFED GOOSE
1202 SW 19th   97205
503 223-6657   Est: 1972
Proprietor: Muriel Walsh
Hours: Mon-Fri, 11-4
Types & Periods: Paintings,
Furniture, China, Silver,
Glass, Rugs, Oriental
Appraisal Service Available
Directions: Corner of 19th
& Madison

CHRIS SWIFT ANTIQUES
7742 SE 13th Ave   97202
503 235-3981   Est: 1960
Proprietor: Chris Swift
Hours: Mon-Sat
Types & Periods: Jewelry,
Glass, China, Silver, Small
Furniture
Specialties: Glass, Silver
Appraisal Service Available
Directions: "Sellwood's
Antique Row", corner of
Lambert

THE TRADERS
7936 NE Glisan St   97213
503 252-8379   Est: 1962
Proprietor: Chas F Norris
& Wm K Hayes
Hours: Tues-Sat, 9:30-6
Types & Periods: General
Line
Directions: SW corner of
NE 80th Ave & Glisan St,
I-5 Frwy to NE 57th Exit,
then E to NE 80th Ave

TREASURE HOUSE ANTIQUES
5812 E Burnside St 97215
503 233-4030   Est: 1972
Proprietor: Viola Clark
Hours: Mon-Fri, 8:30-5;
Sat by appointment
Types & Periods: Glass,
China, Books, Furniture
Specialties: China, Glass

WEATHERVANE ANTIQUES
3115 E Burnside St 97214
503 235-3997   Est: 1962
Proprietor: Lillian & Ervin
Rains
Hours: Tues-Sat, 12-5;
also by appointment

Types & Periods: American
Country & Victorian
Furniture, Primitives,
Copper, Brass, Pottery
Specialties: Chair Caning
Service
Directions: On main E-W
arterial

Prineville

THE POSIE SHOPPE
142 W 3rd   97754
503 447-4397   Est: 1969
Proprietor: Mrs Betty
Mohan
Hours: Daily, 9-5:30
Types & Periods: Primitives,
Glass, China, Collectibles
Specialties: Primitives
Directions: Corner of
Beaver & 3rd

Rickreall

DIXIE ANTIQUES
Box 21 Hwy 99 W   97371
503 623-2739
Proprietor: Joann Harland
Hours: Daily, 10-4:30
Types & Periods: General
Line, Lamp Parts

THE OLD GRANARY ANTIQUES
Hwy 99 W   97371
503 623-2739
Proprietor: Betty
Greenwade & Joann
Harland
Hours: Daily, 10-5
Types & Periods: General
Line, Furniture, Glass,
Jewelry

Roseburg

THE WOODTIQUE
2660 NE Stephens   97470
503 673-8385   Est: 1971
Proprietor: Dick & Glenis
Stratton
Hours: Mon-Sat, 9:30-5
Types & Periods: Primitives,
Furniture, Glass
Specialties: Furniture (Oak)
Directions: Old Hwy 99 at
N Roseburg City Limits

Salem

ACE ANTIQUES
3975 Silverton Rd NE
97303
503 585-8262
Proprietor: Lil Grigsby
Hours: Mon-Sat, 11-4
Types & Periods: Cut & Art
Glass, China, Furniture,
Lamps, Clocks, Jewelry,
Paintings, Pocket Watches
Appraisal Service Available
Directions: Lancaster to
Silverton Rd & go W

**ASSISTANCE LEAGUE GIFT
SHOP**
533 Commercial SE
97301
503 364-8318   Est: 1962
Proprietor: Assistance
League of Salem
Hours: Tues-Fri, 10-4; Mon
& Sat, 12-4
Types & Periods: Furniture,
Silver, Jewelry, Porcelain,
Crystal
Directions: Across from
civic center

THE COUNTRY QUAIL
8321 Macleay Rd SE
97301
503 581-1168
Hours: Daily, 9-5; evenings
by appointment
Types & Periods: General
Line, Collectibles

ET CETERA ANTIQUES
4721 Liberty Rd S   97302
503 581-9850   Est: 1971
Proprietor: Mrs L B Day
Hours: Mon-Sat, 11-3, by
chance
Types & Periods: Glass,
China, Jewelry, Primitives,
Dolls, Oriental & Navajo
Rugs, Furniture
Specialties: Oriental Items,
Antique Jewelry, Glass
Appraisal Service Available
Directions: Sunnyslope
Shopping Center,
Commercial to Liberty
Rd S

**EVANS HOUSE OF
ANTIQUES**
4765 River Rd W   97303
503 393-6620   Est: 1972
Proprietor: Delight Evans
Rost

Hours: By appointment, by
chance
Types & Periods:
Turn-of-the-Century Oak,
Victorian Walnut, Cut
Pressed & Art Glass,
Primitives, Clothing
Appraisal Service Available
Directions: Take
Brooks-Keizer Exit from
I-5, follow signs to Keizer,
2½ blocks S of light

HALEY'S ANTIQUES
7820 River Rd N   97302
503 393-2897
Hours: By appointment, by
chance
Types & Periods: Depression
Glass, Furniture, Clocks

JAN'S ANTIQUES
1890 18th St NE   97303
503 363-5842   Est: 1974
Proprietor: Jan Wood
Hours: By appointment
Types & Periods: Glass, Art
Nouveau, Art Deco, R S
Prussia
Specialties: Glass (R S
Prussia, Art)
Appraisal Service Available
Directions: Market St Exit
off Frwy to 18th, right to
middle of block

LANA AVE 2ND HAND
1880 Lana Ave NE   97303
503 588-1376   Est: 1972
Proprietor: Marvin D
Stanton
Hours: Mon-Sat, 9-6
Types & Periods: Oak
Furniture, Pressback Chairs
& Rockers, Tools, Knives,
Razor, Toys, Collectibles
Specialties: Furniture
(Winchester), Keen Kutter
Tools
Directions: NE Salem

LOU'S ANTIQUES
2455 Salem-Dallas Hwy
97304
503 588-1362   Est: 1974
Proprietor: Lou Banta
Hours: Tues-Sat, 10-5
Types & Periods: Furniture
Specialties: Furniture
Directions: Hwy 22, 1 mile
W of Salem

**MACLEAY COUNTRY
STORE**
8342 Macleay Rd SE
97301
503 362-0282   Est: 1916
Proprietor: Jerry D. Miller
Hours: Daily, 9-8
Types & Periods: General
Line, Collectibles
Specialties: Books on NW
History
Appraisal Service Available
Directions: 6 miles E of
Salem, in Macleay village

POLLY'S BARN ANTIQUES
4137 Center St NE   97301
503 362-8174   Est: 1964
Proprietor: Marie Schmidt
Hours: Daily, 9-9
Types & Periods: Victorian
Furniture, China Glassware,
Primitive Furniture & Kitchen
Ware, Tin, Enamel, Iron,
Copper, Brass, Lamps, Toys,
Doll Furniture
Specialties: Primitives
Directions: 3 miles E of
downtown

RED CARPET ANTIQUES
4792 Lancaster Dr NE
97303
503-393-7640
Hours: Mon-Sat, 10-5; Sun
by appointment
Types & Periods: Old
Carnival, Cut & Pressed
Glass, Silver

RUTH'S ANTIQUES
1496 Court St NE   97301
503 362-7090
Hours: By appointment
Types & Periods: Crockery,
Kitchen Utensils, American
& English Furniture

**SCOTTY'S STARLITE
AUCTION HOUSE**
4744 Center St NE   97302
503 364-6433   Est 1950
Proprietor: Dick Borchers
Hours: Weekends
Types & Periods: Oak,
Primitives, European,
Victorian
Appraial Service Available
Directions: Left on 45th,
1/2 mile to Center, turn
left for 3 blocks

| Salem | Cont'd | Sunriver | Woodburn |

Salem Cont'd

WAYSTATION ANTIQUES
9130 Portland Rd   97305
503 393-7262
Hours: Tues-Sun, 11-5
Types & Periods: General
Line
Specialties: Furniture (Oak)

WEBSTER HOUSE
901 13th SE   97303
Hours: Tues-Sat, 10-5:30;
Sun, 12-4
Types & Periods: General
Line, Stoneware, "Elegant
Junk"

Shady Cove

VICTORIAN AGE ANTIQUES
20847 Crater Lake Hwy
97539
503 878-2322   Est: 1973
Proprietor: Doris & Earl
Heidt
Hours: Daily
Types & Perods: Victorian
Furniture, Glass; China,
Lamps, Clocks, Accessories,
Period 1830-1910
Specialties: Restored
American Oak & Walnut
Furniture
Directions: 20 miles N of
Medford, Hwy 62 (Crater
Lake Hwy), located 1/2
mile S of Shady Cove

Sheridan

**OLSON'S FURNITURE &
ANTIQUES**
1444 W Main St   97378
503 843-3272   Est: 1965
Proprietor: Richard E &
Margaret E Olson
Hours: Mon-Sat; Sun by
appointment
Types & Periods: General
Line, Furniture, Primitives,
Glass
Specialties: Furniture (Oak
Restoration)
Appraisal Service Available
Directions: 50 miles SW of
Portland on Hwy 18

Sunriver

PAST TENSE INC
Sunriver Country Mall
97701
503 593-1637   Est: 1974
Proprietor: Ruth E
Maynord & Ellen S Davis
Hours: Mon-Sat,
10:30-5:30, Sun 'til 2;
closed weekends during
winter
Types & Periods:
Turn-of-the-Century Oak,
Furniture, Glass
Specialties: Early American
Primitives
Appraisal Service Available
Directions: 15 miles S of
Bend

Warren

**ELLISON'S COUNTRY
ANTIQUES SHOP**
Rte 1 Box 275   97053
503 397-3660
Proprietor: Ruth Ellison
Hours: Daily
Types & Periods: Art &
Colored Glass, General
Line

Welches

JENNIE WELCH ANTIQUES
Welches Rd Box 52
97067
503 622-4750   Est: 1953
Proprietor: Jennie Welch
Hours: Daily
Types & Periods: Orientals,
French, English
Directions: 40 miles E of
Portland on Hwy 26, turn
right at Bowman's Golf
Course sign, drive 1 mile

Woodburn

99 E-ANTIQUE USED
17207 Hwy 99 E   97071
503 981-0200   Est: 1978
Proprietor: Marv & Lani
Stanton
Hours: Mon-Sat, 10-6
Types & Periods: Oak
Furniture, Pressback Chairs
& Rockers, Tools, Knives,
Razors, Toys & Collectibles
Specialties: Furniture,
Winchester & Keen Kutter
Tools
Directions: On old 99 E,
1½ miles N of Woodburn,
1/2 mile S of Hubbard

**THE 214 BOUTIQUE-
ANTIQUE**
Mt Angel Hwy   97071
503 981-5173
Hours: Tues-Sat, 10-4;
also by appointment
Types & Periods:
Collectibles, General Line
Diretions: 1 mile E of
Woodburn on Mt Angel Hwy

STATE OF PENNSYLVANIA

Abbottstown

WALLACE ANTIQUES
320 W King St   17301
717 259-7021   Est: 1967
Proprietor: James H
Wallace
Hours: Daily, 1-5
Types & Periods: Primitives,
Furniture, Dishes, General
Line
Specialties: Primitives
Directions: Rte 30, W End
of Town

Abington

ABINGTON ANTIQUE SHOP
1165 York Rd   19001
215 884-3204
Proprietor: Charles
Steinberg
Hours: Daily
Types & Periods: American
& English Furniture, Silver,
Art

Adamstown

TEX JOHNSON ANTIQUES
40 Willow St   19501
215 484-4005
Proprietor: Mrs. William L
Johnson
Hours: By Appointment
Types & Periods: General
Line

**RENNINGERS ANTIQUE
MARKET**
Adamstown   19501
Proprietor: Rita R & Lester
Benson
Hours: Sunday
Types & Periods: Antique
Jewelry
Specialties: Jewelry
Appraisal Service Available
Directions: Just off the Pa
Turnpike at the
Lebanon/Lancaster
Interchange

RENNINGER'S NO 1
Rte 222   19501
215 267-2177

Proprietor: 372 Dealers
Hours: Sun, 8-5
Types & Periods: General
Line
Directions: 1/2 Mile N of
PA Turnpike Exit 21

WEST-WYND
19501
Proprietor: Nina & Robert
Maust
Types & Periods: Furniture,
Primitive & Toleware
Directions: At Black Angus
Antique Mall

Alburtis

JANET'S ANTIQUE SHOP
R D 1   18011
215 395-5013   Est: 1958
Proprietor: Janet Schick
Hours: By Appointment,
by Chance
Types & Periods: 18th &
19th Century Furniture &
Accessories
Specialties: "Fractur",
Textiles, Primitives
Directions: Weiler's Rd,
1/2 Mile off Rte 222 & Rte
100

Allentown

IRENE BIER ANTIQUES
Rte 222   18102
215 398-3000
Proprietor: Irene Bier
Types & Periods: "From
Tools to Tiffany"
Directions: In Antique
Village, 2 Miles W of Town

THE BLUE VICTORIAN
945 Walnut St   18102
215 433-8138
Proprietor: Sallie S & Ron
Murray
Hours: By Appointment;
Sat at Renningers,
Kutztown, Pa
Types & Periods: Victorian
Antiques & Estate Jewelry
Specialties: Jewelry
Appraisal Service Available

**NORMA BORGMAN
ANTIQUES**
2717 South St   18103
215 433-1466
Proprietor: Norma
Borgman
Types & Periods: General
Line, Collectibles

GOLDEN EAGLE ANTIQUES
1425 Gordon St   18102
215 432-1223
Proprietor: Eugene &
Nancy Missmer
Hours: Daily, 10-6
Types & Periods: General
Line, Curios, Primitives,
Collectibles, Period Furniture

**GREENBERG & BARNYAK
INC**
801 Chew St   18102
Est: 1921
Types & Periods: China,
Glass, Clocks, Early Queen
Anne, Chippendale,
Hepplewhite & Sheraton
Furniture
Specialties: Furniture
Appraisal Service Available
Directions: Corner of 8th
& Chew St; 3 Blocks N
from 8th; 7 Hamilton Mall

L & J ANTIQUES
1808 Chew   18104
215 435-1868
Proprietor: James &
Elizabeth Luhman
Hours: Daily
Types & Periods: General
Line; Advertising
Directions: In Rear

**DAVID & BARBARA MEST
ANTIQUES**
Star Rte   18104
215 797-0275
Proprietor: David Mest
Hours: Daily
Types & Periods: Primitives,
Folk Art, Country Furniture

Allenwood

**ALLENWOOD AMERICANA
ANTIQUES**
Box 116   17810
717 538-1440

ALLENWOOD AMERICANA ANTIQUES Cont'd
Proprietor: Gloria Munsell & Kenneth Kipp
Types & Periods: Azalea China, Jewelry, Coins, Toys, Country Store Items, Wicker
Directions: Rte 15, 3 1/2 Miles N of I-80

Altoona

COLLECTOR'S CORNER
W Chestnut Ave & 31st St
16601
814 946-1732   Est: 1970
Proprietor: Jerry Mikolajczyk
Hours: Daily
Types & Periods: General Line
Specialties: Glass, Furniture
Directions: On Mill Run Rd

JUNIATA ANTIQUES
1105 Broadway   16601
814 943-8454   Est: 1970
Proprietor: Raymond Zeak
Hours: Daily; By Appointment
Types & Periods: Collectibles, Advertising Items, Beer Trays
Specialties: Clocks, Railroad Items, Brass Lamps
Appraisal Service Available

SCHULTZ'S ANTIQUE SHOP
1909 E Pleasant Valley Blvd   16602
814 944-9681   Est: 1936
Proprietor: Otto Schultz
Hours: Daily; By Appointment; 9-5; Also by Chance
Types & Periods: General Line
Directions: On Rte 220 between Altoona & Tyrone

Andreas

EBERTS ANTIQUES
Rte 895   18211
717 386-4273
Hours: Daily, 9-6
Types & Periods: Brass Beds, Furniture, Cut Glass, Carnival Lights, Clocks

RED BARN ANTIQUES
Rte 1   18211
717 386-4563   Est: 1967
Proprietor: Gary L Frantz
Hours: Daily; By Appointment, By Chance
Types & Periods: Large Selection of Oak Furniture, Glassware, Etc
Specialties: Oak Furniture
Appraisal Service Available
Directions: Rte 895, 4 Miles E of Rte 309

Annville

AUNT ESTHER'S ANTIQUES
Box 230, RD 1   17003
717 838-1257
Hours: Weekends; Weekdays by Chance
Types & Periods: Primitives, Furniture, General Line
Directions: 1/2 Mile E of Rte 117 on 322

HARPER GENERAL STORE
RD 2   17003
717 865-3456
Hours: Daily
Types & Periods: General Line
Directions: 1/2 Mile S of Exit 29 Off I-81

Ardmore

THE SILVER SHELF
323 W Lancaster Ave
19003
215 649-2035
Proprietor: Edwin H Fitler
Hours: By Appointment
Types & Periods: American Coin Silver

Ashland

WINTERS' ANTIQUES
936-938 Centre St   17921
717 875-2476
Types & Periods: General Line
Appraisal Service Available

Avondale

THE CARPENTER'S TOOL CHEST
40l Pennsylvania Ave
P O Box 426   19311
215 268-3488   Est: 1971
Proprietor: Mr & Mrs Robert R Dean
Hours: By Appointment
Types & Periods: Antique Woodworking Tools, Sewing Accessories, Primitives, Country Furniture, Etc
Specialties: Tools, Sewing Tools
Directions: On Rte 41, Midway between Wilmington, Del & Gap, Pa

Bala Cynwyd

JOAN MEYER
104 Colwyn Lane   19004
215 664-2183   Est: 1967
Proprietor: Joan Meyer
Hours: By Appointment
Types & Periods: Art Nouveau, Tiffany Lamps
Specialties: Restoration of Tiffany Lamps
Appraisal Service Available

Bangor

FEHR'S ANTIQUES
323 Broadway   18013
215 588-4140
Proprietor: Donald J Fehr
Types & Periods: China, Glass, Primitives

Bath

FRANK TOMASITS
406 W Main St   18014
215 837-0448
Proprietor: Frank Tomasits
Hours: Daily, 9-5
Types & Periods: Furniture, China, Glass, Pottery
Directions: On Rte 248

THE TREASURE CHEST ANTIQUES & GIFTS
Benders Drive,
RD 1, Box 349   18014
215 759-0695

Proprietor: Rita Miller
Hours: By Chance or
Appointment
Types & Periods: General
Line, including Glass, China,
Jewelry, Prints, Primitives
Directions: Near
Evergreen Lake off Rte
512 between Bath &
Wind Gap

Beach Lake

DRUMMER BOY ANTIQUES
Rte 652   18405
717 729-7190
Proprietor: Craig & Byron
C White
Hours: Daily, 12-5
Types & Periods: American
Primitive Furniture &
Accessories
Specialties: Cupboards,
Chests, Blanket Chests,
Tables & Chairs
Appraisal Service Available
Directions: NE Corner of
Pa; 25 Miles W of
Monticello, NY, 7 Miles E
of Honesdale, Pa

Beaver

**MARY ROBBINS'
ANTIQUES**
1040 3rd St   15009
412 775-3638   Est: 1941
Proprietor: Mary B
Robbins
Hours: Daily
Types & Periods: Furniture,
Dishes, Primitives
Specialties: Frames,
Miniatures
Appraisal Service Available
Directions: 1 1/2 Blocks
from Court House

Bellefonte

ANN E SMITH'S ANTIQUES
371 E Lamb St   16823
814 355-3532
Proprietor: Ann E Smith
Types & Periods: Glass,
China, Kerosene Lamps,
Primitives

Berks County

CHAPEL ANTIQUE SHOP
Rte 29, Palm RD 1   18070
215 679-5640
Proprietor: George
Kleppinger & Son
Types & Periods: Furniture,
China

Berlin

ANTIQUE AUTOS
RD 1   15530
814 267-3250
Proprietor: R Donald
Williams
Hours: By Appointment
Types & Periods: Autos,
Auto Parts
Directions: E of Somerset
on the Brotherton Rd

EAST END ANTIQUES
1400 E Main St   15530
814 267-3478
Proprietor: R Paul Saylor
Hours: Mon-Sat,
12:30-4:30 & 7-9:30; Sun,
1:30-6 & 7-9:30
Types & Periods: General
Line

Bethel Park

WOODMASTERS
3191 Industrial Blvd
          15102
412 833-7887   Est: 1971
Proprietor: G S Austen
Hours: Daily, 8-4:30
Types & Periods: General
Line, Victorian Period
Directions: 8 Miles SW of
Pittsburgh off S Park Rd

Bethlehem

C & D COIN & GUN SHOP
125 E Broad   18018
215 865-4355
Hours: Daily
Types & Periods: Guns,
Coins, Collectibles
Appraisal Service Available

**HAWTHORN HOUSE
ANTIQUES**
RD 4   18015
215 865-1257
Proprietor: Margaret
Sickeler
Hours: By Appointment,
By Chance
Types & Periods: Country
Furniture, Accessories
Directions: Located on Rte
378, 1 Mile N of Center
Valley

MAIN SHOPPE
823 Main St   18018
215 868-0141
Proprietor: Doris
Schneider
Types & Periods: General
Line

RICE ANTIQUES
818 Broad   18018
215 866-4122   Est: 1960
Proprietor: Margaret &
Edward Rice
Hours: By Appointment
Types & Periods: China,
Glass, Collectibles, Furniture
Directions: "10 Blocks of
Center City Mall"

**SHIRLEY'S OLD
TREASURES 'N THINGS**
734 Linden St   18018
215 865-5858
Hours: Daily
Types & Periods: General
Line, Collectibles

**TOONERVILLE JUNCTION
ANTIQUES**
7 E Church St   18018
215 691-6736
Proprietor: Genie & Bob
Lowe
Types & Periods: Furniture,
Lamps
Specialties: Toys &
Automata, Banks, Trains;
Early American & European

Biglerville

**STRAUSBAUGH'S NEW &
USED FURNITURE**
E Hanover   17307
717 677-7474   Est: 1969
Proprietor: Charles W
Strausbaugh
Hours: Mon-Fri, 9-9; Sat
9-5; Sun by Chance

STRAUSBAUGH'S   Cont'd

Types & Periods: Oak,
Softwood, Glassware,
General Line
  Directions: On 394 E of
  Biglerville off Rte 15 at
  Hunterstown Exit

Bird-in-Hand

BETTY BURKHART
  2637 Old Philadelphia Pike
                      17505
  717 394-2591   Est: 1967
  Proprietor: Betty M
  Burkhart
  Hours: Daily, by Chance
  Types & Periods: General
  Line, Tin, Glass, Furniture,
  Primitives
  Appraisal Service Available
    Directions: Rte 340, 6
    Miles E of Lancaster

HOUSE OF ANTIQUES
  2634 Old Philadelphia Pike
                      17505
  717 394-6564   Est: 1971
  Proprietor: Frances Woods
  Hours: Mon-Wed, Fri &
  Sat; By Chance
  Types & Periods: Early
  Country Things: Quilts,
  Baskets, Iron, Tin-tole,
  Redware, Stoneware,
  Wooden Articles, all in
  Original State
  Specialties: Quilts, Amish &
  Mennonite
    Directions: On Rte 340, 7
    Miles E of Lancaster

Birdsboro

SUSIE HUBER'S ANTIQUES
  1521 Benjamin Franklin
  Hwy   19508
  215 582-8906
  Proprietor: Susie Huber
  Hours: By Appointment
  Types & Periods: Primitives,
  Country

SCARLETS MILL ANTIQUES
  Box 416 RD 1   19508
  215 582-3445
  Proprietor: Rosemary &
  Tony Schorr

Hours: By Appointment
Types & Periods: General
Line, Primitives, Brass

THE SHADOW BOX
  329 Corys Court   19508
  215 582-1781
  Proprietor: Elizabeth
  Lenich
  Hours: By Appointment
  Types & Periods: General
  Line

Blairsville

SHADLE'S ANTIQUES
  RD 1 Box 389A   15717
  412 676-5605
  Proprietor: Sally & Al
  Shadle
  Hours: Tues-Sun, 10-5;
  Eves by Appointment
  Types & Periods: Furniture,
  China, Glass, Lamps,
  Collectibles
    Directions: On US 22
    between Blairsville &
    Clyde

Bloomsburg

DR HAROLD LANTERMAN
  125 W 11th St   17815
  717 784-1176   Est: 1974
  Proprietor: Dr H H
  Lanterman
  Hours: Mon-Sat; Sun &
  Eves by Appointment
  Types & Periods: All types
  Art Glass: Tiffany, Steuben,
  Quezal, Satin, Sandwich,
  Cut, Pattern, Paper Weights,
  Etc; Old China:
  Staffordshire, Chelsea,
  Spatterware; Pottery &
  Stoneware, Lamps of all
  Types, Chinese Art; Oriental
  Rugs; Clocks; Small
  Furniture
  Specialties: Glass; Invisible
  Repair of China, Hard or
  Soft Paste, Pottery (Studied
  under Karl Klein & Son)
  Appraisal Service Available
    Directions: Shop beside
    Home on W 11th St, 11
    Blocks S from Town
    Square, Past Soldiers
    Monument

Boalsburg

GATES ANTIQUES
  RD Box 151   16827
  814 466-6333
  Proprietor: Bob & Betty
  Gates
  Hours: Mon-Sat, 1-5; Eves
  by Appointment
  Types & Periods: Pattern
  Glass, Azalea Glass,
  Furniture
  Appraisal Service Available

Boiling Springs

MARION S SWEENEY
  111 Front St   17007
  717 258-6807
  Proprietor: Marion S
  Sweeney
  Hours: By Appointment
  Types & Periods: Oriental
  Porcelain, Hard Stone
  Carvings
  Appraisal Service Available

Bowmanstown

STAHLER'S ANTIQUES
  627 Ore St   18030
  215 852-2951
  Hours: By Chance " Open
  Whenever I'm Home"
  Types & Periods: Glass,
  China, Furniture, General
  Line
    Directions: On Rte 248

Boyertown

THE BASHFUL BARN
  1 E Philadelphia Ave
                    19512
  215 367-2631   Est: 1969
  Proprietor: Phil Cowley
  Hours: Daily, 9-5; By
  Appointment
  Types & Periods: General
  Line, Furniture
  Specialties: Refinishing
    Directions: Corner 562
    & 73

BOYERTOWN ANTIQUES
  RD 4   19512
  215 367-2452   Est: 1965
  Proprietor: Richard & Lois
  Malmberg

Hours: Mon-Sat, 9-5
Types & Periods: 18th
Century American Furniture
& Clocks, Art Glass, Soft
Paste China, Chippendale
Mirrors, Paintings
Specialties: Clocks
(American Tall Case)
Appraisal Service Available
Directions: Follow Signs
on either Rtes 100 or 73

COUNTRY CORNER
RD 2, Frog Hollow Farm
19512
215 367-8234
Proprietor: Mrs. Sandra
Rhoads
Hours: By Appointment
Types & Periods: Primitives,
Americana, Bottles, General
Line

**YE OLDE RAM RUN
ANTIQUES**
RD 4, Hill Church 19512
215 367-2875 Est: 1973
Proprietor: Nancy M Christ
Hours: Daily, 9-5
Types & Periods: 18th &
19th Century Country &
Period Furniture,
Accessories, Pewter, China,
Iron, Prints, Paintings,
General Line
Directions: Follow Signs
from Rte 100 & from Rte
73; Located 6 Miles N of
Boyertown in Hill Church;
Unusual Display of
Antiques in Old Barn

Braddock

J ROY ANTIQUES
903 Braddock Ave 15104
412 351-0255 Est: 1970
Proprietor: J Roy
Hours: Mon-Sat
Types & Periods: '' We Buy
& Sell Almost Anything''
Specialties: Almost
Everything
Directions: When in the
Pittsburgh Area, Call for
Directions

Brodheadsville

WILLOWBROOK ANTIQUES
Rte 115 18322
717 992-4090 Est: 1971
Proprietor: Ruth & Rudy
Blatt
Hours: Thurs-Tues
Types & Periods: General
Line
Specialties: Oak Furniture
Directions: 1 Mile N of
Brodheadsville

Brookville

PARK COIN & GUN SHOP
124 Main St 15825
814 849-8988 Est: 1965
Proprietor: James Park
Hours: Daily
Types & Periods: General
Line
Specialties: Arms & Armor,
Coins
Appraisal Service Available
Directions: Across from
YMCA

Bryn Mawr

HAYESTOCK HOUSE
19 N Merion Ave 19010
215 527-4282 Est: 1946
Proprietor: T L Hayes & L
J Stock
Hours: Daily, 10:30-5;
Closed Sat, June-Aug;
also by Chance
Types & Periods: Chests,
High Boys, Secretary Desks,
Silk Embroideries, Samplers,
Oriental Export, Lamps
Appraisal Service Available

Buck Hill Falls

SCHNEIDER'S ANTIQUES
18323
717 595-7638
Proprietor: Mabel L
Schneider
Types & Periods: Signed Cut
Glass, Books, Prints,
Jewelry, Satsuma, Art Glass
Appraisal Service Available

Bushkill

SUN HILL FARM ANTIQUES
Rte 209 18324
717 588-6404
Proprietor: Grayce Lenga
Types & Periods: Cherry &
Pine Furniture, Pressed
Glass, China, Primitives
Appraisal Service Available

Butler

**STERN'S ANTIQUES &
CANDLE SHOP**
336 S Main St 16001
412 287-1105 Est: 1967
Proprietor: John R Stern
Hours: Tues-Sat, 9-5
Types & Periods: Primitives,
Accessories
Specialties: Candles, Rings
Appraisal Service Available
Directions: Across from
Post Office

Cambridge Springs

THIESS ANTIQUES
165 Church St 16403
814 398-441/
Proprietor: Viola Thiess
Hours: Daily; 10-5
Summer, 1-4 Winter
Types & Periods: Lamps &
Lamp Service, Glass Shades

Campbelltown

BETTY WOLF ANTIQUES
71 E Main St 17010
717 838-1233
Hours: By Appointment,
by Chance
Types & Periods: General
Line, Brass Beds, Furniture
Directions: Shop in the
barn

Camp Hill

**DOROTHY M ETTLINE
ANTIQUES**
26 S 29th St 17011
717 737-3838

**DOROTHY M ETTLINE
ANTIQUES** Cont'd
Proprietor: Dorothy M
Ettline
Hours: By Appointment
Types & Periods: Primitives,
China, Glass, Furniture

HOLLISTER ANTIQUES
1292 Kingsley Rd   17011
717 737-1972
Proprietor: Frank & Betty
Hollister
Hours: By Appointment
Types & Periods: Art & Cut
Glass, Art Pottery, China

Carlisle

THE BOBB'S ANTIQUES
82 E Ridge St   17013
717 243-3187
Proprietor: Joan &
Raymond C Bobb, Jr
Hours: By Appointment
Types & Periods: Pattern
Glass, Pottery, Primitives,
Country Furniture

ELIZABETH SCHIFFMAN
551 S Hanover St   17013
717 243-1530
Proprietor: Elizabith
Schiffman
Hours: By Appointment
Types & Periods: Georgian,
Victorian, Estate Jewelry
Specialties: Georgian,
Victorian, Estate Jewelry
Appraisal Service Available

THE SCHWIEBERT'S
RD 9 Box 389   17013
717 243-9173
Proprietor: Anne E
Schwiebert
Hours: By Appointment,
by Chance
Types & Periods: Primitives,
& General Line
Directions: Rte 641, 7
Miles W of Carlisle
between Plainfield &
Newville; from Handy Mkt
in Plainfield, 2 1/2 Miles

SNUG HARBOR ANTIQUES
505 Cavalry Rd   17013
717 243-5880
Proprietor: Kermit &
Carolyn Lackey
Types & Periods: Cut Glass;
General Line

THE WOODSHOP
RD 5, Pine Rd   17013
717 486-7549
Proprietor: Barbara & Don
Wood
Hours: Daily
Types & Periods: Primitives,
Country Furniture, Quilts,
Tools
Directions: Between Mt
Holly Springs & Huntsdale

Castle Shannon

SHILLING'S ANTIQUES
1225 Saxonwald Ave
15234
412 882-4596   Est: 1968
Proprietor: Ruth & Jack
Shilling
Hours: Mon-Sat, 10-5;
Also by Appointment
Types & Periods: Early
American thru Victorian
Furniture & Accessories
Specialties: Lighting
Devices, Repair
Directions: 7 Miles SW of
Pittsburg off Rte 88, 1
Block from Grove Rd &
Rte 88

Central City

MARTHA'S FLEA MART
RD 1 Box 129B   15926
814 754-5803
Proprietor: Martha E
Eastwood
Hours: Mon-Sat, 10-6;
Sun, 10-7
Types & Periods: General
Line, Glass, Furniture,
Collectibles
Directions: 3 Miles E of
Reels Corners on Rte US
30; 18 Miles W of Bedford

Chadds Ford

**BRANDYWINE HOUSE
ANTIQUES**
US Rte 1   19317
215 388-6060
Proprietor: Elinor F
Holsinger
Types & Periods: Glass,
China, Furniture, Lamps
Directions: 2 Miles SW of
Chadds Ford

**BRANDYWINE VALLEY
ANTIQUES**
Rte 1 Box 149   19317
215 388-6393
Proprietor: June &
Maurice Conner
Types & Periods: Dolls, Art
& Pattern Glass, Guns &
Accessories, Rare
Scrimshaw & Powder Horns,
Indian Artifacts, Primitives
Directions: US 1, 4 Miles
S of Jcr I & 202

Chalfont

GUTHRIE & LARASON
4 E Butler Ave   18914
215 822-3987   Est: 1975
Proprietor: Patti Guthrie &
Lew Larason
Hours: By Appointment,
by Chance
Types & Periods: American
Country Furniture (before
1840) & Accessories
Specialties: American
Country Items
Directions: In Bucks
County, on US 202 at the
Traffic Light of Rte 152N;
across from the Chalfont
Inn

Chambersburg

HOLLY AMBER SHOP
33 S Second St   17201
717 263-8967   Est: 1977
Hours: By Appointment,
by Chance
Types & Periods: Glass,
China, Reference Books on
Antiques
Directions: On US 11-N, in
Downtown Chambersburg

KELLY'S ANTIQUES
49 Woodland Way   17201
717 263-3789   Est: 1972
Proprietor: Gloria R Kelly
Hours: By Appointment
Types & Periods: General
Line
Specialties: George Ohr
Pottery
Directions: Guilford Hills
South, Use Overhill Dr
Entrance; Woodland Way
is 3rd Rd to Right

KATHERINE MARTIN'S ANTIQUES & COLLECTIBLES
Rte 1 Box 145   17201
717 264-5755
Proprietor: Katherine Martin
Hours: By Appointment
Types & Periods: Ironstone, Pattern Glass, General Line

Cherryville

ARDLE'S HEARTH
Rte 248   18035
215 767-8430
Hours: Tues-Sat, 10-6
Types & Periods: " A Country Store with a Lil' Bit of Everything"

STUDIO G & HOUSE OF THE WHITE ELEPHANT
Rte 248   18035
215 262-3613
Hours: Daily
Types & Periods: General Line, Collectibles, Art, Wall Decor

Chester Heights

DOTTIE'S ANTIQUES
Box 82   19017
215 459-5265
Proprietor: Dottie Freeman
Hours: By Appointment
Types & Periods: General Line
Specialties: Glass (Heisey)

Clearfield

STONEBRAKER'S ANTIQUES
424 S 2nd St   16830
814 765-8715   Est: 1943
Proprietor: L D Stonebraker
Hours: Daily, By Appointment, By Chance
Types & Periods: China, Glass, Bric-a-Brac, Funiture
Appraisal Service Available
Directions: On Main Hwy in Center of Town

Collegeville

EARLY AMERICAN ANTIQUES
1646 Main St   19426
215 489-9783
Proprietor: Frank & Lilla Peirce
Types & Periods: Country Furniture, Primitives

JAMES GALLEY
Box 64   19426
215 489-2828   Est: 1970
Proprietor: James Galley
Hours: By Appointment
Types & Periods: Chinese Export Porcelains
Specialties: Chinese Export Porcelains
Appraisal Service Available
Directions: 30 Minutes NE of Philadelphia, in Rahns

Columbia

PENDULUM 1776
241 Locust St   17512
717 684-2883
717 426-1282   Est: 1970
Proprietor: E Jane Reisinger
Hours: Mon, Thurs-Sat; Also by Appointment
Types & Periods: Early American Furniture, Clocks, Collectibles, Tin, Wood & General Line
Specialties: Clocks & Old Watches, Dutch Cupboards
Appraisal Service Available
Directions: Lancastor County, Approx 12 Miles W of Lancaster, 3 Miles S of Marietta, 15 Miles W of York; just off 441 & 3rd St Exit of Rte 30

SOURBEER & LOCKARD ANTIQUES
277 S 8th St   17512
717 684-7982   Est: 1943
Proprietor: Daniel Morgan Sourbeer
Hours: By Appointment, By Chance
Types & Periods: American Pattern Glass before 1900, French Dolls
Specialties: Glass (Pattern)
Appraisal Service Available
Directions: Corner of 8th & Hwy 482 (Old US 30)

Conneaut Lake

JANE'S ANTIQUES
Aldenia Dr   16316
814 382-8475   Est: 1962
Proprietor: Mildred G & Jane E McKenry
Hours: Tues-Sun, Mon by Chance
Types & Periods: Lamps, Chimneys, Shades, Flow Blue

Connellsville

BRADLEY HOUSE ANTIQUES
127 Witter Ave   15425
412 628-2623
Proprietor: Margaret L Molinaro
Hours: Eves & Weekends, Also by Chance or Appointment
Types & Periods: General Line, Lamps, Furniture, Wicker, Primitives, Glassware, Pictures, Collectibles
Directions: Off US 119

Conshohocken

THE SPRING MILL ANTIQUE SHOP
Spring Mill   19428
215 828-0205   Est: 1945
Proprietor: Matthew & Elisabeth Sharpe
Hours: By Appointment
Types & Periods: 18th Century Furniture, Ceramics, Brass
Specialties: American Furniture, Chinese Export Porcelain
Directions: Near Pa Turnpike Exits 24 & 25, 25 Min from Philadelphia

Coopersburg

SUMMER KITCHEN ANTIQUES
Rte 3   18036
215 797-0275
Proprietor: Barbara & David Mest
Hours: Daily

SUMMER KITCHEN   Cont'd
Types & Periods: Primitives,
Folk Art, Country Furniture
Directions: In Lanark, S of
Allentown on Limeport Rd

Coraopolis

SMITH'S ANTIQUES
Broadhead Rd   15108
412 457-8717   Est: 1964
Proprietor: Mable M Smith
Hours: Mon-Sat, By
Appointment, By Chance
Types & Periods: Lamps,
Quilts, China, Cut & Art
Glass
Specialties: Furniture
(Victorian)
Directions: 4½ Miles NW
of Greater Pittsburgh
Airport

Cornwells Heights

THE STABLE
5936 Hulmeville Rd   19020
215 757-6646
Proprietor: Marie Bond
Types & Periods: Furniture,
China, Glass, Primitives,
Automatic Musical
Instruments

Creamery

**CREAMERY CORNER
ANTIQUES**
Rte 113 & Cressman Rd
19087
215 489-9974
Proprietor: Ken Karstetter
Types & Periods:
Collectibles, Furniture,
General Line

Curwensville

PAT ERRIGO ANTIQUES
848 State St   16833
814 236-3403   Est: 1950
Proprietor: Pat Errigo
Hours: Mon-Sat 9-5, By
Appointment
Specialties: Furniture &
Rugs

Appraisal Service Available
Directions: Exit 19 from
I-80, 9 Miles, 879 W

WOODHURST
201 McLaughlin St   16833
814 236-1053
Proprietor: George & Anne
Thacik
Types & Periods: General
Line

Dallas

**ANTIQUES &
COLLECTABLES**
Country Club Rd, RD 4
18612
Proprietor: Ed & Ann
Yadisky
Hours: By Appointment
Types & Periods: General
Line

CAMEO ANTIQUES
18612
717 675-3061
Proprietor: Edith Hacker
Types & Periods: General
Line, Furniture, Glassware,
China
Directions: Applewood
Manor, Upper Demunds
Rd

COUNTRY CLUB ANTIQUES
Country Club Rd, RD 4
18612
717 675-3425
Proprietor: Ed & Ann
Yadisky
Types & Periods: General
Line, Furniture, Art Glass,
China

**THE GOLDEN EAGLE
ANTIQUES & GIFTS**
Upper Demunds Rd
18612
717 675-0493
Proprietor: Grace
Bachman
Hours: Tues-Sun, 10-8
Types & Periods: General
Line

HITCHING POST ANTIQUES
61 Church St   18612
717 675-0721
Proprietor: Diana Getz
Types & Periods: General
Line, Country Furniture,
Glass, China, Jewelry

MAJOR ANTIQUES
RD 2 Box 315   18612
717 675-2991   Est: 1968
Proprietor: T Bryce Major
Hours: Daily, by Chance;
There is Almost Always
Someone Here
Types & Periods: General
Line, Lamps, Glassware,
Clocks, Woodenware
Specialties: Oak Furniture,
Primitives
Appraisal Service Available
Directions: 1 Mile off Rte
118 on Lehman-Huntsville
Rd; Follow Signs for
Wilkes-Barre Campus of
Penn State College

MANOR ANTIQUES
Hildebrand Rd, Rte 309
18612
717 675-5646
Proprietor: Vern Collura
Hours: Fri-Wed
Types & Periods: General
Line

Denver

**RENNINGER'S ANTIQUE
MARKET**
RD 3   17517
215 267-2177
Proprietor: Terry Heilman
Types & Periods: General
Line

Dillsburg

GROVE'S ANTIQUES
RD 2, Rte 74S   17019
717 432-3465
Proprietor: Edgar Grove,
Jr
Types & Periods: General
Specialties: Clocks

Douglassville

MERRITT'S ANTIQUES INC
RD 2   19518
215 689-9541
Proprietor: Robert J
Merritt
Hours: Mon-Sat, 7-5:30
Types & Periods: General
Line

SCHOOL HOUSE ANTIQUES
Rte 22, Box 395A   19518
215 323-4582   Est: 1974
Proprietor: Robert D & Juanita Taylor
Hours: By Appointment
Types & Periods: General Line

Downingtown

PHILIP H BRADLEY CO
Lancaster Ave.   19335
Proprietor: Philip H Bradley
Hours: Mon-Sat
Types & Periods: Early American Antiques & Accessories
Appraisal Service Available
Directions: Rte 30, 4 Miles W of Rte 100

ECHO GLEN ANTIQUES
RD 1   19335
215 269-0729
Proprietor: Ronald & Beatrice L Beebe
Types & Periods: Primitives, General Line

Drexel Hill

ANN N DOWNEY & DANIEL HARE
807-A Burmont Rd   19026
215 449-9107
Proprietor: Ann N Downey & Daniel Hare
Types & Periods: General Line
Specialties: Silver (Coin & Sterling)

Duncannon

DELACYS ANTIQUES
RD 1   17020
717 824-3589   Est: 1930
Proprietor: L B DeLancy
Hours: Daily
Types & Periods: 18th & 19th Century Furniture, Glass, Brass, Iron
Directions: 2 Miles N of Duncannon on Rte 849

CLAYTON FREY ANTIQUES
701 N High St   17020
717 834-3752   Est: 1964
Proprietor: Clayton Frey Jr
Hours: By Appointment
Types & Periods: Oak & Primitives
Appraisal Service Available
Directions: 16 Miles N of Harrisburg on Rtes 22 & 322; 1 Mile N of Duncannon, 1/2 Mile S of Amity Hall Inn

Duncansville

DODSON'S ANTIQUES
614 3rd Ave   16635
814 695-1901   Est: 1948
Proprietor: Mrs Marian Dodson
Hours: Mon-Sat, 9-5
Types & Periods: Glass, China, Pottery, Furniture
Specialties: China, Glass, Lamps
Directions: Main Hwy Rte 22

JACK'S ANTIQUES
RD 2   16635
814 695-0031   Est: 1962
Proprietor: Jack B Colbert
Types & Periods: Oak Furniture, Primitives, Collectibles, Wicker
Specialties: Oak Furniture
Directions: 2 Blocks W from the Intersection of Rtes 22 & 220; Turn L at Old Rte 22

KINZLE GALLERIES
1002 3rd Ave   16635
814 695-3479   Est: 1957
Proprietor: Dorothy Kinzle
Hours: Mon-Sat, 9-5; Appointment Suggested
Types & Periods: 18th & 19th Century American Furniture & Accessories, Paintings, Prints
Appraisal Service Available
Directions: At Crossroads of Rtes 220 & 22; 30 Miles N of Pa Trpk at Bedford, 85 Miles E of Pittsburgh on Rt 22, 53 Miles SW of Rte 80 at Milesburg

PATTON'S ANTIQUE SHOP
1504 3rd Ave   16635
814 695-0812   Est: 1926
Proprietor: Gerald M Patton
Hours: Daily
Types & Periods: Furniture, Glass, China, Primitives
Specialties: Advertising, Catalogues
Appraisal Service Available
Directions: Rte 22, 6 Miles W of Altoona, 95 Miles E of Pittsburgh

East Berlin

BUFFALO ENTERPRISES, 18TH CENTURY SHOP
308 W King St   17316
717 259-9081
Proprietor: Carole S Roberson
Hours: Tues-Sun
Types & Periods: Country Furniture & Items along the Primitive Line, Early Craftsmen Tools (Woodworking, Blacksmithing, Coopers & Farm), Firearms
Specialties: Custom Made Period Clothing of both the 18th & 19th Centuries; Civilian & Military
Appraisal Service Available
Directions: Between York & Gettysburg, 4 Miles off U S Rte 30 (Lincoln Way)

Easton

MICHAEL S HANDLOVIC
4200 Wm Penn Hwy   18042
215 253-5601
Types & Periods: General Line

YE OLDE TOBY SIGN
2121 Hackett Ave   18042
215 253-7326
Proprietor: Carolyn M Kichline
Types & Periods: General Line, Collectibles

Elizabethtown

AZALEA ANTIQUES & GIFTS
230 N Mt Joy St   17022
717 367-1418
Proprietor: Harry & Kathryn Raymond
Types & Periods: White Pattern Ironstone, Roseville Pottery

TRADING POST CENTER
451 W High St   17022
717 838-5278   Est: 1975
Proprietor: Tony & Donna Szafranic
Hours: Sat & Sun, 9-5
Types & Periods: Complete Collectible Line; Over 600 Tables of Antiques & Collectibles, Specialty Show in Show Bldg
Directions: 1/2 Mile S on Rte 241

Elverson

STALLFORT ANTIQUES
RD 1   19520
215 286-5882   Est: 1965
Proprietor: G Robert Stallfort
Hours: Mon-Sat
Types & Periods: 18th Century American Furniture & Accessories
Specialties: Country Furniture
Appraisal Service Available
Directions: Off Rte 23, 5.8 Miles W of Rte 110 in Chester County

Emmaus

ANNA M BENNER ANTIQUES
Box 477, Rte 1   18049
215 967-1412
Proprietor: Anna M Benner
Hours: By Appointment
Types & Periods: Carnival Glass, China, Primitives

IRON KETTLE ANTIQUES
127 N 2nd St   18049
215 967-4448   Est: 1970

Proprietor: B J Schaefer
Hours: Daily, by Appointment, by Chance; At Shows
Types & Periods: Carnival Glass, China, Art Pottery, General Line
Specialties: Oak Furniture & Refinishing
Directions: Downtown

Enola

M & S ANTIQUES
17 Lancaster Ave   17025
717 732-2118
Proprietor: Merlin Shellenberger
Hours: By Appointment
Types & Periods: Bisque Dolls, Azalea China

Ephrata

LAUSCH'S DUTCH BARN
222 Steinmetz Rd, Box 367   17522
717 733-2659   Est: 1930
Proprietor: R Drewlausch
Hours: By Appointment, by Chance
Types & Periods: General Line
Specialties: Furniture
Appraisal Service Available
Directions: Corner of Mohler Church Rd & Church Ave

ARLENE MINNICH ANTIQUES
1369 W Main St   17522
717 733-2077
Proprietor: Arlene Minnich
Types & Periods: General Line

Equinunk

THE RED HOUSE ANTIQUES
Rte 191   18417
717 224-4650
Proprietor: H Conley Sr
Hours: "Open All Year"
Types & Periods: General Line
Directions: 2 Miles N of Equinunk

SHANGRI LA
Rte 191   18417
717 224-4669
Proprietor: Lillian & Douglas Dixon
Types & Periods: General Line
Appraisal Service Available

Erie

BROWN'S ANTIQUE MANOR
4180 W Lake Rd   16505
814 838-6269   Est: 1972
Proprietor: Dorothy & Robert Brown
Hours: Daily, 12-5
Types & Periods: Victorian & Oak Furniture, Wicker, Leaded Lamp Shades, Clocks, Dolls, Cut & Pattern Glass, Hand Painted China
Appraisal Service Available
Directions: Rt 5 near Airport

TREGLER GALLERY
301 Cascade St   16507
814 454-0315   Est: 1972
Proprietor: Robert Tregler
Hours: Mon-Sat
Types & Periods: Tiffany & Handel Lamps, Art & Cut Glass, Estate Diamonds & Jewelry, Oil Paintings, Sculpture, Sterling Silver, Rare Violins
Specialties: Estate Diamonds & Precious Stone Jewelry
Appraisal Service Available
Directions: Corner of W 3rd St & Cascade near the Shore of Lake Erie

Espyville Station

PYMATUNING ANTIQUES
Rte 285   16414
412 927-2194
Proprietor: Mary Ellen Conlon
Hours: Daily 9-5
Types & Periods: Primitives, China, Clocks

Evans City

ROBERT & JESSIE POWELL
Rd 1 16033
412 776-2333 Est: 1945
Proprietor: Robert & Jessie Powell
Hours: Tues-Sun 10-4
Types & Periods: 18th & 19th Century Furniture & Appointments
Specialties: Furniture (Refinished)
Directions: Rtes 19 & 228 Intersection of I-79 at Traffic Signal

Exton

JOHN W BUNKER & SON
411 E Lincoln Hwy 19341
215 363-7436 Est: 1946
Proprietor: John W Bunker
Hours: Daily
Types & Periods: Queen Anne, Chippendale, Early American
Specialties: Restoration
Appraisal Service Available
Directions: 30 Miles W of Philadelphia, 30 Miles E of Lancaster, 10 Miles S of Valley Forge

HERBERT F SCHIFFER ANTIQUES
Box E 19341
215 363-6889 Est: 1960
Proprietor: Herbert F Schiffer
Hours: Mon-Sat
Types & Periods: American, English 18th & 19th Centuries Furniture, Chinese Porcelains, Delft, Leeds, Straffordshire, Brass, Pewter
Appraisal Service Available
Directions: 30 Miles W of Philadelphia on Rte 30, 2 Miles W of Town

Fairview Village

MARGARET SCHAFER
Box 292 19409
215 584-4239
Proprietor: Margaret Schafer
Hours: Shows Only

Types & Periods: 18th & 19th Centuries Country Furniture, Primitives, Flow Blue, Quilts
Specialties: Same as above

Fayetteville

JACOBY'S ANTIQUES
150 Lincoln Way W 17222
717 352-2035
Proprietor: Don & Cynthia Jacoby
Types & Periods: General Line, Furniture, Cut & Art Glass

RITTER'S ANTIQUES
Rte 1, Box 229 17222
717 352-3320
Proprietor: Janet C Ritter
Types & Periods: Glass, China

Fleetville

TOWN 'N LAKE AUCTION GALLERY PLUS WHOLESALE & RETAIL SHOPS
Box 125 18420
717 945-5295 Est: 1972
Proprietor: Thomas O Motter
Hours: By Appointment
Types & Periods: " Oak & Victorian plus Lamps & Glassware, Etc"
Directions: Corner of Rtes 107 & 407; Exit 61 from Rte 81

Fleetwood

PALMER & VIRGINIA SMELTZ
RD 3 19522
215 987-6129
Proprietor: Palmer & Virginia Smeltz
Hours: By Appointment
Types & Periods: Furniture, Potter, Tinware
Directions: Near Oley

PAM ZIMMERMAN'S ANTIQUES
RD 2 19522
215 944-8414

Proprietor: Pam Zimmerman
Hours: By Appointment
Types & Periods: General Line

Flourtown

ANTIQUES TWO
1407 Bethlehem Pike 19031
215 836-9187 Est: 1971
Proprietor: Elizabeth Joyce & Jane Spadofora
Hours: Daily, 11-5
Types & Periods: Victorian & Turn-of-the-Century Furniture
Directions: 2 Miles N of Chestnut Hill

Fort Washington

MEETINGHOUSE ANTIQUE SHOP
509 Bethlehem Pike 19034
Proprietor: Irvin & Dolores Boyd
Hours: Daily, 9-5; By Appointment
Types & Periods: 18th & 19th Century American Furniture & Accessories
Specialties: Slant Front Desks, Highboys, Corner Cupboards, Dutch Cupboards, Windsor Chairs, Chests of Drawers
Appraisal Service Available
Directions: Exit 26 Penna Turnpike, 90 Miles from New York City, 25 Minutes from Center of Philadelphia

Gettysburg

BATTLEFIELD MILITARY MUSEUM
Box 192, Rte 140 17325
717 334-6568 Est: 1962
Proprietor: George W Marinos
Hours: Daily, May-Sept; By Appointment, Oct-Apr
Types & Periods: Civil War to WWII: Guns, Swords, Uniforms, Hats, Helmets, Military Medals, Books

BATTLEFIELD MILITARY
MUSEUM   Cont'd
Specialties: Arms & Armor
(Civil War to WWII)
Appraisal Service Available
Directions: Rte 140 on
Battlefield Across from
300 Foot Tower

THE BRICK HOUSE
RD 4   17325
717 528-4298
Proprietor: Mary Heltibridle
Types & Periods: General
Line
Directions: In Heidlersburg

HESS ANTIQUES
239 Chambersburg St
                        17325
717 334-5931   Est: 1920
Proprietor: S H Hess
Hours: Daily; By
Appointment, by Chance
Types & Periods: Furniture,
Glass, China
Appraisal Service Available
Directions: 2 1/2 Blocks
W of Center of Town on
Hwy 30W

HESS ANTIQUES WEST
15 Seminary Ridge   17325
717 334-5931
Proprietor: S H Hess
Hours: Daily; By
Appointment, by Chance
Types & Periods: Glass,
China, Furniture, Pattern
Glass
Appraisal Service Available

RED SCHOOLHOUSE
Rte 2   17325
717 334-4771   Est: 1946
Proprietor: Maxwell
Barach
Hours: Daily
Types & Periods: 18th &
19th Century Country &
Period
Directions: 4 Miles S of
Gettysburg on US
Business 15

Green Lane

COLONIAL HOUSE
ANTIQUES
Corner Rtes 63 & 29
                        18054
215 234-4113

Proprietor: Stephen &
Helen Szegda
Hours: Mon-Fri, 9-8; Sat,
9-5
Types & Periods: Large
Selection of Furniture,
Period to Oak, China,
Glassware, Ironware,
Bric-a-Brac
Appraisal Service Available
Directions: SE Pa;
Turnpike Exit No E,
Lansdale Exit; Follow Rte
63 W

Greensburg

ANTIQUE NOOK
135 E Pittsburgh St 15601
412 834-8096   Est: 1974
Proprietor: Betty Freeman
Hours: Daily, Eves by
Chance
Types & Periods: Furniture,
General Line
Specialties: China, Glass,
Silver
Directions: 2 Blocks
"below" Court House
going E on Rte 130

SEVEN OAKS
RD 8, Box 133   15601
412 837-8351   Est: 1975
Proprietor: Mary Lou
McWilliams
Hours: By Appointment,
by Chance
Types & Periods: Primitives,
Country Furniture,
Glassware, Oak
Specialties: Country
Furniture
Directions: 200 Yards off
Rte 30 & Mt View Inn
Intersection

Greentown

SINGER'S ANTIQUES
Rte 1   18426
717 676-3215   Est: 1964
Proprietor: Mrs Ethel
Singer
Hours: Daily
Types & Periods: 1890-1915;
Pattern, Art, Cut Glass;
Lamps; Furniture

Directions: 2 Miles from
Newfoundland, near Lake
Wallenpaupack; Off Rte
507, 1 Mile E of
Newfoundland; Pass Flea
Mkt, Located on Brink Hill

Grove City

CAMPBELL'S ANTIQUES
217 N Broad   16127
412 458-8680
Proprietor: Mrs Robert
Campbell
Hours: By Appointment,
by Chance
Types & Periods: Jewelry,
Collectibles

PINE GROVE ANTIQUES
541 S Center St   16127
412 458-8937   Est: 1971
Proprietor: M Hodge
(Manager)
Hours: By Appointment
Types & Periods: Primitives,
Early American, Paintings
Specialties: Primitives
Appraisal Service Available
Directions: I-79 Grove City
Exit, 208 E or I-80 Grove
City Exit, then 173 S to
208 W; S Center St is Rte
208

Hamburg

THOMAS ANTIQUES
N 4th   19526
215 562-2309   Est: 1956
Proprietor: Dorothy M
Thomas
Hours: Tues-Sun
Types & Periods: General
Line, Primitive Furniture,
Copper, Brass, Tin, China,
Glass, Lamps, Pottery
Specialties: Country
Furniture
Directions: Off Rte 61 &
22-78

Hanover

ANTIQUES OF
DISTINCTION
                        17331
717 637-2039

Proprietor: Weniger &
Rebert
Hours: By Appointment
Types & Periods: Majolica,
Lustre, Miniatures, Glass

BY CHANCE ANTIQUES
429 Baltimore St   17331
717 632-0487   Est: 1973
Proprietor: Mrs Shirley B
Gist
Hours: Thurs-Tues
Types & Periods: Dolls,
Jewelry, Wash Bowl &
Pitcher Sets, Rockers,
Wooden Tub Tables,
Carnival & Depression Glass
Specialties: Dolls
Directions: 4 Blocks from
Square

THE MILLER'S
621 McCosh St   17331
717 633-6119
Proprietor: Harry F &
Romaine E Miller
Hours: By Appointment
Types & Periods: Glass,
China, Primitives, General
Line

Harford

**RANDALL C KRITKAUSKY
& CAROLYN SCHMIDT
ANTIQUES**
Rte 547   18823
717 434-2095   Est: 1971
Hours: Daily
Types & Periods: 18th-Early
1900; American Furniture,
Pottery, Fabrics; European
Furniture
Specialties: Country
Furniture
Directions: 1 1/2 Miles off
I-81 at Exit 65

Harleysville

**HILLTOP ANTIQUES
"HOUSE OF ELEGANT
JUNQUE"**
423 Main St   19438
215 256-8143
Proprietor: Walter Wilcox
Hours: Daily
Types & Periods: Country
Furniture

A LUDWIG KLEIN & SON
683 Sumneytown Pike
19438
215 256-9004   Est: 1786
Proprietor: W Karl &
Byron G Klein
Hours: Mon-Fri, 9-6;
Weekends by Appointment
Types & Periods: Porcelain,
Glass
Specialties: Porcelain, Glass,
Supplies for Repairing China
& Glass without Firing; Free
Catalog for Supplies
Appraisal Service Available
Directions: Rte 63,
Vernfield Village

Harrisburg

BENNEY'S ANTIQUE SHOP
100 N 67th St   17111
717 564-1002
Proprietor: George W
Benney
Types & Periods: Glass,
China, Primitives

DEATRICH'S ANTIQUES
3524 Walnut St   17109
717 545-8466
Proprietor: Martha & Paul
Deatrich
Types & Periods: Buttons,
Military Items, Postcards,
Books, Political Items,
General Line

DITLOW'S ANTIQUE SHED
5103 Jonestown Rd
17112
717 545 4602   Est: 1974
Proprietor: Harold B
Ditlow
Hours: Daily, 10-7
Types & Periods: General
Line
Appraisal Service Available
Directions: 5 Miles E of
Town on Rte 22

DOEHNE'S OX BOW SHOP
N Progress Ave &
Doehne Rd   17110
717 545-7930   Est: 1956
Proprietor: Elsie G Doehne
Hours: Tues-Sat, 12-4:30;
Tues & Thurs Eves, 7-9
Types & Periods: General
Line, Lamps, Doll House
Furniture & Accessories

Specialties: Pattern Glass,
Doll House Accessories
Directions: 2 Miles N of
Rte 22 on Progress Ave;
N Mile off I-81, Exit 25
(Progress Ave)

DOWNTOWN ANTIQUES
1931 Derry St   17104
717 232-0162   Est: 1972
Proprietor: Georgetta S
Strohecker
Hours: Daily
Types & Periods: General
Line
Specialties: Clocks, Lights
Directions: Hill Section of
Harrisburg

C MERLE DUBS
231 North St   17101
717 232-9622
Proprietor: C Merle Dubs
Hours: Daily
Types & Periods: Clocks,
Jewelry, Silver

D I ESHLEMAN
3820 Bolinger Rd   17109
717 545-8826
Proprietor: D I Eshleman
Hours: By Appointment
Types & Periods: General
Line

FOX CHASE ANTIQUES
Fox Chase Rd   17111
717 566-3411
Proprietor: Gerald C Boltz
Types & Periods: Country
Furniture, Primitives
Specialties: Furniture &
Refinishing

HOFFMAN LANE BOOKS
4713 Queen Ave   17109
717 545-2349   Est: 1978
Proprietor: Mrs Deanna
Beeching (Manager)
Hours: Mon-Sat, Noon til
Early Evening
Types & Periods: Books,
Used & Rare, with Special
Emphasis on Pa History,
Civil War, Children's Books,
Hunting & Fishing
Specialties: Books
Directions: Colonial Park
Area; Exit 30E from Hwy
83; Take Rte 22E; Turn S
(right) at Prince St (3rd
light); 1st Cross St is
Queen, Turn L; Shop at
end of Short St on Right

Harrisburg   Cont'd

JENNINGS ANTIQUES
104 N Franklin St   17109
717 469-2594
Hours: Tues, Thurs & Sat,
9-3; Also by Appointment
Types & Periods: Glass,
China, Pottery, Primitives;
Country, Victorian & Oak
Furniture

UPSTAIRS ANTIQUES
404 N 2nd St   17101
717 233-5219
Proprietor: Jane First &
Anne Lowengard
Hours: Tues-Fri, 11:30-4
Types & Periods: Small
Furniture, China, Glass,
Silver
Directions: 1 1/2 Blocks
from State Capitol

Harrison City

THE BUTERBAUGH'S
P O Box 367   15636
412 744-3512
Proprietor: The
Buterbaughs
Hours: By Appointment
Types & Periods: Jewelry,
Wedgewood, Cut Glass,
Cards, Doulton Jugs
Appraisal Service Available

Hartstown

HERITAGE ANTIQUES
Rte 18 & 322   16131
814 382-2438
Proprietor: Phillip M Hans
Types & Periods: General
Line, Collectibles

Harvey's Lake

TRADING POST
RD 1, Box 503   18618
717 639-1949
Proprietor: Pat Passer
Types & Periods: General
Line, Furniture, Collectibles

Hatboro

VALERIE BERNSTEIN
218 Oak Hill Dr   19040
215 672-3152
Proprietor: Valerie
Bernstein
Types & Periods: General
Line, China, Glass, Silver,
Primitives
Appraisal Service Available

WM PENN SHOP
1341 W County Line Rd
                    19040
215 675-6974   Est: 1925
Proprietor: Barry S
Slosberg
Hours: Shop open Sat &
Sun, Warehouse open by
Appointment
Types & Periods: General
Line of Antique Furniture,
Glass, China, Clocks, Silver
& Jewelry
Specialties: Autioneer
Service Available
Appraisal Service Available
Directions: Warehouse
located at above Address;
Shop located in the
Golden Nugget Flea
Market (1st Floor), Rte 29,
Lambertville, NJ

Havertown

**AGNES DU BOSQUE
ANTIQUES**
44 W Wimot Ave   19083
215 449-5349
Proprietor: Agnes Du
Bosque
Types & Periods: Pattern
Glass, China

**RITA ORONS ANTIQUE
ACCESSORIES**
22 Castle Rock Dr   19083
215 449-2653
Proprietor: Rita Orons
Types & Periods: General
Line, Glass, China, Dolls,
Bronze, Silver

Hawley

R J LATOURNOUS
475 Welwood   18428
717 226-9251
Hours: " Open All Year"
Types & Periods: American
Cut Glass
Specialties: Glass
Directions: On Rte 6, 1/2
Mile from the
Wallenpaupack Dam

Hazleton

THE GENERAL STORE
163 N Church St   18201
717 454-3256
Proprietor: Mariene Kroll
Hours: By Appointment
Types & Periods: Furniture,
Primitives, Glass, China,
Quilts, Jewelry

Hellam

MARY MAC'S ANTIQUES
130 W Market St   17406
717 755-5741   Est: 1973
Proprietor: Mary G
McKinley
Hours: Daily; Eves by
Appointment
Types & Periods: General
Line, Furniture, Lamps,
Glass, Sterling, China, Dolls,
Miniatures
Directions: On 462, E Side
of Town

**RUNNING BROOK
ANTIQUE SHOP**
5 E Market St   17406
717 755-3844   Est: 1963
Proprietor: Guy C Keemer,
Jr
Hours: Mon-Sat, 9-5
Types & Periods: 18th &
19th Century Furniture
Specialties: Clocks

Hellertown

RED BARN ANTIQUES
RD 1   18055
215 838-8931

Types & Periods: Primitives, Furniture, Military, Nautical, Americana, General Line
Directions: 3 Miles E of Hellertown on Easton-Hellertown Rd

Henryville

PATRICK HENRY ANTIQUES
Box 275   18332
717 629-0171   Est: 1961
Proprietor: Katherine J Tolman
Hours: By Appointment, by Chance
Types & Periods: Furniture, Primitives, Country Store Items, Early Tools
Directions: Rte 191 N of Stroudsburg, Pa

Hereford

SCHMIDT'S ANTIQUES
Box 125   18056
215 679-5287
Proprietor: Ann & Walter Schmidt
Hours: By Appointment, by Chance
Types & Periods: Primitives, General Line
Directions: 1 1/2 Mile off Rte 100

Hershey

COLONIAL HOUSE OF ANTIQUES
43 W Areba Ave   17033
717 533-7054   Est: 1975
Proprietor: Paul R Aldridge
Hours: Open upon Request (Daily)
Types & Periods: General
Specialties: Refinished & Unfinished Furniture
Appraisal Service Available (Limited)
Directions: Located at Hershey Colonial Motel 3 Blocks S of Sq on Rte 743 (Cocoa Ave) in Downtown Hershey

MY WIFE'S ANTIQUES INC
Rtes 322 & 743   17033
717 533-4267   Est: 1972
Proprietor: Ginny & Harry Stoddart
Hours: Daily
Types & Periods: Primitives, Glass, China, Furniture, Americana
Specialties: Printing Equipment
Directions: 13 Miles E of Harrisburg on Rte 322

Hickory

ROBERT B WILSON
                    15340
412 356-2203   Est: 1930
Proprietor: Robert B Wilson
Hours: By Appointment
Types & Periods: 18th & 19th Century American
Specialties: Clocks, Rugs (Oriental)
Appraisal Service Available
Directions: 10 Miles N of Washington near Rtes 18 & 50

Highspire

HOUSE OF ANTIQUES
13 Roop St   17034
717 939-3064
717 939-9032   Est: 1977
Proprietor: Richard E Chubb
Hours: By Appointment or by Chance
Types & Periods: General Line
Specialties: Roseville Pottery
Directions: 6 Miles E of Harrisburg

Hollidaysburg

BURKHOLDER'S ANTIQUE SHOP
RD 2, Box 619   16648
814 695-1030   Est: 1943
Proprietor: T H Burkholder
Hours: Mon-Sat
Types & Periods: Complete Line of Early to Oak Furniture, Glass, China, Etc

Appraisal Service Available
Directions: 3 Miles E of Hollidaysburg on US Rte 22

Hollsopple

ZOOKS COUNTRY SHOPPE
RD 2   15935
814 629-5479
Proprietor: Jean Zook & Kay Bazley
Hours: Wed-Sun, 1-7; June 1 to Nov 1
Types & Periods: General Line
Directions: 6 Miles N of Jennerstown on Old US 219

Honesdale

THE CARRIAGE HOUSE
312 10th St   18431
717 253-4226
Proprietor: Rose & Bill Martin
Hours: By Appointment
Types & Periods: General Line

THE EVERGREEN ANTIQUE SHOP
622 Church St   18431
717 253-5424   Est: 1974
Proprietor: Miss M Alice Casey
Hours: Mon-Fri; By Appointment
Types & Periods: Usual & Unusual Fine Art Glass, Objets D'Art, Collector Items, Small Figurine, Furniture, China & Glass
Specialties: Cut Glass & China
Appraisal Service Available
Directions: Central City, Rte 6

THE HITCHING POST
1037 Main St   18431
717 253-2050
Proprietor: Miriam Van Horn
Types & Periods: General Line, Objets d'Art
Directions: "In the Alley"

HOLLY CORNER
"ANTIQUES"
   1400 West St   18431
   717 253-2864   Est: 1964
   Proprietor: Herbert M
   Harvey
   Hours: Mon-Sat; Sun by
   Appointment; Closed in
   Winter
Types & Periods: General
Line
Specialties: Oil Lamps,
Country Furniture of Mid
19th Century
   Directions: 1 Block W of
   Main St

KEMMANN'S COUNTRY
EMPORIUM
   959 Main St   18431
   717 253-4312   Est: 1971
   Proprietor: Hazel & Dick
   Kemmann
   Hours: Mon-Sat, Summer;
   By Appointment or
   Chance, Fall, Winter &
   Spring
Types & Periods: General
Line, Country Store, Tins,
Advertising, Primitives
   Directions: US Rte 6 is
   Main St

Hostetter

PUSKAR'S CENTER
   Box 83   15638
   412 539-9942
   Proprietor: Hilde E Puskar
   Hours: Daily, 9-6
Types & Periods: Art Glass,
Silver, Stamps, Coins,
Victrolas, Jewelry,
Collectibles, Flea Market

Hummelstown

HARRY J MENEAR
ANTIQUES
   112 E Main St   17036
   717 566-2802
   Proprietor: Harry J Menear
   Hours: Tues-Sat, 9-5
Types & Periods: General
Line, Furniture
Appraisal Service Available

SCHONEWOLF'S
ANTIQUES
   RD 3, Hummelstown-
   Middletown Rd   17036
   717 566-3015
   Proprietor: Rose &
   Stephen Schonewolf
   Hours: Tues-Sun, 10-5
Types & Periods: Furniture,
Pictures, Lamps, Clocks,
Primitives
   Directions: In Dutch
   Village

BETTY F SMITH
   116 E Main St   17306
   717 566-2057   Est: 1924
   Proprietor: Betty Smith
   Hours: Tues-Sat, 9-5
Types & Periods: General
Line
Appraisal Service Available
   Directions: 4 Miles W of
   Hershey, 9 Miles E of
   Harrisburg

OLIVE R WAGNER
   507 W Main St   17036
   717 566-8247   Est: 1956
   Proprietor: Olive R
   Wagner
   Hours: Tues-Fri
Types & Periods: Early
American Country Furniture,
Primitives

Huntingdon

ZABISKIE'S ANTIQUES
   Mc Alevy's Fort   16652
   814 667-3577
   Proprietor: Franklin P &
   Sara H Zabriskie
   Hours: Wed, Sat, Sun
Types & Periods: General
Line

Huntingdon Valley

COPPER EAGLE ANTIQUES
   Box 164   19006
   215 947-1254   Est: 1971
   Proprietor: Mary L Purdy,
   Edna C Smith
   Hours: By Appointment;
   Shows
Types & Periods: American
Primitives
Specialties: Coin Silver,
Quilts, Glass Cups & Plates,
Small Furniture

Indiana

RUBY & ROY'S ANTIQUES
   20 Stevenson Ave   15701
   412 465-8897
   Proprietor: Ruby & Roy
   Wells
   Hours: Daily; By Chance
Types & Periods: Glass,
China, Brass

Indian Orchard

THE INDIAN ORCHARD
SHOPPE
   Intersection Rtes 6 & 652
                      18431
   Proprietor: Ann & Dan
   Sanfilippo
   Hours: By Appointment
Types & Periods: General
Line, Collectibles
   Directions: 2 Miles E of
   Honesdale

Jennerstown

THE EMPORIUM
   Somerset Pike   15547
   (Mailing): Rte 4 Box 322
   Johnstown   15905
   814 288-2843   Est: 1974
   Proprietor: Jack Roseman
   Hours: Daily, 10-9
Types & Periods: Stained
Glass Windows & Lamps
Specialties: Stained Glass
Work
   Directions: 4 Miles N of
   Johnstown

Jersey Shore

RIVER HOUSE ANTIQUES
   135 N Main St   17740
   717 398-1286
   Proprietor: Marge Kamus
   Hours: Daily, 9-5
Types & Periods: Primitives,
General Line

SCHOOLMASTER'S
ANTIQUES
   225 Thompson St   17740
   717 398-2872
   Proprietor: Charles Phillips

Hours: Daily, 10-10
Types & Periods: Country
Furniture, Primitives, Tin,
Iron, Brass

**JANE SPANGLER
ANTIQUES**
1324 Allegheny St   17740
717 398-1306
Hours: Daily, 1-5
Types & Periods: General
Line

Johnstown

CURIOSITY CORNER
570 Grove Ave   15902
814 535-5210   Est: 1971
Proprietor: George & Sue
Walko
Hours: Daily
Types & Periods: Primitives,
Furniture, Glassware
Appraisal Service Available
Directions: Moxham
Section, about 3 Miles
from Rte 219

GALLAGHER & CO
736 Railroad St   15901
814 535-1111
Proprietor: Barry
Gallagher
Hours: By Appointment,
by Chance
Types & Periods: American
Oak & Walnut, Glassware,
China & Art Pottery
Specialties: Oak Furniture
Directions: Bedford St Exit
off Rte 56 in Downtown;
Turn R at the Light onto
Adams St; Go 2 1/2
Blocks & Veer R onto
Railroad St; 1st Block

Kennett Square

WILLOWDALE ANTIQUES
RD 1, Willowdale   19348
Proprietor: Margaret S
Wallace
Hours: Mon-Sat, 10-5
Types & Periods: Prior to
1840; Furniture, Iron,
Copper, Brass, Silver, Quilts,
Woven Coverlets, Children's
Furniture, Miniature
Furniture

Specialties: Dated and or
Decorated Early Wrought
Iron
Directions: At Rtes 82 &
926, 1 Mile N of Rte 1

Kimberton

WEAVER'S ANTIQUES
                    19442
215 935-1879
Proprietor: Kenneth &
Barbara Weaver
Hours: By Appointment
Types & Periods: Primitives,
Furniture, Lamps
Appraisal Service Available

King of Prussia

W GRAHAM ARADER, III
1000 Boxwood Court
                    19406
215 825-6570   Est: 1972
Proprietor: W Graham
Arader, III
Hours: Mon-Fri; By
Appointment on Weekends
Types & Periods: Rare
Maps, Prints, & Books
(Atlases); 15th-19th
Centuries, Strong in
Americana; Also Material
Dealing with the New World,
Colonial Period of America,
Revolutionary War,
Westward Expansion
Specialties: Maps, Prints,
Books; Restoration of Paper
& Hand Bookbinding
Available
Appraisal Service Available

Kingston

ABIGAIL
43 Park Pl   18704
717 288-8009
Hours: By Appointment
Types & Periods: General
Line

Kittanning

**BRIAR HILL MANOR
ANTIQUES**
RD 7, Pony Farm Rd
                    16201
412 545-1431
Proprietor: Clarence &
Zella West
Types & Periods: Victorian &
Cut Glass Lamps, Orientals,
Cut Glass

Knox

HARRIS ANTIQUES
Main St   16232
814 797-5008   Est: 1976
Proprietor: Ronald W &
Carol A Harris
Hours: By Appointment
Only
Types & Periods: 16th, 17th
& 18th Century: All Types:
Early Oriental Porcelain,
Swords & Other Civil War &
Military Items, Oils, Relics
(Indian, etc), Oriental Rugs
Specialties: Early Oriental
Porcelain, John H Belter
Furniture, Colored Gemstone
& Diamond Jewelry,
Japanese Swords
Appraisal Service Available
Directions: Exit 7 off I-80;
Knox is 3 Miles from Exit;
L at Blinker, R on Main at
Red Light

Knoxdale

VILLAGE ANTIQUES
Box 14   15847
814 849-8230   Est: 1961
Proprietor: Louise Miller
Hours: By Appointment,
by Chance
Types & Periods: Pattern
Glass, Clocks, Jewelry,
General Line
Appraisal Service Available
Directions: Rte 236
between Brookville &
Punxsutawney, I-80 Exits
13-15

Kutztown

AMERICAN CLASSICS
Krumsville Rd   19530
215 683-7866
Proprietor: Erna &
Kenneth Snyder
Hours: By Appointment
Types & Periods: 18th &
19th Century Furniture,
Paintings

ROBERT BURKHARDT
RD 1, Box 304   19530
215 683-8100   Est: 1928
Proprietor: Robert
Burkhardt
Hours: By Appointment,
When at Home
Types & Periods: Period
American & English
Furniture; China
(Staffordshire) Accessories,
Pa Primitives, Pewter &
Glass, Etc
Specialties: Furniture
Directions: At Monterey, 3
Miles E of Kutztown, US
Rte 222

**BUTTONWOOD HOLLOW
ANTIQUES**
RD 3, Box 296   19530
215 562-7927
Proprietor: Gwendolyn &
Richard Crosscup
Hours: By Appointment
Types & Periods: China,
Country Furniture, Primitives
Appraisal Service Available

GREENWICH MILLS
Kutztown-Krumsville Rd
19530
215 683-7866   Est: 1969
Proprietor: Ken & Erna
Snyder
Hours: By Appointment;
No Appointment Needed
Sat
Types & Periods: Furniture,
Primitives
Specialties: Furniture
Directions: 3 Miles N of
Kutztown on Rte 737

**KUTZTOWN GALLERY OF
ANTIQUES**
19 E Main St   19530
215 683-8089
Proprietor: Betty & Phillip
Rossi Jr
Types & Periods: Furniture,
Glass, Dolls, Jewelry,
Paintings, Objets d'Art

RENNINGER'S NO 2
Noble St   19530
Proprietor: 250 Dealer
Hours: Sat, 9-5
Types & Periods: General
Line
Directions: 1 Mile S from
the Middle of Town

Lahaska

**LYNNE-ART'S GLASS
HOUSE INC**
Rte 202,
P O Box 242   18931
215 794-7800
Proprietor: Lynne Block &
Art Hartman
Types & Periods: General
Line
Specialties: Glass (Heisey)

**OAKLAWN METALCRAFT &
ANTIQUE SHOP**
Rte 202,
P O Box 13   18931
215 794-7387   Est: 1946
Proprietor: Dallas,
Florence & David John
Types & Periods: Lighting,
Hardware, Tools, Primitives,
Tin, Toys

PICTURE FRAME GALLERY
Rte 202,
P O Box 75   18931
215 794-7022
Proprietor: Eve & Ben
Bianco
Types & Periods: General
Line, Prints & Frames,
Sterling
Specialties: Custom &
Creative Framing

Lake Ariel

STONE CHAIR ANTIQUES
Rte 3   18436
717 698-5482   Est: 1961
Proprietor: Fanny
Spangeberg
Hours: Daily
Types & Periods: General
Line
Directions: At Lake Ariel
Take Rte 296; 1 Block
Past School

Lampeter

**VILLAGE GIFT & ANTIQUE
SHOP**
Box 236   17537
717 464-3221
Proprietor: Dee Shaeffer
Types & Periods: Lamps,
Pressed Glass, Country
Furniture

Lancaster

**ANTIQUES & DIGNIFIED
JUNK**
Lincoln Hwy E   17602
717 393-8773   Est: 1950
Proprietor: Frank Charles
Hours: Daily, 10-5
Types & Periods: Primitives,
General Line
Directions: Across from
Amish Farm

**THE BENSON GALLERY
INC**
Host Farm Resort   17600
717 234-2209   Est: 1963
Proprietor: Rita R & Lester
Benson
Hours: Saturday
Types & Periods: Fine Gold
Jewelry, Bronzes, Oil
Paintings, Marble Sculpture,
Fine Arts of all Kinds
Specialties: Antique Jewelry
Appraisal Service Available
Directions: 2300 Lincoln
Way East; Also have Shop
at Renningers in
Adamstown on Sundays

BUCHTERS ANTIQUES
6 Pilgrim Dr   17603
717 872-5052   Est: 1954
Proprietor: Victor M
Buchter
Hours: By Appointment
Types & Periods: 19th
Century Furniture, Dolls,
General Line
Specialties: Furniture, Dolls
Directions: Midway on Rte
999 to Millersville, Quaker
Hills

THE GLASSTIQUE
2479 Lincoln Hwy East
17602
717 397-2504   Est: 1965
Proprietor: George Kamm

Hours: Mon-Fri, 11-8; Sat 10-5; Sun by Appointment, Jan & Feb, Mon-Sat, 11-5
Types & Periods: Glass of the Past
Specialties: Glass Paperweights & Contemporary Art Glass
Directions: On Rte 30, just W of Rte 896, 5 Miles E of Lancaster

HEATHER VALLEY ANTIQUES
1072 Centerville Rd   17601
717 898-7875
Proprietor: Mrs Joyce Bowes
Types & Periods: Country & Period Furniture, Primitives, Samplers, Quilts, Weathervanes, Trade Signs, Decoys

CLARENCE HINDEN JR
2475 Lincoln Hwy E
      17602
717 392-0943   Est: 1944
Proprietor: Clarence Hinden Jr
Hours: Daily
Types & Periods: American
Specialties: Furniture
Appraisal Service Available
Directions: 6 Miles E of Town, 1/2 Mile of '' Host Farm Resort''

JANET'S ANTIQUES
145 Strasburg Pike   17602
717 397-9723   Est: 1964
Proprietor: Glenn & Janet Parker
Hours: By Appointment, by Chance
Types & Periods: Country Furniture, Primitives
Appraisal Service Available
Directions: 1Mile S of Rte 462 on Strasburg Pike

RESH'S ANTIQUES
331 N Mary St   17603
717 392-5974
Proprietor: Harry & Erma Resh
Hours: By Appointment
Types & Periods: Art & Cut Glass, China, Victorian Furniture

RUTT'S ANTIQUES
2180 Old Philadelphia Pke
      17602
717 392-8751   Est: 1967

Proprietor: Rhoda Mae Rutt
Hours: Mon-Sat, Eves by Chance
Types & Periods: Country & Period Furniture, Glass, China, Lamps, General Line
Directions: On Rte 340 E; from Rte 30 Bypass take Exit 340, R on 340 1 Mile

SHIRLEY & ARTHUR SHEPHERD
104 Yale Ave   17603
717 393-1914
Proprietor: Shirley & Arthur Shepherd
Hours: By Appointment
Types & Periods: Primitives, Accessories

Landisville

LESTER & FLORENCE GOOD
51 Main St   17538
717 898-2341
Proprietor: Lester & Florence Good
Types & Periods: Ironstone China, Lamps & Shades, Pottery, Primitives

Lansdowne

PHILIP E HARBACH
P O Box 324   19050
215 622-6434
Proprietor: Philip E Harbach
Hours: By Appointment
Types & Periods: Early American Pattern Glass
Specialties: Glass

La Plume

TALL SPRUCE ANTIQUES
Rtes 6 & 11   18440
717 945-5432
Proprietor: Diane K Philbin
Hours: Daily
Types & Periods: Country Furniture, Soft Paste, Pewter, Jewelry

Laughlintown

ANKNEY'S TODAY & TOMORROW ANTIQUES
US 30   15655
Hours: Tues-Sun, 10:30-6:30
Types & Periods: Furniture, China, Glass, Collectibles, General Line

JACK MILLER'S ICE CREAM PARLOUR & COUNTRY STORE
Box 79   15655
412 238-2090   Est: 1974
Proprietor: Jack Miller
Hours: Tues-Sun
Types & Periods: Country Furniture, Primitives, Advertising
Appraisal Service Available
Directions: Rte 30, 3 Miles E of Ligonier

Lebanon

VIOLET L GINGRICH
3116 Tunnel Hill Rd
      17042
Proprietor: Violet L Gingrich
Types & Periods: Country Store Items, General Line

Lederach

JEAN W CLEMMER
Hickery Tree Farm,
Rte 113   19450
215 256-6375   Est. 1970
Proprietor: Jean W Clemmer
Hours: By Appointment or by Chance
Types & Periods: Country Furniture & Decorative Accessories
Specialties: Furniture, Accessories
Directions: SE Penna, 5 Miles from Exit 31, Pa Turnpike

Leeper

LEEPER ANTIQUE MART
Rte 36   16233
814 744-9994
814 752-2629   Est: 1976
Proprietor: Herbert Iman
Hours: Daily
Types & Periods: All Periods
of Furniture, Glass (Cut,
Crystal, Art, Depression),
Good Selection Crocks,
Jugs & Primitives
Specialties: 1894 Ten Tune
Street Piano (P Pomeroy &
Co)
Appraisal Service Available
Directions: Pa I-80 to Exit
8; N on 66 to Leeper;
Turn L at Caution Light, 1
1/2 Blocks, 1st Bldg on
Left across RR Tracks

Leesport

JULIETTE BEST ANTIQUES
80 N Centre Ave   19533
215 926-1333
Proprietor: Juliette Best
Hours: By Appointment,
by Chance
Types & Periods: Paintings,
General Line

Leetsdale

**MARGARET MUTSCHLER
ANTIQUES**
25 Ferry St   15056
412 266-3238   Est: 1958
Proprietor: Margaret
Mutschler
Hours: Wed-Sat, 10-5
Types & Periods: General
Line
Specialties: Lamps
Directions: 15 Miles W of
Pittsburgh, Rte 65 near
Greater Pittsburgh
International Airport

Leighton

**BEERS' ANTIQUES &
COUNTRY STORE**
Rte 209   18325
215 377-5495
Hours: Daily, 10-5

Types & Periods: Clocks,
Watches, Furniture,
Glassware

Lenhartsville

JANE AHRENS ANTIQUES
RD 1, Box 177   19534
215 756-6250
Proprietor: Jane Ahrens
Types & Periods: Books, Art,
General Line

HEX BARN ANTIQUES
Rte 22   19534
215 562-8433
Proprietor: Robert &
Rosalin Ensminger
Hours: Daily
Types & Periods: Country
Furniture, Primitives, Tin &
Iron
Directions: 1/3 Mile W of
Lenhartsville

Lewisburg

WENRICK'S ANTIQUES
610 Buffalo Rd   17837
717 523-3872
Proprietor: Beatrice A
Wenrick
Hours: By Appointment or
by Chance
Types & Periods: Glass,
China, Primitives,
Depression Glass

Lewistown

**THERESA REDMOND
CULBERTSON**
RD 5, Box 307   17044
717 543-5674   Est: 1947
Proprietor: Theresa
Redmond Culbertson
Hours: By Appointment
Only
Types & Periods: American
Glass, Pottery, Porcelain &
Small Items of Furniture;
Also American Pewter &
Penna Primitives
Specialties: Canton &
Jewelry
Appraisal Service Available
Directions: 30 Miles from
Penn State, in the Center
of Penna

RISHEL'S ANTIQUES
164 Valley St   17044
717 248-8830   Est: 1970
Proprietor: Gladys Rishel
Hours: Mon-Sat,
Sometimes Sun
Types & Periods: Oil & Early
Electric Lamps, Cut &
Pressed Glass, China, Small
Primitives, Furniture,
Especially Oak
Directions: Main St from
322 to Lewistown

SMITHERS ANTIQUES
24 Chestnut St   17044
717 248-4617   Est: 1943
Proprietor: Mae E
Smithers
Hours: Daily; Phoning
Ahead is Advised
Types & Periods: The Best
of Rarities: Lamps, Cut
Glass, China, Dolls, Jewelry,
Paintings, Furniture,
Primitives, Etc; Dating
1700's, 1800's, 1900's
Specialties: The Best of the
above Listing
Appraisal Service Available
Directions: Downtown
Lewistown, Just off Five
Points

Ligmier

THE ANTIQUE CLOSET
122A N Market St   15658
412 238-6223   Est: 1974
Proprietor: Matilda L
Egner
Hours: Mon-Sat: Apr-Dec,
10-5; Jan-Mar, 1-5; Sun by
Chance
Types & Periods: General
Line, Collectibles, Victorian
Glass & Furniture
Directions: Across from
Municipal Parking Lot

Ligonier

**THE
FORGET-ME-NOT-SHOP**
107 W Loyalhanna St
                     15658
412 238-6880
Hours: Mon-Sat, 10-5;
Sun, 1-5
Types & Periods: Pewter,
Brass, Glassware, General
Line

LAUREL VALLEY ANTIQUE COTTAGE
PA 711   15658
412 593-7597
Proprietor: Margaretta
Roadman & Betty
Freeman
Hours: Mon-Wed, 9-6;
Thurs-Sat, by
Appointment; Sun, 1-5
Types & Periods: General
Line
Directions: 6 Miles S on
PA 711

MARKY'S OLD FORT ANTIQUES
116 W Main St   15658
412 238-4465
Proprietor: Betty Marky
Hours: Mon, Tues, Thurs
& Sat, Apr-Dec
Types & Periods: Country
Furniture, & Accessories
Specialties: Furniture, Silver,
Pattern Glass
Appraisal Service Available
Directions: Diamond Bldg
next to Library, on the
Square

OLD MILL ANTIQUES
108 N Fairfield St   15658
412 238-4968   Est: 1975
Proprietor: Anne Neff
Hours: Mon-Sat, 10-5;
Sun, 12-5; Appointment
Recommended,
occasionally shop is
closed for a few days at a
time due to buying, shows
or emergency; Closed
Jan, Feb & Mar
Types & Periods: Glass,
China, Collectibles, Some
Smaller Pieces of Furniture,
General Line
Appraisal Service Available
Directions: N Fairfield St is
1 Block NW of "Diamond"
Square

Linesville

BAKER'S ANTIQUE BARN
W Erie Exit   16424
814 683-4780
Proprietor: Marie Baker
Hours: Sun-Fri
Types & Periods: General
Line

Lititz

CHARLOTTE HECK ANTIQUES
22 E Main St   17543
717 626-0100   Est: 1972
Proprietor: Charlotte Heck
Hours: Mon-Sat
Types & Periods: Antique
Jewelry, Silver, Pewter,
Wedgewood, Period
Furniture
Appraisal Service Available
Directions: On Rte 772; 5
Miles N of Lancaster

OLD TOWNE STORE & ANTIQUES
122 E Main   17543
717 626-4040   Est: 1967
Proprietor: Bill Hazlett
Hours: Mon-Sat
Types & Periods: General
Line
Specialties: Country
Furniture
Appraisal Service Available
Directions: 7 Miles Rte
501 N from Lancaster;
Turn Right at Square, go
2 Blocks

Luzerne

COLLECTOR'S CORNER
224 Main St   18709
717 288-3094
Proprietor: Freda Doyle
Hours: Mon-Wed, Fri &
Sat, 11-5; Sun, 1-5
Types & Periods: General
Line, Furniture, Dolls, Glass,
China
Directions: Rte 309

Macungie

COLUMBINE ANTIQUES
                         18062
215 395-9459
Proprietor: Bob & Carol
Baker
Types & Periods: General
Line
Directions: Call for
Directions

FOX HOLLOW FARM ANTIQUES
RD 1   18062
215 679-7023

Proprietor: Mary L Morris
Types & Periods: Tin, Wood
& Country Furniture
Directions: In Hereford
Township

HELEN B HENRY
190 Mountain Rd   18062
215 966-2875   Est: 1952
Proprietor: Helen B Henry
Hours: Mon-Sat, By
Appointment, by Chance
Types & Periods: General
Line
Specialties: Musical
Instruments, Piano Rolls,
Jewelry, China Closets,
Glassware, China
Directions: From Rte 100
Turn into Church St; 1
1/2 Miles to 190 Mt Rd

Mainesburg

GRAY VALLEY ANTIQUES
Box 6 RD   16932
717 549-5483   Est: 1968
Proprietor: John & Claire
Blood
Hours: Daily, by
Appointment, by Chance
Types & Periods: General
Line, Primitives, Pine, Cherry
& Walnut Furniture
Specialties: Country
Furniture
Appraisal Service Available
Directions: 9 Miles E of
Mansfield & 9 Miles W of
Troy on Rte 6

Manheim

COWART'S PRIMITIVE HOUSE
133 Main St   17545
717 665-5524
Proprietor: Lloyd B Cowat
Types & Periods: China,
Glass, Primitives

KOCEVAR'S ANTIQUES
907 Lancaster Rd   17545
717 665-2981   Est: 1958
Proprietor: C J Kocevar
Hours: By Appointment,
by Chance
Types & Periods: Primitives
& Pattern Glass
Directions: One Rte 72, S
of Manheim

Both rocking chairs are Late Victorian. The one on the left is collapsible.

GERALD & MIRIAM NOLL
Rte 7   17545
717 898-8677   Est: 1965
Proprietor: Gerald & Miriam Noll
Hours: Daily; by Appointment, by Chance
Types & Periods: Victorian, Period; Glass, Furniture, Lamps
Specialties: Glass (RS Prussia & Cut)
Directions: 2 1/2 Miles off Rte 283 from Lancaster to Harrisburg; Go N on Colebrook Rd

Mansfield

COUNTRY STORE GIFTS & ANTIQUES
45 E Wellsboro St   16933
717 662- 2561   Est: 1973
Proprietor: Iloe Farrer
Hours: Weekends; by Chance
Types & Periods: Primitives, Collectibles
Appraisal Service Available

Maple Glen

THE ALLERS' ANTIQUES
618 Bell Lane   19002
215 646-5177
Proprietor: Paul Aller
Types & Periods: General Line

Marietta

THE OLIVER HOUSE
104 E Front   17547
Est: 1972
Proprietor: Gene G Cohen
Hours: Daily
Types & Periods: General Line, Glass, China, Furniture
Directions: Corner of Front & New Haven

WHITE SWAN TAVERN ANTIQUES
14 E Front St   17547
717 426-2189   Est: 1973
Proprietor: Jay & Jayne Howell
Hours: Tues-Sat, 10-5:30; Sun, 1-5:30

Types & Periods: 19th Century Furniture, Primitive & Formal, & Accessories
Specialties: Pottery, Baskets, Tin, Wood, Iron
Directions: 30 E from York, Pa, 30 W from Lancaster, Pa: Exit 441 at Columbia, Pa; 3 Miles N on 441 to Marietta (Market St) Rte 23

McKeesrocks

J T M DECORATORS ANTIQUES & THINGS
5633A Stubenville Pike
15136
412 787-1160   Est: 1974
Proprietor: John T Marpes
Hours: Daily; by Appointment
Types & Periods: Oak, Primitives; Early Victorian
Appraisal Service Available
Directions: Rte 79 N to Moon-Crafton Exit; L at Stop Sign; 1/2 Mile L Side in Shopping Center

McMurray

THE CAMPBELLS
740 N Washington Rd
15317
412 941-6505   Est: 1972
Proprietor: Elizabeth K
Campbell
Hours: Mon-Wed, 12-4,
Also by Appointment
Types & Periods: China,
Glass, Furniture, Art Glass,
Paintings
Specialties: Cut Glass,
Bronzes
Appraisal Service Available
Directions: Rte 19 S of
Pittsburgh 15 Miles

McSherrystown

MCKINNEY'S ANTIQUES
212 Stombach St   17344
717 637-1037
Types & Periods: Lamps,
China, Furniture

Meadowbrook

REVA LEVITT JEWELRY
P O Box 69   19046
215 884-5454
Proprietor: Reva & LeRoy
Levitt
Hours: By Appointment
Types & Periods: Jewelry

Meadville

**BREST'S RED BARN
ANTIQUES**
Cutter Rd
RD 4, Box 640   16335
Est: 1968
Proprietor: Sam & Ginny
Brest
Hours: Wed-Sat
Types & Periods: General
Line
Specialties: Furniture
Directions: 4 Miles W of
Meadville on Rte 322

**GRANNY'S CURIOSITY
SHOP**
992 Park Ave   16335
814 724-3092
Proprietor: Pat West &
Valerie Wentz
Hours: Daily, 11-4
Types & Periods: Depression
Glass, General Line

**MARGUERITE'S ANTIQUES
& USED FURNITURE**
RD 4, Cutter Rd   16335
814 336-4673   Est: 1966
Proprietor: Margaret Lyons
Hours: By Appointment,
by Chance
Types & Periods: General
Line

MC QUISTON'S ANTIQUES
789 Park Ave   16335
814 724-7420
Proprietor: Bernetta
McQuiston
Types & Periods: Dolls,
Lampshades, Furniture,
Jewelry, General Line

Both pressed back chairs represent Late Victorian to Turn-of-the-Century. The rocker has mother-of-pearl inlay in the design.

ALDEN LEE MILLER
RD 6   16335
Proprietor: Alden Lee
Miller
Hours: By Appointment,
by Chance
Types & Periods: General
Line, American, Lamps

PINE ANTIQUE SHOP
272 Pine St   16335
814 336-2466
Proprietor: Clara & Nick
Theobald
Hours: Mon-Sat
Types & Periods: General
Line

UNGER'S ANTIQUE SHOP
1193 Penna Ave   16335
814 336-4262
Proprietor: Robert &
Virgilia Unger
Types & Periods: General
Line
Directions: At the Bridge
in Keertown

Mechanicsburg

ARMSTRONG ANTIQUES
RD 3 Arcona Rd   17055
717 766-9103
Proprietor: Thelma Smith
Types & Periods: China,
Glass, Primitives

HEMLOCK HOUSE
306 Thomas Dr   17055
717 761-2726
Proprietor: R Dean
Souders
Hours: By Appointment
Types & Periods: China,
Glass, Silver, Furniture

**SILVER SPRING ANTIQUE
& FLEA MARKET**
Carlisle Pike   17055
717 732-9394   Est: 1968
Proprietor: J C Smith
Hours: Sun, 8-5
Types & Periods: General
Directions: 7 Miles W of
Harrisburg, Rte 11

VERONIQUE'S ANTIQUES
124 S Market St   17055
717 697-4924

Proprietor: Romayne Shay
Miller
Types & Periods: General
Line

WHITE BARN ANTIQUES
RD 1 Trindle Rd   17055
717 766-8727
Proprietor: H D Pries
Hours: By Chance
Types & Periods: Country
Furniture, Primitives

Mehoopany

HEATH HILL ANTIQUES
RD 2   18629
717 833-5950
Proprietor: Josephine G &
William G Ohme Jr
Types & Periods: General
Line, Furniture

Mendenhall

SALLY BORTON ANTIQUES
Kennett Pike   19357
215 388-7687   Est: 1968
Proprietor: Sally Borton
Hours: Mon-Sat
Types & Periods: 18th &
19th Century Furniture &
Accessories
Specialties: Silver
(American)
Appraisal Service Available

MENDENHALL ANTIQUES
Rte 52 Kennett Pike
                       19357
215 388-6408   Est: 1965
Proprietor: T G Firestone
Hours: Daily, 8-5
Types & Periods: Country
Furniture, Oriental Objets
d'Art
Appraisal Service Available
Directions: 1 Mile from
Winterthur Museum, 3
Miles from Brandywine
Museum

Mercer

RICE ANTIQUES
S Pitt St Ext   16137
412 662-3538   Est: 1970
Proprietor: Mrs Lucille
Rice

Hours: By Appointment,
by Chance
Types & Periods: Penn
Country & Victorian
Furniture, Lamps, Dolls,
China, Cut Glass, Quilts
Directions: S Pitt St
Extension, off Rte 258S

Middletown

EISENHAUER'S ANTIQUES
649 Briarcliff Rd   17057
717 944-4990
Proprietor: William &
Agnes Eisenhauer
Hours: Daily
Types & Periods: Furniture,
Tools, Glass, Primitives,
Lamp Parts & Wiring
Directions: 1 1/2 Blocks N
of Rte 230 at Race St
Light

Mifflintown

HELEN M BANKS
Box 145   17059
717 436-2615
Proprietor: Helen M Banks
Types & Periods: General
Line
Directions: Rte 35E

Milanville

**BYRON C WHITE
ANTIQUES**
Box 33   18443
717 729-7190
Proprietor: Byron C White
Types & Periods: Country &
Period Furniture &
Accessories
Appraisal Service Available

Milford

**FLORENCE & GEORGE
GEE**
200 Sawkill Ave   18337
717 296-6373
Proprietor: Florence &
George Gee
Hours: By Appointment
Types & Periods: Jewelry
Specialties: Jewelry

THE ROSS'S ANTIQUES
Rte 6   18337
717 828-7017
Hours: Daily
Types & Periods:
Collectibles, General Line
Specialties: Glass (Cut Glass
Repairs, Replacement of
Shaker Tops)
Directions: In Apple Valley
Village

Millerstown

RHEAM'S ANTIQUES
RD 1   17062
717 589-3739
Proprietor: Mildred I
Rheem
Hours: Daily; By
Appointment, by Chance
Types & Periods: General
Line, Furniture
Directions: On Old Rte 22,
3/4 Mile S of Millerstown
Exit of New 22-322 Expwy
W

Mill Run

**CENTURY SHOPPE
ANTIQUE'S**
Penna 381   15464
412 455-3400
Hours: Tues-Sat, Summer,
11-7; Winter, 11-5
Types & Periods: Glassware,
Furniture, Primitives

Millville

DALE'S ANTIQUES
Mill-View Lane   17846
717 458-6689   Est: 1971
Proprietor: Dale & Rose
Stackhouse
Hours: Daily; By
Appointment
Types & Periods: Old
Furniture, Dishes, Lamps,
Collectibles
Specialties: Old Cook Stoves
before 1900
Directions: Exit 34 I-80; 9
Miles N on Rte 42 to
Millville; 254W to 1st Road
to R, 1/2 Mile on the
Right

Monroeville

CANDLEWOOD ANTIQUES
4509 Northern Pike 15146
412 372-7744
Proprietor: Sybil Bahnak
Hours: Daily, 1-5; Morns &
Eves by Appointment or
Chance
Types & Periods: Furniture,
China, Glass, Primitives,
Hummels
Directions: 1 Mile E of PA
48

Montgomery

CHASE'S ANTIQUE SHOP
Rte 2, Box 397A   17752
717 547-6940   Est: 1935
Proprietor: Mary Evelyn
Chase
Hours: Daily
Types & Periods: General
Line, Furniture, Glass,
China, Lamps, Bric-a-Brac,
Jewelry
Appraisal Service Available
Directions: US 15 S 10
Miles "below"
Williamsport

Mountoursville

**DO FISHER BOOKS &
ANTIQUES**
Rte 15   17754
717 494-1825
Hours: Daily, 10-5
Types & Periods: Books,
Paintings, Paper, Americana,
General Line
Directions: 6 Miles N of
Williamsport

**LYCOMING ANTIQUE
CENTER**
111 N Montour St   17754
717 368-3200
Proprietor: 10 Shops
under 1 Roof
Hours: Daily, 10-5
Types & Periods: General
Line, Collectibles
Directions: Rte 87

TOLE HOUSE
502 Monour St   17754
717 368-8707

Proprietor: Mrs Emerson
Probst
Types & Periods: General
Line

**YANKEE TRADER
ANTIQUES**
RD 2   17754
717 433-3666
Proprietor: John & Peg
Daniels
Hours: Daily, 10-9
Types & Periods: Primitives

Montrose

THE COUNTRY STORE
Grow Ave   18801
717 278-1371   Est: 1956
Proprietor: William Van
Steenburg
Hours: Daily
Types & Periods: Furniture,
Glass, China
Directions: Exit 67 off I-81
to Rte 115 to Rte 706

Morton

THE VILLAGE MALL
Morton Ave   19070
215 543-5566   Est: 1974
Proprietor: Albert A
Yannelli
Hours: Daily
Types & Periods: 50 Shops
open Weekends, 10 Shops
open Daily; General Line,
Arts, Crafts, Collectibles,
Gifts
Specialties: Carousel
Mechanical Music Museum
Appraisal Service Available
Directions: Rte 420,
midway between I-95 &
US 1 near Media

Mount Joy

BIRCHLAND ANTIQUES
306 Birchland Ave   17552
717 653-5969
Proprietor: William P
Neyer
Hours: By Appointment
Types & Periods: Primitives,
Country Wares, Tools

Mt Pleasant

SHERWIN'S ANTIQUES & COLLECTIBLES
Valley View Farm,
480 Quarry St   15666
412 547-6737   Est: 1972
Proprietor: Harry W &
Catherine Sherwin
Hours: Mon-Sat, 9-7; Sun
by Chance or Appointment
Types & Periods: General
Line, Primitives, Collectibles,
Furniture, Glass; All Periods
Appraisal Service Available
Directions: Turn at
Crossroads between
Scottsdale & Mt Pleasant
Exits on US 119; Make 1st
R or Pa 31 to Quarry St; 1
Mile make L to Red Barn

Mt Pocono

POTPOURRI
102 Main St   18344
717 839-7950
Proprietor: Marie
Travisano
Types & Periods: Furniture,
Prints, Jewelry, Accessories

VINTAGE YEARS' ANTIQUES & CURIOS
39 Fairview Ave   18344
717 839-8153
Proprietor: Violet Standish
Hours: Daily, 10-6
Types & Periods: Furniture,
Lamps, Prints, General Line

Mount Union

SMITH'S ANTIQUES
P O Box 278   17066
814 542-4331   Est: 1944
Proprietor: R K Smith
Hours: Daily, 9-8
Types & Periods: American
& English Furniture, Glass,
China
Appraisal Service Available
Directions: On Rte 522 &
22, 1/2 Mile E of Mt
Union

Muncy

RIVERSTONE ANTIQUES
RD 3 Pepper St   17756
717 546-6078
Hours: Daily
Types & Periods: Furniture,
Primitives, Tin, Wood

WHALEN'S ANTIQUES
104 Green St   17756
717 546-3336
Proprietor: Jack & Mary
Whalen
Types & Periods: General
Line, Country Furniture, Folk
Art, Quilts, Pottery

Nazareth

OLDE RED SCHOOL HOUSE
Cherry Hill   18064
215 759-6622
Proprietor: Robert J
Reborts
Hours: Daily
Types & Periods: Furniture,
Collectibles, Primitives,
Brass Beds

THE SHED
10 W Center St   18064
215 759-2335
Types & Periods: General
Line, Primitives, Victorian
Furniture, Lamps,
Decorating Items

New Bloomfield

MAGEE'S
54 Church St   18068
717 582-4030
Proprietor: Boyd A Magee
Hours: By Appointment,
by Chance
Types & Periods: Household
Items

New Britain

BUCKS COUNTY CABINET SHOP
134 Iron Hill Rd   18901
215 345-1725

Proprietor: Frank J
Udinson
Types & Periods: Tiffany
Lamps, General Line

New Castle

BACK DOOR ANTIQUES
Rte 422 East   16101
412 924-9052   Est: 1966
Proprietor: Judy Giangiuli
Hours: Daily; By
Appointment, by Chance
Types & Periods: Furniture,
Glass, China
Specialties: Castleton China
Replacements
Appraisal Service Available
Directions: 7 Miles W of
I-79 or 5 Miles E of
Newcastle

New Holland

BUTERBAUGH'S ANTIQUES
319 S Railroad Ave 17557
717 354-8811   Est: 1966
Proprietor: Rankin
Buterbaugh
Hours: By Appointment,
by Chance
Types & Periods: Early
Country & American Period
Furniture & Accessories
Directions: 12 Miles E of
Lancaster, 2 Blocks off
Rte 23

New Hope

H & R SANDOR, INC
Rte 202   18938
Proprietor: Herbert &
Richard Sandor
Hours: Mon-Sat, 10-12 &
1-4
Types & Periods: American
18th Century Formal
Furniture, Country or
Primitive Furniture
Specialties: American 18th
Century Formal Furniture
Appraisal Service Available
Directions: Approx 2 Miles
S of New Hope, on US
Rte 202

New Kensington

MILLER'S ANTIQUES
721 5th Ave   15068
335-9886   Est: 1966
Proprietor: Mitz & Elaine
Miller
Hours: Mon-Sat, 10-4
Types & Periods: General
Line
Appraisal Service Available
Directions: 6 Miles from
Exit 5 Pa Turnpike

New Kingstown

HARLACHER'S ANTIQUES
Box 78   17072
717 766-3473   Est: 1941
Proprietor: Lawrence &
Evelyn Harlacher
Hours: Daily
Types & Periods: General
Line
Directions: 2 Miles E of
Exit 17E on I-81; 3 Miles E
of Carlisle Exit of the
Penna Turnpike

New Milford

THE CURIOSITY SHOP
165 Main St   18834
717 465-3462
Proprietor: Tom & Linda
Weiss
Hours: By Appointment,
by Chance
Types & Periods: Country &
Golden Oak
Specialties: Clocks, Cherry
Furniture
Directions: Exit 67 off I-81
onto Main

Newport

FENNER'S ANTIQUES
217 Walnut St   17074
717 567-3796
Proprietor: Mrs Dorcas A
Fenner
Types & Periods: Furniture,
Pottery, Dishes, Children's
Items, Primitives

THE OX YOKE
Rd 1, 111 Market St
                    17074
717 567-6173
Proprietor: James R
Chism
Types & Periods: General
Line

Newtown

REN'S ANTIQUES
14 S State St   18940
215 968-5511   Est: 1971
Proprietor: Mrs Mitchell
Spector
Hours: Mon-Sat, 10-5;
Other Times by
Appointment
Types & Periods: Mostly
18th & 19th Century; Glass,
China, Lamps, Primitives,
Important Collectors' Items
Directions: Follow Rte 413
N of US I or Newtown Exit
I-95

Newtown Square

**WHITE ELEPHANT
ANTIQUES**
67 S Newtown St Rd
                    19073
215 356-8032
Proprietor: Elsie B Fuller
Types & Periods: General
Line, Primitives

Normalville

BARGERS BARN
RD 1   15469
412 455-3471   Est: 1970
Proprietor: Mrs Euceba
Barger
Hours: Daily, 11-8
Types & Periods: General
Line, Primitives
Directions: 12 Miles from
PA Turnpike Exit 9 in
Indian Head

Norristown

ANGELL'S ANTIQUES
10 Potts Ave   19401
215 539-1764

Proprietor: Walter &
Elmira Z Angell
Types & Periods: General
Line
Specialties: Chairs Caned,
Dolls Strung

Northampton

IRONS ANTIQUES
Rd 2   18067
215 262-9335
Proprietor: Dave & Sue
Irons
Hours: Daily
Types & Periods: Primitives,
Folk Art, Country Furniture,
Collectibles
Directions: 2 Miles N of
Northampton, N End of
Covered Bridge Rd

NORTHAMPTON ANTIQUES
2650 Cherryville Rd 18067
215 262-0437
Types & Periods: Early
American; Accessories,
Primitives

Northumberland

BIL-MAR ANTIQUES
449 Sheetz Ave   17857
717 473-8540   Est: 1954
Proprietor: John W &
Margaret E Smith
Hours: Mon-Fri, 9-5; Sun,
1-5
Types & Periods: Penna
Primitives, Furniture, Dishes,
Glassware, Composition
Dolls, Lighting
Appraisal Service Available
Directions: Near Junction
of Rtes 11 & 15, 10 Miles
off Interstate 80 via Milton
Exit

North Versailles

JOHN GACS ANTIQUES
3214 5th Ave   15137
412 673-5469   Est: 1950
Proprietor: John Gacs
Hours: Daily; by Chance
Types & Periods: Furniture,
Glass, Brass, Lamps
Appraisal Service Available
Directions: Rte 148 off Rte
30 from Pittsburgh

Norvelt

MANOR HOUSE ANTIQUES
15666 Hecla Rd
RD 1, Box 117,
Mt Pleasant (Mailing)15674
412 423-5348   Est: 1975
Proprietor: Conrad C
Donovan
Hours: By Appointment or
Chance
Types & Periods: Early
American & Victorian; Oil
Paintings, Rugs &
Accessories
Directions: 1 block past
"Open Pantry" Store, 1
block off Rte 981 N

Oley

RALPH & KATHRYN HEIST
Box 195, Rd 2   19547
215 689-9242
Proprietor: Ralph &
Kathryn Heist
Hours: Thurs-Tues
Types & Periods: Furniture,
Primitives, General Line
Directions: On Rte 73

Orefield

QUILL PEN ANTIQUES
Rte 309   18069
215 398-2877
Hours: Daily during
Summer, Weekends 9-5,
By Appointment
Types & Periods: General
Line

Orwigsburg

BENJAMIN SCHNERRING
201 Antique Lane   17961
717 366-2615   Est: 1964
Proprietor: Benjamin
Schnerring
Hours: By Chance
Types & Periods: 19th
Century Glass, China,
Furniture
Directions: On Rte 61, 8
Miles N of Intersection of
I-78 & 61

Palmyra

THE CLOCK SHOP
650 S Green St   17078
717 838-4865
Proprietor: Willis Hartman
Hours: By Appointment
Types & Periods: Clocks,
Reed Organs

JENNINGS ANTIQUES
104 N Franklin St   17078
717 838-5911
Proprietor: Ralph & Evelyn
Jennings
Hours: Tues, Thurs & Sat
9-3, By Appointment
Types & Periods: Pattern
Glass, China, Furniture

STACKS ANTIQUES
406 W Maple St   17078
717 838 3016
Hours: By Appointment
Types & Periods: Early
American

Paradise

**WHITE ELEPHANT
ANTIQUES & GIFTS**
Rte 30, Lincoln Hwy E
                     17562
717 687-6612   Est: 1969
Proprietor: Ralph V
Darrah, Jr
Hours: Daily
Types & Periods: General
Line
Directions: 10 Miles E of
Lancaster

Perkasie

J & J ANTIQUES
Rd 2, Box 486   18944
215 795-2557
Proprietor: Jay & Jackie
Maxson
Types & Periods: General
Line

REEVE'S ANTIQUES
                     18944
215 257-4019
Proprietor: Carl Reeve
Types & Periods: General
Line, Furniture, Oil
Paintings, Glass, China,
Primitives

Perkiomenville

JOHN JEREMICZ, JR
Rte 29, P O Box 89 18074
215 234-8570   Est: 1970
Proprietor: John Jeremicz,
Jr
Hours: Sat, Sun & Mon
11-5, By Appointment
Types & Periods: General
Line
Specialties: Clocks, Stained
Glass Windows, Stoneware
Directions: Follow Rte 29
N, 1/4 Mile before
Montgomery Cty Park, in
Green Lane, Pa

Philadelphia

PHILADELPHIA CLUSTER
Directions: Antique Row
along Pine St between 9th
& 13th Sts

ALMOST ANTIQUES
4311 Main St   19127
215 483-7954   Est: 1964
Proprietor: Stan Muffs
Hours: Mon-Sat, 10-6;
Sun, 12-6
Types & Periods:
Turn-of-the-Century &
Victorian
Directions:
"Manayunk-Only Main St
in Phila"

ANTIQUE FAIR INC
2218 Market St   19103
215 563-3682
Hours: Daily, 9-5
Types & Periods: French,
Chandeliers
Specialties: Baker Racks

THE ARCHIVE
259 S 21st St   19103
215 545-2766
Hours: Tues-Sat, 11-7
Types & Periods:
Turn-of-the-Century Oak &
Country Furniture;
Restoration

ATTIC GALLERIES
1330 E Washington Lane
                     19138
215 548-2434   Est: 1946
Proprietor: Joseph &
Cecilia Feldman

Hours: Mon-Sat, 1-5;
Closed Sat during June,
July & Aug; Also by
Appointment
Types & Periods: Furniture,
China, Glass, Bronze,
Lamps
Specialties: China, Bronze,
Lamps
Directions: In E
Germantown, Mount Airy;
NW Section of Phila

BARTER & CO
1116 Pine St   19107
Hours: By Chance
Types & Periods: Victorian
Bentwood Wicker, Oak
Furniture, American Art
Glass, Art Pottery

SIL BERNARD
1112 Locust St   19107
215 922-2767   Est: 1961
Proprietor: Sil Bernard
Hours: Mon-Sat, 5-9
Types & Periods:
Collectibles such as Post
Cards, Baseball Cards,
Trade & Stereo View Cards,
Political Items, Etc, Mostly
50-60 Yrs Old
Specialties: Above Listing
Appraisal Service Available
Directions: 3 Blocks S of
Market St, 2 1/2 Blocks E
of Broad St

BLUM'S ANTIQUE SHOP
1608 Pine St   19103
215 546-1020   Est: 1935
Proprietor: Alfred Blum
Hours: Daily, 10-5
Types & Periods: 18th
Century American
Specialties: Furniture
Appraisal Service Available

**BLUM'S CHESTNUT HILL
ANTIQUES**
43-45 E Chestnut Hill Ave
19118
215 242-8877
Proprietor: Alfred Blum
Hours: Daily, 10-5
Types & Periods: 18th
Century English & American
General Line
Specialties: Furniture
Appraisal Service Available

**SYLVIA BROCKMON
ANTIQUE DOLLS**
6333 Wayne Ave   19144
215 438-4511   Est: 1941
Proprietor: Sylvia
Brockmon
Hours: By Appointment
Types & Periods: Dolls, Doll
Houses, Toys, Paper Dolls,
Children's Books

ERICA BROOKS ANTIQUES
1038 Pine St   19107
215 922-7717
Hours: Mon-Sat, 11-5:30
Types & Periods: Oriental
Art
Directions: E of Broad St

**ALFRED BULLARD
INC-HELEN MC GEHEE**
1604 Pine St   19103
215 735-1879
Hours: Mon-Fri, 10-5;
Weekends by Appointment
Types & Periods: 18th
Century English Furniture &
Accessories, Chinese
Porcelain, Early Meissen, 1st
Period Worcester, Whieldon
Pottery, Battersea

HARRY BURKE
NE Corner of 20th &
Chestnut Sts   19103
215 564-1869
Hours: Tues-Sun, 9-5:30
Types & Periods: Jewelry,
Silver, Paintings, Oriental Art

**CANDLELIGHT ANTIQUE
SHOP**
2001 Locust St   19103
215 567-0735   Est: 1966
Proprietor: Wm Hardy &
Jim Casto
Hours: By Appointment,
by Chance
Types & Periods: Fine
Antique & Used Furniture,
Porcelain, Silver, Curios,
Orientals
Specialties: Furniture

CAPRICORN
104 S 21st St   19103
215 567-8415
Hours: Daily, 11-7
Types & Periods: Jewelry,
Clothes, Art Deco, Paper
Americana

ROBERT CARLEN
323 S 16th St   19102
215 735-1723   Est: 1936
Proprietor: Robert Carlen
Hours: Mon-Sat; By
Appointment
Types &Periods: American
18th,19th & 20th Centuries
Specialties: Chinese Export
Appraisal Service Available
Directions: NE Corner of
16th & Delancey Sts

**WILLIAM H CHANDLEE III
ANTIQUES**
7811 Germantown Ave
19118
215 242-0375   Est: 1974
Proprietor: William H
Chandlee III
Hours: Mon-Sat, 10-5
Types & Periods: General
Line, 18th & 19th Centuries
Appraisal Service Available
Directions: 15 Minutes
from Independence Hall,
15 Minutes from Exit 26
Penn Turnpike; Chestnut
Hill

COINHUNTER
1616 Walnut St   19103
215 735-5517   Est: 1952
Proprietor: C E Bullowa
Hours: Mon-Sat; By
Appointment
Types & Periods: Coins,
Medals
Appraisal Service Available
Directions: Downtown

RAY CRAFT ANTIQUES
404 S 20th St   19146
215 732-3572   Est: 1975
Proprietor: Ray Craft
Hours: By Appointment
Types & Periods: Orientalia;
18th & 19th Century Export,
Ivory & Jade
Specialties: Chinese &
Japanese Export, Jade &
Fine Ivory
Appraisal Service Available
Directions: Between Pine
& Lombard on 20th (3
Doors S of Pine)

**DAVID DAVID ART
GALLERY**
260 S 18th St   19103
215 735-2966
Hours: Mon-Fri, 9-5; Sat,
10-3
Types & Periods: Old Master
Paintings, Works of Art

Philadelphia   Cont'd

JOSEPH DAVIDSON ANTIQUES
924 Pine St   19107
215 563-8115
Hours: Mon-Sat, 9:30-5:30
Types & Periods: Furniture,
Paintings, China, Cut Glass,
Silver, Jewelry
Directions: E of Broad St

DOUGLAS-MARTIN
1618 Pine St   19103
215 735-8684
Hours: Daily, 9:30-5
Types & Periods: French &
English Furniture,
Accessories, Chandeliers

SHIRLEY DRY ANTIQUES
1135 Pine St   19107
215 923-3913
Hours: Tues-Sat, 11-5
Types & Periods: Country
Furniture, Accessories

FAITH POTTER DUVEEN
336 S 17th St   19103
                Est: 1964
Proprietor: Faith Potter
Duveen
Hours: Mon-Fri & Sat
Afternoon
Types & Periods: 18th
Century Portraits, 18th
Century Chinese Export
Porcelain & Some Small
Furniture
Directions: Just off
Pine St

HARRY A EBERHARDT & SON INC
2010 Walnut St   19103
215 568-4144   Est: 1888
Proprietor: William R
Eberhardt
Hours: Mon-Fri, 9-5
Types & Periods: 18th &
19th Century English,
European & Chinese
Porcelains; Cut Glass, Art
Glass, Ivory
Specialties: Porcelains &
Glass
Appraisal Service Available
Directions: 1 Block W of
Rittenhouse Square

FANFARES ANTIQUES
242 S 22nd St   19103
215 732-5774   Est: 1976

Proprietor: Jean L Rapp
Hours: Mon-Sat, Noon
to 5
Types & Periods: Folk Art,
General Line

MARC FARNESE ANTIQUES
1602 Pine St   19103
215 732-5487
Hours: Wed-Fri, 11-4:30;
Sat, 10-12
Types & Periods: Oriental
Art, Paintings

JUDITH FINKEL ANTIQUES
1030 Pine St   19107
215 923-3094
Hours: Mon-Sat, 10-5
Types & Periods: Fireplace
Equipment
Specialties: Metalwork
Directions: E of Broad St

M FINKEL
936 Pine St   19103
215 627-7797   Est: 1947
Proprietor: Morris Finkel
Hours: Mon-Fri, 9-5:30
Types & Periods: 18th &
19th Century Furniture,
Paintings, Folk Art, Quilts
Appraisal Service Available
Directions: Downtown

M FIORILLO ANTIQUES
1120 Pine St   19107
215 923-3173
Hours: Mon-Sat, 9-5
Types & Periods: Early
American & European
Furniture, Pottery

FRANK'S ANTIQUES INC
1004 Pine St   19107
215 923-4250
Hours: Mon-Fri, 8-5; Sat,
8-1
Types & Periods: English &
American Furniture, General
Line
Directions: E of Broad St

FREIHEITER'S ANTIQUE SHOP
115 S 18th St   19103
215 563-9323
Hours: Mon-Sat 9-5
Types & Periods: Furniture,
Silver, Fine China, Glass,
Bric-a-Brac

GALLERY OF FINE ARTS & ANTIQUES
1506 Lombard St   19146
215 545-7425   Est: 1974
Proprietor: Adeline
Shapirio
Hours: Weekends; By
Appointment
Types & Periods: General
Line
Directions: 5 Blocks S of
Market & 1 Block W of
Broad

GARGOYLES LTD
512 S 3rd St   19147
215 629-1700   Est: 1970
Hours: Daily; By
Appointment
Types & Periods:
Architectural & Decor Items
Appraisal Service Available
Directions: Society Hill
Just a few Blocks from
Independence Hall

GERMANTOWN ANTIQUES
6333 Wayne Ave   19144
215 438-4511   Est: 1931
Proprietor: William
Brockman
Hours: By Appointment
Types & Periods: Collectors
Items, Oriental Rugs,
Chinese Objects, Art & Cut
Glass, Furniture
Appraisal Service Available
Directions: Germantown
Section, near Washington
Lane

FLORENCE HOCKSTEIN ANTIQUES
138 S 17th St   19103
215 567-6663
Hours: Daily, 11-5
Types & Periods: French,
English, Oriental Porcelain,
Bric-a-Brac

INVESTMENT ANTIQUES
3541 Kensington Ave
                19149
215 744-3985   Est: 1965
Proprietor: Mr Joseph B
Hastings
Hours: Mon-Fri, 9-5; Sat,
10-5
Types & Periods: Bronzes,
Ivories, Porcelains, Art
Glass, Oils
Appraisal Service Available
Directions: 1 Block N of
Tioga in Kensington
Section of City

JOHNSTONE-FONG, INC
1710 Locust St   19103
Proprietor: Dr Colin
Johnstone & Dr John K
Fong
Hours: Sun, Tues &
Thurs-Sat, 11-5; Wed,
11-9; By Appointment
Types & Periods: Chinese
Porcelains & Works of Art
from the Han, Tang, Sung &
Ming Dynasties & Ching
Porcelain before the 18th
Century; 18th Century
English Furniture
Specialties: Chinese Works
of Art & 18th Century
English Furniture
Appraisal Service Available
Directions: In Central
Philadelphia, 1/2 Block
from Rittenhouse Square
& Directly across from the
Warwick Hotel

**IRWIN B JOLLES
ANTIQUES**
11th & Pine St   19107
215 923-6675
Hours: Daily, 10-5
Types & Periods: Furniture
Directions: E of Broad St

MARTIN JOLLES CORP
1012 Pine St   19107
215 923-7777
Hours: Mon-Sat, 9:30-5:30
Types & Periods:
Philadelphia Centennial
Antiques
Directions: E of Broad St

**SYDNEY JOLLES
ANTIQUES, INC**
1010 Pine St   19107
215 922-3450
Hours: Daily 9:30-4:30
Types & Periods: 18th &
19th Century Furniture,
Paintings
Directions: E of Broad St

JUDY'S PLACE
255 S 20th St   19103
Hours: Daily, 11-5:30
Types & Periods: Linens,
Laces, Glassware, China

**KINGSLEY & O'BRENNAN
ANTIQUES**
1127 Pine St   19107
215 923-4814   Est: 1975
Proprietor: Garrison G
Kingsley
Hours: Mon-Sat, 9-5

Types & Periods: 19th
Century American Classical
Furniture & Decorative
Accessories
Specialties: Quality
American Empire Furniture
Appraisal Service Available
Directions: Pine St Cluster

KOHN & KOHN
1112 Pine St   19107
215 627-3909
Hours: Mon-Sat, 9-5; Sun,
1-5
Types & Periods: American,
English, French, Italian

LOCUST ANTIQUES
244 S 22nd St   19103
215 732-0534   Est: 1965
Proprietor: Wm Krumboldt
Hours: Mon-Sat, by
Chance
Types & Periods: Art
Nouveau, Art Deco,
Bronzes, Unique Lamps,
Chinese, Etc
Directions: Center City of
Philadelphia

LOVE OF PAST ANTIQUES
205 S 17th St   19103
215 735-5565   Est: 1970
Proprietor: Allen Wexler
Hours: Mon-Fri,
10:30-5:30; Sat, 10:30-4:30
Types & Periods: American
Collectibles, Memorabilia
Specialties: Paper
Americana, Toys, Comic
Items, Advertising Items &
Other Fun Antiques
Directions: Center of
Town, S of Corner of 17th
& Walnut Sts

TERRY LOW
646 South St   19147
215 923-6758   Est: 1978
Proprietor: Terry Low
Hours: Daily
Types & Periods: 17th
Century European Furniture
& Contemporary American
Art
Specialties: 17th Century
European Furniture; Also
Restoration of Period
Furniture Museum
references include The Frick
Museum in New York, the
Smithsonian Institute in
Washington & Hill Physick
Kieth House, Philadelphia

Appraisal Service Available
Directions: Just SE of the
Pine St Shops

ALBERT MARANCA
1100 Pine St   19107
215 925-8909
Hours: By Appointment
Types & Periods: 19th
Century French Furniture

MARIO'S ANTIQUE SHOP
1020 Pine   19017
215 922-0230   Est: 1957
Proprietor: Mario J Zulli
Hours: Mon-Sat, 11-6
Types & Periods: Victorian
Furniture, China, Mettlach
Beer Steins
Specialties: Clocks, Beer
Steins
Appraisal Service Available
Directions: Between 10th
& 11th Sts, 5 Blocks from
Main St Market

L J MORETTINI ANTIQUES
262 S 20th St   19103
215 561-0370   Est: 1971
Proprietor: L J Morettini
Hours: Mon-Sat, 11-6
Types & Periods: Oriental
Works of Art, European &
English Americana, Art
Nouveau & Art Deco,
Jewelry; 18th & 19th
Century
Specialties: Oriental:
Chinese, Japanese, Tibetan
Appraisal Service Available
Under Special
Circumstances
Directions: Center City,
Rittenhouse Square

M J NESCO
1002 Pine St   19107
215 923-4323
Hours: Mon-Fri
Types & Periods: Orientals
Directions: E of Broad St

OLD CURIOSITY SHOP
1621 Sansom St   19103
Hours: Mon-Sat, 10-6
Types & Periods:
Memorabilia "If you collect,
we have it"

PAETSCH & NOLL
1042 Pine St   19107
215 922-5594
Hours: By Appointment;
By Chance

Philadelphia   Cont'd

PAETSCH & NOLL   Cont'd
Types & Periods:
Continental
Directions: E Of Broad St

MIRIAM F RAYVIS
6320 Wissahickon Ave
                    19144
215 843-1386   Est: 1943
Proprietor: Miriam F
Rayvis
Hours: By Appointment
Types & Periods: Jewelry,
"Objets De Verth"
Appraisal Service Available
Directions: In Historic
Germantown Area, Corner
Wissahickon & Cliveden

REESE'S ANTIQUES
928-930 Pine St   19107
215 922-0796
Hours: Mon-Sat, 10-5:30
Types & Periods: 18th &
19th Century American &
European Furniture,
Paintings, Clocks, Cut Glass,
China
Directions: E of Broad St

REMEMBER WHEN
422 South St   19147
215 923-4120
Hours: Tues-Sun, 1-5
Types & Periods:
Chandeliers, Furniture,
Lamps

RENE ANTIQUES
1029 Pine St   19107
215 922-6738
Hours: Mon-Sat, 9:30-5:30
Types & Periods: French
Furniture, Accessories;
General Line
Directions: E of Broad St

MARTIN ROSE ANTIQUES
1022 Pine St   19107
215 922-4090
Hours: Mon-Sat, 11-5:30
Types & Periods: 19th
Century Bric-a-Brac
Directions: E of Broad St

G B SCHAFFER ANTIQUES
1014 Pine St   19107
215 923-2263
Hours: Mon-Sat, 10-5

Types & Periods:
Bric-a-Brac, Furniture,
Leaded & Stained Glass
Windows
Directions: E of Broad St

IRWIN SCHAFFER
1032 Pine   19107
215 923-2949   Est: 1935
Proprietor: Irwin &
Dorothy Schaffer
Hours: Mon-Sat, 11-5;
Closed Sat during July &
Aug
Types & Periods: General
Line
Specialties: Stained Glass
Appraisal Service Available
Directions: Between 11th
& 12th Sts, 5 Blocks
"below" Market St S; On
Antique Row

FRANK S SCHWARZ & SON
1806 Chestnut St   19103
215 563-4887   Est: 1930
Proprietor: Frank S, Marie
D & Robert D Schwarz
Hours: Sept-June,
Mon-Fri, 9:30-5:30; Sat,
10-5; July & Aug, Mon-Fri,
9:30-5
Types & Periods: American
Decorative Arts, Silver,
Jewelry
Specialties: XIXth Century
Paintings

JACK SHAPIRO ANTIQUES
1506 Lombard St   19146
215 545-7425   Est: 1956
Proprietor: Jack Shapiro
Hours: By Appointment,
by Chance
Types & Periods: General
Line
Directions: 5 blocks S of
Market & 1 block W of Broad

CHARLES B SMITH
2043 Chestnut St   19103
215 567-3410   Est: 1949
Proprietor: Charles B
Smith
Hours: Mon-Sat, 10-6
Types & Periods: General
Line; 18th, 19th & Early 20th
Century
Specialties: Wedgewood
China, Oriental

Appraisal Service Available
Directions: Center City
Philadelphia, 10 Blocks
from Expwy

SOUTHWOOD HOUSE
1732 Pine St   19103
215 545-4076
Hours: Daily, 8:45-4:45
Types & Periods: English,
French & American General
Line
Specialties: Lamps

SPICES OF LIFE INC
1039-1040 Pine St   19107
215 922-2420
Types & Periods: General
Line
Directions: E of Broad St

**JOSEPH SPRAIN
ANTIQUES**
1606 Pine St   19103
215 732-1771
Hours: By Appointment
Types & Periods: 18th
Century American Furniture

**LEON F S STARK
ANTIQUES INC**
210 S 17th St   19103
215 735-2799   Est: 1934
Proprietor: Leon F S Stark
& Irene Stark
Hours: Mon-Fri; Holidays
by Chance
Types & Periods: 18th &
19th Century American
Furniture, English & Oriental
Porcelain, Decanters, Bottle
Tickets, Corkscrews
Specialties: " Anything
related to 'Booze'"
Appraisal Service Available
Directions: " 2 Doors
above the Warwick Hotel"

**ANTHONY A P STUEMPFIG
ANTIQUES**
2213 St James St   19103
215 735-2421   Est: 1965
Proprietor: Anthony A P
Stuempfig
Hours: By Appointment
Types & Periods: American
Empire Masterpieces
1805-1835, 19th Century
American Furniture & Art
1810-1900
Specialties: Furniture
(Classical American Empire)

Appraisal Service Available
Directions: Between 22nd
& 23rd Sts Just S of
Walnut St; Take Schuylkill
Expwy to Phila 23rd St
Exit, Cross 23rd & Take a
L on St James

**SWEET VICTORIA'S
EMPORIUM**
1614 Spruce St   19103
215 732-4997
Hours: Daily, 11-5
Types & Periods: Arcade
Machines, Toys,
Advertisements

TRANSUE & CLARKE
926 Pine St   19107
215 925-1684
Proprietor: Peter J Clarke,
James Transue
Hours: Mon-Sat
Types & Periods: Victorian
Furniture, Gas Chandeliers,
Art Nouveau, Lighting &
Accessories, Stained Glass
Windows
Specialties; Highly Carved
Walnut, Mahogany & Oak
Furniture, Complete Sets &
Individual Pieces

VAN PARYS STUDIO
6338 Germantown Ave
                  19144
215 844-1930   Est: 1951
Proprietor: George &
Elaine Van Parys
Hours: Mon-Fri, 10-5:30;
Eves by Appointment
Types & Periods: Full Line:
European China, Crystal,
Brass, Bronzes, Silver,
Porcelain, Chandeliers;
Paintings; American &
Continental Cut Glass;
Chinese, Etc
Specialties: "Expert
Repairers & Restorers of
China, Porcelain & Glass,
Jade, Ivory, Wood; Custom
Lamp & Lamp Shade Work"
Appraisal Service Available
Directions: Near
Intersection of Washington
Lane & Germantown Ave

THE WAY WE WERE
419 S 20th St   19146
215 735-2450
Hours: Wed-Sat, 11-5

Types & Periods: 19th
Century American Country
Furniture, Armoires, Tables,
Chairs

EDWARD G WILSON INC
1802 Chestnut St   19103
215 563-7369   Est: 1929
Proprietor: Edward G
Wilson
Hours: Daily
Types & Periods: Jewelry,
Silver, China, Glass,
Collectibles
Directions: Center of City

ZENA'S ANTIQUE SHOP
1804 Chestnut St   19103
215 567-7355
Hours: By Appointment
Types & Periods: Small
Collectibles, Art Objects

Pittsburgh

PITTSBURGH CLUSTER
Directions: No Tight
Cluster, Most Shops NE
Section Radiating out from
Mellon Park

ART'S SHOP
531 Brownsville Rd 15210
412 431-9948   Est: 1963
Proprietor: Arthur J
Brickner
Hours: Sun-Fri
Types & Periods: General
Line
Directions: Mt Oliver Boro,
near Mt Oliver Theater &
Farmsworth Funeral Home

**BLACKBURN'S ANTIQUES
& FURNITURE**
2010 E Carson St   15203
412 381-6688   Est: 1973
Proprietor: Mary Louise
Blackburn
Hours: Mon-Sat,
11:30-5:30
Types & Periods:
Collectibles
Directions: 5 Minutes by
Bus or Car from
Downtown Pittsburgh on S
Side

BRANDEGEE ANTIQUES
5639 Bartlett St   15217
412 521-7583   Est: 1969
Proprietor: Rob Brandegee

Hours: By Appointment
Types & Periods: 17th &
18th Century Furniture,
Oriental Rugs, Accessories
Appraisal Service Available
Directions: Squirrel Hill
Section, near Corner
Forbes & Murray Aves

**MARTHA BROWN
ANTIQUES**
3610 Fifth Ave   15213
412 681-6055   Est: 1940
Proprietor: Martha Brown
Hours: Daily, 10:30-4:30;
Also by Appointment
Types & Periods: Paintings,
Oriental Rugs, Art Glass,
Silver, Primitives, General
Line
Appraisal Service Available
Directions: In Oakland,
near University of
Pittsburgh

**DELP'S PINK CAROUSEL
ANTIQUES**
4933 Penn Ave   15224
412 441-2110   Est: 1950
Proprietor: Magdalynn
Delp
Hours: Daily; By
Appointment
Types & Periods: Cut Glass,
China, Porcelain; Early
1700-1800
Specialties: Furniture
Appraisal Service Available
Directions: Straight out
Penn Ave from the Point

BETTY GAINES ANTIQUES
1687 Washington Rd
                  15228
412 341-4333   Est: 1965
Proprietor: Betty B Gaines
Hours: Tues-Sat, 1-5
Types & Periods: Chinese,
English, French, American
Porcelains, Pewter, Brass,
Paintings, Jewelry
Appraisal Service Available
Directions: On Rte 19
across St from Steak n
Ale Restaurant

**MARGERY B GEORGE
ANTIQUES**
1408 S Negley Ave 15217
Proprietor: Margery B
George
Hours: Tues-Sat
Types & Periods: Formal
American & English
Antiques

Pittsburgh   Cont'd

MARGERY GEORGE Cont'd
Specialties: Furniture &
Early English Pottery &
Porcelain
Appraisal Service Available
Directions: Center City,
Squirrel Hill Section

MARIE REITER ANTIQUES
1000 Killarney Dr   15234
412 881-6012   Est: 1968
Proprietor: Marie Reiter
Hours: By Appointment,
by Chance
Types & Periods: General
Line
Directions: Rte 88 (Library
Rd) & Killarney Dr in
Castle Shannon Boro
(near Bob Smith Ford
Agency)

**ROCKMAN'S ANTIQUES &
FURNITURE**
5022 Penn Ave   15224
412 661-3343   Est: 1939
Proprietor: Mike Rockman
Hours: Mon-Sat, 9-5
Types & Periods: Victorian &
Oak Furniture, Glass, Lamps
Specialties: Furniture
Appraisal Service Available
Directions: 6 Blocks from E
Liberty, 4 Blocks from St
Francis Hospital

SALT BOX ANTIQUES
3778 Willow Ave   15234
412 344-4443
Proprietor: Carol Felty
Hours: Wed-Sat, 12-4;
Also by Appointment
Types & Periods: General
Line, China, Glassware,
Furniture
Specialties: Clocks, Flow
Blue China
Directions: Located in
Castle Shannon in the
South Hills; 3 Doors from
Vitte's Hardware

**THE TOLL HOUSE
ANTIQUES**
Brookside Farms   15241
412 833-7484   Est: 1971
Proprietor: Mr & Mrs
Richard Getty
Hours: By Appointment
Types & Periods: Glass,
Early American Pattern

Specialties: Chair Caning
Appraisal Service Available
Directions: Directions
When Calling for
Appointment

THE TUCKERS
2236 Murray Ave   15217
412 521-0249   Est: 1973
Proprietor: Esther J
Tucker
Hours: Sun-Fri, 1-5; Sat,
10-5
Types & Periods:
Out-of-Print & Rare Books,
Old Prints, Paper Ephemera
Specialties: Books, Paper
Appraisal Service Available
Directions: Pa I-376
(Parkway East) to Squirrel
Hill Exit 8; L on Murray
Ave; In 1st Block of
Stores on L

WARBURTON'S ANTIQUES
1121 Swissvale Ave
                      15221
412 731-6642   Est: 1940
Proprietor: Marie & Sara
Warburton
Hours: Wed-Sat, 11-4; By
Appointment, by Chance
(Usually open Other Days,
also)
Types & Periods: Primitives,
Tools, Crocks, Baskets,
Paper Nostalgia, Chairs, A
few Handcrafts; 4 Resident
Dealers
Specialties: Chair Seat
Weaving & Wicker Repair
Directions: Pa Turnpike to
Exit 6; Parkway to
Wilkinsburg Exit; 1 Mile,
Then R onto Swissvale

Plymouth

HENRY'S ANTIQUE SHOP
163 E Main St   18651
717 287-8302   Est: 1945
Proprietor: Henry Zolenski
Hours: Mon-Sat, 9-5
Types & Periods: Primitives,
Furniture, Oak, Lamps,
Bric-a-Brac
Specialties: Oak Furniture
Directions: Rte 11 near
Kingston

**OX-BOW ANTIQUES &
GIFTS**
324 E Main St   18651
717 779-3276   Est: 1966
Proprietor: Verna
Waligorski
Hours: Daily; By
Appointment, by Chance
Types & Periods: General
Line, Furniture, Art & Cut
Glass
Directions: Located on Rte
11 near Kingston; Off
Exits of I-81: Nanticoke
Exit-go N on Rte 11,
Wilkes-Barre Exit-go S on
Rte 11

Pottstown

**COUNTRY PEDLAR
ANTIQUES**
Rte 23 Bucktown   19464
215 469-6252   Est: 1964
Proprietor: John &
Blanche Ott
Hours: Mon-Sat, 11:30-5;
Sun, 1-4; April to
Christmas
Types & Periods: General
Line
Specialties: Primitives
Directions: Rte 23, 3/4
Mile E of Rte 100,
Bucktown

WALTER S ELLIOTT
568 High St   19464
215 326-2373   Est: 1922
Proprietor: W S Elliott
Hours: Daily; By
Appointment
Types & Periods: Primitives,
Chippendale, Queen Anne &
Federal Furniture
Appraisal Service Available
Directions: Located on the
Main St (Rte 422), near
Hill School

SEMINARY ANTIQUES
1194 E Schuylkill Rd
                      19464
215 326-9651
Proprietor: Raymond S
Seminary Jr & Marinna
Tull
Types & Periods: General
Line

MERLE WENRICH
1319 High St   19464
215 326-5940   Est: 1935
Proprietor: Merle Wenrich
Hours: By Appointment,
by Chance
Types & Periods: Primitive
Furniture, Lamps, Shades
Appraisal Service Available
Directions: Rte 422 is
Main St through Town

Pottsville

BLUM'S ANTIQUES
605 W Market St   17901
717 622-3089   Est: 1963
Proprietor: George F Blum
Hours: By Appointment
Types & Periods: General
Line, Furniture, Toys,
Advertising
Appraisal Service Available
Directions: Rte 209 & 61
in Central Pennsylvania

KENNETH C STUMPF
535 Prospect St   17901
717 622-5719   Est: 1965
Proprietor: Ken Stumpf
Hours: Daily
Types & Periods: General
Line
Specialties: Furniture, Glass
Directions: '' Ask
Directions''; Live on End
of St next to Warehouse

**TOWNE & COUNTRY
UPHOLSTERY & ANTIQUES**
207 N Center   17901
717 622-2958   Est: 1956
Proprietor: Joseph D &
Josephine Motta
Hours: Daily, 9-5
Types & Periods: Dishes,
Pictures, Early 1900
Furniture
Specialties: Furniture
Appraisal Service Available
Directions: Main St of
Town, 1 Block from City
Hall

Pt Pleasant

RIVER RUN ANTIQUES
River Road (Rte 32)
                     18950
215 294-9488
Proprietor: Julia Bartels

Hours: Wed-Sun, 11-5
Types & Periods: General
Line, Country Store Items,
Tins, Advertising Weapons,
the Unusual
Specialties: The Unusual in
Antiques
Directions: 16 Miles N of
New Hope

Quakertown

**TALL CHIMNEYS
ANTIQUES**
RD 4   18951
215 536-3437
Proprietor: George
Beshore
Types & Periods: 18th &
19th Century American
Furniture & Accessories

WEBBER'S ANTIQUES
Thatcher Rd   18951
215 536-5155
Proprietor: Lawrence
Webber
Types & Periods: Glass,
China, Jewelry, Furniture

Reading

ANTIETAM ANTIQUES
3100 St Lawrence Ave
                     19606
215 779-0600
Proprietor: Rebe Kozak
Hours: Daily, 10-5
Types & Periods: General
Line

THE CORNER CUPBOARD
11 Lorane Rd   19606
215 779-8011   Est: 1975
Proprietor: F Scott Goetz
& Kathy L Rolland
Hours: Daily
Types & Periods: Country &
Period Furniture
Directions: 5 Miles E of
Reading on Rte 422

**BARRY B DOBINSKY
ANTIQUES**
1229 Oley St   19604
215 373-5351   Est: 1970
Proprietor: Barry Dobinsky

Hours: By Appointment,
by Chance
Types & Periods: Penna
Primitive Furniture, Pottery,
Baskets, Quilts, Blue
Spongeware
Specialties: Blue
Spongeware
Appraisal Service Available

**MOSELEY'S ANTIQUES &
CURIOS**
859 Acacia Ave   19605
215 929-9642   Est: 1965
Proprietor: Harry A
Moseley, Jr
Hours: By Appointment
Types & Periods: Glass,
China, Primitives, Jewelry

THE OUTGROWN SHOPPE
525 Court St   19601
215 372-1860   Est: 1946
Proprietor: Millicent O
Keiser
Hours: Daily
Types & Periods: General
Line, Glass, Jewelry
Appraisal Service Available

**PENNYPACKER AUCTION
CENTRE**
1540 New Holland Rd,
Kenhorst   19607
215 777-6121   Est: 1946
Proprietor: Catherine M
Pennypacker
Hours: Daily
Types & Periods: General
Line; Sale by Auction Only
Appraisal Service Available
Directions: Approx 4 Miles
SW of Reading on Rte 625
between Rtes 222 & 724

PETE'S ANTIQUES
1318 N 10th St   19604
215 372-5911   Est: 1952
Proprietor: Clarence
Schlegel
Hours: By Chance
Types & Periods: Jelly
Cupboards, Dry Sinks,
Dutch Cupboards, Oak
Furniture, China, Glass,
Tools
Specialties: Pocket Watches
Appraisal Service Available
Directions: Rte 422 N on
11th St to Pike, L to 10th

STERNBERGH ANTIQUES
Box 865, RD 2   19605
215 926-3898   Est: 1954

STERNBERGH   Cont'd

Proprietor: Arlene F
Sternbergh & Quentin C
Sternbergh
Hours: Mon-Sat, 9-5
Types & Periods: General
Line, China, Glass,
Furniture, Ironstone
Specialties: Jewelry, Clocks,
Furniture
Appraisal Service Available
Directions: 7 Miles N of
Center of Reading on US
Rte 222

TROUTMAN ANTIQUES

325 N 6th St   19601
215 374-0181
Proprietor: Emily & Robert
Troutman
Hours: By Appointment
Types & Periods: Early Flint
& Lacy Sandwich Glass,
Pattern Glass
Specialties: Glass

Reinholds

JOYCE LEIBY

Rte 897   17569
215 267-3331
Proprietor: Joyce Leiby
Hours: By Appointment
Types & Periods: Primitives
Directions: Near
Blainesport

Roslyn

FLORADORA ANTIQUES

P O Box 36   19001
215 885-6729   Est: 1972
Proprietor: Doris Kaplan &
Florence Birnbaum
Types & Periods: Jewelry,
China, Silver, Furniture

Ruffsdale

STILLWAGON'S ANTIQUES

RD 1   15679
412 547-6847
Hours: Mon-Fri, 10-4; Sat
& Sun, 10-5
Types & Periods: General
Line
Directions: State Rte 31, 8
Miles W of Mt Pleasant

Saegertown

WHITE CAT ANTIQUES

Rte 19   16433
814 398-8682
Proprietor: Milton Sipple
Hours: Fri & Sat, 10-3;
Sun by Chance
Types & Periods: Furniture,
Paintings, Collectibles
Directions: 3 Miles N of
Saegertown

Saltsburg

MARY BUCK

Box 408, RD 1   15681
412 726-5773   Est: 1969
Proprietor: Mary Buck
Hours: Daily
Types & Periods: Oak,
Cherry, Pine, Walnut
Furniture; Glassware,
Clocks, Primitives

TOWN & COUNTRY ANTIQUES

M R 1   15681
412 639-9374   Est: 1954
Proprietor: Dorman
Cunkelman
Hours: Daily
Types & Periods: Country
Furniture, General Line,
Collectibles, Staffordshire,
Pewter
Directions: Along Rte 286

Schwenksville

TRIMBLE'S ANTIQUES

Swamp Pike
Box 80, RD 2   19473
215 287-8460   Est: 1968
Proprietor: Connie L
Trimble
Hours: By Appointment
Types & Periods:
Pennsylvania Primitives, &
Country Furniture &
Accessories
Specialties: Original Painted
& Decorated Furniture
Appraisal Service Available
Directions: 4 Miles E of
Pottstown on Rte 422 to
Limerick; L at Traffic Light
on Swamp Pike; Go 1 1/2
Miles, 1st Farmhouse on
the R

Scranton

MARY P CAMPION

724 N Irving Ave   18510
717 342-6473   Est: 1937
717 489-2687 (Summer)
Proprietor: Mary P
Campion
Hours: By Appointment,
for Specific Wants Only;
Mdse Can be Seen at
Shows Only
Types & Periods: Cut &
Pattern Glass, China, Dolls,
Oil Paintings, General Line
Appraisal Service Available

DEN OF ANTIQUITY

1322 E Gibson St   18510
717 347-8026
Proprietor: Esther &
Seymour Schwartz
Types & Periods: Antique
Dolls
Specialties: Doll Hospital

MARJORIE & JOHN EVANICK

523 Taylor Ave   18510
717 347-4967
Proprietor: Marjorie &
John Evanick
Types & Periods: General
Line, Art Glass, China,
Furniture

G T W ANTIQUES

409 Prospect Ave   18505
717 343-1741   Est: 1971
Proprietor: Garth T
Watkins
Hours: Weekends, 1-5;
Also by Appointment
Types & Periods: Cut Glass,
China, 19th & Early 20th
Century Post Cards,
Turn-of-the-Century
Specialties: Cut Glass,
American
Directions: S Side of
Scranton, I-81 N, River St
Exit, S Moosic St Exit; 6
Blocks toward Center of
City

SEVEN TWENTY ONE ANTIQUE SHOPPE

721 N Washington Ave
                      18509
717 346-6914   Est: 1969
Proprietor: Sydelle O'Neal
& Yvette Lichtman

Hours: Mon-Fri, 11-4; Sat & Sun, 2-5; Also by Chance
Types & Periods: Oak, Wicker, Victorian, Limoges, China, Cut Glass
Specialties: Furniture
Appraisal Service Available
Directions: "Off Rte 81 to Downtown Scranton Exit, to Adams Ave, Turn R; We are 5 Blocks Down"

PHYLLIS UHL
115 Putnam St   18508
717 347-7779   Est: 1966
Proprietor: Phyllis Uhl
Hours: By Appointment
Types & Periods: Porcelains
Specialties: China, Glass; Repairing & Restoration
Directions: North End

Seelyville

THE GREEN BARN ANTIQUES
Locust St   18431
717 253-1164   Est: 1963
Proprietor: Hope D Fowler
Hours: Daily, from Noon on
Types & Periods: Jewelry, Cut Glass, China, Miniatures, Primitives, Furniture
Specialties: China, Furniture, Glass
Directions: 2 Miles W of Honesdale on Rte 6

Sewickley

JOHN D LEWIS
421 Broad St   15143
412 741-6100   Est: 1951
Proprietor: John D Lewis
Hours: Daily, " Suggest Appointments"
Types & Periods: 18th & 19th Century Paintings, 18th Century Furniture
Specialties: Queen Anne & Chippendale Furniture
Appraisal Service Available
Directions: Middle of Town at Beaver & Broad Sts

OUR ANTIQUE SHOP
428 Walnut St   15143
412 741-3130   Est: 1970

Proprietor: Joan R & George B Samolis
Hours: Mon-Sat, 10-4
Types & Periods: Furniture, Glassware, Lamps, Clocks, Quilts, Treenware, Frames, China, Pictures, Copper, Brass, Art Pottery
Specialties: Cut Glass

SECOND ADDITIONS
419 Walnut St   15143
412 741-4051   Est: 1973
Proprietor: Cecyl Thaw & Anne Bauer
Hours: Mon-Sat; By Appointment
Types & Periods: Mahogany, Walnut & Cherry Traditional Furniture, Primitives; Silver, Porcelain, Crystal, Prints & Paintings
Appraisal Service Available
Directions: Ohio River Blvd Rte 65, Turn at Sewickley to Beaver St (Main St) Then L at Walnut

Shillington

COUNTRY CLUTTER HOUSE
301 W Lancaster Ave, Rte 222   19607
215 775-1835   Est: 1974
Proprietor: Kathleen S Nester
Hours: Mon-Sat, 9:30-3:30; Sun by Appointment
Types & Periods: Early American; Collectors Items, General
Directions: On Rte 222, 3 Miles SW of Reading; Parking in Rear

Shippensburg

MARY A GUYER
RD 3   17257
717 532-9546
Proprietor: Mary A Guyer
Hours: By Appointment
Types & Periods: Pattern Glass
Directions: Roxbury Rd

K & A TREASURES
Rice Rd, RD 3   17257
717 263-838
Proprietor: Kay Wolfe
Hours: By Appointment
Types & Periods: General Line, Limoges

WILLIAM & MARY ANTIQUES
101 S Queen St   17257
717 532-5342   Est: 1970
Proprietor: Mary Lou & Bill Beyers
Hours: By Appointment, by Chance & at Shows
Types & Periods: General Line of English & American Furniture; Primitives, Glass, China, Etc; Delivery within 25 Miles

Shiremanstown

HOLLENBAUGH'S ANTIQUES
405 W Main St   17011
717 737-2592
Proprietor: Anna E Hollenbaugh
Types & Periods: Cut, Pressed & Art Glass, China, Miniatures, Carnival Glass, Cards, General Line

Sigel

AUNT MARY'S COLLECTIBLES
RD 1   15860
814 752-2729   Est: 1975
Proprietor: Mrs Mary Marshall
Hours: Daily, 10-?; by Chance
Types & Periods: Primitives, Depression Glass, Pattern Glass, General Line
Directions: Exit 12, I-80 N on 949; 1 Mile S of Sigel

SIGEL ACRES ANTIQUES
RD 1   15860
814 752-2629   Est: 1968
Proprietor: Herbert Iman
Hours: By Chance or Appointment
Types & Periods: Furniture, Glass, China, Tools, Horse

SIGEL ACRES Cont'd
Wagon & Buggy Wheels,
Store Items
Specialties: Advertising &
Country Store Items
Appraisal Service Available

Sinking Spring

**CACOOSING FARMS
STORE**
Box 165, RD 5, Faust Rd
19608
215 678-8642 Est: 1968
Hours: Daily
Types & Periods: General
Line, Formal & Informal
Furniture & Accessories
Directions: 1 Mile W of
Town on Rte 422

Somerset

**BAKERSVILLE BRASS
WORKS**
RD 6 15501
814 445-8357 Est: 1969
Proprietor: Richard M
Bowman
Hours: Tues-Sun, 11-5
Types & Periods: General
Line, Brass & Copper Items,
Clocks; (Brass & Copper
Polishing, Lamp Repairing)
Directions: 10 Miles E of
Donegal; Rte 31 on Old
Rd; From Somerset W Rte
31, 7 Miles

THE CELLAR ANTIQUES
425 W Patriot St 15501
814 443-3125
Hours: Eves & Weekends
by Chance or Appointment
Types & Periods: Country
Furniture, Primitives, Pattern
Glass, General Line
Directions: On Pa 281

THE SPRING HOUSE
RD 4, Box 19 15501
814 445-9815
Hours: April-Dec, Mon-Sat,
10-6; Sun, 1-7; Jan, Feb &
Mar, Weekends Only
Types & Periods: Quilts,
Ceramics, Woodware, Toys,
Jewelry, Woven Articles,
Rugs

Spring City

**RICHARD WRIGHT
ANTIQUES**
807 Schuylkill Rd 19475
215 948-9696
Proprietor: Richard Wright
Hours: Mon-Sat, 9:30-5
Types & Periods: Dolls, Art
& Cut Glass, Art Pottery,
Silver

Strasburg

COLLECTORS' TOYS
Rte 896, Box 22 17579
717 687-8326 Est: 1944
Proprietor: Henry & Jane
Schlosser
Hours: Mon-Sat, 10-5
Types & Periods: Toys,
Games, Dolls, Miniatures,
Children's Books
Specialties: Antique Toys
Appraisal Service Available
Directions: From Rte 30
Take Rte 896 N 1 1/2
Miles

Stroudsburg

KAREN L LARSEN
Box 1369, RD 1,
Cherry Valley Rd 18360
717 992-4335 Est: 1960
Proprietor: Karen L Larsen
Hours: By Chance
Types & Periods: General
Antiques & Collectibles

Swarthmore

TAYLOR ANTIQUES
209 Riverview Rd 19081
215 543-8746
Proprietor: Jehane Taylor
Types & Periods: Oriental,
English, American Furniture;
Porcelains
Directions: In the Village
Mall

THE TICK! TOCK! SHOP
Yale & Rutgers Ave
19081
215 543-9600 Est: 1971
Proprietor: Lea R Gregory
Hours: Mon-Sat, 10-3

Types & Periods: Clocks
Specialties: Clocks
Directions: 2 Blocks off
Rte 320; Yale Crosses 320
5 Blocks from Swarthmore
College

Tafton

CIRCA ANTIQUES
Rte 507 18464
717 226-2300 Est: 1972
Proprietor: Teresa &
Gaston Cescot
Hours: May-Oct, Daily;
Oct-May, by Appointment
(Call 226-4440)
Types & Periods: All Original
Kerosene Lamps, Other
Lighting, Clocks, General
Specialties: Kerosene Lamps
& Clocks
Directions: 1.2 Miles off
Rte 6, 6 Miles off I-84
(Exit 7)

Tarentum

CC'S ANTIQUES
5th Ave & Lock St 15084
412 224-9966 Est: 1966
Proprietor: Mrs Gerald
Costanzo
Hours: Mon-Sat, 11-3:30;
Sun & Eves by
Appointment
Types & Periods: Furniture,
Glassware, Gas Chandeliers,
Victorian & Oak, Brass Beds
Specialties: Art Glass,
Leaded Dome & Stained
Glass Shades
Appraisal Service Available
Directions: Corner 5th &
Lock, 4 Blocks from
Rte 28

Temple

**COUNTRY KITCHEN
ANTIQUES**
403 N Temple Blvd 19560
215 929-8918
Proprietor: Louise
Eschenbach
Hours: Daily, 9-5
Types & Periods: Primitives,
Pewter, Tinware, Copper,
Furniture

Thomasville

GREENSLEEVES
Pine Rd   17364
717 792-1783
Proprietor: Donald & Mary
Frank
Types & Periods: American
Country Furniture &
Accessories, Pottery, Tin

HAROLD'S ANTIQUES
RD 1   17364
717 792-1433
Proprietor: Doris & Clifford
Harold
Hours: By Appointment
Types & Periods: General
Line

HELEN'S ANTIQUE SHOP
Box 107, RD 1   17364
717 225-5121   Est: 1961
Proprietor: Helen & Luther
Hobaugh
Hours: Daily; By
Appointment
Types & Periods: General
Line
Appraisal Service Available
Directions: W of York on
US 30 at 10 Mile House

Topton

INTERIORS LTD
228 S Home Ave,
PO Box 96   19562
215 682-2847   Est: 1972
Proprietor: J Park &
Florence F Smith
Hours: By Appointment,
by Chance
Types & Periods:
Continental, American &
Chinese, Circa 1720-1900
Directions: Half Way
between Reading &
Allentown, 2 Miles S of
Rte 222

STUMP ANTIQUES
214 Barclay St   19562
215 682-2318
Proprietor: Evelyn P
Stump
Hours: Mon-Sat, 8-6
Types & Periods: Copper,
Brass, Tinware, Furniture,
General Line

Trucksville

PICKWICK ANTIQUES
89 Warden Ave   18708
717 696-3475   Est: 1972
Proprietor: Jane
Tomassetti
Hours: Daily, 11-4; Also by
Appointment
Types & Periods: General
Line
Specialties: Jewelry
Appraisal Service Available
Directions: 1 Block off Rte
309, N of Wilkes-Barre

Tunkhannock

ANTIQUES
RD 5, Rte 309   18657
Proprietor: Dale K Myers
Types & Periods: General
Line, Art Glass, Oil
Paintings, Silver, Furniture
Directions: Evans Falls

RED BARN ANTIQUES
Rte 29, Lake Carey 18657
717 836-2614   Est: 1965
Proprietor: Frances
VanAuken
Hours: Daily, by
Appointment or by Chance
Types & Periods: General
Line of China, Glass,
Primitives, Furniture &
Collectibles
Directions: On Rte 29N, 3
Miles from Traffic Light in
Tunkhannock

SILVER SLEIGH ANTIQUES
RD 5   18657
717 298-2360
Proprietor: Bob Davis &
Gene Hanley
Types & Periods: General
Line
Appraisal Service Available
Directions: Rte 309
Dallas-Tunkhannock Hwy

Tyler Hill

**TYLER HILL ANTIQUE
SHOP**
Rte 371   18469
717 224-4793

Proprietor: Fred & Wanda
Burley, Pauline Abraham
Hours: Closed in the
Winter
Types & Periods: General
Line

Union City

BATES ANTIQUES
38-40 S Main St   16438
814 438-2610   Est: 1961
Proprietor: Eleanor W
Bates
Hours: Mon-Sat
Types & Periods: General
Line, Some Collectibles,
Some Depression
Specialties: Paperweights;
Custard, Carnival, Cut Glass
Main St of Town

**SEE MORE ANTIQUES &
GIFTS**
RD 4, Rte 6   16438
814 438-2702   Est: 1969
Proprietor: Mrs Roger
Seymour
Hours: Mon & Tues,
Thurs-Sat
Types & Periods: General
Line
Directions: 1 Mile F of
Town on Rte 6

Ursina

**THE OLD COMPANY
STORE**
State Rte 281   15485
814 395-5012
Proprietor: George &
Virginia L Bowser
Hours: Tues-Sun, April 1
to Nov 1, 12-5
Types & Periods: Primitives,
Coins, Furniture, Glass

Valencia

OLEXEN'S ANTIQUES
Rte 8, RD 3   16059
412 898-2810   Est: 1970
Proprietor: Frances J
Olexen
Hours: Daily
Types & Periods: Victorian
Furniture, General Line

OLEXEN'S   Cont'd
Specialties: Victorian
Furniture, Dolls
Appraisal Service Available
   Directions: Rte 8, 10 Miles
   from Pa Turnpike

Villanova

ELINOR GORDON
   Box 211   19085
   215 525-0981
   Proprietor: Elinor Gordon
   Hours: By Appointment
Types & Periods: Chinese
Export Porcelain
Specialties: Chinese Export
Porcelain
Appraisal Service Available

Washington

JOHN'S ANTIQUES
   445 W Chestnut St   15301
   412 222-9646
   Proprietor: John Florida
   Hours: Daily
Types & Periods: General
Line, Guns
Appraisal Service Available
   Directions: Exit 4 from
   I-70, 1/2 Mile on
   Old Rte 40

Waverly

FAMILY TREE ANTIQUES
   Box 75   18471
   717 587-1114
   Proprietor: Dora Cigarran
Types & Periods: Orientals

Wayne

**DALLAS W & GLADYS H
LITTLE**
   280 S Devon Ave   19087
   215 688-5824
   Proprietor: Dallas W &
   Gladys H Little
Types & Periods: China,
Glass, Primitives,
Collectibles

Wernersville

MARILYN J KOWALESKI
   Grandview Rd   19565
   215 678-9948
   Proprietor: Marilyn J
   Kowaleski
   Hours: By Appointment
Types & Periods: Patchwork,
Applique & Amish Quilts
   Directions: RD 3

Wescosville

ANTIQUE VILLAGE
   Rte 222   18106
   215 398-3000
   Proprietor: 5 Separate
   Shops
   Hours: Wed, Fri &
   11-5; Thurs, 1-9
Types & Periods: General
Line
   Directions: 2 Miles W of
   Allentown, or Hamilton
   Blvd Exit W off 309

IRENE BIER'S ANTIQUES
   Rte 222   18106
   215 398-3000
   Proprietor: Irene Bier
   Hours: Wed, Fri & Sat,
   11-5; Thurs, 1-9
Types & Periods: "The old,
the odd, the unusual &
more; You'll find them here"
Appraisal Service Available
   Directions: At Antique
   Village

THE COUNTRY SHOP
   RD 2, Box 675   18106
   215 395-3425
   Proprietor: Teloir M
   Checksfield
Types & Periods: Advertising
& Country Store Items, Tin,
Primitives

DALLY'S ANTIQUES
   Rte 222   18106
Types & Periods: Art, Glass,
Dolls, Furniture, Collectibles
   Directions: At Antique
   Village, W off 309N

GOLDEN OAK ANTIQUES
   Rte 222   18106
   215 435-1798
   Hours: Wed, Fri & Sat,
   11-5; Thurs, 1-9

Types & Periods: Oak &
Early Victorian Furniture,
Clocks, American Indian
Jewelry
   Directions: At Antique
   Village

RHEA MITTMAN ANTIQUES
   Rte 222   18106
   215 398-1500
   Hours: Wed, Fri & Sat,
   11-5; Thurs, 1-9
Types & Periods: Decorator
Items, General Line
   Directions: At Antique
   Village

West Chester

MACK & NICHOLSON
   Rd 4   19380
   215 793-1312   Est: 1970
   Proprietor: Don Nicholson
   De Marino
   Hours: By Appointment
Types & Periods: English
Period Furniture &
Accessories Circa
1650-1800
   Directions: "Please call for
   directions, difficult to find"

ELIZABETH L MATLAT
   1300 Wilmington Pike
                              19380
   Proprietor: Elizabeth L
   Matlat
   Hours: Mon-Sat 9-5; Sun
   1-5
Types & Periods: 18th &
19th Century Furniture &
Accessories
Specialties: Furniture, Tools
& Fireplace Equipment
Appraisal Service Available
   Directions: 5 Miles S of
   Town, Rtes 202 & 322

Wexford

RUTH ARNOLD ANTIQUES
   Baur Dr   15090
   412 935-3217   Est: 1967
   Proprietor: Ruth Arnold
   Hours: Daily 11-5
Types & Periods: Country
Furniture, Primitives &
Victorian
Specialties: "Making our
own lamps & very unusual
items from old antiques"

Directions: Heading N on Rte 19, Turn R onto Wallace Rd, go 1/2 Mile; Turn R onto English Rd, go 1 Mile; Turn R onto Baur Dr & go to the Dead End

White

COFFMAN ANTIQUES
Box 49   15490
412 455-3147   Est: 1973
Proprietor: Beverley Coffman
Hours: Daily, By Appointment, By Chance
Types & Periods: General Line of Antiques
Specialties: Furniture, Glassware, Primitives
Appraisal Service Available
Directions: 4 Miles S of Donegal Exit 9, Pa Turnpike

Whites Valley

THE ELIZABETH HOUSE
Star Rte 670   18453
717 448-2746
Proprietor: Louise R Carbone
Hours: "Open all Year"
Types & Periods: General Line

Whitney

WHITE BARN ANTIQUES
Box 57   15693
412 423-3086
Proprietor: Morna M Huffman
Hours: June 1-Nov 1, Thurs-Sat 1-5, Otherwise by Chance or By Appointment
Types & Periods: Furniture, Clocks, Blue Crocks, Bottles, Tools, Primitives, Lamps, Boxes, Musical Items, Collectibles
Directions: 2 Miles straight S of Latrobe Airport, off Pa 981

Wilkes-Barre

HART ANTIQUES
476 Hazle Ave   18702
717 823-2393   Est: 1948
Proprietor: Peter P Loeffler, Jr
Hours: Daily, 8-4
Types & Periods: General Line, Coins, Collectibles
Specialties: Art Glass
Appraisal Service Available
Directions: 1 Mile from Blackman St Exit I-81

Williamsport

PATTY & BOB BARTO ANTIQUES
2100 Mosser Ave   17701
717 323-1854   Est: 1970
Proprietor: Patty & Bob Barto
Hours: By Appointment, by Chance
Types & Periods: General Line, Collectibles
Directions: Newberry, 1 Block West of Arch St

LEE CILLO
234 Market   17701
717 322-8384
Proprietor: Lee Cillo
Hours: Mon-Sat, 10-5
Types & Periods: Coins, Old Guns, Diamonds

MARTY'S ANTIQUES
315 Brown St   17701
717 326-9992   Est: 1948
Proprietor: Mrs F W Mankey, Jr
Hours: Daily
Types & Periods: Victorian Jewelry, Cut Glass, Silver, Lamps
Specialties: Hand Made Lamp Shades, Lamps Repaired, Lamp Parts
Directions: 4 Blocks N of Maynard St Bridge in S Williamsport

Wireton

THREE MAPLES ANTIQUES
McGovern Blvd   15092
412 457-8710

Proprietor: Bessie Snyder Hainley
Hours: Tues-Sat, 10-5:30
Types & Periods: Furniture, Glass, China

Yardley

GERALDINE LIPMAN ANTIQUES
5 Byron Lane   19067
215 295-6142
Proprietor: Geraldine Lipman
Types & Periods: General Line
Specialties: Belleek China

York

MARY DELHAMER ANTIQUES
RD 9   17402
717 755-3811
Proprietor: Mary Delhamer
Types & Periods: Early Americana, Period Furniture, Glass, China, Primitives

PAUL L ETTLINE'S ANTIQUES
3790 E Market St   17402
717 755-3927
Proprietor: Paul L Ettline
Types & Periods: Furniture, Glassware, China

GOLDEN EAGLE
349 S George St   17403
                Est: 1961
Proprietor: Larry Smith
Hours: Mon & Thurs, 4-9; Sat, 8-5
Types & Periods: General Line, Furniture
Specialties: China, Glass
Appraisal Service Available
Directions: 3 Blocks S of the Square

KENNEDY'S ANTIQUES
4290 W Market St   17404
717 792-1922   Est: 1956
Proprietor: Georgiana Clay Kennedy
Hours: Daily; By Appointment
Types & Periods: General Line, Victorian
Directions: 5 Miles out of York on Gettysburg Hwy

York   **Cont'd**

RICHBAR ANTIQUES
151 Strathcona Dr S
                    17403
717 843-9774
Proprietor: Bill & Dottie
Richardson
Types & Periods: General
Line, Cut Glass

YELLOW BIRD CAGE
11 S Beaver St   17401
717 846-0648
Proprietor: Augusta R
Cohen
Types & Periods: General
Line, Folk Art

Zelienople

OLDE ATTIC ANTIQUES
204 S Main St   16063
412 452-6585   Est: 1972
Proprietor: Edward &
Marion Sankovic
Hours: Tues-Sat, 11-4:30;
Sun, 1-4:30
Types & Periods: Glass,
China, Pottery, Collectibles,
Crocks, Victorian & Primitive
Furniture
Appraisal Service Available
Directions: 5 Miles N Pa
Turnpike; Perry
Interchange on Rte 19

TREEN SHOP ANTIQUES
Zehner School Rd   16063
412 452-9271   Est: 1963
Proprietor: Helen P Witney
Hours: Tues-Sat, 9-5; Sun,
1-5
Types & Periods: Primitives,
Country Furniture,
Treenware
Specialties: Treenware
Directions: 2 Miles S of
Zelienople; Turn W off Rte
19, Go 1/2 Mile

Zieglerville

THANEWOLD
Box 104   19492
215 287-9158   Est: 1957
Proprietor: Elizabeth R
Gamon
Hours: Appointment
Preferred

Types & Periods: 18th &
Early 19th Century Furniture,
Linens, Coin Silver & Tools,
House Hardware, Iron
Specialties: Coin Silver &
Tools
Appraisal Service Available
Directions: Approx 45
Minutes NW of
Philadelphia; On Little Rd
in Zieglerville (Rtes 29 &
73)

Zionsville

THE BEDPOST
Rte 100   18092
215 967-1300
Hours: Sat, 11-5; Sun, 1-4
Types & Periods: Iron &
Brass Beds, Rolltops,
Dressers, Round Tables,
Chairs
Specialties: Furniture (Brass
Beds)

**FREEMAN & GORDON
ANTIQUES**
RD 1   18092
215 967-3443
Hours: By Appointment
Types & Periods: American
Country Furniture, Tin,
Wood, Primitives
Directions: 1 1/2 Miles W
of Shimerville off Rtes
100 & 29

MOSHEIM'S ANTIQUES
Box 87, RD   18092
215 679-5183
Proprietor: Marilyn
Mosheim
Hours: By Appointment
Types & Periods: Primitives,
Country Furniture
Directions: Near Hereford

This Early American side chair design was
periodically reproduced throughout the Victorian Era.

STATE OF RHODE ISLAND

Ashaway

ASHAWAY ANTIQUES STORE
4 Main St   02804
401 377-8116   Est: 1977
Proprietor: Sally E Van
Den Bossche
Hours: Daily
Types & Periods: Country
Furniture, Primitives,
Woodenware, Tinware, Iron,
Ironstone, Yelloware,
Brownware, Soft Paste
Pottery, Quilts, Coverlets,
Paintings, Baskets, Brass,
Copper
Appraisal Service Available
Directions: Rte 216, 1 Mile
off I-95 at R I-Conn Line

Carolina

JAMES E SCUDDER
Rte 112   02012
401 364-7228   Est: 1954
Proprietor: James E
Scudder
Hours: Daily, Sun & Mon
By Appointment
Types & Periods: Furniture,
Glass, China, Silver
Appraisal Service Available
Directions: From I-95, Exit
3E, 2 Miles E on Rte 138
& 2 Miles on 112

Chepachet

BROWN & HOPKINS COUNTRY STORE
Putnam Pike   02814
401 568-4830
Proprietor: Raymond &
Claire Borowski
Hours: Wed-Sat 10-5, Sun
12-5
Types & Periods: Primitives,
Country Store Items
Directions: Rte 44

CHESTNUT HILL ANTIQUES
RFD 2, Box 406, Main St
Rte 44   02814
401 568-4365   Est: 1978
Proprietor: Robert
Anderson & Edward
Grasso
Hours: Sun, Wed-Sat, By
Appointment
Types & Periods: Victorian
Furniture, Primitives,
Kerosene Lamps (Table &
Hanging), Art Glass,
Depression Glass, Porcelain,
Oil Paintings
Specialties: Hanging
Kerosene Lamps, Banquet
Lamps, Victorian Furniture
Appraisal Service Available
Directions: Follow Rte 44
from Providence or E on
44 from Putnam Conn

Cranston

BARBS ANTIQUES
1982 Broad St   02905
401 467-5930   Est: 1974
Proprietor: Barbara
Gornstein
Hours: Daily, Weekends
11-5, Closed Sun & Mon
Types & Periods: General
Line, Wicker, Oak,
Mahogany & Anything
Unusual
Specialties: Wicker
Appraisal Service Available
Directions: Rte 95,
Cranston Exit, Park Ave E
to Broad St

MAGI DECO TO DYNASTY ANTIQUES
2166 Broad St   02905
401 781-6222   Est: 1968
Proprietor: Margaret
Motola
Hours: Mon, Wed-Fri &
Sat 11-5, Closed Tues,
Thurs & Sun, By
Appointment
Types & Periods: Art Deco,
Bronzes, Jewelry, Furniture,
Oriental, Pottery, Turkish,
Chinese, Japanese

Specialties: Oriental, Deco
Items
Appraisal Service Available
Directions: Rte 95 S, Exit
Allens Ave to Narragansett
Blvd, Right on Columbia
to Broad

East Providence

ESTATE LIQUIDATIONS
159 Waterman Ave   02916
401 434-5162   Est: 1976
Proprietor: Cheryl Williams
Hours: Tues-Fri, By
Appointment
Types & Periods: Dolls,
Hummels, Oriental Objects,
Toys
Specialties: Dolls
Appraisal Service Available
Directions: Taunton Ave
Exit off 195 E of
Providence, Follow
Taunton Ave 5 blocks, left
on James to Light, Turn
Right on Waterman

SARA CARLETON
38 James   02914
401 434-2747   Est: 1934
Proprietor: Sara Carleton
Hours: Daily
Types & Periods: Glass,
Furniture, General Line
Specialties: Lamps,
Sconces, Chandeliers
Appraisal Service Available
Directions: Rte 195 E, 1st
E Providence Exit, 2nd
Left after 1st Red Light

Esmond

HELEN E BROOK ANTIQUES & APPRAISER
268 Waterman Ave   02917
401 231-4118
Proprietor: Helen E Brook
Hours: By Appointment
Types & Periods: General
Line

Exeter

MURPHY'S ANTIQUES
Rte 3 Nooseneck Hill Rd
                              02822
401 397-7838
Proprietor: Bob & Dale
Murphy
Hours: Daily 9-5, Closed
Fri
Types & Periods: General
Line

Manville

HARRIS ANTIQUES
60 Spring St   02838
401 769-3920-4466
                         Est: 1965
Proprietor: Bud & Lucille
Kredenser
Hours: By Appointment,
By Chance
Types & Periods: Oak,
Victorian, Glass, China,
General Line
Appraisal Service Available
Directions: Rte 95 to 295,
Rte 122 N or Rte 146 N,
Take Cutoff to Manville

Newport

THE ANTIQUE CENTER
42 Spring St   02840
401 847-3968
Types & Periods: General
Line, Art Glass, Silver,
China, Furniture, Prints

BETSY'S PARLOR
221 Spring St   02840
401 846-7338
Types & Periods: Clothing of
the Gay Nineties to the 50's,
Fabrics, Furs, Jewelry, Art
Deco Accessories

CHINA TRADE ANTIQUES
18 Elm St   02840
401 849-3511   Est: 1970
Proprietor: Bensont Smith
LTD
Hours: Daily
Types & Periods: "China
Trade Objects"

Specialties: Furniture,
Lighting Fixtures
Appraisal Service Available
Directions: 3 blocks from
Washington St Near Goat
Island Causeway

**COLONIAL ANTIQUES
SHOP**
Franklin & Spring Sts
                              02840
401 847-2700   Est: 1964
Proprietor: Edna G Evans
Hours: By Appointment,
By Chance
Types & Periods: 18th &
19th Centuries Furniture,
Collectibles
Specialties: Rose Medallion
& Other Porcelains
Appraisal Service Available
Directions: "Rte 138 to
Memorial, Right turn 2nd
traffic light, go 1 block"

THE CRANBERRY LAMP
35 Franklin St   02840
401 846-8689
Types & Periods: General
Line, Books, Prints,
Collectibles

THE GALLERY
225 Spring St   02840
Types & Periods: "Antiques
& Uniques"
Directions: Corner of
Franklin St, Second Floor

**GALLERY '76 ANTIQUES
INC**
83 Spring St   02840
401 847-4288   Est: 1972
Proprietor: Barbara Leis
Hours: Daily 10-5
Types & Periods: Furniture
& Accessories from 1776 to
1876, General Line

HARVINIDGE
78 Spring St   02840
Proprietor: Mr & Mrs
Vincent Smith & Henry S
Grew
Hours: By Appointment,
By Chance
Types & Periods: British
Historical Items

**JOHN CODDINGTON
HOUSE**
2 Marlborough St   02840
401 846-4821
Types & Periods: Furniture,
Porcelains, Paintings in an
18th Century Setting
Directions: Corner of
Thames St

JOHN GIDLEY HOUSE-1744
22 Franklin St   02840
401 846-8303
Types & Periods: Furniture,
Lighting Fixtures, Objects of
Decoration

LA FONTAINE ANTIQUES
148 Spring St   02840
401 846-1717
Proprietor: Dorothy & Obie
Ross
Hours: Daily 1-5
Types & Periods: 18th &
19th Centuries Items,
European & American
Directions: Across from
Trinity Church

MC DONOUGH & LARNER
26 Franklin St   02840
401 849-2680
Types & Periods: General
Line, Furniture
Specialties: Glass (Leaded)

OLD COLONY SHOP
517 Thames St   02840
401 846-4918, 847-4509
                         Est: 1963
Proprietor: Marian V
Curran
Hours: Mon-Sat
Types & Periods: Chinese
Exports, Glass, China, Coin
Silver & Victorian Silver,
Collectibles, Bells, Brass,
Copper, Fireplace Tools
Specialties: Coin Silver
Directions: Lower Thames
St on the Waterfront in
one of the Busiest Tourist
Towns in New England

OLD FASHION SHOP
4 Franklin St   02840
401 847-2692
Types & Periods:
Americana, Furniture &
Accessories, Oriental Rugs,
Porcelains

ALICE SIMPSON ANTIQUES
24 Franklin St   02840
401 849-4254
Proprietor: Alice Simpson
Types & Periods: Silver, Steins, Jewelry

TREASURE TROVE ANTIQUES
40 Franklin St   02840
401 847-3829
Types & Periods: Nautical Items, General Line, Curios

North Kingstown

NORTH KINGSTOWN ANTIQUE CENTRE
1121 Ten Rod Rd   02852
401 294-9887
Proprietor: Alice, Bill, Dale, Esther & Jane
Hours: Daily 10-4, Closed Mon & Fri
Types & Periods: General Line
Directions: 5 Dealers Under 1 Roof

POTPOURRI
20 Main St   02852
401 295-0891   Est: 1970
Proprietor: Paul C Carlson
Hours: Tues-Sat 11-5, By Appointment
Types & Periods: General Line
Appraisal Service Available

North Scituate

HICKORY HOLLOW ANTIQUES
Trimtown Rd   02857
401 647-5321   Est: 1968
Proprietor: Liz & Cal Dexter
Hours: By Appointment, By Chance
Types & Periods: Country Furniture, Primitives, Glass, China, Books, Collectibles, General Line
Appraisal Service Available
Directions: 1/4 Mile off Business Rte 6

Pascoag

THE ANTIQUARIAN
110 Church   02859
401 568-8125   Est: 1963
Proprietor: Donald A & Margaret B Kemp
Hours: Daily, Weekends 10-6, By Appointment
Types & Periods: General Line
Specialties: Glass (Sandwich), Tools
Appraisal Service Available
Directions: 23 Miles SE of Old Storbridge Village, 45 Miles NW of Providence off US 44

Portsmouth

CORY FARM ANTIQUES
3124 E Main Rd   02871
401 683-4991   Est: 1974
Proprietor: Ann Garfield
Hours: Daily, Weekends 11-5
Types & Periods: General Line
Directions: Off Rte 24 Near Newport

TEX'S AUCTION HOUSE & BARGAIN MALL
1678 E Main Rd   02871
401 683-9870   Est: 1970
Proprietor: Henry Violette
Hours: By Appointment
Types & Periods: Furniture, Brass Beds, Round Oak Tables, China Closet, Tools, Jewelry
Directions: Rte 138 in Back of Roller Rink

Providence

PROVIDENCE CLUSTER
Directions: Wickenden, Governor, Benefit, Thayer & Hope Sts, Also Westminster Mall & Pine St

AARON GALLERY
166 Wickenden St   02903
401 421-5215   Est: 1960
Proprietor: John Aaron
Hours: Daily

Types & Periods: General Line
Specialties: Rugs (Oriental), Paintings, Prints
Appraisal Service Available
Directions: Rte 95 to 195 E, Take 2nd Exit

MARSH-ACKERMAN ANTIQUES LTD
Box 2402   02906
401 751-3168   Est: 1973
Proprietor: Lawrence Marsh & Laurie Ackerman
Hours: Winter, By Appointment
Types & Periods: Silver, Jewelry, Late 19th & 20th Centuries Decorative Arts, Silver Collectibles

NEW ENGLAND ANTIQUES
1487 Broad St   02905
401 781-2870   Est: 1955
Proprietor: Italo L Pellini
Hours: Daily 9-5
Types & Periods: All Collectibles
Appraisal Service Available

PRE-AMBLE ANTIQUES
738 Hope St   02906
401 274-1322   Est: 1969
Proprietor: Fred Luchesi
Hours: Mon-Sat 10-5:30
Types & Periods: Chippendale, Empire, Victorian
Directions: Near Corner of Rochambeau Ave & Hope St

EDWARD & JOAN STECKLER
168 Governor St   02906
Proprietor: Edward L Steckler
Hours: By Appointment
Types & Periods: American Country Furniture, Copper, Brass, Iron, Tin Accessories, Early Lighting, Needlework Tools, Snuff Boxes, Doll House Miniatures, Fireplace Accessories
Directions: Corner of Pitman & Governor

Warren

THE DEACON'S ANNEX
77 Water St   02885
401 245-6938   Est: 1969
Proprietor: Fane Couper &
Susan Mannion
Hours: Daily, Weekends
11-5, Closed Sun, Eve by
Appointment
Types & Periods: Oak,
Mahogany, Pine Furniture,
Pewter, Brass, Bronze, Key
Wind Clocks, Jewelry
Specialties: Brass Beds,
Lighting, Gas Shades
Appraisal Service Available
Directions: Rte 114

West Kingston

THE WAY WE WERE
10 Railroad Ave   02892
401 884-5730
Proprietor: P H Merdinyan
Hours: Sun 12-5, Sat 10-5,
By Appointment
Types & Periods: Nostalgic
Furnishings
Directions: Across the
Green from Kingston
Railroad Station

West Warwick

GROVE FARM ANTIQUES
194 Phenix Ave   02893
401 821-4057
Proprietor: J Foss Magoon
& Gary H Peterson
Hours: By Appointment
Types & Periods: General
Line

**SECOND HAND ROE'S
SHOPPE**
1616 Main St   02893
Est: 1973
Proprietor: Roe BeLeau
Hours: Daily, Weekends
6-9, Also by Appointment
or By Chance
Types & Periods: Dolls,
Jewelry, General Line
Specialties: Jewelry, Toys
(Dolls)
Directions: Btwn Rtes 3 &
117

Drop front secretary, Late Victorian.

STATE OF SOUTH CAROLINA

Abbeville

NOAH'S ARK
301 Washington   29620
803 459-4126   Est: 1941
Proprietor: J C Wiley
Hours: Daily, Closed Sun
& Mon
Types & Periods: Furniture,
Bric-A-Brac, Books
Specialties: Furniture,
Bric-A-Brac, Books

Anderson

THE BEE HIVE
510 N Main   29621
803 225-2377   Est: 1969
Proprietor: Polly Wright &
Frances Johnson
Hours: Daily, Weekends
10-5:30, Closed Sun
Types & Periods:
Bric-A-Brac, Primitive &
Imports, Clocks, Art Glass
Directions: Downtown
"Look for the Old Gray
House"

Bennettsville

DANIS FURNITURE STORE
Gibson Hwy   29512
803 479-2531   Est: 1947
Proprietor: John H Danis
Hours: Daily
Types & Periods: General
Line, Furniture
Appraisal Service Available
Directions: 5 Miles N of
Bennettsville on Hwy 385

Camden

THE ANVIL
1625 Jefferson Davis Hwy
29020
803 432-2639   Est: 1968
Proprietor: Kenneth P
Daniels
Hours: Daily, Weekends
10-5, Sat 10-1, Closed
Wed & Sun

Types & Periods: Tools,
American Primitives &
Victorian Furniture
Specialties: Tools for
Woodworking &
Blacksmithing
Directions: 2 Miles N of
Camden on US 1

THE COURT YARD
208 Laurens St   29020
803 432-7361   Est: 1960
Proprietor: Anne C West
Hours: Daily 10-4, Sun
10-1, Closed Sat & Sun
Types & Periods: General
Line, Mostly English
Directions: 3 blocks off
Rte 1 btwn Fair & Mill Sts

**SHAYLOR'S ON THE HILL
ANTIQUE SHOP**
Jefferson Davis Hwy 29020
803 432-4795   Est: 1971
Proprietor: Sadie & Ed
Shaylor
Hours: Mon-Sat,
Types & Periods: Primitives,
Victorian, Queen Ann,
Chippendale, Clocks
Directions: Hwy 1 N 3
Miles from Town

Charleston

ANSON HOUSE
89 Broad St   29401
803 577-5196   Est: 1976
Proprietor: John H
Beckroge & Norman E
Brown
Hours: Mon-Sat, By
Appointment, By Chance
Types & Periods: English &
American Antiques, Gift
Items, Reproductions

ELIZABETH AUSTIN INC
165 King St   29401
803 722-8227   Est: 1965
Proprietor: Susan Ellen
Austin
Hours: Mon-Sat 10-5, By
Appointment

Types & Periods: Early
American Silver, Sterling,
Period Furniture,
Accessories
Specialties: Silver, American
Furniture
Appraisal Service Available

**BESS & BESS OF
CHARLESTON LTD**
185 King St   29401
803 722-7951   Est: 1977
Proprietor: K B Bess Jr
Hours: Mon thru Sat, By
Appointment, 577-9209
Types & Periods: Scientific
Instruments, Nautical
Antiques, Ships, Models,
Campaign Furniture
Specialties: All Items from
England
Directions: Located in
Middle of Historic Section
of S Carolina in
Charleston

**BETTY'S DOLL HOUSE &
ODDTIQUES**
1307 Ashley River Rd
29407
803 556-2331   Est: 1975
Proprietor: Betty Geisler
Hours: Mon-Sat 9-6
Types & Periods: Wicker
Carriages, Old Cribs,
Cradles, Highchairs, Glass &
Lamps from 1700 to Present
Specialties: Complete
Restoration of Antiques &
Collector's Dolls, Buy & Sell
Dolls, Handmade Dolls
Appraisal Service Available
Directions: On SC Rte 61,
3 Miles from W Ashley
River Bridge & 10 Miles E
of Magnolia Gardens

**BRASS AND SILVER
WORKSHOP**
28 Cumberland St   29407
803 723-7606   Est: 1968
Proprietor: A L Crabtree
Hours: Mon-Fri, By
Appointment
Types & Periods: Brass &
Silver, Restoration, Cleaning,
Repairs, Silver Plating,
Lamps made to order
Specialties: All metal
services available

Charleston   Cont'd

BRASS & SILVER   Cont'd
Appraisal Service Available
Directions: Downtown in
Old Charleston, 1 block
from Market Place

BRICK KITCHEN ANTIQUES
21 Wentworth St   29401
803 577-4944   Est: 1976
Proprietor: Phyllis P Miller
Hours: By Appointment,
By Chance
Types & Periods: American
Country Furniture &
Accessories
Directions: Located in
Historic "Anson Borough"
Section of Downtown
Charleston, 3 blocks North
of Old Market Place

CLOCKMAKERS OF
CHARLESTON
1307 Ashley River Rd
                    29407
803 556-2331   Est: 1975
Proprietor: Martin Geisler
Hours: Mon-Sat 9-6
Types & Periods: Repair &
Restore Cases &
Movements, Clocks
Appraisal Service Available
Directions: On SC Rte 61,
3 Miles W of Ashley River
Bridge & 10 Miles E of
Magnolia Gardens

COLES & COMPANY, INC
84 Wentworth St   29401
803 723-2142 or
723-3111   Est: 1970
Proprietor: William H
Coles
Hours: Mon-Sat, By
Appointment
Types & Periods: 18th &
Early 19th Centuries English
Furniture, Oil Paintings,
Porcelain, Brass
Specialties: Furniture, Oil
Paintings, Porcelain, Brass
Appraisal Service Available
Directions: 1st block to
the right off King St

GARDEN GATE ANTIQUES
96 King St   29401
            Est: 1973
Proprietor: Wallace
Frampton

Hours: Mon-Sat
10:30-5:30, Closed Sat
June, July & Aug, By
Appointment, By Chance
Types & Periods: 18th &
19th Centuries American &
English Furniture &
Accessories
Specialties: Brass
Candlesticks & English
Chests
Appraisal Service Available
Directions: 1 block S of
Broad St on King, in
Historic Charleston

GEO C BIRLANT & CO
191 King St   29401
803 722-3842   Est: 1929
Proprietor: Phil and
Marian Slotin
Hours: Mon-Sat
Types & Periods: 18th &
19th Centuries English
Furniture, Silver, China,
Crystal, Brass, Gifts &
Lighting Fixtures
Appraisal Service Available
Directions: Located at
Corner of King &
Clifford Sts

JOHN GIBSON COMPANY
183 King St   29401
803 722-0909   Est: 1972
Proprietor: John D Gibson
Hours: Mon-Sat 10-5
Types & Periods: Period
Furniture, Oriental Rugs,
Silver, Paintings, Porcelain,
Wholesale & Retail,
Pre-1830
Appraisal Service Available
Directions: In Heart of
Antique District in Old
Charleston

HAMILTON HOUSE
27 State   29401
803 722-4028   Est: 1953
Proprietor: George
Hamilton Bailes
Hours: Mon-Sat
Types & Periods: English,
French, Oriental, Early
American, Porcelains,
Lamps & Accessories
Directions: In Heart of Old
Historic Charleston, 2
blocks from Mills-Hyatt
House, 2 blocks from
Market Sq

KELLOGG ANTIQUES
23-25 Vendue Range
                    29401
            Est: 1966
Proprietor: Paul Kellogg
Hours: Tues thru Sat
Types & Periods: Broad
Range of Periods, Furniture,
Paintings, Decorative Items
Specialties: Antiques to
"Live With"
Appraisal Service Available
Directions: In "French
Quarter" of Old
Charleston just off
E Bay St

LIVINGSTON & SONS
ANTIQUES, INC
2137 Savannah Hwy
(US Hwy 71)   29407
803 556-3502,
556-6162   Est: 1970
Proprietor: John A
Livingston Jr
Hours: Mon-Sat
Types & Periods: General
Line
Specialties: Direct European
Importer & Estate Buyer
Appraisal Service Available
Directions: 5 Miles S of
historic Charleston on
Savannah Hwy (US Hwy
17)

ORIENTAL RUG AND
ANTIQUE CO
192 King St   29401
803 722-2309   Est: 1971
Proprietor: Impex
International Co
Hours: Mon-Sat
Types & Periods: Persian &
Caucasian Rugs, Guns,
Paintings, Silver, Chinese
Silk Embroidery
Specialties: Rugs and Guns
Appraisal Service Available
Directions: Downtown
Charleston

TRADER JOE'S INC
1724 Hwy 61   29407
803 766-2347   Est: 1952
Proprietor: Robert A
Murray
Hours: Mon-Sat
Types & Periods: General
Line
Directions: Near
Wappoo Rd

Cheraw

ANTIQUE IMPORTS INC
92 Power   29520
803 537-5762   Est: 1970
Proprietor: Orrie B
Thomas
Hours: Daily, Weekends
9-5, Closed Sun & Thurs
Types & Periods: American
Furniture, Glass, Clocks,
Paintings
Directions: On Hwy 52 S

Columbia

COLUMBIA CLUSTER
Directions: Gervais St
(700-1000 Blocks), Devine
St (2000 Block), Meeting
St (7000 Block)

**CHARLTON HALL
GALLERIES INC**
930 Gervais Ct   29201
803 252-7927   Est: 1935
Proprietor: Charlton F
Hall Jr
Hours: Mon-Fri 9-5, By
Appointment
Types & Periods: 18th &
19th Centuries French &
English Furniture
Specialties: Furniture,
(Reproduction & Custom
Made)
Appraisal Service Available
Directions: 1 block W of
State Capital

LITTLE BIT ANTIQUES
701 Gervais St   29201
803 779-6488   Est: 1972
Proprietor: Randolph
Gregory
Hours: Daily
Types & Periods: Art Glass,
Chippendale Furniture,
Queen Anne, Hepplewhite,
Art Deco, Georgian, Cameo
Glass, Cut Glass
Appraisal Service Available
Directions: Hwy 1, 4
blocks from State Capitol
on Same Road

ONE THOUSAND GERVAIS
1000 Gervais St   29201
803 252-1499   Est: 1968
Proprietor: Isola Sherrerd
Hartness & George B
Hartness

Hours: Mon-Fri
Types & Periods: 18th &
Early 19th Centuries
Furniture, Porcelains,
Paintings, Rugs,
Accessories
Appraisal Service Available
Directions: 1 block S of
SC State Capitol Bldg,
Corner of Gervais &
Park Sts

Florence

**CHARLES WATERS
INTERIOR DESIGN**
404 S Dargan St   29503
803 662-2433   Est: 1893
Proprietor: Charles Waters
Hours: Mon-Fri, By
Appointment, By Chance
Types & Periods: 18th &
19th Centuries Furniture
Specialties: Interior Designer
Appraisal Service Available
Directions: Downtown, 1
block off US 301 & 76

**FLORENCE FURNITURE
BARN**
1309 Interstate Blvd 29501
803 665-8668   Est: 1974
Proprietor: R L Sheppard
Hours: Daily
Types & Periods: General
Line

HOUSE OF OLE-TIQUES
1001 Kalmia St   29501
803 662-4119   Est: 1964
Proprietor: Mrs Margaret L
Broadway
Hours: Daily 11-5, Closed
Sun & Mon
Types & Periods: General
Line, Handmade Plantation
Pieces (Pine)
Appraisal Service Available

Greenville

**PIEDMONT FURNITURE &
ANTIQUE SHOPPE**
115 N Brown St   29601
803 232-5304   Est: 1922
Proprietor: J H Cannon Jr
Hours: Tues-Sat 9-5:30,
Sat 9-4, Closed Sun
& Mon

Types & Periods: Victorian &
Pennsylvania Pine,
Bric-A-Brac, Vases, Brass
Appraisal Service Available
Directions: 1 block off
Main St, btwn Coffee St &
E North St

**TOWN HOUSE GALLERIES
INC**
206 E North St   29601
803 242-5538   Est: 1967
Proprietor: Kirby Quinn Jr
Hours: Daily 9-5:30
Types & Periods: English
1750-1900

Greenwood

BREWINGTONS ANTIQUES
Hwy 25 North   29646
803 229-3086   Est: 1965
Proprietor: Earl & Betty
Brewington
Hours: Daily, By
Appointment, 1-5:30, All
Day Sat
Types & Periods: China,
Glass, Furniture
Appraisal Service Available
Directions: Near Holiday
Inn & New Cross Creek
Mall

THE RAINBO
Rte 1, Box 159   29646
803 223-3715   Est: 1960
Proprietor: Hilton & Evelyn
Dodgen
Hours: Daily
Types & Periods: Glass,
Furniture, Jewelry, Primitives
Directions: Hwy 25 S

Liberty

KELLEYS ANTIQUES
Hwy 178, Rte 1   29657
803 843-6882   Est: 1974
Proprietor: Charles L &
Sandra G Kelley
Hours: Daily 9-6
Types & Periods: Early
American & English
Specialties: Early American,
Tools
Appraisal Service Available
Directions: 5 Miles S of
Town

Liberty Hill

KOUNTRY KORNER
Hwy 97   29074
803 273-8615   Est: 1972
Hours: Daily, Weekends,
By Appointment
Types & Periods: General
Line
Specialties: Clocks, Glass
Directions: 19 Miles N of
Camden

Manning

FRAN'S ANTIQUE SHOP
Sunset Dr   29102
803 435-8023   Est: 1966
Proprietor: Frances B
Broadway
Hours: Daily
Types & Periods: Victorian,
Oak, Glass, China,
Miniatures, Dolls, Primitives
Specialties: China, Glass
(Pressed), Dolls
Directions: Hwy 301 S

Murrells Inlet

OLD HOUSE ANTIQUES
17 Bypass   29576
803 236-7888   Est: 1973
Proprietor: Alma Robinson
Hours: Daily
Types & Periods: General
Line
Specialties: China, Glass
(Cut)
Directions: Rte 17 Bypass,
10 Miles S of Myrtle
Beach, 20 Miles N of
Georgetown

Mt Pleasant

THE GREEN DOOR
Sea Island Shopping Ctr
                29464
803 884-7610   Est: 1976
Proprietor: James R
Edwards
Hours: Mon-Sat 10-6

Types & Periods: Wood
Accent Pieces (Small),
1800's & English, Some
Consignment Items
Specialties: Gifts
Directions: Hwy 17 N to
Sullivan's Island

Myrtle Beach

CLUB HOUSE ANTIQUES
Deerfield Plantation 29577
803 651-3100   Est: 1975
Proprietor: Norman &
Doris Stegall
Hours: Tues-Sat, By
Appointment, By Chance
Types & Periods: Art Glass,
Lamps, Furniture, Jewelry,
Orientals, Collectibles,
Bronzes, Silver
Specialties: Total Antique
Directions: 6 Miles S on
Hwy 17 from Myrtle
Beach, in Clubhouse of
Deer Track Golf & Country
Club

North Augusta

**THE TIN PALACE
ANTIQUES**
1702 Georgia Ave   29841
803 278-1611   Est: 1968
Proprietor: Charles F
Minor
Hours: Daily, Weekends
10-6, Sun by Appointment
Types & Periods: General
Line, Art & Pressed Glass,
Oak Furniture
Appraisal Service Available
Directions: Hwy 25
Business, 3 Miles off I-20

Pelzer

LITTLE RED HOUSE
Rte 3, Box 458   29669
803 243-3726   Est: 1965
Proprietor: Floyd Janzen
Hours: Daily 10-5,
Weekends by Appointment
Types & Periods: Silver,
China, Glass, Brass,
Furniture
Specialties: Brass, Fireplace
Equipment
Appraisal Service Available

Directions: Going S on
I-85 from Charlotte to
Atlanta Turn Left on US
25 toward Greenwood, Go
10 Miles S

Rock Hill

**FRANKLIN HOUSE
INTERIORS**
1517 Ebenezer Rd   29730
803 328-5106   Est: 1974
Proprietor: Charles F
Steele Jr
Hours: Daily, By
Appointment
Types & Periods: English,
18th Century, French,
General Line

Spartanburg

CHESTNUT GALLERIES
144 Chestnut St   29302
803 585-9576   Est: 1969
Proprietor: Paul Allen
Dunbar Jr
Hours: Mon-Sat
Types & Periods: 18th &
19th Centuries Furniture &
Accessories, Southern
Country Furniture
Specialties: Furniture, Brass,
Porcelain
Directions: Exit 585-176
off I-85, 3.8 Miles to Main
St, Turn Right on Main,
1 block, turn Left on
Chestnut

Sumter

CAROLINA CHINA MARKET
3210 Broad St   29150
803 494-8393   Est: 1970
Proprietor: Kenneth F
Duffy
Hours: Daily
Types & Periods: Early 20th
Century Country Store Items
Specialties: China, Glass
Directions: 5 Miles W on
Hwys 76 & 378

DAN'S ANTIQUE CLOCK SHOP
   210 Broad St   29150
   803 773-7826   Est: 1973
   Proprietor: Dan Owens
   Hours: Mon thru Tues,
   Thurs-Sat 10-5, By
   Appointment
Specialties: Clocks
Appraisal Service Available
Directions: Downtown

THE SNAIL'S PACE
   210 Broad St   29150
   803 773-4214   Est: 1971
   Proprietor: Shirley Tate &
   Abe Newman & Frances
   Matthews
   Hours: Daily 10-5
Types & Periods: English,
Victorian, American,
Turn-of-the-Century
Furniture, Bric-A-Brac,
Stained Glass

STRAWBERRY MANSION ANTIQUES
   252 Broad St   29150
   803 773-7038   Est: 1976
   Proprietor: Shirley Tate &
   Abe Newman
   Hours: By Appointment
Types & Periods. English
Imports

Ware Shoals

BOB'S ANTIQUES
   Rte 1, Box 199   29692
   803 861-2362   Est: 1950
   Proprietor: Robert W
   Finethy
   Hours: By Appointment,
   By Chance
Types & Periods: American,
Early American, Victorian,
Sheraton, Empire 19th
Century Oak, China,
Paintings, Rugs, "Anything
& Everything"
Appraisal Service Available
   Directions: 32 Miles S of
   Greenville on Hwy 25 or 3
   Miles N of Ware Shoals on
   Hwy 25

Dresser with mirror, Late Victorian. This was one of the less expensive pieces being manufactured at that time.

STATE OF SOUTH DAKOTA

Aberdeen

TRADING POST
123-8th Ave NW   57401
605 229-4452   Est: 1971
Proprietor: Gina L Witte
Hours: Daily
Types & Periods: Furniture,
Glass, Primitives, Books,
Magazines, General Line,
Lamps
Appraisal Service Available

Big Stone City

NOLL'S ANTIQUES
Main St   57216
605 862-8395   Est: 1969
Proprietor: Patty Noll
Hours: Daily, By
Appointment, By Chance
Types & Periods: General
Line, Primitives, China,
Jewelry, Clothing, Furniture
Directions: Behind the
Bank on Hwy 12

Black Hawk

NEW PLACE
913 Hwy 79,
Box 148   57718
605 342-9928   Est: 1968
Proprietor: Marvin &
Janice Reiners
Hours: Mon-Fri 8-5, Sat by
Chance
Types & Periods: Furniture
as is or will restore, From
1870-1940
Specialties: Bix Furniture
Stripping & Restoring
Directions: 1 Mile N of
Dog Track, Hwy 79

Freeman

COUNTRY ANTIQUES
R R 3, Box 141   57029
605 925-7203   Est: 1962
Proprietor: Calvin J
Preheim
Hours: Mon-Sat, Sun by
Appointment, By Chance

Types & Periods: Furniture,
Lamps, Clocks, Glass,
Primitives, Many Small Items
Directions: 1½ Miles S
and 3½ Miles E of
Freeman

Gettysburg

**MIDWEST MUSEUM &
ANTIQUE SHOP**
601 W Garfield   57442
605 765-2762   Est: 1976
Proprietor: Gene Sloat
Hours: Daily, By
Appointment, By Chance
from Dec to Feb
Types & Periods: All Types
from any period,
Turn-of-the-Century
Specialties: Primitives,
Glassware, Furniture
Directions: W Hwy 212
near edge of city

Hot Springs

BESSIE'S ANTIQUES
321 N River St   57747
605 745-3482   Est: 1969
Proprietor: Lyle & Alice
Reis
Hours: Mon-Sat,
Sometimes Gone
Types & Periods: General
Line
Directions: On Hwy 385,
Main St

PIONEER TRADING CO
346 S Chicago   57747
605 745-5252   Est: 1976
Proprietor: John W
Stanley
Hours: Mon-Sat 8-5:30
Types & Periods: Indian &
Western Art, Primitives
Specialties: Buyers of Gold,
Silver, Indian, Western Items

Piedmont

PIEDMONT EMPORIUM
PO Box 126   57769
605 787-4700   Est: 1973

Proprietor: James A &
Dorothy C Schmitendorf
Hours: Daily
Types & Periods: Western,
Early American
Appraisal Service Available
Directions: On I-90
Service Road

Rapid City

CALICO CAT ANTIQUES
810 Columbus   57701
605 343-1350   Est: 1976
Proprietor: Barbara & Dick
Shilvock
Hours: Mon-Sat
Types & Periods: Furniture,
Primitives, Paper Goods
(Victorian)
Appraisal Service Available

MORVILLE ANTIQUES
1406 Mt Rushmore Rd
    57701
605 342-5017
Proprietor: W Peterson G
Corning
Hours: Mon & Sat
Types & Periods: General
Line

Sioux Falls

**ANTIQUES GALLERY
MIDWEST**
1502 W 10th St   57104
605 334-3051   Est: 1964
Proprietor: Dean & Mary
Nasser
Hours: Mon-Sat 10-5
Types & Periods: Glassware,
China, Furniture, Books,
Oriental Rugs, General Line
Appraisal Service Available
Directions: Corner of 10th
St & W Ave

CAROLYN ANTIQUES
434 W 5th St   57104
605 335-6035   Est: 1966
Proprietor: Carolyn
Steensma
Hours: Mon-Sat 12-5
Types & Periods: Furniture,
General Line

Appraisal Service Available
Directions: Near
Downtown Business Area

CAROLYN ANTIQUES
Rte 2, Box 54 C   57104
605 338-8919   Est: 1978
Proprietor: Carolyn
Steensma
Hours: By Appointment,
By Chance
Types & Periods: Furniture,
General Line
Appraisal Service Available
Directions: E of City on
Hwy 11 N

**CUMMINGS ENTERPRISES
INC**
300 S Lewis   57103
605 336-3398   Est: 1959
Proprietor: E J Cummings
Hours: Mon-Fri 8-6, Sat
9-12, By Appointment
Types & Periods:
Coin-Operated Slot
Machines, Juke Boxes,
Counter Games, Vendors,
Advertising of all types,
unusual items
Specialties: Coin-Operated
Machines
Appraisal Service Available
Directions: I-229 to 10th
St Exit, Go W 7 blocks to
Lewis Ave, Go S 1 block
to 300 Lewis

**HATTIE'S STAINED GLASS
AND THINGS**
4200 S Minnesota   57105
605 339-1111   Est: 1978
Proprietor: Gary
Hartenhoff
Hours: Daily 10-8, Sun
11-5

Types & Periods: Stained &
Beveled Glass, Furniture
Directions: 3 blocks S of
I-229 on S Minnesota Ave,
S Edge of Sioux Falls

**KOLBE'S CLOCKS &
REPAIR**
1301 S Duluth   57105
605 332-9662   Est: 1971
Proprietor: Robert Kolbe
Hours: Mon-Fri,
Afternoons & Mon Night
Types & Periods: Clocks,
Watches, General Line
Appraisal Service Available

**MAXWELL HOUSE
ANTIQUES**
612 W 4th St   57104
605 334-3640   Est: 1960
Proprietor: Paul Maxwell
Hours: Daily 12-5, Closed
Sun
Types & Periods: Cut Glass,
Sterling Flatware, General
Line
Appraisal Service Available

TUCKERS ANTIQUES
2100 N Drive   57101
                  Est: 1972
Proprietor: Steve & Lore
Tucker
Hours: Daily
Types & Periods: Oak,
Primitives, Walnut,
Glassware
Specialties: Oak, The
Unusual
Appraisal Service Available
Directions: 2 blocks past
Pen on Hwy 77 N of Sioux
Falls

Spearfish

**ANTIQUE AND UNIQUE
SHOPPE**
745 5th St   57783
605 642-4941   Est: 1974
Proprietor: Lawrence &
Terry Larive
Hours: Sun 1-6, Tues-Sat
10-6, Closed Dec 24,
April 1st, By Appointment
Types & Periods:
Depression, Cut, Pressed
Pattern Glass, Oak
Furniture, Aladdin Lamps,
Primitives, Pottery, Indian
Artifacts, Persian Rugs,
Books, Guns, Cars,
European Antiques
Directions: I-90 Exit 12

Bentwood chair.
Pressed wood bottom.

STATE OF TENNESSEE

Adams

BELL WITCH VILLAGE
37010
Est: 1976
Proprietor: Ken & Nina
Seeley
Hours: Mon-Fri, 10-6; Sun,
2-6
Types & Periods: Victorian
in Walnut, Cherry &
Mahogany, Oak Furniture,
Primitives, Accessories,
Glassware, Silver Tea
Services, Punch Bowl Sets
Appraisal Service Available
Directions: 40 miles N of
Nashville

Chattanooga

CATHY'S ANTIQUES
5520 Hwy 153   37443
615 877-7340   Est: 1969
Proprietor: Mr & Mrs C E
Bailey
Hours: Mon-Sat, 10-5
Types & Periods: Early
American, Victorian
Specialties: Player Pianos,
Brass Cash Registers,
Wicker
Directions: 1 mile N of
Northgate Mall Shopping
Center

DWIGHT'S AUCTION
2100 Chamberlain Ave
37404
615 622-9333   Est: 1970
Proprietor: Col Dwight
Branham & Col Terry
Branham
Hours: By chance, Auction
on Fri Twice a Month
Types & Periods: General
Line, Glassware, Furniture &
Collectibles
Directions: Corner of
Chamberlain & Willow St

REED & SON ANTIQUES
2435 S Broad St   37408
615 267-2535   Est: 1951
Proprietor: Travis S Reed
Hours: Mon-Sat, 9-5:30;
Sun, 12-5:30
Types & Periods: Oriental
Rugs, Furniture, Clocks,
Bric-A-Brac
Specialties: Rugs (Persian)
Directions: 24 Expwy to
Broad St Exit, turn right

WHEELER'S ANTIQUES
Chattanooga Valley Rd
37409
404 820-2528   Est: 1955
Proprietor: C H Wheeler
Hours: Mon-Sat
Types & Periods: Primitives,
General Line
Specialties: Primitive
Furniture
Directions: S on St Elmo
Ave to Chattanooga Valley
Rd

Clarksville

**NEW PROVIDENCE
ANTIQUES**
1300 Ft Campbell Blvd
37040
615 647-0809
Hours: Mon-Sat, 9-5
Types & Periods: General
Line

Collegedale

**THE OLDE ENGLISH
COTTAGE**
128 Cliff Dr   37315
615 396-2703   Est: 1970
Proprietor: Mrs Charles E
Read
Hours: Sun-Tues,
Thurs-Fri, 10-6, Wed by
appointment
Types & Periods: 19th
Century English, American,
French Furniture, China,
Glass
Directions: Apison Pike to
Tallant Rd to Collegeview
Dr to Cliff Dr

Franklin

**HERITAGE HOUSE
ANTIQUES**
646 Columbia Ave   37064
615 794-8024   Est: 1971
Hours: Mon-Sat
Types & Periods: Period
Pieces, European, American,
Silver, China, Accessories
Appraisal Service Available
Directions: Next door to
Historical "Carter House"

PEBBLESTONE COURT
Town Sq   37064
615 794-3618   Est: 1965
Proprietor: Marjorie Ewin
Hours: Daily, 9:30-5:30
Types & Periods: 17th, 18th
& 19th Century English &
American

RACK & RUIN INC
237 2nd Ave S   37064
615 790-0691   Est: 1974
Proprietor: George Zeigler
Hours: Mon-Sat, 9:30-5;
also by appointment; Sun
by chance
Types & Periods: Stained
Glass Windows, Mantels,
Doors
Specialties: Architectural
Antiques
Appraisal Service Available
Directions: 3 blocks S of
city square

RED CARPET ANTIQUES
915 Columbia Ave   37064
615 794-7003   Est: 1965
Proprietor: Mrs S Ralph
Brown
Hours: Mon-Sat; Sun and
evenings by appointment
Types & Periods: 18th &
19th Century English &
Continental Furniture, Art
Objects, Accessories
Directions: 2 blocks S of
Post Office on Columbia
Ave, across from College
Grove Bank

SINCLAIR ANTIQUE SHOP
136 4th Ave S   37064
615 794-6968   Est: 1928
Proprietor: Linie Sinclair
Hours: Daily
Types & Periods: Primitives,
Collectors Items

Gallatin

GALLATIN ANTIQUE MALL
450 W Main St   37066
615 452-6538   Est: 1975
Proprietor: Dr Thos
Arrendale & Dr Jas
Bowman
Hours: Mon-Sat, 10-5;
Sun, 1-5
Types & Periods: General
Line, Primitives,
Reproduction Cherry
Specialties: Oak, Custom
Framing
    Directions: 31 E, 1/2 mile
    from town square

Germantown

**MICHELLE B BABCOCK
ANTIQUES & INTERIORS**
7715 Dogwood Rd   38138
901 754-9806   Est: 1972
Proprietor: Michelle B
Babcock
Hours: By appointment
only
Types & Periods: 18th &
19th Century Furnishings
Appraisal Service Available
    Directions: 100 yards E of
    intersection of
    Germantown Rd &
    Dogwood

**MILDRED & CHARLES A
BAIRD**
2206 Johnson Rd   38138
901 754-6700   Est: 1973
Proprietor: Charles A
Baird
Hours: Daily, anytime by
appointment
Types & Periods: Middle
1800's to 1910, General Line
    Directions: Hwy 72 E thru
    Germantown, left on
    Johnson Rd

**NELSIE ANDERSON
MULKINS**
9336 Poplar   38138
901 754-7909   Est: 1906
Proprietor: Mrs Nelsie
Mulkins
Hours: Mon-Sat, Sun by
appointment
Types & Periods: Victorian,
Queen Anne, Chippendale,
General Line
Specialties: Furniture (Dining
Chairs)
    Directions: 4 miles E of
    town, corner of Johnson &
    Poplar

Hixson

CLEMENTS ANTIQUES INC
7022 Dayton Pke   37343
615 842-4177
Proprietor: Charles W
Clements
Hours: Mon-Fri, 9-6; Sat,
9-1
Types & Periods: 18th, 19th
Century English & French

Jackson

ANTIQUES ET CETERA
929 N Highland   38301
901 422-1392
Proprietor: Betty Y Harris
Hours: Daily, 10-5
Types & Periods: Furniture,
Glassware, General Line

Knoxville

KNOXVILLE CLUSTER
    Directions: Chapman Hwy
    SW, Kingston Pike NW
    (5000 Block), Kingston
    Pike SW (5000 Block),
    other shops scattered
    throughout city

AB & REX TRADING POST
817-819 Winona St NE
            37917
615 525-8543   Est: 1966
Hours: Mon-Sat, 9-4:30
Types & Periods: Furniture,
Glassware, Ironware,
Jewelry, Clocks, Knives
    Directions: 1 mile from
    I-40 & 1 mile NE of Gay St

**BROADWAY BARGAIN
BARN**
1931 N Broadway   37917
615 524-5221   Est: 1971
Proprietor: Fern Worley
Hours: Mon-Fri, 5:30-9:30;
Sat-Sun, 12-9
Types & Periods: Collector
Items, Primitives, Old
Records, Literature,
Furniture, Dolls
Specialties: Collectible Dolls
    Directions: Entrance to
    Broadway Shopping
    Center, 10 minutes from
    downtown area; Take
    Broadway Exit from I-40

CANNON ANTIQUES
4812 Asheville Hwy   37914
615 546-1844   Est: 1975
Proprietor: John Moulton
& Vernon Wohland
Hours: Daily
Types & Periods: Primitives,
Period Furniture in Walnut,
Oak & Mahogany, Art Glass,
Silver, Paintings, Jewelry
Appraisal Service Available
    Directions: Across from
    Holiday Inn

CATON'S ANTIQUE MART
6410 Chapman Hwy
            37920
615 577-9147   Est: 1975
Proprietor: Betty & Jim
Caton
Hours: Sun-Mon,
Thurs-Sat
Types & Periods: General
Line
    Directions: Henley St to
    Chapman Hwy off I-40 &
    I 75 junction S, out of
    Gatlinburg straight to
    Chapman

DOMINICKS ANTIQUES
5119 Kingston Pk   37919
            Est: 1967
Proprietor: Paul J
Dominick
Hours: Mon-Tues,
Thurs-Sat, 9:30-6
Types & Periods: English,
American, French (19th &
Early 20th Centuries)
Specialties: Furniture,
Restorations, Framing, Art
Objects, Accessories,
Antique Reproductions

Knoxville   Cont'd

DOMINICKS   Cont'd
Appraisal Service Available
  Directions: Kingston Pk at
  Bearden going W, Exit
  I-40 at Northshore Dr to
  Kingston Pk, turn left, 1
  mile on left

LITTLEWOOD ANTIQUES
  6004 Littlewood Terrace
                         37918
  615 688-2993   Est: 1971
  Proprietor: James H
  Barton
  Hours: Mon-Fri, 10-6; Sat
  & Sun, 2-6
Types & Periods: Walnut,
Victorian & American
Country Furniture
  Directions: Take
  Littlewood Terrace at E
  corner of
  Jacksboro-Broadway (US
  44) intersection, follow to
  dead end

NANNY AND SON
  5037 Park Glen Dr   37921
  615 584-3893   Est: 1975
  Proprietor: Henry G
  Waggoner Jr
  Hours: Fri-Sat, by
  appointment
Types & Periods: Glassware,
Antique Jewelry
Appraisal Service Available
  Directions: Off
  Middlebrook Pike across
  railroad

SELFE'S ANTIQUES
  4305 Chapman Hwy
                         37920
  615 577-0766   Est: 1963
  Proprietor: Joan H Selfe
  Hours: Mon-Sat, 9-5
Types & Periods: General
Line, Manufacture Round
Oak Tables, Pressed Back
Chairs
Appraisal Service Available
  Directions: US 441 S

**THIEVES MARKET
AUCTION & ANTIQUES**
  4900 Chambliss St   37919
  615 584-9641   Est: 1975
  Proprietor: Charles G
  Changas
  Hours: Daily
Types & Periods: Victorian,
Primitives, General Line

Appraisal Service Available
  Directions: 4900 block of
  Kingston Pike, next to
  Pero's Restaurant

Maryville

TIMELESS TREASURES
  1406 E Broadway   37801
  615 983-2424   Est: 1975
  Proprietor: Freda H
  Bennett
  Hours: Daily
Types & Periods: Victorian &
European Furniture, Glass,
Clocks, Lamps
  Directions: Old Knoxville
  Hwy near Five Points

Memphis

MEMPHIS CLUSTER
  Directions: City full of
  Antique Shops, especially
  on the following streets:
  Poplar (200-5000 Blocks),
  Sumner Ave (3000-5000
  Blocks), Madison Ave
  (1000 Block), as well as S
  Cooper, Union Ave, S
  Idlewild, Adams Ave &
  Lamar Ave

ANTIQUES WAREHOUSE
  544 Haymarket   38138
  901 767-9380
  Proprietor: Jean Ward
Types & Periods: English &
American Furniture, Oriental
Porcelain, Silks

BABCOCK GALLERIES INC
  2262 Germantown Rd S
                         38138
  901 754-7950   Est: 1977
  Proprietor: Bernice &
  Richard Hussey
  Hours: Mon-Sat, 9-5
Types & Periods: English
18th & Early 19th Centuries

CHINA TOWN IMPORTS
  1975 Union Ave   38104
  901 726-4272   Est: 1972
  Proprietor: William Y C
  Yan
  Hours: Mon-Sat, 9-6; by
  appointment
Types & Periods: Chinese
Antiques, Han, Ming &
Ching Dynasties

Specialties: Ivory, Cloisonne,
Jade, Bronze, Porcelain,
Clothing, Furniture, Jewelry
Appraisal Service Available
  Directions: Main E-W
  street in midtown

DENAUX INC
  1723 Union Ave   38138
  901 274-0037   Est: 1904
  Proprietor: Robert Dolan
  Hours: Mon-Fri, by
  appointment or by chance

ERNIE'S ANTIQUES
  1517 Madison Ave   38104
  901 272-3341   Est: 1968
  Proprietor: Ernest Heath
  Hours: Mon-Sat, 9:30-5
Types & Periods: Brass
Beds, Oak & Walnut
Wardrobes, Glassware,
China, Sterling, Dining
Room Tables, Chairs,
Buffets, China, Cabinets,
Dressers, Bric-A-Brac
Appraisal Service Available
  Directions: Midtown

JULIUS GOODMAN & SON
  113 Madison Ave   38103
  901 526-8528   Est: 1862
  Proprietor: Joseph A
  Goodman
  Hours: Sun-Fri, 9:30-5
Types & Periods: Sterling
Silver Flatware & Hollow
Ware, Jewelry
Appraisal Service Available
  Directions: Between
  Mid-American Mall &
  Second St

**H & R ANTIQUE
GALLERIES INC**
  1359 Madison Ave   38104
  901 725-9370   Est: 1968
  Proprietor: Howard &
  Rosenberg
  Hours: Mon-Sat, 10-5; also
  by appointment
Types & Periods: 17th &
18th Century Victorian,
Edwardian, French
Furniture, Brass, Copper,
Orientals, Paintings
  Directions: Corner of
  Madison & Cleveland, 3
  minutes W of Overton Sq

THE IDLEWILD HOUSE
  1044 S Yates Rd   38117
  901 682-1165   Est: 1974
  Proprietor: Virginia Barron
  Hours: Mon-Sat, 10-5

Types & Periods: 18th &
19th Century Furniture &
Accessories, English
Directions: E Memphis, S
of Poplar Ave, near I-240

**ISBELL, GERHARDT,
WOLFE INC**
162 S McLean Ave 38104
901 278-2290 Est: 1975
Proprietor: John Isbell,
Roland Gerhardt & Archie
Wolfe
Hours: Mon-Fri, 9-5
Types & Periods: Period
Furniture, Antique
Accessories, Porcelains,
American & European
Paintings & Bronzes,
Oriental Rugs
Specialties: Interior Design
Services
Appraisal Service Available
Directions: Midtown
Memphis at McLean &
Union Aves

KIMBROUGH INC
1400 Union Ave 38104
901 725-7154 Est. 1950
Proprietor: K C Kimbrough
Hours: Daily, 9-5; also by
appointment or by chance
Types & Periods: Georgian,
Early English Oak, French
Specialties: Chinese
Lacquers, Porcelains,
Screens
Directions: On main
thoroughfare

MASTERPIECE GALLERIES
2266 Central Ave 38104
901 272-1804 Est: 1966
Proprietor: David M
Parrish
Hours: Mon-Sat, 10-5
Types & Periods: Queen
Anne, Chippendale, English,
American, Stained Glass,
Bronzes, Brass
Specialties: Furniture
Directions: Midtown, I-240
to Poplar Ave to Central
Ave

THE MATCHMAKERS INC
1466 Harbert 38104
901 274-0310 Est: 1968
Proprietor: Aimee Alden
Hours: Mon-Sat; by
appointment
Types & Periods: Haviland &
Noritake China.

Discontinued & Antique
Patterns
Specialties: Sets & Matching
Pieces (China)
Appraisal Service Available
Directions: Central Garden
Area, phone for
appointment & directions

J H MEDNIKOW & CO INC
474 S Perkins Ext 38117
901 767-2100 Est: 1895
Proprietor: Robert M
Mednikow
Hours: Daily, 10-5
Types & Periods: Jewelry
Appraisal Service Available
Directions: E Memphis in
Laurelwood, vicinity of
Poplar & Perkins

THE OLD BARN ANTIQUES
5850 Summer 38128
916 388-4343 Est: 1969
Proprietor: Joseph E
Giaroli
Hours: Daily
Types & Periods: Brass
Beds, Glass, Furniture
Specialties: Brass Beds
Appraisal Service Available
Directions: 1 mile beyond
Penal Farm

**ROUND CORNER GIFT
SHOP**
191 N Belvedere 38104
901 726-5505 Est: 1965
Proprietor: Mr & Mrs F H
Mills
Hours: Mon-Sat
Types & Periods: Early
American & European
Specialties: Jewelry
Directions: Midtown area,
at the corner of Poplar &
Belvedere

**SISTER'S ANTIQUES &
GIFTS**
1971 Madison Ave 38104
901 725-4820 Est: 1966
Proprietor: Mary Arnette
Tagg
Hours: Mon-Sat, 10-5; Sun
by appointment
Types & Periods: Furniture,
Silver, Porcelain, Collectibles
Directions: 2 blocks W of
Overton Square

**SLENKER & KIRKPATRICK
INC**
1500 Union Ave 38104
Est: 1969

Proprietor: Joe L
Kirkpatrick
Hours: Daily
Types & Periods: 18th &
19th Century English,
Oriental Screens,
Porcelains, Accessories
Appraisal Service Available

**SOUTHERN GENTLEMEN'S
ANTIQUES**
1695-99 Poplar Ave 38104
901 726-9671 Est: 1976
Proprietor: John W
Schuerman
Hours: Tues-Sat, 9:30-5:30
Types & Periods: General
Line
Specialties: Refinishing
Directions: S side of
Poplar between Evergreen
& Belvedere

SPIVACK'S ANTIQUES
1712 Madison Ave 38104
901 726-5633 Est: 1926
Proprietor: Mrs Dean
Jordan
Hours: Mon-Fri, 10-4:30;
weekends by appointment
Types & Periods: English &
American 18th Century
Furniture, Accessories,
Bric-A-Brac
Specialties: Furniture
Directions: Madison at
Belvedere, about 10
blocks E of I-240, Exit
Union E or Madison W

SPRINGER ANTIQUES
1708 Union Ave 38104
901 726-4585 Est: 1968
Proprietor: Henry N &
Grace R Springer
Hours: Mon-Sat, 9-5
Types & Periods: 18th &
19th Century American &
English Furniture
Specialties: Furniture
(Queen Anne &
Chippendale)
Appraisal Service Available
Directions: 3 miles from
downtown on the main
artery running E-W

STATEN'S ANTIQUES
1965 Madison 38104
901 726-5358 Est: 1935
Proprietor: Mr & Mrs W E
Staten
Hours: Daily, 9-5

Memphis   Cont'd

STATEN'S   **Cont'd**

Types & Periods: American,
English, French, Oriental
Specialties: Furniture
Appraisal Service Available

**SURATT'S ANTIQUES &
INTERIORS**
1830 Poplar Ave   38104
901 726-4521   Est: 1967
Proprietor: Bob R Suratt
Hours: Mon-Sat, 9-6; Sun,
1-6
Types & Periods: Antique
Jewelry, Cut Glass, Art
Glass, Lamps, Clocks,
China, American Furniture
Specialties: Antique Jewelry
Appraisal Service Available
Directions: Midtown near
Overton Square &
Memphis Zoo

**SURATT'S ANTIQUES &
INTERIORS**
34 S McLean Blvd   38104
901 725-6602
Proprietor: Bob R Suratt
Hours: By appointment
only
Types & Periods: Antique
Jewelry, Cut Glass, Art
Glass, Lamps, Clocks,
China, American Furniture
Specialties: Antique Jewelry
Appraisal Service Available

WHAT NOT SHOP
2607 Broad   38112
901 327-8551   Est: 1969
Proprietor: Bonner &
Rodgers
Hours: Mon, Thurs & Sat,
10-4; also by appointment
Types & Periods: Period
Clothing, Furniture, Books
Directions: Near Overton
Park

Murfreesboro

**ARNETTE ANTIQUE
GALLERIES**
300 W Castle St   37130
615 893-3725   Est: 1960
Proprietor: C B Arnette
Hours: Daily
Types & Periods: Furniture,
European Imports, China,
Glass, Clocks, Paintings

Specialties: Furniture,
Paintings
Appraisal Service Available
Directions: Hwy 231 Exit
from I-24, go
approximately 1½ miles to
Castle

JONES ANTIQUES
Riverside Rte 3   37130
615 893-8583
Proprietor: Sarah &
Claude Jones
Hours: Daily, 9-6
Types & Periods: Furniture,
China, Cut Glass, Mirrors,
Jewelry

Nashville

NASHVILLE CLUSTER
Directions: Heavy
concentration of shops on
Hillsboro Rd (3000-4000
Blocks), fair number on
Gallatin Rd (1000-4000
Blocks), Nolensville Rd
(2000-3000 Blocks), 8th
Ave S (1000-2000 Blocks),
Marfreesboro Rd
(600-1000 Blocks), &
others scattered
throughout city

**EVELYN ANDERSON
GALLERIES**
6043 Hwy 100   37205
615 352-6770   Est: 1956
Proprietor: Evelyn
Anderson
Hours: Mon-Sat, 10-5
Types & Periods: 18th &
19th Century English &
French Furniture, Porcelain,
Paintings, Accessories,
Lamps, Gifts
Specialties: Furniture,
Porcelain, Paintings
Directions: Intersection of
70 & 100 on the W side of
city, in Westgate Center

BEE GEE'S
2225 Bandywood Dr
                      37204
615 269-9378   Est: 1973
Proprietor: Gennette
Norman
Hours: Mon-Sat
Types & Periods: English
Furniture, Beveled & Stained
Glass Windows, Ivory &

Jade Jewelry, Crystal,
Porcelain, Oriental Rugs
Directions: Green Hills
area, Hillsboro Rd to
Abbott Martin, turn right,
first street on left is
Bandywood, in back of
Jac's Gallery

**BRADFORD FURNITURE CO
INC**
4100 Hillsboro Rd   37215
615 297-3541   Est: 1889
Proprietor: Corporation
Hours: Mon-Sat
Types & Periods: Primarily
18th Century English
Furniture
Directions: Green Hills,
Rte 231 to Franklin

BRIC-A-BRAC SHOP
629 W Iris Dr   37204
615 292-8581   Est: 1977
Proprietor: Earl W Hicks
Hours: Mon-Sat
Types & Periods: Furniture,
Glassware, Bric-A-Brac
Directions: Near 100 Oaks
Shopping Center, turn off
Thompson Lane at
Plantlan

ELDER'S BOOK STORE
22nd & Church Sts 37203
615 327-1867   Est: 1951
Proprietor: Charles Elder
& Randy Elder
Hours: Mon-Sat
Types & Periods: Old & Rare
Books, Memorabilia of the
Civil War, Antique
Glassware, Brass
Specialties: Books &
Memorabilia of the Civil War
Appraisal Service Available
Directions: Corner of 22nd
& Church, Exit on Church
W from I-40-265, turn W, 9
blocks on the left

FAIRBANKS ANTIQUES
7330 Charlotte Ave 37209
615 352-1692   Est: 1955
Proprietor: Harry
Fairbanks
Hours: Daily, by
appointment
Types & Periods: General
Line
Directions: 2 blocks off
I-40 W on Hwy 70 N

FARM HOUSE ANTIQUES
1101 Otter Creek Rd
        37220
615 832-1611
Proprietor: Eloise Jeffries
Hours: Fri, Sat & Sun;
weekdays by appointment
Types & Periods: Period
Country Furniture, Pewter,
Folk Art, Early Pottery
Specialties: Rugs (Hooked),
Weather Vanes, Samplers
Directions: Halfway
between Franklin Pike,
above Radnor Lake, "Best
to call & get directions"

**FOREHAND'S ANTIQUE
SHOP**
4120 Gallatin Rd   37216
615 262-2215   Est: 1946
Proprietor: Mrs Bessie
Forehand
Hours: Daily
Types & Periods: Furniture,
China, Lamps, Pictures
Specialties: China, Furniture
Directions: Hwy 31 E, 4
blocks S of Briley Pkwy, 1
mile from Opry Lane, 5
miles from city of
Nashville

GRANNY'S ATTIC
2911 Granny White Pike
        37204
615 297-8633   Est: 1965
Proprietor: Beatrice
Austell
Hours: Tues-Sat, 12-6;
other times by
appointment
Types & Periods: Primitives,
China, Glass, Jewelry
Appraisal Service Available
Directions: Across road
from Sevier Park

**GREEN HILLS ANTIQUE
MALL**
3716 Hillsboro Rd   37215
615 292-4691   Est: 1973
Proprietor: Frank St
Charles Jr
Hours: Tues-Sat,
9:30-5:30; Sun, 2-5
Types & Periods:
Americana, Imports,
Engravings of Revolutionary
War Patriots
Appraisal Service Available
Directions: Lower level of
Coleman Bldg, behind
Fidelity Federal

TED LELAND INC
4012 Hillsboro Rd   37215
615 385-0612   Est: 1965
Proprietor: Ted Leland
Hours: Daily, 9-5
Types & Periods: 17th, 18th
& 19th Century French &
English
Specialties: Art, Georgian,
Silver
Directions: Green Hills
area

**NASHVILLE VENTAGE
DEPT STORE**
1905 W End Ave   37203
615 329-1751   Est: 1977
Proprietor: Randy Rogers
& John Bell
Hours: Mon-Sat, by
appointment
Types & Periods: Clothing,
Furniture, Glassware,
Accessories, Books,
Jewelry, Furs
Specialties: Florist & Plant
Shop
Directions: Across from
Flaming Steer Restaurant
opposite side of the street,
at 19th & W End Ave

**NICHOLS GARDEN
CENTER**
3950 Dickerson Rd   37207
615 865-1472
Proprietor: Mrs Sam O
Nichols
Hours: Daily
Types & Periods: Glass,
Walnut Furniture, Spinet
Desks, Dressers
Specialties: Cut Glass,
Pattern Glass
Directions: Hwy 31 N, 1/4
mile N of Old Hickory
Blvd, left side of Hwy

THE OLD & NEW HOUSE
2320 W End Ave   37203
615 329-2016   Est: 1975
Proprietor: Howard J Tellis
Hours: Mon-Sat, 9-6; Sun,
1-5
Types & Periods: Victorian
Era & Earlier
Specialties: Glass (Art &
Cut)
Appraisal Service Available
Directions: On Rte 70 thru
Nashville, across from
Vanderbilt University

**OUT-OF-DATE: ANTIQUES
AND COLLECTIBLES**
1803 Church St   37203
615 327-0628   Est: 1977
Proprietor: James L
Collins
Hours: Mon-Sat, 10-6
Types & Periods: Art Deco,
American & English
Furniture, Jewelry, Records,
Framed Prints, Brass, Glass,
Porcelain, Pottery
Specialties: Art Deco, Oriental
Appraisal Service Available
Directions: 10 blocks from
downtown Nashville at
18th Ave N & Church St

KEATH POYNER ANTIQUES
4012 Hillsboro Rd   37215
615 269-6230   Est: 1970
Proprietor: Keath Poyner
Hours: Tues-Sat, 10-5
Types & Periods: 18th &
19th Century English &
American Furniture,
Accessories, Paintings,
Oriental Rugs, Nostalgia
Directions: In Morehead
Center Rear Ct, next to
Bavarian Village, in the
Green Hills Shopping Area

**TEMPTATION INTERIORS &
ANTIQUE GALLERY**
2410 Belmont Blvd   37212
615 297-7412   Est: 1961
Proprietor: Rodd Nelson &
Jay Bradley
Hours: Mon-Sat, 9:30-5;
Sun by appointment
Types & Periods: 18th &
19th Century Furniture,
Silver, Porcelain, Bronze,
Paintings, Oriental Rugs
Appraisal Service Available
Directions: Music City &
University area

TRACE TAVERN ANTIQUES
8456 Hwy 100   37221
615 646-5600   Est: 1969
Proprietor: Malvern &
Delle Brown
Hours: Mon-Sat, 10-5;
Sun, 1-5
Types & Periods: American
Antique Furniture of 18th &
19th Centuries (William &
Mary through Empire)
Specialties: Antique Silver
Appraisal Service Available
Directions: From I-40 W,
take Exit 192, then S on
McCrory Lane 4 miles to
shop

Oak Ridge

LOHREY'S ANTIQUES
Box 426   37830
615 435-0228   Est: 1972
Proprietor: Donald D
Lohrey
Hours: Tues-Sun, 10-8
Types & Periods: General
Line, Collectibles, Primitives
Appraisal Service Available
Directions: Junction Hwy
62 & 61, between Oak
Ridge & Oliver Springs

Oliver Springs

J'S ANTIQUE MALL
875 Tri County Blvd 37840
615 435-0018
Proprietor: J B & Sara
Ogle
Hours: Tues-Sun, 10-8
Types & Periods: General
Line, 30 Dealers
Directions: On Hwys 61 &
62, just outside Oak
Ridge, just across from
the Tri County Shopping
Center in Oliver Springs

Ridgely

ANNE'S ANTIQUES
454 W College   38080
901 264-5967
Proprietor: Jere H & Anne
W Lucas
Hours: By appointment
Types & Periods: Cut & Art
Glass, Porcelain, General
Line

Springfield

**ANNE'S BEAUTY SHOP &
ANTIQUES**
708 Main   37172
615 384-3074
Proprietor: Anne G Hand
Hours: Mon-Tues,
Thurs-Sat, by appointment
Types & Periods: Country
Pieces, Brass, Iron, Copper,
Glassware, Picture Frames,
General Line
Directions: 30 miles N of
Nashville, off I-65 &
I-24 W

Union City

**SALLY MC ADOO
ANTIQUES**
Old Lake Rd   38261
901 885-3446
Proprietor: Sally McAdoo
Hours: Daily, 9-5
Types & Periods: General
Line

Halltree, cast iron,
Late Victorian.

STATE OF TEXAS

Abilene

BIVENS ANTIQUES
625 E N 18th   79601
915 677-1200   Est: 1970
Proprietor: A J Bivens
Hours: Daily
Types & Periods: Clocks,
Furniture
Specialties: Clocks (Repair)
Directions: 1 Block W of
Abilene Christian Univ

LAS MARGIE'S ANTIQUES
7 Burro Alley   79605
915 673-7512   Est: 1966
Proprietor: Margie Wells
Hours: Daily 10-5
Types & Periods: Furniture,
Glass, China, Dolls, Oriental
Items, Jewelry
Specialties: Jewelry
Appraisal Service Available
Directions: W Side of
Abilene on S 1st St, In
Burro Alley Shopping
Center

MARBLE INC
5425 E Hwy 80   79604
915 673-7909   Est: 1957
Proprietor: A D Lewis, Jr
Hours: Mon-Sat
Types & Periods: English,
Early American, Depression
Glass, Primitives
Specialties: Cut Marble Tops
Or Any Type Of Marble
Work
Directions: E On E Hwy 80
to Entrance onto I-20,
Marble Inc is on Right
Opposite Entrance

THE MILL ANTIQUES
239 Locust   79602
915 672-1432   Est: 1970
Proprietor: Earle &
Eualice McMillan
Hours: Tues-Sat 12-5,
Also By Appointment
Types & Periods: Furniture,
Glass, Brass, Clocks,
Imported European Antiques
Specialties: Largest
European Importer of
Antiques in West Texas

Appraisal Service Available
Directions: 2 Blocks E of
Old Court House, Located
in an Old Converted 5
Story Feed Mill

Addison

**HOWARD GREEN
ANTIQUES**
15289 Addison Rd   75001
214 239-1610   Est: 1951
Proprietor: Howard & Judy
Green
Hours: Tue-Sat 8:30-5,
Closed Sun, Mon By
Chance
Types & Periods: Furniture,
Mirrors, Copper, Brass,
Accessories
Specialties: Refinishing
Directions: 2 Miles W of
Preston Rd, 1/2 Block N
of Belt Line Rd, S of
Addison Airport

Alvin

THE ARBOR
Hwy 35 Bypass N   77511
713 331-5670   Est: 1977
Proprietor: Catherine
Coker
Hours: Tues-Sat 10-4
Types & Periods:
Collectibles, American Oak,
European
Directions: Hwy 35
Bypass, Just N of F M 528

Amarillo

AMARILLO CLUSTER
Directions: Amarillo Blvd
to W 16th Ave (3000
Block)

ANTIQUES & NOSTALGIA
3317 W 6th   79106
806 373-0185   Est: 1972
Proprietor: John T
Gassaway
Hours: Mon-Sat 11-6,
Closed Sun

Types & Periods: Furniture,
Nostalgic Items, Comics
Specialties: Magazines,
(Comic)
Appraisal Service Available
Directions: Old Rte 66,
Down 6th St

GOLDEN ANTIQUES
1006 Amarillo Blvd E
79107
806 372-0933   Est: 1973
Proprietor: Dean & Don
Wagner
Hours: Mon-Sat
10:30-5:30, Closed Sun
Types & Periods: Queen
Anne, Sheraton, Louie XV,
Victorian, Chippendale, Oak,
Furniture, Figurines, Clocks,
Cut, Art, Pressed Glass,
China, Jewelry, Lamps
Specialties: Jewelry, Glass,
Furniture
Appraisal Service Available
Directions: Amarillo Blvd,
or Old Hwy 66, Across the
St from Casa De Real
Motel

MILLER'S ANTIQUES
205 Western   79106
806 359-1001   Est: 1972
Proprietor: Bill & Barbara
Miller
Hours: Mon-Sat 9:30-5:30,
Closed Sun
Types & Periods: General
Line, Furniture, Clocks,
Glassware, Primitives
Specialties: Service Available

THIS'N THAT
5503 Andrews   79106
806 355-3285
Proprietor: Kathryn
Shapiro
Hours: By Appointment
Types & Periods: Art & Cut
Glass, General Line

THE THREE PINES
2901 Julian Blvd   79102
806 374-4959
Proprietor: F L & G H
Matthews
Types & Periods: Cut & Art
Glass

Arlington

BEA'S COUNTRY SHOP
4200 S Cooper   76015
817 274-0110   Est: 1966
Proprietor: Robert C
Woltemate
Hours: Daily, Weekends
Types & Periods: Primitives,
Art Glass, Copper, Brass
Directions: 150 Ft N of
I-20

LE VI'S ANTIQUES
1106 W Abram St   76013
817 261-8109   Est: 1975
Proprietor: Leland & Vida
Spencer
Hours: Mon-Sat, Also By
Appointment
Types & Periods: General
Line, Glass & Ceramics,
Depression Glass, Inkwells,
Furniture
Specialties: Depression
Glass
Directions: 2 Blocks S of
Division (Old Hwy 80)
Between Cooper St &
Davis Dr

**NOEL'S ANTIQUES &
GIFTS**
2230 W Park Row   76013
817 275-9323   Est: 1974
Proprietor: Noel Smith
Hours: Daily
Types & Periods: General
Line
Specialties: Clocks,
Primitives
Directions: 2 Blocks E of
Bowen & W Park Row, N
of 303

FAYE PATTERSON
1406 Cherokee   76012
Proprietor: Faye Patterson
Hours: Shows Only

**BETTYE SWEENEY
ANTIQUES**
6110 Ken Ave   76016
817 572-0225
Proprietor: Bettye & Dave
Sweeney
Hours: Mon-Sat 10-5,
Closed Sun
Types & Periods: General
Line, Glass, Primitives,
Furniture

Athens

OLDEN DAZE ANTIQUES
717 E Tyler   75751
214 675-1991   Est: 1977
Proprietor: Holly & John
Jones
Hours: Mon-Sat 9-5, Also
By Appointment
Types & Periods: 18th, 19th,
& 20th Century Pieces With
An Emphasis On Decorative
Potential
Appraisal Service Available
Directions: Hwy 31 E, 2
Blocks E of Courthouse

Austin

AUSTIN CLUSTER
Directions: Funnelling N
from Business District
around W 6th St, Along
Lamar Blvd (N-S) to Jct
183 & W Anderson Ln

ACCENT ALLEY
2207 Hancock Dr   78756
512 454-6565   Est: 1975
Proprietor: Irene S
Johnson
Hours: Tues-Sat 10-5,
Closed Sun & Mon
Types & Periods: General
Line, Foreign Collector
Dolls, Primitives,
Collectibles, Prints,
Paintings, Contempory Art
Specialties: Small Furniture,
Accessories, Antique &
Estate Jewelry,1850-Art Deco
Directions: 1 Block W of
Burnet Rd, Across From
American Theater

ANABLEPS-ANABLEPS
507 W 17th   78701
512 474-4107   Est: 1975
Proprietor: Ralph J Moore
Hours: Mon-Sat 11-6,
Closed Sun, Also By
Appointment
Types & Periods: Artifacts,
Art Imports
Specialties: Jewelry,
(Tibetan), Oriental Art
Directions: Btwn San
Antonio & Nueces Sts

ANTEDILUVIAN ANTIQUES
1002 Rio Grande   78701
512 476-5183   Est: 1973
Proprietor: Bruce A Safley
Hours: Wed-Sat 11-5, Also
By Appointment
Types & Periods: 18th &
19th Century American &
Texas Furniture &
Accessories
Specialties: American
Painted Country Furniture,
Folk Art, Quilts
Directions: 6 blocks W of
the Capitol & 2 blocks S

**DEACON'S BENCH
ANTIQUES**
701 W St Johns   78752
512 454-1090   Est: 1974
Proprietor: John F Hunter
Hours: Mon-Sat 9-6
Types & Periods:
Turn-of-the-Century
American Oak, Pine,
Handmade Eastern & Texas
Preen, Clocks, Tins, Quilts
Directions: N Austin Area,
4 Blocks off I-39

F B'S JEWELS & THINGS
4211 Duval   78751
Est: 1967
Proprietor: Frances
Blakemore
Hours: By Chance
Types & Periods: Jewelry,
Bisque & China Dolls
Specialties: Toys (Dolls &
Costumes for Dolls)
Appraisal Service Available
Directions: I-35 to 38 1/2
St Exit W to Duval

FANNTIQUES
1502 Princeton Ave 78757
512 459-5237   Est: 1970
Proprietor: Keeler Fann
Hours: By Appointment,
By Chance
Types & Periods:
Collectibles, Furniture,
Pattern Glass, Jewelry,
Lighting, Primitives
Directions: Exit I-35 at E
Anderson Ln, W to
Woodrow Ave then 3
Blocks S

HAMPTON HOUSE GALLERIES
504 W 12th St   78745
512 476-4987   Est: 1972
Proprietor: R H Johnson
Hours: Tues-Fri 10-5, Sat 10-2, Closed Sun-Mon, Also By Appointment
Types & Periods: 18th & 19th Century French & English Objets d'Art
Directions: 5 Blocks W of State Capitol Bldg

HURT'S HUNTING GROUNDS
712 Red River   78701
512 472-7680   Est: 1971
Proprietor: Brian & Brenda Hurt
Hours: Mon-Sat 10-5, Closed Sun
Types & Periods: General Line
Specialties: Furniture
Directions: Between 7th & 8th Sts

I E BOUQUET
1802 La Vaca   78701
512 474-1248   Est: 1972
Proprietor: Jane Thomas
Hours: Tues-Sat 10-4, Closed Sun & Mon, Also By Appointment on Mon
Types & Periods: 18th, 19th & 20th Century French Furniture, Bric-A-Brac
Specialties: Porcelains
Directions: 4 Blocks N & 2 Blocks W of the Capitol

N E MERCANTILE CO
4526 Red River   78751
512 451-4986   Est: 1971
Proprietor: Jay & Helen Knowles
Hours: By Appointment, By Chance
Types & Periods: Paper Americana, Books, Comic Books, Big Little Books, Art Deco, Art Nouveau Prints
Appraisal Service Available
Directions: Corner of Red River & 46th St

RUE DE LAMAR GALLERY
5115 N Lamar   78751
512 451-3322   Est: 1969
Proprietor: Wm O & Mary McCluskey
Hours: Daily

Types & Periods: Louis XV Furniture, Oriental Rugs, China, Glass, Sideboards, Etageres, Mirrors
Specialties: Fern Stands, Piano Benches, Sideboards
Appraisal Service Available
Directions: At 51st St

SANDY'S ANTIQUES
506 Walsh   78703
512 478-3346   Est: 1972
Hours: Mon-Fri 8-5:30, Sat 8-4, Closed Sun
Types & Periods: Brass Beds, Rolltop Desks, Furniture
Directions: 1200 Block W 6th St

SOUTHWEST ANTIQUE GALLERY
3310 Red River   78705
512 476-3634   Est: 1964
Proprietor: W C Attal Jr
Hours: Mon-Sat, Closed Sun
Types & Periods: Early Texas Furniture, Victorian, Turn-of-the-Century Oak
Specialties: Books, Prints, Audubon Lithographs, Maps
Appraisal Service Available
Directions: 1 Block W of 32nd & I-35

MARY STINCHCOMB ANTIQUES
608A W 12th   78701
512 476-1638
Proprietor: Mary Stinchcomb
Hours: Tues Sat 11-5 & Appointment Advisable
Types & Periods: Oriental Rugs, 18th & 19th Century Furniture
Specialties: Rugs (Oriental)
Appraisal Service Available
Directions: I 35, Exit at 11th, W on Nueces, Left on 12th

T'S ANTIQUES
2314 Rutland Dr   78758
512 837-3424
Proprietor: Harrell Mahan
Hours: Daily
Types & Periods: Early American Furniture, Mostly Oak & Pine, Glassware, Clocks

Specialties: American Furniture
Appraisal Service Available
Directions: N on Burnet Rd to Rutland & 2 Blocks E

THREE GEESE ANTIQUES
1412 W 9th St   78703
512 478-1465   Est: 1971
Proprietor: Brooks & Corcoran
Hours: Tue-Sat 10:30-5:30, Closed Sun & Mon
Types & Periods: General Line, Bric-A-Brac, Furniture
Directions: 6 Blocks W of Lamar Blvd

VICTORIANA
6215 Walnut Hills   78723
512 926-7017   Est: 1972
Proprietor: Billie Masters
Hours: By Appointment
Types & Periods: American Cottage Furniture, European Imports Circa 1800
Specialties: China, Prints, Glassware, Lithographs
Appraisal Service Available
Directions: Off Manor Rd

WATERLOO COMPOUND
600 E 3rd   78701
512 476-2590   Est: 1967
Proprietor: Cowley & Nease
Hours: Wed-Sat 10:30-5
Types & Periods: American, Texas & European Furniture, Jewelry, Tools, China
Specialties: Fine Vintage Clothes
Appraisal Service Available
Directions: Corner of Red River & 3rd Sts

WESTLAKE ARCHITECTURAL ANTIQUES
3315 WestLake Dr   78746
512 327-1110   Est: 1968
Proprietor: Virginia S Blewett
Hours: Mon-Sun, By Appointment
Types & Periods: Architectural Antiques, Beveled Leaded Glass, Doors, Door Sets, Panels, Stained Glass (American & European) All Sizes & Prices

Austin Cont'd

**WESTLAKE
ARCHITECTURAL Cont'd**
Specialties: Carved & Marble
Mantles, Chandeliers,
Carved Doors, Front & Back
Bars, Armoires, Dining Table
& Dining Chairs

Beaumont

BEAUMONT CLUSTER
Directions: Calder Ave

COUNTRY LANE ANTIQUES
1425 Calder   77701
713 832-5800   Est: 1965
Proprietor: Beth Shaw
Hours: Tue-Sat 10-4
Types & Periods: General
Line, American
Specialties: American
Pattern Glass, Victorian
Furniture, American Oak &
Pine
Appraisal Service Available
Directions: I-10 to Calder
Exit, Turn E

CROPPER'S ANTIQUES
1495 Calder   77701
713 832-2002   Est: 1944
Proprietor: Bernice
Cropper
Hours: Mon-Sat
Types & Periods: General
Line, American Furniture,
18th Century to Oak
Specialties: Cut Glass, Art
Glass, Cloisonne, Bronze,
Haviland
Appraisal Service Available
Directions: Off Calder Exit
or Mariposa on IH 10

**FINDER'S FAYRE QUALITY
ANTIQUES**
1485 Calder   77701
713 833-7000   Est: 1960
Proprietor: James
Steinmeyer
Hours: Tue-Sat 10-5,
Closed Sun & Mon
Types & Periods: 18th &
19th Century English,
French & American, Persian
Rugs
Appraisal Service Available
Directions: Calder at
Mariposa

JUST LOOKIN' SHOP
565 W Lucas   77706
713 892-6543   Est: 1970
Proprietor: "Four Women"
Hours: Daily
Types & Periods: General
Line
Directions: Corner of W
Lucas & Calder

**LARRY'S ANTIQUE MALL &
TRADE MARKET**
7150 Eastex Frwy   77708
713 892-4000   Est: 1975
Proprietor: Larry P Tinkle
Hours: Sat 9-6, Sun 1-6
Types & Periods: Furniture,
Primitives, Coins, Paper
Americana, Clocks, China,
Pottery, Jewelry, Dolls,
Collectibles, Stamps
Appraisal Service Available
Directions: 105 Exit on 69,
96, 287, N Beaumont

LYN'S ANTIQUES
2579 Calder   77702
713 835-1927   Est: 1970
Proprietor: Dr & Mrs Jerry
Johnson
Hours: Mon-Sat 9:30-5
Types & Periods: American
& European Period Furniture
& Accessories
Appraisal Service Available
Directions: Calder Exit, E
4 Blocks off I-10

MELANGE
2325 Calder   77702
713 833-2751   Est: 1968
Proprietor: Doris Mabry
Hours: Tues-Sat 11-6,
Closed Sun & Mon, Also
By Appointment
Types & Periods: General
Line, Art, Gifts
Specialties: Jewelry
Appraisal Service Available
Directions: Little Yellow
Cottage Between 7th &
8th Sts

TRAYLOR REESE INC
1945 Calder Ave   77701
713 832-9221   Est: 1910
Proprietor: Roger &
Jimmie Reese
Hours: Mon-Sat 9-5:30
Types & Periods: Porcelain,
Brass, Silver, Glass, Copper,
Ivories, Carvings, Any Period
We Can Find From Old
Chinese On
Appraisal Service Available
Directions: IH-10 Take
Calder Exit

TINK'S ANTIQUES
2894 Magnolia Ave 77703
713 832-8044   Est: 1962
Proprietor: Gene Tinkee
Hours: Daily, Weekends,
By Appointment
Types & Periods: Oak
Furniture, Bric-A-Brac,
"Antiquax" Polish
Specialties: English Imports
Directions: 8 Blocks Off
I-10

Beeville

ROBERTS ANTIQUES
Hwy 59 W Blueberry Hills
78102
512 358-3556   Est: 1956
Proprietor: Mr & Mrs
Denny Roberts
Hours: Mon-Sat 9-5,
Closed Sun
Types & Periods: American,
Walnut, Victorian & Oak
Furniture, European, Cut
Glass, Art Glass, China
Specialties: Furniture,
Ceramics, Cut Glass
Directions: 1 1/2 Miles
from Courthouse on US
Hwy 59 S Toward Laredo
on Right at Large Oil
Derrick

Bellville

THE CARRIAGE SHOP
301 E Main St   77418
713 865-5171   Est: 1975
Proprietor: Karen &
Dennis Nobrega
Hours: Thurs-Sun
10:30-5:30
Types & Periods: American
& European Furniture,
Accent Pieces, Glass
Specialties: Reproduce &
Repair Stained Glass
Windows
Directions: 2 Blocks S of
the Court House on
Hwy 36

Big Spring

CURIOSITY ANTIQUE SHOP
500 Gregg   79720
915 267-9055   Est: 1971

Proprietor: Mrs Lloyd
McLeod
Hours: Daily
Types & Periods: Depression
Glass, Jewelry, Pottery,
Primitives
Specialties: Pattern Glass
Directions: Downtown

Blum

**MORFORD'S & SON
ANTIQUES**
5th St, Box 44   76627
817 874-3842   Est: 1968
Proprietor: Peter M
Morford II
Hours: Sun, Mon & Fri,
Also By Appointment
Types & Periods: General
Line, American Victorian,
Walnut & Oak Furniture,
Primitives, Small Items
Specialties: We Cater to
Dealers & Can Load or Help
You Load Almost Any Size
Truck
Appraisal Service Available
Directions: Short Drive
from Ft Worth-Dallas
Metroplex, 14 Miles from
Cleburne, Signs on Hwy
174 & FM 933, 12 Miles
from Lake Whitney

Boerne

THE ACCENT SHOP
104 San Antonio   78006
512 249-3741
Types & Periods: "The
Unusual in American
Antiques & Primitives"

THE GARDEN GATE
316 Main   78006
512 249-3482
Proprietor: Mary Travis
Wilcox
Types & Periods: General
Line, Primitives, Collectibles,
Gifts

Brenham

STRAWBERRY PATCH
1301 S Day   77833
713 836-9021   Est: 1974

Proprietor: Mary Gayle
Williams
Hours: Thur-Sun 1-5,
Closed Mon, Tues & Wed
Types & Periods: Country,
French, Pine, Walnut & Oak
Furniture, Glassware,
Handmade Dolls
Specialties: Haviland China
Directions: 1 Block N of
Tom Green St on Hwy 36

**YANKEE PEDDLER
ANTIQUES**
Rte 4 Box 76 Hwy 36 N
                     77833
713 836-4442   Est: 1968
Proprietor: Kaylor Coonse
Hours: Mon-Sun, Closed
Holidays
Types & Periods: General
Line
Directions: 6 Miles N of
Brenham

Bridge City

**INTERNATIONAL
ANTIQUES**
3146 Hwy 87   77611
713 735-3706   Est: 1971
Proprietor: R J C Becke
Hours: Daily
Types & Periods: General
Line
Directions: Hwy 87, N of
Bridge City

Brownsville

COBWEBS & CALICO
1725 Central Blvd   78520
512 542-4644   Est: 1973
Proprietor: Eula Marquis
Hours: Tue-Sun 10-5,
Closed Mon
Types & Periods: General
Line, Glassware,
Collectibles, Nostalgia
Directions: Business
Hwy 77

Brownwood

**BERNELL'S KOUNTRY
KOTTAGE**
1300 Early Blvd   76801
915 646-8429   Est: 1969

Proprietor: Bernell
Guyness
Hours: Daily, Weekends
Types & Periods: Victorian &
Primitive Furniture,
Glassware, Kitchen
Primitives, Bottles
Directions: Ft Worth Hwy
377, NE of Downtown

MARY'S ANTIQUES
1101 Early Blvd   76801
915 646-9503   Est: 1973
Proprietor: Paul & Mary
Waldrop
Hours: Daily
Types & Periods: General
Line
Directions: 1 Mile E of
Early School on Ft Worth
Hwy

Bryan

**COBBS MARKET
ANTIQUES**
608 W 27th St   77801
713 822-2021   Est: 1973
Proprietor: Gerald & Joan
Maffei
Hours: Mon-Fri 10-4, Also
By Appointment
Types & Periods: 18th &
Early 19th Century Furniture,
Flasks, Lacy Glass, Pattern
Glass, Jewelry, Folk Art
Specialties: Furniture
Directions: Corner of
Randolph & W 27th, 5
Blocks W from Downtown

THE PLANTATION SHOP
2024 Texas   77801
713 822-6220   Est: 1947
Proprietor: Eugenia W
Terry
Hours: Daily, Also By
Appointment
Types & Periods: 18th
Century English
Directions: Hwy 67
Between Bryan & College
Station

Calvert

THE BOLL WEEVIL
Main St   77837
713 364-2318
Proprietor: Mrs Wesley E
Anderson

BOLL WEEVIL   **Cont'd**
Hours: Mon-Sat 10-5, Sun
1-5
Types & Periods: Period
American & English
Furniture, Victorian & Texas
Primitives, Jewelry

Canton

CANTON TRADES DAY
Hwys 19 & 64   75103
214 567-2991   Est: 1925
Proprietor: City of Canton
Hours: Sunrise to Sunset,
the prior Friday through
The First Monday of each
month
Types & Periods: Impossible
to describe, Perhaps 2,000
dealers offering wares
ranging from Primitives such
as Wire & Old Tools through
Gone-With-The-Wind Lamps
& Furniture
    Directions: About 60 miles
    E of Dallas on I-20. Use
    Canton Exit 19 and go S 1
    Mile. The selling ground
    covers many acres and
    some dealers use lights at
    night

Canyon

WILLIAMS ET CETERA
1519 4th Ave   79015
806 655-2002
Proprietor: Jerry O
Williams
Hours: Mon-Sat 9-5,
Closed Sun
Types & Periods: General
Line

Carrollton

THE OLD CRAFT STORE
1110 W 3rd   75006
214 242-9111   Est: 1971
Proprietor: J Richard
Fleming
Hours: Mon-Sat 10-5:30
Types & Periods: Primitive
Furniture, Tools, Printers
Trays & Print, Wooden
Spools & Bobbins

Directions: Off I-35 N from
Dallas, on the Old
Downtown Square of
Carrollton

**THE PAINTED PARSON
ANTIQUES**
1300 S Broadway   75006
214 242-3113   Est: 1974
Proprietor: Kitty & Jack
Staes
Hours: Tues-Sat 10:30-4
Types & Periods: American
Country Furniture &
Primitives
    Directions: Belt Line Exit
    Off I-35

Castroville

**VICK'S CASTROVILLE
EMPORIUM**
Angelo & Mardrid   78009
512 538-3115   Est: 1972
Proprietor: Donald W
Belcher
Hours: Tues-Sat 8:30-5:30,
Closed Sun & Mon
Types & Periods: General
Line
Specialties: Lighting
Fixtures, Clocks
    Directions: 25 Miles W of
    San Antonio on Hwy 90

Channelview

THE WHITE ELEPHANT
15662 I-10   77530
713 452-9022   Est: 1971
Proprietor: John & Ad
McDaniel
Hours: Sat & Sun Only
Types & Periods: All Flea
Market, Public Garage
Sales, Antiques
    Directions: I-10 E, Take
    Sheldon Exit

Chapman Ranch

RUE'S COUNTRY STORE
PO Box 103   78347
512 854-7292   Est: 1969
Proprietor: Rue Walker
Hours: Mon-Fri 7-3, Sat
8-12, Closed Sun

Types & Periods: American
Furniture, Primitives,
Collectibles
    Directions: S of Corpus
    Christi on Hwy 286

Coleman

THE BARGAIN HOUSE
711 Concho St   76834
915 625-4331   Est: 1969
Proprietor: Doyle Glasson
Hours: Daily 8-5
Types & Periods: English,
American, Primitives
Appraisal Service Available

College Station

THE GAZEBO ANTIQUES
Box 1122   77840
713 625-5469   Est: 1970
Proprietor: John A. Otts, Jr.
Hours: Thur-Mon, 10-5, &
By appointment
Types & Periods: Furniture;
Pattern, Pressed & Cut Glass;
Musical Items, Decorative
Accessories
Specialties: Music Boxes,
Phonographs
Appraisal Service Available
    Directions: 6 miles S of
    Texas A & M on Hwy 6

Collinsville

BOB McKNIGHT
        76233
214 429-6583
Hours: By appointment
Types & Periods: Pocket
Watches

Conroe

**COPPER KETTLE
ANTIQUES**
209 E Davis   77301
713 756-1892   Est: 1973
Proprietor: Dorothy Pyle
Hours: Mon-Sat 10-5,
Closed Sun, Also By
Appointment
Types & Periods:
Depression, Cut & Carnival
Glass, Lamps, Clocks, Oak

Furniture, Pine, Collectibles,
Stained Glass Doors, Fine
China
Appraisal Service Available
Directions: From I-45 Turn
Off on Conroe Exit, Go E
Thru Town, Cross RR
Track, Go to 1st Traffic
Light

DIAMOND F ANTIQUES
508 York   77356
713 539-2520   Est: 1976
Proprietor: Vickie Fallin
Hours: Tues-Sat 10-3:30
Types & Periods: Oak,
Turn-of-the-Century
Furniture (Restored)
Directions: 5 Blocks S of
Hwy 105, York Crosses
Frazier

EDITH'S ANTIQUES
910 Cable   77301
713 756-3711   Est: 1973
Proprietor: Edith Clanton
Hours: Mon -Sat 10:30-5,
Closed Sun
Types & Periods: American
& English Furniture, Glass,
China
Directions: 1 Block N of
Hotel Conroe, Left off N
Frazier onto Cable

**HEINTZ FURNITURE &
ANTIQUES**
701 N Frazier   77301
713 756-3024   Est: 1945
Proprietor: Mrs J P Heintz
Hours: Mon-Sat
Types & Periods: All
Periods, Including New
Appraisal Service Available
Directions: Old Hwy 75

POT LUCK ANTIQUES
312 N San Jacinto 77301
713 756-1355   Est: 1970
Proprietor: Lee Adams &
Hazel Covey
Hours: Mon-Sat 10-5,
Closed Sun
Types & Periods: Cut &
Depression Glass, Country
Junque, Furniture,
Collectibles
Directions: 40 Miles N of
Houston, Exit at FM 105E,
Go to 2nd Traffic Light &
Go Right 1/2 Block

TIC-WIC SHOP
502 Wilson   73701
713 756-2029

Proprietor: S F Willis
Hours: By Appointment,
By Chance
Types & Periods: Furniture,
Glass, Large Stock of
German Clocks
Specialties: German Clocks,
Box, Post & Weighted
Clocks
Directions: Take Conroe
Exit off of I-45, 40 Miles N
of Houston, Follow Wilson
Rd Signs

Converse

CHISM TRAIL ANTIQUES
616 S Sequin St   78109
512 658-3357   Est: 1973
Proprietor: Mr & Mrs
Leonard Dallas
Types & Periods: General
Line
Specialties: Depression
Glass
Directions: 1 Mile from
Randolph Air Force Base

Corpus Christi

**CORPUS CHRISTI
CLUSTER**
Directions: Kostoryz Rd
(4000-5000 Blocks), Ayers
(1000 Block), Leopard
(4000-10000 Blocks)

E O ANTIQUES
1706 S Staples   78404
512 008 6442   Est: 1974
Proprietor: James J Elliott
Hours: Tues-Sat, By
Appointment
Types & Periods: General
Line
Specialties: Art & Cut Glass,
Paintings
Appraisal Service Available
Directions: Located at Six
Points, 5 Blocks off
Ocean Dr

GRESHAM ANTIQUES
10901 Leopard   78410
512 241-7062   Est: 1964
Proprietor: Betty Gresham
Hours: Daily, By Chance
Types & Periods: Pressed &
Cut Glass, Furniture, Barbed
Wire, Bric-A-Brac, China

Specialties: Barbed Wire
Appraisal Service Available

**JEAN & ELWOOD HESS
ANTIQUES**
4345 Kostoryz   78415
512 853-8430   Est: 1962
Proprietor: Jean & Elwood
Hess
Hours: Mon-Sat 10-5, Also
By Appointment
Types & Periods: American
Country, Pressed Glass,
China, Paintings, Dolls,
Victorian
Specialties: American
Country, Pressed Glass,
Paintings, Dolls
Directions: Kostoryz off of
S Padre Isl Dr, or from S
Staples St, With Several
Adjoining Shops Nearby

THE PUMPKIN PATCH
609 S Staples   78404
512 884-0932   Est: 1975
Proprietor: Jerry Horsman
Hours: Mon-Sat

THE QUAINT SHOP
815 S Staples   78404
512 884-9541   Est: 1967
Proprietor: Ruth Lemmon
& Melissa Hill
Hours: Tues-Sat
Types & Periods: Country
Furniture, Kitchen &
Carpenter Tools, Copper,
Primitives, Early 1900's
Matted Magazine Ads
Specialties: Childrens
Furniture, Wicker, Country
Furniture
Directions: Between Six
Points & the Courthouse

TIN BARN ANTIQUES
4201 Brett   78411
512 855-7621   Est: 1976
Proprietor: Bette L Harris
Hours: Tues-Sat
Types & Periods: Any &
Everything, German,
English, & American,
Furniture, Primitives, Silver,
Glass, Paintings, Prints,
Original Art
Specialties: Furniture,
Cabinetmaking, Furniture
Restoration
Appraisal Service Available
Directions: Off Padre Isl
Expy, Between Weber &
Everhart, Behind Stewart
Title Co

Coupland

THE MARKETPLACE ANTIQUES
                                78615
512 856-2413 or 856-2690
                        Est: 1970
Proprietor: Phyllis Petrus
Hours: Fri, Sat & Sun
Evenings 5-11, Also By
Appointment
Types & Periods: American
Oak, Country Pine, Texas
Primitives
Appraisal Service Available
Directions: Above Old
Coupland Inn Downtown

Cuero

THE EPERGNE ANTIQUES
417 E Newman St   77954
512 275-5356   Est: 1971
Proprietor: Elizabeth C
Stone
Hours: Mon-Sat, Sun By
Appointment
Types & Periods: General
Line, Furniture, China,
Glassware, Lamps (New &
Old), Primitives, Jewelry
Directions: 4 Blocks off
Hwy 87 Coming into Town
Sign on Hwy Showing
Direction

Daingerfield

GREEN HORSES ANTIQUES
208 Jefferson St   75638
214 645-3211   Est: 1969
Proprietor: Bob & Rita
West
Hours: Tues-Fri 10-5
Types & Periods: Glassware,
Carnival Glass, Clocks,
Miniatures
Directions: Behind Old
Court House

Dallas

DALLAS CLUSTER
Directions: Many shops on
Fairmount and Routh Sts
W from McKinney Ave to
RR Tracks. Shops spread
along McKinney Ave
northward to Knox-N
Henderson Sts where
another cluster exists in
surrounding area. Many
shops on 2 blks of Sale
St. Some shops at Snider
Plaza, Hillcrest at Lovers
Ln

AMERICAN HERITAGE CO OF DALLAS
6438 Bordeaux   75209
214 352-3049   Est: 1974
Proprietor: Orman M
Livezey
Hours: By Appointment
Types & Periods:
Newspapers 1600-1800
Appraisal Service Available

ANN'S FURNITURE & ANTIQUES
4238 Maple Ave   75219
214 528-1415   Est: 1956
Proprietor: Lillian
"Ann"Shelby
Hours: Daily 9:30-5:30,
Closed Sat, Sun & Wed
Types & Periods: General
Line, Collectibles
Specialties: Furniture,
Primitives
Appraisal Service Available

ANNS'TIQUES
2318 Oates Dr   75228
214 327-9159   Est: 1966
Proprietor: Mr & Mrs H E
Wade
Hours: Tues-Sat 11-5,
Closed Sun & Mon
Types & Periods: Oak,
Glassware, Primitives,
Collectibles, Books, Papers
Directions: In Oates Plaza
Shopping Center

ANTIQUE ALLEY
2925 N Henderson   75206
214 827-0430   Est: 1965
Proprietor: Col James P
Caston
Hours: Mon-Sat 10-10,
Sun 1-10
Types & Periods: English &
French
Appraisal Service Available
Directions: 1 Block off
Central Expy

ANTIQUE HOUSE
3903 Lemmon Ave   75219
214 528-1270   Est: 1972
Proprietor: James Chow
Hours: Daily
Types & Periods: French,
English & Oriental Furniture,
Glass, Christmas Plates,
China
Specialties: China, Furniture,
Glass
Appraisal Service Available
Directions: Corner of
Reagan & Lemmon, 1
Block N of Oak Lawn

THE ANTIQUE SHOPPE
Suite 100
2800 Routh   75201
214 747-1371 or 653-1930
                        Est: 1968
Proprietor: Cathy Camplen
& Sue Mitz
Hours: Mon-Sat 10-5:30,
Also By Appointment
Types & Periods: French,
Victorian, English Furniture,
Oriental Rugs, Paintings,
Porcelain (Meissen), Sevres,
Dresden, Wedgwood,
Oriental Porcelain, Estate
Jewelry, Silver
Specialties: Estate Jewelry
Appraisal Service Available
Directions: Quadrangle
between McKinney &
Cedar Springs

ANTIQUES FOR INTERIORS
2201 Cedar Springs
                                75201
214 742-2081   Est: 1970
Proprietor: John A Perkins
Hours: Mon-Fri 9-5,
Closed Sat & Sun
Types & Periods: English &
French Furniture,
Porcelains, Paintings,
Chandeliers, General Line,
Collectibles

BAMBERG ANTIQUES
2907 Sale St   75224
214 526-5551   Est: 1973
Proprietor: Mrs Frances R
Bamberg
Hours: By Chance
Types & Periods: Glass,
China, Porcelain, Furniture
Directions: Near
Intersection of Oak Lawn
& Cedar Springs in Oak
Lawn Area, N of
Downtown

BECK-MALLIES ANTIQUES & INTERIORS
2800 Routh St   75201
214 714-1073   Est: 1974
Proprietor: Carl Mallies
Hours: Mon-Sat 10:30-5,
Closed Sun
Types & Periods: 16th-18th
Century Oriental Porcelains,
17th-18th English & French
Furniture, 17th-19th Century
Silver & Paintings
Appraisal Service Available
Directions: Suite 100 in
The Quadrangle, Cedar
Springs & Routh

GEORGE O BOYTE & ASSOC
2335 Dallas Trade Mart
               75207
214 748-4046   Est: 1954
Proprietor: George O
Boyte
Hours: Mon-Fri
Types & Periods: Oriental &
French, Imported & Export,
French & Oriental
Reproductions
Directions: 2100
Stemmons Freeway

BRANTLEY'S GLASS & ANTIQUES
8330 Scyene   75227
214 388-4515   Est: 1970
Proprietor: Elizabeth
Brantley
Hours: Daily, Closed Sun
& Thurs
Types & Periods: Glass,
Furniture, Lamps, Iron,
Wood What-Nots, Chinese

TOMMIE CARTER ANTIQUES
2727A Routh St   75201
214 747-3481   Est: 1961
Proprietor: Tommie & Van
Carter
Hours: Daily
Types & Periods: General
Line, Oriental, French
Directions: Corner of
Routh & Howell Between
Cedar Springs &
McKinney Ave

CHERIE'S ANTIQUES
3719 McKinney   75204
214 521-2832   Est: 1946
Proprietor: Cherie
Lawrence
Hours: Tues-Sun 2-6,
Closed Mon

Types & Periods: Furniture,
China, Silver, Copper
Specialties: Wicker
Directions: Between
Lemon & Haskell across
from Lemon Park Office
Buildings

THE CHINA CUPBOARD
3316 Knox St   75205
214 528-6250   Est: 1970
Proprietor: Mrs May Ree
Bell
Hours: Mon-Sat 10-5:30,
Closed Sun
Types & Periods: China, Cut
& Art Glass, Silver,
Collectibles
Specialties: French Haviland,
Meissen, Dresden, Flow Blue
Directions: N Side of St,
Exit 5 off N Central Expy,
3 1/2 Blocks W of Central

THE COLLECTOR'S ANTIQUES
2817 Routh   75201
214 741-2281 or 526-7177
Proprietor: Vivian Young
Hours: Mon-Sat, Also By
Appointment
Types & Periods: Imported
Elegant to Country &
Painted Styles of Furniture &
Accessories, Georgian, Early
Oak, Primitives
Specialties: Suppliers to the
Designers & Trade
Directions: 2 Blocks off
McKinney & 1/2 Block off
Cedar Springs, Directly
across St from
Quadrangle Shopping
Center & Next Door to
The Sample House

COUNTRY CORNERS ANTIQUES
3015 Sale St   75219
214 521-6760   Est: 1969
Proprietor: Ann Zeman
Hours: Daily
Types & Periods: General
Line

COUNTRY ROAD ANTIQUES
2625 Oak Lawn   75219
214 522-3120   Est: 1970
Proprietor: Jessie Welborn
Hours: Mon-Sat 10-6,
Closed Sun, Also By
Appointment & By Chance

Types & Periods:
Turn-of-the-Century
Furniture, General Line,
Collectibles
Specialties: Primitives
Appraisal Service Available

DALLAS GALLERIES
8414 Preston Rd   75225
214 368-7504   Est: 1951
Proprietor: H L Fetterman
Hours: Mon-Sat 9:30-5:30
Types & Periods: French &
English 18th Century

DENTON-GRANT
1444 Oak Lawn   75207
214 651-1937   Est: 1968
Proprietor: Conley Denton
& Thomas Grant
Hours: Daily, By
Appointment
Types & Periods: 18th &
19th Century French &
English
Specialties: Chandeliers
Directions: Oak Lawn
Plaza, Suite 316

ROSE DRIVER ANTIQUES
2916 Sale St   75219
214 521-7012
Proprietor: Rose Driver
Hours: Mon-Fri 10-4:30,
1/2 Day on Sat
Types & Periods: 17th &
18th Furniture, English,
Continental & Oriental
Porcelains
Specialties: English
Furniture
Appraisal Service Available
Directions: Off Cedar
Springs near Oak Lawn
Area

DONALD EMBREE ANTIQUES
2915 Fairmount St   75201
214 748-3549   Est: 1962
Proprietor: Donald Embree
Hours: Mon-Fri 9-5, Sat By
Appointment Only
Types & Periods: English &
French Furniture &
Accessories
Specialties: Chinese
Porcelains, European
Bronzes

Dallas Cont'd

**JAMES Q ERWIN
ANTIQUES**
2913 Sale St   75219
214 528-2417   Est: 1945
Proprietor: James Q Erwin
Hours: Mon-Sat
Types & Periods: English,
French, American & Chinese
Specialties: Pewter
Appraisal Service Available
Directions: 3 Blocks S of
Melrose Hotel on Cedar
Springs

**WILLIAM FERRELL
ANTIQUES**
3003 N Henderson 75206
214 826-2980   Est: 1974
Proprietor: William R
Ferrell & Bernard Bowman
Hours: Mon-Fri, Sat By
Appointment
Types & Periods: English &
French Furniture, Export
Porcelain & General
Decorations
Appraisal Service Available
Directions: Off N Central
Expy at Knox-Henderson
Exit

**WILLIAM FERRELL
ANTIQUES INC**
2913 Fairmount St   75201
214 651-8861
Proprietor: W R Ferrell &
B L Bowman
Hours: Mon-Fri, Sat By
Appointment
Types & Periods: American,
English & French Furniture,
Chinese Export Porcelain
Specialties: Chinese Export
Porcelain
Appraisal Service Available

FLORENTINE SHOP
4347 Lovers Ln   75225
214 528-4515   Est: 1953
Proprietor: B J Teiber
Hours: Daily, Also By
Appointment
Types & Periods: English,
Continental
Appraisal Service Available
Directions: On Miracle
Mile

GOBLETS ETC ANTIQUES
6920 Snider Plaza   75205
214 368-0313   Est: 1961
Proprietor: Mrs N T
Dunlap & Mrs D J
Killingsworth
Hours: Mon-Sat 10-5,
Closed Sun
Types & Periods: Sebino
Opalescent Figurines,
Christmas, Mother's Day &
Royal Copenhagen Plates,
Small Furniture, Collectibles
Specialties: Glass (Early
American Pressed Glass
Goblets)

HARRY'S ANTIQUES
5615 Alta   75206
214 823-4023   Est: 1962
Proprietor: Harry Holstun,
Jr
Hours: By Appointment,
By Chance
Types & Periods: General
Line
Appraisal Service Available
Directions: Off Greenville
Ave, 2 Blocks N of Ross

HEIRLOOM HOUSE INC
2521 Fairmount   75201
214 748-2087   Est: 1946
Proprietor: O Martel
Bowen & W T Rogers
Hours: Daily
Types & Periods: 18th
Century English & American
Furniture, English & Oriental
Porcelains, Oriental Rugs
Directions: Btwn McKinney
& Cedar Springs

INGALLS LAMPS
2610 Fairmount   75201
214 742-2795   Est: 1936
Proprietor: H W Larson
Hours: Mon-Fri 9-5, Sat
10-2, Closed Sun
Types & Periods: Oriental &
European Porcelains,
Cloisonne, Brass
Directions: 1 Block off
McKinney, 2 Blocks off
Cedar Springs, (2nd Shop
at 6124 Berkshire Ln)

JACKSON ARMS
6209 Hillcrest Ave   75205
214 521-9929   Est: 1950
Proprietor: Leon C
Jackson
Hours: Tue-Sat, Closed
Sun & Mon
Types & Periods: Arms &
Armor, Military, Indian
Artifacts
Specialties: Arms
Appraisal Service Available
Directions: In University
Park, Opposite SMU
Campus

JAMIE'S ANTIQUES
3001 W Davis   75211
214 337-6258   Est: 1971
Proprietor: W Erwin
Hendrix
Hours: Tues-Sat 10-5,
Also By Appointment
Types & Periods: American,
Oak & Pine Furniture, Brass,
Copper, Primitives,
Collectibles
Specialties: Furniture,
Primitives, Brass, Copper
Appraisal Service Available
Directions: Hwy 80 W,
Davis at Ravinia Rd

KARAT TOP
12215 Coit   75215
214 661-3686   Est: 1972
Proprietor: Margaret
Gronberg
Hours: Mon-Sat 10-5:30,
Closed Sun
Types & Periods: Jewelry
1880-1930, Jewelry Repair
Appraisal Service Available
Directions: 1 Block from
Central Expy & I-635, In
Olla Podrida

**KISSIN' COUSINS
ANTIQUES**
2616 Worthington   75204
214 826-8643   Est: 1960
Proprietor: Mrs Helen
DeShong
Hours: Daily
Types & Periods: General
Line, American Primitives
Specialties: Toys &
Automata
Appraisal Service Available
Directions: Btwn 2800
McKinney Ave &
Quadrangle

THE LACQUER DOOR
2905 Sale St   75219
214 528-4414   Est: 1972
Proprietor: E C Dicken
Hours: Daily, By
Appointment
Types & Periods: English &
French Furniture,
Porcelains, Paintings, Rugs
Directions: 1 Block W of
Cedar Springs

LAGNIAPPE SHOP
5009-A W Lovers Ln
                       75209
214 357-2941   Est: 1974
Proprietor: J D Hite & C T
Eaton
Hours: Mon-Sat 10-5
Types & Periods: All Types
& Periods, Gifts, House
Plants & Just Plain Junk
Specialties: Victoriana &
1930's Nostalga
Directions: 2 Blocks W of
Inwood Rd

**ELIZABETH LE CONEY
ANTIQUES**
3115-3117 Knox St 75205
214 522-2366   Est: 1973
Proprietor: Elizabeth K
Le Coney
Hours: Mon-Sun 11-4,
Also By Appointment
Types & Periods: 18th &
19th Century American &
English Furniture &
Accessories, Oriental &
English Porcelain, Willow
Ware, Brass, Copper
Specialties: Furniture,
(Nautical Furniture Made
From Old Ships), Marine
Accessories
Directions: Near
Downtown, 1 1/2 Blocks
Off Central Expy, Hwy 75,
Knox-Henderson Exit

LOYD-PAXTON INC
530 Decorative Center
                       75207
214 651-1999   Est: 1960
Proprietor: Loyd Taylor &
Paxton Gremillion
Hours: Mon-Fri, Also By
Appointment
Types & Periods: 17th, 18th
& 19th Century English,
Continental & Oriental
Furniture & Accessories,
Chandeliers, Sconces,
Tapestries, Mantles,

Fireplace Equipment,
Chinese & Japanese
Screens, Architectural Items,
Planters, Objet de Vertu
Specialties: Import & Buy
From Estates, Always A
Large Selection & Variety
Directions: Off Stemmons
Freeway at 1500 Oak
Lawn Ave

LYDIA'S ANTIQUES
3128 McKinney   75204
214 522-1742   Est: 1960
Proprietor: Lydia Gibbs
Hours: Tues-Sat 11-5,
Closed Sun & Mon
Types & Periods: General
Line
Directions: Btwn Bowen &
Travis Schools

MAMIE'S ANTIQUES
2708 Fairmount   75201
214 651-0587   Est: 1973
Proprietor: Mamie Vertel
Hours: Mon-Sat
Types & Periods: American
Primitives & Accessories,
Furniture, Stoneware,
Ironware, Kitchen Items,
Quilts & Homespun
Specialties: American
Primitives
Directions: Near
Downtown, 1 Block from
Quadrangle, Accessible
from Central Expy & North
Dallas Tollway

MANHEIN GALLERIES
2520 Fairmount St 75201
214 742-2364   Est: 1960
Proprietor: A G Manheim
Hours: Mon-Fri 9-5,
Closed Sat & Sun
Types & Periods: Silver, Fine
Paintings, Chandeliers,
Mantels, English,
Continental & Oriental
Furnishings & Accessories
Specialties: Boehm Birds

MC KINNEY GALLERIES
3312 McKinney Ave
                       75204
214 526-2632   Est: 1970
Proprietor: Desmond A
Wilcox & G Brents Davis
Hours: Daily, Closed Mon
& Major Holidays
Types & Periods: General
Line, Art Deco, Domestic &
European Furniture &

Accessories, Collectibles
Directions: "Located in
Dallas' Oldest Antique
Shopping District Btwn
Hall St & Lemmon Ave,
2 Blocks W of Central
Expy"

MIKE'S THINGS
3136 Routh St   75201
214 748-0210   Est: 1970
Proprietor: Mike Niebuhr
Hours: Mon-Sun 10:30-6
Types & Periods: Art Deco
(1925-1939), Louis Icart
Etchings
Specialties: Furniture,
(French Fine Art Deco
1925-1939), Art Deco
Bronzes
Directions: Chelsea Sq,
2 Blocks W of Cedar
Springs

BILL MILLER'S ANTIQUES
3709 McKinney   75204
214 528-6210   Est: 1962
Proprietor: Bill Miller
Hours: Mon-Sat 9-5:30,
Closed Sun
Types & Periods: Furniture,
General Line, Collectibles,
"Big Variety"
Specialties: Furniture,
(Desks), Brass Beds

**MIYASHITA ART &
ANTIQUE TRADING CO**
8588 Northwest Plaza Dr
                       75225
214 369-4379   Est: 1972
Proprietor: Shoza
Miyashita
Hours: By Appointment
Types & Periods: Orientals,
Porcelain, Objets d'Art,
Paintings, Bronze, Samurai
Sword, Cloisonne, Furniture
Specialties: Japanese
Samurai
Appraisal Service Available
Directions: NW Hwy &
Hillcrest

MONDAYS
2819 N Henderson 75206
214 823-7992   Est: 1974
Proprietor: Ann C Evans
Hours: Mon-Sat, Also By
Appointment
Types & Periods: 17th &
18th Century English
Country Furniture

Dallas   Cont'd

MONDAYS   Cont'd
Specialties: Oak, Elm, &
Pine, Selected Accessories
Directions: 3 Blocks E of
North Central Expy at
Knox Henderson Exit

NADINE'S ANTIQUES
2013 Abrams Rd   75214
214 826-5660   Est: 1973
Proprietor: Nadine Smith
Hours: Tue-Sat 8:30-5:30,
Closed Sun & Mon
Types & Periods: China,
Bric-A-Brac, Furniture
Appraisal Service Available
Directions: In Lakewood
Shopping Center, NE
Dallas

THE NEVER AGAIN SHOP
2710 Routh St   75201
214 832-6870   Est: 1977
Proprietor: Paulina Wilson
Daniels
Hours: Tues-Sat l0-5
Types & Periods: General
Line, American Glass

OL' TYMER CLOCK SHOP
2543 Valley View Ln
75234
214 247-2812   Est: 1970
Proprietor: Joe & Ruth
Grissom
Hours: Tues-Fri 9:30-5,
Sat 9:30-2, Closed Sun &
Mon
Types & Periods: Clocks,
Mostly 18th & 19th Century
Furniture
Specialties: Clocks (Repair)
Directions: 4 Blocks E of
I-35

OLD ENGLAND ANTIQUES
4311 Oak Lawn   75219
214 522-8451   Est: 1972
Proprietor: W R Withey
Hours: Daily, Weekends
Types & Periods: English
Furniture, 18th & 19th
Century Edwardian, Art
Deco, Architectural, Clocks,
Chandeliers, Prints, Oils,
Street Signs
Specialties: Furniture
(Commercial Size)
Appraisal Service Available
Directions: Oak Lawn Exit
Off I-35

OLDE CURIOSITY SHOPPE
2990 Walton Walker
75211
214 337-4377   Est: 1977
Proprietor: Edith Blair
Hours: Mon-Sun 9-5
Types & Periods: Cut Glass,
China, Silver, Art Glass, 18th
Century Furniture
Appraisal Service Available
Directions: On Loop 12
Btwn Illinois & Kiest, At
the Sign on the Covered
Wagon

ONE OF A KIND ANTIQUES
15075 Inwood   75240
214 661-1122   Est: 1976
Proprietor: Cleo Neiman
Hours: Tues-Sat
Types & Periods: 18th &
19th Century Furniture &
Accessories
Specialties: Unusual
Furniture
Appraisal Service Available
Directions: Corner of
Beltline Rd & Inwood Rd

ORIENTAL ART SHOP
218 Inwood Village 75209
214 352-0992   Est: 1952
Proprietor: W Y Hsueh
Hours: Mon-Sat
10:30-5:30, Closed Sun
Types & Periods: Chinese
Art Objects
Specialties: Snuff Bottles,
Cloisonne, Furniture
Appraisal Service Available
Directions: Inwood &
Lovers Ln

ORION ANTIQUES
1628 Oak Lawn   75207
214 748-1177   Est: 1975
Proprietor: David Stevens
& Hinri Chansolme
Hours: Mon-Sat, also by
appt
Types & Periods: French
Imports, Mainly Furniture, All
Periods, Art Objects
Appraisal Service Available
Directions: 35E N to Oak
Lawn Exit, S on Oak Lawn

DORRACE PEARLE ANTIQUES
2736 Routh   75201
214 827-1116   Est: 1960
Proprietor: Dorrace Pearle
Hours: Mon-Sat 9:30-5

Types & Periods: General
Line
Appraisal Service Available
Directions: Across from
Quadrangle Center

PFLASTER'S INC
1532 Hi-Line   75207
214 747-0458   Est: 1951
Proprietor: Lola J
Zygmend Pflaster
Hours: Daily
Types & Periods: Furniture,
Oriental Items, WHOLESALE
ONLY
Directions: Dallas
Wholesale Decorative
Center Area

PHEASANT ANTIQUES
2909 Sale St   75219
214 521-1554   Est: 1977
Proprietor: David Richard
Pheasant
Hours: Tue-Sat 12-4, Also
By Appointment
Types & Periods: English
Period & Victorian Furniture,
Ceramics, Porcelain, Silver,
Bronzes, Brass, Copper,
Prints, Paintings
Specialties: English & Irish
18th Century Furniture,
Silver & Porcelain
Appraisal Service Available
Directions: Off Oak Lawn
& Cedar Springs

PHILLIPS ANTIQUE SHOP
3321 McKinney   75204
214 526-8155   Est: 1949
Proprietor: Mrs Jack
Phillips
Hours: Mon-Sat 10-4:30,
Closed Sun
Types & Periods: General
Line
Specialties: Wicker, English
Iron Beds

A PICKET FENCE DOLL HOUSE
2815 N Henderson 75206
214 827-9422   Est: 1974
Proprietor: Millie Seaton
Hours: Wed-Sat 11-5
Types & Periods: Dolls, Doll
Clothes, Wigs, Shoes, Etc
Specialties: Doll Repair, Doll
Costuming
Appraisal Service Available
Directions: 3 Blocks E of
N Central Expy, Exit 5

REYNOLDS ANTIQUES
11515 Harry Hines Blvd
75229
214 247-2700
Proprietor: Bob & Frankie
Reynolds
Hours: Daily
Types & Periods: Furniture
& Accessories
Appraisal Service Available
Directions: 1 Block Off
LBJ & 1 Block Off
Stemmons Frwy

**LOUIS ROSENBACH
ANTIQUES INC**
1518 Slocum St   75207
214 748-0906   Est: 1950
Proprietor: Louis
Rosenbach
Hours: Mon-Fri 9-5:30,
Closed Sat & Sun
Types & Periods: French,
English & Belgium Furniture,
Oil Paintings, Decorative
Accessories
Specialties: Shipments
Monthly
Appraisal Service Available
Directions: Off Oak Lawn
Ave

THE SAMPLERS
Suite 105
6615 Snider Plaza   75205
214 363-0045   Est: 1972
Proprietor: Jeanne
Jackson & Ruth Brooks
Hours: Mon-Sat
Types & Periods: American,
Dolls, Quilts, Baskets,
Jewelry
Directions: Near SMU
Campus, 1 Block W of
Hillcrest, Off Lovers Lane
in the Craft Compound
Bldg

SID'S ANTIQUES & GIFTS
306 S Beckley   75203
214 941-6781   Est: 1974
Proprietor: J R McSwain
Hours: Tue-Sat 10:30-4,
Closed Sun & Mon
Types & Periods: American,
English
Specialties: Clocks
Directions: At Intersection
of Beckley & Jefferson

**JOHN HENRY STERRY
ANTIQUES**
2906 Sale St   75219
214 241-5951   Est: 1975
Proprietor: John H Sterry

Hours: Mon-Sat
Types & Periods: English,
17th, 18th, & 19th Century
American, Country
Specialties: Gift Items, Pine,
Art
Appraisal Service Available
Directions: Near Oak Lawn
& Turtle Creek Area

STONE'S
4821 W Jefferson   75211
214 331-5851   Est: 1967
Proprietor: A C Stone
Hours: By Appointment,
By Chance
Types & Periods: Furniture,
Copper
Specialties: Brass, Bronze,
Schrimshaw
Directions: 3/4 Mile E of
Loop 12, Take Jefferson
Exit

THE TEA LEAF
2617 McKinney   75204
214 821-1654   Est: 1974
Proprietor: Mr & Mrs S W
Freeman & Mr & Mrs G N
Parrott
Hours: By Appointment,
By Chance
Types & Periods: 17th &
18th Century Orientals
Specialties: Cloisonne
Directions: McKinney at
Routh, 10 Blocks from
Fairmont Hotel, 7 Blocks
Off Akard

TEASEL GALLERIES
2533 McKinney Ave
75201
214 651-0600   Est: 1948
Proprietor: Lucille Teasel
de Albeniz
Hours: Mon 11-5,
Tues-Sat 10-5, Sun 2-5,
Also By Appointment
Types & Periods: Period &
Country French & English
Furniture, English Silver,
Oriental
Specialties: French &
English Porcelain 18th &
Early 19th Century, Silver
Appraisal Service Available
Directions: Corner of
Routh St & McKinney Ave

UNCOMMON MARKET
2701 Fairmount   75201
214 747-0165   Est: 1971
Proprietor: Ward & Don
Mayborn

Hours: Mon-Sat 10-5:30,
Closed Sun
Types & Periods:
Advertising, Shop Fixtures,
Brass Hardware, Light
Fixtures, Circus & Arcade
Items
Specialties: Stained &
Leaded Glass, Advertising
Items
Directions: Near
Downtown, N Side Off
McKinney

**VISUAL ART & GALLERIES
INC**
6333 Gaston Ave   75214
214 821-1616   Est: 1962
Proprietor: Kurt Niven
Hours: Tue-Sat, Closed
Sun & Mon
Types & Periods: Master
Paintings, Engravings &
Graphics, Sculptures
Appraisal Service Available
Directions: Corner of
Abrams Rd

**THE WALLACE HOUSE
ANTIQUES**
2619 McKinney Ave
75227
214 821-3470   Est: 1965
Proprietor: Pat Wallace
Hours: Tues-Sat 10:30-5,
Closed Sun & Mon
Types & Periods: Early
Americana to Empire &
Chippendale, European
Imports,
Gone-With-The-Wind-Lamps,
Clocks, China, Glass
Specialties: Country Store
Items, "Everything from lye
Soap to Coffee Mills"
Appraisal Service Available
Directions: McKinney at
Routh, 2 Blocks from
Quadrangle

WILSON'S ANTIQUES
3636 N Buckner   75228
214 271-0687   Est: 1977
Proprietor: Buddy & Becky
Wilson
Hours: Fri, Sat & Sun
Types & Periods: American
& European, Unusual
Decorative & Accent
Furniture
Directions: Loop 12 at
I-30 E

Dallas   Cont'd

THE WRECKING BAR INC
2601 McKinney   75204
214 826-1717   Est: 1962
Proprietor: Mrs Jo
McDonald
Hours: Mon-Sat 9-5,
Closed Sun
Types & Periods: Mantels,
Doors, Leaded Glass,
Paneling, Columns, Lighting,
Hardware
Directions: NE Section of
Town, Near Quadrangle

YESTERYEAR UNLIMITED
3005 Swiss Ave   75204
214 821-3636   Est: 1973
Proprietor: Mary Rowe
Hours: Wed-Sat 11-6,
Closed Sun, Mon & Tues
Types & Periods: Primitives,
Collectibles
Directions: Near Baylor
Hospital, Central Expy to
Pacific/Gaston, Left on
Hall St 2 Blocks, Left on
Swiss

Darrouzett

POTPOURRI ANTIQUES
12649 Memorial   79024
713 467-6556   Est: 1968
Proprietor: Lois Lee
Richardson
Hours: Tue-Sat 10-5,
Closed Sun & Mon
Types & Periods: English
Furniture, Collectibles,
American Nostalgia,
Bric-A-Brac, Copper, Brass,
Glass, Porcelain, Oriental
Directions: Btwn Lantern
Ln & Town & Country
Shopping Areas

Del Rio

QUAINT SHOP ANTIQUES
1305 E 1st   78840
512 775-6916   Est: 1968
Proprietor: Carl & Anne
Zickefoose
Hours: Daily 10-6

Types & Periods: French,
English & American
Furniture, China, Glass,
Metals, Primitives
Specialties: Glass
Directions: 1 Block off
San Antonio Hwy 90 E

Denison

COLONIAL HOUSE
ANTIQUES
1008 S Austin   75020
214 465-7593
Proprietor: Henry & Hazel
Smythe
Hours: Mon-Sun 10-5
Types & Periods: Furniture,
Glassware, Clocks,
Primitives

ANTIQUES FROM EUNYCE
ALLEN COOKE
518 N Austin Ave   75020
214 465-1339   Est: 1960
Proprietor: E A Cooke
Hours: By Appointment,
By Chance
Types & Periods: General
Line
Directions: Hwy 75, on E
Side

GLIMPSE OF YESTERYEAR
ANTIQUES
106 W Sears   75020
214 463-1950   Est: 1972
Proprietor: Mr & Mrs John
H Phillips
Hours: Mon-Sat, Sun By
Chance or By
Appointment
Types & Periods: Victorian,
Art Nouveau, Art Deco,
American Oak, China,
Pattern & Depression Glass
Specialties: Displayed in
1879 Historical Home, Italian
Villa Architecture
Appraisal Service Available
Directions: 3 Blocks N of
Main St & 1 Block E of
Hwy 69 & 75

TUCKER FURNITURE
422 W Main St   75020
214 465-3630   Est: 1936
Proprietor: Severne
Tucker
Hours: Mon-Sat 8-5:30,
Closed Sun
Types & Periods:
Collectibles

Specialties: Furniture
(Restoring)
Directions: 3 Blocks W of
Hwy 75, E of the Rialto
Theater

Denton

CHANDLER ANTIQUES
617 Sunset   76201
817 382-1117   Est: 1975
Proprietor: Paul Chandler
Hours: Mon-Sat
Types & Periods: 19th
Century New England
Country Furniture, American,
Victorian, Walnut, Oak,
Lighting, Rugs, Jewelry,
Watches
Appraisal Service Available
Directions: Sunset Center,
2 Miles E of I-35 on 380
Hwy

KEN RINEY ANTIQUES &
JEWELRY
617 Sunset Center 76201
817 382-1631   Est: 1966
Proprietor: Ken Riney
Hours: Daily
Types & Periods: American
& French, Jewelry
Specialties: Jewelry
Appraisal Service Available
Directions: 1 Mile E of I-35
on Hwy 380

Duncanville

TOWN & COUNTRY
ANTIQUES
1415 N Duncanville Rd
                      75116
214 298-4003   Est: 1973
Proprietor: Evelyn
Armistead
Hours: Mon-Sat 8:30-4:30,
Closed Sun
Types & Periods: General
Line
Directions: Hwy 20, Exit
Duncanville Rd, go 6/10
Mile N

TRASH & TREASURE
ANTIQUES LTD
312 N Main St   75116
214 296-2177   Est: 1975
Proprietor: Linda Leibrock
Hours: Daily, Weekends,
By Appointment

Types & Periods: English
Regency Period, Victorian,
Brass, Copper, Bric-A-Brac,
Curios, Collectibles
Appraisal Service Available
Directions: 3 Miles From
Red Bird Mall

Eagle Lake

THE FARRIS 1912
201 N McCarty 77434
713 234-2546 Est: 1959
Proprietor: Bill & Helyn
Farris
Hours: Mon-Sat 9-5, Sun
By Appointment
Types & Periods: American,
European 1800-1930,
Furniture, Glass,
Collectibles, Lamps
Directions: Downtown, NW
Corner of Town Sq

Edna

**JUDGE & WORTH
ANTIQUES**
Lower Cordele Rd 77957
512 782-3001 Est: 1963
Proprietor: Elsworth
Williams
Hours: By Appointment,
By Chance
Types & Periods:
Turn-of-the-Century,
Primitives, Old Store Items,
Baskets, Crockery
Specialties: Hummel Plates,
Figurines
Appraisal Service Available
Directions: Exit Hwy 111
W off Hwy 59

El Paso

EL PASO CLUSTER
Directions: Shops
Scattered along Alameda
(3000-10000 Blocks), N
Mesa, E Yandel

ALAMEDO TRADING POST
3501 Alameda Ave 79905
915 533-2363 Est: 1965
Proprietor: Rodney
Davenport
Hours: Daily

Types & Periods: Furniture,
Glass, Cash Registers, Slot
Machines, Primitives
Appraisal Service Available
Directions: I-10 to Copin
St Exit, S to Alameda

**ANTIQUES
INTERNATIONAL**
Suite 110
Coronado Tower 79912
915 584-7271 or 584-7970
Est: 1968
Proprietor: Marian
Burrough
Hours: Tues-Sat, Closed
Sun & Mon, Also By
Appointment
Types & Periods: Silver,
Furniture, Orientals,
Glassware, Silk Flowers,
Gifts
Appraisal Service Available
Directions: I-10 W to
Sunland Park Cut-Off, to
Mesa St, Left to 11 Story
Building

ANTIQUES & JUNK
3726 Alameda 79905
915 532-3894 Est: 1977
Proprietor: Frank Fox &
Mary McNellis
Hours: Mon-Sat
Types & Periods:
Advertising, Documents,
Primitives, Spanish Colonial,
Artifacts
Specialties: Pre-Columbian,
Religious Art of Mexico
Directions: I-10 Exit Copia,
S on Copia to Alameda,
Left on Alameda

**CALDARELLA'S SOCORRO
TRADING POST**
10180 Socorro Rd 79927
915 859-4777 Est: 1970
Proprietor: Jack M
Caldarella
Hours: By Appointment
Types & Periods: Mennonite
& Primitive Pine, Spanish
Colonial Furniture, Pool
Tables, Juke Boxes
Specialties: Saints Painted
on Tin & Wood Carved
Appraisal Service Available
Directions: Exit I-10, S on
Ave of Americas, Pass 3
Signal Lights, E on
Socorro Rd 1 Mile

CIRCA ANTIQUES
3507 Alameda St 79905
915 533-1389
Proprietor: Ken & Helen
Hicks
Hours: Daily
Types & Periods: General
Line
Specialties: Glass, Furniture,
Porcelain
Directions: I-10 to Copia
St Exit, S to Alameda

COUNTRY ANTIQUE SHOP
1806 E Yandell Dr 79902
915 532-2504 Est: 1972
Proprietor: Mrs Oscar
Weissinger
Hours: Tue-Fri 9-5, Sat
9-4, Closed Sun & Mon
Types & Periods: American
Country Furniture,
Collectibles, Primitives
Specialties: Country Store
Tins
Directions: W on I-10 to
Cotton St Exit, Right on
Cotton St 2 Blocks, Left
on Yandell I Block, E on
I-10 to Dallas St

ESTHER'S ANTIQUES
5977 Montoya 79932
915 584-0638 Est: 1976
Proprietor: Esther L
Atzberger
Hours: Mon-Sun
Types & Periods: Victorian &
Oak Furniture, Glass, China,
Primitives
Specialties: Refinished
Furniture
Directions: Mesa N to
Country Club Rd (Montoya
runs off of Country Club
Rd) turn N, 2 Miles on
Montoya

LAS BONITAS CASAS
3131 Pershing Dr 79903
915 565-9342 Est: 1972
Proprietor: Nelda Brown
Hours: By Appointment,
By Chance
Types & Periods: Victorian
Oak, Depression Glassware
Appraisal Service Available
Directions: Exit I-10 at
Raynor St, N 6 Blocks, 2
Blocks Right

El Paso   Cont'd

THE LOOKING GLASS
3737 N Mesa   79902
915 532-8448   Est: 1976
Proprietor: Nancy M Miles
Hours: Mon-Sat
Types & Periods: American,
Rolltops, File Cabinets,
Chairs, European, Side
Boards, Tables, Bookcases,
Armoirs, Dressers, Mirrors,
Hat Racks, Desk,
Accessories, Pictures,
Frames
Specialties: European
Furniture
   Directions: Take Mesa W
   past Sun Bowl, we are to
   the Left (Past Lubby's) in
   Mesa Village

SCHNADIG ANTIQUES
2616 Montana   79903
915 566-1885   Est: 1970
Proprietor: Si Beulah &
Victor Schnadig
Hours: Tues, Wed, Fri &
Sat
Types & Periods: Objets
D'Art, English, Continental,
Oriental
Specialties: Bronzes, Silver,
Porcelains
Appraisal Service Available
   Directions: W on I-10 Exit
   Dallas St, E Exit Copia St

THIS N' THAT ANTIQUES
7549 Alameda   79915
915 778-4511   Est: 1968
Proprietor: Rose M Horst
Hours: Mon-Sat 10-4:30
Types & Periods: General
Line, Glass, China, Art
Glass, Western Relics,
Furniture, You Name It, We
Have It
Specialties: Pre Columbian
Artifacts, Authenic American
(Pueblo) Indian Relics,
Primitives
   Directions: Old Hwy 80, 1
   Block E of Carolina Dr, 8
   Long blocks W of
   Yarbrough Dr, lower valley

Electra

EMANUEL ANTIQUES &
CABINET SHOP
105 Cleveland St   76360
817 495-2715   Est: 1960

Proprietor: Lewis & Datie
Emanuel
Hours: Daily
Types & Periods: Glass,
China, Furniture
Specialties: Furniture
(Restoring & Upholstering)
   Directions: 1 Block Off
   Hwy 287 Business, Next to
   City Hall

Forney

CLEMENTS ANTIQUES OF
TEXAS INC
PO Box 727   75126
214 226-1520   Est: 1971
Proprietor: Charles W
Clements
Hours: Mon-Fri 9-6, Sat
9-1, Closed Sun
Types & Periods: 18th
Century Furniture, Paintings,
China, Porcelains
Appraisal Service Available
   Directions: I-20 E of Dallas
   at the 740 Farm Rd Exit

RED'S ANTIQUE SUPER
MARKET
I-20   75126
214 226-1033   Est: 1955
Proprietor: Red Whaley
Hours: Daily, Weekends
9-6
Types & Periods: Furniture,
Glass, Copper, Bread Racks,
Round Tables, China
Specialties: Clocks
Appraisal Service Available
   Directions: 20 Miles E of
   Dallas

REDS ANTIQUES-PARIS
FLEA MARKET
I-20   75126
214 552-3839   Est: 1960
Proprietor: Glenn Red
Whaley
Hours: Daily, Weekends
Types & Periods: Clocks,
Furniture, Glass, Pianos,
Organs
Specialties: Clocks
   Directions: I-20 to Forney
   Exit

Fort Worth

FORT WORTH CLUSTER
Many Antique Shops
throughout City, Heavy
Concentration on E
Lancaster (3000-6000
Blocks), Hemphill (2000
Block), Camp Bowie Blvd
(3000-6000 Blocks)

ALCOLE ANTIQUES &
INTERIORS
PO Box 9697   76107
817 268-3490
Proprietor: Mrs Oneta D
Cole
Hours: By Appointment
Types & Periods: Paintings,
Prints, Rugs, Furniture,
Accessories

ANTIQUES & ALMOST INC
1630 Park Pl   76110
817 927-7771   Est: 1973
Proprietor: Rowan & Doris
Shaw
Hours: Tues-Sun 11-5,
Closed Mon
Types & Periods: Furniture,
Glass
Appraisal Service Available

NORMA BAKER ANTIQUES
3311 W 7th St   76107
817 335-1152   Est: 1973
Proprietor: Norma J Baker
Hours: Mon-Sat 10-5,
Closed Sun
Types & Periods: General
Line
Specialties: Sterling Flatware
Matching Service
   Directions: W of
   Downtown Area, 2 Blocks
   from Museum Complex,
   1/2 Mile N of E-W
   Freeway

BG'S BELKNAP ANTIQUES
5026 E Belknap St   76117
817 834-4451   Est: 1973
Proprietor: Betty M Greer
Hours: Mon-Sat 10:30-6
Types & Periods: Primitives,
Glassware, Furniture
   Directions: At Haltom Rd
   & Belknap, Just a Few
   Blocks off Hwy 121 Airport
   Frwy

KENNETH BORTZ ANTIQUES
2812 Hemphill St   76110
817 924-3991   Est: 1959
Proprietor: Kenneth Bortz
Hours: Mon-Sat, Also By
Appointment, Closed
July-Aug
Types & Periods: French,
English, American,
Continental Furniture &
Accessories, Oriental,
Victorian, Memorabilia
Appraisal Service Available
Directions: 2 1/2 Blocks N
of the Intersection of W
Berry St & Hemphill St in
the Heart of Ft Worths Old
South Side

CENTRAL ANTIQUES
401 S Freeway   76104
817 332-5981   Est: 1968
Proprietor: J D & Kitty
Brown
Hours: Mon-Sat 10-5:30,
Auctions Each 1st Monday
Night
Types & Periods: American
Oak, Victorian Walnut
Furniture, Dolls, Glass,
China, Orientals, Primitives,
Toys, Paper Items,
Advertising, Books, Lighting
Specialties: American
Furniture, Dolls, Toys,
Glassware, Lighting
Appraisal Service Available
Directions: Hattie Exit off
I-35 W, Near Downtown

THE CHAMBERS
3851 Camp Bowie   76107
817 732-7111   Est: 1974
Proprietor: Larue H
Chambers
Hours: Daily, Weekends,
By Appointment
Types & Periods: Clocks,
Porcelains, Lap Desks,
Chairs, Candlesticks, Desks,
Chests, Copper
Specialties: Imari
Directions: 3 Blocks W of
Will Rogers Colliseum

THE CLOCK GALLERY
6333 Camp Bowie   76116
817 731-0471   Est: 1975
Proprietor: John L Juniker
Hours: Daily 10-6
Types & Periods: Clocks
Appraisal Service Available
Directions: E Side of 6333
Mall

CORA'S ANTIQUES
4512 E Lancaster   76103
817 535-7419
Proprietor: Mr & Mrs
James R Simpson
Hours: Mon-Sat 10-6,
Types & Periods: Glass, Art,
Furniture

THE CORNUCOPIA ANTIQUES
1225 Clara St   76110
817 926-0747
Proprietor: Drs Sue &
Dewey Mays
Hours: By Appointment
Types & Periods: Glass,
General Line

J & J CRAINE ANTIQUES
6712 Glenview Dr   76118
817 284-2001   Est: 1968
Proprietor: Jean Craine
Hours: Tues-Sat 10-4,
or By Appointment
Types & Periods: Imports
Specialties: China
(Staffordshire)
Directions: Loop 820 to
Rte Snow, N Richland
Hills Area

CROSS-EYED CRICKET
7630 Glenview   76118
817 284-8961   Est: 1968
Proprietor: Jeanette Steen
Hours: Mon-Sat 10-5
Types & Periods: Primitives,
China, Art Nouveau,
Specialties: Miniatures
(New), Primitives
Directions: Loop 820 to
Glenview Exit, W on
Glenview about 6 Blocks,
Blue House Sits Back
from St

ELSIE'S ANTIQUES
3901 Bellaire Dr S   76109
923-8681
Proprietor: Elsie Pease
Hours: By Appointment
Appraisal Service Available

THE EMPORIUM
4708 W Bryce   76107
817 738-5651   Est: 1976
Proprietor: Bunelle
Gresham
Hours: Tues-Sat, Also By
Appointment
Types & Periods: Unique
Clocks & Quilts

Specialties: Clocks, Quilts
Directions: I-20 W to
Hulen, N to Camp Bowie,
W to Bryce

ESTATE GALLERIES
2824 W 7th St
PO Box 9856   76107
817 336-3296   Est: 1966
Proprietor: Marie Roos
Hours: Mon-Fri
Types & Periods: English,
French & American
Furniture, China, Art,
Paintings

GRAY'S ANTIQUES
1561 W Berry   76110
817 921-2431   Est: 1973
Proprietor: Don Gray
Hours: Mon-Sat 10-5,
Closed Sun
Types & Periods: General
Line, American, European,
Continental, British
Specialties: Collectibles
Appraisal Service Available
Directions: W on Berry St
Exit From I-35 W

GOLDEN ERA ANTIQUES
2744 Hemphill   76110
817 927-0921   Est: 1972
Proprietor: Tom R Stewart
Hours: Mon-Sat 10-6
Types & Periods: Furniture,
Glass, Lamps, Vintage
Clothing
Appraisal Service Available
Directions: I-35 to Berry
St, W to Hemphill, N 3
Blocks

HARRIS ANTIQUES & GIFTS
3625 E Loop 820 S   76112
817 451-8906   Est: 1961
Proprietor: G L Buck
Harris
Hours: Mon-Sat 8:30-5:30,
Closed Sun
Types & Periods: English,
Belgium, French, German,
Denmark, American
Directions: Loop 820 S at
the E Berry St Exit

HAZEL'S ANTIQUES
3759 E Lancaster   76103
817 531-3541   Est: 1972
Proprietor: Hazel & John
Fergusen

Fort Worth   Cont'd

HAZEL'S   Cont'd
Hours: Mon-Sun
12:00-5:00
Types & Periods: Furniture
of all types

HEMPHILL ANTIQUES
2929 Hemphill   76110
817 926-0081   Est: 1973
Proprietor: Ola Finley &
Ralph Linscott
Hours: Mon-Sat 10-5
Types & Periods: General
Line, American Furniture,
Art Glass, China, Clocks,
Primitives
Appraisal Service Available
Directions: From I-35 Take
Berry St Exit W for 1 1/2
Miles to 2nd Traffic Light,
Turn Right 1 1/2 Blocks

JESSIE'S SHOWCASE
3959 E Lancaster   76103
817 535-7611   Est: 1973
Proprietor: Jessie Hall
Hours: Daily, By
Appointment
Types & Periods: Period
Furniture, China, Art Glass,
Clocks
Specialties: Clocks, Glass
Directions: Close to
Dallas/Ft Worth Turnpike,
On old Dallas Hwy

**JOHNSON'S ANTIQUES
INC**
2201 Scott Ave   76103
817 469-1212   Est: 1974
Proprietor: Fred Ernest
Johnson
Hours: Mon-Sat, 9-5:30
Types & Periods: European
& American
Appraisal Service Available
Directions: Beach St Exit
off Trnpke, S 1 Block to
Scott Ave, Turn W

LA VERNE'S ANTIQUES
5909 E Lancaster Hwy 80
76112
817 451-2141   Est: 1977
Proprietor: La Verne Davis
Hours: Tues-Sat 10-5,
Closed Sun & Mon
Types & Periods: General
Line, Glass, China, Small
Primitives, Pottery

Directions: 2nd Block W of
Loop 820 at Dallas-Ft
Worth Trnpke (I-20) to
Handley Exit, Take 820 to
E Lancaster Exit, Right 2
Blocks

MARJORIE'S ANTIQUES
4116 Belknap   76117
817 834-0441   Est: 1971
Proprietor: Marjorie J
Phillips
Directions: Daily, By
Appointment, Closed
Thurs & Sun
Types & Periods: General
Line, Furniture, Glass,
Brass, Silver, Lamps, Clocks
Directions: 1 1/2 Blocks E
from N Beach St

MEEKINS GALLERIES
3501 W 7th St   76107
817 731-7409   Est: 1977
Proprietor: Lew Meekins
Hours: Mon-Sat 11-4:30
Types & Periods: 17th, 18th
& 19th Century Italian,
French, English & Oriental,
North American Indian Arts
Directions: 3 Blocks N of
Carter Museum

NOTHING NEW ANTIQUES
152 N Sylvania   76111
817 834-8571   Est: 1969
Proprietor: Lorraine
Gilliland
Hours: Daily
Types & Periods: Primitives,
Furniture, Glass, China
Directions: 4 Doors S of
Airport Frwy Hwy 121

OAKLAND ANTIQUES
3955 E Lancaster   76103
817 534-9441   Est: 1973
Proprietor: Bobby &
Janelle Downs
Hours: Mon-Sat 10-5, Sun
By Appointment
Types & Periods: American
Oak Furniture, Ceiling Fans,
Advertisements
Specialties: Ceiling Fans
Directions: From Old Ft
Worth-Dallas Trnpk S on
Oakland to E Lancaster W
4 Blocks

OLDE TYMERS ANTIQUES
4611 Bryce   76107
817 732-6751   Est: 1971

Proprietor: Dorothy
Sweger
Hours: Tue-Sat 11-5,
Closed Sun & Mon
Types & Periods: Victorian,
Art & Cut Glass, Jewelry,
Lamps, Furniture, China,
Orientals
Specialties: Clocks
Directions: 7 Blocks N of
I-20, Off Hulen & Camp
Bowie

ORIENTAL ACCENTS
5513A W Rosedale   76107
817 738-9871   Est: 1971
Proprietor: Richard D
Gordon
Hours: Tues-Fri 10-4
Types & Periods: Orientals,
Ming thru Ching
Specialties: Oriental
Appraisal Service Available
Directions: I-20 to Merrick
St Exit, Turn Left to
Rosedale, Right on
Rosedale for 3 Blocks

PATTY'S CORNER
3623 Decatur   76106
817 624-3511   Est: 1975
Proprietor: Bill & Patty
McGee
Hours: Tues-Sun, Closed
Mon
Types & Periods: General
Line, Collectibles, Period &
Turn-of-the-Century
Specialties: Furniture
(American Oak), Coca Cola
Items

PENN STATION
4706 Camp Bowie   76107
817 738-5111   Est: 1977
Proprietor: Patricia Penn
Goss
Hours: Tues-Sat, By
Appointment
Types & Periods: General
Line, Primitives
Specialties: Unusual
Decorative Accessories
Directions: 4 Blocks N of
I-20 Exit at Hulen St to
Camp Bowie Blvd, W 2
Blocks

THE SMITH SHOP
4704-4706 Bryce
76107
817 737-4307   Est: 1962
Proprietor: James A &
Bernadine Smith

Hours: Mon-Sat, Closed
Sun
Types & Periods: English &
American
Specialties: Furniture
Appraisal Service Available
Directions: At Intersection
of Bryce & Camp Bowie, 1
Block W of Hulen St

**FORREST SMITH &
COMPANY INC**
1628 Fifth Ave   76104
817 924-2293   Est: 1937
Proprietor: Forrest T Smith
Hours: Mon-Fri 8-4:30, Sat
8-12, Closed Sun &
Holidays
Types & Periods: General
Line, American & Imported
Directions: 10 Blocks S of
Harris Hospital Parking
Garage

**STONE HOUSE TRADING
POST INC**
4332 W Vickery Blvd
                      76107
817 738-5631   Est: 1972
Proprietor: Perry
Chamblioc
Hours: Mon-Sat 10-5, Also
By Appointment
Types & Periods: Furniture,
Primitives, Glass, China,
Bric-A-Brac
Specialties: Furniture,
Refinished
Directions: N on Hulen
from 820 to W Vickery, Off
I-20 on Hulen to W
Vickery

THIS OLD HOUSE
2516 Hemphill   76110
817 921-4691   Est: 1976
Proprietor: Ms Mary Ruth
Boone
Hours: Mon-Sat, Also By
Appointment
Types & Periods: Glass,
China, Pictures, Furniture,
Clothing, American Oak,
Dolls, Lamps, Cut & Pressed
Glass, Quilts, Jewelry, Furs
Appraisal Service Available
Directions: Take
Morningside Exit off I-35
S, W to Hemphill, 3rd
House N, on the W Side
of St

**TOWN PUMP ANTIQUES &
COLLECTIBLES**
6201 E Lancaster   76112
817 457-0870   Est: 1972
Proprietor: Mr & Mrs
James A Keller
Hours: Mon-Sat 9:30-5:30
Types & Periods: General
Line, Glassware
Specialties: American Oak
Furniture, Primitives
Appraisal Service Available
Directions: 1 Block E of
Loop 820

TREASURES OF ALL AGES
7630 Glenview Dr   76118
817 284-8961   Est: 1975
Proprietor: Janice Sue
Anderson
Hours: Mon-Sat
Types & Periods: American
Oak, Primitives
Specialties: Doll Furniture
Directions: 4 Blocks W off
Airport Freeway (121), Exit
Glenview-Pipeline Rd

Fredericksburg

**THE CONNECTICUT
YANKEE**
7075 Washington US 87
                      78624
512 997-4992   Est: 1965
Proprietor: Bruce & Norma
Benway
Hours: By Appointment,
By Chance
Types & Periods: Glass,
Clocks, Brass, Copper,
Lamps, Jewelry, Early
American
Specialties: Glass (Heisey &
Colored Pattern)
Appraisal Service Available

JACK'S EMPORIUM
103-109 E Main St   78624
512 997-7455   Est: 1972
Proprietor: Jack &
Frances Estes
Hours: Mon-Sat 9:30-5:30,
Sun 11-4 Summer till
Labor Day, Closed other
Sun During Year
Types & Periods: Gifts,
Collectibles, Nostalgia,
Memorabilia, Minatures,
Primitives, Books, Canning
Jars, Over 25,000 Different
items

Specialties: Primitives,
Collectibles, German
Imports, Toys, Beer Steins
Directions: Corner US 290
& State 16, Kerrville Hwy,
Downtown

THE TULIP & THE BIRD
602 W Main   78624
512 997-7444   Est: 1973
Proprietor: Joe & Von
Bolin
Hours: Tues-Sun, Closed
Mon
Types & Periods: Early
Country Furniture, Copper,
Pewter, Quilts & Coverlets
Specialties: Early Texas
Furniture
Directions: On Main St
Past the Business District,
Next Door to "Immigrants
Landing Restaurant"

Gainesville

ANTIQUES ETC
216 Ritchey   76240
817 665-5724
Proprietor: Patsy Murrell
Hours: By Appointment,
By Chance
Types & Periods: General
Line

HENLEY HOUSE ANTIQUES
205 N Commeroe   76240
817 665-2025   Est: 1977
Proprietor: Eldon & Edna
Henley
Hours: Tues-Sat 12-5
Types & Periods: General
Line
Specialties: Pump Organs,
Player Pianos (Restored)
Directions: 1 1/2 Blocks N
of Court House

**I REMEMBER MAMA
ANTIQUES**
109 Davis St   76240
817 665-2264
Proprietor: Mrs Eula
Gardner
Types & Periods: General
Line

PRITCHETT ANTIQUES
421 N Grand   76240
817 668-7915
Proprietor: George
Pritchett
Hours: Mon-Sat 8-6
Types & Periods: General
Line

**WATTS ANTIQUES &
INTERIORS**
1010 E California   76240
817 665-5381   Est: 1969
Proprietor: B N Watts, Jr
Hours: Tues-Sat 10-5:30,
Closed Sun & Mon
Types & Periods: 18th &
19th Century Oriental,
French, English & American
Furniture, Oriental
Porcelains & Rugs, Clocks
Appraisal Service Available
Directions: Exit California
St Off I-35 or Hwy 82, 70
Miles N of Dallas/Ft Worth

Garland

BETTY'S ANTIQUES
4345 Chaha Rd   75043
214 226-1539   Est: 1965
Proprietor: Betty Macon
Hours: Mon-Sun
Types & Periods: American
Architectural, Bevelled &
Stained Glass 1870-1920,
And The Unusual Only, We
Wholesale
Specialties: Bevelled Entries,
Slot Machines, Circus Items,
"Bawdy" House Items, Cash
Reg, Country Store Eqpt
Directions: I-30 E on Lake
Ray Hubbard, 15 Miles
from Downtown Dallas

**COUNTRY COTTAGE
ANTIQUES**
2214 Royal Crest   75043
214 271-4253   Est: 1974
Proprietor: Alaine Adams
Hours: Tue-Sat, Also By
Appointment
Types & Periods: 18th &
19th Century Country
Furniture & Accessories,
American
Specialties: Pine Furniture
Appraisal Service Available

Goliad

**ANTIQUES ON THE
GOLIAD SQUARE**
218 Commercial   77963
Est: 1972
Proprietor: David & Elmer
Davis
Hours: Mon-Fri 10-5
Directions: 2 Blocks Off
Hwy 59 & 77 On the
Square

Granbury

IMO'S POLLY ANTIQUES
109 E Bridge   76048
817 573-4444   Est: 1968
Proprietor: Imogene &
Leon Meissner
Hours: Tues-Sat 10-5
Types & Periods: Art Glass,
China, Furniture
Directions: On the Square

Grand Prairie

**ABBY'S ATTIC &
ANTIQUES**
208 E Main   75050
214 262-7828   Est: 1973
Proprietor: Ann Schroeder
Hours: Tues-Thurs 10-5,
Closed June, July & Aug
Types & Periods: Primitives,
Clocks
Directions: Btwn Dallas &
Ft Worth, S off I-30 to
Main St

**FINDERS KEEPERS
ANTIQUES**
202 E Main   75050
214 262-3039
Proprietor: Dorothy Ballard
Hours: Thurs-Sat 10-5
Types & Periods: Primitives,
Collectibles, Advertising
Directions: Exit Belt Line
S to Hwy 80, Turn Right 6
Blocks W

**TRADERS VILLAGE FLEA
MARKET & SHOPPERS
BAZAAR**
2602 Mayfield Rd   75051
214 647-2331   Est: 1974
Proprietor: Irving Taggart
Hours: Sat & Sun

Types & Periods: General
Line, Collectibles
Directions: 5 Miles S of
Six Flags Over Texas

Groesbeck

THE JUNQUE SHOPPE
Rte 2 Box 52   76642
817 729-5726   Est: 1972
Proprietor: Juanita
McLemore
Hours: Tues-Sat, Closed
Sun & Mon
Types & Periods: General
Line, Collectibles
Specialties: Dolls Restored
Directions: Buffalo Hwy
164 E at Groesbeck City
Limits

Hallsville

KATHERINE'S ANTIQUES
102 W Main St   75650
214 668-2936   Est: 1971
Proprietor: Mrs Chas L
Brown
Hours: Tues, Thurs, Fri &
Sat 1-5, Also By
Appointment, By Chance
Types & Periods:
Mid-Victorian, General Line
Directions: Downtown

Hamlin

**TOM'S TRADING POST &
ANTIQUES**
330 E Lake Dr   79520
915 576-2121   Est: 1966
Proprietor: Tom & Mary
Brady
Hours: Mon-Sat, Closed
Sun
Types & Periods: General
Line, Furniture
Specialties: Clocks, Brass
Directions: US Hwy 92,
Corner of E Lake Dr & NE
Ave C

Harlingen

ANTIQUES ETC
Rte I Box 303   78550
512 423-2882   Est: 1974

Proprietor: Ruth S &
George Lamborn
Hours: Tues-Thurs, Also
By Appointment
Types & Periods: General
Line, Glassware, China,
Brass, Collectible Items,
Nippon, Heisey, Pottery,
Some Music Boxes
Directions: SW Corner
Business 83 & Bass Blvd

CARRIE'S ANTIQUES
412 E Tyler   78550
512 423-0683   Est: 1957
Proprietor: C C & Carrie
Ramert
Hours: Mon-Fri 9-5, Sat
9-4
Types & Periods: Glass,
China, Furniture, Clocks,
American & European
Directions: 1/2 Block E of
Chamber of Commerce on
Hwy 83

**YANKEE PEDDLER
ANTIQUES**
1121 E Harrison   78550
512 423-7326   Est: 1973
Proprietor: Michael Hooks
Hours: Mon-Fri 10 6
Types & Periods: Primitives,
Stained Glass, Brass,
Copper, Furniture, Ceiling
Fans

Haskell

BARBER SHOP ANTIQUES
17 N Ave E   79521
817 864-2575   Est: 1974
Proprietor: Gayla Nanny &
Ruby Turner
Hours: Mon-Sat 10-5, Sun
By Appointment
Types & Periods: Depression
Glass, Furniture, Primitives,
Stoneware
Specialties: Glass, Pie
Safes, Washstands
Directions: Downtown on
W Side of Sq

Hempstead

PIGEON HOUSE ANTIQUES
716 12th St   77445
713 826-2261   Est: 1972
Proprietor: Albert & Myrtle
Somerford

Hours: By Appointment
Types & Periods: Americana
Furniture 1875-1915,
Glassware, Lamps, Political
Buttons
Directions: 1 Block from
City Hall Downtown

Henderson

**FAULKNERS' ANTIQUES
INC**
108 Hwy 64 W   75652
214 657-3481   Est: 1968
Proprietor: Vernon & June
Faulkner
Hours: Mon-Sat, Closed
Sun & Wed
Types & Periods: Direct
Importers of Quality English
Antiques & Accessories
Specialties: Oak, Jacobean,
Stripped Pine, Clocks,
Accessories
Directions: At the Traffic
Circle

Hillsboro

THE VICTORIAN SHOP
110 W Elm   76645
817 582-5201   Est: 1967
Proprietor: Margaret
Ballard
Hours: Mon-Sat
Types & Periods: General
Line
Directions: 1 Block off of
Town Sq, Hwy 22 W

Houston

HOUSTON CLUSTER
Directions: Westheimer
(300-1800 Blocks), Heights
Blvd (1500-1800 Blocks),
Washington (3400-4500
Blocks), Main (3500-4000
Blocks)

**ABSSI & HALL-THE ISHTAR
GATE GALLERY**
3265 The Galleria
5015 Westheimer   77056
713 622-0114   Est: 1959
Proprietor: Ali & Florence
Al-Abssi

Types & Periods: Antiquities,
Pre-Columbian, Egyptian 50
AD-2500 BC, Chinese 1200
BC-1800 AD, Southeast
Asian 1200 AD-1800 AD
Appraisal Service Available
Directions: The Galleria

ACCENT ANTIQUES
5534 Truett Ave   77023
713 923-7118
Proprietor: Grant L Payne
Hours: Eves 5-10 ,
Weekends 8-6
Types & Periods: General
Line, Bottles, Primitives

ALLART GALLERIE
2023 S Shepherd   77019
713 526-3631   Est: 1953
Proprietor: R T Auera
Hours: Mon-Fri 9-5, Sat
9-1, Closed Sun
Types & Periods: 18th &
19th Century, Furniture,
Clocks, Accessories
Specialties: Clocks
Directions: Off Hwy 59 S,
Btwn Westheimer & San
Felipe, River Oaks Area

**ALMOST NEW FURNITURE
& ANTIQUES**
14610 Hiram Clarke
                     77045
713 434-2980   Est: 1977
Proprietor: Fred G Hagans
Hours: Mon-Sat
Types & Periods: British,
American
Directions: Corner of W
Fuqua & Hiram Clarke in
SW Houston, Approx 3
Miles W of S Main St

AMCO JEWELRY CO
1010 Jefferson   77002
713 659-2769   Est: 1935
Hours: Mon-Fri 9:30-5:30
Types & Periods: Jewelry
Appraisal Service Available
Directions: Suite 1006,
First International Bank
Bldg

**AMERICAN DECORATIVE
ARTS**
2002 Peden St
River Oaks Center   77019
713 526-0095   Est: 1969
Proprietor: Robert E
Kinnaman & Brian A
Ramaekers
Hours: Tues-Sat 10-5

Houston Cont'd

AMERICAN DECORATIVE ARTS Cont'd
Types & Periods: 18th &
19th American Furniture &
Related Decorative Art
Appraisal Service Available
Directions: Corner of
Shepard Dr & W Gray in
the River Oaks Center,
Near Downtown Houston,
Easily reached from all
Points in Town by the
Freeways

ANCIENT AGE ANTIQUES
6718 Chetwood   77081
713 665-0047   Est: 1971
Proprietor: Marion Sword
Hours: Mon-Fri, Also By
Appointment
Types & Periods: English &
Continental, Georgian,
Victorian & Edwardian,
Mahogany, Walnut,
Rosewood & Pine Furniture,
Copper, Brass, Bric-A-Brac
Directions: 1 Block W of
Chimney Rock & 1/2
Block N of Bellaire Blvd

ANTIQUE HOUSE
1010 Wirt Rd   77055
713 686-1250   Est: 1965
Proprietor: Gordon & Ella
Mae Hayslip
Hours: Tues-Sat 10-4,
Closed Sun & Mon, Also
By Appointment
Types & Periods: 18th, 19th
& Early 20th Century
Directions: 1 Block N Katy
Frwy at Wirt Rd

ANTIQUES & COLLECTIBLES
621 Town & Country
Village   77024
713 464-3186   Est: 1970
Proprietor: Gerry Bradley
& L T Griffin, Jr
Hours: Tues-Sat, Also By
Appointment
Types & Periods: General
Line, American, Texas,
European, Primitives,
Accessories
Specialties: Unusual Items,
Brass
Directions: In Town &
Country Village, Off I-10 at
W Belt, N of Joske's in
the Mall of Fountains

AVALON ANTIQUES
2615 Westheimer   77098
713 528-6855   Est: 1931
Proprietor: Don M James
Hours: Mon-Fri 9-5, Sat
10-4, Also By Appointment
Specialties: Refinished
American Antiques
Directions: Westheimer at
Kirby

BIT OF YESTERYEAR
10114 FM 1960 W   77070
713 469-0331   Est: 1971
Proprietor: Charlotte M
Vincent
Hours: Wed-Sat 9:30-4,
Also By Appointment
Types & Periods: Country
Furniture, Primitives
Specialties: Musical
Instruments, Arcade
Machines, Country Store
Appraisal Service Available
Directions: I-45

BLECHMAN GALLERIES
518 Shepherd Dr   77007
713 869-0634 or 864-7844
                    Est: 1976
Proprietor: Mark Blechman
Hours: Mon-Fri
Types & Periods: General
Line, Hand Woven Oriental
Carpets
Specialties: Wholesale To
The Trade Only
Directions: Btwn
Washington Ave &
Memorial

THE BOARDING HOUSE INC
1653 Blalock   77080
713 461-1773   Est: 1973
Proprietor: Ms Jacqueline
W Cassidy
Hours: Mon-Sat
Types & Periods: Jewelry
Pre-Columbian & Classic
Stones Gold & Silver, Early
1840 British, Pine, Primitive,
Art Glass Windows
Specialties: Decorator
Accent Pieces, All Antique
Pieces Completely Restored
on Our Premises
Directions: Take Blalock
Exit Off I-10 W, N on
Blalock past 2 Traffic
Signals

BRIGUGLIO ANTIQUES
3626 N Braeswood Blvd
                    77025
713 667-8029
Proprietor: Anthony &
Mary Briguglio
Hours: By Appointment
Types & Periods: Cut & Art
Glass, China, General Line

BRITISH ANTIQUE PLACE INC
4410 W 12th St   77055
713 681-1180   Est: 1970
Proprietor: James D Black
Hours: Mon-Fri 9-5, Sat
9-12
Types & Periods: Victorian
Furniture, Pianos, Clocks
Specialties: Brass, China,
Wooden Reproductions
Directions: 1 Block W 610
Loop

BROWNSTONE GALLERY
2803 Westheimer   77098
713 523-8171   Est: 1974
Proprietor: Beau Theriot
Hours: Mon-Fri 9-5, Also
By Appointment
Types & Periods: Imari,
Cloisonne, General Line
Directions: Btwn River
Oaks Blvd & Kirby Dr

CAROLINE ANTIQUE SHOP
521 Westheimer St   77006
713 529-7192
Proprietor: Mrs Jessie
Mathews
Hours: Mon-Sat 8:30-5:30,
Closed Sun
Types & Periods: General
Line

THE CENTER OF HOME FURNISHINGS INC
4316 Westheimer   77027
713 840-1480   Est: 1977
Proprietor: Nancy
Goodrich
Hours: Mon-Sat
Types & Periods: American,
French, English, Victorian,
Armoires, Chests, Chairs,
Tables
Appraisal Service Available
Directions: Westheimer at
Mid Lane in New
Westheimer Oaks Village

CHANDLER'S NOSTALGIA
1832 Westheimer   77098
713 668-7864 (After 6 PM)
Est: 1969
Proprietor: Ceil, Henry &
Edy Chandler
Hours: Mon-Sat 10-4
Types & Periods: Paper
Goods, Comic Books, Beatle
& Rock Items of the 60's &
70's, Post Cards, Occupied
Japan Collectibles, Toys,
Advertising Items
Specialties: Beatle & Rock
Items of the 60's & 70's,
Paper Goods, Occupied
Japan Collectibles
Directions: Btwn Shepherd
Dr & Montrose, Across
from Lanier Jr High
School

CHEN ORIENTAL CO
631 Town & Country
77024
713 467-4802   Est: 1970
Proprietor: Philip C Chen
Hours: Tues-Sat 11-5,
Closed Sun & Mon
Types & Periods: 1700 BC
to 1890 AD Oriental Arts
Specialties: Bronze, Jade,
Porcelain
Appraisal Service Available
Directions: I-10 at W Belt
Exit, Behind Joske's Dept
Store

COLLECTORS EXCHANGE
1200 S Post Oak Rd
Suite 200   77056
Est: 1971
Proprietor: A B Cass, Jr
Hours: Mon-Fri, Also By
Appointment
Types & Periods: Bronzes,
Cloisonne, Paintings, Prints,
Glassware, Stueben
Specialties: 19th Century
Bronzes
Appraisal Service Available
Directions: Galleria Area

**COLLECTOR'S FIREARMS
INC**
3301 Fondren   77063
713 781-5812 & 781-1960
Est: 1974
Proprietor: Mike Clark &
Jerry Fountain
Hours: Mon-Sat
Types & Periods: Weapons
& Related Antiques, Modern
Advertising, Promotional
Items from Gun Mfg

Appraisal Service Available
Directions: Corner of
Fondren & Richmond in
SW Houston

**THE COLLECTORS HOUSE
OF ANTIQUES INC**
3900 Montrose Blvd
77006
713 526-6296   Est: 1967
Proprietor: Herb Wiener
Hours: Mon-Fri, Also By
Appointment
Types & Periods: General
Line, American Cut Glass
Specialties: Cut Glass
Appraisal Service Available
Directions: Near
Downtown Astrodome

**ALEX CONSTANTINO
ANTIQUES**
3631 University Blvd
77005
713 664-8840
Proprietor: Dorothy & Alex
Constantino
Hours: Tues-Sat 10:30-5,
Closed Sun & Mon
Types & Periods: Art Glass,
Art Nouveau & Deco, Silver,
Furniture

COPPER PENNY ANTIQUES
2406 Bessonnet   77005
Est: 1975
Hours: Mon-Sat 9:30-3:30
Types & Periods: English,
Gifts & Plants
Directions: Btwn Kirby &
Morningside

CURIOSITY CHOP
4712 Telephone   77087
713 644-7571   Est: 1971
Proprietor: H G Simmons
Hours: Mon-Sat
Types & Periods:
Miscellaneous, Located with
Flower Shop
Specialties: Buy, Sell Flo
Blue
Directions: Gulf Frwy at S
Loop

FISHER SHOP
4320 Yale   77018
713 692-0057   Est: 1974
Proprietor: Mrs Ruth
Fisher
Hours: Sat-Sun

Types & Periods: Furniture,
Glassware
Directions: I-45
Crosstimbers Exit W to
Yale

FOR EXAMPLE INC
2702 Westheimer   77098
713 523-2293   Est: 1977
Proprietor: Sue R Pittman
& Merrick C Brants
Hours: Mon-Sat
Types & Periods: American
Primitives, Late 1700's to
Late 1800's, Texas
Primitives, American
Accessories, Pottery, Rugs
Specialties: We also Carry
Special Order Items, Rag
Rugs (New), Tin Ceilings, &
Offer an Interior Design
Service
Directions: Corner of
Westheimer & Lake Sts,
1 Block W of Kirby Dr

**FORGET ME NOT
ANTIQUES**
957 Brittmoore Rd   77079
713 468-3551   Est: 1970
Proprietor: George &
Shirley Finnell
Hours: Mon-Sat 10-5,
Closed Sun
Types & Periods:
Turn-of-the-Century Oak,
Victorian & Primitives, Salt
Glazed Stoneware, Kitchen
Items Restored, Quilts
Specialties: American
Antiques Only
Appraisal Service Available
Directions: S of Katy Frwy
Btwn N Wilcrest Dr & W
Belt

**ELIZABETH FOWLER
ANTIQUES & BOOKS**
2290 W Holcombe   77025
Proprietor: Helen Matsu
Hours: Tues-Sat 10:30-5,
Closed Sun & Mon
Types & Periods: General
Line, Post Cards, Books
Directions: Holcombe at
Greenbriar

FULSHERA'S ANTIQUES
2227 Fairview Ave   77019
713 529-2021   Est: 1962
Proprietor: Mrs G N
Fulshear
Hours: Mon-Fri
Types & Periods: Pressed,
Cut & Art Glass, China

(From page 455). In today's world of collecting, one might find them being sold as pieces "of the period". Their quality is excellent, but obviously one must be aware of whether he is looking at a piece "of the period" or one made a century later. A little attentiveness to the presence of hand tool marks or machine tool marks can make all the difference in determining its age. When thinking about buying a piece attributed to the 18th Century, do not hesitate to pull out drawers. If necessary, crawl underneath to look. Pull it away from the wall and look at the tool marks on the back. Be certain it was made by hand tools in the 1700's rather than machinery in the 1800's.

Back to the Late Victorian Period. A few eccentricities should be noted. An item or two of papier mache was expected. In America it was usually made into sewing or jewelry boxes, but sometimes into such things as game tables. There were also chairs made from buffalo and cow horn as well as candlesticks and chandeliers made from antlers.

Brass beds had their first surge of real popularity in this period although they existed at an earlier time. Cast iron furniture came into vogue during this period too. Extremely ornate garden seats were cast in pieces, assembled and painted. Park benches were made, but so were other things as we show on page 552.

By the end of the century and the close of the Victorian Era, the factory was dominant in this country. This period introduced an incredible variety of styles to bemuse the collector. Very fine woods and excellent craftsmanship are present. Only my often repeated warning is necessary. Victorian furniture can be of a large scale which might pose problems for the modern home.

The next identifiable period remains only loosely jumbled together in what is called by some "Turn of the Century". It includes Art Nouveau, the Mission Oak, Age of Golden Oak and the Bird's-eye Maple furniture vogues. Turn of the Century has a range of time from the 1880's into the 1920's, but there is no clear beginning nor ending.

Art Nouveau is the result of an effort in the late 19th Century to devise a new way of living as well as new things with which to live. It traveled around Europe, flowered in Belgium and finally reached America. It was espoused primarily by artists who professed to be free from all old tradition and sought inspiration from nature alone. Some say it had roots in the ancient Celtic culture. Characterization is difficult, but the asymmetrical or sinuous line may be the most reliable. (Continued, page 623).

Houston Cont'd

FULSHERA'S Cont'd
Specialties: Celery Vases
Directions: SW Houston,
2 Blocks N of Westheimer,
Btwn S Shephard & Kirby,
Corner of Westgate &
Fairview

GEORGE-SHIA & SONS INC
1744 Norfolk 77098
713 522-5224 & 529-9072
Est: 1972
Proprietor: George C C
Lee
Hours: Mon-Sat
Types & Periods: Chinese,
Ch'ing Dynasty, Porcelain,
Wood Carving, Jade Trees,
Screen
Directions: At Woodhead
off Richmond, Btwn
Shepherd & Montrose,
About 10 Minutes Drive
from Downtown Houston

ISABELL GERHART PRECIOUS STONES & ANTIQUES
6015 Westheimer 77027
713 626-3700
Proprietor: Michael
Hughes
Hours: Daily 10-6, Until 9
Thurs & Fri, Closed Sun
Types & Periods: General
Line, Jewelry

GOLD MINE ANTIQUES
9743 Katy Freeway 77024
713 461-7493 Est: 1972
Proprietor: Mrs Verle
Rivers, Mrs Julie Myers,
Mrs Jeanne Milton
Hours: Mon-Fri 11-4:30,
Sat By Chance or By
Appointment, Closed Sun
Types & Periods: American
& English Furniture of the
18th & 19th Century,
Accessories, Collectibles
Specialties: Brass, Copper,
Tinware, Rugs
Directions: Off I-10 W at
Bunker Hill Exit, Located
on S Side of Shopping
Center which is Adjacent
to Holiday Inn

THE GREAT EXCHANGE
9102 W Park 77063
713 789-0590 Est: 1977

Proprietor: Nurick's,
Felsen's, Reis's
Hours: Sat & Sun, Thurs
& Fri By Chance
Types & Periods: Oriental,
French, English, American
from 1700's, Glassware,
Collectibles
Specialties: Fine Antiques,
Diamonds, Gold
Directions: Btwn Fondren
& Gessner

GREAT EXPECTATIONS ANTIQUES
618 Town & Country
Village 77024
713 465-7622 Est: 1974
Proprietor: Karey
Bresenhan
Hours: Tues-Sat 11-5:30,
Closed Sun & Mon
Types & Periods: Quilts,
Furniture 1800-1900,
American Cut Glass, Art
Nouveau, Bentwood
Specialties: Needlework
(Quilts)
Directions: 3 Doors Down
from Joske's Back Door,
Go S on W Belt Off I-10

GREAT THINGS
2515 Morse 77019
713 522-7996 Est: 1977
Proprietor: J R Arnold
Hours: Mon-Sat 10-5
Types & Periods:
Reproductive, Beveled Glass
Directions: Off 1800
Westheimer, Across the St
from Lanier Jr High
School

THE GREEN BOTTLE ANTIQUE SHOP
701 Colquitt Ave 77098
713 528-4483 Est: 1927
Proprietor: Elizabeth
Morford
Hours: Mon-Fri, Sat By
Appointment
Types & Periods: American
Period Furniture
Specialties: Only Genuine
Antiques of the Period
Appraisal Service Available
Directions: 5 Blocks W of
4200 Main St

GRUMPY GRUNTS ANTIQUES
1512 Westheimer 77006
713 529-9092 Est: 1975

Proprietor: James F Lynch
Hours: Tues-Sat, Also By
Appointment, By Chance
Types & Periods: European
Furniture, 19th Century &
Later
Specialties: Collectibles,
Glassware, Men & Womens
Vintage Clothes
Directions: Btwn Montrose
Blvd & Shepard

HEIGHTS GIFTS & ANTIQUES
1811 Heights Blvd 77008
713 869-8391 Est: 1973
Proprietor: Betty & Lloyd
Leusing, Jane Zieliwski,
Lou Kukes
Hours: Tues-Sat 11-5:30,
Closed Sun & Mon
Types & Periods: General
Line, Furniture, Flow Blue,
Primitives, Wood Type &
Type Trays

HEIGHTS STATION
121 Heights Blvd 77007
713 868-3175 Est: 1977
Proprietor: Linda, Wayne
& Hasle Richards, Tim &
Sharon Hattenbach
Hours: Wed-Sun 10-6,
Closed Mon & Tues
Types & Periods: Bev Glass
Mirrors, Glassware,
Collectibles
Directions: Btwn I-10 &
Washington Ave

HEIRLOOM HOUSE
10224A Westheimer
77042
713 780-0772 Est: 1977
Proprietor: Betty W Boyd
& Beth B Matthews
Hours: Mon-Sat, Sun By
Appointment
Types & Periods: 18th &
19th Century Furniture,
Bric-A-Brac, Chandeliers,
Old & New Oriental Rugs,
Lamps made from Antique
Porcelain or Tin, Country,
French & English, Some
American
Specialties: Furniture
Directions: Westheimer at
Seagler, Jumbo Food
Market Shopping Center

Houston   Cont'd

HOME ANTIQUES
515 Richmond Ave   77006
713 522-5072
Proprietor: Myles & Ruth
Cogan
Hours: Mon-Fri 8-6
Types & Periods: Cut Glass,
Souvenir Spoons, Christmas
Plates

HOMESTEAD HEIRLOOMS
7415 Marinette   77074
713 774-6984   Est: 1965
Proprietor: Kay & Max
Stansbury
Hours: At Antique Shows,
Also By Appointment
Types & Periods: Postcards,
Tins, Rural Relics

**HOUSTON ANTIQUE & ART
CENTER**
7560 Harwin Dr   77036
713 789-7393   Est: 1977
Proprietor: Linda Weddle
& Patti Weddle Collins
Hours: Mon-Sat 10-6
Types & Periods: English &
Scottish, Varying Greatly in
Style & Type from Fine
Period Pieces to Good
Furniture through the Art
Deco Period
Specialties: Wardrobes,
Sideboards, Table & Chair
Sets
    Directions: Off Hwy 59,
    Hillcroft Exit Right to
    Harwin, then Left about
    1 Mile, at the Back of a
    Warehouse Complex

**THE HOUSTON FLEA
MARKET INC**
6116 Southwest Freeway
                    77057
713 782-0391   Est: 1968
Proprietor: John & Mary
Wright
Hours: Fri 8-5 for
Reservations, Sat & Sun
8-6
Types & Periods: 40 Shops
Plus 350 Transient Spaces,
Also known as the
"Common Market" & the
"Antique Barn"
    Directions: SW Frwy is
    Hwy 59, Exit at Westpark

**HOUSTON INTERNATIONAL
ANTIQUES INC**
1120 Lockwood Dr   77020
713 675-1704   Est: 1978
Proprietor: Manning A
Mann
Hours: Mon-Fri 8-5
Types & Periods: Imported
European & American 18th
& 19th Walnut, Oak &
Mahogany, Victorian, Wide
Variety
Specialties: Designer,
Decorator Items,
Architectural Items, All
Restored
Appraisal Service Available
    Directions: I-10 E to
    Lockwood Exit, S 5 Blocks

**INTERNATIONAL ANTIQUE
& AUCTION CENTER INC**
7415 Hillcroft   77081
713 981-0877   Est: 1977
Proprietor: Mr & Mrs Sami
S Shehata
Hours: Tues-Sun, Closed
Mon
Types & Periods: Queen
Anne, Victorian, Early
American, European
Primitives, British, Austrian,
German
Specialties: Austrian China
Cabinets, Clocks
Appraisal Service Available
    Directions: Btwn Bellaire &
    Bissonnet, almost to the
    Corner of Bissonnet in
    Large Red Brick
    Warehouses

JENNIE'S ANTIQUES
2039 W Gray   77019
713 528-2767   Est: 1972
Proprietor: Jennie S
Schneider
Hours: Mon-Sat 10:30-5:30
Types & Periods: European,
Oriental, Porcelains,
Furniture, Accessories
Specialties: Oriental,
Porcelains
    Directions: River Oaks
    Shopping Center, Corner
    W Gray & Shepherd Dr

KAY-LEN DOLLS
5414 W Bellfort   77035
713 729-6648   Est: 1965
Proprietor: Mrs Kay
Woodward
Hours: Tues-Sat 11-4,
Closed Sun & Mon

Types & Periods: Antique &
Heirloom Dolls
Specialties: Buy, Sell,
Appraise, Repair
Appraisal Service Available
    Directions: SW Houston,
    Btwn Chimney Rock &
    Hillcroft

**LITTLE'S ANTIQUES &
COUNTRY JUNK**
1246 Wirt Rd   77055
713 682-3222   Est: 1968
Proprietor: Mrs W E Little
Hours: Mon-Fri 10-4, Also
By Appointment, By
Chance, Closed Sat & Sun
Types & Periods: Furniture,
Early American, Primitive,
Quilts, Crocks, Kitchen
Pieces, Ironstone, Victorian,
18th Century
Specialties: Primitives,
Quilts, Decoys
    Directions: Off I-10 W
    Spring Branch Area

**MAI YIN ORIENTAL
ANTIQUES**
2301 Westheimer   77098
713 529-5385   Est: 1973
Proprietor: Andrew Hsueh
Hours: Mon-Sun
Types & Periods: Oriental
Snuff Bottles, Porcelains,
Jade, Furniture
Specialties: Oriental
Appraisal Service Available

**MAPLE LEAF ANTIQUE
SHOP**
1239 Blalock   77080
713 465-4843   Est: 1967
Proprietor: Mercedes & J
D Maples
Hours: Mon-Sat 10-5:30,
Closed Sun
Types & Periods: Glassware,
Clocks, Early Victorian
Walnut to
Turn-of-the-Century Oak,
Lamps, Bric-A-Brac
Specialties: American
Walnut, Victorian &
Turn-of-the-Century Oak
Furniture
Appraisal Service Available

**NORTH MAIN
UPHOLSTERING &
ANTIQUE CO**
4425 Pinemont   77018
713 686-5218   Est: 1947
Proprietor: Charles P Ellis

Hours: Mon-Fri
Types & Periods: General
Line
Directions: NW Area

PEYTON PLACE ANTIQUES
819 Lovett Blvd   77006
713 523-4841
Proprietor: Bill Peyton &
Dewey Gregg
Hours: Mon-Sat 9:30-5:30,
Closed Sun
Types & Periods: Furniture,
Art Objects, Orientals

PINE HOUSE
9035 Lariat   77055
713 461-1621   Est: 1953
Proprietor: Mrs Avis
Behrens
Hours: Tues-Sat 10-5,
Closed Sun & Mon
Types & Periods: Primitive
Pine, Cherry, Maple &
Walnut Early American,
Accessories
Directions: 1 Block N of
Katy Frwy (I-10) Off
Campbell Rd, Turn R at
West Tex

POST OAK ANTIQUES
4410 Morningside   77098
713 523-5661   Est: 1974
Proprietor: Virginia
Sonderegger, Maudean
Fowler, Mary Colbeck
Hours: Mon-Sat, Also By
Appointment
Types & Periods: American,
European Furniture, Art,
Glass, China, Collectibles
Specialties: Furniture
Directions: 1/2 Block N of
the 2300 Block of
Bissonnet

PRICE & COMPANY
2208 Fairview   77019
713 522-8746   Est: 1977
Proprietor: Steve Price
Hours: Tues-Sat 11-5,
Closed on Sat During
Summer Months
Types & Periods: Oriental,
European, Decorative
Accessories
Specialties: Neoclassical
Designs
Directions: 2 Blocks N of
Westheimer Btwn Kirby Dr
& S Shepherd

THE QUILT COLLECTOR
1724 Bissonnet   77005
713 524-8281   Est: 1977
Proprietor: Diane Giles
Hours: Tues-Sat 10-4
Types & Periods: Quilts,
American Primitive
Furniture, Brass, Wood,
Pottery, Candlestands
Specialties: Quilts, Fiber
Wallhangings
Directions: 7 Blocks W of
the Museum of Fine Arts

R & F ANTIQUES
4411 Washington Ave
                        77007
713 861-7750   Est: 1969
Proprietor: R Stohr & J
Baroski
Hours: Mon-Fri
Types & Periods:
Turn-of-the-Century
American Oak
Specialties: Furniture,
Spindle Back Chairs,
Wooden Iceboxes, Radios
Appraisal Service Available
Directions: Centrally
Located off I-10, 3 Blocks
E of Shepherd Dr

THE RED LION
7315 S Main St   77025
713 666-7000
Proprietor: George &
Marjorie Crowder
Hours: Mon-Fri 11-5
Types & Periods: European

**ROBERT RICE GALLERY
INC**
2010 S Post Oak Rd
                        77056
713 960-8003   Est: 1974
Proprietor: Robert Rice
Hours: Mon-Sat
Types & Periods: American
& French Paintings of the
19th & 20th Century
Specialties: American
Paintings
Appraisal Service Available
Directions: Near Post Oak
Central Bldg

RICHARD'S ANTIQUES
3500-3506 & 3709 S Main
St   77002
713 528-5651   Est: 1962
Proprietor: Richard
Coucroun
Hours: Mon-Fri 9:30-5:30

Types & Periods: Louis XV,
Louis XVI & Empire,
Chandeliers, Statues,
Accessories
Specialties: Glass

**ALMA H ROBINSON
ANTIQUES**
500 Westheimer Rd 77006
713 522-6806
Proprietor: Alma H
Robinson
Hours: Tues-Sat 11-5,
Closed Sun & Mon
Types & Periods: Wicker,
Brass Beds, General Line

ROSEY'S ANTIQUES
939 Robbie St   77009
713 862-8529   Est: 1968
Proprietor: Eugene & Ruth
Rosenquist
Hours: Mon-Sat 9-5,
Closed Sun
Types & Periods: American
Oak & Walnut Furniture,
Glass
Directions: Off 900 Block
of W Cavalcade

ROSEY'S ANTIQUES
939 Robbie St   77009
713 862-8529   Est: 1968
Proprietor: Eugene & Ruth
Rosenquist
Hours: Mon-Sat 9-5,
Closed Sun
Types & Periods: American
Oak & Walnut Furniture,
Glass
Directions: Off 900 Block
of W Cavalcade

SANDERS ANTIQUES
315 Fairview   77006
713 522-0539   Est: 1960
Proprietor: W M Sanders
Hours: Mon-Fri, Also By
Appointment
Types & Periods: 18th &
19th Century American
Furniture, Oriental
Porcelains, Coin Silver
Directions: Inner City
Area, Near Downtown

TOM SKELTON ANTIQUES
3219 S Main   77002
713 523-9996   Est: 1964
Proprietor: Tom & Joe
Skelton
Hours: Mon-Fri

Houston Cont'd

TOM SKELTON Cont'd
Types & Periods: General
Line, Collectibles
Appraisal Service Available
Directions: Near
Downtown

TOM SKELTON ANTIQUES
3700 S Main 77002
713 523-9996 Est: 1964
Proprietor: Tom & Joe
Skelton
Hours: Mon-Fri
Types & Periods: General
Line, Collectibles
Appraisal Service Available
Directions: Near
Downtown

SHOP IN YESTERYEAR
4656 FM 1960 W 77069
713 444-0572 Est: 1973
Proprietor: Hal & Gladys
Mossberger
Hours: Mon-Sat 10-5
Types & Periods: American
Oak, Pine Furniture,
Primitives, Woodenware,
Accessory Items
Specialties: Wooden Store
Boxes
Directions: 4656 FM 1960
W, Across the St from
Target Discount Store &
Next to Pizza Inn in the
Woods Shopping Center
The Woods Center is
located next to Paul's
Green Thumb Nursery

THE SILVER SHOP
2288 W Holcombe Blvd
77030
713 661-2051 Est: 1978
Proprietor: Steven
Sommers
Hours: Mon-Sat
Types & Periods: Sterling
Silver Flatware & Holloware
Specialties: Matching
Obsolete & Discontinued
Patterns
Directions: Braeswood
Shopping Center at the
Corner of Greenbriar &
Holcombe Blvd

**SWEENEY & CO
JEWELERS**
820 Fannin St 77002
713 222-8080

Proprietor: Aron S Gordon
Hours: Mon-Fri 8-6
Types & Periods: General
Line, Jewelry

**KING-THOMASSON
ANTIQUES**
1213 Berthea St 77006
713 529-9768 Est: 1975
Proprietor: Judy King
Thomasson
Hours: Tues-Sat 10-4,
Closed Sun & Mon
Types & Periods: 17th &
18th Century English
Country Furniture, Copper,
Brass, Porcelains, Ironstone
Specialties: Period Oak
Furniture
Directions: Near Museum
of Fine Arts, There is no
Sign But Large Number
on Lattice Gate

**GLENN TILLOTSON
ANTIQUES**
4413 Mt Vernon 77006
713 524-9049 Est: 1972
Proprietor: Glenn Tillotson
Hours: Tues-Fri, Also By
Appointment
Types & Periods: 18th &
19th Century English,
Continental, Oriental
Furniture, Accessories
Directions: 1 Block S of
Richmond & Mt Vernon
Intersection

TIVEL ANTIQUES
2537 S Gessner 77063
713 783-9079 Est: 1974
Proprietor: George LeVit
Hours: By Appointment
Types & Periods: Custom
Buying for Commercial
Operation Deco, Estate &
Job Lot Purchasing, Office
Decoration, Restaurants &
Clubs

TRASH & TREASURE SHOP
1716 Westheimer Rd
77098
713 522-7415 or 522-5601
Est: 1954
Proprietor: Nelson Ray
McClendon
Hours: Mon-Sat 8-4:30,
Closed Sun
Types & Periods: '' All
Things Our Name Implies'',
Book Dealers

Appraisal Service Available
Directions: Near River
Oaks

USED TO BE NEW
1115 Dumble 77023
713 926-0135 Est: 1977
Proprietor: Anita Bechaud
Hours: Mon-Fri 12-5, Sat
9-5
Types & Periods:
Collectibles, Furniture,
Glassware
Directions: At Polk in the
E End off the Gulf Frwy

VILLAGE ANTIQUES
5601 Morningside 77005
713 523-7067 Est: 1973
Proprietor: Robin Morris
Hours: Mon-Sat, Also By
Appointment
Types & Periods: General
Line
Specialties: Furniture,
Turn-of-the-Century Oak &
Earlier, Eclectic Collectibles
Directions: Near Rice Univ
& Shamrock Hotel, SW
Frwy Kirby Exit, S on
Kirby, E on Amherst, Shop
Located where Amherst
Dead Ends into
Morningside

**WASHINGTON AVENUE
ANTIQUES**
4330 Washington 77007
713 862-1605 Est: 1970
Proprietor: Ms Lynn Hall
Hours: Mon-Sat 10-5, Sun
12-5
Types & Periods: Furniture,
Glass, American, Mahogany,
Walnut
Specialties: Victorian
Furniture
Appraisal Service Available
Directions: Near Heights
Area Btwn Heights Blvd &
Sheppard Dr, N of Allen
Pkwy

**WESTHEIMER FLEA
MARKET**
1731-1735 Westheimer
77098
713 528-1015 Est: 1975
Hours: Tues-Sun 10-6,
Closed Mon
Types & Periods: 25 Shops
Of Antiques & Collectibles
Directions: Btwn Montrose
& Shepherd

WICKET IMPORTERS INC
2431 Westheimer 77098
Proprietor: B E Hibbert &
J L Belchic
Hours: Mon-Fri, 10-5
Types & Periods: 18th &
19th Century English
Furniture & Accessories
Directions: Close to the
Intersection of Kirby &
Westheimer, Town West
Shopping Center

**EVELYN WILSON
INTERIORS**
3917 Main 77002
713 523-5561 Est: 1964
Proprietor: Evelyn Wilson
Hours: Mon-Fri 9-5:30, Sat
10-5, Closed Sun
Types & Periods: 18th
Century, Queen Anne,
Chippendale, Sheraton,
English, American
Specialties: Furniture, Silver,
Paintings, Chandeliers,
Imari
Appraisal Service Available
Directions: Off US 59
Btwn Richmond &
Alabama

WINEDALE ANTIQUES
10001 Westheimer 36
77042
713 789-4560 Est: 1973
Proprietor: Betty Jane
Hindman
Hours: Mon-Sat
Types & Periods: Collectors
Clocks, Period Furniture,
Rare Jewelry, Oriental, Cut
Glass, Porcelain
Specialties: Collectors
Clocks, American, German,
French, Dutch, English,
Welsh
Directions: In Shopping
Village, Carillon W, Btwn
Gessner & W Belt

YORK ANTIQUES
3504 Yoakum Blvd 77006
713 529-5275
Proprietor: Helen M York
Hours: Mon-Sat 10-5,
Closed Sun
Types & Periods: Glass,
Porcelain, Furniture

Howe

**LINKER'S ANTIQUES &
GIFTS**
400 W Hanning 75059
214 532-6102 Est: 1968
Proprietor: L H Linker
Hours: Mon-Sat, Closed
Sun
Types & Periods: Furniture,
Clocks, Glassware
Specialties: Clocks
Directions: Howe Exit Off
Hwy 75 N, turn Right at
Texaco Station, Howe Exit
Off 75 S, go Under
Underpass

Hurst

NITA JO'S ANTIQUES
124 S Norwood Dr 76053
817 282-4180
Proprietor: Mrs H L Merrill
Hours: Mon-Sat, Closed
Sun
Types & Periods: Furniture,
Glassware, Jewelry,
Primitives

**THE PENDULUM CLOCK
SHOP**
112 Norwood Dr 76053
817 282-1831 Est: 1969
Proprietor: J A Larson
Hours: Mon-Sat 10-5
Types & Periods: Mantel,
Wall & Floor Clocks, Both
Antique & New, Clocks of
All Kinds
Specialties: Clock Repair
Appraisal Service Available
Directions: Btwn Ft Worth
& Dallas on Hwy 183, 1/2
Block N of Hwy 183 on
Norwood Dr Which
Intersects 183

Irving

GLASS SLIPPER ANTIQUES
2109 Red Oak Dr 75060
214 253-7940 Est: 1976
Proprietor: Mrs H A Vavra
Hours: By Appointment
Types & Periods: Depression
Glass, Glassware, Lamps
Specialties: Glass
Directions: Nursery Rd S
to Oakdale, W on Oakdale
to Red Oak Dr

J'S ANTIQUES
311 N Jefferson 75061
214 438-1465 Est: 1976
Proprietor: Joe Tarver
Hours: Mon-Fri, Also By
Appointment
Types & Periods: American,
European, Furniture,
Depression Glass
Specialties: American Oak
Furniture

Jacksonville

B & J ANTIQUES
Hwy 69 N 75766
214 586-3047 Est: 1966
Proprietor: Mr & Mrs Bob
Barber
Hours: Mon-Fri, Also By
Appointment,
Types & Periods: Furniture,
Glass, Primitives, Pottery,
Collectibles
Specialties: Depression
Glass
Appraisal Service Available
Directions: Jacksonville on
Hwy 69 N

Karnes City

THE COLONIAL ANTIQUES
315 E Crockett 78118
512 780-3151
Proprietor: Joyce Kimble
Hours: By Appointment
Types & Periods: General
Line, Victorian, Cut Glass
Directions: Corner of N
Esplanade & E Crockett

Keller

OLD TIMEY SHOPPE
108 Wall Price Rd 76248
817 431-1537 Est: 1970
Proprietor: Mildred Jones
& Judy West
Hours: Mon-Fri, Sun By
Appointment or By
Chance
Types & Periods: Glassware,
Furniture, Jewelry,
Collectibles
Specialties: Depression
Glass
Directions: Corner Hwy
377 & Wall Price, 1 Mile S
of Town

Kemah

PINE KNOT ANTIQUES IN THE MEETING HOUSE
805 Harris   77565
713 334-3121   Est: 1968
Proprietor: Doris Morris
Hours: Mon-Sun 10-5
Types & Periods: Country Pine & Primitive Furniture, Baskets, Quilts, Stoneware, Copper, Brass
Directions: On Hwy 146 in Old Church, Six Dealers

Kemp

WRIGHT'S ANTIQUE IMPORTS
Hwy 175 Drawer F   75143
214 498-6425   Est: 1968
Proprietor: Ella Mae Wright
Hours: Mon-Fri, By Chance
Types & Periods: Furniture, Art Objects, Orientals
Specialties: Cut Glass
Directions: 45 Miles E of Dallas

Kennedale

SUSIE R SMITH ANTIQUES
Box 597   76060
817 478-5557   Est: 1970
Proprietor: Robert & Susie R Smith
Hours: Mon-Sat 10:30-5, Also By Appointment
Types & Periods: Oak Furniture, Collectibles, Wicker, Ceiling Fans
Specialties: American Oak, Wicker
Directions: Call For Directions

Kilgore

COX'S ANTIQUES
922 E Main   75662
214 984-6026   Est: 1962
Proprietor: J M Cox
Hours: Mon-Fri
Types & Periods: General Line

Specialties: Furniture
Directions: 1 Block N of Kilgore Jr College on Hwy 259

PALMERS
325 N Kilgore St   75662
214 984-3144   Est: 1962
Proprietor: Mr & Mrs Jimmie Palmer
Hours: Mon-Fri
Types & Periods: General Line, Furniture, Glass
Directions: Old City Hall Bldg

La Marque

BUTTERMILK JUNCTION ANTIQUES
1220 Hwy 3   77568
713 938-0439   Est: 1973
Proprietor: Marilyn R Steele
Hours: Tues-Sat 10-5, Closed Sun & Mon
Types & Periods: American & European
Specialties: Stained Glass
Directions: Hwy 3 Btwn Houston & Galveston

JEANIE'S ANTIQUES
1020 Hwy 3   77568
713 938-0301   Est: 1969
Proprietor: Jeanie Balez
Hours: Mon-Sat, Open 11:30, Closed Sun
Types & Periods: Pressed, Cut & Art Glass, Furniture, China, Clocks, Silver, Jewelry
Specialties: Victorian Jewelry
Appraisal Service Available
Directions: Btwn Houston & Galveston E from I-45 to Hwy 3

Lancaster

ROSEBUD ANTIQUES OF LANCASTER
Town Sq   75136
214 227-1705   Est: 1973
Proprietor: Jean & Walter Clark
Hours: Tues-Fri 1-5, Sat 11-5, Closed Sun & Mon

Types & Periods: Primitives, Furniture, Glass, China, Collectibles
Directions: 14 Miles S of Dallas, NW Corner of the Old Town Sq

Laredo

OSCAR'S ANTIQUES
604 Zapata Hwy   78040
512 723-0765   Est: 1972
Proprietor: Oscar & Emma Cardenas
Hours: Tues-Sun
Types & Periods: American & European Furniture, Primitives, Glass, Collectibles
Appraisal Service Available
Directions: Located on US 83 S

League City

GAIDO'S COUNTRY LANE ANTIQUES
814 Louisiana Ave   77573
713 332-4308   Est: 1973
Proprietor: Don & Sheryl Gaido
Hours: Daily, By Chance
Types & Periods: American Golden Oak, Circa 1900
Specialties: Fancy Oak Refinished
Directions: Off FM 518, 1 Mile S off Louisiana Ave

THE UNIQUE ANTIQUES
104 N Hwy 3   77573
713 332-6114   Est: 1967
Proprietor: Dovie Hanson
Hours: Mon-Sun
Types & Periods: General Line, Collectibles
Specialties: Glassware, Victorian Period Furniture
Appraisal Service Available
Directions: League City where Hwy 3 & Hwy 518 Intersect

Lewisville

LEWISVILLE FLEA MARKET
I-35 at Roundgrove Rd
                    75067
214 436-7211   Est: 1973

Proprietor: James H
Robbs
Hours: Sat & Sun
Types & Periods: Furniture,
Glass, Dishes, Jewelry
Directions: I-35 E towards
Denton, 12 Miles from
Dallas

Lindale

ANNEX ANTIQUES INC
200 N Main   75771
214 882-6911   Est: 1972
Proprietor: Bill & Evelyn
Regian
Hours: Mon-Fri, Also By
Appointment
Types & Periods: English,
French & American
Furniture, Primitives, Cut &
Art Glass, China
Specialties: Cut Glass
Appraisal Service Available
Directions: 1 Block N of
4-Way Stop in Downtown
on Hwy 69

Longview

**THE ANTIQUE EMPORIUM
INC**
701 B E Methvin St 75601
214 753-4891   Est: 1975
Proprietor: Etoile Dan
Forth
Hours: Tues-Sat
Types & Periods: American,
European Furniture,
Bric-A-Brac, Custom Silk &
Dried Floral Arrangements,
Paintings, Stained Glass
Specialties: Victorian,
Golden Oak Furniture,
Primitives, English, Belgian
Appraisal Service Available
Directions: 1 Mile E of
Downtown, From Hwy 80
take 4th St S, 3 Blocks to
Methvin then E, From I-20
take Business Exit, Go E
thru Town to Green St, N
on Green to Tyler St, E on
Tyler to Methvin Appx 4
Blocks

BRASS RINGS ANTIQUES
4704 Judson Rd   75605
214 663-0951   Est: 1977
Proprietor: Jimmy Thomas
Hours: Mon-Sat

Types & Periods: Brass,
Copper, Lighting Fixtures,
Ceiling Fans
Specialties: Polishing &
Repair of Metals & Lighting
Fixtures, Fan Restoration,
Plating
Directions: 2 Miles N of
Loop 281

**FREDERICK-NILA
GALLERIES**
306 N 4th St
PO Box 2563   75601
214 753-2902   Est: 1947
Proprietor: Nila Boatner
Hours: Mon-Sat
Types & Periods: Small
Furniture Items, Glass,
Silver, Frames, Prints,
Paintings
Specialties: Antique & Estate
Jewelry
Directions: 3 Blocks from
Downtown, Going E on
Methvin St Turn on 4th St,
1st Bldg after you turn off
onto 4th St

TURNER ANTIQUES
211 E College Ave   75602
214 758-2562   Est: 1966
Proprietor: Mrs Harold R
Turner
Hours: Mon-Sat 12-5,
Closed Sun, Also By
Appointment
Types & Periods: American
& English Furniture,
American, Art & Cut Glass,
Coin, Sterling & Quad Plate
Silver, Orientals, China,
Porcelain, Pottery,
Primitives, Jewelry, Dolls
Specialties: Early American
Pattern Glass, Items Of
Interest To Collectors, Texas
Furniture, Ten Rooms Of
Quality Merchandise
Appraisal Service Available
Directions: 3 Blocks S of
Downtown, Btwn S
Fredonia & S Green St

Lorena

THE ANTIQUE BANK
Borden & Center Sts
                    76655
817 857-4432   Est: 1975
Proprietor: Candy Hauser
Hours: Wed-Sat

Types & Periods: American,
Oak, Primitives, Wicker
Directions: 10 Miles S of
Waco off I-35

Lubbock

LUBBOCK CLUSTER
Directions: 34th St
(2000-4000 Blocks),
Ave H (2000-4000 Blocks)

ARTS & ANTIQUITIES
4810 W 16th St   79416
806 799-4491
Proprietor: Martha J Mack
Hours: By Appointment
Types & Periods: Paintings,
French Glass, Porcelains,
Art Glass

COLONIAL ANTIQUES
1947 Nineteenth St 79401
806 763-5533
Proprietor: Mrs Jerry
Milburn
Hours: Mon-Fri 9:30-4:30
Types & Periods: General
Line

COTTAGE ANTIQUES
2247 34th St   79412
806 744-3927   Est: 1973
Proprietor: Ina May
Stewart
Hours: Mon-Sat 10-5:30
Types & Periods: General
Line, American, Primitives,
Art Nouveau, Victorian
Furniture, Bric-A-Brac,
Clocks, Dolls, Leaded &
Beveled Glass
Specialties: Leaded &
Beveled Glass, Primitives,
Clocks, Furniture
Appraisal Service Available
Directions: Center of
Town, Btwn University &
Ave Q

DAISY'S ANTIQUES
4013 34th   79410
806 792-3686
Proprietor: Mr & Mrs Ed
Hughes
Hours: Mon-Fri
Types & Periods: Glassware,
Furniture, Primitives, Clocks,
Jewelry
Specialties: Wooton Desks
Appraisal Service Available
Directions: Across from
Wolfe Nursery

Lubbock   Cont'd

FRAN'S ANTIQUES
2301 58th St   79412
806 795-1387
Proprietor: Francis & Jack
Walker
Hours: Mon-Fri After 2,
Sat & Sun By
Appointment
Types & Periods: Glass

C A "LUCKY" HENSON
3612 Ave P   79412
806 744-2524   Est: 1959
Proprietor: Lucky Henson
Hours: Mon-Sun
Types & Periods: Small
Carved Furniture, Items
Unusual & Different, General
Line
Specialties: Old "Found"Iron
Farm & Ranch Items, Bits,
Spurs, Branding Irons,
Wagon Wheels, Horse
Collars & Harness
Appraisal Service Available
Directions: Corner 37th St
& Ave P

LEGACIES
2716A 50th St   79413
806 792-0607   Est: 1973
Proprietor: Gladys
Plowman
Hours: Mon-Fri
Types & Periods: American,
English & French Furniture,
Oriental Porcelains,
Cloisonne, Jade, Clocks,
Copper, Brass
Directions: Across from
Caprock Shopping Center,
Btwn Boston & Canton Sts

LEONA'S ANTIQUES
4601 Ave H   79404
806 744-1893
Proprietor: Mr & Mrs
William C Kent
Hours: Mon-Sat 10-5:30,
Closed Sun or By
Appointment
Types & Periods: Furniture,
Silver, China, Crystal, Clocks

**RUTH LITTLE ART &
ANTIQUES**
3430 34th St   79410
806 792-1809   Est: 1967
Proprietor: Ruth Little &
Billie Ruth McCarty
Hours: Mon-Sat 10-5:30,
Closed Sun

Types & Periods: Art, R S
Prussia & Cut Glass, Lamps,
White China, Hummel
Figures & Plates
Specialties: Hand Painted
China
Appraisal Service Available
Directions: In Indiana
Gardens Shopping Center
in SW Lubbock

Lufkin

**KINARDS ANTIQUES &
COLLECTABLES**
Rte 3 Box 322   75901
713 634-6933
Proprietor: Arline &
Murray Kinard
Hours: Tues-Sat 9:30-5,
Closed Sun & Mon
Types & Periods: General
Line, Furniture, Art Glass,
China

Mansfield

FLOWERS ETC
103 Main   76063
817 473-1165   Est: 1975
Proprietor: Charlotte Holly
Martin
Hours: Mon-Fri 8-5, Sat
8-1, Closed Sun
Types & Periods: Depression
Glass, Furniture
Directions: S of Arlington
12 Miles on 157, S of Ft
Worth 20 Miles on 287

Marble Falls

ANTIQUA UNLIMITED
Box 211   78654
512 693-2136
Proprietor: Dr & Mrs R H
Schaper
Hours: By Appointment
Types & Periods: General
Line
Specialties: Pattern Glass

Marshall

**FRANKS ANTIQUE SHOP &
DOLL MUSEUM**
211 W Grand Ave   75670
214 935-3065   Est: 1948

Proprietor: Mr & Mrs
Francis W Franks
Hours: By Appointment,
By Chance
Types & Periods: Cut & Art
Glass, China, Early Victorian
& Early American Furniture,
Dolls
Specialties: China, Cut
Glass, Dolls
Appraisal Service Available
Directions: On US 80 W,
Near Business District

RED BARN ANTIQUES
Hwy 80 W   75670
214 938-4011   Est: 1973
Proprietor: Leonard &
Dorothy Nash
Hours: Mon-Sat 9-6, Sun
1-6
Types & Periods: Furniture,
Glassware, Lamps,
Collectibles
Specialties: Oak Furniture
Directions: US Hwy 80 W

McAllen

**SERVIERE'S ANTIQUES &
COLLECTIBLES**
N 10th St   78501
512 686-4566   Est: 1974
Proprietor: Salli Serviere
Hours: Mon-Sat 10-6
Types & Periods: General
Line
Specialties: Clocks, Glass

**TRIFLES & TREASURES
ANTIQUES**
707 Pecan St   78501
512 682-6669
Proprietor: Hattie McLellan
Hours: Mon-Sat 10:30-5
Types & Periods: Furniture,
Brass, Glassware

VAN'S ANTIQUES
1201 Jonquill Ave 78501
512 682-4783
Proprietor: Dolores
Vanlandingham
Hours: By Appointment
Types & Periods: Glass,
Silver, Jewelry

McKinney

SIDE DOOR ANTIQUES
401 W Louisiana St 75069
Proprietor: Sue
McClintock
Hours: Tues, Thur & Sat
10-5, Sun 1-5
Types & Periods: American
& English Furniture

TAYLOR'S ANTIQUES
1006 N Graves   75069
214 542-7417
Hours: Daily, Closed Wed,
Weekends By Chance
Types & Periods: Paintings,
Copper, Brass, Furniture

Mesquite

**CHRIS VAN DAMME
ANTIQUES INC**
I-20   75182
214 226-3594   Est: 1976
Proprietor: Pieter Van
Damme
Hours: Mon-Fri
Types & Periods: Clocks,
Bronzes, Dutch Furniture,
Cut Glass, Copper &
Brassware Period from 18th
Century to present
Directions: 10 miles E of
Dallas

**FISHERS ANTIQUES
MARKET**
                   75149
                   Est. 1965
Proprietor: Wamon Fischer
Hours: Sat & Sun
Types & Periods: General
Line, 40 Dealers
Directions: I-20 at E Fork
Rd, 8 miles E of Big Town

Midland

DECORATING CENTER INC
1608 N Big Spring 79701
915 684-7525   Est: 1961
Proprietor: Ethel Howell
Hours: Mon-Fri
Types & Periods: General
Line, American, French &
English Furniture

Specialties: Oriental
Directions: 2 Blue Houses
on Corner of Wall St & N
Big Spring

MARY HOOVER ANTIQUES
503 S F St   79701
915 682-1209   Est: 1947
Proprietor: Mary Hoover
Langley
Hours: By Appointment
Types & Periods: Furniture,
China, Copper, Brass, Silver
Appraisal Service Available
Directions: Corner of F &
Kentucky St, S on F Off
Wall St

HYDE'S
1909 Holloway   79701
915 684-4971   Est: 1970
Proprietor: Lou Ella Hyde
Hours: By Chance
Types & Periods: European,
American, Glass, Furniture
Specialties: Clocks

TALL CITY ANTIQUES
1801 N Big Spring St
                   79701
                   Est: 1963
Proprietor; Mr & Mrs L A
Snodgrass
Hours: Mon-Sat 9-5,
Closed Sun
Types & Periods: Furniture,
Glassware, Primitives, Books
Directions: Turn Off I-20
at 1st Midland Sign, Come
to N Big Spring St, Turn N

Morton

THE BACK FORTY
Rte 2   79346
806 266-5166   Est: 1978
Proprietor: Cherry Thomas
& Marilyn Greener
Hours: Tues-Sat 10-4:30
Types & Periods: General
Line, Primitives, Collectibles,
Handwrapped Silk Flowers,
Art Work
Directions: 1/2 Mile E of
Morton Mfg off Hwy 114

Muleshoe

THE MULESHOE ART LOFT
1529 W American Blvd
                   79347
806 272-3485   Est: 1965
Proprietor: Arline Phelps,
Marie Lenau & Inez F
Bobo
Hours: Mon-Sat
Types & Periods: General
Line
Specialties: Furniture &
Accessories
Directions: American Blvd
is a State Hwy Passing
through Muleshoe

Nacogdoches

IMPRESSIONS
122 N Mound   75961
713 569-0105   Est: 1973
Proprietor: Betsy Shaw
Hours: By Appointment
Types & Periods:
Collectibles, Accessories
Specialties: Brass Plated
Wooden Milk Crates

New Braunfels

**PALACE HEIGHTS
ANTIQUES**
1175 Hwy 81 E   78130
512 625-0612   Est: 1972
Proprietor: Jerry M & Judy
A Johnson
Hours: Mon-Sun
Types & Periods: Brass &
Iron Beds
Specialties: Furniture,
Renovation of Beds
Directions: Across from
the New Braunfels
Smokehouse

Normanna

MADE IN TEXAS CENTER
US Hwy 181   78142
                   Est: 1972
Proprietor: Lin Cox
Hours: Sat & Sun, Also By
Chance
Types & Periods: General
Line

MADE IN TEXAS   Cont'd
Directions: US 181, 9
Miles N of Beeville,
"Building with the Bars &
1909 on Top"

Odessa

RED DOOR ANTIQUES
2818 Yukon Rd   79762
              Est: 1962
Proprietor: Delora & Doyle
Kirby
Hours: Mon-Fri 9:30-5
Types & Periods: Glass,
China, Furniture
Specialties: Jewelry, Silver
Appraisal Service Available
  Directions: NW of Odessa,
  3 Miles Out County Rd W

Orange

HAZEL M RAWLS
ANTIQUES
2117 Monterrey   77630
713 886-2554   Est: 1964
Proprietor: Hazel M Rawls
Hours: By Appointment
Types & Periods: Early
American, Flint & Pattern
Glass, Matching Service
Specialties: Flint & Pattern
Glass, Matching Serivce,
Furniture
Appraisal Service Available
  Directions: Call First

Palacios

CLAXTON'S ANTIQUES
308 5th   77465
512 972-3534   Est: 1974
Proprietor: Mary Sue
Claxton
Hours: Mon-Sat 9-5,
Closed Sun
Types & Periods: Victorian,
American Oak, Imports,
General Line
  Directions: 1/2 Block Off
  Business Hwy 35,
  Downtown

EULA'S ANTIQUES & GIFTS
1601 First   77465
512 972-3231   Est: 1960
Proprietor: Eula Pore

Hours: Sat & Sun,
Weekdays By Chance
Types & Periods: Furniture,
Glassware, Specimen
Seashells
Appraisal Service Available
  Directions: Hwy 35 City
  Limit N, 1 Mile from
  Center of Town

Palestine

BETH'S ORIGINALS
1305 N Queen St   75801
214 729-1262 or 723-0127
              Est: 1976
Proprietor: Beth &
Deannette Johnston
Hours: Mon-Sat 9-5, Sun
During Dogwood Trails
March or April Each Year
Types & Periods: Glassware,
Furniture, Primitives, Crocks,
Churns, Weather Vanes,
Lightning Rods, Tools,
Reproductions in Furniture,
Glass, Arts & Craft Supplies,
Jewelry, Gifts
Specialties: Glassware
Appraisal Service Available
  Directions: Corner of Hwy
  79 & Queen St, Across
  from Sonic Drive Inn

GERRY CONE ANTIQUES
320 W Oak St   75801
214 729-1903   Est: 1966
Proprietor: Geraldine J
Cone
Hours: Mon-Sat, By
Appointment Sun &
Holidays
Types & Periods: General
Line, Glass, Furniture,
Sabino Figurines
Specialties: Sabino Figurines
  Directions: Downtown

VICTORIAN ANTIQUES
400 N Queen   75801
214 729-4178   Est: 1977
Proprietor: Jean Laughlin
Hours: Mon-Sun
Types & Periods: General
Line, Collectibles
Specialties: Industrial
Artifacts, Textile Spools,
Bobbins, Wooden Shoe
Lasts, Ceiling Fans
  Directions: Exit S on
  Queen St from Hwy 79, At
  Oak & Queen, Downtown

Pampa

FAYE'S ANTIQUE & GIFT
SHOP
914 S Osborne   79065
806 669-6408   Est: 1965
Proprietor: Faye Messer
Hours: By Chance
Types & Periods: General
Line
Specialties: Depression
Glass
  Directions: Turn S on Hwy
  60 at S & J Grocery, Go
  to Stop Sign, Turn E 4
  Blocks, Turn Back S

Pasadena

GLORIA'S ANTIQUES
1514 E Southmore   77502
713 472-6613   Est: 1967
Proprietor: Gloria Sale
Hours: Mon-Sat, By
Chance, Sun By
Appointment
Types & Periods: General
Line
Specialties: Depression
Glass, Clocks
  Directions: 5 Blocks E of
  Bank, 300 Yards E of
  Strawberry Rd
  Intersection, S Side of St

HOUSE OF RUTH
3205 Federal St   77504
713 944-2304   Est: 1970
Proprietor: Bob & Ruth
Roberts
Hours: Mon-Sun 10-5
Types & Periods: American
& European Furniture &
Glassware from 1800 to
1920
Specialties: American Oak,
Victorian, Restoration Shop
Appraisal Service Available
  Directions: I-45 to College
  Ave, College Changes
  Name at Hwy 2 to
  Spencer Hwy, Follow
  Spencer to 3100 Block
  take a Left

Pharr

ADKINS ANTIQUES
PO Box 718   78577
512 787-1857 or 383-9337
              Est: 1960

Proprietor: Don Adkins
Hours: Mon-Sat 9-5:30
Types & Periods: General
Line, Furniture, "3 Acres of
Antiques"
Directions: 3 Miles S of
Court House on Hwy 281
(Edinburg), 4 Miles N of
Pharr

Pilot Point

PAPERWHITE INN
Box 592   76258
Proprietor: Earl Meador
Hours: Fri, Sat & Sun 10-6
Types & Periods: Furniture,
Collectilbes, Memorabilia
Directions: SW Corner of
Square

Plainview

KATHLEEN BARKER
ANTIQUES
1306 W 6th   79072
806 293-1582
Proprietor: Kathleen
Barker
Hours: Mon-Fri 9-6
Types & Periods: Lamps,
Victorian Fixtures

LAIRDS COLONIAL
ANTIQUES
722 Ash St   79072
806 293-1974
Proprietor: Fern Laird
Hours: Mon-Sat 9-5,
Closed Sun
Types & Periods: General
Line

Plano

MAGNOLIA HOUSE
ANTIQUES
1206 14th   75074
214 423-3822   Est: 1973
Proprietor: Fred & Dortha
Scoles
Hours: Wed-Sun, Closed
Mon & Tues
Types & Periods: Oak &
Mahogany Furniture,
Glassware, Primitives
Specialties: Old Wood &
Lead Type, Type Trays

Directions: Plano Exit off
Hwy 75, Uptown to Ave K,
1 Block S & E

Port Arthur

SNOOPER'S PARADISE
1701 Bluebonnet   77640
713 982-6461   Est: 1951
Proprietor: Jon Hampton
Hours: Mon-Sat 9-5,
Closed Sun
Types & Periods: European
Furniture, Bric-A-Brac, Late
18th thru 19th Century
Specialties: Furniture
Directions: 1 Block from
Gilliam Circle

Port Lavaca

JAMES L & NELLIE M
DAVIS ANTIQUES
Rte 2 Box 158C   77979
512 552-5429   Est: 1975
Proprietor: James L &
Nellie M Davis
Hours: Mon-Fri
Types & Periods: Bottles,
Dolls, Coins, Knives
Specialties: Bottles, Dolls
Directions: Across from
State Park at Indianola

Raymondville

SHANGRI-LA
PO Box 275   78580
512 689-3761   Est: 1965
Proprietor: Mrs Frank T
Williams
Hours: Mon-Fri 9-5
Types & Periods: General
Line
Directions: 1 Mile W on
Hwy 186

Richardson

BAIN'S ANTIQUES
200 S Interurban   75080
214 238-0963   Est: 1970
Proprietor: Mr & Mrs Wm
D Bain
Hours: Tues-Sat 10-5,
Closed Sun & Mon

Types & Periods: Furniture,
China, Glass
Specialties: Clocks, Lamps
Directions: Exit 24 from
Central Expwy, 1 Block E
on Belt Line, 1 Block S on
Interurban to Polk, Corner
of Polk & Interurban

FRONTIER GUNS
104 E Main   75081
214 238-7434
Proprietor: Tommy Rholes
Hours: Mon-Sat By
Chance
Types & Periods: American
Percussion & Cartridge
Arms
Specialties: Arms & Armor,
Colt Single Action &
Winchester Lever Action
Appraisal Service Available
Directions: 4 Blocks E of
N Central Expwy (75),
Exit 24

TOM NOBLE
1323 Comanche Dr 75080
214 235-4301   Est: 1971
Proprietor: Tom Noble
Hours: Sat-Sun By
Appointment, Also Eves
Types & Periods: General
Line
Specialties: Repairing,
Restoring & Refinishing
Appraisal Service Available
Directions: Exit Off Hwy
75 N, W on Arapho to
Mimosa, N 4 Blocks

THE RED HUT
203 W Polk   75080
214 235-7756   Est: 1973
Proprietor: Sheryl Young
Hours: Tues-Sat 10-5,
Closed Sun & Mon
Types & Periods: General
Line
Directions: Exit on Belt
Line from Hwy 75, 2
Blocks then Turn Right on
Polk

THE TINKERS DAM
2181 Promenade
Shopping Center   75080
214 234-0737   Est: 1970
Proprietor: Linda
Hendrickson
Hours: Mon-Sat 10-6, Thur
10-9, Closed Sun
Types & Periods: General
Line, Collectibles

TINKERS DAM   **Cont'd**

Specialties: Americana
Primitives
  Directions: Promenade
  Shopping Center, At Coit
  & Belt Line Rds, 2 Miles N
  of I-635

Rockwall

THE CURIOSITY SHOP
  1009 S Goliad   75087
  214 722-6051   Est: 1974
  Proprietor: Don & Lalla
  Lauderdale
  Hours: Tues-Sat 10-5,
  Closed Sun & Mon
Types & Periods: General
Line, China, Glass, Furniture
Specialties: Depression
Glass
  Directions: 1 Mile N of
  I-30 on TX 205

San Angelo

ANTIQUE BARN
  431 E Ave C   76901
  915 655-4887   Est: 1972
  Proprietor: Sara DeMoville
  & Lamoine Helton
  Hours: Mon-Thur 1-5, Fri
  & Sat 10-5, Closed Sun
Types & Periods: General
Line, Furniture
Specialties: European
Imports
  Directions: Around the
  Corner from Ft Concho
  Museum

THE ANTIQUE MALL
  19 E Concho   76901
  915 653-8832   Est: 1973
  Hours: Tues-Sat, Sun PM,
  Closed Mon
Types & Periods: Furniture,
Clocks, Glassware, Jewelry
Specialties: Clocks,
Furniture, Jewelry
  Directions: Btwn
  Chadbourne & Oakes Sts,
  Ten Shops at This
  Location

CHRIS' OLD HOUSE
  116 E Twohig   76901
  915 653-1796   Est: 1968
  Proprietor: Chris Jaehne
  Hours: Mon-Fri, Also By
  Appointment

Types & Periods: Cut & Art
Glass, China, Silver,
Furniture
Specialties: American Cut
Glass
Appraisal Service Available
  Directions: 1/2 Block E of
  Post Office & Cactus
  Hotel

San Antonio

SAN ANTONIO CLUSTER
  Directions: Concentration
  of Shops on W Hildebrand
  (500-1000 Blocks), S
  Hackberry (300-2000
  Blocks) & Broadway,
  Many Shops Scattered

ALISON'S ANTIQUES
  1815 Blanco Rd   78212
  512 735-6261
  Proprietor: Mr & Mrs J B
  Cearly
Types & Periods: General
Line

**ALLENS ANTIQUES & ART
GALLERIES**
  2101 McCullough   78212
  512 734-6441   Est: 1950
  Proprietor: Charles H Allen
  Hours: Mon-Fri 8-5, Sat
  8-1 June-July-Aug, Closed
  Sun
Types & Periods: Queen
Anne Chairs, Louis XVI
Cabinets, Pier Mirror,
Napoleonic Chairs, Sheraton
Couches, Victorian Chairs,
Country French Sideboards
Specialties: Furniture
  Directions: Btwn Loop 410
  By Airport & Downtown

**AMERICANA NOSTALGIA
SHOP**
  PO Box 10150 Hackberry
  Station   78210
  512 532-5873 or 533-5214
                  Est: 1972
  Proprietor: Stella & Robert
  Morehead
  Hours: By Appointment,
  By Chance
Types & Periods: Nostalgia,
Curios, Collectibles from
1900's

Specialties: Toys, Movie &
Radio Memorabilia, Pinball
Machines
  Directions: 3520 S New
  Braunfels

ANTIQUE COTTAGE
  508 Dallas St   78215
  512 227-5821
  Proprietor: Martha
  Chancellor
  Hours: Mon-Fri 11-5
Types & Periods: General
Line

THE ANTIQUE GALLERY
  4211 McCullough Ave
                  78212
  512 824-5555   Est: 1973
  Proprietor: C Parnell
  Hours: Tues-Sat 10-5:30,
  Closed Sun & Mon
Types & Periods: Cut & Art
Glass, Sterling Silver,
Porcelains, Furniture,
Objets d'Art
Specialties: Furniture,
American Cut Glass, Sterling
Silver
Appraisal Service Available
  Directions: McCullough S
  Exit Off of Loop 410, 2
  Blocks S Olmos Dr to
  McCullough

BEDLAM BRASS BEDS
  3123 Broadway   78209
  512 824-6925   Est: 1971
  Proprietor: Tex & Judy
  Ellis
  Hours: Tues-Sat 10-7, Sun
  12-3, Closed Mon
Types & Periods: General
Line, Brass Beds
Specialties: Handrails &
Footrails for Bars, Brass
Accessories
  Directions: Near
  Brackenridge Park, Across
  from Christies Restaurant

BESS' ANTIQUES
  5450 Old Seguin Rd
                  78219
  512 661-5582   Est: 1966
  Proprietor: Bess Palmire
  Hours: Tues-Sat 10-5,
  Closed Sun & Mon
Types & Periods: Victorian &
Turn-of-the-Century Oak
Furniture, Glass, China
Specialties: Pattern Glass

Directions: Rittman Rd
Exit E off 410, Go to
Woodlake Golf Course,
Turn Right on 78 & Go
About 2 Miles to Sign

BILLS ANTIQUES
2110 McCullough 78212
512 736-5521 Est: 1970
Proprietor: Wm A Baucum
Hours: Tues-Sat
Types & Periods: Clocks,
Jewelry, Furniture, Lamps

**CHARLOTT'S ANTIQUES &
CLOCKS**
2017 Austin Hwy 78218
512 655-6661 Est: 1966
Proprietor: C Whisenhunt
Hours: Mon-Fri
Types & Periods: German,
English & American
Furniture, Clocks,
Bric-A-Brac
Specialties: Clocks
Appraisal Service Available
Directions: Follow US 81
Business Rte from N

COFFEE MILL ANTIQUES
5859 Randolph Blvd
78233
512 655-9848 or 225-4716
Est: 1976
Proprietor: Katharine D
Siege
Hours: Wed-Sat 11-4
Types & Periods: Oak &
Walnut Victorian, Country
Furniture, Primitives,
Collectibles, Iron, Wood,
Copper, Brass
Specialties: Carousel
Horses, Roll Top Desks
Directions: Exit I-35 at
Wiedner Rd, E 3 Blocks to
Randolph Blvd, Turn Left,
Go 1/4 Mile, Shop on Left

**COLONIES NORTH MALL
ANTIQUE SHOP & FLEA
MARKET CO**
3719 B Colony Dr 78230
512 691-1283 Est: 1967
Proprietor: Manuel D
Garza
Hours: Tues-Sat, Closed
Mon, Flea Market Open
Every Sun
Types & Periods:
Collectibles, Imports
Specialties: 20 Dealers
Directions: I-10 at
Wurzbach Rd

**MARY F DAUGHTRY
ANTIQUES**
5524 Daughtry 78238
512 684-0344 Est: 1958
Proprietor: Mary F
Daughtry
Hours: Mon-Sat
Types & Periods: American,
European, Oriental
Specialties: China Repair
Appraisal Service Available
Directions: Loop 410 &
Bandera Rd Area

THE DIFFERENT DRUMMER
1020 Townsend 78209
512 826-3764 Est: 1971
Proprietor: Dorothy L Katz
Hours: Mon-Fri
Types & Periods: Copper,
Brass, Wood Pieces,
Primitives, Staffordshire
Specialties: Embroidery &
Needlework, Quilts, Indian
Rugs
Directions: 1 Block off
Broadway in Alamo
Heights

**DUNN'S NOSTALGIA
GALLERY**
2520 N Main 78212
512 735-8835 Est: 1976
Proprietor: Martin M Dunn
Hours: Mon-Sat, Closed
Sun, Also By
Appointment, By Chance
Types & Periods: Furniture,
Collectibles, Nostalgia Items,
Toys, Glassware, China
Specialties: Nostalgia-Type
Collectibles
Appraisal Service Available
Directions: N of Woodlawn
Ave

EUROPA
205 W Summit 78212
512 732-0823 Est: 1972
Proprietor: Mrs Wm A
Johnson
Hours: Mon-Fri 10:30-4,
Also By Appointment
Types & Periods: French,
English, German & American
Furniture, Bronzes, Art
Glass
Specialties: Porcelains, Ivory
Appraisal Service Available
Directions: 2409 N Main
Ave

**GASLIGHT ANTIQUE
SHOPPE**
1525 McCullough 78212
512 227-4803
Proprietor: James J
Slaughter
Hours: Mon-Fri 3:50-5:45,
Sat & Holidays 10-6
Types & Periods: Furniture,
Art Glass, Objets D'Art

GRABO ANTIQUES
2934 Austin Hwy 78218
512 655-5141 Est: 1952
Proprietor: Grace & Bob
Hoeller
Hours: Thurs-Sat 10-6,
Also By Appointment
Types & Periods: French,
English, German & American
Furniture, Art & Cut Glass,
China
Specialties: Collectibles
Appraisal Service Available
Directions: Frontage Rd of
Austin Hwy at Jct of 410
E & Business Rte 81

GREAT THINGS
1020 Townsend 78209
512 828-5555 Est: 1971
Proprietor: Dorothy Katz
Hours: Mon-Sat
Types & Periods: Folk Art
From Around The World
Directions: 1 Block off
5900 Block of Broadway
in Alamo Heights

GRIFFAY'S ANTIQUES
1303 Roosevelt Ave
78210
512 533-1171
Proprietor: Mr & Mrs F N
Griffay
Hours: Mon-Fri 10-6
Types & Periods: Victorian,
French & Primitive Furniture,
Glass

HELETIQUES
2716 McCullough 78212
512 734-3796 Est: 1972
Proprietor: Helen Hargis
Hours: Mon-Fri
Types & Periods: Orientals,
Collectibles, Furniture,
Paintings, Bric-A-Brac
Specialties: Orientals &
American
Appraisal Service Available
Directions: N Central San
Antonio, On Main N-S
Thoroughfare About 30
Blocks from Downtown

San Antonio   Cont'd

HORSE OF A DIFFERENT COLOR
140 W Sunset Rd   78209
512 824-9762
Types & Periods: Country Furniture, Accessories

IRON FENCE ANTIQUES
115 E Ashly   78212
512 732-5529   Est: 1962
Proprietor: Mr & Mrs Joseph B Jolliffe
Hours: Mon-Fri
Types & Periods: Primitives, Early American
Specialties: Brass, Copper, Pewter, Tin
Directions: Near N Main St

J KAHN & ASSOCIATES INC
5096 Blanco   78216
512 342-4822   Est: 1949
Proprietor: John Wm Jones
Hours: Mon-Fri
Types & Periods: American & Oriental Rugs, Period, European
Specialties: Oriental Rugs
Appraisal Service Available
Directions: Btwn Jackson Keller & Bassie, 17 Blocks S of Loop 410

LAND OF WAS ANTIQUES
3125 Broadway   78209
512 822-5265
Proprietor: Helen & Donna Spear
Hours: Mon-Sat 9:30-5:30, Closed Sun
Types & Periods: General Line

MILNE ANTIQUES
5554 Randolph Blvd
78233
512 655-9892   Est: 1978
Proprietor: Pat Milne
Hours: Mon-Sat 10-6
Types & Periods: American, European Furniture & Glassware, Victorian & Later
Appraisal Service Available
Directions: Corner of Randolph Blvd & Weidner Rd, Exit I-35 at Weidner Rd, E to Randolph, or Take Access Road from Windsor Park Mall, N to Randolph Blvd

MORAN ANTIQUES
2119 San Pedro   78212
512 734-5668   Est: 1968
Proprietor: Phil & Carolyn Moran
Hours: Tues-Sat, Closed Sun & Mon, Also By Appointment, By Chance
Types & Periods: American Victorian Furniture, Pressed, Cut & Depression Glass, Sterling Silver, Clocks, Records, Collectibles, Nostalgia Items
Specialties: Victorian & Empire Furniture, Estate Liquidations
Appraisal Service Available
Directions: San Pedro is Also US Hwy 281, on Corner of Magnolia Near Downtown

WONG NGONG ANTIQUE SHOP
1202 Nogalitos St   78204
512 226-6642   Est: 1973
Proprietor: Wong Ngong
Hours: Mon-Sun, Also By Appointment, By Chance
Types & Periods: Chinese Screens, Bamboo Paneling, Jade, Ivory, Furniture, Bric-A-Brac
Appraisal Service Available
Directions: S End of City, Take Laredo Hwy

OLD TIME ANTIQUES
519 W Hildebrand   78212
512 733-7559   Est: 1970
Proprietor: Karin Londono
Hours: Mon-Fri 10-5, Sat & Sun 10-3
Types & Periods: Furniture, Art Glass, Porcelains, Clocks, Stained Glass Lamps
Specialties: Estate Sales
Appraisal Service Available
Directions: Btwn San Pedro Ave & Blanco

M PAGENKOPF ANTIQUES
5312 Broadway   78209
512 826-8222   Est: 1935
Proprietor: Mrs Peggy Ewing
Hours: Mon-Sat, Closed Sun
Types & Periods: 18th & 19th Century Furniture, Orientals, Cut Glass, Silver, Canes & Umbrellas, Clocks, Music Boxes, Ivories, China, Jewelry

Specialties: Jewelry
Appraisal Service Available
Directions: In Tree House Shopping Center, Near Austin Hwy Turnoff

REGENCY ANTIQUES
3014 Broadway   78216
512 822-5440   Est: 1973
Proprietor: Rick Brenner
Hours: Mon-Fri 10-5:30, Also By Appointment
Types & Periods: French & American Furniture, Bronze, Jewelry, Clocks, Objets d'Art
Appraisal Service Available
Directions: Across from Breckenridge Park

MISS ROBERTSON'S SHOP
202 Alamo Plaza   78205
512 226-4091
Proprietor: Medora Robertson
Hours: Mon-Fri
Types & Periods: Silver, Porcelain, Jewelry, Bronzes, Crystal
Specialties: Silver, Sabino, Meissen
Appraisal Service Available
Directions: 1 Block S of Alamo

M SMITH ANTIQUES
235 Army Blvd   78215
512 223-4862   Est: 1960
Proprietor: Morrell & Margaret Smith
Hours: Mon-Sat 10-5, Closed Sun
Types & Periods: European & Oriental Porcelain, Furniture, Silver, 18th & 19th Century Paintings
Specialties: Silver, Porcelain, Meissen & Oriental
Directions: Off the 2500 block of Broadway

THE STONEHENGE ANTIQUES
4101 S Presa   78223
512 544-3275
Proprietor: Jimye Hurt
Hours: Wed-Sat 12-5, Closed Sun, Mon & Tues
Types & Periods: General Line

THREE WIVES ANTIQUES
705 Ivy Ln   78209
512 822-3463   Est: 1962
Proprietor: Mrs John N McCamish

Hours: By Appointment
Types & Periods: Estate
Sales
Appraisal Service Available

TOWN AND COUNTRY ANTIQUES
3609 Broadway   78209
512 826-2749   Est: 1958
Proprietor: Phil Willborn
Hours: Mon-Sat 10-5:30
Types & Periods: American,
European & Oriental
Furniture, Bric-A-Brac, Rugs
Appraisal Service Available
Directions: Near Town,
1/2 Block from Whitte
Museum, Next to
Brackenridge Park

WINDMILL ANTIQUES
10075 Bandera Rd   78228
512 695-8229
Proprietor: George &
Carolyn Terry
Hours: Wed-Sat, Closed
Sun, Mon & Tues, Also By
Appointment
Types & Periods: General
Line

San Benito

THE GIZMO
Hwy 77   78586
512 399-1639
Proprietor: Iva Lee Luttes
Hours: Wed-Fri 10 -4, Sat
10-12
Types & Periods: Jewelry,
Furniture, Glass
Directions: 1/4 Mile N of
Town on 140

San Juan

THE TOM DAWSON COLLECTION
611 Nebraska Ave   78589
512 787-5632
Proprietor: Tom & Deloy
Dawson
Hours: Tues-Fri 9-5, Sat
9-12, Closed Sun & Mon
Types & Periods: "Browse
In Nostalgic Americana"

THIS & THAT ANTIQUES
507 S Nebraska   78589
512 787-8661   Est: 1966
Proprietor: Frankie Jones

Hours: Tues-Fri 10-5
Types & Periods: Furniture,
Glass, Primitives, Toys, Old
Nostalgia
Specialties: Furniture, Glass,
Primitives
Directions: Lower Rio
Grande Valley, 4 Miles E
of McAllen on Old Hwy 83

Schertz

LONE OAK ANTIQUES
225 Valley Oak   78154
512 658-3088
Types & Periods: General
Line

Seabrook

THE COUNTRY MARKET
1401 2nd St   77586
713 474-2347   Est: 1976
Proprietor: Mrs Jean
Cloyd
Hours: Mon-Sun
Types & Periods: General
Line, Collectibles, Gift Items,
Old Fashioned Penny Candy
Counter
Specialties: Collectibles,
Decorator Pieces
Directions: Cross Hwy 146
& NASA I (2nd St)

Seguin

PEARL'S ANTIQUES & GIFTS
202 S King   78155
512 379-2553
Proprietor: Pearl & Jesse
Talley
Types & Periods: General
Line

Seymour

COLONIAL HOUSE ANTIQUES
100 S Hill Dr   76380
817 888-2500   Est: 1974
Proprietor: Phyllis Walker
Hours: By Appointment,
By Chance
Types & Periods: Glassware,
China, Silver

Specialties: RS Prussia, Irish
Belleek
Directions: 1 Block S of
the Seymour Hospital

Sherman

THE BARN
309 N Willow   75090
214 892-2632
Proprietor: Russell & Lota
Lee Norrell
Hours: Tues-Sat, 10-5
Types & Periods: Furniture,
Glassware, China, Silver,
Pottery, Primitives

BRITTON'S ANTIQUES
611 E Lamar   75090
214 892-2823
Proprietor: Lewis J Britton
Hours: Mon-Fri 8-5
Types & Periods: General
Line

CINDY'S CURIOSITY SHOP
500 E Evergreen St 75090
214 893-0482
Proprietor: Cindy Rice
Hours: Mon-Fri 11-5
Types & Periods: Glass,
Primitives, Furniture

LYON HOUSE ANTIQUES
716 N Crockett   75090
214 893-6711   Est: 1976
Proprietor: Awilda Baker &
Doris Boyd
Hours: Mon-Fri 9:30-4:30,
Closed Wed, Sat, & Sun
or By Appointment, By
Chance
Types & Periods: English,
French & American
Furniture
Directions: 2 Blocks Off
Hwy 75, Washington St
Exit

RAY BOB ANTIQUES
220 W Houston   75090
214 892-2092
Proprietor: Ray Brown &
Bob Hargesheimer
Hours: Mon-Fri 4-5:30, Sat
9-5:30, Also By
Appointment
Types & Periods: Clocks,
Furniture, Glass

TWO-TEN ANTIQUES
210 W Houston   75090
Proprietor: Byron Rice
Hours: Tues-Sat 10-5
Types & Periods: Primitives,
Furniture, Glassware

Snyder

**THE ANTIQUE CLOCK
SHOP**
Rte 2 Box 209   79549
915 573-5327   Est: 1969
Proprietor: Lowell K
Marble
Hours: Mon-Sat 9:30-6,
Sun 2-6, Also By
Appointment
Types & Periods: Early
American, Victorian,
Primitives, Clocks, Furniture
Specialties: Restoring
Clocks
Directions: Hwy 84
By-Pass, 1 1/2 Miles N of
Hwy 180

Stephenville

JO & TOMMY'S ANTIQUES
666 N Neblett   76401
817 965-4798   Est: 1948
Proprietor: Mrs Jo Collins
Hours: Mon-Fri 10-5, Also
By Appointment
Types & Periods: General
Line
Specialties: Art & Cut Glass,
Porcelain, Paintings
Directions: 1 Block N of
Tarleton State Univ

Tatum

J & J ANTIQUES
Hwy 149 N   75691
214 947-2228   Est: 1970
Proprietor: Jerry & Jessie
Nunn
Hours: Mon-Sun
Types & Periods:
1880's-1930's
Specialties: Depression
Glass
Directions: Longview Hwy
at City Limits

Temple

**SPEYER'S ANTIQUE &
AUCTION GALLERIES INC**
108 N Main   76501
817 773-3900   Est: 1977
Proprietor: Pauline &
Lanny Speyer
Hours: Mon-Sat, Also By
Appointment, Open For
Auction Once A Month On
Sun, Closed Sat Before
Types & Periods: American,
English, French & Oriental
Furniture, Porcelains, Glass,
Silver
Specialties: English
Furniture, Bric-A-Brac
Appraisal Service Available
Directions: Exit 301 on
I-35, Take Adams St to
Main St, Shop Across
from Kyle Hotel & Public
Library

Texas City

JONES ANTIQUES
609 4th Ave N   77590
713 945-7933   Est: 1970
Proprietor: Bess Jones
Hours: Tues-Sat, Closed
Sun & Mon
Types & Periods: Art & Cut
Glass, China, Refinished
Furniture, Oak & Walnut
Victorian
Specialties: RS Prussia,
Lamps, Art Glass
Appraisal Service Available
Directions: Downtown,
Across the St from J C
Penney's

Tioga

ARCHER'S ANTIQUES
        76271
817 437-2219
Proprietor: Wanda Archer
Hours: Wed-Sun 10-7
Types & Periods: Furniture,
Glass, Primitives, Clocks,
Silver

**THE CONVERSATION
PIECE**
PO Box 121   76271
        Est: 1976
Proprietor: Hazel Silliman

Hours: Tues-Fri
Types & Periods: Early
American Pine, Pressed
Glass, Turn-of-the-Century
1890-1910
Directions: 50 Miles N of
Dallas on Hwy 377, 20
Miles From Denton

THE GILDED CAGE
201 S Main St   76271
817 437-2219   Est: 1970
Proprietor: Jim Wendover
Hours: Tues-Sun, Closed
Mon
Types & Periods: General
Line, English Imports
Specialties: Shakertown
Directions: 45 Miles N of
Dallas, 20 Miles NE of
Denton on US 377

Tomball

GOLDEN CHANCES
26050 Rimwick Forest Dr
PO Box 1146   77375
713 356-2286   Est: 1964
Proprietor: Ruth Schippers
Hours: By Appointment
Types & Periods: English &
Continental Furniture &
Decorative Accessories,
18th, 19th & Early 20th
Century
Directions: Rte 149, Take
Hardin Store Rd, Follow
Over RR Tracks, Then
Left Turn at Rimwick
Forest Sign, 3 Brick Gate
Post, 2nd House on Right

Tyler

**THE BRASS LION
ANTIQUES**
5935 S Broadway   75703
214 561-1111   Est: 1959
Proprietor: Paul Grubb
Hours: Mon-Sat 10-5
Types & Periods: 18th &
19th Century English
Furniture, Chinese Export
Porcelains, Oriental Rugs
Specialties: Hand Made
Reproductions 18th Century
Chandeliers, Sconces in
Solid Brass
Directions: US Hwy 69, 1
Mile S of Loop 323

Uvalde

LOESSBERG'S
524 E Pecos   78801
512 278-3958   Est: 1946
Proprietor: A J Loessberg
Hours: Mon-Fri
Types & Periods: Victorian,
Brass, Glass
Specialties: Restoration
Appraisal Service Available
Directions: Hwy 83 N

Van Alstyne

ANTIQUES DOWNTOWN
Box 874   75095
214 482-5230   Est: 1974
Proprietor: Lee & Bill
Jordan
Hours: Tues-Sat 9-6,
Closed Sun & Mon
Types & Periods: Ceramics,
Bronzes, Furniture,
Primitives
Specialties: Clocks
Directions: 35 Minutes N
of Dallas Off US 75 E a
few Blocks

**GRADY LANGFORD
ANTIQUES**
Hwy 5 Box 66   75095
214 482-5809   Est: 1970
Proprietor: Grady & Fay
Langford
Hours: Mon-Sat Day &
Eve
Types & Periods: Victorian,
Primitives, Lamps, Clocks,
Decorative Pieces
Specialties: Wholesale,
Retail
Directions: 1006 S Waco

Victoria

**CHRISTY DONOGHUE
ANTIQUES**
2424 N Navarro   77901
512 573-7895   Est: 1951
Proprietor: Christy & Bill
Donoghue
Hours: Mon-Fri 9-5, Sat,
Sun & Eves By
Appointment
Types & Periods: 18th &
19th Century European
Furniture, Paintings, Objets
d'Art, Oriental Rugs

Specialties: Formal French &
English Furniture
Appraisal Service Available
Directions: Hwy 77, 10
Blocks N of Hwy 59

GRIFFITH'S ANTIQUES
605 Larkspur   77901
512 573-6467
Proprietor: Mr & Mrs S W
Griffith
Hours: Mon-Fri 9-6, Also
By Appointment
Types & Periods: Furniture,
China, Glass

**SALEM HOUSE OF
ANTIQUES**
501 E Rio Grande   77901
512 575-7984   Est: 1970
Proprietor: Jack & Dorothy
Bleeker
Hours: Mon-Sat, Closed
Sun
Types & Periods: Primitives,
American Walnut & Oak
Furniture, European, China,
Pressed, Crystal & Carnival
Glass
Specialties: Glass, China
Plates
Directions: Corner of
Hwy 59 & 77

VICTORIA ANTIQUE SHOP
804 Berkman Dr   77901
512 575-2203   Est: 1930
Proprietor: Mrs Billy W
Hardegree
Hours: Mon-Sat, Also By
Appointment, By Chance
Types & Periods: American
Furniture
Specialties: Restorations,
Repairs & Refinish of
American Furniture, Chairs
Caned
Appraisal Service Available
Directions: 1/4 Mile Off
US 77 N, Sign at Turn

Waco

AIMEE'S ANTIQUES
3720 W Waco Dr   76710
817 752-2672   Est: 1975
Proprietor: Audrey &
Aimee Chernoff
Hours: By Appointment,
By Chance

Types & Periods:
Wedgwood, Cut Glass,
Belleek, Cloisonne, Furniture
Specialties: Wedgwood
Directions: Hwy 84 &
38th St

**ALMA'S DAUGHTER'S
ANTIQUE SHOP**
600 N 22nd St   76707
817 752-2111   Est: 1958
Proprietor: Mrs Dorothy
Hall
Hours: Mon-Sat 9-3, Also
By Appointment, By
Chance
Types & Periods: China,
Silver, Lamps, Art & Colored
Glass, Oriental Rugs,
Bric-A-Brac, American
Furniture
Specialties: Glass
Appraisal Service Available
Directions: 22nd & Fort St
(Fort St is Side St of 18th
St) Fort St Dead Ends Into
My Drive

**ANTIQUES THIS THAT &
THE OTHER**
1823 Austin Ave   76701
817 754-0881 or 772-6597
                Est: 1972
Proprietor: Mrs Ruth
Shipp
Hours: Mon-Fri 10-4, Also
By Appointment, By
Chance
Types & Periods: Men &
Women's Clothing Late
1800's, Hats, Purses, Shoes,
Fans, Linens, Bed Spreads,
Fiesta, China, Silver, Crystal
Specialties: Clothing, Silver
Flatware, China, Crystal
Directions: From I-35 Take
17th St Exit to Austin Ave,
Left 1 1/2 Blocks on the
Right

COLLIER'S ANTIQUES
2311 N 18th St   76708
817 756-2424   Est: 1938
Proprietor: D L Collier
Hours: Mon-Fri
Types & Periods: Period
Furniture
Specialties: Glass
Appraisal Service Available
Directions: At 18th &
Herring Ave

Waco　　　　Cont'd

THE COUNTRY SHOP
4108 Compton Ln　76705
817 799-0934　Est: 1970
Proprietor: Mrs Esther
Mathews
Hours: Mon-Fri, Also By
Appointment
Types & Periods: General
Line, Primitives, Glassware,
China, Pottery
Specialties: Glass
Directions: In Bellmead,
On Loop 340 &
Compton Ln

DOWNTOWN MARKET
617 Austin Ave　76703
817 753-9467　Est: 1977
Proprietor: Jack & Mary
Vinson
Hours: Tues-Sat 10-5
Types & Periods: General
Line
Directions: Austin Ave
Mall

MAGNOLIA ANTIQUES
1416 Sunset　76710
817 753-4469　Est: 1974
Proprietor: Lee Kramer
Hours: Mon-Sat, Closed
Tues & Sun
Types & Periods: Furniture,
Lamps, Glass, Primitives
Appraisal Service Available
Directions: 38th St Turns
into Sunset, Store In
Fairgate Shopping Center

NELL'S ANTIQUES
509 N 14　76702
817 756-2725　Est: 1960
Proprietor: Nell Morris
Hours: Mon-Fri 1-5, Sat
9-5, Closed Sun
Types & Periods: Primitives,
Clocks, Small Furniture,
China, Glass
Directions: Waco Dr at
14th St

THE TWO "Q'S"ANTIQUES
2511 Colonial　76710
817 753-9071　Est: 1964
Proprietor: Mrs Frank
Quinius
Hours: Mon-Fri, Also By
Appointment, By Chance
Types & Periods: Primitives,
Glass, China, Metals,
Furniture, Fixtures

Appraisal Service Available
Directions: W Waco Dr to
N 25th St, Left after 7
Blocks

Whitewright

THE BACK DOOR
　　　　　　　75491
214 364-2662
Proprietor: Aleva & Earl
Blanton
Hours: By Appointment,
By Chance
Types & Periods: Primitives,
English & American
Furniture, General Line
Directions: Corner of
Carter & Maple

HOUSE'S ANTIQUES
Main St　75491
214 364-2591
Proprietor: Buford House
Hours: Sat & Sun, Also By
Appointment
Types & Periods: Primitives,
Aladdin Lamps, Pocket
Watches, Knives

MURPHY'S ANTIQUES
Hwy 11　75491
214 364-2642　Est: 1963
Proprietor: Pat & Patsy
Murphy
Hours: Mon-Sat, Also By
Appointment, By Chance
Types & Periods: Furniture,
Clocks, Glass, Metals
Appraisal Service Available
Directions: W of Hwys 69,
160 & 11, On Hwy 11 S
Side

TATER BUG
　　　　　　　75491
214 364-2221
Proprietor: Dick & Lurline
Walker
Hours: Mon-Sat, Closed
Sun
Types & Periods: Furniture,
Glassware
Directions: Downtown

Wichita Falls

CENTIME ANTIQUES
1010 10th St　76301
817 723-1711
Proprietor: Paul & Pearle
Collins
Hours: Mon-Sat 10-5,
Closed Sun
Types & Periods: General
Line

MOLLIE STIPE ANTIQUES
2011 McGregor St　76301
817 766-3041
Proprietor: Mrs Mollie
Stipe
Hours: Mon-Fri 9-5:30
Types & Periods: General
Line, Glass, China, Furniture

Wimberley

THE DOUBLETREE
PO Box 285　78676
512 847-9733　Est: 1973
Proprietor: Rose & Al
Flocke
Hours: Mon-Sun 10-5,
Closed Tues
Types & Periods: Primitives,
Glassware, Furniture 1890's-
1930's, Collectibles
1920's-1940's
Specialties: Collectibles &
Unusual Items, Primitives
Appraisal Service Available
Directions: Wimberley Sq

J & J COUNTRY STORE
Ranch Rd 12　78676
512 847-2285　Est: 1968
Proprietor: Jean Garland
Hours: Mon-Sun
Types & Periods: Primitives,
Collectibles, Early 1900
Specialties: Milk Bottles,
Raggedy Ann Dolls, Tools
Appraisal Service Available
Directions: 1 Mile S of
Wimberley on Banks of
Pierce Creek

East Layton

COTTAGE GIFT SHOP
1361 N Hwy 89   84041
801 766-0520   Est: 1975
Proprietor: Sheila A Raitt
Hours: Mon-Sat, 12-6
Types & Periods: Country
Antiques

Lehi

THE OUTPOST ANTIQUES
197 East State St   84043
801 768-9083   Est: 1967
Proprietor: Wallace B &
Arlene Olsen
Hours: Tues-Sun, 10-5;
Closed Holidays
Types & Periods: General
Line
Specialties: Western Frontier
Items
Directions: Between SLC
& Provo on Hwy 89

Nephi

C & D'S ANTIQUES
298 South Main   84648
801 623-0179   Est: 1977
Proprietor: Clair & Delores
Daniels
Hours: Mon-Sat, 10:30-6
Types & Periods: American
Antiques, Furniture &
Primitives

Ogden

ANTIQUE HOUSE
406 Canyon Rd   84401
801 394-4749   Est: 1963
Proprietor: O C & Lee
Budge
Hours: Wed-Sat, 12-5; By
Chance
Types & Periods: Mormon
Pine, Primitives, Oak, Walnut
Specialties: Furniture
Appraisal Service Available
Directions: Between 16th
& 17th Sts at Washington
Blvd

ERIKA MARTIN ANTIQUES
3480 Washington Blvd
84401
801 393-5963   Est: 1973
Proprietor: Erika M Martin
Hours: Tues-Sat
Types & Periods: Glass,
Porcelain, Clocks, Brass,
Copper, Furniture, Paintings;
Victorian Era
Appraisal Service Available
Directions: From I-15, take
31st St Exit to Washington
Blvd; Turn S; Approx 4
Blocks to Shop, Located
on " Washington Square"

Payson

MAIN STREET ANTIQUES
66 South Main   84651
801 465-9442   Est: 1975
Proprietor: MacArthur
Whitelock
Hours: Mon-Sat; Sun by
Appointment
Types & Periods: American
Oak, Pine, Walnut: Full Line
Specialties: Fully Restored
Black & Nickel Cook &
Parlor Stoves
Appraisal Service Available
Directions: Off I-15, on
Main St

Provo

QUIGLEY'S ANTIQUES
119 N University Ave
84057
801 373-3226   Est: 1968
Proprietor: Maxine L Davis
Hours: Mon-Sat, 10-6; and
by Appointment Ph 801
225-0500
Types & Periods: Primitives,
Glassware, China, Dolls,
Bottles, Furniture
Specialties: American Oak &
Walnut Victorian Furniture
Appraisal Service Available

Salt Lake City

SALT LAKE CITY CLUSTER
Directions: S State St
(300-1000 Blocks) &
Adjacent Sts; E 9th South
St; S 11th East St; Others
scattered throughout Area

ANTIQUE SHOPPE
2016 South 11th East
84106
801 466-2171
Proprietor: Ione Hughes
Hours: Mon-Sat, 10-6
Types & Periods: Glass,
Furniture, Books, Primitives
Appraisal Service Available
Directions: Sugarhouse
Area; 1/2 Block North of
21st South & 11th East

BASIL'S ANTIQUES & ART
515 E 3rd S   84102
801 355-1011   Est: 1974
Proprietor: Marcia C &
Brent K Evans
Hours: Wed-Sat, also by
Chance
Types & Periods: 18th &
19th Century Furniture,
Decorative Pieces, Bronze
Sculpture
Directions: 5 Blocks E of
Main on 3rd St S of LDS
Temple

**BEEHIVE COLLECTORS
GALLERY**
368 E Broadway   84111
801 533-0119   Est: 1955
Proprietor: Nyal W
Anderson
Hours: Tues-Sat, 11-5
Types & Periods: Stamps,
Coins, Historical Western
Americana, Militaria,
Jewelry, Paintings, Prints,
Autographs, Photographs,
Political, Postcards, Books,
Indian Items, Currency
Specialties: Stamps, Paper
Americana, Mormon Items

JOHANN BEKKER
903 South 10th East 84105
801 359-5185   Est: 1966
Proprietor: Johann Bekker
Hours: Mon-Sat, 9-6

Salt Lake City   Cont'd

JOHANN BEKKER   Cont'd
Types & Periods: Glass,
Porcelain, Prints (Hand
Colored), Weavings
Specialties: Rare Books,
Early as 14th Century
Appraisal Service Available
   Directions: 9 Blocks from
   Mormon Temple

BRASS KEY ANTIQUES
   43 W 300 S   84101
   801 532-2844   Est: 1969
   Proprietor: Wally &
   Margaret Dodds
   Hours: Mon-Sat
Types & Periods: American
Oak Furniture, Architectural
Detail, Glass, Collectibles
Appraisal Service Available
   Directions: Downtown SLC

COBBLESTONE ANTIQUES
   1228 S 9th E   84105
   801 467-1557   Est: 1967
   Proprietor: Wilma McAffee
   Hours: Daily, By
   Appointment
Types & Periods: Glass,
China, Toys, Jewelry,
Collectibles, Furniture
   Directions: 9 Blocks E &
   almost 13 Blocks S of
   Center of Town

FIRE HOUSE ANTIQUES
   1135 E 21st South   84106
   801 484-1481   Est: 1976
   Proprietor: John Guild
   Hours: Mon-Sat
Types & Periods:
Turn-of-the-Century, Art
Nouveau, Art Deco,
Furniture, Dutch
Copperware
Specialties: French Louis XV
Furniture, Inexpensive Oak
Furniture & Dutch
Copperware
   Directions: In Old Fire
   House 3, Downtown
   Sugarhouse Area

HONEST JON'S ANTIQUES
   167 Broadway   84108
   801 359-4852   Est: 1972
   Proprietor: Jonathon
   Sweet
   Hours: Mon-Sat, 10-5:30

Types & Periods: Victorian,
Oak, Primitive Furniture, &
19th Century Furnishings
Specialties: Quality
American Furniture
   Directions: 300 South 167
   East

THE STOVE KING
   4651 S Riverside Dr
   (500 W)   84107
   801 261-2495
   Proprietor: Clarence B
   Froman
   Hours: Mon-Fri; Sat, 1/2
   Day; Anytime by
   Appointment
Types & Periods: Cook,
Heating & Parlor Stoves
from Early 1800's to 1920's;
Also Stove Related Items,
Cast Iron, Brass & Copper
Items
Specialties: Unusual Ornate
Antique Stoves
Appraisal Service Available
   Directions: Off I-15 at 45th
   S Exit; 2 Blocks W to
   Riverside Dr (500 W); 1
   1/2 Blocks S, in Riverside
   Plaza

Springville

PIONEER CENTER
   391 Main St   84663
   801 489-6853   Est: 1963
   Proprietor: Norma L &
   Betty Suth
   Hours: Mon-Sat
Types & Periods: Indian,
Glass
Appraisal Service Available
   Directions: Downtown, on
   Hwy 89

Woods Cross

ANTIQUES ET-CETERA
   980 S 800 W   84087
   801 295-4214   Est: 1974
   Proprietor: Stephen M Holt
   Hours: Daily, Also by
   Appointment
Types & Periods: General
Line
Appraisal Service Available
   Directions: 10 Miles N of
   SLC to Bountiful; 5th S
   Exit, W to 800 W

Grandfather Clock,
ca. 1850 (Hanlin &
Robert, Dublin).

Since the original
conception, a
variation has existed
in every period.

597

STATE OF VERMONT

Addison

OLD STONE HOUSE ANTIQUES
Rte 22A 05491
802 759-2134
Proprietor: Walter & Helen Washburn
Hours: Daily
Types & Periods: Furniture, Glass, China, Orientals, Primitives
Directions: 1 mile N of Addison, 4 Corners

Alburg

GAM'S & GAMP'S ANTIQUES
Rte 2 05440
802 796-3521
Proprietor: C D & A C Ashline
Hours: By chance
Types & Periods: General Line
Specialties: Furniture (Early)
Directions: In Alburg Village

Arlington

BERNHARDY'S ANTIQUES
Warm Brook Rd 05250
802 375-9953
Proprietor: Dorothy & Roy Bernhardy
Hours: By appointment, by chance
Types & Periods: Country Furniture, Accessories, Paintings, Folk Art
Specialties: China (Flow Blue)
Directions: On road to E Arlington, 1 mile E of Rte 7

Barre

ARNHOLM'S ANTIQUES
891 N Main St 05641
802 476-5921
Proprietor: Rachel Arnholm

Hours: By appointment, by chance
Types & Periods: China, Glass, Silver, Jewelry

BONNIE MEAKER
186¼ N Main 05641
802 479-2474 Est: 1974
Proprietor: Mrs Bonnie Meaker
Hours: Mon-Sat
Types & Periods: Glass, China, Clocks, Pocket Watches, Jewelry, Prints, Books, Laces
Directions: "Shop is a covered-over alley"

MUSIC BOX ANTIQUES
50 Prospect St 05641
802 476-4841
Proprietor: E Hilton Holmes
Hours: Mon-Sat, 8-4:30; closed at noon during July & Aug
Types & Periods: Glassware, China, Jewelry, Clocks, Furniture, Silverware, Lamps, Music Boxes

THE SAMPLER SHOP
176 Washington St 05641
802 479-2865
Proprietor: Richard & Joyce Sample
Hours: By appointment, By chance, May 1-Nov 1
Types & Periods: Country Furniture, Wooden Items, Iron, Brass, Copper, Tin, Crockery

Belmont

BELMONT ANTIQUES
Box 63 05730
802 259-2338 Est: 1958
Proprietor: Fran Sitterly
Hours: By appointment, by chance
Types & Periods: Primitives, Cherry, Pine & Maple Country Furniture, Glass, China, Oil Lamps, General Line

Specialties: Woodstock Workshop Handmade Lampshades
Directions: 1 mile off Rte 155, or 3 miles off Rte 103 in Belmont Village

Bennington

FOUR CORNERS-EAST INC
802 Main St 05201
802 442-2612
Proprietor: R Cox & R Bagley
Hours: Daily, 9-5
Types & Periods: 18th & Early 19th Century American Furniture, Painting, Accessories
Specialties: Bennington Pottery & Porcelain
Appraisal Service Available
Directions: 3/8 mile E of Intersection of Rtes 9 & 7

MATTESON ANTIQUES
  05201
802 442-9596
Proprietor: Bob Matteson
Hours: Daily, 11-5
Types & Periods: American Furniture & Accessories
Directions: South St at Grandview, Rte 7

BETTY TOWNE ANTIQUES
520 South St Rte 7 S
  05201
802 442-9204
Proprietor: Betty Towne
Hours: Mon-Sat, 9-5; Sun by chance or by appointment
Types & Periods: Pressed Glass, Cut Glass, Art Glass, Lamps, Furniture, Fine China, General Line

Bomoseen

IRON HORSE ANTIQUES INC
    Star Rte   05732
    802 273-2000
    Proprietor: Vernon Ward
    Hours: Mon-Sat, 9-6
Types & Periods: Tools,
Utensils, American Country
Furnishings

Brandon

THE ANTIQUE SHOP
    Rte 7 S   05733
    802 247-6320
    Proprietor: Sally & Pen
    Reed
Types & Periods: Primitives,
Furniture, Nautical Items

AGNES AND BILL FRANKS ANTIQUES
    Rte 7 55 Franklin St
                  05733
    802 247-3690   Est: 1958
    Proprietor: Agnes & Bill
    Franks
    Hours: Daily
Types & Periods: Country
Furniture & Accessories,
Folk Art, Primitives, Textiles
    Directions: 15 miles N of
    Rutland

H CRAY GILDERSLEEVE ANTIQUES
    57 Park St   05733
    802 247-6684
    Proprietor: H Cray
    Gildersleeve
    Hours: By appointment, by
    chance
Types & Periods: Primitives,
Wood, Iron, Tin, Early
Lighting, Folk Art

HOLLAND HOUSE ANTIQUES
    25 Franklin St   05733
    802 247-5765   Est: 1970
    Proprietor: Cecil Holland
    Hours: By appointment, by
    chance
Types & Periods: Lamps,
Ironstone, Tools,
Woodenware, Iron, Country
Furniture
    Directions: Rte 7

LORRAINE & WARREN KIMBLE
    77 Park St   05733
    802 247-3026
    Proprietor: Lorraine &
    Warren Kimble
    Hours: By appointment, by
    chance
Types & Periods: Primitives,
Country Furniture, Original
Decoration
Specialties: Original Painted
& Decorated Furniture &
Accessories
    Directions: E end of Park
    St

ROSEMARY ANTIQUES
    16 Grave St   05733
    802 247-3055
    Proprietor: Andrew
    Larabee & Mary Oerther
    Hours: By appointment, by
    chance
Types & Periods: General
Line, Tools
    Directions: Rte 7

STONEY FIELDS ANTIQUES INC
    RD 2   05733
    802 247-6711   Est: 1962
    Proprietor: Walter Cerf
    Hours: Daily 10-5,
    June-Oct; By appointment,
    Nov-May
Types & Periods: Paintings,
Formal & Country Furniture,
Porcelain, Silver, Rugs,
American, English,
Continental, Oriental, William
& Mary to Early Victorian
Specialties: 19th Century
Works of Art (Paintings,
Sculptures, Engravings)
Appraisal Service Available
    Directions: 2 miles E of
    Rte 7, near Fern Lake in
    Leicester

Brattleboro

BROOKS HOUSE ANTIQUES
    Brookside   05301
    802 257-7100
    Proprietor: Norma L
    Chase
    Hours: Daily, 10-5,
    April-Dec; Daily, 11-4,
    Jan-March

Types & Periods: Jewelry,
Silver, China, Glass,
Paintings, Primitives,
Furniture, Orientals

HOLDENS ANTIQUE SHOP
    Putner Rd   05301
    802 254-4725   Est: 1922
    Proprietor: Mrs S V
    Holden
    Hours: By appointment, by
    chance, June-Oct
Types & Periods: General
Line
Specialties: Primitives
    Directions: Rtes 5 & 9, 2
    miles N of Brattleboro,
    200 feet off I-91 at Exit 3

Bristol

COUNTRY ANTIQUES
    Rte 116   05443
    802 453-2014
    Proprietor: David & Marion
    Murray
    Hours: Tues-Sun,
    May-Nov; off season by
    appointment
Types & Periods: Early
American Furniture, China,
Flint Glass, Primitives
    Directions: Between Rtes
    17 & 125

Burlington

ETHAN ALLEN ANTIQUE SHOP INC
                  05401
    802 863-3764
    Proprietor: Nathan &
    Margaret Merrill
    Hours: Mon-Sat, 11-4:30;
    Sun by appointment
Types & Periods: Early
American Furniture,
Primitives, Prints, China,
Glass, Folk Art
    Directions: On US 2 E of
    Burlington, Exit 14 E from
    I-89 (1 mile)

CORINNE HARRINGTON ANTIQUES
    81 Black Lantern Ln
                  05401
    802 862-7250
    Proprietor: Corinne
    Harrington

Hours: By appointment, by
chance
Types & Periods: Early
American Furniture,
Accessories
Directions: Laurel Hill, S
of Burlington off Rte 7

**THE WHITE HOUSE
ANTIQUES**
914 North Ave   05401
802 863-3348
Proprietor: Marjorie M
Graves
Hours: Daily, May-Sept; By
chance or appointment
during winter
Types & Periods: Furniture,
Primitives, China, Glass,
Quilts, Children's Things
Directions: 2 miles from
center of town on Rte 127

Castleton

EILEEN'S ANTIQUES
Main St   05735
802 468-5820
Proprietor: John & Eileen
Smart
Hours: Daily, 9-6
Types & Periods: General
Line, Early American &
Victorian, Primitives,
Stoneware, Lamps, Country
Store Items, Glass, China,
Quilts
Directions: Rte 4A

THE WEATHERVANE
South S   05735
802 468-5527
Proprietor: Natalie & Paul
Sweitzer
Hours: By appointment, by
chance, May 1-Nov 1
Types & Periods: Folk Art
Directions: 8th house on
left

Castleton Corners

**OLD HOMESTEAD
ANTIQUES**
Castleton Corners   05732
802 468-2425
Proprietor: Alma Gibbs
Donchian
Hours: By appointment, by
chance, May-Nov

Types & Periods: Lamps,
Oriental Rugs, Glass, China,
Primitives, Furniture, Early
Americana
Directions: Corner of Rtes
4A & 30, 4th house on left
on Rte 4A going toward
Rutland

Charlotte

THE CHESTNUT TREE
Rte 7   05445
802 425-2811   Est: 1975
Proprietor: Judy Pascal
Hours: By chance
Types & Periods: Country
Furniture, Baskets, Quilts,
Primitives
Specialties: Quilts
Directions: 4½ miles S of
Shelburne Museum on Rte
7, at the F H Horsford
Nursery

**NEW ENGLAND SHOPPE
ANTIQUES**
Rte 7   05445
802 425-3219   Est: 1975
Proprietor: Rita Masso
Hours: By chance
Types & Periods: Early
American Primitives
(Accessories & Furniture)
Specialties: Yelloware
Appraisal Service Available
Directions: 4 miles S of
Shelburne Museum on
Rte 7

Chelsea

**CHELSEA GREEN
ANTIQUES**
Junction Rtes 110-113
      05038
802 685-4845
Proprietor: Arthur &
Bernice Gill
Hours: Tues-Sat, 9-5,
May-Nov 1; also by
chance or appointment
Types & Periods: Pattern,
Sandwich & Art Glass

Chester

FIELDFARM
Rte 11 W   05143
802 875-2454
Proprietor: Arthur Bratton
Hours: Mon-Sat
afternoons
Types & Periods: Country
Items, Tiles

Colchester

MILL POND GALLERY
Main St   05446
802 879-7079   Est: 1973
Proprietor: Vernon & Jean
Krause
Hours: By chance
Types & Periods:
Collectibles, Furniture,
Glass, Pictures
Directions: In the center
of village on the main
street

SCANLON'S ANTIQUES
Colchester Village   05446
802 878-5992
Proprietor: Larry & Martha
Scanlon
Hours: Daily, afternoons;
mornings by chance or
appointment
Types & Periods: Furniture,
China, Tin, Decoys, Glass
Directions: Rte 2A, 1/2
mile E of Rtes 2 & 7

Coventry

YESTERYEAR SHOP
      05825
802 754-6623
Proprietor: Marion C
Conway
Hours: Daily, May 15-Oct
15; also by appointment
Types & Periods: General
Line, Collectibles

Cuttingsville

HEARTHSIDE ANTIQUES
      05738
802 492-3464
Proprietor: Ruth Lindholm

HEARTHSIDE Cont'd
Hours: By appointment, by chance
Types & Periods: General Line

J W MC CULLOUGH
Rte 103 05738
802 492-3317
Proprietor: W J McCollough
Hours: By appointment, by chance, April-Dec
Types & Periods: American
Appraisal Service Available

Danby

RED WAGON ANTIQUES
4 Corners Rd 05739
802 293-5404 Est: 1965
Proprietor: George & Anna Burdine
Hours: Daily, 10-5, May 15-Oct 15
Types & Periods: Silver, Cut Glass, Pottery, General Line
Specialties: Silver Flatware
Directions: 2 miles W of Rte 7 on Danby Four Corners Rd towards Pawlet

Dorset

COLONIAL ANTIQUES
Rte 30 05251
802 867-4480
Proprietor: Gertrude Bickel
Hours: Sun-Mon, Wed-Sat, April 20-Oct
Types & Periods: Historical China, Staffordshire, General Line

East Arlington

ICE POND FARM ANTIQUES
05252
802 375-6448
Proprietor: Mary C Shafer
Hours: Mon-Sat, 9-5:30
Types & Periods: American Country Furniture, Accessories
Directions: 1¼ miles E of Rte 7

East Barre

FARR'S ANTIQUES
05641
802 476-4308
Proprietor: Edward & Alice Farr
Hours: Daily, 10-4
Types & Periods: Vermont Primitives & Furniture, Glass, China, Tools
Directions: Take Rte 302 4 miles E of Barre City, 1/4 mile on Rte 110

East Montpelier

ANTIQUES
Rte 14 05651
802 223-5502
Proprietor: Joe & Margaret Lonergan
Hours: Daily, 9-5:30; off season by appointment
Types & Periods: General Line, Clocks, Lamps, Furniture, Glass, China

East Thetford

MEADOW GREEN ANTIQUES
05043
802 785-2882
Proprietor: Ronald & Charlotte Shaffer
Hours: Daily, 10-6, May-Oct
Types & Periods: General Line, Collectibles
Directions: Directly off Rte 5, 1 mile S of village of East Thetford, 10 minutes from Hanover, NH

East Wallingford

GOLDEN CHANCES
05742
802 259-2305
Proprietor: Ruth Schippers
Hours: Daily, 9-5, May-Nov
Types & Periods: English & Continental Furniture, Decorative Accessories
Directions: Follow state signs to Sugar Hill Rd, then follow signs 2½ miles bearing right all the way

Essex Junction

BACK DOOR ANTIQUES
178 Old Stage Rd 05452
802 878-2093 Est: 1970
Proprietor: Jean Tudhope
Hours: Mon-Sat, by appointment or by chance; closed holidays & deer season
Types & Periods: Out of Print & Rare Books, Country Furniture, Advertising, Tin, Containers, Signs, Sporting Items
Specialties: Books & Paper, Country Furniture, Advertising Items
Directions: Take Rte 15 E, 2 miles from Essex Junction, turn left on Old Stage Rd, 1½ miles

BRIGHAM HILL FARM ANTIQUES
126 Brigham Hill Ln 05452
802 878-2143 Est: 1970
Proprietor: Lois Kenney
Hours: By appointment, By chance
Types & Periods: Glass, China, Collectibles, Dolls, Prints, Books, Pottery, "Vermontiana"
Specialties: Glass (Art)
Directions: Off Rte 15 to Old Stage Rd, left to Brigham Hill Rd, left up hill to Brigham Hill Ln

Fairfax

GLENORTON COUNTRY ANTIQUES
Rte 104 05454
Proprietor: Stuart & Joanna Orton
Hours: Daily, July & Aug; Spring & Fall by chance
Types & Periods: American Country Furniture & Accessories, Iron, Decoys, Primitives, Buggies, Sleighs
Directions: Next to Village Bridge

Grafton

**ANTIQUES AT
STRONGHOLD COTTAGE**
Rte 121   05146
802 843-2254
Proprietor: Mary E Hinkle
(Mrs Walter M Hinkle)
Hours: Daily, by
appointment, by chance
Types & Periods: Period &
Country Furniture, Folk Art,
Delft, Chinese Export, Metal,
Wooden Primitives
Directions: 6/10 mile from
Grafton Inn, opposite side
of road & 2 houses from
Woodshed Antiques

GABRIEL'S BARN
Woodchuck Hill Farm
Middletown Rd   05146
802 843-2398   Est: 1968
Proprietor: Anne & Frank
Gabriel
Hours: Daily, 10-6
Types & Periods: Country
Furniture, Pine, Farm, Barn,
Country Kitchen, Blue Salt
Glaze Stoneware Pottery,
Jugs & Crocks
Specialties: Country
Furniture, Stoneware Pottery
Appraisal Service Available
Directions: 2 miles W of
village of Grafton off
Middletown Rd (follow
signs from village)

Grand Isle

MC GARITY'S GARRET
                              05458
802 372-8849
Proprietor: Velva McGarity
Hours: Daily, 8-5,
May-Sept
Types & Periods: General
Line
Directions: Rte 2, 30 miles
from Burlington

Hardwick

HIGH MOWING ANTIQUES
Woodbury Rd Rte 14
                              05843
802 472-6035   Est: 1971
Proprietor: Mrs Polly
Pelletier

Hours: By appointment, by
chance
Types & Periods: Country
Furniture, Lamps, Tables,
Glass from Sandwich to Art,
Oriental, Ivory, Glass,
Porcelain
Appraisal Service Available
Directions: Rte 14 from
blinker in Hardwick village,
1¼ miles S toward
Montpelier

Harmonyville

THE GABLES ANTIQUES
Rte 30   05353
802 365-7909   Est: 1977
Proprietor: Leete Ekstrom
Hours: Daily, all year
Types & Periods: Furniture
& Accessories from 17th to
Early 19th Centuries
Specialties: Formal Furniture
Appraisal Service Available
Directions: Right on Rte
30, between Newfane &
Townshend

Hartland

BARBARA E MILLS
Rte 5   05048
802 436-2441   Est: 1963
Proprietor: Barbara E Mills
Hours: Daily, by chance,
June-Oct
Types & Periods: New
England, General Line, Early
19th Century, some 18th
Century
Specialties: Furniture
Appraisal Service Available
Directions: I-91 to Exit 9 N
on Rte 5, 2 miles to shop

Highgate Springs

**TREASURE HOUSE
ANTIQUES**
Highgate Center Rd
                              05460
802 868-4158
Proprietor: Mrs Madeline
McCarthy
Hours: Daily, May 15-
Oct 31
Types & Periods: General
Line

Directions: Rte 7, turn at
overpass on Highgate
Center Rd, watch for sign

Hubbardton

**IRON HORSE ANTIQUES
INC**
Rte 30   05764
802 273-2000   Est: 1970
Proprietor: Corporation
Hours: Mon-Sat, 10-5:30,·
May 1-Oct 30
Types & Periods: Antique
Tools, Implements &
Utensils, Primitives,
Furniture (Country)
Specialties: Antique Tools,
In Print Books on Traditional
Crafts & Collectibles
Appraisal Service Available
Directions: 7 miles N of
Castleton Corners on Rte
30

Jamaica

DORE B MC KENNIS
Rte 30   05343
802 874-7191
Proprietor: Dore B
McKennis
Hours: By appointment, by
chance
Types & Periods: 18th &
19th Century American
Furniture, Accessories,
Glass, Primitives

Johnson

AL'S ANTIQUES
Railroad St   05656
802 635-7771
Proprietor: Albert Dolan
Hours: 8-5
Types & Periods: China,
Furniture, Glass
Directions: Just 50 ft off
Hwy 15

FARRELL'S ANTIQUE SHOP
Rte 15   05656
Proprietor: Roger & Helen
Farrell & Jean Crisp
Hours: Mon-Sat, 9-6
Types & Periods: Furniture,
China, Glass

Londonderry

YESTERDAY SHOP
Rte 100   05148
802 824-5964
Proprietor: Alta F Roberts
Hours: June-Oct
Types & Periods: General
Line

Lower Waterford

**WATERFORD HILLS
ANTIQUES**
Town Hwy 19   05848
802 748-9456
Proprietor: Mrs Roger W
Olds
Hours: Daily, May-Oct;
other times by chance
Types & Periods: Country
Furniture, Primitives, Quilts,
Paper, General Line, Glass
& China
Specialties: Furniture,
Lamps
  Directions: Between St
  Johnsbury & Littleton NH,
  off Rte 18 on Hwy 19

Ludlow

**BAKER'S VILLAGE BARN
ANTIQUES**
57 Depot St   05149
802 228-4461
Proprietor: A T & M S
Baker
Hours: Mon-Sat, May-Nov
Types & Periods: Lamps,
Silver, Tin, Dolls, Furniture

Manchester

THE INCREDIBLE TREE
Rte 7 at the Jelly Mill
                     05254
802 362-3629   Est: 1973
Proprietor: Phyllis Dunn &
William Herrick
Hours: Daily
Types & Periods: General
Line, American, French &
English Furniture &
Decorative Accessories
  Directions: 3rd floor in the
  Jelly Mill, right in heart of
  Manchester, on Rte 7

OLD WORLD ANTIQUES
Village Mall Rte 7   05254
802 362-2729
Proprietor: Mary E Combe
Hours: Daily, 10-5; closed
Tues during winter
Types & Periods: European
& Oriental Imports

**PARAPHERNALIA
ANTIQUES**
Box 451 Rte 7 S   05254
802 362-2421   Est: 1960
Proprietor: Anne Alenick
Hours: By appointment, by
chance
Types & Periods: European
& Continental Circa 1850 to
1900, Bronzes, Orientals, Art
Glass, Lamps, Furniture,
Collectibles
Specialties: Boxes, Clocks,
Victorian Sewing
Paraphernalia
Appraisal Service Available
  Directions: 2 miles S on
  Rte 7, on grounds of
  Weathervane Motel

SKYLINE ANTIQUES
                     05254
802 362-2377
Proprietor: Kay Parsons
Sweets
Hours: Mon-Sat, 11-5,
May-Oct
Types & Periods: Glass,
China, American Historical,
Soft Paste, Primitives, Silver,
Oriental, Furniture
Specialties: Collectibles

Manchester Center

BREWSTER ANTIQUES
Bonnet St Rte 30 N 05255
802 362-1579   Est: 1945
Proprietor: Mrs Cecile
Brewster
Hours: Daily, 10-5
Types & Periods: Jewelry,
Sterling Flatware, Decorator
Items
Specialties: Jewelry
Appraisal Service Available
  Directions: Rte 30, corner
  of Bonnet & School Sts

COACH HOUSE ANTIQUES
PO Box 815   05255
802 362-1436
Proprietor: Louise Marvin

Hours: By appointment, by
chance, May 1-Nov 1
Types & Periods: Glass,
China, Toys, Furniture,
Paintings
  Directions: Rte 7, 2 miles
  N of Center

Marlboro

GREENRIVER GLASS CO
Rte 9   05344
802 254-2195
Proprietor: Kit Barry
Hours: By appointment,
9-5
Types & Periods: Flasks,
Bitters, Pontil, Inks,
Medicines, All Bottles
  Directions: 8 miles W of
  Brattleboro

Marshfield

**ANTIQUE TOOLS &
PRIMITIVES**
US 2   05667
802 426-3381   Est: 1972
Proprietor: John D &
Pauline Welch
Hours: Mon-Sat, by
chance
Types & Periods: Primitives,
Tools
  Directions: On US 2
  halfway between Plainfield
  & Marshfield

Middlebury

**BIX ANTIQUES &
TREASURES**
RD 3 Rte 116   05753
802 388-2277   Est: 1970
Proprietor: John & Laurie
Wetmore
Hours: Mon-Sat, 8-5
Types & Periods: General
Line
Specialties: Furniture
  Directions: 1½ miles N of
  E Middlebury on Rte 116

REBA B BLAIR
                     05753
802 388-2970
Proprietor: Reba B Blair
Hours: By appointment

Types & Periods: Miniature
Furniture, Doll Furnishings,
Toys, Collectibles

LITTLE OAKEN BUCKET
74 Main St   05753
802 388-2928   Est: 1970
Proprietor: Mr & Mrs E M
Gipson
Hours: Tues-Sat
Types & Periods: Glass,
China, Furniture, Tools
   Directions: Near Cannon
   Pk

**THE VILLAGE STORE OF
MIDDLEBURY**
Rte 7   05753
802 388-6476
Proprietor: Jean & Ted
Panicucci
Hours: Mon-Sat; Sun by
appointment
Types & Periods: Country
Furniture, Primitives,
Accessories
   Directions: 4 miles S of
   Middlebury

Middletown Springs

NIMMO & HART ANTIQUES
Rte 133   05757
802 235-2388
Hours: By appointment, by
chance
Types & Periods: 18th
Century NE Country
Furniture, Faience,
Porcelain, Accessories
   Directions: 11 miles S of
   W Rutland or 11 miles W
   of Wallingford

Montpelier

**FIRST REPUBLIC
ANTIQUES**
24 Liberty St   05602
802 223-5175   Est: 1976
Proprietor: Jeffrey &
Margaret Cueto
Hours: Daily, by
appointment or by chance
Types & Periods: General
Line, American Furniture,
Clocks, Accessories,
Country Store Items
Appraisal Service Available
   Directions: Turn right off
   Main St

MULLALLY'S ANTIQUES
183 State St   05602
802 223-7700
Hours: Mon-Sat, 9-5,
April-Oct
Types & Periods: General
Line

Newbury

VALMONT VIEW ANTIQUES
                          05051
802 866-7331
Proprietor: George &
Dorothy Ebeling
Hours: Mon-Sat, 10-5, by
chance or appointment,
Late June to Mid Oct
Types & Periods: General
Line, Clocks, Lamps, Town
& Country Furniture
   Directions: In the village
   on Rte 5

Newport

HYLAND'S ANTIQUES
Star Rte Derby Rd   05855
802 334-2662   Est: 1962
Proprietor: Mr & Mrs
Bernard E Hyland
Hours: Daily, 8-8
Types & Periods: Furniture,
Glass, China, Primitives,
Tinware, Boxes, Baskets,
Bottles, Tools
Specialties: Furniture
   Directions: Approximately
   3 miles N of last red light
   in city of Newport, near
   Derby Center Exit Rte
   91 S

THE SALT BOX
Derby Rd   05855
802 334-2901   Est: 1956
Proprietor: E C Humphrey
Hours: Daily
Types & Periods: Early
American Furniture,
Lanterns, Cast Iron Kettles,
Wood Tools, Glass, Mirrors
   Directions: 1/2 mile from
   I-91, Derby-Newport Exit

North Hero

THE GRANARY
                          05474 .
802 372-4211
Proprietor: Marion Howes
Hours: By appointment,
June-Oct
Types & Periods: "Odds &
Ends & All Sorts of Old
Things"
   Directions: On US 2 at
   Block House Point Rd

**ROMA KNIGHT WEANER
ANTIQUES**
                          05474
802 372-4215
Hours: Mon-Sat, 10-4:30,
May 15-Oct 1
Types & Periods: General
Line, Furniture, Lamps,
Primitives,
Specialties: China (Canton)

Perkinsville

MRS AUDREY R CONNIFF
                          05151
802 263-5273
Proprietor: Mrs Audrey R
Conniff
Hours: By appointment, by
chance
Types & Periods: Early
Americana Furniture,
Paintings, Collectibles
   Directions: 19 miles S of
   Woodstock on Rte 106

JEANNE COUTS ANTIQUES
                          05151
802 263-5770
Proprietor: Jeanne Couts
Hours: 'Open All Year'
Types & Periods: Glass,
China, Furniture, Prints,
Lamps, Decorator Items
   Directions: Rte 106,
   Between Springfield
   & Woodstock

Pittsford

VINTAGE VALUE
Rte 7   05763
802 483-2229   Est: 1970
Proprietor: Virgie Fish
Hours: Daily, 9-5

VINTAGE VALUE   Cont'd
Types & Periods: Furniture,
Glass, Pewter, Iron, Period
Clothing, Paintings, Brass,
Bronze, Jewelry, Paper
Americana, Advertising
Items, Books
Appraisal Service Available
    Directions: 7 miles N of
    Rutland on Rte 7 at only
    blinking light

Poultney

ELBOW BEND II
    Rte 30 Lake Rd   05764
    802 287-9192   Est: 1970
    Proprietor: Ruth L
    Anderson
    Hours: By appointment, by
    chance
Types & Periods: Small
Furniture, Country Things,
Tin, Wood, Iron, China &
Glass
    Directions: 2 state signs
    on Rte 30

OLD CHINA SHOP
    71 Main St   05764
    802 773-9039
    Proprietor: Edith Martin
    Hours: Daily, 10-5
Types & Periods: General
Line

VARGISH ANTIQUES
                05764
    802 287-5852
    Proprietor: Andrew
    Vargish
    Hours: By appointment, by
    chance
Types & Periods: Early
American Furniture
    Directions: Off Rte 22A,
    halfway between Poultney
    & Fair Haven

Proctorsville

THIS & THAT SHOP
                05153
    802 388-6763
    Proprietor: Webster &
    Susan Slack
    Hours: Wed afternoons,
    July & Aug; Weekends by
    chance, Spring & Fall

Appraisal Service Available
    Directions: Rte 131 in
    village

Randolph

BETTY STERLING
    Peth Rd   05060
    802 728-5054
    Proprietor: Betty Sterling
    Hours: By appointment,
    June 15-Oct 30
Types & Periods: American
Country Formal Furniture &
Accessories, 18th-19th
Centuries
Specialties: Painted
Furniture, Hooked Rugs,
Early Iron, Lighting, Primitive
Water Color Painting
Appraisal Service Available
    Directions: 4 miles N of
    Randolph, off Rte 12

Randolph Center

**COLONIAL HOUSE
ANTIQUES**
    Main St   05061
    802 728-5571
    Proprietor: William Dupras
    Hours: By appointment, by
    chance
Types & Periods:
Cupboards, Early American,
Victorian, Clocks

THE RED BRICK HOUSE
                05061
    802 728-5843
    Proprietor: Bill Mather
    Hours: By appointment, by
    chance
Types & Periods: Clocks for
Beginning & Advanced
Collectors
    Directions: 1/2 mile off
    I-89

Rawsonville

THE RUSTY HORSESHOE
    Rte 100
    802 824-3805
    Proprietor: Bill McMillen &
    David Hamman
    Hours: 9-5, May 15-Oct
    30; Nov-May by
    appointment

Types & Periods: Primitives,
Country Furniture
    Directions: 8/10 mile N
    Rawsonville

Reading

MILL BROOK ANTIQUES
    Rte 106   05062
    802 484-5942   Est: 1975
    Proprietor: John & Nancy
    Stahura
    Hours: Daily, spring,
    summer & fall; winter by
    chance or appointment
Types & Periods: Antiques &
Collectibles
Specialties: Country
Furniture, Stoneware,
Kitchen & Country Store
Items, Tin, China, Tools
    Directions: On Rte 105, 2
    miles N of Reading Post
    Office, 10 miles S of
    Woodstock

WEATHERWELL ANTIQUES
                05062
    802 484-7489
    Proprietor: Harland A
    Cass
    Hours: Daily, 8-6, July &
    Aug
Types & Periods: Early
Country Furniture &
Accessories, General Line
    Directions: In 18th Century
    Red Saltbox on Rte 106, 1
    mile S of Reading

Ripton

**BREAD LOAF MOUNTAIN
ANTIQUES**
                05766
    802 388-2436
    Proprietor: Mildred Inskip
    Hours: By chance or
    appointment, June 1 to
    Oct 12
Types & Periods: General
Line
    Directions: A mountain
    shop in Middlebury area,
    1/4 mile off Rte 125 at
    Ripton Memorial Marker
    Triangle

Rutland

EAGLES NEST ANTIQUES
53 Prospect St   05701
802 773-2418
Proprietor: Mrs James
Lemmo
Hours: Mon-Fri; Sat & Sun
by chance or appointment
Types & Periods: Fine
China, Lamps, Dolls, Kettles,
Jewelry, Sterling Silver,
Furniture
Appraisal Service Available
Directions: 2 short blocks
from Rte 7, 1 block from
downtown shopping plaza

HANNIBAL HODGES
79 Center St   05701
Hours: By appointment
Types & Periods: General
Line, Pre 1915 Postcards

OLD CHINA SHOP
55 N Main St   05701
802 773-9039
Proprietor: Edith Martin
Hours: By appointment, by
chance
Types & Periods: China,
Silver, Brass, Jewelry,
Lamps, Clocks, Oriental
Items
Directions: Rte 7

WHAT-NOT-SHOP
25 N Main St   05701
802 773-8950
Proprietor: Joseph E
Provost
Hours: Daily, 9-7, summer;
9-5 winter
Types & Periods: General
Line
Directions: Intersection of
Rtes 4 & 7

WINDY LEDGE ANTIQUES
64 N Main   05701
802 775-5251
Proprietor: Mrs Barbara
Chiolino
Hours: By appointment
Types & Periods: Quilts,
Stoneware, Dolls, Primitives
Directions: Rte 7, just N of
Rte 4

St Albans

DUST & COBWEBS
43 Diamond St   05478
802 524-4476
Proprietor: Bonnie
Wersebe
Hours: Daily, 11-5,
June-Oct
Types & Periods: Glass,
China, Primitives, Furniture
Directions: Off Main St

Saxtons River

SCHOOLHOUSE ANTIQUES
Rte 121   05154
802 869-2332   Est: 1972
Proprietor: Faith Boone &
Sandy Saunders
Hours: Daily by
appointment or by chance
Specialties: Country
Furniture
Directions: 2.2 miles W of
Saxtons River on Rte 121,
look for sign & blue
mailbox

Shaftsbury

COPPER LAMP ANTIQUES
RD 1 US 7   05262
802 375-2769
Proprietor: Ethelyn &
Howard Grassel
Hours: Tues-Sun, by
appointment or by chance
Types & Periods: Early Pine,
Cherry, Maple, Walnut
Specialties: Cupboards in
the rough
Appraisal Service Available
Directions: 10 miles N of
Bennington, 14 miles S of
Manchester on Hwy 7

STEPHEN/ DOUGLAS ANTIQUES
Rte 7   05262
802 442-6659
Proprietor: Stephen
Corrigan & Douglas
Jackman
Hours: By appointment or
chance anytime
Types & Periods: 18th &
19th Century Furniture, Folk
Art, Textiles, Rag Dolls,
Decorations, Toys, Primitives

Specialties: Early Rag Dolls,
Sewing Items, Textiles
Directions: Rte 7, across
from Medical Center

Shelburne

THE ANTIQUE CLOCK & GUN SHOP
Rte 7 Harrington Bldg
        05482
802 985-3000   Est: 1974
Proprietor: James C
Raymond
Hours: Mon-Fri, 2:30-9;
Sat, 10:30-6 by chance
Types & Periods: Clocks,
Watches, Firearms &
Swords, Banks, Cash
Registers, Scales
Specialties: Arms, Clocks &
Watches
Appraisal Service Available

GADHUES ANTIQUES
Rte 7   05482
802 985-2682   Est: 1939
Proprietor: Helen & Rene
Gadhue
Hours: By appointment, by
chance
Types & Periods: Furniture,
Glassware, China, Textiles,
Primitives

Shoreham

LAPHAM & DIBBLE GALLERY INC
Main St   05770
802 897-5531
Proprietor: Rick & Martha
Lapham
Hours: Tues-Sat, 9-5
Types & Periods: 19th &
20th Century American
Paintings, Prints & Maps

South Dorset

THE ANGLOPHILE ANTIQUES
The Old Schoolhouse
        05263
802 362-1621
Proprietor: Dorothy R
Jones
Hours: Sun-Tues,
Thurs-Sat

THE ANGLOPHILE Cont'd
Types & Periods: English
18th & 19th Century, China,
Silver, Small Furniture,
Jewelry, Brass, Copper
Specialties: Miniature China
 Directions: Rte 30, 4 miles
 N of Manchester Center, 2
 miles S of the Dorset
 Green

South Londonderry

HEARTHSTONE ANTIQUES
Rte 100   05155
802 824-3126
Proprietor: Barbara Trask
Hours: Mon-Sat, 9-5
Types & Periods: Country
Furniture & Accessories
 Directions: Between
 Londonderry & S
 Londonderry

South Newfane

ATTIC ANTIQUES
E Dover Rd   05351
802 348-7707   Est: 1967
Proprietor: Nancy Weiss
Hours: By appointment, by
chance; closed winters
Types & Periods: Country &
Victorian Furniture, Quilts,
Mirrors, Primitives, China,
Books
 Directions: 3 miles from
 General Store on E Dover
 Rd

Springfield

FRASER'S ANTIQUES
Rte 143   05156
802 885-4838
Proprietor: Bob & Mary
Fraser
Hours: Daily, by
appointment, by chance
Types & Periods: Country
Furniture, Textiles, Early
American
Appraisal Service Available
 Directions: ½ mile W on Rte
 143 from the Junction of
 Rtes 5 & 143

SKITCHEWAUG ANTIQUES
Rte 143   05156
802 885-4063
Proprietor: The Crandalls
Hours: By appointment, by
chance, May-Oct
Types & Periods: Books,
General Line
 Directions: 3.2 miles from
 square, Rte 143, turn right
 on Spencer Hollow Rd,
 700 ft from Rte 5, 2.7
 miles

THE SUMMER HILL SHOP
80 Summer Hill   05156
802 885-3294
Proprietor: Julia Currie
Hours: 10-4, by
appointment or by chance,
May-Nov
Types & Periods: Dolls,
Toys, Prints, Coverlets,
Quilts, Furniture, Clocks

Stowe

GREEN MT ANTIQUES OF
STOWE
Main St   05672
                       Est: 1974
Proprietor: Russell & Judy
Foregger
Hours: Sun-Tues,
Thurs-Sat, 10-5
Types & Periods: Furniture,
Primitives, Quilts, Paintings,
Silver, Toys
 Directions: Exit from Rte
 89 at Waterbury & Stowe
 Exit, N on Rte 100

Sunderland

KAAREN JEAN ANTIQUES
Rte 7   05250
802 362-1651
Hours: Daily, 9-5, April-Oct
Types & Periods: Glass,
China, Furniture
Specialties: Clocks
 Directions: Between
 Manchester & Arlington

Thetford

REGINA MUSIC BOX CO
INC
Sawnee Bean Rd   05074

802 785-2669   Est: 1938
Proprietor: Lloyd G Kelley
Hours: Daily
Types & Periods: Swiss &
Disc Type Music Boxes
Specialties: Restoration
Mechanical Music
Appraisal Service Available
 Directions: Off Rtes 91 &
 113

Thetford Center

L G KELLEY
Sawnee Bean Rd   05075
802 785-2669   Est: 1939
Proprietor: Lloyd G Kelley
Hours: Daily, 8-5; also by
appointment
Types & Periods: Music
Boxes
 Directions: Off Rte 113

Underhill

J LEE MURRAY JR
Rte 15 Box 38   05489
802 899-4013
Proprietor: J Lee Murray
Jr
Hours: By appointment
Types & Periods: Antique
Woodworking Tools

Vergennes

THE OWL IN THE ATTIC
123 Main St   05491
802 877-2231
Proprietor: Grace
Bottamini
Hours: By appointment, by
chance
Types & Periods: General
Line, Fascinators

Waitsfield

THE VERSATILE SHOP
Appalachina Gap Rd
                          05763
Proprietor: Mrs Francis A
Martin
Hours: By appointment, by
chance

Types & Periods: Pewter, Copper, Brass, Ironwork, Furniture, China, Glass, Chinese Pieces
Directions: Fayston-1½ miles from Rte 100

Wallingford

THE 1805 HOUSE
Rte 7 05773
802 446-2745
Proprietor: Liza & Gaston Oxemaar
Hours: Daily, May-Nov
Types & Periods: Furniture, Primitives, Glass, China, Silver, Clocks, Toys, Paintings
Directions: Just S of Twin Bridges

YANKEE MAID ANTIQUES
Rte 7 05773
802 446-2463
Proprietor: Lynne N Gallipo
Hours: By chance
Types & Periods: Early Country Furniture, Primitives, General Line

Waterbury

UPLAND ACRES ANTIQUES
05676
802 244-7197
Proprietor: Rebecca T Iiggino
Hours: Daily, 9-5 during summer; winter by appointment
Types & Periods: Early Rough Furniture, Copper, Pewter, Brass, Primitives, Wooden Items, Glass, China, General Line
Directions: Off Rte 100 up Blush Hill, across from Country Club

Waterbury Center

SIR RICHARD'S ANTIQUES
Rte 100 05677
802 244-8879
Proprietor: Richard & Barbara Woodard

Hours: By appointment, by chance
Types & Periods: Country Furniture & Decorative Items, Early American & Art Nouveau Glass, General Line
Appraisal Service Available

Wells River

THE VILLAGE TRADER
05081
802 757-2716
Proprietor: S H Kaiser
Hours: Daily, 8:30-5
Types & Periods: Lamps, Clocks, Dishes, Furniture

West Brattleboro

UPPERWAY ANTIQUES
Ames Hill Rd 05301
802 254-9445
Proprietor: The Blackburns
Hours: By appointment, by chance
Types & Periods: American Furniture, Stoneware, Quilts, Samplers

Weston

AMAPOLA ANTIQUES INC
Rte 100 05161
802 824-3572
Proprietor: Dolores Bersell
Hours: Daily, 10-6
Types & Periods: Victoriana, Country Store Items, Advertising, Stained Glass Windows
Specialties: Paper Memorabilia of the 19th Century
Directions: S end of town

GAY MEADOW FARM ANTIQUES INC
Trout Club Rd 05161
802 824-6386
Proprietor: Harriet Sisson
Hours: Daily, 10-5; also by appointment
Types & Periods: Country & Period Furniture, Brass, Copper, General Line

Directions: Turn at Post Office, follow signs to 2nd left

Whiting

VILL-EDGE ANTIQUES
Rte 30 05778
802 623-7911 Est: 1969
Proprietor: Margaret R Anzalone
Hours: Daily
Types & Periods: Primitives, Early American, Victorian, Jewelry, Silver, China
Directions: Rte 30

Wilmington

DEERFIELD VALLEY ANTIQUES
Marlboro Rd 05363
802 464-8221
Proprietor: Henri & Cato Logcher
Hours: Daily, 9-6, May 1-Oct 31; other times by appointment
Types & Periods: Period Furniture, Clocks, Lamps, China, Glass
Appraisal Service Available
Directions: 3 miles E of Wilmington on Rte 9 & Lake Raponda Rd

ED JAFFE STUDIO INC
Shearer Hill Rd 05363
802 464-8516 Est: 1975
Proprietor: Ed & Sandy Jaffe
Hours: By chance or appointment
Types & Periods: Fine Victorian Pieces, Oriental Export, Early Pieces
Directions: 1 mile from Rte 9 off Shearer Hill Rd, which is 2 miles E of the light in Wilmington

Windsor

THE COVERED BRIDGE ANTIQUE SHOP
RFD 2   05089
                   Est: 1940
Proprietor: John L Nichols
Hours: Daily, by
appointment
Types & Periods: 1760-1860,
General Line
Specialties: Furniture
(Windsor Chairs & Harvest
Tables)
Appraisal Service Available
  Directions: S on Rte 12A,
  1/2 mile, keep left at
  Chabots Gas Station, 1
  mile to bridge

Woodstock

STEPHEN CORRIGAN ANTIQUES
                          05091
Proprietor: Stephen
Corrigan
Hours: Daily, 10-8
Types & Periods: Furniture,
Textiles, Primitive Art,
Decorations

MARION FIELD
2 Church St Rte 4   05091
802 457-2740
Proprietor: Marion Field
Hours: By chance; closed
Jan-March
Types & Periods: New
England Furniture &
Accessories, Garden
Furniture, Silver

THE LAMP SHOP
49 Central St   05091
802 457-1320
Proprietor: Sheila D
Barton
Hours: Mon-Sat, 9-5
Types & Periods: Custom
Made Lampshades, General
Line
Specialties: Custom Wiring
& Lamp Mounting

ELSA ROSS ASID
7 The Green   05091
802 457-1700
Proprietor: Elsa Ross (Mrs
E G)
Hours: Mon-Tues,
Thurs-Sat, 10-4:30
Types & Periods: Choice
Period Furniture, Formal &
Country, Chinese Export
Porcelain, Fine China, Glass,
Paintings & Prints,
Collectors Items, Primitives,
Lamps
  Directions: Brick house on
  the Green in Woodstock

HILLARY UNDERWOOD
21 Pleasant St   05091
802 457-1750
Hours: Summer, 10-6, by
chance; winter, 10-5
Types & Periods: Informal
Furniture, Folk Art,
Paintings, Crude Items

THE WOODSHED
                          05091
802 457-2490
Proprietor: Emerson &
Mary Johnstone
Hours: Mon-Sat, 9-6
Types & Periods: Farmhouse
Furniture & Country Items
from Attic, Shed & Barn

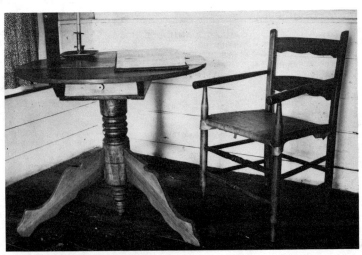

Pedestal table and rawhide bottomed chair. While city furniture was
being made, rural pieces existed as well.

STATE OF VIRGINIA

Accomac

SERENDIPITY
Rte 13   23301
804 787-1371
Proprietor: John &
Kathleen Jones & Wilma
Jones, Mgr
Hours: Mon-Fri, 12-9; Sat,
10-6; Sun, 1-6; by
appointment or chance
Types & Periods: "The gift
of finding unforseen things
of value"

Aldie

VINTAGE ANTIQUES
PO Box 16   22001
703 327-6965   Est: 1971
Proprietor: Susan M
Cromer
Hours: Weekends; also by
appointment
Types & Periods: Early
American, Queen Anne,
Chippendale, Chinese
Artifacts
Directions: W on Rte 50
about 6 miles E of
Middleburg

Alexandria

ALEXANDRIA CLUSTER
Directions: Waterfront thru
Washington St (100 & 700
Blocks), Duke St thru
Ocean St

ABRACADABRA ANTIQUES
917 Prince St   22314
703 549-8937
Proprietor: Anne Woodley
Jones
Hours: Daily, 10-4; also by
appointment
Types & Periods: Pottery,
Furniture, Miscellanea
1840-1940

AMANDA'S ANTIQUES
104B S Alfred St   22314
703 549-1855   Est: 1971
Proprietor: Catherine
Reynolds

Hours: Tues-Sat, 11-4;
also by appointment
Types & Periods:
Autographs, Americana,
Bronzes, Collectibles

ANTIQUES
1520 King St   22304
703 683-9436
Proprietor: Ruth Duckett,
Mgr
Hours: Thurs-Sat, 11-5
Types & Periods: Furniture,
China
Specialties: China Plates,
Unique Furniture
Directions: Upper part of
King St towards Masonic
Monument

APOTHECARY SHOP
105 S Fairfax St   22314
703 836-3713
Hours: Mon-Sat, 10-4:30
Types & Periods: General
Line

C & M ANTIQUES
311 Cameron St   22314
703 548-9882   Est: 1969
Proprietor: Len Harmon,
Partner
Hours: Daily, evenings by
appointment
Types & Periods: 18th &
19th Century American,
European, Oriental
Furnishings, Glass
Appraisal Service Available
Directions: Old Town
Alexandria in the Old
Norford Inn

THE CAROUSEL ANTIQUES
907 King St   22314
703 836-0028   Est: 1969
Proprietor: Robin K
Ruffner
Hours: Mon-Sat, 11-4; also
by appointment or chance
Types & Periods: American
Country Antiques of Late
18th & Early 19th Centuries,
Coin Silver, Stoneware
Specialties: Stoneware, Coin
Silver
Directions: 1 block E off
US Rte 1 on King St (Rte
7) in downtown

THE CARRIAGE HOUSE
ANTIQUES LTD
112A S Royal St   22314
703 549-1291
Hours: Mon-Fri, 10:30-5;
Sat, 10-6
Types & Periods: Traditional
& Country Furniture, Old
Prints, Silver, Accessories

CAVALIER ANTIQUES
400 Prince St   22314
703 836-2539
Hours: Tues-Sat, 1-3:30;
also by appointment
Types & Periods: 18th &
19th Century American
Furniture & Accessories

A COLLECTOR'S SHOP
222½ S Washington St
                        22314
703 836-8690
Proprietor: Kay Fries
Hours: Mon-Sat, 10-5:30
Types & Periods: Art Glass
to Period Furniture

CUPBOARD ANTIQUES OF
ARLINGTON &
ALEXANDRIA
106-114 N Henry St
                        22314
703 548-5914
Hours: Mon-Sat, 10-6;
Sun, 12:30-6
Types & Periods: American,
English, Austrian, General
Line, Collectibles, Civil War,
Decorator Items

DECOR ANTIQUES
6228 Richmond Hwy
US 1   22303
703 765-5500   Est: 1967
Proprietor: Decor
Furniture Corporation
Hours: Mon-Fri, 10-9; Sat,
10-6; Sun, 12-5; also by
appointment
Types & Periods: Furniture,
Oriental Rugs
Specialties: Furniture
Directions: 2 miles S of
city

DIANE'S ANTIQUES
7704 Richmond Hwy
                        22306
703 780-4413   Est: 1966
Proprietor: Diane Thulin

Alexandria   Cont'd

DIANE'S   Cont'd
Hours: Daily
Types & Periods: Christmas
Plates, Paintings, Silver,
Jewelry, Glass
    Directions: 4 miles S on
    Hwy 1 from 495 Beltway

BLANCHE DOBKIN ANTIQUES
7704 Richmond Hwy
                    22306
703 360-3166   Est: 1926
Proprietor: Blanche
Dobkin
Hours: Daily
Types & Periods: Chinese &
Japanese Scrolls, Netsukes,
Figurines, Porcelains,
Bronzes, Sterling & Plated
Silver, Jewelry, Objets d'Art,
Books
Specialties: China, Furniture,
Glass
Appraisal Service Available
    Directions: US Hwy 1

THE DUSTY ATTIC
106 N Patrick St   22314
703 548-1919
Proprietor: Frances Jarvis
Types & Periods: General
Line, Collectibles

EAGLE ANTIQUES
311 Cameron   22314
703 549-7611   Est: 1972
Proprietor: Shirley
Uffelman
Hours: Mon-Sat, 11-5;
Sun, 12-5
Types & Periods: 18th &
19th Century Furniture,
Glassware, Silver
Specialties: Clocks

EILEEN'S ANTIQUES
311 S Washington St
                    22314
703 549-1312
Hours: By appointment, by
chance
Types & Periods: Primitives,
Sewing Items

FIREHOUSE SQUARE ANTIQUES
908 King St   22314
703 683-9892
Proprietor: Betty & Larry
Cohen
Hours: Daily, 11-5

Types & Periods: Flea
Market with 10 Shops at one
location

KEN FORSTER ANTIQUES
7704 Richmond Hwy
                    22306
703 780-9663   Est: 1971
Proprietor: Kenneth C
Forster
Hours: Mon-Sat
Types & Periods: Glass,
Pottery, Porcelain, Silver,
Pewter, Bronze, Lamps,
Graphics, Jewelry of the
Period 1865-1939
Specialties: Art Nouveau, Art
Deco, Arts & Crafts
Movement (Including
American Art Pottery,
European & American Art
Glass)
Appraisal Service Available
    Directions: In the Thieves'
    Market on US Rte 1, 3
    miles S of Alexandria Old
    Town

BETTY GAINES ANTIQUES
222 S Washington St
                    22314
703 548-7446   Est: 1965
Proprietor: Betty Gaines
Hours: Tues-Sun, 12-5
Types & Periods: 18th &
19th Century English,
Chinese, American
Porcelains, Silver, Furniture,
Paintings, Jewelry
Specialties: Oriental
Appraisal Service Available
    Directions: In heart of Old
    Town 1 block from center
    of town

GLOUCESTER ANTIQUES
311 Cameron St   22314
703 549-9505
Hours: Mon-Sat, 10-5;
Sun, 12-5
Types & Periods: 18th &
19th Century Country
Furniture & Accessories

GRANDMOTHER'S ANTIQUES
1510-1512 King St   22314
703 836-1174
Types & Periods: Brass,
Copper, Crystal, Glass,
Furniture

C KING & CO ANTIQUES
403 S Washington   22314
703 549-0638

Hours: Mon-Sat, 10-5; also
by appointment
Types & Periods: 18th
Century Porcelain, American
Furniture

LIROS GALLERY INC
628 N Washington St
                    22314
703 549-7881   Est: 1966
Proprietor: Serge L Liros
Hours: Mon-Sat
Types & Periods: 17th-20th
Century American &
European Paintings, Prints,
Maps, Russian Icons
Appraisal Service Available
    Directions: 5 minutes S of
    National Airport

THE LIVING ROOM
1305 King St   22314
Types & Periods: Furniture,
China, Silver

LLOYD'S ROW
222 S Washington St
                    22314
703 549-7517   Est: 1971
Proprietor: R J Mraz
Hours: Tues-Fri, 1-6; Sat,
11-6
Types & Periods: 18th
Century American & English
Furniture, Silver, Books,
Brass Candlesticks, Chinese
Export
Specialties: Furniture
(Formal American & English
18th Century Queen Anne &
Chippendale)
Appraisal Service Available
    Directions: On the second
    floor

MIDAS TOUCH ANTIQUES
2301 Mt Vernon Ave
                    22301
703 549-3472   Est: 1973
Proprietor: Marjorie
Langford
Hours: Tues-Sat, 11-5
Types & Periods: China,
Silver, Crystal, Furniture,
Jewelry
Specialties: Glass (Silver
Deposit & Cut), Satsuma,
Cloisonne
    Directions: Del Ray area,
    between Crystal City &
    Old Town

**MIMI OF OLD TOWN
ANTIQUE MEWS**
220 S Washington St
22314
703 548-6884
Proprietor: 4 shops, 1
location
Hours: Wed-Fri, 11-4; also
by appointment & by
chance
Types & Periods: Period &
Country Furniture, Paintings,
Accessories

MONUMENT ANTIQUES
1638 King St   22314
703 683-5566
Hours: Wed-Sat, 11-5
Types & Periods: American
Glass, Silver, Collectibles

**SHIRLEY MYERS
ANTIQUES**
201 N Fairfax St   22314
703 548-9882   Est: 1972
Proprietor: Shirley Myers
Hours: Daily, 10-5:30
Types & Periods: Oriental,
American & European
Objets d'Art, Jewelry
Specialties: Oriental
(Furniture & Porcelains)
Appraisal Service Available
Directions: Old Town
Alexandria, corner of N
Fairfax & Cameron Sts

**THE NOT NEW SHOP OF
ALEXANDRIA**
125 S Fairfax St   22314
703 549-0649   Est: 1946
Proprietor: Marion P
Robertson
Hours: Mon-Sat, 9-4:30
Types & Periods: Silver,
Crystal, Jewelry, China,
Small Furniture
Specialties: Jewelry, Silver
Directions: In Old Town,
3 blocks from river

ODDS & ENDS SHOPPE
1511 Mt Vernon Ave
22301
703 836-9522   Est: 1973
Proprietor: Earl & Denise
Webb
Hours: Tues-Sat, 11-6;
Sun & Mon by
appointment
Types & Periods:
Collectibles, Unique
Furniture, All Periods,
Curios, Prints, China, Silver,
Grandfather Clocks,

Depression Glass, Other
Glassware, Records, Bottles
Specialties: Oak Furniture,
Depression Glassware
Directions: Corner of
Monroe Ave & Mt Vernon
Ave, 4th store to the right,
between Rte 1 &
Commonwealth Ave,
before King St downtown
if going S

OLDE TOWNE ANTIQUES
320 Prince St   22314
703 836-0250   Est: 1973
Proprietor: George W &
Agnes G Spicer
Hours: Mon-Fri, 10-4; Sat,
10-6; Sun, 11-5
Types & Periods: Victorian,
Walnut & Oak Furniture,
Glassware, Primitives, Tools
Directions: 1 block from
City Hall in Old Town,
corner of Prince & Royal

**PETTICOAT LANE
GALLERY**
7704 Richmond Hwy
22306
703 360-7003   Est: 1967
Proprietor: Yusef H
Rooddary
Hours: Daily
Types & Periods:
Collectibles, Reusables, Lots
of Interesting Junk
Specialties: Chandelier
Prisms
Directions: In the Thieves'
Market, located on Rte 1,
between Alexandria & Fort
Belvoir

THE PINEAPPLE
311 Cameron St   22314
703 549-7611   Est: 1976
Proprietor: Joan P Alger
Hours: Mon-Sat, 11-5,
Sept-May
Types & Periods: 18th &
19th Century American &
English Furniture &
Accessories
Directions: In Old Town,
from Washington DC
come S on George
Washington Pkwy & turn
left on Cameron St

**PRESIDENTIAL COIN AND
ANTIQUE CO INC**
6204 Little River Trnpk
22312
703 354-5454   Est: 1971

Proprietor: Gail B & H
Joseph Levine
Hours: Mon-Sat
Types & Periods: General
Line, Art Nouveau, Art Deco,
Jewelry, Silver, Political
Americana
Specialties: Art Nouveau &
Art Deco, Jewelry, Silver,
Political Americana
Appraisal Service Available
Directions: 236 W Exit off
395 in Virginia Plaza
Shopping Center

**G RANDALL FINE
ANTIQUES & WORKS OF
ART**
229 N Royal St   22314
703 549-4432   Est: 1952
Proprietor: Glenn C
Randall
Hours: Mon-Sat, 11-6;
appointment advisable
Types & Periods: Fine 17th
& 18th Century English &
American Furniture,
Paintings, Silver, Export
China
Specialties: English Queen
Anne & William & Mary
Period Walnut
Appraisal Service Available

**E SEMONIAN ORIENTAL
RUGS**
613 S Washington St
22314
703 683-5744
Proprietor: E Semonian
Hours: Tues-Sat, 10-5
Types & Periods: Oriental
Rugs, General Line

SILVERMAN GALLERIES
110½ N St Asaph St
22314
703 836-5363   Est: 1958
Proprietor: Maurice B
Silverman
Hours: Tues-Sat, 11-5; by
appointment
Types & Periods: 18th &
19th Century Furniture,
Paintings, Silver, Jewelry,
Some Archaic Pieces
Appraisal Service Available
Directions: 1 block E of
Washington between King
& Cameron Sts

Alexandria   Cont'd

THE SLEIGH BELL
2014 Mt Vernon Ave
          22301
703 765-7509   Est: 1965
Proprietor: C V Rehmert
Sr
Hours: Thurs-Sat, by
appointment
Types & Periods: Fine
China, Furniture, Glass,
Farm & Kitchen Items,
Lamps, Old Tools, Pottery,
Metals, Primitives,
Collectibles
Specialties: Replace Tiffany
Type Lamp Shade Panels,
Curved Glass in China
Cabinets, Aladdin Lamp
Parts
Directions: I-395 to Glebe
Rd S to Mt Vernon Ave,
right on Mt Vernon to
2014

STABLER-LEADBEATER
APOTHECARY MUSEUM &
ANTIQUE SHOP
105-107 S Fairfax St
          22314
703 836-3713   Est: 1939
Proprietor: Donald C
Slaugh
Hours: Mon-Sat
Types & Periods: General
Line
Appraisal Service Available
Directions: Near corner of
King & Fairfax Sts

TARNISHED TREASURES
ANTIQUES
7704 Richmond Hwy
          22306
703 780-7225   Est: 1972
Proprietor: Robert &
Elizabeth Carr
Hours: Daily, 10-5
Types & Periods: Furniture
Specialties: Glass, Musical
Instruments
Appraisal Service Available
Directions: 5 miles S of
Capitol Beltway 495 on
Richmond Hwy, Thieves'
Market

TISH & TRACY
105 S Alfred   22314
703 683-6338
Proprietor: Tish
Mannsman & Tracy
Colgan

Hours: Tues-Sat, 11-4
Types & Periods: General
Line, Collectibles

UNIQUE IMPORTS INC
610 Franklin St   22314
703 549-0775   Est: 1972
Proprietor: Thomas E
Nelson
Hours: Mon-Fri, 8:30-5;
Sat, 10-4
Types & Periods: Military
Collectibles
Specialties: WWII German
Collectibles
Appraisal Service Available
Directions: Exit 1 N from
Rte 495 to 1st traffic light,
turn right, 4 blocks to
store

VICTORIA'S ANTIQUES
910 King St   22314
703 836-4399
Proprietor: Bev & Ed
O'Brien & Douglas
Clement
Hours: Mon-Fri, 12-4; Sat,
11-5; Sun, 1-4
Types & Periods: Tiffany
Type Lamps, Stained Glass,
Victorian & Oak Furniture,
Sterling, Decorator Pieces

WILLSON HOUSE
311 Cameron St   22314
703 549-9505
Hours: Mon-Sat, 10-5;
Sun, 12-5
Types & Periods: Books,
Furniture, Needlework

WOLFF ANTIQUES & GIFTS
1311 King St   22314
703 548-8618
Types & Periods: Mirrors,
Pewter, Brass, Crystal,
Prints, Lamps, Glass,
Furniture
Specialties: Restoration

Arlington

A ADCOCK YANKEE
PEDLAR
1108 N Irving St   22201
703 527-3060   Est: 1950
Proprietor: Shirley M
Adcock
Hours: Daily, 12-4
Types & Periods: Oriental,
Glass

BOOKHOUSE
805 N Emerson St   22205
703 527-7797   Est: 1970
Proprietor: Natalie &
Edward Hughes
Hours: Tues & Thurs,
11-7; Wed, Fri & Sat, 11-5;
Sun, 1-5
Types & Periods: Used &
Rare Books
Specialties: Illustrated Books
Directions: In heart of
Arlington, 3 miles from
Potomac River

BOULEVARD ANTIQUES
2818 Washington Blvd
          22201
703 525-8622   Est: 1935
Proprietor: Emile Meyers
Hours: Daily, By
appointment
Types & Periods: Furniture,
French, Chinese
Specialties: Chinese &
Japanese Arts, Porcelains,
Paintings
Directions: Near Arlington
National Cemetery, 1
block from entrance of
Fort Meyer on Rte 50

CHEAP FRILLS
1112 N Irving St   22201
703 538-5875   Est: 1967
Proprietor: Maria E
Chresottos
Hours: Daily; by
appointment
Types & Periods: Clothes,
Jewelry, General Line
Directions: 3 miles from
Georgetown

CUPBOARD ANTIQUES
2645 N Pershing Dr
          22201
703 527-2894   Est: 1967
Proprietor: J J Riordan &
R E Smith
Hours: Mon-Tues,
Thurs-Sat, 10-5:30; Sun,
12:30-5:30
Types & Periods: General
Line, Direct Importers of
British Antiques (1750-1950)
Specialties: Clocks,
Glassware, Copper & Brass
Furniture, China
Appraisal Service Available
Directions: 2 blocks off
Rte 50 (Arlington Blvd) at
the corner of Washington
Blvd & Pershing Dr

GASPARD'S
1110 N Irving St   22201
703 525-6511   Est: 1964
Proprietor: G P Mazzie
Hours: Daily
Types & Periods: Jewelry,
Silver, Brass, Collectibles
Specialties: Lamp Repair
Directions: Off Wilson
Blvd, approximately 10
minutes from Washington
DC on the Virginia side

PETTICOAT LANE
INTERIORS & ANTIQUES
4522 Lee Hwy   22207
703 524-0131   Est: 1969
Proprietor: C Rae Salazar
Hours: Mon-Sat, 10-5:30
Types & Periods: 17th &
18th Century Decoratives
Specialties: Interior Design
Service, Accessories,
Carpets, Drapery
Directions: 3 miles from
Georgetown, DC & Key
Bridge

RED BENCH ANTIQUES &
GIFTS
900 N Kansas   22201
703 527-1816   Est. 1900
Proprietor: Ethel H
Edwards
Hours: Weekends; also by
appointment
Types & Periods: General
Line
Specialties: China, Glass
Directions: Corner of
Wilson Blvd &
N Kansas St

Ashland

COPPER KETTLE
COUNTRY STORE
23005
804 798-4400
Hours: Daily, 1-6
Types & Periods: Country
Furniture, Glass, Primitives
Directions: Approximately
1 mile S of Ashland
stoplight on US Rte 1

FARMER'S INN ANTIQUES
Rte 1 Box 33   23005
804 798-7036   Est: 1972
Proprietor: Ed & Louise
Walton
Hours: Weekends &
evenings by appointment

Types & Periods: Glass,
China, Country Furniture
Appraisal Service Available
Directions: Near
intersection of Rtes 657 &
626, SW of Ashland

Atlantic

DERBY'S ANTIQUES
Rte 175 Box 133   23303
804 824-5268
Proprietor: Ann & Henry
Derby
Hours: By appointment, by
chance
Types & Periods: Pattern
Glass, Furniture
Directions: Near NASA's
Wallop's Island, from US
Rte 13 turn right, 3.4 miles
(Just before Satellite
Motel) on Rte 679, .03
mile on right

Barboursville

ANTIQUES AT
BURLINGTON
Burlington Farm   22923
Proprietor: Ken & Dolores
Colby
Hours: Daily, by
appointment or by chance
Types & Periods: 18th &
Early 19th Century Formal
Furniture, Clocks, Period
Accessories
Specialties; Architectural
Pieces (Highboys, Chests &
Secretaries with
Architectural Features)
Directions: Rte 20, 1.5
miles NE of village of
Barboursville

Bedford

PEGGY'S ANTIQUES
804 E Main St   24523
703 586-8716   Est: 1964
Proprietor: Mr & Mrs A T
Phillips
Hours: Tues-Sat
Types & Periods: Period &
Victorian Furniture, China,
Glass, Lamps

Appraisal Service Available
Directions: Business Alt
460, off Bypass

Cape Charles

CHARMAR'S ANTIQUES
213 Mason Ave   23310
804 331-1488
Proprietor: Charles &
Margaret Calson
Hours: Mon-Sat, 10-5; also
by appointment
Types & Periods: Clocks,
Glass, Furniture, Guns,
China, Lamps, Collectibles

Centreville

INTERNATIONAL
ANTIQUES
13826 Lee Hwy   22020
703 830-2329   Est: 1972
Proprietor: Joy Lee Powell
Hours: Daily
Types & Periods: American,
Oriental, French, English,
Jewelry
Appraisal Service Available
Directions: 3 miles W of
Fairfax, 5 miles S of
Dulles Airport

OBSESSION ANTIQUES
INC
13848 Lee Hwy   22020
703 830-8423   Est: 1974
Proprietor: James W
Smith
Hours: Fri-Sun, also by
appointment
Types & Periods: Furniture,
Lamps, Clocks, Glass
Directions: Take I-495
(Washington DC Beltway)
to Exit 9, I-66 to Rte 28
Centerville Exit, go to
traffic light & turn left on
Rtes 29 & 211 to next
traffic light

Charlottesville

THE BALOGH GALLERY
1018 W Main St   22903
Proprietor: Eva G Balogh
Hours: Mon-Sat, 10-5;
appointment advisable

Charlottesville   Cont'd

BALOGH GALLERY   Cont'd
Types & Periods: Fine Arts,
Old Master Prints, 17th &
18th Century Furniture
Appraisal Service Available
    Directions: Near University
    of Virginia, Fidelity
    American Bank Bldg

**BERNARD M CAPERTON
ANTIQUES**
    1113 W Main St   22903
    804 293-2383   Est: 1954
    Proprietor: Bernard M
    Capterton
    Hours: Mon-Thurs by
    appointment; Fri & Sat,
    10-5
Types & Periods: 17th, 18th
& 19th Century European,
American & Oriental
Furniture & Accessories
Appraisal Service Available
    Directions: About 5 blocks
    E of the University of
    Virginia

**COCHRAN'S MILL
ANTIQUES**
    Rio Rd   22901
    804 295-5509   Est: 1966
    Proprietor: Mrs George
    Lyons
    Hours: Wed-Sat, 1-5:30
Types & Periods: American
18th Century Furniture,
Copper, Brass, Pewter,
Porcelain
Appraisal Service Available
    Directions: Park St Exit off
    250 Bypass, turn left to
    end

THE CORNER SHOPPE
    1405 University Ave
                            22903
    804 295-0085   Est: 1970
    Proprietor: Jo Ann S
    Braswell
    Hours: Daily
Types & Periods:
Collectibles, Jewelry
    Directions: Corner 14th &
    University Ave, across
    from University of Virginia

SALEM M EWAYS INC
    1417 N Emmet St   22901
    Proprietor: Corporation
    Hours: Mon-Sat, 9-5:30,
    evenings by appointment

Types & Periods: Antique &
New Oriental Rugs
Appraisal Service Available
    Directions: Rte 250 W &
    29 N

HENSLEY'S ANTIQUES
    101 E Water St   22901
    804 977-3185   Est: 1972
    Proprietor: William L
    Hensley
    Hours: Daily
Types & Periods: General
Line
    Directions: 1 block S of
    Mall at corner of 1st &
    Water Sts

**PAULA LEWIS-COURT
SQUARE**
    4th & Jefferson Sts   22901
    804 295-6244   Est: 1975
    Proprietor: Paula L Lewis
    Hours: Mon-Sat, 10-5:30
Types & Periods: Quilts,
Coverlets, Primitives
    Directions: Downtown in
    Historic Court Square

**OBSESSION ANTIQUES
INC**
    201 E High St   22901
    804 295-0671   Est: 1970
    Proprietor: R Stedman
    Oakey Jr
    Hours: Mon-Fri, 9-5; Sat,
    10-5
Types & Periods: 18th &
19th Century English
Specialties: Furniture,
Accessories
    Directions: 5th St Exit
    from I-64, go N, turn at
    Preston Ave, immediate
    left to High St

RIDGEFIELD ANTIQUES
    1 Village Green Circle
                            22901
    804 296-8078   Est: 1969
    Proprietor: William Garrett
    Hodges
    Hours: Daily, also by
    appointment
Types & Periods: 17th &
18th Century Furniture &
Accessories, Art
Specialties: Clocks,
Porcelains, Art
Appraisal Service Available
    Directions: 2 miles W of
    Charlottesville on Rte 250

SANDRA'S BOUTIQUE
    1203 W Main St   22903
    804 296-1070   Est: 1976
    Proprietor: Sandra
    MacGregor
    Hours: Mon-Sat, 9-5
Types & Periods: Formal
Period Furnishings &
Accessories, Country
    Directions: Near the
    University of Virginia

THE WINDMILL ANTIQUES
    1018 W Main St   22906
    804 977-6101   Est: 1971
    Proprietor: Neil & Helen
    Hevener
    Hours: Daily, by
    appointment or by chance
Types & Periods: American
Period Furniture, Art Glass,
Collectibles
Appraisal Service Available
    Directions: 2 blocks from
    University of Virginia

ANNE WOODS
    1215 W Main St   22903
    Proprietor: Anne Woods
    Hours: Daily
Types & Periods: 18th
Century China, Silver, Glass,
Furniture
    Directions: 1 block E of
    University of Virginia

Chesapeake

DRURY ANTIQUE SHOP
    1944 S Military Hwy
                            23320
    703 545-9837   Est: 1937
    Proprietor: Fannie Drury
    Hours: Mon-Sat, 10:30-4
Types & Periods: General
Line
    Directions: Off I-64
    Battlefield Blvd N, 1 block

**HUGHES HOUSE OF
ANTIQUES**
    3021 S Military Hwy
                            23323
    804 485-1142   Est: 1974
    Proprietor: Beverly G
    Hughes
    Hours: Weekends by
    appointment or by chance
Types & Periods: General
Line
Specialties: Furniture
(Country), Primitives

Appraisal Service Available
Directions: Rte 13
Broadmoor Section near
Canal Dr

**OAK GROVE FLEA
MARKET**
910 Oak Grove Rd   23320
804 482-1030   Est: 1973
Proprietor: Robert &
Winnie Larmore
Hours: Sat & Sun, 10-6
Types & Periods:
Collectibles & Antiques
Specialties: Depression
Glass, Crystals, Roseville
Pottery, Antique Furniture,
Other Antique Pottery
Appraisal Service Available
Directions: 2 miles S from
I-64 on Rte 168, left on
Oak Grove Rd

VIOLET'S ANTIQUES
3008 S Military Hwy
23323
703 485-1713   Est: 1970
Proprietor: Violet Melton
Hours: Weekends, by
appointment
Typoc & Periods; General
Line
Specialties: Glass
(Depression)
Directions: Rte 13
between Norfolk & Suffolk,
Eagle House Center

Ellenson

THE MILLSTONE
US 301   23111
804 746-3988
Hours: Tues-Sat, 9:30-5
Types & Periods: American
Period & Country Furniture,
Lamps, China, Glass,
Primitives
Directions: 9 miles N of
Richmond

Falls Church

**COUNTRY PEDDLER
ANTIQUES**
418 S Washington St
22046
703 241-2708   Est: 1965
Proprietor: Lorn & Leola
Dumont

Hours: Mon-Fri, 12-4; Sat
& Sun, 10-5; evenings by
appointment
Types & Periods: Refinished
American Oak from
1880-1920
Appraisal Service Available
Directions: Between Rte 7
& 795 on 29 & 211, Lee
Hwy

**DAUBE'S OLD BRICK
HOUSE**
2814 Graham Rd   22042
703 560-0900   Est: 1962
Proprietor: Robert W
Daube
Hours: Daily, 10-6
Types & Periods: General
Line
Appraisal Service Available
Directions: Corner Graham
Rd & Lee Hwy (US 29 &
211) in Lee Graham
Shopping Center

THE MARTIN ANTIQUES
706 S Washington St
22046
703 533-9278   Est: 1969
Proprietor: Joseph C
Martin
Hours: Tues-Sat, 10-5;
other times by
appointment
Types & Periods: Victorian
(Early, no East Lake or
Oak), Fine Period Formal
Furniture, Country Pieces,
China, Glass, Silver & Brass
Specialties: Chandeliers,
Sconces, Candlesticks,
Lamps
Directions: S Washington
St is the same as Lee
Hwy, which is also Rte
29-211

Fork Union

HOLLY HILL ANTIQUES
Box 397   23055
804 842-3063
Proprietor: Merilee H Ward
Hours: Weekends, 1-5;
appointment anytime
Types & Periods: Decorative
Accessories

Fort Defiance

DEAN WILSON ANTIQUES
PO Box 102   24437
Proprietor: Mark Wilson
Hours: Mon-Sat, 10-4:30
Types & Periods: 18th &
Early 19th Century American
Furniture
Directions: Exit 58 off US
I-81, 3 miles N of
Staunton, in Verona, next
to Wilco gasoline station

Fredericksburg

KENDALL'S ANTIQUES
Rte 1 Box 122-K   22401
703 786-6161
Hours: Daily, 10-5
Types & Periods: Primitives,
Glass, China, Toys, Period
Furniture
Directions: On Rte 3, 6
miles W of I-95

**STARS & BARS TRADING
POST**
Rte 3   22401
703 972-7171
Types & Periods: Civil War
Relics, Radios, Phonos,
Music Boxes, Collectibles,
General Line
Directions: 11 miles W of
Fredericksburg

**THIS AND THAT SHOP AND
DOLL HOUSE**
1725 Single Oak Rd
22401
703 786-7972   Est: 1971
Proprietor: J F Turnley
Hours: Mon-Fri, 10-9; Sat
& Sun, 2-7, by chance
Types & Periods: Depression,
Heisey, Cambridge, Dolls,
Toys, Glass, Collectibles
Specialties: Depression,
Dolls
Appraisal Service Available
Directions: W of
Fredericksburg 4 miles on
Rte 3 to Rte 688, then 1
mile

Glen Allen

THE ANTIQUE HOUSE
US Hwy 1   23060
804 798-4505

ANTIQUE HOUSE   Cont'd

Proprietor: Peggy Hayes &
Alice Allen
Hours: Weekends, also by
appointment
Types & Periods: Furniture,
Glassware, China
Directions: At the Wigwam
Reservation, 6 miles N of
Richmond

ITZHERE
US Hwy 1   23060
804 798-9891   Est: 1975
Proprietor: Eliz Holden
Slipek
Hours: Tues-Sat
Types & Periods: Paintings,
China, Glass, Primitives,
Collectibles
Directions: At the Wigwam
Reservation, 6 miles N of
Richmond

THE MC KINNEY'S
US Hwy 1   23060
804 798-9981
Proprietor: Mr & Mrs
McKinney
Hours: Weekends
Types & Periods: Jewelry,
Cut Glass, Silver, Clocks
Directions: At the Wigwam
Reservation, 6 miles N of
Richmond

PAST TIME ANTIQUES
US Hwy 1   23060
804 798-9981
Proprietor: Judy & Mike
Cornelison
Hours: Weekends
Types & Periods: Furniture,
Collectibles
Directions: At the Wigwam
Reservation, 6 miles N of
Richmond

WIGWAM RESERVATION
US Hwy 1   .   23060
804 798-5956
Proprietor: 12 Shops
Hours: Weekends
Types & Periods: General
Line
Directions: 6 miles N of
Richmond

Hamilton

ALEXANDER'S ANTIQUES
Rte 1 Box 16A   22068
703 338-4619   Est: 1971
Proprietor: Evelyn R Sims
Hours: Daily
Types & Periods: 18th &
19th Century Furniture &
Accessories
Directions: Rte 7, 6 miles
W of Leesburg

Hanover

**THE OLD STORE
ANTIQUES**
Rte 301   23069
804 798-6734
Hours: Fri, Sat & Sun,
9:30-5:30
Types & Periods: General
Line, Primitives
Directions: At Rte 54

Hillsboro

SCHENCKIES ANTIQUES
PO Box 43   22132
304 754-3429   Est: 1972
Proprietor: Lenora
Schenck
Hours: Sun-Tues,
Thurs-Sat, 10-6:30
Types & Periods: General
Line (1700-1900)
Specialties: Corner
Cupboards, Dry Sinks, Show
Cases
Directions: Rte 9 near
Hillsboro Post Office

Irvington

**THE GLORY BOX AT KING
CANTON INN**
Tidewater & King
Canton Rd   22480
Proprietor: Trudy Dinneen
Hours: Daily, by chance
Types & Periods: General
Line
Specialties: Furniture,
Primitives
Directions: From
Fredericksburg take Rte 3
to Kilmarnock, 4 miles to
Irvington

**SHIP & SEA NAUTICAL
ANTIQUES INC**
Rte 3   22480
804 438-5855   Est: 1970
Proprietor: Ned Kidwell
Hours: Daily
Types & Periods: Items from
17th Century on up, Ship
Lights, Compasses,
Sextants, Spyglasses,
Wheels, Bells, Ship Models,
Hatchcover, Grating Tables
Specialties: Nautical
Antiques & Accessories
Appraisal Service Available
Directions: State Rte 3,
where the Rappahanock
River & Chesapeake Bay
meet

Jenkins Bridge

WAVELAND ANTIQUES
                   23399
804 824-4878
Proprietor: Kitty & Bob Hill
Hours: Sun-Wed, Fri-Sat,
10-5
Types & Periods: General
Line
Directions: From
Temperanceville take Rte
695, turn right in town

Lovingston

CHESTNUT LOG STORE
Rte 29   22949
                Est: 1969
Proprietor: Von Matthews
Hours: Daily
Types & Periods: General
Line
Appraisal Service Available
Directions: Rte 29, 7 miles
N of town

Lynchburg

**THE LITTLE SHOP AT
PLAIN DEALING**
Wiggington Rd   24502
804 384-6011   Est: 1965
Proprietor: Elinor H
Jackson
Hours: Mon-Sat, 10-5; Sun
by appointment
Types & Periods: American
18th & 19th Centuries,
Bric-A-Brac, Collectibles

Specialties: Carpets & Rugs
(Oriental)
Directions: 2.4 miles on
Wiggington Rd, off 291,
off 221

**MC CRAW'S FURNITURE
CO**
1210-1214 Main St   24504
804 845-8812   Est: 1967
Proprietor: Bussey T
McCraw Jr & Sr
Hours: Mon-Sat
Types & Periods: Rustics,
Brass Beds
Specialties: Lamp Parts &
Repairs

TIMBROOK ANTIQUES
9223 Timberlake Rd
24502
804 239-0134   Est: 1969
Proprietor: Mrs L A
Crickenberger
Hours: Tues-Sat; Sun &
Mon by appointment
Types & Periods: Furniture,
Glassware, Bric-A-Brac
Directions: 1 mile W of
Lynchburg on Rte 460

**WARDS ROAD BARGAIN
SHOP**
4439 Wards Rd   24502
804 239-4516   Est: 1964
Proprietor: Glenna D
Smith
Hours: Mon-Sat, 10-4; also
by appointment
Types & Periods: General
Line
Specialties: Dolls, Jewelry,
Silver
Directions: 29 S, 1 mile
past Lynchburg Airport
going S

Manassas

**THE VILLAGE WATCH &
CLOCK SHOP**
8466 Centreville Rd,
Rte 28   22110
703 369-5674   Est: 1966
Proprietor: Robert B
Dahmer
Hours: Mon-Sat, 12-6; also
by appointment
Types & Periods: Clocks &
Watches, Repairs,
Restoration, Bought & Sold

Specialties: Antique Clocks
& Watches, Repairs,
Restoration
Appraisal Service Available
Directions: Manassas Park
Shopping Center, Beltway
66 W to Centreville Rd,
Rte 28 Exit, 5 miles on
Rte 28 to Shopping Center
on right

WORLDWIDE ANTIQUES
7217 Centerville Rd   22110
703 533-8152   Est: 1969
Proprietor: Michael &
Ingrid Kelly
Hours: Wed-Sun, 10:30-5
Types & Periods: Oriental
Furniture, Cloisonne,
Porcelains, Ivories, Jade
Appraisal Service Available
Directions: Laws Antique
Center, Rte 28-495 to I-66
W to 28 S, 4 miles on left

McLean

**THE CHESTERBROOK
CONSIGNMENT SHOP**
6222A Old Dominion Dr
22101
725 536-4763   Est: 1970
Proprietor: Hilda Merritts &
Mildred Winston
Hours: Tues-Sat, 11-5
Types & Periods: Antiques,
China, Glass, Silver,
Furniture, Collectibles
Directions: Exit at 123
from 495, N to Old
Dominion, 4 miles to
Chesterbrook Shopping
Center, back of High's

**EVANS FARM INN
COUNTRY STORE**
1696 Chain Bridge Rd
22101
703 356-8000   Est: 1957
Proprietor: Ralph B Evans
Hours: Daily
Types & Periods: 18th
Century Primitives, Civil
War, Glass
Specialties: 18th Century
Decor-Restaurant
Directions: Rte 123, Hwy
495 Exit 11 or 12E

Mechanicsville

GOVERNOR'S ANTIQUES
6240 Meadowbridge Rd
23111
804 746-1030   Est: 1970
Proprietor: Stuart Gary
Thomas
Hours: Mon-Sat, 9-5; Fri
'til 9; Sun by appointment
Types & Periods: Victorian
Period Furniture, Primitives,
Oak, Wicker, Brass Beds,
Lamps
Specialties: Guns, Swords &
Civil War Relics
Appraisal Service Available
Directions: 4½ miles on
Meadowbridge Rd E from
Richmond

Middleburg

ANTIQUES CENTER
Box 984   22117
703 687-2211   Est: 1972
Proprietor: Mrs John
Freeman Brown
Hours: Daily
Types & Periods: American,
English & French Furniture,
Oriental Rugs, Mirrors, Silver
Appraisal Service Available

Midlothian

GATES ANTIQUES LTD
12700 Old Buckingham Rd
23113
804 794-8472   Est: 1967
Proprietor: Jo E & John A
Gates Jr
Hours: Tues-Sat, 10-4
Types & Periods: 18th &
19th Century Furniture &
Accessories, American &
English
Specialties: Furniture
Appraisal Service Available
Directions: Go 6½ miles W
of Richmond city limits on
Rte 60, turn right on Old
Buckingham Rd

Mount Holly

AMERICAN FOLK ART CO
22524
804 472-3510
Proprietor: Jeffrey Camp
Hours: By appointment
Types & Periods: General
Line

New Church

WORCESTER HOUSE
ANTIQUES
US 13   23415
804 824-3847   Est: 1963
Proprietor: Thelma &
Melvin Arion
Hours: Daily, 10-6
Types & Periods: 18th &
19th Century Furniture &
Accessories, Brass, Copper,
Silver, Pewter
Specialties: American
Furniture
Directions: 1/4 miles S
Maryland-Virginia line on
Virginia's Eastern Shore
on Rte 13

Newport News

NEWPORT
NEWS/HAMPTON
CLUSTER
Directions: Many shops
throughout area, heavy
concentration on Warwick
Blvd (9000-15000 Blocks),
also W Mercury Blvd, Hwy
17, Jefferson Ave, W
Pembroke Ave

FINE ARTS SHOP
10178 Warwick Blvd
23601
804 595-7754   Est: 1940
Proprietor: David N
Sherman
Hours: Daily
Types & Periods: General
Line
Specialties: Oils,
Watercolors, Etchings
Appraisal Service Available

VILLAGE ANTIQUES
10221 Warwick Blvd
23601
804 596-1142   Est: 1976
Proprietor: Mrs James
Yonkos
Hours: Tues-Sat, 10-3
Types & Periods: Southern
Antiques, American
Primitives, Occassional
English Country Pieces
Specialties: Bull's Eye Glass
Panes
Directions: Hwy 60, 25
miles S of Williamsburg,
2 miles S of Mariner's
Museum

Norfolk

NORFOLK CLUSTER
Directions: City with many
antique shops, especially
on S Military Hwy
(300-3000 Blocks), Granby
St (400-800 Blocks),
Colley Ave (100 Block),
Virginia Beach Blvd (800
Block), Princess Anne Rd
(400 Block)

AMERICAN ANTIQUE
IMPORTERS & AUCTION
ROOMS
242 W 21st   23517
804 623-1718   Est: 1960
Hours: Daily
Types & Periods: 18th
Century Furniture,
Porcelains, Clocks,
Brassware, Bric-A-Brac,
Glass
Specialties: Furniture (18th
Century)
Appraisal Service Available
Directions: Corner 21st &
Llewellyn, opposite Sears

DECOR DESIGN
912 W Little Creek Rd
23505
804 423-3503   Est: 1968
Proprietor: Kenneth M
Lenhart
Hours: Mon-Fri, 1-5; Sat,
10-5; also by appointment
Types & Periods: Nautical
Items, Artifacts,
Accessories, Furniture, Hand
Crafted Items

Specialties: Furniture
(Hatchboard Coffee Tables),
Cobblestones, Slate
Directions: Midway
between Granby St &
Hampton Blvd, both main
arteries running N-S thru
Norfolk

HAASE'S NAUTICAL
ANTIQUES
6150 Virginia Beach Blvd
23502
804 461-2465   Est: 1971
Proprietor: Daniel A Haase
Hours: Daily, 10-7
Types & Periods: Sextants,
Binnacles, Wood & Brass
Engine Order Telegraphs,
Compasses, Clocks
Appraisal Service Available
Directions: 5 miles E of
downtown on Virginia
Beach Blvd

LEMON TREE ANTIQUES
1506 Colley Ave   23517
804 625-9322   Est: 1970
Proprietor: Helen
McMahon Pope
Hours: Mon-Fri, 11-5; Sat,
10-5; by appointment
Types & Periods: Primitives,
Early Americana, Pocket
Watches, Lamps, Furniture
Specialties: Primitives
Directions: Heart of Ghent
Neighborhood, near
downtown Norfolk, Old
Dominion University

NEWEL POST ANTIQUE
GALLERY
7454 Tidewater Dr   23505
804 583-5000   Est: 1966
Proprietor: Margery C
Raymond
Hours: Daily, 1-5; also by
appointment
Types & Periods: Paintings,
Porcelains, Furniture,
Jewelry, Chandeliers,
Clocks, Pewter, Silver,
Brass, Copper
Specialties: Accent Pieces,
Paintings
Appraisal Service Available
Directions: Off Rte 64,
take Tidewater Dr N, in
center of city between
Portsmouth & Newport
News Tunnels

SCOPE ANTIQUES BAZAAR
723-733-737 & 817
Granby St   23510
804 622-9040   Est: 1956
Proprietor: Paul J Hirtz &
Miki Kirkbride
Hours: Mon-Sat, by
appointment
Types & Periods: General
Line, Marble, Oak,
Architectural Items,
Restaurant, Hotel, Motel,
Church & Store Fixtures
Appraisal Service Available
  Directions: Center of
  downtown

Portsmouth

DESKS INC
800 Crawford St   23705
804 393-0091   Est: 1969
Proprietor: Lamar J
Schlegel
Hours: Mon-Fri, 9-5; Sat,
9-4
Types & Periods: Victorian
Desks, Roll Tops, Cylinder
Tops, Partners Desks
Specialties: Wooton Desks
(Wells Fargo)
Appraisal Service Available
  Directions: Downtown
  Portsmouth, South &
  Crawford Sts

**THE MOUNT VERNON
ANTIQUE SHOP**
258 Mt Vernon Ave 23707
804 399-9585   Est: 1971
Proprietor: Jim & Connie
Wynn
Hours: Daily during winter
months, Weekends during
summer months
Types & Periods: Furniture
to Period Pieces
Specialties: Furniture
(Rocking Chairs), Lamp
Parts, Refinishing
  Directions: Port Norfolk
  section of Portsmouth,
  about 1 mile from I-64,
  downtown

Purcellville

COCHRAN'S ANTIQUES
10th St   22132
703 338-7395   Est: 1958
Proprietor: Phillip W &
Sybil B Cochran
Hours: Daily
Types & Periods: 18th &
19th Century Country &
Primitive Furniture,
Accessories
Specialties: Furniture
Appraisal Service Available
  Directions: From
  Washington, W on Rte 7,
  approximately 40 miles to
  Purcellville, turn left at
  first traffic light (10th St)

Richmond

RICHMOND CLUSTER
  Directions: Beginning E
  Main through 100 Block,
  some on W Main, W Cary
  St (2000-3000 Blocks), W
  Broad St (300-800
  Blocks), Midlothian Trnpk
  (6000-10000 Blocks) &
  many adjacent streets

WILLIAM C ADAMS JR
PO Box 8364   23226
Proprietor: William C
Adams Jr
Hours: By appointment
only
Types & Periods: 18th &
Early 19th Century Furniture,
Paintings, High-Style
American Empire
Specialties: Southern 18th &
Early 19th Century Furniture
Appraisal Service Available

**AMERICA HURRAH!
ANTIQUES**
405 Libbie Ave   23226
804 285-7971   Est: 1969
Proprietor: Maurice &
Anne Costello
Hours: Mon-Sat, 11-5:30
Types & Periods: Primitives,
Light Wood Furniture,
Collectibles
Specialties: Antique
Advertising
Appraisal Service Available
  Directions: In W end of
  Richmond near University
  of Richmond

ANNE'S ANTIQUES
10601 Midlothian Trnpk
                    23235
804 794-8458   Est: 1971
Proprietor: Anne H May
Hours: Mon-Sat, 10-5;
Sun, 2-5, by chance
Types & Periods: American
Furniture, Glassware,
Lamps, Decorative Items,
Collectibles
Specialties: American
Furniture
Appraisal Service Available
  Directions: US 60 W of
  Richmond between
  Cloverleaf Mall &
  Chesterfield Mall

**THE ANTIQUES
WAREHOUSE**
1310 E Cary St   23219
804 643-1310   Est: 1973
Proprietor: Roy M Blanks
Hours: Daily
Types & Periods: 17th, 18th
Century English
Specialties: Carpets
(Persian), English Oak
Appraisal Service Available
  Directions: In Historic
  Shockoe Slip

BERRY'S ANTIQUES
318 W Broad St   23220
                Est: 1968
Proprietor: Berry Family
Hours: Mon-Sat, 9:30-5;
also by appointment
Types & Periods: Treasures
& Collectors Items
Specialties: Brass Beds &
Brass Items
  Directions: 2 blocks E US
  I-301 in downtown

BRADLEY'S ANTIQUES
103 E Main St   23219
804 644-7305   Est: 1954
Proprietor: Malcolm B
Bradley
Hours: Daily
Types & Periods: American
& European & Decorative
Arts
Specialties: American &
European Paintings
Appraisal Service Available
  Directions: Belvidere Exit
  off I-95 going S, 5 blocks
  to Main

Richmond Cont'd

CYNTHIA'S ANTIQUE SHOPPE
1203 W Main St   23220
804 353-7249   Est: 1936
Proprietor: Mrs C K Quinn
Hours: Daily, Weekends, by appointment
Types & Periods: Period Furniture & Accessories

GOODWILL INDUSTRIES OF CENTRAL VIRGINIA
7 S 14th St   23219
804 643-6734   Est: 1945
Hours: Mon-Sat
Types & Periods: Bicentennial, Victorian, Early 20th Century (1900-1940)
Directions: Other shops at 607 McGuire Center & 809 W Broad St

GRESHAM'S COUNTRY STORE
6725 Midlothian Pike   23225
804 276-5323   Est: 1964
Proprietor: Ann Gresham
Hours: Mon-Sat, 10-5
Types & Periods: Country Wares & Primitives
Specialties: Bottles, Kitchen, Advertising
Directions: Rte 60 W, E of Chippenham Pkwy (150)

M KAMBOURIAN SONS INC
13 W Grace St   23220
804 644-0306   Est: 1896
Proprietor: Jerome M Kambourian
Hours: Mon-Sat, 10-2
Types & Periods: Oriental Rugs
Specialties: Rugs
Appraisal Service Available
Directions: Grace St between Adams & Fouschee, from I-64 E Exit 5th St & turn right at Grace, from I-95 N Exit Broad St, turn left at 10th & right at Grace

LUNDIN'S
211 E Grace   23219
804 643-1413   Est: 1946
Proprietor: J C Lundin
Hours: Mon-Fri, 9-5; Sat, 1/2 Day
Types & Periods: Jewelry, Gems

Specialties: Jewelry (Old & New, Estate)
Appraisal Service Available
Directions: Downtown

MARY-LEW'S ANTIQUE SHOPPE
5232 Brook Hill-Azalea Shopping Center   23227
804 266-1245   Est: 1973
Proprietor: Mrs Mary T Schmuck
Hours: Mon-Fri, 10:30-5; Sat, 10-5; evenings by appointment
Types & Periods: Victorian, Walnut & Oak Furniture, Glass & China
Specialties: Oil Lamps, Reproduction Glass Shades, Lamp Repair
Directions: On N side of Richmond at intersection of 301 N & Azalea Ave in Brook Hill-Azalea Shopping Center, across parking lot of A&P store

REESE ANTIQUE COMPANY
207 E Main St   23219
804 644-0781   Est: 1932
Proprietor: Mac Reese
Hours: Mon-Sat, 9-5
Types & Periods: American & English Period Furniture & Accessories
Specialties: Virginia Furniture
Appraisal Service Available
Directions: At the corner of 2nd & Main Sts in downtown Richmond, located behind the city Library

RICHMOND ART COMPANY INC
101 E Grace St   23219
804 644-0733   Est: 1900
Proprietor: J Alton Joel
Hours: Mon-Fri, 10-5:30; Sat, 10-5
Types & Periods: 16th to Early 19th Century
Specialties: Furniture
Appraisal Service Available
Directions: Downtown

SHAMBURGER'S INC
5208 Brook Rd   23227
804 266-8457   Est: 1932
Proprietor: M E Shamburger III

Hours: Mon-Fri, 8:30-4:30; Sat, 8:30-12; also by appointment
Types & Periods: Late 18th Century & Early 19th Century Furniture & Accessories
Directions: Going N on 95 take Exit 16, Rte 1, turn left, go 1 block

JAYNE SPURR GALLERIES
2201 E Cary St   23223
804 643-5468   Est: 1977
Proprietor: Jane B Rehrig
Hours: Tues-Sat, 10-4
Types & Periods: 17th, 18th & Early 19th Century English Furniture, 18th Century English Porcelain & Silver, Chinese Porcelain, Yuan, Sung Dynasties, Kang Hsi, Chieu Lung
Directions: 4/5 mile off I-95

THOMAS-HINES ANTIQUES & INTERIORS
3027 W Cary St   23221
804 355-2782   Est: 1972
Proprietor: Mr & Mrs Robert L Hines Jr
Hours: Daily
Types & Periods: 18th Century & Centennial Pieces in Queen Anne, Chippendale, Sheraton, Hepplewhite Styles, Reproductions & Accessories
Directions: W end of Richmond near Cary Court Shopping Center

Roanoke

MIKE'S TRADING POST
1805 Orange Ave NW   24017
703 345-9395   Est: 1967
Proprietor: Victor M Attalla
Hours: Daily, 10-5:30
Types & Periods: Furniture, Glassware, Primitives, Collectibles
Specialties: Lamps, Lamp Repair, Hand Painted Glass Shades
Directions: On 460 at 18th St NW

THE VIRGINIA GALLERIES LTD
1402 Grandin Rd 24015
703 342-4279 Est: 1940
Proprietor: Charles B Farrelly
Hours: Mon-Sat, 9-5; also by appointment
Types & Periods: Early American, French, English, Oriental Rugs
Specialties: Lamp Shades
Appraisal Service Available
Directions: Rte 11 thru city, about 2 miles from downtown

Ruther Glen

BOONE'S ANTIQUES
Hwy 207 E 22546
804 448-2500 Est: 1969
Proprietor: John W Burke Jr
Hours: Tues-Sat, 9-4
Types & Periods: Furniture, Glassware, General Line
Directions: Between Richmond & Washington

REBEL HILL ANTIQUES
Rte 3 Box 32 22546
804 448-3432 Est: 1965
Proprietor: Ruth B Harbold
Hours: Wed-Sun, 9-5
Types & Periods: Refinished Furniture, Country Pine, Victorian, Lamps, China, General Line
Specialties: Pattern Glass, Pine Furniture
Directions: US Rte 1, 25 miles S of Fredericksburg, 25 miles N of Richmond

Salem

SMITH'S ANTIQUES & LAMP SHOP
1800 W Main St 24153
703 389-3163 Est: 1940
Proprietor: Douglas C Smith
Hours: Daily
Types & Periods: Furniture, Dishes
Specialties: Lamps, Shades & Parts, Brass Cleaning
Directions: Exit 40 from I-81, left at Main, next door to Salem Motel

Scottsville

SCOTTSVILLE FOLK ART
24590
804 286-3434
Proprietor: Julie Duff
Hours: By appointment
Types & Periods: Country Furniture, Quilts, Coverlets, Paintings

Staunton

AAA ANTIQUES
Rte 4 Box 90-B 24401
703 886-9800 Est: 1970
Proprietor: M M Deffenbaugh
Hours: Daily
Types & Periods: Furniture, China, Glass, Guns, Coins, Money, Books, Paintings, Swords, Knives, Razors, RR Items, Militaria, Jewelry
Directions: Exit 57 E off I-81 on US 250, near Rowe's Steak House

JOLLY ROGER HAGGLE SHOP
27 Middlebrook Ave
24401
703 886-9527 Est: 1962
Proprietor: M M Deffenbaugh
Hours: Daily, 10-8
Types & Periods: Furniture, China, Glass, Indian Artifacts, Coins, Guns, War Items, Primitives, Jewelry, RR Items
Specialties: Military, Indian Items

Stephens City

THE WHITNEYS
Rte 631 22655
703 869-1713 Est: 1968
Proprietor: Mrs Phil Whitney
Hours: Sun-Wed, Fri-Sat
Types & Periods: China, Glass, Clocks, Furniture, Dolls, Lamps, Miniatures
Specialties: Clocks, Cut Glass, Flow Blue
Appraisal Service Available
Directions: Rte 631 (Lime Kiln Rd), 2 miles W of I-81 & US 11

Thornburg

BOB'S COUNTRY STORE
Rte 1 22565
703 582-5755
Types & Periods: Country Furniture, Advertising, Collectibles
Directions: At Eastern Antique Mart

D'MARIE'S ANTIQUES
Rte 1 22565
Types & Periods: Handcrafted Pine, Cherry & Walnut Furniture, Roseville, Rookwood & Weller Pottery, Cambridge, Heisey, Degenhart & Depression Glass
Directions: At Eastern Antique Mart

EASTERN ANTIQUE MART
Rte 1 22565
703 582-5755
Hours: Tues-Fri, 9-5; Sat open at 10; Sun, 12-5
Types & Periods: General Line
Directions: Located at Eastern Sales & Auction Oo

THE PEDDLER
22565
703 582-5965
Hours: Mon-Sat, 10-6
Types & Periods: Some of everything
Directions: US 1, approximately 1 mile N of Thornburg

Vienna

BIRD-IN-THE-CAGE ANTIQUES
130 Maple Ave E 22180
703 281-2268 Est: 1972
Proprietor: Vivian Temes
Hours: Mon-Sat
Types & Periods: American, French, Oriental, Other European, Glass, Furniture, Prints, Lamps, Jewelry, Art Nouveau, Early American Quilts

BIRD-IN-THE-CAGE   Cont'd
Specialties: Special
Requests
Appraisal Service Available
Directions: On Rte 123 in
center of town, across
from Public Library

Virginia Beach

ANTIQUES UNIQUE
2224 N Great Neck Rd
23451
804 481-7188   Est: 1974
Proprietor: Kay DeArmond
& Jackie Acree
Hours: Mon-Sat, 11-5
Types & Periods: General
Line
Specialties: Art Glass,
Wicker, Children's Items
Directions: 2 blocks off
Shore Dr

BAY BRIDGE ANTIQUES
4516 Shore Dr   23455
804 464-4029   Est: 1972
Proprietor: Irene & Jim
Agles
Hours: Mon-Sat, 10-5;
Sun, 1-5; also by
appointment
Types & Periods: China,
Glass, Silver, Furniture
Appraisal Service Available
Directions: Crossroads of
Rte 13 & 60, follow the
blue sign with the "White
Gull" to Chesapeake Bay
Bridge Tunnel

**BEHL'S SPORTS MARINA &
ANTIQUES**
320 S Military Hwy   23462
804 420-3000   Est: 1949
Proprietor: Howard D &
Lucille R Behl
Hours: Mon-Sat
Types & Periods: Furniture,
Glass, Silver, Frames
Specialties: Furniture
(Victorian), Frames &
Pictures
Directions: 1 mile S of
Military Circle Shopping
Mall on Military Hwy
(Rte 13)

BOOTS' THRIFT SHOP
4345A Princess Anne Rd
23465
804 499-6255   Est: 1972
Proprietor: Boots Jones
Hours: By appointment
Types & Periods: General
Line
Directions: Get off
Interstate on Newton Rd,
turn left, go to first stop
light, turn left

**DOLLY'S ANTIQUES & GIFT
SHOP**
418 Virginia Beach Blvd
23451
804 486-1286   Est: 1965
Proprietor: Dollie Blount
Hours: Daily
Types & Periods: General
Line
Specialties: Glass, Furniture
(Oak)
Appraisal Service Available
Directions: 3 blocks from
Boardwalk, across street
from the Van House

THE IRON GATE
3600 Atlantic Ave   23451
804 428-1402   Est: 1974
Proprietor: Sarah L Wilson
& Nancy Reynolds
Hours: Mon-Sat, 10-5
Types & Periods: 18th &
19th Century American &
English Furniture,
Accessories, Brass, Pewter,
Copper
Specialties: Silver, Rugs
(Oriental)
Appraisal Service Available

**NEWEL POST ANTIQUE
GALLERY**
2973 Virginia Beach Blvd
23452
804 340-6262   Est: 1966
Proprietor: Margery C
Raymond
Hours: Tues-Sat, 12-5;
Sun by chance or
appointment
Types & Periods: Paintings,
Porcelains, Furniture,
Jewelry, Chandeliers,
Clocks, Pewter, Silver,
Brass, Copper
Specialties: Accent Pieces,
Paintings, Boxes

Appraisal Service Available
Directions: Take
Lynnhaven Exit off Expwy
44 to feeder road on
Virginia Beach Blvd, then
W short distance to
Gallery

**PRINCESS ANNE
ANTIQUES**
626 Hilltop W   23451
804 425-6401   Est: 1967
Proprietor: Charles L
Kelley
Hours: Daily
Types & Periods: 18th
Century Furniture &
Accessories, Chinese
Porcelain, Oriental Rugs
Specialties: Restorations
Appraisal Service Available
Directions: Lakkin Rd &
1st Colonial Rd at Hilltop

Williamsburg

**TK ORIENTAL ART &
ANTIQUES**
1784 Jamestown Rd 23185
804 229-7720   Est: 1972
Proprietor: Michael C
Teller IV
Hours: Wed-Mon, 10:30-
5:30, May 15-Oct 31,
Closed Tues; Other months
By appointment or
By chance
Types & Periods: Fine Oriental
Prints, Paintings, Porcelains,
Jade, Ivory, Furniture,
Lacquer, 12th-19th Centuries
Specialties: Japanese Wood-
Block Prints, Oriental
Porcelains
Appraisal Service Available
Directions: 4½ miles
out Jamestown Rd from
center of town

Yorktown

**THE SWAN TAVERN
ANTIQUES**
   104 Main St   23185
   804 887-5078
   Proprietor: Frank P
   Dickinson
   Hours: Daily
Types & Periods: 18th Century
English Furniture &
Accessories
Specialties: Furniture
(Formal Chippendale & Queen
Anne Period Pieces)
   Directions: Follow Colonial
   Pkwy to Yorktown from
   Williamsburg. Pkwy ends
   at Main St

Victorian Era.

A rural cabinetmaker.

(From page 576). In Scotland and Germany there was an opposing group devoted to the rectilinear. Since designers of this persuasion disdained mass production methods, a very few pieces of furniture are found which may be attributed to Art Nouveau. Some of the designers did striking things, but each item was to be by the school's philosophy a unique piece of art. This style has a more prevalent representation in jewelry and glassware. The glass of Louis Comfort Tiffany is of this period.

     Grand Rapids turned to oak, a wood not used for more than a century, and out poured Golden Oak furniture. The Golden in Golden Oak is possibly the earliest example of an attempt to enhance the acceptability of a material in a mass furniture market. Oak is an excellent wood, but they wanted it to seem more exotic. It may be seen in the roll-top desk, oak icebox and the frame of the Morris chair, the forerunner of today's recliner. It may also be seen in the ever popular oak pedestal dining table that expands by using many leaves, in pressed back chairs, the desk bookcase, parlor and bedroom sets. A few decades ago these were looked upon as simply used furniture, but today they are eagerly (Continued, page 650).

STATE OF WASHINGTON

Arlington

BRADLEY'S ANTIQUES
Rte 3, Box 315   98223
206 435-3597
Hours: Mon-Sat, 11-4;
Closed Sun
Types & Periods: Furniture,
Clocks, Glass, China

Bainbridge Island

**MARIAN'S EAGLE HARBOR
ANTIQUES**
11025 NE Wing Point
98110
206 842-2770   Est: 1974
Proprietor: Marian Hansen
Hours: Daily
Types & Periods: Glass,
Porcelain, & Primitives of
the 19th & Early 20th
Century
Specialties: Open Salts;
Primitive Kitchenware
Appraisal Service Available
Directions: Wing Point
Way

Bellevue

**OLD AND ELEGANT
DISTRIBUTING**
10203 Main St Lane
98004
206 455-4660   Est: 1965
Proprietor: Dennis True
Hours: Mon-Sat, 10-6;
Sun, 12-5; Thurs 'til 9
Types & Periods: Jewelry,
Cabinet, Door, Bath &
Lighting Hardware, Fine Art
Appraisal Service Available
Directions: 4 blocks S of
Bellevue Square, rear side
of city of Paris Bldg on
102nd & Main

Bellingham

BRISTOL ANTIQUES
318 W Champion St
98225
206 733-7809   Est: 1972

Proprietor: Estella G
Gelder
Hours: Mon-Sat,
10:30-5:30
Types & Periods: Broad
General Line, Old Books,
Over 400 New Books About
Antiques and Collectibles
Specialties: Old and rare
Books, New Books About
Antiques
Appraisal Service Available
Directions: Downtown,
Across from the Whatcom
Museum of History and
Art

CHERYL LEAF ANTIQUES
2828 Northwest Ave
98225
206 734-2880
Proprietor: Elmer &
Cheryl Leaf
Hours: Mon-Sat, 10-5;
Closed Sun
Types & Periods: Jewelry,
Furniture, Christmas Plates,
General Line

Buckley

**DAVE'S FURNITURE AND
ANTIQUES**
127 N River Road   98321
206 829-0471   Est: 1960
Proprietor: Jim Werner
Hours: Wed-Sun, 10-5;
Closed Mon & Tues
Types & Periods: Early &
Late Victorian, China, Glass,
Primitives, Collectibles, Cut
Glass
Directions: I-5 to Auburn
Exit, Hwy 18 to Enumclaw
Exit, Hwy 164 to Hwy 410
to Buckley

Carnation

SHEPPARD'S EMPORIUM
32122 NE 8th   98104
206 333-4909   Est: 1974
Proprietor: Ralph &
Wanda Sheppard
Hours: By Appointment,
By Chance
Types & Periods: Early
Americana Through 1900

Specialties: Furniture,
Primitives, Glass, Nautical,
Over 1200 Titles of
Reference Books on
Antiques & Collectibles
Directions: 3 1/2 Miles
North of Fall City on Hwy
(Fall City Carnation Road)

Des Moines

HEARTHSIDE ANTIQUES
2228 Pacific Hwy S 98188
206 878-4364
Proprietor: Tom &
Audrey Backes
Hours: Daily
Types & Periods: Cloisonne,
Nippon, Bronzes, Ivory,
Satsuma, Cinnabar,
Porcelain
Specialties: Oriental
Directions: Two Miles S of
Sea-Tac Airport

Edmonds

ANDERBERG ANTIQUES
109 Main St   98020
206 775-3770
Hours: Mon-Sat, 8:30-5:30
Types & Periods: Tiffany,
Handel, Quezel, Oriental
Specialties: Furniture

AYERS ANTIQUES
560 Bell St   98020
206 774-0773
Hours: Wed-Sat, 11-5
Types & Periods: Cut Glass,
Orientals, General Line

**THE CORNER STORE
COMPANY**
18502 76th Ave W   98020
206 776-0001
Types & Periods: American
Oak, Furniture, Glassware,
Collectibles

DOROTHY'S ANTIQUES
204 5th Ave S
In the Caboose
206 775-1735   Est: 1970
Proprietor: Dorothy &
Doreen Suran
Hours: Daily

Types & Periods: Bisque
Dolls, Victorian Doll Houses,
Toys, Furniture, Jewelry
Specialties: Bisque Dolls
Appraisal Service Available
Directions: Downtown
Edmonds

EARLY ATTIC ANTIQUES
201 5th Ave S   98020
206 775-2332   Est: 1972
Proprietor: Patricia K
Pettelle
Hours: Mon-Sat, 10-6; Sun
12-5
Types & Periods:
Turn-of-the-Century
Collectibles, Oak Furniture
Specialties: Repairs,
Refinishing, Chair Caning
Directions: In 'Old
Milltown', A Turn-Of-The
Century Shopping Center,
Downtown

**REMEMBER WHEN-
SYLVIA'S ANTIQUES**
9713 Firdale Ave   98020
206 546-1886
Hours: Mon-Sat, 10-6
Types & Periods: Furniture,
Primitives, Collectibles
Directions: Firdale Village

Everett

A BIT O' EVERYTHING
11011 Hwy 99 S   98204
206 353-7826   Est: 1976
Proprietor: Richard D
White
Hours: Tues-Sat, 10-5;
Closed Sun & Mon
Types & Periods:
1800-1900's
Specialties: Books, Oak
Furniture, Tools
Directions: I-5 N Toward
Everett, Exit at 28th St,
West to Hwy 99, N to
Stop-Light

ANDY'S ANTIQUES
14307 Old Everett-
Bothell Hwy   98204
206 337-4007
Hours: Mon-Sat, 11-5:30,
Sun 12-5:30
Types & Periods: Stoves,
Furniture, Clocks,
Glassware, Lamps

**ANTIQUES OF THE
FUTURE**
2931 Broadway   98201
206 252-5777   Est: 1974
Proprietor: Donald &
Virginia Washena; Gary &
Gladys Horner
Hours: Tues-Sat,
10:30-4:30
Types & Periods: Furniture,
Glassware, Collectibles,
Junque, Etc
Directions: 1/2 Block
South of Hewitt and
Broadway

BRASS NUT ANTIQUES
1308 Hewitt Ave   98201
206 252-9600   Est: 1974
Proprietor: Rodger Gilbert
Hours: Daily
Types & Periods: Brass,
Copper, Light Fixtures,
Advertising, General Line
Directions: Downtown at
Hewitt & Rucker Ave

**CLUTTER COTTAGE
ANTIQUES**
2919 Oakes Ave   98201
206 252-0078   Est: 1973
Proprietor: Sandra Willard
Hours: Mon-Fri, 10-5,
Closed Weekends
Types & Periods: Primitives,
Collectibles
Specialties: Oriental

COLLECTORS' CUPBOARD
1816 Hewitt Ave   98201
206 252-7521   Est: 1969
Proprietor: Rose Frazier
Hours: Thurs & Fri, 12-5;
Sat, 10-5
Types & Periods: Furniture,
China, Glassware, Silver
Appraisal Service Available
Directions: Everett Exit I-5
to Hewitt Ave; West to
1816

**DEAR AND NEAR
ANTIQUES**
10127 36th St SE   98205
206 334-6226   Est: 1970
Proprietor: Mary A Snyder
Hours: Mon, Tues, Wed,
Thurs, Fri, Sun; By
Appointment
Types & Periods:
Pennsylvania Colonial
Furniture, Brasses, Iron and
Primitives, Clocks, Molds

Specialties: 150 to 200 Year
Old Items; Copper & Brass
Pudding Molds, Butter
Molds, Penna Speciality
Items
Appraisal Service Available
Directions: Two Miles
North of Snohomish,
Washington; Off Highway
9 on 36th Street

THE RED HOUSE
2532 Broadway   98201
206 259-2982   Est: 1971
Proprietor: Doris Bassett
Hours: Sun-Sat
Types & Periods: Furniture,
Tins, Small Primitives,
Wicker, Pine, Misc.
Appraisal Service Available
Directions: Take Exit 192
Off I-5 To Shop In Everett

SOMETHING SPECIAL
Eastmont Interchange
                  98203
206 355-7994
Directions: Sat, Sun, Mon,
10-4
Types & Periods: Oak
Furniture, Clocks, Wicker
Directions: Exit 189 Off I-5

**SPINNING WHEEL
ANTIQUES**
4824 Evergreen Way
                  98203
206 252-2922
Directions: Wed-Sat, 10-5
Types & Periods: General
Line, Americana, Railroad,
Marine, Brass Lighting
Fixtures

Gig Harbor

**NARROWS BRIDGE
ANTIQUES**
1601 Stone Drive NW
                  98335
206 858-3300
Proprietor: Leslie &
Landra Skelly
Hours: Mon-Sun
Types & Periods: Furniture,
Glass, China, Dolls,
Primitives
Specialties: Furniture
Directions: W End of
Narrows Bridge

ROADSIDE ANTIQUES
3008 14th Ave NW   98335
206 858-2922   Est: 1968
Proprietor: Betty Skidmore
Hours: Mon-Fri, 11-5; Sat
& Sun 11-6
Types & Periods: General
Line, American Oak,
European Pieces, Glass,
Silver, Primitives
Appraisal Service Available
Directions: W End
Narrows Bridge on Hwy 16

Issaquah

BROWSE & BARTER, INC
155 E Sunset Way   98027
206 392-2424   Est: 1964
Proprietor: Thelma I
Erickson
Hours: Daily
Types & Periods: China,
Glass, Silver, Furniture,
Collectibles
Directions: Exit 17 Off
I-90; Right at Stop Sign

**COCKLEBERRY
GALLERIES**
38 Front St N   98027
206 392-1990   Est: 1972
Proprietor: Dean &
Dorothy Nylin
Hours: Daily, By
Appointment
Types & Periods: American
18th & 19th Century
Furniture, Glass, Porcelain,
Paintings, Lighting,
Primitives
Specialties: Art Glass
Appraisal Service Available
Directions: Nine Miles E
on Hwy I-90 of Bellevue;
12 Miles from Seattle

**PILGRIM'S PRIDE
ANTIQUES**
58 Front St N   98027
206 392-7404   Est: 1973
Proprietor: Michael &
Donna Bishop
Hours: Thurs-Sun, 12-5
Types & Periods: 19th &
20th Century Furniture,
Copper, Brass
Directions: Front St Exit
from I-90 at Issaquah,
Eight Blocks East

Kennewick

THE CLOCKWORK DUCK
21410 84th Ave S   98031
206 852-5452
Proprietor: T V Clark & R
J Wanner
Hours: By Appointment;
By Chance
Types & Periods: General
Line
Specialties: Brass, Copper

Kirkland

THE WOODSHED
5918 Lake Washington
Blvd   98033
206 822-8600   Est: 1958
Proprietor: Mrs Mildred W
Brown
Hours: Tues-Sat, 11-5
Types & Periods: Primitive,
Pine Pieces, Early & Late
Victorian, Some Pine Pieces
Appraisal Service Available
Directions: Follow Blvd
along the lake to
Houghton Park, located
directly across the street

Lynnwood

ALMOST ANTIQUES
16406 Hwy 99   98036
206 743-5087
Hours: Wed-Sun, 12-5
Types & Periods: Leaded
Glass, Mirrors, Furniture,
Glassware, Clocks, General

**CALICO
COTTAGE-SCOTTY'S**
13806 Hwy 99   98036
206 743-3141
Hours: Daily, Weekends
Types & Periods: Primitives,
Collectibles, Oak

**COUNTRY PLACE
ANTIQUES**
13815 Hwy 99   98036
206 745-1110   Est: 1972
Proprietor: C L Beddoe &
L B Seim
Hours: Daily, 10-5
Types & Periods: Oak,
Walnut, Pine, Stained Glass,
Lamps

Appraisal Service Available
Directions: Four Miles N of
Lynnwood on Old Hwy 99,
or Exit 164th from I-5

KEELER'S KORNER
16401 Old U S 99   98036
206 743-0608
Hours: Tues-Sat, 11-5
Types & Periods: Furniture,
Juke Boxes, Signs, Auto
Parts

PARAPHERNALIA WEST
6625 212th SW   98036
206 778-0713   Est: 1969
Proprietor: Mrs Sue
Vassart
Hours: Daily, Weekends,
10-5; Closed Tues
Types & Periods: Glass,
Porcelain, Prints, Furniture
Directions: Two Blocks
East of Hwy 99

VAN'S TRADING POST
19716 Hwy 99   98036
206 775-2430
Proprietor: M L Van Zandt
Hours: Mon-Sat
Directions: Hwy 99 South
of 196th St, 1/2 Block

Marysville

EVELYN'S ANTIQUES
3301 140th NE   98270
206 659-6114
Hours: Mon-Wed,
Weekends, 10-5
Types & Periods: General
Line

MIDWAY ANTIQUES
14925 35th Ave NE   98270
206 659-8812   Est: 1966
Proprietor: Norman
Sarazin
Hours: Daily
Types & Periods: Furniture,
Glassware, Primitives
Directions: Five Miles N of
Marysville on Hwy 99

THE PLANT SHACK
9208 Old Hwy 99   98270
206 659-9331
Hours: Mon-Sat, 10-6; Sun
12-6
Types & Periods: General
Line, Collectibles

Mount Vernon

**MAGNOLIA LANE
ANTIQUES**
1345 Memorial Hwy 98273
206 424-7767
Proprietor: Bernadine
Lefeber
Hours: By Appointment;
By Chance
Types & Periods: Art Glass,
General Line
Specialties: Cameo

Naches

**HODGE-PODGE ANTIQUES
'N THINGS**
308 Moxee Ave 98937
509 653-2411
Proprietor: Dewey H &
Phyllis L Baker
Hours: Mon-Sat; Closed
Sun
Types & Periods: 1890-1930
Primitives, Oak, China,
Glass, Silver, Brass
Directions: Twelve Miles W
of Yakima On Hwy U S 12

Olympia

THE ANTIQUERIE
201 West 4th Ave 98501
206 357-5005 Est: 1967
Proprietor: V E Wilson
Hours: Mon-Fri; Weekends
By Appointment
Types & Periods: Oriental,
European and American
Porcelain, Art Glass, and
Objets De Vertu
Specialties: Oriental
Directions: Downtown
Olympia

BROWSERS' BOOK SHOP
522 S Washington 98501
206 357-7462 Est: 1970
Proprietor: Ilene Yates
Hours: Daily, Weekends,
10-5:30; Closed Sun
Types & Periods: Books,
China, Glassware
Specialties: Books
Appraisal Service Available
Directions: Downtown

OLD AGE ANTIQUES
Rte 8 Box 19 98502
206 943-4227 Est: 1967
Proprietor: Gordon & Jan
Madden
Hours: Daily, Weekends;
By Appointment
Types & Periods: Primitives,
Clocks, Watches, Furniture,
Collectibles
Appraisal Service Available
Directions: Tumwater on
Trosper Road, 1 Mile W of
Tyee Motel

THE WHITE HOUSE
1431 11th E 98501
206 352-3212
Proprietor: Evelyne & W M
McBee
Hours: Weekends; By
Appointment
Types & Periods: Victorian
Furniture & Artifacts
Appraisal Service Available
Directions: Corner of S
Central & 11th

Port Townsend

BOLAND'S ANTIQUES
1025 Lawrence St 98368
206 385-2228
Proprietor: Claude & Jo
Boland
Hours: Daily, 1-5
Types & Periods: Pine,
Walnut, Oak Furniture &
Accessories

**STARRETT HOUSE
ANTIQUES**
821 Water St 98368
206 385-0008 Est: 1974
Proprietor: Pat & Bo
Sullivan
Hours: Mon-Sun
Types & Periods: Clocks,
Oak & Victorian Furniture,
Silver, Coins, Lamps,
Carnival, Cut & Pressed
Glass, China, Firearms,
General Line
Specialties: Clocks
Appraisal Service Available
Directions: On the Water
Historic Point, Townsend
on Washington's Olympic
Pennisula

Poulsbo

ANTIQUE FARM
Rte 4, Box 138 98370
206 779-4849
Proprietor: David Burnham
& R Oakley
Hours: Daily, By Chance,
By Appointment
Types & Periods: Paintings,
Primitives, General Line
Appraisal Service Available

Puyallup

COACH HOUSE ANTIQUES
14104 Meridian S 98371
206 845-3573 Est: 1965
Proprietor: Dorothy
Hillistad
Hours: Thurs-Sat, 11-5
Types & Periods: China,
Furniture, Primitives
Specialties: Clocks
Directions: Four Miles S
Puyallup on Hwy 161

LOYD's OF PUYALLUP
7812 River Road 98371
206 848-6151 Est: 1974
Proprietor: Vern & Lois
Loyd
Hours: Daily, Weekends,
9-5, Closed Sun
Types & Periods: Early
American, Oak & Pine
Furniture, Primitives,
Depression Glass,
Collectibles
Specialties: Refinishing,
Caning
Directions: On Puyallup
River Between Tacoma &
Puyallup, Take Bay
St-Puyallup Cut-off from
I-5

PERIOD HOUSE ANTIQUES
527 W Pioneer 98371
206 845-6805 Est: 1973
Proprietor: Don Dunnigan
Hours: Sun-Sat
Types & Periods: 18th &
19th English Furniture,
American Victorian Cherry &
Walnut Furniture, Choice
Ornate American Oak
Specialties: Oriental
Antiques, Choice Cloisonne,
Imari, Kutani, Chinese
Export Porcelain

PERIOD HOUSE   **Cont'd**
Appraisal Service Available
   Directions: East of
   Tacoma, Major Hwy 512,
   or Take River Road From
   Tacoma to Puyallup

Redmond

COBWEB ANTIQUES
   12045 140th Ave NE 98052
   206 885-2174   Est: 1968
   Proprietor: Wallace &
   Loretta Johnson
   Hours: By Chance, By
   Appointment
Types & Periods: 1860
Walnut, Cherry & Pine to
1920 Oak, Lots of Primitives,
Wicker, Glassware
Specialties: Oak, Wicker,
Primitives, & Reproduction
Antique Furniture, Hardware
Appraisal Service Available
   Directions: Hwy 405 to
   124th Exit, East 1 Mile to
   140th Ave NE (Willow
   Road), Turn Right 3rd
   Driveway

**VIELLIE MAISON
ANTIQUES**
   7830 & 7979 Leary
   Way NE   98052
   206 885-4433   Est: 1970
   Proprietor: Bob & Polly
   Anderson
   Hours: Daily, Weekends,
   Closed Sun & Mon
Types & Periods: American
& European Furniture
1700-1900
Appraisal Service Available
Specialties: English Art
Nouveau, Mackintosh, Vosey
   Directions: Exit 18 off Rte
   405 E to Redmond

Roy

OZYMANDIAS ANTIQUES
   Rte 1 Box 53   98580
   206 458-5245   Est: 1973
   Proprietor: John & Kathy
   White
   Hours: Daily
Types & Periods: Oak
Pieces, 1850-1890; General
Line

Specialties: Documented Va
Pieces
   Directions: 'Best To Call &
   Get Directions First Hand'

Seattle

SEATTLE CLUSTER
   Directions: Downtown;
   Seneca to Stewart Sts,
   Between 1st & 8th Ave;
   1st Ave S to Union Station
   Bounded By S King;
   Denny Way W bounded By
   Olive Way on E Between
   6th Ave N & 8th Ave N;
   Green N (600-9000
   Blocks)

**THE ANCHORAGE MARINE
ANTIQUES**
   6518 15th Ave NE   98115
   206 524-7017   Est: 1964
   Proprietor: William C Little
   Hours: Mon-Sat, 10-5;
   Closed Sun
Types & Periods: Marine
Artifacts, Instruments,
Lamps, Lanterns, Cannons,
Furniture, Hardware, Ship's
Wheels, Diving Gear
Appraisal Service Available
   Directions: One Mile N of
   the University of
   Washington

ANEX ANTIQUES
   145 SW 178th   98166
   206 243-3055   Est: 1972
   Proprietor: Miny Anex
   Hours: By Appointment,
   By Chance
Types & Periods: Oriental,
Furniture, Wicker, Silver,
Jewelry, Cut Glass
Specialties: Silver
Appraisal Service Available
   Directions: Between
   Burien & Des Moines

ANITA'S ANTIQUES
   4743 University Village
   Plaza NE   98105
   206 524-0070   Est: 1970
   Proprietor: Anita R Fornia
   Hours: Mon-Sat, 10-6,
   Closed Sun
Types & Periods: Early
Victorian Thru 30's, Jewelry,
Silver, Glass, China, Lighting
Fixture, Furniture
Specialties: Wicker, Quilts

Appraisal Service Available
   Directions: In University
   Village Shopping Center

**ANTIQUES & ART
ASSOCIATES**
   2113 Third Ave   98121
   206 624-4378   1970
   Proprietor: Mr & Mrs
   George Harder
   Hours: Mon-Sat, 10-5
Types & Periods: Antiques,
Rare Prints, Antiquarian
Books
Appraisal Service Available
   Directions: Downtown, 2
   Blocks N of The Bon
   Marche

THE ANTIQUE COMPANY
   1054 N 39th   98103
   206 522-5103   Est: 1975
   Proprietor: Jerry Johnson
   Hours: Daily, Weekends,
   12-6, Closed Mon
Types & Periods: Art Glass,
American Furniture,
Mahogany, Walnut & Maple
Specialties: Art Glass
   Directions: Two Blocks E
   of N end of the Aurora
   Bridge

THE ANTIQUE WORLD
   4th & Jackson   98104
   206 622-9691   Est: 1976
   Proprietor: James Russell
   Hours: Sun-Thurs & Sat,
   10-6, Fri 10-9
Types & Periods: 19th &
20th Century European and
Oriental Furniture &
Accessories, Architectual
Pieces, Prints, Rugs,
Paintings, Jewelry, China,
Pewter, Copper, Brass,
Stained Glass
Specialties: Brass Beds,
Quantities of Stained Glass,
Oriental Unusual Items,
Desks, Wardrobes, Bedroom
and Dining Room Suites
   Directions: Located in the
   Historic Union Pacific R R
   Station; 4th & Jackson
   Sts, Just Off Pioneer
   Square in Downtown
   Seattle; Interstate 5 to
   Dearborn St Exit, West to
   4th Ave, North to Jackson

**BAMBOO HUT CURIO
SHOP**
   1914 3rd Ave   98101
   206 622-4090   Est: 1955

Proprietor: Benjamin
Gorlick
Hours: Daily, Weekends
Types & Periods: Military
Nautical, Indian & Eskimo
Artifacts, Orientalia
Specialties: Militaria;
Nautical
Appraisal Service Available
Directions: Downtown; 1/2
Block N of the Bon
Marche

BLANCHE'S ANTIQUES
307 NE 71st   98115
                Est: 1968
Proprietor: Blanche C
Gregg
Hours: Wed-Sat, 11-5
Types & Periods: Art Glass,
China, Silver, Furniture,
Collectibles
Specialties: China, Glass,
Silver
Directions: Ravenna Blvd
& E Greenlake Way Near
Freeway

CAP'N SAM'S LOFT
2702 1st Ave S   98134
206 624-1478   Est: 1973
Proprietor: Dave Tuss, Jim
Pelham, John Ramm
Hours: Mon-Sat, 11-6
Types & Periods: Furniture,
Vintage Building Materials,
Old Plumbing & Lighting
Fixtures, Hardware, Clocks
Specialties: Refinishing,
Restoration Service
Directions: Corner 1st Ave
S and Lander; Across
from Main Sears Store;
Enter on 1st Ave (No
Longer On 2nd Floor-Have
Moved Entrance)

**CARRIAGE HOUSE
GALLERIES OF SEATTLE**
5611 University Way N.E.
                98105
206 523-4960   Est: 1958
Proprietor: Robert Bernard
Shaw
Hours: Mon-Sat, 12-5;
Closed Sun, By
Appointment
Types & Periods:
Continental Period Piece,
Paintings, Jewelry
Specialties: Fine Early
Oriental
Appraisal Service Available
Directions: NE Vicinity of
Seattle, 6 Blocks E of
Freeway at 50th St Exit

**CATHERINE TYRELL
ANTIQUES**
208 First Ave   98104
206 623-1093
Proprietor: Catherine &
Robert Tyrell
Hours: Daily; Weekends;
Closed Sun & Mon in
Winter
Types & Periods: Art Glass,
Dishes, Porcelains, Silver,
Pewter, Oriental Objects of
Art
Specialties: Restore Oil
Paintings
Appraisal Service Available
Directions: Pioneer Square

CHELSEA ANTIQUES
3622 NE 45th   98105
206 525-2727   Est: 1971
Proprietor: Ellen McMurry
& Suzanne Ries
Types & Periods: Fine 18th
& 19th Century Silver and
Porcelain, American &
English Furniture, Dolls &
Commemorative Blue And
White Pottery
Specialties: Silver And
Porcelain
Appraisal Service Available
Directions: Exit Freeway
on NE 45th; Go East; Near
University of Washington

COLLECTOR'S CORNER
6203 15th NW   98107
206 782-5950   Est: 1966
Proprietor: Anabelle Rapp
Hours: Thurs, Fri, & Sat;
Also By Appointment
Types & Periods: Cut Glass
Orientals, Silver, Pictures,
Plates, Dishes, Furniture
Directions: One Mile North
of Ballard Bridge on
West Side

**THE CONNOISSEUR
GALLERY**
115 S Jackson St   98104
206 622-3249   Est: 1976
Proprietor: William H
Swigart
Hours: Tues-Sat, 11-5;
Closed Sun & Mon
Types & Periods: Paintings
from the 17th Century thru
the Early 20th; 18th & Early
19th Century Furniture,
Period Accessories
Specialties: Paintings,
Wedgewood Basalt, Bronzes

Directions: Adjacent to
Pioneer Square,
Downtown Seattle

CRANE GALLERY, INC
1326 6th   98101
206 622-7185   Est: 1975
Proprietor: Cheney Cowles
Hours: Mon-Sat;
Closed Sun
Types & Periods: Antique
Asian Art, Pre-Victorian
English and American
Furniture, Antiquities
Specialties: Asian Art,
Antiquities
Appraisal Service Available
Asian Art Only
Directions: Downtown
Seattle, 6th Street
Between Union &
University Streets

WM L DAVIS COMPANY
1300 5th Ave   98101
206 622-0518   Est: 1890
Proprietor: D W Bailey
Hours: Mon-Fri, 9-5;
Sat, 9-12
Types & Periods: Furniture
from England, France, Italy,
and Japan
Directions: Corner of 5th
Avenue & University
Street, Near the Olympic
Hotel

FOX'S GEM SHOPS, INC
1324 5th Ave   98101
206 623-2528   Est: 1912
Proprietor: Sidney R Thal
Hours: Daily
Types & Periods: Oriental
Art; Jewelry
Specialties: Bottles, (Snuff),
Jade, Ivory
Appraisal Service Available

FURNITURE SPA
7557 15th NW   98117
206 784-0011   Est: 1966
Proprietor: J N Brookes
Hours: Tues-Sat, 9-5;
Closed Sun & Mon
Types & Periods: 1900
American Furniture
Specialties: Furniture
Stripping
Directions: North Ballard
Area

Seattle   Cont'd

GALLERY ANTIQUES
8003 Greenwood Ave N
98108
206 782-2028   Est: 1969
Proprietor: Jay Steensma
& R K Brown
Hours: Daily
Types & Periods: 18th &
Early 19th Century
Furnishings
Specialties: Porcelain
Appraisal Service Available
Directions: 85th St Off
Ramp From I-5; West to
Greenwood Ave; Approx
1/2 Mile

HEARTHSIDE ANTIQUES
22228 Pacific Hwy 98188
206 878-4364   Est: 1948
Proprietor: Tom & Audrey
Backes
Hours: Tues-Sun, 11-5
Types & Periods: Oriental,
French Cameo and Art
Glass
Specialties: Vast Selection
of Quality Antiques
Directions: 2 1/2 Miles
South of Sea-Tac Airport
on Hwy 99 Or Exit 149
Off I-5

HOTEL LOBBY ANTIQUES
4350 Leary Way NW
98107
206 784-5340   Est: 1972
Proprietor: Roger Ligrano
& David Marzullo
Hours: Daily
Types & Periods: Toys,
Jewelry, Paper, Art Deco,
American & European
Pottery, Vintage Clothing
Appraisal Service Available
Directions: Between
Ballard & Fremont district
on Main Road in city of
Seattle's N end

**KILBORN'S ANTIQUES &
COLLECTIBLES**
2400 NW 61st   98107
206 789-0717   Est: 1973
Proprietor: Mary & Peter
Kilborn
Hours: Mon-Sat, 11-5
Types & Periods:
Turn-of-the-Century & Later,
Glass, China, Silver, Dolls,
Furniture
Directions: Six Blocks N of
NW Market St in Ballard

LADYBUG ANTIQUES
8001 Greenwood N 98103
206 783-3342   Est: 1972
Proprietor: Billie
Buckingham & Carolyn
Lehman
Hours: Tues-Sat, 11-5;
Closed Sun & Mon
Types & Periods: General
Line
Specialties: Oak Furniture;
Primitives

THE LEGACY, LTD
71 Marion Viaduct 98104
206 624-6350   Est: 1933
Proprietor: Mardonna
Austin-McKillop
Hours: Mon-Sat, 10-6
Types & Periods: Historic &
Contemporary North
American Indian & Eskimo
Art, Artifacts & Books
Appraisal Service Available
Directions: NE Block from
the Colman Ferry Terminal
Downtown

LITTLE HOUSE ANTIQUES
7330A 15th Ave NE 98117
206 783-4131   Est: 1966
Proprietor: Genevieve
Gislason
Hours: Thurs-Sat, 11-5
Types & Periods: 19th &
Early 20th Century Furniture,
Lamps, Clocks, Victorian &
Art Glass, China, Silver
Specialties: Glass, Silver
Directions: Exit 172 Off I-5
to 15th Ave NW, Then Left

MARIKO TADA, INC
519 Olive Way   98101
206 624-7667   Est: 1968
Proprietor: Mariko Tada
Hours: Daily, 9:30-5:30;
Closed Sun; Also By
Appointment
Types & Periods: Oriental
Fine Arts, Ceramics,
Furniture & Prints
Specialties: Oriental,
(Japanese Imari)
Appraisal Service Available
Directions: Corner of 6th
& Olive

NANCY'S NOOK
8400 Greenwood Ave N
98103
206 782-6636   Est: 1973
Proprietor: Nancy & David
Amdal

Hours: Daily; Weekends;
Evenings By Appointment
Types & Periods: Primitives,
Bottles, Jars, Jewelry, Art
Glass, Tools, Collectibles,
Furniture
Directions: W on 85th to
Dayton; Left 1 Block to
84th; Right for 1 Mile

NOW & THEN ANTIQUES
202 1st Ave South 98104
206 622-3421
Proprietor: Virginia Walton
Hours: Tues-Sat,
10:30-4:30, Closed Sun &
Mon; By Appointment
Types & Periods: Furniture,
Decorator Items, Jewelry,
Clocks, Stained Glass, Glass
& Silver
Specialties: General
Directions: 1st S &
Washington Street,
Pioneer Square

OAK EMPORIUM
8005 Greenwood Ave N
98103
206 783-5040   Est: 1972
Proprietor: J W Conner &
Wanda Martin
Hours: Tues-Sun
Types & Periods: Oak
Furniture
Appraisal Service Available
Directions: 80th &
Greenwood

**OAK EMPORIUM NEW
WAREHOUSE**
6500 24th NW   98117
Call Oak Emporium
Types & Periods: Oak
Furniture

THE OAK PARLOR
5405-07 Ballard Ave NW
98107
206 783-2327   Est: 1973
Proprietor: David
Baumchen
Hours: Sun-Sat, 11-5
Types & Periods: American
Furniture, Oak, Chestnut,
Ash, Mahogany, Walnut,
Maple, Pine & Cherry
Specialties: Complete Line
of Refinishing Supplies &
Replacement Hardware
Appraisal Service Available
Directions: In Old Historic
Ballard, One Block Off
Market Street

OASIS-ORIENTAL RUGS
5655 University Way NE
98105
206 525-2060   Est: 1969
Proprietor: Douglas
Barnhart
Hours: Daily 12-6
Types & Periods: Oriental
Rugs, Collectibles, Furniture
Specialties: Oriental
Appraisal Service Available

PELAYO ANTIQUES
5758 35th Ave NE   98105
206 523-5105   Est: 1973
Proprietor: Pedro &
Wanda G Pelayo
Hours: Daily,
Weekends, 11-6
Types & Periods: 18th, 19th
& Early 20th Century
Furniture, Brass, Copper,
Cast Iron, Stained Glass,
Clocks
  Directions: NE of U of
  Washington Campus &
  University Village
  Shopping Center

THE PLAYER PIANO SHOP
75 Yesler Way   98104
206 622-4204   Est: 1968
Proprietor: M Silver
Hours: Daily, Closed Sat;
Sun By Chance or By
Appointment
Types & Periods: Player
Pianos, Nickelodeons, Pump
Organs, Automatic Pipe
Organs
Appraisal Service Available
  Directions; Take Janes St
  Exit, Turn West, Drive
  Along Hill Toward Puget
  Sound to Yesler Way, 1/2
  Block West, Next to
  Yesler Hotel

RITCHIE'S PLANTS &
ANTIQUES
14900 Ambaum Blvd SW
98166
206 243-3055   Est: 1976
Proprietor: Miny Anex
Hours: Mon-Tues,
Thurs-Fri, 11-5; also by
appointment
Types & Periods: Jewelry,
Wicker, Silver, Oriental, Cut
Glass
Specialties: Jewelry, Cut
Glass, Silver, Furniture,
1870-1930 Oriental Objects

Appraisal Service Available
  Directions: Burien Exit off
  I-5 to Ambaum Blvd SW

ROSEN-COLGREN
GALLERY
1814 7th Ave   98101
206 623-3230   Est: 1972
Proprietor: Ralph Rosen &
Monte Colgren
Hours: Daily, Closed Sun
Types & Periods: 18th &
Early 19th Century
American, English &
Continental Furniture,
Porcelains, Silver, Glass,
Paintings, Prints, Jewelry,
Textiles, Art
Specialties: Furniture,
Oriental Rugs, Soft Paste,
Porcelains
Appraisal Service Available
  Directions: Downtown,
  One Block East of
  Washington Plaza Hotel;
  In 7th Ave Theater Bldg
  Just N of the Crepe De
  Paris Restaurant

SHEPARD'S EMPORIUM
2120 2nd Ave   98121
206 623-3844   Est: 1974
Proprietor: Ralph & Lana
Shepard
Hours: Tues-Sat, 11-5, By
Appointment
Types & Periods: Early
American thru 1900
Specialties: Furniture,
Primitives, Glass, Nautical,
Over 1200 Titles of
Reference Books on
Antiques & Collectibles
  Directions: Downtown
  Between Lenora and
  Blanchard

SIXTH AVENUE ANTIQUES
1330 6th Avenue   98033
206 622-1110   Est: 1976
Proprietor: Jean Williams
& Bob Alsin
Hours: Mon-Sat, 10-5:30,
Closed Sun
Types & Periods: 17th, 18th
and 19th Century French
and English Country
Furniture and Accessories;
Also Architectural Items
Specialties: Fireplace
Equipment, Mantles and
Fine Boxes
  Directions: Across From
  the Washington Athletic
  Club

THIRD HAND SHOP
11 W McGraw   98119
206 284-3011   Est: 1967
Proprietor: Dale R
Rutherford
Hours: Daily, 12-6
Types & Periods: Primitives,
Brass, Copper, Stained
Glass, Furniture
Specialties: Furniture (Brass
Beds, Rolltop Desks, Round
Oak Tables, Wicker)
  Directions: On Queen
  Anne Hill

THOMPSON ANTIQUES
7531 11th   98115
206 524-4722   Est: 1951
Proprietor: Kenneth &
Lucile Thompson
Hours: Tues-Sat, 11-5
Types & Periods: Frames,
Cut Glass, Haviland
Specialties: Toys (Dolls)
  Directions: University
  District

TO THE TRADE, INC
500 E Pike   98104
206 324-7191   1960
Proprietor: Ken Weeks
Hours: Daily, 9-5;
Closed 12-1
Types & Periods: Wholesale
Only
Specialties: Furniture
  Directions: Near
  Broadway, 2nd Floor

TRUST HOUSE ANTIQUES
4105 E Madison   98112
206 329-7944
Proprietor: Casey Hannum
Hours: Daily, 11-5; By
Appointment
Types & Periods: American
& English, Georgian,
Victorian, Shaker,
Chippendale, Hepplewhite
Specialties: Furniture,
(Chests, Dining Sets)
Appraisal Service Available
  Directions: 41st & Madison
  in Madison Park

UPSTART CROW &
COMPANY
164 S Washington   98104
206 622-7636   Est: 1974
Proprietor: R Breese
Jones
Hours: Tues-Sat, 12-5; By
Appointment

Seattle   Cont'd

UPSTART CROW   Cont'd
Types & Periods: American
& European Furniture, All
Periods
Appraisal Service Available
  Directions: Seattle,
  'Pioneer Square' Area

VANITY FAIR ANTIQUES
  Pier 70   98121
  206 622-9240   Est: 1973
  Proprietor: Karen Lorene
  Hours: Sun-Sat
Types & Periods: General
Line
Specialties: Jewelry,
Collectibles
Appraisal Service Available
  Directions: End of Broad;
  On the Waterfront

**VINTAGE HOUSE
ANTIQUES**
  19918 Aurora Ave N
                      98133
  206 542-2049   Est: 1971
  Proprietor: Rose Marie
  Cattle
  Hours: Tues-Sat, 1-4:30;
  Closed Sun & Mon
Types & Periods: 1800 &
Early 1900; Silver, Art Glass,
China, Wicker & Walnut
Furniture
Specialties: Glass, Silver
  Directions: One Block S of
  Aurora Shopping Center

YE OLDE CURIOSITY SHOP
  601 Alaskan Way   98104
  206 682-5844   Est: 1899
  Proprietor: Joseph R
  James
  Hours: Daily
Types & Periods: Indian,
Oriental
Appraisal Service Available
  Directions: Foot of Yesler
  Way, Pier 51, On the
  Waterfront

Shawano

MEADOWCREST ANTIQUES
  Box 288   54166
  715 526-2210
  Proprietor: Marjorie W
  Klein

Types & Periods: General
Line, Art Glass, Dolls,
Buttons
  Directions: E on Hwy
  29-47-55 at County E

Shelton

BLUE LANTERN ANTIQUE
  Rte 1 Box 245   98485
  206 426-6444   Est: 1967
  Proprietor: Jack & Gwen
  Avery
  Directions: Mon-Sat, 11-5;
  Closed Sun & Holidays in
  Winter
Types & Periods: General
Line, Primitives, Furniture,
Glass
Specialties: Oak Furniture,
Primitives
Appraisal Service Available
  Directions:
  Shelton-Olympia Frwy at
  McCleary Cut Off

Snohomish

ANOTHER ANTIQUE SHOP
  924 First St   98290
  206 568-3629   Est: 1969
  Proprietor: Mary
  Bookwalter, Jan
  Humphrey & Sybil
  Johnson
  Hours: Mon, 11-3; Tues,
  Thurs-Sat, 11-5; Sun, 12-5
Types & Periods: Oak, Pine,
Wicker, Walnut, Pictures,
Glass, Lamps, Clocks
Specialties: Restored
Furniture
  Directions: One Block S
  Hwy 2 from Everett

BAKER'S ANTIQUES
  111 Union Ave   98290
  206 568-3444   Est: 1972
  Proprietor: Shod Baker
  Hours: Tues-Sat, 1-5 or By
  Appointment
Types & Periods: 18th &19th
Century Furniture, Cherry,
Mahogany, Walnut, Silver,
Objets d' Art
Specialties: Haviland China,
& Limoges
Appraisal Service Available
  Directions: Across from
  Post Office

**THE CABBAGE PATCH
CAFE AND ANTIQUE SHOP**
  111 Avenue A   98290
  206 568-9091
  Hours: Daily, Weekends,
  11-7
Types & Periods: General
Line

**WAGONMASTER
ANTIQUES**
  711 First St   98290
  206 259-4488
  Hours: Daily, By Chance
Types & Periods: Oak
Furniture, General Line

Spanaway

RED WAGON ANTIQUES
  26001 Mountain Hwy
                      98387
  206 847-2089   Est: 1974
  Proprietor: Mr & Mrs
  Robert Holshouser
  Hours: Daily, Weekends,
  11-6; Closed Mon; By
  Appointment
Types & Periods: American,
Oak & Victorian Furniture,
Lamps, Primitives
Specialties: Picture Frames
  Directions: 15 Miles S of
  Tacoma on Hwy 7 on the
  Way to Mt Rainer

Spokane

**ANIMAL CRACKERS &
APPLE ANNIES**
  N 217 Division St   99202
  509 624-4775   Est: 1973
  Proprietor: Clay Hibbitt
  Hours: Daily 10-6; Closed
  Sun; By Appointment
Types & Periods: Furniture,
Primitives, Gambling Tables,
Branding Irons, Tins, Toys,
China, Crystal, Advertising
Appraisal Service Available
  Directions: 7 Blocks From
  I-90 Exit Division Street

HAZEL CRANE
  701 N Monroe   99201
  509 327-1392   Est: 1954
  Proprietor: Hazel Crane
  Hours: Daily, 10-4
Types & Periods: Glass,
China, Dolls
Specialties: Dolls

Appraisal Service Available
Directions: Cross Monroe
St Bridge Going N 2
Blocks

ENGELS FLEA MARKET
N Division St   99207
            Est: 1978
Hours: Fri-Sun, 8-5
Types & Periods: General
Line, Dolls, Jewelry,
Primitives
Specialties: Furniture,
Glassware
Directions: Take Division
St N to the Y where the
roads branch to Newport

KAY MC CORMICK
S 1224 Grand Blvd   99202
509 747-2523   Est: 1962
Proprietor: Kay
McCormick
Hours: Mon-Sat, 9:30-5:30
Types & Periods: General
Line
Specialties: Oriental
Directions: Top of the hill,
across from the Cathedral

LESLIE'S ANTIQUES
W 621 Mallon   99201
509 327-3804   Est: 1973
Proprietor: Leslie Mattson
Directions: Mon-Thurs,
11-6, Fri, 11-9, Sat, 11-6,
Sun 12-5
Types & Periods: General
Line of Victorian, Art
Nouveau, Art Deco
Specialties: Service
Advertising Items
Directions: Located Within
'Flour Mill' Shopping
Complex

MC LEOD'S ANTIQUES
2118 Sprague E   99202
509 535-6032
Proprietor: Roy E McLeod
Hours: Tues-Sat,
10:30-5:30; Closed Sun
& Mon
Types & Periods: Glass,
China, Furniture, General
Line

PARAPHERNALIA GALORE
223 N Division   99203
509 747-3596   Est: 1973
Proprietor: Rich
Hieronymus
Hours: Mon-Sat,
11:30-5:30, Closed Sun

Types & Periods: Clothes,
Linen, Jewelry
Specialties: Clothing
Directions: Between Main
& Spokane Falls Blvd SE
of the Sheraton Hotel

PHILIP EDGE ANTIQUES
1022 W First St   99204
509 624-2568   Est: 1956
Proprietor: Phillip Edge
Hours: Daily
Types & Periods: 18th &
Early 19th Century Furniture,
Paintings, Chess Sets,
Persian Rugs
Appraisal Service Available
Directions: 1 1/2 Blocks
W of Davenport Hotel
on 1st

**ROOD'S ALL AMERICAN
ANTIQUES**
2134 Grand Blvd S   99203
206 624-0347
Proprietor: Floyd & Lee
Rood
Hours: By Appointment;
By Chance
Types & Periods: Art & Cut
Glass, Haviland, Furniture,
Early American Items

THE WOODEN NICKEL
N 207 Division   99201
509 747-6887   Est: 1972
Proprietor: Bob & Becky
Somes
Hours: Tues-Sat, Closed
Sun & Mon
Types & Periods: American
Oak, Collectibles
Specialties, Roll Tops,
Ceiling Fans, Stoves
Appraisal Service Available
Directions: Two Blocks SE
of Sheraton Inn

Tacoma

TACOMA CLUSTER
Directions: No Real
Cluster, Many Shops
Scattered Throughout
City; a Number of Shops
on N Pearl (5000 Block);
Steilacoom Blvd
(5000-6000 Blocks);
McKinley (3000-5000
Blocks)

ANTIQUES ET CETERA
5929 Steilacoom Blvd SW
            98499
206 588-7715   Est: 1969
Proprietor: A Rex Bennett
Hours: Daily, 10-5
Types & Periods: English &
American Furniture,
Advertising, Bottles
Specialties: Early American
Appraisal Service Available
Directions: Lakewood
District

**DOROTHY OLSEN
ANTIQUES**
8807 Bridgeport Way SW
            98499
206 584-1121   Est: 1970
Proprietor: Dorothy &
Harold Olsen
Hours: Daily, Weekends,
Evenings By Appointment
or By Chance
Types & Periods: Furniture,
Sterling, Cut & Art Glass,
Porcelains, Orientals
Specialties: China (Belleek &
Royal Doulton)
Appraisal Service Available
Directions: Lakewood
Area, 72nd St Exit From
I-5, W to Bridgeport, Few
Blocks South

**DRAHOLD'S OLD TACOMA
ANTIQUE SHOP**
2223 N 30th St   98403
206 627-2743   Est: 1958
Proprietor: Lucille & Otto
Drahold
Hours: Weekends; By
Appointment; By Chance
Types & Periods: Art & Cut
Glass, Indian Artifacts, Dolls,
Furniture, Tiffany Shades
Specialties: Clocks, China,
French Dolls
Appraisal Service Available
Directions: Corner of N
30th St & Schuster
Parkway Drive

MANDARIN ENTERPRISES
5929 Steilacoom Blvd SW
            98499
206 582-3355   Est: 1969
Proprietor: Howard
Welborn
Hours: Mon-Sat;
Appointment During
Evening Hours

Tacoma   Cont'd

MANDARIN ENT.   Cont'd
Types & Periods: Orientals,
Architectural Items, Stained
and Beveled Glass Doors,
Player Pianos
Specialties: Lectures and
Free Appraisals
Appraisal Service Available
  Directions: Outside
  Tacoma, South on I-5,
  Take Exit 125 and
  proceed 2 Miles on
  Bridgeport Way SW, Turn
  right on Steilacoom Blvd

MANDARIN GALLERY
8821 Bridgeport Way
                    98499
206 582-3355   Est: 1969
Hours: Mon-Sat; Mon &
Fri Evenings till 9; By
Appointment
Types & Periods: Stained
and Beveled Glass Windows
& Doors
Specialties: Restoration and
Appraisals
Appraisal Service Available
  Directions: Outside
  Tacoma, South on I-5,
  Take Exit 125 and
  proceed 2 Miles on
  Bridgeport Way

**MC KINLEY FURNITURE
COMPANY**
3502 McKinley Ave   98404
206 6276932   Est: 1969
Proprietor: D G Lane
Hours: Mon-Sat, 10-6;
Closed Sun & Holidays
Types & Periods: American
Oak, 1800-Early 1900
  Directions: NW Corner of
  35th & McKinley Ave

**OLD TACOMA ANTIQUES
SHOP**
2223 North 30th   98403
206 627-2743
Proprietor: Otto & Lucille
Drahold
Hours: Daily, 10-6;
Evenings & Sun By
Appointment
Types & Periods: Dolls,
China, Furniture, Haviland

PACIFIC GALLERIES
8218 Pacific Ave   98408
206 475-5955   Est: 1972
Proprietor: B Terry Payson

Hours: Auctions Held
Every 4-6 Weeks
Types & Periods: European,
Rugs, Clocks, Art
Appraisal Service Available
  Directions: 1 1/2 Miles Off
  I-5, Take Exit 129 (S 72nd
  St) E to Pacific Ave

ROYAL OAK ANTIQUES
6411 Steilacoom Blvd
                    98499
206 588-0030   Est: 1968
Proprietor: Chad Hinckley
Hours: Mon-Sat, 10-6
Types & Periods: Dolls,
Glass, Jewelry, China,
Furniture, Phonographs,
Music Boxes, Weapons,
Clocks, Silver, Circa
1700-1930's
Specialties: Dolls
Appraisal Service Available
  Directions: Off I-5, North
  on Bridgeport Way Left 4
  Blocks on Steilacoom Blvd

**SIXTH AVENUE HOUSE OF
ANTIQUES**
3620 6th Ave   98406
206 759-2999   Est: 1971
Proprietor: Georgia C
Ginnis
Hours: Sun-Wed, Fri-Sat,
10-5:30
Types & Periods: Victorian
Furniture, Silver, Glass,
Hand Painted Plates, Brass,
Pictures
Specialties: Furniture (Tea
Carts)
Appraisal Service Available
  Directions: Bremerton
  Cut off from 5 Frwy, 1 mile
  to Union Ave, N to 6th
  Ave, left 1 block

T & G ANTIQUES
5320 McKinley Ave   98404
206 474-1172   Est: 1974
Proprietor: Gary & Terrie
Holmes
Hours: Mon-Fri, by
appointment; Sat-Sun,
10-5
Types & Periods: American
Oak & Pine Furniture,
Aladdin Parts & Service,
Nauticals
Specialties: Stripping &
Refinishing Furniture
  Directions: Exit 56th E off
  I-5 to McKinley

THE TIME MACHINE
765 Broadway   98402
206 272-6254   Est: 1973
Proprietor: Douglas
Bassett
Hours: Tues-Sat, 10-5
Types & Periods: American,
Collectibles
Specialties: Arcade
Equipment, Coin Operated
Devices
  Directions: Downtown off
  Broadway Plaza

Toppenish

DAISY ANTIQUES
807 Adams Ave   98948
509 865-4240
Proprietor: Mr & Mrs
Henry Arens
Hours: Mon-Sat, 9-5; Sun
and evenings by
appointment
Types & Periods: Furniture,
Western Equipment, Dolls,
Art & Cut Glass

Valleyford

**YANKEE PEDDLER
ANTIQUES**
Rte 1   99036
509 535-7929   Est: 1974
Proprietor: Vallarie Walter
Hours: Tues-Sun
Types & Periods: General
Line
Specialties: Jewelry,
Primitives
Appraisal Service Available
  Directions: 8 miles S of
  KHQ TV on Old
  Palouse Hwy

Vancouver

HART'S ANTIQUES
715 South St   98661
206 694-2134
Proprietor: Ted & Hazel
Hart
Hours: By appointment, by
chance
Types & Periods: Indian
Artifacts, Weapons, Stoves,
General Line

SERENDIPITY
9713 NW 31st Ave 98665
206 573-6313
Proprietor: Wanda W
Wigginton
Hours: By appointment
Types & Periods: China,
Glass, Silver, Primitives,
Quilts

Waitsburg

WEIR'S HOUSE OF GLASS
220 E 10th St 99361
509 337-6528
Proprietor: Carol C Weir
Hours: By appointment, by
chance
Types & Periods: Cut Glass

Walla Walla

DAVIS ANTIQUES
1958 Pleasant 99362
509 529-4030
Proprietor: Jim & Dixie
Davis
Hours: Tues-Sat, 10-5
Types & Periods: General
Line

Wenatchee

CHARBY'S PIXIES
204 S Wenatchee Ave
98801
509 662-2451
Proprietor: Clair & Isabella
C Warren
Hours: Mon-Sat, 11-5
Types & Periods: China,
Glass, Danish Plates,
Primitives

Yakima

THE FORD GALLERY
19 N Front St 98901
509 452-1770 Est: 1974
Proprietor: Bill Ford
Hours: Daily
Types & Periods: English &
French Primitives

SAGARS ANTIQUES
4002 Summitview Ave
98908
509 966-8480 Est: 1973
Proprietor: Joyce Sagar
Hours: Daily
Types & Periods: Brass,
Glass, Pewter, China,
Steins, Collectibles, Jewelry
Specialties: Clocks, Old
Cameras & Accessories
Directions: W Park
Shopping Centre, 40th &
Summitview

THE SHOPKEEPER LTD
807 W Yakima Ave 98902
509 452-6646 Est: 1972
Proprietor: Dean W
Hammermeister
Hours: Daily, 8:30-5:30
Types & Periods: Primitives,
American & European
Furniture, Wicker, Glass
Appraisal Service Available
Directions: The Main Ave
in Yakima

Kitchen Safe,
Victorian Era.

A rural
cabinetmaker
at work.

STATE OF WEST VIRGINIA

Charles Town

RINALDI'S ANTIQUES
Jefferson Terrace   25414
304 725-7343   Est: 1969
Proprietor: Dorothy &
Robert Rinaldi
Hours: Daily
Types & Periods: Victorian,
Oak, Walnut
Directions: Jefferson
Terrace is just off Rte 340,
1/4 Mile from Charles
Town Race Track

Charleston

BELLE'S ANTIQUES
714 Patrick St   25312
304 343-3930   Est: 1970
Proprietor: Belle Withrow
Hours: Mon-Thurs 10-3,
Sat 10-5
Types & Periods: General
Line, Collectibles, No
Imports
Appraisal Service Available
Directions: 7 blocks N of
Patrick St, Bridge on
Kanawha River, Corner
7th Ave & Patrick St

**KANAWHA COIN &
ANTIQUES**
712 Fife St   25301
304 342-8081   Est: 1962
Proprietor: Doug
Bumgardner
Hours: Mon-Fri 10-4
Types & Periods: Coins,
Small Antiques, (Pocket
Watches, Rings, Etc)
Appraisal Service Available
Directions: Downtown
Charleston

WINE CELLAR ANTIQUES
1317 Hansford St   25301
304 343-1965   Est: 1974
Proprietor: Nancy K Wells
Hours: Daily 10-4, Closed
during Summer Except by
Appointment or by Chance
Types & Periods: 1790-1860,
American

Specialties: English
Directions: W of E
Washington to Morris,
Turn Right, Cross RR, 1st
St on Right, Turn Right

**WOODEN BRIDGE
ANTIQUES**
1026 Bridge Rd   25314
304 342-9552   Est: 1976
Proprietor: Tom
Blankenship
Hours: Mon-Sat
Types & Periods: Furniture
of all Periods
Specialties: Oriental Rugs
Appraisal Service Available
Directions: From
Charleston cross
Southside Bridge, 1 Mile
up Bridge Rd

Harpers Ferry

JOHN C NEWCOMER
1141 Washington St 25425
304 535-6902   Est: 1960
Proprietor: John C
Newcomer
Hours: Sat 11-5, Sun 1-5,
By Appointment, Also by
Chance
Types & Periods: 18th &
Early 19th Century American
Country & Formal Furniture
Specialties: Textiles, Pottery,
Folk Art
Appraisal Service Available
Directions: Main St of
Bolivar, Adjoining Harpers
Ferry, Approx 1 Mile
above the National Park

**THOMAS MILLER
ANTIQUES**
High St   25425
304 535-6910   Est: 1964
Proprietor: Thomas W
Miller
Hours: Thurs-Sun
Types & Periods: 19th
Century Furniture, Mirrors,
Frames, Tools, Crockery

**WILLIAM PAYNE
ANTIQUES AT CANAL
HOUSE**
Washington St   25425
304 535-2406

Proprietor: William H
Payne
Hours: Weekends 11-5
Types & Periods: 19th
Century American Country
Furniture, Folk Art, Books,
Accessories
Specialties: Maps,
Daguerreotypes, Decorated
Stoneware
Directions: In Bolivar at
Harpers Ferry, Just off US
Rte 340

Huntington

BIX FURNITURE SERVICES
1645 Spring Valley Dr
    25704
304 429-4395   Est: 1971
Proprietor: Joe & Sandy
Pyle
Hours: Daily 8:30-5
Types & Periods: Furniture,
Glassware
Specialties: Furniture
(Refinishing)

**COLLINSWORTH
INTERIORS & ANTIQUES**
824 8th St   25701
304 525-1954   Est: 1956
Proprietor: Hershel &
Frances Collinsworth
Hours: Daily, Weekends,
Sun & Eves by
Appointment
Types & Periods: Oil
Paintings, Ivories, Cameo,
Glass, Tiffany, Jade,
Cloisonne
Specialties: Oriental
Directions: From I-64 Take
5th St Exit & Follow 52
Signs

THIS 'N THAT ANTIQUES
2935 Auburn Rd   25704
304 429-1736   Est: 1973
Proprietor: Irma Watts
Kidd
Hours: Daily
Types & Periods: General
Line
Directions: US Rte 60 in
W End of City

Morgantown

POTPOURRI INC
229 Chestnut St   26505
304 292-0868   Est: 1970
Proprietor: S Morasco
Hours: Mon-Fri
Types & Periods:
Neo-Renaissance,
Biedermeier, Victorian,
Jugendstil (Art Nouveau),
Turn-of-the-Century
(Furniture, Linens,
Porcelains, Knickknacks,
Musical)
Specialties: Unique &
Beautiful from Europe
    Directions: In the Middle
    of Morgantown, in Knights
    of Columbus Bldg, Just
    behind Courthouse

St Albans

**ATTIC ANTIQUES &
CHERISHABLES INC**
6735 MacCorkle Ave SW
                                    25177
304 766-9015   Est: 1976
Proprietor: Joan B Rollins
Hours: Mon, Tues,
Thurs-Sat 10-4, Sun By
Appointment, Wed By
Chance (For Appt, phone
727-9500)
Types & Periods: Civil War
Period, Turn-of-the-Century
Items & Collectibles
Specialties: Depression
Glass, China, Small
Antiques, Collectibles
Appraisal Service Available
    Directions: US Rte 60 at
    Old Rte 60 Jct beside
    Deputy Sheriff's Dept

GOEBEL'S ANTIQUES
108 MacCorkle Ave 25177
304 727-4120   Est: 1963
Proprietor: Eleanor &
Elmer Goebel
Hours: By Appointment,
By Chance
Types & Periods: Country &
Period Furniture, Clocks,
Silver
Specialties: Clocks,
Furniture, Silver
    Directions: 4 Miles from
    I-64 on US 60

St Marys

ALPINE ANTIQUES
Box 263, Rte 2   26170
304 684-3702   Est: 1976
Proprietor: Kay & Jane
Buck
Hours: Daily, Weekends,
By Appointment
Types & Periods: "All types
& periods"
Appraisal Service Available
    Directions: 1 Mile S of
    Town

BUCK'S AUCTION SALES
Rte 2   26170
304 684-3702   Est: 1971
Hours: Weekends, By
Chance, By Appointment
Types & Periods: General
Line
Appraisal Service Available
    Directions: 1 Mile S of St
    Marys, 24 Miles N of
    Parkersburg on Rt 2

Triadelphia

ANTIQUES BY HAGEDORN
173 National Rd   26059
304 547-1835   Est: 1957
Proprietor: Bill Hagedorn
Hours: By Appointment
Types & Periods: "We sell
primarily at auction,
liquidation of estates,
collections"
Appraisal Service Available
    Directions: 2 Miles E on
    Rte 40 off Exit 5 I-70

Wheeling

FIX 'N STRIP & ANTIQUES
1114 McColloch St 26003
304 233-1640   Est: 1969
Proprietor: Pat Miller
Hours: Mon-Sat 9-5
Types & Periods: Furniture
& Miscellaneous
Appraisal Service Available
    Directions: 16th St Exit off
    I-70

Side Chair, Golden Oak.
Reminiscent of Mission style.

STATE OF WISCONSIN

Abbotsford

DOUBLE ACRES ANTIQUES
Hwy 13   54405
715 654-2313
Proprietor: Dorothy Mazza
Hours: Fri, Sat, Sun, Other
Days by Chance or
Appointment
Types & Periods: General
Line
Directions: 2 Miles N on
Hwy 13 & 1 Mile W

Appleton

ABOUT TIME ANTIQUE
115½ E College Ave
54911
414 734-3555   Est: 1978
Proprietor: M T Dreke, B
Smeester & J Schubert
Hours: Mon-Sat, By
Appointment, Eves
Types & Periods: Furniture,
China, Glass, Orientals,
Primitives, Jewelry
Appraisal Service Available
Directions: Downtown, a
Step Above the
Avenue-Across from
Gimbels

THE HODGE-PODGE
106 E Franklin St   54913
414 733-5901   Est: 1972
Proprietor: Robert L Geyer
Hours: Mon-Sat
Types & Periods: General
Line
Specialties: Antique Dolls
Appraisal Service Available
Directions: Right by City
Hall

ZOELK'S ANTIQUE & IRON
SHOP
3818 E Wise Ave   54911
414 733-9154   Est: 1967
Proprietor: C D Zoelk
Hours: By Chance
Types & Periods: General
Line, Glass, Primitives
Specialties: Iron Plant
Stands
Directions: On Rte 96
Btwn Appleton & Little
Chute

Berlin

FEATHER FIN & FOX
Rte 2   54923
414 361-1833   Est: 1962
Proprietor: Louis M Weiss
Hours: Daily, Closed Mon
Types & Periods: General
Line
Specialties: Lamps,
Furniture, Repair & Refinish
Appraisal Service Available
Directions: 2 Miles E on
Hwy 116 then N 3 Miles to
end of Willard Rd

Boulder Junction

ARVILLA'S ANTIQUE SHOP
54512
715 385-2143
Proprietor: Arvilla M Doss
Hours: Daily, Weekends
10-5, Sun 10-4
Types & Periods: Pine
Country Furniture, Copper,
Brass, Primitives

Burlington

ANNE STOFFEL'S
ANTIQUES
RR 5, Box 58   53105
414 537-2335
Hours: By Appointment,
By Chance
Types & Periods: Primitives,
Lamps, Furniture
Directions: On Hwy 83 at
the Schall Rd, Halfway
between Burlington &
Hwy 50

Cedarburg

DOROTHY GALLUN
ANTIQUES
1034 E Bridge St   53012
414 377-9250
Proprietor: Dorothy Gallun
Types & Periods: General
Line

EVIE'S ANTIQUES
Cleveland & Madison Ave
53012
414 377-3456
Proprietor: Evelyn Ritter
Hours: Daily, By Chance
Types & Periods: Furniture,
Glassware, Primitives,
Lamps, China

GRANDPA'S BARN
ANTIQUES
W 61 N 510 Washington
Ave   53012
414 377-7710   Est: 1969
Proprietor: Pat Boeck
Hours: Tues-Sat 11-5,
Fri Eve 7-9
Types & Periods: Furniture
(19th Century) Country &
Victorian
Specialties: Antique
Fashions, Furniture
Restoration & Refinishing
Appraisal Service Available
Directions: South end of
Downtown Area, On East
Side of St

STONE MILL ANTIQUE
CORNER INC
W 53 N 684 Washington
53012
414 377-9240   Est: 1973
Proprietor: Lois Gara
Hours: Daily, Weekends
Types & Periods: Primitives,
Tools, Toys, General Line
Directions: N End of
Cedarburg, 3 doors S of
General Store

Chippewa Falls

WHITE COTTAGE
ANTIQUES
Rte 5, Box 543   54729
715 382-4242
Proprietor: Marianna
Hanson
Hours: By Appointment,
By Chance
Types & Periods: General
Line

Cleveland

RAVEN NEST ANTIQUES
Rte 1   53015
414 693-8428
Proprietor: Gerald
Shafranski
Types & Periods: General
Line

Colgate

**BRAEBURN VIEW
ANTIQUES**
                               53017
414 246-3878
Proprietor: The Willard
Melvilles
Hours: By Appointment,
By Chance, Closed Sun
Types & Periods: Primitives,
Pattern Glass, China, Danish
& Limited Edition Plates
Directions: 2½ Miles E of
J, 5 Miles W of US 41

Delafield

THE ENCORE SHOP
630 Milwaukee St   53018
414 646-8738   Est: 1968
Proprietor: Evelyn M
Schoen
Hours: Daily 11-5:30,
Sun 1-5, Closed Tues
Types & Periods: Press &
Art Glass, China, Furniture,
Frames, Clocks, Collectibles,
Lamps
Directions: 30 Miles W of
Milwaukee off I-94

THE STEEPLE
606 Genesee St   53018
414 646-8565
Proprietor: Ray & Ruth
Brehmer
Hours: Daily, Weekends
9:30-5:30, Sun 1-5
Types & Periods: Furniture,
Clocks, Brass, China, Lamps

Dodgeville

**THE WOODSHED
ANTIQUES**
                               53533
608 935-3896

Proprietor: William
Treweek
Types & Periods: General
Line
Directions: 5 Miles N on
Hwy 23

Eagle

**EAGLE ANTIQUES &
STRIPPERS**
Rte 2, Box 82   53119
414 594-2362
Proprietor: The
Armentrouts
Types & Periods: Furniture,
China, Primitives,
Depression Glass
Specialties: Furniture
Stripping

**KETTLE MORAINE
ANTIQUES**
Hwy 59   53119
414 594-2326
Proprietor: Mary Berglund
Hours: Daily 10-6, Closed
Tues
Types & Periods: Furniture,
Glassware, China, Primitives,
Collectibles, Wagon Wheels
Directions: 12 Miles W of
Waukesha, 2½ miles N of
Eagle

Eagle River

THE HOUSE OF ANTIQUES
Hwy 70   54521
715 479-8650
Proprietor: Mrs Evelyn
Miller
Hours: Daily, Weekends,
May 1-Nov 1, Closed Sun
Types & Periods: General
Line

Eau Claire

COLLECTORS III
1009 E Lexington Blvd
                   54701
715 832-6319
Proprietor: Ed, Flip &
Candy Davis
Hours: By Appointment
Types & Periods: China,
Glass, Quilts, Accessories

Edgerton

MILDRED'S ANTIQUES
20 N Henry St   53534
608 884-3031   Est: 1940
Proprietor: Mildred
Harrison
Hours: Mon-Sat
Types & Periods: Glass,
China, Oil Paintings,
Jewelry, Furniture
Appraisal Service Available
Directions: Downtown,
1 block W of US 51

WARTMANNIA ANTIQUES
Box 336A, Rte 2   53534
608 884-8414   Est: 1973
Proprietor: William J
Wartmann
Hours: Tues-Sat
Types & Periods: Early 19th
Century to Art Deco
Specialties: China, Glass,
Brass, Silver, Oriental Rugs,
Pictures
Appraisal Service Available
Directions: W of 184,
1 Mile on Caladonia Rd

Elkhart Lake

**SIEBKEN RESORT
ANTIQUE SHOP**
                   53020
414 876-2600
Proprietor: Mrs O S
Moeller
Types & Periods: General
Line
Directions: On the Lake,
2 blocks from Hwy 67

Ephraim

RED BARN ANTIQUES
Hwy 42   54211
414 854-2045
Proprietor: Ms Binder,
McAghan & Wright
Hours: Summer Only
Types & Periods: Primitives,
Silver, Glass, Furniture, Toys

Evansville

**CHARLES
SHANNON-MAGNOLIA
HOUSE**
Hwy 213, Rte 2   53536
608 882-5666
Proprietor: Charles
Shannon
Hours: Daily, Weekends
8-9
Types & Periods: Art Glass,
Period Furniture, Clocks,
Paintings, Metals
Specialties: Lamps,
Paperweights
Appraisal Service Available
    Directions: 4½ Miles S on
    Hwy 213

THE RED DOOR SHOP
Hwy 138   53536
608 882-5911
Proprietor: Eunice &
George Mattakat
Hours: Daily, 1-5,
Closed Mon & Tues
Types & Periods: China,
Glass, Lamps, Pottery,
Furniture
    Directions: Rte 1 at
    Cooksville, Hwy 138

Fountain City

**THE RED LANTERN &
STRIPPERS**
                    54629
608 687-9751/8346
Proprietor: Norm & Mary
Berube
Hours: Daily, 10-5,
Closed Sun thru Tues
Types & Periods: Furniture
& Miscellaneous
    Directions: On the Great
    Mississippi

Franklin

**GEORGIAN HOUSE OF
ANTIQUES**
10209 W Loomis Rd
                    51132
414 425-7330
Hours: Daily, Closed Mon,
By Appointment

Types & Periods: Victorian &
Primitive Furniture, Clocks,
Brass, Copper, Cut Glass,
Steins, Lamps
    Directions: 2 blocks W of
    Hwy 100

Friendship

FRIENDSHIP ANTIQUES
Main St   53934
608 339-3130   Est: 1960
Proprietor: Foy, Eloise,
Kneisel
Hours: Daily, 9-5,
Sun 1-5
Types & Periods: Glass,
China, Silver, Dolls,
Furniture, Victorian
Specialties: "Big Selection
of Most Types of Antiques"
Appraisal Service Available
    Directions: Right on
    Hwy 13

Galesville

THE LITTLE RED SHED
RFD 1   54630
608 539-2621
Proprietor: Jackie Siefkas
Hours: Daily 10-6, Closed
Mon & Thurs, By
Appointment
Types & Periods: Primitives,
General Line, "Featuring
The Loft Gallery in June thru
Aug"

Genesee Depot

**THE WEATHERVANE
ANTIQUES**
W 313 S 4343, Hwy 83
                    53118
414 968-2886   Est: 1974
Proprietor: Rosemary
Beutner
Hours: Daily, Weekends
Types & Periods: Empire
Furniture, Oak, General Line
Specialties: Needlework,
(Quilts), Weather Vanes
    Directions: In Post Office
    Bldg on Hwy 83

Germantown

BLACK HORSE ANTIQUES
Box 85   53022
414 251-8315
Proprietor: Betty & Vern
Barquist
Hours: By Appointment
Types & Periods: Furniture,
Primitives, Collectibles
    Directions: On Hwy 145

MARDI'S ANTIQUES
Pilgrim Rd   53022
414 251-1244
Proprietor: Kurt & Mardi
Westenberger
Hours: By Appointment,
By Chance
Types & Periods: Country
Furniture & Accessories
    Directions: 1 block N of
    Hwy 145

Grafton

THE JUNE BUG SHOP
Hwy C Stonecroft   53024
414 377-5730
Proprietor: June Greasby
Hours: Daily, 10-5,
Sun 1-5, Closed Mon
Types & Periods: General
Line
    Directions: 2 Miles S of
    Port Washington in
    Stonecroft

Green Bay

BARNEY'S ANTIQUES
901 W Mason   54303
414 435-1208   Est: 1974
Proprietor: Dee & Art
Rassner
Hours: Daily, Sun by
Appointment
Types & Periods: Furniture,
Glassware, Lamps,
Ironstones
Specialties: Dolls
Appraisal Service Available
    Directions: Corner of W
    Mason & 11th St

DE WITT'S ANTIQUES
1739 University Ave
54302
414 432-2234   Est: 1944
Proprietor: Bob De Witt
Hours: Daily 9-5, Closed
Sun
Types & Periods: Art Glass,
Victorian Furniture, Jewelry
Specialties: Jewelry
Appraisal Service Available
Directions: Hwy 51 N

HIS AND HERS RED BARN ANTIQUES
1860 Cardinal Ln   54303
414 434-1790   Est: 1973
Proprietor: Bonnie & Bill
Kanzenbach
Hours: Daily 1-Sundown
Types & Periods: Refinished
Primitives, General Line
Specialties: Stained Glass
Windows, Antique & Made
to Order
Directions: US 41-141 N,
West on Lineville 2 Miles

900 SOUTH JACKSON ANTIQUES
900 S Jackson   54301
414 435-7909   Est: 1973
Proprietor: Jonathan Alk
Hours: Daily, Weekends,
By Appointment
Types & Periods: Country
Store Fixtures, Scientific
Instruments, Leaded
Windows, Architectural
Items, Lighting Fixtures,
Paper Material
Appraisal Service Available
Directions. Corner Porlier
at Jackson, 2 blocks E of
Hwy 57

PALMER'S B PALMER'S COLLECTOR'S CORNER
898 Elmore   54303
414 437-7831   Est: 1961
Proprietor: James Palmer
Hours: Daily 10-5:30, Sat
9:30-5:30
Types & Periods: Ancient
Primitive to Modern
Collectibles
Specialties: Glass
(Iridescent), Military Relics,
Lamps
Appraisal Service Available
Directions: W Side of
Green Bay, Dousman to
Ashland, 2 blocks N to
Elmore

SCHWARTZ ANTIQUE SHOP
1013 Main St   54301
414 432-3832   Est: 1935
Proprietor: Art & Ruth
Schwartz
Hours: Daily, By
Appointment
Types & Periods: Primitives,
General Line
Specialties: Furniture
(Refinishing & Lamp Repair)
Appraisal Service Available
Directions: Near Webster
Hwy 141

SHIRLEY-RED'S ANTIQUES
1344 Main St   54302
414 437-3596   Est: 1959
Proprietor: Shirley Brosig
Hours: Daily, By
Appointment
Types & Periods: Glass,
China, Furniture, Oriental,
Dolls, Jewelry, Lamps,
Decorator Items
Specialties: Glass,
Primitives, Advertising,
Brewiana
Appraisal Service Available
Directions: "At Three
Corners"

Hartford

ERIN ANTIQUES
1691 Hwy 83 S   53027
414 673-4680
Proprietor: Audrey Marty
Hours: Daily
Types & Periods: General
Line
Specialties: China, Glass
Directions: On Hwy 83 1/2
block S of Hwy 167, Holy
Hill Area

FURNITURE DOCTORS INC
25 S Main   53027
414 673-3100   Est: 1972
Proprietor: Galen Brunner
Hours: Daily, Closed at
Noon Sat & All Day Sun
Types & Periods:
Midwestern Country
Furniture,
Turn-of-the-Century Oak,
General Line
Directions: 25 S Main to
the Rear of the Shell
Station

Hartland

THE BIRD CAGE
3115 Hwy 83   53029
414 367-6084   Est: 1967
Proprietor: Leah G
Wolcott
Hours: Daily, Weekends,
12-5
Types & Periods: General
Line, Collectibles, Furniture
Directions: On Hwy 83 3
miles N of I-94, 1½ miles
S of Hwy 16

MONCHES COUNTRY STORE
Rte 2, Box 118   53029
414 628-1680
Proprietor: Nancy Woll
Types & Periods: General
Line
Directions: N of Hartland
on E, W of Meno Falls
on Q

Hustisford

THE COUNTRY PEDDLER
312 W Juneau St   53034
414 349-3423
Proprietor: Sally & Walter
Schockmel
Hours: Daily 9:30-5, Sun
11-5
Types & Periods: China,
Glass, Furniture, General
Line
Directions: Hwy 60 &
Hwy E

Janesville

CENTURY FARM ANTIQUES
5331 Cemetery Rd, Rte 5
53545
608 752-0092   Est: 1965
Proprietor: Dorothy &
Charles Risch
Hours: Daily 10:30-5:30,
Sun 1-5:30
Types & Periods: General
Line, Pine, Walnut, Cherry,
Oak, Rough & Refinished
Furniture, China, Glass, Tin,
Primitives, Pottery
Specialties: Lamp Parts,
Shades for Kerosene &
Aladdin Lamps
Directions: 2 Miles W of
Afton Rd btwn Janesville
& Beloit on Rte 5

**COLONIAL ACRES
ANTIQUES**
Rte 2, Hwy 14   53545
608 752-8101   Est: 1974
Proprietor: D R Graham
Hours: Daily
Types & Periods: "Whatever
we can find"
Directions: 1 Mile SE of
I-90 on Bypass 14

THE EVERYTHING SHOPPE
407 W Milwaukee St
53545
608 754-7031   Est: 1971
Proprietor: Loretta
Krueger
Hours: Daily 10-5, Sat
10-4, Closed Mon
Types & Periods: General
Line, Collectibles, Furniture
Directions: Downtown

JAEGER ANTIQUES
459 S Randall Ave   53545
608 754-8585
Proprietor: Josephine
Jaeger
Hours: Mon-Sat 12-4:30,
Sun 1-4:30
Types & Periods: Period
Furniture, Pennsylvania
Country-All over 100 years
old, Art & Cut Glass,
Pewter, Brass, Silver, China
Specialties: Furniture
Appraisal Service Available
Directions: Exit 11, W off
I-90, 2nd Turn Left

Lake Geneva

**THE HOUSE OF
TREASURES**
P O Box 89   53147
414 248-8333
Proprietor: Alyce & Lou
Nesslar
Hours: By Appointment
Types & Periods: General
Line

Land o' Lakes

PHIL ELSCHNER
Box 224   54540
715 547-3301
Proprietor: Phil Elschner
Hours: WHOLESALE
ONLY
Types & Periods: Art Glass,
Porcelain, Imports

SNOW GOOSE ANTIQUES
54540
715 547-3820   Est: 1972
Proprietor: Marilyn Nagel
Hours: Mon-Sat 9-5
Types & Periods: General
Line, Furniture
Directions: 2 blocks W on
B Off US 45, Across from
Golf Course

Lannon

BETTI ANNE'S ANTIQUES
7291 N Lannon Rd   53046
Hours: Daily, Weekends
11-5
Types & Periods: Primitives,
Glassware, Furniture,
Collectibles
Directions: Hwy Y & Hwy
74, Corner of Main St &
Lannon Rd

Lomira

MARTIN HOUSE
Rte 1, Box 15   53048
414 269-4455
Proprietor: Joe & Cindy
Martin
Hours: By Appointment,
By Chance
Types & Periods: Furniture,
Country Things
Directions: On Hwy 175,
1/2 Mile S of Lomira

Madison

THE ANTIQUE GALLERY
702 N Midvale Blvd 53705
608 238-6600   Est: 1973
Proprietor: W
Bogdanowicz
Hours: Daily 11-4, Closed
Sun
Types & Periods: Prints,
Maps, From 1600-1900
Directions: Hilldale
Shopping Center

KAPPEL'S CLOCK SHOP
2250 Sherman Ave   53704
608 244-6165   Est: 1970
Proprietor: Karl K Kappel
Hours: Daily, Weekends
10-5, Closed Mon

Types & Periods: Clocks,
Furniture
Specialties: Clocks (Repair
& Restoration)
Appraisal Service Available
Directions: Off Hwy 30 1/2
Mile Corner of Sherman
Ave & Fordem

THE LAST STRAW
9 Grey Birch Trail   53717
608 831-0103   Est: 1971
Proprietor: Joanna B
Pruess
Hours: By Appointment,
Show Dealer
Types & Periods: Country &
Formal Furniture, 1800-1920,
Glassware, Jewelry
Specialties: Furniture
(Restored)

**NEWPORT
GALLERIES-PLOUGH INN**
3402 Monroe St   53711
608 231-1881   Est: 1970
Proprietor: Lorraine Wilke
& Rita Wlodarczyk
Hours: Daily
Types & Periods: China,
Glass, Kimonos, Lead
Soldiers, Furniture,
Primitives
Appraisal Service Available
Directions: "In landmark
house built in 1853, From
downtown, W toward UW
Stadium, W on Monroe"

**WHAT WOULD MOTHER
SAY? ANTIQUE SHOPPE**
422 North St   53704
608 241-0453   Est: 1974
Proprietor: James F
Babcock
Hours: By Appointment,
By Chance
Types & Periods: Wisc
Primitives & Ethnic Items,
Period Furniture, Folk Art,
Quilts
Appraisal Service Available
Directions: 2 blocks from
E Johnson St

Manitowish Waters

THE COUNTRY STORE
54545
715 543-8461   Est: 1972
Proprietor: E Wanatka III
Hours: Daily

Types & Periods: 19th
Century Furniture
Specialties: Early & Rare
Stoneware
  Directions: 1/4 Mile off
  Hwy 51 on County
  Trunk W

Mazomanie

AMERICAN ANTIQUES
  Hwy 14   53560
  608 767-2608   Est: 1962
  Proprietor: Karen & Dick
  Rahn
  Hours: Weekends, By
  Appointment, By Chance
Types & Periods: Furniture,
Glass, Jewelry, Indian, Folk
Art, Lamps, China
Specialties: Furniture
(Country)
Appraisal Service Available
  Directions: 24 Miles W of
  Madison

Menasha

THE WOOD SHED
  540-544 Broad St   54952
  414 725-3347   Est: 1971
  Proprietor: Ted O Kloehn
  Hours: Daily, Weekends,
  Sat 12-6
Types & Periods:
Collectibles, Primitives,
Furniture,
Turn-of-the-Century
Specialties: Furniture
(Restoration)
  Directions: Downtown 1
  block from Post Office

Menomonee Falls

LIESEL'S ANTIQUE
  Mill St   53051
  414 251-3736
  Proprietor: Mrs W
  Salzmann
  Hours: By Appointment,
  By Chance
Types & Periods: Lamps,
Bric-A-Brac, Christmas
Plates, Glassware, China
  Directions: Btwn Main St
  (Hwy 74) & Appleton Ave
  (Hwy 175)

Milton

LIGMAN'S ANTIQUE SHOP
  100 Front St   53563
  608 868-7506   Est: 1972
  Proprietor: Harley &
  Marlene Ligman
  Hours: By Appointment,
  By Chance
Types & Periods: Victorian &
Oak Furniture
Appraisal Service Available
  Directions: 4 Miles off I-90
  Janesville Exit

Milwaukee

MILWAUKEE CLUSTER
  Directions: Shops
  scattered throughout City
  with heavier concentration
  on E Section bounded on
  E by N Downer
  (2000-3000 Blocks),
  Moving W to N Oakland
  (4000 Block), Bounded by
  E Capitol Dr (1000 Block)
  on N & E Park Pl (1000
  Block) on S

**ASTOR GALLERIES
VICTORIAN SHOP**
  2630 N Downer Ave
                  53211
  414 962-0272   Est: 1972
  Proprietor: Larry L Stussy
  & Thomas Gomez
  Hours: Daily, By
  Appointment
Types & Periods: General
Line, Glass, Furniture,
Printings, Silver, Jewelry, Art
Glass
Specialties: Tiffany, Art
Glass
Appraisal Service Available
  Directions: E Side near
  Lake Michigan, 4 blocks S
  of Univ of Wisc

**BRAUN'S ANTIQUES
WHOLESALE FURNITURE**
  3327 W National   53215
  414 671-0060   Est: 1973
  Proprietor: Richard Braun
  Hours: Weekends, 10-4,
  By Appointment
Types & Periods: American
Furniture Wholesale Only

COLES ANTIQUES
  1404 S 11th St   53204
  414 645-3610   Est: 1964
  Proprietor: Veronica A
  Cole
  Hours: Daily 12-6, Sat 9-5,
  Closed Sun
Types & Periods: Furniture,
Telephones, Watches
  Directions: 11th &
  Greenfield, Next to Post
  Office

**CONSIGNMENT CENTER
OF MILWAUKEE**
  5032 W Burleigh   53210
  414 447-0777   Est: 1974
  Proprietor: Mr & Mrs L
  Zampino
  Hours: Daily, Sun & Mon
  by Appointment
Types & Periods: Furniture,
Glass, China, Primitives,
Collectibles, Jewelry
Specialties: Furniture,
American & European
Appraisal Service Available
  Directions: NW Area of
  Milwaukee at 51st &
  Burleigh

EAST-WAY ANTIQUE SHOP
  845 N Marshall St   53202
  414 272-2640
  Proprietor: Carol Paulson
Types & Periods: Steins,
General Line

**FABULOUS FINDS
ANTIQUES**
  4018 N Oakland Ave
                  53211
  414 332-0201   Est: 1970
  Proprietor: Froda B Kanter
  Hours: Daily
Types & Periods: Primitive,
Country, American, French,
English, Wall Pieces, Small
Furniture

GABRIEL RUG CO INC
  420 E Wells St   53202
  414 276-2840   Est: 1924
  Proprietor: Lee N Gabriel
  Hours: Mon-Sat 9-5, Sat
  9-4, Eves by Appointment
Types & Periods: Oriental
Rugs, Persian, Caucasian,
Turkish, Turkoman, Chinese,
India
Appraisal Service Available
  Directions: Downtown 2½
  blocks E of City Hall or
  1½ blocks N of Pfister
  Hotel

Milwaukee Cont'd

GALLERY II INC
2563 N Downer Ave
53211
414 332-9570   Est: 1964
Proprietor: Bernard A
Brown
Hours: Daily, 10-5,
Closed Sun
Types & Periods: Primitive
Art, African Sculpture,
Oceanic, American Indian
Artifacts, Pre-Columbian &
Antiquities

THE GOOD OLDE DAYS
1209 E Brady St   53202
414 278-9403   Est: 1972
Proprietor: Teresita C
Ward
Hours: Daily 11-7,
Weekends 11-5
Types & Periods: Furniture,
Jewelry, Stained Glass,
Lamps, Glassware
Directions: Lower E Side
1 Mile E of Downtown

GRAF'S ANTIQUES
3018 W Lincoln   53215
414 384-1210   Est: 1967
Proprietor: Joe Graf
Hours: By Appointment,
By Chance
Types & Periods: General
Line
Specialties: Oriental
Appraisal Service Available
Directions: I-94 E to 35th
St Exit, S to 2300 block,
Left on Lincoln Ave

**GRACE GRAVES-HAVILAND
MATCHING SERVICE**
3939 N Harcourt Place
53211
414 964-9180   Est: 1975
Proprietor: Grace Graves
Hours: By Appointment,
By Chance
Types & Periods: French
Haviland China, Collectibles
Specialties: "I will identify
Haviland patterns & seek
replacement pieces"
Directions: 15 Minutes N
of Downtown, 1 block W
of Intersection of E
Capitol & N Lake Drives

**MID AMERICA ANTIQUE
CENTER**
341 N Milwaukee   53202
414 276-0605   Est: 1974
Proprietor: Incorporated
Hours: Daily 10-5, Sun
12-5
Types & Periods: 75 Dealers
Under One Roof, General
Line, Collectables
Appraisal Service Available
Directions: Downtown Just
Off Expressway

**MILWAUKEE AUCTION
GALLERIES**
4747 W. Bradley Rd
53223
414 355-5054   Est: 1956
Proprietor: Janice Kuhn
Hours: By Appointment
Types & Periods: Furniture,
Glassware, Porcelains,
Silver, Oriental Art & Rugs,
Master Paintings,
Engravings, Estate
Furnishing and Jewelry.
Appraisal Service Available
Directions: 5 Minutes West
of Expressway, Good
Hope Exit.

PICCADILLY ANTIQUES
1732 S Muskego Ave
53204
414 645-6750   Est: 1970
Proprietor: Blanche
Kaczmarek
Hours: Daily, Closed Sun,
By Appointment
Types & Periods: Pewter,
Brass, Primitive, Victorian,
Art Noveau, Art Deco,
Silver, Copper, China,
Glassware, Furniture,
Lamps, Dolls
Specialties: Clocks
Directions: Approx 15
blocks W of Freeway 194
Mitchell St Exit

**RUELLE'S FURNITURE
CENTER**
905 S 16th St   53204
414 383-0260   Est: 1973
Proprietor: Ambrose
Ruelle
Hours: Daily, 9-6,
Closed Sun
Types & Periods: Furniture

SECOND HAND ROSE
4600 W Burleigh   53021
414 272-5795   Est: 1971
Proprietor: C Kumferman

Hours: Mon-Sat 10-6
Types & Periods: English,
French, American, Victorian
Specialties: Doll Houses,
Miniatures
Appraisal Service Available
Directions: Near NW Side
of Town

SECOND HAND ROSE
1221 W Vliet   53021
414 272-5795   Est: 1971
Proprietor: C Kumferman
Hours: Mon-Sat 10-6
Types & Periods: English,
French, American, Victorian
Specialties: Doll Houses,
Miniatures
Appraisal Service Available
Directions: Downtown

**VERONA SUNVOLD
ANTIQUES-AMERICAN**
2867 N Marietta Ave
53211
414 962-2566
Proprietor: Verona
Sunvold
Hours: By Appointment
Types & Periods: Lamps,
Shades, Antique Fabric

**VILLAGE ANTIQUE
CENTER**
1800 E Capitol Dr   53211
414 332-8484   Est: 1972
Proprietor: Arnold J
Porchep
Hours: Daily 10:30-5,
Closed Sun
Types & Periods:
Collectibles, Prints,
Engravings, Etchings
Specialties: Postcards,
Currier & Ives, Frames
Appraisal Service Available
Directions: NE Corner of
Oakland & Capitol Dr

**DONALD M WALL ART
GALLERIES INC**
631 N Milwaukee St
53202
414 276-9611   Est: 1847
Proprietor: Gerald F Wall
Hours: Daily 9-4
Types & Periods: General
Line, Estate Liquidations,
Auctions every 5-6 weeks
Specialties: Rugs (Persian),
Bronzes

**WHITE SHUTTERS
ANTIQUE SHOP**
771 N Jefferson St   53202
414 271-8866
Proprietor: Dorothy M
Taylor
Hours: Daily 11-5, By
Appointment
Types & Periods: General
Line, Collectibles

Monona

JEAN LINEWEBER
5216 Mesa Rd   53716
608 222-3787
Proprietor: R H & Jean
Lineweber
Hours: By Appointment
Types & Periods: 18th &
19th Century Country
Furniture & Accessories
Directions: Near Madison

Mount Horeb

KELLER TRADING CO
132 E Main   53572
000 437 5071   Est: 1971
Proprietor: Wallace Keller
Hours: Daily
Types & Periods: From 1800
to Reproductions, Primitives,
Glassware, General Line
Specialties: Furniture
Directions: On Hwy 18-151
Middle of Town

Mukwonago

ANTIQUES 'N THINGS
Rte 3, Box 324   53149
414 594-2544
Proprietor: Thea R
Tannert
Hours: Daily, 10-5,
By Appointment, By
Chance, Closed Jan 15-
April 15
Types & Periods: Furniture,
Lamps, China, Pressed &
Cut Glass, Frames
Directions: On Hwy 99, 5
Miles W of Mukwonago,
1/2 Mile E of Hwy E

New Berlin

FLORENTINE'S ANTIQUES
18715 W Greenfield
                   53515
414 782-5080
Proprietor: Florentine
Ruck
Hours: Daily 11-5
Types & Periods: English,
American, General Line

North Lake

**OLD NORTH CHURCH
ANTIQUES**
Hwy 83   53064
414 966-2182
Proprietor: Dale A
Sorensen
Hours: Daily 1-5
Types & Periods: Country &
Victorian Furniture, Brass
Beds, Oak Tables,
Cupboards, Coins, Dolls,
Coin Operated Devices,
Collectibles

Oconomowoc

LINCOLN ANTIQUES
291 Lincoln Rd   53066
414 474-4274
Proprietor: Robert Egbert
Hours: Daily
Types & Periods: Furniture,
Primitives, Glassware
Directions: From
Oconomowoc Take Hwy
67 N 8 Miles to Ashippun,
Then 1 Mile E on Lincoln

MAPLETON ANTIQUES
8755 Brown St   53066
414 474-4514   Est: 1971
Proprietor: Bob & Lorraine
Christenson
Hours: Daily, By Chance
Types & Periods: General
Line

YE OLD ANTIQUES
38726 McMahon Rd
                   53066
414 474-4380
Proprietor: The Weides
Hours: Daily, 9-5

Types & Periods: Primitives,
Rough & Fine Furniture,
Crocks, General Line
Directions: From
Oconomowoc take Hwy 67
N for 3½ Miles, Then W
on McMahon Rd

Omro

ANN'S ANTIQUES
132 W Main St   54963
414 685-5555   Est: 1972
Proprietor: Mrs Ann M
Kuhnz
Hours: Thurs-Sat 1-5, By
Appointment
Types & Periods: Glassware,
Furniture, Primitives, Clocks,
Lamps
Directions: On Hwy 21, 9
Miles W of Hwy 41 at
Oshkosh

Oshkosh

ANTIQUE CORNER
1132 N Main St   54901
414 231-7644
Proprietor: P K Williams
Hours: Mon-Sat 1-4:30,
Mornings by Appointment
Types & Periods: China,
Glass, Furniture, Books,
Clocks, Collectibles
Appraisal Service Available

ATTIC ANTIQUES
132 W Sixth Ave   54901
414 236 1623
Proprietor: Fred Rates
Hours: Daily 10-5, Sun by
Appointment
Types & Periods: Glassware,
Clocks, Military Items

BEE'S ANTIQUES
1023 S Main St   54901
414 231-4938
Proprietor: Beatrice Van
Der Kellen
Hours: Daily, Weekends
9-5
Types & Periods: General
Line, Curios, Collectibles

Oshkosh   Cont'd

MARLEY'S ANTIQUES
256 W 8th Ave   54901
414 231-1320
Proprietor: Marlene Faust
Hours: By Appointmemt,
By Chance
Types & Periods: Furniture,
Glass, China, Brass, Copper,
Depression Glass,
Collectibles

RATES ANTIQUES
711 Oregon St   54901
414 231-5622
Proprietor: Harvey &
Margaret Rates
Hours: Daily, 10-5, Fri 'til 9,
Closed Sun
Types & Periods: China,
Glass, Furniture, Clocks,
Dolls, Pottery, Paintings,
Guns, Primitives

**THE RIGHT ANTIQUE &
AUCTION CO**
1606 Oregon St   54901
414 231-6616
Proprietor: Col R C
Behnke
Hours: Daily 9-5, By
Appointment
Types & Periods: General
Line, Auctions

**SAWYER CREEK
ANTIQUES**
501 Ohio St   54901
414 231-1492   Est: 1973
Proprietor: Vi Richards,
Mae Cobb, Marie Leach
Hours: Mon-Sat 10-5, Sun
By Appointment
Types & Periods: Furniture,
China, Glassware, Copper,
Brass & Lighting Fixtures
Specialties: Primitives
Appraisal Service Available
Directions: Take Hwy 41
to 9th St Exit, Then E on
9th to Ohio St, Then Left
to 5th

THE TRADING POST
400 E Irving   54901
414 235-5375
Proprietor: Dorothy
Glidden
Hours: Mon, Tues & Thurs
11:30-5, Wed & Fri
11:30-4, Sat 10-4

Types & Periods: Primitives,
Furniture, Dishes,
Collectibles, General Line
Directions: At Grand

Park Falls

DIXIE'S TREASURE CHEST
119 N 2nd   54552
715 762-4771   Est: 1958
Proprietor: Erika Carden
Hours: Mon-Sat 10-5, By
Appointment
Types & Periods: General
Line
Specialties: European China
Appraisal Service Available
Directions: Downtown

Pewaukee

A SUMMER PLACE
Duplainville Rd   53071
414 691-1120
Proprietor: Joan Griswold
& Bea Kehoss
Hours: June-Oct
Types & Periods:
Collectibles, General Line
Directions: S off Hwy 190
or Springdale Rd, W on
Green Rd to Duplainville
Rd

CANDLESTICK ANTIQUES
Edgewood   53072
414 691-3490
Proprietor: Mary J
Kerrigan & Virginia
Stuhlman
Hours: Daily 11:30-4:30,
Closed Mon
Types & Periods: General
Line
Directions: 1 Mile N of
I-94

**COLLECTORS WAYSIDE
HAVEN**
Duplainville Rd   53072
414 691-2432
Proprietor: Charlotte &
William Harland
Hours: By Appointment,
By Chance
Types & Periods: US
Calendar Plates, Souvenir
China, Glass, Dolls Dishes,
Masonic China & Glass,
Paperweights, Paperiana
Directions: Btwn Hwys V &
190 (Capitol Dr)

Phelps

**HACKLEY HOUSE
ANTIQUES**
Box 117   54554
715 545-2759
Proprietor: Mary Jean
Myers
Hours: Daily, 10-5,
Closed Sun
Types & Periods: Primitives,
Victorian Furniture

Portage

**MALONEY'S ANTIQUE
SHOP**
127½ W Cook St   53901
608 742-3133   Est: 1925
Proprietor: William H
Maloney
Hours: Daily 9-5, Closed
Mon
Types & Periods: Glassware,
Furniture
Specialties: Glass (Art &
Sandwich), Paintings
Appraisal Service Available
Directions: In Main Block

Random Lake

THE SALT BOX HOUSE
Rte 1   53075
Proprietor: W Allan &
Bernice Wendel
Hours: By Appointment,
By Chance
Types & Periods: Pattern
Glass, Collectibles
Directions: 9 Miles N of W
Bend, Hwy 144 & 28

Rubicon

WEST WIND ANTIQUES
154 A Hwy P   53078
414 474-4593
Proprietor: Nancy Andrich
Hours: Mon, Wed-Thurs
1-5
Types & Periods: General
Line
Directions: 4 Miles N of
Mapleton, 6 Miles S of
Rubicon on Hwy P

Shawano

MATHIE'S WHITEHOUSE FARM ANTIQUES
Box 242   54166
715 524-4421
Proprietor: Doreen Mathie
Hours: Daily, Closed Winter
Types & Periods: General Line, Furniture
Specialties: Primitives
Directions: County Trunk A off Hwy 47-55

MEADOWCREST ANTIQUES
1403 E Green Bay St,
P O Box 288   54166
715 526-2210   Est: 1968
Proprietor: Marjorie Klein
Hours: Daily
Types & Periods: General Line, Primitives, Furniture
Appraisal Service Available
Directions: On Hwy 55-47-29 at County HH

SALT CELLAR ANTIQUES
1345 Zingler Shawano
                     54166
715 526-5645
Proprietor: Jacky Popp & Phyllis Tinsman
Hours: By Appointment, By Chance
Types & Periods: Victorian Jewelry, Pattern Glass, Paper & General Line
Specialties: Victorian Jewelry (Largest Selection in Area)
Appraisal Service Available
Directions: Hwy 47 N to H

SALT CELLAR ANTIQUES
Pinemead Rd   54166
715 526-3814
Proprietor: Jacky Popp & Phyllis Tinsman
Hours: By Appointment, By Chance
Types & Periods: Victorian Jewelry, Pattern Glass, Paper & General Line
Specialties: Victorian Jewelry
Appraisal Service Available
Directions: 1 Mile E on H to Pinemead Rd

Sister Bay

THE RAIL FENCE
Hwy 57   54234
414 854-4654
Proprietor: Ethel & Ron Bitters
Hours: Daily 10-5, Summer Only
Types & Periods: General Line
Directions: 1 Mile S Jct Hwy 42

Stoughton

ONLY YESTERDAY SHOP
Box 476   53589
608 873-7766   Est: 1968
Proprietor: Jon & Ada Irving
Hours: By Chance, Daily
Types & Periods: Furniture, Lamps, Pottery, Porcelain, Pressed & Cut Glass, Paintings, 1820-1920
Specialties: Glass
Appraisal Service Available

Superior

ATTIC ANTIQUES
4101 E 2nd St   54880
715 398-7051   Est: 1972
Proprietor: Don Love
Hours: Mon-Sat 9-5, By Appointment
Types & Periods: Glassware, Primitives, Paintings, Stained Glass, Art Glass, General Line
Appraisal Service Available
Directions: On Hwy 2 & 53 just as you enter town

CURIOSITY SHOP ANTIQUES
2331 Tower Ave   54880
715 394-4080   Est: 1956
Proprietor: Vivian & Bob Plunkett
Hours: Daily 12-5, By Chance
Types & Periods: China, Glassware, Silver, Lamps, Toys, Linens, Primitives
Directions: S on Hwy 35

KLINE'S KOLLECTABLES KORNER
701 Ogden Ave   54880
715 392-3251   Est: 1936
Proprietor: Karl Kline
Hours: Daily
Types & Periods: General Line
Specialties: Furniture

Sussex

MINDY'S ANTIQUES
W 220 N 5651 Townline Rd   53089
414 246-3183   Est: 1960
Proprietor: Betty & Reuben Mindemann
Hours: Daily
Types & Periods: New England Furniture & Accessories of 18th & Early 19th Centuries
Specialties: Furniture
Appraisal Service Available
Directions: "Corner of Silver Spring Dr Hwy V & Townline Rd Hwy VV, 2 Miles E of Sussex"

Theresa

THE WEAVING LOOM
Rte 1, Box 38   53091
414 488-3961
Proprietor: Catherine A Fleisner
Hours: Tues, Wed, Thurs 9-5, Sat & Sun 1-5
Types & Periods: Furniture, Collectibles, General Line
Directions: On Hwy 28 1/2 Mile W of Theresa

Tomahawk

LAURETTA'S ANTIQUES
Hwy 51   54481
715 282-5743
Proprietor: Gordon & Lauretta Shea
Hours: Open May 15-Oct 15 Daily, Closed Sun,
Types & Periods: Furniture, Art Glass, China, Primitives, Country Pieces
Directions: 10 Mile N of Town

Trempealeau

WEST PRAIRIE SQUARE
54661
608 539-2582
Proprietor: Janet Ecker
Hours: Daily 10:30-5:30,
Mon by Appointment
Types & Periods: Carnival &
Pressed Glass, Primitives
Directions: 3 Miles W of
Centerville

Wales

TY CARREG ANTIQUES
323 E Summit Rd   53183
414 968-2191
Proprietor: Geraldine
Henry
Hours: Daily
Types & Periods: "Browse
thru nostalgia", Primitives,
Period Furniture, China
Accessories
Directions: 7 Miles W of
Waukesha on Hwy 18,
1/4 Mile E of Hwy 83

Waukesha

**AIRPORT ANTIQUES &
RESALE SHOP**
Hwy JJ & Hwy F   53186
414 542-9105
Proprietor: Marie A
McDermott
Hours: Daily, 10-6,
Closed Mon
Types & Periods: China,
Glassware, Clocks, Dolls
Directions: Across from
the Airport

AUCTION DEPOT
301 N Grand   53186
414 542-8797   Est: 1968
Proprietor: Freddie Plehn
Types & Periods: Estate
Auctions
Appraisal Service Available
Directions: Downtown, 25
Miles W of Milwaukee

ROBERT H KRUGER
401 Madison St   53136
414 542-7722
Proprietor: Robert H
Kruger

Hours: Daily, 9-5,
Closed Sun
Types & Periods: Furniture,
Lamps, Fixtures, China,
Glass, Iron
Directions: Inbound Hwy
164 at Hwy 18

JUDIE PIEPER ANTIQUES
437 E North St   53186
414 544-6136   Est: 1969
Proprietor: Judie Pieper
Hours: Daily 10:30-5, Sun
1-5
Types & Periods: Country
Store, Advertiques, Saloon,
Ice Cream Parlour Fixtures
Specialties: Restoration of
Country Store Items
Directions: 2½ Miles S of
I-94 on Hwy 164

SNOW BIRD ANTIQUES
1596 E North St   53186
414 544-1240
Proprietor: Karla Johnson
& Rose Ann Tomasini
Hours: Daily, 10:30-5,
Sun 12-5, Closed Mon
Types & Periods: New
England, Pennsylvania
Dutch, Wisconsin Country
Furniture & Accessories
Directions: Just outside of
City on Hwy 164, 1 block
N of Moreland Blvd or 2
Miles S of I-94

Waunakee

MUENCHOW ENTERPRISES
119 W Main   53597
608 849-4774   Est: 1969
Proprietor: Eugene C
Muenchow
Hours: Daily, Weekends,
Closed on Sun
Types & Periods: General
Line, Furniture
Appraisal Service Available
Directions: On Hwy 113
Downtown 3 Miles from
Madison

**SCHALLES ANTIQUES &
TURQUOISE**
205 W Main St   53597
608 849-4690
Proprietor: Eleanore
Schalles & Katy Milling

Hours: Daily, Closed Sun
& Mon, By Appointment
Types & Periods: Art & Cut
Glass, Porcelain, Pottery,
Hand-Painted Plates &
Bowls, Primitives, Furniture,
Rugs
Specialties: Rugs, Jewelry
(Indian), Pictures
Appraisal Service Available
Directions: 12 Miles NW of
Madison, On Hwys 113 &
19

Waupun

**THE DONALD WM
HALLOCKS**
222 Carrington St   53963
414 324-2209
Hours: By Appointment
Types & Periods: General
Line

Wauwatosa

THE ANTIQUE LANTERN
1413 N 60th St   53208
414 771-7580
Proprietor: Ginny & Russ
Gonnering
Types & Periods: Lighting &
Accessories

**ARCHITECTURAL
ANTIQUES**
7014 W State St   53213
414 475-1073   Est: 1974
Proprietor: Tom Schaffer
Hours: Daily, Weekends,
"Late Morn 'til Early Eve"
Types & Periods: Light
Fixtures, Doors, Hardware,
Woodwork, Stonework,
Leaded Glass
Specialties: Glass (Stained
Windows)
Directions: 1st Western
Suburb of Milwaukee

THE CROW'S NEST
7008 W State St   53213
414 257-9996   Est: 1973
Proprietor: Elizabeth A
Woest
Hours: Daily, 11-3,
By Appointment,
Closed Sun

Types & Periods:
Collectibles, General Line
Specialties: Metalwork,
Woods, Primitives
    Directions: Suburb of
    Milwaukee

West Allis

ALCORN'S ANTIQUES
    1729 S 81st St   53214
    414 771-9167   Est: 1971
    Proprietor: Charles Alcorn
    Hours: Daily, Weekends
Types & Periods: General
Line, Brass, Copper,
Collectibles
Specialties: Furniture,
Clocks, China
    Directions: 3 blocks S of
    State Fair Park Entrance
    on 81st

West Bend

KILBY'S ANTIQUES
    131 Island Ave   53095
    414 334-2602
    Hours: Daily 8-5, Sat 9-12
    Noon
Types & Periods: Glassware,
China, Lamps, Bottles,
Pewter, Clocks, Dolls, Brass,
Iron
    Directions: 1 block E of
    Main St (Hwy 45), 3
    blocks S of Hwy 33

STARKS ANTIQUES
    240 South 12th Ave
        53095
    414 334-7416
    Hours: Daily, 12-5,
    By Appointment,
    Closed Sun
Types & Periods: China, Cut
& Pressed Glass, Clocks,
Lamps, Primitives, Cherry,
Pine & Walnut Furniture
    Directions: 3 blocks N of
    Hospital

West DePere

**PAY LESS
FURNITURE-NEW-USED
ANTIQUES**
    348 Main Ave   54115
    414 336-6123   Est: 1965
    Proprietor: Jack & Ceil
    Hofmeister
    Hours: Mon-Thurs 10-5,
    Fri 10-9, Sat 10-1
Types & Periods: General
Line, Furniture & Collectibles
    Directions: Exit G Off
    Hwy 41

Whitewater

THE GREEN SHUTTERS
    507 W Main St   53190
    414 473-4878   Est: 1977
    Proprietor: Marj Simandl,
    Trudy Macharen
    Hours: Tues-Fri 11-3,
    5:30-9
Types & Periods: General
Line, Collectibles
Specialties: In 1841 Mansion
& Furnishings
    Directions: Hwys 12, 59 &
    89 Intersection

Williams Bay

HOUSE OF TWO LIONS INC
    Hwy 67 & Bailey Rd
        53191
    414 245-6598   Est: 1953
    Proprietor: Marcelle
    Fischer
    Hours: Daily 9:30-5
Types & Periods: American,
European, Collectibles,
General Line
Appraisal Service Available
    Directions: 6 Miles W of
    Lake Geneva

Winneconne

THE FOLLY
    311 W Main St   54986
    414 582-4409

Proprietor: Linda
Thompson
Hours: By Appointment,
By Chance, Wed & Sun
11-7
Types & Periods: General
Line, Collectibles

Wisconsin Dells

**THE CHICKEN
COOP-ANTIQUES**
    Box 65, Rte 2   53965
    608 254-7820   Est: 1975
    Proprietor: Maggie
    Dahlquist
    Hours: Daily
Types & Periods: General
Line, Collectibles
    Directions: 6½ Miles N of
    Wi Dells on Hwy 13

**EDMONDS-CLASEN
ANTIQUES**
    Rte 2, Box 73   53965
    608 253-5162   Est: 1961
    Proprietor: C Edmonds &
    L Clasen
    Hours: Daily 9-5
Types & Periods: China,
Glass, Primitives
Specialties: China, R S
Prussian, Cut Glass,
Primitives
    Directions: 7 Miles N on
    Hwy 13

Woodruff

THE MILL ANTIQUES
    Hwy 47, Box 45   54560
    715 356-5468
    Hours: Daily 9-6, Sun
    10-6, By Appointment, By
    Chance
Types & Periods: Furniture,
Collectibles, Breweriana,
Advertiques, Coins, Glass,
China, Copper, Brass,
Books, Bottles, Silver,
Jewelry, Primitives, Indian
Artifacts
    Directions: On Hwy 47 S
    Just 5 blocks from the
    Stoplight at Jct 51 & 47

(From page 623). sought as collectibles. They are made of solid wood, and the Age of Golden Oak lives again after a very short time of languishing. (See page 637).

The Mission Oak style was created by Dustav Stickley. It was an attempt to recreate furniture used in the early missions of California and Mexico. Because he manufactured furniture and published periodicals, his styles met with favor but were not long lasting.

As the last of the "Turn of the Century", we must mention the Bird's-eye Maple furniture vogue of the 1920's. The bird's-eye effect is a freak condition in the growth of maple trees. Because of its relative scarcity, it was used as a veneer and for some reason mostly in bedroom sets. It is a very decorative wood, and a dramatic effect could be achieved.

We have progressed through the styles of furniture that have been with us for centuries, have influenced our preferences and therefore our heritage. What will be the collectible antique for the future? With continuing and increasing scarcity of hardwoods for manufacturing furniture, the future becomes unclear. Economics has always played a large part in the choice of furniture. An inexpensive line seen in stores today is made of sawdust pressed into a particle board upon which a photographically processed finish is applied to its surfaces. Are the bonding agents in particle board of good enough quality? If the particle board absorbs too much moisture, it will literally disintegrate. However, if the finish on natural wood is neglected, moisture will cause its deterioration as well. What furniture of today's manufacture will also exist 100 years from now? That is still to be learned, but experience shows that natural woods may last for centuries.

There are three elemental criterion to be found in prized antiques. One is the excellence of craftsmanship in its execution. Another is the excellence of its design. The final ingredient is wide acceptance of that design, therefore popularity. We have seen styles from the Golden Age of the late 18th Century remain with us. Remember always, that good things will always be good. Good examples in furniture only continue to rise in esteem and therefore value. Other examples advance very slowly. Always take your time when buying an antique. Examine it thoroughly. Be certain that you can be happy with what you are getting, and that it is at a price you can afford. With this approach, collecting can contribute a joy to your life.

My best wishes for your good hunting.

STATE OF WYOMING

Buffalo

UPSTAIRS ANTIQUES
58 S Main   82834
307 684-7230   Est: 1975
Proprietor: Virginia R
Keith
Hours: Daily, By
Appointment
Types & Periods: China,
Glass, Furniture
Directions: Downtown

Casper

ANTIQUES AND GIFTS
1830 Burlington   82601
307 237-7844,
234-7686   Est: 1977
Proprietor: Margaret E
Farrar
Hours: Mon-Sat 9-5
Types & Periods: Glass, Cut,
Pressed, Art, Primitives,
Furniture, Gifts-Fenton &
Goebel Items, Hummels
Directions: Btwn E
Yellowstone & I-25. Bryan
Stock Trail Exit, come to
Burlington off I-25; Or
come to end of Lennox

GOLDEN DOOR, INC
130 N Ash   82601
307 234-7475   Est: 1978
Proprietor: Marlene &
Oscar Anderson
Hours: Mon-Sat 10-5:30
Types & Periods: Furniture,
1800's Primitives, Walnut,
Mahagony, Victorian Oak,
Brass Beds, Hall Trees,
Lamps, Carnival Glass,
China, Depression & Cut
Glass, Dolls, Clocks, Jewelry
Directions: Ash St is off
1st St in Downtown Area

Cheyenne

AGEE'S ANTIQUES &
FURNITURE
714 S Greeley Hwy 82001
303 638-8455   Est: 1940
Proprietor: Mrs William
Agee
Hours: Mon-Fri, By
Chance
Types & Periods: General
Line
Appraisal Service Available
Directions: On Old Greeley
Hwy

GOLDENKEY ANTIQUES
1609 Central Ave   82001
307 634-6024   Est: 1971
Proprietor: Bill & Barbara
Curran
Hours: Mon-Fri 10-5, Sat
10-4
Types & Periods: Furniture,
Glassware, Primitives, Dolls,
& More
Appraisal Service Available
Directions: One block off
16th St in Downtown
Cheyenne

HIGH PLAINS ANTIQUES
724 S Greeley Hwy 82001
307 634-6440   Est: 1976
Proprietor: Tom Daugherty
& John Tabor
Hours: By Appointment,
By Chance
Types & Periods:
Architectural Antiques,
Gambling Devices, Gaming
Machines, Unusual & Fine
Furniture, Office Furniture,
Wholesale to trade "Only"
Appraisal Service Available
Directions: Off I-80 at
Greeley Exit

MANITOU GALLERY
1718 Capitol Ave   82001
307 635-0019   Est: 1977
Proprietor: Bob Nelson
Hours: Mon-Sat
Types & Periods: Indian
Material, Paintings, Bronzes
Directions: S of the
Capitol Bldg in middle of
Downtown

SUE'S ANTIQUE & GIFT
SHOP
307 W 16th St   82001
307 634-4578   Est: 1965
Proprietor: Sue Patrick &
Millicent Sims
Hours: Daily 9-5
Types & Periods: Furniture,
Primitives

Douglas

JACKS ANTIQUES & USED
FURNITURE
123 S 2nd St   82633
307 358-2487   Est: 1978
Proprietor: John & Jeanne
McIntosh
Hours: Mon-Sat
Types & Periods: General
Line
Directions: One block S
off Main St

Laramie

ANTIQUES FROM FORT
SANDERS
219 Garfield   82070
307 742-5120   Est: 1976
Proprietor: Mrs Pat
Rogers
Hours: Mon-Sat, By
Appointment
Eves-742-2720
Types & Periods: Victorian
Glass, China, Lamps, Parts
Western Relics, Primitives,
Bottles, Insulators, License
Plates, Civil War Items
Specialties: Bottles,
Insulators, Relics
Appraisal Service Available
Directions: Downtown
across from Bank of
Laramie

NEW LISTINGS

This information was received so recently
that it could not be properly incorporated.

ILLINOIS

Rock Island

IRON HORSE ANTIQUES & GIFTS
533 30th St   61201
309 793-1869   Est: 1962
Proprietor: Phil & Jean Hutchison
Hours: Tues-Sat
Types & Periods: Primitives, General Line, Post Cards & Paper Items, Furniture
Specialties: Primitives, Paper Items
Appraisal Service Available

INDIANA

New Harmony

CARRIAGE TRADE STUDIO
The Mews   47631
812 682-4488   Est: 1953
Proprietor: Jack Holland
Hours: Mon-Sat 9-5, Sun 1-5
Types & Periods: Oriental, including Puppets & Furniture
Directions: Russell Carrell Antique Showrooms, in the Mews

IOWA

Fertile

OLD MILL ANTIQUES
Main Street   50434
515 797-2490
Proprietor: Ann Hargrave
Hours: Daily, by Appointment, by Chance
Types & Periods: Pattern Glass, Lamps, Walnut Furniture, Stoneware, Dolls, Jewelry, Wood Trunks

Specialties: Pattern Glass
Directions: 5 Miles W of I-35 at the Forest City Exit

Des Moines

VALLEY JUNCTION MALL
333 Fifth St   50265
515 255-9600   Est: 1973
Proprietor: 14 Dealers
Hours: Mon-Sat
Types & Periods: Furniture, Art Glass, Depression Glass, Pottery, Coins, Primitives, Books, Jewelry, Stoneware, General
Specialties: Depression Glass; Mail-order & Searching Service
Appraisal Service Available
Directions: On Fifth St between Railroad & Walnut

MARYLAND

Gaithersburg

CRAFT SHOP
405 S Frederick Ave   20760
301 926-3000   Est: 1946
Proprietor: Grace C & Helen Becraft
Hours: Tues-Sat, 10-5
Types & Periods: General Line
Specialties: Early Blown Glass, Early China
Directions: Rte 355, Opposite Gaithersburg High School

MASSACHUSETTS

Newburyport

GALLERY 7
98 Water St   01950
617 462-8682   Est: 1970
Proprietor: Rhoda E. Ranshaw
Hours: Mon-Sat, also by Appointment
Types & Periods: General, Paintings, Prints, Canadian Eskimo Art
Specialties: Paintings, Prints, Canadian Eskimo Art
Directions: Water St Follows the Merrimac River in Downtown Newburyport; 3 Blocks S of Rte 1A

Upton

PATRICIA HAVEN ANTIQUES
23 Pleasant St   01568
617 529-3948   Est: 1976
Proprietor: Patricia Haven
Hours: By Appointment
Types & Periods: General Line
Specialties: Art Deco
Directions: Corner of Fiske & Pleasant Sts off Rte 140

NEW YORK

Sunnyside

OLD CHINA CUPBOARD
40-14 Greenpoint Ave   11104
Proprietor: Ruth Waldman
Hours: Mon-Sat, by Appointment
Types & Periods: China, Glass, Brass, Bric-a-Brac, Pictures

Directions: 1 Mile E of
59th St Bridge, 2 Blocks
S of Queens Blvd

NORTH CAROLINA

Fayetteville

HOUSE OF ANTIQUES
908-A Laurel St   28303
919 484-1245
Proprietor: Mamie Lenker
Hours: Tues-Sat 10:30-5
Types & Periods: Furniture,
China, Glass, Clocks
Directions: Eutaw Village

OKLAHOMA

Oklahoma City

**THE PINE SHOP & CALICO
CORNER**
12020 NE Expressway
I-35   73111
405 478-0220   Est: 1967
Proprietor: Jack & Helen
McMahan
Hours: Mon-Sat 10-6;
Sunday 1-5:30
Types & Periods: Glass,
Tables, Chairs, Beds
Specialties: Early Primitives
Directions: In Hummel
Village

PENNSYLVANIA

Campbelltown

**STAUFFER HOUSE
ANTIQUES**
Hwy 322   17010
717 838-2502   Est: 1977
Proprietor: Weldine
Dossett
Hours: Mon-Sat,
by Chance or by
Appointment
Types & Periods: Primitives
& Quilts
Directions: 4 Miles E of
Hershey on US Rte 322,
across the Rd from the
Village Motel

TENNESSEE

Memphis

COMMON MARKET, INC.
364 S Front St   38103
901 526-4501
Proprietor: Srend Nielsen
Hours: Mon-Fri 9-5;
Sat 10-5; also by
Appointment
Types & Periods: "Imported
Architectural Antiques: all
Types of Mantels;
Numerous Doors, including
fine stained glass, etched
glass, French & many more;
We have a large selection
of old iron works: Gates,
Fencing, Panels, etc;
Our shutter selection is
complete; Large inventory
of unusual Objets d'Art;
Furniture of all Periods;
Bric-a-brac; Brass
Hardware"
Specialties: Mantels, Doors
& Shutters; Brass
Hardware; Stained Glass
Appraisal Service Available
Directions: 1 Block W of
Main St & 1 Block E of
Riverside Drive

VERMONT

Grafton

EDWARDS OF GRAFTON
Box 123   01540
802 843-2271   Est: 1971
Proprietor: Donald E.
Edwards
Hours: Mon-Sat 9:45-5;
Sun 9-12
Types & Periods: 18th &
Early 19th Century
Furniture, Glass, Porcelain,
Copper, Brass, Prints,
Pictures, General
Appraisal Service Available
Directions: Directly
behind the Grafton
Tavern on Townshend St

VIRGINIA

Arlington

SERENDIPITY ANTIQUES
2901 Columbia Pike
22204
703 920-6000
Proprietor: Orville B. Lynn
Hours: Mon-Sun
Types & Periods: General
Line, Furniture, Glass,
Oriental, Decorator Items,
Etc.
Appraisal Service Available
Directions: At the Corner
of Walter Reed Dr

BIBLIOGRAPHY

The Basics of Antique Furniture

Butler, Joseph T., *American Antiques, 1800-1900*, Odyssey Press, New York, 1965.

Christensen, Erwin O., *The Index of American Design*, MacMillan Company, New York, 1950.

Comstock, Helen, *American Furniture*, The Viking Press, New York, 1962.

Downs, Joseph, *American Furniture, Queen Anne and Chippendale Periods*, MacMillan Company, New York, 1952.

Iverson, Marion, *The American Chair, 1630-1890*, Hastings House, New York, 1957.

Miller, Edgar, *American Antique Furniture*, two volumes, Baltimore Press, Baltimore, 1937.

McClinton, Katherine M., *Collecting American Victorian Antiques*, Wallace Homestead, Des Moines, Iowa, 1966.

Nutting, Wallace, *Furniture Treasury*, three volumes, MacMillan Company, New York, 1933. (Reprint).

Pain, Howard, *The Heritage of Country Furniture*, Van Nostrand, New York, 1978.

Yates, Raymond F. and Marquerite W., *A Guide to Victorian Antiques*, Harper & Brother, New York, 1949.

SPECIALTIES INDEX

ARMS & ARMOR

ARIZONA
HOUSE OF TRASH &
TREASURE,
   Sedona

CALIFORNIA
JAMES WASTE ANTIQUES,
   San Francisco

CONNECTICUT
LEISURE HOUSE COUNTRY
STORE,
   Oxford

DELAWARE
THE HUDSON HOUSE,
   Dover

FLORIDA
FRANK D GUARINO,
   DeBary
ANGEVINES ANTIQUES,
   DeLand
MARQUETTE'S GIFTS &
ANTIQUES,
   Lake Worth
TROPICAL TRADER,
   Miami

GEORGIA
WOODLIEF'S MILITARY
ANTIQUES,
   Kennesaw

KANSAS
LEASURES TREASURE CHEST,
   Manhattan

MAINE
MARITIME ANTIQUES,
   York

MARYLAND
FUNKSTOWN ANTIQUE MART,
   Funkstown
ANTIQUES BOUTIQUE,
   Kensington
POTOMAC TRADING POST,
   Kensington

MASSACHUSETTS
COUNTRY ANTIQUES,
   Phillipston
KELLEY'S,
   Woburn

MICHIGAN
BOB HARRIS ANTIQUES,
   West Bloomfield

MINNESOTA
MILT'S ANTIQUES,
   Blue Earth

MISSOURI
BUSY BEE ANTIQUES,
   New Franklin

MONTANA
MONTANA OUTFITTERS,
   Great Falls

NEW JERSEY
AUDRAY'S BEST OF THE WEST,
   Barnegat
BERMAN'S AUCTION BARN,
   Dover
THE COLLECTOR,
   Garfield

NEW MEXICO
BORDERTOWN ANTIQUES,
   Texico

NEW YORK
CRAIG ADAMSON,
   Genesco
MAIN STREET EXCHANGE,
   Ilion
ROBERT L BROOKS,
   New York City
YANKEE PEDDLER ANTIQUE
SHOP,
   Saratoga Springs
WILLIAM J JURGENSEN,
   Stony Point

OHIO
MT WASHINGTON,
   Cincinnati
THE E CHRISTOPHER
FIREARMS COMPANY,
   Miamitown

OREGON
SILAS MESSER,
   Eugene

PENNSYLVANIA
PARK COIN & GUN SHOP,
   Brookville
BATTLEFIELD MILITARY
MUSEUM,
   Gettysburg
HARRIS ANTIQUES,
   Knox

SOUTH CAROLINA
ORIENTAL RUGS & ANTIQUE
CO
   Charleston

TEXAS
JACKSON ARMS,
   Dallas
FRONTIER GUNS,
   Richardson

VERMONT
THE ANTIQUE CLOCK & GUN
SHOP,
   Shelburne

VIRGINIA
GOVERNOR'S ANTIQUES,
   Mechanicsville

BOOKS, MAGAZINES & POST CARDS

ALABAMA
IRON ART INC,
 Birmingham
ANTIQUE EMPORIUM & GIFT
SHOP,
 Mobile
HANEYS ANTIQUES,
 Ozark

ARIZONA
UNEEDA ANTIQUES,
 Phoenix

ARKANSAS
YESTERDAY'S BOOK, ETC,
 Hot Springs
OX YOKE,
 Mountain Home

CALIFORNIA
KEN PRAG,
 Burlingame
BRETON HOUSE,
 Los Angeles
MARTHA'S ANTIQUES,
 Pasadena
ANDER'S ATTIC,
 Riverside
WITHERSPOON &
POSTLETHWAITE,
 San Anselmo
THE HAWTHORN'S ANTIQUES,
 San Diego
BLANCHE KOEHMSTEDT
ANTIQUES,
 San Diego
ARGONAUT BOOK SHOP,
 San Francisco
THE PAPERMILL,
 Santa Rosa

COLORADO
BEE'S ANTIQUES,
 Denver
ASHLEE'S ANTIQUES,
 Denver
GRANDMA'S HOUSE,
 Denver
GRANDPA SNAZZY'S
ANTIQUES,
 Denver
THE PROSPECTOR,
 Littleton

CONNECTICUT
JAN & LARRY MALIS,
 New Canaan
SCARLET LETTER ANTIQUES &
BOOKS,
 New Milford
PLAINVILLE RAILROAD
STATION ANTIQUE CENTER,
 Plainville
BOOKS FOR COLLECTORS,
 Stamford
THE ANTIQUE SHOP,
 Stratford

DISTRICT OF COLUMBIA
GEORGETOWN TEMPTATIONS,
 Washington

FLORIDA
LIBERTY ANTIQUES COINS &
STAMPS,
 Miami

GEORGIA
YESTERYEAR BOOK SHOP,
 Atlanta

IDAHO
STAGE STOP,
 Pocatello

ILLINOIS
MARSHALL FIELD & COMPANY,
 Chicago
FLY-BY-NITE GALLERY,
 Chicago
MARK & LOIS JACOBS
AMERICANA
COLLECTIBLES-ANTIQUES,
 Chicago
THE TURQUOISE BUTTERFLY,
 Chicago
ROOM 102,
 Richmond
PRAIRIE ARCHIVES,
 Springfield
STOREYBOOK ANTIQUES,
 Sycamore

INDIANA
JERRY'S JUNKATIQUE,
 Anderson
GOLDEN RULE ANTIQUES,
 Indianapolis
OLE CORRAL ANTIQUES,
 North Vernon
MARTIN'S ANTIQUES,
 Terre Haute
ANTIQUES & THINGS,
 Williamsport

IOWA
HEDGEPETH ANTIQUES,
 Burlington
HEDGEPETH ANTIQUES,
 Fort Madison
THE EARLY ATTIC,
 Imogene

KANSAS
DETRICH ANTIQUES,
 Great Bend
LEASURES TREASURE CHEST,
 Manhattan
HITCHING POST ANTIQUES,
 Sabetha

LOUISIANA
WIND HAVEN ANTIQUES
 Mandeville

MAINE
SOMEPLACE ELSE ANTIQUES &
BOOKS,
 Alfred
CHARLES ANTIQUES & BOOKS,
 Augusta
MOLL OCKETT ANTIQUES,
 Bryant Pond
JEFFERSON BORDEN 5th,
 Deer Isle
THE SAIL LOFT,
 Newcastle

MARYLAND
OLD BOWIE ANTIQUE MARKET,
 Bowie
ODDS & ENDS SHOP,
 Frederick
THIS 'N' THAT SHOP,
 Kensington
THE LOOKING GLASS
ANTIQUES,
 Keymar
PICK & POKE,
 Owings Mills

MASSACHUSETTS
DONALD B HOWES ANTIQUES,
 Brewster
GOLD DIGGERS OF 1933,
 Cambridge
JOHNSTON'S ANTIQUES,
 Franklin
VALLADOA'S ANTIQUES,
 Mattapoisett
JUDITH CRONIN-ANTIQUES,
 Orleans
GALLERY ONE SEVENTEEN
ANTIQUES,
 Rockport

MICHIGAN
AQUARIAN BOOK SERVICE,
 Birmingham
MCKEE MEMORIAL WORKS,
 Marshall
SUNFLOWER SHOP
 Northville
HOWARD SHAPIRO ANTIQUES,
 Okemos

MINNESOTA
OLD VILLAGE SHOP,
 Lanesboro
BARGAIN CENTER,
 Mankato
BLACK SWAN COUNTRY
STORE,
 Minneapolis
MARY TWYCE ANTIQUES &
BOOKS,
 Winona

MISSISSIPPI
SILVER KNIGHT ANTIQUE'S,
 Ocean Springs

MISSOURI
BLACK FLAG ANTIQUES,
 Independence
LINDA'S LOFT ANTIQUES,
 Windsor

NEW HAMPSHIRE
ELDERBERRY ANTIQUES,
 Claremont
THE OLD EMERY PLACE,
 Derry
MAYFIELD,
 Goffstown
THE SHADOW SHOP,
 Hillsboro
YANKEE STOREKEEPER,
 Milford

NEW JERSEY
AUDRAY'S BEST OF THE WEST,
 Barnegat
THE COLLECTOR,
 Garfield

NEW MEXICO
THE SILVER SUNBEAM
GALLERY
 Albuquerque

NEW YORK
GRANDMA'S DUSTED
TREASURES,
 Auburn
FREDONIA WOODS & WARES,
 Fredonia
BLAINE A HILL,
 Harriman
JAMES PUGLIESE,
 New Paltz
GOOSE HILL ANTIQUES,
 Nyack
JOHN B HENDRICK,
 Rochester
DOROTHEA F BERTRAM,
 Westfield
VIRTU ANTIQUES & ART,
 Woodstock

NORTH CAROLINA
BOOK SHOP
 Winston-Salem

OHIO
MAD MONEY,
 Akron
SIGNS OF THE TIME,
 Athens
MT WASHINGTON,
 Cincinnati
WEE SCOT ANTIQUES,
 Cincinnati
THE LUCAS COUNTRY STORE,
 Lucas
HILO FARM ANTIQUES,
 Mentor
IRVING M ROTH ANTIQUES,
 Norwalk
ONTARIO ANTIQUE & COIN
SHOP,
 Ontario
THE BIRD HOUSE ANTIQUES,
 Oxford
SENECA SALES,
 Tiffin
SHARON CENTER ANTIQUES,
 Wadsworth
WAYSIDE ANTIQUES,
 Zanesville

OREGON
HILLSBORO NOSTALGIA
CENTER,
 Hillsboro
MACLEAY COUNTRY STORE,
 Salem

PENNSYLVANIA
HOFFMAN LANE BOOKS,
 Harrisburg
W GRAHAM ARADER, III,
 King of Prussia (Norristown)
SIL BERNARD
 Philadelphia
LOVE OF PAST ANTIQUES,
 Philadelphia
THE TUCKERS,
 Pittsburgh

SOUTH CAROLINA
NOAH'S ARK
 Abbeville

TENNESSEE
ELDER'S BOOK STORE,
 Nashville

TEXAS
SOUTHWEST ANTIQUE
GALLERY,
 Austin

UTAH
JOHANN BEKKER,
 Salt Lake City

VERMONT
BACK DOOR ANTIQUES,
 Essex Junction
AMAPOLA ANTIQUES INC,
 Weston

VIRGINIA
BOOKHOUSE,
 Arlington

WASHINGTON
BRISTOL ANTIQUES,
 Bellingham
A BIT O' EVERYTHING,
 Everett
BROWERS' BOOK SHOP,
 Olympia

WISCONSIN
VILLAGE ANTIQUE CENTER
 Milwaukee

ARKANSAS
MR CHRISTOPHER SHOP,
Hardy

COLORADO
ASHLEE'S ANTIQUES,
Denver

CONNECTICUT
A LITTLE BEFORE YOUR TIME,
Hartford
SCHAFER ANTIQUES,
Madison
BARREDO'S ANTIQUES & USED
FURNITURE,
Torrington

DISTRICT OF COLUMBIA
GEORGETOWN TEMPTATIONS,
Washington
ROSE BROS JEWELERA,
Washington

FLORIDA
HARTMAN GALLERIES,
Palm Beach

GEORGIA
TEMPTATIONS-UPSTAIRS-
DOWNSTAIRS,
Savannah

HAWAII
CREATIVE DECORATING,
Honolulu
ANTIQUES & JUNQUE AT
KAHALULU,
Kaneohe

IDAHO
STAGE STOP,
Pocatello

ILLINOIS
GRANDA'S EARLY AMERICANA,
Trenton
SUZANNE ANTIQUE
ACCESSORIES,
Winnetka

INDIANA
DEE'S ANTIQUES,
Somerville

IOWA
HIRSCHY'S USED FURNITURE &
ANTIQUES,
Wayland
OLD MILL,
West Union

KENTUCKY
E S TICHENOR CO,
Louisville

LOUISIANA
WIND HAVEN ANTIQUES
Mandeville
PETERS' TRADING POST
New Orleans

MAINE
BONNEY'S ANTIQUES,
Kennebunkport

MARYLAND
RUXTON IMPORTS,
Ruxton

MASSACHUSETTS
NOVACK GALLERY,
Newton Centre

MICHIGAN
GOOD-OL-DAYS ANTIQUES,
Holly

MISSISSIPPI
OUIDA'S ANTIQUES,
Clinton
LILL'3 ANTIQUES.
Pascagoula

MISSOURI
IRON GATE ANTIQUES,
Pacific

NEW HAMPSHIRE
RALPH K REED,
Wolfeboro

NEW YORK
JIM'S BOTTLE SH
Ardsley
MEADOWOOD SHO.
Ashville
CHRISTOPHER'S
COLLECTABLES,
Newark
ISI FISCHZANG,
New York City
JOHN B HENDRICK,
Rochester

OREGON
GENERATION III ANTIQUES,
Portland

TEXAS
ORIENTAL ART SHOP,
Dallas
JAMES L & NELLIE M DAVIS
ANTIQUES,
Port Lavaca
J & J COUNTRY STORE,
Wimberley

VERMONT
PARAPHERNALIA ANTIQUES,
Manchester

VIRGINIA
GRESHAM'S COUNTRY STORE,
Richmond
NEWEL POST ANTIQUE
GALLERY,
Virginia Beach

WASHINGTON
FOX'S GEM SHOPE,
Seattle

WYOMING
ANTIQUES FROM FORT
SANDERS
Laramie

ANTIQUES,
ALABA
THE KI FLYING
B
CA
C
UES & ORIENTAL

NTIQUES,

ZADE GALLERIES

o
SPOON &
THWAITE,
an Anselmo
MB ANTIQUES & APPRAISAL
SERVICE,
San Diego
JOHN HUDSON AVERY,
San Francisco

COLORADO
THE CARPET SHOPS LTD,
Boulder
NEUHART'S ANTIQUES &
IMPORTS,
Denver

CONNECTICUT
HAIG RUGS,
New Haven

FLORIDA
H & H ANTIQUES,
Largo
GARTH'S ANTIQUES,
Pensacola
O'NEAL ANTIQUE SHOP,
Tampa

ILLINOIS
ANTIQUE MART,
Bloomington
ALLEGRETTI ORIENTAL RUGS,
Chicago
ALLEGRETTI ORIENTAL RUGS,
Evanston

INDIANA
CAROL'S ANTIQUES,
Chesterton
MILDRED BOINK'S BRASS BELL
SHOP,
Evansville
FERN'S ANTIQUES,
French Lick
GYPSY POT ANTIQUES,
Nashville
ANTIQUE ART,
New Albany
MAX'S WATERTOWER
ANTIQUES,
Westfield

IOWA
RED ROBIN FARM,
Marengo

KENTUCKY
BURCH INTERIOR'S,
Frankfort
BOONE'S ANTIQUES OF
KENTUCKY INC,
Lexington
E S TICHENOR CO,
Louisville

LOUISIANA
R L MAYBERRY GALLERIES,
Bastrop
SAROUK SHOP,
New Orleans

MARYLAND
PEACOCK & PARRETT,
Baltimore
JAMSHID ANTIQUE RUGS,
Chevy Chase
KENDELL'S ANTIQUES,
Fork

MASSACHUSETTS
ACADIA SHOP,
Cambridge
CHARLEMONT HOUSE
GALLERY,
Charlemont
ELMWOOD BOOKSHOP AND
GALLERY,
East Bridgewater

MICHIGAN
MADELINE'S ANTIQUE SHOPPE,
Birmingham

MINNESOTA
COBBLESTONE ANTIQUES,
Minneapolis

MISSISSIPPI
AD-MIXTURE,
Itta Bena

NEW HAMPSHIRE
PEDERSEN ANTIQUES,
Grafton
CONSTANCE BERGENDOFF
ANTIQUES,
Lyme
DOW'S CORNER SHOP,
Tuftonboro Corner
THE UNICORN ANTIQUE SHOP,
West Nottingham

NEW JERSEY
THE COLLECTOR,
Garfield
ANTIQUE ASSOCIATES,
Wayne

NEW MEXICO
PACKARDS OF ALBUQUERQUE
Albuquerque

NEW YORK
EATON GALLERIES,
Buffalo
ANTIQUE BUYERS OF AMERICA
INC,
New York City
BARBARA N COHEN,
Pittsford
PANCHRONIA ANTIQUES,
Warners

NORTH CAROLINA
G S MCKENNA GALLERY,
Charlotte
WILLIAM-KEITH ANTIQUES,
Raleigh
MIRIAM'S ORIENTAL RUGS,
Tarboro

OHIO
JAMES H WELCH & SONS
TRADING CO
Canton
A B CLOSSON JR CO,
Cincinnati

OKLAHOMA
AMIR'S PERSIAN IMPORTS
Tulsa

OREGON
LEE FARR ORIENTAL RUGS,
Portland

PENNSYLVANIA
PAT ERRIGO ANTIQUES,
Curwensville
ROBERT B WILSON,
Hickory

RHODE ISLAND
AARON GALLERY,
Providence

SOUTH CAROLINA
ORIENTAL RUGS &
ANTIQUE CO
Charleston

TENNESSEE
REED & SON ANTIQUES,
Chattanooga
FARM HOUSE ANTIQUES,
Nashville

TEXAS
MARY STINCHCOMB,
Austin
ANTIQUES DOWNTOWN,
Van Alstyne

VERMONT
BETTY STERLING,
Randolph

VIRGINIA
PETTICOAT LANE INTERIORS &
ANTIQUES,
Arlington
THE LITTLE SHOP AT PLAIN
DEALING,
Lynchburg
THE ANTIQUES WAREHOUSE,
Richmond
M KAMBOURIAN SONS INC,
Richmond
THE IRON GATE,
Virginia Beach

WASHINGTON
ROSEN-COLGEN GALLERY,
Seattle

WEST VIRGINIA
WOODEN BRIDGE ANTIQUES,
Charleston

WISCONSIN
WARTMANNIA
Edgerton
DONALD M WALL ART
GALLERIES, INC
Milwaukee
SCHALLES ANTIQUES &
TURQUOISE
Waunakee

CERAMICS & CHINA

ALABAMA
KILGROE'S ANTIQUES,
Pell City

ARIZONA
UPTOWN ANTIQUES,
Phoenix
PAUL-MAR ANTIQUES,
Prescott
REDDY'S ANTIQUES,
Scottsdale
THE ROSEMARY ANTIQUE
SHOP,
Scottsdale
RED LAMP ANTIQUES,
Thatcher
LASTENIA'S ANTIQUES,
Tucson
PHYLISS C SPAGNOLA,
Tucson

ARKANSAS
MARGARET'S ANTIQUES,
Batesville
MILLER'S ANTIQUES,
Carlise
FERNE'S ANTIQUES,
Fort Smith

MR CHRISTOPHER,
Hardy
CLINTON'S ANTIQUES,
Hot Springs
WATSON'S ANTIQUES,
Hot Springs
ANTIQUE HOUSE,
Little Rock
KAYLIN'S ANTIQUES,
Little Rock
RED HOUSE,
Marvel
NINA'S ANTIQUES & GIFTS,
Paragould

CALIFORNIA
SHADOW HILLS ANTIQUES &
FINE ARTS GALLERY,
Beverly Hills
ROAD RUNNER ANTIQUES,
Columbia
SUNDBORG'S ANTIQUE BARN,
Jamestown
WEATHERVANE ANTIQUES,
Jamestown
JOANNA'S CURIOSITY SHOPPE,
La Canada

GALLERY ONE,
Laguna Beach
THOSE WERE THE DAYS,
Pasadena
LAMB ANTIQUES & APPRAISAL
SERVICE,
San Diego
UNIQUE ANTIQUES & GIFTS,
San Diego
DILLINGHAM & BROWN LTD,
San Francisco
RONALD JAMES,
San Francisco
NGAN'S ANTIQUES,
San Francisco
NOSTALGIA EXPRESS,
San Francisco
OLD WAGON WHEEL,
San Francisco
R & FH POSTLETHWAITE,
San Francisco
RED ANCHOR,
San Francisco
CLASSIC ANTIQUES,
San Jose

RICHARD GOULD ANTIQUES
LTD,
  Santa Monica
INTERNATIONAL ANTIQUES,
  Solano Beach
OLDEN TYMES,
  Solvang

COLORADO
EUROPA ANTIQUES,
  Aurora
REVA'S MOUNTAIN HOME,
  Lyons
LEIGH ANTIQUES & GALLERY,
  Snowmass Village
MC KINLEY & HILL ANTIQUES,
  Wheatridge

CONNECTICUT
NONE OF A KIND,
  Chester
CHARLES STUART & CO,
  Darien
JAMES E ELLIOTT ANTIQUES,
  Essex
THOMAS D & CONSTANCE R
WILLIAMS,
  Litchfield
ANTIQUES ET CETERA,
  Manchester
DOLLY'S ANTIQUES,
  Meridan
BUTTONSHOP ANTIQUES,
  Newton
WILSON'S ANTIQUES,
  Old Saybrook
THE ANTIQUE SHOP,
  Stratford

DELAWARE
OLD DOVER ANTIQUES,
  Dover
EILEEN GANT ANTIQUES,
  Smyrna

DISTRICT OF COLUMBIA
PETER MACK BROWN
ANTIQUES,
  Washington
CALVERT GALLERY,
  Washington
VIP ANTIQUES OF
GEORGETOWN,
  Washington

FLORIDA
KAREN'S KORNER,
  Clearwater
PORTOBELLO ANTIQUES,
  Clearwater
PAT'S ANTIQUES,
  Cocoa
THE VILLAGE PLATE
COLLECTOR,
  Cocoa

WEDGEWOOD OF CANTEBURY,
  Dania
LUCILLE'S ANTIQUES,
  Delray Beach
ROSS-PLUMMER LTD,
  Fort Lauderdale
TREASURES OF THE WORLD,
  Fort Lauderdale
EARLY ATTIC,
  Jupiter
I CHING ORIENTAL ANTIQUE
GALLERY,
  Miami
TROPICAL TRADER,
  Miami
ANTIQUE TREASURES,
  North Miami
THE ANTIQUE MUSEUM,
  Ocala
ANTIQUE MEISSEN,
  Palm Beach
DOUGLAS LORIE, INC,
  Palm Beach
FOSTER'S TRADING CENTER,
  Sebring
GOLDEN EAGLE,
  Tampa

GEORGIA
ANTIQUES LIMITED,
  Atlanta
ATLANTA ANTIQUES
EXCHANGE,
  Atlanta
A COLLECTORS CHOICE INC,
  Atlanta
J H ELLIOTT ANTIQUES,
  Atlanta
GERALD'S ANTIQUES,
  Atlanta
INTERNATIONAL ART
PROPERTIES LTD,
  Atlanta
JOSEPH KONRAD, INC,
  Atlanta
THE LITTLE SHOPPE
(ANTIQUES), INC,
  Atlanta
JANE J MARSDEN ANTIQUES &
INTERIORS,
  Atlanta
THE TOBY HOUSE ANTIQUES,
  Atlanta
HAY'S MILL ANTIQUES,
  Carrollton
CENTURY ANTIQUES,
  Columbus
PAUL BARON CO,
  Decatur
WEBB'S ANTIQUES & ACCENTS,
  Decatur
BRANNON ANTIQUES INC,
  Grantville
OAK WOOD ANTIQUES,
  La Grange

AUNTIES ANTIQUES,
  Riverdale
MEETING HOUSE ANTIQUES,
  Roswell
ARTHUR G SMITH ANTIQUES,
  Savannah
DREAM HOUSE ANTIQUES,
  Sylvester
BARRY'S JUNKTION,
  Warner Robbins

HAWAII
THE CARRIAGE HOUSE,
  Honolulu

ILLINOIS
THE TURQUOISE BUTTERFLY,
  Chicago
STRAW FLOWER INC,
  Decatur
ALLEN'S ANTIQUES,
  Frankfort
THE ANTIQUE GALLERY,
  Glen Ellyn
GALERIE DE PORCELAIN,
  Glen Ellyn
A LITTLE BIT ANTIQUES LTD,
  Glenview
CAT & FIDDLER INC,
  Lake Bluff
OWENS COUNTRY CORNER
ANTIQUES,
  Litchfield
THE OLD TOLL GATE
ANTIQUES,
  Milan
STOREYBOOK ANTIQUES,
  Sycamore

INDIANA
EASTBURG LAMPLITER
ANTIQUES,
  Brownsburg
CUSTER HOUSE ANTIQUES,
  Centerville
WOOD & STONE ANTIQUES,
  Columbus
ORIENTAL GARDEN ANTIQUES,
  Forest
KINNETT ANTIQUES,
  Mooresville
BETTY'S ANTIQUES,
  Nashville
CORNER CUPBOARD
ANTIQUES,
  Spencer
MIDWAY ANTIQUES &
COUNTRY STORE,
  Washington
VIVIAN'S ANTIQUES,
  Waveland

IOWA
HEDGEPETH ANTIQUES,
Burlington
HEDGEPETH ANTIQUES,
Fort Madison
ORIGINAL ANTIQUE SHOP,
Marion
MAXINE'S HEN HOUSE,
Oskaloosa
GAS LIGHT ANTIQUES,
Sioux City
THE VICTORIAN ANTIQUE
SHOP,
Sioux City

KANSAS
FISHER'S ANTIQUES &
FURNITURE STRIPPING,
El Dorado
PLOWSHARES & POLKA DOT
CORNER ANTIQUES,
Harper
LOU'S LOT NO 2,
Morganville
BISHOP ANTIQUES,
Topeka
THE COBWEB,
Topeka
SPENCER
ANTIQUES-ODDTIQUES INC,
Topeka

KENTUCKY
BOONE'S ANTIQUES OF
KENTUCKY INC,
Lexington
THE CENTURY SHOP,
Louisville
THE STRASSEL CO,
Louisville
THOMPSON'S ANTIQUES & GIFT
SHOP,
Paducah
LENA'S ANTIQUES,
Richmond

LOUISIANA
PECQUET'S BROCANTURE
ANTIQUE SHOPPE
Baton Rouge
COUNTRY CABIN ANTIQUES
Benton
CAIN'S INC
Bossier
BEL'S ANTIQUES & GIFTS INC
Harahan
THE BROWN HOUSE
Lafayette
WIND HAVEN ANTIQUES
Mandeville
A-ANTIQUES
New Orleans
HAMILTON HOUSE ANTIQUES
New Orleans

ST CHARLES ANTIQUES LTD
New Orleans
ARNETT'S ANTIQUES
Pouchatoula
SHADETREE ANTIQUES
St Francisville

MAINE
CAMPBELLS ANTIQUES,
Augusta
GOLD COAST ANTIQUES,
Belfast
THE CHAMBERLAIN CARRIAGE
HOUSE & NOT,
Brewer
DELFT BOWL ANTIQUES,
Bryant Pond
JEFFERSON BORDEN 5TH,
Deer Isle
MARY IRENE BIRMINGHAM,
Frankfort
PHIPPS OF PITTSTON,
Gariner
KENNEBUNK ANTIQUES,
Kennebunk
DUCK TRAP ANTIQUES,
Lincolnville
THE SAIL LOFT,
Newcastle
THE CHATFIELDS ANTIQUES,
Pemaquid Harbor
DECON'S LOT ANTIQUES,
Union

MARYLAND
ANNE ARUNDEL ANTIQUES,
Annapolis
ANTIQUES BY WALLACE INC,
Bethesda
EVELETH & SUMMERFORD,
Bethesda
FLEUR-DE-LIS ANTIQUES,
Bethesda
JONES ANTIQUES,
Cambridge
CRAFT SHOP,
Gaithersburg

MASSACHUSETTS
DON FRENCH ANTIQUES,
Athol
THE LOVING CUP ANTIQUES,
Belchertown
CROSS & GRIFFIN,
Belmont
ALBERTS-LANGDON INC,
Boston
SONIA PAINE ANTIQUES
GALLERY,
Chestnut Hill
SYLVIA H HOSLEY,
Dennis
THE HOUSE OF THE CLIPPER
SHIP,
East Sandwich

DONNA & JOE MELLO,
Gloucester
VICTORIAN HOUSE ANTIQUES,
Kingston
STAGECOACH ANTIQUES,
Lincoln
CHRISTINE VINING ANTIQUES,
Marblehead
THE BUTCHER BLOCK,
Orleans
THE ANTIQUE LADY,
Randolph
PINXIT,
Rockport
ANTIQUES OF RIVERSIDE INC,
Sheffield
DEN OF ANTIQUITY,
Wellesley

MICHIGAN
DOUBLE L ANTIQUES,
COLLECTORS DIVISION LTD,
Berkley
SALLY THOMAS & COMPANY,
Brighton
CLARKSTON MAIN STREET
ANTIQUES,
Clarkston
DROVERS EAST ANTIQUES,
Detroit
THE HINTER HAUS ANTIQUE &
GIFT SHOP,
Eastport
CHINA CUPBOARD,
Easton Rapids
CURIOSITY SHOPPE LTD,
Franklin
SALLY THOMAS & COMPANY,
Hartland
THE DUTCH BARN,
Holland
THE VILLAGE STORE
ANTIQUES,
Ironwood
41 ANTIQUES,
Ishpeming
HARBOR HILLS ANTIQUES,
Macatawa
LONGTON HALL GALLERIES,
Petoskey

MINNESOTA
ARDEN HILLS ANTIQUE SHOP,
Arden Hills
STAN'S ANTIQUES,
Bemidji
ELSA'S ANTIQUES,
Dodge Center
SUMMER KITCHEN ANTIQUES,
Lake City
STAN'S ANTIQUES,
Lake Park
GOSSE'S ANTIQUES,
Minneapolis
GEORGE ENZ ANTIQUES,
Red Wing

IRIDESCENT HOUSE,
Spring Valley

MISSISSIPPI
JEAN BROWN ANTIQUES,
Columbus
ANTIQUE BROWSE SHOP,
Jackson
JACKSON COIN SHOP,
Jackson
LILL'S ANTIQUES,
Pascagoula
HOWAT ANTIQUES,
Ripley
MURPHEY ANTIQUES LTD,
Tupelo

MISSOURI
GEORGE'S ANTIQUES,
Cape Girardeau
COUNTRY ROAD ANTIQUES,
Centralia
LONG'S ANTIQUES,
Higginsville
EDNAMAY'S ANTIQUES,
Macon
CYRIL'S ANTIQUES,
Manchester
HELEN'S ANTIQUES,
St Joseph
DOROTHY'S ANTIQUES INC,
Sedalia

MONTANA
GOLDEN LEAF ANTIQUES,
Butte

NEBRASKA
ANDERSONS ANTIQUES,
Holdrage
COACH HOUSE ANTIQUES,
Lincoln
MILLER'S USED FURNITURE,
ANTIQUES & DOLLS,
Lincoln
WAGON WHEEL ANTIQUES,
Lincoln
PHILLIPS ANTIQUES,
Nebraska City
YE OLDE JUNQUE SHOPPE,
Nebraska City
THE ANTIQUE BROKERAGE,
Omaha

NEW HAMPSHIRE
CRICKET FARM ANTIQUES,
Amherst
PEDERSEN ANTIQUES,
Grafton
CONSTANCE BERGENDOFF
ANTIQUES,
Lyme
BURLWOOD ANTIQUE MARKET,
Meredith

MILL ROAD ANTIQUES,
Rumney
THE STONE HOUSE,
Spofford
PEPPERSAUCE ANTIQUES,
West Ossipee

NEW JERSEY
REESE PALLEY,
Atlantic City
TRIFLES & TREASURES,
Buttzville
STAGE COACH INN ANTIQUES,
Ocean View
THE CRYSTAL SHOPPE,
Perth Amboy
LEE DAVIS ANTIQUES,
Sergeantsville
CONTI REALTY & AUCTION
SERVICE,
Trenton

NEW MEXICO
CATES ANTIQUES & SELECT
USED FURNITURE
Las Cruces
ATTIC ANTIQUES
Las Vegas
REID'S ANTIQUES
Roswell
ADELENE B MC LAUGHLIN
Santa Fe
TRAILS END TRADING POST
Santa Fe

NEW YORK
THE HEIRLOOM SHOP,
Bayside
BEARSVILLE ANTIQUES,
Bearsville
EXQUISITE ANTIQUES LTD,
Bellmore
IRONSTONE ANTIQUES,
Binghamton
BROWNER ANTIQUES &
GALLERY INC,
Brooklyn
TESS AND ALLEN USATIN,
Brooklyn
VI & SI'S ANTIQUES,
Clarence
JUNE BIGGAR ANTIQUES,
Cooperstown
BUTTER HILL ANTIQUE SHOP,
Cornwall-on-Hudson
FIRE HOUSE ANTIQUES CO-OP,
East Aurora
LILLIAN ASCH ANTIQUES,
Flushing
BRICKWOOD ANTIQUES,
Gloversville
JO ANNE BLUM INC,
New York City
SARAH POTTER CONOVER INC,
New York City

LEO KAPLAN LTD,
New York City
ERE 'N AFT,
Nyack
HOLLY'S ANTIQUES,
Ogdensburg
ANNABEGH ANTIQUE & GIFT
SHOP,
Pearl River
PHILIP & SHIRLEY GORDON
ANTIQUES,
Plattsburgh
THE INTERIORS PLACE,
Rochester
DORIS E WALKER & JAMES A
WALKER,
St Johnsville
GALLOW'S ANTIQUES,
Unadilla
FRANCES ANTIQUE SHOP,
Warrensburg
DOROTHEA F BERTRAM,
Westfield
VOGUE DECORATORS INC,
White Plains
BERNAL ANTIQUES INC,
Whitestone

NORTH CAROLINA
CLARA'S ANTIQUES
Charlotte
EM'S LOOK-A-NOOK ANTIQUES
Charlotte
TYLER-SMITH ANTIQUES
Greensboro
THE EMPORIUM
Old Fort
GARNIER ANTIQUES INC
Pinehurst
ARTHUR H DANIELSON
ANTIQUES LTD
Raleigh
L & S ANTIQUES
Reidsville
JOHN E TYLER,
Roxobel

OHIO
A B CLOSSON, JR CO,
Cincinnati
ANTIQUES AT OLD IRONSTONE,
Dayton
MC DONALD'S ANTIQUES,
East Liverpool
GYPSY MOTH ANTIQUES,
Lucas
THE ANTIQUE SHOWCASE,
Ravenna
GLUCK'S GIFT & ANTIQUE
SHOP INC,
Youngstown
WAYSIDE ANTIQUES,
Zanesville

OKLAHOMA
PAULINE'S ANTIQUES
Bethany

THE CRANBERRY SHOPPE
Canton
FRANCES ANTIQUES
McAlester
LAURA'S ANTIQUES & GIFTS
Oklahoma City
TOM'S ANTIQUES
Tulsa

OREGON
COLD COMFORT FARM
ANTIQUES,
Arch Cape
ROTAY'S ANTIQUES,
Hubbard
ANTIQUES FOR INTERIORS,
Portland
CHOWN SHOWCASE,
Portland
CONKLIN'S ANTIQUES,
Portland
GENERATION III ANTIQUES,
Portland
TREASURE HOUSE ANTIQUES,
Portland

PENNSYLVANIA
KELLY'S ANTIQUES,
Chambersburg
JAMES GALLEY,
Collegeville
THE SPRING MILL ANTIQUE
SHOP,
Conshohocken
DODSON'S ANTIQUES,
Duncansville
MARGARET SCHAFER,
Fairview Village
ANTIQUE NOOK,
Greenburg
A LUDWIG KLEIN & SON,
Harleysville
HOUSE OF ANTIQUES,
Highspire
THE EVERGREEN ANTIQUE
SHOP,
Honesdale
HARRIS ANTIQUES,
Knox
THERESA REDMOND
CULBERTSON,
Lewistown
SMITHERS ANTIQUES,
Lewistown
HELEN B HENRY,
Macungie
WHITE SWAN TAVERN
ANTIQUES,
Marietta
BACK DOOR ANTIQUES,
New Castle
JOHN JEREMICZ, JR,
Perkiomenville
ATTIC GALLERIES,
Philadelphia

ROBERT CARLEN,
Philadelphia
RAY CRAFT ANTIQUES,
Philadelphia
HARRY A EBERHARDT & SON
INC,
Philadelphia
CHARLES B SMITH,
Philadelphia
MARGERY B GEORGE
ANTIQUES,
Pittsburgh
SALT BOX ANTIQUES,
Pittsburgh
BARRY B DOBINSKY ANTIQUES,
Reading
PHYLLIS UHL,
Scranton
THE GREEN BARN ANTIQUES,
Seelyville
ELINOR GORDON,
Villanova
GERALDINE LIPMAN ANTIQUES,
Yardley
GOLDEN EAGLE,
York
TREEN SHOP ANTIQUES,
Zelienople

RHODE ISLAND
COLONIAL ANTIQUES SHOP
Newport

SOUTH CAROLINA
COLES & COMPANY INC
Charleston
FRAN'S ANTIQUE SHOP
Manning
OLD HOUSE ANTIQUES
Murrells Inlet
CHESTNUT GALLERIES
Spartanburg
CAROLINA CHINA MARKET
Sumter

TENNESSEE
CHINA TOWN IMPORTS,
Memphis
KIMBROUGH, INC,
Memphis
THE MATCHMAKERS, INC,
Memphis
EVELYN ANDERSON
GALLERIES,
Nashville
FOREHAND'S ANTIQUE SHOP,
Nashville

TEXAS
VICTORIANA,
Austin
STRAWBERRY PATCH,
Brenham
ANTIQUE HOUSE,
Dallas

THE CHINA CUPBOARD,
Dallas
WILLIAM FERRELL ANTIQUES
INC,
Dallas
JUDGE & WORTH ANTIQUES,
Dallas
J & J CRAINE ANTIQUES,
Dallas
BRITISH ANTIQUE PLACE INC,
Houston
RUTH LITTLE ART & ANTIQUES,
Lubbock
MARY F DAUGHTRY ANTIQUES,
San Antonio
JONES ANTIQUES,
Texas City
SALEM HOUSE OF ANTIQUES,
Victoria

VERMONT
BERNHARDY'S ANTIQUES,
Arlington
FOUR CORNERS-EAST INC,
Bennington
GABRIEL'S BARN,
Grafton
ROMA KNIGHT WEANER
ANTIQUES,
North Hero
MILL BROOK ANTIQUES,
Reading
THE ANGLOPHILE ANTIQUES,
South Dorset

VIRGINIA
ANTIQUES,
Alexandria
THE CAROUSEL ANTIQUES,
Alexandria
BLANCHE DOBKIN ANTIQUES,
Alexandria
KEN FORSTER ANTIQUES,
Alexandria
MIDAS TOUCH ANTIQUES,
Alexandria
SHIRLEY MYERS ANTIQUES,
Alexandria
BOULEVARD ANTIQUES,
Arlington
CUPBOARD ANTIQUES,
Arlington
RED BENCH ANTIQUES &
GIFTS,
Arlington
RIDGEFIELD ANTIQUES,
Charlottesville
OAK GROVE FLEA MARKET,
Chesapeake
THE WHITNEYS,
Stephens City
TK ORIENTAL ART & ANTIQUES,
Williamsburg

WASHINGTON
PERIOD HOUSE ANTIQUES,
  Puyallup
BLANCHE'S ANTIQUES,
  Seattle
CHELSEA ANTIQUES,
  Seattle
THE CONNOISSEUR GALLERY,
  Seattle
GALLERY ANTIQUES,
  Seattle
ROSEN-COLGREN GALLERY,
  Seattle
BAKER'S ANTIQUES,
  Snohomish

DOROTHY OLSEN ANTIQUES,
  Tacoma
DRAHOLD'S OLD TACOMA
ANTIQUE SHOP,
  Tacoma

WEST VIRGINIA
JOHN C NEWCOMER,
  Harpers Ferry
WILLIAM PAYNE ANTIQUES AT
CANAL HOUSE,
  Harpers Ferry
ATTIC ANTIQUES &
CHERISHABLES, INC,
  St Albans

WISCONSIN
WARTMANNIA ANTIQUES
  Edgerton
ERIN ANTIQUES
  Hartford
THE COUNTRY STORE
  Manitowish Waters
GRACE GRAVES-HAVILAND
MATCHING SERVICE
  Milwaukee
DIXIE'S TREASURE CHEST
  Park Falls
ALCORN'S ANTIQUES
  West Allis
EDMONDS-CLASEN ANTIQUES
  Wisconsin Dells

CLOCKS, WATCHES & BAROMETERS

ALABAMA
THE COLLECTORS SHOP,
  Cullman
MC CRORY'S JEWELRY &
ANTIQUES,
  Mobile
COACH & CARRIAGE,
  Ozark

ALASKA
BLACK EAGLE ANTIQUES,
  Anchorage

ARIZONA
COLLECTOR'S CORNER,
  Mesa
LILLIAN'S ANTIQUES,
  Phoenix

ARKANSAS
THE HOUSE OF TIME,
  Fort Smith

CALIFORNIA
TREASURE HOUSE ANTIQUES,
  Carpinteria
CHEAP CASH STORE,
  Columbia
ROAD RUNNER ANTIQUES,
  Columbia
ARELL'S ANTIQUES N' THINGS,
  Culver City
GALLERY ONE,
  Laguna Beach
THE CHIMES,
  Lake Elsinore

LOCKEFORD CLOCK COMPANY,
  Lockeford
BEAUSEJOUR ANTIQUES,
  Los Angeles
LEISURE TIME INC,
  Los Angeles
SACRAMENTO ANTIQUE
CENTER,
  Sacramento
SAN ANSELMO ANTIQUES,
  San Anselmo
SKI'S TRADING POST,
  San Diego
UNICORN COMPANY ANTIQUES,
  San Diego
FILIPELLO ANTIQUES,
  San Francisco
URBAN ANTIQUES AT
SEAWALL B,
  San Francisco
WALLACE EDWARD ANTIQUES,
  San Francisco
THE BLUE CANDLESTICK,
  Saratoga
ROBERT M SOARES,
  Stockton
CLOCKS UNLIMITED,
  Yountville

COLORADO
IGOTATHINGABOUT ANTIQUES,
  Denver
D C ALMQUIST JEWELERS &
WATCHMAKERS,
  Evergreen
SARAH'S ANTIQUES,
  Greeley

CONNECTICUT
HARRY HOLMES ANTIQUES,
  Cornwall Bridge
RUSTY HINGE ANTIQUES,
  Cromwell
MRS MC GILLICUDDY'S
SHOPPE,
  Danbury
YE OLDE CLOCK SHOPPE,
  Guilford
A ANTIQUES,
  Hartford
THE FERRY SLIP,
  New London
FALCONS ROOST ANTIQUES,
  Old Lyme
GEORGE'S JEWELERS ARTS &
TREASURES,
  Stamford
ANTIQUES OF CONNECTICUT,
  Waterford
ROGER S DAVIS INC,
  Woodbury

FLORIDA
THE BIZARRE BAZAAR,
  Bradentown
TREASURES OF TIME,
  Delray Beach
MITCHELL'S HOUSE OF
ANTIQUES & COLLECTIBLES,
  Fort Lauderdale
ANTIQUE PARADISE,
  South Miami
GARDINER'S GARRET,
  South Miami

GEORGIA

HENSEL'S ANTIQUES,
   Tampa
WALTER'S MEMORY LANE
ANTIQUES,
   Tampa

GEORGIA

GEORGIA-CAROLINA SALES CO,
   Augusta
MILLER'S ANTIQUES &
WHAT-KNOTS,
   Columbus
THE MOUNTAIN HOMESTEAD,
   Hiawasee
CENTURY HOUSE ANTIQUES,
   Jackson
ROSWELL CLOCK &
ANTIQUE CO,
   Roswell

IDAHO

GLORIA'S ANTIQUES,
   Boise

ILLINOIS

MINDY'S MEMORIES,
   Alton
WHITE FENCE ANTIQUES,
   Chatham
FISHER'S ANTIQUES,
   Chicago
ANTIQUE CORNER,
   East Dubuque
IT'S ABOUT TIME,
   Glencoe
ALLADIN'S LAMP ANTIQUES,
   Highland Park
EARLY ATTIC ANTIQUES,
   Mattoon
THE LITTLE CORNER, INC,
   McHenry
VILLAGE EMPORIUM ANTIQUE
& GIFT SHOPPE,
   Oak Park
LENOR'S ANTIQUES,
   Oswego
AARDVARK CLOCKS &
ANTIQUES,
   Springfield

INDIANA

THE ANTIQUE GALLERY,
   Fort Wayne
KIRKS FINE CLOCKS AND
ANTIQUES,
   Fort Wayne
THE WEBER CLOCK SHOP,
   Indianapolis
BROWN'S CLOCK SHOP,
   Morgantown
HARTLEY BELL & WHISTLE
ANTIQUES,
   Portland

IOWA

ALLEN'S ANTIQUES,
   Davenport
BANOWETZ ANTIQUES,
   Maquoketa

KANSAS

VIRGINIA'S ANTIQUES,
   Hoyt
PIN OAK ANTIQUES,
   Topeka

LOUISIANA

KLOCK KRAFTS
   Monroe

MAINE

SIMPSON'S ANTIQUES,
   Kennebunkport
HILL ANTIQUE GALLERY,
   Northeast Harbor
FOXHOLE ANTIQUES,
   Ogunquit
SCOTCH HILL ANTIQUES,
   Ogunquit

MARYLAND

ANTIQUE WHOLESALERS INC,
   Kensington

MASSACHUSETTS

WEINER'S ANTIQUE SHOP,
   Boston
THE FRENCH'S,
   Boylston
TREASURE CHEST ANTIQUES,
   Chatham
CUMMAQUID ANTIQUES,
   Cummaquid
GIDEON PUTNAM "TAVERN
ANTIQUES",
   Danvers
YE OLDE TYME SHOPPE,
   East Bridgewater
OLD POST OFFICE CLOCK
SHOP,
   Ipswich
ANTIQUES AT TOM CAREY'S
PLACE,
   Stockbridge
WAKEFIELD ANTIQUES,
   Wakefield
JOSEPH CONWAY ANTIQUES,
   West Newton

MICHIGAN

VARADI'S ANTIQUE SHOP,
   Bay City
SILVER STAR ANTIQUES,
   Fenton
WOODEN SKATE ANTIQUES,
   Okemos
RIVER REST ANTIQUES,
   Saint Ignace

MR & MRS VICTOR
BISSONNETTE,
   Standish

MINNESOTA

SCHMITT ANTIQUES
FURNITURE & JEWELRY,
   Aitkin
STOECKEL'S ANTIQUE CLOCKS
& DOLLS,
   Faribault

MISSISSIPPI

GENE'S ANTIQUES,
   Greenwood
YOUR BARGAIN SHOP,
   Jackson

MONTANA

THE TIME SHOP,
   Great Falls

NEBRASKA

ANDERSON'S ANTIQUES
   Holdrege
CITY CLOCK COMPANY, INC
   Lincoln
JOELLA'S HOUSE-ANTIQUES &
HEIRLOOMS
   Omaha

NEW HAMPSHIRE

THE CARRIAGE SHED,
   Amherst
THE CHURCH ANTIQUES,
   Exeter
OCTOBER STONE ANTIQUES,
   Exeter
MAYFIELD,
   Goffstown
H G WEBBER ANTIQUES,
   Hampton
HARBOR VIEW ANTIQUES,
   Portsmouth

NEW JERSEY

THE COLLECTOR,
   Garfield
THE GOLD MAN,
   Hackensack
PUMLEYE'S ANTIQUES SHOP,
   Lafayette
GOVERNORS ANTIQUE MARKET
AND OUTDOOR FLEA MARKET,
   Lambertville

NEW YORK

MORMARK ENTERPRISES INC,
   Baldwin Place
DONNA'S ANTIQUES,
   Bath
PAST TIMES,
   Bay Shore

RAY'S ANTIQUES,
  Bellmore
IRONSTONE ANTIQUES,
  Binghamton
SAXTON ANTIQUES,
  Brocton
ALAN & JEAN SMITH,
  Chazy
THE LEDGES,
  Cooperstown
BUTTER HILL ANTIQUE SHOP,
  Cornwall-on-Hudson
REMEMBER WHEN? ANTIQUES,
  Floral Park
LILLIAN ASCH ANTIQUES,
  Flushing
DAWN ANTIQUES,
  Flushing
FREDONIA WOODS & WARES,
  Fredonia
WHITNEY ANTIQUES,
  Garden City
HOUSE OF ANTIQUES,
  Hudson
EDDIE ANTIQUE JEWELERS,
  Liberty
TIME WAS ANTIQUES,
  Mineola
ISI FISCHZANG,
  New York City
ANCHORAGE ANTIQUES,
  Poughkeepsie
WHITE'S ANTIQUES,
  Skaneateles
PANCHRONIA ANTIQUES,
  Warners

NORTH CAROLINA
CLOCK BOUTIQUE
  Fayetteville
RHODY'S ANTIQUES
  Hendersonville

OHIO
TRADING POST ANTIQUES,
  Akron
V & R ANTIQUES,
  Bucyrus
ANTIQUE WORLD LTD,
  Cincinnati
INDIAN MOUND ANTIQUES,
  Cincinnati
VILLAGE CLOCK SHOP,
  Hudson
MARKHAM'S ANTIQUES,
  Massillon
TIME CONTINUIM,
  Massillon
NOW N' THEN SHOP,
  Springfield
WESTERVILLE,
  Westerville

OKLAHOMA
DUVALL'S CLOCKS & ANTIQUES
  Altus
WARDEN'S ANTIQUES &
CLOCKS
  Claremore
LINAM WHOLESALE ANTIQUES
  Marlow
ARNOLA SCHRODER ANTIQUES
& DECORATIVES
  Oklahoma City

OREGON
DORMAN'S ANTIQUES,
  Jacksonville
ANTIQUES FOR INTERIORS,
  Portland

PENNSYLVANIA
JUNIATA ANTIQUES,
  Altoona
BOYERTOWN ANTIQUES,
  Boyertown
PENDULUM 1776,
  Columbia
GROVES ANTIQUES,
  Dillsburg
DOWNTOWN ANTIQUES,
  Harrisburg
RUNNING BROOK ANTIQUE
SHOP,
  Hellman
ROBERT B WILSON,
  Hickory
THE CURIOSITY SHOP,
  New Milford
JOHN JEREMICZ, JR,
  Perkiomenville
MARIO'S ANTIQUE SHOP,
  Philadelphia
SALT BOX ANTIQUES,
  Pittsburgh
PETE'S ANTIQUES,
  Reading
STERNBERGH ANTIQUES,
  Reading
THE TICK! TOCK! SHOP,
  Swarthmore
CIRCA ANTIQUES,
  Tafton

SOUTH CAROLINA
KOUNTRY KORNER
  Liberty Hill
DAN'S ANTIQUE CLOCK SHOP
  Sumter

TEXAS
BIVENS ANTIQUES,
  Abilene
NOEL'S ANTIQUES & GIFTS,
  Arlington

VICK'S CASTROVILLE
EMPORIUM,
  Castroville
TIC-WIC SHOP,
  Converse
OL' TYMER CLOCK SHOP,
  Dallas
SID'S ANTIQUES & GIFTS,
  Dallas
RED'S ANTIQUE SUPER
MARKET,
  Forney
REDS ANTIQUE-PARIS FLEA
MARKET,
  Forney
THE EMPORIUM,
  Ft Worth
JESSIE'S SHOWCASE,
  Ft Worth
TOM'S TRADING POST &
ANTIQUES,
  Hamlin
FAULKNER'S ANTIQUES INC,
  Henderson
ALLANT GALLERIE,
  Houston
INTERNATIONAL ANTIQUE &
AUCTION CENTER INC,
  Houston
WINEDALE ANTIQUES,
  Houston
LINKER'S ANTIQUES & GIFTS,
  Howe
THE PENDULUM CLOCK SHOP,
  Hurst
COTTAGE ANTIQUES,
  Lubbock
FRANKS ANTIQUE SHOP &
DOLL MUSEUM,
  Marshall
HYDE'S,
  Midland
GLORIA'S ANTIQUES,
  Pasadena
THE ANTIQUE MALL,
  San Angelo
CHARLOTT'S ANTIQUES &
CLOCKS,
  San Antonio
THE ANTIQUE CLOCK SHOP,
  Snyder

VERMONT
PARAPHERNALIA ANTIQUES,
  Manchester
THE ANTIQUE CLOCK & GUN
SHOP,
  Shelburne
KAAREN JEAN ANTIQUES,
  Sunderland

VIRGINIA
EAGLE ANTIQUES,
  Alexandria

CUPBOARD ANTIQUES,
Arlington
RIDGEFIELD ANTIQUES,
Charlottesville
THE VILLAGE WATCH & CLOCK
SHOP,
Manassas
THE WHITNEYS,
Stephens City

WASHINGTON
STARRETT HOUSE ANTIQUES,
Port Townsend
COACH HOUSE ANTIQUES,
Puyallup
DRAHOLD'S OLD TACOMA
ANTIQUE SHOP,
Tacoma
SAGARS ANTIQUES,
Yakima

WEST VIRGINIA
GOEBEL'S ANTIQUES
St Albans

WISCONSIN
KAPPEL'S CLOCK SHOP
Madison
PICCADILLY ANTIQUES
Milwaukee
ALCORN'S ANTIQUES
West Allis

EMBROIDERY & NEEDLEWORK

ALABAMA
SUZIE'S ANTIQUES,
Midway

ARIZONA
SADIE'S QUILTS & ANTIQUES,
Phoenix

ARKANSAS
THE PRIMITIVE HOUSE,
Jasper

CALIFORNIA
ROBERT K BORMAN ANTIQUES,
San Francisco

CONNECTICUT
THE QUILT PATCH,
Avon
HOBART HOUSE,
Haddam

DISTRICT OF COLUMBIA
CANAL CO OF GEORGETOWN,
Washington
CHERISHABLES,
Washington

FLORIDA
GARDINER'S GARRET,
South Miami
DECOR INC,
Surfside

GEORGIA
THE LITTLE SHOPPE
(ANTIQUES) INC,
Atlanta

THE FENCE RAIL,
Clayton
THE MOUNTAIN HOMESTEAD,
Hiawasee
MEETING HOUSE ANTIQUES,
Roswell

ILLINOIS
WILD GOOSE CHASE QUILT
GALLERY,
Evanston

INDIANA
ALCORN ANTIQUES,
Centerville
CAROL'S ANTIQUES,
Chesterton
WOOD & STONE ANTIQUES,
Columbus
HEAVILON'S ANTIQUES,
Frankfort
PRAIRIE HOUSE ANTIQUES,
Prairieton
MIDWAY ANTIQUES &
COUNTRY STORE,
Washington

KANSAS
LAND M SHOPPE,
Wichita

LOUISIANA
COLLECTOR ANTIQUES,
New Orleans
CABIN CRAFTS,
St Francisville
SHADETREE ANTIQUES,
St Francisville

MAINE
JORGENSONS OF HALLOWELL,
Hallowell
TOWN SHOP ANTIQUES,
Rockport

MARYLAND
PEACOCK & PARRETT,
Baltimore
PHYLLIS VAN AUKEN
ANTIQUES,
Kensington
CREATIVE CORNER,
Walkersville

MASSACHUSETTS
CONWAY HOUSE,
Conway
SOUTH RIVER PRIMITIVES,
Marshfield
NOVACK GALLERY,
Newton Centre

MICHIGAN
CLARKSTON MAIN STREET
ANTIQUES,
Clarkston

MINNESOTA
AMERICAN CLASSICS,
Minneapolis
BLACK SWAN COUNTRY
STORE,
Minneapolis
OLSON'S ANTIQUES,
Pennock

MISSISSIPPI
THE COCKY CROW,
Belzoni

MISSOURI
DEN OF ANTIQUITY,
   Columbia
ROBINWOOD INN ANTIQUES &
CRAFTS,
   Moberly

NEW HAMPSHIRE
CONSTANCE BERGENDOFF
ANTIQUES,
   Lyme

NEW JERSEY
LEONARD BALISH,
   Englewood

NEW YORK
DAVISON ANTIQUES,
   Delhi
AMERICA HURRAH ANTIQUES,
   New York City
ERNEST TROGANOWAN INC,
   New York City
THOMAS K. WOODARD
AMERICAN ANTIQUES &
QUILTS,
   New York City
THE MEATING PLACE
ANTIQUES,
   Port Washington

NORTH CAROLINA
PEMBEE ANTIQUES
   Lumberton

OHIO
THE BIRD HOUSE ANTIQUES,
   Oxford

OKLAHOMA
BUCKBOARD ANTIQUES &
GIFTS,
   Oklahoma City

OREGON
COLD COMFORT FARM
ANTIQUES,
   Arch Cape

PENNSYLVANIA
HOUSE OF ANTIQUES,
   Bird-in-Hand
MARGARET SCHAFER,
   Fairview Village
COPPER EAGLE ANTIQUES,
   Huntingdon Valley
MARILYN J KOWALESKI,
   Wernersville

TENNESSEE
FARM HOUSE ANTIQUES,
   Nashville

TEXAS
MILLER'S ANTIQUES,
   Amarillo
ANTEDILUVIAN,
   Austin
THE EMPORIUM,
   Ft Worth
GREAT EXPECTATIONS
ANTIQUES,
   Houston
THE QUILT COLLECTOR,
   Houston
THE DIFFERNET DRUMMER,
   San Antonio

VERMONT
THE CHESTNUT TREE,
   Charlotte
PARAPHERNALIA ANTIQUES,
   Manchester
STEPHEN/DOUGLAS ANTIQUES,
   Shaftsbury

WASHINGTON
ANITA'S ANTIQUES,
   Seattle

WISCONSIN
THE WEATHERVANE ANTIQUES
   Genesee Depot

FURNITURE

ALABAMA
IRON ART INC,
   Birmingham
THE KING'S HOUSE ANTIQUES,
   Birmingham
THE WRENS NEST ANTIQUES,
   Birmingham
DANCY-POLK HOUSE
ANTIQUES,
   Decatur
THE GASLIGHT,
   Decatur
MURPHY CUSTOM CRAFTS,
   Decatur
LEJON'S ANTIQUES & LAMPS,
   Enterprise
SARA ANN'S ANTIQUE SHOPPE,
   Florence
SOLOMONS ANTIQUES,
   Greenville

FOUR SEASONS ANTIQUES,
   Hueytown
COLLECTORS II,
   Montgomery
BETTY'S BARN,
   Opelika
HERITAGE HOUSE ANTIQUES,
   Opelika
JACKSON ANTIQUES,
   Opelika
B & S ANTIQUES,
   Owens Cross Roads
COACH & CARRIAGE,
   Ozark

ALASKA
SPINNING WHEEL ANTIQUES,
   Anchorage
YE OLDE PINE SHOP,
   Anchorage

ARIZONA
BROWN HOUSE ANTIQUES,
   Mesa
COLLECTOR'S CORNER,
   Mesa
FLORENCE'S UNIQUE COUNTRY
ANTIQUES,
   Mesa
RED SLEIGH ANTIQUES,
   Mesa
PHOENIX LAMPS & ANTIQUES,
   Phoenix
SEVENTH STREET SHOPPE,
   Phoenix
TOY COTTAGE ANTIQUES,
   Phoenix
UPTOWN ANTIQUES,
   Phoenix
ANTIQUES FOREVER,
   Scottsdale

THE ANTIQUE GALLERY,
Sedona
THINGS UNLIMITED,
Sedona
HAYDEN'S DISTINCTIVE
FURNITURE COMPANY,
Tucson

ARKANSAS
DEN OF ANTIQUITY,
Benton
BOB WHITE'S ANTIQUES,
Blytheville
ANTIQUES IN THE RED BARN,
Conway
EDELWEISS ANTIQUES,
Helena
WATSON'S ANTIQUES,
Hot Springs
DORA DAVIS' ANTIQUES,
Lake Hamilton
ANTIQUES LIMITED,
Little Rock
FIELD'S SELECT ANTIQUES,
Little Rock
KAZUKO ORIENTAL ARTS,
Little Rock
BETTY'S ANTIQUES,
North Little Rock

CALIFORNIA
BETTY'S BARN OF ANTIQUES,
Bakersfield
SAM'S,
Bakersfield
SHADOW HILLS ANTIQUES &
FINE ARTS GALLERY,
Beverly Hills
BRAWLEY ANTIQUES,
Brawley
THE GRAND MANOR,
Buellton
LA MARINA ANTIQUES LTD
Dana Point
CORBETTS ANTIQUES,
Fairfax
GEORGE GEORGES & SONS,
Hollywood
ANTIQUE MART OF LOS
ANGELES,
Los Angeles
BEAUSEJOUR ANTIQUES,
Los Angeles
BRETON HOUSE,
Los Angeles
HAMMOND HOUSE ANTIQUES,
Los Angeles
KINGS CABINET,
Los Angeles
MR RICK'S ANTIQUES,
Los Angeles
OLDEN TYMES OFFICE
INTERIORS,
Los Angeles
THE ANTIQUE SHOPPE,
Mammoth Lakes

GOLD TRAILS ANTIQUES,
Murphy
MARTHA'S ANTIQUES,
Pasadena
THE SOHO SHOPPE ANTIQUES,
Pasadena
ODOM'S ANTIQUES,
Sacramento
SACRAMENTO ANTIQUE
CENTER,
Sacramento
SACRAMENTO FLEA MARKET,
Sacramento
SAN ANSELMO ANTIQUES,
San Anselmo
THE CHOPPING BLOCK
ANTIQUES,
San Diego
NOSTALGIA,
San Diego
NEWCOMB'S ANTIQUES,
San Diego
THE RED LION ANTIQUES,
San Diego
ALESIA,
San Francisco
DILLINGHAM & BROWN,
San Francisco
HOUSE OF WICKER,
San Francisco
TOM KAYE ANTIQUES,
San Francisco
KINGS ANTIQUES,
San Francisco
OLD WAGON WHEEL
ANTIQUES,
San Francisco
RED ANCHOR,
San Francisco
SHINGLE SHACK ANTIQUES,
San Francisco
JAMES HENRY WALKER
ANTIQUES,
San Francisco
INDIANA ANTIQUES & DOLLS,
San Jose
THE BLUE CANDLESTICK,
Saratoga
COUNTRY ANTIQUES,
Studio City
ANTIQUE FAIR,
Yountville
THE VICTORIAN LADY,
Yountville

COLORADO
NANNY'S LITTLE SHACK,
Cortez
ANTIQUE TRADER,
Denver
DENVER ANTIQUE MARKET,
Denver
IGOTATHINGABOUT ANTIQUES,
Denver

SECOND NATURE
RESTORATION & ANTIQUES,
Denver
ANTIQUE MERCANTILE,
Lamar
THE ANTIQUE PLACE,
Niwot
THE LITTLE RED SLEIGH
ANTIQUES,
Steamboat Springs

CONNECTICUT
OLE' LAMPLIGHTER ANTIQUES,
Bristol
HEIRLOOM ANTIQUES,
Brooklyn
BRASS BED BOUTIQUE,
Canton
ONE OF A KIND,
Chester
NATHAN LIVERANT & SONS,
Colchester
HOLMES ANTIQUES,
Cornwall Bridge
HARRY HOLMES ANTIQUES,
Cornwall Bridge
MICHAEL FRIEDMAN ANTIQUES,
Easton
LILLIAN BLANKLEY COGAN,
Farmington
JUNE'S ANTIQUES &
COLLECTIBLES,
Groton
LEWIS W SCRANTON,
Killingworth
THOMAS D & CONSTANCE R
WILLIAMS,
Litchfield
LORETTA ROVINSKY,
Marble Dale
DOLLY'S ANTIQUES,
Meriden
WANDERERS DEN,
New Britain
HILBERT BROS,
New Canaan
THE ANTIQUE MARKET,
New Haven
PENNY PINCHER ANTIQUES,
New Milford
SAM & LEE SMITH-BONDED
WHOLESALE IMPORT
MERCHANTS,
Niantic
ANTIQUES AND,
Old Lyme
FALCONS ROOST ANTIQUES,
Old Lyme
ROBERT T BARANOWSKY
ANTIQUE SHOP,
Plainville
PLAINVILLE RAIL ROAD
STATION ANTIQUES,
Plainville

BARREDO'S ANTIQUES & USED
FURNITURE,
  Torrington
MILL HOUSE ANTIQUES,
  Woodbury

DELAWARE
CULVER'S ANTIQUES,
  Laurel
THE HUDSON HOUSE,
  Rehoboth Beach
THE COLLECTOR,
  Wilmington

DISTRICT OF COLUMBIA
THE CANAL CO OF
GEORGETOWN,
  Washington
THE CANDLER COMPANY,
  Washington
EARLY AMERICAN SHOP,
  Washington
MARKET ROW ANTIQUES,
  Washington
SEGAL'S ANTIQUES,
  Washington
UNIVERSITY ANTIQUES,
  Washington

FLORIDA
THE CHESTNUT TREE,
  Apalachicola
WEE BIT O'HEATHER,
  Clearwater
HEART OF THE ARTICHOKE,
  Coconut Grove
JOSEPH TUDISCO ANTIQUES,
  Coral Gables
KAY'S ANTIQUES,
  Daytona Beach
SERENDIPITY ANTIQUES &
FURNITURE,
  DeLand
GARRISON ANTIQUES,
  Delray Beach
BRASS BEDS LTD,
  Fort Lauderdale
R SINES ANTIQUES,
  Ft Lauderdale
RUTH BAILEY'S ANTIQUES,
  Ft Walton Beach
EARLY ATTIC,
  Jupiter
H & H ANTIQUES,
  Largo
BISHOP'S ANTIQUES,
  Lutz
I CHING ORIENTAL ANTIQUES
GALLERY,
  Miami
NORTH MIAMI ANTIQUE &
FURNITURE EXCHANGE,
  North Miami
ANTIQUE ACCENTS,
  Orlando

IVANHOE ANTIQUES MINI-MALL,
  Orlando
GARTH'S ANTIQUES,
  Pensacola
VEASIE'S ANTIQUE SHOP,
  Pensacola
WAYSIDE ANTIQUES,
  Reddick
METHUSELAH'S ANTIQUES,
  Sarasota
BEAUFEL'S ANTIQUES INC,
  Tampa

GEORGIA
RAY'S ANTIQUES,
  Albany
ANTHONY & STICKNEY,
  Atlanta
BENCHMARK ANTIQUES,
  Atlanta
SHARON BENNETT,
  Atlanta
THE BRASS GALLERY,
  Atlanta
J H ELLIOTT ANTIQUES,
  Atlanta
GOLD ANTIQUES & AUCTION
GALLERY,
  Atlanta
HOLLAND & COMPANY INC,
  Atlanta
NOBLE PIECES LTD, ANTIQUES,
  Atlanta
BEVERLY SCOTT,
  Atlanta
SLATER'S ANTIQUES,
  Atlanta
THE TOBY HOUSE ANTIQUES,
  Atlanta
TRADER DOY'S,
  Atlanta
WILLIAM WORD ANTIQUES INC,
  Atlanta
FLO'S ANTIQUES,
  Bogart
BRICE ANTIQUES,
  Bolingbroke
HAY'S MILL ANTIQUES,
  Carrollton
SARA HORNDON'S COLONY
HOUSE,
  Clermont
CENTURY ANTIQUES,
  Columbus
JACK THE STRIPPER,
  Decatur
MITCHEM'S ANTIQUES,
  Gay
HALL ANTIQUES & FLEA
MARKET,
  Indian Springs
CENTURY HOUSE ANTIQUES,
  Jackson
OAK WOOD ANTIQUES,
  LaGrange

THE EMPORIUM,
  Marietta
AUNTIE'S ANTIQUES,
  Riverdale
THE ANTIQUE INN,
  Smyrna
BARRY'S JUNKTION,
  Warner Robbins
GRIFFIS ANTIQUES,
  Woodbine

HAWAII
CREATIVE DECORATING,
  Honolulu

ILLINOIS
THE BELL JAR ANTIQUES,
  Chicago
BROWN BEAVER ANTIQUES,
  Chicago
CAVALIER ANTIQUE STUDIOS,
  Chicago
MARSHALL FIELD & COMPANY,
  Chicago
MALCOLM FRANKLIN INC,
  Chicago
GRIGGS ANTIQUE LAMPS,
  Chicago
LINCOLN AVE ANTIQUES,
  Chicago
JILL'S,
  Crete
COLONEL DANHELKA'S
ANTIQUES, INC,
  Downers Grove
BARN ANTIQUES,
  East Moline
SOMETHING ELSE LTD,
  Forest Park
UNIQUE ANTIQUES,
  Galena
HICKORY HILL ANTIQUES,
  Galesburg
D GRUNWALD ANTIQUES,
  Geneva
SHIRLEY MC GILL ANTIQUES,
  Geneva
THE HOUSE IN THE GLEN,
  Glen Ellyn
NADINE P MARTENS,
  Glen Ellyn
HERRINGS ANTIQUES,
  Greenville
FREIDARICA LTD,
  Highwood
THE LIAR,
  Hinsdale
THE ANTIQUE EMPORIUM,
  Kenilworth
OWEN'S COUNTRY CORNER
ANTIQUES,
  Litchfield
NOSTALGIA ANTIQUES,
  McHenry
ACORN ANTIQUES,
  Oak Park

BEV'S JUNTIQUES,
   Oakley
TOWPATH HOUSE,
   Ottawa
ED'S ANTIQUES,
   Richmond
HALFWAY HOUSE ANTIQUES
LTD,
   Rock Island
WHISTLER'S ART & ANTIQUE
SHOP,
   Rossville
ANTIQUE & CUROSITY SHOP,
   Sadorus
FRITZ GALLERY,
   St Charles
AARDVARK CLOCKS &
ANTIQUES,
   Springfield
NOSTALGIA ANTIQUES,
   Springfield
CHRIS L HILL ANTIQUES INC,
   Tuscola
VIOLETTA'S,
   Villa Park
VILLAGE STORE ANTIQUES,
   Wauconda
HELLO DOLLY SHOPPE,
   Waukegan
THINGS IN GENERAL,
   Waukegan
OLDIES BUT GOODIES,
   Wilmington
CALEDONIAN,
   Winnetka
SUZANNE ANTIQUE
ACCESSORIES,
   Winnetka
WEST END ANTIQUES LTD,
   Winnetka

INDIANA
BEAL'S ANTIQUES SHOP,
   Anderson
ACORN FARM ANTIQUES INC,
   Carmel
CUSTER HOUSE ANTIQUES,
   Centerville
SUBURBAN ANTIQUES,
   Centerville
WEBB'S ANTIQUES,
   Centerville
THE ANTIQUE SHOP,
   Chesterton
FIVE GABLES ANTIQUES,
   Chesterton
TREE HOUSE ANTIQUES,
   Chesterton
EDNA'S TREASURES,
   Columbus
WOOD & STONE ANTIQUES,
   Columbus
BILL & FAYE'S ANTIQUES,
   Crawfordsville
MICHELS JONES STUDIO,
   Crawfordsville

GASKILL'S ANTIQUES &
AUCTIONS,
   Fort Wayne
STATE STREET ANTIQUES,
   Fort Wayne
MOZELLES ANTIQUES,
   Frankfort
FERN'S ANTIQUES,
   French Lick
MC NEELEY'S ANTIQUES,
   Hardinsburg
WHISPERING WINDS ANTIQUES,
   Indianapolis
CANDLE CUPBOARD ANTIQUES,
   Knightstown
FULLER POLISHING COMPANY,
   Morgantown
JAY & ELLEN CARTER
ANTIQUES,
   Nashville
THE GARRET,
   Nashville
SCARCE O' FAT HOUSE,
   Nashville
THE 'WAGGIN' WHEELER,
   New Harmony
CENTURY HOUSE ANTIQUES,
   Richland
DEE'S ANTIQUES,
   Somerville
PRIMROSE ANTIQUES,
   South Bend
THE ATTIC,
   Terre Haute
MARTIN'S ANTIQUES,
   Terre Haute
BARBER'S ANTIQUES &
COLLECTIBLES,
   Thorntown
VERSAILLES ANTIQUES,
   Versailles
CURRY'S ANTIQUES,
   Waterloo
BROWN'S ANTIQUES,
   Zionsville

IOWA
HOBERT'S ANTIQUES,
   Charles City
J & M SHOPPE,
   Clarence
RED BARN ANTIQUES,
   Corydon
D & D ANTIQUES,
   Council Bluffs
A & D ANTIQUES,
   Davenport
RIVERBEND ANTIQUES, GIFTS &
RESTORATION,
   Davenport
K G ANTIQUES,
   Dexter
SCHOENS ANTIQUES,
   Dubuque
COUNTRY LANE ANTIQUES,
   Fort Madison

RED & WHITE ANTIQUE
SHOPPE,
   Fort Madison
INA-MARY SHOP,
   Fremont
PRESLER ANTIQUES,
   Gilmore City
STOFFER'S ANTIQUES,
   Hazleton
DAVE & MARY'S ANTIQUES,
   Iowa City
THE LANTERN ANTIQUES,
   La Porte City
SWANSON'S FARMHOUSE
ANTIQUES,
   Lehigh
BANOWETZ ANTIQUES,
   Maquoketa
ANTIQUES BY THE BULLARDS,
   Marion
RUNNING WATERS ANTIQUES,
   McGregor
COUNTRY STORE ANTIQUES,
   Mondamin
LION'S DEN ANTIQUES,
   Ogden
ISLAND CITY ANTIQUES,
   Sabula
RED WHEEL ANTIQUES,
   Sioux City
HIRSCHY'S USED FURNITURE &
ANTIQUES,
   Wayland
A B C ANTIQUE SHOPPE,
   West Des Moines
CENTURY SHOPPE LTD,
   West Des Moines

KANSAS
HORSE TRADERS ANTIQUES,
   Atwood
HIME'S YESTERDAY'S
ANTIQUES,
   Augusta
SUNFLOWER ANTIQUES,
   Belleville
FURNITURE WORKSHOP
ANTIQUES,
   Derby
DETRICH ANTIQUES,
   Great Bend
PLOWSHARE & POLKA DOT
CORNER ANTIQUES,
   Harper
QUANTRILL'S FLEA MARKET,
   Lawrence
VILLAGE BAZAAR,
   Lindsboro
LOU'S LOT NO 2,
   Morganville
FENNER'S ANTIQUES,
   Neodesha
GEORGE HAAS ANTIQUES,
   Ottawa
OLD & KLASSIC,
   Ottawa

HITCHING POST ANTIQUES,
Sabetha
GEORGE BENGE SR,
Topeka
NELSON'S ANTIQUES,
Topeka
WOODS SHED ANTIQUES,
Topeka
LUCILLA ANTIQUES,
Valley Center
COUNTRY ANTIQUES,
Wichita

KENTUCKY
TRASH & TREASURE SHOP,
Lebanon
BOONE'S ANTIQUES OF
KENTUCKY INC,
Lexington
DONALD MC GURK INC,
Lexington
BITTNERS,
Louisville
THE CENTURY SHOP,
Louisville
B A MAHANEY,
Louisville
E S TICHENOR COMPANY,
Louisville
HENDRICKSON'S ANTIQUES,
Maysville
THOMPSON'S ANTIQUES & GIFT
SHOP,
Paducah
BRENT'S ANTIQUE SHOP,
Paris
LONG BRANCH ANTIQUES,
Pendleton
RUSSELLVILLE ANTIQUE MALL,
Russellville
CORNER ANTIQUE SHOP,
Versailles

LOUISIANA
NOEL WISE ANTIQUES
Arabi
THE ANTIQUE WAREHOUSE
Baton Rouge
CRACKER BARREL ANTIQUES
Baton Rouge
OLD HOMESTEAD ANTIQUES &
COUNTRY THINGS
Baton Rouge
PECQUET'S BROCANTURE
ANTIQUE SHOPPE
Baton Rouge
SUNCO-SUN TRADING
COMPANY
Duson
ANTIQUE HAVEN
Harahan
ANTIQUES & INTERIORS
Lafayette
LAFITTE'S TREASURE ATTIC
Lafayette

LEBLANC'S ANTIQUES
Lafayette
BARBARA'S ANTIQUES
Lake Charles
WIND HAVEN ANTIQUES
Mandeville
B & F UPHOLSTERY
Metairie
HOUSE OF EUROPE
Monroe
COLLECTOR ANTIQUES
New Orleans
FLEUR DE LIS ANTIQUES
New Orleans
MANHEIM GALLERIES
New Orleans
MORTON'S AUCTION & SALES
CO
New Orleans
OLOE TOWNE ANTIQUE
SHOPPE,
New Orleans
M S RAU, INC
New Orleans
ST CHARLES ANTIQUES LTD
New Orleans
SHIRLEY'S ANTIQUES
New Orleans
NINA SLOSS ANTIQUES &
INTERIORS
New Orleans
WHISNANT GALLERIES
New Orleans
ARNETT'S ANTIQUES
Ponchatoula
EMILY ZUM BRUNNEN INC
Shreveport

MAINE
SOMEPLACE ELSE ANTIQUES &
BOOKS,
Alfred
PADDY'S COVE ANTIQUES,
Cape Porpoise
DAVIS ANTIQUES,
Farmington
FROST'S ANTIQUES,
Farmington
CRIMSON CRICKET,
Kennebunk
RANDS ANTIQUES,
Kennebunkport
J & J ANTIQUES OF MAINE,
Mexico
JACK PARTRIDGE,
North Edgecomb
THE CHATFIELDS ANTIQUES,
Pemaquid Harbor
MAC DOUGALL-GIONET
ANTIQUES GALLERY,
Wells

MARYLAND
CAROL TRELLA ANTIQUES,
Annapolis

ANTIQUE CENTER,
Baltimore
BRASS TOWNE,
Baltimore
THE DUSTY ATTIC,
Baltimore
PEACOCK & PARRETT,
Baltimore
THE J S PEARSON COMPANY,
Baltimore
JANE ALPER ANTIQUES,
Bethesda
WM BLAIR LTD,
Bethesda
EVELETH & SUMMERFORD,
Bethesda
OLD BOWIE ANTIQUE MARKET,
Bowie
MENDELSOHN GALLERIES,
Chevy Chase
LEN'S COUNTRY BARN
ANTIQUES,
College Park
GRANNY'S WORKSHOP,
Cordova
RUTH'S ANTIQUE SHOP, INC,
Funkstown
PINK DOMAIN ANTIQUES,
Galesville
STAGE COACH STOP,
Joppa
KRAMER & SCOTT, INC,
Kensington
THE VICTORIAN PARLOR,
Kensington
TRELA ANTIQUES,
Reistertown
HOLLY RIDGE ANTIQUES,
Salisbury
RED'S ANTIQUES,
Union Bridge
FOLEY'S ANTIQUES,
White Marsh

MASSACHUSETTS
DAM' YANKEE ANTIQUE
SHOPPE,
Bridgewater
HARVEST HILL ANTIQUES,
Bridgewater
BRIMFIELD ANTIQUES,
Brimfield
HARVARD ANTIQUES,
Cambridge
CHESHIRE VILLAGE ANTIQUES,
Cheshire
REDCOATS LTD,
Chestnut Hill
CREATION ANTIQUES &
INTERIORS,
Cohasset
THE OWL'S NEST ANTIQUES,
Cummaquid
GLASKOWSKY & COMPANY,
Easthampton

HOWARD'S ANTIQUES,
Essex
HOWARD'S FLYING DRAGON,
Essex
ANTIQUES AND INTERIORS,
Fairhaven
GRAIN MILL ANTIQUES,
Falmouth
SOPHISTICATED JUNK &
ANTIQUE SHOP,
Falmouth
JOHNSTON'S ANTIQUES,
Franklin
ANTIQUES-A JOINT VENTURE,
Hadley
GOOD TIME STOVE COMPANY,
Haydenville
WHOLESALE ANTIQUES,
Lancaster
PAUL WEISS ANTIQUES,
Leverett
STAGECOACH ANTIQUES,
Lincoln
THE HOBBY HORSE,
Marion
SOUTH RIVER PRIMITIVES,
Marshfield
MUSHROOM ANTIQUES,
Natick
HOUSE OF BRASS,
New Bedford
ROGER WILLIAMS AT THE OLD
CURIOSITY SHOP,
Newbury
THE CARRIAGE STOP,
Northfield
CAPE COD ANTIQUES
EXPOSITION,
Orleans
ENGLISH MANOR ANTIQUES,
Prides Crossing
COBWEB CORNER ANTIQUES,
Reading
LEONARD'S ANTIQUES INC,
Seekonk
TO EACH THEIR OWN,
Somerville
TOOMEY'S HAVEN ANTIQUES,
Southboro
GALLERIE DES JARDINS,
Sudbury
BIX FURNITURE STRIPPING
SERVICE,
Uxbridge
ANTIQUE CORNER,
West Newton
KING PHILLIP ANTIQUES,
Wrentham

MICHIGAN
ANDY'S ANTIQUES,
Allen
VARADI'S ANTIQUE SHOP,
Bay City
THE OLD PIONEER STORE,
Big Rapids

CLARKSTON MAIN STREET
ANTIQUES,
Clarkston
MILLSTONS ANTIQUE SHOP,
Coloma
THE HINTER HAUS ANTIQUE &
GIFT SHOP,
Eastport
SILVER STAR ANTIQUES,
Fenton
ERMA'S ANTIQUE SHOP,
Flint
THE SIGN OF THE PEACOCK,
Grand Ledge
BRASS SMITH SHOP,
Grand Rapids
THE DUTCH BARN,
Holland
O & B ANTIQUES,
Holly
KORNWOLF'S ANTIQUES,
Ironwood
41 ANTIQUES,
Ishpeming
HARBOR HILLS ANTIQUES,
Macatawa
WOODEN SKATE ANTIQUES,
Okemos
JOHN A MCGUIRE,
Pontiac
THE WHIPPOORWILL,
Whitehall

MINNESOTA
CURIOSITY SHOP,
Faribault
OLDE TYME SHOPPE,
Kennedy
BEEHIVE ANTIQUES,
Long Lake
BARGAIN CENTER,
Mankato
COBBLESTONE ANTIQUES,
Minneapolis
WICKERWORKS,
Minneapolis
YANKEE PEDDLER,
Minneapolis
GEORGE ENZ ANTIQUES,
Red Wing
STRUCK'S ANTIQUE SHOP,
Red Wing
GRAND HOUSE ANTIQUES,
St Paul
J & E ANTIQUES,
St Paul
ROBERT J RIESBERG,
St Paul
THE BARN WITH THE RED
DOOR,
Stillwater
THE TURNING POINT,
Willmar
BREMERS' ANTIQUES &
COLLECTIBLES,
Zumbro Falls

ZUMBRO VALLEY ANTIQUES,
Zumbro Falls

MISSISSIPPI
HOBBY HOUSE ANTIQUES,
Biloxi
GENE'S ANTIQUES,
Greenwood
WALKER MCINTYRE ANTIQUES,
Greenwood
EARLY TIMES ANTIQUES,
Gulfport
ROSE'S RELIC ROOM,
Gulfport
VADA'S ANTIQUE SHOP,
Hattiesburg
ANTIQUES GALLERY,
Jackson
JO'S ANTIQUES,
Jackson
YOUR BARGAIN SHOP,
Jackson
MARY'S FUTURE ANTIQUES,
Madison
HELEN B FIGURA ANTIQUES,
Natchez
THE CURIOSITY SHOP,
Ocean Springs
MURPHEY ANTIQUES LTD,
Tupelo
MCNUTT HOUSE ANTIQUES,
Vicksburg
YESTERYEAR ANTIQUES,
Yazoo City

MISSOURI
CENTURY HOUSE ANTIQUE'S,
Blue Springs
CAMERON'S ANTIQUES,
Halltown
LONG'S ANTIQUES,
Higginsville
LASATER'S ANTIQUES,
Independence
MARY & MONTY'S ANTIQUES,
Independence
ANTIQUE WORLD,
Kansas City
BLUE VALLEY ANTIQUES,
Kansas City
STREET'S ANTIQUES,
Laclede
SILVER DOLLAR TRADING CO,
Mexico
THE OLD N' YOU ANTIQUE
MART,
Riverside
WOOD'N THINGS SHOPPE,
Robertsville
CREVERLINGS ANTIQUES &
TREASURES BOUTIQUE,
St Joseph
DALSING'S,
St Joseph

GRAVOIS-ANTIQUES & FLEA
MARKET,
St Louis
CAROUSEL ANTIQUES,
Springfield
BROWNSVILLE STATION
ANTIQUES,
Sweet Springs
HOHN'S ANTIQUES,
Warrensburg
RED DOOR ANTIQUE SHOP,
Warrenton

MONTANA
TRAILS END ANTIQUES,
Ronan
PUYEAR'S ANTIQUES,
Stevensville

NEBRASKA
CEDAR HILLS ANTIQUES,
Beatrice
THE ANTIQUE SHOP LTD,
Bennington
EL-BI-GON ANTIQUES,
Columbus
KNISLEY'S ANTIQUES,
Goehner
BARGAIN JOHN'S ANTIQUES,
Lexington
HAUGH'S ANTIQUES,
Lexington
THE HERITAGE HOUSE,
Lincoln
WAGON WHEELS,
Lincoln
HOMESTEAD ANTIQUES,
McCook
YE OLDE JUNQUE SHOPPE,
Nebraska City
KATELMAN COMPANY, INC,
Omaha
WAREHOUSE ANTIQUES,
Omaha

NEVADA
PURPLE BOTTLE ANTIQUES,
Gardnerville
A TO Z MART,
Las Vegas
BUZZ AND COMPANY,
Las Vegas
THOMSON'S ANTIQUES,
Reno
HERITAGE ANTIQUES,
Virginia City

NEW HAMPSHIRE
FERN ROCK ANTIQUES,
Ashland
CRAWFORD CORNER
ANTIQUES,
Bristol
FERN ROCK ANTIQUES,
Campton

OLDE CHESTER ANTIQUES,
Chester
1680 HOUSE ANTIQUES,
East Kingston
OCTOBER STONE ANTIQUES,
Exeter
FERN ROCK ANTIQUES,
Gilford
PEDERSEN ANTIQUES,
Grafton
THE COBBS,
Hancock
FELSEN'S ANTIQUES,
Henniker
MEADOW HEARTH ANTIQUES,
Hopkinton
WHEAT & CHAFF ANTIQUES,
Hopkinton
FERN ROCK,
Laconia
BEAL HOUSE INN & ANTIQUES,
Littleton
CONSTANCE BERGENDOFF
ANTIQUES,
Lyme
BURLWOOD ANTIQUE MARKET,
Meredith
THE LOG CABIN ANTIQUES,
North Conway
BLUE BOAR ANTIQUES,
Northhampton
COUNTRY ANTIQUES,
Pittsfield
NELSON'S ANTIQUES,
Rumney
HARRISON HOUSE ANTIQUES,
South Weare
THE OLDE TANNERY
ANTIQUES,
Stratham
THE TIN DRUM ANTIQUES,
Stratham
DOW'S CORNER SHOP,
Tuftonboro Corner
HALF-MOON ANTIQUES,
Washington
PEPPERSAUCE ANTIQUES,
West Ossipee

NEW JERSEY
ANTIQUERY,
Clifton
PUMLEYE'S ANTIQUES SHOP,
Lafayette
GOVERNORS ANTIQUE MARKET
AND OUTDOOR FLEA MARKET,
Lambertville
ANTHONY & ELLEN BARRETT
ANTIQUES,
Mullica Hill
ROBERT & ANN SCHUMANN
ANTIQUES,
Mullica Hill
STONE HEARTH ANTIQUES
VILLAGE,
Pemberton

HAWTHORN & GRAY DESIGN
STUDIO,
Sergeantsville
SOMERS POINT CURIOSITY
SHOP,
Somers Point
ANTIQUE ASSOCIATES,
Wayne
YESTERYEAR TREASURES,
Whitehouse

NEW MEXICO
THE DEPOT ANTIQUES
Alamogordo
OZARK COUNTRY ANTIQUES
Albuquerque
SUE'S ANTIQUES
Hillsboro
CATES ANTIQUES & SELECT
USED FURNITURE
Las Cruces
WILSON GALLERIES
Santa Fe

NEW YORK
LITTLE BROWN JUG,
Acra
GRANDMA'S DUSTED
TREASURES,
Auburn
DONNA'S ANTIQUES,
Bath
THE HEIRLOOM SHOP,
Bayside
BEARSVILLE ANTIQUES,
Bearsville
RAY'S ANTIQUES,
Bellmore
CONE HOUSE ANTIQUES,
Binghamton
BROWNER ANTIQUES &
GALLERY INC,
Brooklyn
A TIME TO REMEMBER
ANTIQUES,
Brooklyn
EDWARD E DAVIS,
Canandaigua
HARVEST MILL,
Canandaigua
HEIRLOOM GALLERY,
Canandaigua
ALAN & JEAN SMITH,
Chazy
OLD STORY TAVERN
ANTIQUES,
Cherry Valley
ROUND MOUNTAIN ANTIQUES,
Cold Spring
COOPERSTOWN COUNTRY
STORE & ANTIQUES,
Cooperstown
THE LEDGES,
Cooperstown

STAGE COACH LANE
ANTIQUES,
  Cooperstown
BUTTER HILL ANTIQUE SHOP,
  Cornwall-on-Hudson
ACKERLY AUCTION BARN,
  Delhi
DAVISON ANTIQUES,
  Delhi
FIRE HOUSE ANTIQUES CO-OP,
  East Aurora
THE STRABELS,
  East Aurora
DE LAP'S ANTIQUES,
  Fairport
EVELYN NORBERG ANTIQUES,
  Falconer
FREDONIA WOODS & WARES,
  Fredonia
THE VICTORIAN HOUSE,
  Hartwick
CANASTAR'S ANTIQUES,
  Herkimer
THE CARROUSEL,
  Huntington
HOUSE OF HOFFMAN,
  Ithaca
FRED J JOHNSTON,
  Kingston
COLDSTREAM ANTIQUES,
  Larchmont
MONT VERT ANTIQUE
FURNITURE,
  Larchmont
THOMAS E TREMER,
  Lima
DOT'S ANTIQUES AND
UPHOLSTERY SHOP,
  Lockport
HAVEN HOUSE,
  Lockport
THE VILLAGE SHOP,
  Long Eddy
GARY P GUARNO,
  Mamaroneck
YE OLDE SHOPPE ANTIQUES,
  Mohawk
MONROE ANTIQUES,
  Monroe
JA-CO ANTIQUES,
  Monticello
MYRTLE'S WHAT NOT SHOP,
  Mount Morris
R H ELLSWORTH LTD,
  New York City
LANDRIGAN & STAIR,
  New York City
PIERRE DEUX ANTIQUES INC,
  New York City
SHOPKEEPER ANTIQUES,
  Otego
ANTIQUES ET CAETERA,
  Plattsburgh
HOUSE OF WELTZ,
  Port Chester

THE MEATING PLACE
ANTIQUES,
  Port Washington
VILLAGE INTERIORS &
ANTIQUES,
  Port Washington
JACK GRECO,
  Rochester
MONROE ANTIQUE CENTER,
  Rochester
TRADE WINDS EAST ANTIQUES,
  Saranac Lake
BURTON & HELAINE
FENDELMAN,
  Scarsdale
TIBBITS ANTIQUES,
  Southampton
THE GRACE SHOPPE,
  South Durham
BALL TAVERN ANTIQUES,
  Stanley
WALKER-MURPHY INC,
  Staten Island
ATWOOD TREASURE COVE,
  Stone Ridge
SCHOOLMASTER ANTIQUES,
  Tappan
THE COUNTRY COLLECTOR,
  Tuxedo
EDWARD & CAROL PETERS,
  Watkins Glen
CHICKEN COOP ANTIQUES,
  Webster
DOROTHEA F BERTRAM,
  Westfield
YANKEE TRADER ANTIQUE
SHOPPE,
  Westfield
THE TREASURE CHEST,
  Worcester

NORTH CAROLINA
BEHIAVILLE ANTIQUES &
FURNITURE CO
  Beulaville
CLARA'S ANTIQUES
  Charlotte
GLORY BE!
  Charlotte
THOMPSON ANTIQUE CO
  Charlotte
AMERICAN INTERNATIONAL
FURNITURE & ANTIQUES
  Durham
HELENE'S ANTIQUES
  Etowah
ADAMS ANTIQUES-THE
CAROLINIANS
  Greensboro
AMERICAN INTERNATIONAL
FURNITURE & ANTIQUES
  Greensboro
B & B TREASURES
  Greensboro
THELMA B HARRISON
  Greensboro

LINK'S ANTIQUE SHOP
  Lexington
AMERICAN INTERNATIONAL
FURNITURE & ANTIQUES
  Raleigh
L & S ANTIQUES
  Reidsville
BOONE'S ANTIQUES INC
  Wilson
COLONIAL HOUSE OF
ANTIQUES
  Wilson
TREASURES'-TRASH ANTIQUES
& GIFTS
  Wingate
SUMMIT ANTIQUES
  Winston-Salem

NORTH DAKOTA
MAC'S PLACE ANTIQUES,
  Bowbells

OHIO
RED BARN ANTIQUES,
  Amlin
TYGERT HOUSE ANTIQUES,
  Chillicothe
ANTIQUE WORLD LTD,
  Cincinnati
HIDDEN HERITAGE,
  Cincinnati
INDIAN MOUND ANTIQUES,
  Cincinnati
YORK'S OLDE THING,
  Cincinnati
A-R-M APPRAISAL SERVICE,
  Columbus
MARGE PIPER ET CETERA
ANTIQUES,
  Fairhaven
THE SHOE STRING,
  Greenville
GARRETT'S ANTIQUES,
  Hamilton
ROCK CHIMNEY,
  Huntsville
DUTCHMAN'S 2ND ANTIQUES,
  Marietta
AMERICAN GENERAL STORE
CO,
  Marysville
ANNE GROH'S ANTIQUE
GALLERY,
  Massillon
THE SARGENT HOUSE
ANTIQUES,
  Medina
COOPER'S GENERAL STORE &
AUCTION GALLERY,
  Northfield center
KEMBLE'S ANTIQUES,
  Norwich
MARGE PIPER ET CETERA
ANTIQUES,
  Oxford

HEIRLOOMS ETCETERA,
Sandusky
KING 50,
Toledo
GLUCK'S GIFT & ANTIQUE
SHOP INC,
Youngstown

OKLAHOMA
LACY ANTIQUES GIFTS &
JEWELRY
Claremore
VENTRIS ANTIQUES
Claremore
FRANCES ANTIQUES
McAlester
DAVE'S NEW & USED
FURNITURE
Miami
KING'S ANTIQUES
Norman
ANDERSON ANTIQUES & ART
GALLERIES
Oklahoma City
ARNOLA SCHRODER ANTIQUES
& DECORATIVES
Oklahoma City
THE CONNOISSEUR SHOP
Oklahoma City
COTTAGE ANTIQUES
Oklahoma City
MEMORIES MALL
Oklahoma City
THE RUSHLIGHT
Oklahoma City
JOHNIE'S ANTIQUES
Tulsa

OREGON
FORT DALLES ANTIQUES,
The Dalles
LAKE'S ANTIQUES,
Eugene
B LOWD AND SON,
Hubbard
TOLLEFSON'S ANTIQUES
(TOLLY'S),
Oakland
THE GENERAL STORE,
Portland
THE WOODTIQUE,
Roseburg
LANA AVE 2ND HAND,
Salem
LOU'S ANTIQUES,
Salem
WAYSTATION ANTIQUES,
Salem
99 E-ANTIQUE-USED,
Woodburn

PENNSYLVANIA
GREENBURG & BARNYAK INC,
Allentown
COLLECTOR'S CORNER,
Altoona

EBERTS ANTIQUES,
Andreas
DRUMMER BOY ANTIQUES,
Beach Lake
WILLOWBROOK ANTIQUES,
Brodheadsville
THE SPRING MILL ANTIQUE
SHOP,
Conshohocken
SMITH'S ANTIQUES,
Coraopolis
PAT ERRIGO ANTIQUES,
Curwensville
MAJOR ANTIQUES,
Dallas
JACK'S ANTIQUES,
Duncansville
STALLFORT ANTIQUES,
Elverson
IRON KETTLE ANTIQUES,
Emmaus
LAUSCH'S DUTCH BARN,
Ephrata
ROBERT & JESSIE POWELL,
Evans City
MARGARET SCHAFER,
Fairview Village
MEETINGHOUSE ANTIQUE
SHOP,
Fort Washington
SEVEN OAKS,
Greensburg
THOMAS ANTIQUES,
Hamburg
RANDALL C KRITKAUSKY &
CAROLYN SCHMIDT ANTIQUES,
Harford
FOX CHASE ANTIQUES,
Harrisburg
COLONIAL HOUSE ANTIQUES,
Hershey
HOLLY CORNER ANTIQUES ,
Honesdale
COPPER EAGLE ANTIQUES,
Huntingdon Valley
GALLAGHER & CO,
Johnstown
HARRIS ANTIQUES,
Knox
ROBERT BURKHARDT,
Kutztown
GREENWICH MILLS,
Kutztown
BUCHTERS ANTIQUES,
Lancaster
CLARENCE HINDEN,
Lancaster
JEAN C CLEMMER,
Lederach
SMITHERS ANTIQUES,
Lewistown
MARKY'S OLD FORT ANTIQUES,
Ligonier
OLD TOWNE STORE &
ANTIQUES,
Lititz

HELEN B HENRY,
Macungie
GRAY VALLEY ANTIQUES,
Mainesburg
BREST'S RED BARN ANTIQUES,
Meadville
H & R SANDOR, INC,
New Hope
THE CURIOSITY SHOP,
New Milford
THE ARCHIVE,
Philadelphia
BLUM'S ANTIQUE SHOP,
Philadelphia
BLUM'S CHESTNUT HILL
ANTIQUES,
Philadelphia
CANDELIGHT ANTIQUE SHOP,
Philadelphia
JOHNSTONE-FONG, INC,
Philadelphia
KINGSLEY & O'BRENNAN,
Philadelphia
TERRY LOW,
Philadelphia
ANTHONY A P STUEMPFIG
ANTIQUES,
Philadelphia
TRANSUE & CLARKE,
Philadelphia
THE WAY WE WERE,
Philadelphia
DELP'S PINK CAROUSEL
ANTIQUES,
Pittsburgh
MARGERY B GEORGE
ANTIQUES,
Pittsburgh
ROCKMAN'S ANTIQUES &
FURNITURE,
Pittsburgh
HENRY'S ANTIQUE SHOP,
Plymouth
WALTER S ELLIOTT,
Pottstown
KENNETH C STUMPF,
Pottsville
TOWN & COUNTRY
UPHOLSTERY & ANTIQUES,
Pottsville
STERNBERGH ANTIQUES,
Reading
TRIMBLE'S ANTIQUES,
Schwenksville
SEVEN TWENTY ONE ANTIQUE
SHOPPE,
Scranton
THE GREEN BARN ANTIQUES,
Seelyville
JOHN D LEWIS,
Sewickley
OLEXEN'S ANTIQUES,
Valencia
ELIZABETH L MATLAT,
West Chester
COFFMAN ANTIQUES,
White

THE BEDPOST,
Zionsville

RHODE ISLAND
CHESTNUT HILL ANTIQUES
Chepachet
BARBS ANTIQUES
Cranston
CHINA TRADE ANTIQUES
Newport
THE DEACON'S ANNEX
Warren

SOUTH CAROLINA
NOAH'S ARK
Abbeville
ELIZABETH AUSTIN INC
Charleston
COLES & COMPANY INC
Charleston
GARDEN GATE ANTIQUES
Charleston
KELLEYS ANTIQUES
Liberty
CHESTNUT GALLERIES
Spartanburg

SOUTH DAKOTA
MIDWEST MUSEUM & ANTIQUE
SHOP,
Gettysburg
TUCKERO ANTIQUES,
Sioux Falls

TENNESSEE
WHEELER'S ANTIQUES,
Chattanooga
NELSIE ANDERSON MULKINS,
Germantown
DOMINICKS ANTIQUES,
Knoxville
CHINA TOWN IMPORTS
Memphis
MASTERPIECE GALLERIES,
Memphis
THE OLD BARN ANTIQUES,
Memphis
SPIVACK'S ANTIQUES,
Memphis
SPRINGER ANTIQUES,
Memphis
STATEN'S ANTIQUES,
Memphis
ARNETTE ANTIQUE GALLERIES,
Murfreesboro
EVELYN ANDERSON
GALLERIES,
Nashville
FOREHAND'S ANTIQUE SHOP,
Nashville

TEXAS
GOLDEN ANTIQUES,
Amarillo

ACCENT ALLEY,
Austin
ANTEDILUVIAN ANTIQUES,
Austin
HURT'S HUNTING GROUNDS,
Austin
RUE DE LAMAR GALLERY,
Austin
T'S ANTIQUES,
Austin
WESTLAKE ARCHITECURAL
ANTIQUES,
Austin
COUNTRY LANE ANTIQUES,
Beaumont
ROBERTS ANTIQUES,
Beeville
COBBS MARKET ANTIQUES,
Bryan
THE QUAINT SHOP,
Corpus Christi
TIN BARN ANTIQUES,
Corpus Christi
ANN'S FURNITURE &
ANTIQUES,
Dallas
ANTIQUE HOUSE,
Dallas
CHERIE'S ANTIQUES,
Dallas
ROSE DRIVER,
Dallas
JAMIE'S ANTIQUES,
Dallas
ELIZABETH LE CONEY
ANTIQUES,
Dallas
MIKE'S THINGS,
Dallas
BILL MILLER'S ANTIQUES,
Dallas
MONDAYS,
Dallas
OLD ENGLAND ANTIQUES,
Dallas
ONE OF A KIND ANTIQUES,
Dallas
ORIENTAL ART SHOP,
Dallas
PHEASANT ANTIQUES,
Dallas
TUCKER FURNITURE,
Dallas
CIRCA,
El Paso
ESTHER'S ANTIQUES,
El Paso
THE LOOKING GLASS,
El Paso
EMANUEL ANTIQUES &
CABINET SHOP,
Electra
CENTRAL ANTIQUES,
Ft Worth
THE SMITH SHOP,
Ft Worth

STONE HOUSE TRADING POST
INC,
Ft Worth
THIS OLD HOUSE,
Ft Worth
THE TULIP & THE BIRD,
Frederickburg
COUNTRY COTTAGE ANTIQUES,
Garland
FAULKNER'S ANTIQUES INC,
Henderson
HEIRLOOM HOUSE,
Houston
HOUSTON ANTIQUE & ART
CENTER,
Houston
INTERNATIONAL ANTIQUE &
AUCTION CENTER INC,
Houston
MAPLE LEAF ANTIQUE SHOP,
Houston
POST OAK ANTIQUES,
Houston
R & F ANTIQUES,
Houston
KING-THOMASSON ANTIQUES,
Houston
WASHINGTON AVENUE
ANTIQUES,
Houston
EVELYN WILSON INTERIORS,
Houston
J'S ANTIQUES,
Irving
SUSIE R SMITH ANTIQUES,
Kennedale
COX'S ANTIQUES,
Kilgore
GAIDO'S COUNTRY LANE
ANTIQUES,
League City
THE UNIQUE ANTIQUES,
League City
TURNER ANTIQUES,
Longview
THE ANTIQUE EMPORIUM INC,
Longview
COTTAGE ANTIQUES,
Lubbock
RED BARN ANTIQUES,
Marshall
THE MULESHOE ART LOFT,
Muleshoe
PALACE HEIGHTS ANTIQUES,
New Braunfels
HAZEL M RAWLS ANTIQUES,
Orange
HOUSE OF RUTH,
Pasadena
SNOOPER'S PARADISE,
Port Authur
TOM NOBLE,
Richardson
THE ANTIQUE MALL,
San Angelo

ALLENS ANTIQUES & ART
GALLERIES,
  San Antonio
THE ANTIQUE GALLERY,
  San Antonio
COFFEE MILL ANTIQUES,
  San Antonio
MORAN ANTIQUES,
  San Antonio
THIS & THAT ANTIQUES,
  San Antonio
SPEYER'S ANTIQUE & AUCTION
GALLERIES INC,
  Temple
VICTORIA ANTIQUE SHOP,
  Victoria

UTAH
ANTIQUE HOUSE,
  Ogden
QUIGLEY'S ANTIQUES,
  Provo
FIRE HOUSE ANTIQUES,
  Salt Lake City
'' HONEST JON'S ANTIQUES''
  Salt Lake City

VERMONT
GAM'S & GAMP'S ANTIQUES,
  Alburg
LORRAINE & WARREN KIMBLE,
  Brandon
BACK DOOR ANTIQUES,
  Essex Junction
GABRIEL'S BARN,
  Grafton
THE GABLES ANTIQUES,
  Harmonyville
BARBARA E MILLS,
  Hartland
WATERFORD HILL ANTIQUES,
  Lower Waterford
BIX ANTIQUES & TREASURES,
  Middlebury
HYLAND'S ANTIQUES,
  Newport
BETTY STERLING,
  Randolph
MILL BROOK ANTIQUES,
  Reading
SCHOOLHOUSE ANTIQUES,
  Saxtons River
COPPER LAMP ANTIQUES,
  Shaftsbury
THE COVERED BRIDGE
ANTIQUE SHOP,
  Windsor

VIRGINIA
ANTIQUES,
  Alexandria
DECOR ANTIQUES,
  Alexandria
BLANCHE DOBKIN ANTIQUES,
  Alexandria

LLOYD'S ROW,
  Alexandria
SHIRLEY MYERS ANTIQUES,
  Alexandria
ODDS & ENDS SHOPPE,
  Alexandria
G RANDALL FINE ANTIQUES &
WORKS OF ART,
  Alexandria
THE SLEIGH BELL,
  Alexandria
CUPBOARD ANTIQUES,
  Arlington
ANTIQUES AT BURLINGTON,
  Barboursville
OBSESSION ANTIQUES INC,
  Charlottesville
HUGHES HOUSE OF ANTIQUES,
  Chesapeake
OAK GROVE FLEA MARKET,
  Chesapeake
SCHENCKIES ANTIQUES,
  Hillsboro
THE GLORY BOX AT KING
CANTON INN,
  Irvington
GATES ANTIQUES LTD,
  Midlothian
WORCESTER HOUSE
ANTIQUES,
  New Church
AMERICAN ANTIQUE
IMPORTERS & AUCTION
ROOMS,
  Norfolk
DECOR DESIGN,
  Norfolk
DESKS INC,
  Portsmouth
THE MOUNT VERNON ANTIQUE
SHOP,
  Portsmouth
COCHRAN'S ANTIQUES,
  Purcellville
WILLIAM C ADAMS JR,
  Richmond
ANNE'S ANTIQUES,
  Richmond
THE ANTIQUES WAREHOUSE,
  Richmond
BERRY'S ANTIQUES,
  Richmond
REESE ANTIQUE COMPANY,
  Richmond
RICHMOND ART COMPANY INC,
  Richmond
REBEL HILL ANTIQUES,
  Ruther Glen
BEHL'S SPORTS MARINA &
ANTIQUES,
  Virginia Beach
DOLLY'S ANTIQUES & GIFT
SHOP,
  Virginia Beach
THE SWAN TAVERN ANTIQUES,
  Yorktown

WASHINGTON
SHEPARD'S EMPORIUM,
  Carnation
ANDERBERG ANTIQUES,
  Edmonds
A BIT O' EVERYTHING,
  Everett
NARROWS BRIDGE ANTIQUES,
  Gig Harbor
COBWEB ANTIQUES,
  Redmond
ANITA'S ANTIQUES,
  Des Moines
THE ANTIQUE WORLD,
  Seattle
COBWEB ANTIQUES,
  Seattle
FURNITURE SPA,
  Seattle
LADYBUG ANTIQUES,
  Seattle
THE OAK PARLOR,
  Seattle
RITCHIE'S PLANTS AND
ANTIQUES,
  Seattle
ROSEN-COLGREN GALLERY,
  Seattle
SHEPARD'S EMPORIUM,
  Seattle
THIRD HAND SHOP,
  Seattle
TO THE TRADE, INC,
  Seattle
TRUST HOUSE ANTIQUES,
  Seattle
BLUE LANTERN ANTIQUES,
  Shelton
ANOTHER ANTIQUE SHOP,
  Snohomish
ENGEL'S FLEA MARKET,
  Spokane
THE WOODEN NICKEL,
  Spokane
SIXTH AVENUE HOUSE OF
ANTIQUES,
  Tacoma

WEST VIRGINIA
GOEBEL'S ANTIQUES
  St Albans

WISCONSIN
SCHWARTZ ANTIQUE
  Green Bay
JAEGER ANTIQUES
  Janesville
THE LAST STRAW
  Madison
AMERICAN ANTIQUES
  Mazomanie
THE WOOD SHED
  Menasha

CONSIGNMENT CENTER OF
MILWAUKEE
  Milwaukee
KELLER TRADING CO
  Mount Horeb

KLINE'S KOLLECTABLES
KORNER
  Superior
MINDY'S ANTIQUES
  Sussex
ALCORN'S ANTIQUES
  West Allis

GLASS

ALABAMA
IRON ART INC,
  Birmingham
FARMER'S ANTIQUE SHOP,
  Elba
EUFAULA ANTIQUE SHOP,
  Eufaula
SUZIE'S ANTIQUES,
  Midway
MEMORY LANE ANTIQUES,
  Montgomery

ARIZONA
THE GLASS URN,
  Phoenix
KAY'S ANTIQUES,
  Phoenix
LILLIAN'S ANTIQUES,
  Phoenix
SEVENTH STREET SHOPPE,
  Phoenix
JOANNA'S ANTIQUES,
  Scottsdale
REDDY'S ANTIQUES,
  Scottsdale
THE ROSEMARY ANTIQUE
SHOP,
  Scottsdale
THINGS UNLIMITED,
  Sedona
ANTIQUE FURNITURE GALLERY,
  Tucson
LASTENIA'S ANTIQUES,
  Tucson
NETTIE'S TREASURES,
  Tucson
PHYLISS C SPAGNOLA,
  Tucson
BARBARA SKILTON'S
ANTIQUES,
  Tucson

ARKANSAS
MARGARET'S ANTIQUES,
  Batesville

CAMP ANTIQUE SALES,
  Brinkley
COOK'S ANTIQUE HOUSE,
  Carlisle
MILLER'S ANTIQUES,
  Carlisle
GALLERY 'G' ANTIQUES,
  De Witt
MR CHRISTOPHER SHOP,
  Hardy
GWALTNEY'S,
  Heber Springs
WORTHEY'S ANTIQUES AND
GIFTS,
  Hope
CLINTON'S ANTIQUES,
  Hot Springs
WATSON'S ANTIQUE,
  Hot Springs
SCHRAND'S GIFTS AND
ANTIQUES,
  Judsonia
BLACKBURN'S ANTIQUES,
  Little Rock
RED HOUSE ANTIQUES,
  Marvel
NINA'S ANTIQUES AND GIFTS,
  Paragould
HOUSE OF VALUE,
  Rogers

CALIFORNIA
BUSTAMENTE ENTERPRISES,
INC,
  Atwater
CLEO'S ATTIC,
  Bakersfield
DR ANN'S ANTIQUES,
  Bakersfield
SHADOW HILLS ANTIQUES &
FINE ARTS GALLERY,
  Beverly Hills
MARY K'S ANTIQUES,
  Big Pine
BRAWLEY ANTIQUES,
  Brawley

THIS 'N THAT SHOPPE,
  Buellton
ROAD RUNNER ANTIQUES,
  Columbia
NINA'S ANTIQUES,
  Glendale
JOANNA'S CURIOSITY SHOPPE,
  LaCanada
GALLERY ONE,
  Laguna Beach
RICK'S RELICS,
  Lemon Grove
LAKESIDE ANTIQUES,
  Lodi
GLORIA'S POTPOURRI,
  Los Angeles
OLD WORLD IMPORTS,
  Los Angeles
UNUSUAL ANTIQUES, A TO Z,
  Los Angeles
LOVELL'S WINDO-ART,
  Sacramento
PERRAULT'S ANTIQUES,
  Sacramento
WILLIAM'S ANTIQUES,
  Sacramento
BLANCHE KOEHMSTEDT
ANTIQUES,
  San Diego
LAMB ANTIQUES & APPRAISAL
SERVICE,
  San Diego
NOSTALGIA EXPRESS,
  San Francisco
CLASSIC ANTIQUES,
  San Jose
WAY BACK WHEN ANTIQUES,
  Santa Cruz
BOUTIQUE ANTIQUES,
  Yucca Valley

COLORADO
ARIEL'S ANTIQUES,
  Boulder
COBWEB ANTIQUES,
  Colorado Springs

DENVER ANTIQUE MARKET,
Denver
MEMORABILIA/COLORADO ART
GLASS WORKS,
Denver
GATEWAY ANTIQUES,
Englewood
LITTLE RED HOUSE ANTIQUES,
Greeley
REVA'S MOUNTAIN HOME,
Lyons
MC KINLEY & HILL ANTIQUES,
Wheatridge

CONNECTICUT
J THOMAS MELVIN,
Bethel
ONE OF A KIND,
Chester
THE BRASS BUGLE,
Cornwall Bridge
OLD EASTON CENTER
ANTIQUES,
Easton
BUTTONSHOP ANTIQUES,
Newton
EAST LYNN ANTIQUES,
Niantic
OLD MYSTIC ANTIQUES,
Old Mystic
PLAINVILLE RAIL ROAD
STATION ANTIQUES,
Plainville
YESTERDAY ANTIQUES,
Rowayton
THE ANTIQUE SHOP,
Stratford
TURN O' THE CENTURY,
Woodbury

DELAWARE
FLAMM ANTIQUES INC,
Dover

FLORIDA
KAREN'S KORNER,
Clearwater
WEE BIT O'HEATHER,
Clearwater
PAT'S ANTIQUES,
Cocoa
LONGFRITZ'S ANTIQUES,
Dade City
ROBERTS BARN ANTIQUES,
Dade City
BROWNER ANTIQUES,
Dania
SERENDIPITY ANTIQUES &
FURNITURE CO, INC,
DeLand
TRASH 'N TREASURES,
Largo
ANTIQUE COLLECTORS MALL,
Malabar

LYNN'S ANTIQUES,
Malabar
SIDNEY SCHAFFER ANTIQUES,
Miami
ANTIQUE ACCENTS,
Orlando
ST ANDREW ANTIQUE SHOP,
Panama City
MAGIC DREAM CASTLES,
Pompano Beach
CAMPBELL'S COUNTRY STORE,
Princeton
GRANDMA'S ATTIC ANTIQUES,
St Petersburg
FOSTER'S TRADING CENTER,
Sebring
ANTIQUE PARADISE,
South Miami
GOLDEN EAGLE,
Tampa

GEORGIA
THE MAXWELL HOUSE,
Atlanta
HAY'S MILL ANTIQUES,
Carrollton
PAUL BARON CO,
Decatur
THE MAN OF KENT INC,
Savannah
DREAM HOUSE ANTIQUES,
Sylvester
BETTY'S VARIETY & ANTIQUES,
Winder

HAWAII
THE CARRIAGE HOUSE,
Honolulu

IDAHO
VICTORIA ONE,
Boise
RON'S EMPORIUM,
Garden City

ILLINOIS
MAGIC LAMP,
Chicago
THE TURQUOISE BUTTERFLY,
Chicago
LITTLE BARN
ANTIQUES-CHURCH STORE,
Elizabeth
WOOD 'N' WONDERS,
Elmhurst
H L ENTERPRISES,
Flossmoor
ALLEN'S ANTIQUES,
Frankfort
GRUNWALD ANTIQUES,
Geneva
WINDSOR MANOR,
Glen Ellyn

OWENS COUNTRY CORNER
ANTIQUES,
Litchfield
J DARTER'S ANTIQUE
INTERIORS,
Manteno
KERIN DEE ANTIQUES,
Oak Park
LENORE'S ANTIQUES,
Oswego
ANTIQUE & CURIO SHOP,
Palmyra
MY HOUSE ANTIQUES,
Prospect Heights
RAIL FENCE FARM,
Rochelle
CHRIS L HILL ANTIQUES, INC,
Tuscola
VIOLETTA'S,
Villa Park
GRANNY'S ANTIQUES,
Wauconda
VILLAGE STORE ANTIQUES,
Wauconda
THINGS IN GENERAL,
Waukegan
OLDIES BUT GOODIES,
Wilmington

INDIANA
CUSTER HOUSE ANTIQUES,
Centerville
PINK PANTRY,
Centerville
SHANNON'S ANTIQUES,
Connersville
LOUISE'S ANTIQUES,
Converse
MARCHAND'S ANTIQUES,
Evansville
EVELYN'S ANTIQUES,
Fort Wayne
KINNETT ANTIQUES,
Mooresville
AGE OF ELEGANCE,
Nashville
THE GARRET,
Nashville
SCARCE O' FAT HOUSE,
Nashville
OLE CORRAL ANTIQUES,
North Vernon
B J'S ANTIQUES,
Plymouth
THE DOWNSTAIRS ANTIQUES,
Terre Haute
MARTIN'S ANTIQUES,
Terre Haute
ROST'S CARRIAGE HOUSE
ANTIQUES,
Terre Haute
BARBER'S ANTIQUES &
COLLECTIBLES,
Thorntown
VIVIAN'S ANTIQUES,
Waveland

MAX'S WATERTOWER
ANTIQUES,
Westfield

IOWA
CELLAR ANTIQUES,
Cedar Rapids
AGNES KOEHN ANTIQUES,
Cedar Rapids
HOBERT'S ANTIQUES,
Charles City
J & M SHOPPE,
Clarence
A & D ANTIQUES,
Davenport
RIVERBEND ANTIQUES, GIFTS &
RESTORATION,
Davenport
K G ANTIQUES,
Dexter
INA-MARY SHOP,
Fremont
STOFFER'S ANTIQUES,
Hazleton
FRANK'S FOLLY ANTIQUE
SHOP,
Hinton
BROWN'S ANTIQUE SHOP,
Ottumwa
GAS LIGHT ANTIQUES,
Sioux City
RED WHEEL ANTIQUES,
Sioux City
MRS B'S ANTIQUES,
Waterloo
EVELYN'S ANTIQUES,
Waverly
HARGRAVE ANTIQUES,
Webster City
PUMP HOUSE ANTIQUES,
West Branch

KANSAS
DUMLER'S HOUSE OF
DEPRESSION,
Russell
HITCHING POST ANTIQUES,
Sabetha
THE COBWEB,
Topeka
DENNETT'S ANTIQUES,
Towanda
CELLAR ANTIQUES,
Washington
NORTH END FLEA MARKET,
Wichita
ESTHER'S JUNQUE,
Winfield

KENTUCKY
BOONE'S ANTIQUES OF
KENTUCKY INC,
Lexington

LOUISIANA
BROWSER DOWSER
Harahan
LILLIAN'S ANTIQUE SHOP
Homer
THE BROWN HOUSE
Lafayette
A-ANTIQUES
New Orleans
THE BANK ARCHITECTURALS
New Orleans
HERITAGE GALLERIES
ANTIQUES
New Orleans
M S RAU INC
New Orleans
SHADETREE ANTIQUES
St Francisville
MANNING'S ANTIQUES
Shreveport

MAINE
CUSHNOC SHOP,
Augusta
DELFT BOWL ANTIQUES,
Bryant Pond
MARY IRENE BIRMINGHAM,
Frankfort
OLD FARM ANTIQUES,
Kezar Falls
THE SAIL LOFT,
Newcastle
THE MATHEWS ANTIQUES,
Ogunquit
GOLD COAST ANTIQUES,
Searsport

MARYLAND
ANTIQUE CENTER,
Baltimore
THINK 'N THINGS ANTIQUES,
Baltimore
TREASURE HOUSE ANTIQUES,
Bowie
MENDELSOHN GALLERIES,
Chevy Chase
END OF THE LINE ANTIQUES,
Churchville
CRAFT SHOP,
Gaithersburg
THE LOOKING GLASS
ANTIQUES,
Keymar
SUE W'MSON-MICHAELS
ANTIQUES,
New Market
CARL'S ANTIQUES,
Olney
CELE'S OLD MILL ANTIQUES &
INTERIORS,
Savage
YE OLE MILL ANTIQUES,
Trappe
RED'S ANTIQUES,
Union Bridge

ANTIQUES 'N THINGS,
Wheaton

MASSACHUSETTS
DON FRENCH ANTIQUES,
Athol
HOUSE OF BURGESS
ANTIQUES,
Athol
CHERRY WATSON,
Barnstable
CROSS & GRIFFIN,
Belmont
ERNEST J REPETTI III
ANTIQUES,
Boston
ANTIQUES III,
Brookline
SUITSUS II,
Chatham
TREASURE CHEST ANTIQUES,
Chatham
SONIA PAINE ANTIQUES
GALLERY,
Chestnut Hill
THE ANDERSONS,
Cochituate
HOWARD'S ANTIQUES,
Essex
HOWARD'S FLYING DRAGON,
Essex
FANTASY HOUSE ANTIQUES,
Fairhaven
JOHNSTON'S ANTIQUES,
Franklin
DONNA & JOE MELLO,
Gloucester
GOOD TIME STOVE COMPANY,
Haydenville
STONE'S ANTIQUE SHOPPE,
Hyannis
HILDA KNOWLES ANTIQUES
AND COLLECTABLES,
Ipswich
ANTIQUES AT THE SIGN OF
THE BLUEBIRD,
Littleton
THE BERGENDAHLS,
Lynn
TREASURE HIGHLAND,
Marstons Mills
BLUE LAMP ANTIQUES,
Millers Falls
NEW BEDFORD ARTS AND
ANTIQUES,
New Bedford
JUDITH CRONIN-ANTIQUES,
Orleans
BLACK LANTERN ANTIQUES,
Oxford
DILLINGHAM HOUSE ANTIQUES,
Sandwich
THE HAWKES,
Sandwich
CLEVELAND'S ANTIQUES,
Somerset

THE JOE'S ANTIQUES,
South Easton
HOLLY HILL ANTIQUES,
Waltham
ARMEN AMERIGIAN ANTIQUES,
West Bridgewater
ANTIQUE CORNER,
West Newton
RENEE'S ANTIQUE SHOPPE,
Winthrop
BUTLER ANTIQUES,
Worcester

MICHIGAN
ANDY'S ANTIQUES,
Allen
ANTIQUES UNLIMITED,
Bessemer
CLARKSTON MAIN STREET
ANTIQUES,
Clarkston
THE HINTER HAUS ANTIQUE &
GIFT SHOP,
Eastport
CHINA CUPBOARD,
Easton Rapids
GOOD-OL-DAYS ANTIQUES,
Holly
THE VILLAGE STORE
ANTIQUES,
Ironwood
41 ANTIQUES,
Ishpeming
HINKLEY'S ATTIC,
Jackson
ADA'S TREASURE VAULT,
Lansing
1849 HOUSE ANTIQUES,
Okemos

MINNESOTA
ARDEN HILLS ANTIQUE SHOP,
Arden Hills
DORI ANTIQUES,
Brownsdale
ELSA'S ANTIQUES,
Dodge Center
YE OLDE ANTIQUE SHOPPE,
Hokah
BEEHIVE ANTIQUES,
Long Lake
MINNEHAHA ANTIQUES,
Minneapolis
THE IRIDESCENT HOUSE,
Rochester
THE ANTIQUE STORE,
St Cloud
313 ANTIQUES,
St James
GRAND HOUSE ANTIQUES,
St Paul
IRIDESCENT HOUSE,
Spring Valley
GENNETTE'S ANTIQUES,
Willmar

MISSISSIPPI
HOBBY HOUSE ANTIQUES,
Biloxi
FRANCES PARKE ANTIQUES,
Canton
BETTY'S TREASURE SHOP,
Gulfport
DEN OF ANTIQUITY,
Gulfport
HANDSBORO TRADING POST,
Gulfport
ROSE'S RELIC ROOMS,
Gulfport
DRAGONWYCK ANTIQUES,
Jackson
BARGAIN BARN,
Ocean Springs
COUNTRY STORE ANTIQUES,
Oxford
LILL'S ANTIQUES,
Pascagoula
HOWAT ANTIQUES,
Ripley
YESTERYEAR ANTIQUES,
Yazoo City

MISSOURI
LARSONS ANTIQUES,
Ballwin
OLD TRAIL HOUSE ANTIQUES
INC,
Camdenton
PLATTE PURCHASE ANTIQUES,
Gower
LONG'S ANTIQUES,
Higginsville
ANTIQUE WORLD,
Kansas City
BROOKSIDE ANTIQUES,
Kansas City
RUMMERFIELDS ANTIQUES,
La Plata
EDNAMAY'S ANTIQUES,
Macon
CYRIL'S ANTIQUES,
Manchester
SEEK & FIND ANTIQUES,
Marceline
THE OLD N' YOU ANTIQUE
MART,
Riverside
ROBBIE MORGAN'S ANTIQUES
& GIFTS,
Roach
AUNT HEIDI'S CORNER,
St Charles
DALSING'S,
St Joseph
HELEN'S ANTIQUES,
St Joseph
ROTHSCHILD-WOOD ANTIQUES,
St Louis
DOROTHY'S ANTIQUES INC,
Sedalia

MONTANA
LEFLER'S ANTIQUES,
Billings
GOLDEN LEAF ANTIQUES,
Butte
JEANS ANTIQUES,
Missoula
TRAILS END ANTIQUES,
Ronan

NEBRASKA
BITS & PIECES,
Broken Bow
YEUTTER'S ANTIQUES,
Cozad
BERDINA'S TREASURE TROVE,
Hastings
COACH HOUSE ANTIQUES,
Lincoln
THE COUNTRY STORE,
Lincoln
THE HERITAGE HOUSE,
Lincoln
WAGON WHEEL ANTIQUES,
Lincoln
PHILLIPS ANTIQUES,
Nebraska City
THE YESTERDAY SHOPPE,
North Platte
BEAUTY & THE BEAST,
Omaha
FROSTED LION ANTIQUES,
Omaha
KATELMAN COMPANY, INC,
Omaha
ANTIQUES MARTELLE,
Pierce

NEVADA
THE GLASS SHACK,
Las Vegas
IRON FENCE ANTIQUES,
Minden
DEN OF ANTIQUITY,
Reno
FAUST'S ANYTHING
COLLECTIBLE,
Reno
HERITAGE HOUSE ANTIQUES,
Virginia City
SILVER STOPE ANTIQUE SHOP,
Virginia City
HAAS ANTIQUES, LTD,
Zephyr Cove

NEW HAMPSHIRE
WHEAT & CHAFF ANTIQUES,
Hopkinton
THE LOG CABIN ANTIQUES,
North Conway
KAY'S ANTIQUE SHOP,
Plaistow
ANN'S ANTIQUE SHOP,
Salem

HAINES HILLTOP ANTIQUES,
Wolfeboro

NEW JERSEY
TRIFLES & TREASURES,
Buttzville
THE ROADRUNNER,
Cape May
THE COLLECTOR,
Garfield
EAGLES NEST ANTIQUES,
Mullica Hill
THE CRYSTAL SHOPPE,
Perth Amboy
THE CELLAR SHELF,
Yardville

NEW MEXICO
LEE & MAVIS BRICKER
Clovis
ARMSTRONG'S ANTIQUES
Deming
CATES ANTIQUES & SELECT
USED FURNITURE
Las Cruces
ATTIC ANTIQUES
Las Vegas
LAS LOMAS ANTIQUES
Roswell
REID'S ANTIQUES
Roswell
ADELENE B MC LAUGHLIN
Santa Fe
BORDERTOWN ANTIQUES
Texico

NEW YORK
RILEY'S ROADSIDE ANTIQUES,
Aberdeen
THE ANTIQUERY,
Amherst
DONNA'S ANTIQUES,
Bath
BERNARD'S ANTIQUES LTD,
Bellmore
EXQUISITE ANTIQUES LTD,
Bellmore
BRINKER'S ANTIQUES,
Binghamton
BROWNER ANTIQUES &
GALLERY,
Brooklyn
DEJA VU ANTIQUES,
Brooklyn
EATON GALLERIES,
Buffalo
IRIS COTTAGE,
Canaan
JUNE BIGGAR ANTIQUES,
Cooperstown
THE LEDGES,
Cooperstown
THE EAGLE GLASS BARN,
Cornwall

MERRIWOLD ANTIQUES,
Forestburgh
MARC & MARY HILDERBRAND,
Franklin
THE OLD OYSTER WHARF,
Freeport
ELIZABETH SEAGERS
ANTIQUES,
Groton
GA-NUN-DA-SA-GA ANTIQUE
SHOP,
Himrod
HERKIMER FAMILY TREASURE
HOUSE,
Ilion
VILLAGE ANTIQUES,
Kenmore
LIMA ANTIQUES,
Lima
THE GOLDEN PAST,
Macedon
LIBERTY BELL ANTIQUES,
Margaretville
PETERSEN'S EXCHANGE,
Middletown
WICKER'S ANTIQUES,
Millbrook
MERE PITTANCE,
Mineola
CHRISTOPHER'S
COLLECTABLES,
Newark
LEO KAPLAN LTD,
New York City
JAMES ROBINSON INC,
New York City
HOLLY'S ANTIQUES,
Ogdensburg
PHILIP & SHIRLEY GORDON
ANTIQUES,
Plattsburgh
GINNY'S HUTCH,
Schoharie
ARTIFACTS,
Sea Cliff
THE BRASS EAGLE BARN,
Shokan
WHAT NOT SHOP,
Sidney
THE GRACE SHOPPE,
South Durham
THUMBPRINT ANTIQUES,
Stone Ridge
JUNE & CAROL AMES
ANTIQUES,
Webster
DOROTHEA F BERTRAM,
Westfield
THE TREASURE CHEST,
Worcester

NORTH CAROLINA
RILEY'S ROADSIDE ANTIQUES
Aberdeen

BEULAVILLE ANTIQUES &
FURNITURE CO
Beulaville
CLARA'S ANTIQUES
Charlotte
EM'S LOOK-A-NOOK ANTIQUES
Charlotte
THE CORNER CUPBOARD
Durham
HELENE'S ANTIQUES
Etowah
HAYMOUNT ANTIQUES
Fayetteville
B & B TREASURES
Greensboro
ADAMS ANTIQUES
Raleigh
TREASURES'-TRASH ANTIQUES
& GIFTS
Wingate

NORTH DAKOTA
MAC'S PLACE ANTIQUES,
Bowbells
GRANDPA'S GRANARY,
Fargo
S & S ANTIQUES,
La Moure

OHIO
WALNUT HOUSE ANTIQUES,
Bucyrus
BLACK ROOSTER ANTIQUES,
Cambridge
HAROLD & JUDY'S ANTIQUES,
Cambridge
HERITAGE ANTIQUES,
Cambridge
INDIAN MOUND ANTIQUES,
Cincinnati
PLAIN 'N' FANCY ANTIQUES
WEEKEND SHOP,
Cincinnati
A-R-M APPRAISAL SERVICE,
Columbus
BUSY BEE ANTIQUES,
Columbus
ANTIQUES AT OLD IRONSTONE,
Dayton
GREENFIELD ACRES ANTIQUES,
Findley
DANBAR'S DISTANT VIEW FARM
ANTIQUES,
Massillon
GIBSON ANTIQUES,
Massillon
MARKHAM'S ANTIQUES,
Massillon
MAIL POUCH ANTIQUES IN THE
BROOM FACTORY,
Maumee
BERT'S BUDGET SHOP,
Newark
FLORAL ARTS & ANTIQUES,
Port Clinton

THE ANTIQUE SHOWCASE,
  Ravenna
HEIRLOOMS ETCETERA,
  Sandusky
THE CHESHIRE CAT,
  Toledo
MECCA FOR COLLECTORS,
  Toledo
APPLEWOOD ANTIQUES,
  Trotwood
COPPER KETTLE ANTIQUES,
  Urbana
MAE THOMPSON ANTIQUES,
  Washington Court House

OKLAHOMA

HOBBY HORSE ANTIQUES
  Ardmore
FRAN'S ANTIQUES
  Chickasha
FRONTIER ANTIQUES
  Claremore
A H & PAULINE GREEN
  Durant
MARTIN'S ANTIQUES
  Elk City
YE OLDE ANTIQUE SHOPPE
  Grove
ISOM'S ANTIQUES &
COLLECTABLES
  Muskogee
KUNTRY KORNER
  Ninnekah
ANDERSON ANTIQUES & ART
GALLERIES
  Oklahoma City
LAURA'S ANTIQUES & GIFTS
  Oklahoma City
THE WHAT NOT SHELF
ANTIQUES
  Oklahoma City
JANKEY'S ANTIQUES
  Oologah
DOWELL ANTIQUE SHOP
  Tulsa
TOM'S ANTIQUES
  Tulsa
MILLER'S ANTIQUES
  Vinita

OREGON

WAY STATION ANTIQUES,
  Brooks
STIX & STONZ ANTIQUES,
  Grants Pass
ROTAY'S ANTIQUES,
  Hubbard
CATHY'S ANTIQUE SHOP,
  Portland
MORE OR LESS
COLLECTIBLES,
  Portland
OAK TREE ANTIQUES,
  Portland

CHRIS SWIFT ANTIQUES,
  Portland
TREASURE HOUSE ANTIQUES,
  Portland
ET CETERA ANTIQUES,
  Salem
JAN'S ANTIQUES,
  Salem

PENNSYLVANIA

COLLECTOR'S CORNER,
  Altoona
DR HAROLD LANTERMAN,
  Bloomsburg
DOTTIE'S ANTIQUES,
  Chester Heights
SOURBEER & LOCHARD
ANTIQUES,
  Columbia
DODSON'S ANTIQUES,
  Duncansville
ANTIQUE NOOK,
  Greensburg
A LUDWIG KLEIN & SON,
  Harleysville
DOEHNE'S OX BOW SHOP,
  Harrisburg
R J LATOURNOUS,
  Hawley
THE EVERGREEN ANTIQUE
SHOP,
  Honesdale
COPPER EAGLE ANTIQUES,
  Huntington Valley
THE EMPORIUM,
  Jennerstown
LYNNE'ART'S GLASS HOUSE
INC,
  Lahaska
THE GLASSTIQUE,
  Lancaster
PHILIP E HARBACH,
  Lansdowne
SMITHER'S ANTIQUES,
  Lewistown
MARKY'S OLD FORT ANTIQUES,
  Ligonier
HELEN B HENRY,
  Macungie
GERALD & MIRIAM NOLL,
  Manheim
THE CAMPBELLS,
  McMurray
THE ROSS'S ANTIQUES,
  Milford
JOHN JEREMICZ, JR,
  Perkiomenville
HARRY A EBERHARDT & SON
INC,
  Philadelphia
IRWIN SCHAFFER,
  Philadelphia
KENNETH C STUMPF,
  Pottsville
TROUTMAN ANTIQUES,
  Reading

G T W ANTIQUES,
  Scranton
PHYLLIS UHL,
  Scranton
THE GREEN BARN ANTIQUES,
  Seelyville
OUR ANTIQUE SHOP,
  Sewickley
MARY A GUYER,
  Shippensburg
CC'S ANTIQUES,
  Tarentum
BATES ANTIQUES,
  Union City
COFFMAN ANTIQUES,
  White
HART ANTIQUES,
  Wilkes-Barre
GOLDEN EAGLE,
  York

RHODE ISLAND

MC DONOUGH & LARNER
  Newport
THE ANTIQUARIAN
  Pascoag

SOUTH CAROLINA

KOUNTRY KORNER
  Liberty Hill
FRAN'S ANTIQUE SHOP
  Manning
OLD HOUSE ANTIQUES
  Murrells Inlet
CAROLINA CHINA MARKET
  Sumter

SOUTH DAKOTA

MIDWEST MUSEUM & ANTIQUE
SHOP,
  Gettysburg

TENNESSEE

COMMON MARKET, INC,
  Memphis
NICHOLS GARDEN CENTER,
  Nashville
THE OLD & NEW HOUSE,
  Nashville

TEXAS

GOLDEN ANTIQUES,
  Amarillo
LE VI'S ANTIQUES,
  Arlington
VICTORIANA,
  Austin
COUNTRY LANE ANTIQUES,
  Beaumont
CROPPER'S ANTIQUES,
  Beaumont
ROBERTS ANTIQUES,
  Beeville

THE CARRIAGE SHOP,
  Bellville
CURIOSITY ANTIQUE SHOP,
  Big Spring
E O ANTIQUES,
  Corpus Christi
JEAN & ELWOOD HESS
ANTIQUES,
  Corpus Christi
ANTIQUE HOUSE,
  Dallas
GOBLETS ETC ANTIQUES,
  Dallas
UNCOMMON MARKET,
  Dallas
QUAINT SHOP ANTIQUES,
  Del Rio
JUDGE & WORTH ANTIQUES,
  Edna
CIRCA,
  El Paso
CENTRAL ANTIQUES,
  Ft Worth
JESSIE'S SHOWCASE,
  Ft Worth
THIS OLD HOUSE,
  Ft Worth
GRUMPY GRUNTS ANTIQUES,
  Houston
RICHARD'S ANTIQUES,
  Houston
B & J ANTIQUES,
  Jacksonville
OLD TIMEY SHOPPE,
  Keller
WRIGHT'S ANTIQUE IMPORTS,
  Kemp
BUTTERMILK JUNCTION
ANTIQUES,
  La Marque
ANNEX ANTIQUES INC,
  Lindale
TURNER ANTIQUES,
  Longview
COTTAGE ANTIQUES,
  Longview
ANTIQUA UNLIMITED,
  Marble Falls
FRANKS ANTIQUE SHOP &
DOLL MUSEUM,
  Marshall
HAZEL M RAWLS ANTIQUES,
  Orange
BETH'S ORIGINALS,
  Palestine
GLORIA'S ANTIQUES,
  Pasadena
THE CURIOSITY SHOP,
  Rockwall
THE ANTIQUE MALL,
  San Angelo
CHRIS' OLD HOUSE,
  San Angelo
THE ANTIQUE GALLERY,
  San Antonio

BESS' ANTIQUES,
  San Antonio
THIS & THAT ANTIQUES,
  San Antonio
JO & TOMMY'S ANTIQUES,
  Stephenville
J & J ANTIQUES,
  Tatum
SALEM HOUSE OF ANTIQUES,
  Victoria
ALMA'S DAUGHTER'S ANTIQUE
SHOP,
  Waco
COLLIER'S ANTIQUES,
  Waco
THE COUNTRY SHOP,
  Waco

VERMONT
BRIGHAM HILL FARM
ANTIQUES,
  Essex Junction

VIRGINIA
BLANCHE DOBKIN ANTIQUES,
  Alexandria
KEN FORSTER ANTIQUES,
  Alexandria
MIDAS TOUCH ANTIQUES,
  Alexandria
ODDS & ENDS SHOPPE,
  Alexandria
THE SLEIGH BELL,
  Alexandria
TARNISHED TREASURES
ANTIQUES,
  Alexandria
CUPBOARD ANTIQUES,
  Arlington
RED BENCH ANTIQUES &
GIFTS,
  Arlington
OAK GROVE FLEA MARKET,
  Chesapeake
VIOLET'S ANTIQUES,
  Chesapeake
THIS AND THAT SHOP AND
DOLL HOUSE,
  Fredericksburg
VILLAGE ANTIQUES,
  Newport News
MARY-LEW'S ANTIQUE
SHOPPE,
  Richmond
MIKE'S TRADING POST,
  Roanoke
REBEL HILL ANTIQUES,
  Ruther Glen
THE WHITNEYS,
  Stephens City
ANTIQUES UNIQUE,
  Virginia Beach

DOLLY'S ANTIQUES & GIFT
SHOP,
  Virginia Beach

WASHINGTON
SHEPARD'S EMPORIUM,
  Carnation
COCKLEBERRY GALLERIES,
  Issaquah
THE ANTIQUE COMPANY,
  Seattle
ANTIQUE WORLD,
  Seattle
BLANCHE'S ANTIQUES,
  Seattle
LITTLE HOUSE ANTIQUES,
  Seattle
RITCHIE'S PLANTS AND
ANTIQUES,
  Seattle
SHEPARD'S EMPORIUM,
  Seattle
VINTAGE HOUSE ANTIQUES,
  Seattle
ENGELS FLEA MARKET,
  Spokane
MANDARIN GALLERY,
  Tacoma

WEST VIRGINIA
ATTIC ANTIQUES &
CHERISHABLES INC
  St Albans

WISCONSIN
WARTMANNIA ANTIQUES
  Edgerton
HIS AND HERS RED BARN
ANTIQUES
  Green Bay
PALMER'S COLLECTOR'S
CORNER
  Green Bay
SHIRLEY-RED'S ANTIQUES
  Green Bay
ERIN ANTIQUES
  Hartford
ASTER GALLERIES VICTORIAN
SHOP
  Milwaukee
MALONEY'S ANTIQUE SHOP
  Portage
ONLY YESTERDAY SHOP
  Stoughton
ARCHITECTURAL ANTIQUES
  Wauwatosa
EDMONDS-CLASEN ANTIQUES
  Wisconsin Dells

688

JEWELRY

ALABAMA
THE WRENS NEST ANTIQUES,
  Birmingham
LAZY DAZY ANTIQUES,
  Florence
FRIENDSHIP HOUSE,
  Gulf Shores
MEMORY LANE ANTIQUES,
  Montgomery

ARIZONA
ANN CLARK SHOWCASE,
  Phoenix
REDDY'S ANTIQUES,
  Scottsdale
THE DELIGHTFUL ANTIQUES,
  Sedona
NANCY'S TRADING POST &
ANTIQUES,
  Wickenburg

ARKANSAS
GALLERY 'G' ANTIQUES,
  De Witt
ANTIQUES LIMITED,
  Little Rock
LAMPS-N-TIQUES,
  Little Rock
RED HOUSE ANTIQUES,
  Marvel
SISSY'S LOG CABIN, INC,
  Pine Bluff

CALIFORNIA
GOLDBERG & LAND LTD,
  Bakersfield
LUNDIN HOUSE,
  Benicia
SHADOW HILLS ANTIQUES &
FINE ARTS GALLERY,
  Beverly Hills
DESERT AUCTION GALLERY,
  Cathedral City
GALLERY ONE,
  Laguna Beach
WARREN IMPORTS-FAR EAST
FINE ARTS,
  Laguna Beach
HOUSE OF SECONDS,
  Laguna Niquel
CENTURY HOUSE ANTIQUES,
  La Jolla
THE CHIMES,
  Lake Elsinore
DON QUIXOTE ANTIQUES,
  Los Angeles
MARY AYER INTERIORS &
ANTIQUES,
  Pasadena

THE OLD & THE YOUNGS,
  San Anselmo
KELLY'S RELICS,
  San Diego
LAMB ANTIQUES & APPRAISAL
SERVICE,
  San Diego
BETTIE BOOPS,
  San Francisco
BLACKWELL ANTIQUES,
  San Francisco
PAINTED LADY,
  San Francisco
DOROTHY'S ANTIQUES,
  Santa Ana

COLORADO
DENVER ANTIQUE MARKET,
  Denver
MANSION ANTIQUES,
  Monte Vista

CONNECTICUT
TRANQUIL ACRES ANTIQUES,
  Goshen
TROLLEY BARN ANTIQUES,
  Mystic
BUTTONSHOP ANTIQUES,
  Newton
OLD MYSTIC ANTIQUES,
  Old Mystic
RAWBURN HALL,
  Warren
SILVER GUILD MEMORABILIA,
  Washington Depot

DELAWARE
THE COLLECTOR,
  Wilmington

DISTRICT OF COLUMBIA
DEJA VU,
  Washington
VICTORIA FORTUNE INC,
  Washington

FLORIDA
MASTER JEWELERS,
  Belleair Bluffs
CHARLOTTE FERRARA
ANTIQUES & COLLECTIBLES,
  Clearwater
FORGET-ME-NOT,
  Cocoa
ANGEVINES ANTIQUES,
  DeLand
ANTIQUES BY DAVID &
PATRICIA,
  Delray Beach

MITCHELL'S HOUSE OF
ANTIQUES & COLLECTIBLES,
  Fort Lauderdale
LIBERTY ANTIQUES COINS &
STAMPS,
  Miami
MAIN JEWELRY & TRADING CO,
  Miami
CIRCLE ART & ANTIQUES,
  Miami Beach
WAYSIDE ANTIQUES,
  Reddick
JANET F POST JEWELRY INC,
  Sarasota
LARRY R ENGLE ANTIQUES,
  Tampa
A TIFANEY & SON,
  Tampa

GEORGIA
THE MOUNTAIN HOMESTEAD,
  Hiawasee
LEVY JEWELERS,
  Savannah

HAWAII
THE GALLERY LTD,
  Lahaina

IDAHO
VICTORIAN SHOP,
  Boise

ILLINOIS
THE BELL JAR ANTIQUES,
  Chicago
MARSHALL FIELD & COMPANY,
  Chicago
FISHER'S ANTIQUES,
  Chicago
GALLAI LTD, INC,
  Chicago
NEVA'S ANTIQUES 'N THINGS,
  East Peoria
D GRUNWALD ANTIQUES,
  Geneva
GRUNWALD GALLERY OF
ANTIQUES,
  Geneva
SHIRLEY RYAN'S ANTIQUES,
  Gilman
CARDAY ANTIQUES,
  Glencoe
THE GENERAL STORE,
  Homer
SHOW-GATE ANTIQUES,
  Lake Forest

ANTIQUES OF ORLAND,
Orland Park
HODGE PODGE LODGE,
Shelbyville
VIOLETTA'S,
Villa Park
THE LITTLE CORNER,
Wauconda
THINGS IN GENERAL,
Waukegan

INDIANA
SUGAR 'N' SPICE ANTIQUES,
Bristol
HEIRLOOM ANTIQUE SHOP,
Eaton
MARCHAND'S ANTIQUES,
Evansville
EVELYN'S ANTIQUES,
Fort Wayne
KENNETH BENNETT,
Hartford City

IOWA
PARLOR ANTIQUE INC,
Davenport
RUNNING WATERS ANTIQUES,
McGregor

KANSAS
THE WAGON WHEEL
El Dorado
DIVINES ANTIQUES,
Parsons

KENTUCKY
OLD CLARK HOUSE,
Henderson

LOUISIANA
MANY MANSIONS ANTIQUES &
GIFTS
Baton Rouge
COLLECTOR ANTIQUES
New Orleans
SHADETREE ANTIQUES
St Francisville

MAINE
ESTELLES ANTIQUES,
Cape Neddick
FOXHOLE ANTIQUES,
Ogunquit
POTPOURRI ANTIQUES,
Ogunquit

MARYLAND
CHRIS EVANS ANTIQUES,
Baltimore
ANTIQUES ANONYMOUS,
Kensington
BOBB'S TRADING CO,
Mount Rainer

E J CANTON ANTIQUES,
Reisterstown
HEIRLOOM JEWELS,
Stevenson

MASSACHUSETTS
ALLSTON ANTIQUES,
Allston
BRODNEY ART GALLERY,
Boston
MARCOZ ANTIQUES,
Boston
ERNEST J REPETTI III
ANTIQUES,
Boston
ANTIQUE MART,
Buzzards Bay
BERNHEIMER'S ANTIQUE ARTS,
Cambridge
ANTIQUE HOUSE,
Plymouth
SMALL PLEASURES LTD,
Provincetown
THE ANTIQUE LADY,
Randolph
ANTIQUES 'N ODDITIES,
Waltham

MICHIGAN
DROVERS EAST ANTIQUES,
Detroit
THE SIGN OF THE PEACOCK,
Grand Ledge
SUNFLOWER SHOP,
Northville
WOODEN SKATE ANTIQUES,
Okemos

MINNESOTA
BRUDA COLLECTABLES,
Hopkins
JEANNIE'S PLACE
Litchfield
ANTIQUE FINDS,
Minneapolis
THE STUDIO,
Minneapolis
LEBLANC ROCK & ANTIQUE
SHOP,
Royalton
ATHENA ANTIQUES,
Wayzata

MISSISSIPPI
THE CABIN ANTIQUES,
Kosciusko
HARPER'S ANTIQUES,
Natchez

MISSOURI
KARGO ANTIQUES,
Kansas City
BRAUN GALLERIES,
St Louis

DOROTHY'S ANTIQUES INC,
Sedalia

NEVADA
POW WOW TRADING POST,
Las Vegas

NEW HAMPSHIRE
LOFT ANTIQUES,
Lancaster
SANDI'S ANTIQUES,
Manchester
PINE SHED ANTIQUES,
Milford
HARTLEY'S BARN,
Pelham

NEW JERSEY
DISCOVERY HOUSE,
Boonton
COLONY ANTIQUE SHOP,
Englewood
THE COLLECTOR,
Garfield
GOVERNORS ANTIQUE MARKET
AND OUTDOOR FLEA MARKET,
Lambertville
HALO,
Newark
MURIAL'S ANTIQUE GALLERY
LTD,
Summit
ANTIQUE ASSOCIATES,
Wayne

NEW MEXICO
R & B TRASH & TREASURES
Alamogordo
TRAILS END TRADING POST
Santa Fe

NEW YORK
ALTHEA'S ANTIQUES JEWELRY,
Baldwin
ABBEY'S ANTIQUES,
Bath
IRIS MARNELL ANTIQUE
JEWELRY LTD,
Bellmore
TESS AND ALLEN USATIN,
Brooklyn
SABINE LAW,
Buffalo
BUTTER HILL ANTIQUE SHOP,
Cornwall-on-Hudson
L & J KNIGHT ANTIQUE
JEWELRY LTD,
Great Neck
CANASTAR'S ANTIQUES,
Herkimer
HERKIMER FAMILY TREASURE
HOUSE,
Ilion

AROUND THE CORNER
ANTIQUES,
  Liberty
DINGLE DAISY ANTIQUES,
  Monticello
CONTINENTAL CRAFTS,
  Mount Vernon
ISI FISCHZANG,
  New York City
EDITH WEBER,
  Oceanside
PHILIP & SHIRLEY GORDON
ANTIQUES,
  Plattsburgh
ANCHORAGE ANTIQUES,
  Poughkeepsie
BELL HAGAR ANTIQUES,
  Schenectady
GINNY'S HUTCH,
  Schoharie
THE COUNTRY COLLECTOR,
  Tuxedo
GALERIE OBJECTS D'ART,
  Tuxedo
MY MOTHER'S PLACE,
  Wantagh
FRANCES ANTIQUE SHOP,
  Warrensburg
ANTIQUE GOLD & SILVER
SHOPPE,
  Webster

NORTH CAROLINA
THE VAGABOND SHOP
  Blowing Rock
SCUDDER'S GALLERY
  Highlands
PEMBEE ANTIQUES
  Lumberton
GARNIER ANTIQUES INC
  Pinehurst

OHIO
VILLAGE JEWEL,
  Columbus
APPLEWOOD ANTIQUES,
  Trotwood

OKLAHOMA
LACY'S ANTIQUES GIFTS &
JEWELRY
  Claremore
ISOM'S ANTIQUES &
COLLECTABLES
  Muskogee
AMIR'S PERSIAN IMPORTS
  Tulsa
THE LAMPOST ANTIQUES &
SILVER CO
  Tulsa

OREGON
ET CETERA ANTIQUES,
  Salem

PENNSYLVANIA
RENNINGERS ANTIQUE
MARKET,
  Adamstown
THE BLUE VICTORIAN,
  Allentown
ELIZABETH SCHIFFMAN,
  Carlisle
TREGLER GALLERY,
  Erie
HARRIS ANTIQUES,
  Knox
THE BENSON GALLERY,
  Lancaster
THERESA REDMOND
CULBERTSON,
  Lewistown
SMITHERS ANTIQUES,
  Lewistown
HELEN B HENRY,
  Macungie
REVA LEVITT JEWELRY,
  Meadowbrook
FLORENCE & GEORGE GEE,
  Milford
MIRIAM F RAYVIS,
  Philadelphia
STERNBERGH ANTIQUES,
  Reading
PICKWICK ANTIQUES,
  Trucksville

RHODE ISLAND
SECOND HAND ROE'S SHOPPE
  West Warwick

TENNESSEE
CHINA TOWN IMPORTS,
  Memphis
ROUND CORNER GIFT SHOP,
  Memphis
SURATT'S ANTIQUES &
INTERIORS,
  Memphis

TEXAS
LAS MARGIE'S ANTIQUES,
  Abilene
GOLDEN ANTIQUES,
  Amarillo
ACCENT ALLEY,
  Austin
ANABLEPS-ANABLEPS,
  Austin
MELANGE,
  Beauont

THE ANTIQUE SHOPPE,
  Dallas
THIS OLD HOUSE,
  Ft Worth
JEANIE'S ANTIQUES,
  La Marque
FREDRICK NILA GALLERIES,
  Longview
RED DOOR ANTIQUES,
  Odessa
M PAGENKOPF ANTIQUES,
  San Antonio

VERMONT
BREWSTER ANTIQUES,
  Manchester Center

VIRGINIA
THE NOT NEW SHOP OF
ALEXANDRIA,
  Alexandria
PRESIDENTIAL COIN AND
ANTIQUE CO INC,
  Alexandria
WARDS ROAD BARGAIN SHOP,
  Lynchburg
LUNDIN'S,
  Richmond

WASHINGTON
MAGNOLIA LANE ANTIQUES,
  Mount Vernon
RITCHIE'S PLANTS AND
ANTIQUES,
  Seattle
VANITY FAIR ANTIQUES,
  Seattle
YANKEE PEDDLER ANTIQUES,
  Valleyford

WISCONSIN
DE WITT'S ANTIQUES
  Green Bay
SALT CELLAR ANTIQUES
  Shawano
SCHALLES ANTIQUES &
TURQUOISE
  Waunakee

METALWORK

ARIZONA
SUDEE'S ANTIQUES,
  Chandler
COLLECTOR'S CORNER,
  Mesa
THE SELECTIVE SALVAGE
COMPANY,
  Phoenix

ARKANSAS
PERSIAN MARKET,
  Bentonville

CALIFORNIA
ANTIQUES INVESTMENTS
(HOLDINGS) LTD,
  Lemon Grove
DILLINGHAM & BROWN, LTD,
  San Francisco

DELAWARE
JACKSON-MITCHELL/WILLIS
MOORE INC,
  New Castle
IRON AGE ANTIQUES,
  Ocean View

FLORIDA
HEART OF THE ARTICHOKE,
  Coconut Grove
ST JAMES ENGLISH ANTIQUES,
  Delray Beach

IDAHO
HAPPYS ANTIQUES,
  Boise
THE WHISTLE STOP,
  Boise

ILLINOIS
ANTIQUE MART,
  Bloomington
MARK & LOIS JACOBS
AMERICANA-COLLECTIBLES,
  Chicago
THE SWAN HOUSE,
  Genoa
THE ELF SHOP,
  Kenilworth
THE SPARROW,
  Kenilworth
J DARTERS ANTIQUE
INTERIORS,
  Manteno
PUFFABELLY STATION
ANTIQUES,
  McLean

RELIANCE UPHOLSTERY &
ANTIQUES,
  Midlothian
IRON GATE ANTIQUES,
  Trenton
ROBERT & SMITH,
  Wauconda

INDIANA
KIRKS FINE CLOCKS AND
ANTIQUES,
  Fort Wayne
HEAVILON'S ANTIQUES,
  Frankfort
AGE OF ELEGANCE,
  Nashville

IOWA
HEDGEPETH,
  Burlington
RED ROBIN FARM,
  Marengo

KANSAS
LOU'S LOT NO 2,
  Morganville
WHARF ROAD
  Newton
PARK ANTIQUES,
  Ottawa

KENTUCKY
OLD CLARK HOUSE,
  Henderson
ANTIQUITIES,
  Lexington
BOONE'S ANTIQUES OF
KENTUCKY INC,
  Lexington

LOUISIANA
NOEL WISE ANTIQUES
  Arabi
BROWSER DOWSER
  Harahan
LEBLANC'S ANTIQUES
  Lafayette
WIND HAVEN ANTIQUES
  Mandeville
CASS-GARR COMPANY
  New Orleans
HAMILTON HOUSE ANTIQUES
  New Orleans
MAINE S RAU INC
  New Orleans
THE CHAMBERLAIN CARRIAGE
HOUSE & NOT,
  Brewer

MARYLAND
CREST ANTIQUES,
  Baltimore
TREASURE HOUSE ANTIQUES,
  Bowie
FIN-COR,
  Braddock Hts
CROSSROADS ANTIQUES,
  Galena
COMUS ANTIQUES,
  New Market

MASSACHUSETTS
H CLAYMAN & SON INC,
  Boston
REDCOATS LTD,
  Chestnut Hill
CUMMAQUID ANTIQUES,
  Cummaquid
GRAY COTTAGE ANTIQUES,
  Deerfield
BERNARD PLATING WORKS,
  Florence
THE WINDLE SHOPPE,
  Hardwick
STONE'S ANTIQUE SHOPPE,
  Hyannis
THE VILLAGE BARN,
  Mansfield
THE HOBBY HORSE,
  Marion
SOUTH RIVER PRIMITIVES,
  Marshfield
MUSHROOM ANTIQUES,
  Natick
HOUSE OF BRASS,
  New Bedford
THE BUTCHER BLOCK,
  Orleans
TWIN FIRES ANTIQUES,
  Sheffield
RICHARD W SHAW ANTIQUES,
  West Acton

MICHIGAN
THE OLD PIONEER STORE,
  Big Rapids
DOROTHY THOMPSON
ANTIQUES,
  Farmington
BRASS SMITH SHOP,
  Grand Rapids
GOOD-OL-DAYS ANTIQUES,
  Holly
BOB HARRIS ANTIQUES,
  West Bloomfield

MINNESOTA
THE WAGGIN' WHEELER,
  Maple Plain
ALBATROSS ANTIQUES AND
RESTORATION WORKSHOP,
  Minneapolis
DUANE'S ANTIQUES & THINGS
INC,
  Minneapolis
OLSON'S ANTIQUES,
  Pennock

MISSISSIPPI
JEAN BROWN ANTIQUES,
  Columbus
THE DEN OF ANTIQUITY,
  Gulfport

NEBRASKA
COACH HOUSE ANTIQUES, INC,
  Lincoln
THE ANTIQUE BROKERAGE,
  Omaha

NEVADA
TREASURES ET CETERA,
  Reno

NEW HAMPSHIRE
THE OLD EMERY PLACE,
  Derry
KENSINGTON HISTORICAL
COMPANY,
  East Kingston
1680 HOUSE ANTIQUES,
  East Kingston
THE COBBS,
  Hancock
HARDINGS OF HANCOCK,
  Hancock
KAY MC GOWAN,
  Laconia
YANKEE STOREKEEPER,
  Milford
THE SLOP CHEST ANTIQUES,
  Pequaket

NEW JERSEY
HAWTHORN & GRAY DESIGN
STUDIO,
  Sergeantsville

NEW YORK
ANTIQUES IN A BROWNSTONE,
  Brooklyn
DANTONE ANTIQUES,
  Brooklyn
BUTTER HILL ANTIQUE SHOP,
  Cornwall-on-Hudson
ANDY'S ANTIQUES,
  Herkimer
PARKER'S ANTIQUES,
  Lyons
GRAHAM GALLERY,
  New York City
GRAMERCY GALLERIES LTD,
  New York City
MAN-TIQUES,
  New York City
JACK GRECO,
  Rochester

OHIO
BUGGY WHEEL ANTIQUES,
  Waldo
GLUCK'S GIFTS & ANTIQUE
SHOP INC,
  Youngstown

OKLAHOMA
AMIR'S PERSIAN IMPORTS
  Tulsa
BARBER ANTIQUES
  Tulsa

OREGON
DOTSON'S COBURG ANTIQUES,
  Coburg

PENNSYLVANIA
WILLOWDALE ANTIQUES,
  Kennett Square
WHITE SWAN TAVERN
ANTIQUES,
  Marietta
JUDITH FINKEL ANTIQUES,
  Philadelphia

SOUTH CAROLINA
BRASS & SILVER WORKSHOP
  Charleston
COLES & COMPANY INC,
  Charleston
LITTLE RED HOUSE
  Pelzer
CHESTNUT GALLERIES
  Spartanburg

TENNESSEE
CHINA TOWN IMPORTS,
  Memphis
COMMON MARKET, INC,
  Memphis
THE OLD BARN ANTIQUES,
  Memphis

TEXAS
GLENN TILLOTSON ANTIQUES,
  Houston
BRASS RING ANTIQUES,
  Longview

VERMONT
BETTY STERLING,
  Randolph
MILL BROOK ANTIQUES,
  Reading

VIRGINIA
CUPBOARD ANTIQUES,
  Arlington
BERRY'S ANTIQUES,
  Richmond

WASHINGTON
DEAR AND NEAR ANTIQUES,
  Everett
THE CLOCKWORK DUCK,
  Kennewick

WISCONSIN
WARTMANNIA ANTIQUES
  Edgerton
THE CROW'S NEST
  Wauwatosa

MUSICAL INSTRUMENTS

CALIFORNIA
EDISON ANTIQUES,
Bakersfield
THE DIALS,
Benicia
NORMAN SOLGAS,
Sacramento
TUCKER'S MUSIC BOX,
San Diego
URBAN ANTIQUES AT
SEAWALL B,
San Francisco
BRASS WASHBOARD,
San Jose

COLORADO
ANTIQUE MERCANTILE,
Lamar

FLORIDA
H & H ANTIQUES,
Largo
THE ANTIQUE MUSEUM,
Ocala

GEORGIA
M RINGEL & SON ANTIQUE CO,
INC,
Kennesaw

ILLINOIS
HAYLOFT ANTIQUES,
Champaign
TAYMAN'S TIN TO TIFFANY,
Jacksonville

IOWA
MIKE & BERTHA'S,
McGregor
RUNNING WATERS ANTIQUES,
McGregor

MAINE
BEEHIVE ANTIQUES,
Alfred
EASTMOOR ANTIQUES,
Wells

MASSACHUSETTS
ALLSTON ANTIQUES,
Allston
ABRAHAMS ANTIQUES &
ACCESSORIES,
Amherst
ACADIA SHOP,
Cambridge

MICHIGAN
RIVER REST ANTIQUES,
Saint Ignace

MISSISSIPPI
STEWARTS ANTIQUES & GIFTS,
Yazoo City

NEW JERSEY
THE COLLECTOR,
Garfield

NEW YORK
VI & SI'S ANTIQUES,
Clarence
ANDY'S ANTIQUES,
Herkimer

WHITE'S ANTIQUES,
Skaneateles
PANCHRONIA ANTIQUES,
Warners

NORTH CAROLINA
RHYNE'S CORNER CUPBOARD
ANTIQUES INC,
Greensboro

OKLAHOMA
SMITH'S ANTIQUES
Bache
DOWELL ANTIQUE SHOP
Tulsa

PENNSYLVANIA
LEEPER ANTIQUE MART,
Leeper
HELEN B HENRY,
Macungie
THE VILLAGE MALL,
Morton

TENNESSEE
CATHY'S ANTIQUES,
Chattanooga

TEXAS
BIT OF YESTERYEAR,
Houston
THE GAZEBO ANTIQUES,
College Station

VIRGINIA
TARNISHED TREASURES
ANTIQUES,
Alexandria

ORIENTAL

ALABAMA
COX ANTIQUES,
Birmingham
GRIER ANTIQUES,
Birmingham
CABIN ANTIQUES/FLYING
CARPET,
Florence
KILGROE'S ANTIQUES,
Pell City

HOUSE OF EXOTICA,
Prattville
BLOSSOM TOP FARM,
Tuscaloosa

ARIZONA
TOY COTTAGE ANTIQUES,
Phoenix

JOANNA LOKEY ANTIQUE
FURNITURE,
Scottsdale

ARKANSAS
KAZUKO,
Little Rock

CALIFORNIA
GALLERY ONE,
 Laguna Beach
CENTURY HOUSE ANTIQUES,
 La Jolla
GALLERY ARTASIA,
 Los Angeles
LOREN'S ANTIQUES,
 Los Angeles
THE NEW MANILA IMPORTING
CO,
 Los Angeles
PERSIAN GALLERY & BIAZAR'S
ANTIQUE SHOP,
 Los Angeles
ROBERT SCOTT & ASSOCIATES
INC,
 Los Angeles
SCHEHERAZADE GALLERIES
INC,
 Los Angeles
DRAGON ARTS,
 Oakland
NETTIE WOLF ANTIQUES,
 Palm Desert
T L SUN CO,
 Pasadena
SACRAMENTO ANTIQUE
CENTER,
 Sacramento
ASIAN ART,
 San Francisco
FABULOUS THINGS LTD,
 San Francisco
FAR EAST FINE ARTS INC,
 San Francisco
FILIA,
 San Francisco
JEAN MILLER,
 San Francisco
THE NEW MANILA IMPORTING
CO,
 San Francisco
SERVICE-KNOLLE,
 San Francisco
T Z SHIOTA,
 San Francisco
ANTIQUES FROM FREUND'S,
 San Jose
WAY BACK WHEN ANTIQUES,
 Santa Cruz

COLORADO
NEUHART'S ANTIQUES &
IMPORTS,
 Denver

CONNECTICUT
J THOMAS MELVIN,
 Bethel
BETTY & WALT KILLAM,
 Chester
JOSEPH WEI GALLERY INC,
 Farmington

HAIG RUGS,
 New Haven
HEMPSTEAD HOUSE ANTIQUES,
 New London

DISTRICT OF COLUMBIA
PETER MACK BROWN,
 Washington

FLORIDA
KAY'S ANTIQUES,
 Daytona Beach
ANTIQUES BY DAVID &
PATRICIA,
 Delray Beach
GULF ROYAL IMPORTS,
 Largo
THE ORIENTAL SHOP,
 Margate
I CHING ORIENTAL ANTIQUE
GALLERY,
 Miami
RIKKI'S STUDIO, INC,
 Miami
HARTMAN GALLERIES INC,
 Palm Beach
STARITA ANTIQUES,
 Palm Beach
ANTIQUES & THINGS,
 Sebring
DECOR INC,
 Surfside
BEAUFEL'S ANTIQUES INC,
 Tampa

GEORGIA
ANTIQUES LIMITED,
 Atlanta
INTERNATIONAL ART
PROPERTIES LTD,
 Atlanta
BRANNON ANTIQUES INC,
 Grantville

HAWAII
ANSTETH LIMITED,
 Honolulu
ANTIQUES & OBJETS D'ART,
 Honolulu
FABULOUS THINGS LTD,
 Honolulu
FAR EAST ANTIQUITIES,
 Honolulu
THE LANTERN SHOP
ANTIQUES,
 Honolulu
ANTIQUE & JUNQUE AT
KAHALUU,
 Kaneohe

IDAHO
VICTORIAN SHOP,
 Boise

ILLINOIS,
ANTIQUE MART,
 Bloomington
ALLEGRETTI ORIENTAL RUGS,
 Chicago
ALLEGRETTI ORIENTAL RUGS,
 Evanston
THE ANTIQUE GALLERY,
 Glen Ellyn
RELIANCE UPHOSTERY &
ANTIQUES,
 Midlothian
BLUE MING ANTIQUE SHOP,
 Springfield

INDIANA
ORIENTAL GARDEN ANTIQUES,
 Forest

KENTUCKY
BURCH INTERIORS,
 Frankfort
BOONE'S ANTIQUES OF
KENTUCKY INC,
 Lexington

LOUISIANA
R L MAYBERRY GALLERIES
 Bastrop
THE COLONY LTD
 New Orleans
MANHEIM GALLERIES
 New Orleans
SAROUK SHOP
 New Orleans
NINA SLOSS ANTIQUES &
INTERIORS
 New Orleans
WHISNANT GALLERIES
 New Orleans

MAINE
FOXHOLE ANTIQUES,
 Ogunquit

MARYLAND
EVELETH & SUMMERFORD,
 Bethesda
BILL BENTLEY'S ANTIQUE
SHOW MART,
 Cockeysville
KENDELL'S ANTIQUES,
 Fork

MASSACHUSETTS
MARCOZ ANTIQUES,
 Boston
PHOEBE,
 Boston
BROOKLINE VILLAGER,
 Brookline
ACADIA SHOP,
 Cambridge

CHARLEMONT HOUSE
GALLERY,
    Charlemont
HOUSE OF ORIENT,
    Chestnut Hill
SONIA PAINE ANTIQUES
GALLERY,
    Chestnut Hill
ELEPHANT WALKS ANTIQUES,
    Rehoboth
RO-DAN ANTIQUES,
    Rockport
THE BLUE LADY ANTIQUES,
    Wellesley
DEN OF ANTIQUITY,
    Wellesley

MICHIGAN
MADELINE'S ANTIQUE SHOPPE,
    Birmingham
THE SIGN OF THE PEACOCK,
    Grand Ledge
HARBOR HILLS ANTIQUES,
    Macatawa

MINNESOTA
BRUDA COLLECTABLES,
    Hopkins
ARTS OF ASIA,
    Rochester

MISSISSIPPI
OUIDA'S ANTIQUES,
    Clinton
WALKER MCINTYRE ANTIQUES,
    Greenwood
THE DEN OF ANTIQUITY,
    Gulfport
AUSTIN TIKI HOUSE,
    Hattiesburg
AD-MIXTURE,
    Itta Bena
ANTIQUE BROWSE SHOP,
    Jackson
IRMA FELTS ANTIQUES,
    Pascagoula

MISSOURI
ANTIQUE WORLD,
    Kansas City
DRAPER ANTIQUES,
    St Louis

NEBRASKA
VILLAGE FOLK SHOP,
    Brownville

NEW JERSEY
MURIAL'S ANTIQUE GALLERY
LTD,
    Summit

NEW MEXICO
JAMIL ORIENTAL CARPETS
    Albuquerque

NEW YORK
EATON GALLERIES,
    Buffalo
BUTTER HILL ANTIQUE SHOP,
    Cornwall-on-Hudson
MAH JONG ORIENTAL
ANTIQUES,
    Geneva
ARLINE INTERIORS INC,
    Great Neck
VAN DEUSEN HOUSE,
    Hurley
EASTLAKE ANTIQUES,
    Mineola
FRANK CARO CO,
    New York City
R H ELLSWORTH LTD,
    New York City
BARBARA N COHEN,
    Pittsford
TIBBITS ANTIQUES,
    Southampton
KIRKLAND GALLERIES,
    Utica
PANCHRONIA ANTIQUES,
    Warners
EAST WEST SHOP,
    Victor

NORTH CAROLINA
G S MC KENNA GALLERY
    Charlotte
ARTHUR H DANIELSON
ANTIQUES LTD
    Raleigh
SARA GREENE ART &
ANTIQUES
    Raleigh
WILLIAM-KEITH ANTIQUES
    Raleigh
JOHN E TYLER
    Roxobel

OHIO
JAMES H WELCH & SONS
TRADING CO,
    Canton
A B CLOSSON JR CO,
    Cincinnati
THE CELLAR DOOR,
    Dayton
ANNE GROH'S ANTIQUE
GALLERY,
    Massillon

OKLAHOMA
FRANCES ANTIQUES
    McAlester

OREGON
GENERATION II ANTIQUES,
    Portland
ET CETERA ANTIQUES,
    Salem

PENNSYLVANIA
ROBERT CARLEN,
    Philadelphia
RAY CRAFT ANTIQUES,
    Philadelphia
JOHNSTONE-FONG, INC,
    Philadelphia
L J MORETTINI ANTIQUES,
    Philadelphia
M J NESCO,
    Philadelphia
CHARLES B SMITH,
    Philadelphia

RHODE ISLAND
MAGI DECO TO DYNASTY
ANTIQUES
    Cranston
AARON GALLERY
    Providence

SOUTH CAROLINA
ORIENTAL RUG & ANTIQUE CO
    Charleston

TENNESSEE
KIMBROUGH INC,
    Memphis
OUT-OF-DATE: ANTIQUES &
COLLECTIBLES,
    Nashville

TEXAS
ANABLEPS-ANABLEPS,
    Austin
MARY STINCHCOMB ANTIQUES
    Austin
DONALD EMBREE ANTIQUES,
    Dallas
MIYASHITA ART & ANTIQUE
TRADING CO,
    Dallas
ORIENTAL ACCENTS,
    Ft Worth
CHANDLER'S NOSTALGIA,
    Houston
JENNIE'S ANTIQUES,
    Houston
MAI YIN ORIENTAL ANTIQUES,
    Houston
DECORATING CENTER INC,
    Midland
HELETIQUES,
    San Antonio
J KAHN & ASSOCIATES INC,
    San Antonio

VERMONT
REGINA MUSIC BOX CO INC,
  Thetford
L G KELLEY,
  Thetford Center

VIRGINIA
BETTY GAINES ANTIQUES,
  Alexandria
SHIRLEY MYERS ANTIQUES,
  Alexandria
THE LITTLE SHOP AT PLAIN
DEALING,
  Lynchburg
THE IRON GATE,
  Virginia Beach
TK ORIENTAL ART & ANTIQUES,
  Williamsburg

WASHINGTON
HEARTHSIDE ANTIQUES,
  Des Moines
CLUTTER COTTAGE ANTIQUES,
  Everett
THE ANTIQUERIE,
  Olympia
PERIOD HOUSE ANTIQUES,
  Puyallup
ANTIQUE WORLD,
  Seattle
CARRIAGE HOUSE GALLERIES
OF SEATTLE
  Seattle
CRANE GALLERY,
  Seattle
MARIKO TADA,
  Seattle
OASIS-ORIENTAL RUGS,
  Seattle

RITCHIE'S PLANTS AND
ANTIQUES,
  Seattle
ROSEN-COLGREN GALLERY,
  Seattle
KAY MC CORMICK,
  Spokane

WEST VIRGINIA
WOODEN BRIDGE ANTIQUES
  Charleston
COLLINSWORTH INTERIORS &
ANTIQUES
  Huntington

WISCONSIN
WARTMANNIA ANTIQUES
  Edgerton
GRAF'S ANTIQUES
  Milwaukee

PEWTER

CALIFORNIA
ANTIQUE INVESTMENTS
(HOLDINGS) LTD,
  Lemon Grove

CONNECTICUT
HERITAGE ANTIQUES,
  Avon
OLD PECK PLACE,
  Hamden
THOMAS D & CONSTANCE R
WILLIAMS,
  Litchfield
GRAMPA SNAZZY'S LOG CABIN
ANTIQUES,
  New Preston

FLORIDA
ROSS-PLUMMER LTD,
  Fort Lauderdale

ILLINOIS
MARSHALL FIELD & COMPANY,
  Chicago

IOWA
RED ROBIN FARM,
  Marengo

KENTUCKY
SOMETHING OLD,
  Louisville

MAINE
THE SAIL LOFT,
  Newcastle
THE MATHEWS ANTIQUES,
  Ogunquit

MASSACHUSETTS
THE BOSTON ANTIQUE SHOP
INC,
  Boston
GORDON AND GENEVIEVE
DEMING,
  Duxbury
THE HOUSE OF THE CLIPPER
SHIP,
  East Sandwich
BERNARD PLATING WORKS,
  Florence

JOHNSTON'S ANTIQUES,
  Franklin
THE WINDLE SHOPPE,
  Hardwick

MINNESOTA
ROBERT J RIESBERG,
  St Paul

NEW HAMPSHIRE
COLE HILL FARM ANTIQUES,
  Alexander

NEW JERSEY
CAPE MAY COUNTRY STORE,
  Cape May

TEXAS
JAMES Q ERWIN ANTIQUES,
  Dallas
IRON FENCE ANTIQUES,
  San Antonio
M SMITH ANTIQUES,
  San Antonio

SCIENTIFIC INSTRUMENTS

CALIFORNIA
THE CABOOSE ANTIQUES,
Niles

CONNECTICUT
VILLAGE STORE,
Hadlyme

SILVER

ALABAMA
MEMORY LANE ANTIQUES,
Montgomery
HERITAGE HOUSE ANTIQUES,
Opelika

ARIZONA
LASTENIA'S ANTIQUES,
Tucson

ARKANSAS
RUBYE BARBER,
Hot Springs

CALIFORNIA
BEVERLY ANTIQUES,
Los Angeles
THE VILLAGE FLORIST,
Ojai
LAMB ANTIQUES & APPRAISAL
SERVICE,
San Diego
JOHN HUDSON AVERY,
San Francisco
OLD WAGON WHEEL ANTIQUES
San Francisco
RED ANCHOR,
San Francisco
SYLVAR GALLERY,
San Francisco
CLASSIC ANTIQUES,
San Jose

COLORADO
MAJORIE'S BARN,
Aspen

CONNECTICUT
CHARLES STUART & CO,
Darien
TRANQUIL ACRES ANTIQUES,
Goshem
HARRY W STROUSE ANTIQUES,
Litchfield

OLD MYSTIC ANTIQUES,
Old Mystic
RAWBURN HALL,
Warren
SILVER GUILD MEMORABILIA,
Washington Depot

DISTRICT OF COLUMBIA
MARTIN'S OF GEORGETOWN,
Washington
SEGAL'S ANTIQUES,
Washington

FLORIDA
ANGEVINES ANTIQUES,
DeLand
THE ARGO GALLERY,
Ft Lauderdale
EARLY ATTIC,
Jupiter
I CHING ORIENTAL ANTIQUES
GALLERY,
Miami
SIDNEY SCHAFFER,
Miami
WESCHE'S ANTIQUES,
Orlando
AUNT BESSIE'S,
Pompano Beach
LARRY R ENGLE,
Tampa
THE GOLDEN EAGLE,
Tampa
A TIFANEY & SON,
Tampa

GEORGIA
J N ELLIOTT ANTIQUES,
Atlanta
LEVY JEWELERS,
Savannah
APPLE TREE ANTIQUES,
Tifton

HAWAII
THE CARRAIGE HOUSE,
Honolulu

ILLINOIS
MARSHALL FIELD & COMPANY,
Chicago
KINGS 3 ANTIQUES,
Evanston
D GRUNWALD ANTIQUES,
Geneva
GRUNWALD GALLERY OF
ANTIQUES,
Geneva
MANOR HOUSE ANTIQUES,
Kenilworth
HOUSE OF ANTIQUES,
Springfield
THE PACK RATS,
Springfield
STOREYBOOK ANTIQUES,
Sycamore
VIOLETTA'S,
Villa Park
VIVIAN C HEFFRAN ANTIQUES,
Winnebago
THE LION MARK,
Winnetka

INDIANA
HEIRLOOM ANTIQUE SHOP,
Eaton
KINNETT ANTIQUES,
Mooresville

KANSAS
LOU'S LOT NO 2,
Morganville

KENTUCKY
BOULTINGHOUSE & HALL
ANTIQUES,
Lexington

LOUISIANA
COLLECTOR ANTIQUES
New Orleans
PETERS' TRADING POST
New Orleans

MAINE
ESTELLES ANTIQUES,
Cape Neddick

MARYLAND
ANTIQUE CENTER,
Baltimore
IMPERIAL HALF BUSHEL,
Baltimore

MASSACHUSETTS
ERNEST J REPETTI III
ANTIQUES,
Boston
BERNARD PLATING WORKS,
Florence
SHIRLEY VAN ANTIQUES,
Newton Centre
THE BUTCHER BLOCK,
Orleans

MICHIGAN
DROVERS EAST ANTIQUES,
Detroit
TRASH & TREASURES,
Escanaba
HARBOR HILLS ANTIQUES,
Macatawa
RIVER REST ANTIQUES,
Saint Ignace

MISSISSIPPI
WALKER MCINTYRE ANTIQUES,
Greenwood
THE CABIN ANTIQUES,
Kosciusko
MURPHEY ANTIQUES LTD,
Tupelo

MISSOURI
DEN OF ANTIQUITY,
Columbia
CORBIN & SON,
Kansas City
CYRIL'S ANTIQUES,
Manchester

MONTANA
JEANS ANTIQUES,
Missoula

NEVADA
TREASURES ET CETERA,
Reno

NEW HAMPSHIRE
LOFT ANTIQUES,
Lancaster
SANDI'S ANTIQUES,
Manchester
HARTLEY'S BARN,
Pelham

NEW JERSEY
THE COLLECTOR,
Garfield
ANTIQUE ASSOCIATES,
Wayne

NEW MEXICO
LAS LOMAS ANTIQUES
Roswell

NEW YORK
STAGE COACH LANE
ANTIQUES,
Cooperstown
REMEMBER WHEN? ANTIQUES,
Floral Park
LILLIAN ASCH ANTIQUES,
Flushing
BRICKWOOD ANTIQUES,
Gloversville
CANASTAR'S ANTIQUES,
Herkimer
BARTLETT ANTIQUES,
Johnson City
PARKER'S ANTIQUES,
Lyons
AMBERGRIS,
New York City
JAMES ROBINSON INC,
New York City
PHILIP & SHIRLEY GORDON
ANTIQUES,
Plattsburgh
HOUSE OF WELTZ,
Port Chester
THUMBPRINT ANTIQUES,
Stone Ridge

OHIO
A B CLOSSON JR CO,
Cincinnati
ROGERS & CO,
Mansfield
MECCA FOR COLLECTORS,
Toledo

OKLAHOMA
THE CONNOISSEUR SHOP
Oklahoma City
THE LAMPOST ANTIQUES &
SILVER CO
Tulsa
MILLER'S ANTIQUES
Vinita

OREGON
ROTAY'S ANTIQUES,
Hubbard
CHRIS SWIFT ANTIQUES,
Portland

PENNSYLVANIA
ANN N DOWNEY & DANIEL
HARE,
Drexel Hill
ANTIQUE NOOK,
Greensburg
MARKY'S OLD FORT ANTIQUES,
Ligonier
SALLY BORTON ANTIQUES,
Mendenhall

SOUTH CAROLINA
ELIZABETH AUSTIN INC
Charleston

TENNESSEE
TED LELAND INC,
Nashville
TRACE TAVERN ANTIQUES,
Nashville

TEXAS
PHEASANT ANTIQUES,
Dallas
SCHNADIG ANTIQUES,
El Paso
NORMA BAKER ANTIQUES,
Ft Worth
EVELYN WILSON INTERIORS,
Houston
SWEENEY & CO JEWELERS,
Houston
RED DOOR ANTIQUES,
Odessa
THE ANTIQUE GALLERY,
San Antonio
M SMITH ANTIQUES,
San Antonio
MISS ROBERTSON'S SHOP,
San Antonio

VERMONT
RED WAGON ANTIQUES,
Danby

VIRGINIA
THE CAROUSEL ANTIQUES,
Alexandria
THE NOT NEW SHOP OF
ALEXANDRIA,
Alexandria
PRESIDENTIAL COIN AND
ANTIQUE CO INC,
Alexandria
WARDS ROAD BARGAIN SHOP,
Lynchburg
THE IRON GATE,
Virginia Beach

WASHINGTON
ANEX ANTIQUES,
   Seattle
BLANCHE'S ANTIQUES,
   Seattle
CHELSEA ANTIQUES,
   Seattle

LITTLE HOUSE ANTIQUES,
   Seattle
RITCHIE'S PLANTS AND
ANTIQUES,
   Seattle
VINTAGE HOUSE ANTIQUES,
   Seattle

WEST VIRGINIA
GOEBEL'S ANTIQUES
   St Albans

WISCONSIN
WARTMANNIA ANTIQUES
   Edgerton

TOYS & AUTOMATA

ALASKA
BLACK EAGLE ANTIQUES,
   Anchorage

ARIZONA
LILLIAN'S ANTIQUES,
   Phoenix
SYLVIAS' DOLLS & ANTIQUES,
   Phoenix
THINGS UNLIMITED,
   Sedona

ARKANSAS
SCHRAND'S GIFTS,
   Judsonia

CALIFORNIA
WITS END,
   Los Angeles
INDIANA ANTIQUES & DOLLS,
   San Jose
THE RAGAMUFFIN,
   Santa Cruz
TRINKETS 'N TREASURES,
   Sonora

COLORADO
NANNY'S LITTLE SHACK,
   Cortez
REVA'S MOUNTAIN HOME,
   Lyons

CONNECTICUT
GRACE DYAR DOOLS,
   Hartford
ELIZABETH WINSOR MCINTYRE
ANTIQUES,
   Hitchcocksville
LORETTA ROVINSKY,
   Marble Dale
JAN & LARRY MALIS,
   New Canaan
DOROTHY'S DOLL HOSPITAL,
   West Cornwall

DISTRICT OF COLUMBIA
THE COLLECTORS GALLERY,
   Washington

FLORIDA
PORTOBELLO ANTIQUES,
   Clearwater
CORNELIA MOSELEY
ANTIQUES,
   DeLand
MITCHELL'S HOUSE OF
ANTIQUES & COLLECTIBLES,
   Fort Lauderdale
ALEXANDRA'S ANTIQUES,
   Mt Dora
COLONIAL ANTIQUES &
COLLECTABLES,
   Nokomis
THE YELLOW BIRD OF ST
ARMAND'S INC,
   Sarasota
FOSTER'S TRADING CENTER,
   Sebring

GEORGIA
LILA BINTON ANTIQUE DOLLS,
   Atlanta
THE MOUNTAIN HOMESTEAD,
   Hiawasee
TEMPTATIONS-UPSTAIRS-
DOWNSTAIRS,
   Savannah

IDAHO
STAGE STOP,
   Pocatello

ILLINOIS
LITTLE BARN
ANTIQUES-CHURCH STORE,
   Elizabeth
BETTY PITTS ANTIQUES,
   Glen Ellyn
LENORE'S ANTIQUES,
   Oswego

GRACE OCHSNER DOLL
HOUSE,
   Niota
VIOLETTA'S,
   Villa Park
THE LITTLE CORNER,
   Wauconda
THINGS IN GENERAL,
   Waukegan

INDIANA
FERN'S ANTIQUES,
   French Lick
MARY'S ANTIQUES,
   Nashville

IOWA
AGNES KOEHN ANTIQUES,
   Cedar Rapids
ALLADINS' LAMP ANTIQUES,
   Davenport
MAXINES LIMITED,
   Des Moines
MIKE & BERTHA'S,
   McGregor
THE VICTORIAN ANTIQUE
SHOP,
   Sioux City

KANSAS
DETRICH ANTIQUES,
   Great Bend
ERMEY'S ANTIQUES,
   Ottawa
SPENCER
ANTIQUES-ODDTIQUES INC,
   Topeka

KENTUCKY
STRAWBERRY HILL ANTIQUES,
   Lexington

LOUISIANA
THE FIELD HOUSE ANTIQUES
   Alexandria

MANY MANSIONS ANTIQUES &
GIFTS
 Baton Rouge
CAMILLE MAHER ANTIQUES &
GIFTS
 New Orleans
THE OLD MINT RUMMAGE
SHOP
 New Orleans

MAINE
GOLD COAST ANTIQUES,
 Searsport
RED KETTLE ANTIQUES,
 Searsport

MARYLAND
THE COLLECTOR'S ITEM,
 Baltimore
HORNE'S ANTIQUES,
 Baltimore
MARGIE'S ANTIQUES,
COLLECTIBLES & DOLLS,
 Reisterstown
DAISY TRADING POST,
 Woodbine

MASSACHUSETTS
CROSS & GRIFFIN,
 Belmont
SUNSMITH HOUSE ANTIQUES,
 Brewster
GOLD DIGGERS OF 1933,
 Cambridge
STEELE'S TINY OLD NEW
ENGLAND,
 Cummington
RUTH FALKINBURG ANTIQUES,
 Seekonk
YANKEE ANTIQUE SHOP,
 Westport
MOUSE HOUSE FARM
ANTIQUES,
 Yarmouth Port

MICHIGAN
DROVERS EAST ANTIQUES,
 Detroit
THE GINGERBREAD HOUSE BY
ROHAMA,
 Lake Orion
ANN BATTISTELLA,
 Lowell
CRANBERRY URN
ANTIQUES-BORGERSON,
 Lowell

MINNESOTA
SCHMIDT'S ANTIQUES
FURNITURE & JEWELRY,
 Aitkin
STOECKEL'S ANTIQUE CLOCKS
& DOLLS,
 Faribault

STAN'S ANTIQUES,
 Lake Park
J & E ANTIQUES,
 St Paul
BUSY "B" ANTIQUES,
 Zumbro Falls

MISSOURI
BETHEL'S ANTIQUES,
 Camdenton
ANTIQUE BARN,
 Grandview
SERENDIPITY,
 Independence
ANTIQUES BY WELTE,
 Kirksville
RUMMERFIELDS ANTIQUES,
 La Plata

NEBRASKA
PLAIN & FANCY ANTIQUES
IMPORTS,
 Fremont
MILLERS USED FURNITURE,
ANTIQUE & DOLLS,
 Lincoln
RAGGEDY ANN'S ANTIQUE &
GIFT SHOPPE,
 Lincoln
SWAPPERS PARADISE,
 Lincoln

NEW HAMPSHIRE
SILENT WOMEN ANTIQUES,
 Candia
KAY MC GOWAN,
 Laconia
WHERE THE RAINBOW ENDS,
 Portsmouth

NEW JERSEY
CAPE MAY COUNTRY STORE,
 Cape May
LEONARD BALISH,
 Englewood
THE COLLECTOR,
 Garfield
PORT MURRAY EMPORIUM
ANTIQUES,
 Port Murray

NEW MEXICO
THE ANTIQUE PARLOR
 Albuquerque

NEW YORK
COLLECTOR'S CORNER,
 Bellmore
DEJA VU ANTIQUES,
 Brooklyn
THE DOLL SHOP,
 Clyde
FISHKILL TRADING POST INC,
 Fishkill

BLAINE A HILL,
 Harriman
ISLIP ANTIQUES AND DOLL
HOSPITAL,
 Islip
J & R FERRIS,
 Madison
PICK & POKE ANTIQUES,
 Maryland
MILNE MINIATURES,
 New York City
PAST TENSE INC,
 Nyack
ROCK CITY ANTIQUES,
 Red Hook
MONROE ANTIQUE CENTER,
 Rochester
WHITE'S ANTIQUES,
 Skaneateles
GRANNY'S ATTIC,
 Valley Stream
JOAN & LARRY KINDLER
ANTIQUES INC,
 Whitestone

NORTH CAROLINA
THE COUNTRY STORE
 Charlotte

OHIO
NOW & THEN SHOP,
 Greentown
THE LUCAS COUNTRY STORE,
 Lucas
BONNIE ROWLANDS,
 Medina
GEM ANTIQUES &
COLLECTIBLES,
 Toledo
SHARON CENTER ANTIQUES,
 Wadsworth

OKLAHOMA
HOBBY HORSE ANTIQUES
 Ardmore
GWEN HARRISON ANTIQUES
 Cushing
ZIGLER ANTIQUES & DOLL
STUDIO
 Oklahoma City

OREGON
MIKE'S GOLD ANVIL ANTIQUES,
 Portland

PENNSYLVANIA
TOONERVILLE JUNCTION
ANTIQUES,
 Bethelhem
BY CHANCE ANTIQUES,
 Hanover
DOEHNE'S OX BOW SHOP,
 Harrisburg
BUCHTERS ANTIQUES,
 Lancaster

SMITHERS ANTIQUES,
  Lewistown
ANGELL'S ANTIQUES,
  Norristown
LOVE OF PAST ANTIQUES,
  Philadelphia
DEN OF ANTIQUITY,
  Scranton
COLLECTOR'S TOYS,
  Strasburg
OLEXEN'S ANTIQUES,
  Valencia

RHODE ISLAND
ESTATE LIQUIDATIONS
  East Providence
SECOND HAND ROE'S SHOPPE
  West Warwick

SOUTH CAROLINA
BETTY'S DOLL HOUSE &
ODDTIQUES
  Charleston
FRAN'S ANTIQUE SHOP
  Manning

TENNESSEE
BROADWAY BARGAIN BARN,
  Knoxville

TEXAS
F B'S JEWELS & THINGS,
  Austin
KISSIN' COUSINS ANTIQUES,
  Dallas
CENTRAL ANTIQUES,
  Ft Worth
JACK'S EMPORIUM,
  Frederickburg

VERMONT
STEPHEN/DOUGLAS ANTIQUES,
  Shaftsbury

VIRGINIA
THIS & THAT SHOP & DOLL
HOUSE,
  Fredericksburg
WARDS ROAD BARGAIN SHOP,
  Lynchburg

WASHINGTON
DOROTHY'S ANTIQUES,
  Edmonds
THOMPSON ANTIQUES,
  Seattle
HAZEL CRANE,
  Spokane
DRAHOLD'S OLD TACOMA
ANTIQUE SHOP,
  Tacoma
ROYAL OAK ANTIQUES,
  Tacoma

WISCONSIN
THE HODGE-PODGE
  Appleton
BARNEY'S ANTIQUES
  Green Bay
SECOND HAND ROSE
  Milwaukee

To All Owners of Antique Shops
And Dealers In Antiques

LET US KNOW OF YOU

We are seeking out shops or newly opened shops at all
times. Very new establishments are extremely difficult
to locate by conventional means. We wish to solicit your
help so that we may come to know of you. Should you
not be listed in this edition, or should our search group
have failed to find you, please send us a post card with
your name and mailing address. Simply ask that we send
our listing material to you, and it shall be done. Our mailing
address is

Antique Shops & Dealers, U. S. A.
Driverdale Company
P. O. Box 12577
Dallas, Texas 75225